Navigation in your pocket
Charts as Apps for the iPad

Imray have joined forces with software developer Tucabo to produce this fully functioning chart navigation package based on high quality images of Imray and official charts.

Available in the following languages:
English, Dutch, French, German, Italian and Spanish

Download the free Marine Imray Chart App 2.5 which contains the navigation software and demo charts from the App Store and then the following chart areas can be downloaded:

- **Imray Charts North Sea**
- **Imray Charts British Isles West coast and Ireland**
- **Imray Charts English Channel**
- **1800 series Netherlands Small Craft Charts,**
- **German BSH Charts for the North and Baltic Seas**
- **Danish (DGA) Charts**
- **Swedish Charts**
- **Imray Charts Atlantic Europe**
- **Imray Charts Western, Central and Eastern Mediterranean**
- **French (SHOM) charts for Mediterranean France and Corsica**
- **Caribbean Sea**
- **Australian Hydrographic Office charts for East and South Australia with Tasmania**

Imray Chart Navigator Apps feature

Waypoints
Routes: distances, targets, bearings
Position and destination
Course to steer, speed and bearing
Magnetic compass
Distances, bearings from any point to any point
Electronic bearing line
GPS and instruments
Tides with full functionality from Tides Planner
Aerial photographs (subject to coverage) and harbour plans
Tracks which you can share with friends
GPX import/export

IMTA Gold Award 2012 'Best Digital Data Product'

Delivery is simple and Apps are downloaded from the Apple iTunes App Store

IMRAY/TUCABO APPS FOR IPHONES

A series of inexpensive Apps providing quick reference for crews and anyone involved in navigation

Marine Rules and Signals
Topics include buoyage, motor and sailing lights and shapes, rules of the road, safety and life saving signals.

Tides
This App provides active tidal data and tidal curves for ports around the UK and further afield.

RYA Racing Rules
A simple guide to the racing rules produced in partnership with the RYA.

Symbols and abbreviations
A quick reference to the signs, symbols and abbreviations used on nautical charts

Port of Ramsgate

Royal Harbour Marina

SAIL IN & SEE US

Have you considered a permanent mooring at the Royal Harbour Marina, Ramsgate?

The Cruising Almanac
2014

Imray Laurie Norie & Wilson Ltd
and The Cruising Association

THE CRUISING ALMANAC 2014

Published by
Imray, Laurie, Norie & Wilson Ltd
Wych House, The Broadway, St Ives,
Cambridgeshire PE27 5BT England
℡ +44 (0)1480 462114, *Fax* +44 (0)1480 496109
www.imray.com
2013

The Cruising Association
CA House, 1 Northey Street, Limehouse Basin,
London E14 8BT
℡ +44 (0)20 7537 2828, *Email* office@cruising.org.uk
www.cruising.org.uk

First edition 2002
Second edition 2004
Third edition 2006
Fourth edition 2008
Fifth edition 2010
Sixth edition 2011
Seventh edition 2012
Eighth edition 2013

British Library Cataloguing in Publication Data.
A catalogue record for this book is available from the British
Library.

ISBN 978 184623 512 2

Originally published as Sailing Directions within the *Cruising
Association Handbook 1909*
Editions 1920, 1928
Fifth edition 1971
Sixth edition 1981
Seventh edition 1990
Seventh edition revised 1992
Eighth edition 1996

CAUTION

The plans in this almanac should not be used for navigation except
in conjunction with the proper up-to-date charts of appropriate
scale, together with the latest *Notices to Mariners*.

The Cruising Association, its officers, members, the editor and
individual authors make no warranty as to the accuracy or
reliability of any information contained in this publication and
accept no liability for any loss, injury or damage occasioned to any
person acting or refraining from action as a result of the use of
such information or any decision made or action taken in reliance
or partial reliance on it save that nothing contained in this
publication in any way limits or excludes liability for negligence
causing death or personal injury or for anything which may not
legally be excluded or limited.

This book contains selected information and thus is not definitive
and does not include all known information on the subject in
hand; this is particularly relevant to the plans, which should not be
used for navigation. The publisher and author believe that its
selection is a useful aid to prudent navigation, but the safety of a
vessel depends ultimately on the judgement of the navigator, who
should assess all information, published or unpublished, available
to him/her.

The cut-off date for information was April 2013

Printed and bound in Singapore by
Star Standard Industries PTE Ltd

CORRECTIONS

Cumulative corrections are published on the CA website
www.cruising.org.uk at approximately two monthly intervals.
These take into account *Notices to Mariners*, information received
from Harbourmasters, changes to buoyage and lights as well as
new developments that have taken place during the life of the
Almanac. These may also be obtained as printed copies from The
Cruising Association, CA House, 1 Northey Street, Limehouse
Basin, London E14 8BT at a nominal charge.

The editor would be glad to receive any corrections, information
or suggestions which readers may consider would improve the
book, as new impressions will be required from time to time.
Letters should be addressed to the Editor, care of the publishers or
Email almanac@cruising.org.uk. The more precise the information
the better, but even partial or doubtful information is helpful, if
the nature of the doubt is made clear.

Foreword

It's over 100 years since the foundation of the Cruising Association, a gathering of like minded adventurers of the seas. They wanted to help each other by sharing their experiences to enjoy this wonderful world with as much fore knowledge as could be gleaned from those who had been before.

This almanac is an evolution of the notes and messages passed between those earlier members. Today the Cruising Association is able to draw methodically on the best and most up to date information from its members, now over 4,000 strong, and all other sources to produce a compact guide to the waters of NW Europe.

The Cruising Association almanac is still compiled by members with special knowledge of each area. I commend it to cruisers and wish you all the joy of the seas I have had the good fortune to experience.

Sir Robin Knox-Johnston CBE
Patron Cruising Association

The Cruising Almanac
2014

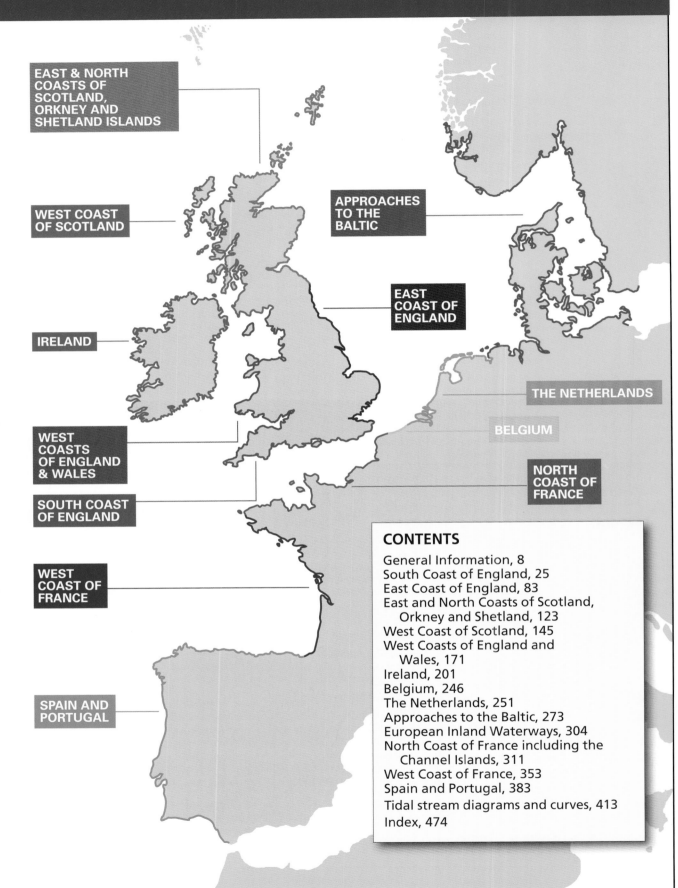

EAST & NORTH COASTS OF SCOTLAND, ORKNEY AND SHETLAND ISLANDS

WEST COAST OF SCOTLAND

APPROACHES TO THE BALTIC

EAST COAST OF ENGLAND

IRELAND

THE NETHERLANDS

BELGIUM

WEST COASTS OF ENGLAND & WALES

SOUTH COAST OF ENGLAND

NORTH COAST OF FRANCE

WEST COAST OF FRANCE

SPAIN AND PORTUGAL

CONTENTS

Preface

The Cruising Association places great weight on maintaining the standards set over the years for this publication. Our members contribute most of the content and many hours are spent creating a volume that succinctly informs on passage making and safe landfalls in some of the busiest waters in the world. We are pleased to present our insights and observations for those discerning cruisers who value a compendium created specifically for the cruiser.

Revising work never ceases. This year, parts of the sections covering N Netherlands, Approaches to the Baltic and Northern Ireland have been rewritten, new ports and plans have been added, all with a view to encouraging more cruisers to venture into attractive but less visited areas. Likewise other sections have been brought up to date. The expertise of Imray is evident in the plans; we have several new plans and many have been redrawn.

I am very grateful to our Regional Editors for the assistance they give and also to the many readers for the information and suggestions which they send in; without this help, production of the *Cruising Almanac* would be impossible. Members of the CA should please send information as a Cruising Report which they can post directly on the CA website, other readers please email almanac@cruising.org.uk.

For over 100 years members of the Cruising Association have revelled in the outstanding variety of cruising grounds just a few days journey away in NW Europe. So, above all, our editors want this volume to be a good read. We hope you find it so.

Acknowledgements

The key contributors to this 2014 edition are:

S ENGLAND
John Robinson, John Parsons, and Adrian Wilkins

SE ENGLAND
David Sadler

E ENGLAND AND E SCOTLAND
John Calver

W AND N SCOTLAND
Mike Henderson

NW ENGLAND AND ISLE OF MAN
Richard Collier

N AND W WALES
Sue Phillips

S WALES AND BRISTOL CHANNEL
Roger Lloyd

IRELAND
Peter Poole

APPROACHES TO THE BALTIC
Hans Jakob Valderhaug

HOLLAND AND BELGIUM
Peter Gibbs

EUROPEAN INLAND WATERWAYS
Roger Edgar

NW FRANCE AND CHANNEL ISLANDS
David Burden

W FRANCE
Judith Grimwade

ATLANTIC COAST OF SPAIN AND PORTUGAL
Tony Montgomery-Smith

METEOROLOGY
Frank Singleton

John Calver
Honorary Editor

General Information

CONVENTIONS

Passage notes are easily identified in the text by their distinctive type and blue background.

HW is given in relation to the 47 standard ports in the attached Tide Table. With every standard port a list of secondary ports with their tidal characteristics is given with the tidal curves. This tidal information is based on direct observation by the Hydrographic Office and not solely on rhythmic calculations from the moon and sun. The actual tidal height may vary considerably from that calculated because of the effects of barometric pressure and wind.

Courses and bearings are given TRUE unless stated otherwise. Bearings of lights, etc. are as seen from the position of the observer.

Depths are in metres below Lowest Astronomical Tide which usually coincides with Chart Datum.

Chart datum. Drying heights are given as such in the text but on plans the number is underlined. On the plans depths more than 2m are coloured dark blue and depths less than this are coloured light blue. On many of the plans on the continent the light blue extends out to the 5m contour. Drying heights are coloured brown and land is green. No distinction is made in dredged areas although the depth may be reduced by silting.

Bridges and lights have their height in metres above MHWS in the UK but on the continent this is related to Mean Tidal Level.

Distances are given in Nautical Miles (M), equal to a minute of latitude. Lesser distances are tenths of this, called a cable (ca) which is equal to 185·2m.

Winds are given as the compass point from which they blow unless they are described as off or onshore.

Tidal streams are described by the direction in which they are running, for example a south-flowing stream.

Index pages on these plans at the start of each section, page references are shown after each location. If bold type is used it means that there is a plan near that page.

Other navigational information The prudent navigator must not rely on the Cruising Almanac alone. It is essential to use up-to-date British Admiralty, Imray or official foreign charts and refer to Admiralty *Pilots*, *Lists of Lights* and *Notices to Mariners*.

BA charts are best updated by using UKHO *Notices to Mariners* available at www.ukho.gov.uk/nmwebsearch.

For Imray charts go to www.imray.com and follow the link to corrections.

For this *Cruising Almanac* go to www.cruising.org.uk/almanac/corrections.

Passage lights are numbered according to the BA *Lists of Lights* and only selected principal lights are included. The Lists of Lights are:

Vol A	*UK, Ireland and N Coast of France*
Vol B	*Netherlands, Belgium and the N Sea Coasts of Denmark, Germany and Norway.*
Vol C	*Approaches to the Baltic*
Vol D	*W Coast of France, Spain and Portugal*

Pilot books Suitable books are recommended for each area.

Telephones The area code is given with the first telephone number but not repeated.

International dialing codes

UK	+44	Norway	+47
Republic of Ireland	+353	Sweden	+46
Belgium	+32	France	+33
Netherlands	+31	Spain	+34
Germany	+49	Portugal	+351
Denmark	+45	Gibraltar	+350

ABBREVIATIONS

Abbreviations found in BA 5011 and the Admiralty *List of Lights* are used in the text and the plans. Some additional abbreviations are also used. Whenever there is doubt the word is printed in full.

Tides

DS	Direction of Stream
HW	High Water
kn	Knot(s)
HAT	Highest Astronomical Tide
LAT	Lowest Astronomical Tide
LW	Low Water
CD	Chart Datum
MHWS	Mean High Water Springs
MHWN	Mean High Water Neaps
MLWN	Mean Low Water Neaps
MLWS	Mean Low Water Springs
HWD	High Water Dover
Np	Neap
Sp	Spring

Direction

N, Nly	North, Northerly
E, S, W	East, South, West

Lights

Lt, lt	Light
Al	Alternating
Dir	Directional
F	Fixed
Fl	Flashing
Fl(3)	Group Flashing
Intens	Intensified sector
IPTS	International Port Traffic Signals
Iso	Isophase
IQ	Interrupted Quick Flashing
Ldg Lts	Leading Lights
LtF	Light Float
LtHo	Light House
LtV	Light Vessel
LFl	Long Flashing
Mo	Morse
Oc	Occulting
Oc(2)	Group Occulting
Occas	Occasional
Q	Continuous Quick Flashing
VQ	Very Quick Flashing
(hor)	Horizontal
(vert)	Vertical

Colours

W	White (Lts assumed White unless coloured)
R	Red
G	Green
Y	Yellow
Vi	Violet
Bu	Blue
B	Black

Miscellaneous

AIS	Automatic Ship Indentification
ATT	Admiralty Tide Tables
bn	Beacon
br(s)	Bridge(s)
ca	Cable
con	Conical
CG	Coastguard
conspic	Conspicuous

Dn	Dolphin
dr	Dries
EC	Early closing
F5	Beaufort wind scale Force 5
FS	Flagstaff
HM	Harbourmaster
hbr(s)	Harbour (s)
hPA	Hectopascal (=millibar)
h	Hour(s)
ht	Height
I, Is	Island
IPTS	International Port Traffic Signals
kn	Knots
LB	Lifeboat station
ldg	Leading
M	Miles (nautical)
m	Metre(s)
mkt	Market
PH	Public House
PO	Post Office
Pt	Point
rk	Rock(s)
rly	Railway
s	Second
SC	Sailing Club
sph	Spherical
stb	Starboard
tel	Telephone
tfc	Traffic
tr	Tower
TSS	Traffic Separation Scheme
VHF	VHF channel
VTS	Vessel Traffic Service
wk	Wreck(s)
YC	Yacht Club

Charts

BA	British Admiralty
SC	Small Craft
I	Imray
B	Belgian
D	Danish
F	French
G	German
N	Netherlands
N	Norwegian
P	Portuguese
S	Spanish, Swedish

SYMBOLS

- ⚓ Marina
- ⚓ Yacht berthing, no facilities
- Ⓥ Visitors' mooring
- ⚓ Harbourmaster/Reception
- ⊖ Customs office
- ➤ Slip
- ♦ Fuel
- ▶ Yacht club
- Pump out
- Laundry
- Boat hoist
- ♦ Lifeboat

YACHT SAFETY

Regulations

Yachts are regulated under **SOLAS V** (The International Convention for the Safety of Life at Sea). Although most of the regulations only apply to large ships, parts of Chapter V apply to small, privately owned, pleasure craft. These regulations are mostly those which any prudent skipper would take anyway but it may be prudent to record in the Ship's Log that you have complied for legal and insurance purposes in case you have an accident.

V/34 Passage Planning

Weather Check the weather forecast and get regular updates.

Tides Check the time of HW, tidal gates and other predictions.

Craft: Is your boat seaworthy for the intended trip? Do you have the right safety equipment: flares, harnesses, life jackets, radio, fire extinguishers, liferaft, tools, bilge pumps, first aid kit, charts and other navigation equipment?

Crew Is your crew fit, warm? Have you enough food? Are they sufficiently experienced and briefed to relieve you? Are they liable to be seasick?

Dangers Are there any hazards such as shoals, rocks, tidal races or overfalls or are you likely to meet large vessels in traffic lanes or constrained by their draught?

Ports of Refuge On any long trip when the weather may deteriorate, it is wise to have an alternative plan to allow you to take shelter. You might also consider what action you might take if someone is ill or injured.

System Failure Are you able to navigate if the electrical system goes down or the GPS fails? Can you cope with engine failure, a major leak or a defect in the steering? We can all get a rope or a piece of fishing gear round the propeller; have you the means to disentangle yourself?

Overdue It is important that someone ashore knows your plans and that you complete a CG66 so that Search and Rescue Services (SAR) know who they are looking for. Reporting your departure on a long trip means that the CG have logged this but will not monitor your trip unless alerted.

V/19 Radar

Large ships rely a great deal on radar. All small craft are required to fit a radar reflector if practical. Boats longer than 15m are required to fit a reflector to IMO standards of 10cm². The reflector should be fitted as recommended and be as high as possible. (Some vessels have an active radar transponder which shows up clearly on a radar screen).

V/29 Lifesaving signals

A copy of the lifesaving signals should be kept accessible to the helmsman.

V/31/32/33

Report any hazards to navigation to the coastguard and to any vessels in the vicinity. You must respond to any distress signal and render assistance if you can.

V/35 Misuse of Distress Signals

It is prohibited to misuse distress signals as it places lives at risk and severe penalties are imposed on those who fire flares or send malicious radio messages.

Briefing

The prudent skipper will explain the trip to his crew. The location of safety equipment, fire extinguishers/blankets; the procedures for use in emergency and the grab-bag to take in the life raft (with spare water, flares and a torch) should be described. Each member of the crew should have his own harness and life-jacket and know how to put them on and adjust them. He should be told the rules for wearing them and clipping on.Finally, they should each know how to make a distress call on the radio. A distress procedure card should be displayed near the radio.

Out of date pyrotechnics

Out of date pyrotechnics should be landed ashore as soon as possible after the date of expiry, for safe disposal. It is an offence to fire them at sea or on land for practice or as fireworks, nor may they be disposed of as household waste. Possible methods of disposal are:

a. through your supplier

b. liferaft service station

c. harbour or marina where your vessel is berthed (a charge may be made)

d. coastguard, your MRCC may accept them but they have limited storage facilities. Contact them in advance

MARINE COMMUNICATIONS

Usage is intended to be brief, clear and to allow others to use it in turn. You may send a message to another vessel, a water-taxi or an authorised shore station such as the coastguard, hbr control or marina. You must not call an individual person but must use a vessel's name or call-sign and your boat name. Low power (1watt) should be used in harbours and is compulsory on European inland waterways.

VHF Ch 16 Calling and Distress only. Call on a working channel if you can, most harbours and marinas listen on Ch 12, 14, 37 (M) or 80. From Ch 16 transfer to a working channel as soon as you have made contact. Monitor Ch 16 for Distress calls.

Boats with a DSC radio should enter the MMSI number of the coastguard station for the area in which they are sailing. Mayday calls alert all DSC radios within range.

Boats with or without DSC may call the coastguard on VHF Ch 16 switching to Ch 67 or another channel as directed. Solent CG should be contacted directly on VHF Ch 67 not Ch 16 (except for Security messages.) The CG have expressed a preference for the use of DSC calling.

MAYDAY is the International Distress Call on VHF Ch 16 using high power (25 watt). All radio traffic must cease until the emergency is over unless related to distress working. It may only be used when a person or a vessel is in immediate, grave and imminent danger. All vessels are required to monitor VHF Ch 16 and, if practical, proceed to the casualty to render assistance. The dangers could be fire, sinking or drifting onto a lee shore without control. Heart attack, haemorrhage and man overboard would be similar life-threatening emergencies.

DISTRESS CALL

Turn on the radio, tune to Channel 16, HIGH POWER, turn up the volume, adjust the SQUELCH, lift the microphone, press the transmit button firmly and say, for example:

'MAYDAY, MAYDAY, MAYDAY
This is SAILING YACHT BOAT NAME, BOAT NAME, BOAT NAME
Call-sign 2GBH4, MMSI 235899982
MAYDAY BOAT NAME, Call sign 2GBH4, MMSI 235899982
My position is 50°13'.20N 002°44'.30W
(or give bearing and distance from headland etc)
Serious engine fire. I require immediate assistance
Three persons on board are preparing to abandon to the life raft.
OVER'

Release the transmission button. Listen.

If the radio is fitted with Digital Selective Calling it is only necessary to ensure that both it and the GPS are switched on. Slide or lift the cover and press the RED button for 10 seconds. This will send your boat identity and GPS position to the CG and all ships within range. The screen will show that the alert has been sent. Wait no more than 15 seconds and send a voice MAYDAY as above.

NOTE You must only use a MAYDAY call if the vessel, or a person, is in grave and imminent danger and needs immediate assistance. It is not justified for engine breakdown, running out of fuel or seasickness. In these circumstances use an urgency call with the words PANPAN replacing MAYDAY in the message. On DSC sets this is an Urgency call. Do not use the red button. Use the boat's MMSI number after the name. Each DSC fitted boat is allocated a 9-figure Maritime Mobile Service Identity (MMSI) number similar to a telephone number. These are also allocated to the CG.

During security working the following pro-words are in use:

SEELONCE MAYDAY is a sharp rebuke from the controlling rescue centre to remind all stations not to transmit.

PRUDONCE MAYDAY Some emergencies take considerable time and to permit safety of navigation, the controlling coastguard may announce *PRUDONCE MAYDAY*. This means that although the emergency is continuing, priority VHF calls concerned with the safety of navigation may be made.

SEELONCE FEENEE means that normal transmissions may resume.

Urgency messages are prefaced by PANPAN repeated three times on VHF Ch 16. These go straight to the Rescue Centre. These calls are made when a vessel is in urgent need of assistance or there is a major casualty on board. Such emergencies could be loss of power or steering. Individuals might have appendicitis. The Rescue centre will arrange lifeboats, helicopters or advice as necessary, in some cases they will make an ALL SHIPS call asking any vessel in the vicinity of the casualty to render assistance such as a tow.

ALL SHIPS SECURITAY messages are usually used by the coastguard to indicate hazards to navigation. They may also be used by tugs, seismic ships and similar vessels. Small craft seldom have cause to use this type of call but it would be justified if for example you found a floating container which was a hazard to shipping. It would also be correct to report this hazard to the coastguard who have a greater VHF range and would investigate and log it.

LIFERAFT AND HELICOPTER RESCUE

If at all possible, avoid inflating and entering the liferaft. You are usually better off to stay with the yacht. Liferafts are cold, wet, difficult to enter, cause sea-sickness and are difficult to see from air or sea and are a last resort if the boat is on fire or about to sink. As they have no mast helicopter rescue may be easier.

If a helicopter is expected, be ready. Lower all sails, get the topping lift and any running back stays out of the way, lash the boom to the stb quarter. Put one competent person on the VHF and the other on the helm. Wear lifejackets. The helicopter will tell you what to do. When the Hi-line comes down, let it earth on the boat or in the water then hold it with some tension but DO NOT FASTEN IT TO THE BOAT. Flake it into a bucket.

MAN OVERBOARD

If someone goes over, shout for help, watch the casualty all the time, press the MOB buttons on the GPS, throw a lifebelt and release the Danbuoy. Take all way off the boat, if under sail heave-to, if under engine go astern and then to neutral. Drop the sails.

Do not run the casualty down, try to drift down on him across wind. A boat without power or sails may still make 1–2 knots through the water.

Every boat is different but the following points need consideration. The person will be very heavy to lift, the boarding ladder with a scoop stern may be attractive in calm water but it is close to the propeller and in a seaway, as the stern rises and falls it may inflict a head injury. There is least movement at the shrouds and there may be a halyard and a winch to assist with the lifting. Commercial aids provide either a sling or a raft but these are not easy to get under the casualty. A person in the water rapidly becomes hypothermic. Ideally the casualty should be lifted horizontally and kept flat until warm. Treat the casualty for hypothermia, and drowning (if necessary): see First Aid. If a casualty is lifted in the upright position, then, without the support of the water, blood can pool in the legs and the brain is starved leading to rapid death.

The Rescue Services are keen that you put out a distress call (MAYDAY) before manoeuvring.

It is a good test of boat manoeuvrability and often humbling to attempt to retrieve a bucket tied to a fender. It is so difficult to get someone back on board that it is worth preventing it by the proper use and maintenance of lifejackets, harnesses and jackstays. Regular practice is advised, especially with a new crew aboard.

VHF AND GMDSS

Ship's Radio

OFCOM issues free lifetime licences for ship's radios online (with an alternative hard copy for a fee). These must carried on board but not displayed and list all the radio and radar equipment. A fixed penalty of £100 will be payable for not registering or carriage. Details at www.ofcom.org.uk/consult/condocs/src/statement/

All radios and radio-operators must be licensed although a VHF can be operated by a non-licensed person under the supervision of a radio-operator or in an emergency.

The Global Maritime Distress and Safety System (GMDSS) includes INMARSAT, Search and Rescue Transponders, EPIRBs and Navtex. It provides for a worldwide co-ordinated Search and Rescue Service of coastguards, lifeboats and helicopters. In Europe there are Centres every 100M with VHF aerials every 25M. Vessels in distress contact a centre on HF, MF or VHF emergency frequencies. The VHF Channel is 16 but there may only be a loudspeaker watch at the Search and rescue centre.

Small craft going more than 3M offshore are recommended to have a fixed VHF set, fitted with DSC which may be used to contact MRCC.

Coastguard and MRCC

Station	MMSI	Telephone
United Kingdom		
Falmouth	002320014	+44 1326 317575
Brixham	002320013	+44 1803 882704
Portland	002320012	+44 1305 760439
Solent	002320011	+44 23952552100
Dover	002320010	+44 1304 210008
London	002320063	+44 020 83127300
Thames	002320009	+44 1255 675518
Humber	002320007	+44 1262 672317
Aberdeen	002320004	+44 1224 592324
Shetland	002320001	+44 1595 692976
Stornoway	002320024	+44 1851 702013
Liverpool	002320019	+44 1519 313341
Holyhead	002320018	+44 1407 762051
Milford Hn	002320017	+44 1646 690909
Swansea	002320016	+44 1792 366534
Belfast	002320021	+44 2891 463933
Channel Islands		
Guernsey	002320064	+44 1481 720085
Jersey	002320060	+44 1534 447704
Republic of Ireland		
Dublin	002500300	+353 1 620922
Malin Hd	002500100	+353 74930103
Valentia	002500200	+353 669476109
Belgium		
Oostende	002050480	+32 59 701100
Netherlands		
Den Helder	002442000	+31 223 542300
Norway		
Rogaland	002570300	+47 51517000/+47 120
Tjøme	002570100	+47 120
Germany		
Bremen	002111240	+49 42 15 36 8714
Denmark		
Lyngby	002191000	+45 66 63 48 00
Sweden		
Göteborg	002653000	+46 31 64 80 20
France		

There are four marine rescue and coordination centres known as CROSS (Centres régionaux opérationnels de surveillance et de sauvetage)

Station	MMSI	Telephone
Gris-Nez	002275100	+33 3 21 87 21 87
Jobourg	002275200	+33 2 33 52 72 13
Corsen	002275300	+33 2 98 89 31 31
Étel	002275000	+33 2 97 55 35 35
Spain		
Bilbao	002241021	+34 94 483 9286
Gijon	002240997	+34 985 326 050
Finisterre	002241022	+34 981 967 320

DSC sets have a push button facility to send repeated distress messages, which include the vessel's identity and GPS position, to the coastguard. This transmission has a slightly greater range than normal VHF and should carry 50M. It will also switch all DSC radios to VHF Ch 16 on ships within range. Because VHF 16 is increasingly crowded, it is recommended that working channels are used wherever possible, and also that HMCG are contacted by DSC for routine traffic.

VHF Ch 0 private channel reserved for rescue services
VHF Ch 09 most continental marinas
VHF Ch 10 Oil Pollution or UK CG MSI broadcast
VHF Ch 12, 14, 68 ports and harbours
VHF Ch 13 bridge to bridge
VHF Ch 16 emergency and calling
VHF Ch 23 UK CG MSI broadcast
VHF Ch 67 UK CG working channel, call on this channel in the Solent, otherwise call on Ch 16 or DSC.
VHF Ch 70 must not be used for voice transmission. It is used by DSC.
VHF Ch 73 UK CG overload on Ch 67
VHF Ch 79 and 80 in France for CROSS
VHF Ch 80 UK and Ireland, Marinas (Ch 37, M may be used)
VHF Ch 84, 86 UK CG MSI broadcast
Intership channels are Ch 06, 08, 72, 77.
Ch M, 37 and 80 should not be used outside the UK or Republic of Ireland.

There are no Coast Radio Stations in the UK, France or the Netherlands and link calls are not possible. CRS still function in some other countries including Channel Islands.

In an emergency VHF is preferred to mobile phones because the latter:
- only have a range of about 10M,
- cannot be located by direction finding equipment.
- do not alert nearby vessels.

Navtex is described in the section on meteorology.

THE INTERNATIONAL REGULATIONS FOR PREVENTING COLLISION AT SEA

COLREGS are mandatory for all vessels on tidal waters and are contained in RYA booklet G2. The following notes are only explanatory but emphasize points of particular relevance to all small vessels under sail or power. They apply to vessels within sight of each other by day and night and to vessels detected by radar. You should refer to a copy of the full Regulations.

It should be noted that no-one at sea has right-of-way. In some situations some vessels are designated stand-on vessels and others give-way vessels, however this is relative and even stand-on vessels should be prepared to make an early and substantial alteration of course to avoid a collision.

All vessels should be navigated with prudence and at a safe speed for the prevailing conditions. As a rule of thumb, all powered vessels pass port to port, vessels crossing or in a nearly head-on situation make an early and substantial turn to stb to avoid collision. When vessels are crossing, a risk of collision exists when the other vessel is on a constant bearing, the vessel on your stb bow stands on and your vessel is the give-way vessel which turns to stb and passes astern of it.

Vessels in a narrow channel keep to the stb side as far as their draught allows.

Overtaking vessels give way to the overtaken until safely past and clear.

An all-round watch should be kept at all times but attention should be particularly paid to ships on the stb bow or to port-hand navigation lights. There is a moral and legal difficulty about keeping watch if the vessel is single-handed and the helmsman needs to go below.

Give a wide berth to:
- fishing vessels (two cones points together, R over W or G over W),
- sailing boats,
- vessels restricted in their ability to manoeuvre (ball-diamond-ball vert, RWR vert), vessels not under command (two balls vert),
- tugs (diamond, two or three W vert and Y stern Lt) and tows, dive boats showing an 'A' flag (W Bu chevron),
- minesweepers (three balls in a triangle, three green lts at night)
- vessels flying 'Romeo Yankee' (Y cross on R and RY oblique stripes).

In some countries dive boats are marked by a red flag with a white stripe from upper left to lower right corners.

If your craft creates wash, slow down for moored boats and in crowded waters.

Avoid yacht races unless you are participating.

Sail A yacht which is motor-sailing is classed as a powered craft and should display a cone point down and obey the above rules. In some places in UK and abroad spot fines are imposed for not displaying this cone correctly.

Sailing vessels should stand on and powered craft should give way. There are problems about this, in shallow water a ship is often constrained by its draft and has to maintain speed for steerage way. Five short blasts warn you that you are in the way. At sea there may be single-man bridge-manning and the watch-keeper may be very busy. His vision may be obscured by deck cargo or the forecastle. He may be travelling at 25kn and you are making 5kn. He may have been used to the Baltic where leisure traffic always gives way to commercial ships. The motto 'Discretion is the better part of Valour' springs to mind and a 360° turn away from the ship will usually put you behind him and indicate your intentions.

Sailing vessels which meet other sailing vessels have special rules:
- A yacht on the port tack – with the wind coming over the port side) gives way to a yacht on the stb tack. Usually it will bear off the wind and pass astern.

- Yachts on the same tack, the yacht to windward gives way to the leeward boat.
- Unless racing, a yacht with a spinnaker should be cleared; in theory a spinnaker set on a pole to stb is on a stb tack, whether it has the mainsail set or not.
- In German territorial waters a sailing vessel taking up a fairway has to give way to a vessel (even a motor yacht) travelling along the fairway.

In reduced visibility

In fog, snow and heavy rain according to the rules, a vessel should reduce speed, post a lookout in the bows to listen and if under power give a 4–6 second blast on the foghorn not less frequently than every two minutes.

Under sail the signal is a long and two short blasts every two minutes. In practice one suspects that a yacht horn cannot be heard on a ship but it could on another yacht. Stay in port but if caught outside, get out of the shipping lanes and if accessible make for shallow water where a large ship cannot follow and consider anchoring.

Traffic Separation Schemes (TSS)

Ships are obliged to use these where they are shown on the chart. They must keep in the stb lane and enter or leave at an oblique angle. No-one may anchor in a lane.

Vessels less than 20m should use the Inshore Shipping Zone when navigating along the coast and should keep well clear of the TSS. Off N Germany it is an offence to sail within 1M of a TSS except at designated crossing places.

When crossing a TSS, cross on a HEADING at right angles to the lane and do so as fast as possible, keeping a good lookout and give way to vessels using the lane. Rule 10 states 'A vessel of less than 20m in length or a sailing vessel shall not impede the safe passage of a power-driven vessel following a traffic lane.' As many TSS are monitored by radar or patrol craft infringements could be expensive.

Sound signals

A short blast is 1 second; a long blast is 4–6seconds.

•	I am turning to stb
••	I am turning to port
•••	My engines are going astern
•••••	I am uncertain of your intentions
—	I am coming round the bend
– – –	I am overtaking on stb
– – ••	I am overtaking on port
– • – •	I agree you can overtake

In restricted visibility, at intervals of not more than 2 minutes

—	I am making way through the water
——	I am underway, but stopped
– ••	I am restricted in my ability to manoeuvre or sailing

Vessels at anchor or aground ring bells, sound gongs or sound • – • for five seconds every minute.

Radar

In reduced visibility, vessels are required to use all available means to detect other ships including the use of radar when so equipped. Formerly the Collision Regulations applied only to vessels within sight of each other but now Rule 19 states that 'when a close-quarters situation is detected by radar a vessel shall take avoiding action in ample time. An alteration of course shall avoid when possible an alteration of course to port or an alteration of course towards a vessel abeam or abaft the beam'. If a fog signal is heard

WINDFARMS

The government is committed to renewable sources of energy. Several windfarms have been built on offshore shoals and are operational while others are under construction. Their positions are shown on the latest charts and those under construction are recorded in *Notices to Mariners*. The blades are 22m above MHWS. Except when they are under construction there is no prohibited area or guard ship but they are marked by cardinal buoys Fl.Y and display F.R lights on masts. Their influence on wind and radar is under investigation. It would seem prudent to avoid these farms. There are three main UK groups; the Thames Estuary, the Greater Wash which extends E to Cromer and N to the Humber and the NW group off Morecambe and North Wales.

IALA BUOYAGE SYSTEM REGION A

Lateral marks
Port hand
All red
Topmark (if any): can
Light (if any): red

Starboard hand
All green
Topmark (if any): cone
Light (if any): green

Preferred channel to port
Green/red/green
Light (if any): Fl(2+1)G

Preferred channel to starboard
Red/green/red
Light (if any): Fl(2+1)R

Isolated danger marks
(stationed over a danger with navigable water around)
Black with red band
Topmark: 2 black balls
Light (if any): Fl(2) (white)

BRB BRB

Special mark
Body shape optional, yellow
Topmark (if any): Yellow X
Light (if any): Fl.Y etc

Y Y Y Y

Safe water marks
(mid-channel and landfall)
Red and white vertical stripes
Topmark (if any): red ball
Light (if any): Iso, Oc, LFl.10s
or Mo(A) (white)

RW RW RW

Emergency Wreck Marking buoy
Yellow and blue vertical stripes
Topmark: upright yellow cross
Light (if any): Fl.Bu/Y.3s

Cardinal marks

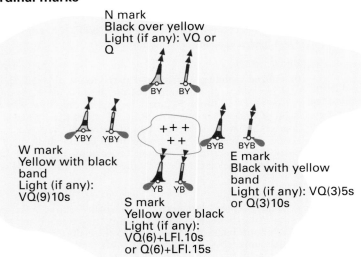

N mark
Black over yellow
Light (if any): VQ or Q

BY BY

W mark
Yellow with black band
Light (if any): VQ(9)10s

YBY YBY

E mark
Black with yellow band
Light (if any): VQ(3)5s or Q(3)10s

BYB BYB

S mark
Yellow over black
Light (if any): VQ(6)+LFl.10s or Q(6)+LFl.15s

YB YB

Spar buoys that are unlit have distinctive colouring, but may lack a topmark, particularly in the Baltic and the Netherlands.

INTERNATIONAL PORT TRAFFIC SIGNALS (IPTS)

MAIN MESSAGE		
1	Flashing	Serious emergency - all vessels to stop or divert according to instructions
2		Vessels shall not proceed
3	Fixed or slow occulting	Vessels may proceed; One-way traffic
4		Vessels may proceed; Two-way traffic
5		A vessel may proceed only when it has received specific orders to do so
EXEMPTION SIGNALS AND MESSAGES		
2a	Fixed or slow occulting	Vessels shall not proceed, except that vessels which navigate outside the main channel need not comply with the main message
5a		A vessel may proceed only when it has received specific orders to do so, except that vessels which navigate outside the main channel need not comply with the main message

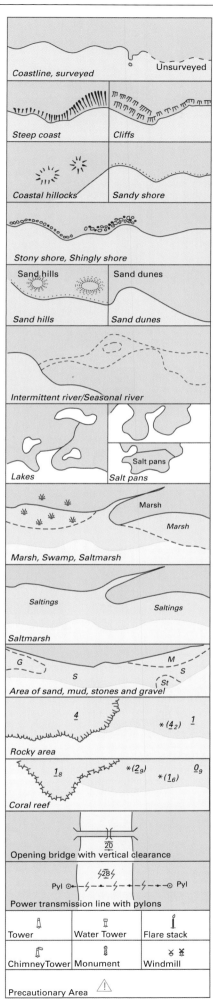

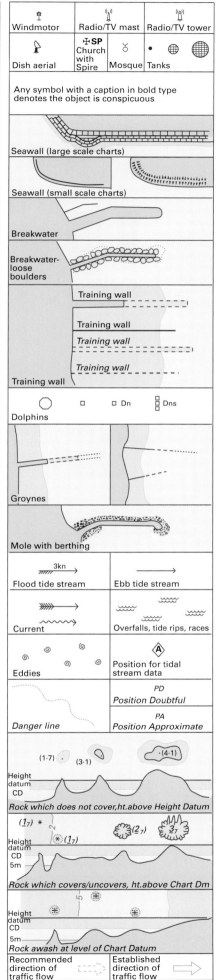

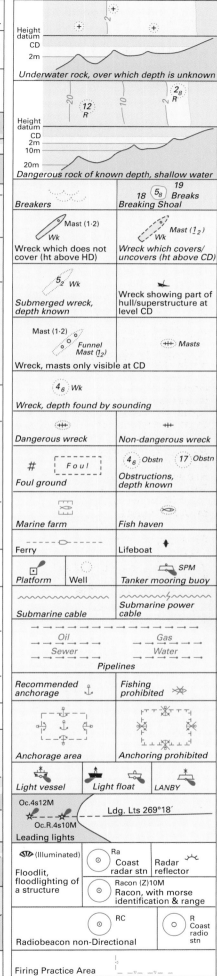

Morse code and Phonetic Alphabet

Morse code may be used on lights, racons, and fog signals. Ensure that you can spell your yacht's name and radio call sign phonetically without hesitation.

A	·—	Alfa	Al fah
B	—···	Bravo	Brah voh
C	—·—·	Charlie	Char lee
D	—··	Delta	Dell tah
E	·	Echo	Eck oh
F	··—·	Foxtrot	Foks trot
G	——·	Golf	Golf
H	····	Hotel	Hoh tell
I	··	India	In dee ah
J	·———	Juliet	Jew lee ett
K	—·—	Kilo	Key Loh
L	·—··	Lima	Lee mah
M	——	Mike	Mike
N	—·	November	No vem ber
O	———	Oscar	Oss Cah
P	·——·	Papa	Pah pah
Q	——·—	Quebec	Keh beck
R	·—·	Romeo	Roh me oh
S	···	Sierra	See air rah
T	—	Tango	Tang go
U	··—	Uniform	You nee form
V	···—	Victor	Vik tah
W	·——	Whiskey	Wiss key
X	—··—	X-Ray	Ecks ray
Y	—·——	Yankee	Yang key
Z	——··	Zulu	Zoo loo

Numbers

1	·————	Wun	6	—····	Six
2	··———	Too	7	——···	Sev en
3	···——	Tree	8	———··	Ait
4	····—	Fow er	9	————·	Nin er
5	·····	Fife	0	—————	Zero

National flags

 United Kingdom    Norway

 Ireland   Sweden

Belgium   France

Netherlands    Spain

Germany    Portugal

Denmark   Gibraltar

Navigational lights and shapes

Rule 25 Motor Sailing
Cone point down, forward

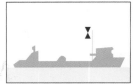

Rule 26 Fishing/Trawling
A shape consisting of two cones point to point in a vertical line one above the other

Rule 26 Vessel Trawling
All round green light over all-round white, plus side-lights and sternlight when making way

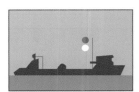

Rule 26 Vessel Fishing
All-round red light over all-round white, plus side-lights and sternlight when making way

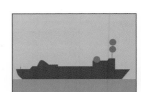

Rule 27 Not under command
Two all-round red lights, plus sidelights and stern-light when making way

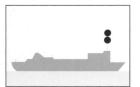

Rule 27 Not under command
Two black balls vertically

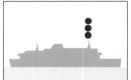

Rule 30 Vessel aground
Three black balls in a vertical line

Rule 30 Vessel aground
Anchor light(s), plus two all-round red lights in a vertical line

Rule 30 Vessel at anchor
All-round white light: if over 50m, a second light aft and lower

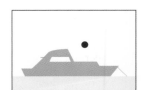

Rule 30 Vessel at anchor
Black ball forward

Rule 24 Towing by day - Length of tow more than 200m
Towing vessel and tow display diamond shapes

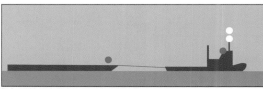

Rule 24 Vessels being towed and towing
Vessel towed shows side - lights (forward) and sternlight
Tug shows two masthead lights, sidelights, stern-light, yellow towing light

Rule 27 Dredger

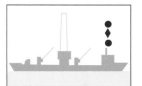

Rule 27 Vessel restricted in her ability to manoeuvre
Three shapes in a vertical line - ball, diamond, ball

Rule 27 Vessel restricted in her ability to manoeuvre
All-round red, white, red lights vertically; plus normal steaming lights

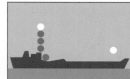

Rule 28 Constained by draught
Three all round red lights in a vertical line, plus normal steaming lights.
By day-a cylinder

Rule 29 Pilot boat
All-round white light over all-round red; plus side-lights and sternlight when underway or anchor light

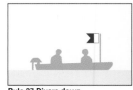

Rule 27 Divers down
Letter 'A' International Code

from forward of the beam or if radar shows a close-quarters situation to exist, then all way should be taken off consistent with staying on course. Great care should be taken when crossing hbr mouths, sea-lanes, fairway buoys or other places where vessels might gather to await entry. Vessels under way, but stopped, are unpredictable as they may move to remain on station.

Radar shows a reflected beam from ships, buoys or the coast which is displayed on a screen in which the transmitter is at the centre and in the 'head-up' mode, the vessels heading is vertically upwards (other modes are sometimes employed). The reflections are called 'targets'. Some targets reflect beams better than others, vertical surfaces at right-angles to the beam give a large echo, such as the beam of a ship or a cliff. The bows of a ship, a wooden or fibreglass hull or a beach give a poor reflected beam. The range and bearing of a target is given with great accuracy. A VESSEL ON A FIXED BEARING AND A DIMINISHING RANGE IS ON A COLLISION COURSE. To determine whether a vessel is on a fixed bearing, it is necessary to use the electronic bearing line (EBL) and the Range Rings on the radar screen. By plotting on a special radar chart at timed intervals the speed and course of the target can be determined. On sophisticated sets this can be done electronically. The Collision Regulations state that when there is a risk of collision 'an early and substantial change of course to STARBOARD is required' provided that there is not a vessel or other hazard in that direction. If it is necessary to continue on course or turn to port it is important to communicate your intentions to the other vessel.

Small vessels may disappear from the screen for several minutes in a swell. Heavy rain or waves may cause 'clutter' on the screen the operator can reduce this by adjusting the gain but this reduces the sensitivity of the radar.

ELECTRONIC NAVIGATION

Experienced navigators prefer the name 'electronic aids to navigation' implying that the navigator should use all the aids at his disposal and not rely on one system alone.

GPS

The Global Positioning System has revolutionised navigation and can give an accuracy of less than 20m. Differential GPS using land-based corrections can improve this to 1m. It is provided free by the United States government and is based on timed radio-signals from geostatic satellites. In spite of reassurances, it could be turned off and the fairly weak radio-signals can be blocked electronically or by strong electromagnetic radiation experienced near warships. Alternative systems are proposed but not yet available.

On any boat the receiver may develop a fault or there may be an electrical power failure.

Old surveys, old charts and outdated chart datum may mean that the accuracy of the GPS may be greater than the chart in use.

HORIZONTAL CHART DATUM AND GPS

All plans and geographical positions in this Almanac refer to WGS 84 (effectively the same as ETRS 89). Most new charts refer to WGS 84, however some charts of the West coast of Ireland refer to Ordnance Survey Ireland and a few European charts refer to ED50. Mariners are advised to look at the small print on the chart under the title, especially if using old charts, since there could well be a 100m error. GPS sets can be adjusted to the appropriate datum, otherwise a correction can be applied.

Position, waypoints and routes

A GPS fix gives a position in latitude and longitude to a second or third place of decimals. It may confirm a dragging anchor but allowance should be made for the scope of the chain and any yaw. The computer software can find the co-ordinates of any other point called a 'Waypoint' and link several of these to form a 'Route'. It will measure course and distance between waypoints on the route. Simple manipulation can edit or reverse the route. Speed over the ground (SOG) and course over the ground (COG) are displayed and deviation from the course is shown by 'Cross Track Error'.

Precautions

A ruler or straight edge should always be laid between adjoining waypoints to ensure that the course does not cross land, shoals, rocks or other hazards. Except by cross-track error, the GPS has no feeling for leeway or tidal set. Allowance must always be made for these, both in advance and by monitoring progress and correcting cross track error when appropriate to avoid the boat being set into a hazard. In a close-quarters situation it is often more accurate to rely on visual transits than GPS. In some circumstances such as

crossing the Channel, it may be counterproductive to use cross-track error as allowing the tides to cancel out makes the journey shorter rather than using an off-set first one way and then the other.

It is a mistake to position waypoints at buoys as the accuracy is such that collision with the buoy is a possibility. This is particularly likely in poor visibility, when there is the additional hazard of collision with another vessel using the same mark. Care should be taken on approach lines and at geographical features. Although radar and GPS are a great assistance if caught in a fog at sea, they require experience and skill to interpret. The prudent mariner will avoid going to sea in a fog even if he has a dedicated, skilled operator to assist him.

Electronic charts

These enable positions, waypoints, courses and bearings to be presented on a chart. The yacht position is not only shown continuously as an icon but it may also be recorded as an electronic log at set intervals. These systems are difficult for the occasional user. It is sensible to carry paper charts as a back-up and sometimes these show more detail or give a broader perspective. It is now possible to download an application onto Smartphones and tablets for electronic charts.

Even the most sophisticated system may fail and the navigator may need to fall back on traditional methods. It is helpful when this happens to have the last recorded position in the log book and this is best done hourly when away from land.

Waypoint lists

These should be treated with caution as they can lead to serious error. They are subject to editorial, printer's and reader's error and should always be plotted on the chart as a precaution.

Waypoints may be derived from a paper chart using compasses or a plotter, or from an electronic chart. It is prudent to record waypoints in the logbook by number, lat and long, and written description such as '1M N of Cherbourg W Entrance' .

Internet access

Internet access is of increasing importance for the cruising yachtsman and many marinas provide Wi-Fi, sometimes at no extra cost. In some countries, if a long stay is envisaged, it may be more practical to either buy a dongle or subscribe to an individual provider. A Wi-Fi booster will increase the strength of the signal but not its bandwidth, which will also limit the Wi-Fi traffic. If using a USB cable greater than 5m, it must be an active cable (i.e. taking a little power from the computer to avoid signal losses in the cable). Non-directional and directional aerials are available. If you know the direction of the transmitter a directional aerial, when correctly orientated, will offer the greater boost.

Automatic Ship Identification (AIS)

All ships over 300 tonnes are required to carry an AIS transponder which transmits data about its name, MMSI number, position, speed and course over the ground, and heading. AIS transmitters are relatively uncommon on yachts but receivers are readily available for around £250, they all require a VHF aerial and connection to GPS. Best results are obtained if they can be linked to the yacht's radar or chart plotter. Stand alone sets are also available. They display the data received from ships within line of sight and can calculate the closest distance of approach. Some lighthouses and buoys transmit an AIS signal. It is not a foolproof system, it depends on ships having their set switched on, and it should be regarded as another very useful aid to safe navigation.

A recent development is the **Virtual AIS** aid to navigation which is a mark that does not physically exist. There is no structure or light to be seen at the given position of the mark and it does not have a transmitter; it is operated by shore stations. It is likely to be used as a temporary mark e.g. until a buoy can be deployed. It is depicted on a chart by a magenta circle showing that a radio transmission is involved and the words V-AIS. Inside, it contains the description of the physical mark if it were actually at that place. Many AIS receivers used on pleasure craft cannot receive virtual targets.

CUSTOMS

Every skipper travelling across borders should be familiar with the customs and immigration regulations of the state which he is entering. In general, documents to be carried should include:

Ship's papers
Registration document for the boat
Proof of ownership, such as a Bill of Sale
Proof of VAT status
Ship radio licence
Details of insurance cover, including a current receipt.

Personal papers
Passports for all crew members
Proof of Authority to operate maritime radio
EHIC - European Health Insurance Card
Certificate of competence such as the International Certificate of Competence (ICC) – valid for inland waters, if planning to use the inland waterways.

Proof of VAT status An original receipt for VAT paid within the EU on first purchase is required or, for older vessels, evidence that the vessel was in use in the EU before 1992 and was built before 1985. Evidence for the former could be mooring/harbour dues receipt and for the latter Part 1 registry, builder's receipt.

With the exception of the UK and Ireland, all countries covered in this Almanac are signatories to the Schengen Agreement. Passage between the EU countries should be reasonably free from formalities for EU/EEA citizens. There are in general no restrictions on individuals who are citizens of the EU who are carrying goods between EU countries on which tax has been paid. Norway is a member of the EEA but not the EU, there are restrictions on alcohol and tobacco which may be imported, currently one litre of spirits or three litres of wine. Holders of non EU/EEA passports should establish beforehand whether there are any visa requirements: they will normally be required to report to immigration or the police. Yachts arriving from a non Schengen country may be required to complete an entry procedure. Skippers may be asked for a crew list with dates of birth and passport numbers. If intending to sail from the UK to either Belgium or the Netherlands a special form is required to be presented on arrival. It is easiest to download this from www.rya.org.uk before departure. Many states have reduced their customs facilities, an enquiry to the harbourmaster or marina will usually reveal local procedure.

Individuals travelling on non-EU passports should always report to the police or immigration.

Individuals living in the EU but only having visas should check that they will be readmitted before crossing borders.

All countries have strict laws prohibiting the import of addictive drugs, pornography and firearms. The UK prohibits handguns except for licensed signal pistols. Other countries may prohibit various types of miniflares and pyrotechnics. Many countries prohibit the carrying of out of date flares: on the spot fines may be demanded. Many countries have regulations on the transport of animals, meat, dairy produce, fruit and vegetables. These may be very strictly enforced particularly in the UK and Ireland. A ham sandwich, milk, a potato, an apple, a dog or budgerigar may be confiscated. See Customs Notice No.8 of December 2002.

UK Customs allow private users to use red diesel for yacht propulsion within UK waters provided that they make a simple declaration to the supplier and pay the appropriate rate. If going abroad, the regulations of the appropriate country must be obeyed. Keep receipts, do not carry red diesel in cans. It is advisable to record fuel purchases in the yacht's log.

If carrying duty-free goods, be prepared to demonstrate that the onboard stock does not exceed EU allowances. In the event of having a large quantity of dutiable goods on board it is a requirement to report to Customs.

Boats entering the EU from a non-EU country should always fly a yellow flag and contact the Customs when entering territorial waters. (In the UK Yachtline ☎ 0845 723 1110.) They should follow instructions carefully.

For Customs purposes the Channel Islands and Gibraltar are outside the EU and very limited quantities of goods may be imported duty-free. For a comprehensive explanation of British Customs regulations go to www.hmrc.gov.uk and then search for *Notice 8*.

PETS FROM ABROAD

Any dog, cat, or other animal on a vessel arriving from abroad must at all times be restrained and securely confined within a totally enclosed part of the vessel. It must not land nor come into contact with animals ashore. The UK Pet Passport Scheme does not apply to dogs or cats landed from private vessels, and is only intended to include animals being imported via certain commercial sea or air routes. There are no requirements for pets travelling directly between the UK and the Republic of Ireland or the Channel Islands since they are currently both free of rabies. Failure to observe the rules is a criminal offence. Penalties include heavy fines and destruction of the animal. It is not an offence to have a pet aboard a UK-based yacht or vessel, provided it is not taken outside the UK waters. This regulation is found under the Rabies Importation Order. Further information can be found at: www.defra.gov.uk/wildlife-pets/pets/travel/pets/procedures/owners.htm

CONSERVATION AND POLLUTION

By law it is illegal to throw any refuse over the side of your vessel whether it is biodegradable or not and however far you are out to sea. Heavy fines may be enforced. In most harbours and inland waterways, it is illegal to discharge marine toilets. There are no restrictions on the discharge of washing up water. Avoid the use of bleach; choose environmentally favourable detergents. To reduce oily discharge in bilge water, install in-line bilge filters, drip tray or bilge sock. The Helcom Convention prohibited discharges into the Baltic. Individual countries are implementing this. Take recent advice from the CA or RYA.

In the absence of discharge facilities, holding tanks should be pumped out and flushed at least two miles off the coast. In The Netherlands and Denmark, there is a ban on the use of antifouling paint of any sort. Visiting vessels are exempt but new coats should not be applied. Paints based on organic tin compounds are illegal on vessels throughout the world.

Bird and seal preservation areas are marked on new charts. Usually rights of navigation are preserved but landing near nesting sites is usually prohibited. Care should be taken in the Waddensee and in the Baltic to observe the local regulations which are obtainable from harbourmasters. Grounding is usually forbidden.

Marine conservation areas or parks may contain corals, sea grass or other delicate natural features. Anchoring may be forbidden but buoys may be provided. Fishing is usually prohibited in these areas.

Underwater archaeology and wrecks are often protected and local or national law must be respected. On some wrecks diving is completely forbidden; these are marked on the charts.

FIRST AID

Every crew member should have dressings for minor cuts, a seasickness remedy and some suitable pain-relieving tablets, also sun block fluid. If on prescribed medication they should bring enough with them for the journey and discuss this with the skipper. It is desirable to put an ICE (In Case of Emergency) number on your mobile telephone. Everyone with a severe medical condition is advised to wear a medi-alert bracelet or necklace. Diabetes may be difficult to manage on a small boat where meals may be erratic, further those taking anticoagulants where the main adverse effect is haemorrhage may be more at risk following a relatively minor injury.

Seasickness is caused by a combination of motion, cold, hunger, fumes and fear. It is often worse in young people. A heavy meal and/or alcohol is not recommended on the evening before setting sail. It is relieved by fresh air, work, a view of the horizon, and some tablets. Stugeron, hyoscine hydrobromide is the most effective, and is normally given to prevent motion sickness rather than after nausea or vomiting develop. For children over 10 years a transdermal hyoscine patch provides prolonged activity but it needs to be applied several hours before travelling. Other sedating type antihistamines are generally held to be less effective, although some individuals may tolerate these well, and in some cases find them effective. Most will need to be taken two hours in advance of boarding – follow packet directions.

It is highly desirable that anyone going to sea has done a First Aid course, and kept it up to date, often as part of RYA training, otherwise consider for example one of the courses run by the Red Cross (www.redcross.org.uk), or the Cruising Association.

Your plan

In the case of any illness or injury your plan is DR ABC, check for Danger – are there any Dangers to you or the casualty? Check for Response – shake them gently by the shoulder and shout into each ear, check they have an Airway – remove anything you can see in the mouth and tilt the head well back (unless under a year where the tilt is less extended), check for Breathing – if they are breathing place on their side in the recovery position to protect the airway and monitor breathing regularly, treat any injury.

If they are not breathing and you suspect a Heart Attack

MAYDAY call and commence chest compressions as soon as possible.

Cardiac Compression – place your hands on the centre of their chest and with the heel of your hand press down on the breastbone 4–5cms. This is at about the nipple level, kneel down beside the casualty to do this, leaning over and keeping your arms straight. Give 30 (thirty) compressions. (You are aiming for a rate of approx 110–120 compressions per minute).

Then give two breaths, the casualty's head should be well back, you need to pinch the nose firmly, and place your mouth around theirs, keeping a good seal, transfer the air from your lungs to theirs, until you see the chest rise. Do not blow hard or over blow, this may cause lung damage particularly if you are large and the casualty is small.

Continue with 30 compressions and two breaths until help arrives, if there are two of you one could breath and one do compressions. This is Cardio Pulmonary Resuscitation CPR.

In the case of drowning

Once the casualty has been removed from the water, open the airway by tilting the head well back, remove anything you can see in the mouth but do not push your fingers into the throat. Check for breathing if they are not breathing normally give five initial rescue breaths and then commence Cardio Pulmonary Resuscitation as above.

Assess the situation, make a **MAYDAY** call: you need help. In the case of drowning, breathing and chest compressions should be a little slower, do not force air in as this may damage the lung.

If the casualty begins to breath or cough turn at once on their side into the recovery position, their first action may be to vomit up water from the stomach, there is danger here of this entering the airway if the patient is left on their back.

The casualty will usually need oxygen and antibiotics and possibly steroid treatment to prevent the lungs and airways swelling, this usually happens six to 12 hours after recovery and is referred to as secondary drowning. It is important the casualty be taken to hospital even if they seem to make a full recovery initially.

Hypothermia

Suspect this in anyone exposed for long periods to cold, wind, wet or immersion (as in drowning, see Man Overboard box on page 10). Although shivering may occur in the early stages, it tends to be followed by apathy, disorientation or irrational behaviour, this is followed by a progressive diminishing level of response. Eventually into unconsciousness, with slow shallow breathing and a slow pulse, and finally to cardiac arrest. The casualty will lack insight and not appreciate they are in any danger.

To prevent this, use several layers of clothing with an outer wind and waterproof layer. Short watches with ample hot drinks and warm dry conditions below. Single handers are particularly at risk.

Manage this condition by ensuring the casualty is in dry clothing, and put them in a warm sleeping bag with a hat on their head. Also cover with an overblanket. Give warm drinks. Do not give alcohol or use hot water bottles. It is stressed that gradual re warming is safer.

Dangerous injuries

• Head injuries from the boom causing unconsciousness for any length on time.
• Severe chest and rib injury associated with breathlessness and the coughing up of blood.
• Heavy falls either on deck or down into the cabin (particularly where the patient has fallen further than their own height), where the casualty is unable to stand, or appears to have the symptoms of shock, pale cold clammy, feeling faint, nausea or vomiting.
• Heart Attack, where a vice like chest pain is present, the pain will often radiate to the neck, jaw, shoulder and down an arm, commonly the left arm. There may be severe pain between the shoulder blades and shock as described above.

These casualties need urgent evacuation to hospital. You would not be wrong to send a MAYDAY call although a PANPAN or Urgency call would alert the coastguard without diverting ships. In the case of a head injury, while waiting for the helicopter or lifeboat, record the time of the injury, the level of consciousness (response to speech, to command and to pain), every 10 minutes. Also note the pulse rate, the size, equality and response to light of the pupils, and note any discharge from nose or ears. Send this record with the casualty. A diminishing level of response often indicates compression due to bleeding into the brain space. If in any doubt do not hesitate to make a PANPAN call, urgent medical advice can be obtained from any UK coastguard who may then connect you to a doctor.

Intermediate injuries

• Burns and scalds should be cooled with water for at least 10 minutes, do not immerse the casualty in cold water as this will worsen shock. They may then be dressed with clean plastic bag, Clingfilm or other non-fluffy dressing.
• Suspected fracture or broken bone should be immobilised, legs should be tied together with a pad between the knees and ankles. Arms should be supported in a sling, and fastened to the chest by wearing the arm inside a jersey tucked in at the waist.
• Crushed arm or hand should be kept inside a clean plastic bag loosely tied round the wrist.

Following First Aid send a PANPAN call, as extensive burns, fractured bones or any multiple injury may result in fluid loss. If there is a possibility of needing surgical intervention do not give anything to eat, drink or smoke. Keep the patient warm to minimize shock. If there is severe bleeding apply pressure to the area, any object in a wound should be left and pressure applied either side to minimise bleeding. If you do not suspect a fracture you may also elevate a limb above the level of the heart to minimize further blood loss.

Minor injuries

• Sunburn is common, and as with other burns the area should be cooled for at least 10 minutes at time with cool water, wear cotton next the skin. Do not burst blisters, as this is a route for infection, if they do burst treat as open wound and cover with a sterile dressing. Check daily for signs of infection, worsening pain, swelling, pus or any sign of fever. Wounds should be kept clean and dry.
• Sunburn of the conjunctiva may prevent the wearing of contact lenses, so bring a spare pair of glasses.
• Contact lens injuries and corneal abrasions are common on boats. The casualty says he/she has something in their eye. Careful inspection with a bright torch will usually reveal nothing. Close the eye and keep it closed with a sterile pad. Inspect daily for any worsening signs particularly infection. Healing may be assisted with the use of an antibacterial eye ointment Chloramphenical (available over the counter for those over two years). Contact lenses should not be worn for 10 days after healing appears to have taken place.
• Sprains, bruises, and other soft tissue injuries are treated with Ibuprofen, follow the packet instructions carefully and take after food. This medication is not advised for those who have asthma, kidney problems, gastric ulcer, indigestion or are taking some other medications. (It may also relieve gout).
• Rope burns should be kept clean and dry, if open cover with sterile dressing and inspect daily for infection.
• Diarrhoea and Vomiting is usually self-limiting, keep drinking fluids, since the body is loosing them, there is advantage in replacing lost fluids with sachets of Dioralyte, although the casualty should not be kept on this alone for more than 24 hours. Diarrhoea may commonly last for up to a week and relief may be obtained by using Loperamide, again follow the packet instructions carefully. Of utmost importance is the maintenance of good hygiene, especially HANDWASHING, and those experiencing this condition should not prepare food for others. If severe abdominal pain develops with breathlessness, dizziness or fever urgent medical assistance should be sought.
• Dehydration is common on some small boats, it can result in constipation and bladder infections. It is important to keep fresh tap water in readily available plastic bottles. Generally an adult needs two litres of fluid a day to remain healthy. More if they have a fever or in hot weather.
• Any condition likely to last more than 48 hours is not suitable for nursing on a small boat and should be landed and either be admitted to a medical facility or sent home.

METEOROLOGY

SOLAS Regulation V/34 places a legal requirement on all pleasure vessel skippers going to sea to make a passage plan. This includes using relevant weather forecasts and getting regular weather updates, including warnings, whilst at sea via GMDSS Marine Safety Information broadcasts. Texts of these are available from Public Service Radio, MRCC Radio (VHF and MF/SSB), NAVTEX, INMARSAT-C and the internet. Other GMDSS services can be received by HF/SSB radio using voice, Radio Fax or Radio Teletype. With a receive only set the long range certificate is not necessary.

Forecasts broadcast as MSI are necessarily brief and general in nature. However, they are produced by professional meteorologists on the basis of output from their weather prediction computer models. They benefit from human experience and judgement. Sailing decisions for the next 24 to 48 hours should always be made with these forecasts in mind whatever other information is being used.

RYA publication *G5 – Weather Forecasts* gives a very useful summary of terms, some basic meteorology and sources of forecasts but is, inevitably, always likely to be a little out of date. Other useful publications are the MCA *Marine Safety Information* brochure and *Le Guide Marine de Météo France*. Both are available in hard copy and on-line. The MyCA website, http://cruising.org.uk/cruising_info/weather and http://weather.mailasail.com/Franks-Weather are also a useful data sources.

UK Sea Area (Shipping) Forecasts

These are broadcast by the BBC on Radio 4 LW, 198kHz at 0048*, 0520*, 1201 and 1754 LT. Those marked with * are also on FM and MW. All broadcasts comprise a gale warning summary (when appropriate), synopsis and area forecasts of wind, weather and visibility. Areas are shown on the chart below. Parts of the Shipping Forecast are broadcast by MRCCs on VHF, MF/SSB and on NAVTEX 518 kHz. (See page 23.)

In common with many other countries the UK uses the Beaufort scale to describe wind force. The table shows equivalent wind speeds at a standard 10m (33ft) above sea level and an indication of sea state. Other terms having specific meanings in UK Shipping and NAVTEX broadcasts are as follows.

In the synopsis, speeds of movement of lows and highs are given as:

Slowly	<15kn	Steadily	15–25kn
Rather quickly	25–35kn	Rapidly	35–45kn
Very rapidly	>45kn		

In the area forecasts, visibility is described as:

Fog	< 1000m	Poor	1000m–2M
Moderate	2–5M	Good	>5M

Gale and strong wind warnings

Gale warnings are issued when the average wind is currently or is forecast to be Force 8 or above. The UK also warns of gales if the average wind is Force 7 but gusts are expected to exceed 41kn. Warnings are broadcast as soon as possible after receipt by the BBC on 198kHz and by HMCG via VHF, MF and NAVTEX.

Coastguards issue Strong Wind warnings if Force 6 or more is expected in inshore waters but are not included in the latest Inshore Waters Forecast.

The terminology and wind speeds in knots are as in the Beaufort Force table below. Gusts may be stronger than the average by 10kn or more.

A gale warning is described as:

Imminent	Within the next six hours
Soon	Within 6–12 hours
Later	Within 12–24 hours

In case of uncertainty the term 'perhaps ... later' can be used in forecasts but with no warnings issued. HOWEVER, a gale warning MUST be issued if it may occur within the next 12 hours, even if the forecast uses words like 'perhaps locally' or 'perhaps at times'.

HM Coastguard Forecasts on VHF, MF/SSB and the BBC LW

HMCG broadcasts parts of the shipping forecast on VHF and MF/SSB – twice a day, at the times shown in the table on page 20. Inshore Waters forecasts are broadcast on VHF every three hours. There are 18 Inshore Waters areas including Shetland and the Isle of Man. The Met Office and the Isle of Man Met service issue new Inshore Waters forecasts for this purpose at about 0600, 1200, 1800 and 0000 LT.

VHF broadcasts are preceded by a brief announcement on Channel 16 and then transmitted on one of Channels 23, 84 or 86, except for the Western Isles of Scotland and Southwest England where Channel 10 is also used. MF/SSB broadcasts are announced on 2182 kHz.

Inshore Waters forecasts including the Channel Islands are broadcast on the national NAVTEX frequency, 490kHz. See page 23 for details. Inshore Waters forecasts are broadcast after the 0048 and 0521 shipping forecasts on Radio 4. They cover up to 12 miles offshore starting from Cape Wrath clockwise around the UK in 18 sections. They are valid for 24 hours and have a 24 National outlook.

Coastal Station Reports

The 0520 forecast on Radio 4 is followed by reports of actual wind, weather, visibility, barometric pressure and tendency from coastal stations and light vessels. Reports are from Tiree, Stornoway, Lerwick, Leuchars, Bridlington, Sandettie LV, Greenwich LV, Jersey, Channel LV, Scilly, Valentia, Ronaldsway and Malin Head. Locations are shown on the UK sea area chartlet. Some of the stations are automatic and measure visibility but not 'weather' ie there are no reports of rain, drizzle, showers etc.

The 0048 forecast on Radio 4 is followed by an extended list. These lists may change from time to time.

In coastal reports, pressures are given in hectoPascals (hPa) the scientifically correct unit. One hPa = one millibar (mb). Pressure changes relate to the three hours previous to the time of the report and are described as

Steady	<0·1 hPa
Rising or falling slowly	0·1 to 1·5 hPa
Rising or falling	1·6 to 3·5 hPa
Rising or falling quickly	3·6 to 6·0 hPa
Rising or falling very rapidly	>6·0 hPa

BEAUFORT WIND SCALE

B'fort No.	Wind Description	Effect on Sea	Effect on Land	Wind speed (knots)	Ave/max Wave Ht (m)
0	Calm	Sea like a mirror	Smoke rises vertically	<1	–
1	Light air	Ripples like scales, no crests	Direction of wind shown by smoke	1–3	0·1
2	Light breeze	Small wavelets, crests do not break	Wind felt on face, leaves rustle	4–6	0·2/0·3
3	Gentle breeze	Large wavelets, some crests break	Wind extends light flags	7–10	0·6/1·0
4	Moderate breeze	Small waves, frequent white horses	Small branches move	11–16	1·0/1·5
5	Fresh breeze	Moderate waves, many white horses	Small trees sway	17–21	2·0/2·5
6	Strong breeze	Large waves form, white crests	Large branches move	22–27	3·0/4·0
7	Near gale	Sea heaps up, white foam from breaking waves	Whole trees in motion	28–33	4·0/5·5
8	Gale	Moderately high waves some spindrift. Foam blown with wind	Twigs break from trees, difficult to walk	34–40	5·5/7·5
9	Strong gale	High waves, dense foam, wave crests topple, spray may affect visibility	Slight structural damage	41–47	7·0/10·0
10	Storm	Very high waves, sea appears white, visibility affected	Trees uprooted, structural damage	48–55	9·0/12·5
11	Violent storm	Exceptionally high waves, long white patches of foam, crests blown into froth	Widespread damage	56–63	11·5/16·0
12	Hurricane	The air is filled with foam, visibility very seriously affected	Widespread structural damage	64+	>14

Note – to get m/sec divide knots by two ie 5m/sec =10kn.

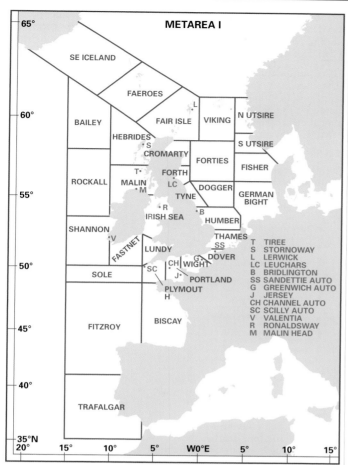

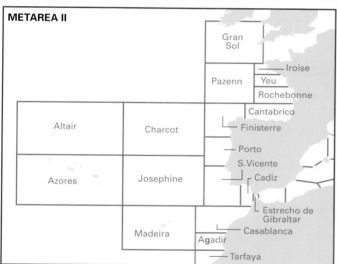

usually fairly recognisable with some practice. Useful multi-language glossaries are found in the *Yachtsman's 10 Language Dictionary* (Adlard Coles Nautical) and *RYA G5*.

Sea Areas

A common set of sea areas is used by countries bordering the North Sea although the names may differ slightly from the English. Note that French broadcasts covering METAREA I (north of 48°27'N) use the same areas as the UK except that the names of Channel Sea areas are Tamise, Pas-de-Calais, Antifer, Casquets and Ouessant, for Thames, Dover, Wight, Portland and Plymouth. Similarly, France, Spain and Portugal use common areas in METAREA II (south of 48°27'N). Spain adds an area known as Gran Sol, effectively Plymouth, Lundy, Fastnet, and east Sole.

Countries surrounding the Baltic also use common sea areas. The chartlet shows areas for the entrance to the Baltic.

GMDSS HF/SSB Radio Broadcasts

Voice broadcasts from Monaco Radio, in slow, clear French and English, include the NAVTEX areas used by France to the south of 48°27'N (METAREA II). NOTE: This is now a request-only service.

Analyses, forecast charts and sea state charts can be received on Radio Fax from the DWD (Hamburg/Pinnenburg) and from the Royal Navy, Northwood. However, note that the latter are not part of the GMDSS and transmissions may cease from time to time.

Inshore waters forecasts for the Northern North Sea and Southern Baltic (Ostsee) and open sea area forecasts can be received in text from Hamburg on Radio Teletype. Hamburg also broadcasts forecasts of wind at specific points for up to five days ahead. For schedules and broadcast content see the DWD website www.dwd.de, *Admiralty Marine Communications* manuals, RYA G5 and http://weather.mailasail.com/Franks-Weather.

Other sources of forecasts

All the countries in the area of this almanac broadcast weather forecasts on their Public Service FM and MF frequencies. Schedules and content vary greatly and the latest available details are in Admiralty manuals and RYA G5.

The Internet

The internet is a valuable source of information that supplements and complements the GMDSS. Access to mobile data networks and Wi-Fi hotspots has made the internet easily accessible to all using smartphones, tablets or laptop computers. Even without dedicated aerials the internet can often be accessed several miles out to sea.

Now falling (rising) means that the pressure has changed from rising (falling) within the last three hours.

Other terms used in the coastal reports are self evident. Some coastal reports are broadcast on NAVTEX 490kHz, see page 23.

GMDSS Services from other countries

All the countries in the area of this almanac broadcast Inshore Waters and Sea Area forecasts on VHF and/or MF/SSB. Varying from country to country, there are usually between two and eight forecasts a day.

NAVTEX weather broadcasts are available throughout except for local areas of poor reception.

Some information will be found in the various sections of this almanac and fuller details can be found in *Admiralty Marine Communications* manuals, RYA G5, *Votre Livre de Bord (Bloc Marine), Le Guide Marine of Météo France.*

Bulletins for open sea areas will usually be in English, the international maritime language. Some Inshore Waters forecasts will be in English but meteorological terms in other languages are

The internet is an additional source of GMDSS MSI forecasts and synoptic charts. Weather pages on MyCA, www.cruising.org.uk/cruising_info/weather, provide fast direct links to information provided by National Weather Services. Alternatively, see http://weather.mailasail.com/Franks-Weather/Weather-Forecasts-On-The-Internet.

For those with limited bandwidth there is a free service offered by Saildocs using email to provide text, including forecasts, from web pages. For details send a blank email to info@saildocs.com.

The UK Met Office has a free App for iPad and Android tablets that gives 36 hour forecasts of rain, wind and other parameters. The same information but including gust speed forecasts is on the Met Office Public site, choose *Weather* then, from the drop down menu, select *UK Forecasts* and *Map*.

For rainfall radar and satellite images select *Weather* then from the drop down menu, *Observations* and *Map*.

An alternative source for rainfall radar and satellite images is www.sat24.com/en/eu and for Europe at http://meteox.co.uk/h.aspx?r=&soort=loop1uur.

Satellite cloud picture using infra-red and visible light can be found at www.metoffice.gov.uk/satpics/latest_uk_vis.html for the British Isles and western Europe. Rainfall radar images for the British Isles are at www.metoffice.gov.uk/weather/uk/radar and for Europe at http://meteox.co.uk/h.aspx?r=&jaar=-3&soort=loop1uur.

GRIB Files

GRidded Information in Binary files are output direct from Numerical Weather Prediction computers. These can be obtained at no cost apart from communications, in four ways:
- Direct transfer to an on-board computer using free software – zyGrib or Ugrib
- On a tablet using low cost Apps for an iPad (eg Weathertrack, Weather4D, PocketGrib, iGrib) or Android (mobileGRIB)
- Web browser eg XCWeather, Passageweather, Magic Seaweed, Weatheronline, Windfinder etc
- By email via Saildocs or MailASail.

See http://weather.mailasail.com/Franks-Weather/Grib-Files-Getting-And-Using.

The data are usually from the US NOAA Global Forecast System. The only differences in the various services are in the parameters available and the presentation. Wind vectors and isobars are always available. Other parameters include precipitation, air and sea temperatures, cloud cover, sea state and swell.

Forecasts in GRIB form are usually available up to eight days ahead and provide useful planning tools. These should be updated on, at least, a daily basis. GRIB forecasts can help in interpreting GMDSS forecasts. Because there is no human interpretation or vetting of them, GRIB files should always be used in the light of GMDSS forecasts.

Other automatically produced forecasts

There are many other forecasts on the internet and sometimes seen as printouts in marinas. The majority are produced automatically based on the NOAA GFS GRIB files. Some are free, others are on prepayment. These also should always be used in the light of GMDSS MSI forecasts.

Understanding Weather Charts

Weather charts can be found on the Internet, displayed in some marinas or produced by software packages from coded weather

Meteorological chart symbols

observations broadcast by Hamburg. Weather observations plotted on charts are in a part numeric and part symbol form.

Wind arrows 'fly' with the wind with the feathers, by convention, pointing at low pressure. One long feather means 10kn, one short feather means 5kn, a triangle means 50kn. In these examples the wind is NW 15kn, SW 25kn, E 50kn.

Total cloud cover is indicated by filling in the centre circle as appropriate. Temperature is given in whole degrees, usually Celsius. Pressures are shown in hPa and tenths but with the first nine or 10 and the decimal point omitted. Pressures shown as 876 and 105 will be 987·6 and 1010·5 respectively. The pressure change is given in tenths of a hPa with a symbol showing whether rising, falling or now rising (falling). (The US still uses inches of mercury and degrees Fahrenheit!)

HM Coastguard Forecasts on VHF and MF/SSB

MRCC	B	C	A	C	B	C	A	C	Shipping forecast areas included in transmissions
		Times & schedules							
Shetland 1770kHz	0110	0410	0710	1010	1310	1610	1910	2210	Faeroes, Viking, Cromarty, Fair Isle
Aberdeen 2226kHz	0130	0430	0730	1030	1330	1630	1930	2230	Forties, Cromarty, Forth, Tyne, Fair Isle
Humber 2226 kHz	0150	0450	0750	1050	1350	1650	1950	2250	Tyne, Dogger, Humber, German Bight, Thames
Thames** Dover	0110	0410	0710	1010	1310	1610	1910	2210	Humber, Thames, Dover, Wight
Solent* Portland*	0130	0430	0730	1030	1330	1630	1930	2230	Wight, Portland, Plymouth
Brixham* Falmouth 2226 kHz	0110	0410	0710	1010	1310	1610	1910	2210	Portland, Plymouth, Shannon, Fastnet, Sole
Swansea** Milford Haven Holyhead	0150	0450	0750	1050	1350	1650	1950	2250	Lundy, Fastnet, Irish Sea Irish Sea
Liverpool**	0130	0430	0730	1030	1330	1630	1930	2230	Irish Sea
Belfast	0210	0510	0810	1110	1410	1710	2010	2310	Irish Sea, Rockall, Malin, Hebrides, Bailey
Stornoway 1743kHz	0110	0410	0710	1010	1310	1610	1910	2210	Malin, Hebrides, Bailey, Rockall, Fair Isle, Faeroes, SE Iceland

The working channel is given after an initial announcement on VHF Ch 16. All times are **local time**.

* These stations are expected to close 2013/14

** These may close 2014/15

Visibility is given as a coded number to the left of the weather symbol. Values of 0 to 50 are in 100s of metres, ie 20 means 2km, 45 means 4·5km. From 55–80, subtract 50 to give the value in km, ie 60 means 10km, 72 means 22km. Above 80 means over 30km. Some weather symbols used are as shown. Symbols for intermittent, continuous, moderate or heavy drizzle or snow follow the convention for rain.

The observation shown here says six oktas of cloud (¾ cover), SW wind at 15kn, pressure 1008·3 hPa falling 1·9 hPa in three hours, temperature 9°C, shower, visibility 15km.

UK Inshore Forecast Areas

Except for Shetland, the forecasts are to 12 miles out to sea, Areas and MRCC responsible for broadcasting are:

MRCC	Inshore areas
Shetland	Shetland and Cape Wrath to Rattray Head
Aberdeen	Cape Wrath to Rattray Head including Orkney, Rattray Head to Berwick
Humber	Berwick to Whitby, Whitby to Gibraltar Point, Gibraltar Point to North Foreland
Thames & Dover	Gibraltar Point to North Foreland & North Foreland to Selsey Bill
Solent & Portland	North Foreland to Selsey Bill & Selsey Bill to Lyme Regis, Lyme Regis to Lands End
Brixham & Falmouth	Lyme Regis to Lands End & Lands End to St Davids Head
Swansea & Milford Haven	Lands End to St David's Head and, St David's Head to Great Orme Head
Holyhead	St David's Head to Great Orme Head & Great Orme Head to Mull of Galloway
Liverpool	Great Orme Head to Mull of Galloway & Isle of Man
Belfast	Lough Foyle to Carlingford Lough & Mull of Galloway to Mull of Kintyre and Isle of Man
	Mull of Galloway to Mull of Kintyre, Mull of Kintyre to Ardnamurchan Point and Ardnamurchan Point to Cape Wrath. The Minch, from South Uist and Rum in the south to Butt of Lewis and Lochinver in the north
Stornoway	Ardnamurchan Point to Cape Wrath, excluding the Minch: The Minch, from South Uist and Rum in the south, to Butt of Lewis and Lochinver in the north

Schedule A Full Maritime Safety Information broadcast, including new Inshore Forecast and Outlook, Gale Warnings, Shipping Forecast, WZ Navigation Warnings, SUBFACTS and GUNFACTS where appropriate, Three-day Fisherman's Forecast (October to March).

Schedule B New Inshore Forecast new Outlook, Gale Warnings.

Schedule C Repetition of Inshore Forecast and Gale Warnings as per previous Schedule A or B broadcast plus new Strong Wind Warning.

MF Broadcasts (times as schedule B) Three-day Fisherman's forecast (October to March) and repetition of Inshore Forecast, Gale Warnings (if any in force).

VHF Schedules for Western Europe

The following are VHF broadcasts as listed in Admiralty publications. MF/SSB broadcast details will be found in the same manuals and are not shown here except for the UK. Times are UTC except where stated.

Channel Isles, Ireland, Belgium, Netherlands, Germany

(*Note* Denmark only broadcasts on MF. Portugal broadcasts weather forecasts on MF although there are some port forecasts on Ch 11 and Radionaval may be heard on Ch 11 from Monsanto, (try 0805 and 2005 UTC), or Sagres, (try 0835 and 2035 UTC.) If you do not hear them, then call on VHF.

Most coast coastguard stations will broadcast warnings. Routine forecasts are as in the table below.

Station	VHF Ch and Times	Areas
Jersey Radio	25, 82 at 0645,0745,0845 (all LT) and 1245,1845,2245 (all UTC)	Area bounded by 50°N, 3°W and the French Coast. 24 hour forecast and 24 hour outlook
Irish Coastguard	02, 04, 23, 24, 26, 28, 83 (3 hourly LT from 0103)	24 hour forecast for coastal waters to 30M and Irish Sea
Oostende	27, at 0820,1720 UTC	Dover and Thames
Dutch Coastguard	0940,2140 UTC	Dover, Thames, Humber, German Bight, Dogger, Fisher, Forties and Viking in English. 24 hour forecast.
Dutch Coastguard	23, 83 at 0805, 1305,1905,2305 LT	Coastal waters in Dutch and English
German Coastguard	23, 83 at 0630, 1730 UTC	Fisher and German Bight (in German)

German Traffic Centres give regular and frequent updates of weather conditions in the approaches to ports and harbours

France

French, CROSS, stations broadcasting Inshore waters forecasts (in French). Forecasts cover up to 20M offshore. Transmissions are pre-recorded and broadcast from each transmitter in sequence.

Area	Transmitter, VHF Ch	Times (LT)
The Belgian frontier to Baie de Somme (Gris-Nez)	Dunkerque VHF 79	0720, 1603, 1920
	Gris-Nez VHF 79	0710, 1545, 1910
The Baie de Somme to Cap de la Hague (Gris-Nez)	Ailly VHF 79	0703, 1533, 1903
Cap de la Hague to Pointe de Penmarc'h (Jobourg)	Antifer VHF 80	0803, 1633, 2003
	Port-en-Bessin VHF 80	0745, 1615, 1945
	Jobourg VHF 80	0733, 1603, 1933
Warning for sea areas Antifer to Casquets	Jobourg VHF 80	on receipt, at every half hour H+20 and H+50 (in English)
Cap de la Hague to Pointe de Penmarc'h (Jobourg)	Jobourg VHF 80	0715, 1545, 1915
	Granville VHF 80	0703, 1533, 1903
Cap de la Hague to Pointe de Penmarc'h (Etel)	Raz VHF 79	0445, 0703, 1103*, 1533, 1903
	Stiff VHF 79	0503, 0715, 1115* 1545, 1915
	Batz VHF 79	0515, 0733, 1133*,1603, 1933
	Bodic VHF 79	0533, 0745, 1145*, 1615, 1945
	Fréhel VHF 79	0545, 0803, 1203*, 1633, 2003

* from 1 May to 30 September

Area	Transmitter, VHF Ch	Times (LT)
Pointe de Penmarc'h to Anse de l'Aiguillon (Etel)	Penmarc'h VHF 80	0703, 1533, 1903
	Groix VHF 80	0715, 1545, 1915
	Etel VHF 63	Continually repeated
	Belle-Ile VHF 80	0733, 1603, 1933
	Saint-Nazaire VHF 80	0745, 1615, 1945
	Yeu VHF 80	0803, 1633, 2003
	Les Sables d'Olonne VHF 80	0815, 1645, 2015
Anse de l'Aiguillon to the Spanish Frontier (Etel)	Chassiron VHF 79	Continually repeated
	Soulac VHF 79	0715, 1545, 1915
	Cap-Ferret VHF 79	0733, 1603, 1933
	Contis VHF 79	0745, 1615, 1945
	Biarritz VHF 79	0803, 1633, 2003

GENERAL INFORMATION

Spain

Spanish stations broadcasting Sea Area forecast in English and Inshore waters forecasts, sometimes in English

Station	VHF Ch	Times
Bilbao	10	Even hours +33
Santander	11	0245, 0645, 1045, 1445, 1845, 2245
Gijón	10, 15, 17	Even hours +15
A Coruña	13, 67, 15	Even hours +15
Finisterre	11	Even hours +33
Vigo	10, 67, 15	Even hours +15
Tarifa	10, 67,73	Even hours +15
Algeciras	74	0315, 0515, 0715, 1115, 1515, 1915, 2315

Spanish stations broadcasting Inshore Waters forecasts, in Spanish only.

Station	VHF Ch	Times
Pasajes	27	0840, 1240, 2010
Bilbāo	26	0840, 1240, 2010
Santander	24	0840, 1240, 2010
Cabo Peñas	26	0840, 1240, 2010
Navia	60	0840, 1240, 2010
Cabo Ortegal	2	0840, 1240, 2010
A Coruña	26	0840, 1240, 2010
Finisterre	22	0840, 1240, 2010
Vigo	65	0840, 1240, 2010
La Guardia	21	0840, 1240, 2010
Cádiz	26	0833, 1133, 2003
Tarifa	21	0833, 1133, 2003

Other Fax services

Weather radar sequence	09060 100 425
Surface analysis chart	09060 100 444
User guide to surface charts	09060 100 445
UK plotted chart	09060 100 447

Talk to a forecaster

Met Office: for details see www.metoffice.gov.uk/services/talkfc
Weatherweb: for details see www.weatherweb.net/weatherlive.htm

Actual weather information

For those with Internet access, useful data can be obtained from: www.metoffice.gov.uk/weather/marine/observations/index.html This gives the latest Marine hourly observations around UK coasts and including open ocean buoys to the west pf the British Isles and Biscay. Updated hourly.

www.met.ie/latest/buoy.asp for a very handy collection of data buoys around Ireland and coastal stations.

For the latest three-hourly reports from useful locations around German coasts go to www.dwd.de look for Wetter, Seewetter, Aktuell or Stationmeldungen.

The most comprehensive source of actual wind data for weather observing sites over the British Isles and France is www.xcweather.co.uk. This gives latest wind data from airfields, data buoys, light vessels etc.

CONTACTS

Canals Canal and River Trust
  ☎ +44(0)303 040 4040
  www.canalrivertrust.org.uk also www.waterscape.com
Cruising Association, CA House, 1 Northey Street, Limehouse
  Basin, London E14 8BT
  ☎ +44(0)20 7537 2828
  Email office@cruising.org.uk,
  www.cruising.org.uk
HM Customs www.hmrc.gov.uk
  National Yachtline (to report arrival or departure)
  ☎ 0845 723 1110
  Helpline service ☎ 0845 010 900
  or +44(0)208 929 0152 from abroad.
  Customs Confidential Hotline
  If you see any suspicious activity (drugs, smuggling, etc) around the UK coastline, don't ignore it, report it to
  ☎ 0800 595 000
Imray Laurie Norie and Wilson
  ☎ +44(0)1480 462114
  Email ilnw@imray.com, www.imray.com
Maritime and Coastguard Agency, Spring Place, 105 Commercial
  Road, Southampton SO15 1EG
  ☎ 0870 6006505 *Email* infoline@mcga.gov.uk
  www.mcga.gov.uk
Registry of Shipping and Seamen, 12 Anchor Court, Ocean Way,
  Cardiff CF24 5JW
  ☎ 029 2044 8800
  www.mcagency.org.uk
Royal Yachting Association, RYA House, Ensign Way, Hamble
  Southampton SO31 4YA
  ☎ 0845 345 0400 Cruising ☎ 0845 345 0370
  www.rya.org.uk
Seastart
  ☎ 0800 885500 VHF M/37 or M2
  From France ☎ +44 2380 457245
Clyde Cruising Club Suite 101 Pentagon Centre, 36 Washington
  Street, Glasgow G3 8AZ
  ☎ +44(0) 141 221 2774 *Email* office@clyde.org
  www.clyde.org
CHIRP confidential hazardous incident reporting programme (for
  poorly marked fishing gear
  ☎ Freefone 0808 1003237 or +44(0)1252 393348
  www.chirp.co.uk
National Coastwatch Institution (NCI) provide a visual lookout
  by day along many parts of the UK coastline, often from recently closed coastguard stations. They are volunteers who call themselves the 'Eyes along the coast'
  www.nci.org.uk

NAVTEX Broadcast content and schedules (Times in UT)

Stations broadcasting weather forecasts on the International Frequency 518 kHz, in English

Station	Times	Content	Areas
Niton (E)	0840, 2040	Warning Summary, 24h forecast and brief outlook	Thames, Dover, Wight, Portland, Plymouth, Biscay, Fitzroy, Sole, Lundy, Fastnet
	0040	Extended Outlook	Thames, Dover, Wight, Portland, Plymouth, Biscay, Sole, Lundy, Fastnet
Portpatrick (O)	0620, 1820	Warning Summary, 24h forecast and brief outlook	Lundy, Fastnet, Irish Sea, Rockall, Malin, Hebrides, Bailey, Fair Isle, Faeroes and SE Iceland
	0220	Extended Outlook	Lundy, Fastnet, Irish sea, Rockall, Malin, Hebrides, Bailey, Fair Isle, Faeroes and SE Iceland
Cullercoats (G)	0900, 2100	Warning Summary, 24h forecast and brief outlook	Viking, Forties, Cromarty, Forth, Tyne, Dogger, Humber, Thames and Fair Isle
	0100	Extended Outlook	Fair Isle, Viking, North Utsire, South Utsire, Forties, Cromarty, Forth, Tyne, Dogger, Fisher, German Bight, Humber, Thames, Dover and Wight
Valentia (W)	0740, 1940	24h forecast and brief outlook	Sole, Fastnet and Shannon
	1140, 2340	High Seas Bulletin	East Central section of METAREA I, High Seas
Malin Head (Q) *see Note 1*	0640, 1840	24h forecast, brief outlook and High Seas Bulletin	Shannon, Rockall, Malin Hebrides and Bailey, East Northern and East Central sections of METAREA I, High Seas
Thorshavn (D)	Every 4 hours from 0030	24h forecast and brief outlook	Outer Banks, The Munk, Fugloy Banks, Iceland Ridge
Rogaland (L)	0150 and 1350	24h forecast and brief outlook	North Utsire, South Utsire, Fisher and German Bight
Jeløy (M)	0200, 1400	24h forecast	Skagerrak
Grimeton (I)	0520, 1720	24h forecast	Kattegat and The Belts
Ørlandet (N)	0210, 1410	24h forecast	Norwegian Sea Areas to the north of 61°N
Vardo (C)	0820, 2020	Sea Area Forecast	Baltic Sea Areas
Gislövshammar (J)	0530, 1730	Sea Area Forecast	Baltic Sea Areas
Grimeton (I)	0520, 1720	Sea Area Forecast	Baltic Sea Areas
Oostende (T)	0710, 1910	24h forecast	Coasts of Belgium and Sea Areas Thames and Dover
Hamburg (S) (Pinneberg)	Every 4h from 0300	24h forecast	German North Sea Areas
IJmuiden (P)	Every 4h from 0230	Warning Summary. Forecasts for next 12h and 12h outlook	German Bight, Humber, Thames and Dogger
Corsen (A)	0000, 1200	Warning summary. Forecasts for next 24h and brief outlook	Iroise, Yeu, Rochebonne, Cantabrico, Finisterre and Pazenn
A Coruña (D)	0030,1230	Sea Area Forecasts for next 24h (in English and Spanish)	Gran Sol, Pazenn, Iroise, Yeu, Rochebonne, Altair, Charcot, Finisterre, Cantabrico, Azores, Josephine, Porto, São Vicente, Cádiz, Estrecho, Madeira, Casablanca and Agadir
Monsanto (R)	0550, 1750	Sea Area Forecasts for next 24h	Charcot, Josephine, Finisterre, Porto, São Vicente and Cádiz
Tarifa (G)	0900, 2100	Sea Area Forecasts for next 24h (in English and Spanish)	São Vicente, Cádiz, Casablanca, Agadir, Gibraltar, Strait/Estrecho, Alborán, Palos, Argelia (NB. The last three are in the Mediterranean)

Stations broadcasting weather forecasts on the national frequency of 490 kHz

Station	Times	Content	Areas
Niton (I)	0120, 0520 1320, 1720	Inshore Waters Forecast and 24h Outlook	North Foreland to St David's Head including the Channel Islands, the Isles of Scilly and the Bristol Channel
	0920, 2120	Latest observations	South coast
Niton (T)	0710, 1910	Warning summary and Sea Area Forecasts for next 24h and a brief outlook (in French)	Humber, Tamise, Pas de Calais and Antifer
Portpatrick (C)	0200, 0820 1220, 2020	Inshore Waters Forecast and 24h Outlook	The Channel Islands, Lands End and coastal waters of Wales, W England, Northern Ireland, W Scotland and the Shetland Islands
	0420, 1620	Latest observations	West coast
Malin Head (A)	Every 4h from 0000	Inshore Waters Forecast and 24h outlook	Lough Foyle to Carlingford Lough, Mull of Galloway to Mull of Kintyre including the Firth of Clyde and North Channel, Mull of Kintyre to Ardnamurchan Point, The Minch, Ardnamurchan Pt to Cape Wrath, Isle of Man, the Channel Islands
Cullercoats (U)	0720, 1120 1920, 2320 0320, 1520	Inshore Waters Forecast and 24h outlook	Shetland Isles, coastal waters of Eastern Scotland and Eastern England and from North Foreland to Selsey Bill East coast
Hamburg (L)	0550, 2150	24h forecast (In German)	German Bight and German coastal waters.
Corsen (E)	0840, 2040	Warning summary. 24h forecast and brief outlook (in French)	Casquets, Ouessant, Iroise, Yeu, Rochebonne, Cantabrico, Finisterre, Pazenn, Sole, Shannon, Fastnet, Lundy and Irish Sea
A Coruña (W)	1140, 1940	Sea Area Forecasts for next 24h (In Spanish)	Gran Sol, Pazenn, Iroise, Yeu, Rochebonne, Charcot, Finisterre, Cantabrico, Josephine, Porto, São Vincente, Cádiz, Estrecho
Monsanto (G) *See Note 2*	0500, 1700	Sea Area Forecasts for next 24h (In Portuguese)	Charcot, Josephine, Finisterre, Porto, São Vicente and Cádiz

Note 1 On W coast of Scotland, Malin Head may give better reception.
Note 2 Monsanto broadcasts two separate forecasts in each slot, the second is for Madeira, Casablanca and Agadir.

ENGLAND – SOUTH COAST

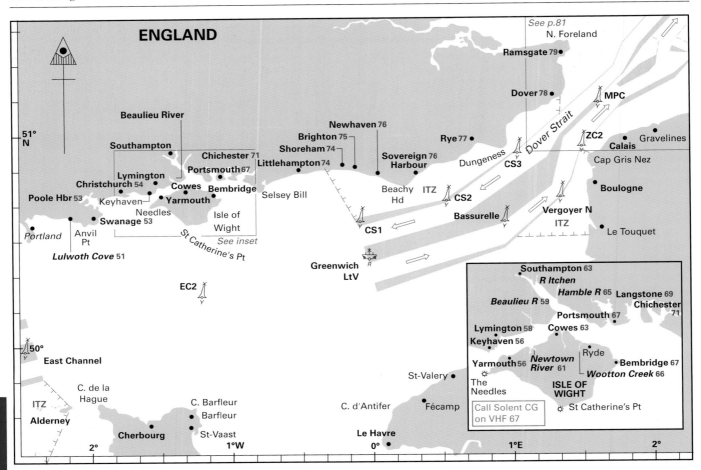

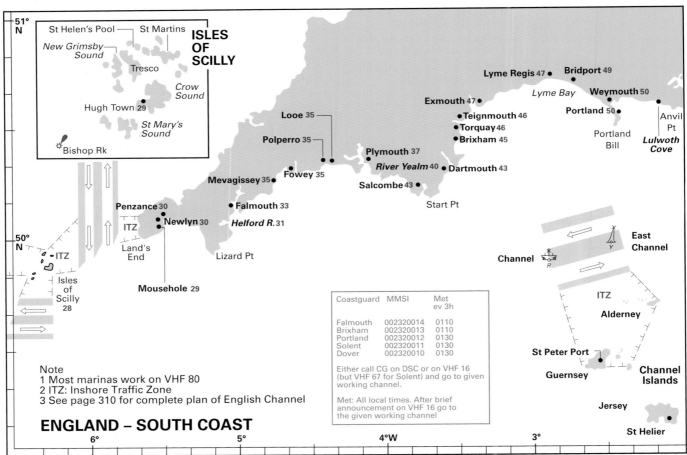

Note
1 Most marinas work on VHF 80
2 ITZ: Inshore Traffic Zone
3 See page 310 for complete plan of English Channel

Coastguard	MMSI	Met ev 3h
Falmouth	002320014	0110
Brixham	002320013	0110
Portland	002320012	0130
Solent	002320011	0130
Dover	002320010	0130

Either call CG on DSC or on VHF 16 (but VHF 67 for Solent) and go to given working channel.

Met: All local times. After brief announcement on VHF 16 go to the given working channel

ENGLAND – SOUTH COAST

Page references are shown after locations, for example:
Falmouth 33. Bold type indicates that it is accompanied by a plan.
Italics are used for rivers, lochs, bays, seas etc.

England – South Coast
Isles of Scilly to Ramsgate

The S coast of England has a great variety of beautiful sailing areas varying from the exposed and rugged W parts with their sheltered and extensive rivers and relatively little commercial traffic to the very popular and attractive Solent, busy with ships, cruising boats and yacht racing. Here, though the waters are more sheltered, there are strong tidal streams. Care has to be taken when negotiating unfamiliar port entrances as the Solent has interesting tidal stands in parts. There are many yacht havens some of which can become overcrowded at weekends at the height of the season. E of the Solent the ports are well spaced, there are fewer boats and the chalk cliff scenery is spectacular. The prevailing winds are from the SW and the Channel generates its own particular sort of choppy seas in strong winds. When going from one area to another careful plans need to be made to negotiate the headlands with their tidal gates and take advantage of the tidal streams which can run fast, bearing in mind that the sea may become treacherous in wind over tide conditions.

PASSAGES AROUND LAND'S END

Pedn-an-Laaz means the end of the earth and is appropriate to this inhospitable but beautiful, most westerly point of mainland England. It is usually a lee shore. It has many rocks in addition to the Longships. To the north one cannot pass inside the Brisons and to the south the passage inshore of Runnel Stone is not recommended. Weather forecasts are less reliable here than elsewhere and SE winds can quickly veer to the W and freshen. It is also a tidal gate, especially if southbound

Carn Brae, the most westerly of the Longships on which the LtHo stands, is steep to on its seaward side and the TSS lies 3M offshore. Kettle's Bottom (dr 5·2m) lies halfway between the lt ho and the shore. There is a

GENERAL

Some useful reference books:
The Shell Channel Pilot Tom Cunliffe (Imray)
British Admiralty Channel Pilot NP 27

For more details refer to:
Isles of Scilly RCC Pilotage Foundation (Imray)
The West Country Carlos Rojas & Susan Kemp-Wheeler (Imray)
West Country Cruising Mark Fishwick (Wiley Nautical)

passage ½M wide between Kettle's Bottom and a rock, The Peel, close to shore. N (high) Brison just open W of S (low) Brison on 001° leads through. The shore should be given a berth of 400m and Kettle's Bottom one of 100m, almost awash at HW, Kettle's Bottom can always be identified by swell breaking on it. The Longships Passage should not be attempted in bad weather and never at night.

Working the tides which run at up to 4kn.

Northbound. This is the easier direction. W of Longships the tide turns N at HW Dover +0100 (HW Devonport –0500 approx). However, close inshore it turns much earlier. If off Runnelstone S card Lt buoy 3hrs before HW Dover one has a fair tide through the Longships Passage up to the Brisons in time to catch the NE going stream along the N Cornwall coast. 10hrs of fair tide can be worked. Locking out of Penzance up to 1hr after local HW one can reach Padstow to lock in at HW. Alternatively, if bound further NE the contrary tide can be dodged in Widemouth Bay to catch the next fair tide at Hartland Pt. From Falmouth it is more difficult as slack water off Lizard Pt is at HW Dover ±0300 and it is 18M to Runnel Stone buoy although tides in Mount's Bay are weak. If late the tide in the Longships Passage will be contrary. When passing W of

Longships on a N going tide you will be carried towards the Lt ho while making an offing. This can be very disconcerting at night after you lose sight of Tater Du Lt Ho and cannot get a cross bearing.

Southbound. Timing is more critical. Tides are weak off the N Cornwall coast but strengthen W of St Ives. Leaving St Ives on the first of the SW stream the tidal gate will shut on you off Gwennap Hd. You need to be there at HW Dover +0500 (HW Devonport –0100) to have 2hrs of fair tide to get into Mount's Bay. Leave St Ives at HW Dover (HW Devonport +0600) keeping well inshore to take advantage of a SW going eddy but avoiding the rocks, especially the Wra (reef off Cape Cornwall) and passing to seaward of the Brisons. Overfalls may be encountered off Pendeen. Then, if possible, use the Longships Passage. If bound from Milford Haven to W Brittany and making a landfall well to the west the timing is less crucial.

ISLES OF SCILLY TO PENZANCE

Charts BA 2565, 1148, 777, SC 5603;
Imray 2400, C7, C10

Passage lights	BA No
Bishop Rock Fl(2)15s44m20M	0002
Round Is Fl.10s55m18M Horn(4)60s	0018
Peninnis Head Fl.20s36m9M	0006
Seven Stones LtV Fl(3)30s15M Horn(3)60s Racon(O) (–––)	0020
Longships Fl(2)WR.10s35m15/11M Horn 10s	0028
Wolf Rk Fl.15s34m16M Horn 30s Racon(T) (–)	0030
Tater-Du Fl(3)15s34m20M+F.R (over Runnel Stone)	0032

Streams related to HW Dover

Scilly Is to Land's End +0100NW, +0300N; +0500NE; –0400SSE; –0100SSW

Runnelstone –0600 to –0300E; –0300 to +0600NW

Land's End HWD N; –0500S

When going E from the Scillies to Penzance make for the Wolf Rock LtHo, deep water up to ½M off on all sides. Then pass well S of the Runnel Stone, S card Lt buoy liable to drift, and follow the coast at least 1M offshore.

England South Coast: Isles of Scilly to Ramsgate distances (miles)

	Hugh Town	Newlyn	Lizard (2M S)	Falmouth	Fowey	Plymouth BW	Salcombe	Start Point	Dartmouth	Portland Hbr	Poole	Yarmouth	Portsmouth	St Catherine's	Nab Tower	Chichester	Brighton	Beachy Head	Dungeness	Dover	Ramsgate
Hugh Town	0																				
Newlyn	41	0																			
Lizard (2M S)	44	18	0																		
Falmouth	63	25	18	0																	
Fowey	51	49	34	20	0																
Plymouth BW	85	68	47	38	22	0															
Salcombe	104	77	60	50	36	20	0														
Start Point	108	81	63	55	41	25	7	0													
Dartmouth	117	90	73	65	50	35	16	9	0												
Portland Hbr	164	137	103	111	97	81	63	56	53	0											
Poole	185	157	140	131	117	102	79	77	72	32	0										
Yarmouth	202	169	148	144	129	114	95	88	84	38	20	0									
Portsmouth	219	186	165	161	146	131	112	105	101	55	37	17	0								
St Catherine's	200	171	155	147	132	117	99	92	88	42	26	19	20	0							
Nab Tower	215	188	170	162	148	132	114	107	103	57	42	35	10	15	0						
Chichester	221	192	171	167	152	137	118	112	108	62	43	24	10	22	7	0					
Brighton	248	220	204	196	181	166	147	140	137	91	75	64	41	49	33	41	0				
Beachy Head	260	232	215	208	193	178	159	152	149	102	87	69	54	60	46	48	15	0			
Dungeness	290	261	245	237	223	208	190	183	179	133	117	100	84	90	77	79	46	31	0		
Dover	308	279	263	255	241	226	208	201	197	151	135	118	102	108	95	97	64	48	18	0	
Ramsgate	325	296	280	272	257	242	224	217	213	167	151	134	118	125	111	113	80	65	33	15	0

ENGLAND – SOUTH COAST

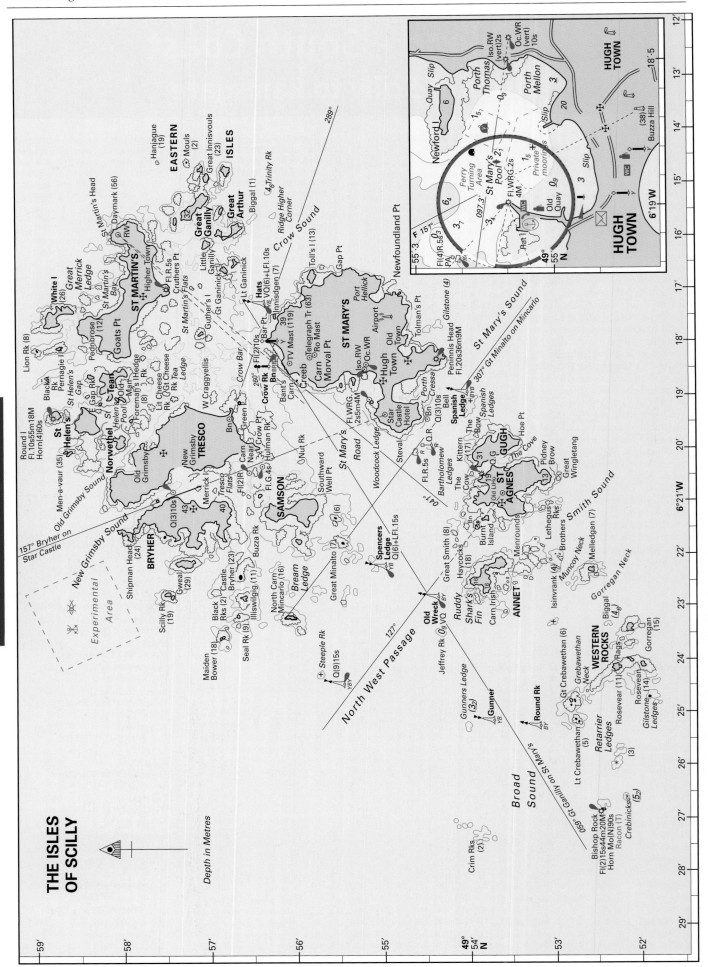

THE ISLES OF SCILLY

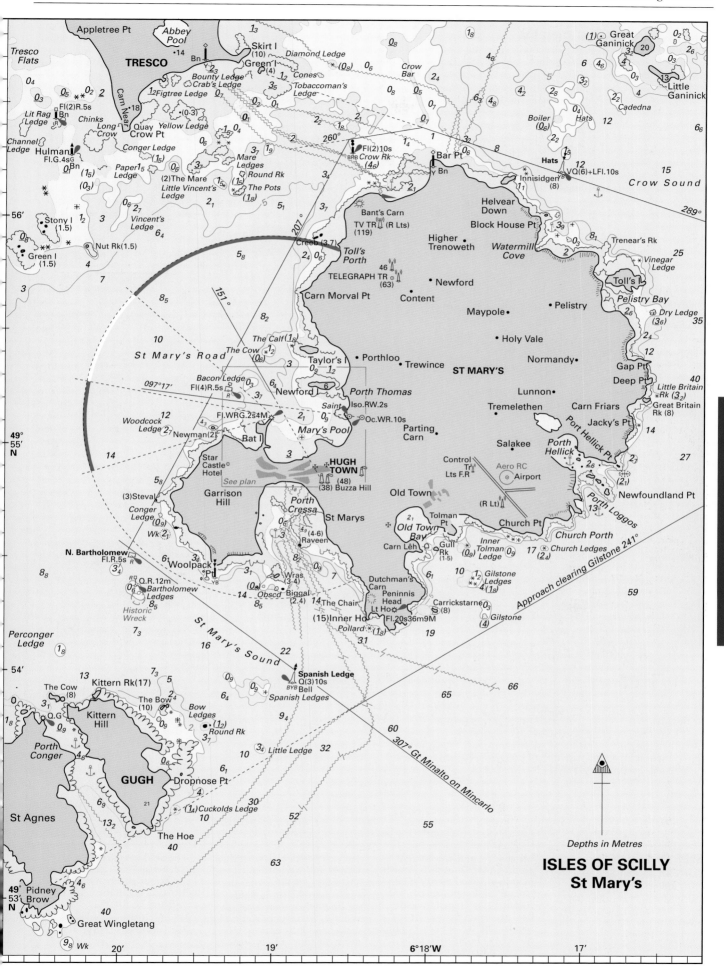

ISLES OF SCILLY
St Mary's

Depths in Metres

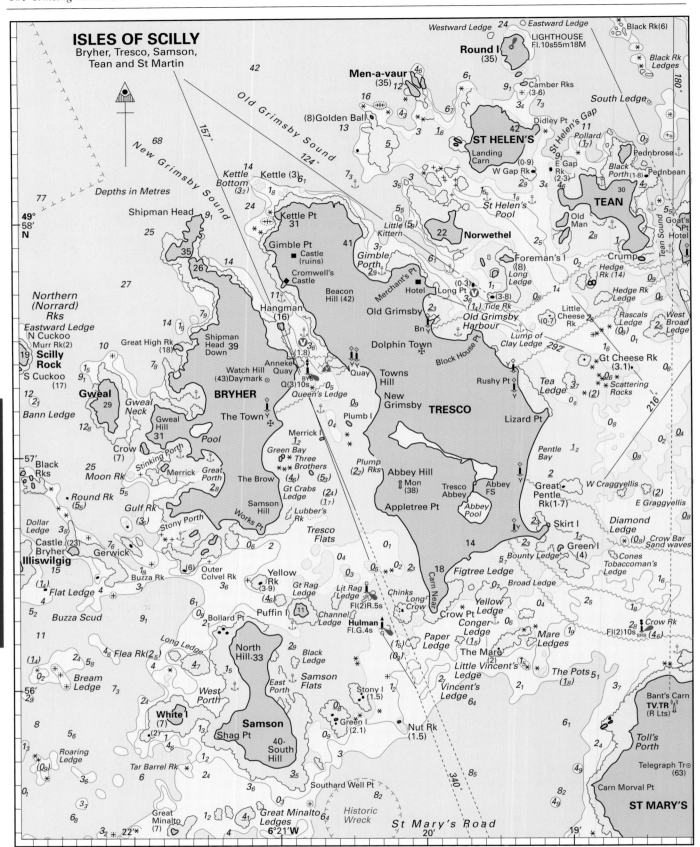

ISLES OF SCILLY
Bryher, Tresco, Samson,
Tean and St Martin

ENGLAND – SOUTH COAST

ISLES OF SCILLY

Charts BA 34, 883, SC 5603;
Imray 2400, C7, C10

HW St Mary's Plymouth –0055

MHWS	MHWN	MLWN	MLWS
5·7m	4·3m	2·0m	0·7m

The Isles of Scilly are made up of five inhabited islands and many smaller islets and rocky outcrops. They are exposed, low lying, the highest land being 46m, and are situated about 28M SW of the Cornish mainland. Their rotary tidal streams and exposure to Atlantic swell mean they are liable to rough seas in strong winds. The weather can change quickly so boats need to be prepared to change their anchorage fast, as none of the anchorages are protected from all directions. However, they are well worth a visit for their beauty and wild life.

The Isles of Scilly are most easily approached in light weather when there is good visibility in daylight so that Ldg marks and lobster pots are more obvious. The intricacies of navigating all the islands are well covered in the pilot books mentioned above.

The tidal streams are rotary clockwise ¾ to 1½kn but more at various points. Off St Martin's Head there is a tide rip to S and SE for 3M.

DS off Gilstone: Dover +0245 NE 1·8kn; –0415 SW 2·5kn.

St Mary's Road: Dover +0145E –0545W (varies between SW and NW), both about 1kn.

St Mary's Sound: Dover +0245SE; –0400NW, both 2kn.

Crow Sound: weak and irregular except from Dover −0145 to +0515 when it runs SE at first, changing through E to N; max 1·4kn at 0245 NE.

New Grimsby Harbour: Dover −0400N; +0040S, both 1kn. Off the entrance: +0115E; −0515W, both 2½kn.

N of Round Is, streams are up to 4kn ½M off.

Approaches Principal landmarks are:
St Mary's Is – TV mast 118m, radio masts and telegraph tr 63m, and Peninnis Head LtHo (W circular iron 36m with a black cupola). There is an aero radio bn on St Mary's, 49°54'·8N 6°17'·4W, 321kHz continuous, call sign STM, range 15M. St Agnes is disused LtHo (W stone 23m). Bishop Rock LtHo (grey circular 44m). Round Is LtHo (W circular 55m). St Martin's Is daymark (R & W horizontal bands 56m). From E, St Martin's daymark comes up first; from S, St Mary's TV mast.

Main approaches arranged in clockwise order:
From SE – St Mary's Sound.
From S – Smith's Sound W of St Agnes. Not recommended because of unmarked dangers, distant Ldg marks and difficulty in identifying recognisable points for fixing a position.
From SW – Broad Sound close N of Bishop Rock.
From W – North Channel between Annet and Mincarlo.
From NNW
• to New Grimsby Harbour, between Bryher and Tresco.
• to Old Grimsby Harbour on NE side of Tresco.
From N – E of Round Is to St Helen's Pool and Old Grimsby.
From E – Crow Sound.

Approach and Entrance
• **St Mary's Sound** Easiest, buoyed but beware of set to stb and unlit lobster pot markers. Exposed in any SW swell. Round S of St Mary's keeping ½M off Tolman Point to clear Gilstone; close round Peninnis Head Fl.20s leaving Spanish Ledge (E card) and Bartholomew Ledge Fl.R.5s to port with N Carn of Mincarlo in line with W extreme of Gt Minalto 308° until NW corner of St Mary's is in line with St Martin's daymark; follow this line (040°) and enter St Mary's Pool on line 097° of Lt bns, F.R, front white topmark, rear orange X.
• **Broad Sound** Buoyed, unlit. Enter 4ca N of Bishop Rock LtHo and S of Flemings Ledge. Ldg line 059° Gt Gannilly summit (8½M off) just open N of Bants Carn.
• **North Channel** Cross tide, outlying rks. Keep on approach Ldg line, 127° keeping St Agnes

old LtHo in line with Tins Walbert bn until on Ldg line for Broad Sound (*see above*).
• **New Grimsby Sound** Beware cross stream in approach. Round Is Lt is 1½M to port (Ro Bn), otherwise unlit. Keep the W side of Hangman Is (conspic pinnacle 19m) in line with Star Castle on St Mary's 157°.
• **Old Grimsby Sound** Overfalls exist over Kettle Bottom off the point between Old and New Grimsby Sounds and there are strong cross streams in approach, unbuoyed and unlit. From N of Tresco steer 124° for mid-pt between Norwethel and Merchants Point. Beware the Little Kittern (dries 1·9m). Past Merchants Point beware Tide Rock.
• **St Helen's Gap** Beware cross stream in approach. Leave Round Is 1¼ca to W and keep Star Castle in line with E Gap Rock (2m) 182° until past E extreme of St Helen's Is whence steer 201° between E and W Gap Rks into St Helen's Pool.
• **Crow Sound** Crow Bar dries 0·7m 2ca N of Bar Pt, but has 1m to S, unlit. Leave Hats S card buoy close to stb and clear Bar Pt by 1ca; pass 50m either side of Crow bn Fl(2)10s. Follow island round to pass between Bacon and Cow ledges (latter dries 0·6m) by keeping B vert strip on white shelter on promenade in line with Buzza Tr on skyline 151°. This approach is sheltered from the W, with a good anchorage at Watermill Cove to await the tide to get round to Hugh Town.

Interior channels
• St Mary's to New Grimsby. Leave 2hrs after LW for 1·3m draught and at half flood for 1·8m. Leave Nut Rock to port and Hulman Bn 50m to stb until Merrick Is is in line with right-hand edge of Hangman Is. On this transit keep Little Rag Ledge Bn (E of Great Rag Ledge) to port, Chink Rks to stb, Gt Crabs Ledge to port, Plump Rocks to stb, Merrick Is to port and Plumb Is to stb, direction generally 340° but varies.
• To Old Grimsby. At half tide steer on back bearing of Crow Bn in line with middle TV tr on St Mary's (160°) to Lizard Pt whence steer for middle of gap between Tresco and Norwethel.
• To St Helen's Pool. At half tide from Hats anchorage, N of St Mary's, steer on the centre islet of Men-a-vaur in line with the landing cairn on SW corner of St Helen's, 322°. As the anchorage nears, the islet will be obscured by the cairn.

Anchorages and Moorings
None of the following anchorages offer all round shelter, so it is important to consider wind direction, probable wind shift and direction of swell.

• **St Mary's, Hugh Town** No resident customs here but occasional visits by patrol boats. Busy in season. No anchoring is allowed in the hbr. Uncomfortable in winds SW to N. 28+10 Y visitors' moorings, (charged). Moor dinghies alongside pontoon or in the corner between old and new quays. Yachts may lie alongside St Mary's Quay, the harbourmaster will give directions. The ferry *Scillonian* comes in at 1200 and leaves at 1630 weekdays (two calls on summer Saturdays).
• **St Mary's, Porth Cressa**, W side of bay only, V mooring buoys (charged). Untenable in strong winds from SE to SW, sheltered from W through N to E, but swell possible from W or ESE. Markers indicate submarine power cable.
• **St Mary's, Watermill Cove** Sheltered from S through W to NW.
• **New Grimsby Harbour** Best and most sheltered anchorage. Sheltered SSW through W to NW and from NNE through E to SSE. Submarine cables. 22 visitors' moorings (charged) are encroaching on the anchorage. Beware weed when anchoring.
• **Old Grimsby** Sheltered from SSW to W. Subject to swell, even from W. Strong spring tidal streams. Six visitors' moorings.
• **St Helen's Pool** Anchor astride line joining centre of Men-a-vaur to landing cairn on SW tip of St Helen's Is. Comparatively sheltered; some scend at HW.
• **St Agnes/Gugh** These two islands are connected by a bar drying 4·6m, providing anchorages to the S in the Cove for winds from WSW through N to NNE, and to the N in Porth Conger for winds from E by S to W. Bar covers at HW springs when anchorages may

be uncomfortable for HW ±0130.
• Visitors' buoys opposite the hotel in Tean Sound, W of St Martins. No charge if visiting the hotel. Beware rocky bottom if anchoring. If going ashore to St Martin's take the dinghy on to the beach leaving the quay clear.

Facilities Fuel, water and showers on quay at Hugh Town. Water also on quays at Bryher and Tresco. Toilets, showers, and community meeting room above beach at Porth Cressa. Shops at Hugh Town and stores at St Agnes, Bryher and Tresco. Pubs or hotels at Hugh Town, Tresco, Bryher, St Martin's and St Agnes.

☎/VHF HM 01720 422768. VHF 14 in working hours. Customs 22571. Coastguard 22651.

Transport By ferry from Penzance. By air from Exeter, Newquay, and Land's End to St Mary's.

Interest Exotic Tresco Abbey Gardens. Exciting gig races off St Mary's on Wednesdays and Fridays.

MOUSEHOLE

Charts BA 2345, 777, SC 5603; Imray 2400, C7, C10
HW Plymouth −0105

MHWS	MHWN
5·5m	4·6m

A small drying hbr S of Newlyn, 4m springs, 2·6m neaps, access HW±0300. 3F.R(vert) indicates hbr closed. Sand and rock. Entrance closed in S gales. Good anchorage S of entrance. Water, shops. A very picturesque hbr with an RSPB bird sanctuary close by.

☎ HM (01736) 731644.

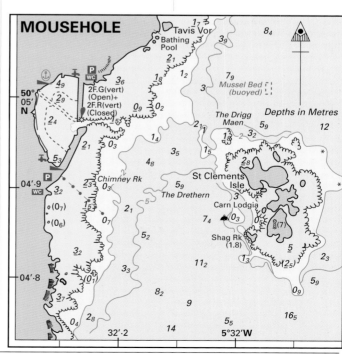

NEWLYN

Charts BA 2345, 777, SC 5603;
Imray 2400, C7

HW Plymouth –0105

MHWS	MHWN	MLWN	MLWS
5·6m	4·4m	2·0m	0·8m

From last quarter flood to first quarter ebb the tide flows NE in the N part of Mount's Bay.

For those coming from the Bristol Channel going S this is a useful port of refuge in the event of a bad weather forecast, affording protection in gales from S through W to NE. SE winds may bring in a heavy swell.

Approach From Penzance leave Gear Rock to stb and steer for pier heads. From S, leave St Clement's Is ½M to port, steer N with Low Lee E card Lt buoy, to port until LtHo on S arm of hbr bears 305°, which course clears Carn Base Rks. By night, keep in W sector of Penzance LtHo (Fl.WR.5s 268°-W-345°) until Newlyn Lt (Fl.5s) bears 305°.

Note W sectors of Penzance and Newlyn are Fl.5s.

Entrance Beware of emerging fishing boats. Turn to stb, leaving to port R spar buoy at end of slipway.

Berthing
• Anchor outside in Gwavas Lake, N of end of North Pier; good holding and sheltered in W winds.
• Berth along W side of central pier, (Mary Williams Pier) rather than alongside Northern Pier which is used by fishing boats which may leave at a very early hour. New pontoon is primarily for fishing vessels. Visiting yachts usually berth on two outer fingers. Crowded in summer.

Facilities Fuel from tanker; water on quays. Fisherman's Mission at root of N pier open to yachtsmen (not weekends). Shops. EC Wednesday. Showers.

☎ /VHF HM 01736 362523. VHF 12.

PENZANCE

Charts BA 2345, 777, SC5603;
Imray 2400, C7, C10

HW Plymouth –0105

MHWS	MHWN	MLWN	MLWS
5·6m	4·4m	2·0m	0·8m

Tide flows NE in N part of Mount's Bay from last quarter flood to first quarter ebb.

There is a wet dock with sheltered berths open HW–0200 to HW+0100 (yachts welcome), an outer drying hbr and outside anchorage. Entrance to drying hbr dangerous in strong S or SE winds.

Approach From the E leave Mountamopus S card buoy to stb. From W clear Low Lee E card Lt buoy and Carn Base Rks off Penlee Pt, the Gear Rock (bn) and the Battery Rocks to SW of South Pier. At night keep in W sector (268°-345°) of Lt Fl.WR.5s on S pier head. Do not confuse with Lt Fl.5s on S pier at Newlyn.

Signals
3F.G(vert) Lts – gates open.
3F.R(vert) Lts – gates closed.
Signal mast on N side of dock entrance.

Entrance Keep clear of Cressar Rocks to N of approach and be prepared to stand off if ship arrival or departure is imminent. When waiting for dock opening either anchor (in fair weather) E of end of Albert Pier, or wait in tidal hbr, or alongside LtHo pier if not required by the *Scillonian*. In bad weather and at weekends the ship may use the Albert Pier, but her normal berth is alongside the LtHo pier and she occupies this only from 1900–0930 and on Saturdays in summer from 1230–1400. The berth is therefore usually available while awaiting the opening of the dock gates between 1000 and 1830. There is 1·8m alongside between the LtHo and the ladder halfway along the pier. The S wall is swept by seas in S and SE gales and it may not be possible to

open the dock gates in winds of storm force from those directions. Otherwise they open HW–0200 to HW+0100. 10 R visitors' waiting buoys on the S side of the S pier (seasonal).

Berthing
• Anchor in fair weather, with winds SW–W–N, 2ca or more off the LtHo pier, clear of fairway but not E of LtHo because of swell.
• Drying moorings may be available in tidal hbr.
• Visitors alongside berths in wet dock.
• 10 R visitors' moorings on S side of pier.

Facilities Diesel from hbr staff day or night when dock gates are open. Water on quay. Chandlery and 10-ton crane. All facilities, incl cycle hire.

Transport Rly, buses to Land's End, St Ives. Ferry and Skybus flights to Isles of Scilly.

☎ /VHF HM 01736 366113. VHF 12 *Penzance Harbour*, during office hours and HW–0200 to HW+0100.

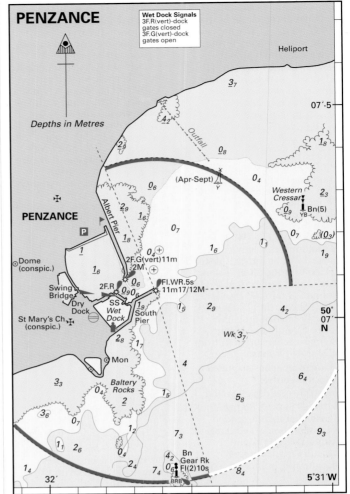

ST MICHAEL'S MOUNT

Charts BA 2345, 777, SC 5603;
Imray 2400, C7, C10

HW Plymouth –0105

MHWS	MHWN	MLWN	MLWS
5·6m	4·4m	2·0m	0·8m

The outline of St Michael's Mount, a drying hbr, is a distinctive landmark in Mount's Bay.

Approach The E and N sides are foul with shoals so the approach should be made either from the S or SW. Give the Mount an offing of 1½ca to clear Maltman Rock, (dr 0·9m), Guthen Rock and the obstruction to its N, until E side of Chapel Rock is in line with the Marazion clock tr on 053°. From the W, avoid Outer Penzeath Rk (awash at LAT) ½M to W, and the Great Hogus (dr 4·9m) 1ca NW of the W pier head.

Entrance The ferries berth alongside to the E of the hbr mouth in the deepest water. There are many small fishing boat moorings in the hbr.

Berthing Good anchorage in offshore wind 1–1½ca W of W arm of hbr (or, with permission, visitors berth alongside the N end of the W arm to dry out).

☎ HM 01736 710265.

Interest Beautiful NT property and garden with café.

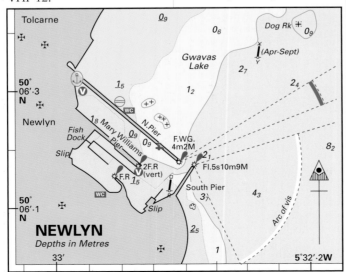

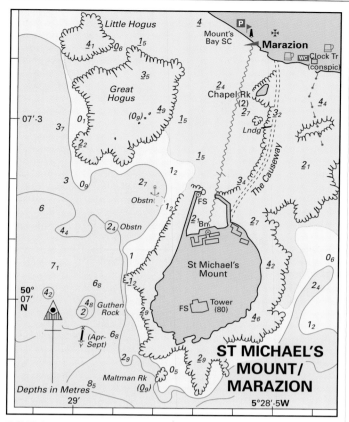

ST MICHAEL'S MOUNT/ MARAZION

Depths in Metres

PENZANCE TO FALMOUTH

Charts BA 777; Imray 2400, C7

Passage Lights	*BA No*
Lizard	0060
Fl.3s70m26M Horn 30s	
St Anthony Hd	0062
Iso.WR.15s22m16/14M Horn 30s	

Streams related to HW Dover

Mount's Bay (middle): rotary clockwise. –0600E; +0030W (weak)

Lizard –0330W; +0200E

Lizard to Falmouth –0300 SW; +0300 to –0400 NE

Bound to Falmouth from Mount's Bay it is desirable to reach the Lizard at the turn of the tide to the E because the ebb stream out of Falmouth makes progress slow. Avoid the Boa, an 11m shoal 3½M W of the Lizard LtHo, in strong SW winds because of breaking seas. Off the Lizard dangers extend ½M to seaward, and a race extends to the S and SE for 3M. The violence of the seas varies with the tide and wind, but it is particularly bad in strong westerlies against an ebb tide. In bad weather keep at least 3–4M offshore. Otherwise, to clear Lizard dangers keep Godolphin Hill open of Rill Head, 337°, until Lowland Point opens E of Black Head, 036°.

Black Head should be cleared by ½M and the Manacles E card Lt buoy given a wide berth to seaward. In E winds a confused sea builds up between Black Head and the Manacles; with

the flood tide a race may develop, dangerous at springs. In such conditions if heading for Falmouth it is best to keep about 4M off Black Head and then steer N, not steering for Falmouth until due S of St Anthony Lt.

From the Manacles to Helford River and Falmouth the passage is straightforward.

Anchorages

Loe Pool Good anchorage ¾M SSW of Pool. There is no navigable water between the sea and the Pool.

Mullion Good anchorage in E wind N of the island.

Housel Bay between Lizard Pt and Bass Pt, 6ca ENE. Large hotel conspic at head. Two RW striped bns on Bass Pt bear 292°.

Parn Voose Balk Bn RW mast, W diamond top, at head of cove in line with a W patch 4½ca SSE bears 325°. This transit's intersection with 292° transit of Bass Point bns marks Vrogue Rk.

Cadgwith Cove SW of lifeboat station at Kilcobben Cove. (N.B. It is imperative to get out to sea from the above three anchorages if onshore wind is expected.)

Coverack Cove has a small drying harbour protected by a pier extending NW from Dolor Point. Anchorage possible in offshore winds ENE of the pier.

Porthoustock Cove midway between Manacle Pt and Pencra Hd, ½M N with conspic RW radar tr. Beware rks awash on N side of entrance for 1ca offshore.

PORTHLEVEN

Charts BA 2345, 777, SC 5603; Imray 2400, C7, C10

HW Plymouth –0057

MHWS	MHWN	MLWN	MLWS
5·5m	4·3m	2·0m	0·8m

A drying hbr 8M NW of Lizard. Entrance closed in bad weather. Used mainly by small fishing boats but room for a few yachts. 3·6m on sill at springs, 2·7m at neaps. Visitors' berth is along E quay immediately to stb. Access HW±0300. Water, shops, boat and engine repairs.

☎ 01326 574270.

HELFORD RIVER

Charts BA 147, 154, SC 5603; Imray 2400, C7, C10

HW Plymouth –0032

MHWS	MHWN	MLWN	MLWS
5·3m	4·2m	1·9m	0·6m

A sheltered river, except in E winds, with several creeks, navigable to Gweek at the top of the tide, 4½M within entrance.

Approach from NE: to clear the Gedges keep Pennance Point well open of Rosemullion Head until Bosahan Point on S side of the entrance is well open of Mawnan Shear on N side. From S, bring N extremity of the point, ¼M NNW of Helford Point, just open of Bosahan Point, 270°.

Entrance is between Rosemullion Head in N and Nare Point in S. G con buoy (seasonal) lies about 1ca SE of the Gedges (August Rock). Give Nare Pt a wide berth at all states of the tide. Keep Helford Pt open of Bosahan Pt to clear a reef off the E end of the latter. To port a N card buoy marks the Voose, a drying ledge 1M

WNW of Dennis Head. NW of the Bosahan Narrows a G con buoy is moored on the edge of the N bank; it is difficult to see among moored craft.

Gillan Creek is entered S of Dennis Head. Enter to N of E card buoy, midway between the buoy and Dennis Hd. The buoy marks a rock (dries 1m) almost in the centre of the entrance.

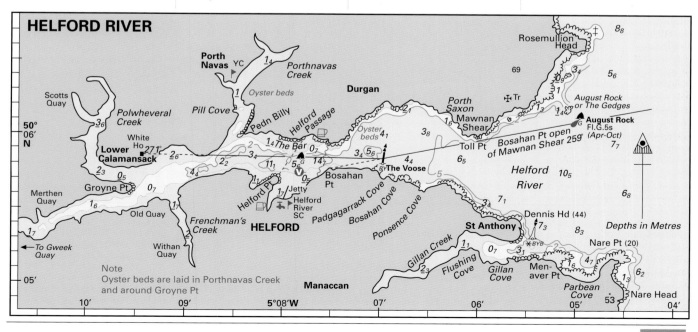

HELFORD RIVER

Note
Oyster beds are laid in Porthnavas Creek and around Groyne Pt

Depths in Metres

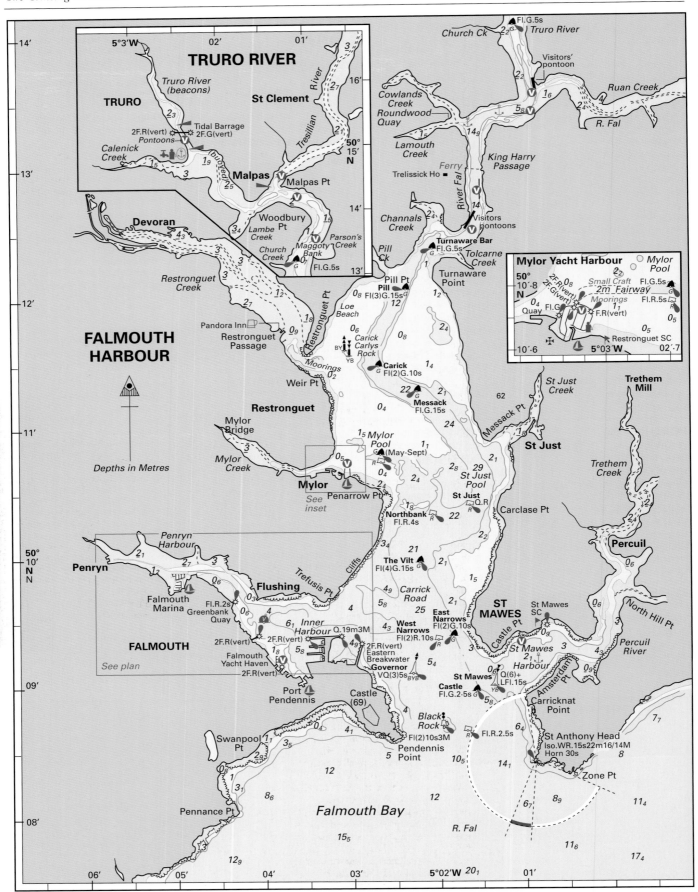

ENGLAND – SOUTH COAST

The passage S of the buoy is not
recommended without local
knowledge, due to off-lying rks.

Berthing
Oyster beds lie in river and
creeks. Anchor
• Off Durgan or Grebe Rocks,

2½–3½m, disturbed in S to E
winds; restricted due to eelgrass
under water.
• Off Helford, 5½–11m, among
or at W end of moorings; very
limited room, strong tide. Edge
of mud across Penarvon Cove

(W of Helford Point) is steep-to.
• Near entrance to Navas Creek
along the N shore out of the
tide, 1¾m or more.
Uncomfortable if far out in the
stream in fresh E or W winds.
Holding poor W of the entrance,

better to E, inshore of moorings.
• Quiet anchorage inside Navas
Creek, among moorings, in
Abraham's Bosom pool, 2m,
but space very limited. NB
0·9m bar at entrance. Land at
Oyster Fisheries Quay. No

anchoring in River W of Navas Creek because of oyster beds.
• Gweek Quay. Dries; hard level bottom (beyond plan).
• Gillan Creek. Pool with 1½–2m inside the entrance but no shelter in E winds unless on the mud 1M up the creek. There is 1½–3m either side of and just beyond the mid-channel rk, shoaling rapidly to under 1m.

Moorings Visitors' moorings (those with green pick-up buoys) off Helford. Consult Sailaway, St Anthony, for Gillan Creek.

The river may be explored at HW to Gweek, Mawgan and Polwheveral.

Facilities Fuel (not in bulk) and water at St Anthony (Sailaway), Gillan Creek and at Porth Navas YC. Water at Durgan and Helford River SC. Stores at Helford. Landing at pontoon on Helford Pt (charge) or at SC.

☾/VHF
Moorings 01326 250749, VHF 80, M.

FALMOUTH AND TRURO RIVER

Charts BA 18, 32, 154, SC 5602; Imray 2400, Y58, C6, C10

HW Plymouth –0035

DS Dover –0300SW +0300NE

Falmouth

MHWS	MHWN	MLWN	MLWS
5·4m	4·3m	2·1	0·8m

Truro

MHWS	MHWN
3·5m	2·4 (dries)

The Fal estuary provides excellent shelter and beautiful anchorages, with several drying creeks and navigation at HW via Truro River to Truro.

Approach From E, St Anthony Lt is not visible until it bears NW. From SW, coast between Pennance and Pendennis Pts has drying rks up to 1ca from shore.

Entrance is divided into two channels by Black Rock conspic B bn and red can Lt buoy. When this rock is covered there is 2·7m over the banks inside the river as far as Trelissick.

Inner Harbour, Falmouth and Penryn River The river continues 1M to W above Falmouth to Penryn but there are moorings on the mudflats on both sides of the channel. Above the wharf at Boyer's Cellars the river dries. At Penryn, Town Quay has 4·3 to 3·0m at HW.

Anchorage Anchor off Custom House Quay, close NE of Visitors Yacht Haven (buoy anchor and keep clear of approach to docks).

Moorings
• There is one trot of bookable Harbour Authority moorings for visitors between Greenbank Quay and Prince of Wales Pier, green buoys marked K1 to K7 and T3 to T5.
• RCYC have some buoys marked for visitors; others may be had from local yards.

Berthing Marinas at Falmouth: Visitors Yacht Haven, North Quay: 40 yachts on pontoons, 1·5–2·5m; best for shopping in town, water and short stays. Port Pendennis marina has pontoons in 3m outside a locked basin, access HW±0300. No fuel available in marina. Yacht Marina, North Parade, ½M above Greenbank Quay: 30 pontoon berths for visitors; dredged access channel 2m, Lt buoys Q; drying pipeline across middle of basin – take outside berth and enquire. Free standing pontoon off entrance.

Landing places at Custom House Quay or Visitors Yacht Haven, Fish Strand Quay, Prince of Wales Pier, R Cornwall YC and Greenbank Quay all on S side of the channel (do not leave dinghies moored at Custom House Quay or Prince of Wales Pier); and at Old and New Quays at Flushing on the N side. Hard at Flushing Quay and several good ones both sides of hbr.

St Mawes Creek: from Castle G con buoy, leave St Mawes S card buoy (Lugo Rock) well to port. At half tide there is not less than 1·8m between the buoy and the Point. There is about 1·2m up to Porthcuel but channel is tortuous, unmarked, with many moorings and oyster beds off both banks.

Anchorage Anchor off two beaches beyond the pier, in 2m or more. In SW wind there is good shelter round Amsterdam Point clear of moorings, dries. Avoid Black Rock close inshore abreast N end of wood on E side.

St Mawes SC has moorings also HM operates visitors' buoys. Landing on slipway at SC at Polvarth except LWS.

St Just Creek Good anchorage in 3m inside Messack Point under N shore.

Mylor Creek Navigable to Mylor Br by dinghy. Mylor Yacht Harbour has 30 moorings and four pontoon berths for visitors.

Restronguet Creek Anchor off entrance; no room inside. Landing at **Ferry Ho** or **Pandora Inn** pontoon. Devoran (1½M) may be reached by dinghy on the tide.

Truro River There is plenty of water up to Malpas except at Maggoty Bank (G con buoy). Concrete mooring clumps, drying, are reported near the W bank 3ca S of the ferry at King Harry Passage. They are marked by a W post. Malpas is the limit of LW navigation. With a draught of less than 3m (springs) or 2m (neaps), Truro can be reached on the tide following the lit buoyed channel.

Flood Barrier in the approaches to Truro closes (2F.R Lts) when very high tides (5·6m Falmouth datum) are accompanied by a tidal surge or heavy river flood water. Gates will then be closed to all traffic for about HW±0230; waiting pontoon on downstream end of gate.

Berthing
• Off Loe beach. Good, clean, quiet anchorage in 2m inshore off Loe Vean. Summer moorings are laid all the way between Restronguet and Loe Beach: anchor outside these. Riding Lt necessary.
• Channels Creek.
• Above King Harry Ferry off the entrance to Cowlands Creek on the N side.
• Off the mouth of the River Fal (Ruan Creek) where it joins River Truro near Tregothnan. Beware of drying concrete blocks close inshore off ruined cottage on N side of entrance to Ruan Creek.
• On Maggoty Bank according to tide.

Moorings off thatched restaurant at Tolverne, opposite entrance to Cowlands Creek; four Carrick visitors' buoys off Malpas Point; and at Malpas Marine. Visitors' pontoons on W side of channel N of Turnaware Pt at (50°12′N), and off E bank just N of entrance to Ruan Creek. Also

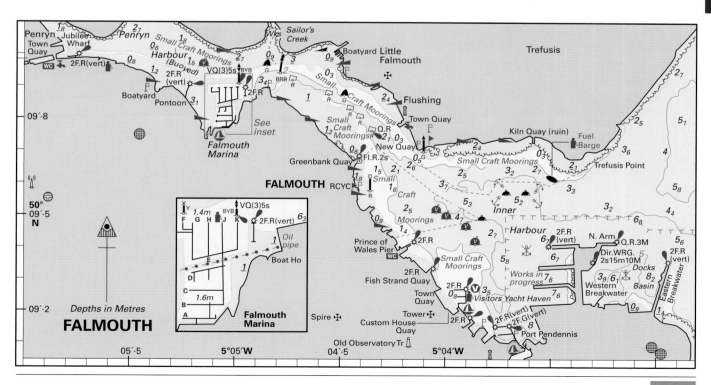

FALMOUTH

Depths in Metres

Falmouth Marina

ENGLAND – SOUTH COAST

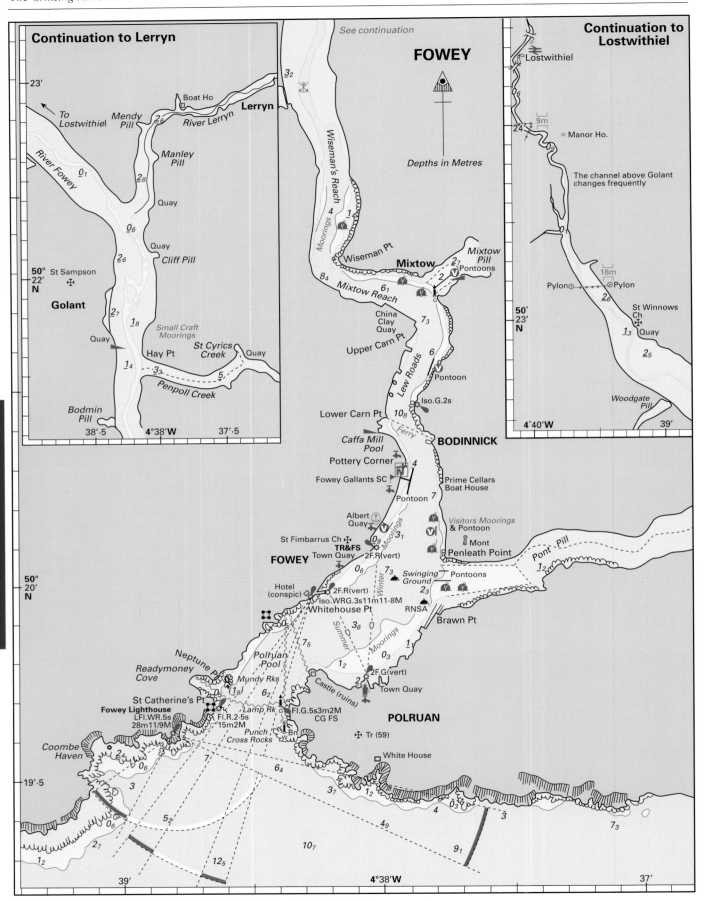

Continuation to Lerryn

To Lostwithiel
23′
Boat Ho
Mendy Pill
Lerryn
River Lerryn
Manley Pill
River Fowey
Quay
0₁
0₆
2₆
Cliff Pill
2₈
50° 22′ N
St Sampson
Golant
Quay
2₇
1₈
Quay
Hay Pt
St Cyrics Creek
Quay
Small Craft Moorings
1₄
3₃
5₃
Penpoll Creek
Bodmin Pill
38′·5
37′·5
4°38′W

Continuation to Lostwithiel

Lostwithiel
0₆
24′
9m
Manor Ho.
The channel above Golant changes frequently
18m
Pylon
Pylon
2₆
50° 23′ N
St Winnows Ch
1₃
Quay
2₅
Woodgate Pill
4°40′W
39′

FOWEY

Depths in Metres

See continuation

3₂

Wiseman's Reach
Moorings
4
1₄
Wiseman Pt
8₄
Mixtow Reach
Mixtow
Mixtow Pill Pontoons
2₇
2
6₁
7₃
China Clay Quay
Upper Carn Pt
Lew Roads
6
Pontoon
Iso.G.2s
Lower Carn Pt
10₈
Ferry
BODINNICK
Caffa Mill Pool
Pottery Corner
4
Fowey Gallants SC
Prime Cellars Boat House
Pontoon
7
Albert Quay
Moorings
3₁
Visitors Moorings & Pontoon
Mont
Penleath Point
St Fimbarrus Ch
0₉
TR&FS
FOWEY
Town Quay
2F.R(vert)
Pont Pill
1₂
0₆
7₃
Swinging Ground
Pontoons
2₃
Hotel (conspic)
2F.R(vert)
Iso.WRG.3s11m11-8M
Whitehouse Pt
RNSA
Brawn Pt
Winter Moorings
Summer Moorings
3₆
0₃
1₁
7₅
1₂
Neptune Pt
Polruan Pool
Readymoney Cove
Mundy Rks
(1₈)
6₂
2F.G(vert)
Castle (ruins)
2
Town Quay
St Catherine's Pt
Lamp Rk
Fl.G.5s3m2M CG FS
POLRUAN
Fowey Lighthouse
LFl.WR.5s 28m11/9M
Fl.R.2·5s 15m2M
Punch Cross Rocks
Bn
Tr (59)
Coombe Haven
2₄
0₆
White House
3
6₄
3₇
1₂
2₇
5₂
7
12₅
6₄
4₉
10₇
4
0₃
3
9₁
7₃
1₂
19′·5
39′
4°38′W
37′

---

at W of channel at Woodbury Point and Malpas.

Mooring possible alongside Town and Worths quays and Garras Wharf at Truro; dries, soft mud.

Facilities Fuel and water at Falmouth Yacht Haven and Yacht Marina, Falmouth Boat Const Co, Mylor Yacht Hbr. Water at RCYC, St Mawes (tap opposite hbr steps), Porthcuel,

Truro and Malpas Marine. Sailmaker and chandler at Falmouth. When Falmouth is crowded in the season it is interesting to go to Truro at HW for water and supermarket.

☎/VHF Falmouth hbr office 01326 312285, 314379, VHF 12, 14. HM Launch VHF 12. Falmouth Visitors' Yacht Haven, deep water moorings and slipway as for hbr office. Port Pendennis Marina 211211.

FALMOUTH TO PLYMOUTH

Charts BA 1267; Imray 2400, C6, C10

Passage Lights		BA No

St Anthony Hd 0062
Iso.WR.15s22m16/14M
(R over Manacles) Horn30s

Eddystone 0098
Fl(2)10s41m17M+Iso.R.10s 110°-vis-133° Horn(1)30s

Streams related to HW Dover

Rectilinear in W, rotary clockwise in E

5M E of St Anthony Head: Dover +0300NE; –0330SW

Plymouth +0400E –0200W

Leaving Falmouth bound E, keep at least 1M offshore to clear the Bizzies, a shoal patch off Greeb Point, and the Whelps off Nare Head. In bad weather keep at least 2M off Dodman Pt (conspic stone cross) because of overfalls. There is a naval firing range off Dodman Point and Gribbin Head VHF FOST OPS Ch 74. It is 2·5M S of the point, marked by three special Y Lt buoys. If going inshore to Fowey, give a wide berth to Gwineas and Yaw Rks (E card Lt buoy) ¾M S of Chapel Point, and Cannis Rock (S card Lt buoy) 4ca SE of Gribbin Head. E-bound from Fowey keep well clear of Udder Rock (S card, bell) 3M to E, and Ranneys Rocks off Looe Is. Rame Head appears conical and has a small chapel on its summit. No off-lying dangers.

Bound up-channel offshore give a wide berth to Eddystone Lt Ho, especially in bad weather; also avoid Hand Deeps, 3¾M to NW (in F.R sector), dangerous overfalls, (W card Lt buoy).

With light winds along the shore it is often possible to carry a breeze close inshore by the Dodman and Fowey, while a direct course to Plymouth might end in being becalmed.

Bound from Fowey or Plymouth to Falmouth, there is a considerable set into the bight E of Falmouth. Remember St Anthony Lt first appears when bearing NW.

Anchorages

Gorran Haven 1M WSW of Gwineas Rock. Good anchorage in W winds in 6m.

Portmellon a small sandy cove in SW corner of Mevagissey Bay. Good anchorage in W winds, 5m.

St Austell Bay in S corner, 5m. In SW winds anchor off Ropehaven, good holding. Polkerris 1½M N of Gribbin Head: good anchorage in E winds, 5m. Water skiers; harbour dries.

Whitesand Bay (W of Rame Head) offers a long stretch of clear coast with shelving shore in which to close the land in poor visibility. Good anchorage in calm weather and offshore winds.

THE WEST COUNTRY TO L'ABERWRAC'H

See page 351.

Falmouth Yacht Marina 316620, VHF 80, 37. Falmouth Boat Const Co 374309. RCYC 311105, VHF 37 (for boatman). St Mawes SC 270686 or 270808 for moorings. Mylor Yacht Hbr 372121, VHF 37, 80. Truro hbr office 01872 272130, 224231. VHF 12 *Carrick*. Fal River patrol VHF 16, 12 *Carrick 3*. Penryn HM 01326 373352. Malpas Marine 01872 271260.

Transport Railway at Truro with branch to Falmouth. National Express coaches. Hire cars at Falmouth Yacht Haven.

Interest National Maritime Museum Cornwall on Discovery Quay at Falmouth close by Port Pendennis.

MEVAGISSEY

Charts BA 147, 148, 1267, SC 5602;
Imray 2400, C6

HW Plymouth –0017

DS Dover +0300NE –0300SW

MHWS	MHWN	MLWN	MLWS
5·4m	4·3m	2·0m	0·7m

Mevagissey is a fishing hbr which can accept only a few visiting yachts. It provides good shelter except in strong E winds when it is dangerous to approach.

Entrance Beware of Black Rk (dries 0·3m) to N of entrance 20m wide and 2·1m depth.

Outer Harbour has 2m alongside S pier with drying rocks along S and N sides. Inner Harbour dries and is reserved for fishing boats except when taking on fuel or water.

Berthing Call HM on VHF before berthing. If unable to contact moor alongside S Pier, clear of steps, and report to HM (or car park attendant in hut at root of quay). There are two sets of fore and aft moorings for visitors. Do not pick up a vacant buoy without HM's consent. There is a good anchorage in offshore winds off Porthmellon ½M S of hbr.

Supplies Fuel and water at W side of Inner Harbour. Diesel delivery to S pier. Boatyard and slip.

☎/VHF HM (01726) 843305. VHF 16, 14 (working hours); Harbourmaster out of hours 842496.

Interest Visit The Eden Project close by.

FOWEY

Charts BA 31, 148, SC 5602;
Imray 2400, C6, C10

HW Plymouth –0012
DS Dover +0400E –0200W

MHWS	MHWN	MLWN	MLWS
5·4m	4·3m	2·0m	0·6m

Fowey has many sheltered moorings for yachts but is also a commercial port used by large ships for the export of china clay. Gales from the S cause

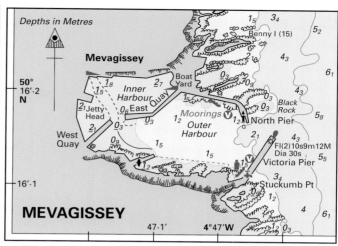

Depths in Metres

MEVAGISSEY

swell in the hbr especially on the ebb.

Approach from E: keep RWHS tr on Gribbin Hd bearing more than 273° to clear the Udder Rock 3M E of Fowey (S card bell buoy). To pass between the Udder and the mainland keep Looe Is shut in by Nealand Pt. From SW to clear the Cannis Rock, ¼M SE from Gribbin Hd daymark RWHS, keep Dodman Pt open to seaward of Gwineas until tower of Fowey Parish church is open of St Catherine Point. To pass between Cannis and the mainland (1·2m) keep the old castle on Polruan Point in line with conspic memorial on Penleath Point (048°).

At night from E keep a mile offshore and alter course N when in G sector of Whitehouse Point Lt (Iso.WRG.3s) and bring W Lt ahead steering 025°. From SW bring W Lt bearing 025° and keep in W sector.

Entrance Fowey church tr in line with Whitehouse Point, 028°, leads in mid-channel. To clear Lamp Rk on E side, keep the houses in Bodinnick shut in by Fowey town quay. To clear Mundy Rk on W side, keep the FS at the YC open of the end of Whitehouse Point breakwater. The River is often crowded with shipping and it is inadvisable to attempt to reach Wiseman's Pt without reliable power. The upper reaches can be explored by dinghy to Lostwithiel and Lerryn. Overhead cable (9m) crosses river ½M S of Lostwithiel.

Berthing Anchoring is allowed only with permission of HM. Anchoring off Polruan, clear of the swinging area, is normally allowed only when pontoons or moorings are full or with no shipping movements. Give 90m berth to large can mooring buoy, used for swinging, off Pont Pill. Avoid anchoring between Penleath Point and Wiseman's Point as large ships swing in channel. There are no floating anchorages in upper reaches.

Moorings Pontoon at Albert Quay is short-stay (max 2½hrs) and for water only. There are

W visitors' buoys, marked R or Y Visitors for craft up to 12m, and a 120ft pontoon just N of Penleath Point; pontoon and buoys are uncomfortable in SW winds above Force 4 (and removed in winter). There is more shelter in Pont Pill on trots of fore and aft moorings (each taking two boats) and another 120ft pontoon. There is a third pontoon, with the W section nominated for visitors, further upriver at Mixtow Pill (dredged), but the surrounding landing places are private except for the head of the Pill, accessible at HW. Otherwise land on slip by hotel opposite Bodinnick.

Facilities Fuel on Polruan Quay or from barge *Fowey Refueller* at entrance to Pont Pill; Water on pontoons at Albert Quay (max 2h) and S of Pottery Corner, and Polruan Quay. All stores. Showers at RFYC and Fowey Gallants YC, available 24h.

☎/VHF HM 01726 832471/2, VHF 12, 11. Hbr Patrol Boat (April–September) VHF 12. Water taxi VHF 6. Fuel Barge *Fowey Refueller* 01836 519341, VHF 10.

Interest Visits to The Eden Project can be arranged via the tourist information office.

POLPERRO

Charts BA 148, SC 5602;
Imray 2400, C6, C10

HW Plymouth –0010

MHWS	MHWN	MLWN	MLWS
5·4m	4·3m	2·0m	0·6m

An attractive small drying hbr with visitors' buoys for four. Uncomfortable in onshore winds and swell. A fair weather anchorage outside the pier. Entrance closed in bad weather. Fuel, water, shops.

LOOE

Charts BA 147, 148, SC 5602;
Imray 2400, C6, C10

HW Plymouth –0010

MHWS	MHWN	MLWN	MLWS
5·4m	4·2m	2·0m	0·6m

A drying hbr with 3·4m alongside E quay at HW and 1·2m–3m along W one.

ENGLAND – SOUTH COAST

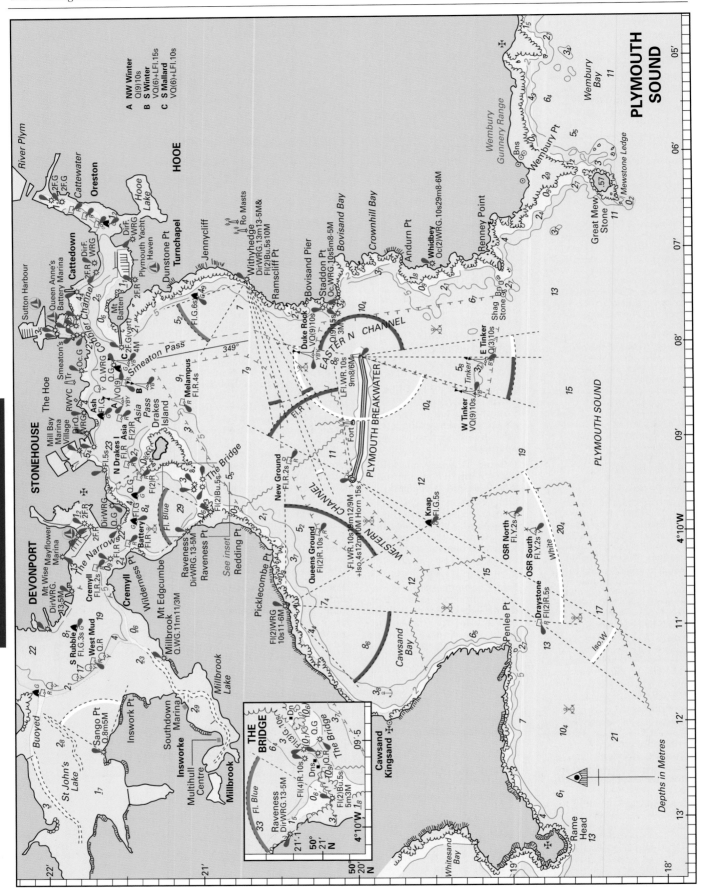

PLYMOUTH SOUND

A NW Winter   Q(9)10s
B S Winter   VQ(6)+LFl.15s
C S Mallard   VQ(6)+LFl.10s

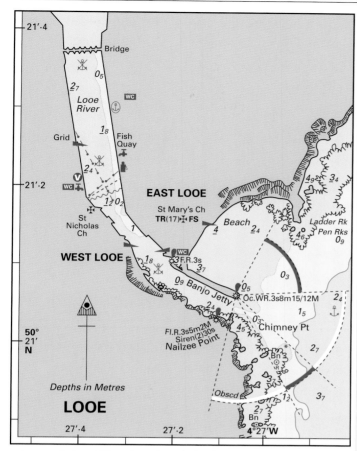

LOOE

Depths in Metres

Approach from W to clear the Ranneys keep the mainland showing above the top of Looe Is; overfalls S of the Is on the ebb. Steer in when E Looe church is well open of W point of the entrance. At night, coming from W, keep in W sector of pier head Lt Oc.WR which opens at 313°. If beating in from E, remember that rocks run out 1½ca from the shore NE of the entrance. Passage between the Is and the mainland should not be attempted except at HW with local knowledge. Dangerous half-tide rock (Dunker) ½ca off NW corner of Is.

Entrance Stream runs at 3kn through the narrows on both flood and ebb. On the flood there is an out-going eddy on both sides of the river from the inner end of the narrows to beyond the visitors' berth on the W side of the hbr, causing problems coming alongside. A bank runs down the centre of hbr from the br to opposite St Nicholas Church giving ½m less water.

Berthing Anchorage outside. Sheltered in W winds, open to SE and E, and S by W. Bring pier head on with St Nicholas Church, W Looe, and anchor in 3m, sand and mud, abreast the W marks on the rock at W entrance of the hbr. Inside mooring: hbr is crowded when fishermen are in and yachts are not allowed to lie alongside fishing boats. Visitors' berth is immediately up-river of the third set of steps on the W side of the hbr by a fishermen's shelter. 2–3 berths abreast. Fender board essential.

Facilities Water on quays; fuel in cans at E Looe. Shops EC Thursday. Transport: Rly to Liskeard for main line.

☎ HM 01503 262839.

PLYMOUTH

Charts BA 30, 1900, 1901, 1267, 1902, SC 5602;
Imray 2400, C14, C10
HW Plymouth HW
DS Dover +0400E −0200W

MHWS	MHWN	MLWN	MLWS
5·5m	4·4m	2·2m	0·8m

At Cotehele Quay HW is up to HW Plymouth +0020; LW is LW Plymouth +0045.

Plymouth is a Naval Dockyard Port, under a QHM, with considerable commercial traffic as well as extensive yachting facilities. The hbr is protected by a breakwater with E and W entrances.

In E entrance streams are rotary clockwise, Dover +0500 N; −0330 S.

In W entrance, streams are rectilinear, Dover +0215 NE; −0430 SE.

Internally the streams run strongly NNW and SSE across The Br. In Asia Pass the flood (1kn springs) sets towards the shoal running NE from Drake's Is; the ebb sets towards Winter Shoal. S of Vanguard Bank the flood (2kn) sets towards Barn Pool, the ebb SE towards The Br. In The Narrows at the S end the flood (2¾kn) sets NE out of Barn Pool and the ebb towards Vanguard Bank. At the N end the flood sets towards Mount Wise and the ebb towards Devil's Point. In Hamoaze S of Rubble Bank the ebb starts local HW+0030 and sets towards Millbrook Lake.

Approach From E, round the Great Mewstone and steer on summit of Rame Head bearing 290° until Tinker Q(3)10s bears 325° then steer to leave it a cable to port. From W, in bad weather or with wind against tide, give Rame Head at least ½M clearance and steer to leave breakwater LtHo (Fl.WR.10s+Iso.4s) well clear to stb.

Entrance In strong S winds the sea breaks heavily on Knap and Panther shoals, to SSW of breakwater LtHo, and on the ebb in the E entrance, which also has a dangerous sea in strong W winds. E entrance: bring the Lt bn, LFl.WR.10s, on E arm of breakwater in line with Smeaton's tr (RW bands) on the Hoe, 355° (at night keep in W sector of breakwater East Head Lt). Give breakwater end 1ca clearance. W entrance: leave the breakwater West Head LtHo well clear to stb.

Signals Signals to control the movement of ships longer than 20m in the main channels may be displayed at a mast on Drake's Is or at FS at Devonport N Dockyard:

3R Fl – Emergency. All unauthorised movements stopped.

1R Oc over 2G Oc – Outgoing traffic only may proceed on recommended track.

2G Oc over 1R Oc – Incoming traffic only may proceed on recommended track.

2G Oc over 1W Oc – Give wide berth to HM vessels on recommended track.

Craft under 20m may proceed in the contrary direction so long as they do not impede the main channels.

In daytime wind warning signal Lts are shown from Drake's Is mast when there is no traffic Lt signal:

1 Lt Oc – Wind Force 5–7

2 Lts Oc(vert) – Wind greater than Force 7.

North of the breakwater, craft longer than 45m have right of way over smaller craft whether under power or sail.

The main channels have W bns 9m high with Or/W day marks, mostly lit: W on course; Al.WR or Al.WG slightly off channel; F.R or F.G further off channel.

Lt QY is displayed at all major Dir Lts when main power supplies are interrupted.

The Sound

Anchorages Yachts can approach to 1½ca of the shore, apart from the area of The Br, SW of Drake's Is.

• **Cawsand Bay**, W of breakwater, except in E and SE winds. Anchor close inshore on S side of bay.

• **Jenny Cliff Bay**, E side of The Sound, near to Withyhedge dir Lt to avoid off-lying reefs. Keep clear of skiing area. Sheltered from NE through E to SE.

To Cattewater, Sutton Harbour and Cobbler Channel Pass ½ca W of Mount Batten breakwater 2F.G(vert) to Fisher's Nose Fl(3)R.10s W of entrance to Sutton Harbour. At night pick up Dir Lts at Queen Anne's Battery F.R (front) Oc.WRG.7·5s (rear), 049°. For Sutton Harbour Marina steer N, when abreast of Fisher's Nose, for entrance between pier heads Fl.R and Fl.G.3s, with Queen Anne's Battery Marina to stb marked by four pairs of 2F.G(vert) Lts on breakwater and pontoon heads. For Cattewater continue to steer 049° on Dir Lt on Queen Anne's Marina, then Cattedown Ldg bns 102° followed by Turnchapel Ldg bns 129°, depth 4·9m. Laira Br, at the N end of Cattewater, has clearance of 4·9m in the centre.

Berthing Anchoring in Cattewater is difficult: space may be found in Clovelly Bay. There are Cattewater Harbour Commissioners visitors' buoys S of Sutton Harbour entrance (exposed to S and SW winds; wash) and four belonging to RWYC (Or with W tops) S of QAB breakwater; moorings may also be available from Turnchapel yacht yards. Two marinas at Sutton: Sutton Harbour Marina in N (lock 24hrs; free flow HW±0200; boats up to 45ft) and Queen Anne's Battery Marina (visitors' berths, up to 100ft), and Plymouth Yacht Haven in Clovelly Bay.

To Millbay Docks From Melampus R can Lt buoy either steer NNW over Asia Knoll shoal, 5·5m, or follow Asia Pass round Asia buoy (Fl(2)5s). By night approach from The Sound with Millbay dir Lt (DirQ.WRG) bearing 326°, within W sector to Asia Lt buoy and NW Winter (W card Lt buoy) and thence to entrance between pier heads (Q.R and Q.G).

Berthing Anchor off W Hoe, 3½–7½m, in all but S winds, very uncomfortable in SE wind. Bottom foul, buoy anchor. Steamer wash day and night.

Hamoaze and Mayflower Marina From Melampus R can buoy make for Asia Pass buoys and follow buoyed channel round to the Narrows where Mayflower Marina is to stb. By night follow Dir Lts (all F) from Asia Pass: Western King 271°, Ravenness 225°, Mount Wise 343°.

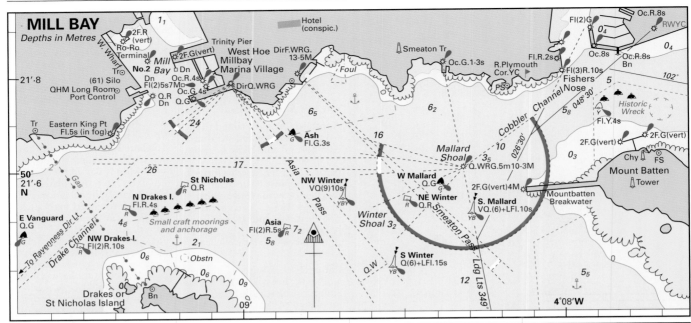

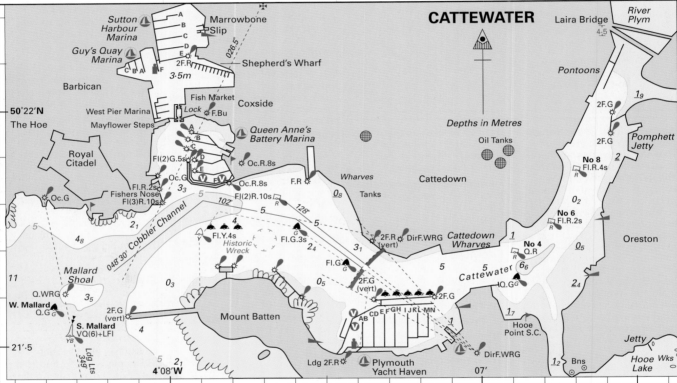

Another route by day is via The Br to SW of Drake's Is. The passage is marked by four Lt bns and has only 1·5m. There are obstructions on the bottom close to the channel either side of the bns and in bad weather the sea breaks heavily in the approach. Across The Br the streams run strongly NNW and SSE. There are depth gauges on the NW and SE bns showing ht above CD.

St John's Lake dries but a narrow channel, buoys and bns, has 0·4 to 1·8m to Trevol Point, jetty with 1·9m at head.

Anchorage
• In NW corner of Barn Pool at W end of Drake Channel, bottom very steep-to; good shelter from W winds. Beware fouling anchor on wreck (*see plan*).
• N of Drake's Is to E of private pier – buoy anchor.
• Millbrook Lake, 3ca W of Mashford's Yard at Cremyll.

Moorings available in Stonehouse Pool from yard adjoining Admiral's Hard; and at Ballast Pound Yacht Harbour off Torpoint, 2ca S of chain ferry. This yacht hbr has also drying quayside berths accessible HW±0200.
Mayflower Marina at Ocean Quay has berths for craft up to 19·8m long, 3m draught
Passage beneath the Tamar bridges (50°24'·5N) is best taken at LW Devonport +0100.
The Hamoaze has many large unlit mooring buoys for warships extending from Cremyll to the Tamar Br. Passage in poor visibility is not recommended.
The Tamar has Lt bns as far as Warren Point 50°25'N. Above Skinham Point LW depths are generally less than 2m but some stretches have more (*see notes below on mooring*). Calstock can be reached at HW and craft with 1·5m draught can reach ¼M off the head of navigation at Weir Head at HWS. Navigation in this area at LW (even LWN) is not recommended owing to debris (water-logged tree trunks) and the unreliability of charts. Channel winds through mud-banks and is unmarked.
Although the Torpoint chain ferry between Torpoint and Devonport is required to give way, yachts should avoid impeding its passage. The ferries carry four Lts, one at each corner, showing W ahead or astern, and R on the beam. Underway they show a VQ Or Lt at the leading end. When in use by the emergency services they also show VQ Bu below the Or Lt in direction of progress. In transit in fog they sound a bell for five seconds each 30 seconds.

Overhead cables cross 4ca below Cargreen with 19m clearance and 1¼M above Cargreen, 16m.
St German's or Lynher River is buoyed for 2¼M and is navigable by yachts to St German's Quay and with 2m draught to Tideford at MHWS; also to Notter Br on River

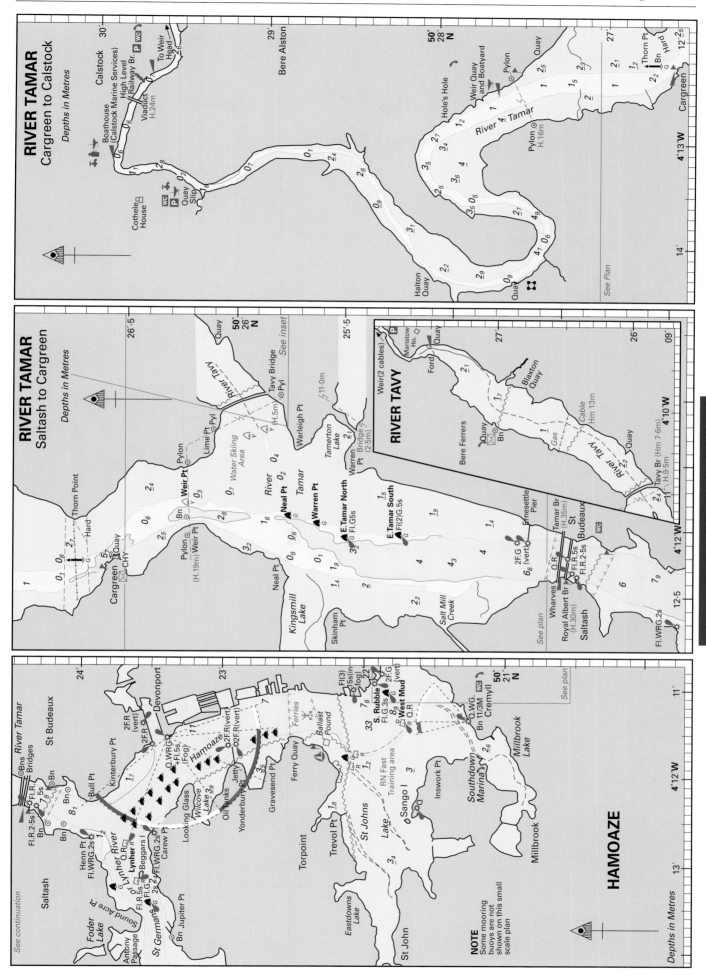

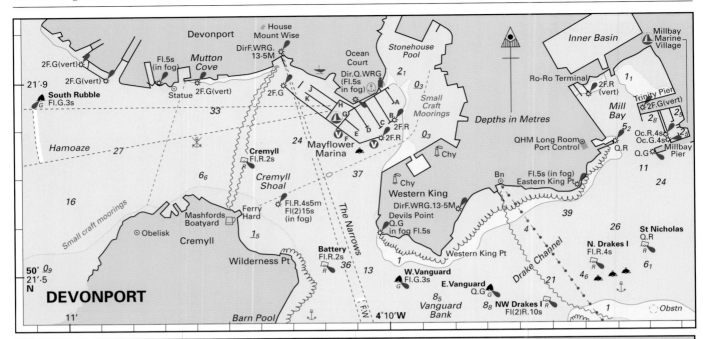

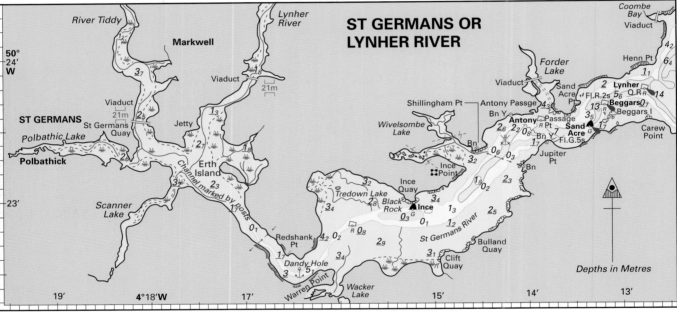

Lynher. Cables cross each route with clearance to Tideford of 20m 1ca S of Morvah Quay and 3m at the quay; and 26m S of Notter.

Anchorages in St German's River: Off Antony Village or Dandy Hole off S tip of Erth Hill, 3m, sheltered but landing difficult at LW. Keep clear of bend at W end of reach, used by salmon fishermen with nets.

River Tavy has an overhead cable at its entrance with 5m clearance. Craft with 1·5m draught can reach the falls (2½M) at MHWS.

Berthing
• Saltash Bay on W side below the bridges in 3½m.
• Cargreen. Good holding in 3–3½m except opposite quays. Several deep-water holes may be found in this area, good holding but stream strong.
• Cotehele ¼M above quay but spring streams strong.

• In pools above Calstock.

Facilities Alongside fuel and water at the marinas and Calstock Boatyard; water at St Germans SC. All facilities in Plymouth; PO and shop at Cargreen.

☎/VHF (all 01752).
Longroom Port Control 836528, VHF 14 (private and commercial craft), VHF 13 (military). Cattewater Harbour Commissioners 665934, VHF 14 (Monday–Friday). Marinas VHF 80. Plymouth Yacht Haven 404231. Mayflower Marina 556633. Millbay Marina Village 226785. Queen Anne Battery Marina 671142. Sutton Harbour Marina 204702, *Mobile* 07785 986921, Lock VHF 12. River Plymouth Corinthian YC 664327. RWYC 660077.

Interest Particularly National Marine Aquarium, Plymouth.

RIVER YEALM

Charts BA 30, 1613, 1900, SC 5602;
Imray 2400, C14, C10
HW Plymouth +0006

MHWS	MHWN	MLWN	MLWS
5·4m	4·3m	2·1m	0·7m

In the river the flood starts at Plymouth –0545 (1½kn) and the ebb at +0015 (2kn but 4kn off Warren Point).

Approach To clear outlying rks on E and W of approach, keep Cawsand open of the Mewstone 298° until, coming from W, Wembury church (St Werburgh's on BA charts) bears 030° which clears Slimers Rocks on W of approach; or, coming from E, Wembury church bearing 006° clears Ebb Rocks on the E of the approach. Misery Pt well open of Season Pt clears Church Ledge. Stand in between these limits until the outer marks are

identified. Entry should not be attempted in strong SW winds.

Entrance A sand bar runs S from Season Point leaving a narrow channel close along the S shore. The outer Ldg marks (BW bns, topmarks) lead over the S end of the bar where it dries 0·6m and lead 089° into Cellar Bay. To clear Mouthstone Ledge do not stray S of the line until past Mouthstone Point. After this the best water is midway between the line and the rocks on the S shore leaving the Bar buoy, R can Fl.R.5s to port. There is a gap of 40m between the buoy and the S shore with a least depth of 1·5m. A second R can buoy marks the inner edge of the bar. When past, transit on RW can bns on N shore leads clear of shallows off Misery Point. Thence keep mid-channel leaving to port R can buoy marking drying spit SE of Warren Point.

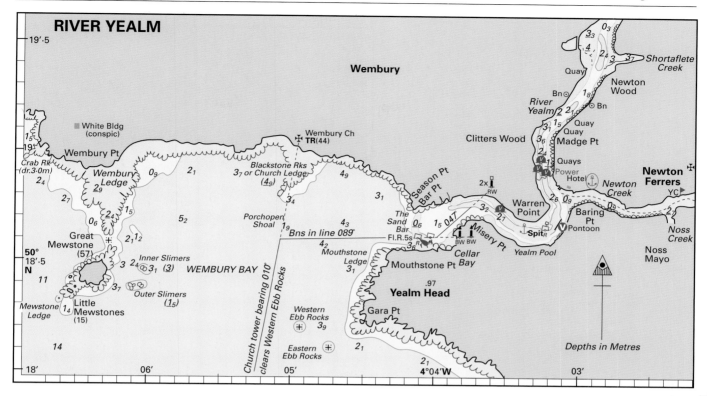

RIVER YEALM

Berthing Anchor in fine weather in Cellar Bay (open from W to NW). The river is crowded with moorings. No anchoring east or north of RW can bns on N shore, except by arrangement with HM. For visitors there is a mooring for craft up to 75ft off Misery Point, further in are two moorings each taking three craft or 25 tonnes. There is a line of pontoons in the Pool with some 25 berths and a further pontoon on the W shore providing 20 berths; and a trot of fore and aft moorings

(yachts may moor up to five abreast) on W side N of Yealm Hotel. Residents' moorings may be picked up if they are vacant.

Facilities Water at slip near Yealm Hotel; no fuel. Newton: PO/Store, grocer, butcher, chemist, pub, YC; Noss: PO/Store, two pubs. EC Thursday. Bus to Plymouth.

☎/VHF HM 01752 872533, VHF 10. Water taxi VHF 08.

- Folios of charts in a plastic wallet
- Small format A2 size sheets – 594mm x 420mm
- Yeoman plotter points
- All WGS 84 Datum
- Corrected to date of issue with free updating service from www.imray.com

2400 The West Country
Start Point to the Isles of Scilly and Padstow

PLYMOUTH TO TORBAY

Charts BA 1613, SC 5602; Imray 2300, 2400, C6, C5

Passage Lights	BA No
Start Point	0228

Fl(3)10s62m25M+F.R (over Skerries) Horn 60s

Berry Head	0244

Fl(2)15s 58m19M

Streams related to HW Dover

Bolt Tail to Bolt Head +0500E –0200W

3M S of Start Point +0500ENE –0115WSW 2kn

Start Point inshore +0430E –0145W 4kn

Start Bay: +0415NE –0115SW

Berry Head: +0545N –0100S

Between Plymouth and Bolt Tail keep at least ½M offshore in fine weather to clear rocky ledges. In strong onshore winds keep well out to sea.

From Bolt Tail to Bolt Head there are cliffs up to 120m; conspic radio masts 1¼M E of Bolt Tail. Heavy swell possible, keep at least ½M offshore.

In strong winds the race off Start Point may be severe for

1M or more SE, and up to 2M with strong SW wind against tide. There is a set into West Bay especially in S winds. Bound for Dartmouth either pass outside the Skerries (Berry Head bearing 021° between Scabbacombe Hd (Downend Pt), 50°21′N, 3°31′W and E Blackstone Rock to the S, clears Skerries to SE) or take the inner passage, usually smoother, between Start Pt and Skerries, ¾M wide. Keep at least 4ca off LtHo until it bears 320°, at least 2ca S of Start Rocks, thence pass close to the Pt. Southernmost white ho (conspic) at Beesands bearing 320° leads through.

In fog do not try to make the land between Bolt Tail and Start Pt: aim for Start Bay or Torbay.

Start Bay may be entered in a calm with no swell if position known within 2M. From SE aim for Torcross, sounding continuously. 40+m depth up to 5ca off Skerries, 2·3m on its SW end, 5m in the middle and over 4½m on its NE end. Start Point fog signal often inaudible here. When soundings reach 14m you are over the bank: steer WNW

and anchor in 8·9m. Sand, good holding, little traffic and sheltered between SSW and N. If shallow soundings not met when expected, stand off to E and wait for it to clear, N of shipping lane. With any swell keep away from the Skerries.

E-bound from Dartmouth keep ¾M offshore to clear E Blackstone and Nimble Rock and keep 1M offshore of Hope's Nose to clear Ore Stone. Coast is then free of dangers to Exmouth apart from Dawlish Rock, 3·5m, ½M off the town.

Anchorages

R Erme Keep close to port on entry to avoid reef off Fernycombe Point on starboard. Anchor off cove W of pine-clad hill. Keep clear of historic wreck restricted area.

Burgh Is Pool N of Murrays Rock (R beacon, cross top) 2m, sand. Exposed at HW, otherwise protected from W to N. Keep well to E in approach as there is an underwater rock E of Murrays.

River Avon 1ca E of Murray Rocks head 060° towards two most E'ly houses on Mount Folly hilltop. These lie conveniently above one another. A W mark is painted on the cliffs just to the N of the houses mentioned above. When this point is reached turn onto 030° and head towards point of Lower Cellars Bank steep to on starboard. Once past boat houses keep close under cliff to find the deepest water. Anchor 1¼ca W of thatched boat house for flat bottom. Breaking waves add interest and diversion to the entrance to this beautiful anchorage.

Hope Cove Anchor in offshore winds only. Poor holding. Beware rock drying 2·7m ¼ca offshore.

Start Bay in offshore winds off Hall Sands or Torcross close inshore. Run for Dartmouth if wind backs S.

Torbay Elberry Cove in SW corner of bay in 5m, 3ca offshore.

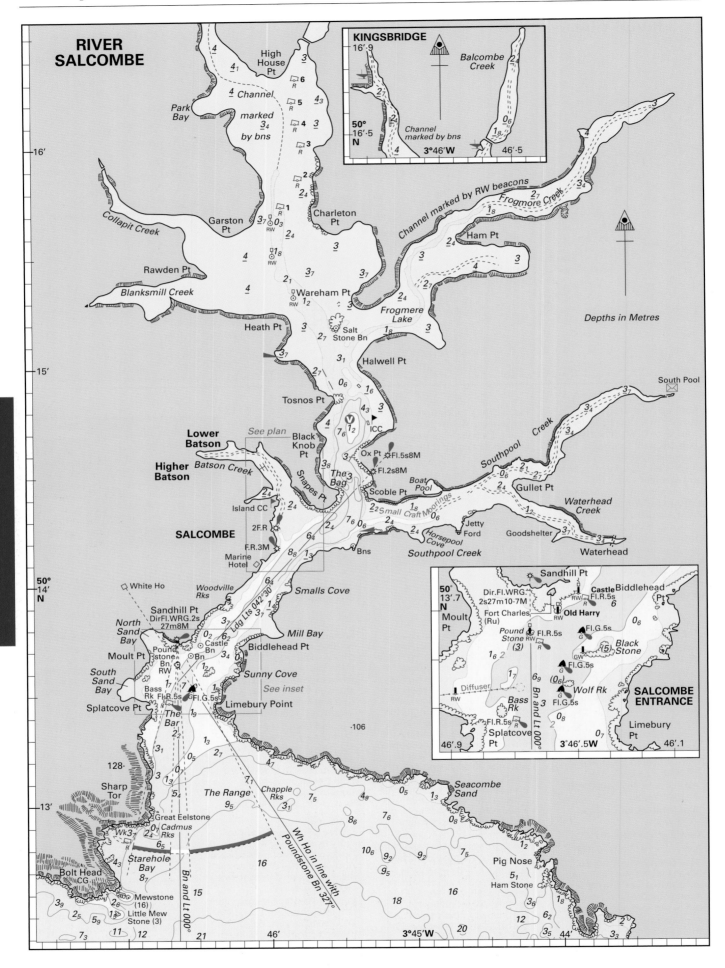

RIVER SALCOMBE

KINGSBRIDGE

Park Bay

High House Pt

Channel marked by bns

Balcombe Creek

Channel marked by bns

50° 16'·5 N

3°46'W

46'·5

Collapit Creek

Garston Pt

Charleton Pt

Channel marked by RW beacons

Frogmore Creek

Ham Pt

Rawden Pt

Blanksmill Creek

Wareham Pt

Frogmere Lake

Depths in Metres

Heath Pt

Salt Stone Bn

Halwell Pt

Tosnos Pt

South Pool

Lower Batson

Higher Batson

Black Knob Pt

Batson Creek

Ox Pt Fl.5s8M

Fl.2s8M

Southpool Creek

Gullet Pt

Waterhead Creek

Island CC

Snapes Pt

The Bag

Scoble Pt

Boat Pool

Small Craft Moorings

2F.R

SALCOMBE

F.R.3M

Marine Hotel

Horsepool Cove

Jetty Ford

Southpool Creek

Goodshelter

Waterhead

Bns

White Ho

Woodville Rks

Smalls Cove

North Sand Bay

Sandhill Pt DirFl.WRG.2s 27m8M

Ldg Lts 042°30

Mill Bay

SALCOMBE ENTRANCE

Moult Pt

Pound stone Bn RW

Castle Bn

Biddlehead Pt

Sunny Cove

See inset

Sandhill Pt Dir.Fl.WRG. 2s27m10-7M

Castle Fl.R.5s Biddlehead Pt

Fort Charles (Ru)

Old Harry

South Sand Bay

Bass Rk Fl.R.5s

Fl.G.5s

Limebury Point

Pound Stone RW

Fl.R.5s

Black Stone

Fl.G.5s

Splatcove Pt

The Bar

Moult Pt

50° 13'·7 N

Diffuser RW

Fl.G.5s

Wolf Rk Fl.G.5s

·106

Bass Rk

Sharp Tor

128·

Fl.R.5s

Splatcove Pt

Limebury Pt

46'·9

3°46'·5W

46'·1

The Range

Chapple Rks

Seacombe Sand

Great Eelstone

Cadmus Rks

Starehole Bay

Bolt Head CG

Pig Nose

Mewstone (16)

Little Mew Stone (3)

Ham Stone

Wh Ho in line with Poundstone Bn 327°

Bn and Lt 000°

3°45'W

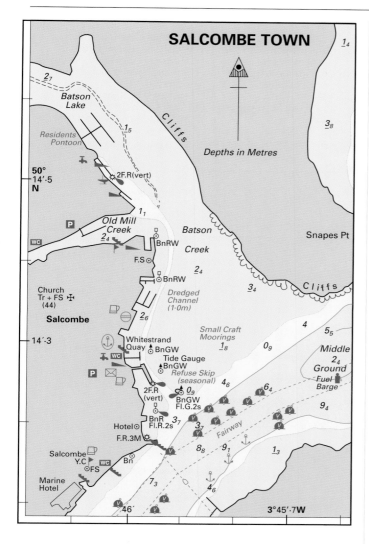

SALCOMBE TOWN

Depths in Metres

Batson Lake

Residents Pontoon

Old Mill Creek

Batson Creek

Snapes Pt

Cliffs

Church Tr + FS ⛪ (44)

Salcombe

Dredged Channel (1·0m)

Small Craft Moorings

Whitestrand Quay

Tide Gauge

Refuse Skip (seasonal)

Middle Ground

Fuel Barge

Fairway

Salcombe Y.C

Marine Hotel

Hotel

50° 14'·5 N

14'·3

3°45'·7W

SALCOMBE

Charts BA 28, 1634, SC 5602; Imray 2400, C5, C10

HW Plymouth +0005

MHWS	MHWN	MLWN	MLWS
5·3m	4·1m	2·1m	0·7m

Salcombe is a very attractive hbr, but The Bar is very dangerous in strong onshore winds with the ebb tide. With a swell of 1m, crossing should not be attempted until there is a considerable rise in tide, HW –0200 is recommended. Inside the stream can reach 3kn below the ferry landing. If in doubt contact the HM. The wind is fluky off the cliffs and as cruising yachts are prohibited from sailing inside the hbr in July and August, it is best to be under engine with the sails stowed before crossing The Bar. Yachts may not sail in the fairway during July and August.

Approach From W give the Mewstone and Cadmus Rocks clearances of 2ca and 1ca respectively. Starehole Bay provides temporary anchorage in W winds to wait for a suitable time to cross the bar. From E give Prawle Point clearance of 2ca and steer 298° for the pinewood S of Bar Lodge, a tall narrow building with a red roof. (Note also Ldg line on plan for clearing Chapple Rock, 3·1m). From 2ca off Mewstone steer N for about 4ca to a position about 1ca off the Eelstones and follow entry directions.

Entrance At the N end of the gradually shoaling range is The Bar (0·7m), extending SW from Limebury Point. The deepest water is ¾ca W of the Ldg line, Poundstone Bn (RW with R can top) in line with Sandhill Point bn (RWHS, diamond top) to W of red-roofed house, 000°. Leave Bass Rocks to port, and follow the buoyed channel. Round up to 042° with Ox Point Lts in line once Blackstone Rk is abeam.

By night enter in W sector (358°-003°) of Sandhill Point Dir Lt, Fl.WRG.2s. Follow the buoyed channel leaving Bass Rock R. can, Fl.R.5s to port, and then bring Ox Point Ldg Lts front Fl.2s (may be obscured by anchored vessels), rear Fl.5s, in line 042°.

The river is marked by bns to Kingsbridge where Squares Quay dries 3·4m and has 1·3m HWS and 0·2 HWN.

Berthing Anchorages
• In settled weather with modest draught, off Sunny Cove and Mill Bay on the E side. If anchoring in Smalls Cove, give the YC racing start line a wide berth.
• In settled weather, in deep water to E of fairway off the town.
• N of Halwell Point.
• W of Salt Stone bn.
• Frogmore Lake: Narrow pool (2m) just before bay on S side.
• For Kingsbridge by dinghy, anchor off junction to Balcombe Lake.

Moorings Visitors' pontoon at Whitestrand allows short-stay (30 minutes) for shopping; no double banking. Overnight stays incur charges.

Visitors' moorings mostly R (up to 30ft) and Y (over 30ft), marked 'V', off the town, N of the fairway, and off entrance to Southpool Creek.

With strong winds from SE to W, it is well worth going beyond The Bag where there is complete shelter. No anchoring in The Bag.

Alongside: two berths, overnight only (depart by 0800) on northern pontoon at Whitestrand; pre-booking essential; also visitors' pontoon on W side of Bag, not connected to shore. Half-tide pontoon in Frogmore Creek.

Drying berths at Kingsbridge alongside car park on W bank or pontoon on E. Check availability with the HM. Navigable HW±0230.

Facilities Landing at Ferry Pier (dinghies cannot be left), at Whitestrand pontoon and at Creek Boat Park Slip (1m). Boatyards at Salcombe and Lyncombe. Water from Whitestrand pontoon. Refuse barge off Whitestrand (April–October). Showers at Salcombe YC and ICC Egremont. Sailmaker at Kingsbridge.

☎/VHF HM 01548 843791, VHF 14. Hbr water taxi VHF 12. Island Cruising Club 843481, VHF 37, M. Salcombe YC 842872.

DARTMOUTH

Charts BA 2253, 1634, SC 5602; Imray 2300, C5, C10

HW Plymouth +0020

DS outside Dover –0100SW +0545NE; both 1½kn max

MHWS	MHWN	MLWN	MLWS
4·6m	3·8	2·0m	0·6m

Approaches SW set may be experienced on the flood and NE on the ebb, except near the ends of both. To the E above Froward Pt there is a truncated stone pyramid bn 24m (177m above HW).

From E, give Mewstone Rock (35m) a clear berth to stb (crab pots) and then keep E Blackstone well open of it to clear rocky ledge extending 3ca WSW. After this make for Castle Ledge G con buoy (Fl.G.5s). From W, keep outside the Homestone buoy (R can) and keep E of W Blackstone Rock (2·4m). Keep away from Coombe Pt at all times. From S, Skerries bell buoy, 3½M from the entrance, is a good guide.

At night, from E keep Lts of Berry Head and Start Pt both just visible until Castle Ledge buoy, G con (Fl.G 5s), is visible. Steer for this until in W sector of Kingswear (*see below*). From W, keep both Berry Head and Start Point lights visible until in Kingswear W sector.

Entrance is easy under power but squalls off the high land either side of the entrance may make sailing difficult, particularly with winds from SW through W to NW. Checkstone buoy is just E of a rocky ledge and must be left well to port. At springs localised streams up to 3kn may be experienced off Battery and Castle Pts with associated heavy swell in the entrance. The swell and fast tides disappear inside the estuary.

At night keep in W sector of Kingswear Lt (Iso.WRG.3s9m8M; 325°-W-331°) until within W sector of Bayards Cove Lt, Fl.WRG.2s, 289°-W-297°. (There is a F Lt NNW of Kettle Point for vessels leaving; it is useful to keep it astern on this leg). Keep in the Bayards Cove W sector until the G Lts on Kingswear pontoon are well open, when course should be altered to pass through the fairway to the anchorage E of the main hbr buoys.

The River Dart is navigable to Dittisham at any state of the tide and to Totnes after half-flood. It is controlled all the way by the Harbour Authority; dues are levied on all vessels. The S-most ferry has right of way and the cable ferry should be given a clear berth as under strong wind or tide the cables can be very close to the surface. Do not pass between the ferry and the shore unless the ferry is at least one third of the river's width clear of the side in question. Between Noss Point and the Anchor Stone the channel hugs the E bank. Dittisham Lake, ½M wide, has two navigable channels separated by Flat Owers (dries 2m). Large vessels use the W channel. Above this the channel is winding, marked to Totnes by buoys and bns. Keep High Gurrow and Blackness Pts close to port, Pighole and Mill Points close to stb; alter course to port to cross the river, pass close N of White Rock and make for buoys off Langham Wood Pt, leaving latter close to port. Then follow the buoys, keeping to outside of bends. At springs the river dries for 2M below Totnes but yachts of 1m draught can proceed there at LW+0130.

Berthing During working hours the River Officers (VHF 11, *Dart Nav*) are on duty near the town jetty and up-river at Dittisham. Dinghies may be left at pontoons adjacent to Dartmouth YC and at pontoons N of Lee Court Flats.
• Anchor E of the town and of the ships' buoys in 4½m. Good holding but beware the chains of large moorings.

• Visitors' buoys marked with a blue flag or blue with a V, and pontoons between buoys: enquire of river officers.
• Visitors' pontoons adjacent to Dartmouth YC (max 30ft) W bank; yachts may use S end of inshore side of town jetty for 1hr free; also for craft under 26ft at pontoons on W bank N of Court Flats.

• Darthaven Marina pontoons (E side).
• Dart Marina pontoons (W side, just above cable ferry).
• Fore and aft moorings sometimes available at River Dart YC on E bank.
• Noss-on-Dart Marina on W side of river.
• Anchor on W side of river below Anchor Stone (R can) off

Parson's Mud clear of moorings and out of main channel.
• Visitors' moorings off Dittisham, clearly marked with holding capacity which must be observed.
• Above Dittisham, including Totnes, consult river officer, VHF 11 *Dart Nav*, waiting for him at Dittisham if necessary.

Facilities Diesel and petrol from Dartmouth Fuel Barge, VHF 06, call sign *Dart Crusader* or *Dart Fuel Barge*. Water at North Embankment (by WCs) and South Embankment, Dartmouth YC, Dittisham, Galmpton. Water and stores at Dittisham, Galmpton and Totnes.

☎/VHF (all 01803). HM 832337, VHF 11. Dartmouth YC 832305. Coastguard 882704, VHF 67; R Dart YC 752272; Dart Marina 833351. VHF 80, 37. Darthaven Marina 752545, VHF 80. Noss-on-Dart Marina 833351. Dartside Quay, Galmpton 845445, VHF 37, 80. Yacht Taxi 833727, VHF 6, 8, 73. Fuel Barge 07801 798861, VHF 06.

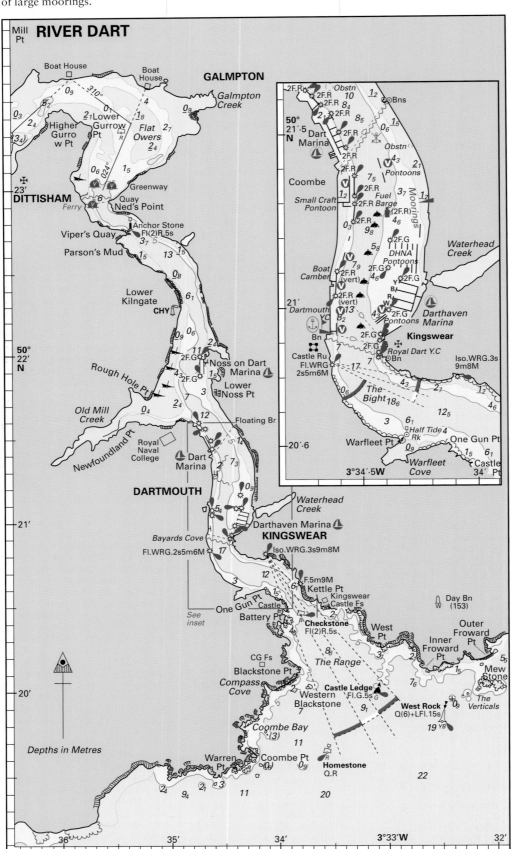

BRIXHAM

Charts BA 26, 1634, 1613, SC 5602;
Imray 2300, C5, C10

HW Plymouth +0035

DS Dover –0100SW +0500NE

MHWS	MHWN	MLWN	MLWS
4·9m	3·7	2·0m	0·7m

Brixham is a busy fishing port with marina accommodation for yachts. In N–NE winds there is considerable scend in outer hbr.

Approach Steer for safe water sph Lt buoy, Mo(A)10s (·−), bearing 308°, 1·2ca, from Victoria Breakwater LtHo.

From N, clear rocks off Hope's Nose by keeping W edge of Cod Rock, off Berry Head, bearing more than 195° and open E of Berry Head. From S, clear dangers S of Berry Head by keeping Hope's Nose open E of Berry Hd, 359°. From Berry Head (25m depth close inshore) steer 284° for Safewater Buoy.

Signals 3R balls or Lts at the inner harbour entrance indicate hbr is closed.

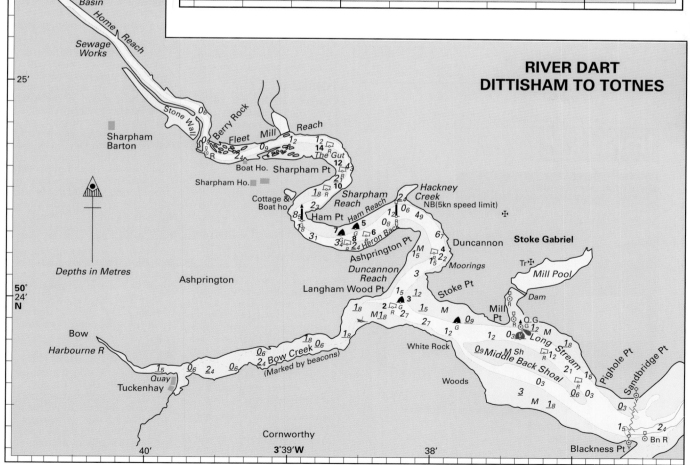

BRIXHAM HARBOUR

Depths in Metres

Totnes

RIVER DART
DITTISHAM TO TOTNES

Depths in Metres

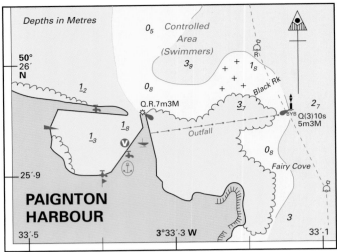

PAIGNTON HARBOUR

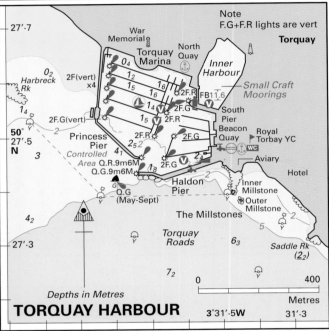

TORQUAY HARBOUR

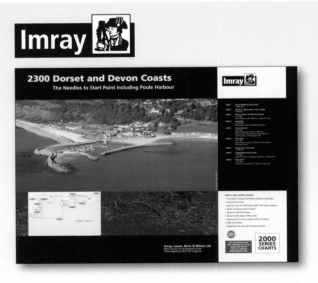

Imray

2300 Dorset and Devon Coasts
The Needles to Start Point including Poole Harbour

2000 SERIES CHARTS

- Folios of charts in a plastic wallet
- Small format A2 size sheets – 594mm x 420mm
- Yeoman plotter points
- All WGS 84 Datum
- Corrected to date of issue with free updating service from www.imray.com

Entrance Give the breakwater end a wide berth, as large beam trawlers can often emerge from behind it: you should then keep to the stb side of the Main Fairway, marked by two pairs of lateral Lt buoys. Give way to the LB when showing emergency signals.

Berthing Marina in SE corner of hbr. In summer a pontoon is moored off Brixham YC, subject to MFV wash. There is no room to anchor in the hbr and holding in Fishcombe Cove is very poor.
Leaving the marina, give way to fishing vessels leaving the MFV basin or manoeuvring off fuel berth, and to craft entering hbr from seaward.

Facilities Diesel at marina, pontoon C; water at end of pier, breakwater hard, new pier and oil jetty. All facilities. EC Wednesday.

☎ /VHF (all 01803) HM 853321, VHF 14, (*Brixham Port*). Coastguard 882704. YC 853332. Marina 882929, VHF 80.

PAIGNTON

Charts BA 26;
Imray 2300, C5, C10

Tidal data as for Torquay. A small drying hbr with very limited accommodation for smaller yachts. Visiting vessels may secure alongside East Quay for a short stay only. Alongside berthing is very limited, so vessels should contact Harbour Office on VHF 14 for permission and specific berthing instructions. Water, fuel at garage, shops.

TORQUAY

Charts BA 26, 1613, SC 5602;
Imray 2400.3, C5, C10
HW Plymouth +0035
DS Dover –0100W +0500E

MHWS	MHWN	MLWN	MLWS
4·9m	3·7	2·0m	0·7m

A sheltered hbr with marina, commercial traffic and passenger launches. Busy in summer.

Approach From E a church tr and a spire stand out on the skyline above Babbacombe. There is a safe passage between the Orestone and the Flat Rock off Hope's Nose. It is not safe for strangers to pass inside the Thatcher even at HW. The Orestone with its own length open of the Thatcher will clear all shoals along the N shore of Torbay.

Signals 3R balls or Lts vert: hbr closed, or incoming traffic must wait until entrance is clear.

Entrance faces W. G con buoy Q.G is moored (May–September) off W end of Haldon Pier. Much traffic in summer: keep well to stb in entrance.

Berthing 500-berth marina occupies W half of outer harbour with some 50 berths for visitors (signposted). Harbour Authority pontoons northwards of Haldon Pier. Call *Torquay Harbour* on VHF 14.
Haldon Pier is used by commercial vessels. Tidal gate HW±3hrs approx to inner harbour for small local craft. Good anchorage outside the hbr: keep clear of buoyed fairway. Landing inside Haldon and Princess piers. Short stay visitors may remain on visitors' pontoons for up to two hours free of charge.

Facilities Fuel at South Pier. Small to medium craft may dry against wall in inner harbour. All facilities.

☎ /VHF HM 01803 292429, VHF 16, 14.
Marina 200210, VHF 80.
Royal Torbay YC 292006.

TEIGNMOUTH

Charts BA 26, 3315, SC 5602;
Imray 2300, C5, C10
HW Plymouth +0032
DS Dover –0030W +0515E

MHWS	MHWN	MLWN	MLWS
4·8m	3·6	1·9	0·6m

A commercial port with limited accommodation for yachts. Entrance difficult and not accessible in strong onshore winds from NE to S.

Approach River Teign is N of the Ness, a red sandstone headland with pines at summit.

Entrance The bar is dangerous in onshore winds and with a swell. It is wise to seek local guidance to approach even when there are offshore winds at the last quarter of the flood. The bar is constantly changing. It extends from the Ness, a distinctive red sandstone cliff, to Teignmouth Pier. Tides scour channels which are marked by buoys for the use of pilots but because of constant changes in the channel, should not be used by visitors for navigation. There is a dredged channel, (least depth 1m above CD) marked by a Ldg line (Lucette Lt Oc.R.6s on the training wall on the left of the entrance with W black W stripes on the hbr wall behind) on approx 270°.
Note The 2F.R Lts on the shore bearing 334° are not Ldg Lts but show the dangers off the Ness and visitors should keep E of this line.
Past The Point steer 021° for New Quay leaving R can buoys well to port. Beware of set along the Shaldon shore and unmarked shoals above the quay on stb side. The stream off The Point runs at 4kn and is strong throughout the hbr especially for last half of the ebb.

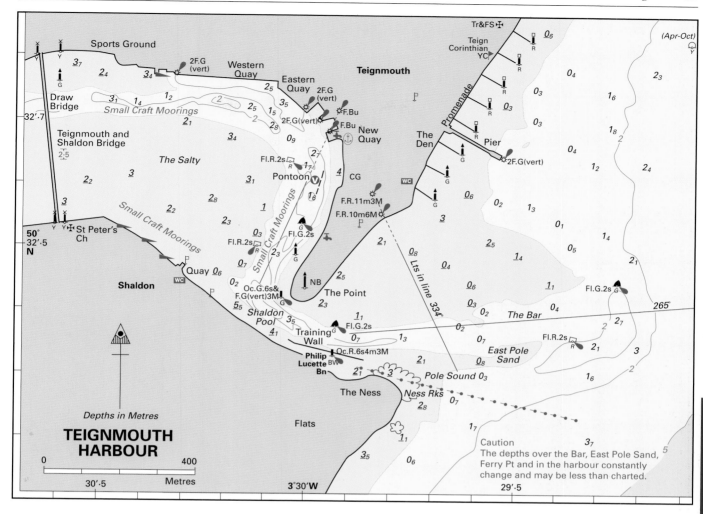

TEIGNMOUTH HARBOUR

Depths in Metres

0   400
Metres

Inadvisable to attempt entrance at night or to leave when ebb is running strongly.

Berthing In settled weather anchor outside 2ca E of end of pier, 2m. Fore and aft mooring for visitors 1ca N of The Point. Quiet anchorage above the br, clearance 3m. Drawbridge section has 2m depth at MHWS.

Facilities Water at quays. Fuel by tanker. Scrubbing hard on S side of New Quay. Shops: EC Thursday.

☎/VHF HM 01626 773165, VHF 12 (office hours).

☎/VHF HM River and Canal 01392 274306, VHF 12 (*Port of Exeter*). Exmouth Dock HM VHF 14, 16. Yacht Basin 01395 269314. Trout's Boatyard Topsham 01392 873044. Ferry service from river to Dock. VHF M (*Conveyance*).

RIVER EXE

Charts BA 2290, 3315, SC 5601; Imray 2300, C5, C10

HW Plymouth +0040

DS Dover +0445E HWD W

MHWS	MHWN	MLWN	MLWS
4·6m	3·4	1·7	0·5m

A pleasant estuary with many moorings (few for visitors) but still places to anchor. Exmouth Dock now closed to

commercial traffic. Approach dangerous in strong onshore winds.

Approach and Entrance Make for Exe RW safewater buoy Mo(A)10s, at 50°35'·9N 3°23'·7W, then follow buoyed channel, on approx 340°. Turn to port at R can buoy Q.R. No.8. After passing buoy No.10, head for a point just S of the pierhead. At night, after passing No.10, pick up Ldg Lts 305° Iso.2s+Q. For an assessment of current weather and sea conditions at river entrance, call duty watchkeeper at National Coastwatch Institution, ☎ 01395 222492 (daylight hours).

River Exe Proceeding up-river follow the curves of the centre of the channel rather than straight lines between the buoys. Bull Head obtrudes between 13 and 15 buoys. The channel is buoyed to Topsham. Turf lock gives access to a canal leading to Exeter, used by commercial craft. Daily convoy to Exeter (max headroom 11m under M5), lock opening HW Exmouth −0100.

Berthing
• Opposite Warren Point. Visitors' pontoon £10 per night.
• In the Bight, 3–5½m, sand.

• Off Starcross S of pier, but many moorings.
• In Lympstone Lake.
• Off Turf lock, clear of fairway and entrance (strong ebb).
• Marina in Exmouth Dock – contact Dock Master for update on depths in entrance. There are yellow visitors' buoys near No.15 buoy, one to E of line between Nos.17 and 19 buoys, and two S of Starcross Pier. (Ferry service from yachts in river to the Dock.) Limited mooring in Exmouth Dock and in canal via Turf Lock (opens HW Exmouth −0100). Limited buoys and pontoon berths for visitors (shallow at springs, sand/mud) at Topsham (Trout's boatyard). Land at dock entrance pontoon, Starcross or on the beach S or N of hbr entrance. It is dangerous to anchor off the point especially with spring tides or SE wind against tide as streams may reach 5kn.

Facilities Water from Dock and Topsham. Shops at Exmouth and Topsham. Water taxi VHF 37 *Mobile* 07970 918418.

☎/VHF Dock Master 01395 269314 Exmouth Docks VHF 14; HM 274 306; NCI Exmouth 222492.

AXMOUTH

Charts BA 3315;
Imray 2300, C5, C10

HW Plymouth +0050

Entrance depths

MHWS	MHWN
2·8m	1·3m

A small drying hbr in mouth of River Axe. Enter HW±0030, dangerous in more than moderate onshore wind. Bar dries 1m; entrance channel 2m. Spring ebb 6kn. Moorings from Axe YC ☎ 01297 20043, bilge keels, max 8·5m LOA and 1·2m draught. Anchorage offshore 2ca W of entrance.

LYME REGIS

Charts BA 3315, SC 5601;
Imray 2300, C5, C10

HW Plymouth +0050

MHWS	MHWN	MLWN	MLWS
4·3m	3·1m	1·7	0·6m

Approach Lyme lies 22M NW of Portland Bill. The approach is straightforward. Comfortable in offshore winds but bad in heavy weather from S to E as swell enters the hbr.

Entrance The hbr is protected from the W by a stone pier, the Cobb, surrounded by rocks, with a R bn marking the extension of rocks at the E end which cover at ½ tide. The inner arm of the hbr and its entrance are to the NW. The leading line

ENGLAND – SOUTH COAST

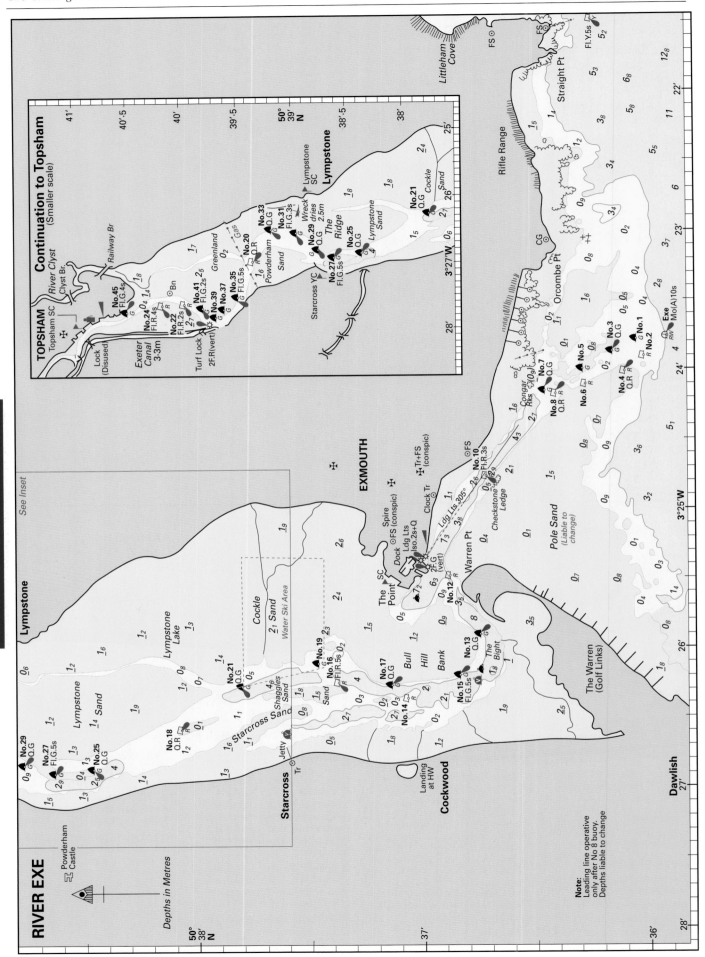

RIVER EXE

Powderham Castle

Depths in Metres

50°
38'
N

Continuation to Topsham (Smaller scale)

TOPSHAM

Note:
Leading line operative
only after No 8 buoy.
Depths liable to change

LYME BAY (TORBAY) TO WEYMOUTH

Charts BA 3315, 2615; SC 5602; Imray 2300, C5, C10

There is a Firing Practice Area extending from Exmouth to Chesil Beach.

Caution In Lyme Bay if S–SW gales blow up there is no refuge in onshore winds.

Passage Lights	*BA No*
Portland Bill	0294

Fl(4)20s43m25M+
Dia 30s (From 221° to 244° gradually changes 1 Fl to 4 Fl, then 4 Fl to 117°, gradually changing from 4 Fl to 1 Fl by 141°) + F.R.13M (over Shambles)

W Shambles W card buoy
Q(9)15s Bell

E Shambles
E card buoy 0300
Q(3)10s Bell

Portland Harbour
A Pier head 0314
Fl.2.5s22m10M

Streams related to HW Dover

Inshore off Bridport: +0600E; HWD W.

On W-going stream Portland Bill produces an eddy in West Bay with a N set felt up to 10M off the Bill and a S set felt as far as 6M S of the Bill.

Portland Bill Streams

(*Caveat* Yachtsmen approaching Portland Bill from E may be using BA Charts with streams related to HW Portsmouth or Dover; but for the Bill they are shown on charts 2615 and 3315 related to HW Plymouth. See page 418 for tidal stream chart related to Plymouth. Those below are related to Dover).

W of the Bill
From +0200 to −0345 (about 9½hrs) S, 3kn
From −0015 to +0200N, 1.1kn

Off the Bill
From +0500E to SE (max 6kn at −0500)
From −0100SW to W (max 7+kn at +0100)

E of the Bill
From −0515 to +0500 (about 10¼hrs) S, 4½kn
From +0500 to −0515N, 1.8kn
From Exmouth to Portland Bill there are two conspic features: Beer Head 130m, the W-most chalk cliff on S coast; and 3M before Bridport is Golden Cap 187m.

Portland Bill

The strong S streams either side of the Bill, running for nine or 10hrs, meet the main Channel streams causing violent turbulence on Portland Ledge. The resultant race is dangerous for yachts and should be avoided either by passing at least 5M S of the Bill and outside E Shambles E card buoy; or in good conditions by the 5ca-wide passage between the Bill and the Race. Timing is important or the yacht may be set out of the channel into the Race.

For passing inshore the best time E-bound is at Dover +0500 and is possible to −0500. Between these times the S stream is running out of W Bay and the land must be closed to 1.2ca well N of Is of Portland: keep close to Chesil Beach in the approach and round the Bill at 1.2ca off.

W-bound the best time is Dover −0100 (earlier risks being set in to the last of the E-going Race) and is possible until +0200. During this period the yacht will have a strong fair stream down the E side of the peninsula; the land should be kept within 1.2ca down to the pitch of the Bill. If the tide has turned to the W when the pitch is reached, steer NW into West Bay to avoid being set into the Race.

Caution

• In winds of Force 6+, and in weaker E winds, the inshore passage ceases to be relatively smooth.
• Lobster pots and their buoys are a hazard in the passage and along the E coast as are divers and their support boats.

The Shambles

The passage between the Race and the Shambles needs extreme care. Strong tidal streams may cause heavy seas; allow for strong set into the race or onto the Shambles. Ldg marks are Portland Harbour 'A' pier head Lt in line with Grove Point 358°, leading 3ca W of The Shambles.

Anchorages

Babbacombe (close N of Long Quarry Point) clear of local moorings in offshore winds.

Exmouth, outside anchorage near Fairway buoy if waiting for the tide in fair weather.

Littleham Cove just N of Straight Point.

Beer Roads E of Beer Head, good anchorage in offshore winds through W to SW in Bay of Beer.

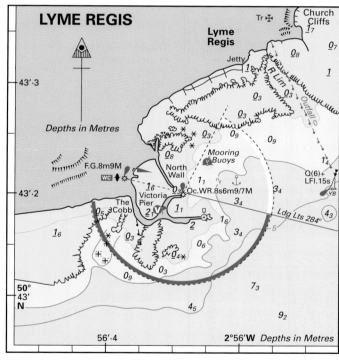

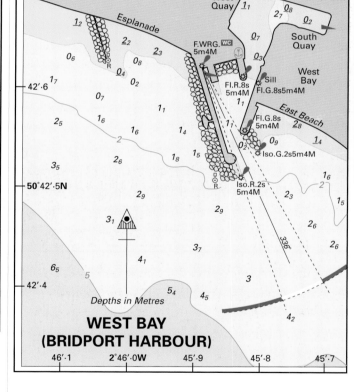

284°, is Lt with a sectored RW Lt. It is safest to keep just inside the W sector until the hbr begins to open.

Berthing The hbr dries (0.3m to 1.3m, hard sand) with limited accommodation for visitors in boats under 9m alongside the Victoria Pier. HM may reserve moorings for intending visitors. *Mobile* 07870 240645. Enter HW±0230. Anchor to the N of the Ldg line opposite the Victoria Pier. R visitors' buoys lie to the NW of the anchorage.

There are many moorings for local boats. There is a pontoon (May–September), check depth with HM, usually 2m at outer end.

Facilities Fuel, water, shops.

☎/VHF HM 01297 442137, VHF 14 (*Lyme Regis Harbour Radio*).

Interest A very attractive town famous for the fossils to be found on the beaches under the cliffs.

WEST BAY (BRIDPORT)

Charts BA 3315, SC 5601; Imray 2300, C5, C10

HW Plymouth +0050

MHWS	MHWN	MLWN	MLWS
4.1m	3.0m	1.6	0.6m

A small artificial hbr, recently extended to improve shelter and provide 200m of berthing for visitors (approx. 1.5m). Dredging is frequently necessary. Enter HW±0200. Pontoon access to new quay.

Facilities Water, electricity. Showers in nearby camp-site.

☎/VHF HM 01308 423222, *Mobile* 07870 240636, VHF 11.

PORTLAND HARBOUR

Charts BA 2268, 2255, SC 5601;
Imray 2300, C4, C10

HW Plymouth +0106 sp
+0025 np

MHWS	MHWN	MLWN	MLWS
2·1m	1·4m	0·8m	0·1m

A spacious hbr but not well sheltered now has good facilities for visiting yachts.

Streams are imperceptible in the hbr but run up to 1kn in the entrances, with eddies.

Approach The hbr is on the E side of Portland peninsula. From the W the main hazard is Portland Race; from S the Shambles and from E, Lulworth gunnery ranges. *Study Passage Notes Lyme Bay*

to Weymouth (above) and Weymouth to Poole (page 51).

Entrance The South Ship Channel is closed. Yachts must use the North Channel and follow the buoyed safety fairway. Observe 6kn speed limit at S end of the fairway. Use engine. Monitor *Portland Harbour Radio* VHF 74 while entering. Observe Port Traffic Signals.

Signals (IPTS) when shown from North and East Ship Channels.

Berthing Ferrybridge Marine Service moorings, marked FMS, in vicinity of New Channel bn, or anchor nearby, clear of moorings. Visitors' moorings may also be obtainable from Royal Dorset YC or Castle Cove SC. Uncomfortable in southerlies. Portland Marina at southern end of Safety Fairway. All facilities. Call *Marina Control* on VHF 80.

Facilities Fuel from garages. Water from SC dinghy park. Shops.

☎ HM (01305) 824 044; Royal Dorset YC 786 258; Castle Cove SC 783 708; Ferrybridge Marine Services *Mobile* 07780 610 997. Portland Marina 0845 430 2012. www.portland-port.co.uk

WEYMOUTH

Chart BA 2172, 2268, 2255, SC 5601;
Imray 2300, C4, C10

HW Plymouth +0106 sp
+0025 np
DS Dover +0545E HWD W

Tides 4hrs flood, 4hrs ebb, 4hrs slack

MHWS	MHWN	MLWN	MLWS
2·1m	1·4m	0·8m	0·1m

Owing to an eddy, stream in Weymouth Roads is W-going (not more than ½kn) at all times except Dover −0515 to −0315.

Weymouth is a commercial port and cross-channel ferry terminal with friendly

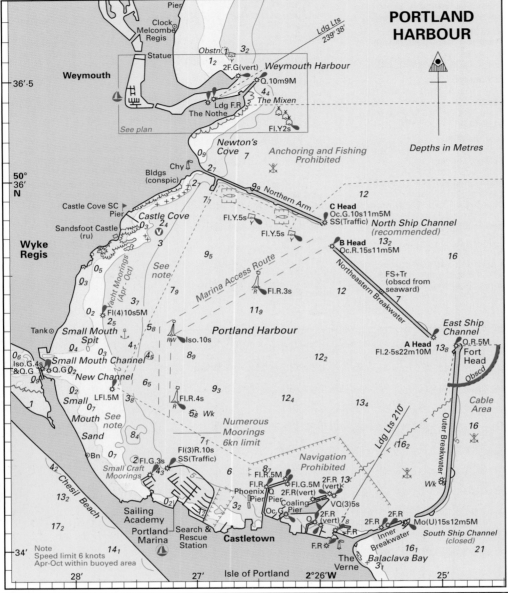

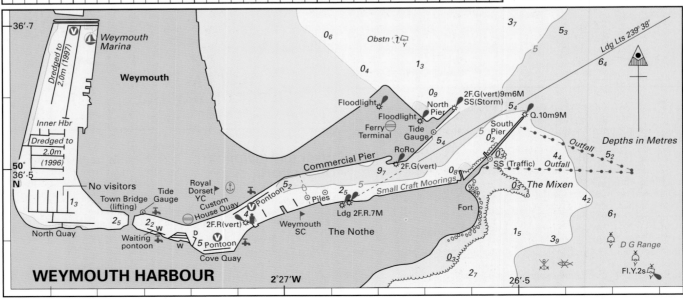

accommodation and good facilities for yachts.

Approach As for Portland Harbour. High speed cross-channel ferries use the hbr. Before closing entrance, observe traffic signals and call *Weymouth Harbour* VHF 12 (not 24hrs).

Signals, non-directional, on pole at root of S pier, all vert:
3Fl.R – All vessels await instructions
3R – Vessel leaving pierheads area, keep clear
3G – Vessel approaching pierheads area from seaward, do not leave hbr
G/W/G – A vessel may proceed only if instructed to do so
No signal Proceed with caution

Entrance Keep to N of transit through the ends of hbr piers and steer in as soon as entrance is wide open. Two R diamonds (R Lts at night) on S side of hbr in line 240° lead between the piers.

Berthing instructions may be given from office on N pier, or on VHF 12, or by piermaster in Cove area; otherwise berth as convenient until instructed by staff. Visitors' berths on pontoon in The Cove and, for craft over 10m, off Custom House Quay opposite LBS. Anchoring in the hbr is forbidden. Swell runs up the hbr with winds from E–NE. Pontoon berths for local yachts above the br; beyond them, Weymouth Marina may have some visitors' berths. Depth 2·5m. Br opens every 2hrs between 0800 and 1800 with later openings in summer (consult HM); R and G traffic Lts.

In fine weather there is a good anchorage outside the hbr 3 or 4ca N of S pier-head, 2½–3½m.

Facilities Water at pierhead and at fuel pontoon. All facilities.

☎ /VHF Berthing officer 01305 838 423; HM 838 386, VHF 12 (working day or when vessels expected), Royal Dorset YC 786 258; Weymouth Marina 767 576.
www.harbour.weymouth.gov.uk

LULWORTH COVE

Chart BA 2172, SC5601; Imray 2300, C4, C10
HW Plymouth +0110 sp +0040 np
DS Dover +0545E HWD W

MHWS	MHWN	MLWN	MLWS
2·2m	1·5m	1·0m	0·2m

A popular tourist spot comprising a circular basin with a narrow entrance. In S winds a heavy swell rolls in, dangerous with strong winds; and in NE winds katabatic effects reported in E part of the cove. Otherwise a yacht with good ground tackle may ride out bad W weather safely but uncomfortably.

WEYMOUTH TO POOLE

Charts BA 2610, 2615, SC 5601; Imray 2300, C4, C10
Hazards are Lulworth Gunnery Ranges and St Alban's Race.

Passage Light	BA No
Anvil Point	0496
Fl.10s45m9M	

Streams related to HW Dover
Lulworth to St Alban's Head, close inshore: +0500E –0200 W
W side of St Alban's Head SE almost continuously.
3½M S of St Alban's Head +0545E –0015W, 4·5kn
Durlston Head +0530NE –0030, 3kn
Peveril buoy: +0500NNE, (1½kn) –0215SSW, (3kn)
Old Harry: +0500E; –0115W

When coming from S or W of Portland Race study Passage Notes – Lyme Bay to Weymouth (page 49).

Inshore E of Weymouth there is an obstruction, least depth 4m, 3ca SE of Redcliffe Point, and rocks running out 3ca from Ringstead Point with wreck dries 2·5m. There are no dangers outside 2ca as far as Lulworth Cove. E of that avoid Kimmeridge Ledge extending seaward more than ½M.

Lulworth Gunnery Range for army firing extends from St Albans Head to a point 5M S of Lulworth Cove. In addition there is a naval gunnery range, firing from 2°17'·5W (approx) at targets marked by three DZ Lt buoys (Fl.Y, from W to E, 2s, 10s, 5s) 2½M S to SW of St Alban's Head.

Army firing is mainly in the daytime, Monday–Friday, but occasionally there is night and weekend firing. No firing in August. Information obtainable from ☎ 01929 404819 (recording) or 404700.

Naval firing is less regular. Warships patrol S of Lulworth Banks and fly R flags during firing.

When firing is in progress, range safety boats, VHF Ch 08 and 16, are stationed at the edges of the danger area. Firing times are made available to Portland Coastguards and HMs and are broadcast by Radio Solent.

Legally yachts may pass through the firing area; some do. The range officer is responsible for ceasing fire, but as this disrupts the firing schedule, yachtsmen may find themselves under very considerable pressure from the safety boats to pass clear of the area on the recommended tracks: from Weymouth Pierhead 121° to a turning point at 50°30'N 2°09'W, thence 062° to clear Anvil Point, a course which clears St Alban's Race.

St Alban's Head is easily identified with chapel and CG hut on top. Off the head the dangerous race varies in position and severity. It extends 3M seaward, less in S winds.

Overfalls extend 2½M further SW on the ebb than on the flood and are much more dangerous. Either avoid the race by giving the head a berth of 3½M or in good weather and offshore winds use the ½M-wide passage between the head and the race (passage can narrow to 50m in some conditions).

Close inshore the E-going stream starts at Dover +0500, offshore at Dover +0600. The W-going stream starts at Dover –0020.

There is deep water to close inshore between the hd and Anvil Point (W LtHo). From Anvil Point to Peveril Point rough water is frequent. Durlston Head has a castellated building on top; Peveril Point (CG and FS) has a rocky ledge running ¼M to seaward with R can buoy at end. Stream sets towards the ledge. In bad weather a dangerous race runs seaward of the buoy especially to SE with W-going stream. Between Swanage and Poole lobster-pot buoys are frequent.

On sp ebb tides the tidal streams around Anvil and Peveril Points are stronger close inshore than further out.

Anchorages

Worbarrow Bay 1M E of Lulworth Cove, sheltered from WNW·ESE. Approach on line of W ldg beacons on high ground in NE corner, front ▲, rear ◆, 043°. Anchor in E half of the bay to avoid pipe-line running SSE from Arish Mell Gap: inshore end marked by BY bn, can top. This is in the Gunnery Range area and mooring is forbidden when firing is in progress.

Chapman's Pool W of St Alban's Head. 1·6m in centre of Pool; depths inshore unreliable due to cliff falls. Open from S to SW and swell from SE. If becalmed, W of Kimmeridge Ledge, clear of rocky bottom, may be preferable.

See also separate entries for Lulworth, Swanage and Studland.

LULWORTH COVE
37'·2
Black Rks 0·4
Ramp 0·6 0·3
Moorings 0·6
Little Beach 0·9
50° 37' N
West Point
East Point
Depths in Metres
2°14'·9W 14'·7
East Over
2·7 3 0·3
4·9 3
0·3 +

Approach From W keep ½M offshore to clear Ringstead Ledge. Lulworth lies 3M E of White Nothe where the cliffs change from clay to chalk. Near the hbr the shore is steep-to. From E, Arish Mell Gap open of Worbarrow Head clears Kimmeridge Ledges.

Entrance Channel is 80m wide with 4·8m depth. The wind may be fluky or squally in the entrance. Rocky ledges extend into the hbr NNW and ENE from each side of the entrance. The W ledge obtrudes more into the entrance and a yacht

LULWORTH FIRING RANGES

Weymouth
The Bear White Nothe
Lulworth Cove
Worbarrow Bay
Kimmeridge Bay
Q.9M
Iso.R.2s (occas)
St Alban's Head
Iso.R.2s (occas)
Lulworth Banks
Firing Practice Area
Fl.Y.2s DZA
Fl.Y.5s DZC
Isle of Portland
To/from Weymouth S Pierhead Lt 302°-122° 12.6M
Fl.Y.10s DZB
35'
50° 30' N
Bill of Portland
Q(3)10s Bell E Shambles BYB
50°30'·00N 2°10'·00W
To/from 1M off Anvil Point Lt 061°-241° 9M
2°20'W 10'

should therefore keep a third of the way over from the E cliff and head for the junction of green and white cliffs on N side of hbr. Do not deviate to port or stb until fully halfway across the cove.

Anchorage in NE corner of Cove in 3m, good holding (but dragging reported in E part, SE of Y MoD mooring). Avoid obstructing the fairway to NW corner of the bay, used by

tourist boats to land passengers. Mooring buoy in NE part is for MoD vessels. If there is any suggestion of the wind going into S, get out.

Facilities Garage, hotel, stores, PO. Water at car park.

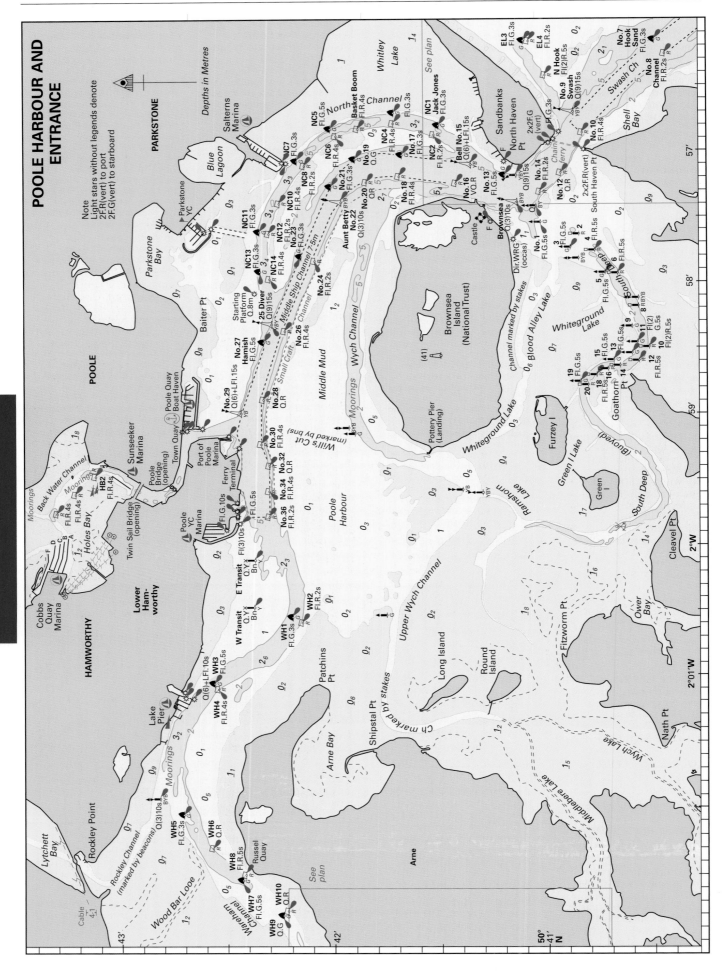

POOLE HARBOUR AND ENTRANCE

Note
Light stars without legends denote
2F.R(vert) to port
2F.G(vert) to starboard

Depths in Metres

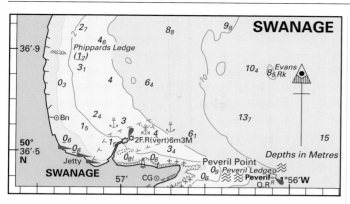

SWANAGE

SWANAGE

Chart BA 2172, SC 5601;
Imray C4, C10

LW Poole –0050
Double HW at sp
DS Dover +0500E –0100W

MHWS	MHWN	MLWN	MLWS
2.0m	1.4m	1.2m	0.3m
& 1.5m	& 1.6m		

Approach From W give Peveril
Ledge buoy a good berth as tide
sets across the ledge. There can
be a sharp race off the Pt
extending beyond the buoy.

Anchorage There is good
shelter from W winds. Anchor
1ca WNW of head of pier, good
holding but foul in places. Land
on beach.

Facilities Water at pier. Shops,
EC Thursday.

STUDLAND BAY

Chart BA 2172, SC 5601;
Imray 2300, C4, C10

Tidal data as Swanage. A
popular, very pleasant
anchorage, sheltered from S
through W to WNW. Good
holding except on visible weed
patches. Anchor about 2ca off
the beach, 2½m abreast the
Yards, three prominent
projections in the cliff. In

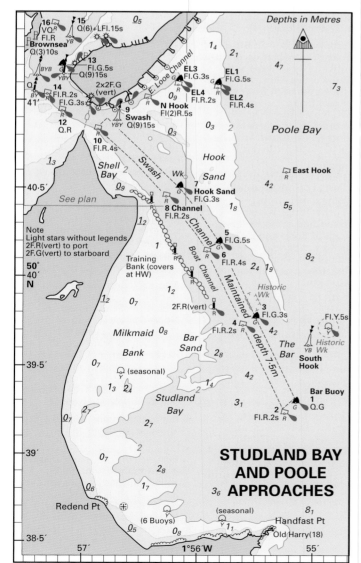

STUDLAND BAY
AND POOLE
APPROACHES

sounding to find suitable depth,
be aware of abnormal tide
heights; see tidal curves for
Poole, page 450. Riding Lts
desirable but many yachts do
not hoist them – care needed if
entering at night. Water skiers
in E half of Bay.

Supplies Shops up steep hill.
Pub nearer at hand.

POOLE HARBOUR

Chart BA 2611, SC 5601;
Imray 2300, Y23, C4, C10

An extensive natural hbr with
quays at the town, many
channels and islands, several
marinas and anchorages. There
is considerable commercial
traffic, including that from the
oil-field base at Furzey Is.

LW (Town Quay) Poole LW See
tidal curves, page 450.

HW sp (when LW is between
0230 and 0830 or 1430 and
2030) is about 5hrs after LW; a
second, lesser, HW is 4hrs after
that, 3hrs before next LW.

HW np (LW between 2030 and
0230 or 0830 and 1430) is just
over 3hrs before the next LW.
There may also be a first, lesser,
HW at nps or there may be a
rise, a stand for 2hrs and then
another rise to main HW. Range
only 0.5m.

HW related to Town Quay is:
Entrance –0030, Russel Quay
+0015, Wareham Quay +0030.
Variations in tide levels above
CD in different parts of the area
are small and levels can be
taken as:

MHWS	MHWN	MLWN	MLWS
2.2m	1.7m	1.2m	0.6m

but Wareham:

MHWS	MHWN	MLWN	MLWS
2.2m	1.7m	1.2m	0.9m

These heights are subject to a
variation of ±0.3m according to
barometric pressure and wind
direction.

Streams in entrance are ingoing
Dover –0600 3kn; outgoing
–0115, 4¾kn. Outgoing stream
is weak for first 3hrs.

Approach From W, to clear
shoals off Handfast Point, keep
Anvil Point LtHo open until
you pick up the Poole Lts, then
head up the Swash Channel.
Avoid Handfast Point tide-rip
on the ebb or in a breeze. From
the E, in reasonable conditions,
small craft need not round Bar
Buoy but should join the Swash
Channel well S of No.3 buoy,
Fl.G.3s, according to draft and
rise of tide.

Bar

MHWS	MHWN	MLWN	MLWS
5.5m	5.2m	3.7m	

Strong winds between S and E
cause a heavy sea.

Entrance Swash Channel,
buoyed and lighted and
dredged to 7.5m, leads to the
entrance between Sandbanks
and S Haven Pt. A chain ferry,

that has right of way, runs
between these two points and it
must be given a clear berth as
the chains are near the surface
at each end of the ferry. Use
engine.

W of Swash Channel is a
training bank which covers at
half tide and is marked by five
bns, R can tops. A subsidiary
Boat Channel, 3m, for small
craft, between the training
bank and Swash Channel, runs
from the port-hand bn,
2F.R(vert), to rejoin Swash
Channel just before the
entrance.

East Looe is another subsidiary
channel for small craft from E
parallel to the shore close to S
side of Sandbanks. Outer end,
marked by EL1 and EL2 buoys
(*see plan*), may have less than
1m. Only use with sufficient
rise of tide and do not attempt
in swell or onshore winds.

For commercial shipping
entering the hbr the centre of
the channel may occasionally
be shown by a DirWRG
sectored light, the W sector
bearing 299°.

Signal Orange flashing warning
light at South Haven Pt when
large vessel navigating between
Swash Channel and Aunt Betty
buoy in Middle Ship Channel.

Interior Channels It is advisable
to keep to the marked channels:
outside them the water is
generally shallow. However
recreational craft are advised to
avoid using the main channel
when leaving hbr and keep
close to Brownsea and No.14
buoys.

South Deep Channel is to port
after No.14 buoy, Fl.R.5s, and
leads to the network of
channels S of Brownsea Is and
the oil base on Furzey Is, to
which pt there are Lt bns
(mainly stb).

Anchoring Avoid oyster beds,
marked by YW buoys and
stakes, and mussel beds at W
end of Blood Alley Lake.
Otherwise anchor:
• Between Brownsea E Cardinal
and first green beacon at
entrance of South Deep. Keep
out of channel.
• In South Deep W of Goathorn
Pt or W of Green Is; tripper
boats, keep out of fairway.
• For shallow bilge-keel craft,
Blood Alley Lake, 0.3m, mud.

**Middle Ship, Small Craft,
Northern and Little Channels**
The main channel bears NNE
round N Haven W card Lt bn
after which the array of buoys,
bns and moored yachts may
appear confusing. At No.15
Middle Ground S card Lt buoy
the Northern Channel (marked
as Main Channel on some
charts) is to stb, NE; and
Middle Ship Channel (used by
large vessels) to port, due N.
Both are buoyed and lit and
bear round to W to Poole,

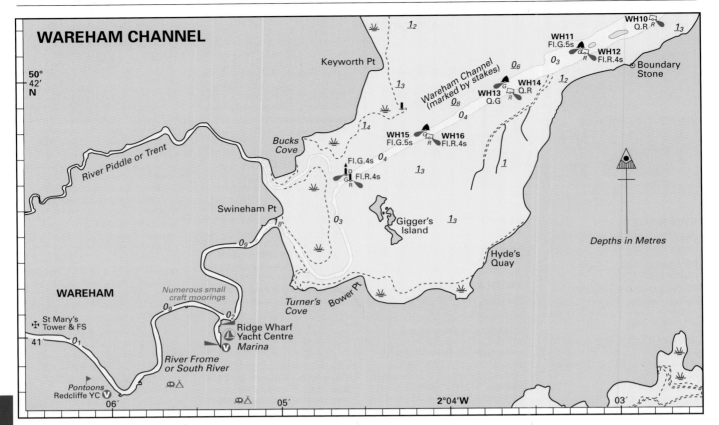

WAREHAM CHANNEL

joining again at No.25 (Diver) W card Lt bn.

Small craft are advised to take the Northern, rather than Middle Ship, Channel; but if following the latter there is on SW side, from No.18 R can buoy, a Small Craft Channel running alongside Middle Ship Channel. It is marked on its south side by R stakes with R can tops and on its north side by the Middle Ship Channel port-hand buoys, mostly Fl.R.4s. It is 30m wide, for craft with up to 1·5m draught, and goes as far as No.28 R can buoy.
Entrance to Poole Quays is via Little Channel after No.29 (Stakes) S card Lt buoy. Little Channel is buoyed N of the lifting br.

Poole Bridge and new Twin Sail Bridge Call *Poole Bridge* on VHF 12 for opening times. IPTS Traffic Lts. Only 2m clearance when closed.

Berthing Anchoring is forbidden in Middle Ship, Northern and Little Channels. Moorings are sometimes available from yards.
• Salterns Marina, entered from NC7 buoy in North Channel, may have visitors' berths.
• Parkstone Haven (part of Parkstone YC), entered via a channel dredged to 1·5m from NC11 buoy in North Channel, welcomes visitors. Call Parkstone Haven on VHF 80 or 37.
• Port of Poole Marina.
• Town Quay entered via Little Channel. Can be crowded and difficult to clear on ebb with several craft outside; very

uncomfortable with strong winds from S to E. Berth in vacant space or alongside another vessel of similar size to yours. Vessels under 15m should use Poole Quay Boat Haven below if space is available.
• Poole Quay Boat Haven, immediately E of Town Quay. For both Port of Poole Marina and Poole Quay Boat Haven call *Poole Quay Boat Haven* on VHF 80. You will then be directed to an available berth. Call Poole Quay Boat Haven before entering from N end of Little Channel. 100 berths, all for visitors, but at peak times phone in advance to reserve berth. W half has 3·5m, E half 2·5m.

Wych Channel Adjacent to No.18 R can buoy a bn marks the S edge of the entrance to Wych Channel, rounding Brownsea Is to N, marked with stakes. There are two shallow (1m) short-cuts across the mud linking Wych to the main channel: Ball's Lake, near the NE tip of Arne peninsula, and Wills Cut from NW corner of Brownsea Is. Each is marked by stakes.

Berthing Anchor
• Clear of moorings (e.g. to NW of Brownsea Is) clear of oyster beds or off Pottery Pier.
• Shipstal Point 1m.

Wareham Channel is the continuation of the main channel after the entrance to Poole Quay and leads to the entrance to River Frome and thence to Wareham. It is buoyed and staked and is lit at the main turning pts as far

Gigger's Island; it is navigable at HW to Wareham for craft up to 1·5m draught. Channel subject to silting.

Berthing Anchor off Russel Quay or elsewhere according to draft and oyster beds S of Hamworthy. Alongside berths:
• Ridge Wharf in River Frome
• Redcliffe YC
• Wareham Town Quay is not recommended except for very short stay as tourist launches are liable to berth alongside.

Supplies
• Diesel in Parkstone Haven;
• Fuel at Corals, oposite Town Quay, just below br;
• Fuel at Ridge Wharf on River Frome, and at most yards. Shops at Poole and Wareham. Visitors to Parkstone Haven are temporary members of Parkstone YC, with bar and restaurant.

✆ /VHF HM 01202 440 230, VHF 16, 14 (24hrs); Salterns Marina 709 971, VHF 80, 37; Parkstone Haven 743 610, VHF 80, 37 *(Parkstone Haven)*; Poole Quay Boat Haven 649488, VHF 80 *(Poole Quay Boat Haven)*; Cobb's Quay 674299, VHF 80, 37 *(CQ Base)*; Ridge Wharf 01929 554434; for moorings: Sandbanks Boatyard and Marina (01202) 708068; Stevenson Moorings and Marine Services 675738; Dorset Yacht Co (Hamworthy) 674531. www.phc.co.uk

CHRISTCHURCH
Charts BA 2172, 2035, SC 5601.5; Imray 2200, C4, DS Dover +0500E; –0115 W
LW Entrance Portsmouth –0035. At sps there is 5hrs rise, 3½hrs stand, 4hrs ebb. At nps there is 5½hrs flood, 2¾hrs stand and 4¼hrs ebb. The ebb in the entrance is fierce after the second HW. In the hbr, tide height can be critical – see *Poole tidal curves*.

MHWS	MHWN	MLWN	MLWS
1·8	1·4m	0·7m	0·6m
& 1·5m			

Entry safe during HW stand for draughts up to 1·1m (1·3m at sps) except in fresh winds between S and E.

Beware of changing depths in entrance from those charted.

Approach Entrance lies about ¾M NE of Hengistbury Head. From E, leave the Solent via North Channel. From W give groyne off Hengistbury Head ¾M berth to clear Beerpan Rocks. Beware of Clarendon Rocks, a groyne of stones running 1½ca offshore, 3ca SSW of entrance. Keep offshore to make approach from SE.

Bar has normally 0·3 to 0·6m but varies in depth and position.

Entrance over the bar is marked in season by two lateral buoys and about four pairs of sph buoys. There is a Lt Fl.G.2s at NE end of Mudeford Quay. Best times to enter: sps from 2hrs before first HW to second HW; nps at or between the two HWs. Streams in The Run are

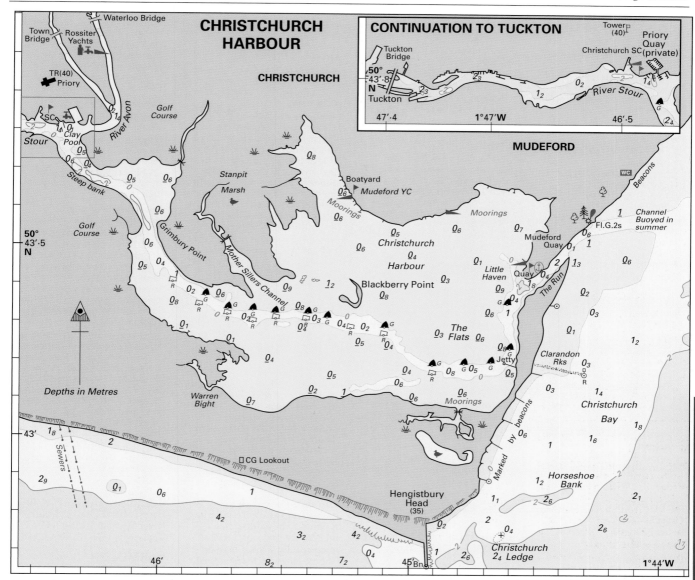

strong. The ebb there and in the hbr continues until 1½hrs after LW. Beware fishermen shooting nets in The Run.

Inside, after Mudeford Quay bear sharply to port and give first G sph buoy a wide berth to stb. The channel is well buoyed to Grimsbury Pt after which moorings indicate it. Leave moored boats to stb until the pontoon jetty, after which leave them to port. Depths in the two rivers vary from 0·6m to 1·3m.

Berthing Anchoring room is limited but possibilities are:
• In reach running SSW from Mudeford Quay between Black House and pontoon jetty; restrict swing with two anchors.
• In unmarked pool (0·6m) close to N side of Hengistbury Hd, entered from reach above pontoon jetty.
• At SE end of Steepbank on W side immediately below moorings in approach to rivers.
• In Clay Pool at junction of the rivers.

Moorings enquire at Christchurch SC, G Elkins or Christchurch Marine.

Supplies Fuel at Christchurch Marine; water from Mudeford beach or Christchurch SC. Limited supplies from Mudeford beach café. Shops at Mudeford village and Christchurch.

☎ Harbour Authority Christchurch Borough Council 01202 486 321; Christchurch SC 483 150; Christchurch Marine 483 250.

NEEDLES CHANNEL

Charts BA 2035, SC 5600; Imray 2200, C3, C15

DS (Needles entrance) Portsmouth +0520E; –0045W

For lights see Poole to Chichester Passage Notes, above.

With wind against the ebb, the entrance is uncomfortable, at times dangerous, and N Channel is then to be preferred. Even at other times conditions can be difficult for small craft when there are strong winds. The tide sets across the Shingles on both the ebb and flood; this

calls for extreme care when SW-bound with the ebb. The Bank is encroaching into the channel, parts drying as much as 1·2m; after severe gales there can be deposits above HW level which gradually disperse.

Needles Channel The main entrance is made between SW Shingles port-hand pillar buoy, Fl.R.2·5s, and Br W card buoy, VQ(9)10s Racon(T) (–), in the W sector (041°) of Hurst Point Lt Iso.WRG.4s. The Br can be very turbulent and small craft will generally find it smoother to cross 3ca E of the Br buoy, about a third of the distance to Needles Lt ho, just E of the IsoG sector of Hurst Point Lt. (Note that a W sector of the Fl(4)WR.15s Lt on the same tr is visible when Hurst Point bears less than 053°).

Beware of the Goose Rock and wrecks, awash at LW, which extend nearly 2ca W from Needles LtHo.

Once over The Br, steer towards the Island side of the channel. At night this brings you into a W sector of Needles Lt, Ldg to Warden G con buoy, Fl.G.2·5s, clear of dangers off the Island shore.

North Channel From Christchurch Ledge make good to NE (flood setting onto Shingles to stb) in the northern W sector of Hurst Point Lt (Fl(4)WR.15s) to North Head buoy, G con Fl(3)G.10s, then steer SE with Golden Hill Fort (white) on with Brambles Chine, parallel with Hurst Spit to leave NE Shingles E card Lt buoy to stb. Streams run strongly in the channel, mainly in its direction.

Caution There are nearly always overfalls in Hurst narrows. The Trap is a spit which runs S from Hurst Point with 0·2m at its inshore end which the tide sets onto.

Anchorages: Off the Needles Channel in Alum Bay (mind drying rocks 1 and 2ca W of coloured cliffs) and in Totland Bay where the 2F.G(vert) Lts on the pier provide a guide at night; also a good anchorage NW of Hurst Pt (*see Keyhaven plan*). These anchorages are useful when waiting for a fair stream through the channel.

POOLE TO CHICHESTER

Charts BA 2450, SC 5600;
Imray 2200, 2300, C4, C3, C9,
C12, C15

The main hazards are
Christchurch Ledge and the
Shingles Bank on NW side of the
Needles Channel.

Passage lts	BA No
Bridge Lt buoy	0527.6
VQ(9)10s5M, Racon(T) (–)	
The Needles	0528
Oc(2)WRG.20s24m17/13M	
Horn(2)30s (R sector over	
Shingles) and dangers to S of	
Island	
Hurst Point	0538.1
Fl(4)WR.15s23m13/11M	
DirIso.WRG.4s19m21–17M	
(W sector 041° over Needles	
Channel)	
St Catherine's Point	0774
Fl.5s41m25M	
(+F.R.13M 099°-vis-116°)	
Nab Tower	0780
Fl(2)5s28m5M	

Tides

From Christchurch to
Southampton there is a stand
around the time of HW
Portsmouth during which some
places have a small fall followed
by a second HW; others have a
second HW only at sps.

Streams related to HW Dover

Poole Bay,
offshore +0530NE –0030SW,
inshore +0500E –0115W, 1kn

Needles entrance
+0530E; –0030W

North Channel to Hurst approx
+0500E –0100W

Ryde Pier, N of +0415E –0130W

S of Isle of Wight +0530ENE
–0045WSW, 5kn between St
Catherine's Point and Dunnose.

Nab Tower HWD W +0100SW
+0615E –0400ENE –0245NE
–0030N

The E stream sets towards
Christchurch ledge and across
the Shingles. The W stream sets
well S of Durlston Head and
Anvil Point. Streams are weak
inside the line Handfast Point to
Hengistbury Head and in
Christchurch Bay but are strong
across Christchurch Ledge and
the Shingles. Between Poole
and Wight the flood sets
strongly into Poole Bay.

North Channel to Hurst approx
+0500E –0100W

Ryde Pier, N of +0415E –0130W

S of IoW +0530ENE –0045WSW,
5kn between St Catherine's
Point and Dunnose.

Nab Tower HWD W
+0100SW +0615E –0400ENE
–0245NE –0030N

The E stream sets towards
Christchurch ledge and across
the Shingles. The W stream sets
well S of Durlston Head and
Anvil Point. Streams are weak
inside the line Handfast Point to
Hengistbury Head and in
Christchurch Bay but are strong
across Christchurch Ledge and
the Shingles. Between Poole
and Wight the flood sets
strongly into Poole Bay.

Hengistbury Head is prominent
with dark red cliffs, 18m high
and a lookout, conspic, with FS
4½ca to W.

There are overfalls on
Christchurch Ledge on the ebb.
Christchurch Priory open SW of
the lookout on Warren Hill (W
side of Hengistbury Head), 333°
leads SW of it. If crossing the
Ledge in fair weather aim for a
point about 1½M SE of
Hengistbury Head. Close inshore
there are rocks, awash at LW,
½ca off the head of the groyne.

In fog the position of Needles Lt
can often be gauged from the
fact that fog lies lightly to W of
the entrance, but hangs in a
dark and heavy patch on the
cliff overlooking the Lt.

The Solent

Entrance to the Solent is via the
Needles Channel or the North
Channel (*see separate entry
below*).

Within the Solent

Hazards are the mud flats along
the N side of West Solent,
Gurnard Ledge on the S side W
of West Cowes, Bramble Bank
(dries 1·1m) in the entrance to
Southampton Water, the
submerged obstruction running
inshore from N of Horse Sand
Fort, and the remains of the

submerged barrier, least depth
2m, extending 3·5ca SW from
No Man's Land Fort.
Movements of large ships
present another Hazard – *see
Shipping Movements under
Central Solent on page 61*.

East of Isle of Wight

Note that the Nab Channel, N
of Nab Tower, is for deeply-
laden inbound tankers; further
south, deep draft vessels
manoeuvre to enter the
channel and there are pilot
boarding areas SE and SW of
Nab Tower.

South of Isle of Wight

At night, rounding St
Catherine's Point from NW,
keep in Needles W sector until
St Catherine's Lt bears 064° and
keep S of latter's F.R sector. To
clear the worst of the race (bad
in strong wind against tide
conditions, severe to SE of the
Point with W gales) keep 2M
offshore.

Anchorages are to be found in
suitable conditions off the coast
in Poole and Christchurch Bays,
and off the Isle of Wight in
Freshwater Bay on the SW coast
and N of St Helen's Fort on the
E coast. Within the Solent there
are good anchorages NW of
Hurst Point (*see Keyhaven
plan*), and in Osborne Bay.

KEYHAVEN

Chart BA 2021;
Imray 2200, C3

At Hurst Pt

LW Portsmouth –0030

Sps: rise for 6½hrs to 1st HW,
fall for 1hr, stand and small rise
to 2nd HW for 1½hrs, fall for
3½hrs. Nps: Rise for 7½hrs,
followed by fall, with no stand
or 2nd HW.

MHWS	MHWN	MLWN	MLWS
2·7	2·3m	1·4m	0·7m
& 2·5m			

DS (Hurst Narrows) Portsmouth
+0515NE –0100SW, 4kn

A small attractive creek with
limited room for anchoring.

Approach From E, keep Hurst
Point Lt tr bearing not less than
225°. From W, give The Trap
off S side of Hurst Castle a
berth of 1½ca.

Entrance The bar changes. Do
not attempt entrance in strong
E winds. The leading line,
marked by two small RW
horizontally striped boards
(inconspic) which are moved
from time to time, is generally
about 285°. The entrance is
marked by two small buoys, G
and R. Inside, the channel is
marked by a few stb buoys, one
port buoy just inside the
entrance and the line of private
moorings. Pass round the bows
of all moored craft as the areas
astern are shallow.

Berthing The river is congested
with private moorings but
space to anchor may be found
in the bay just inside the
entrance. The heavy mooring
there is used by the tender for
maintenance at the castle. Land
on the spit or at Keyhaven
hard. Short-term mooring is
generally possible at HW at
Keyhaven Quay.

In favourable conditions it may
be preferable to anchor outside
the entrance where there is
more room. Sound to find a
suitable depth with Hurst Lt tr
bearing about 220°. Land on
beach near ferry pier. Riding Lt
essential at night.

Facilities Fuel at W Solent Boat
Builders in emergency only;
otherwise by can from Milford.
Water at Keyhaven YC and at
River Warden's Office. Inn at
Keyhaven; shops at Milford.
EC Wednesday.

① Harbour Authority: New
Forest DC, 023 80285 000.
River Warden 01590 645 695;
Keyhaven YC: 01590 642 165.

YARMOUTH
(ISLE OF WIGHT)

Charts BA 2021, SC 5600;
Imray 2200, C15, C3

LW Portsmouth –0030. Sps rise
for 6¾hrs to 1st HW, fall for
1¼hrs, stand and small rise to
2nd HW for 1hr, fall for 3½hrs.
Nps rise for 8hrs, followed by
fall. No stand or 2nd HW.

MHWS	MHWN	MLWN	MLWS
3·0m	2·6m	1·6m	0·8m
& 2·8m			

DS Portsmouth +0500E –0100W.
Stream runs hard across the
outer half of pier but weaker
near the entrance where hbr
stream takes over.

A very popular hbr, likely to be
full early on Saturday
afternoons in season.

Approach From W keep 2ca
offshore to clear Black Rock
(dries) until abreast Y buoy,
Fl.Y.5s, then aim for the pier,
about a third of its length from
the head, until Ldg marks in
line. From E beware anglers'
lines in rounding pier.

Entrance Ldg Lts F.G front and
rear, W diamonds black band
on W posts, 188°. There are
2F.R(vert) each side of the ferry
ramp and Fl.G.5s on dolphin at
W side of entrance. Illuminated
notice 'Harbour Full' or R flag

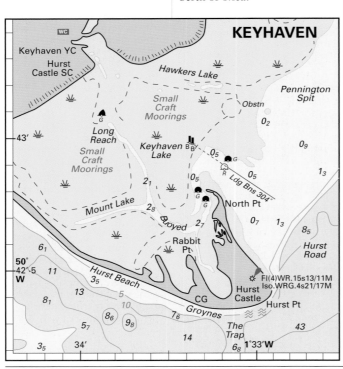

KEYHAVEN

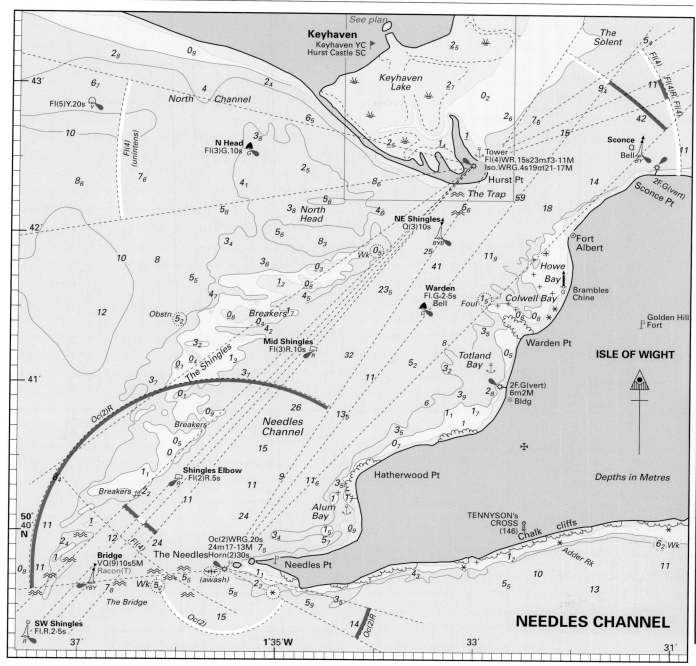

SOLENT – CHERBOURG PASSAGE NOTES

Cherbourg Passe de l'Ouest is 59M from the Needles, 65M from Nab Tower, so the open water passage will typically take 10 to 15 hours. There are no traffic separation zones on either route but you will cross fairly busy shipping lanes just N and S of 50°N lat.

Starting from Cowes or Southampton Water, the course via the Needles is usually the better choice because it is shorter and, with the prevailing SW'ly wind, you are more likely to complete the crossing in a single reach. In deciding your departure time, it is important to ensure that you get through the Needles channel before the end of the ebb (HW Dover+0400). Also, you will probably want to aim to reach Cherbourg before dusk or after dawn.

In setting a course to steer across the channel, it is best to start by estimating what the direction of the tidal stream will be when you reach the French coast and to set a course to arrive a couple of miles upstream of your destination, taking account of the net tidal vector for the whole crossing. You will need to correct the course as you close the French coast.

Additional considerations apply to the return crossing, from Cherbourg to the Solent. If heading for the Needles it is important to arrive on the flood, with at least an hour in hand to get through Hurst Narrows before the stream turns foul. With strong W or SW winds it may be better to avoid the Needles and enter the Solent through the North Channel (*see above*) or even via the Nab.

by day at end of ferry jetty (R flag also at Pierhead) mean no spare berths inside, but there is usually room outside on the visitors' moorings N of breakwater. Failing that, anchor N of moorings, but stream is strong. It is inadvisable to enter under sail because of ferry movements and, in season, congestion. At the dolphin beware of traffic emerging on stb hand from outer line of piles.

Berthing Walk-ashore berths are bookable in advance through the Harbour Office. Otherwise on arrival moor as directed by Berthing Master or find space on a visitors' pontoon, rafting up if necessary. Berthing on S quay only, with permission, for loading and unloading. Moorings sometimes available from the two yards for a longer stay. Br opens about every two

hrs in summer; by arrangement in winter. River navigable by dinghy at HW to Freshwater Causeway.

Outside visitors' moorings following 3m contour except two at W end in 2m. Anchor outside according to height of tide, clear of entrance to W of pier. Sand, shingle.

Facilities Fuel and pumpout facilities at E end central pontoon, water also at Town Quay. Good shops, including chandlers (EC Wed), also at Freshwater (EC Thurs).

Water taxi serves all moorings, including those outside and anchored craft. Scrubbing berths alongside breakwater – *see plan*. Buses to Freshwater and Newport. Ferry to Lymington. New administrative, shower, toilet and laundry block on S quay.

ENGLAND – SOUTH COAST

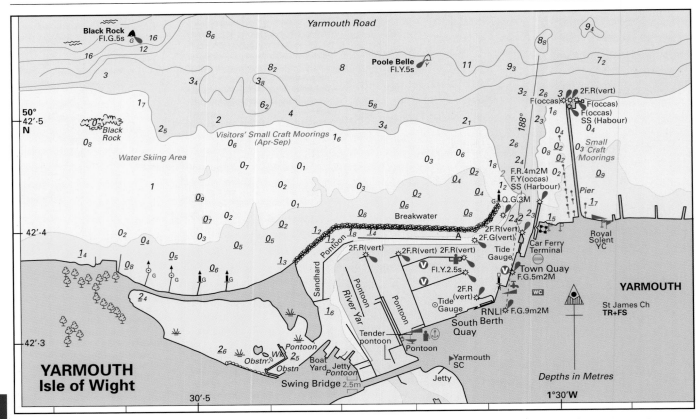

YARMOUTH
Isle of Wight

Depths in Metres

1°30'W

✆ /VHF HM 01983 766 130. Harbour office 760 321. VHF 68; R Solent YC 760 256; Harold Hayles Boatyard 760 373; River Yar Boatyard 760 521; Water taxi VHF 15; Bridge requests VHF 68, *Yar Bridge.*

CENTRAL SOLENT

Charts BA 2038; SC 5600; Imray 2200
HW (Calshot Castle) Southampton +0015
DS W app Ch Portsmouth +0500E –0115W

Shipping movements Large vessels navigating between Spithead and Southampton invariably use the Western Approach Channel (SW of Bramble Bank), Thorn Channel (W of the Bank) and Calshot Reach (N of the Bank) and have to make two turns, one of them through 120°. These channels are designated a **Precautionary Area** (*see plan*). Within the area, vessels over 150m in length display a black cylinder by day, 3 F.R(vert) Lts by night, and may be preceded by a patrol launch showing a Fl.Bu Lt. Such vessels are deemed to be enclosed by a Moving Prohibited Zone (MPZ), 200m wide and extending 1000m ahead. Small craft are required to remain outside the MPZ.

Small craft skippers are advised to monitor Southampton VTS, VHF Ch 12, to keep informed of shipping movements. They can also hear warnings of large vessel movements and other information broadcast on VHF Ch 14 on the hour between 0600 and 2200 Fridays to Sundays and Bank Holidays from Easter Good Friday to end of October, and daily between 1 June and 30 September.

The North Channel connects Calshot Reach with the East Solent and is used by smaller commercial shipping.

High Speed Craft mainly plying between Southampton and Cowes, generally use the recognised main channels but may navigate outside them to avoid risk of collision. In good visibility during daylight in the summer they may take a more direct route across the Bramble Bank area. They are not allowed to pass inshore of Calshot Reach and Thorn Channel between Black Jack and Bourne Gap Lt buoys.

Cowes – Southampton Water The three mile crossing between Cowes and Southampton Water deserves careful planning to take account of shipping movements, Bramble Bank (dries 1·2m), East Knoll (least depth 0·6m) and strong tidal streams, especially between Cowes and the Bramble where the spring rate can reach nearly 4kn. It is best to keep out of the Precautionary Area as far as possible, particularly the Western Approach Channel where large vessels may turn through 120° and the stream can exceed 2·5kn. The Bramble beacon, Y, unlit, can be hard to see but once spotted is an invaluable guide both to the position of the drying bank and to how one is being set by the stream.

Racing buoys There are several Y racing buoys (*not shown in plan*) in the area, many of which are lit Fl.Y.4s.

LYMINGTON

Chart BA 2021, SC 5600; Imray 2200, C15, C3

LW Portsmouth –0020 Sps rise for 6¾hrs to 1st HW, fall for 1¼hrs, stand and small rise to 2nd HW for 1hr, fall for 3½hrs. Nps: Rise for 8hrs, followed by fall. No stand or 2nd HW.

DS Portsmouth +0430NE –0130SW

MHWS	MHWN	MLWN	MLWS
3·0 & 2·9m	2·6m	1·4m	0·7m

Approach Keep Hurst Lt tr bearing not less than 225° to clear the mud banks either side of the entrance; at night do not go N of W sector of Hurst Point Fl(4)WR.15s until on line of F.R Ldg Lts, 319°. The RLYC starting platform on E corner of entrance is conspic landmark by day.

Entrance All craft must give way to Wightlink ferries which take up much of the channel. They pass abreast between Cocked Hat pile and Seymours Post on parallel Ldg lines 008° and 188°. Keep well to stb but

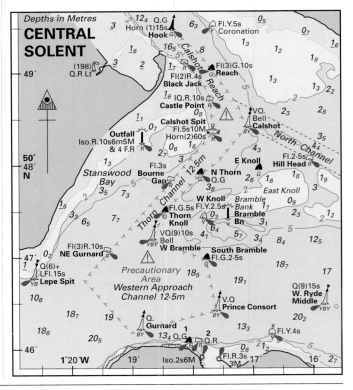

Depths in Metres

CENTRAL SOLENT

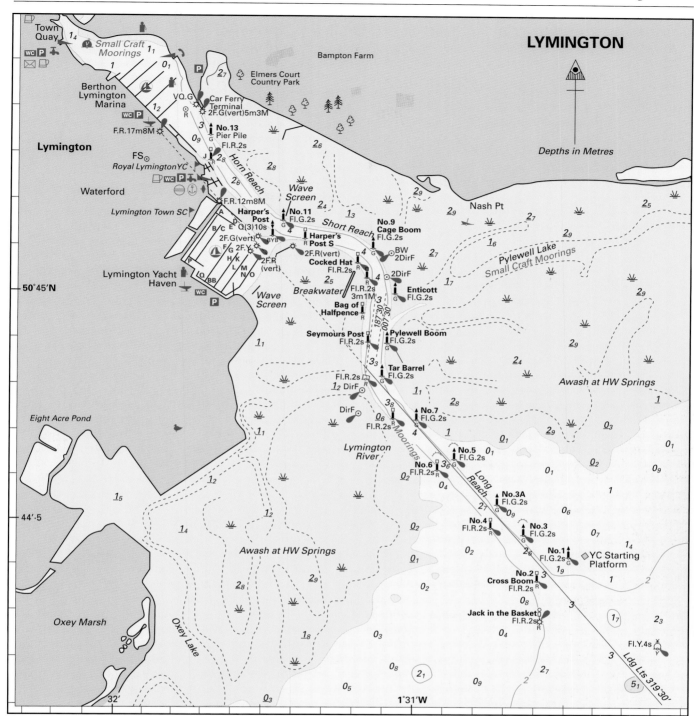

LYMINGTON

Depths in Metres

remember that in passing they lower the water level and the mud flats are steep-to. The channel is marked by Lt bns as far as ferry terminal opposite Berthon Lymington Marina. The bns are on the edge of the drying mud flats. It is important to follow the natural curves of the river rather than going in a straight line from bn to bn, especially above Cage Boom and Cocked Hat bns. The final stretch to Town Quay is not lit but is navigable at night with care by following lines of moored boats. Entrance to Lymington Yacht Haven is marked by Harper's Post E card Lt bn and 2F.G(vert) on S end of breakwater. Leave both to stb on Ldg Lts F.Y 244°.

Berthing Anchoring in hbr is prohibited. Visitors' berths at Lymington Yacht Haven, Berthon Lymington Marina and at Town Quay (pontoons alongside and fore and aft buoys). Hbr very busy. Seek advice from HM if berthing near Town Quay.

Facilities Fuel at marinas, water but no electricity at Town Quay; all facilities. Chandlers and good shops. Rly.

☎ /VHF HM 01590 672 014; R Lymington YC 672 677; Lymington Yacht Haven 677 071. VHF 80, 37; Lymington Marina 647 405. VHF 80, 37. No VHF for Town Quay.

BEAULIEU RIVER

Chart BA 2021, SC 5600; Imray 2200, C15, C3

LW (entrance) Portsmouth –0100
Rise for 7hrs (sps), 7½hrs (nps)
DS Portsmouth –0115W +0500E

At entrance

MHWS	MHWN	MLWN	MLWS
3·9m	3·3m	1·6m	0·7m

At Buckler's Hard

MHWS	MHWN	MLWN	MLWS
3·7m	3·0m	1·7m	0·5m

See plan on page 60.

A beautiful, natural river, winding its way down through wooded countryside, past Buckler's Hard, a historic village with maritime museum, hotel and marina, past Gull

Island and mud flats to emerge into the West Solent at Lepe.

Approach From the SW, keep well off the Beaulieu Spit mudbanks until abreast of East Lepe R can buoy, Fl(2)R.5s, to stb and the conspicuous boathouse to port. By day, this boathouse on with the W-most cottage beyond it, heads towards the entrance, intercepting the Ldg line Lepe House in line with No.2 bn, 324°. By night follow in the W sector, 334°, of the DirOc.WRG.4s Lt on the Millennium Bn. From the NE, leave Lepe Spit S card Lt buoy to stb and head SW to intercept one or other Ldg line.

ENGLAND – SOUTH COAST

BEAULIEU RIVER

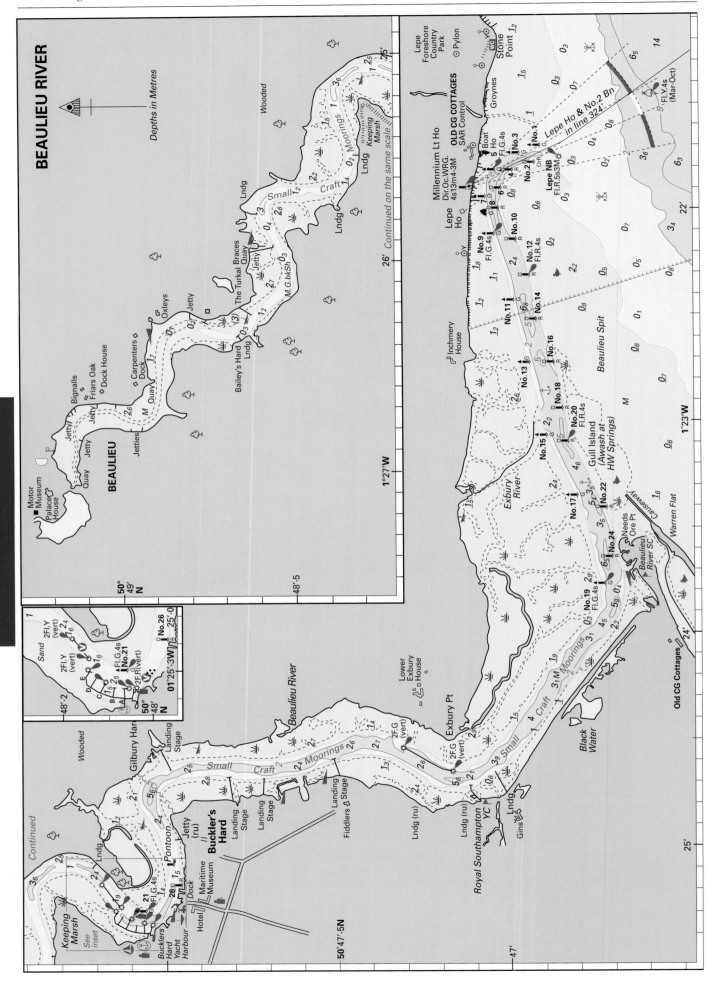

Depths in Metres

BEAULIEU

Motor Museum
Palace House

Jetty
Bignalls
Friars Oak
Dock House
Carpenters Dock

Quay
Quay
Jetty
Jetty
Jetties

Wooded

Oxleys
Jetty
Jetty

The Turkal
Braces Quay
M.G.bkSh
Jetty
Bailey's Hard

Wooded

Small Craft

Moorings

Keeping Marsh

Lndg
Lndg
Lndg

Continued on the same scale

50° 49' N

48'·5

1°27'W

26'

25'

Inset:
Sand
2Fl.Y
2Fl.Y (vert)
2Fl.Y (vert)
2F.R(vert)
Fl.G.4s
No.21
No.26
E D C B A
01'25'·3W
50° 48' N
25'·0

Continued

Keeping Marsh

Buckler's Hard Yacht Harbour
See inset
21 Fl.G.4s
26

Maritime Museum
Hotel
Dock
Jetty (ru)
Pontoon

Buckler's Hard

Gilbury Hard
Landing Stage
Landing Stage
Landing Stage
Landing Stage
Fiddlers Stage

Wooded

Beaulieu River

Small Craft Moorings

Lower Exbury House

Exbury Pt
2F.G (vert)
2F.G (vert)

Lndg (ru)
Lndg (ru)
Royal Southampton YC
Gins
Lndg
Beaulieu River SC
Needs Ore Pt
Causeway
Warren Flat

Small Craft Moorings

Black Water

Old CG Cottages

50° 47'·5N
47'
25'
24'
1°23'W

Exbury River

Lepe Foreshore Country Park
Pylon
Stone Point 1₂
Groynes

OLD CG COTTAGES
SAR Control
Lepe Ho & No.2 Bn in line 324°
Millennium Lt Ho
Dir.Oc.WRG. 4s13m4-3M
Lepe Ho
Boat Ho
5 Ho
Fl.G.4s
No.3
No.1
No.2
No.4
6
7
8
Lepe NB
Fl.R.5s3M
No.9 Fl.G.4s
No.10
No.12 Fl.R.4s
No.11
No.13
No.14
No.16
No.15
No.18
No.20 Fl.R.4s
No.22
No.17
No.24
No.19 Fl.G.4s

Inchmery House

Beaulieu Spit

Gull Island (Awash at HW Springs)

Fl.Y.4s (Mar-Oct)

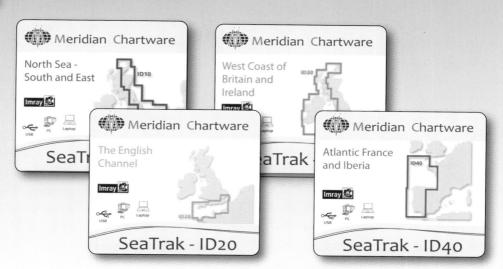

Imray Digital Charts

Imray Digital Charts are electronic editions of standard Imray charts published on USB sticks in PC format with integrated GPS plotter software.

Each Chart Pack comes with on line corrections and upgrades for a year.

Imray Digital Charts are now published by Meridian Chartware as Meridian Digital Charts

Meridian Chartware — North Sea – South and East — ID10

Meridian Chartware — West Coast of Britain and Ireland — ID30

Meridian Chartware — The English Channel — SeaTrak – ID20

Meridian Chartware — Atlantic France and Iberia — SeaTrak – ID40

Full support to users at **www.meridian-chartware.co.uk**

Entrance should not be attempted approx 2hrs either side of LW depending on tide and draught of boat. The entrance is well marked by closely spaced bns and the outermost mark is a port-hand dolphin with directional Lt Fl.R.5s, visible from seaward. Channel is well marked, initially by bns with R and G reflectors, of which three stb and two port are lit; after the bns there are perches. Least depth 1·5m to Buckler's Hard.

Berthing Anchor in first reach up to Needs Oar Point clear of fairway; strong stream.

Anchoring prohibited within 1M either side of Buckler's Hard. Marina (2m) and pile moorings at Buckler's Hard. At marina, visitors berth on outer pontoons above marina; beware of stream setting across pontoons. Report to HM within 24hrs of arrival.

Facilities Water and fuel, hotel, shop and Maritime Museum at Buckler's Hard. Shops at Beaulieu, 2M by footpath or, depending on tide, by dinghy.

✆ HM and Yacht Harbour 01590 616 200 or 616 234.

NEWTOWN RIVER (ISLE OF WIGHT)

Charts BA 2021, SC 5600; Imray 2200, C15, C3

LW Portsmouth –0015. Rise for 6¾hrs (sp), 7¼hrs (np).

Solent Banks

MHWS	MHWN	MLWN	MLWS
3·4m	2·8m	1·6m	0·7m

An unspoilt sheltered natural hbr renowned for its bird life, especially in winter. Owned by the National Trust who give discounts on anchoring fees to NT members.

Approach The entrance lies ¾M E of Hamstead Ledge G con buoy Fl(2)G.5s. From E, Yarmouth Pierhead open of Hamstead Pt skirts the edge of Newtown Gravel Banks (3½m).

Entrance Ldg bns (130°): front RW, Y-shaped top, rear W bn, W circle with black surround at top, off Fishhouse Point lead over the bar (1·1m) with a W card buoy Q(9)15s to port in approach. Within, channels are marked by R and G stakes with can or pointed topmarks. Beware of overhead power lines near the head of Clamerkin Lake, clearance 9m.

Berthing W visitors' buoys on both sides of entrance. HM allows double rafting if first occupant agrees. HM may also allocate vacant R buoys to visitors. Anchorage in main channel before the moorings or in Clamerkin Lake as far as the two 'Anchorage Prohibited' notice boards (oyster beds). Poor holding on clay unless anchor well dug in. Anchoring possible E or W of entrance, clear of banks. Landing on Fishhouse Point is prohibited (nature reserve). Land at Shalfleet Quay, Newtown Quay (both dry) or Lower Hamstead on W side of entrance.

Facilities Fuel and bottled gas at Shalfleet Garage. Food at Shalfleet PO/shop and New Inn, or farm produce at Coleman's Farm; bus to Yarmouth or Newport. Water at Newtown and Shalfleet Quays and Lower Hamstead. Small yard at Shalfleet Quay.

✆ HM 01983 531 424, no VHF. Shalfleet Garage 531 315. New Inn 531 314.

ENGLAND – SOUTH COAST

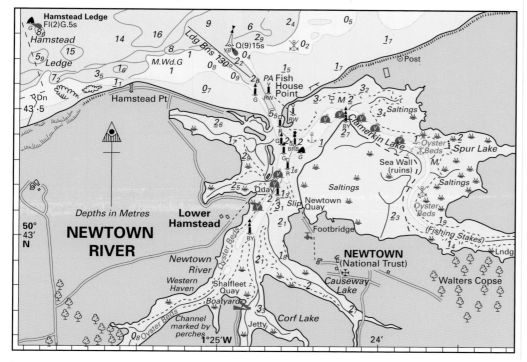

NEWTOWN RIVER — Depths in Metres — 50° 43' N — 1°25'W

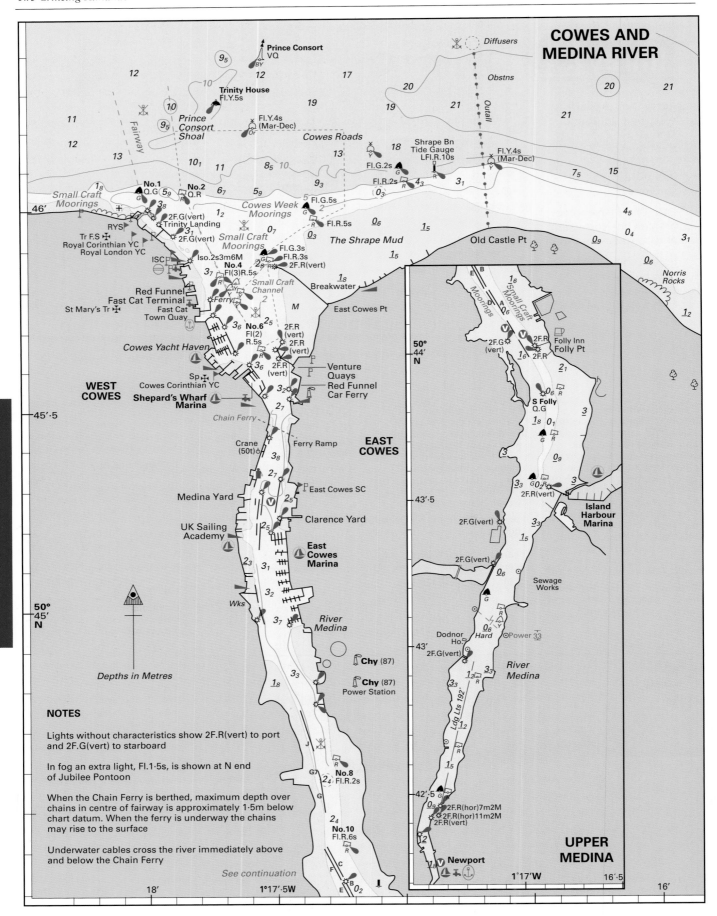

COWES AND MEDINA RIVER

ENGLAND – SOUTH COAST

NOTES

Lights without characteristics show 2F.R(vert) to port and 2F.G(vert) to starboard

In fog an extra light, Fl.1·5s, is shown at N end of Jubilee Pontoon

When the Chain Ferry is berthed, maximum depth over chains in centre of fairway is approximately 1·5m below chart datum. When the ferry is underway the chains may rise to the surface

Underwater cables cross the river immediately above and below the Chain Ferry

See continuation

Depths in Metres

UPPER MEDINA

COWES AND RIVER MEDINA (ISLE OF WIGHT)

Chart BA 2793, SC 5600; Imray 2200, C15, C3, 2200.6

HW Portsmouth +0015

DS Portsmouth +0430E –0115W In R Medina, Portsmouth +0515 flood, +0015 ebb

Cowes

MHWS	MHWN	MLWN	MLWS
4·2m	3·5m	1·8m	0·8m

Folly Inn

MHWS	MHWN	MLWN	MLWS
4·1m	3·4	1·8m	1·0m

Newport

MHWS	MHWN	MLWN	MLWS
4·1m	3·4	2·0m	1·6m

A busy port and yachting centre with ferries and cat to Southampton. Accessible at all states of tide and with good all-round shelter in upper reaches.

Extensive hbr works, new outer breakwater, new entrance channels planned 2013/14.

Approach Restrictions apply in the area N of line Gurnard buoy to Prince Consort buoy. See Shipping Movements entry for Southampton.

E side of entrance is occupied by Shrape Mud, covered at half-flood, leaving only a comparatively narrow channel along W Cowes shore. From E, keep 2ca off Old Castle Point.

Entrance Enter between the first G (No.1 Q.G) and R (No.2 Q.R) buoys. From HW Cowes –0130 to +0300 there is a strong W-going set in the entrance extending as far as No.4 buoy, Fl(3)R.5s. The channel is straight and well marked by lit port-hand buoys as far as Red Funnel Ferry Terminal on the E Cowes side.

For vessels arriving from the east a small craft channel allows passage from the Shrape Bn, LFl.R.10s, through the moorings to the end of the E breakwater. It is marked by three pairs of lit lateral buoys. Note limited depth at LW and strong tide in harbour.

Beware of the chain ferry. Here the sp ebb can reach 4kn – special care needed if heading N past the ferry under these conditions. Below the ferry the ebb runs hardest on E side, above it hardest on the W side.

Cowes

Berthing Anchoring in Cowes Roads. Contact Harbourmaster for swinging moorings in hbr and in Cowes Roads E. Visitors' pontoons on E side ¼M S of chain ferry. No shore access. Marinas on stb, Cowes Yacht Haven and Shepard's Wharf Marina, and port, East Cowes Marina. Short stop allowed at Trinity Landing.

Supplies Fuel from Lallows yard ½ca S of Cowes Yacht Haven, and from fuel berth 1ca

S of chain ferry. All facilities in Cowes. Water at Trinity Landing. EC Wednesday. Sewage pump out at Shepards Wharf Marina.

River Medina

Above Cowes there are open rural surroundings to Newport. River is navigable for boats up to 2m draught to Folly Inn and boats can reach Newport at –0130 HW Portsmouth to +0230 with 2m draught. Max length 40ft. Channel is buoyed but not lit above Folly Inn. ½M above the inn is Island Harbour Marina entrance lock. Enter alongside jetty.

Berthing Visitors' pontoons opposite Folly Inn; pontoons at Island Harbour Marina, lock open HW±0330, 1·8m draught. At Newport twin-keeled boats tie to a pontoon, fin keels to the quay. Bottom soft mud. Showers and toilets for yachtsmen on quay.

Supplies Island Harbour Marina: Large chandlery, full boatyard facilities. Newport: Water at Town Quay, shops in town.

☎/VHF HM 01983 293 952. VHF 16, 69; Chain Ferry VHF 69; Cowes Yacht Haven 299 975. VHF 80; East Cowes Marina 293 983. VHF 80; Water Taxi 07050 344 818 VHF 77, *Harbour Taxi*. HM Newport (includes Folly Point moorings) 525 994. VHF 16, 69 (office hours); Folly Inn 297 171. Folly Water Bus 07974 864 627. Island Harbour Marina 539 994. VHF 80; For Ferry movements monitor VHF 69.

SOUTHAMPTON WATER

Charts BA 2036, 2041, SC 5600; Imray 2200, C15, C3

HW (Calshot and Southampton) Southampton HW

DS (Calshot) Portsmouth –0100 to +0400 mainly SW, +0500 to –0100 mainly NE; (Southampton) Portsmouth +0530 flood, –0400 slack, –0300 flood, –0300 slack +0200 ebb.

At Southampton

MHWS	MHWN	MLWN	MLWS
4·5m	3·7m	1·8m	0·5m

A very busy commercial hbr and oil terminal with good facilities for yachts.

Approach From E take North Channel, buoyed and lit, entered from E Bramble E card Lt buoy. Coming from Cowes beware Bramble Bank, dries 1·1m. Depending on wind, draft and tidal stream, either keep W of the bank, passing near W Bramble W card Lt buoy and Thorn Knoll G con buoy, Fl.G.5s, or head NE to join the North Channel.

Channel is clearly marked. For River Itchen, head N after passing Weston Shelf G con buoy, Fl(3)G.15s. The entrance to Hythe Marina Village is

immediately opposite, just above Hythe Pier. Town Quay Marina is 1M further on, to stb.

Going up River Itchen, Ocean Village Marina is on W side, below Itchen Br which has 24·4m clearance; Ocean Quay and Shamrock Quay about a mile further up, also on W side, and Kemps Marina ½ mile beyond on N bank.

Anchorages
• Calshot Castle inshore near Activities Centre. Shallow.
• Ashlett Creek (just SE of Fawley oil wharf), below the notice board. (Chart BA *2022*) The creek itself dries and is full of private moorings. Land at Public Quay near HW or at LW hard, 0·3m. All stores, EC Wednesday.
• Netley, outside moorings in 2m.
• Hythe Pier, N of pierhead, 2m, clear of ferry. (These four anchorages are exposed to wash from commercial traffic).
• Marchwood near former power intake at top of permanently navigable water; local YC.
• Clear of moorings in former power station basin.

Marinas Visitors are accommodated in vacant berths as available. Call VHF 80 before entering.
• **Hythe Marina Village.** Entrance, 1·5m, marked by piles, some lit. IPTS. Lock manned 24hrs, waiting pontoon outside. Free flow during HW. Fuel 24hrs. All facilities. Passenger ferries from Hythe Pier to Southampton.
• **Town Quay Marina.** Enter leaving outer wave screen to stb, inner screen to port. Few facilities but shops nearby.
• **Ocean Village Marina.** Few facilities but shops nearby and bus to town centre.
• **Shamrock Quay.** Stream strong on outer pontoons. No fuel but chandlers and all boatyard services. Visitors' pontoon D.
• Berths for shallow draught boats, and those capable of taking the ground, at Kemp's Shipyard above Shamrock Quay to stb.

Supplies Fuel at Hythe Marina Village (through lock, no charge for fuelling stop), Itchen Marine at American wharf (diesel only) and at Kemp's Shipyard.

☎/VHF HM 023 8033 0022. VHF 16, 12; Hythe Marina Village 8020 7073. VHF 80. Town Quay Marina 8023 4397. VHF 80; Ocean Village Marina 8022 9385. VHF 80. Shamrock Quay 8022 9461. VHF 80. Wi-Fi; Itchen Marine 8063 1500; Kemps Quay 8063 2323; R Southampton YC 8022 3352; Ocean Quay Marina 8023 5089.

HAMBLE

Chart BA 2022, SC 5600; Imray C15, C3, 2200.7

HW (Warsash) Southampton +0015

HW (Bursledon) Southampton +0020

DS (off Hillhead) Portsmouth +0400E, –0200W

At Warsash

MHWS	MHWN	MLWN	MLWS
4·5m	3·8m	1·9m	0·8m

Although the Hamble is congested with moorings and marinas, there is provision for visitors. Traffic at weekends is heavy, engines should be used, and wash can be uncomfortable at moorings. There is silting on the inside of bends in the stretch from Mercury Yacht Harbour to Jolly Sailor Hard.

Regulations Vessels over 20m are required to call *Hamble Harbour Radio*, VHF 68, before entering the river or getting under way, and to keep a listening watch while in the river. Speed limit 6kn.

Vessels should keep to stb side of fairway. When crossing the fairway give way to other vessels. Anchoring is prohibited between No.1 bn and M27 br (50°53'.33N).

Approach Steer for Hamble Point S card Lt buoy, then head 352° (W sector of Oc(2)WRG.12s dir Lt) up channel marked by lit bns. After bn 5, steer 028° (W sector of Iso.WRG.6s dir Lt), as far as Warsash Jetty, 2F.G(vert), then head up the river, marked by piles. Some of them are lit, all have R or G reflectors. Do not cut corners, which are shallow, particularly on E side opposite Mercury Y Harbour and on W side approaching Swanwick.

Bridges at Bursledon have 4·0m headroom.

Berthing Short stay berthing at HM's jetty off HM's office (conspic round tr), Warsash and at Hamble-le-Rice Quay. Harbour Authority visitors' moorings on two mid-stream pontoons between Warsash and Hamble Point Marina; also between piles to stb opposite Port Hamble. Marinas (call on VHF to check availability): Hamble Point, Port Hamble, Mercury Y Harbour, Universal Marina, Swanwick Marina. Moorings sometimes available from RAF YC.

Landing on public hards at Warsash, Hamble-le-Rice, Swanwick Shore; on pontoons at HM's jetty, Hamble-le-Rice Quay, and at Jolly Sailor Inn at Bursledon; or at jetty at Hamble S of RAF YC.

Supplies Fuel and water at fuelling berth, Hamble Point Marina. Water at HM's jetty and at all marinas. Provisions and chandlery at Warsash,

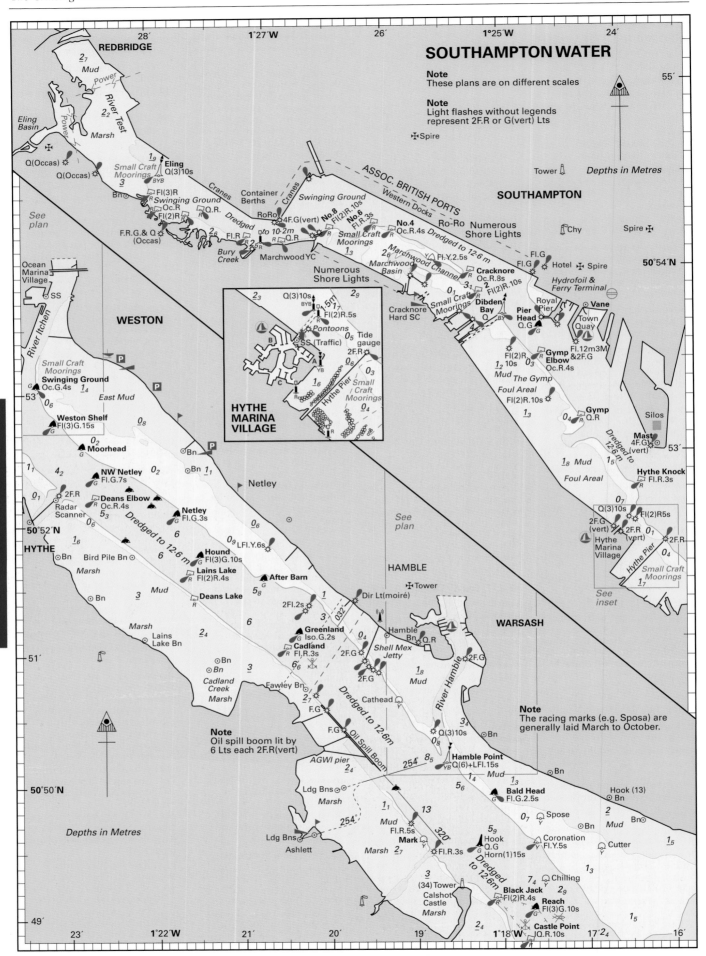

SOUTHAMPTON WATER

Note
These plans are on different scales

Note
Light flashes without legends represent 2.F.R or G(vert) Lts

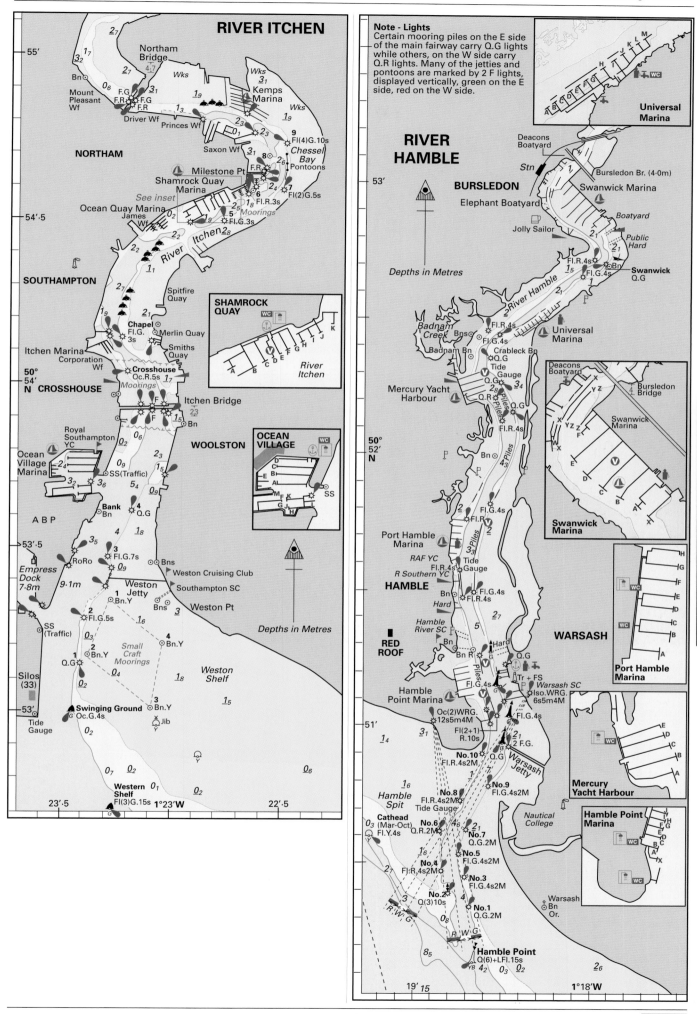

RIVER ITCHEN

RIVER HAMBLE

Note - Lights
Certain mooring piles on the E side of the main fairway carry Q.G lights while others, on the W side carry Q.R lights. Many of the jetties and pontoons are marked by 2 F lights, displayed vertically, green on the E side, red on the W side.

Universal Marina

NORTHAM

BURSLEDON

SOUTHAMPTON

SHAMROCK QUAY

OCEAN VILLAGE

WOOLSTON

Swanwick Marina

HAMBLE

WARSASH

Port Hamble Marina

RED ROOF

Mercury Yacht Harbour

Hamble Point Marina

Depths in Metres

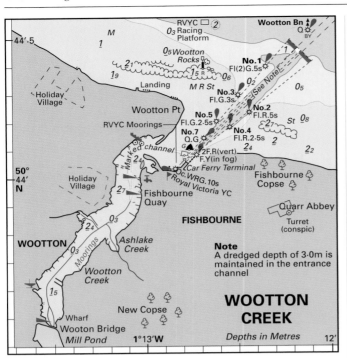

WOOTTON CREEK

Depths in Metres

1°13'W   12'

draught vessels near HW but the fairway is generally not marked after R and G buoys and piles at the N end.

Berthing Some visitors' berths on Royal Victoria YC pontoon, W of the ferry terminal. Pontoon dries to mud at LW and can be used with care by keel boats. Boats may raft up. Mooring can be uncomfortable in strong winds from NW to NE. Pedestrian access to shore and club house. Drying pontoons for local yachts at Fishbourne Quay.

Anchoring, forbidden in fairway, may be possible with care for a short stay over HW just below Wootton Br; landing by public slipway adjacent to br; access to shops, waterside inn and buses. Possible to anchor off the RVYC N and W of the G buoy and clear of the fairway to wait for the tide.

Supplies Water at RVYC; inn/restaurant; papers at ferry terminal; PO and shops at Wootton Br. EC Wednesday.

Facilities Bar, restaurant, showers at RVYC. Good food at Fishbourne Inn, three minute walk.

✆ RVYC 01983 882 325.

RYDE (ISLE OF WIGHT)

Chart BA 2036, SC 5600; Imray 2200, C15, C3

Ryde Harbour is a small craft drying hbr (sand/mud) 300m E of Ryde Pier and Pavilion (conspic). Pontoon berths and quay for fin keels. Max draught 2m. Accessible HW–0230 to +0200 by buoyed drying approach across Ryde Sands, 197°. Entrance Lts 2F.R(vert) and Fl.G.3s7m1M. Look out for fast catamaran and hovercraft ferries.

Visitors welcome. Visitors' pontoon is Pontoon A unless directed elsewhere.

Supplies Water; fuel 200m.

✆ /VHF HM (01983) 613 879, VHF 80 *Ryde Harbour*.

Hamble and Swanwick. EC Wednesday.

Facilities Sewage pump out at HM's jetty. All boatyard facilities available on the river.

✆ /VHF Warsash HM 01489 576 387, VHF 68; Hamble Point Marina 023 8045 2464, VHF 80. Wi-Fi; Port Hamble 023 8045 2741, VHF 80; Hamble Yacht Services 023 8045 4111, VHF 80. Mercury Y Harbour 023 8045 5994, VHF 80. Wi-Fi; Universal Marina 01489 574 272, VHF 80 *Universal Marina*; Swanwick Marina 01489 884081. VHF 80. Wi-Fi; RAF YC 023 8045 2208; R Southern YC 023 8045 0300.

WOOTTON (ISLE OF WIGHT)

Chart BA 2022; SC 5600; Imray 2200, C15, C3

HW Portsmouth HW

DS Portsmouth +0330 –0245E

MHWS	MHWN	MLWN	MLWS
4·5m	3·7m	1·9m	0·9m

An attractive winding creek, most of which dries. No room for single keel boats except during HW.

Approach From W keep N of Peel Wreck, R can, and Y RVYC racing platform. From E keep 5ca off shore. Make for Wootton N card Lt bn or, with sufficient rise of tide, for No.1 bn, Fl(2)G.5s, and turn into the channel, 224°.

Beware of inbound ferries which may at times approach ferry terminal to west (outside) of marked channel.

Entrance Channel, dredged 3m is marked both sides by lit bns and W sector of the dir Lt, Oc.WRG.10s at the terminal for the Portsmouth vehicle ferry. Wootton Br (impassable) can be reached by shallow

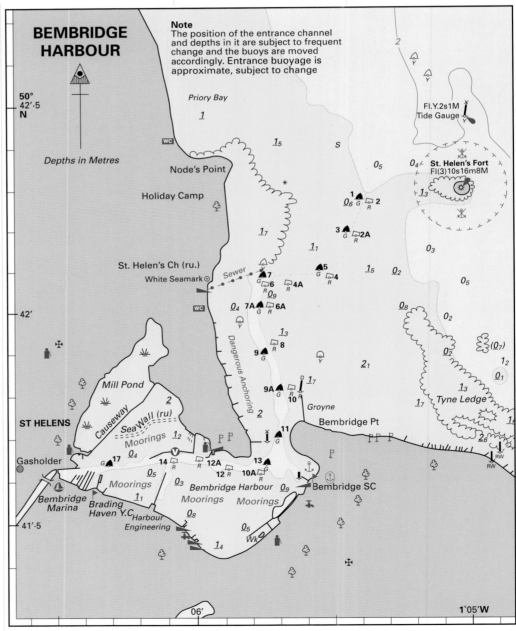

BEMBRIDGE HARBOUR

Depths in Metres

Note The position of the entrance channel and depths in it are subject to frequent change and the buoys are moved accordingly. Entrance buoyage is approximate, subject to change

1°05'W

BEMBRIDGE (ISLE OF WIGHT)

Charts BA 2022, SC 5600; Imray 2200, C15, C3

HW Portsmouth HW

DS Weak and variable except from Portsmouth +0300S for 1hr

MHWS	MHWN	MLWN	MLWS
3·2m	2·4	0·6m	−0·2m

A natural hbr much of it drying, dries 0·9m in entrance.

Approach Aim for N side of St Helen's Fort, Fl(3)10s, making sure the tide has risen enough to clear the gravel banks that surround it. Do not approach within 1·2ca of the fort on seaward side.

Entrance The channel starts at the tide gauge, indicating depth of water on the bar, Fl.Y.2s1M, 2ca N of the fort and is buoyed but unlit. With sp or medium tides vessels with up to 1·8m draught can enter from HW−0300 to +0200, but with tides under 4m, depth on the bar may not exceed 1·5m. There is a minimum depth of 1m between No.10 buoy and the marina; otherwise the channel dries every tide with the least depth between buoys 6 and 8. Max flow across the entrance is 1½kn.

Berthing Anchoring is forbidden except for boats that can dry out, anchored fore and aft, in sandy bay on E side by Bembridge SC. Visitors' pontoon at Fisherman's Wharf and on N side of channel with access to shore on St Helens side and hence, via causeway, to facilities at Bembridge Marina. Bottom is soft and 2m draft can be accommodated. May be some visitors' berths at marina. Buoys are private.

Supplies Fuel at yard, water at marina and quay. Shops up the hill in Bembridge or at St Helens. EC Thursday.

☎/**VHF** Bembridge Marina 01983 872 828, VHF 80; Harbour launch VHF 37, M.

VENTNOR (ISLE OF WIGHT)

Charts BA 2045, SC 5600; Imray 2200, C3

HW Portsmouth −0025

Position 50°35'·6N 1°12'·13W

A small haven, exposed to the SW, with a depth of 0·5m and mooring space for about six 9m craft. Entrance has a sandy bar slightly shallower than the haven.

☎/**VHF** Supervisor 07976 009260, VHF 80 in season.

Charts from Imray for the South Coast

C3 **Isle of Wight**
1:52,500 WGS 84
Plans Continuation of Southampton Water, River Hamble, Lymington River, Bembridge Harbour

C4 **Needles Channel to Bill of Portland**
1:75,000 WGS 84
Plans Weymouth, Portland, Swanage, Lulworth Cove, Christchurch, Studland Bay, Continuation of the River Stour

C5 **Bill of Portland to Salcombe Harbour**
1:100,000 WGS 84
Plans Bridport, Lyme Regis, Exmouth, Tor Bay, Torquay, Brixham, Dartmouth, Teignmouth

C6 **Salcombe to Lizard Point**
1:100,000 WGS 84
Plans Fowey Approaches, Looe, Mevagissey, Charlestown, Polperro, Plymouth Sound, Falmouth, Salcombe

C7 **Falmouth to Isles of Scilly and Trevose Head**
1:120,000 WGS 84
Plans St Mary's Road, Mousehole, Newlyn, St Ives, St Michael's Mount, Porthleven, Penzance, Newquay Bay, Hugh Town, Mullion Cove

C8 **Dover Strait – North Foreland to Beachy Head and Boulogne**
1:115,000 WGS 84
Plans Pegwell Bay, Ramsgate, Dover, Folkestone, Rye, Sovereign Harbour, Calais, Boulogne

C9 **Beachy Head to Isle of Wight**
1:110,000 WGS 84
Plans Newhaven, Shoreham, Littlehampton, Brighton Marina, Portsmouth, Langstone and Chichester Harbours, Sovereign Harbour

C10 **Western English Channel Passage Chart**
1:400,000 WGS 84
Radiobeacons, Lights, Tides

C12 **Eastern English Channel Passage Chart**
1:300,000 WGS 84
Inset Dover Strait
Radiobeacons, Lights, Tides

C14 **Plymouth Harbour and Rivers**
1:20,000 WGS 84
Plans River Tamar to Gunnislake, St German's River, Sutton Harbour and Queen Anne's Battery Marinas, Mayflower Marina, Plymouth, River Yealm

C15 **The Solent — Bembridge to Hurst Point and Southampton**
1:35,000 WGS 84
Plans River Hamble, River Itchen, Yarmouth Harbour, Lymington River, Beaulieu River, Wootton Creek, Newtown River, Cowes Harbour, Bembridge Harbour, Hythe Marina

C18 **Western Approaches to the English Channel and Biscay**
1:1,000,000 WGS 84

PORTSMOUTH

Charts BA 2631, 2628, 2629, SC 5600; Imray 2200, C15, C3

HW Portsmouth HW

DS Portsmouth +0315E −0200W

MHWS	MHWN	MLWN	MLWS
4·7m	3·8m	1·9m	0·8m

A busy naval and commercial port with ferry terminal and marinas, under control of Queen's HM. The town has much to offer in maritime history.

Regulations Small craft under 20m must enter and leave by the Boat Channel and vessels with engines must proceed under power. No loitering in Boat Channel and no overtaking if that means straying into the main channel. Small craft may continue to use the Boat Channel when the main channel is closed for the passage of a large vessel. Prior permission to cross between Ballast bn and Gunwharf Quay must be obtained from QHM VHF 11.

Observe mandatory 50m exclusion zone around all warships and berths in HM Naval Base. Also, when directed by QHM on VHF 11, observe 500m exclusion zone around underway warships. Such warships display two diamond shapes (vert) by day and two Fl.R lts (hor) by night. Craft fitted with engines must use them between the Southsea War Memorial and Ballast Bn.

Listen on VHF 11 but do not transmit on that frequency except in emergency.

Do not stop or linger in the area of Tipner Range in the approach to Port Solent (*see under Portchester Lake, below*).

During busy periods, the Boat Channel and other parts of the port are patrolled by the Queen's HM Harbour Patrol, QHP, a 6m hulled launch, VHF 11 call *Harbour Patrol Launch*. The QHP is tasked with assisting recreational users and, where necessary, enforcing regulations.

Approach A submerged barrier nearly 2M long runs S from the shore 8ca E of Southsea Castle to Horse Sand Fort. From Langstone and Chichester Harbours there is an inshore passage for small craft (0·6m), 12m wide, 1ca from shore, marked to N and S by a stb and port bn respectively. A better passage (1·2m) 8ca offshore is marked by a G pile to N and a dolphin, QR, to S; pass close N of the dolphin. Otherwise pass S of Horse Sand Fort. In all cases cross to W side of main channel and follow port-hand buoys to the Boat Channel.

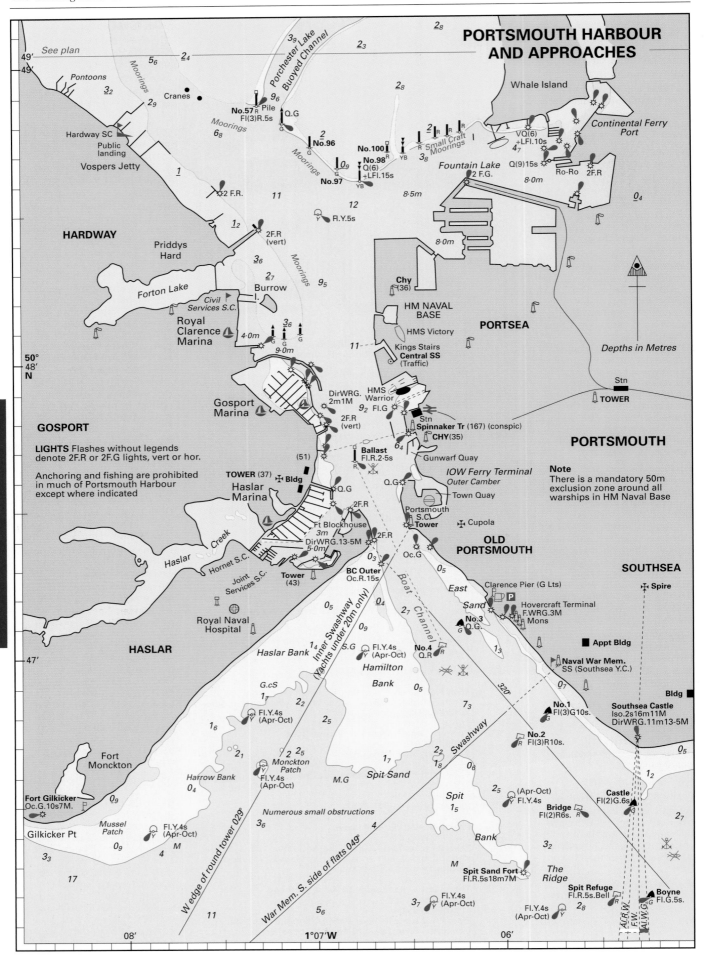

PORTSMOUTH HARBOUR
AND APPROACHES

ENGLAND – SOUTH COAST

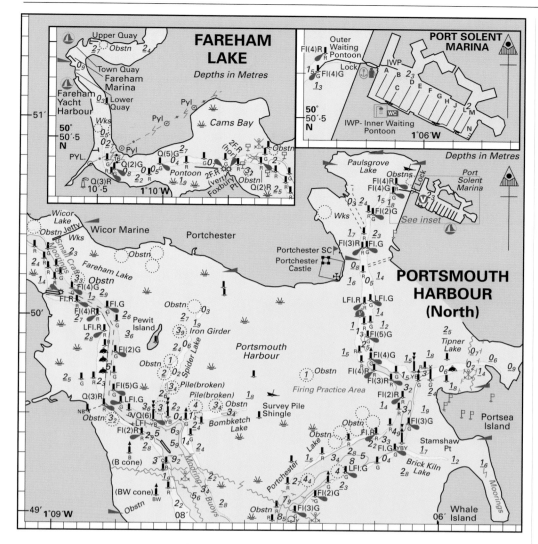

FAREHAM LAKE — Depths in Metres

PORT SOLENT MARINA — Depths in Metres
IWP- Inner Waiting Pontoon

PORTSMOUTH HARBOUR (North)

From W either
• Steer towards Outer Spit S card Lt buoy, turning to port when S of Spit Sand Fort, Fl.R.5s. Follow the main channel port-hand buoys and enter the Boat Channel at No.4, Q.R; or
• Take the Swashway over Spit Bank (1·8m), with War Memorial (unlit) bearing 049°, turning to port when you have come into deep water: or
• Use the Inner Swashway (0·5m, forbidden to craft over 20m), steering on the W edge of round tr (unlit) 029°. This course passes close to the N tip of a drying shoal 2ca S of Fort Blockhouse. The N end of the Inner Swashway is marked by BC Outer, a R Bn, Oc.R.15s, which must be left to port on entering the hbr or on leaving it via the Inner Swashway.

Signals These signals, displayed at Fort Blockhouse, do not apply to craft under 20m long using the boat channel but should be watched for warnings of movements of large ships which must be given a clear berth. Instructions from QHM will be on VHF 11 or 13.
R/G/G Lts – Large vessel underway; other vessels may be ordered to wait

W/G Lts – Large vessel leaving. Vessels may leave; those entering will be kept clear
G/W Lts – Large vessel entering. Vessels may enter; those leaving will be kept clear.

Entrance
Boat Channel Vessels under 20m must use the Boat Channel in the hbr entrance. It is 50m wide and runs from No.4 Bar buoy, Q.R, close along Fort Blockhouse wall (leaving two unlit R stick bns, BC2 and BC4 close to port) to Ballast bn, Fl.R.2·5s, which must be left close to port. Likewise, when leaving the hbr, all vessels under 20m must use this channel, again leaving Ballast bn close to port. Vessels may only cross the entrance N of Ballast bn or S of No.4 Bar buoy. The Oc.R sector of Fort Blockhouse Lt (24hrs) and the Iso.R sector of the Lt on dolphin off Gosport Marina show over Small Boat Channel.
Hbr is difficult to enter on the ebb which runs strongest (5+kn) in third and fourth hours. Flood runs strongest in last two hours (3¼kn) but an eddy runs along E side of hbr during part of the flood. There is slack in entrance for ¾hr during second and third hours of the flood.

Portchester Lake has 4·4m at its lower end and 1·8m near Portchester. Firing from the Tipner Range crosses the channel between piles 63/67 and 70/80. You are not allowed to stop or linger in this area. If R flags are flying, you may still pass but do so quickly. Channel is marked by R and G posts, nine lighted. The channel to Port Solent (dredged 2m, Lt piles) starts just E of Portchester Castle.
Fareham Lake is marked by R and G poles, some are lit. There is a least depth of 5·0m to Bedenham Pier but it dries out ½M below Fareham town. There is also an overhead cable in the same area with clearance of 16m.

Anchorages
• Off Portchester Castle near top of Portchester Lake, 1·8m. Land at hard;
• ¾M below Fareham, 1·5m. Riding Lt necessary.

Marinas
• **Haslar Marina**, just inside entrance to port. No fuel;
• **Gosport Marina**, 4ca further N;
• **Royal Clarence Marina**, 2ca further NW;
• **Port Solent Marina** (lock, 24hrs service) ½M NE of

Portchester Castle; waiting pontoon, lit Fl(4)G.10s. Hardway SC has pile moorings at end of landing stage for craft up to 32ft long.

Berthing Buoys at Wicormarine, Fareham. Short term berthing alongside dock wall in The Camber, 1ca inside entrance to stb. Pontoon berthing 1ca futher N at Gunwharf Quays by prior arrangement; expensive and exposed to wash. For either of these, call *QHM*, VHF 11, for permission before crossing hbr from Ballast Buoy at top of Boat Channel, also before leaving.

Supplies Fuel at Gosport marina, Port Solent, Hardway Marine, Wicormarine, Fareham Yacht Harbour. EC Fareham Wednesday; variable in Portsmouth and Gosport.

☎/VHF QHM 023 9272 3124. VHF 11, or 13 if so instructed; Harbour Control (023) 9272 3694; Camber Berthing Master 9285 5902. VHF 14. Haslar Marina 9260 1201. VHF 80. Gosport Marina 9252 4811. VHF 80, 37; Royal Clarence Marina 9252 3523, VHF 80. Wi-Fi; Gunwharf Quays 9283 6700, VHF 80, *Gunwharf Quays*. Wi-Fi; Port Solent 9221 0765. VHF 80. Hardway Marine 9258 0420; Wicormarine 01329 237 112. VHF 80, 37; Fareham Yacht Harbour 01329 232 854. VHF 80, 37; Fareham Marine 01329 822 445.

LANGSTONE HARBOUR
Chart BA 3418, SC 5600; Imray 2200, Y33, C3, C9
HW Portsmouth HW
DS (Winner) Portsmouth −0300N; +0230S, rotary anti-clockwise, less than 1kn

In entrance stream is strongest for fourth and fifth hours of the flood (3·4kn) and second and third of the ebb (3·1kn).

MHWS	MHWN	MLWN	MLWS
4·8m	3·9m	1·9m	0·8m

A natural hbr with narrow channels lacking anchorages convenient to shore. Has a large water-skiing area.

Approach From Portsmouth there are two inshore passages in the submerged barrier between the shore and Horse Sand Fort. *See Portsmouth Approach* for details. Otherwise from W pass S of Horse Sand Fort and keep No Man's Land Fort open to S of the latter until entrance is open. From Chichester, steer S for 4ca past Bar Bn and then steer for Winner S card buoy, unlit. With a heavy sea or strong S wind the shallows can be dangerous for 1½M offshore.

Entrance is bounded on either side by gravel banks, steep to on E side of fairway. These may

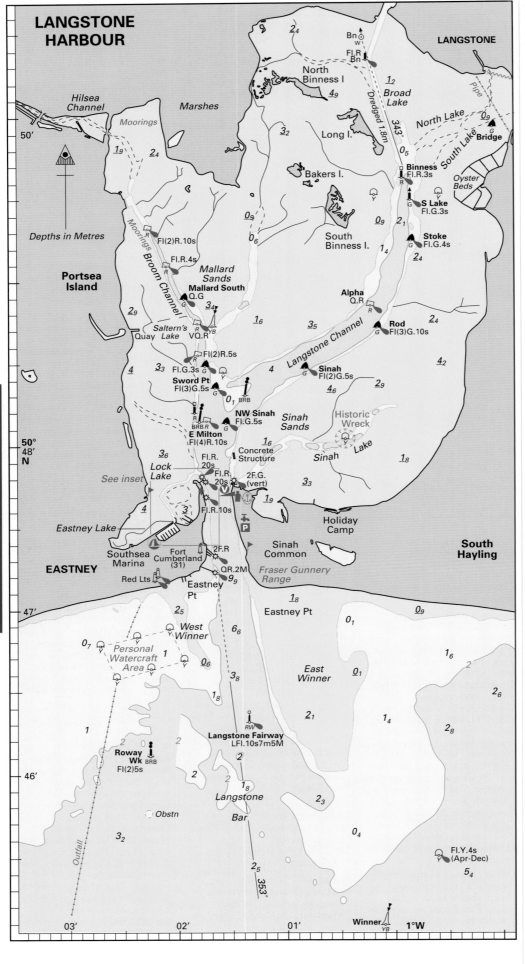

move in gales and their height varies. The connecting bar has a least depth of 1·8m and is dangerous in onshore winds especially near LW on the ebb. Bring Fairway bn, R sph on RW pile, LFl.10s, on with centre of hbr entrance, 354°. Alternatively, concrete dolphin off Eastney Pt, Q.R, in line with outfall jetty to N, 2F.R(vert), 353° has 1·7m on the bar. Inside, Langstone Channel is buoyed, lit and dredged 1·8m at its N end and leads to Havant Quay used mainly by gravel dredgers. The drying channel leading to Chichester Harbour round the N of Hayling Is has 3·7m at MHWS with a br clearance of 1·7m and cables 1·8m.

Channel through Lock and Eastney Lakes to Southsea Marina has lit and unlit piles and is dredged 0·5m.

Berthing All visiting vessels should report to Harbour Office just inside the entrance to stb, on the Hayling Island side. Go alongside pontoon, leaving NW berth clear for ferry. HM's Y visitors' buoys to stb off Ferry Boat Inn for craft up to 30ft – no doubling up; not for use in SE gales. (Advisable to make advance arrangements with HM, especially if staying overnight). Anchor (with HM's approval) in upper reaches of Broom and Langstone Channels, but both are in use by gravel dredgers day and night; the latter channel is a water-skiing area (April–September); mooring may be uncomfortable. Pontoon berths at Southsea Marina (*see plan inset*). Access via automatic sill gate, minimum depth 1·6m when open, giving free flow HW±0300; waiting pontoon (2·5m) with pedestrian access to marina.

Supplies Fuel and water at Marina and HM's office. Diesel on ferry pontoon (do not berth on shore side of latter); petrol on wall (tidal). Provisions in West Town, Hayling Island (1½M).

✆/VHF HM 023 9246 3419, VHF 16, 12 *Langstone Harbour Radio*. Southsea Marina 9282 2719, VHF 80, 37 *Southsea Marina* (24hrs). Wi-Fi.

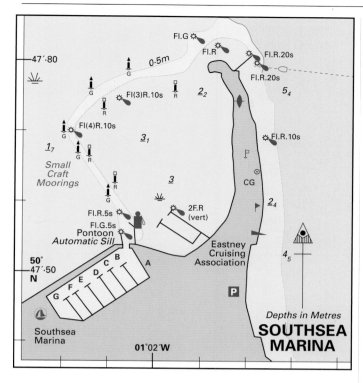

Depths in Metres
SOUTHSEA MARINA

CHICHESTER HARBOUR

Chart BA 3418, SC 5600;
Imray 2200, Y33, C3, C9
HW (entrance)Portsmouth HW
DS (off bar) Portsmouth
+0500SE −0130NW

In entrance flood reaches 2·8kn,
ebb 6·4kn

At entrance

MHWS	MHWN	MLWN	MLWS
4·9m	4·0m	1·9m	0·9m

A major yachting centre in largely unspoilt natural hbr with marinas, moorings and anchorages near pleasant villages. Virtually no commercial traffic except tourist and fishing boats. Bar restricts entry and exit and is dangerous in strong onshore wind against an ebb tide. In quiet weather access is straightforward with care.

Approach Aim to cross Chichester Bar at slack water or between HW−0300 and HW+0100. From E keep 2M offshore (in poor visibility the 5m line); from S keep Nab Tr on a back bearing of 186°; from W stay on 5m line or with old target (N card) in line with Cakeham Tr, 064°. From all three directions get Bar Bn, Fl(2)R.10s, and Eastoke Bn, open to E of West Pole Bn, Fl.R.5s.

Entrance The bar is periodically dredged to 1·5m below datum but shoaling may occur and it is prudent to assume a minimum depth of 0·75m below datum giving a depth of 1·4m at MLWS (0·7m). For the deepest water, leave West Pole tripod Bn, Fl.R.5s, and Bar Bn, Fl(2)R.10s, about ½ca to port and follow a course of 013° to the centre of the entrance. Note that the tide gauge on the West Pole bn, like all other tide gauges in the hbr, reads depth above datum, NOT depth on the bar. Follow the W shore until abreast of Hayling Is SC after which channel divides at Fishery S card Lt buoy.

Chichester Channel goes to stb with three G con buoys (Fl, Fl(2) and Fl(3) all 10s) in an arc marking NW edge of the Winner. Channel to Emsworth and Northney Marina continues to N, buoyed and lit.

Within the hbr anchored yachts must hoist a B ball, and an anchor Lt at night, and must not be left unattended for more than four hours.

Emsworth Channel is free of moorings between the entrance to Mill Rythe and the junction with Sweare Deep. It is marked by half-tide perches and three Lt bns (two port, one stb). Sweare Deep is also lit (Fl(3)R and Fl(4)R both 10s) as far as the entrance to Northney Marina (but near LW follow the moorings to stb rather than going straight from one bn to the other). Although there is a Lt bn, Echo, Fl(3)G.10s, at the head of the Emsworth branch, the stretch between it and Fisherman's Bn (Fl(3)R.10s) to the S is so congested with moorings that night passage for a stranger is not recommended, nor is Emsworth Yacht Harbour easily accessible in the dark. It would be better at night to tie alongside one of the boats on the piles to port or to use the visitors' pontoon 1·5ca SSW of Fisherman's bn Fl(3)R.10s. Landing is possible at Sparkes Marina (approach dredged 2m) or at HW at Mengham Rythe SC and at the head of Mill Rythe; each is navigable at MHWS for draughts up to 1·5m. *For passage through Sweare Deep to Langstone Harbour see entry for that hbr.*

Anchorage in Emsworth Channel: anchor out of the fairway to N of Hayling Is SC moorings (use tripping line). Visitors' buoys available from the club.

Marinas
•**Sparkes Marina**. Enter marked channel, dredged 2m, immediately after outer end of Hayling Is SC, leaving E card bn with tide gauge and stb bn close S of it to stb. Ldg line, 277°, is provided by two dayglo orange crosses. After 3ca turn S, leaving pile mooring to port, and follow port-hand bns into hbr.
•**Northney Marina** Near head of Sweare Deep; entrance sill dries at datum.
•**Emsworth Yacht Harbour** Sill dries 2·4m.

Visitors' pontoon at N end of piles E of Fowley Is. Half-tide buoys and pontoons at Hayling Yacht Co at head of Mill Rythe.

Chichester Channel is buoyed and lit as far as entrance to Chichester Marina. Landing at East Head, Itchenor Hard, hard on Bosham side of Itchenor ferry (dries out for 2ca) and Dell Quay. At entrance junction with Bosham Channel leave Fairway G con buoy, Fl(3)G.10s, (not readily distinguishable against background of moorings) to stb for fairway through the trots.

Anchorage Anchor N and NE of East Head (uncomfortable with winds from NW to NE; swimming dangerous) or W of the Fairway buoy on S side of channel. Anchoring is forbidden in Itchenor Reach. Six Conservancy visitors' buoys, white marked V, off Itchenor take up to six vessels each (depending on size); visitors' pontoon (April–September) on S side above Itchenor SC, at W end of Conservancy fore and aft moorings.

Marinas
•**Birdham Pool** (1·6m draught, lock HW±0300).
•**Chichester Marina** (lock HW±0400).

Thorney Channel Entrance is in gap, marked by port-hand bn, Fl(2)R.10s, in line of broken piles which runs NE from S tip of Pilsey Is. 2ca to N, the channel passes through a gap in a second line of broken piles running E from S tip of Thorney, this gap being marked by an unlit port bn and a stb bn Fl.G.5s. Rest of channel is marked by perches, some well above LW mark. Pilsey Is is a nature reserve and access above HW mark is not allowed. Thorney Is is MoD controlled but the public are allowed to use the foreshore path all round the island. Land at stage by the channel just beyond Thorney Is SC.

Anchorage Anchor off Pilsey in the stretch between the two lines of broken piles. Shore is steep-to and current strong. Sheltered from strong NW winds when East Head is untenable. Anchoring also possible further up the channel clear of moorings.

Visitors' buoy available from SC near channel. Drying berths (jetty and buoy) at Thornham Marina (about HW±0100) at head of channel.

Bosham Channel is unlit and dries near the quay. There are no visitors' buoys (all moorings are private) but it is possible to dry out alongside the quay – charges. Alternatively Bosham, an attractive village, can be reached by dinghy with the tide or, in the season, by the ferry from Itchenor.

Facilities Fuel at Sparkes Marina, Hayling Yacht Co, Northney Marina, Emsworth Yacht Harbour, Birdham Pool (at HW to stb outside lock, diesel only), Chichester Marina (lock dues). Water also at pontoon off HM office (Itchenor), Emsworth landing pontoon and Bosham Quay. Provisions at Emsworth, Mengham, West Wittering, Chichester Marina, Birdham and Bosham (EC Wednesday). None at Itchenor. Chichester (EC Thursday) best reached by train from Emsworth or bus from Bosham, Birdham or Itchenor cross-roads.

①/**VHF** HM 01243 512 301. VHF 14 *Chichester Harbour Radio*; Patrol Launch (when manned) VHF 16, 14 *Chichester Harbour Patrol*; Coastguard 023 9255 2100; Sparkes Marina 023 9246 3572, VHF 80; Hayling Y Co 023 9246 3592; Northney Marina (023) 9246 6321, VHF 80; Hayling Is SC 023 9246 3768, VHF 37, M *Hayling Club*; Emsworth Yacht Harbour 01243 377 727. VHF 80, 37; Thornham Marina 01243 375 335; Birdham Pool 01243 512 310; Chichester Marina 01243 512 731. VHF 80.

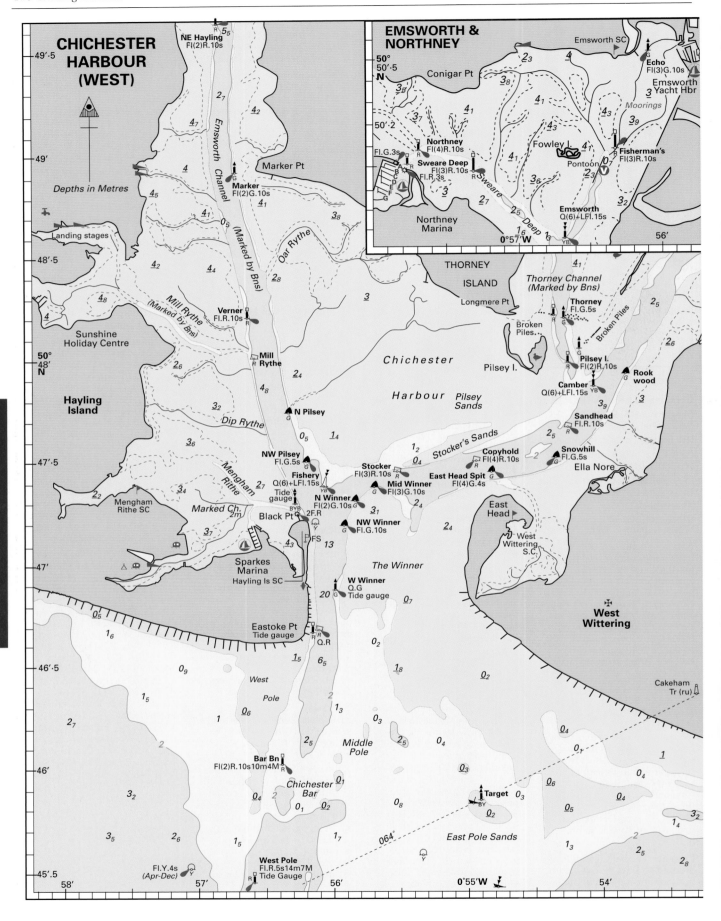

CHICHESTER HARBOUR (WEST)

Depths in Metres

EMSWORTH & NORTHNEY

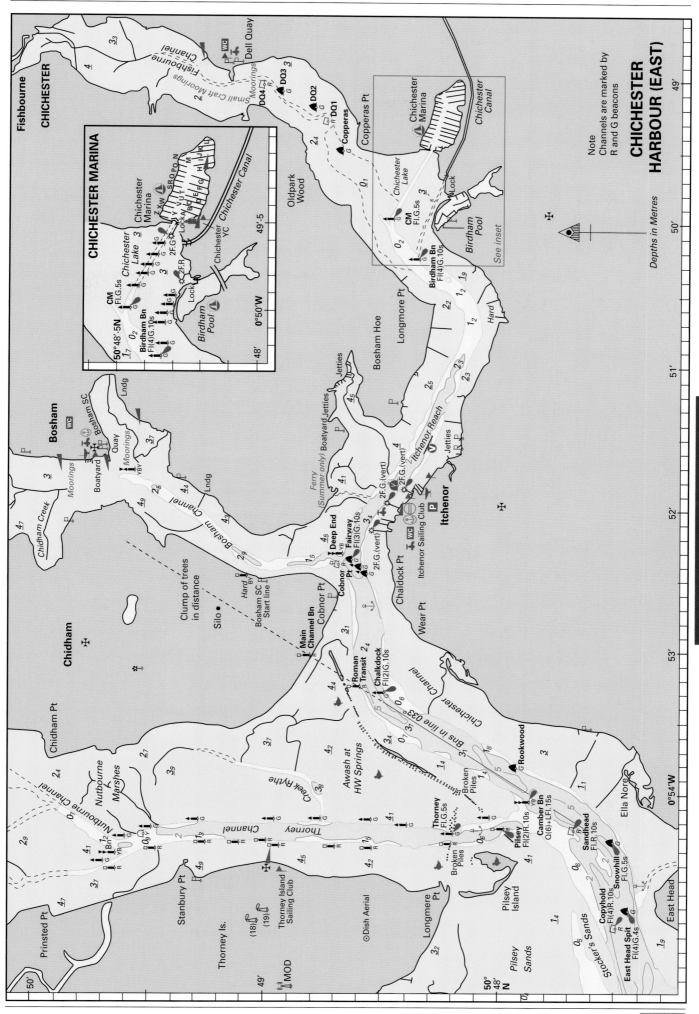

CHICHESTER

Fishbourne

Dell Quay

Fishbourne Channel

Small Craft Moorings

DQ4 G
DQ3 G
DQ2 G
DQ1 G

Copperas

Copperas Pt

Oldpark Wood

Bosham Hoe

Longmore Pt

CHICHESTER MARINA

Chichester Marina

SHOP

LOCK

Chichester YC

Chichester Lake

CM
Fl.G.5s

Birdham Bn
Fl(4)G.10s

2F.R.

2F.G.

Birdham Pool

Chichester Canal

Lock

50°48'.5N

0°50'W

49'.5

48'

Chichester Marina

Chichester Lake

CM Fl.G.5s

Birdham Bn
Fl(4)G.10s

Birdham Pool

See inset

Chichester Canal

Lock

Note
Channels are marked by
R and G beacons

CHICHESTER HARBOUR (EAST)

Depths in Metres

50'

Bosham SC

Bosham

Quay
Boatyard
Moorings

Chidham Creek

Chidham

Chidham Pt

Bosham Channel

Silo

Clump of trees
in distance

Bosham SC
Start line

Hard

Main
Channel Bn

Cobnor Pt

Cobnor
Pt

Deep End

Fairway
Fl(3)G:10s

2F.G.(vert)

2F.G.(vert)

Chaldock Pt

Wear Pt

Itchenor

Itchenor Sailing Club

Itchenor Reach

Jetties

Jetties

Boatyard Jetties

Ferry (Summer only)

Roman Transit

Chaldock
Fl(2)G.10s

Nutbourne
Marshes

Nutbourne Channel

Stanbury Pt

Prinsted Pt

50'

Thorney Is.

Thorney Island
Sailing Club

MOD

Dish Aerial

(18)
(19)

Creek Rythe

Awash at
HW Springs

Thorney Channel

Thorney
Fl.G.5s

Bns in line 033°

Chichester Channel

Broken Piles

Rookwood

Longmere Pt

Pilsey Island

Pilsey Sands

Stocker's Sands

Camber Bn
Ql(6)+LFl.15s

Pilsey
Fl(2)R.10s

Broken Piles

Sandhead
Fl.R.10s

Snowhill
Fl.G.5s

Copyhold
Fl(4)R.10s

East Head Spit
Fl(4)G.4s

East Head

Ella Nore

54'W

52'

53'

0°54'W

49'

50°
48'
N

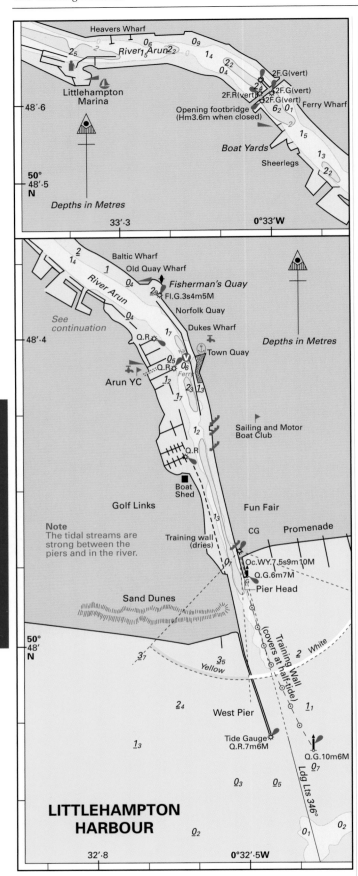

ENGLAND – SOUTH COAST

LITTLEHAMPTON

Charts BA 1991, 1652; SC 5605;
Imray 2100, C9, C12

HW Shoreham +0008

DS Dover –0100W +0430E

MHWS	MHWN	MLWN	MLWS
5·9m	4·4m	1·7m	0·4m

This commercial port is the estuary of River Arun;

navigation is limited by a bar ¾M from the entrance. The bar dries 0·9m.

Approach Leaving Looe Channel at E Borough Head E Card Lt buoy, make good 049° towards the Y sewer buoy, Fl(5)Y.20s9m5M, SSE of entrance. Call HM on VHF 71 before entering. Do not attempt

CHICHESTER TO NEWHAVEN

Charts BA 1652, 2045, SC 5605;
Imray 2100, C9, C12

Passage lights	*BA No*
Nab Tower	0780
Fl(2)5s28m5M	
Owers Lt buoy	
S card Lt buoy Bell Racon(O) (– – –)	
W entrance to Looe Channel	
Boulder buoy Fl.G.2·5s	
Beachy Hd	0840
Fl(2)20s31m8M	

Streams Related to HW Dover

The Looe +0445E –0115W 2hkn

S of Owers +0545E –0045W 2ykn

E-going stream sets onto Outer Owers

Selsey Bill HW Portsmouth –0005

There are three ways of passing Selsey Bill:

• S of the Owers S card Lt buoy, the best route in strong winds when the sea is breaking heavily on the shallows of the Owers, at night, or in poor visibility

• Through the Looe, passing 1½M S of the Bill; for use by day and in good visibility

• Close inshore; only by day around HW in good visibility with light or offshore winds. Beware crab pots in this whole area.

E-bound through the Looe, steer about 097° between the two entrance Lt buoys, R can QR and G con Fl.G.2·5s; when the Mixon bn Fl.R.5s, 9m with square cage, bears N 2ca, alter course to 077° to clear East Borough Head (E card Lt buoy, Bell).

The inshore route should be made within 0230hrs either side of HW. From E approach LB Ho,

entrance in strong onshore winds.

Entrance Littlehampton Bar extends 600m southwards from the end of West Pier and is 0·8m above chart datum. The approach should be made on a bearing of 346°. Tide boards on West Pierhead show height of tide above CD marked in units of 20cm. The height of the bar should be subtracted from this. Ldg Lts on East Pier Head are Oc.WY.7·5s9m10M and F.G.6m7M. From abeam the West Pierhead, keep to E centre of fairway to allow for W-going set.

The swing footbridge has 3·6m closed; requests for opening must be made before 1600 the preceding day (not Sundays or Bank Holidays). 4ca upstream is a fixed br, clearance also 3·6m. Littlehampton Marina to port above the footbridge. River is navigable to Arundel for 1·2m draught and dinghies can get to Amberley.

Berthing Report to HM on Town Quay where there are

½M NE of the Bill, on a bearing of not less than 280° and follow round the line of the Bill, keeping about 40m off the ends of the groynes until windmill (conspic 1M NW of Bill) is abeam; then head out for Nab Tower 238°. Shallowest water will be between the end of the High Street and coastguard tower. When ¾M clear of the shore, course may be set for West Pole bn leaving the unlit S card beacon S of East Pole Sands close to starboard.

For the inshore passage from W, head for the windmill with Nab astern and follow the line of beaconed groynes. The direction of the stream changes considerably earlier than in the Looe; on the early spring ebb there may be a current of 6·7kn just to the E and round the Bill. If going E, the effect may be reduced by a wider sweep offshore.

Pagham Harbour is only a basin of mudflats. Access is difficult, and as it is a nature reserve, landing and anchoring are forbidden.

Between Selsey Bill and Beachy Hd the effect of a foul tide may be escaped by keeping close inshore, where the tide may turn 1½–2hrs before the main offshore stream. But be careful between Littlehampton and Shoreham where shallows extend a considerable way offshore.

Anchorages In W and N weather, in The Run N and S of Selsey LB Ho, clear of moorings (2m).

In offshore winds, on NE side of Bognor Rocks, between them and the shore. SE winds bring in a heavy sea.

marked berths alongside pontoon with depths varying between 1·4m and 1·9m. Hillyards and Arun YC have berths on port side below foot br.

Facilities Fuel at marina above br; water and electricity on pontoon. Fuel at Littlehampton Marina.

☎/VHF HM 01903 721215, *Mobile* 07775 743078 VHF 71. Hillyards 713327. Arun YC 714533, VHF 37, M. Littlehampton Marina 713553, VHF 80, 37.

SHOREHAM

Charts BA 2044, 1652, SC 5605;
Imray 2100, C9, C12

HW Shoreham

DS Dover –0145W +0530E

MHWS	MHWN	MLWN	MLWS
6·3m	4·8m	1·9m	0·6m

Comprises the estuary of River Adur (dries) and a non-tidal basin, approached through locks, with quite busy commercial wharves and a small marina which may have a visitors' berth. If vessel is over 10m call *Shoreham Harbour Radio* before entering.

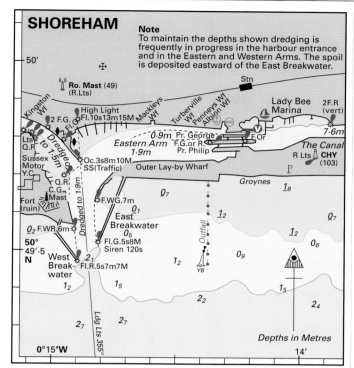

SHOREHAM

Note
To maintain the depths shown dredging is frequently in progress in the harbour entrance and in the Eastern and Western Arms. The spoil is deposited eastward of the East Breakwater.

Approach High Lt is Fl.10s13m15M. Avoid from W, Church Rocks, 0.9m, over ¼M offshore and 1½M W of entrance; from E, Jenny Ground 1½m, 3ca offshore, and 1¾M E of entrance, and S card Lt sewer buoy 3ca ESE of entrance. Shallows in approach can be very rough in strong onshore winds particularly on the ebb, when Newhaven is a better refuge. Keep front Ldg Lt on Middle Pier watch house (Oc.3s) in line with High Light Fl.10s, 355°.

Signals
Traffic signals, shown as below, do not apply to small craft provided they do not impede ship movements. Beware turbulence from ships.

Middle pier control station, Lt Oc.Amber.3s showing seaward:
Major vessel manoeuvring or leaving port. Entry forbidden.

LB Ho Oc.R.3s showing over E arm:
Major vessel entering port or leaving W arm. Navigation in E arm forbidden.

LB Ho Oc.R.3s showing over W arm:
Major vessel entering port or leaving E arm for sea or to W arm. Navigation in W arm forbidden.

IPTS signals for lock opening.

Entrance If vessel over 10m call *Shoreham Harbour Radio* before entering. Keep to middle and avoid eddies along the piers. Turn to port for Adur; beware training wall extending N from W pier, awash at half-tide, marked with port perches. Tide sets against E end of Kingston Wharf. Turn to stb for locks and Lady Bee Marina.

Berthing Yachts, small commercial vessels and fishing boats use E arm and the smaller, northern, Prince George Lock. The lock is open for 2400 except at LWS ± about 0100 as the lock sill 0.26m below CD. Incoming boats 0030 and outgoing on the hr. Small craft waiting for the lock may wait in the approaches to the lock but must remain manned and ready to move. Visitors' moorings by prior arrangement from Lady Bee Marina (to port after lock). Few facilities for visitors.

Facilities Rail service.

☎/VHF Shoreham Harbour Radio 01273 592366, VHF 14. Vessel Notification Form (if over 10m) *Fax* 01273 592492 or *Email* HarbourRadio@shoreham-port.co.uk. Lady Bee Marina 591705, VHF 14.

BRIGHTON

Charts BA 1991, 1652, SC 5605; Imray 2100, C9, C12
HW Shoreham 0000
DS –0130W +0430E Streams weak

MHWS	MHWN	MLWN	MLWS
6·6m	5·0m	2·0m	0·6m

A man-made marina with 1800 berths in tidal hbr; and inner harbour through lock with yard and domestic moorings. Entry not advised in SE gales.

Approach No outlying dangers. Landmarks are Roedean School on cliffs to E and tall hospital block with W vert stripe to W. Entrance LtHo is Fl(4)RW.20s, (R over rocks to E of entrance).

Entrance Avoid shoal obstruction adjacent S and N of E breakwater hd. If approaching from W beware blind corner with much small craft traffic. Channel is very close to W breakwater until well in. Channel turns to E, marked by buoys some of which are unlit. Entrance to marina marked by 2F.R(vert) port and 2F.G(vert) stb Lts. Depths on plan may be less due to silting. Room to lower sails when in hbr.

Berthing Visitors' reception pontoon (No.10) is immediately inside hbr. Max. 30m +2m draught.

Facilities Good rail service to London. Large supermarket nearby.

Interest The Royal Pavilion and The Lanes are worth a visit. They can be reached by the

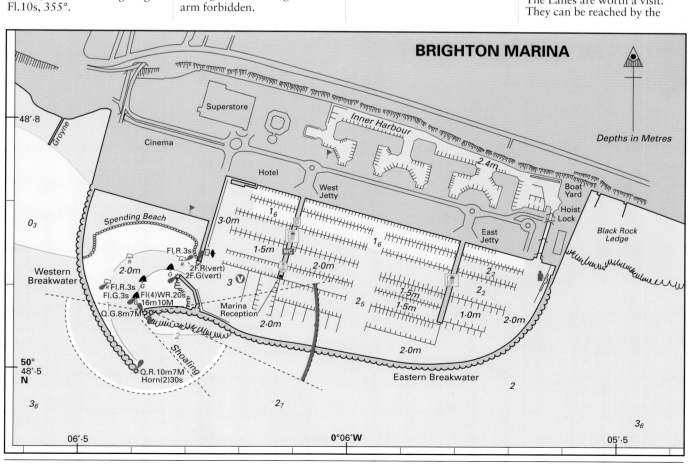

BRIGHTON MARINA

little railway which runs along the beach to the pier.

☎ /VHF HM 01273 819919, VHF 80/37 *Brighton Marina*.

NEWHAVEN

Charts BA 2154, 1652, SC 5605; Imray 2100, C9, C12

HW Shoreham –0012

DS –0530E –0130W

MHWS	MHWN	MLWN	MLWS
6·5m	4·9m	1·8m	0·4m

The estuary of River Ouse. A busy commercial and ferry port with a marina. It is accessible with care in all weathers. Call VHF 12 before entering or leaving.

Approach The hbr lies immediately E of the line of cliffs running from Brighton to Newhaven. To its E the coastline is low. From W at night the lights of Seaford make a good mark to steer on. From E in heavy weather keep breakwater LtHo Oc(2)10s to stb until E pier Lts are open to clear shallows E of entrance.

Signals Entry signals on mast at base of LtHo do not conform to the International System but are as follows:

3Fl.R(vert) Serious emergency. All vessels stop, follow instructions from HM.

3F.R(vert) Vessels may not proceed.

F.GGW(vert). Small vessels may proceed. Two-way traffic.

FGWG(vert) Proceed as instructed. All other vessels keep clear.

Swing br Fl.G – Operating.
F.G pass S to N.
F.R pass N to S.

When R Lts showing on signal mast at N end of marina no vessel may leave.

Entrance Within the breakwater keep in main channel to clear the mud on W side between it and the W pier. Inside, 2½ca N, Newhaven Marina is to port. Swing br opens on demand through Port Radio. Above the br to port is Cantell's Yard. At

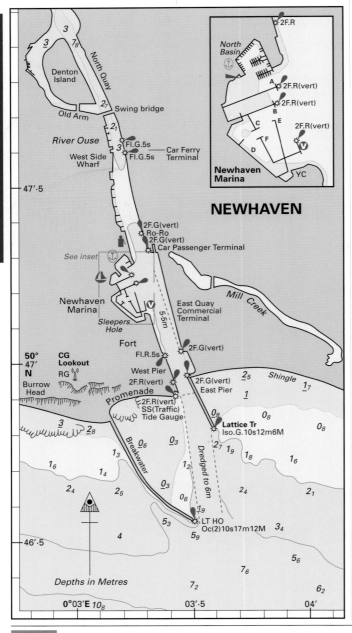

NEWHAVEN

North Basin
2F.R
2F.R(vert)
2F.R(vert)
2F.R(vert)
V
Newhaven Marina
YC

3
3
7₈
Denton Island
North Quay
2₇
Swing bridge
Old Arm
2₁
River Ouse
3 Fl.G.5s
West Side Wharf
Fl.G.5s
Car Ferry Terminal
47'·5
2F.G(vert)
Ro-Ro
2F.G(vert)
Car Passenger Terminal
See inset
Newhaven Marina
V
East Quay Commercial Terminal
Sleepers Hole
Mill Creek
Fort
2F.G(vert)
Fl.R.5s
50°
47'
N
CG Lookout
RG
West Pier
2F.R(vert)
2F.G(vert) East Pier
Shingle 2₅ 1₇
Burrow Head
Promenade
1
2F.R(vert)
SS(Traffic) Tide Gauge
0₈ 0₈
0₈
Lattice Tr Iso.G.10s12m6M
0₈
2₇ 1₉
3 2₈
Breakwater
0₆
0₃
1₈ 1₆
1₃
1₆
1₄
0₃
2₄
2₄
2₁
2₄
2₅
0₆
0₃
1₉
LT HO Oc(2)10s17m12M
5₃
3₄
5₉
4
5₆
Depths in Metres
7₆
7₂
6₂
0°03'E 10₈
03'·5
04'
46'·5

NEWHAVEN TO RAMSGATE

Charts BA 536, 1892, 1828, SC 5605; Imray 2100, C8, C12

Passage Lights	*BA No*
Beachy Head Fl(2)20s31m8M	0840
Royal Sovereign Fl.20s28m12M Horn(2)30s	0843
Dungeness Fl.10s40m21M+F.RG.37m10M (057°-R–073°-G-078°, 196°-R-216°) Horn(3)60s	0876
Lydd Range F.R 2·5M W of Dungeness when firing is taking place	
Dover Admiralty Pier Fl.7·5s21m20M Horn 10s	0900
N Foreland Fl(5)WR.20s57m19/15M. (R over N approach)	0966

Streams Related to HW Dover

Beachy Head (2M S) +0015W –0515E

Dungeness (2M SE) +0430SW 0200NE

Gull Stream +0430SSW –0030NNE

N Foreland (3M SE) +0445SSW –0115NE

Inshore

S Foreland to Deal and Ramsgate to N Foreland +0415S –0145N

Streams run at 2½kn off Beachy Head, Royal Sovereign and Dungeness but at only 1½kn between the latter. Passing Dungeness at the beginning of the W stream, one has only 2hrs of fair tide. It is better to pass with the last of a fair stream, fight the weak foul stream between Rye and Hastings and take the next fair stream off Eastbourne. If faced with foul

HW river is navigable to Lewes, 3m headroom.

Berthing

• Newhaven Marina moor to visitors' pontoon, accessible for 1·5m HW ±0230.
• Cantell's drying pontoons, accessible HW±0200.

Supplies Fuel N of Marina. Shops. Chandlery.

Facilities Rail services. Ferry to Dieppe.

☎ /VHF HM 01273 612926, Port Radio VHF 12. Marina 513881, VHF 80. Cantell 514118. Bridge Control VHF 12.

EASTBOURNE – SOVEREIGN HARBOUR

Charts BA 536, SC 5605; Imray 2100, C8, C12

HW Shoreham –0008

DS 2M S of Beachy Head –0500E 0000W

MHWS	MHWN	MLWN	MLWS
7·4m	5·4m	2·1m	0·7m

A purpose-built yacht hbr with inner non-tidal basin with twin entrance locks and an outer tidal basin, shallow, not used.

tide when W-bound at Beachy Head consider anchoring off Eastbourne or staying at Sovereign Harbour Marina to await the next tide.

E-bound with adequate speed a fair tide can be carried for 10hrs to N Foreland.

Anchorages

Seaford Road ¼M offshore abreast the channel. Sheltered from ESE to NNW, little stream, good holding.

Eastbourne E of pier; sheltered from W by N to NE.

Rye In N winds, anchor 1M·1¼M (according to draught) NNE of Rye Fairway buoy, LFl.10s.

Dungeness W Road In NE winds anchor inside the Ness out of stream, but the best anchorages, 1·3M W of the light, are now in Lydd Range danger area, which extends E to within 8ca from the Ness. Reported uncomfortable scend from E winds. Range control launches may be encountered W or E of the Ness; VHF 73, 13.

E Road Good anchorage NE off the Ness in 5·6m E of water tower (conspic) and Dungeness new LtHo bearing 197°, on W edge of R sector of the Lt. Sheltered with wind from SW through W to N.

Small Downs 1M N of Deal Pier off Sandown Castle, less than ½M offshore. Sheltered from SSW through W to N. Good holding, some stream. Beware wreck 4·4m ¾M NNE of Deal Pier.

Anchoring in Pegwell Bay is not recommended as the fetch from W is too great when flats are covered.

Approach From the W clear Beachy Head by 1½M and head NE past Eastbourne for Langney Point. From the E, approach N of Royal Sovereign shoals. The coast is low, main features being a tr block of flats, 1M NW of Langney Point and a line of five Martello towers NE of the point. However the entrance is not easy to see against a setting sun and may be found most easily with the aid of GPS. The entrance channel is liable to silting so it is prudent to check the depth with the HM before entering.

Entrance Lies between Langney Point, identified by the most SW Martello tr, lit Fl(3)15s12m7M, high intensity strobe flash, and a wreck on the shore. Call VHF 17 on arrival at Safewater buoy SH permanently maintained in its GPS position, LFl.10s, keeping in W sector of Dir Lt Fl.WRG.5s4m1M, 258°, between port and stb bns, Fl(4)R.12s3m6M or G.5s3m6M. Wreck visible at LW Springs. Buoyed channel, some lit, dredged 2·0m. At LW

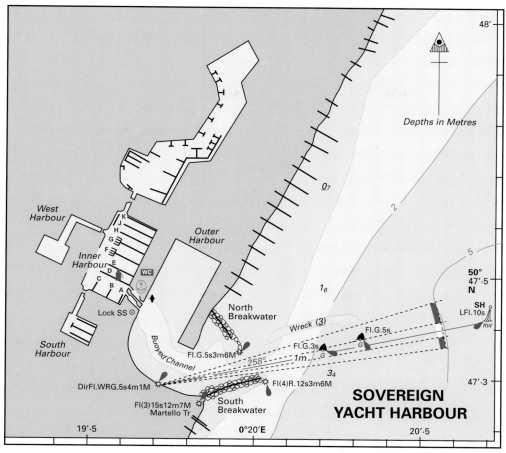

SOVEREIGN YACHT HARBOUR

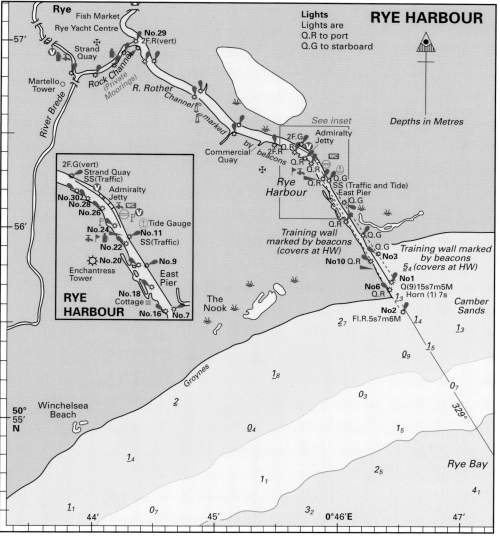

pass close to port of first G con channel buoy Fl.G.5s. Locks work 24hrs; traffic signals. Locks operate on hour and half hour only. Wait in open lock.

Berthing At pontoons, 4m depth. Berthing instructions from Lock-keeper.

Facilities Shops, cafés, boatyard, launderette. Cinema.

☎/**VHF** HM 01323 470099, VHF 17 (locks and bridges).

RYE

Charts BA 1991, 536, SC 5605; Imray 2100, C8, C12

HW Dover –0002

DS –0400E +0300W

MHWS MHWN
5·4m 3·6m

The approach dries and is liable to shifts in depth but generally 7·8m can be found at MHWS, about 6·0m at MHWN.

Harbour

MHWS MHWN
5·4m 3·6m

The Port of Rye dries completely and entry should only be made between HW –0200 and HW + 0100. It should not be attempted in strong onshore winds.

Approach From Dungeness to the east, or from Fairlight to the west, follow the coast keeping at least two miles off shore in a depth of 6m until Rye Fairway RW Sph Lt buoy LFl.10s is sighted, 1·8M from entrance.

Signals near HM office. IPTS. Contact Port Control on VHF 14.

Entrance Only HW–2 to HW+1. From Fairway Buoy steer 329° for R tripod bn Fl.R.5s and G square bn Q(9)15s Horn(1)7s. Floodlit. Follow buoyed channel and report to HM.

Berthing Boats up to 15m berth at Strand Quay upstream in soft mud. Boats over 15m and up to 25m berth near Harbour Office on hard ground. All berths dry. Facilities at both sites.

Facilities Water, shops and yards at Rye. Water, store, inn and PO at Rye Harbour village.

☎/**VHF** HM 01797 225225. VHF 14; Lydd and Hythe Firing Ranges VHF 73, 13.

Interest The town of Rye is a Cinque Port with interesting historical associations.

ENGLAND – SOUTH COAST

77

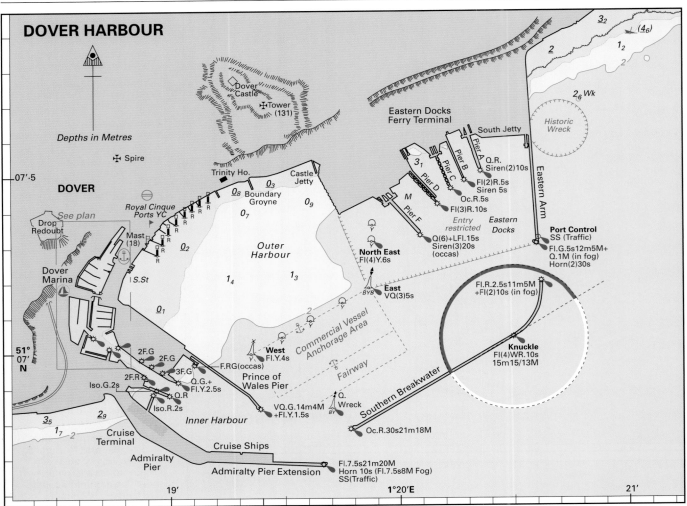

DOVER HARBOUR

Depths in Metres

DOVER

Charts BA 1698, 1892, SC 5605; Imray 2100, C8

HW Dover

DS –0200E +0500W

MHWS	MHWN	MLWN	MLWS
6·8m	5·3m	2·1m	0·8m

A very busy ferry and jet-foil terminal, but with good accommodation for yachts.

Approach From E observe Separation Zone regulations.

Signals International traffic signals (no exemptions) are displayed day and night on the port side of the western entrance and the stb side of the eastern entrance.

Entrance Permission to enter (when two miles from entrance) or leave **must** be obtained from port control on VHF 74. State which entrance you propose to use, and if you intend to anchor. Continue to listen on VHF 74, until you approach the marina area where VHF 80 is used.

Report again on VHF 74 when 200m off entrance and follow instructions. When leaving report to marina VHF 80 before leaving berth, Port Control VHF 74 on entering harbour area and follow instructions (all very helpful).

Both the W and E entrances have strong streams setting across them with overfalls and confused seas. Keep up-tide and clear of entrance until entry is permitted. Enter under power at all times and do not try to pass between the southern breakwater and the N card buoy inside the western entrance.

Berthing Tidal harbour for short-stay with access 24hrs. Wellington Dock (gates open HW±0130). Granville Dock (gates open HW-3·5 to +4·5). Approaching the marina area, keep in the main channel until the Ldg Lt F 324°-333° opens, especially near LW.

Anchorage in the corner on N side of Prince of Wales Pier, inshore of Y buoys. Exposed from NE through S to SW; in gales a heavy sea builds up. Yachts must not be left here unattended; landing on POW pier not allowed.

Facilities 24hr fuel, LPG, pump-out, scrubbing grid and 50-ton boat hoist. Launderette.

☎/VHF Dover Marina 01304 241663. Royal Cinque Ports YC 206262. Port Control VHF 74, 12. Marina VHF 80. Channel Navigation Information Service VHF 11, H+40. Weather VHF 23, 86; 0110 every 3hrs.

Interest Dover Castle. Museum.

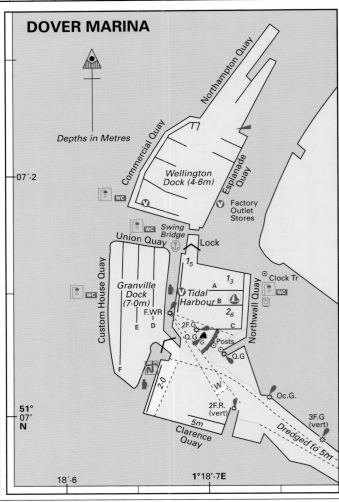

DOVER MARINA

Depths in Metres

RIVER STOUR AND SANDWICH

Charts BA 1827, 1828; Imray 2100, C8, C12

HW Dover +0015

DS (offing): Dover –0215NE +0400SW

Flood in entrance probably starts about Dover –0445; ebb +0200

Sandwich ebb runs for 9hrs, flood for 3hrs

Richborough

MHWS	MHWN	MLWN	MLWS
3·4m	2·7m	0·4m	0·1m

Estuary of River Stour. Entrance dries but 3·4m at HW.

Approach at HW±0200 to avoid berthing with flood. From Ramsgate, steer 255° for RW buoy at 51°18'·93N 1°23'·93E and No.2 N Card bn at 51°23'·14N 1°23'·14E. Follow seasonal buoyed channel to Shellness Point and enter the river.

Entrance Channel buoyed at entrance to R Stour after which buoys mark channel to Sandwich. 3m at springs, 1·9m at neaps. Br at Sandwich has only 1m clearance at HW but opens with 1hrs notice. Above br river is navigable for some miles with 1·8m draught and 3·1m headroom.

Berthing Richborough Quay is used by small tankers and is private. Berth at Town Quay. Limited room to turn, difficult with flood. Sloping bottom is mud on chalk.

☎ /VHF HM 07958 376183, VHF 8; Lifting bridge 01304 826236.

Interest Cinque port. Medieval buildings.

RAMSGATE

Charts BA 1827, 1828, 323, SC 5605; Imray 2100, C1, C8

HW Dover +0030

DS (inshore) Dover –0100N +0500S

2M SW of Gull buoy –0100NE; +0500SSE

MHWS	MHWN	MLWN	MLWS
5·2m	4·0m	1·4	0·6m

Ramsgate Harbour consists of the outer RoRo hbr (known as the Turning Basin) to S and the inner, Royal Harbour, to the N, sharing the same approach channel. Hbr busy with fishing boat and wind farm traffic.

ENGLAND – SOUTH COAST

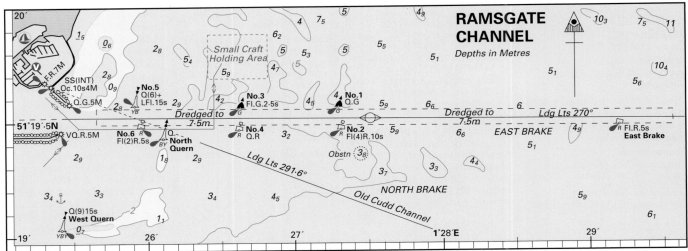

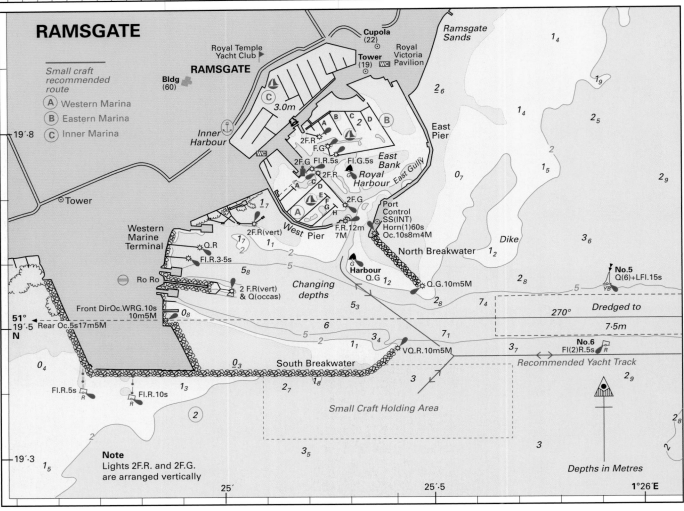

ENGLAND – SOUTH COAST

Approach Yachts must report to *Ramsgate Port Control* on VHF 14 and remain listening, before entering the recommended yacht track (*see plans*) to enter. There are small craft holding areas to N of No.3 buoy and to S of the South breakwater to which yachts may be directed to keep the hbr entrance clear during ship movements. The recommended crossing track is at right angles to the channel on the W side of No.3 and 4 buoys.

Signals IPTS on E pier control movement in and out of Royal Harbour. A Fl.O Lt indicates that a ship is on the move. At this time no vessel may move from the Royal Harbour or enter from the sea.

Entrance There is a dredged approach channel before entrance between N and S breakwaters. This channel is used by ships. At night steer 270° on dir Oc.WRG.10s. After clearing the breakwaters steer to stb for the Royal Harbour whose entrance is 3m or less, variable, giving the hbr G con buoy, Q.G, a wide berth to stb and keeping close to the W Pier as the entrance dries 1m on the E side. Yachts should pass quickly under power through the area between the outer breakwaters and Royal Harbour; do not stop to raise or lower sails.

Berthing With winds from WNW to NNE small craft can anchor near hbr entrance S of breakwater and entrance channel, 2½–3½m. There are three marinas in Royal Harbour, outer marina E mainly used by fishing boats Ⓑ (2m) and outer marina W for yachts Ⓐ, as well as a locked inner harbour (3m) open approx HW ±0200. A red and yellow flag by day and single green light at night indicate the gate is open.

Facilities Boatyard, sail loft, chandlery and launderette.

☎/VHF HM 01843 572100, Marina Office 572110. Port radio VHF 14. Berthing and Lock control VHF 80. Royal Temple YC 591766.

Interest Pugin's Grange open Wed pm ☎ 01628 825925 to book a visit.

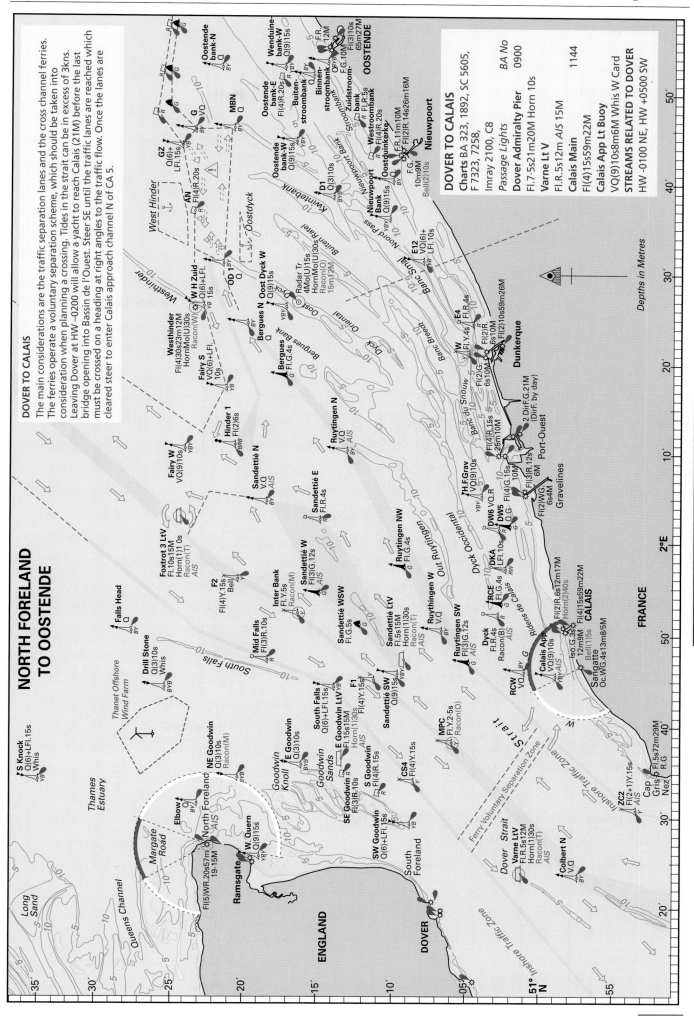

NORTH FORELAND TO OOSTENDE

DOVER TO CALAIS

The main considerations are the traffic separation lanes and the cross channel ferries. The ferries operate a voluntary separation scheme, which should be taken into consideration when planning a crossing. Tides in the strait can be in excess of 3kns. Leaving Dover at HW −0200 will allow a yacht to reach Calais (21M) before the last bridge opening into Bassin de l'Ouest. Steer SE until the traffic lanes are reached which must be crossed on a heading at right angles to the traffic flow. Once the lanes are cleared steer to enter Calais approach channel N of CA 5.

DOVER TO CALAIS

Charts BA 323, 1892, SC 5605,
F 7323, 7258,
Imray 2100, C8   *BA No*

Passage Lights   0900

Dover Admiralty Pier
Fl.7·5s21m20M Horn 10s

Varne Lt V
Fl.R.5s12m *AIS* 15M

Calais Main   1144
Fl(4)15s59m22M

Calais App Lt Buoy
VQ(9)10s8m6M Whis W Card
STREAMS RELATED TO DOVER
HW −0100 NE, HW +0500 SW

Depths in Metres

ENGLAND – SOUTH COAST

ENGLAND – EAST COAST

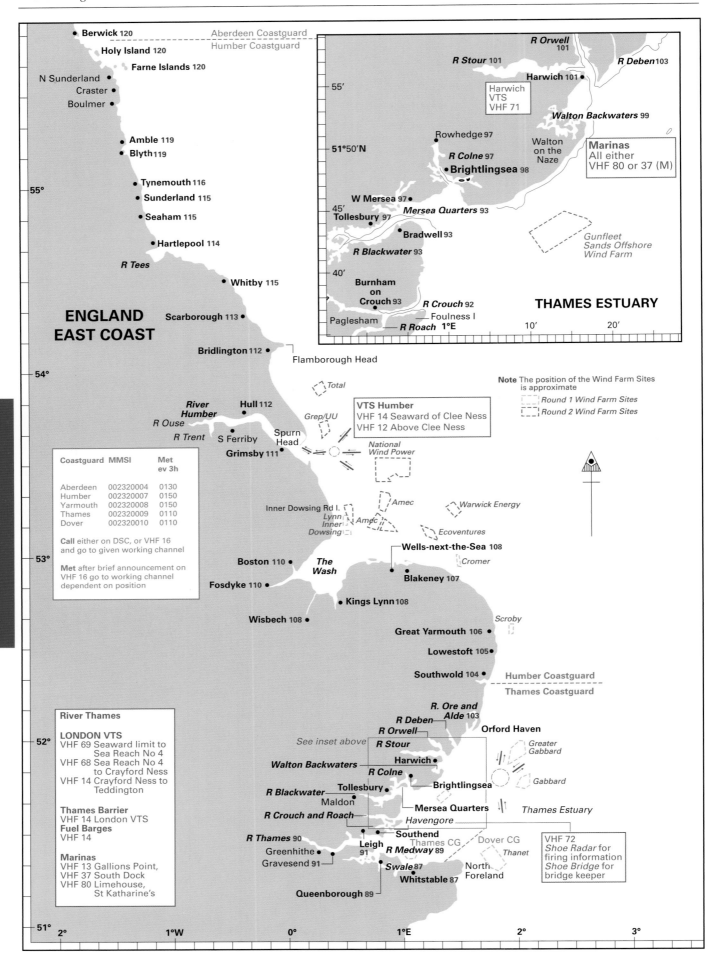

Berwick 120
Holy Island 120
Farne Islands 120
N Sunderland
Craster
Boulmer
Amble 119
Blyth 119
Tynemouth 116
Sunderland 115
Seaham 115
Hartlepool 114
R Tees
Whitby 115

ENGLAND EAST COAST

Scarborough 113
Bridlington 112
Flamborough Head

Total

River Humber
Hull 112
R Ouse
R Trent
S Ferriby
Spurn Head
Grimsby 111

Grep/UU

VTS Humber
VHF 14 Seaward of Clee Ness
VHF 12 Above Clee Ness

National Wind Power

Coastguard	MMSI	Met ev 3h
Aberdeen	002320004	0130
Humber	002320007	0150
Yarmouth	002320008	0150
Thames	002320009	0110
Dover	002320010	0110

Call either on DSC, or VHF 16 and go to given working channel

Met after brief announcement on VHF 16 go to working channel dependent on position

Inner Dowsing Rd I.
Lynn Inner Dowsing
Amec
Amec
Amec
Warwick Energy
Ecoventures

Wells-next-the-Sea 108
Cromer
Boston 110
The Wash
Blakeney 107
Fosdyke 110
Kings Lynn 108
Wisbech 108
Scroby
Great Yarmouth 106
Lowestoft 105
Southwold 104

Humber Coastguard
Thames Coastguard

River Thames

LONDON VTS
VHF 69 Seaward limit to Sea Reach No 4
VHF 68 Sea Reach No 4 to Crayford Ness
VHF 14 Crayford Ness to Teddington

Thames Barrier
VHF 14 London VTS
Fuel Barges
VHF 14

Marinas
VHF 13 Gallions Point,
VHF 37 South Dock
VHF 80 Limehouse, St Katharine's

R. Ore and Alde 103
R Deben
R Orwell
Orford Haven
R Stour
See inset above
Greater Gabbard
Harwich
Gabbard
Walton Backwaters
R Colne
R Blackwater
Tollesbury
Maldon
Brightlingsea
Mersea Quarters
R Crouch and Roach
Havengore
Thames Estuary
R Thames 90
Southend
Leigh 91
Thames CG
Dover CG
Greenhithe
R Medway 89
Thanet
Gravesend 91
Swale 87
North Foreland
Whitstable 87
Queenborough 89

VHF 72
Shoe Radar for firing information
Shoe Bridge for bridge keeper

THAMES ESTUARY

Aberdeen Coastguard
Humber Coastguard

R Orwell 101
R Stour 101
R Deben 103
Harwich 101
55'
Harwich VTS VHF 71
Walton Backwaters 99
Rowhedge 97
51°50'N
R Colne 97
Walton on the Naze
Brightlingsea 98

Marinas
All either VHF 80 or 37 (M)

W Mersea 97
45'
Mersea Quarters 93
Tollesbury 97
Bradwell 93
Gunfleet Sands Offshore Wind Farm
R Blackwater 93
40'
Burnham on Crouch 93
R Crouch 92
Paglesham
Foulness I
R Roach 1°E
10'
20'

Note The position of the Wind Farm Sites is approximate
Round 1 Wind Farm Sites
Round 2 Wind Farm Sites

Page references are shown after locations, for example:
Lowestoft 105. Bold type indicates that it is accompanied by a plan. *Italics* are used for rivers, lochs, bays, seas etc.

England – East Coast
North Foreland to Berwick

The Thames Estuary, from North Foreland to Orfordness with its rich tradition of commercial shipping, is a cruising area in itself. It has many quiet, secluded anchorages, especially in the Essex and Suffolk rivers, but at the same time there is a good selection of marinas. The chart, with its many sandbanks may look daunting, but the buoyage is good. Much of the area is reasonably sheltered but tides are strong and should be used to advantage, however wind against tide rapidly sets up a steep short sea, especially with a NE'ly wind. There is often considerable commercial shipping in the Princes Channel, about five miles north of the Kent coast, and also in the approaches to Harwich/Felixstowe where due attention must be paid to the TSS. Wind farms continue to grow. The N Kent coast has chalk cliffs as far as Westgate and is backed by hills; there are low cliffs on the Isle of Sheppey. If time allows, a visit to London is well worthwhile. The Essex coast is low apart from the sandy cliffs near Walton-on-the-Naze. Major yachting areas include the R. Medway, and the Suffolk and Essex Rivers; they provide excellent sailing in virtually all weathers. Harwich Harbour and its rivers provide a very safe port of refuge. The coastal marshes of Kent, Essex and Suffolk are important for the breeding and overwintering of water birds. There are RSPB sites on the Stour (one mile east of Wrabness), the Ore (Havergate Island), at Elmley Marshes and Cliffe Pools, the latter two both in North Kent. The estuaries of the Stour, Colne, Blackwater, Crouch and Thames have many Sites of Special Scientific Interest which support plants and animals that find it more difficult to survive in the wider countryside.

Between Orfordness and Flamborough Head many yachts tend to be on longer passages. Bound north, Lowestoft is a convenient port of departure for say Scarborough or Whitby. With the exception of the sandy cliffs between Happisburgh and Cromer much of the coastline is low. It is particularly difficult to identify the shore between the Wash and the Humber. Both Lowestoft and Gt Yarmouth provide access to the Broads for sea-going craft. The Wash and the R. Humber provide access to the inland waterways. To enjoy the north Norfolk coast one needs shallow draught, it is dangerous in fresh onshore winds.

Flamborough Head with its high chalk cliffs is very conspicuous. From here to Berwick there are few convenient anchorages, with the exception of Holy Island and the Farnes in suitable conditions. On passage, distances between harbours are such that overnight passages are rarely necessary; there are pontoon berths at Scarborough, Whitby, Hartlepool, Sunderland, Newcastle, Royal Quays marina (River Tyne), Blyth and Amble. The Yorkshire coast with its superb cliff scenery, bays, and ports is delightful in offshore winds, but beware of the swell which may build up after N'ly weather making many harbour entrances dangerous. Tees Bay is an industrial area and there are usually several ships at anchor. Blyth is a safe port in heavy weather, except from the SE. The Northumberland coast with its sandy beaches and views towards the Cheviots is very attractive.

North Foreland to Harwich

Charts BA 1183, 1607, 1975, 2052; SC 5606, 5607; Imray C1, 2000, 2100
DS All related to Dover. The main North Sea and river tides interact in the Estuary. These summarise:

Off N Foreland
Estuary tide runs W,
Downs tide runs S –0445 to –0115
N and W from the Downs to the Estuary –0115 to +0045
Downs tide runs N, Estuary tide runs E +0045 to +0445
E and S from the Estuary to the Downs +0445 to –0445

At intermediary points
The Princes Channel
–0445 W, +0200 E
Tongue Sand Tower
–0500 W, +0130 E
Great Nore
–0430 W, +0145 E

Barrow Deep
–0530 SW, +0015 NE
Whitaker buoy
–0500 WSW, +0115 ENE
Columbine buoy
–0400 W, +0130 E

At N extremity of the Estuary
Sunk Inner Lt F
–0545 SW, +0030 NE
The Naze/N end of the Wallet
–0530 SW, +0045 NE

Passage lights	*BA No*
N Foreland LtHo	0966

Fl(5)WR.20s57m19/15M AIS

Sunk Inner RW Lt Float	2172

Iso.3s12M AIS Horn(1)30s Racon T (–)

Sunk Centre LtV	2170

Fl(2)20s12m16M Horn(2)60s Racon C (–···) AIS

CROSSING THE THAMES ESTUARY
PASSAGE NOTES

Tides should be used to their best advantage. From the S, depending upon destination, it may be best to stem an adverse tide in the Downs to make the first of the flood at N Foreland. A careful analysis of the tidal streams and depths may permit straight line passages but for most boats it is necessary to navigate a way through the sand banks. Alternatively one can pass to seaward of the sand banks, but beware of the Sunk Precautionary Area. Three TSSs lead traffic into and out of the Outer Area. Traffic within the Outer Area flows in a counter-clockwise direction around an area to be avoided, one nautical mile in diameter, centred on the Sunk Centre LtF Fl(2)20s16M in position 51°50'·10N 1°46'·02E. *See plan on page 84–85.* There are many ways to pass through the maze of channels and swathways. Some are indicated on the passage plan (*see page 84–85*).

The London Array wind farm is situated in the area of Long Sand, Kentish Knock and Knock Deep. Foulger's Gat is closed during construction, the buoys have been removed; it may be open in late 2013. London VTS recommend using Fisherman's Gat, with a course just outside the buoyed channel. The whole area is busy with work boats and construction traffic. For latest information see www.londonarray.com.

England, East Coast distances (miles)

	N Foreland,1M E	Harwich	Orfordness	Southwold	Lowestoft	Wells	Grimsby	Flamborough Hd	Scarborough	Whitby	Hartlepool	Sunderland	Blyth	Amble	Holy Island	Eyemouth	Stonehaven
N Foreland,1M E	0																
Harwich	44	0															
Orfordness	45	16	0														
Southwold	58	32	15	0													
Lowestoft	68	43	25	12	0												
Wells	124	101	81	68	56	0											
Grimsby	170	145	127	115	102	54	0										
Flamborough Hd	190	165	147	133	122	77	47	0									
Scarborough	205	180	162	148	137	92	62	15	0								
Whitby	222	197	179	165	154	117	94	31	18	0							
Hartlepool	245	220	202	188	177	141	119	55	42	24	0						
Sunderland	258	233	215	201	190	153	130	67	53	36	17	0					
Blyth	269	244	226	212	202	165	166	78	65	48	29	11	0				
Amble	283	258	240	226	216	179	193	92	79	62	43	26	15	0			
Holy Island	302	277	259	245	235	198	247	111	98	81	61	44	33	23	0		
Eyemouth	320	294	276	262	252	215	291	129	115	98	79	62	51	40	18	0	
Stonehaven	385	359	341	327	317	280	356	194	180	163	144	127	116	105	82	66	0

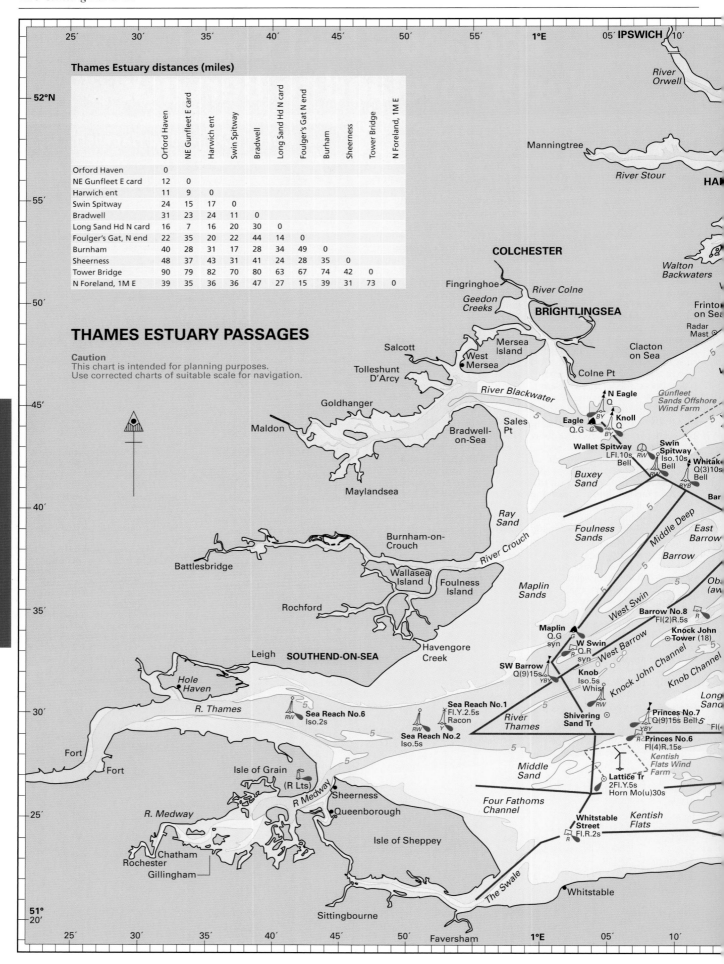

Thames Estuary distances (miles)

	Orford Haven	NE Gunfleet E card	Harwich ent	Swin Spitway	Bradwell	Long Sand Hd N card	Foulger's Gat N end	Burham	Sheerness	Tower Bridge	N Foreland, 1M E
Orford Haven	0										
NE Gunfleet E card	12	0									
Harwich ent	11	9	0								
Swin Spitway	24	15	17	0							
Bradwell	31	23	24	11	0						
Long Sand Hd N card	16	7	16	20	30	0					
Foulger's Gat, N end	22	35	20	22	44	14	0				
Burnham	40	28	31	17	28	34	49	0			
Sheerness	48	37	43	31	41	24	28	35	0		
Tower Bridge	90	79	82	70	80	63	67	74	42	0	
N Foreland, 1M E	39	35	36	36	47	27	15	39	31	73	0

THAMES ESTUARY PASSAGES

Caution
This chart is intended for planning purposes.
Use corrected charts of suitable scale for navigation.

ENGLAND – EAST COAST

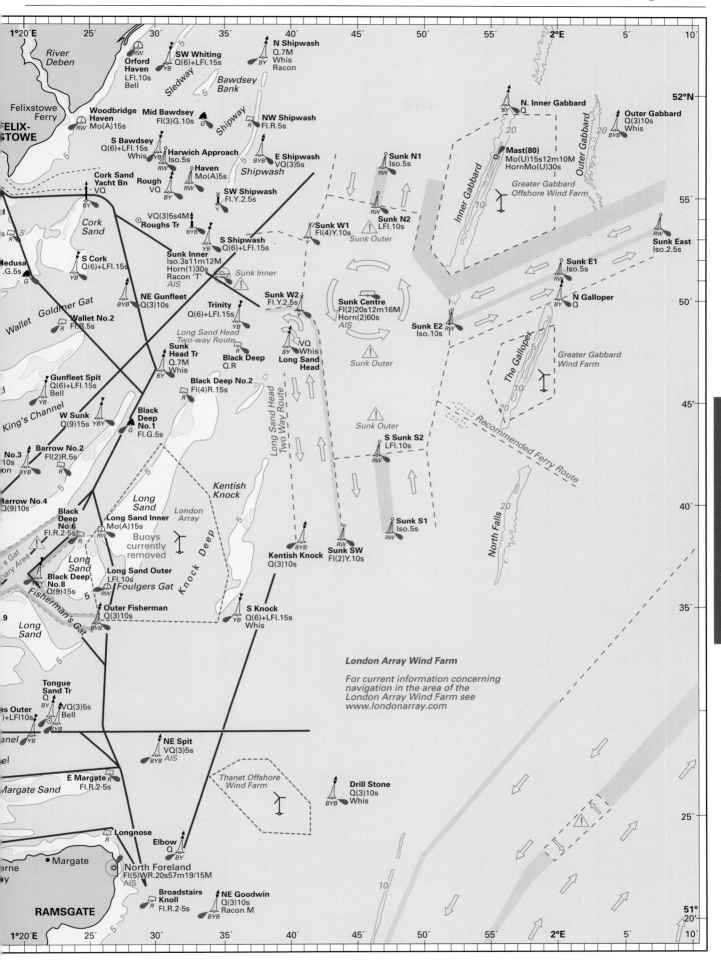

River Deben

FELIX-STOWE

Felixstowe Ferry

Orford Haven
LFl.10s
Bell

SW Whiting
Q(6)+LFl.15s

Sledway

Bawdsey Bank

N Shipwash
Q.7M
Whis
Racon

N. Inner Gabbard
Q

Outer Gabbard
Q(3)10s
Whis

Woodbridge Haven
Mo(A)15s

Mid Bawdsey
Fl(3)G.10s

NW Shipwash
Fl.R.5s

Shipway

S Bawdsey
Q(6)+LFl.15s
Whis

Harwich Approach
Iso.5s

E Shipwash
VQ(3)5s

Sunk N1
Iso.5s

Mast(80)
Mo(U)15s12m10M
HornMo(U)30s

Greater Gabbard Offshore Wind Farm

Outer Gabbard

Cork Sand Yacht Bn
VQ

Rough
VQ

Haven
Mo(A)5s

Shipwash

Medusa
l.G.5s

S Cork
Q(6)+LFl.15s

Cork Sand

Roughs Tr
VQ(3)3s4M

SW Shipwash
Fl.Y.2.5s

Sunk W1
Fl(4)Y.10s

Sunk N2
LFl.10s

Sunk Outer

Sunk East
Iso.2.5s

NE Gunfleet
Q(3)10s

Sunk Inner
Iso.3s11m12M
Horn(1)30s
Racon 'T'
AIS

Sunk Inner

S Shipwash
Q(6)+LFl.15s

Sunk E1
Iso.5s

Sunk W2
Fl.Y.2.5s

Sunk Centre
Fl(2)20s12m16M
Horn(2)60s
AIS

Sunk E2
Iso.10s

N Galloper
Q

Wallet *Goldmer Gat*

Wallet No.2
Fl.R.5s

Trinity
Q(6)+LFl.15s

Long Sand Head Two-way Route

Black Deep
Q.R

Long Sand Head

VQ
Whis

Sunk Outer

The Galloper

Greater Gabbard Wind Farm

King's Channel

Gunfleet Spit
Q(6)+LFl.15s
Bell

Sunk Head Tr
Q.7M
Whis

Black Deep No.2
Fl(4)R.15s

W Sunk
Q(9)15s

Black Deep No.1
Fl.G.5s

No.3
10s
on

Barrow No.2
Fl(2)R.5s

Kentish Knock

Recommended Ferry Route

Barrow No.4
Q(9)10s

Black Deep No.6
Fl.R.2.5s

Long Sand Inner
Mo(A)15s

London Array

Long Sand

Knock Deep

Buoys currently removed

S Sunk S2
LFl.10s

North Falls

Fisherman's Gat

Black Deep No.8
Q(9)15s

Long Sand

Long Sand Outer
LFl.10s

Foulgers Gat

Sunk S1
Iso.5s

Outer Fisherman
Q(3)10s

Kentish Knock
Q(3)10s

Sunk SW
Fl(2)Y.10s

S Knock
Q(6)+LFl.15s
Whis

Long Sand

Tongue Sand Tr
Q

s Outer
)+LFl10s

VQ(3)5s
Bell

London Array Wind Farm

For current information concerning navigation in the area of the London Array Wind Farm see www.londonarray.com

NE Spit
VQ(3)5s
AIS

nel

E Margate
Fl.R.2·5s

Thanet Offshore Wind Farm

Drill Stone
Q(3)10s
Whis

Margate Sand

Longnose

Elbow
Q

RAMSGATE

North Foreland
Fl(5)WR.20s57m19/15M
AIS

• Margate

erne
y

Broadstairs Knoll
Fl.R.2·5s

NE Goodwin
Q(3)10s
Racon M

1°20′E   25′   30′   35′   40′   45′   50′   55′   2°E   5′   10′

52°N   55′   50′   45′   40′   35′   25′   51°   20′

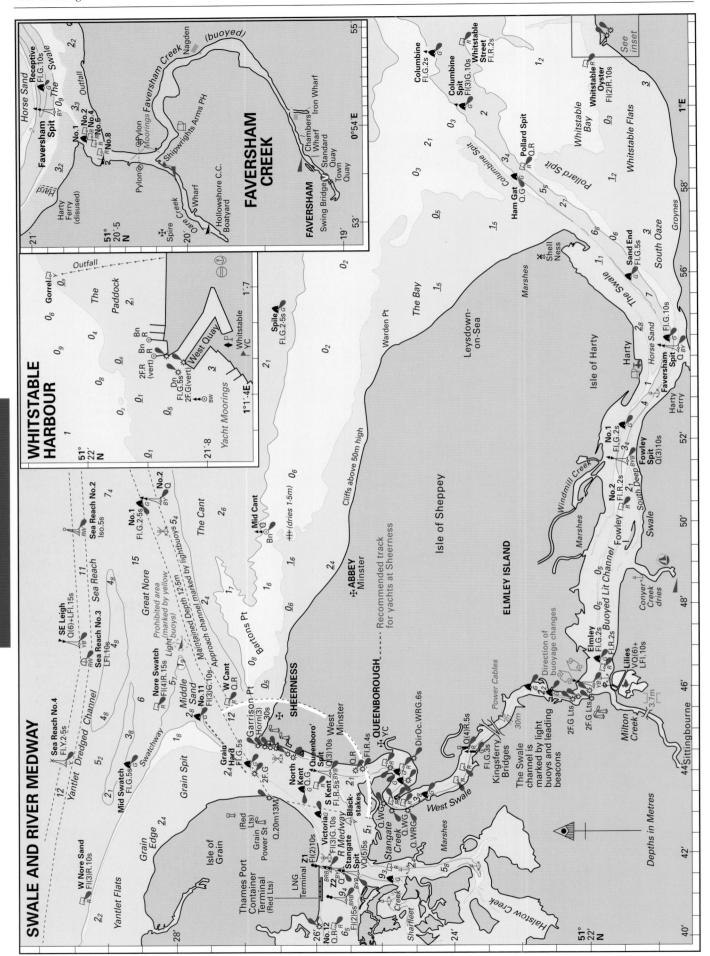

SWALE AND RIVER MEDWAY

WHITSTABLE HARBOUR

FAVERSHAM CREEK

FAVERSHAM

Depths in Metres

CROSSING THE THAMES ESTUARY

PASSAGE NOTES *continued*

• **N Foreland to the Swale, River Medway and River Thames**
Through the Gore and Copperas channels, S of Margate sands. They have few lit buoys and there are unmarked shallows and drying patches. Probably better E of Margate Sand through the Queens or Princes Channels. The latter has lit buoys but considerable commercial traffic. In onshore winds the only secure anchorages are the E Swale and River Medway. Anchored ships will frequently be encountered in Medway Roads.

• **N Foreland to River Crouch, River Blackwater and River Colne** From N Foreland pass E of Margate Sand and through Fisherman's Gat or Foulger's Gat using the buoyed channel through the wind farm to Black Deep. With sufficient height of tide and good conditions Sunk Sand can be crossed close to Barrow No.2 Fl(2)R.5s. Proceed N round E Barrow and N Middle Sands to the Whitaker E card buoy. Be aware that the drying sands in this area have been increasing in recent years. If in doubt take the Knock John Channel SW, pass W of West Barrow Sand into the West Swin and East Swin Channels to the Whitaker Channel for the Crouch or across the Swin Spitway to the Blackwater and the Colne.

• **N Foreland to Harwich** Pass E of Margate Sands and 2M E of the Tongue Sand Tower through Fisherman's Gat or Foulger's Gat using the buoyed channel through the wind farm and Black Deep. In either case leave the Black Deep at Sunk Head Tower N card Lt buoy Q and take the Medusa Channel to Harwich. Alternatively enter Barrow Deep as above following deep water E of the Gunfleet Spit S card Lt buoy until clear of Gunfleet Sand before turning to port for the Medusa channel. There is also the offshore route either through the Knock Deep or outside Kentish Knock to Long Sand Head N card VQ. If passing outside the Kentish Knock be careful to avoid the TSSs and

Sunk Outer Precautionary Area by following the recommended two way route from the Kentish Knock E card buoy to Long Sand Head N card buoy. This route may be used by any vessel less than 20m, or if sailing or fishing. Then make for the Roughs Tower and the Cork Sand N card yacht beacon.

• **Sunk Inner to Rivers Medway and Thames** The main routes are Barrow and Black Deeps but E and W Swins avoid shipping. A few buoys mark the passages.

• **Sunk Inner to River Crouch** Pass SW along the Kings Channel to the Whitaker E card Lt buoy and then into the Whitaker channel.

• **Sunk Inner to Rivers Colne and Blackwater** Pass N of the NE Gunfleet E card Q(3)10s into the Wallet, then SW to the Knoll N card Q and the buoyed channel to Colne Bar G con Fl(2)G.5s for the River Colne or to the Bench Head G con Fl(3)G.10s to enter the River Blackwater.

• **Harwich to the River Crouch** Leave Harwich by the recommended yacht track preferably about LW -0200. Pass close W of Stone Banks R. can buoy towards Medusa buoy. Turn to stb up the Wallet to the Wallet Spitway buoy and then through the Spitway which has least depth of 1.6m. Turn SW up the well buoyed channel to the Crouch. Tides run strongly in both the Wallet and in the approaches to the Crouch, so time of departure is all important.

• **Whitaker Channel to E Swale** From the Whitaker E card Q(3)10s pass through the E and W Swins to the SW Barrow S card Lt buoy Q(9)15s Sand, then given sufficient depth, go to the Whitstable Street R can buoy at the entrance to the E Swale. If there is need to avoid the Red and Middle Sands, from the SW Barrow go first to the Princes No.8 and then around Kentish Flats Wind Farm to Whitstable Street.

• **Thames Estuary to the near Continent** Bound for France head for North Foreland (*see above*). Bound for Belgium see page 246 or for the Netherlands page 251.

WHITSTABLE

Charts BA 1607, 2571, SC 5606; Imray 2100, C1

HW Sheerness +0010

MHWS	MHWN	MLWN	MLWS
5·4m	4·5m	1·5m	0·5m

Small hbr, controlled by Canterbury Council, used commercially. Temporary shelter at discretion of HM for yachts caught in W or SW winds.

Approach There are drying patches at LW in Whitstable Bay. Take care to avoid oyster beds marked by flag buoys. Steer 155° from the Columbine

Spit G con buoy or 182° from the Whitstable Street R can buoy taking care to avoid the Whitstable Street drying spit 3ca to the S. The tide runs across the entrance at a maximum speed of 2kn W on flood, E on ebb. Ebb begins approx HW–0100.

Entrance The hbr dries to 1·2m with shingle between the piers and mud inside. Best water close alongside the W pier. Long fender boards required.

Berthing Limited time for essential services only, with permission of HM. A mooring

---

Whitstable to Queenborough through the Swale

Charts BA 1834, 2482, 2571, 2572, 3683, SC 5606; Imray 2100, C1

Least depth at MLWS 1m. All times relate to Dover.

DS –0430 to –0400: slack everywhere.

Harty Ferry +0130 E, –0400 W.

Fowley Is –0400 to +0130 streams run in at both ends and meet here. From +0130 to +0500 the stream is E-going. From +0500 to –0430 streams separate here and run out at both ends.

Kingsferry –0400 SE, +0330 NW. (i.e. in from Medway for 0730, out towards Medway for 0430).

Streams are strongest soon after they begin and the greatest rates, about 4kn at springs, occur near Kingsferry. It is easier to carry a fair tide when bound E.

Queenborough –0400 S, +0230 N.

Buoyage Inward from Shellness to Milton Creek. Inward from Queenborough to Milton Creek. The Swale is well buoyed and has Ldg lines for large vessels at the W end. It is essential to keep to the marked channels and to be aware of depth at all times.

From Harty Ferry, where there are moorings and good holding,

steer to clear No.1 G con Lt buoy Fl.G.2s well to S, then to No.2 R can Lt buoy Fl.R.2s near Fowley Island. Least water, nearly dries, near Fowley I and just before Elmley Ferry, where a causeway stands ½m above the river bed. Marked by four posts. Best water on N (island) side. At LW channel only a few metres wide bounded by large areas of mud.

Kingsferry Bridge lifts on request, rly traffic permitting. Contact Bridge Keeper well in advance before committing to passage as opening times can be erratic. Clearance at MHWS: closed 3·3m; lifted, up to 27m. Traffic signals are shown only when bridge is about to open or close.

Fl.G+R	Br about to be lifted
F.G	Br open for passage
Fl.R	Br closing
Fl.Or	Br not working – keep clear
No lights	Opening not imminent

Use of Lts variable. Be prepared to move as soon as bridge rises even if no Lts showing.

VHF 10 Bridge keeper.
VHF 74 Message may be passed through Medway Radio.

Beware very bright sectored lights.

in the bay may be obtained from the Secretary of Whitstable YC.

Anchorages Good anchorage in the bay for up to 1·5m draught close by the yacht moorings W of the hbr entrance and clear of fairway, also in Tankerton Bay 1M E of hbr, in suitable winds.

☎ / VHF Whitstable YC 01227 272981; HM VHF 9, for permission to berth, between HW +0300 and –0200 any day 0800–1700 Monday–Friday. HM 274086.

SWALE AND HARTY FERRY

Charts BA 1607, 2571, 2572, SC 5606; Imray 2100

HW Sheerness –0007 Grovehurst Jetty

MHWS	MHWN	MLWN	MLWS
5·8m	4·7M	1·5M	0·6M

Approach and Entrance From the Columbine G con buoy Fl.G.2s on 234° to close N of the Pollard Spit R can Lt buoy Q.R, thence 227° leaving the Sand End G con Lt buoy Fl.G.5s to stb. Thence 237° towards Faversham Spit N card buoy which should be left to port if proceeding up Swale but to stb if entering Faversham Creek. Access HW±0130. Keep to mid channel. For Faversham Creek, continue to port at the fork, leaving the pub to stb. Detailed navigation information is given on guide from Faversham Town Council

☎ 01795 594442 or www.faversham.org.uk.

Faversham Creek Berthing
• **Hollowshore Services** at Oare Creek. Alongside mooring. Access HW±0045. Limited facilities. Uncomfortable in strong NE winds. ☎ 01795 532317.
• **Iron Wharf Boatyard**, Abbeyfields, Faversham. Access HW±0200. Limited facilities. ☎ 537122. VHF 8 *Iron Wharf*.
• **Front Brents Jetty**, Upper Brents, Faversham. Access HW±0200. Limited facilities.
• **Youngboats**, Oare Creek, Faversham. Access HW±0130. Limited facilities, diesel. ☎ 536176.
• **Swale Marina**, Conyer Wharf, Sittingbourne. Pontoon mud berths, access HW±0100. Diesel. ☎ 521562.
• **Conyer Creek Marina**, Conyer Quay, Sittingbourne. Access HW±0200 ☎ 521384.

Anchorages
• Good holding ground (mud) between Fowley Spit buoy and Faversham Creek, avoiding moorings and shellfish beds by Horseshoe Sands. More comfortable shallow-draught anchorages may be found in South Deep. Oare and Faversham are accessible from the hard on the S side. Boatyard and Inn at junction of Faversham and Oare Creeks.
• In the South Deep between Fowley Is and the S shore in 1m. To approach follow the S

ENGLAND – EAST COAST

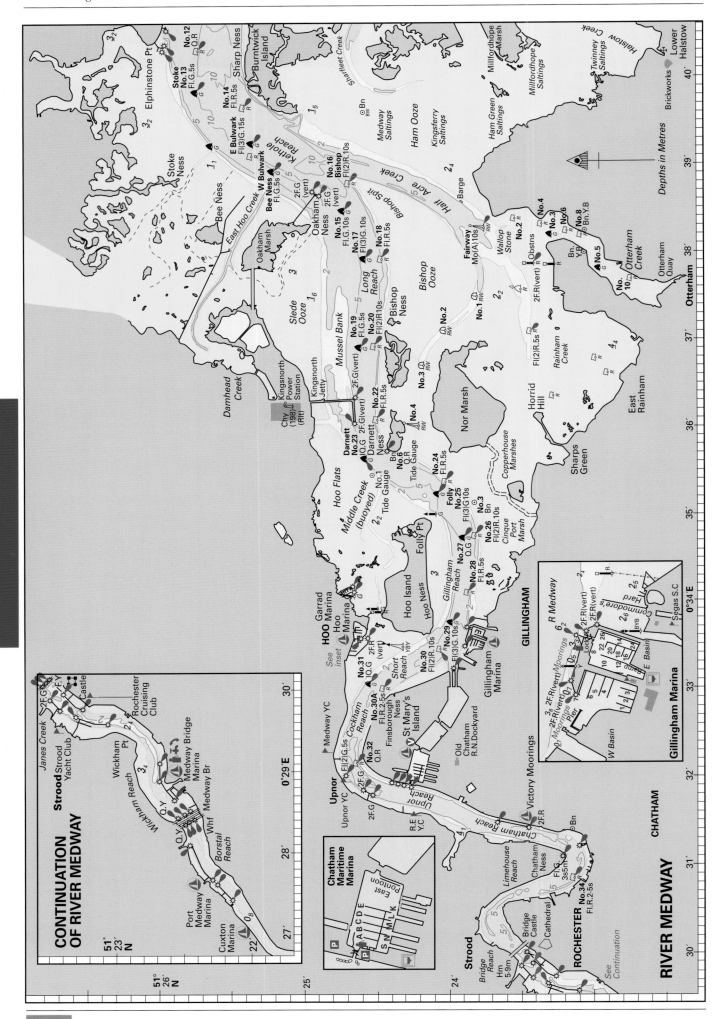

CONTINUATION OF RIVER MEDWAY

RIVER MEDWAY

Depths in Metres

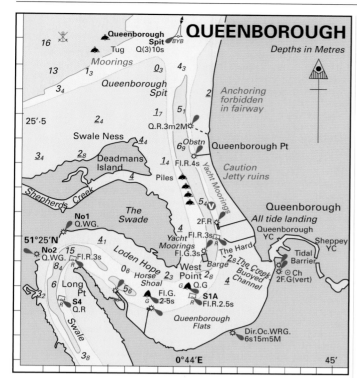

bank for approx 1M from Harty Ferry hard leaving a small Island marked by a E card buoy to stb.

Facilities Faversham is a medieval market town, 10 miles from Canterbury. Rly to London, Canterbury and Ramsgate. Oare and S Swale Nature Reserves.

QUEENBOROUGH

Charts BA 1834, 3683, SC 5606.10; Imray 2100

HW Sheerness
DS Dover −0400 S; +0230N

MHWS	MHWN	MLWN	MLWS
5·8m	4·7m	1·5m	0·6m

A convenient port, easily accessible by day and night. Sheltered except in strong N/NE winds.

Approach and Entrance From the R Medway leave the Queenborough Spit E card Lt buoy close to stb. A course of 178° leads up the fairway; at night keep in the narrow W sector of the Dir.Oc.WRG.6s light. Further into the creek leave to port the ruins of the rly pier; the area of the derelict pier is dangerous and stumps are exposed at half-tide.

Berthing
• 20 yellow visitors' buoys E of fairway to N of all tide landing for up to 11m.
• Two grey visitors' buoys for up to four larger boats near The Hard. Concrete lighter on W side of Swale opposite all tide landing pontoon available for mooring. Do not moor on E/Fairway side overnight.
The Queenborough YC has an all tide landing pontoon. Access gate needs token, available from local stores, pubs and YC.

Vessels may tie up alongside the pontoon, but only briefly to take on water, or overnight with prior authorization. Showers ashore. Visitors should note instructions on the all tide landing notice board.

Facilities Rly to London. Scrubbing berth.

☎ /VHF Queenborough Harbour 01795 662051. VHF 08 Trot boat and water taxi.

RIVER MEDWAY

Charts BA 1185, 1834, 1835, 3683 SC 5606; Imray 2100, Y18

HW Sheerness HW;
Upnor: +0015

DS (Sheerness narrows) Dover −0430S; +0145N

Sheerness

MHWS	MHWN	MLWN	MLWS
5·8m	4·7m	1·5m	0·6m

Upnor

MHWS	MHWN	MLWN	MLWS
6·0m	4·9m	1·4m	0·5m

Sheltered sailing and mooring are available in all winds. The main fairway is clearly marked by lit buoys and is suitable for yachts at all states of tide. At high water, wide areas of ooze and saltings cover deceptively. Three marinas on the Medway welcome visitors, there are numerous buoys and anchoring is possible in Stangate and Half Acre creeks and outside the fairway in the river.

Traffic is controlled by Medway Ports Authority and a listening watch should be kept on VHF 74 for VTS information. There is extensive commercial traffic to the Swale wharves, Sheerness Docks, Thamesport, Chatham Docks, Kingsnorth Power Station and several timber and aggregate

wharves, together with LASH operations and the exercises of Royal Engineers afloat.

The river is tidal up to Allington, but is effectively divided by the bridges at Rochester, which prevent most masted yachts from proceeding upstream.

East Coast Pilot has a chapter on the lower reaches of the Medway with *The River Medway* covering Gillingham to Tonbridge. Both are published by Imray. For local information on the Medway and Swale see www.msba.org.uk.

Approach
• From the E, an inshore passage from Spile G.2·5s to No.6 Q.R of the Medway Approach Channel may be taken on a rising tide, leaving the Mid Cant pile and Cheyney Tripod (N card) posts marking inshore hazards well to port. There is deep water at Garrison Point by the disused ferry terminal.
• From Sea Reach on the Thames, the Nore Swatchway may be taken, leaving Nore Swatch R to stb, then join Medway Approach Channel at No.11 G. Fl(3)10s. The recommended track for leisure craft should be followed to Grain Hard G con Lt buoy Fl.G.5s.
• From N and E, follow the Medway Approach Channel, which runs SW for six miles from Medway safe water buoy, Mo(A)6s to Garrison Point. There is a Medway Secondary Channel, S of the main shipping channel, marked by buoys Fl(2)Y.5s. There is plenty of water outside the marked channel, except to the NW after No.7 Fl.G.10s. where the wreck of the second world war ammunition ship *Richard Montgomery* is still fully loaded. The wreck is extensively buoyed. There are strong tides across the approach channel.

The E side of the Medway is marked by a fort at Garrison Point, from which a bright W light Fl.7s is displayed (both to sea and up river) when big ship movements are in progress. Yachts may proceed with caution.

The W side has Grain tr, marked by a buoy Fl.G.10s and, beyond it, the chimney of Grain Power Station, 244m, displaying red air navigation Lts. A wide berth should be given to large ships containing Liquefied Natural Gas using Sheerness Docks and berthing at LNG terminal at 51°25'·9N 0°42'·55E where there is a 150m exclusion zone.

Entrance Stream may run up to 3kn. On the ebb considerable advantage may be gained from an inflowing eddy that runs

close in by the seaward side of Garrison Point, or the main strength of stream avoided by keeping to the W.

From Garrison Point to Rochester the channel is marked by lit buoys. Beware numerous unlit buoys outside channel. The entrance to the West Swale is marked by the Queenborough Spit E card Lt buoy Q(3)10s. A further 1½M on in Saltpan Reach the entrance to Stangate Creek on the S side of the river is marked by the Stangate Spit E card Lt buoy VQ(3)5s which lies S of the conspic five container cranes on the N side of the Reach. These wharves extend from Victoria to Elphinstone Pt. Large vessel movements take place in this area and small craft must keep well clear. The hbr authority prohibits any unauthorised vessel from coming within 30m of the jetties or the vessels moored there.

From Kethole Reach inwards the river appears deceptively wide towards HW, but the buoyed deep-water channel is only about 2ca wide. Speed limit of 6kn from Gillingham Reach inwards. Large vessels including tugs and lighters use the river below Rochester. Take particular care at bends. Navigation for vessels with high fixed masts stops at Rochester Br. Headroom under the middle span 5·96m above MHWS giving 11·36m at MLWS but with depths of less than 1m in places. For motor cruisers the other key br is the stone br at Aylesford 8·4M upstream from Rochester Br. This has 2·87m clear at MHWS. Passage under Rochester Br is safest at HW±0300. Centre arch has least water, is subject to difficult tidal eddies and leads directly on to shoal patch. When depth is critical take Strood arch obliquely. Line up with end of pier on Rochester bank above br and straighten up into channel along outside line of RCC moorings. If heading for MPA visitors buoy on Strood side, follow same approach, cross river when above these moorings and fall back onto them. Progress beyond this point to Allington Lock 12M, the end of the tidal part of the river, is inadvisable before half flood. The lock is operated from HW−0300 to HW+0200 and manned at all times. Craft proceeding upriver against the stream give way to craft going downriver. ☎ Allington Lock 01622 752864.

Berthing
• **Gillingham Marina** Access HW±0430 to locked basin. Access lock manned 0600 to 2200 April to October, 0800 to 1700 otherwise. Once through the lock be ready to manoeuvre

ENGLAND – EAST COAST

in a confined space and maybe to moor between posts. Fuel pontoon (diesel and petrol) outside but no foot access from these into the Marina. There are also holding moorings and a tidal basin with access HW±0130.

Facilities Supermarket. Heliport ☎ 01634 280022, VHF 80.

• **Chatham Maritime Marina** Access 24 hrs by lock. Waiting pontoon. Restaurants and pubs, many located in historic buildings. Historic Dockyard with museum. RNLI Museum with 15 lifeboats on show. ☎ 899200, VHF 80. Diesel. Launderette. Regular bus to Rly and shops in Chatham.

• **Medway Ports Ltd** maintains six visitors' buoys above Rochester Br on the Strood side. VHF 80.

• **Medway Bridge Marina** Access all tides.

Facilities Shops in Borstal nearby; Rochester Castle and Cathedral are a 15 minute walk. ☎ 01634 843576, VHF 80.

Anchorages

• Stangate Creek and offlying creeks afford a quiet sheltered anchorage clear of traffic, in among the marshes. To enter the creek leave the Stangate Spit E card VQ(3)5s buoy to stb. Proceed in centre of creek keeping large mooring buoy (reserved for vessels carrying explosives) to stb and between port and stb unlit buoys ½M from entrance. Good anchorage on either side beyond this point. Riding Lt essential as creek is used by barges etc. Entrance at night not advisable for strangers.

• Sharfleet Creek leads off on the stb hand ½M from the entrance of Stangate. Good anchorage, probably the best on the Medway, on the S side just inside, or on either shore further in, clear of any oyster beds.

• There are many moorings suitable for yachts between Gillingham and Rochester, mostly controlled by yacht clubs or privately owned. Some commercially available. None are intended for visitors but may be available from Medway Cruising Club, REYC, Upnor SC ☎ 07092 197923 or commercial operators at Gillingham Wharf. Beware fore-and-aft moorings with fixed lines between buoys.

Facilities Diesel from Marinas at Gillingham, Chatham and Medway Br.

RIVER THAMES

Charts BA 1185, 1186, 2151, 2484, 3319, 3337, SC 5606; Imray 2100 (Sea Reach only), C2

HW London Bridge HW

MHWS	MLWS	MLWN	MLWS
7·1m	5·9m	1·3m	0·5m

Sea Reach No2

DS London Br -0055E +0500W

The River Thames is the gateway to London and provides an interesting sail to marinas in the centre of the capital. The Port of London Authority (PLA) controls the river downstream from Teddington. Their website (www.pla.co.uk) gives much useful information and they publish annually *The River Thames Recreational Users Guide* (laminated fold-out chartlet) and *Handbook of Tide Tables and Port Information*. These can be downloaded. They are also available from London River House, Royal Pier Road, Gravesend, Kent DA12 2BG ☎ 01474 562200. Imray publish *The River Thames Book* by Chris Cove-Smith which covers the area upriver from the Thames Barrier and *East Coast Pilot* which covers down river from Tower Br.

Vessels navigating any part of the River Thames must comply with sound signals. Failure to do so may lead to proceedings and a substantial fine. It is advisable to monitor *London VTS*.

VHF 69 Seaward limit to Sea Reach No.4 buoy: VHF 68 Sea Reach No.4 buoy to Crayford Ness: VHF 14 Crayford Ness to Teddington.

The RNLI run a lifeboat service on the Thames. In emergency ☎ 999 and ask for London Coastguard, use VHF 16/67 or the appropriate London VTS working channel.

Tides Tides can run at 3–4kn and it is essential to use them to best advantage. Since the tide off the entrance to R. Medway turns approx 1h before that at London Bridge, up-river one can usually carry a fair tide for 7h but down-river for only 5h.

Sea Reach to Margaret Ness Inward bound, begin the upriver passage at LW in Sea Reach. Queenborough, on the River Medway, is a convenient stopover point to await the tide in all conditions. From there start using the last hour of ebb. Outward bound, e.g. from Limehouse, leave 1h before HW, with average speed one should be in Sea Reach by LW. The Sea Reach deep-water channel is well marked. Keep well clear of commercial vessels by using the N and S navigable margins. It is best to keep to the S side between Southend and Lower Hope Pt.

Margaret Ness to Blackwall Point and Thames Barrier When planning a passage on the Thames, routine closures for maintenance of the Thames Barrier can be found on www.environment-agency.gov.uk. A control zone exists between Margaret Ness and Blackwall Point for regulating traffic; passage of all craft is strictly controlled. Contact *London VTS* on VHF 14 or ☎ 020 8855 0315 for permission to proceed when passing Margaret Ness inward or Blackwall Point outward. London VTS will then allocate a span which will be indicated as being available by the lit green arrows and red crosses. Green arrows will be exhibited from the ends of piers either side of the span(s) open to navigation. The arrows point inwards towards the span open to navigation from a particular direction. Red crosses will be exhibited from the ends of the piers either side of span(s) closed to navigation from one or both directions. Keep a watch on traffic from astern. Spans A, H, J and K are permanently closed to navigation. Maintain a listening watch on VHF 14. London VTS makes regular broadcasts at 15 min before and 15 min after the hour. You may be asked to call again when the barrier is in sight. There are illuminated notice boards indicating Barrier closure at Barking or False Pt, Blackwall Pt, and Blackwall Stairs. Closed spans may be open to navigation in the opposite direction. Before you reach the barrier, keep a close look out for the Woolwich cross river ferries which leave their berths very quickly. Vessels proceeding under sail between the Woolwich Ferry Terminal and Hookness must keep to the stb side of the fairway and are not to impede any other vessels. Whenever possible, such vessels should take in their sails and use the engine to navigate through the Barrier. The tide runs hard through the open spans. No stopping, turning or anchoring within 100m of the Barrier.

Blackwall Point to Tower Bridge There are no special problems here. Sailing is difficult. Beware of high speed ferries.

Berthing and anchorages

• **Gravesend** See separate entry

• **Thurrock YC** welcomes visitors. A member's mooring may be available for vessels less than 10m. ☎ 01375 373720.

• **Erith YC** has moorings for yachts up to 35ft. Larger vessels should anchor above moorings. Smaller, shallow draught vessels below moorings. Water at HW by arrangement. Supermarket ☎ 01322 332943.

• **Greenwich YC** has deep water moorings for yachts up to 12m. Contact HM ☎ 0844 736 5846 prior to arrival.

• **Gallions Point Marina** Access HW±0500. Lock Monday–Friday 0630–1830, weekend 0930–1830. DLR London City Airport ☎ 020 7476 7054. VHF 37/M, 80. Diesel.

• **South Dock Marina** Access HW-0230/+0130. National Maritime Museum, Royal Naval College, Royal Observatory and Cutty Sark. Crane: 20 tonnes. ☎ 020 7252 2244. VHF 37/M.

• **Limehouse Marina** Access HW±0300 approx. 0800–1800 April–September; 0800–1600 October–March. ☎ 020 7308 9930, VHF 80, when passing the Cutty Sark. Out of hours locking available from 0500 or until 2200 at any time of year if prebooked at least 24h in advance. Waiting pontoons may dry at LW. Beware cross tide. Headquarters of the Cruising Association which, with its renowned library, overlooks the basin and welcomes visitors. Cruising Association ☎ 020 7537 2828, www.cruising.org.uk. Docklands Light Railway nearby.

• **Hermitage Moorings** Visitors' mooring may be available on N bank downstream of St Katharine Docks ☎ 020 7481 2122, VHF 80, 37/M www.hcmoorings.org.

• **St Katharine Docks** Access HW–0200 to +0130, lock working hours 0600–2030 April–October, 0800–1800 November–March. ☎ 020 7264 5312, VHF 80, www.skdocks.co.uk. Six Y waiting buoys just downstream. A tranquil place within the City

River Thames Bridges	Headway of Centre Spans in metres			
	Chart Datum	MHWS	MHWN	MLWN	MLWS
QE II Dartford	60·7	54·1	55·2	59·3	60·2
Tower-lowered	15·7	8·6	9·8	14·4	15·3
Tower-raised	49·6	42·5	43·7	48·3	49·2
London Br	16·0	8·9	10·1	14·7	15·5
Cannon Street Rail	14·0	7·1	8·2	12·8	13·6
Blackfriars Rail	13·9	7·0	8·3	12·8	13·5
Westminster	12·2	5·4	6·6	11·1	11·8
Albert	11·5	5·3	6·4	10·9	11·4
Hammersmith	9·2	3·5	4·6	8·9	9·2
Twickenham	8·5	5·9	7·1	8·5	8·5
Richmond	7·9	5·3	6·5	7·9	7·9

of London. Supermarket and Tower of London nearby. Pump out facility.

Fuel Diesel (not petrol) available from fuel barge *Heiko*, usually moored outside St Katharine Docks, but advisable to ☎ 020 7481 1774 (Westminster Petroleum) to confirm current position. Usually open Monday–Friday 0630–1430; closed Saturday and Sunday. VHF 14. Petrol is not available anywhere on the river in central London.

Canals Canal and River Trust (formerly British Waterways) control the canals which connect to the Thames. Information may be obtained from CRT ☎ 0303 040 4040 www.canalrivertrust.org.uk has details of tidal locks, marinas and inland waterways. Limehouse Basin ☎ 020 73089930; Bow Locks ☎ 020 75175570; Thames Lock (Brentford)and Brentford Locks ☎ 0208568 2779. The Grand Union Canal is in Syon Reach and is normally open HW±0200.

GRAVESEND

Chart BA 1186 SC 5606; Imray 2100, C2

HW Sheerness +0010

MHWS	MHWN	MLWN	MLWS
6·4m	5·4	1·4	0·5

Approach Take care when passing through the outer ship moorings as the tide runs very hard.

• **Embankment Marina** Entrance is at the E end of the promenade, approached by a narrow gut between drying banks to the lock. Access HW–0100 to HW. PLA have

yellow small craft moorings upriver of Gravesend Sailing Club which may be available.

• **Gravesend Sailing Club** Visitors' mooring – eastern end of outer trot. Landing at wooden causeway.

• **Anchorage** In Higham Bight, near Shornmead Lighthouse Fl(2)WR.10s. Tripping line essential. Wash uncomfortable.

Facilities Diesel. Marina ☎ 01474 535700, VHF 80. Gravesend SC ☎ 07538 326623.

LEIGH AND SOUTHEND

Charts BA 1185; SC 5606; Imray 2100, C2

HW Sheerness –0003

MHWS	MHWN	MLWN	MLWS
5·8m	4·7	1·4	0·5

An exposed shore. Visitors should ask local advice. The only reasonable moorings are in the Ray Gut which leads to Two Tree Island and Benfleet. This gives sheltered anchorage except in Force 5 SW to E winds. Safe water HW±0200. Comfortable in SW winds, not so in strong E winds with wind over tide. There are drying moorings in Hadleigh Ray. In strong winds best go to Queenborough.

Approach Either make for the moorings E or W of Southend Pier if able to take the ground or enter the Ray Gut channel 8ca WNW of Southend Pier for Leigh, Canvey Is and Benfleet. This has 2·4–4m. Silting occurs. Approach with caution.

Entrance Leave the Leigh G con buoy close to stb. A pair of unlit G con and R can buoys mark the channel. Then head for moored fishing boats

leaving them fine to stb for best water. Benfleet Creek continues W to S Benfleet after ½M marked by stb then numbered port hand marks. Canvey Road Bridge blocks navigation.

Berthing Only for craft able to take the ground.
• **Leigh** Alongside Bell or Victoria Wharf. Both free.
• **Chalkwell** Anchor close in for crew changes etc. Close to stn.
• **Canvey Is E** Island YC and Halcon Marine. Drying mud berths, access HW±0200 from Ray Gut. Limited facilities, diesel, repairs. Maximum 30m length, 1·2m draught. ☎ YC 01268 510360; Halcon Marine 511611.
• **Benfleet YC and boatyard** Access as Canvey Is E but further in. A drying mooring may be available. Apply to moorings manager ☎ 01268 792278.

Anchorages
• **Ray Gut** Suitable in good weather whilst waiting for the tide.
• **Southend** Anchor off Pier end for a short period. Land by dinghy on to Pier. Area is patrolled April–October by Southend BC Launches *Alec White II*, *Sidney Bates* and *Low Way*.

Facilities
• **Leigh** Water Leigh SC or Essex YC. Telephone outside Smack PH, all facilities in town 2M, Rly. Southend Airport.
• **Southend** Water from YCs, all facilities in town. Rly.
• **Canvey Is** Water Island YC, Halcon Marine Boatyard.
• **Benfleet** Water Benfleet YC, Dauntless Boatyard. Rly.

HAVENGORE CREEK

Charts BA 3750, SC5607; Imray 2000, C1

This creek runs between the Rivers Thames and Crouch/Roach. Vessels with less than 1·5m draught may use it near HW when the tides are higher than mean. Navigate only in daylight. At the S end start between HW–0130 to –0030 by crossing the raised causeway, the Roman Broomway, ½M from the Creek entrance. In calm conditions the route has 2m at MHWS, 0·9m at MHWN, reduced by up to 1m by S winds or high barometric pressure.

The Maplin Sand is a very active MoD firing range. The passage of vessels through the area is strictly controlled. Do not enter when red flags fly on the sea wall, hoisted 1hr before firing commences. For latest information on firing VHF 16 or 72 *Shoe Radar* or ☎ 01702 383211.

Entrance Approaching from the Thames, make for S Shoebury G con Lt by Fl.G.5s at HW–0100. Leave the isolated danger mark to port. Make for two unlit MoD radar reflectors on wire stayed posts on the Broomway. Steer towards the Havengore Br, where, once between the sea walls, there is better water on the N side. The br keeper is on duty HW±0200 from sunrise to sunset, less in winter. In the entrance the bottom is mud to the SW and sand to the NE. All dries HW+0230. The ebb and flood meet about ½M inside and, as the Broomway covers, the flood reverses to run from seaward. There is a wreck 1M off the entrance and off the two

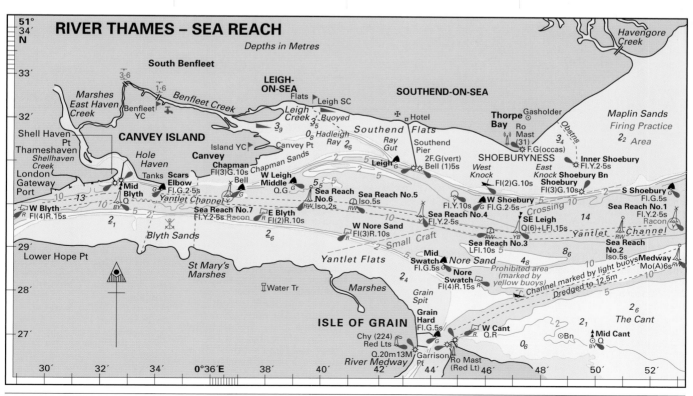

RIVER THAMES – SEA REACH

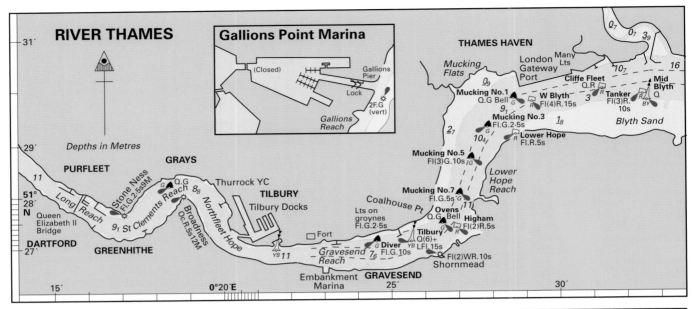

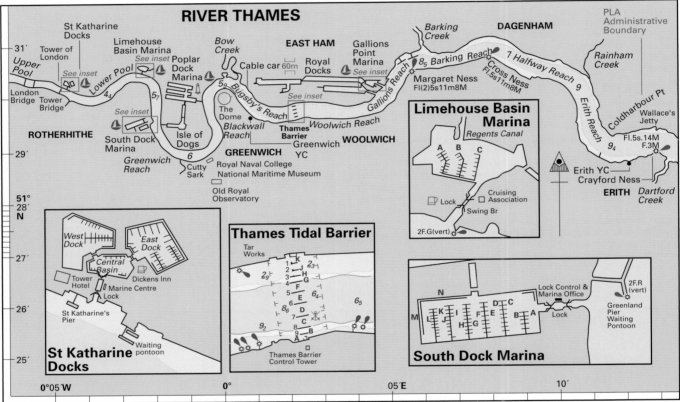

ENGLAND – EAST COAST

approaches above, marked with bn with two ball top mark. Once through the br either turning goes to the Middleway and thence to the River Roach. That to stb is narrow and needs local knowledge. Best go to port, S of Rushley Is, keeping close to the Rushley bank once the br has disappeared astern. On reaching the River Roach turn E for the River Crouch and Burnham. There are two Creeks to the E off the Middleway but both are dammed.

To go S from Burnham take first creek to port in the River Roach and then the third to port again missing the two dammed creeks. The nearest to the br where a vessel can lie

afloat is in the Middleway off the dammed creeks where there is 1·2 to 1·5m at MLWS. When the mud on the bank of the channel at this point is covered there is 1m of water at the entrance to the Haven.

☾/VHF Firing information: 01702 383211, VHF 16, 72 Call sign *Shoe Radar*. Bridge keeper 383436, VHF 72 *Shoe Bridge*.

RIVER CROUCH

Charts BA 1975, 3750, SC 5607; Imray 2000, C1, Y17

HW (Burnham):Walton +0042

MHWS	MHWN	MLWN	MLWS
5·2m	4·2	1·0	0·2

Accessible at all times. The coastline is low with few distinguishing marks; the spire of Foulness Church may be seen inland in good visibility and there are two conspic lattice towers well to the S on Foulness. These form a near transit with the Ray Sand Channel. The tides run up to 3kn on a spring ebb and follow the line of the channel. The river has a least depth of 2m in or close by the channel at the Sunken Buxey. The channel is

narrow in places and shoals rapidly at the edges. Vessels drawing up to 2m can reach Battlesbridge, the upper limit of the river at MHWS, but the upper reaches are crowded and tortuous making passage difficult. Beware streams crossing channels.

Approach
• From the Whitaker E card Lt buoy Bell leave Inner Whitaker S card buoy to stb and follow the well buoyed Whitaker Channel.
• From the Wallet cross the Swin Spitway. From the Swin Spitway safe water buoy Iso.10s Bell steer approx 245° leaving the Y can buoys with cross topmarks close to port. Shoaling has been reported

towards the west end of the Swallowtail bank.

• From the Wallet through the Ray Sand Channel. This channel dries 1·2m at the S end; seasonal variations in the line of deepest water occur. Passage should only be attempted on a rising tide. Take care to avoid Bachelor Spit and other shallow areas and sound across into the Crouch channel.

Entrance From Whitaker Channel follow the buoyed channel, taking care at Buxey No.1 S card Lt buoy and Buxey No.2 N card Lt buoy as the channel is narrow. Alternatively, coming from the Swin Spitway, after Swallowtail W card buoy pass N of Sunken Buxey N card Lt buoy. At the entrance to the Roach there is a GRG buoy, Branklet, leave to stb if entering the Roach, otherwise leave to port.

Continue up the buoyed channel, leaving the moorings to stb. To port, W of Fairway No.1 buoy, beware of ships unloading ballast and perhaps turning in mid-channel; keep well clear of the breaches in the sea wall, into the Wallasea wetlands which are marked by steel tubular piles carrying red port hand topmarks. Burnham Yacht Harbour is at the west end of the town. After Burnham, Essex Marina is situated on the S bank closely followed by Baltic Wharf at which timber ships berth. At the NW end of Cliff Reach, Althorne Creek leads to Bridgemarsh Marina. Between Creeksea and Fambridge, Bridgemarsh Is is completely covered at HW making identification of the channel difficult. Keep to the centre of the channel and do not enter bights in the river bank; the line of the S bank indicates the channel. About ½M E of Fambridge on the N bank there is a sunken sea wall, which is deceptive at HW owing to a bight in the sea wall at this position. At Fambridge moorings line both sides of the river.

Berthing
• **Burnham Yacht Harbour** 350 berths; access 24hrs. Entrance ½M W of Town Quay on N bank marked by a buoy Fl.Y.5s and entrance Lt bns to port Fl.R.10s and stb Fl.G.10s.

Facilities Travel-lift to 35-tonnes. Slip to 100-tonnes. Supermarket within walking distance. VHF 80. ☎ 01621 782150. Wi-Fi *Email* admin@burnham yachtharbour.co.uk
• **Essex Marina** 500 berths; access 24hrs. On S side of river. Ferry to Burnham, Easter to 31 October. ☎ 01702 258531, VHF 80, 37(M).

• **Burnham** on mooring buoy, by arrangement with Burnham Yacht Harbour or one of the yards or YCs. Do not leave boat unattended on buoy without permission.
• **Bridgemarsh Marina** Althorne Creek 120 berths; access HW±0400. Hoist, repairs. ☎ 01621 740414.
• **Fambridge Yacht Station** Visitors' pontoon at Fambridge Yacht Station on N bank at North Fambridge. Ferry Boat Inn. ☎ 01621 742911 *Mobile* 07917 390005
• **Fambridge Yacht Haven** In Stow Creek, on N bank, marked by bn and Wh Lts. Leave Stow Post, Q.Fl(4)8s, to port on entering, follow buoyed channel. Access HW±0500. **Facilities** at both sites. Diesel at marina. ☎ 01621 740370 *Mobile* 07917 390005, VHF 80.

Anchorages
• Burnham, ½M below the town, clear of the fairway and power cables marked by bns on banks and buoys in midstream.
• Cliff Reach. Keep well over to the S bank abeam of the Baltic Wharf to avoid a spit which extends from the N bank a quarter of the way across the river. Anchor in the bay of the S bank beyond the moorings in 5·5m if the wind is W, and off the red cliff further upriver on the N bank in 3·5m if the wind is E.

Anchorage notes
Do not anchor among moorings as the ground is foul. Crouch Harbour Authority Bye-laws prohibit anchoring to obstruct any fairway.

Facilities Burnham, all facilities; rly to London.

RIVER ROACH
Charts BA 3750, SC 5607; Imray 2100, C1, Y17

Entrance From seaward do not cut the corner at Nase Point as the mud is extensive and unmarked. From Burnham do not pass inside the Branklet buoy near LW. 1½M beyond the entrance is Horseshoe Corner where the river turns W; on the port hand in this reach is Yokefleet Creek leading to Havengore. ½M further on the river bears away SW and leads to moorings at Paglesham. Beyond Paglesham the river shoals rapidly. Landing on Foulness is prohibited.

Anchorages
• In W winds close under the W Bank under the high sea wall in the bay. In E winds off the quay on the E side ½M further up.
• Inside the entrance to Yokefleet Creek in 2m.
• Off Paglesham clear of the moorings and S of the fairway marked by G con and R can buoys.

RIVER BLACKWATER
Charts BA 1975, 3741, SC 5607; Imray 2000, C1, Y17

HW Bradwell: Walton +0030; Osea Is +0050; Maldon +0100.
DS Knoll buoy Dover
−0500 W; +0200 E;
Osea Is −0445 in, +0130 out;
Maldon −0415 in, +0130 out

The river is navigable as far as Osea Pier at all times and to Maldon at HW.

Approach From the Wallet approach from Knoll N card Lt buoy or North Eagle N card Lt buoy. Both channels clearly marked and have a least depth of 3·8m.

Entrance From Benchhead G con Lt buoy maintain a course of 290° until Bradwell Power Station barrier stands well clear of land. After passing the barrier and Bradwell Marina to port keep to midstream, leaving Thirslet G con Lt buoy to stb and Stone Point and Marconi Yacht Club to port, both of which have numerous moorings. Leaving Marconi R can Lt buoy to port, follow the buoyed channel with Doctor G con Lt buoy and Osea Island to stb. Lawling Creek, the channel to Maylandsea, is accessed by leaving No.2 R can Lt buoy to stb – it is a port hand mark for the river, not the creek. Keep closely to channel marked by moorings.

On turning to port rounding Northey Island, Heybridge Basin is on the stb side, marked by G con buoy Lock Approach.

Berthing (see also Bradwell and Mersea Quarters)
• **Blackwater Marina**, Maylandsea in Lawling Creek Pontoon mud berths, drying, access HW±0300. Floating moorings. ☎ 01621 740264. VHF 37(M).
• **Heybridge Basin** For access there is a depth of 4m in the approach channel at MHWS. The lock opens at times varying from HW−0100 to HW for any boat visible in the approach channel. Wait until out-going boats are clear of the channel and the green light is showing. Leave Lock Approach G. con buoy close to stb and proceed towards the lock, leaving the withies to port.

Facilities Launderette. Supermarket, by dinghy up the canal to Maldon. Lock ☎ 853506, *Mobile* 07712 079764. VHF 80.
• **Maldon** A drying pontoon berth may be obtained on soft mud. There is 2·5m at MHWS and 1·0m at MHWN at Hythe Quay. ☎ 01621 875837. River Bailiff *Mobile* 07818 013723 for mooring.

Anchorages
• In Latchingdon Hole in 2m. Leave No.4 R can Southey

Creek buoy to stb and follow the channel by sounding.
• E of Osea pier-head.
• Thirslet Creek in 3·3m or less.
• Goldhanger Creek in 2m. Goldhanger Spit is marked by No.1 G con buoy. Leave well to port to enter creek.
• Lawling Creek, opposite Osea Pier; good anchorage in 2m, within 2ca of the entrance.
• Off the Stone. Clean landing on shingle.

Supplies All facilities at Maldon.

BRADWELL
Chart BA 3741, SC 5607; Imray 2000, C1, Y17

HW Walton +0030

MHWS	MHWN	MLWN	MLWS
5·2m	4·2m	1·3m	0·4m

A small inlet on the S side of the River Blackwater inside Pewit Is with the approach channel to Bradwell Marina. The creek is full of small craft moorings with approx 0·6m at MLWS.

Approach Approach from the N then steer to leave the prominent square pile entrance N card Lt Bn Q 'Tidepole' approx 3m to stb. Tide gauge on bn gives available depth in channel to Marina.

Entrance The narrow entrance channel is marked by withies and R can buoys. Leave withies about 3m to stb. At last withy steer for G con buoy. At G con buoy turn sharply to stb and pass between shore and lines of moorings. Then head for R can buoy marking marina entrance channel and follow marked channel into marina.

Berthing
• **Bradwell Marina** Access HW±0400. Regular dredging aims to maintain 1½m at MLWS but less depth at some berths. Visitors moor to end of 'A' or 'B' pontoon on arrival. ☎ 01621 776235. VHF 37(M) and 80.

Facilities Marina club with restaurant and bar; inn in village; Bradwell Quay YC nearby, open at weekends.

MERSEA QUARTERS
Charts BA 3741, SC 5607; Imray 2000, C1, Y17

HW Walton + 0025

MHWS	MHWN	MLWN	MLWS
5·1m	3·8m	1·2m	0·5m

Mersea Quarters has a depth of up to 6m. It is on the N side of the River Blackwater N of the Nass Spit. This is marked by an E card Lt bn VQ(3)5s6m2M. The bn has a tide gauge showing height of water over the sill at Tollesbury Marina. Over the whole area the simplistic advice is where there are no moorings there is no water.

Continued on page 97

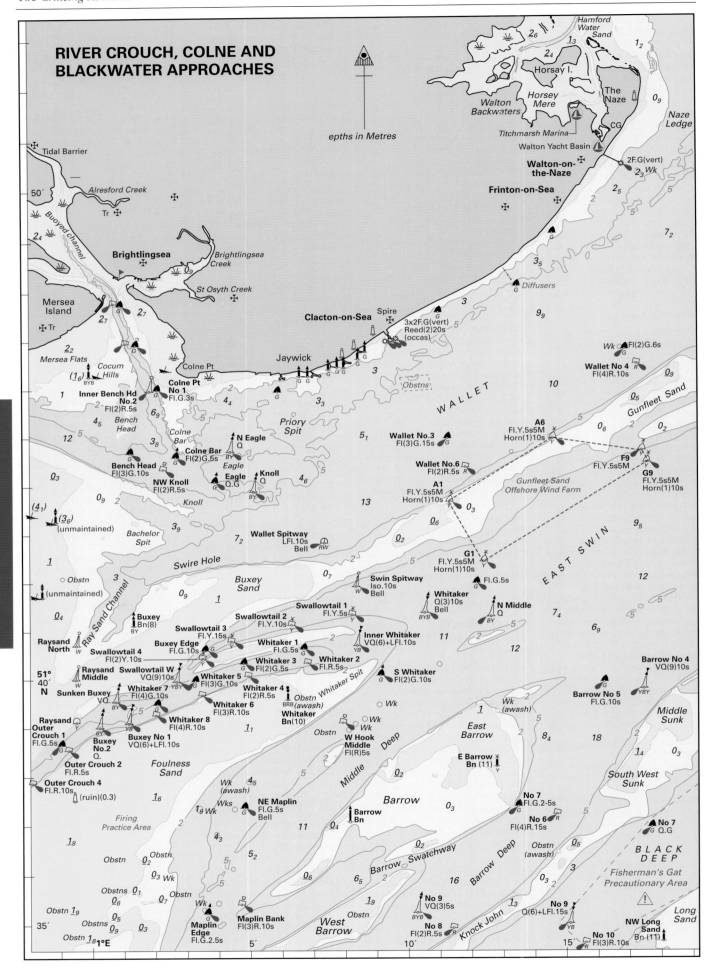

RIVER CROUCH, COLNE AND BLACKWATER APPROACHES

RIVERS CROUCH AND ROACH

Caution
Buoyage may be subject to alteration

Depths in Metres

BURNHAM YACHT HARBOUR AND ESSEX MARINA

Continuation of River Crouch to Battlesbridge

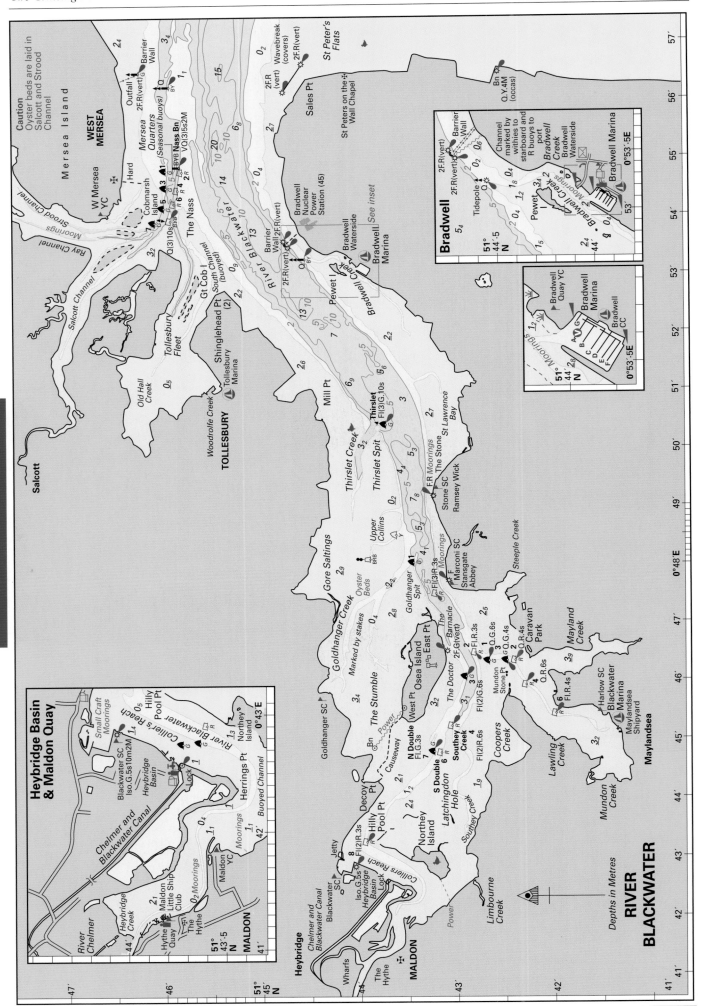

ENGLAND – EAST COAST

Approach From the NW Knoll R can Fl(2)R.5s steer 288° 4½M to the Nass E card Lt bn. This is difficult to pick up from a distance but the church tr and large block of flats in West Mersea give a good line. Outer approach from E or W is across shallows of 0·9–1·4m depending on line taken. After passing through the buoyed channel in Mersea Quarters, the black shed on Packing Marsh Island is then a guide to Thorn Fleet to which visitors are usually directed. Coming from the River Colne, keep the shed well open of the W end of Mersea Is to clear the Cocum Hills shoal, leaving Molliette E card bn to stb.

Entrance Pass at least 2ca to the NE of the Nass Bn particularly at LW, as the spit dries W of the bn and only 1·2m will be found close E. Then follow buoyed channel. After some 4ca from the Nass Bn the channel divides:
• Thorn Fleet, W of Packingmarsh Is, identified by its conspic black shed, has 1·7m. Mersea Fleet, the channel between Cobmarsh Is and Packingmarsh Is and extending N to the Gut, locally called the Creek has 1·5m, but 1m on bar abreast shed. Thorn Fleet is the best channel but care should be taken to follow the line of deep keeled moored craft as many moorings on the E and W edges are half drying. Keep to a general N/S line past Packingmarsh Is to avoid grounding. Salcott Channel is to the W of Thornfleet, bear to

port after No.7 G con buoy; there is 1·8m to Sunken Island.
• For Tollesbury Marina bear to port and follow the buoyed S channel on a SW course into Tollesbury Fleet. This has about 2m for 2M. The S channel leads to Woodrolfe Creek. A small E card buoy, marking the E end of Gt Cob Is, should be left to stb on entering South Channel. The entrance channel to Tollesbury Marina has a tide gauge to indicate depth of water on the Marina sill.

Berthing
• **Tollesbury Marina** Access HW±0200 sp; HW±0100 np Depth over sill 2·9m MHWS, 1·8m MHWN, Cruising Club, restaurant, swimming pool, tennis. Laundry. Scrubbing posts, repair yard. The marina is at the head of the ½M Woodrolfe Creek. Inside hbr is dredged to about 2m below sill level. Waiting buoys marked Tollesbury Marina in Tollesbury Fleet near Woodrolfe Creek. Tide gauge in creek. ☎ 01621 869202, VHF 37(M), 80.
• **W Mersea** No pontoons but otherwise the full facilities of a major yachting centre. The creeks are narrow and too full of moorings to anchor. Beware extensive oyster beds where anchoring prohibited. For best water keep close to moorings. A vacant buoy can usually be found, for which a charge is made – enquire from West Mersea Yacht Club launches and water taxi on VHF 37/M, call sign YC1, or *Mobile* 07752 309435.

• Scrubbing posts: apply to WMYC.
• Mooring piles in Thorn Fleet – contact WMYC launch.
• There are some deep water moorings in Mersea Quarters – exposed from NE to SW.
• West Mersea Marine boat yard.

☎ WMYC 01206 382947; West Mersea Marine 382244.

Facilities Renowned fish restaurant. Store at end of causeway and more extensive shopping facilities in Mersea town, 1M. Shops and pubs in Tollesbury village.

RIVER COLNE
Charts BA 1975, 3741, SC 5607; Imray 2000, C1, Y1

HW +0030

MHWS	MHWN
4·2m	3·1m

Approach into river channel:
• From seaward at any state of tide, by day or night from Knoll N card Q to Eagle G con Q.G; then to Colne Bar G con Fl(2)G.5s and to Inner Bench Head R pillar Fl(2)R.5s.
• From N. Eagle N card Q to Colne Bar buoy.
• If sufficient depth on a rising tide, from N. Eagle direct to Inner Bench Head. Beware that, between the Colne Bar and Inner Bench Head buoys the tide sets strongly E or W up to 1½kn on spring ebb and flood tides respectively.
• From the River Blackwater at any state of tide, from Bench Head buoy to Inner Bench Head buoy gives least depth of 2·3m. Or, if sufficient rise of

tide to clear Cocum Hills, from Nass Bn to ½M S of Molliette E card Bn on Mersea Flats, then enter channel south of No.8 R can Fl.R.3s buoy. This has a least depth of 0·5m.

Entrance From Inner Bench Head buoy follow the buoyed channel. Bateman's Tr Fl(3)20s has a conical roof and is visible from seaward.

Anchorages In Pyefleet Channel, E of Pewit Is and clear of oyster beds marked by withies. 10 W mooring buoys may be available, call Colchester Oyster Fishery ☎ 01296 384141, who will collect dues. If possible avoid anchoring in Brightlingsea Roads, particularly to seaward of R can Lt buoy Fl.R.5s marking wreck on E Mersea shore. This area has deep water and is used by commercial vessels up to 100m long. When anchoring or swinging at low water these can take the full width of the roads. Land at Mersea Stone Point from where a foot ferry runs to Brightlingsea in summer. After half flood, at E Mersea hard and on the beach at Bateman's Tr ½M from Brightlingsea. At Rowhedge, alongside pontoon or quay for short stay near HW. Nearby shop and pub.

Facilities Shops, all facilities at Brightlingsea. Foot ferry *Mobile* 07981 450169.

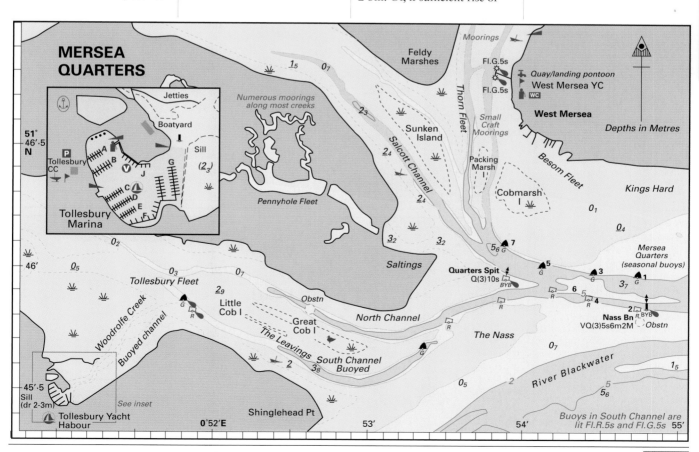

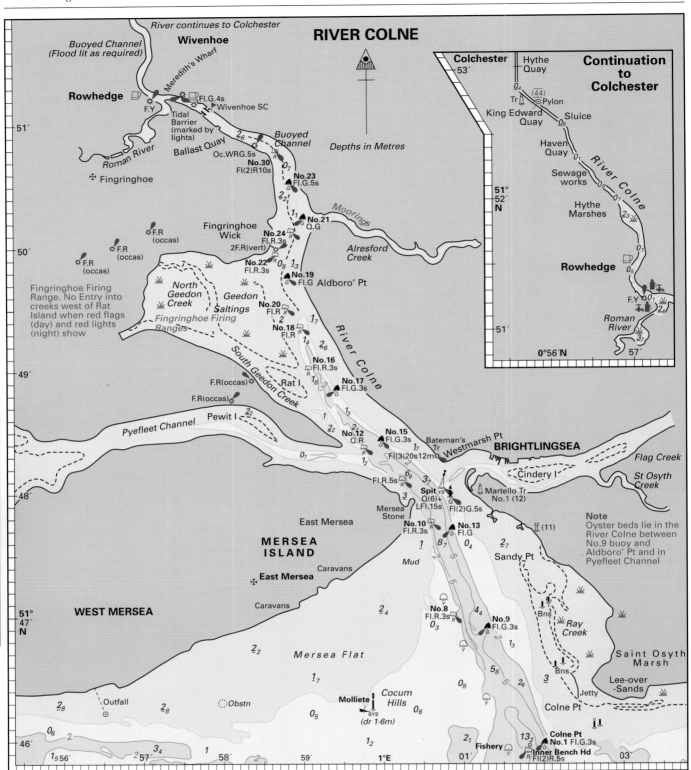

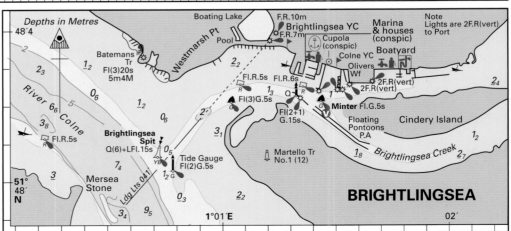

BRIGHTLINGSEA

Charts BA 1975, 3741, SC 5607; Imray 2000, C1, Y17

HW Walton +0023

MHWS	MHWN	MLWN	MLWS
5·0m	3·8m	1·2m	0·4m

Entrance From No.13 G con lt buoy Q.G. stand out in mid channel until abeam of G stb hand post with tide gauge showing depth in entrance channel. Pass between *Brightlingsea Spit* S card lt buoy and the post, keeping ldg bns, rectangular white boards with red vertical lines, on a bearing of 041°. Pass between R can Lt buoy and G con Lt buoy then approach the hbr, leaving N card Lt bn Q to stb and pass to moorings area. By night there are F.R Ldg Lts; two F.R(vert) mark the end of Brightlingsea hard on the N side of the channel; 2F.R(vert) at either end of Colne YC hammer head jetty and 2F.R(vert) at SW corner of Olivers Wharf close E of Colne YC. Watch out for commercial vessels manoeuvring in the vicinity of the quay at Olivers Wharf.

Berthing Call HM on VHF 68 when approaching S Card Lt buoy Brightlingsea Spit for berth on floating pontoons. Waterside Marina (maximum LOA 12m; minimum depth 2m) has some berths – apply to HM in advance. Sill 1m above CD.

Facilities Landing at town pontoon. Mooring allowed for 20 minutes. Water at Colne YC pontoon and at up river facility, where diesel and pump-out is now available by request from

HM. Showers in YC and laundry in Wreck House. Chandleries, boatyard with hoist, scrubbing posts (apply HM). Convenience store near marina.

✆/VHF HM 01206 302200; *Brightlingsea Harbour* VHF 68. Water taxi VHF 37/M; *Mobile* 07535 508537.

WALTON BACKWATERS

Chart BA 2695, SC 5607; Imray 2000, C1, Y16

HW Walton

MHWS	MHWN	MLWN	MLWS
4·2m	3·4m	1·1m	0·4m

Approach Locate *Pye End* RW small pillar buoy LFl.10s at 51°55'·0N 1°17'·9E at NE end of entrance channel.

Entrance Follow the buoyed channel in a southwesterly direction from Pye End RW buoy. After No.8 R can buoy the channel becomes very narrow. Bound into Hamford Water leave Island Point N card

buoy to port. When bound into the Walton Channel, keep Island Point N card to stb and keep close to the R can buoys to avoid the spit running out from Island Pt, but beware of strong cross current on early ebb. Take the buoyed channel until Twizzle Creek bears W towards Titchmarsh Marina. The line of moorings indicates the best water.

Continue S into Foundry Reach, which dries, to the Walton and Frinton YC and boatyards.

Berthing
• **Titchmarsh Marina** Access HW±0500.
Well-equipped marina, with restaurant. Basic provisions at marina chandlery, otherwise shops at Walton-on-the-Naze 1M. Marine engineer. Walton-on-the-Naze 1M.
✆/VHF 01255 672185, 851899, VHF 80.
• **Walton Yacht Basin** located near YC. Craft up to 2m

draught can lie afloat. 60 berths, access HW±0200 most times. Maybe no access at low neaps. Berthing by prior arrangement. ✆ 01255 675873 Bedwell & Co.
• **Walton and Frinton Yacht Club** Drying quay. Visitors limited to 2hrs. Open seven days a week in season.
✆ 678161.

Anchorages Off Stone Point, leaving a fairway to the W side of the channel. If landing on Stone Point respect Nature Reserve. Hamford Water is uncomfortable in NE winds. Heavy pipe reed may impede anchoring. In Kirkby Creek anchor clear of all moorings and oyster beds. Due to movement of ships carrying explosives, Oakley Creek is not a recommended anchorage. Land at the WFYC hard or quay approx HW±0200.

Facilities Shops and Rly in Walton-on-the-Naze.

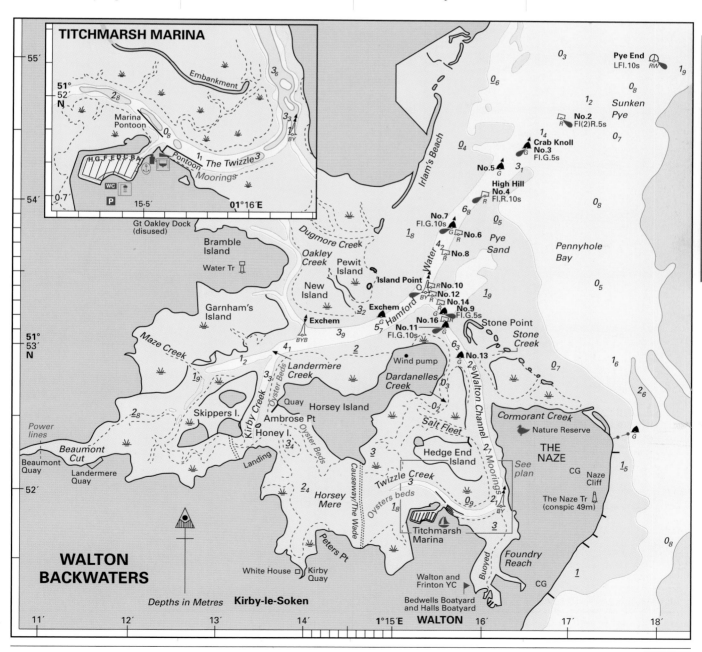

ENGLAND – EAST COAST

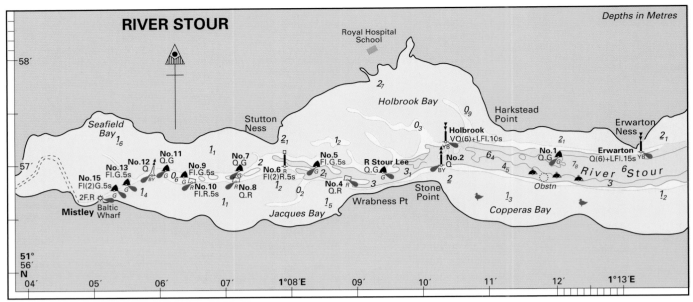

RIVER STOUR

Depths in Metres

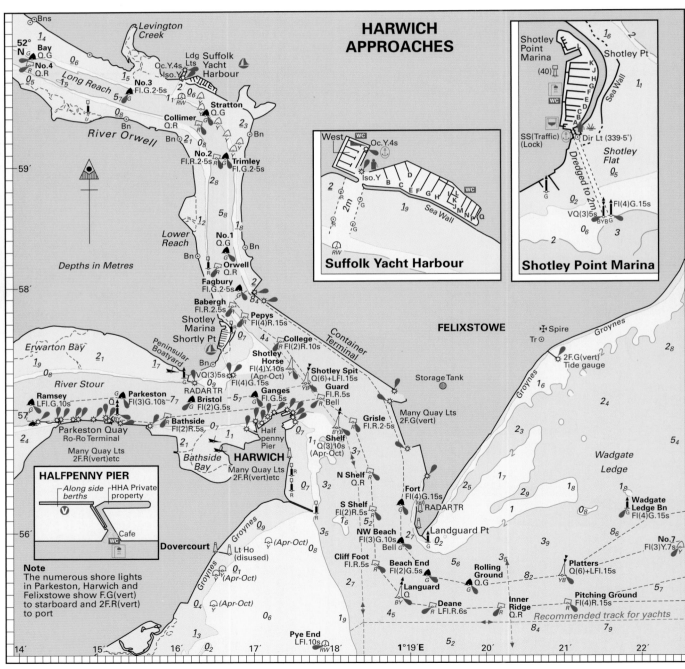

HARWICH APPROACHES

FELIXSTOWE

Suffolk Yacht Harbour

Shotley Point Marina

HALFPENNY PIER

Note
The numerous shore lights in Parkeston, Harwich and Felixstowe show F.G(vert) to starboard and 2F.R(vert) to port

RIVER STOUR

Charts BA 1491, 1594, 2693, SC 5607

Imray 2000, C28, Y16

HW Mistley: Walton +0025

MHWS	MHWN	MLWN	MLWS
4·2m	3·4	1·0	0·3

Entrance Leaving Parkeston Quay to port proceed upriver in a W direction. The river is broad and straight for a distance of 2½M until approaching Wrabness; the channel is buoyed and lit as far as Mistley. The River Stour is navigable as far as Manningtree, 5M upriver of Wrabness, for 1·2m draught at HW.

Berthing
• **Shotley Marina** *see Harwich*.
• **Wrabness** A vacant mooring buoy may be used for a short period but, for many yachts, only the outer row is deep enough at LWS. Yachts should not be left unattended.
• **Mistley Quay** No access to shore.
• **Manningtree Stour SC** has a quay which visitors may use. Access HW±0020 HWS only. Not easy to reach.

Anchorages In the River Stour, clear of the channel.

HARWICH AND FELIXSTOWE

Charts BA 1491, 1594, 2693, SC 5607;

Imray 2000, C28, Y16

HW Walton +0005

DS Landguard Point

Dover +0530 flood, –0030 ebb

Cork buoy

–0600 SW, +0015 NE

Naze: +0615 S, –0015 N

MHWS	MHWN	MLWN	MLWS
4·0m	3·4m	1·1m	0·4m

Accessible at all times. Harwich and Felixstowe are major ports for both ferry traffic and large container vessels. Small craft must at all times keep clear of commercial vessels in the approaches, anchorages and hbr area. The Harwich Haven Authority (HHA) publish an annual Yachting Guide obtainable from Harbour House, The Quay, Harwich CO12 3HH ✆ 01255 243030. See also www.hha.co.uk/leisure HHA patrol the hbr throughout the year.

Harwich VTS VHF 71 is extremely busy with commercial operations. Yachts should monitor but not make calls on this channel, except in an emergency.

Yachts should use the recommended yacht channels and cross the deep water channels at right angles and at the designated crossing points.

Approach Well marked. From the S by night 355° from the Medusa G con Lt buoy Fl.G.5s to join the recommended yacht

track S of the Inner Ridge R can Lt buoy Q.R passing Stone Banks R can Lt buoy Fl.R.5s and avoiding unlit Outer Ridge R can buoy. From the E keep S of the deep water channel to pass S of the Inner Ridge R can Lt buoy Q.R. From the N at or near LW, stand out from shore to pass seaward of the Wadgate Ledge G con Lt bn Fl(4)G.15s before crossing the deep water channel W of the Platters S card Lt buoy to join the recommended yacht track.

Entrance From S of the Inner Ridge R can Lt buoy Q.R follow the recommended yacht track by leaving all channel marker buoys close to stb but the small Harwich Shelf E card Lt buoy (seasonal) to port. At the Guard R can Lt buoy leave the buoy to stb and cross the deep water channel to the Shotley Spit S card Lt buoy. Then take either the N route into the River Orwell, or turn due W for either Shotley Marina, or, staying N of the deep water channel, continue into the River Stour keeping well clear of commercial ships and unlit mooring buoys.

Berthing
•**Shotley Marina** Access 24hrs through lock. Call the Lock Keeper before starting approach. From the Shotley Spit buoy take a course to pass close N of the Ganges G con Lt buoy Fl.G.5s and round to enter approach marked by Lt bns, E card VQ(3)5s to port; Fl(4)G.15s to stb. Traffic lights at lock entrance plus Inogon directional lights (arrows show direction to steer). Channel dredged to 2m MLWS. Lock can be turbulent, good fenders essential.

Facilities. Chandler with supplies. Water taxi to Harwich and Felixstowe. Marina restaurant; convenience store and pub in village. ✆ 01473 788982, VHF 80.
• **Halfpenny Pier, Harwich** At the SW end of the quay. Berth either side of the pontoon, the E end of the N side is reserved for a ferry. Maximum stay 72 hours. Free mooring 0900–1600 hours. Avoid in strong winds. Take advice from HM. Depth 2·5m.

Facilities Harwich town. Rly. Tours of Old Harwich by Harwich Society.

Anchorages Well inshore immediately to seaward of the moorings on the Shelf, otherwise upstream of Parkeston Quay in the River Stour.

RIVER ORWELL

Charts BA 1491, 2693, SC 5607

Imray 2000, C28, Y16

HW Ipswich Walton +0020

MHWS	MHWN	MLWN	MLWS
4·2m	3·4	1·0	0·3

Entrance From close Shotley Spit S card Lt buoy enter the River Orwell in 8m leaving close to stb the R can Lt buoys College, Pepys and Babergh. The channel is dredged to 5·8m as far as Ipswich, the navigable limit 9M from Harwich. It is well marked with Lt buoys. The river narrows above Collimer Point with extensive mud banks on both shores. Pleasure craft must keep clear of commercial shipping. Anchoring in the channel is prohibited.

Berthing
• **Suffolk Yacht Harbour** Access 24hr. Entrance marked by sph RW buoy. Channel, 2·5m, marked by port and stb bns. Ldg Lts Y shown at night. Contact HM for berth.
Facilities Extensive yachting facilities including sailmaker, rigger, electronic and marine engineers. ✆ 01473 659465. VHF 80.
• **Pin Mill** All services, swinging moorings only. Landing at concrete hard at all states of tide except low springs. Muddy.
Facilities Shops at Chelmondiston. Famous pub Butt and Oyster.
• **Royal Harwich Yacht Club** Visitors berth on hammerhead and contact berthing master. Cheaper than commercial marina next door. *Mobile* 07742 145994, VHF 77.
Facilities Yacht club welcomes visitors to their bar and restaurant. Pump out. ✆ 01473 780319.
• **Woolverstone Marina** Access 24hrs, restaurant, no petrol. ✆ 780206, VHF 80.

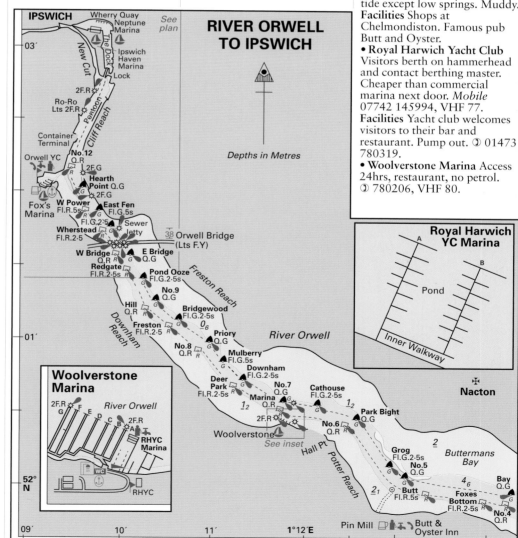

Anchorages All occupied vessels should show a riding light, whether anchored or on a mooring. There is much commercial traffic.

• Above Shotley Point on W side above Orwell QR and R bn, clear of channel. Shore is steep-to, beware tel cable. Landing on isolated beaches at HW. Good shelter in W winds.

• In Long Reach on S side, well clear of main channel.

• In Pin Mill bay below moorings.

IPSWICH

Chart BA 2693, SC 5607; Imray 2000, Y16

HW Walton +0025

MHWS	MHWN	MLWN	MLWS
4·2m	3·4m	1·0m	0·3m

Ipswich is a large town with a historic waterfront which is currently benefiting from a regeneration programme. The town centre has many historic buildings, art galleries and museums which are within walking distance from Ipswich Dock. Rly to London, Cambridge and Norwich. Coach to Stansted.

• **Fox's Marina** At the W side in Ostrich Creek. Access 24hrs. Enter channel S of No.12 buoy, through dredged and buoyed channel with approx 2m MLWS. Visitors' berth by arrangement. ☎ 01473 689111, VHF 80.

• **Ipswich Dock** Inward bound craft, on passing Orwell Br, must contact *Ipswich Lock* VHF 68 for details of lock opening. Waiting pontoon. Access 24hrs. Before departure call the lock for next opening. Floating pontoon on stb side of lock; ropes to port. Pontoon removed when ship expected.

• **Neptune Marina** At the NE end of Ipswich Dock. 150 berths. No chandlery. Berth depths vary 5·8m to 3·5m.

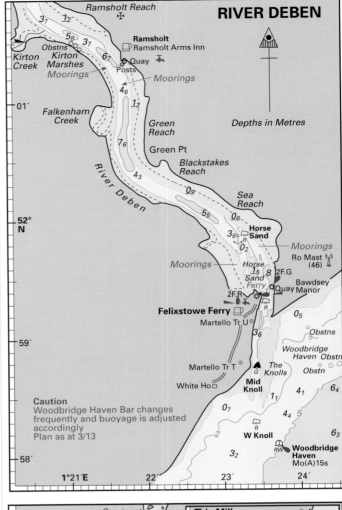

RIVER DEBEN

Depths in Metres

Caution
Woodbridge Haven Bar changes frequently and buoyage is adjusted accordingly
Plan as at 3/13

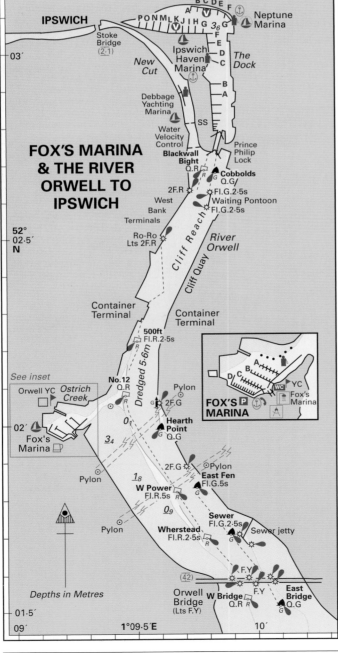

FOX'S MARINA & THE RIVER ORWELL TO IPSWICH

Depths in Metres

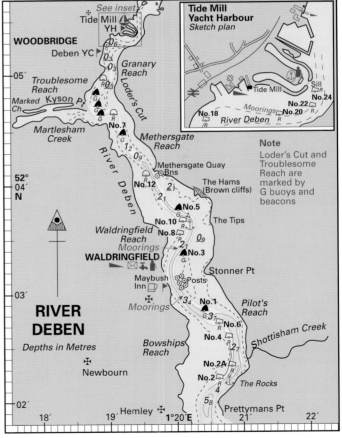

RIVER DEBEN

Depths in Metres

Note
Loder's Cut and Troublesome Reach are marked by G buoys and beacons

Tide Mill Yacht Harbour
Sketch plan

Berths alongside quay available for very large craft.
Facilities Close to town centre shops. ① 01473 215204, VHF 80.
• **Ipswich Haven Marina** On south side of Ipswich Dock. Call on VHF 80 when in the lock. Visitors normally berth on pontoon K, or alongside on L. 270 berths, 30 visitors. Can accommodate vessels up to 6m draft and 20m in length.
Facilities All marina services on site and restaurants close by. ① 01473 236644, VHF 80.

RIVER DEBEN

Charts BA 2052, 2693, SC 5607; Imray 2000, Y16, C28
DS in offing: Dover +0015 NE; −0600SW

HW Walton-on-the-Naze −0002
MHWS	MHWN	MLWN	MLWS
3·7m	2·9m	1·0m	0·5m

Approach The entrance lies between Felixstowe and Bawdsey Cliff between two Martello trs (T and U on the plan) to the W and a radio tr to the N. Make for the Woodbridge Haven safe water buoy from which the W Knoll R can buoy can usually be seen. The bar has least depth 1·0m (2012).

Entrance The banks and lie of the channel alter every winter, sometimes significantly. Advise enter and leave only on the flood. Entry is best in the second half of the flood or up to HW+0100 with caution and sufficient power.

The entrance is rough in onshore winds or swell. Beware strong cross currents in entrance.

Advice from John White, Felixstowe Ferry HM on VHF 08 or *Mobile* 07803 476621. Free download of latest plan from www.eastcoastpilot.com.

From Woodbridge Haven RW buoy steer approx 315° to the R can W Knoll buoy turning upriver at the G con. Beware of being set onto the rocky sea defences.

After leaving the Horse Sand R can buoy close to port follow the channel near mid stream as far as The Rocks. Above this the channel is buoyed.

Berthing
• **Felixstowe Ferry Boatyard** 20-ton slip. A mooring may be available from A. Moore. Limited facilities. ① 01394 282173.
• **Ramsholt** a mooring sometimes may be obtained. Pub, phone, no other facilities. HM George Collins, ① 334318 (evenings). *Mobile* 0775 1034959.
Tide Mill Yacht Harbour Woodbridge On port hand just beyond the Tide Mill. Access for 1·5m draught HW−0230 to +0100 approx at springs. www.tidemillyachtharbour.co.uk

has tide tables giving predicted heights over the sill which dries 1·5m. 2m draught yachts may not be able to pass at neaps. Waiting buoys, dredged entrance channel. If a yacht has enough water to reach Woodbridge, there is usually enough water to enter the yacht hbr. Tide gauge. All facilities, including repairs and laying-up. 12-tonne crane. Diesel. Visitors welcome but advisable to contact in advance. VHF 80, ① 01394 385745.

Anchorages
• Off the west bank above moorings at Felixstowe Ferry.
• Ramsholt, clear of moorings.
• Above Ramsholt at The Rocks.

Facilities Woodbridge all, sailmaker, rly to London. Charity and Taylor (Melton) ① 01394 382600 have a good selection of charts and pilot guides.

ORFORD HAVEN

Charts BA 2052, 2695, SC 5607; Imray 2000, C28
DS in offing: Dover +0030NE; −0530SW

HW at bar: Walton −0028
MHWS	MHWN	MLWN	MLWS
3·2m	2·6m	1·0m	0·4m

There is a shingle bar at the entrance over which the depth at CD is about 0·8m. The bar frequently shifts, especially in the winter. It is essential to

obtain up to date information, free download of latest plan from www.eastcoastpilot.com. Streams run fast, the ebb reaching 5kn at springs. The flood and ebb streams run for about 0115 after local HW and LW respectively. The rivers Ore, Alde, and the Butley River are attractive unspoilt rivers with mainly muddy banks and a few landing places, but many safe anchorages.

Approach The entrance to Orford Haven may be located by a cluster of small white cottages known as Shingle Street and an old CG station about ⅓M to the N. Keep at least ½M offshore to avoid the

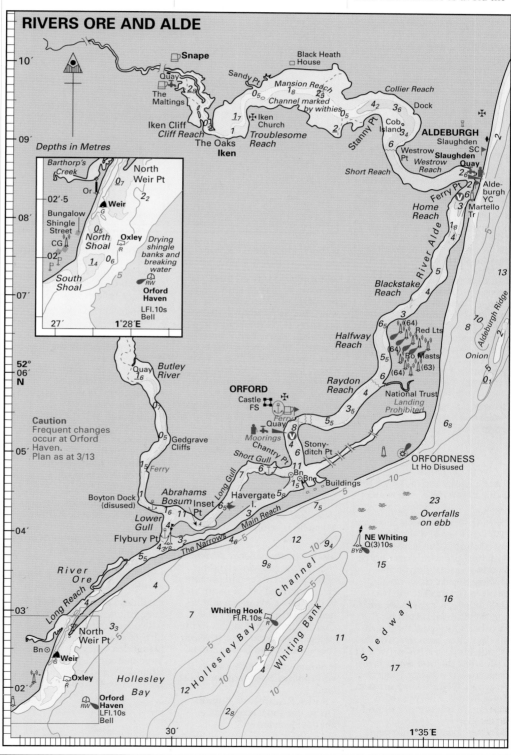

RIVERS ORE AND ALDE

HARWICH TO GREAT YARMOUTH

Charts BA 1536, 1543, 2052, 2693, SC 5607;
Imray 2000, C28, Y16

DS Dover –0600SW +0015NE

Passage lights	*BA No*
Southwold	2272
Fl.10s37m24M AIS	
Lowestoft	2280
Fl.15s37m23M	

Leave Harwich on the recommended yacht track; round Landguard Point S of the buoyed deep water channel; cross W of the Platters S card Lt buoy and proceed NE leaving the Wadgate Ledge G bn close to stb to avoid wreck on the Wadgate Ledge. Then a least offshore distance of ½M will clear outlying dangers as far as Orfordness.

Orfordness is steep-to. An eddy runs close inshore N and S. Tides run hard and with wind over tide a steep, confused sea is raised. Calm water may be found close inshore. Avoid the Aldeburgh Ridge 7ca offshore which nearly dries at LW and cannot be ignored at HW. Stand close inshore or pass E of the Aldeburgh Ridge R can buoy.

Orfordness to Southwold has off-lying sand banks at Sizewell and Dunwich. Conspic Sizewell power stn is the main landmark but beware of its outfall.

Southwold to Lowestoft: keep to the E of Barnard Shoal off Benacre Ness. Southwold LtHo bearing not less than 218° until Kessingland ch bears 297° leads ½M clear of the end of the shoal. If Southwold is not visible, Covehithe channel bearing 240° leads to the same position.

From Lowestoft to Great Yarmouth a safe distance is ½M offshore. The offshore sandbanks are liable to move, it is strongly advised that up-to-date charts are used.

Lobster pots on long floating lines are a hazard in some places on this coast.

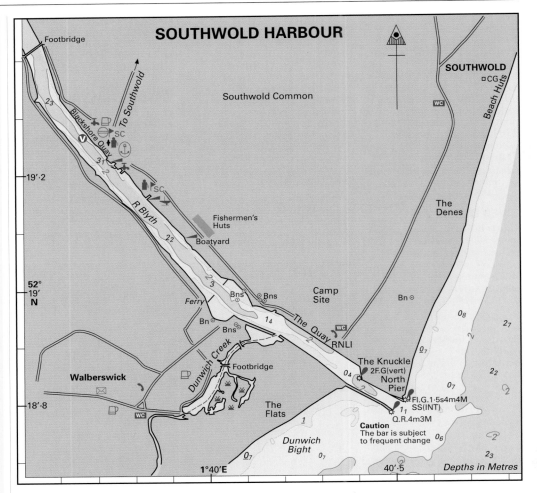

SOUTHWOLD HARBOUR

Depths in Metres

---

shingle banks and make for the Orford Haven RW safe water buoy.

Entrance Entry or exit best local HW –0330 to HW+0130. It is not advisable during the ebb or with onshore winds over Force 5. Wind against tide or an onshore swell can set up a heavy sea at or near the bar. Unlit buoys, R can Oxley and G con Weir are laid April to October. Once past Weir turn up river, then keep towards the W side until past North Weir Pt. Thereafter the best water is on the seaward side until past the Narrows. Water-skiing areas in Long Reach. The W side of Havergate Is has more room for beating up river. Above Westrow Point the channel is marked by withies, R topmarks

to port (unreliable), explore only above half tide and rising.

Moorings At Orford there are six marked visitors' moorings on E side of river below the quay and at Aldeburgh there are three R visitors' moorings on E side of river opposite Martello tr where rafting may be necessary, max 25-tonnes. Other temporary moorings may be possible by application to:
• New Orford Town Trust, Orford Quay. VHF 8, call sign *Chantry* or ☎ 01394 459950 *Mobile* 07528 092635
• RF Upson & co, Slaughden Boatyard ☎ 01728 453047
• D Cable, Slaughden ☎ 01728 452569.

Anchorages Outside, in calm offshore weather, it is possible to anchor S of the Shingle Street Martello tr whilst awaiting the tide.

Inside, one may anchor anywhere clear of the fairway avoiding underwater cables and pipelines clearly marked on the shore and, in particular, avoid anywhere near moorings since ground chains run at right angles to the shore. Holding is poor between the entrance and Havergate Is.

Recommended anchorages
• Abrahams Bosom or the Short Gull
• Butley River below Boyton Dock, use short scope since channel is narrow

• Aldeburgh, below Aldeburgh YC in suitable weather or above moorings
• At Iken Cliff, shallow but there is a hole.

Landings
• Steep shingle bank for approx 3M above N Weir Point, discouraged during the breeding season
• Orford Quay (0·5m LW) 1hr max, slip or Orford SC
• Slaughden Quay (dries), water hose, slip
• Aldeburgh YC
• Iken, The Oaks, small sandy beach near HW
• Snape Maltings Quay (dries to soft sloping mud). Apply Maltings Marine Office ☎ 01728 699303.

Landing prohibited
• Havergate Island, RSPB sanctuary
• National Trust property from Stony Ditch to 1M S of Martello tr at Slaughden.
• In the vicinity of Black Heath House or Iken church.

Facilities Pubs, shops and restaurants at Orford and Aldeburgh. Fuel by can, at Orford garage (½M) or Slaughden Quay (by pipe if large quantity, Upsons). Chandlery and good boatyard facilities at Aldeburgh.

SOUTHWOLD

Charts BA 2695; SC 5614;
Imray 2000, C28

DS Dover +0015N; –0600S

HW Lowestoft +0105

MHWS	MHWN	MLWN	MLWS
2·4m	2·1m	0·9m	0·5m

Southwold is on relatively high land and can be recognised by its conspicuous white lighthouse in the town. The hbr entrance, between two piers 36m apart, is approx ¾M S of the town. Call HM 24h in advance to check berth availability and depth in entrance. Least depth 1m (2012). It can be dangerous to enter with onshore winds greater than Force 5, especially if northeasterly. Go to www.waveney.gov.uk for latest information.

Approach From any direction keep at least 4ca offshore for the last mile. Best approach waypoint is 52°18'·49N 1°40'·80E. Call *Southwold Harbour* on VHF 12. Turn in towards the piers, making good 330°. Take due allowance for the stream.

Entrance Best HW–0330 to HW+0130. 3.F.R.(vert) on N pierhead show that hbr is closed. The channel is narrow. Tides are strong, up to 4kn on flood and 6kn on ebb. Go slowly but fast enough to maintain control. Enter down the centre; pass close to the Knuckle, turn to stb towards the N wall following it within 2–3m, until abeam of the Y bollard, then turn to port towards the black huts on the SW shore until in the centre of the river. The Ferry is a rowing boat and has right of way over all vessels. It is then 3ca to the visitors' berths.

Berthing At busy times it is essential to book in advance. On visitors' staging, as directed, 2m alongside at LWS at W end reducing to 0·5m at E end. Rafting is usual, as many as six deep. Come alongside stemming the tide. Turning can be difficult: if you have suitable stem, put the bow into the mud on the S side and let the current swing you round. Long shore lines (up to 20m) are essential. Moor parallel to the tide, secure tiller amidships. Call *Southwold Harbour* before departure.

Facilities Pub with food. Fresh fish. Electricity. Showers at Sailing Club (when open) or caravan site. Good boatyards. No petrol. Shops, restaurants etc in town 1M.

☎ /VHF HM 01502 724712. *Southwold Harbour* VHF 12.

LOWESTOFT

Charts BA 1535, 1543; SC 5614; Imray 2000, C28
DS Dover –0020N; +0540S
HW Lowestoft HW

MHWS	MHWN	MLWN	MLWS
2·4m	2·1m	1·0m	0·5m

This is a valuable passage port available at all times. There is a small friendly marina to port the seaward side of a lifting br with further marina facilities beyond it.

Approach From the S make E Barnard E card Lt buoy, then follow buoyed Stanford Channel E of Newcome Sand to N Newcome R can Lt buoy Fl(4)R.15s before turning W to hbr. From the E enter the Stanford Channel S of S Holm S Card Lt buoy and then as from S. From the N follow the buoyed Roads to the W of the sandbanks.

With fresh wind against tide a heavy sea gets up off the hbr especially near the N pier. In any event keep well clear of shoal patches near to the sand banks. Vessels should remain inside the buoyed channels since the banks are continuously changing. Buoys may well have been moved since the last correction applied to the chart.

The ebb runs strongly across the entrance. Make the final approach from the SE, keeping closer to the S pier.

Entrance IPTS are shown on the S pierhead. Call *Lowestoft Harbour Control* (VHF 14) for permission to enter. It is also essential to obtain permission to leave the RN & SYC Marina, since vessels leaving cannot see those about to enter.

If waiting for the br opening, yachts must use the waiting pontoon in the Trawl Dock.

A free lifting road br gives access to inner harbour, opening times are: 0300, 0500, 0700, 0945, 1115, 1430, 1600, 1900, 2100, 2400 LT. On Saturday, Sunday and Bank Holidays there is an additional opening at 1800. Call on VHF 14 at least 20 minutes before desired opening. Other openings may occur for commercial traffic, yachts may only use these with prior permission. Whilst waiting, all vessels must listen on VHF 14. Navigation through the br is controlled by R and G lights.

Access to the Broads is via Mutford Lock (a charge is made) about 1½M from the br. Advise 24hrs in advance, the lock gets congested at weekends. When making for the sea ask to enter the lock 2–3hrs before the desired road br opening time.

Berthing
• **RN & SYC Marina,** immediately to port on entering narrow channel to br. Visitors should secure to outside of pontoons, rafting if necessary, but not enter the fingered area. The YC is friendly and makes

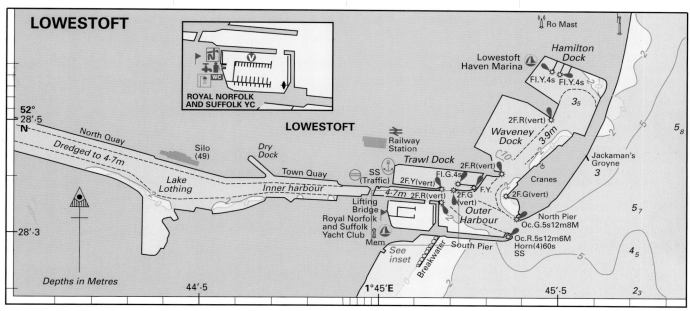

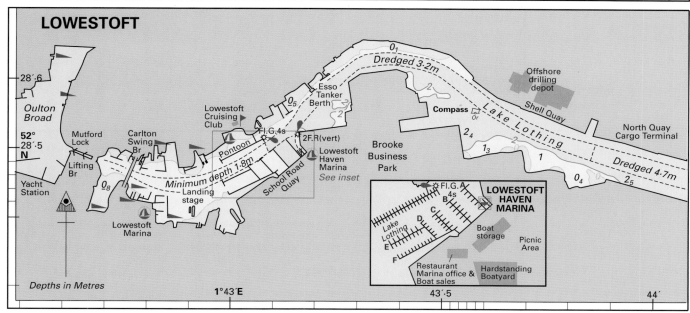

NORTH SEA PASSAGE NOTES

Lowestoft to IJmuiden

Charts BA 1408, 1543, 1631; SC 5614; Imray C25, C28

Leave Lowestoft by the Stanford Channel, preferably avoiding the worst of the N-going tide since the tides are strong along the English coast. Pass to the south of the Brown Ridge which lies just over halfway on this 100M passage. It is marked near its S end by a W card Lt buoy Q(9)15s. The best time to arrive at IJmuiden is soon after dawn so that shore lights can have been identified. The rear Ldg Lt Fl.5s29M is the most powerful light. By day, the tall steelworks chimneys (166m) to the N of the hbr are a useful landmark. It is a busy commercial port. Aim to make the final approach to one side or other of the harbour avoiding the main shipping channel, the Ij-Geul, track 100°, which is well marked by Y Lt buoys for the final 18M to the harbour entrance. Major changes have recently taken place on buoyage. Carry up-to-date charts.

facilities available to visitors. 24hr toilets for visitors, free internet access to weather forecasts, electricity by card from office.
• **Lowestoft Cruising Club** has berths on the N shore at the W end of Lake Lothing. Welcoming and sheltered. Contact moorings officer before arrival if possible. No VHF.
• **Lowestoft Haven Marina** at both School Road Quay and in the Hamilton Dock has 30 visitors' berths with full marina facilities.

Facilities As expected of a major port and town.

☎/VHF Lowestoft Port Control VHF 14, ☎ 01502 572286. Mutford Lock VHF 73, ☎ 01502 531778. RN&SYC VHF 80, ☎ 01502 566726. Lowestoft Cruising Club Moorings Officer ☎ 07913 39150; Club ☎ 01502 574376. Lowestoft Haven Marina VHF 80, ☎ 01502 580300.

NORFOLK BROADS

There are two entrances, Lowestoft to the S into Oulton Broad and Great Yarmouth to the N into Breydon Water and River Yare to Norwich and River Waveney to Lowestoft. Cruising yachts of 1·5m draught and 10m air draught (subject to overhead cables) are able to get to Lowestoft or Norwich. The tidal range is 1·5m at Great Yarmouth to 0·3m at Norwich and 0·6m at Oulton Broad. There is also the R Bure to the N Broads. This has two fixed bridges, headroom about 2m at HW, and unlikely to be of use for

cruising yachts. To enter from the S see Lowestoft. From Great Yarmouth pass the lifting Haven Br at E end of Breydon Water (air draught when closed 4·2m at MLWS, 2·4m at MHWS), preferably at slack water. For Breydon Water also pass the Breydon Br (air draught when closed 4·5m MHWS) which lifts in conjunction with the Haven Br. Yachts must book opening of the bridges, preferably before entry to hbr, by calling the Harbour Office on ☎ 01493 335503. Booking for Saturday, Sunday and Bank Holidays must be made by 1600 or the previous Friday afternoon. The bridges normally open between 0900–1200 and 1300–1600. If waiting for an opening, moor alongside Town Hall Quay. 3F.R(vert) Lts indicates passage is from the other side.

Norfolk Broads temporary licences from The Haven Commissioners, 21 South Quay, Gt Yarmouth ☎ 01603 610734 or from a patrol.

Priority at all times to shipping, yachts must keep clear. There are boatyards and marinas above Haven Br. Keep to marked channel across Breydon Water. Observe speed limits. Discharging forbidden.

Berthing
• **Broads** There are many moorings in the Broads, some free, some offset against food etc. Oulton Broad HM VHF 14, ☎ 01502 574946 may be able to assist.
• **Oulton Broad Yacht Station.** Boatyard JR Wigg. No VHF, ☎ 513087, winter 566479.
• **Broom Boats Ltd**, Brundall on River Yare 100 pontoon berths, access 24hrs. Normal facilities, full repairs, restaurant, no chandlery or launderette. No VHF, ☎ 01603 712334.
• **Burgh Castle Marina** on River Waveney ½M from S end of Breydon water. 93 berths max draught 1·5m, access HW±0300. Full facilities. 32-tonne hoist. One visitor's pontoon. No VHF, ☎ 01493 780331.
• **Riverside moorings** many but use only with local permission. When in doubt tie up but be prepared to move.

GREAT YARMOUTH

Charts BA 1534; SC 5614; Imray C28

DS Dover –0100NW and W; +0600E and SE

HW Lowestoft –0035

MHWS	MHWN	MLWN	MLWS
2·4m	2·1m	1·0m	0·5m

There are two harbours, the new Outer Harbour where yachts are forbidden and the River Harbour. The latter remains busy mainly as an offshore industry support base. No special yacht facilities exist but it does provide a gateway

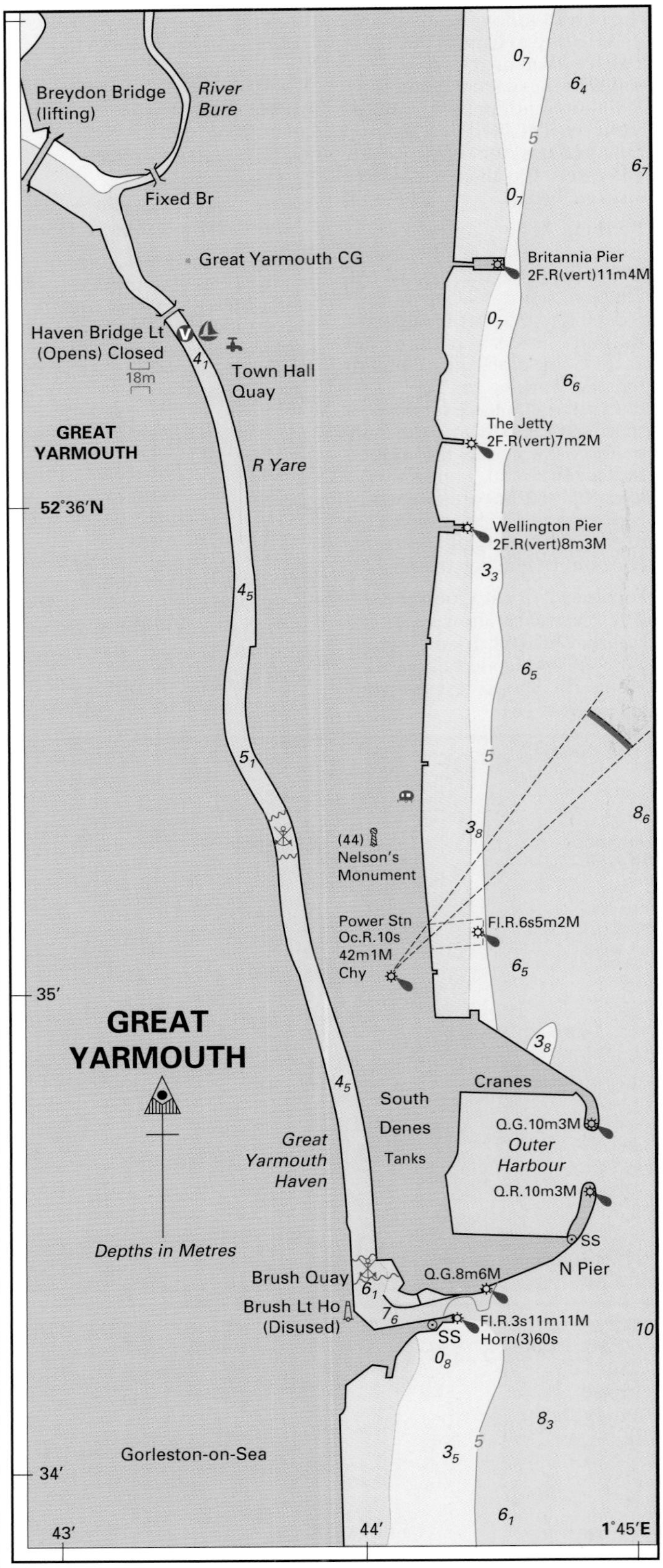

to the Broads, with a mast-up route towards Norwich.

Approach and Entrance From the N avoid passing too close to the Outer Harbour. Call *Yarmouth Radio* before entry or departure and maintain a listening watch. The one-way traffic system at the hbr entrance must be strictly observed. The white rectangular building on the E end of the S pier is illuminated at night.

On its roof there are three vert Lts Oc.12s:
• 3R(vert) entry prohibited
• 3G(vert) enter, if safe
• GWG enter if given permission

At Brush Quay similar lights control vessels leaving the hbr downstream of the lifeboat house.

Q amber tidal signal is displayed from S pier head indicating tide flooding.

Chart labels (Great Yarmouth):
Breydon Bridge (lifting) · River Bure · Fixed Br · Great Yarmouth CG · Haven Bridge Lt (Opens) Closed · 18m · Town Hall Quay · R Yare · GREAT YARMOUTH · 52°36'N · (44) Nelson's Monument · Power Stn Oc.R.10s 42m1M Chy · Fl.R.6s5m2M · 35' · **GREAT YARMOUTH** · Depths in Metres · Great Yarmouth Haven · South Denes Tanks · Cranes · Outer Harbour · Q.G.10m3M · Q.R.10m3M · Brush Quay · Brush Lt Ho (Disused) · Q.G.8m6M · SS · Fl.R.3s11m11M · Horn(3)60s · N Pier · 34' · Gorleston-on-Sea · Britannia Pier 2F.R(vert)11m4M · The Jetty 2F.R(vert)7m2M · Wellington Pier 2F.R(vert)8m3M · 43' · 44' · 1°45'E

There is 4·3m in the entrance. Small craft can enter at most times, but preferably at slack water; the stream runs up to 5kn or more. It makes up the hbr until HW+0130 at the pier head, and out of the hbr until LW+0130. Seas near the entrance are confused. Entrance should not be attempted in strong SE winds, when a dangerous sea occurs especially on the ebb tide. Passage under sail within the port limits is not normally permitted. Anchoring in the hbr prohibited except in emergency. Vessels are strongly advised to keep an anchor cleared ready to drop especially if navigating up-tide of the br.

Berthing Visitors should berth on the east side of the river close to the S side of Haven Br against a ladder. There are vertical wooden piles, large fenders or a fender board desirable.

The streams runs strongly; a spring is essential and it helps to tie the helm to hold the vessel off the piles. Beware of vandalism.

Facilities None on quay, but near town centre.

☎ /VHF *Yarmouth Radio* VHF 12. Port Control ☎ 01493 335511.

BLAKENEY

Charts BA 108; SC 5614; Imray C28, Y9
DS Dover –0100NW & W; +0600E and SE

HW bar: Immingham +0030
MHWS MHWN
5·7m   4·5m

Very exposed to winds from a N direction and conditions in the entrance deteriorate quickly. A poor hbr for cruising yachts: most of it dries and any craft drawing more than 1·0m must expect to take the bottom at LW. Inadvisable in fresh onshore winds and in lighter ones during the ebb or if a swell is running. Without local knowledge this hbr should only be approached under ideal and settled conditions in a shallow draught vessel at the entrance and with full understanding of the risk of stranding in an exposed position. The only guide to the entrance is the appearance of the sea. The bottom is steep-to. Beware tidal set across the entrance during the last quarter flood.

If notified in advance, Blakeney Harbour Boatmen's Association ☎ 01263 740747 may be able to arrange pilotage.

Approach From the E conspic marks are Blakeney church with large and small towers, Langham church tr, and turret above trees on skyline 3M inland. Follow 5m contour until abeam of the Watch House with a conspic chimney standing on the neck of

Blakeney Point (grass topped sand dunes). Then steer due W to the RW Fairway pillar buoy and buoy marked entrance channel. This has G con buoys and, possibly, ldg marks. From the W stand off 1M from the Bink, the low sandy point with a clump of fir trees ½M E of Wells and steer due E to entrance channel.

Entrance Leave G buoys to stb on entering. Leave R can (Q.R) well to port for as entrance changes, it may not give clearance to Wreck *Hjordis*.

Note Buoys are provided by boatmen and are usually drums. Only Nos.2 and 7 reliable, 7 has radar reflector. Channel shallow, and frequently varying in position and depth. Shallow flats run off a long way NW and W of Blakeney Spit, which should be left to port. The whole of Stiffkey Freshes is obstructed by mussel lays standing up to 0·8m above the sand and drying at half tide. They are protected by Fishing Orders and vessels must be certain of sufficient water to pass clear over. Avoid. Channel turns sharp E at No.7 G buoy. Soundings are the best guides here. Inside the hbr keep close to G buoys.

Berthing A mooring may be available in the Pit max 1m, 2M to Blakeney village, 1M to Morston. Morston Ferry operates as tender HW±0230. The flats inside the hbr cover

NORFOLK COAST

Charts BA 108, 106; SC 5614; Imray C28, C29, Y9

Inshore tidal streams run true in the channels parallel to the coast. In the outer channels the streams run true when they are strongest, but there is a set across the shoals towards the beginning and end of each stream. The SE stream changes through SW to NW, and the NW stream changes through NE to SE. On this coast generally the NW stream is strongest at LW by the shore, and the SE stream strongest at HW. The sea breeze often comes from the SE rather than the NE. This helps going N but causes difficulty going S. Offshore, there is a wind farm on the Scroby Sands marked at its extremities by Lt Fl.Y.5s13m Horn Mo(U)30s and an abundance of oil and gas rigs. Beware of frequent changes of depth between Gt Yarmouth and Winterton Ness. Follow buoyed channel.

Caution

Only Wells-next-the-Sea harbour on the N Norfolk coast is accessible during fresh winds appreciably N of E or W and then only near HW. Most become dangerous before this.

approx. 1·5m to 1m at neaps. Shallow-draught craft able to sit upright can anchor and dry out, but it is a long way to the village and muddy. Avoid narrow and crowded gut at quay, land from dinghy at hard near quay or in Morston Creek at HW.

Also all harbours along this coast dry at low water. In poor conditions the outer entrances are a mass of broken water making marks and buoys very difficult to see, some being small or substandard. Grounding can easily result in the loss of the vessel. Conditions in entrances rapidly worsen when the ebb begins or if there is any swell running from offshore. Under these conditions entrances may be unsafe even in a light breeze. The most dangerous conditions are at spring and surge tides. The nearest alternative safe hbrs are 30M or more away and need accurate navigation among the sands to reach them. Passage should not be started, even in fine weather, without recognising this.

It is difficult to assess conditions in the entrances from outside. In poor conditions avoid Blakeney. The choice is between Wells or staying outside. Wells is lit far enough in to reach a safe anchorage if the bar can be crossed and its marks are fairly easy to see. If in doubt it is prudent not to attempt. Wells-next-the-Sea HM will assist. See Wells details.

Facilities Water, stores, petrol, diesel, chandlery, gas, launching hard, hotel at Blakeney. Water, stores and pub at Morston.

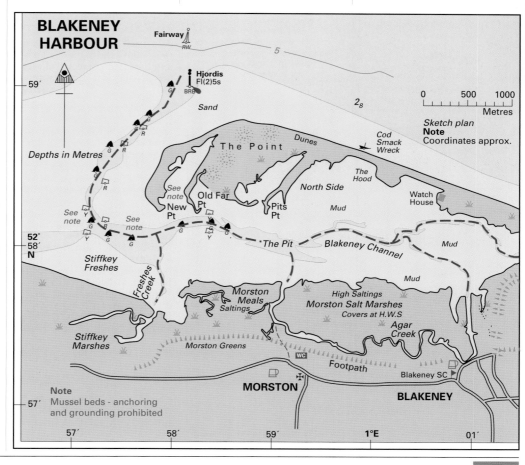

WELLS-NEXT-THE-SEA

Charts BA 108; SC 5614; Imray C28, Y9
DS Dover –0030NW and W; +0600E and SE

HW bar: Immingham +0020

MHWS	MHWN
6·0m	4·8m

Wells is the only lit hbr in N Norfolk and is increasingly busy with wind farm vessels which use the dredged outer hbr, due S of the LB Ho; this hbr is not available for yachts. Otherwise the hbr dries but the quay is accessible to 3m draught craft at MHWS, 1·75m at MHWN. There are drying pontoon berths and visitors' moorings available. With onshore winds over F4 it should not be attempted by strangers. The channel is dredged as far as the Pool, however shifting sands cause frequent changes in buoy positions. Nevertheless, under suitable conditions, this is a delightful hbr. Before entry seek advice from the HM; if necessary the hbr launch will guide you in. A useful website is www.wellsharbour.co.uk.

Approach Make for the R Wells Harbour buoy, Fl(2)R.5s, known locally as the 'Leading Buoy'.

From the E pass Blakeney leaving The Bink, a low sandy point with a clump of fir trees, 1M to port, carefully watching the depth to keep clear of shallows extending up to 2M offshore.

From the W make for the Bridgirdle R can buoy approx 346° 4·5M from the Wells Harbour buoy. Initially the Holkham obelisk and the church tr are visible, but fir trees obscure the town.

Entrance The best time to enter is HW –0200 to +0130. At the Wells Harbour buoy call *Wells Harbour* on VHF 12 for entry and berthing instructions. Thereafter maintain a listening watch on VHF 12/16. The channel is between large No.1 G con Lt buoy Fl.G.3s and No.2 R can Fl.R.3s. Beware of strong tidal set to E for 2h before HW. Recently a bar has extended NW from No.2 buoy and is marked by two additional R can buoys Fl.R.3s. Then follow the smaller Lt buoys.

The hbr mouth has a conspic W LB Ho with R roof on its W point close W of the Lookout. Extending S is a long line of beach huts. Follow the mid-channel course until opposite the LB Ho. There the channel turns from SE to SW as R bns to port indicate. Keep close to R bns and head towards bn by the E shore. Take a long turn to port to pass close to R bns to the quay.

Berthing If an alongside berth is required contact the HM preferably before entering hbr to be certain that a place exists. Mooring maybe permissible along W end of the quay wall of the hbr but do not obstruct fishing boats.

Facilities Electricity, water, diesel from bowser. Repairs, slip, crane, chandlery (closed Thursday). Good restaurants a bit out of town centre.

☎ /VHF *Wells Harbour* VHF 12 Office 01328 711646; HM 07775 507284, or 07881 824912.

THE WASH

Charts BA 108, 1200; SC 5614; Imray Y9
In main channels DS Dover +0130 in, –0445 out

In main channels the tide range is about 7m springs and 2·7m neaps, so that it is possible to find 2m more than charted at MLWN.

Approach The Wash is not easy once out of the main channels and the latest corrected charts are advised. It is best to wait until half flood before entering any of the rivers. Buoys may be moved to conform with frequent depth changes.

From the E
• Docking Channel, well buoyed ship route, to N Docking N card Lt buoy, then SW to the Roaring Middle LtF LFl.10s.
• From Bridgirdle R can buoy off Brancaster to Woolpack R can Lt buoy Fl.R.10s, N of Middle bank. Narrow passage and seas break on both sides in NE winds. Then SW to the Roaring Middle LtF LFl.10s
• From Bridgirdle R can buoy off Brancaster through the Bays, between Middle Bank and Sunk Sand. There is approx 5m at LW between the banks but less than 2m in the approach from the E. The channel is not buoyed and is difficult to follow
• For Kings Lynn leave Sunk W card Lt buoy to port and proceed into Bull Dog Channel

• For Wisbech leave RAF buoys 1 and 2 well to stb and enter the Wisbech Channel. There are visitors' waiting buoys S of RAF No.4
• For Boston or R Welland approach through Freeman Channel and Boston Deep thence Cuts marked by bns.

KINGS LYNN

Charts BA 1200; SC 5614; Imray Y9
HW Immingham +0030

MHWS	MHWN	MLWN	MLWS
6·8m	5·0m	1·8m	1·0m

A commercial port with no facilities for yachts. Useful as a port of refuge, and for vessels heading to Denver Sluice and the inland waterways.

Approach Well buoyed channel is constantly changing. 1·5m draught vessels can get up about 2hrs after LW. www.portauthoritykingslynn. fsnet.co.uk/page69 has details of latest surveys. In the Lynn Cut and the river 9–10hrs ebb and 2–3hrs flood are usual. Ebb in the river may run up to 5kn. Monitor VHF 14.

Berthing Consult HM, preferably 24hrs in advance. ☎ 01553 773411; VHF 14.

WISBECH

Charts BA 1200; SC 5614; Imray Y9
HW Wisbech cut: Immingham +0025

MHWS	MHWN
7·1m	5·2m

Secure marina with pontoon berths close to historic town centre. Access to inland waterways and Peterborough. Vessels of 2·7m draught can reach Wisbech at neaps. Monitor VHF 09 at all times and be aware of commercial ship movements. It is preferable to call Wisbech Yacht Harbour 24hr in advance.

Approach Make for the *Nene Roads* RW Fairway buoy, Mo(A)10s, at 52°54'·2N 0°15'·8E, from there it is 223° 1·1M to the *No.1* G con buoy Fl.G.5s. Once past, report to *Swing Bridge* (VHF 09) and follow the well buoyed Wisbech Channel. There are yacht moorings just SSW of *No.4* E Card buoy. Note that *Kerr* N card buoy is left to stb. The buoys may often be moved to follow the changing channel.

Entrance Once past Big Tom bn Fl(2)R.10s report to *Swing Bridge* with ETA and air draught. The channel is marked by lit bns, G on W bank and R on E bank. A waiting and overnight pontoon is ¼M N of br. Spring tides run at up to 4kn.

Berthing When 1M away from Wisbech Yacht Harbour which is 8M beyond the br, call on

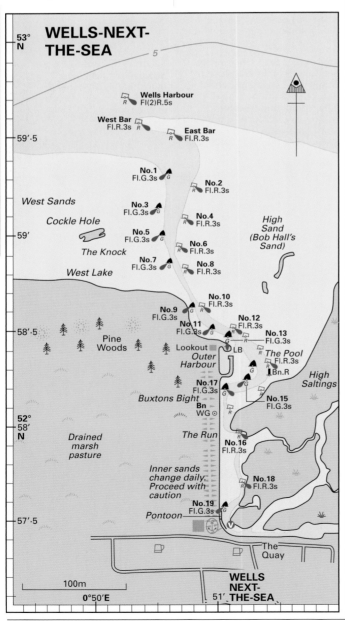

WELLS-NEXT-THE-SEA

53° N

Wells Harbour
Fl(2)R.5s

West Bar
Fl.R.3s

East Bar
Fl.R.3s

59'·5

No.1
Fl.G.3s G

No.2
Fl.R.3s

West Sands

No.3
Fl.G.3s G

No.4
Fl.R.3s

Cockle Hole

59'

No.5
Fl.G.3s G

No.6
Fl.R.3s

High Sand (Bob Hall's Sand)

The Knock

No.7
Fl.G.3s G

No.8
Fl.R.3s

West Lake

No.10
Fl.R.3s

No.9
Fl.G.3s

No.12
Fl.R.3s

58'·5

No.11
Fl.G.3s

No.13
Fl.G.3s

Pine Woods

Lookout

LB

The Pool
Fl.R.3s

Outer Harbour

Bn.R

High Saltings

No.17
Fl.G.3s G

Buxtons Bight

No.15
Fl.G.3s

Bn
WG

52° 58' N

The Run

Drained marsh pasture

No.16
Fl.R.3s

Inner sands change daily. Proceed with caution

No.18
Fl.R.3s

No.19
Fl.G.3s

Pontoon

57'·5

100m

0°50'E

The Quay

WELLS NEXT-THE-SEA

51'

APPROACHES TO KING'S LYNN AND WISBECH

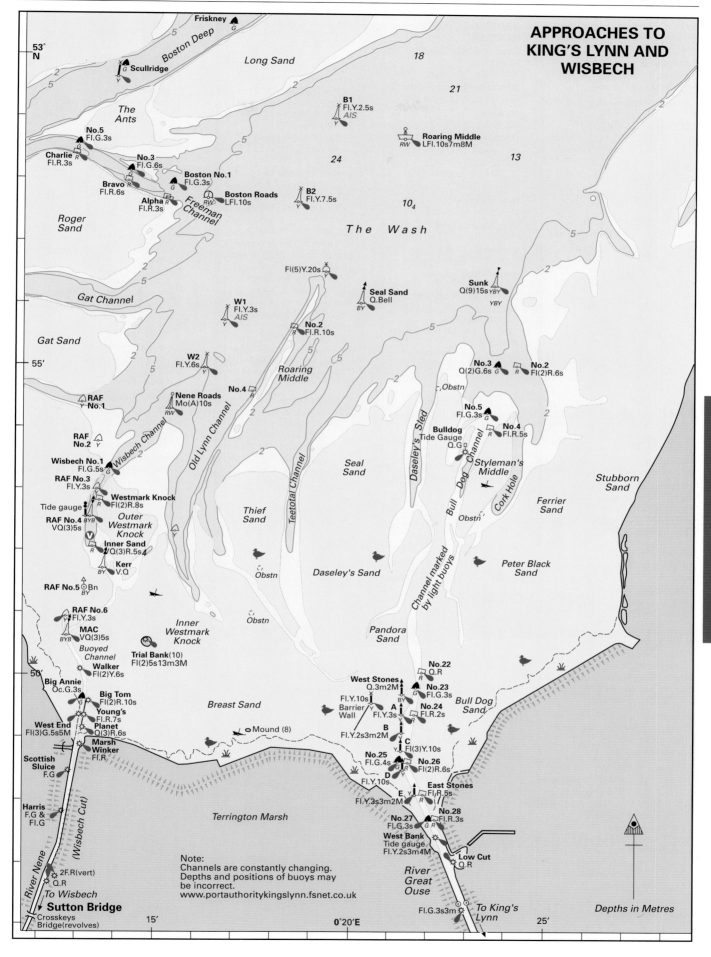

53°
N

Friskney
G

Boston Deep

Long Sand

18

21

Scullridge
G
Y

The Ants

B1
Fl.Y.2.5s
AIS
Y

Roaring Middle
LFl.10s7m8M
RW

24

13

No.5
Fl.G.3s
G

Charlie
Fl.R.3s
R

No.3
Fl.G.6s
G

Boston No.1
Fl.G.3s
G

Bravo
Fl.R.6s
R

Alpha
Fl.R.3s
R

Freeman Channel

Boston Roads
LFl.10s
RW

B2
Fl.Y.7.5s
Y

10₄

Roger Sand

The Wash

5

Gat Channel

Fl(5)Y.20s
X

Seal Sand
Q.Bell
BY

Sunk
Q(9)15s
YBY
YBY

Gat Sand

55'

W1
Fl.Y.3s
AIS
Y

No.2
Fl.R.10s
R

RAF No.1
Y

W2
Fl.Y.6s
Y

Roaring Middle

No.3
Q(2)G.6s
G

No.2
Fl(2)R.6s
R

Nene Roads
Mo(A)10s
RW

No.4
R

Obstn

No.5
Fl.G.3s
G

No.4
Fl.R.5s
R

RAF No.2
Y

Daseley's Sled

Bulldog
Tide Gauge
Q.G

Styleman's Middle

Stubborn Sand

Wisbech No.1
Fl.G.5s
G

RAF No.3
Fl.Y.3s
Y

Wisbech Channel

Old Lynn Channel

Teetotal Channel

Seal Sand

Bull Dog Channel

Cork Hole

Ferrier Sand

Westmark Knock
Fl(2)R.8s
R

Tide gauge

RAF No.4
VQ(3)5s
BYB

Outer Westmark Knock

Inner Sand
Q(3)R.5s
R

Thief Sand

Obstn

Daseley's Sand

Peter Black Sand

Kerr
V.Q
BY

RAF No.5
Bn
BY

Obstn

RAF No.6
Fl.Y.3s
Y

MAC
VQ(3)5s
BYB

Buoyed Channel

Inner Westmark Knock

Trial Bank(10)
Fl(2)5s13m3M

Pandora Sand

Channel marked by light buoys

Walker
Fl(2)Y.6s

50'

Big Annie
Oc.G.3s
G

Big Tom
Fl(2)R.10s
R

Young's
Fl.R.7s
R

Planet
Q(3)R.6s

West End
Fl(3)G.5s5M
G

Marsh Winker
Fl.R

Breast Sand

No.22
Q.R
R

West Stones
Q.3m2M

No.23
Fl.G.3s
G

BY

Bull Dog Sand

A
Fl.Y.3s
Y

Fl.Y.10s
Y

Barrier Wall

No.24
Fl.R.2s
R

Scottish Sluice
F.G

B
Fl.Y.2s3m2M

C
Fl(3)Y.10s

Mound (8)

No.25
Fl.G.4s
G

No.26
Fl(2)R.6s
R

D
Fl.Y.10s

Harris
F.G &
Fl.G

Terrington Marsh

East Stones
Fl.R.5s
Y

E
Fl.Y.3s3m2M

No.28
Fl.R.3s
R

No.27
Fl.G.3s
G

West Bank
Tide gauge
Fl.Y.2s3m4M

River Nene

(Wisbech Cut)

2F.R(vert)
Q.R

River Great Ouse

Low Cut
Q.R

To Wisbech

Sutton Bridge

Crosskeys Bridge(revolves)

Note:
Channels are constantly changing.
Depths and positions of buoys may
be incorrect.
www.portauthoritykingslynn.fsnet.co.uk

Fl.G.3s3m

To King's Lynn

Depths in Metres

15'

0°20'E

25'

VHF 09 for instructions. HW is best time to arrive, i.e. Immingham +0155.

Facilities as expected of a modern marina, incl. laundry. 75-tonne travel hoist.

☎/VHF Swing Bridge ☎ 01406 350364 VHF 09: Wisbech Yacht Harbour ☎ 01945 588059 VHF 09, out of hours call Duty Officer on ☎ 07860 576685 (24hrs).

FOSDYKE

Charts BA 1200; SC 5614; Imray Y9

HW Immingham +0005

Approach From the north via Boston Deep; from the east via Roaring Middle and the Freeman channel: thence to Clay Hole, anchor and await tide if necessary.

Entrance By the Welland Cut which runs SW from the Welland Cut bn QR. It is marked by lighted bns on top of stone banks on either hand, at approx 64m intervals. Tides may reach 4kn at springs. Best to enter HW–0100 so as to arrive at Fosdyke at HW.

Berthing At Fosdyke Yacht Haven which is just to seaward of the Fosdyke Br (clearance 4·5m). Max draught 1·8m, preferable to phone 24h in advance to secure a berth.

Facilities As usual for a small yacht hbr, including travel hoists and repairs. Nearby pub with food, but little else. ☎ HM 01205 260240.

BOSTON

Charts BA 1200; SC 5614; Imray Y9

HW Immingham +0005

MHWS	MHWN	MLWN	MLWS
6·8m	4·8m	1·7m	0·4m

An active small commercial port. Yachts, which can lower their masts, can enter the inland waterways through the Grand Sluice. Contact the Sluice Keeper the day before (☎ 01205 364864).

Approach is best through the Freeman Channel, subject to silting however it is well buoyed.

Entrance at half flood is best. Temporary anchorage to await the tide 5ca SW of No.9 buoy. After No.9 buoy call *Boston Port Control* on VHF 12. Lower masts near the dock. The dock is only available in an emergency. Entry at the Grand Sluice is twice each tide, approx HW±0230, this varies due to variability of levels.

Berthing in Boston Marina, above the Sluice.

☎/VHF Port/Dock 362328, *Boston Port Control* VHF 12; Grand Sluice 364864, VHF 74; Marina 364420, VHF 06.

CROMER TO RIVER HUMBER

Charts BA 107, 108, 109; SC 5614; Imray C29

Standard Port Immingham

Along Lincolnshire coast

DS Dover
+0200 S and SW, –0500 NE and N

Off N Norfolk

DS Dover
+0300 W turning S,
–0300 E turning N

Passage lights	BA No
Newarp Lt buoy	2332
LFl.10s7M Racon O (– – –)	
Happisburgh LtHo	2336
Fl(3)30s41m14M	
Cromer Lt Ho AIS	2342
Fl.5s84m21M, Racon O (– – –)	
Inner Dowsing Lt buoy	
	2351
Q(3)10s7M Racon T(–)	
Dowsing B1D	2420
Fl(2)10s28m22M	
Mo(U) (··–)R 15s Horn(2)60s	
Racon T(–)	
Spurn LtF	2422
Q(3)10s10m8M Racon M (– –)	

RIVER HUMBER

Charts BA 109, 1188, 3497; SC 5614; Imray C29

Approaches The Humber is a busy commercial river. While in the Humber monitor VTS Humber VHF 12 or 14 if below Clee Ness or in the approaches for shipping movements and weather reports. From S see

passage notes. From the N steer for the Spurn LtF and follow recommended yacht track. From seaward leave Spurn LtF between LW and half flood to carry favourable stream to Hull.

Spring tides run at 4·5kn at Immingham, 5kn at Hull. Wind against tide can be very unpleasant and best avoided. In the Humber fairway pass between the Bull N card Lt

With the exception of the sandy cliffs from Happisburgh to Cromer much of the coastline is low. It is particularly difficult to identify the shore between the Wash and the Humber.

Off-lying banks may produce heavily breaking seas in bad weather and should be avoided. To do this:

• Pass E of the Blakeney Overfalls R can Lt buoy Fl(2)R.5s Bell;

• Pass between the E Docking R can Lt buoy Fl.R.2·5s and S Race S card Lt buoy, Bell;

• Pass between the N Docking N card Lt buoy and N Race G con Lt buoy Fl.G.5s Bell;

• Leave the Inner Dowsing E card Lt buoy Q(3)10s approx 1M to port;

• Leave the Protector Lt buoy Fl.R.2·5s 1M to port;

• Make for the Rosse Spit Lt buoy Fl(2)R.5s marking the approach to the R Humber;

• Make for and leave to stb No.2 Haile Sand Lt buoy Fl(3)R.10s to avoid the Haile Sand to port particularly if early on the flood;

• Alter course to W to enter Humber buoyed channel using recommended yacht tracks.

• The Tetney Monobuoy is used by large tankers discharging oil via an underwater pipeline to the shore. They are often held on station by one or more tugs on the end of a long hawser. A wide berth is requested.

There are many gas and oil installations mainly well offshore which must be passed at not less than 500m. At night, these are lit Fl.15s Mo(U) (··–); in fog Horn 30s.

Closer inshore beware of wind farms, some still being developed, round which there are 500m exclusion zones. There is a large windfarm, some 5M north of the Sheringham Shoal: it is marked by lit card buoys at its extremities.

It is highly recommended that up-to-date corrected charts are used.

float VQ.8m6M Horn(2)20s and Spurn Head Fl.G.3s11m on the stb side of the channel. Then follow the well lit and buoyed channels, Bull to Grimsby and Hawke to Hull taking care NW of Immingham to avoid Foulholme Spit and Skitter Sand. Shoaling occurs frequently, buoys are moved as necessary.

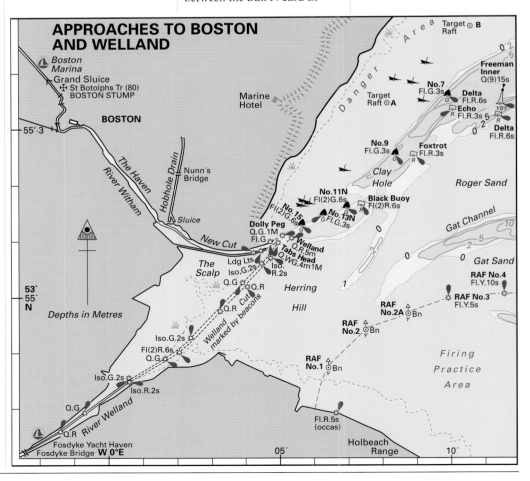

Anchorages

• **Spurn Head** at river entrance in N channel a good anchorage inside Spurn Pt sheltered in N and E winds, uncomfortable in strong NW winds particularly on spring ebb. Anchor in 2–3·5m opposite the LtHo off brickyard chimney N of pilot boat station. Clay bottom gives good holding but strong ebb.

• **Killingholme**, in S or W winds, S off Hawkins Point, opposite Grimsby, sheltered in N winds.

• **Off Cleethorpes** about 1M offshore in fine weather: untenable in strong winds.

• **Humber Mouth Yacht Club** Drying moorings are reached by a channel which runs roughly N–S. The channel is marked by B stb barrel buoys. It is essential to identify them before attempting to reach the moorings. The best approach is on line from the Haile Sand Fort to the Cleethorpes sewer outfall. Following this course will result in crossing the line of marker buoys between Nos.2 and 3. The anchorage is safe for boats which can take the ground though it is uncomfortable at HW springs when the Haile Sand Bank covers.

GRIMSBY

Charts BA 109, 1188; SC 5614; Imray C29

HW Immingham –0012

MHWS	MHWN	MLWN	MLWS
7·1m	5·7m	2·6m	1·1m

Entrance by conspic square brick tr (94m). The western part, Alexandra Dock, is commercial with no facilities for visiting cruising yachts who should enter the Fish Dock by the easterly lock. Call *Fish Dock Island* on VHF 74 for permission to enter or leave. The lock is on free flow HW±0200, beware of strong currents. Access may be possible HW±0400 with a charge of £10. Keep a sharp lookout for shipping entering or leaving Alexandra Dock, immediately to the west. When entry not possible wait in tidal basin, can be difficult, or anchor outside. Uncomfortable in fresh E winds.

Berthing Berth holder marina run by the Humber Cruising Association at Meridian Quay in SW corner of Fish Dock. Visitors' pontoon to port beyond the travel-hoist.

Facilities Diesel, showers, a welcoming club, supplies ¾M in town.

℡ 01472 268424. No VHF.

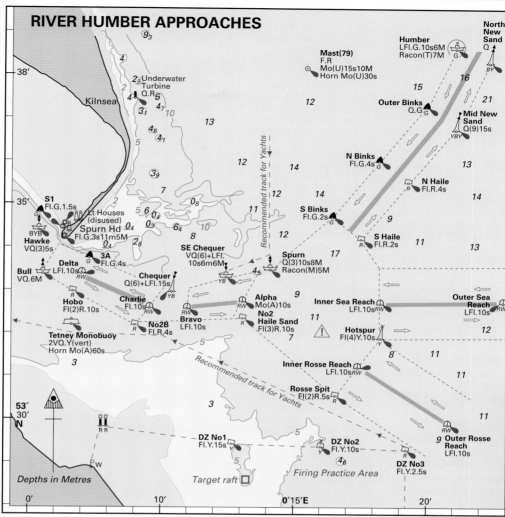

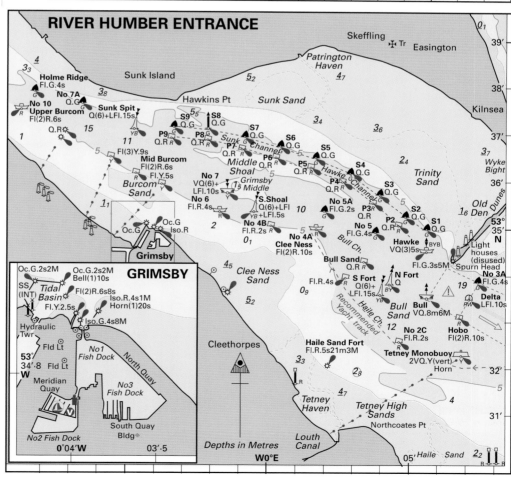

HULL

Charts BA 3497, 109; SC 5614;
Imray C29
HW Immingham +0015

MHWS	MHWN	MLWN	MLWS
7·6m	5·9m	2·5m	0·7m

A major town with excellent
access to city and rly from
marina.
• **Hull Marina** 305 berths,
access HW±0300. Full facilities,
petrol, diesel, sailmaker, 50-ton
travel-hoist and storage ashore.
2m minimum depth over cill. If
waiting better to moor to stb on
inside of outer basin wall, dries
to soft mud. Shore access by
steps and vert ladder.
Alternatively anchor outside
avoiding prohibited areas. Lock
operational 24hrs HW±0300.
Lts, 2G over W to enter. Allow
for strong set past outer
entrance. Call 15 minutes
before arrival VHF 80 or
℡ 01482 609960 (reception),
330508 (lock) or *Mobile* 07789
178501 (lock).

UPPER REACHES

Charts BA 109; SC 5614;
Imray C29
HW Humber Bridge:
Immingham +0025
Goole +0120

For the most up-to-date
information on navigation
above Hull, contact Associated

British Ports ℡01482 327171
who have responsibility for
Humber estuary, as the channel
and its buoyage (light floats)
are constantly changing. Above
the Humber br, VTS works
VHF 15. There can be severe
standing waves above Humber
Br in wind over tide conditions.
• **South Ferriby Marina** S bank,
3M upstream of Humber Br.
120 berths, access HW±0300.
Normal facilities, sailmaker,
shore storage, repairs. Visitors
advised to phone in advance.
VHF 80, ℡01652 635620.
Lock keeper (48hrs notice
required in winter) VHF 74,
℡ 635219.
• **Winteringham Haven** (S
bank) Humber Yawl Club.
Buoyed entrance with R port
spars to channel, useable for
1·5m draught ±0130 HW neaps
to ±0230 MHWS. Drying mud
creek with pontoons. Toilets.
Beware of submerged saltings
downstream of entrance at
HWS. ℡ 01724 733458.
• **Rivers Trent and Ouse** These
rivers provide access to the
extensive inland waterways
network. York Marina is
accessible to yachts 1·2m
draught and 13m air draught.
Useful information can be
obtained from
www.canalrivertrust.org.uk
www.waterscape.com

BRIDLINGTON

Charts BA 1882; SC 5614;
Imray C29
DS in offing Dover +0200SE,
–0400NW
HW River Tyne +0108

MHWS	MHWN	MLWN	MLWS
6·1 m	4·7m	2·3m	1·1m

Access HW±0300 for 2·7m
draught. Sand bar across hbr
entrance, minimum 0·6m
approx. Hbr dries.

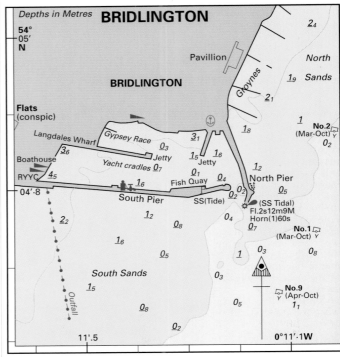

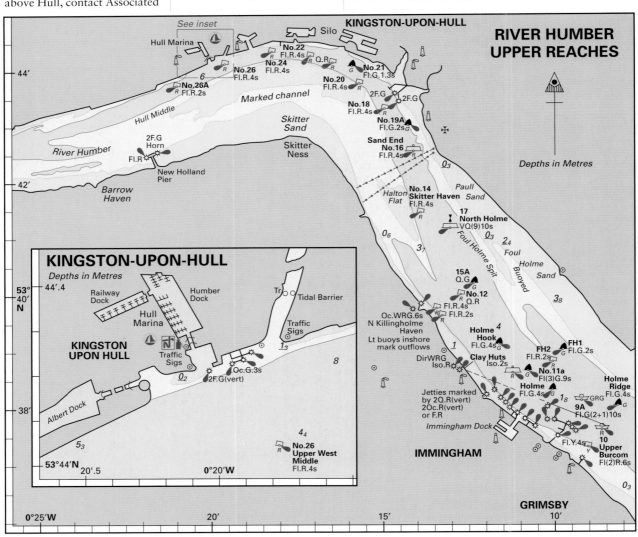

Approach from S so that hbr entrance is open. N pier head Fl.2s12m9M Horn 60s. Depth of water in hbr – signals are by day >2·7m R flag, by night Fl.R. >2·7m, Fl.G. <2·7m. Day signal station 50m W from head of S pier. Light signals at head of N pier.

Berthing Visitors normally berth on S pier W of crane. Enquire of HM VHF 12. ☎ 01262 670148, *Mobile* 07860 275150 before entry.

Anchorage With the wind from NNW to SSW, anchor approx ¼M off the pier end. Winds from NNW round to NE, bring up under Danes' Dyke or near the S landing.

Facilities All supplies, repairs, crane, shipwright. Diesel fuel from tank/hose. Petrol from town in cans. Water from S pier.

The Royal Yorkshire YC ☎ 672041 is situated near the approach to the S pier.

SCARBOROUGH

Charts BA 1612; SC 5614; Imray C24

DS in offing: Dover +0200SE –0400NW

HW River Tyne +0053

MHWS	MHWN	MLWN	MLWS
5·7m	4·6m	2·3m	0·9m

Just to the north of the hbr there is a conspic rocky promontory, Scarborough Rock, on which there are castle ruins.

Scarborough is a vibrant holiday town. Shops near the hbr are mainly fast food outlets and amusements. When approaching or leaving the hbr beware of trip boats and speedboats. No vessel should attempt to enter in strong

onshore winds (NE through E to SSE). When by night a Lt Iso.5s is shown from LtHo, there is at least 3·7m available in the inner harbour. R flag indicates entry forbidden. Call *Scarborough Harbour Watchkeeper* VHF 12 or ☎ 01723 373877 (24hrs) before making an approach.

Approach From the S, make for 54°16'·6N 0°22'·0E then make good a course of 290° for the entrance. From quarter flood to HW an eddy sets NE from 1–2kn. Beware isolated rocks in an area SSW of E pierhead. From the N, keep three ca off Scarborough Rock.

Entrance Entry into the inner harbour possible HW±0400 springs, longer at neaps. Port Control will advise.

Berthing Unless directed otherwise, on SE side of long pontoon in Inner Harbour. Near LW keep close to pontoon, dredged to 1·8m. In season, usually met by berthing master who supplies a key to the marina gate. Berthing master's office is under the lighthouse. The outer harbour, access HW±0300 dries to hard sand, fender plank necessary.

Anchorage 1–3ca from outer pier, keeping E of a line Scarborough Castle-Vincent Pier Lt Ho. Sand over blue clay, good holding. Open to E.

Facilities Water and electricity on pontoon. Showers, toilets, and laundry at Scarborough YC, berthing master will advise. Shops, 10 minute walk up the hill. There is a well stocked chandler, facing the hbr, 50m from the marina gate, who also supplies diesel by can.

SPURN HEAD TO BERWICK

Charts BA 1190, 109, 121, 129, 134, 152, 156, 160, 111; SC 5614; Imray C29, C24

Passage lights	BA No
Flamborough Head	2582

Fl(4)15s65m24M Horn(2)90s

Whitby High	2596

Fl.WR.5s73m18/16M

South Gare – Tees	2626

Fl.WR.12s16m20/17M Horn(2)30s

The Heugh – Hartlepool	2663

Fl(2)10s19m19M

Roker Pier, Sunderland	2681

Fl.5s25m23M Siren 20s

Tynemouth, N pier Hd	2700

Fl(3)10s26m26M Horn 10s

Blyth, E Pier Head	2754

Fl(4)10s19m21M+ F.R.13m13M Horn(3)30s

Coquet	2780

Fl(3)WR.20s25m19/15M Horn 30s

Bamburgh Black Rocks	2810

Oc(2)WRG.8s12m14-11M

Longstone – Farne Is	2814

Fl.20s23m24M

Tidal streams
Spurn Point to Bridlington
DS Dover +0130S, –0445N
Flamborough Head
DS Dover +0015S, –0600N
Tees Bay to Farnes
DS Dover HW –S, –0555N
Farnes, Inner Sound
DS Dover –0010 SE, +0600 NW

North of the Humber the *Royal Northumberland YC Sailing Directions* is excellent. Copies and corrections (s.a.e) from RNYC Tyne, S Harbour, Blyth NE24 3PB ☎ 01670 353636 or from Imray who also publish Henry Irving's *Forth, Tyne, Dogger, Humber, Blakeney to St Abbs*. For most of its length the passage from Spurn Head to Tees Bay offers no particular navigational difficulties or offshore hazards. But in strong NE'ly winds or with a heavy NE'ly swell keep at least 2M offshore. Many harbour entrances become unsafe under these conditions, when Whitby should only be approached with extreme caution and certainly not near LW. However Hartlepool and Blyth are well protected from the NE.

There are well used bombing ranges off the Humber estuary

WHITBY

Charts BA 1612; SC 5614; Imray C24

DS Dover –0430 NW +0130SE

HW River Tyne +0033 sp +0054 np

MHWS	MHWN	MLWN	MLWS
5·6m	4·3m	1·9m	0·8m

Picturesque port of interesting old town. Whitby Abbey, Captain Cook museum, etc.

Approach Avoid entrance in strong onshore winds. Otherwise approach directly except, from SE keep 1M offshore to avoid breaking seas off the Whitby Rock. Make for the Whitby N card Lt buoy Q Bell about ¾M from hbr mouth

which should be avoided. The Humber approaches are very busy with commercial shipping. See plan of TSS and recommended yacht channel, monitor VTS Humber VHF Ch 14. Dangerous seas can be set up over the Binks shoal which extends 4M to the E of Spurn Head. 6M North of Spurn Head, Easington gas and oil terminal is conspicuous in an otherwise bleak, low lying coastline with some crumbling cliffs. Flamborough Head with its high chalk cliffs is very conspicuous. Around it there is a tidal overfall that can be dangerous in strong winds against the tide. In such conditions keep 3M offshore. Care must be taken to avoid Filey Brigg, marked by an E card Lt buoy, and also the Whitby Rock marked by a N card Lt buoy about 1M offshore. The Yorkshire coast with its superb cliff scenery, bays, and ports is delightful in offshore winds. Along this coast the inshore tides often seem to be stronger than those predicted, turning 1½ to ½h earlier than those offshore, until reaching Tees Bay where the tides are weak. In many of the smaller bays there may be an appreciable in-draught. In Tees Bay there are usually several ships at anchor, some may be manoeuvring, waiting for a pilot to board. Once north of Hartlepool the coastline is less industrial. Blyth is a safe port in heavy weather, except from the SE. Do not attempt to pass inside Coquet Is. The Northumberland coast with its sandy beaches and views towards the Cheviots is attractive. Approaching the Farne Is, tides run strongly; in bad weather keep at least 1M E of the Longstone and don't attempt the inshore passage.

In summer months one may encounter the occasional salmon drift net laid across the tide between the fishing boat and usually a large pink buoy; maintain a listening watch on VHF 16.

On passage there are pontoon berths at Scarborough, Whitby, Hartlepool, Sunderland, Newcastle, Royal Quays marina (River Tyne), Blyth and Amble.

(where the tide turns approx HW and LW+0200). Leave it to port. Then approach on 169° to Ldg Bns (W ▲ below a W circle with B stripe) and both Fl.Y.4s (sync) on the SE side of the lower hbr.

Entrance Depth 0·9m min, access HW±0500. Concrete ledge awash on piers gives depth 4m minimum in channel. Entrance can be rough. A strong tidal set may occur across entrance, to E on flood, W on ebb. The ebb stream between piers can reach 5kn when River Esk in flood. On entrance, when abeam of bend in E pier, turn onto 209° with two ldg Lts Fl.Y.2s (sync) astern

SCARBOROUGH

Castle (106) (ru)

Scarborough Rock

Saint Mary's Ch Tower & FS (conspic)

Scarborough

Depths in Metres

Inner Harbour

54°17'N

West Pier

2F.R.5m4M

Vincent's Pier LtHo (tidal)Iso.5s17m9M Dia(1)60s

Old Pier

Outer Harbour

East Pier

South Sands

Ramsdale Scar

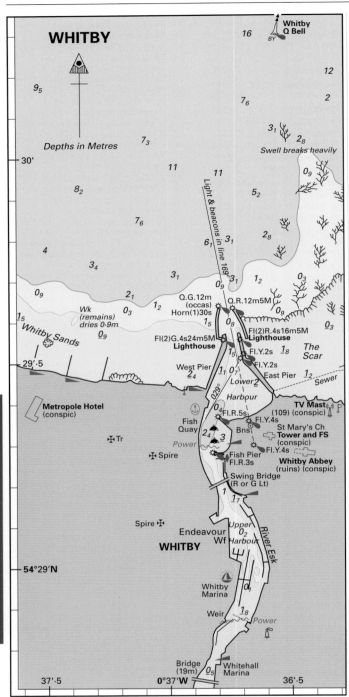

with the wind E of NNE. In winds from W of S anchor 4M S of Filey under Speeton Cliffs.

• **Whitby Bay and Sandsend Bay.** Beware of Up Gang Rocks lying ¾M offshore mid-way between Whitby and Sandsend with 0·5m over them and 11m close by.

• **Runswick Bay.** When entering to anchor, give Kettleness a wide berth.

RIVER TEES

Chart BA 2566; Imray C24

DS in offing: Dover –0430 NW; +0130 SE

HW River Tyne +0012

MHWS	MHWN	MLWN	MLWS
5.5m	4.3m	2.0m	0.9m

In heavy weather, especially with strong winds from NE through N to SE, W Hartlepool with more sea room is preferable to the Tees, the whole river being very heavily industrialised and best avoided.

Approach The main channel, with Ldg Lts on 210° F.R.18m13M, F.R.20m16M from the Tees Fairway safe water pillar buoy, Iso.4s9m8M Horn(1)5s Racon B(–···). The channel has port and stb Lt buoys, leading to the N and S Gare breakwaters.

Entrance The approach leads to No.8 can Fl.G.5s east of which is channel to Bran Sands anchorage. Advice from *Tees Port Control* VHF 14, 22.

Berthing Paddy's Hole in the Bran Sands 6ca in from outer tip of S Gare Breakwater on E side of entrance. Up to 1·2m draught. Call *S Gare Marine Club* ☎ 01642 491039 or HM ☎ 277205 at Tees Dock 2¾M from entrance for advice.

Anchorage Near Pilot jetty on either side of piles. Water from Pilot Station, S Gare Marine Club.

Navigation up river possible but not advised unless essential.

Facilities Buses to Middlesbrough, 2M walk to Seaton Carew; hotel, shops.

HARTLEPOOL

Charts BA 2566, 134, 152; Imray C24

DS in offing Dover –0445N; +0115S

HW River Tyne +0012

MHWS	MHWN	MLWN	MLWS
5.4m	4.2m	1.8m	0.8m

Tidal stream at entrance is rotary Max 1kn.

Hartlepool Marina is a modern development with full facilities. An historic quay with museums and the *Trincomalee*, a fully restored 18th-century warship, are nearby. The marina has 500 berths, with 100 for visitors, up to 50m LOA and 5m draught. Access for 2m draught approx HW±0500: it can be difficult in strong easterly weather, especially near LW, in which case, call *Tees Port Control* VHF 14 for permission to use Victoria Harbour as a temporary refuge.

Approach Conspic landmarks are St Hilda's church 2·5ca WSW of Heugh LtHo. The LtHo lies NE of the hbr entrance. From either N or S make for the Longscar E card Lt buoy, bell. From the N, in heavy weather, give the Heugh a good clearance to avoid the backwash which upsets the swell for some distance E and S of it. From the S avoid the Long Scar shoal lying 6ca SW of the buoy. Fifteen minutes before

---

on the E pier. Proceed to fish quay then turn onto 160° and follow 1·5m channel to upper hbr through swing br. Br control Lts F.G open, F.R closed.

Call *Whitby Bridge* VHF 11, ☎ 01947 602354. Swing br opens HW±0200 on hrs and ½hrs. Some additional openings Saturday and Sunday in summer 0900–1800 regardless of tide. Outside the br opening times wait in the lower hbr alongside the Fish Quay/fishing vessels or the waiting pontoon on E side. Boats on the quay must remain manned at all times.

Berthing

• **Whitby Marina** 12 visitors' berths on N end of W pontoon. Call *Whitby Marina* VHF 11 for allocation of berth.

☎ 600165. Normal facilities. Depths maintained at 1·5m minimum as far as possible but subject to rapid shoaling.

• **Fish Quay** with fishing boats. Short stay only with HM permission.

Anchorage Outside ¼–½M NNW of W pier opposite hotel buildings in 5m, sand.

Facilities Nearby supermarket. Diesel by can from marina.

OFFSHORE ANCHORAGES

• **Filey Bay.** Keep the Flamborough Head Lt open above the cliff tops and stand off the Filey Brigg card Lt buoy. The bottom is clay covered with sand, with foul ground beginning with Scarborough Rock appearing outside Car Naze. Do not remain in the bay

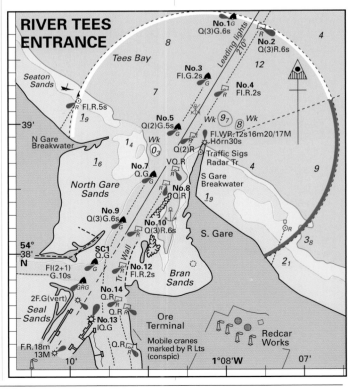

RIVER TEES ENTRANCE

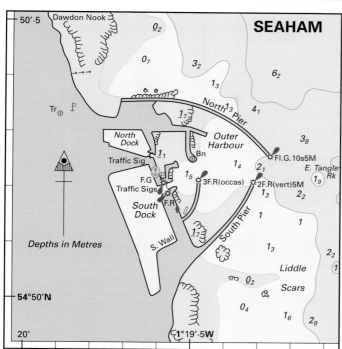

SEAHAM

otherwise entrance is normally easy.

Approach and Entrance Keep ½M offshore until E of hbr entrance. FS at NE corner of S Dock in line with N LtHo (W with B bands) Fl.G.10s leads in 256° clear of E Tangle Rock 1·9m.

Berthing N dock has been dredged. Automatic gate opens when height of tide >2·5m, approx HW±0330. Lts near gate; 3 vert G two-way traffic, 3 vert R stop. Three visitors' berths immediately to stb, max length 10m draught 1·5m.

Larger craft may lock into S Dock HW−0200 to +0100.

Facilities Supermarkets 300m. ☎/VHF Marina: 0191 5818998; *Seaham Marina* VHF 80. Commercial port: HM 0191 5161700; VHF 12 (HW −0230 to +0130).

SUNDERLAND

Charts BA 1627;
Imray C24
DS Dover −0500N; +0100S
HW River Tyne −0002

MHWS	MHWN	MLWN	MLWS
5·2m	4·2m	2·0m	0·8m

Approach If from the S beware of White Stones and Hendon Rock which lie 1·5M offshore to the SE of Roker Pier Lt Ho. The entrance to the River Wear is made between two crescent shaped piers, the N'most Roker Pier has LtHo conspic at its head Fl.5s25m23M Siren 20s. The S pier Fl.10s14m10M has a R can buoy just N of it which must be left to port to avoid underwater pier end.

Entrance Between the inner piers with Lts Q.G on N, Fl.R.5s on S.

Entry signal on old N pier; three Fl.R(vert) = Danger in hbr – no

---

arrival Call *Hartlepool Marina* VHF 37/M or 80, or ☎ 01429 865774.

Entrance To marina by channel dredged to chart datum with Lts Oc.G.5s on N pier and similar R on S. Pass through into W inner harbour through fixed R&G. DirFl.WRG.2s sector Lt on lock N side shows 308°. Enter lock with port side fenders and lines to pontoon. Control Lts; G enter; R keep clear, vessel departing; 2R lock closed. Lock cill is 0·8m below chart datum.

To Victoria Harbour by channel marked by sector Lt Iso.WRG.3s42m on ldg line 325° and buoyed channel.

Berthing
• **Hartlepool Marina** 500 berths up to 50m LOA and 5m draught, 100 visitors, access HW±0500. Call VHF 37(M) or 80, 15 minutes before arrival. ☎ 01429 865744.
• **Victoria Harbour** Private moorings. Call *Tees Port Control* VHF 14 for temporary berthing.

Facilities Diesel and Calor Gas are available 24h near the Lock Office. There are many shops and services in the adjoining development. A 24h hypermarket and retail park is a 10 minute walk.

SEAHAM

Charts BA 1627;
Imray C24
DS Dover −0500N; +0100S
HW River Tyne +0002

MHWS	MHWN	MLWN	MLWS
5·2m	4·1m	2·0m	0·7m

A mainly commercial hbr with marina and leisure facilities in N Dock.

In severe NE and E winds the hbr may be closed but

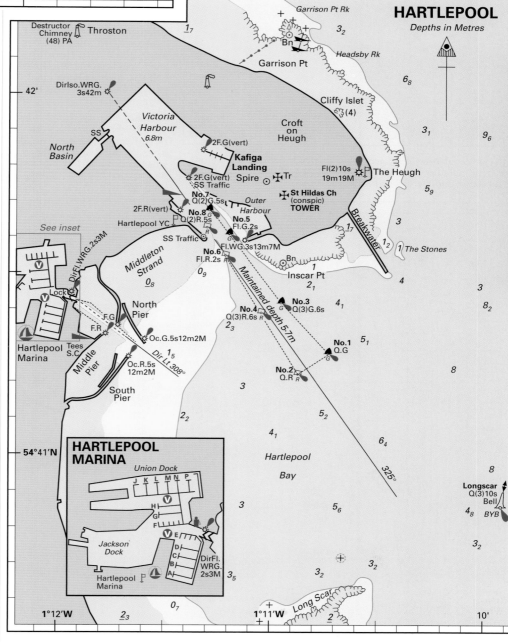

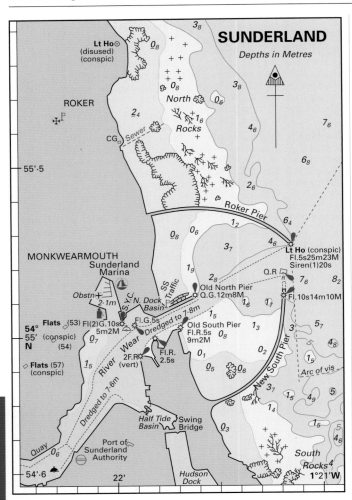

SUNDERLAND

Depths in Metres

Berthing

• **Sunderland Marina** in N Dock, 200 moorings and pontoons, access 24hrs. Fuel berth immediately to port on entering marina. VHF 37(M)/80 or ☎ 514 4721.

Anchorage Clear of fairway inside Roker Pier in 3m.

Facilities Limited, diesel 24h. Town 1M.

RIVER TYNE

Charts BA 1934;
Imray C24
DS Dover –0500 N; +0100S
HW River Tyne HW

MHWS	MHWN	MLWN	MLWS
5·0m	3·9m	1·8m	0·7m

The channel of the River Tyne from the sea to the hbr in Newcastle city centre (Jarrow Quay Corner) is dredged to a minimum depth of 8m. Can be difficult in strong winds from E through N to NE. Inform Tyne Harbour ☎ 0191 257 2080 VHF 12 of arrival and departure.

Approach On 258° pass between LtHo conspic on N pier head Fl(3)10s Horn 10s and S pier head Oc.WRG.10s Bell 10s. Inner light on Herd Groyne Oc.RG.10s+DirOc.10s, (W sector 005°).

Entrance After clearance from Tyne Harbour pass between the piers. Keep to N inward except in strong flood or E winds when mid-channel avoids steep seas beyond N pier. Leaving, keep to S side.

Berthing

• **Fish quay.** Now private. Yachts may berth against river wall just W of fish dock for short stay only. Contact Quay Master ☎ 0191 257 5422 for clearance. VHF 12.

• **Royal Quays Marina** 170 berths in Albert Edward Dock 2M upriver. Contact Marina control 15 min before arrival ☎ 0191 272 8282, VHF 80. Lock in quarter past and quarter to the hour. Use outer pontoon unless otherwise directed. Comprehensive marina facilities including fuel berth outside lock and 30-tonne travel-hoist. Manned 24hrs.

• **St Peter's Marina** 150 berths. 7½M upriver from Tynemouth. ☎ 0191 265 4472, VHF 37, 80 when within 3M. 24hr all tide waiting pontoons and attendance, access HW±0400, 2m min in marina. Good place to visit city, about 1M from centre, best by taxi. Full facilities, boat hoist, small chandlery. Nearby bar/restaurant but no shops.

• **Friers Goose** berths (S side of river) minimum facilities.

• **Newcastle Motor Boat Club** Ouseburn. (N bank within walking distance of town centre) Welcomes yachts on short or overnight stay. ☎ 0191 224 3832, VHF 77 occasionally. Club house.

• **Newcastle City Marina** A security controlled pontoon in the heart of the city. *Mobile* 07435 788426 or ☎ 0191 2211348, preferably 24h in

entry or departure. There are no yacht facilities in S Dock and beware commercial traffic.

Signal Station VHF 14, 16 or ☎ 0191 567 0161.

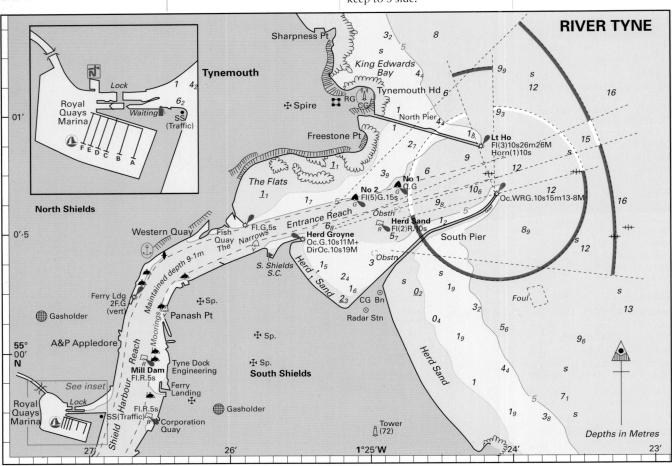

RIVER TYNE

Depths in Metres

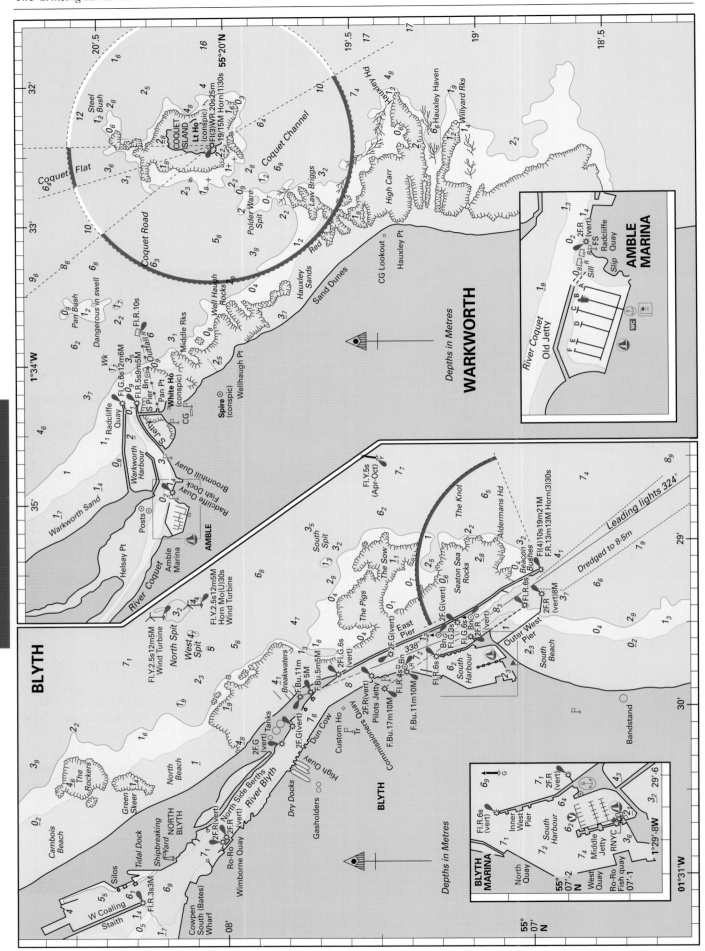

ENGLAND – EAST COAST

55°20'N

Coquet Flat

Coquet Road

Coquet Channel

Steel Bush

COQUET ISLAND

Lt Ho (conspic)
Fl(3)WR.20s25m
19/15M Horn(1)30s

Haxley Hd

Hauxley Haven

Willyard Rks

High Carr

Law Briggs

Polder Ware Spit

Red

Hauxley Sands

Sand Dunes

CG Lookout

Hauxley Pt

WARKWORTH

Depths in Metres

Dangerous in swell

Pan Bush

Fl.R.10s

Well Haugh Rocks

Middle Rks

Outfall

Wk

Fl.G.6s12m6M

Fl.R.5s9m5M

S Pier Bn

Pan Pt

White Ho (conspic)

CG

Spire (conspic)

Wellhaugh Pt

Radcliffe Quay

S Jetty

Warkworth Harbour

Broomhill Quay

Radcliffe Quay

Fish Dock

AMBLE

Helsay Pt

Warkworth Sand

Posts

River Coquet

Amble Marina

AMBLE MARINA

River Coquet

Old Jetty

2F.R (vert)

FS

Radcliffe Quay

Sill

Slip

A B C D E F

WC

BLYTH

Fl.Y.2.5s12m5M
Wind Turbine

North Spit

West Spit

Fl.Y.2.5s12m5M
Horn Mo(U)30s
Wind Turbine

The Rockers

Green Skeer

Cambois Beach

North Beach

NORTH BLYTH

Shipbreaking Yard

Tidal Dock

Silos

W Coaling Staith

Fl.R.3s3M

Cowpen South (Bates) Wharf

Wimborne Quay

Ro-Ro Quay

2F.R (vert)

2F.R (vert)

North Side Berths

River Blyth

High Quay

Dry Docks

Gasholders

2F.G (vert) Tanks

2F.G (vert)

2F.G (vert)

Dun Cow

Custom Ho

Tr Quay

Pilots Jetty

Commissioner's Quay

2F.R (vert)

F.Bu.17m10M

F.Bu.11m10M

Breakwaters

F.Bu.11m 5M

F.Bu.5m5M

2Fl.G.6s

338°

Fl.R.4s Bn

Fl.R.6s

South Harbour

East Pier

The Pigs

The Sow

Seaton Sea Rocks

Beacon Bn

Bushes

2Fl.G (vert)

Fl.G.3s Bn

Fl.G.6s

2F.R (vert)

Fl.R.6s

Outer West Pier

South Beach

Aldermans Hd

The Knot

The Sow

South Spit

Fl.Y.5s (Apr-Oct)

Fl(4)10s19m21M
F.R.13m13M Horn(3)30s

Leading lights 324°

Dredged to 8.5m

Bandstand

BLYTH

Depths in Metres

BLYTH / MARINA

G

Fl.R.6s (vert)

2F.R (vert)

Inner West Pier

North Quay

South Harbour

Middle Jetty

RNVR

West Quay

Ro-Ro Fish quay 07'·1

1°29'·8W

55° 07'·2 N

29'·6

4·3

1°34'W

1°31'W

55° 07' N

08'

35'

32'

33'

30'

29'

19'

18'·5

advance to book berth and opening of the Millenium Bridge.

Anchorage

Tynemouth 200m N of the G con No.1 buoy W of the N pier head or off Herd Sand S of dredged channel. Quiet rural shelter is also available up river beyond Scandinavian ferry terminals and shipyards where grassed areas have replaced industrial buildings.

Upriver Vessels with air draught <4·5m MHWS can proceed upriver through bridges and when raised, <20m. 24hrs notice to Tyne Harbour required.

BLYTH

Charts BA 1626;
Imray C24
DS Dover −0500N +0100S
HW River Tyne +0002

MHWS	MHWN	MLWN	MLWS
5·0m	3·9m	1·7m	0·8m

A commercial hbr and headquarters of Royal Northumberland YC.

Approach Two conspic wind turbines ½M offshore. The entrance opens to the S with sands to W and rocks to E abreast of breakwaters. There are Ldg Lts 2F.Bu in line 324° on lattice towers with Or diamond topmarks. From S, Blyth Bay is clear. After passing St Mary's Is head for the pier. From N, clear the Sow, Pigs and Seaton Sea Rocks to stb and proceed towards the entrance. Seas may break on the bar in heavy weather from SE especially at LW.

Entrance Call *Blyth Harbour Control* VHF 12 or ☎ 01670 352678 before entry or departure. Enter between the piers, turn hard to port round the N end of the inner W pier Fl.R.6s into S hbr.

Berthing Visiting yachts may be accommodated by the Royal Northumberland YC ☎ 353636. Use N side of outer pontoon unless otherwise directed. Apply direct to RNYC and pay dues at bar after 1900.

Anchorage In fair weather in 4m in centre of bay to N of Blyth off Newbiggin. Shelter from SW to N winds. Beware rocks to N and S.

Facilities Showers, bar and weekend food at Royal Northumberland YC. Town 1½M.

AMBLE AND WARKWORTH HARBOUR

Charts BA 1627;
Imray C24
DS Dover −0500N
HW River Tyne −0013

MHWS	MHWN	MLWN	MLWS
5·0m	3·9m	1·9m	0·8m

Amble is the town adjacent to Warkworth Harbour, with all usual facilities. Warkworth is inland.

Approach Avoid entrance in strong N to E winds when Blyth is a port of refuge. From S leave Coquet LtHo Fl(3)WR.30s well to port until N of Lat 55°20′·7N, joining route from E when Coquet LtHo bears 210°. From E steer due W to leave Coquet LtHo 2M to port until able to turn onto 225° direct to hbr entrance leaving Pan Bush shoal 2ca to port. From N steer onto 225° to hbr keeping 2M N of Coquet LtHo. Watch out for lobster pots.

Passage through channel inshore of Coquet Is hazardous without local knowledge except in calmest conditions at HW.

Entrance Two piers 68m apart Fl.R.5s from LtHo, RW horizontal stripes, at end of S pier; Fl.G.6s from W iron LtHo on N pier. Beware S-going stream across entrance and swell over rock covered with sand bar 2·2m at MLWS. 4kn limit. Avoid shoaling N side S pier head and S of N jetty by entering midway between piers and then steering about 5m N of S jetty to stand clear of half tide piled obstruction extending 1·5m for full length of jetty. Wait for marina against Broomhill Quay.

Berthing

• **Amble Marina** 230 berths, access HW±0300 MHWS; HW±0400 MHWN. Normal facilities, most repairs, chandlery. Follow line of quays, keeping well to S, pass R can buoy and turn in S of jetty marked by E card bn. Depth over cill, which dries 0·8m, on tide gauge at entrance. VHF 80 *Amble Marina*, ☎ 01665 712168. Outside office hours collect berthing instructions from reception/fuel pontoon.
• **Broomhill Quay** Yachts may lie in 0·7m MLWS to 2·1m MLWN. Permission from HM ☎ 710306.
• **Coquet YC** Further upriver beyond the quays. May have moorings available with similar depths from Coquet YC to quays. Scrubbing grid. ☎ 711179.

Facilities Laundry, chandlery. Bus to Newcastle and Alnwick. Provisions from town ¼M.

BOULMER, CRASTER AND N SUNDERLAND

Boulmer Small haven almost enclosed by rocks. Narrow (30m) entrance. Only advisable in settled weather. Ldg bns on 262° to entrance. Anchor just inside in 1·5m or dry on sand. No facilities.

Craster Tiny drying hbr for use in settled offshore weather only. 1M S of conspic Dunstanburgh Castle ruins. Anchor just inshore of 40m wide entrance between Muckle Carr (to N), Little Carr (to S) or, if able to take the ground, berth at E pier on sand over rock.

North Sunderland Harbour near Seahouses. Access HW±0300. Dredged to 0·7m above chart datum. Inner harbour, good shelter but used by fishing boats. Outer harbour, swell in onshore winds very uncomfortable and dangerous. Beware rks to W of entrance and NE from breakwater. When dangerous to

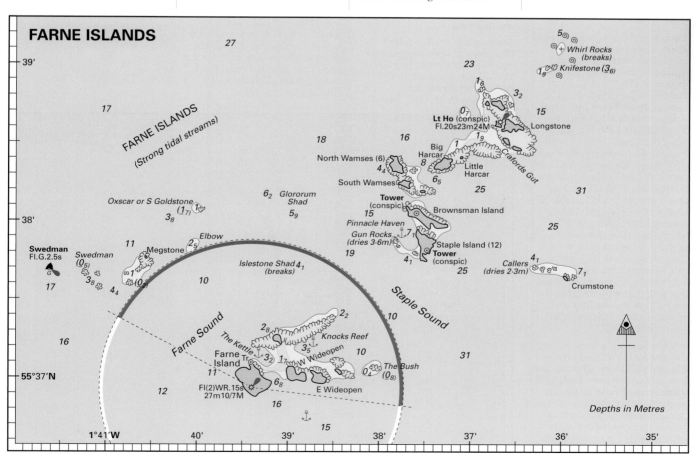

FARNE ISLANDS

enter R Lt over F.G Lt or R over Bu flags on NW pier are shown.

HM ☎ 01665 720033 or 721558, VHF 14, 12.

FARNE ISLANDS

Charts BA 111, 156; Imray C24

Tides. As Holy Island

National Trust nature reserve. Landing prohibited except on Farne, Staple and Longstone. Magnificent wildlife but no facilities. Attempt only in good weather. Beware turbulence over Knivestone and Whirl rocks and eddy S of Longstone in NW tidal stream.

Anchorages
• The Kettle, NE side of Inner Farne near the bridges between Knocks Reef and W Wideopen.
• S of W Wideopen.
• S of Knocks reef.
• Pinnacle Haven between Staple Is and Brownsman.

HOLY ISLAND (LINDISFARNE)

Charts BA 111, 1612; Imray C24

DS in offing: HWD SE; +0600NW; DS in hbr: –0245 flood; +0345 ebb

HW River Tyne –0040

MHWS	MHWN	MLWN	MLWS
4·8m	3·7m	1·5m	0·6m

A natural hbr with 3–7m inside. Strong streams and eddies.

Approach Make for Ridge E card buoy. If coming from the N, at night or in poor visibility, pass to the east of Plough Seat Reef.

Entrance The long and narrow channel is easy in good conditions once the conspic leading marks (stone obelisks 21m and 25m) on Old Law have been identified. The ebb runs at up to 4kn. Least depth 1·3m. Steer on 262° with East Bn Oc.WRG.6s in line with West Bn. Leave Triton G con buoy Q.G. to stb and turn onto 309° when the bn Oc.WRG 6s on the Heugh (caution: do not confuse with the tall narrow stone war memorial further W) comes in line with St Mary's church belfry giving 309° to anchorage. The ebb runs at 4kn in the channel, the entrance is long and narrow but easy in fine weather with the help of Ldg marks. Caution is advised in using the sectored lights by night. East Beacon and the Heugh lights, both Oc.WRG are synchronised.

Anchorages Vessels exceeding 2m draught, bring up off Heugh bn. Vessels drawing 2m can lie 1ca S of Steel End. In W gales boats should lie to two anchors. Buoy anchors as many buried chains. Small craft able to take the ground are more secure in the Ooze, soft mud,

but avoid in S and SE winds. Often crowded.

Facilities Water tap in square, stores at PO, PH.

HM ☎ 01289 89217.

BERWICK

Charts BA 111, 1612; Imray C24

DS Dover –0445N ; +0100S

HW River Tyne –0053

MHWS	MHWN	MLWN	MLWS
4·7m	3·8m	1·3m	0·6m

A commercial hbr with few facilities for yachts but attractive with good shelter and worth a visit.

Approach From S, to clear Holy Island, keep Megstone and Farne Is Lt tr in line astern at 142° turning onto 309° to Berwick when abeam Emmanuel Pt on Holy Island.

From N stand off from shore ¾M until LtHo in line with town hall spire then turn and approach breakwater head on 294°. Call HM VHF 12 or ☎ 01289 307404 before entry.

Entrance Bar 0·6 to 1·8m very variable. Enter parallel with breakwater approx 10m off and head for bn Q.G.W of breakwater. When Spittal Ldg marks (Lt bns F.R with triangular topmarks) come in line turn onto 207° until S of 2nd G con Lt buoy Q.G. Beware ldg bns may not show best water. Then steer for NW end of fish jetty. Do not keep too close to G buoys which are laid in shoal water outside the channel. From here steer for the end of the pier at Tweed Dock. Enter 5m off, well clear of E card bn.

Berthing Tweed Dock is left open and yachts may enter or leave at most states of the tide. Berth alongside E wall which has one ladder or against fishing boats, then as directed by HM ☎ 01289 307404. Do not leave boats unattended without permission from HM. Depth approx 1m at MLWS, 0·6m in entrance, bottom soft mud. 3-tonne mobile crane.

Anchorage In river clear of traffic or may pick up one of few mooring buoys.

Facilities Water on quay. Town 1M, small local shops nearby. Good rail and road transport.

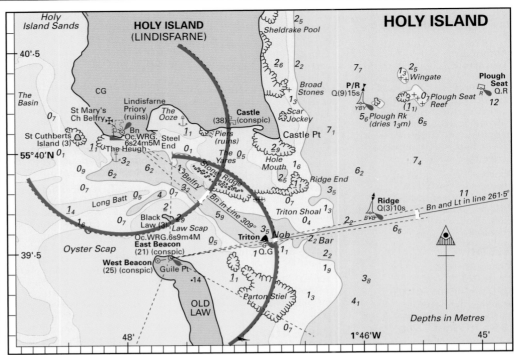

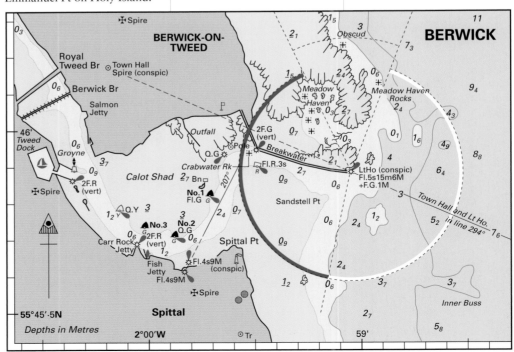

Navigation in your pocket
Charts as Apps for the iPad

TUCABO

Imray have joined forces with software developer Tucabo to produce this fully functioning chart navigation package based on high quality images of Imray and official charts.

Available in the following languages:
English, Dutch, French, German, Italian and Spanish

Download the free Marine Imray Chart App 2.5 which contains the navigation software and demo charts from the App Store and then the following chart areas can be downloaded:

- **Imray Charts North Sea**
- **Imray Charts British Isles West coast and Ireland**
- **Imray Charts English Channel**
- **1800 series Netherlands Small Craft Charts,**
- **German BSH Charts for the North and Baltic Seas**
- **Danish (DGA) Charts**
- **Swedish Charts**
- **Imray Charts Atlantic Europe**
- **Imray Charts Western, Central and Eastern Mediterranean**
- **French (SHOM) charts for Mediterranean France and Corsica**
- **Caribbean Sea**
- **Australian Hydrographic Office charts for East and South Australia with Tasmania**

Imray Chart Navigator Apps feature

Waypoints
Routes: distances, targets, bearings
Position and destination
Course to steer, speed and bearing
Magnetic compass
Distances, bearings from any point to any point
Electronic bearing line
GPS and instruments
Tides with full functionality from Tides Planner
Aerial photographs (subject to coverage) and harbour plans
Tracks which you can share with friends
GPX import/export

IMRAY/TUCABO APPS FOR IPHONES

A series of inexpensive Apps providing quick reference for crews and anyone involved in navigation

Marine Rules and Signals
Topics include buoyage, motor and sailing lights and shapes, rules of the road, safety and life saving signals.

Tides
This App provides active tidal data and tidal curves for ports around the UK and further afield.

RYA Racing Rules
A simple guide to the racing rules produced in partnership with the RYA.

Symbols and abbreviations
A quick reference to the signs, symbols and abbreviations used on nautical charts

IMTA Gold Award 2012 'Best Digital Data Product'

Delivery is simple and Apps are downloaded from the Apple iTunes App Store

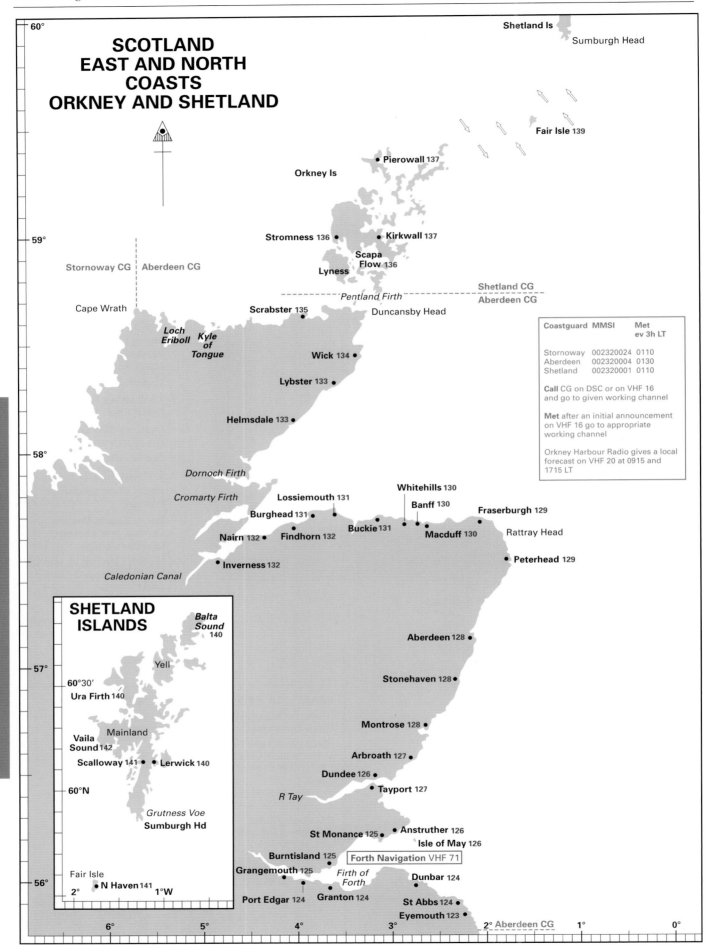

SCOTLAND
EAST AND NORTH
COASTS
ORKNEY AND SHETLAND

Shetland Is
Sumburgh Head

Fair Isle 139

Pierowall 137

Orkney Is

Stornoway CG | Aberdeen CG

Stromness 136 ● ● Kirkwall 137

Scapa
Flow 136

Lyness

Shetland CG
Aberdeen CG

Pentland Firth

Cape Wrath

Scrabster 135 ● Duncansby Head

*Loch
Eriboll* *Kyle
of
Tongue*

Wick 134

Lybster 133

Helmsdale 133

Dornoch Firth

Cromarty Firth

Whitehills 130

Lossiemouth 131
Banff 130

Burghead 131 ● Buckie 131 ● Macduff 130 ● Fraserburgh 129

Nairn 132 ● ● Findhorn 132 Rattray Head

● Inverness 132 ● Peterhead 129

Caledonian Canal

Coastguard	MMSI	Met ev 3h LT
Stornoway	002320024	0110
Aberdeen	002320004	0130
Shetland	002320001	0110

Call CG on DSC or on VHF 16
and go to given working channel

Met after an initial announcement
on VHF 16 go to appropriate
working channel

Orkney Harbour Radio gives a local
forecast on VHF 20 at 0915 and
1715 LT

Aberdeen 128 ●

Stonehaven 128 ●

Montrose 128 ●

Arbroath 127 ●

Dundee 126 ●

● Tayport 127

R Tay

St Monance 125 ● ● Anstruther 126

Isle of May 126

Burntisland 125 Forth Navigation VHF 71

Grangemouth 125 *Firth of
Forth* Dunbar 124

Port Edgar 124 Granton 124

St Abbs 124 ●

Eyemouth 123 ●

SHETLAND ISLANDS

*Balta
Sound*
140

Yell

60°30′
Ura Firth 140

Mainland

**Vaila
Sound** 142

Scalloway 141 ● ● Lerwick 140

60°N

Grutness Voe
Sumburgh Hd

Fair Isle

● N Haven 141

2° 1°W

Page references are shown after locations, for example:
Peterhead 129. Bold type indicates that it is accompanied by a plan. *Italics* are used for rivers, lochs, bays, seas etc.

Scotland – East and North Coasts

The border to Duncansby Head

BA Sailing Directions *North Sea (West)* – NP54

For more details refer to:

The Yachtsman's Pilot – North and East Scotland. The Farne Islands to Cape Wrath Martin Lawrence (Imray).

Forth, Tyne, Dogger, Humber – Blakeney to St Abbs Henry Irving (Imray).

Berwick to Fraserburgh Forth Yacht Clubs Association Pilot Handbook

N and NE coasts of Scotland and Orkney Clyde Cruising Club Sailing Directions (CCC SD) (2003)

Humber to Rattray Head R Northumberland YC Sailing Directions:.

Map of the Inland Waterways of Scotland (Imray).

A yacht cruising this coast needs to be able to make off-shore passages of 100 miles and to keep at sea in adverse conditions. Many of the harbours are unavailable in strong on-shore winds; and a large swell, which may make entrances dangerous, persists for some days after heavy northerly or northeasterly winds have died down.

Nevertheless, with the prevailing offshore wind, it is an interesting cruising area with a coastline varying from spectacular high rocky cliffs, abounding in bird life, to low-lying farming land and sand dunes. The main yachting centres are Port Edgar and Granton in the Firth of Forth, the River Tay and also in the Moray Firth at Lossiemouth and Findhorn. Many harbours on this coast are working harbours, busy with fishing and the oil industry. However with the decline in fishing, yacht facilities are increasing. For yachts on passage, Peterhead, with its good marina facilities, is available in virtually all conditions. Wick, with its marina, is a good port of departure for the Northern Isles.

BERWICK TO ARBROATH

On a direct passage, the crossings of the Forth and Tay estuaries pose no great problems; but bad seas can be experienced off the Forth, particularly in E winds against the tide. The Tay is shoal for several miles out and should be given a wide berth especially with wind or onshore swell against the tide. St Abbs Head (90m) has the appearance of an island from NW and SE.

Passage lights	BA No
St Abbs Head Fl.10s68m26M	2850
Bass Rock Fl(3)20s46m10M	2864
Isle of May Fl(2)15s73m22M	3090
Fife Ness Iso.WR.10s12m21/20M AIS	3102
Bell Rock Fl.5s28m18M	3108

EYEMOUTH

EYEMOUTH

Depths in Metres

EYEMOUTH

Chart BA 1612; Imray C23
HW Leith −0020

MHWS	MHWN	MLWN	MLWS
5·2m	4·1m	2·0m	0·9m

A busy fishing hbr, safe in any weather but not to be approached in strong winds from between N and E or near LW with N'ly swell. Bar varies but normally dredged to 2m MLWS. Yachts welcome.

Signals R flag by day, F.R Lt by night: hbr closed.

Approach Keep ½M offshore until Ldg marks orange poles (F.G) come in line on 174°. E pier head lit Iso.R.2s. If any sea, approach after half flood. Passage S of Hurkar Rocks is unmarked, keep mid-channel, borrowing slightly towards Hurkars.

Entrance 16m wide. Keep to Ldg line until hbr is well open, then round E pier fairly close. Be prepared to stand off for fishing vessels leaving hbr.

North and East Scotland, and the Orkney Islands distances (miles)

	Eyemouth	Granton	Fife Ness	Stonehaven	Peterhead	Whitehills	Lossiemouth	Chanory Point	Helmsdale	Duncansby Head	Scrabster	Cape Wrath, 2M N	Stromness	Kirkwall	Whitehall, Stronsay
Eyemouth	0														
Granton	43	0													
Fife Ness	30	29	0												
Stonehaven	66	71	43	0											
Peterhead	99	105	77	35	0										
Whitehills	137	140	113	71	35	0									
Lossiemouth	158	163	135	93	58	23	0								
Chanonry Point	188	191	163	122	89	52	30	0							
Helmsdale	181	180	151	110	75	43	26	36	0						
Duncansby Head	180	185	158	116	81	60	56	75	42	0					
Scrabster	202	207	181	139	103	82	79	97	64	22	0				
Cape Wrath, 2M N	267	288	223	181	166	145	144	128	107	65	48	0			
Stromness	202	207	180	139	103	82	79	97	67	23	28	56	0		
Kirkwall	213	210	182	141	107	89	91	111	78	34	49	78	37	0	
Whitehall,Stronsay	205	212	185	143	107	95	96	115	82	43	55	87	39	21	0

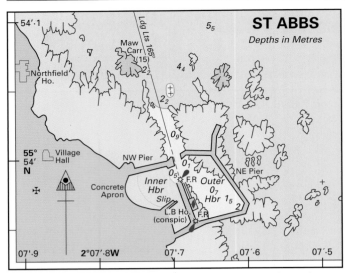

ST ABBS
Depths in Metres

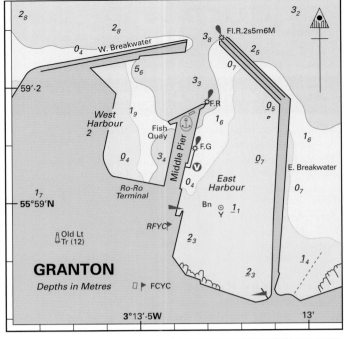

GRANTON
Depths in Metres   □▶ FCYC

Berthing Usually alongside pontoon on SE side of inner hbr. Alternatively alongside quay below lifeboat house.

Facilities Water on quay, stores. Diesel from HM.

☎/VHF HM 01890 750223, *Mobile* 07885 742505, VHF 12.

ST ABBS HARBOUR

Chart BA 160;
Imray C23
HW Leith –0025
MHWS   MHWN
4·8m   3·7m

Small attractive hbr 1M S of St Abbs Head. Inner harbour dries; outer harbour has about 1m LWS. Not to be attempted in strong on-shore wind/seas.

Bar 1m.

Approach From S identify by cliff top village and high SE-facing cliffs whitened by birds; from N round St Abbs Head which is steep-to. Make for Maw Carr, a prominent steep-sided reddish rock (15m) about 120m NNW of entrance. Conspic Y LB Ho identifies hbr.

Entrance Bring E edges of NW pier and centre pier in line and steer exactly on this line. Channel through rocks is narrow but all dangers show. Ldg line lit F.R.

Berthing As directed; best alongside towards S end of NE pier (at springs diagonally across corner).

Facilities Stores, PO, PH.

☎ 07881 767587

DUNBAR

Chart BA 734;
Imray C23
HW Leith –0007

MHWS   MHWN   MLWN   MLWS
5·3m   4·1m   2·0m   0·9m

A pleasant resort town with picturesque hbr. 0·5m MLWS in entrance. Good anchorage outside, sheltered from W through S to E, clean sand, good holding.

Do not approach with winds between NW and E greater than Force 5 or if there is an appreciable onshore swell.

Approach On Ldg line 198°, orange triangles on white posts on grassy slope (Lts Oc.G.6s)

Entrance Enter HW ±0300. 10m cleft cut through rock to port, invisible until open.

HM should be contacted prior to entry.

Berthing In 1·2m alongside as near to castle as possible, sand. N quay dries, uneven, sand at E end. Uncomfortable surge with onshore swell. In bad weather HM will open br admitting to old hbr, dries out, mud.

Facilities Showers at Dunbar SC. Stores. Rly.

☎/VHF HM (office) 01368 865404, *Mobile* 07958 754 858, VHF 12.

GRANTON

Chart BA 735;
Imray C27
HW Leith HW

MHWS   MHWN   MLWN   MLWS
5·6m   4·4m   2·0m   0·8m

Headquarters of River Forth and Forth Corinthian YCs. Hbr

DUNBAR TO GRANGEMOUTH

Between Dunbar and Granton there are a number of anchorages and harbours which dry. Most significant are North Berwick and Fisherrow – both are restricted and subject to surge. Yachts are not normally allowed into Leith Docks. Dunbar entrance can be dangerous even in light winds if any swell. From Dunbar a direct course to Bass Rock, a very conspicuous cone island ht 115m with large gannetry, clears all dangers. If proceeding up the Firth pass at least ¼M outside Fidra, thereafter the coast falls away and becomes low lying. Monitor Forth Navigation Service VHF 71. For Granton make for the South Channel passing at least 1M south of the island of Inchkeith to avoid off-lying drying rocks. For Port Edgar or Grangemouth it is preferable after dark or in poor weather to take the well buoyed North Channel passing to the north of Inchkeith. From Hound Point westwards, on the north side, when large craft are manoeuvring, yachts must keep clear of the navigation channel. On the south side from a point 200m to the north of the unlit bn off Hound Point, keep north of a line between it and the base of the south cantilever of the rail bridge, clearance 44m. Pass at least 30m away from either side of the oil terminal. Pass anywhere between the main N and S towers of the road bridge, clearance 45m. Tides may reach 4kn. Thereafter there are extensive mud flats.

When a tanker is entering or leaving Mortimer's Deep it shall have an exclusion zone of 1M.

A replacement Forth road bridge is being constructed W of existing bridge. There are exclusion zones, marked by Y buoys, round the sites of two new columns. Monitor VHF 71.

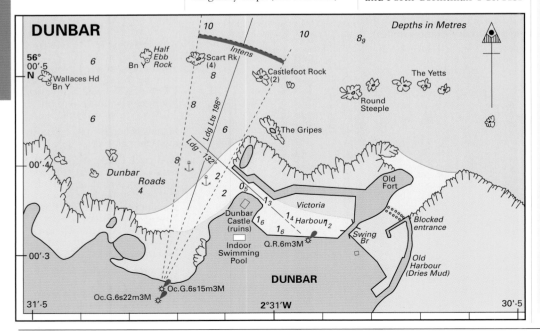

DUNBAR
Depths in Metres

DUNBAR

divided by central pier; yachts use E arm. Much of hbr dries.

Entrance 3m. Beware pilot boats.

Signals Tide signals on middle pier. Red flag W cross (F.G Lt) = No Entry. Yachts drawing less than 3m can ignore these signals with caution.

Berthing Visitors' pontoons (1·5 to 2·0m at LWS) on east side of Middle Pier. Security gate; key fob on payment of dues to RFYC. Information sheets at head of ramp.

Facilities Buses to Edinburgh and Leith. No fuel. No power on pontoon. Welcome to use club.

☎/VHF RFYC: Office 0131 552 8560, Bar 07551 426 813, VHF 80/M.
Port: 523385, VHF 20.
Forth Navigation Service VHF 71.

PORT EDGAR

Chart BA 736;
Imray C27
HW Leith +0010

MHWS	MHWN	MLWN	MLWS
5·6m	4·4m	2·0m	0·9m

Large efficient yachting centre in old naval hbr on S shore immediately above the bridges.

Approach Follow the buoyed shipping channel N or S of Inchkeith as convenient and pass through centre of road and rail bridges.

Entrance Pass W of floating breakwater of lorry tyres (lit 4x Q.Y) leaving W breakwater (Fl.R.4s) to stb.

Berthing Visitors' berths on end of pontoons. Call by VHF/☎ prior to arrival.

Facilities All. Sailboard and dinghy hire and instruction. Restaurant, shops, etc. in S Queensferry, ½M E.

☎/VHF HM 01313 313330, VHF 80 (0900–1930).

FORTH-CLYDE CANAL AND RIVER CARRON

Chart BA 737;
Imray C27
HW Leith +0025sp +0010np

MHWS	MHWN	MLWN	MLWS
5·8m	4·6m	2·0m	0·6m

Passage must be booked in advance (☎ 0845 67766000). Max depth 1·83m. It is advisable to study the *Skipper's Guide*, download from www.waterscape.com/canals-and-rivers.

The entrance to the Forth-Clyde Canal is 2·5M from the mouth of the River Carron; it is immediately to the west of the busy commercial port of Grangemouth, which is not available to yachts. Monitor VHF 14 for shipping movements. As air draft is 3m, masts should previously have been unstepped at Port Edgar, or in River Carron, phone in advance ☎ 07833 953288 (before 1600 on Friday for weekends). Be prepared to handle the lowered mast and set up on deck.

Approach From seaward hold to the north side of the main channel. Prior to arrival at the Carron Approach R can Lt buoy Fl(4)R.12s contact Carron Sea Lock VHF 74 ☎ 07810 794468.

Entrance Navigation is constrained by the Kerse Road Br. When the rise of tide is 4·5m there is 1·8m depth and 3·0m air draught. All depth and air draught gauges are calibrated to this br. It is best to enter at HW–0200, but possible up to HW+0100. Leave Carron bn Fl.G.5s, marking the end of the training wall, close to stb and follow the buoyed channel keeping towards the centre or outside of the curves.

Transit *See Scotland – West Coast section*. Exit and step mast at Bowling. The canal office ☎ 01324 671217 should be contacted for times of opening.

N SHORE FIRTH OF FORTH

Of the harbours on the N shore of the Forth, Pittenweem is a restricted and very busy fishing harbour, yachts unwelcome except weekends. Many of the harbours dry, most are inaccessible in strong E–SE winds but then Methil is available. Burntisland may be convenient for yachts on passage.

BURNTISLAND

Chart BA 733;
Imray C27
HW Leith +0008

MHWS	MHWN	MLWN	MLWS
5·7m	4·4m	2·1m	1·0m

Commercial hbr with oil rig fabrication yard. Outer tidal hbr and two wet docks. Accessible at all states of tide and in most weather, heavy surge in winds SE to SW. Keep clear of pilot boats. Useful for yachts on passage.

Berthing Report to HM. Yachts may sometimes lock into E dock HW–0200 to HW. Outer harbour unsuitable for yachts in strong winds and E dock wide open to W wind. W side of outer harbour shoals to less than 1·5m.

Facilities Water, stores, trains to Edinburgh and Dundee.

☎/VHF HM 01592 87373, VHF 20, 71 *Forth Navigation Service*.

ST MONANS

Chart BA 734;
Imray C27
HW Leith –0010

MHWS	MHWN
5·5m	4·3m

Small pleasant fishing hbr, dries completely, sand and mud. Conspicuous church close W of hbr.

Approach After half tide; avoid in bad weather.

Entrance Between E breakwater (Oc.WRG.6s) and pole bn on rocks to W.

Berthing In E hbr on outer pier. Dries, hard sand. Two reserved visitor berths, contact HM.

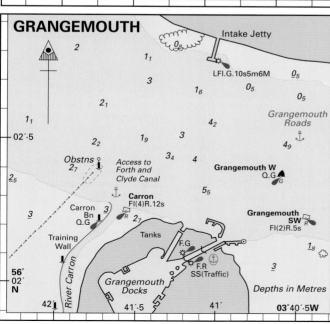

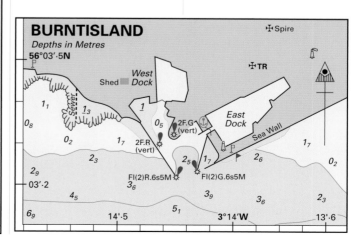

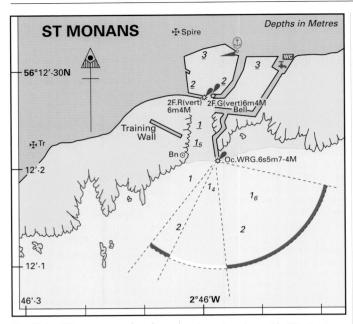

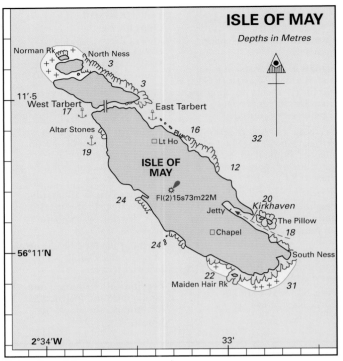

Facilities Water, stores, local buses; boatbuilder. Windmill and saltpans worth a visit. EC Wednesday.

☎ HM (part-time) 07930 869358.

ANSTRUTHER

Chart BA 190;
Imray C27
HW Leith –0015

MHWS	MHWN	MLWN	MLWS
5·3m	4·2m	2·0m	0·8m

A busy holiday town with usual facilities. Admirable fisheries museum. Hbr dries, inner to soft mud, used by leisure and small fishing vessels. Advisable to call HM 24h in advance.

Approach HW±0300. Conspic. white light tr on W breakwater. Enter on line of Ldg lts, F.G. on 019°.

Berthing As directed. Pontoons for bilge keelers <10·5 m,

otherwise alongside W pier in inner harbour just above first knuckle. Shore-side access from the pontoons requires a key provided by HM.

☎/VHF HM 01333 310836, VHF 11 (Office hours only).

OFFSHORE ANCHORAGES

Isle of May Shore is bold except NW end, bottom rocky, holding poor.

Shelter from E winds at W Tarbert and Altar Stones; from W winds at E Tarbert. Kirkhaven small boat hbr requires detailed knowledge; enter on 216° on white Ldg marks just south of the Pillow. The island is a nature reserve, landing restricted.

Largo Bay On N shore of Firth of Forth. Good anchorage in N and E winds.

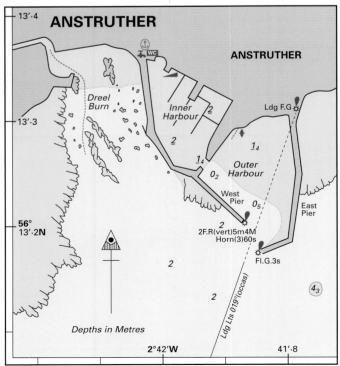

St Andrew's Bay (N of Fife Ness) Good in S winds through W to NW. Anchor about ½M E of St Andrew's harbour pier in suitable depth, sand. Beware of rocks beyond pier head.

RIVER TAY

Chart BA 1481;
Imray C23

HW Aberdeen +0100 (Bar)
+0130 (Dundee)

Bar

MHWS	MHWN	MLWN	MLWS
5·2m	4·2m	1·9m	0·7m

A major river leading to port of Dundee and navigable on tide to the deep-water hbr of Perth. Approaches are shoal a long way offshore. Once in the river ebb stream is stronger on N shore, flood on S.

Approach With draught of 1·5m enter channel between R and G Middle Lt buoys. With deeper draft or in onshore weather enter from Fairway safe water buoy 3½M ENE of Buddon Ness. From S, after half tide and in smooth water, it is possible to join the main channel near Abertay R can buoy (Fl.R.6s). Do not attempt to cross Abertay Sand which extends 5M out from S shore – submerged stakes.

Bar 3·2m between Gaa Spit and Abertay R can buoy. Dangerous in strong E wind or onshore swell, especially on the ebb.

Entrance Channel is buoyed. From Abertay E card Lt buoy steer on steep-to shore at Tayport with Dir LtHo (Iso.WRG.3s) bearing 269°.

Anchorages and Berthing
• Tayport – *see separate entry*.
• Temporary anchorage on S side just N of Lucky Scalp E of Tayport. On N side close

inshore SW of Buddon Ness, out of main ebb stream.
• Good anchorage clear to W of Tayport entrance, to N of line of high and low lights (low Lt disused). Exposed.
• In W Ferry Bay 8ca WNW from Broughty Castle by River Tay YC moorings. Mooring may be available from club; stream runs strongly.
• Broughty Harbour dries; available ±0300hrs, keep to W wall. Slip, crane. Exposed.
• **Dundee Docks:** Entrance 4ca E of Road Br. Anchoring off not recommended. Yachts can enter wet docks by prior arrangement; perfect safety but commercial area. Lock HW–0200 to HW. Strictly no smoking.
• Pleasant anchorages above bridges off Balmerino and further W.

For upper reaches and **Perth** leave rly br 2–2½hrs before HW Dundee.

☎/VHF HM VHF 12 *Dundee Harbour Radio* covers all shipping movements, weather etc ☎ 01382 224121. Royal Tay YC VHF M, ☎ 01382 477516.

TAYPORT

Chart BA 1481;
Imray C23
HW Aberdeen +0140sp
+0120np

MHWS	MHWN	MLWN	MLWS
5·5m	4·3m	2·0m	0·8m

A pleasant small town. Completely sheltered private hbr 7M from the Abertay BYB buoy, offering an excellent passage stop. Mostly dries to very deep soft mud. No commercial activity, visitors welcome.

Approach Just W of Larick Bn (conspic pile Lt) head for hbr

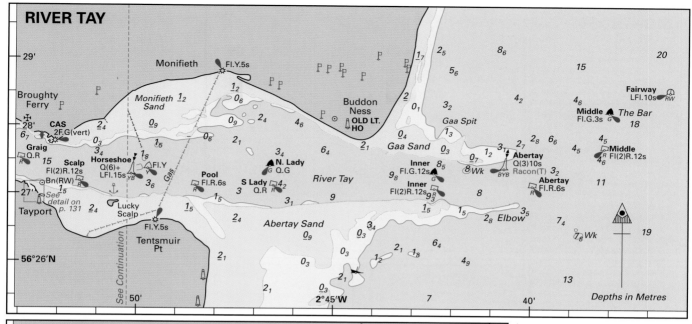

RIVER TAY

Depths in Metres

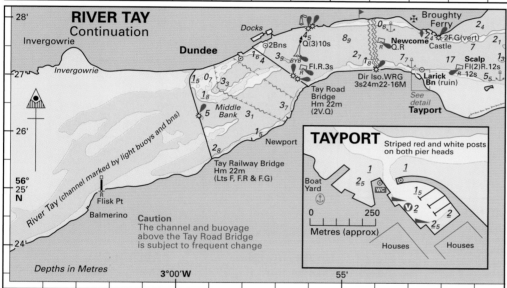

RIVER TAY
Continuation

Caution
The channel and buoyage
above the Tay Road Bridge
is subject to frequent change

Depths in Metres

TAYPORT

Striped red and white posts
on both pier heads

0   250

Metres (approx)

Houses   Houses

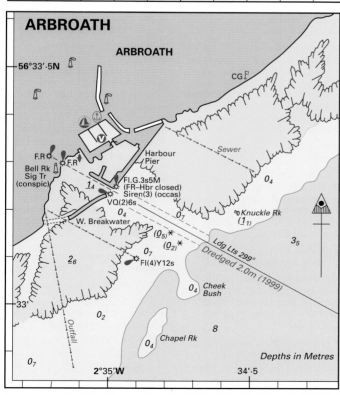

ARBROATH

Depths in Metres

mouth on 180°. Beware strong
cross-stream and moorings W
of entrance.

Entrance Keep close to E quay
wall for best water (3hrs either
side of HW for 1·5m draught).

Berthing On SW wall, or with
permission at private pontoon
berth. Check with HM. Top of
hbr dries very early on ebb.

Facilities Water on quay. Shops.
Bus to Dundee.

☎ Berthing Officer 01382
553799.

ARBROATH

Chart BA 1438;
Imray C23
HW Aberdeen +0045

MHWS	MHWN	MLWN	MLWS
5·3m	4·2m	2·0m	0·8m

Fishing and recreational hbr.
Outer harbour dries; wet dock
gates open approx HW±0300
between 0700 and 2000 –
phone HM for accurate times.
Identified by conspic white
swimming pool ½M W of
entrance and white signal tr W
of entrance.

ARBROATH TO
RATTRAY HEAD

Not a stretch of coast to be
trifled with in on-shore weather.
All vessels, including
recreational craft, must call
Aberdeen VTS (VHF Ch 12) when
3M from Fairway buoy to obtain
permission to enter Aberdeen
VTS area which is within 2M of
Aberdeen N pier and north of
57°07'·7N. An offing of ¾–1M
(but 2M in on-shore weather) is
sufficient as far as 57°20'N. S of
Cruden Bay a reef, 'The Scares',
runs 1M to seaward, buoyed
Fl.R.10s *AIS* off end. In thick
weather the 30m contour gives
clearance of all dangers, closing
the coast at Buchan Ness just S
of Peterhead. Peterhead alone
offers safe entry in almost any
conditions.

Tide The ebb, NE'ly, starts Dover
–0600 off Bell Rock and 2½hrs
earlier (Dover +0400) 5M off
Rattray Head. Similarly the
flood sets in later the further S.
The inshore streams change
some 2hrs earlier than this or
that shown in the *Admiralty
Tidal Atlas*.

Rattray Head Seas can be
dangerous in heavy weather.
Best rounded at slack water, 1M
off (this clears inshore dangers
and leaves area of steepest seas
to seaward). In bad conditions
pass five miles off and if
necessary more.

Passage lights	BA No
Scurdie Ness Fl(3)20s38m23M Racon(T) (–)	3220
Girdle Ness Fl(2)20s56m22M Racon(G) (——·)	3246
Buchan Ness Fl.5s40m18M Racon(O) (———)	3280
Rattray Head Fl(3)30s28m18M Racon(M) (——)	3304

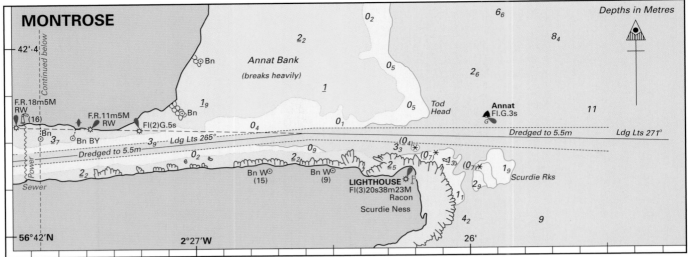

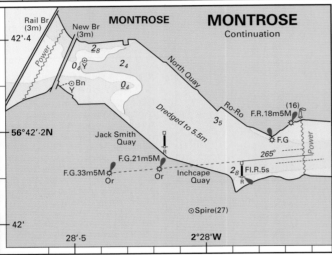

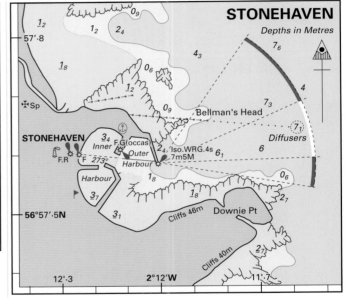

Approach Channel bounded by drying rock ledges for ½M from a bar (0·5m). Outlying dangers Knuckle Rock (stb), Cheek Bush and Chapel Rock (port). Enter HW±0330.

Entrance and Berthing Steer with twin towers of church between the gap in piers until white pole Ldg marks (F.R) located, 299°. Keep strictly to line. Moderate SE swell causes very awkward swell in entrance. Berth at pontoons in inner harbour, minimum depth 2·5m.

Signals F.R on E pier when hbr closed.

Facilities Water and electricity on pontoons, showers, stores, fuel at garage. EC Wednesday. Rly.

☎/VHF HM 01241 872166, VHF 11.

OFF-SHORE ANCHORAGE

Lunan Bay offers temporary anchorage in off-shore winds, either close to S shore (no further W than Ethie village) or under Boddin Point at N end. Subject to swell.

MONTROSE

Chart BA 1438;
Imray C23
HW Aberdeen +0050

MHWS	MHWN	MLWN	MLWS
4·8m	3·8m	1·8m	0·6m

A busy commercial and oil port with ship movements round the clock. No special facilities for yachts. Very strong tides in channel and entrance.

Approach From S or N keep minimum ½M offshore. Enter on Ldg line 271°. 50m-wide channel dredged to a minimum of 4m. Hold Ldg line until abeam inner of two W unlit stone bns on S shore; then alter to 265° on inner Ldg line. Call VHF 12 *Montrose Port Control* 1hr before entry for permission and berthing instructions.

Entrance Best at slack water or first hour of flood. Avoid in strong on-shore weather; seas break in channel.

Berthing As instructed. Fender board essential; risk of damage from effect of tide especially on ebb.

Facilities of a commercial port.

☎/VHF HM 01674 672302, VHF 12.

STONEHAVEN

Chart BA 1438;
Imray C23
HW Aberdeen +0010

MHWS	MHWN	MLWN	MLWS
4·5m	3·6m	1·7m	0·6m

A good small fishing boat and holiday hbr 9ca N of Dunottar Castle (ruins). Outer harbour dredged 1·5m along piers but subject to silting. Inner harbour dries, sand and mud. Inner harbour closed with booms in bad weather.

Avoid in heavy onshore weather. Outer harbour subject to surge with onshore swell.

Approach Steer just S of W, giving good clearance to Downie Point and Bellman's Head. Pierhead lit DirWGR. F.G Lt (B Ball) on S Pier 'unsafe to enter'.

Entrance Keep up to stb after passing outer pier head.

Berthing In offshore weather alongside pier in outer harbour. Otherwise enter inner harbour and dry out against quays as directed.

Facilities Stores, water, showers. EC Wednesday.

☎/VHF HM 01569 762741, VHF 11 (occas).

ABERDEEN

Chart BA 1446;
Imray C23
HW Aberdeen HW

MHWS	MHWN	MLWN	MLWS
4·3m	3·4m	1·6m	0·6m

Busy oil and commercial port; not recommended except as a port of refuge/emergency. Well protected from S but open to NE; do not attempt on ebb in strong NE wind. Harbour works in progress (2013), consult www.aberdeen-harbour.co.uk.

Approach Ldg line 236° from Fairway RW Lt buoy. Keep S face of N pier just open.

Entrance Call *Aberdeen Port Control* for permission to enter or leave. Traffic signals from control tr:
• F.G. no entry
• F.R. no departure
• F.R. & F.G. Port closed

N pier and S breakwater floodlit.

Berthing As directed; usually in Victoria or Upper Dock.

Facilities Large town. Rly. Coaches. Dyce Airport 7M.

☎/VHF Port Control 01224 597000, VHF 12 .

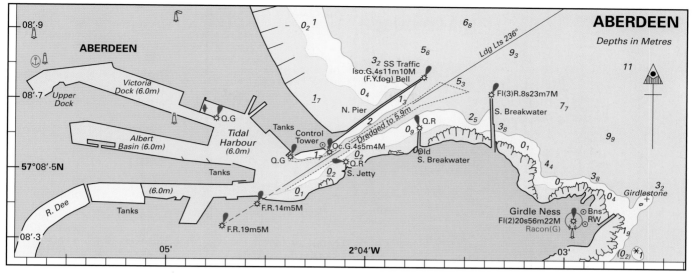

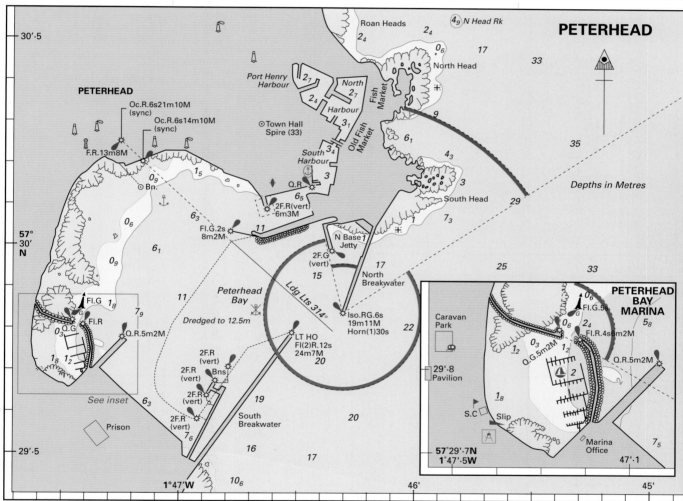

PETERHEAD

Chart BA 1438;
Imray C23

HW Aberdeen –0040

MHWS	MHWN	MLWN	MLWS
3·9m	3·1m	1·5m	0·5m

An invaluable all-weather hbr with modern marina. Much fishing and oil traffic. Power station chimney S of bay makes conspic landmark. Long breakwaters turn whole bay into hbr of refuge available in almost any weather.

Approach Headlands to N and S are foul for ¼M; then approach between SE and NE (Ldg lts 314°). Call *Peterhead Harbour* VHF 14 five minutes before reaching outer breakwater.

Anchorage In NW corner of bay 150m offshore below Ldg marks.

Berthing Marina in W corner of the Bay behind quay and marina breakwater; pontoon berths with water and power. Enter leaving G con buoy close to stb. Yachts may not use the main fishing hbr except with special permission. Call VHF 14 before leaving marina.

Facilities All stores in town 1M. Fuel (bowser) in main hbr or by can from marina; washing/drying at nearby caravan park.

☎/VHF HM 01779 474020 (483600 after hours), VHF 14 (port control and marina).

FRASERBURGH

Chart BA 1462;
Imray C23

HW Aberdeen –0110

MHWS	MHWN	MLWN	MLWS
3·7m	2·9m	1·4m	0·6m

A very busy fishing port, especially Sunday evenings. It has no special facilities for yachts though harbour authorities do their best to find a berth for visiting yachts. Useful as a port of refuge or if waiting for a fair tide. Can be dirty and noisy. Entrance dangerous in onshore gales.

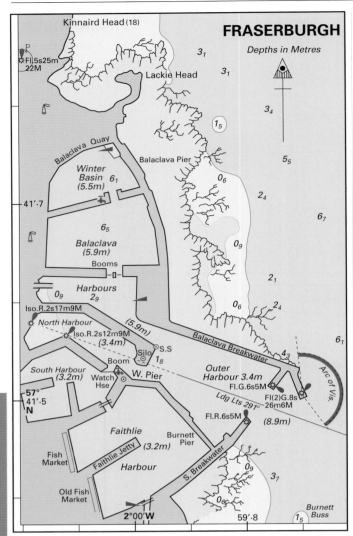

FRASERBURGH

Depths in Metres

Kinnaird Head (18)
Fl.5s25m 22M
Lackie Head
Balaclava Quay
Winter Basin (5.5m) 6₁
41'.7
Balaclava Pier
Balaclava (5.9m) 6₅
Booms
Harbours 2₉
Iso.R.2s17m9M
North Harbour
Iso.R.2s12m9M (3.4m)
(5.9m)
S.S
Silo 1₈
Boom
W. Pier
South Harbour (3.2m)
Watch Hse
57° 41'.5 N
Balaclava Breakwater
Outer Harbour 3.4m
Fl.G.6s5M
Fl(2)G.8s 26m6M
Ldg Lts 291°
Fl.R.6s5M (8.9m)
Arc of Vis.
Faithlie (3.2m)
Burnett Pier
Faithlie Jetty
Fish Market
Harbour
S. Breakwater
Old Fish Market
2°00'W
59'.8
Burnett Buss

Approach on 291°. Ldg Lts Iso.R, or old parish church spire (to S of dome) just open S of Balaclava Pier. Keep W silo on N Pier open S of Lt on Balaclava breakwater. Essential to call *Fraserburgh Harbour* on VHF 12 before entry or departure.

Berthing directions from watch-house or VHF 12; usually in S hbr.

Signals R flag/R Lt – entrance dangerous.
2B Balls/2R Lts vert – port closed.

☎/**VHF** HM 01346 515858, VHF 12 (24hrs).

MORAY FIRTH SMALL HARBOURS

In good weather and with enough time the small hbrs on the Moray Firth are available to yachts willing to dry out: Portsoy, Portknockie (good shelter from E, berth just inside entrance, beware of broken quay), Findochty, Hopeman (popular and crowded in season), Nairn (bars at river mouth and in channel; dredging in progress, pontoon berths; chart BA *1462*). Similarly Portmahomack on S side of entrance to Dornoch Firth, where there is also good anchorage in 2m, sand, with winds from SE to SW.

Beware stake nets and inconspic pot markers in approaches to these harbours.

MACDUFF

Chart BA 1462; Imray C23

HW Aberdeen –0100sp –0150np

MHWS	MHWN	MLWN	MLWS
3.9m	3.2m	1.5m	0.8m

Fishing hbr with three basins, least depth 2m; generally

crowded. Good shelter but entrance very rough in winds from W to N. Not to be attempted in onshore gales or in heavy swell.

Berthing In N-most basin clear of slipway.

Signals Ldg Lts October–March only. B ball/G Lt – hbr closed.

☎/**VHF** HM 01261 833962. VHF 12 (24hrs).

BANFF

Tidal data as Macduff

A flourishing historic town with a recreational hbr and small marina for vessels <10m, though larger vessels can dry out alongside New Quay on clean sand. Access HW±0200. Do not attempt in strong N/NE winds or with heavy onshore swell. A useful hbr if W or NW winds make Macduff dangerous. Silting reported.

Entrance Approach on 295°, ldg Lts Q.R and Fl.R4s on two posts near the building above the beach. Dredged to 0·2m, after entry turn to port and keep towards E quay.

Berthing Six visitors' berths. Middle basin, depths up to 1·8m, Inner basin 1·2m or less. As directed by HM.

Facilities Shops, library, hospital.

☎/**VHF** HM (part time) VHF 12, 01261 815544 or 07770 646115.

WHITEHILLS

Chart BA 222

HW Aberdeen –0122sp –0137np

MHWS	MHWN	MLWN	MLWS
3·9m	3·1m	1·7m	0·7m

A small recreational hbr. Entrance dangerous with strong onshore winds or heavy swell.

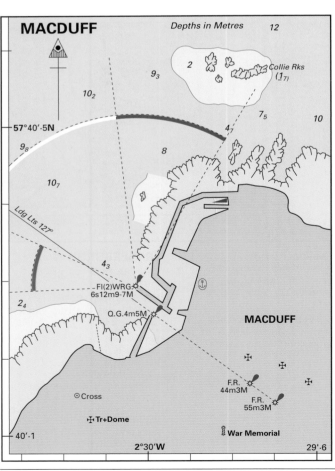

MACDUFF

Depths in Metres

57°40'.5N
Collie Rks (1₇)
Ldg Lts 127°
Fl(2)WRG 6s12m9-7M
Q.G.4m5M
MACDUFF
Cross
Tr+Dome
War Memorial
F.R. 44m3M
F.R. 55m3M
40'.1
2°30'W
29'.6

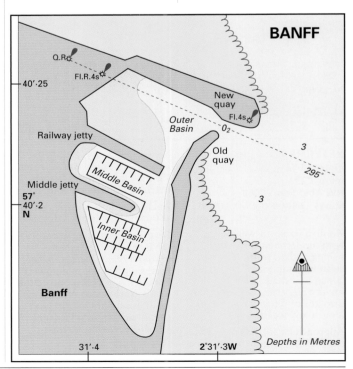

BANFF

Q.R
Fl.R.4s
40'.25
New quay
Fl.4s
Railway jetty
Outer Basin
Old quay
Middle jetty
57° 40'.2 N
Middle Basin
295°
Inner Basin
Banff
31'.4
2°31'.3W
Depths in Metres

MORAY FIRTH
Charts BA 115, 222, 223, 1078
Imray C23
Rattray Head to Inverness Firth

In heavy onshore weather keep 2M off the coast otherwise keep ½M off R Lt bn (Fl.10s10M) marking reef off Cairnbulg Point and at least 1M off Kinnaird Head in wind against tide conditions. Bombing range target float 4M E of Troup Head. W of Lossiemouth, beware of the Halliman Skerries, marked by an unlit beacon; these lie 1M offshore, NE of the conspicuous disused Covesea Skerries white lighthouse.

Tides, once past Kinnaird Head, are relatively weak and complex, except off headlands and in the approaches to the Inverness Firth. Close inshore between Rosehearty and Portknockie the flood tide runs east, not as shown in the *Tidal Stream Atlas*. With strong N'ly winds or large N'ly swell most of the harbours on this coast are

dangerous. Large scale charts are needed for the approach to Inverness Firth and the Caledonian Canal. (*For canal see W coast of Scotland*).

Rattray Head to Wick

Surprisingly heavy seas can be met in W or NW winds, otherwise this 65M passage presents no problem. Once 10M clear of Kinnard Head, tides are weak until approaching the Caithness coast where they reach 2kn at springs between Clyth Ness and Noss Head.

Passage lights	BA No
Kinnaird Head Fl.5s25m22M	3332
Chanonry Point Oc.6s12m12M	3440
Tarbat Ness Fl(4)30s53m24M Racon(T) (–)	3506
Noss Head Fl.WR.20s53m25/21M	3544
Duncansby Head Fl.12s67m22M Racon(T) (–)	3558

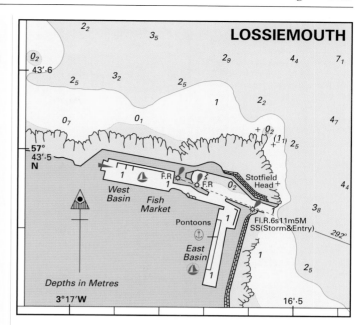

LOSSIEMOUTH

Depths in Metres

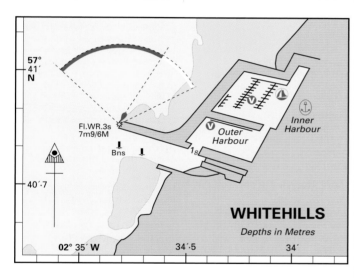

WHITEHILLS

Depths in Metres

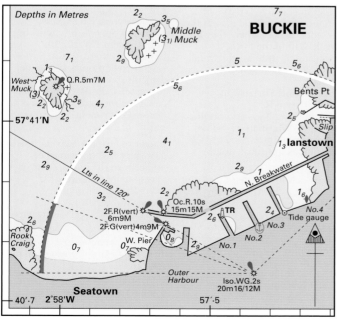

BUCKIE

Seatown

Approach from the N or NW. Head for end of N pier, Fl.WR.3s.

Entrance is narrow, keep close to N pier, leaving bns, which mark drying rocks, to stb. At MLWS min depth is 1·5m. Beware of surge. There is a very sharp turn to port into outer hbr. Then go diagonally across to enter inner hbr.

Berthing On end of pontoons in inner harbour or on pontoon in outer harbour.

Facilities Stores, fuel, laundry, Wi-Fi.

☏/**VHF** HM 01261 861291, *Mobile* 07906 135786, VHF 14.

BUCKIE
Chart BA 1462;
Imray C23
HW Aberdeen –0130sp –0145np

MHWS	MHWN	MLWN	MLWS
4·1m	3·2m	1·6m	0·7m

A busy fishing port with four basins, drawbridge between No.3 and No.4. Safe entry in all weathers. 2·2m minimum in entrance and 3m alongside. Beware of reflected swell in W winds.

Signals Three B balls/3F.R (vert) – hbr closed.

Berthing As directed, usually No.3 basin.

Facilities Shops, water, showers, fuel.

☏/**VHF** HM 01542 831700. VHF 12 (24h).

LOSSIEMOUTH
Chart BA 1462;
Imray C23
HW Aberdeen –0125sp –0200np

MHWS	MHWN	MLWN	MLWS
4·1m	3·2m	1·6m	0·6m

Recreational hbr, identified by Covesea Skerries LtHo to W of town. Avoid in winds Force 6 or over from N to SE.

Entrance 1·2m in entrance MLWS but silting possible; best HW±0400. Beware strong current setting N across entrance. Call before entering.

Berthing Pontoons along W side of inner (S) hbr or on N side of west hbr; visitors' berths.

Facilities Stores. Showers, laundry, key and electricity card from HM or Steam Boat Inn. Diesel by can.

Signals Ldg Lts (F.R 292°) when entrance is safe.

☏/**VHF** HM 01343 813066, VHF 12. Lossiemouth Cruising Club 813767.

BURGHEAD
Chart BA 1462;
Imray, C23
HW Aberdeen –0120sp –0150np

MHWS	MHWN	MLWN	MLWS
4·1m	3·2m	1·6m	0·6m

A commercial hbr used by local fishing and grain vessels. Access can be difficult in onshore winds or swell.

Entrance 1·5m LWS. Tide gauge. Keep 15m off extension of N pier hd then keep mid-channel; at night identify Lts on N pier spur (Q.R) and S pier (Q.G), both vis only from SW, and keep G open S of R.

Berthing Only as directed by HM and may not always be possible.

Facilities Stores, chandler, water, fuel, buses. BL cranes ☏ 01343 835360 will lift a yacht in slings here and elsewhere in the area.

☏/**VHF** HM 01343 835337, VHF 12, 14.

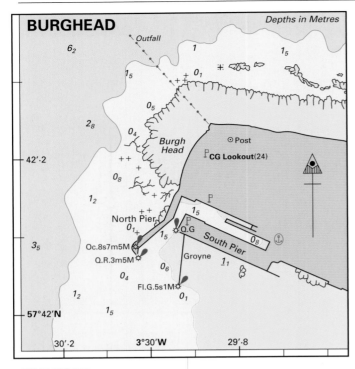

BURGHEAD

Depths in Metres

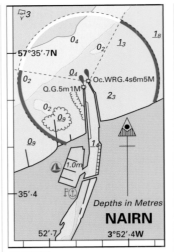

NAIRN

Depths in Metres

FINDHORN

Chart BA 223

HW Aberdeen –0120sp –0150np

MHWS	MHWN	MLWN	MLWS
4·2m	3·2m	1·6m	0·6m

This is the most sheltered natural hbr in the Moray Firth and is a main yachting centre, however there is a bar. Entrance is dangerous in strong NE winds or in a heavy NE swell.

Bar There is more than 1·0m at half tide. Strangers are advised to enter HW–0200 to HW+0100. www.rfyc.net has latest information.

Approach Make for the RW spherical landfall buoy. The land is low, to the west it is wooded and to the east there is a conspicuous windsock. From here it is possible, through binoculars, to see the outermost port-hand buoy.

Entrance From the RW approach buoy make for the outer bar buoy, R can Fl.R. Thence follow the lateral buoys, leaving the three bns, which are on drying sands, about 30m to port.

Anchorage Anchor between the south end of the moorings and the twin stone piers on the east bank. Good holding in sand, but tide may run at up to 4kn. Visitors' moorings or alongside pontoon berths may be available from Findhorn Boatyard, ☎ 01309 690099.

Facilities Water and electricity at N pier (dries). Boatyard with chandlery, slip etc., shop, pubs, showers and restaurant at Royal Findhorn YC ☎ 01309 690247.

NAIRN

Chart BA 223, 1462; Imray C23

HW Aberdeen –0112sp –0153np

MHWS	MHWN	MLWN	MLWS
4·3m	3·3m	1·6m	0·7m

A non-commercial hbr with a drying entrance.

Approach Keep in W sector of Lt Oc.WRG on E pier head. Y waiting buoy 2ca NNW of pier heads.

Entrance HW–0230 to HW+0100, difficult in fresh northerly winds, dangerous with heavy onshore swell.

Berthing In basin, 1m at pontoons, soft mud, three berths 1·8m against E wall.

☎ HM 01667 452877 or 456008.

INVERNESS FIRTH

Chart BA 1078; Imray C23

HW Aberdeen –0050sp –0150np

MHWS	MHWN	MLWN	MLWS
4·6m	3·6m	1·7m	0·8m

DS Chanonry Point W Dover–0410 E Dover+0115

Tides may reach 4kn at Chanonry Point and also at the Kessock Br. Elsewhere they are weak. Within the Firth, if awaiting the tide for the canal, suitable anchorage/berthing can be had:
• Anchor off Fortrose in offshore winds
• Enter River Ness and berth at Inverness Marina (*see below*).
• Anchor temporarily 2ca NW of sea lock entrance, good holding.

Approach From Chanonry Point Oc.6s12m15M with sufficient water and suitable rise of tide there are two passages via Kessock Br to Inverness or Clachnaharry for the Caledonian Canal.
• **Up the middle of the Firth** Steer 220° for Munlochy Safe Water RW buoy(Fl 10s) at 57°32'·9N 4°07'·6W, avoiding Skate Bank to stb, then on approx same course to G con Lt buoy (Fl.G.3s) at 57°30'·2N 4°12'·0W and then head towards the centre of the br.

• **Along the NW side of the Firth** Having passed Chanonry Point turn sharp to stb keeping fairly close to the shore. Leave two red can buoys to port (these mark the NE extremity of Skate Bank) then make for a WP at 57°34'·53N 4°08'·0W which is SW of Fortrose. It may be convenient to anchor near here in offshore winds if awaiting the tide. Follow the NW shore to a WP 57°31'·2N 4°12'·4W which is SW of the ruins of Kilmuir church which can best be detected by a stone wall round the graveyard and some yew trees. Then head 160° SE to G con Lt buoy Fl.G.3s at 57°30'·3N 4°12'·0W, before heading for the br.

INVERNESS

Chart and tidal data as for Inverness Firth

The capital of the Highlands with a modern marina at entrance of River Ness. Close to the Caledonian Canal. Excellent rail and road connections. City centre ¾M.

Entrance River Ness is narrow but deep. Beware of unmarked spit on W side of entrance; there are strong cross tides. Give way to commercial craft, main activity HW–0200 to HW. Call *Inverness Pilots* on VHF 12 to check channel is clear and maintain listening watch.

Berthing In marina as directed or near the end of pontoons close to the entrance.

Facilities As expected of a modern marina. Wi-Fi. City centre ¾M.

☎/VHF 01463 220501. *Inverness Marina* VHF 12 (office hours).

CALEDONIAN CANAL

Entrance Clachnaharry sea lock is 1M beyond River Ness, normally open during working hours except LW ±0200: beware of extensive shoal to W side of river mouth. It may be difficult to wait in the entrance to the sea lock. Waiting in the canal before transiting is best at Seaport Marina in Muirtown basin.

Facilities Seaport Marina. Fuel, gas, showers; supermarkets adjacent to the basin, easy transport to Inverness for trains/coaches. Chandlery, diesel, and repairs at Caley Marina, above the Muirtown flight.

See the Corpach entry, page 154, for further information on the canal.

☎/VHF Clachnaharry Sea Lock 01463 713896, VHF 74; Seaport Marina 233140; Caley Marina 236539.

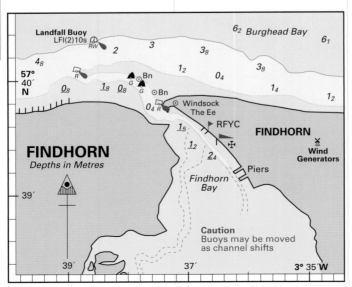

FINDHORN

Depths in Metres

Caution Buoys may be moved as channel shifts

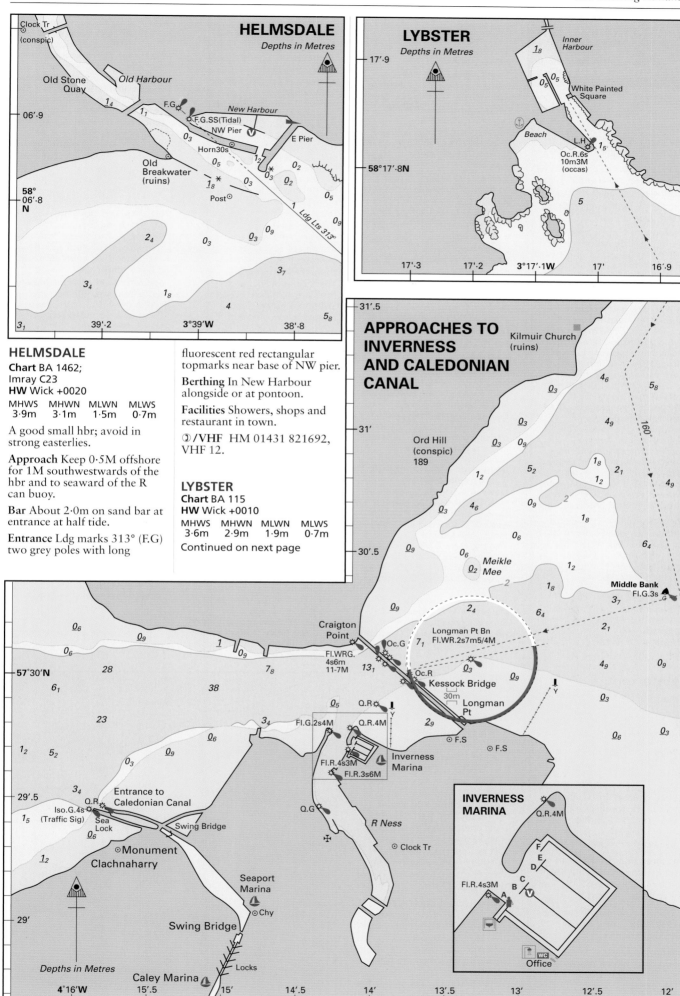

HELMSDALE
Depths in Metres

Clock Tr (conspic)

Old Stone Quay

Old Harbour

F.G.

F.G.SS(Tidal) NW Pier

New Harbour

E Pier

Horn30s

Old Breakwater (ruins)

Post

Ldg Lts 313°

LYBSTER
Depths in Metres

Inner Harbour

White Painted Square

Beach

L.H

Oc.R.6s 10m3M (occas)

HELMSDALE

Chart BA 1462;
Imray C23
HW Wick +0020

MHWS	MHWN	MLWN	MLWS
3·9m	3·1m	1·5m	0·7m

A good small hbr; avoid in strong easterlies.

Approach Keep 0·5M offshore for 1M southwestwards of the hbr and to seaward of the R can buoy.

Bar About 2·0m on sand bar at entrance at half tide.

Entrance Ldg marks 313° (F.G) two grey poles with long

fluorescent red rectangular topmarks near base of NW pier.

Berthing In New Harbour alongside or at pontoon.

Facilities Showers, shops and restaurant in town.

☎/**VHF** HM 01431 821692, VHF 12.

LYBSTER

Chart BA 115
HW Wick +0010

MHWS	MHWN	MLWN	MLWS
3·6m	2·9m	1·9m	0·7m

Continued on next page

APPROACHES TO INVERNESS AND CALEDONIAN CANAL

Kilmuir Church (ruins)

Ord Hill (conspic) 189

Meikle Mee

Middle Bank
Fl.G.3s

Craigton Point

Oc.G

Fl.WRG. 4s6m 11-7M

Oc.R

Kessock Bridge

Longman Pt Bn Fl.WR.2s7m5/4M

30m

Longman Pt

Q.R.

Q.R.4M

Fl.G.2s4M

F.S

F.S

Inverness Marina

Fl.R.4s3M

Fl.R.3s6M

Q.R

Iso.G.4s (Traffic Sig)

Sea Lock

Entrance to Caledonian Canal

Swing Bridge

Q.G

R Ness

Clock Tr

Monument Clachnaharry

Seaport Marina

Chy

Swing Bridge

Locks

Caley Marina

Depths in Metres

INVERNESS MARINA

Q.R.4M

F
E
D
C
B
A

Fl.R.4s3M

Office

Duncansby Head to Cape Wrath

GENERAL

BA Sailing Directions, *North Coast of Scotland* – NP52

BA *Tidal Atlas Orkney and Shetland Is* – NP209

CCC Sailing Directions, N and NE Coasts of Scotland and Orkney (including Pentland Firth)

Charts BA 1954, 2162, 2581, 35, 2250, 2249

Passage through or across the Pentland Firth, which is one of the most dangerous stretches of water in the British Isles, where tidal streams may reach 16kn, requires accurate timing. Reference to the BA *Tidal Atlas* is highly recommended. It should not be attempted at spring tides, wind over Force 4, wind against the tide or swell, or in poor visibility. Flotta in Scapa Flow is an important oil terminal and very large oil tankers use the Firth. However calm it may seem, all yachts should be thoroughly secured, safety harnesses worn etc. A reliable engine is desirable. The Merry Men of Mey is a particularly dangerous race which forms on the W going tide and must be avoided; it consists of an area of breaking seas reaching across the Firth from St John's Point to Tor Ness.

Passage lights	BA No
Duncansby Head Fl.12s67m22M Racon(T) (–)	3558
Pentland Skerries Fl(3)30s52m23M	3562
Stroma Fl(2)20s32m26M	3568
Dunnet Head Fl(4)30s105m23M	3574
C Wrath Fl(4)30s122m22M	3880

Sule Skerry Fl(2)15s34m21M Racon(T) (–)	3868

TIDAL STREAMS

From Freswick Bay (S of Duncansby Head) keep inshore where there is 10hr slack water.

Off Duncansby Head
Dover +0100W -0545E
To Westward of Dunnet Head Dover +0030W -0600E but close inshore W until -0430

Gill's Bay
Stream sets towards St John's Point for 9hr from Dover -0300

Brough Bay
HW Dover NW for 4hrs. Eddy continues to run NW on main E-going stream.

Brims Ness
HW Dover W for 6hrs at up to 8kn at springs

Cape Wrath
Inshore of Duslic (Stag) Rock always W

2M seaward of Duslic Rock
Dover -0145W +0415E

PASSAGE NOTES

All times refer to HW Dover

Pentland Firth E to W: the passage can be hazardous. The RNLI coxswains and HMs at Wick and Scrabster are always helpful. If approaching from the South, Freswick Bay, 3·5M south of Duncansby Head, is a useful anchorage in offshore conditions if waiting for the tide in the Firth. In the bay the tide runs N for 9hrs starting Dover–0545. Round Duncansby Head at Dover+0100 keeping close in with Dunnet Head just open of St John's Point: take the Inner Sound about ½M offshore. Pass the Men of Mey Rocks off St John's Point about 100m off. Do NOT pass these rocks before Dover+0300 or +0500 at springs (i.e. before 2hrs of ebb have run or 4h at springs): by this time the severe Merry Men of Mey Race will have moved north allowing safe passage round the point. If early, anchorage is available in W of Gill's Bay, but beware of fishermen's lines. With wind against the tide, give Dunnet Head a good clearance.

Pentland Firth W to E: this is somewhat easier, as no race forms while tide is favourable and wind with tide is more common. Leave Scrabster at Dover+0430 to arrive off Dunnet Hd at Dover +0530 as stream turns E'ly. Pass mid-way between St John's Point and Stroma steering S to avoid being set onto rocks S of Stroma (bn unlit). Then through middle of Inner Sd and give Duncansby Head a wide berth.

Via Orkneys the worst of the Pentland Firth can be partly avoided by passing through Hoy Sound and Scapa Flow.

Dunnet Head to Cape Wrath: The N coast of Scotland stretches 50M E to W. E of Strathy Point the coast is relatively low-lying and agricultural, beyond this the cliff scenery becomes more spectacular with the Sutherland mountains in the background. In NE winds anchorage can be had in Dunnet Bay behind Dunnet Head, Scrabster provides the only perfect shelter in virtually all conditions. In offshore winds, temporary anchorage may be had in numerous sandy bays but these are very dangerous if the wind changes N'ly and wind changes are often sudden. There are several anchorages in Loch Eriboll but they may be subject to severe squalls. Advantage can be taken of the continuous N going eddy to E of Strathay Point, off which, the W going tide starts at Dover +0030. But beware of turbulent seas off the point in wind against tide conditions. E of Cape Wrath there is a live firing range extending 4M out to sea: contact Stornoway coastguard for firing times. Duslic Rock lies ¾M NE of Cape Wrath Lt Ho; it covers at half tide though it can usually be seen in the swell. In calm conditions it is possible to pass inside the rock where the tide is nearly always W'ly, keeping well towards the steep-to headland, otherwise give it and Cape Wrath a wide berth, especially if a heavy swell is running or if the wind is against swell or tide.

Wick to E coast of Orkney: No special problems – keep at least 6M E of Pentland Skerries.

Wick to Scapa Flow: Reach a point 1M NE of Duncansby Head at Dover +0300 (nearly slack water) then make good a course of 001° to the W coast of S Ronaldsay. This goes across the tidal streams. If wind is in the W the passage can be safely made if less than Force 4.

Scrabster to W coast of Orkney and Stromness: This passage avoids the Firth. Time departure to arrive at Sound of Hoy at slack water (Dover +0530).

Scrabster to Scapa Flow: Time departure to arrive off Dunnet Hd at Dover –0600. Make good a course for a point about 1M S of Tor Ness – a strong favourable tide will then take you past Brims Point, round Cantick Head and E of Switha into Scapa Flow.

Scrabster to E coast of Orkney: This is a fast passage, do not attempt with E'ly winds over Force 3. Time departure to arrive off Dunnet Head at Dover +0530. Pass between Swona and Stroma. Constant updating of position is required to avoid being swept onto the islands or the Pentland Skerries. One should round Old Head by Dover –0330, when the tide turns and overfalls occur.

For more details and other possible passages consult the *CCC Sailing Directions.*

Lybster cont.

Small hbr 2½M WSW of Clyth Ness. Good refuge; entrance needs to be accurate, and difficult in strong easterlies.

Entrance Steer for W pier-head (Oc.R.6s occas) on 330°. Do not stray E of ldg line, rear mark W pole with W topmark above white painted square, front mark R pole with R topmark near LH. Keep up to W pier; beware set onto rocks and first pier to stb.

Berthing In outer harbour on innermost end of W pier using fender plank or in SE corner of inner basin (W part dries).

E or S side of inner basin 1·8m MLWS but only 1·0m at entrance to basin.

Facilities Showers, laundry, key from café. Hotel, stores ½M. EC Thursday.

WICK

Chart BA 1462; Imray C68
HW Wick HW

MHWS	MHWN	MLWN	MLWS
3·5m	2·8m	1·4m	0·7m

The hbr, at the head of Wick Bay 2½M S of Noss Head, consists of three basins. The Inner and Outer Harbours are the main fishing and leisure berths, and the River Harbour is the commercial area which must be avoided. It is an ideal port of departure for the Northern Isles or for timing a passage through strong tides of the Pentland Firth.

Approach and Entrance
Dangerous in strong winds between NE and S; heavy seas run into the bay. Hbr obscured until bay fully opened up. Both shores of Wick Bay are foul. Approach on 289°, DirIso.WRG.4s. Then steer for LtHo on S pier (W tr,

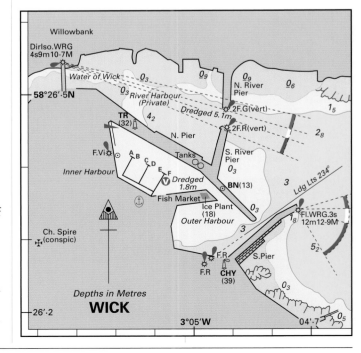

WICK

Fl.WRG.3s) on 270°–285°, i.e. in the W sector. Port Closed Signal: a black ball is hoisted by day, or a fixed Green light shown by night, on a prominent mast at South Head. Pass close N of pierhead and keep along N face (Ldg Lts F.R.234°).

Berthing Visitors should contact *Wick Harbour* by VHF (office hours) or telephone before arrival. Berth as directed, normally on pontoon F. Outside office hours you will be given the security code by telephone.

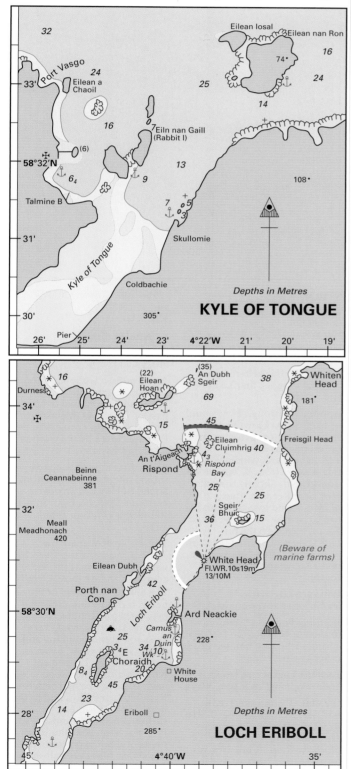

KYLE OF TONGUE

LOCH ERIBOLL

Facilities Electricity and water on pontoons. Showers. Launderette. Wi-Fi. Nearby supermarket. Rly to Inverness. Airport.

☎/**VHF** HM 01955 602030 VHF 14 (office hours or when vessel expected).

SCRABSTER

Chart BA 1462; Imray C68
HW Wick –0255

MHWS	MHWN	MLWN	MLWS
5.0m	3.7m	2.1m	0.8m

Hbr can be entered at all states of tide; complete shelter. It is used by Orkney Ro-Ro ferry,

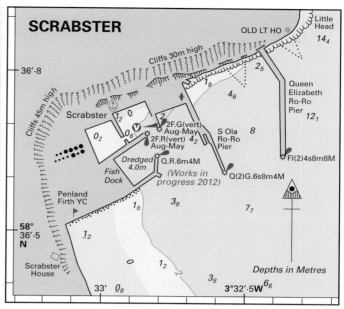

coasters and fishing vessels, and increasingly by service vessels to the oil and renewable energy industry. Development work is in progress (2012); further is planned, involving dredging and quay extension. It is essential to call *Scrabster Harbour* VHF 12 for berthing instructions before entry. www.scrabster.co.uk has the latest information.

Facilities Restaurant. No provisions. Water, diesel. Shops in Thurso, two miles. Bus.

☎/**VHF** HM 01847 892779. VHF 12 (24hr); radio contact poor from N and W until clear of Holborn Head.

KYLE OF TONGUE

Chart BA 1954; Imray C68
HW Wick –0350

MHWS	MHWN	MLWN	MLWS
4.7m	3.5m	1.8m	0.6m

The Kyle of Tongue contains a number of sheltered anchorages but entry during gales or strong N'lies is not recommended.

Anchorages

• Talmine, good protection except from N and E winds. Approach from N, but do not turn S until the W edge of the largest islet of Eiln nan Gaill (i.e. the westernmost) bears no less than 200°. Anchor in 5m S of small islet connected to shore by jetty. Sand. Shop 10 mins. Shelter from W and N in 5m off beach at S side of Eiln nan Gaill.
• Shelter from W and NW off Mol na Coinnle, a small bight on E of Eiln nan Ron. Anchorage is recognised by tin-roofed hut near foreshore. Uninhabited. Landing possible.
• On E side of Kyle just off small hbr of Skullomie. Entrance directly below house on hillside, best seen looking SE from Eiln nan Gaill. Keep well clear of broken wall to stb and towards E shore. Limited supplies at Coldbachie ½M.

LOCH ERIBOLL

Chart BA 2076; Imray C68
HW (Portnancon): Wick –0340sp –0255np

MHWS	MHWN	MLWN	MLWS
5.1m	4.1m	2.2m	1.1m

Loch Eriboll lies on W side of the high cliffs of Whiten Head. Funnelling produces extremely strong winds in SW'ly weather, when the entrance can be very rough; but good sheltered anchorages are available.

Anchorages
On E side
• In bays N and S of Ard Neackie, good shelter.
• In 7m off white house 1M to S. Fish farm cages extend S of Ard Neackie across whole of Camus an Duin. Pass N of cages and anchor inshore. (Fish Farm, VHF 14, helpful).
On W side
• Excellent anchorage in Rispond Bay, sand, but congested by fishing boat moorings.
• Admiralty buoy 4ca NNW of E Choraidh.
• In S of loch. Beware mussel farming; large buoys, long ropes.

Orkney

GENERAL

BA Tidal Atlas, Orkney and Shetland – NP209

For more details refer to:
CCC SD: N & NE Scotland and Orkney and Shetland
(separate volumes)
Shetland Islands Pilot Gordon Buchanan (Imray)

Anyone intending to cruise the islands should carry these sailing directions. Information given here is intended for passage-making boats.

Approaching from the E, Whitehall Harbour, (Stronsay) and Kirkwall are the best 'target' ports.

Though the Northern Isles provide fascinating cruising grounds, sailing here calls for particular attention to barometer trends and weather information. Essentially the flood runs SE and the ebb NW but there are many anomalies and back eddies round headlands and between the isles. In the main channels the tide changes approx Kirkwall +0100. Both tides and winds are stronger than in other UK waters: the avoidance of both wind-over-tide and swell-against-tide conditions take on special importance in entrances, between islands and off major headlands. There are numerous secluded anchorages. In Orkney there are marinas at Stromness, Kirkwall and Pierowall. Many islands have piers or jetties which may be used subject to commercial traffic, visitors mooring buoys are also available. Berthing fees are valid for use in all marinas/harbours, it may be advantageous to pay for a week rather than individual days.

See www.orkneymarinas.co.uk for latest details. This site has a link which provides very useful Sailing Notes.

Lobster pot markers are numerous. Mussel rafts and salmon farms abound in sheltered waters. Salmon farms are marked with Y buoys and flashing lights.

Orkney has probably the highest concentration of archaeological sites anywhere in NW Europe. It is famous for its settlements dating from the 4th or 3rd millennia BC, e.g. Skara Brae, its chambered tombs demonstrating engineering skill and ingenuity, many open to the casual visitor, and its standing stones such as the Ring of Brodgar. Many of these can be visited by sailing to a suitable anchorage and walking or hiring a bicycle.

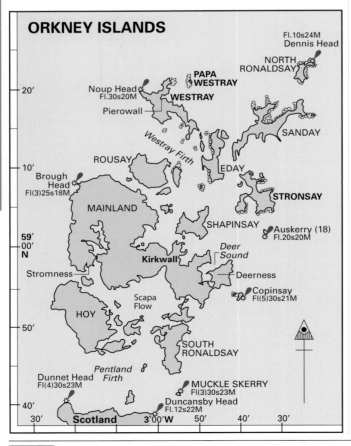

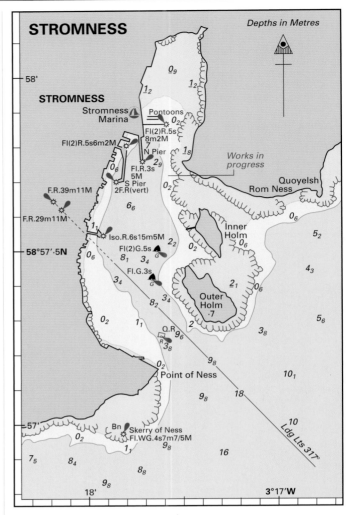

STROMNESS

Chart BA 2568;
Imray C68
HW Wick –0225sp –0135np

MHWS	MHWN	MLWN	MLWS
3·6m	2·7m	1·4m	0·7m

An excellently sheltered port; no tidal streams, marina at N end of bay.

Approach Through Hoy Sound or from Scapa Flow. Very strong tides in approaches, not to be undertaken in bad weather or with wind against tide. Easiest from W with flood tide, keeping slightly towards Hoy side. Keep on transit 104° of Hoy Sound low and high Lts (on Graemsay – *see plan Scapa Flow*), then keep the bn Fl.WG.4s well open of the shore until abeam chapel ruins, then mid-channel or slightly to south.

Entrance Ldg marks lit 317° leading up buoyed channel.

Berthing Pontoon berths in marina to N of Ro-Ro terminal. Visitors >14m on hammerheads otherwise on S fingers.

Facilities Fuel, water, laundry, good shopping, cycle hire. Wi-Fi.

☎/VHF Piermaster 01856 850744. Marina *Mobile* 07810 465825, VHF 14. *Stromness Harbour* VHF 14. *Orkney Harbour Radio* VHF 20 gives local weather forecast and *Notices to Mariners* at 0915 and 1715. *Orkney Harbour VTS* VHF 11.

SCAPA FLOW

Chart BA 35;
Imray C68

An inland sea with many good anchorages, entered from the W through the Sound of Hoy, passing north of Graemsay, or from the South. Passages to the East are closed by the wartime Churchill Barriers.

All yachts entering Scapa Flow should obtain clearance: from Sound of Hoy call *Stromness Harbour* VHF 12, from South call *Orkney Harbour Radio* VHF 11.

The whole of Scapa Flow contains many historic wrecks with surrounding restricted areas particularly near Cava Is. The ebb out of Sound of Hoy is fierce; if conditions allow, it may be better, coming from W, to enter from S keeping very close to the shore of Hoy and South Walls. Lyness, former naval base, has 120m quay with 8m alongside. Good anchorage can be had between Rysa Little and Hoy, and to the north, in Howton Bay, sheltered from all winds. Scapa Pier (tug base) has 80m with 6m depth, but very exposed to the SW. St Mary's (small shop)

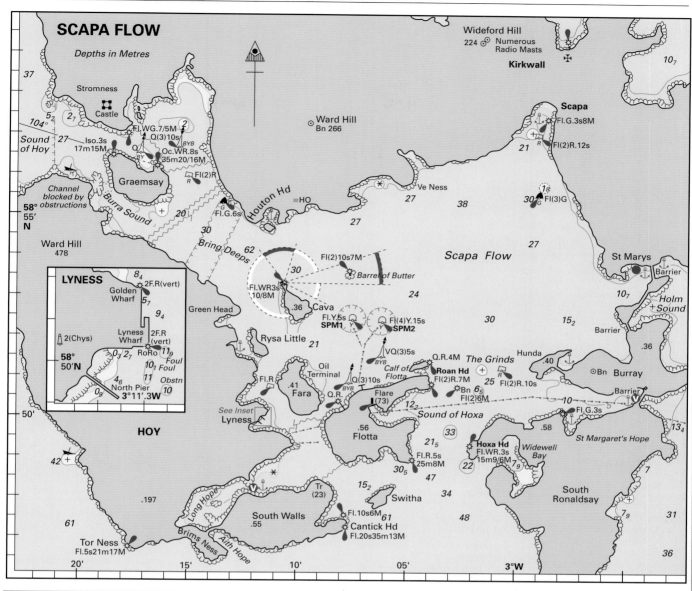

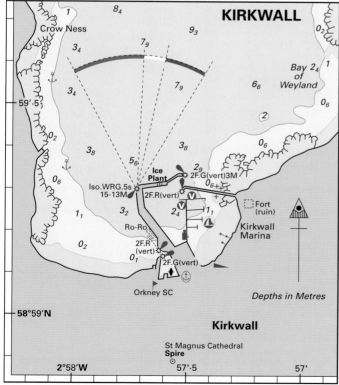

is convenient for a visit to the Italian chapel on Lamb Holm. Long Hope, to the east of the narrows, is useful in order to ensure accurate timing for the Pentland Firth.

KIRKWALL

Chart BA 1553; Imray C68
HW Wick –0042

MHWS	MHWN	MLWN	MLWS
3·0m	2·4m	1·3m	0·6m

Principal town of Orkney. Spire of cathedral conspic.

Approach Easiest from E through Shapinsay Sound, turning S when cathedral bears 190°. By night keep in W sectors of WRG Lts on Helliar Holm and outer pier-head. Tide negligible in Kirkwall Bay.

Berthing In marina to E of Ice Plant. Anchoring possible between W pier-head and Crow Ness Point to W but holding reported poor.

Facilities Most, fuel, no chandler. Showers at SC. Wi-Fi.

☎/VHF Piermaster 01856 872292. Marina *Mobile* 07810 465835, VHF 14. HM 01856 873636, VHF 14 (office hours).

Elwick Bay on Shapinsay, clean sand but weed round edges, offers a peaceful alternative. Approach S and W of Helliar Holm LtHo and anchor in 2½ to 3m off village or use visitors' mooring. E side obstructed by fish farm.

PIEROWALL, WESTRAY

Chart BA 2562, 3299; Imray C68
HW Wick –0150

MHWS	MHWN	MLWN	MLWS
3·7m	2·8m	1·4m	0·6m

See plan on page 138.

Pierowall Harbour at S end of Papa Sound between Westray and Papa Westray comprises a ferry pier with a marina at Gill Pt and anchorages at the head of the bay.

Approach From W and N via Papa Sound keep towards the Papa Westray shore. This entrance requires caution. A tide race forms rapidly at N end of Papa Sound as soon as ebb sets in. From S and E note that

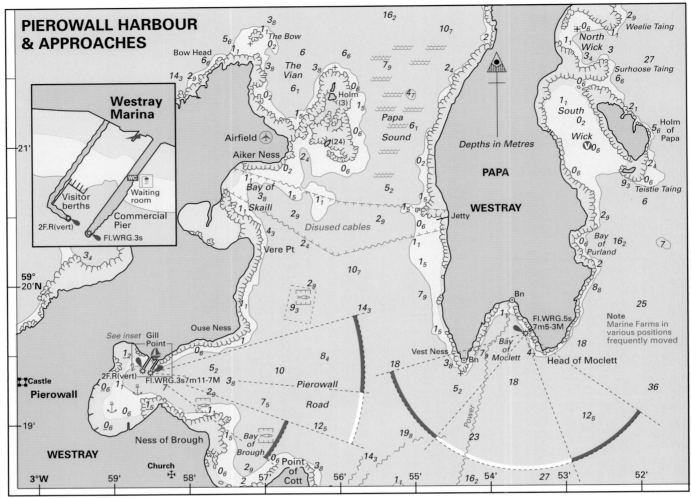

PIEROWALL HARBOUR & APPROACHES

Westray Marina

Skerry of Skelwick (off our plan) extends 6ca N from shore. White sector of Lt on Gill Pt leads in, 280°, but Lt is weak compared with nearby shore lights.

Berthing Pontoon berths (April–October) in small marina at Gill Pier.

Anchorage 50m off Gill Pier close to moorings in least depths 3·7m or on W side of bay in 1·8m.

Facilities Village on W shore of bay, shops, hotel. Diesel from ferry pier. Flights and ferry to Kirkwall.

☏/VHF Piermaster 01857 677216. HM 01857 677273. Marina *Mobile* 07787 364934. VHF 14.

STRONSAY

Chart BA 2562, 3299; Imray C68

HW Wick –0300

MHWS	MHWN	MLWN	MLWS
3·4m	2·8m	1·2m	0·9m

Whitehall Harbour off the village at the N end of Stronsay offers good shelter.

Approach Enter by buoyed N channel, dredged to Ro-Ro terminal. Keep buoys close aboard. Do not attempt E entrance without local knowledge.

Berthing Secure along seaward end of W pier or on W side of E pier, clear of Ro-Ro berth and consult HM; or anchor in 3m between pier ends or elsewhere in bay.

Facilities Provisions. Showers in hostel. Hotel. Flights and ferry to Kirkwall.

☏ HM 01857 616257.

ORKNEY TO SHETLAND

Charts BA 1942, 1119, 2249, 2250, 3283

Passage lights	BA No
Noup Head Fl.30s79m20M	3736
N Ronaldsay Fl.10s43m24M	3722
Start Point Fl(2)20s24m18M	3718
Skaden, Fair Is Fl(4)30s32m22M	3750
Skroo, Fair Is Fl(2)30s80m22M	3756
Foula Fl(3)WR.15s36m18/14M	3860
Sumburgh Head Fl(3)30s91m23M AIS	3766
Bressay Fl(2)20s18m10M	3776

If making the passage from the W of Orkney, give Mull Head at the N end of Papa Westray a berth of 5M since a violent race forms here with tides reaching 6kn. From the North Sound or the E of Orkney the passage is much easier, with Fair Isle making a convenient port of call.

A traffic routing scheme specifies a westbound lane only to the north of Fair Isle, but both eastbound and westbound lanes between Fair Isle and N Ronaldsay.

The tides run generally NW and SE at up to 2kn apart from a race off the S end of Fair Isle and the notorious race off Sumburgh Head which should be given a berth of 3M. If proceeding round the heads from Lerwick to Scalloway the latter can be avoided by keeping close in to Sumburgh Head.

In poorer weather the best route from Westray, once clear of Orkney, is to make for Scalloway. This avoids the worst of the turbulence.

STRONSAY

Shetland

For more details refer to: CCC SD, *Shetland* or *Shetland Islands Pilot* Gordon Buchanan (Imray). It is useful to carry *BA Tidal Atlas, Orkney and Shetland – NP209*. There is useful information on www.shetlandmarinas.com and www.lerwick-harbour.co.uk/yachts. The passage ports covered here comprise Fair Isle; on the east Lerwick, the main port, and Balta Sound, Unst; on the west, Ura Firth (Hillswick), Vaila Sound (Walls) and Gruting Voe, and Scalloway. Grutness Voe on the E coast just N of Sumburgh provides a convenient first anchorage coming from the S. (Beware of two rocks awash at LW in entrance: enter with head of bay on 225° or less, or round S headland very close). Many small boat marinas have been built. Generally they are occupied by local boats but some have one or two visitors' berths, watch out for depth. Some have showers. Charge usually £10/day. Recommended are: Skeld 60°09′N 1°27′W, sheltered. Aith 60°17′N 1°22′W, good facilities, if too shallow use pier. Voe (Olna Firth) 60°21′N 1°16′W. Brae 60°24′N 1°22′W Delta Boating Club, laundry, small chandlery. Burra Voe (Yell), if too shallow use pier or anchor. Vidlin 60°22′N 1°08′W. In addition many piers may be used but don't obstruct ferries or local fishermen. There is a plentiful choice of anchorages, but beware of heavy loose weed; however, the water is usually clear enough to avoid this. Tides are strong around headlands where races, or 'rosts' occur; also, Yell Sound should be avoided in wind over tide conditions.

It is best to stock up with provisions and fuel at either Lerwick or Scalloway. The islands are rich in archaeology, notably near Grutness Voe, the Iron Age village at Old Scratness, and Jarlshof, believed to have been inhabited for more than 4,200 years; also the best broch to be found anywhere is on the island of Mousa. The Shetland Isles are one of the last wilderness areas in Europe and are noted for their wildlife; the coastline is probably more dramatic than that of Orkney.

FAIR ISLE
Chart BA 2562, 3299
HW Lerwick –0010

MHWS	MHWN	MLWN	MLWS
2·2m	1·7m	1·0m	0·6m

The secure anchorage of North Haven on the NE side offers a useful half-way stop between Orkney and the main islands of Shetland, apart from its particular charm and ornithological interest.

Both South Haven and South Harbour are full of rocks and should be avoided except with detailed local knowledge.

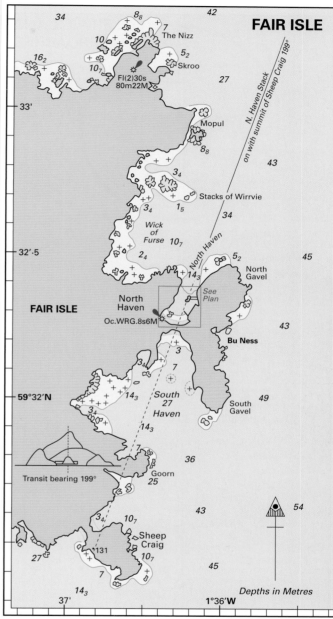

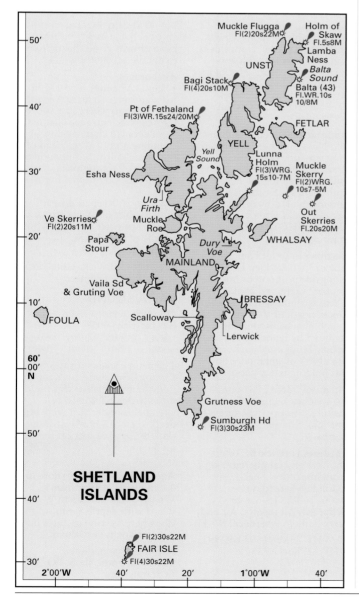

SHETLAND ISLANDS

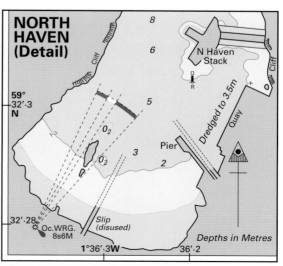

N Haven is uncomfortable in strong NE winds but usually tenable in summer. Enter on 199° keeping N Haven Stack on with summit of Sheep Craig behind. Keep W of Stack now incorporated in rock breakwater. Night entry in white sector of Oc light.

Berthing at quay on port hand inside (N end is used by ferry) or S side of pier.

Facilities Showers and meals at Bird Observatory. Shop 1½M. Water on quay. Large fenders are available on the quay for use by visitors.

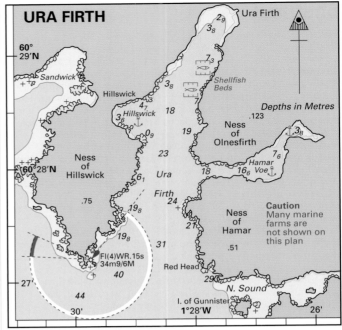

URA FIRTH

Depths in Metres

1°28'W

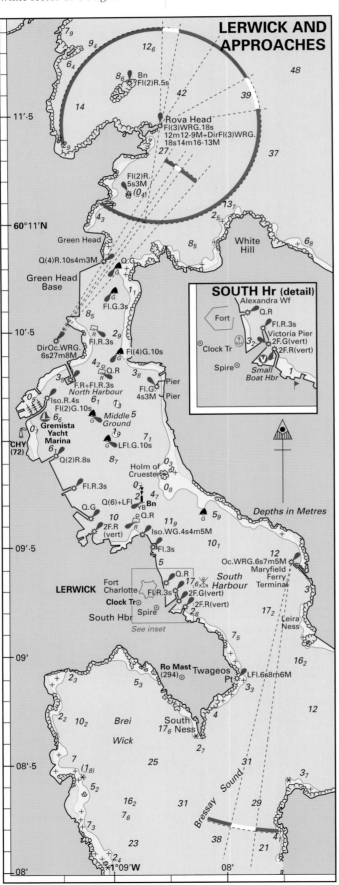

LERWICK AND APPROACHES

SOUTH Hr (detail)

Depths in Metres

LERWICK

Chart BA 3271
HW Lerwick HW

MHWS	MHWN	MLWN	MLWS
2·1m	1·7m	0·9m	0·5m

The capital of the Shetland Isles. A busy hbr with considerable oil, commercial and fishing traffic. Convenient and easy to enter with good berthing for yachts. Hbr of first choice bound to or from Scandinavia. www.lerwick-harbour.co.uk has a useful yacht pack.

Approach High cliffs in Bressay and Noss may be visible from a long way off. Entry S of Bressay is easier, with well lit and sheltered funnel-shaped approach. N channel is narrow and much used by oil rig vessels. Call *Lerwick Port Control* VHF 12 before entering.

Berthing In small boat hbr on S side of Victoria Pier. Lie alongside pontoon or outside another yacht and contact HM. There is a pontoon in Albert Dock, north of Victoria Pier, which may be used if not required by tenders from cruise liners. Temporary anchorage possible S of small boat hbr, but holding is not good.

Gremista Yacht Harbour has NO space or facilities for casual visitors. Bressay (½M across hbr) has two quiet visitors' berths.

Facilities Lerwick BC offers showers and launderette, key from hbr office. Fuel (Monday–Saturday) 0900–1630. Gas can be delivered. All repairs. Air and ferry daily to Aberdeen. Wi-Fi.

☎/VHF HM 01595 692991, VHF 12. Fuel 692379.

URA FIRTH

Chart BA 3295
HW Lerwick –0220

MHWS	MHWN	MLWN	MLWS
2·0m	1·6m	0·8m	0·4m

At NE corner of St Magnus Bay. Wide, lit, S-facing entrance approachable in any weather. Firth affords good shelter. Keep to middle on entering.

Anchorages
• Hamar Voe on E side 1M in from entrance to firth. Anchor in 4–10m anywhere just above the 1ca wide entrance channel. With detailed chart or careful sounding a pool at the head of the Voe, shallow but no hidden dangers, offers complete security. Good holding but no supplies.
• Hillswick. Keep mid-firth until the bay on W shore is well open, then enter steering W for middle of bay. Anchor in 4–6m, holding poor.

Facilities Hillswick. Hotel, PO, stores, diesel, engineer.

BALTA SOUND

Chart BA 3299
HW Lerwick –0055

MHWS	MHWN	MLWN	MLWS
2·3m	1·8m	0·9m	0·4m

The main channel is the S Channel, 3ca wide, lit. Keep in mid-channel. Heavy seas build up in strong SE winds. N Channel is under ½ca wide but deep: keep close to Unst shore on 209° passing ½ca off the reef on Swinna Ness and ½ca E of the G bn.

Anchorage Best off N shore in 4–8m just W of Sandison's Wharf. Small marina to W of wharf with depths 0·6m. Elsewhere as wind dictates but head of Voe is very shoal.

Facilities Water, diesel, boatyard, hotel, shop. PO ¼M. Boat museum.

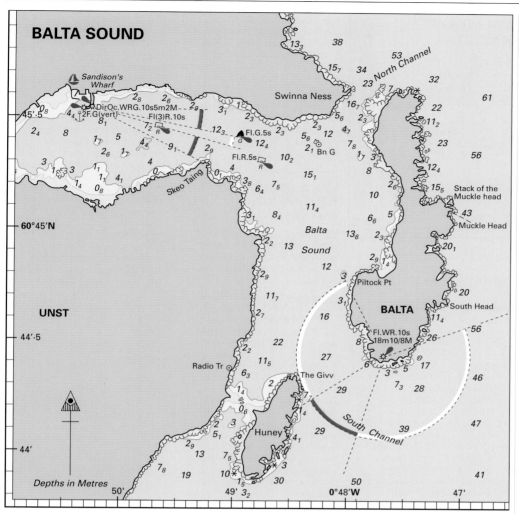

BALTA SOUND

UNST

60°45'N

44'·5

44'

Depths in Metres

(labels within chart)
Sandison's Wharf
DirOc.WRG.10s5m2M
2F.G(vert)
Fl(3)R.10s
Skeo Taing
Fl.G.5s
Bn G
Fl.R.5s
Swinna Ness
North Channel
Stack of the Muckle head
Muckle Head
Balta Sound
Piltock Pt
BALTA
Fl.WR.10s 18m10/8M
South Head
Radio Tr
The Givv
South Channel
Huney

60°45'N · 45'·5 · 44'·5 · 44'
50' · 49' · 0°48'W · 47'

SCALLOWAY

Chart BA 3294
HW Lerwick –0150

MHWS	MHWN	MLWN	MLWS
1·6m	1·3m	0·6m	0·5m

A convenient port of arrival from S and W with sheltered anchorage on W coast of mainland. Hbr protected by numerous islands. Entry should be possible in all weathers, but great care needed in strong SW winds.

Approach Of the two approaches, the North Channel is the easier and safer.

North Channel Enter between Hildasay Island and Sanda Stour keeping in mid-channel to avoid the dangerous rock close north of Hildasay. Pass between Burwick Holm and Langa keeping 2ca off Langa to avoid the fish farm on the island's E side, and then keep 1ca off Point of the Pund to clear the drying Whaleback Skerry to stb.

South Channel Enter between Fugla Ness and Bulia Skerry. Keep the Fugla Ness light between 032° and 082° in the W sector.

Note the two dangers, Bulia Skerry and Helia Baa, which can cause heavy breaking seas across the entrance during southwesterly gales. At such times the South Channel is not recommended.

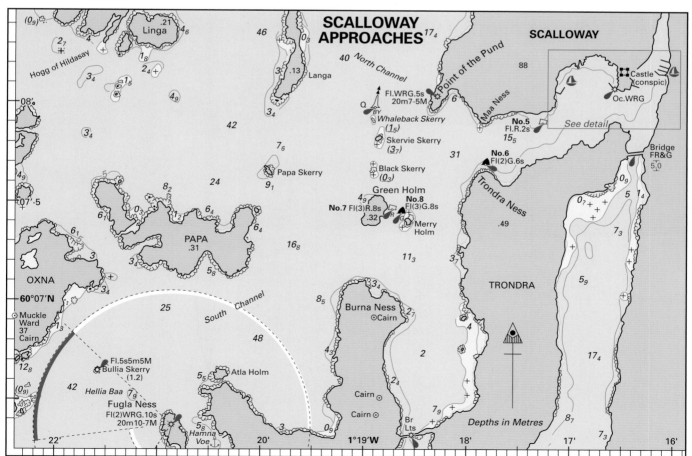

SCALLOWAY APPROACHES

SCALLOWAY

(labels within chart)
Linga
Hogg of Hildasay
North Channel
Langa
Fl.WRG.5s 20m7-5M
Point of the Pund
Maa Ness
Castle (conspic)
Oc.WRG
Whaleback Skerry
Skervie Skerry
No.5 Fl.R.2s
See detail
Papa Skerry
Black Skerry
Bridge FR&G
Green Holm
No.6 Fl(2)G.6s
Trondra Ness
No.7 Fl(3)R.8s
No.8 Fl(3)G.8s
Merry Holm
PAPA
TRONDRA
OXNA
Muckle Ward Cairn
South Channel
Burna Ness Cairn
Fl.5s5m5M
Bullia Skerry
Hellia Baa
Atla Holm
Fugla Ness Fl(2)WRG.10s 20m10-7M
Hamna Voe
Cairn
Cairn
Br Lts
Depths in Metres

60°07'N
08'
07'·5

22' · 20' · 1°19'W · 18' · 17' · 16'

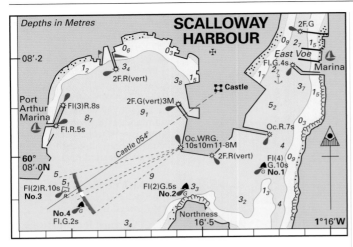

From a position between the two dangers bring Scalloway Castle just open N of Trondra Ness on 054° and pass either between Green Holm and Merry Holm, leaving Green Holm close to port, or turn N to enter N of Whaleback Skerry.

At night LtHos on N Havra Fl(3)WRG.12s and Point of Pund (Fl.WRG.5s) provide easy night-time access via North Channel. For South Channel approach Fugla Ness light in SW'ly white sector to 1½ca and round the point northwards to anchor in Hamna Voe and wait for daylight.

Entrance Keep mid-channel between Maa Ness and Trondra Ness, thence follow the hbr buoyage. Note that a day/night sector light provides a white sector over the deepest part of the bar in depths of 6·6m.

Anchorages and Berthing
• Scalloway BC welcomes visitors to its pontoon on W side of hbr. Showers, Laundry. ☎ 01595 880388 (evenings and weekends).
• Port Arthur Marina. Small local boats, few free berths. Contact Scalloway BC or ☎ 880649.
• Off Scalloway between Gallow Hill and Blacks Ness, 6–10m soft mud. Better shelter in W winds E of the castle.
• East Voe Marina. Well protected. Few visitors' berths by arrangement. ☎ 880476.

• In Hamna Voe on W Burra just inside Fugla Ness. Almost land-locked and safe in bad summer weather (*also night – see above*); but busy fishing hbr, crowded, bottom foul with old moorings.

Facilities Scalloway – water, stores, fuel, repairs, slip, crane, diver. EC Thursday.

☎/VHF Piermaster 01595 744221, *Scalloway Harbour* VHF 12, 16 (office hours).

VAILA SOUND AND GRUTING VOE

Chart BA 3295

An area of good shelter with choice of anchorages to suit wind and mud bottom, on the SW of mainland behind Vaila Island.

Approach Do not use Wester Sound to NW of the island. W and S sides of Vaila Island are clean and any dangers visible; give E shore a berth of ½ca. Easter Sound divides into Vaila Sound to W, and entrance to Gruting Voe to E of Ram's Head (WRG sectored light). Northwards of the narrows keep 1½ca off E side of Vaila Sound, towards the island shore, to clear Galta Skerry, and the Baa of Linga. The Skerry runs NNW from the eastern shore and is marked by a concrete bn; the Baa, a dangerous sunken rock in mid-channel, lies 2ca NW of the

Skerry, and must be passed well to the East if heading for Walls at the top of Vaila Voe.

Entering Gruting Voe keep course 055° or less and favour the West shore. Callie Taing is foul.

Anchorages
• Walls. From Vaila Voe head for the pier and anchor midway between it and the post. There are two visitors' berths in the marina but only for small craft; contact 01595 809311. Shop, PO, and showers on the pier.
• Gruting Voe. Browland, Seli and Scutta Voes offer a choice of anchorages. (Olas Voe is very shallow.) Keep to N entering Scutta Voe. Entrance to Browland Voe is foul on both hands, keep mid-stream but rather nearer N side.

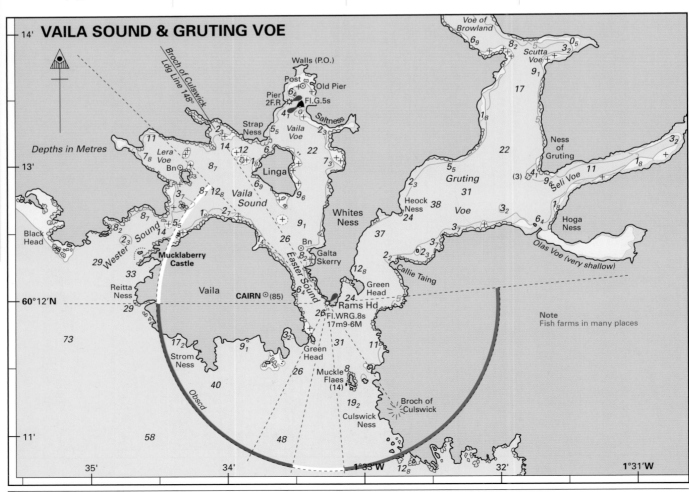

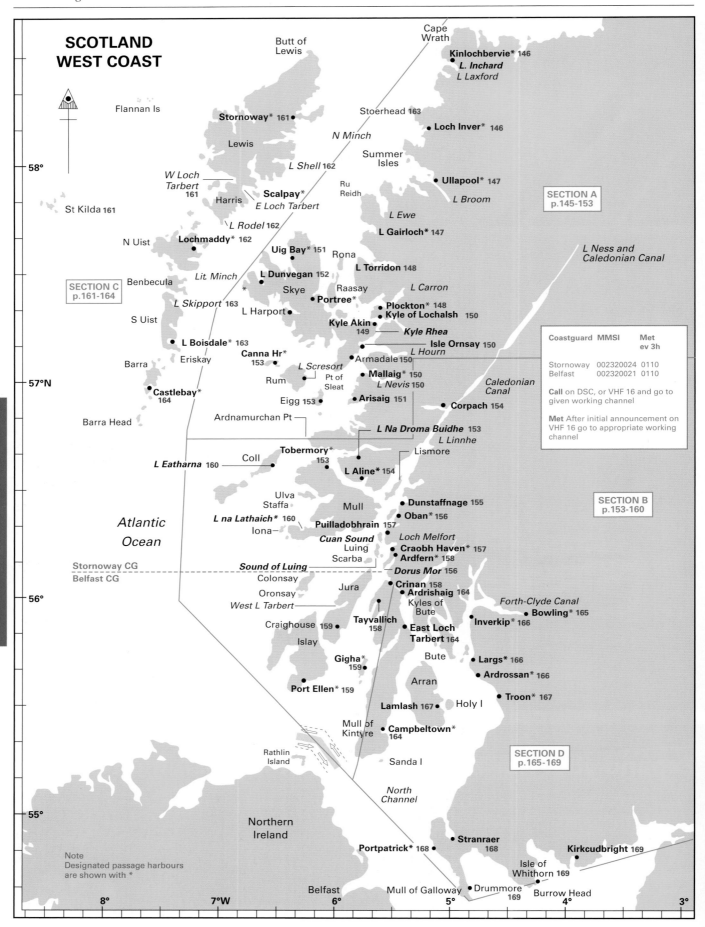

SCOTLAND WEST COAST

SCOTLAND – WEST COAST

Cape Wrath

Butt of Lewis

Kinlochbervie* 146
L. Inchard
L Laxford

Flannan Is

Stoerhead 163

Stornoway* 161

Lewis

N Minch

Loch Inver* 146

Summer Isles

Ru Reidh

Ullapool* 147
L Broom

W Loch Tarbert 161

L Shell 162

St Kilda 161

Harris

Scalpay*
E Loch Tarbert

L Ewe

L Rodel 162

Lochmaddy* 162

N Uist

Uig Bay* 151

Rona

L Dunvegan 152

Benbecula

Lit. Minch

Skye

Raasay

L Torridon 148

L Carron

L Ness and Caledonian Canal

SECTION A
p.145-153

SECTION C
p.161-164

L Skipport 163

L Harport

Portree*

Plockton* 148
Kyle of Lochalsh 150
Kyle Akin
149
Kyle Rhea

S Uist

L Boisdale* 163

Eriskay

Canna Hr*
153

Rum

L Scresort

Pt of Sleat

Armadale 150

Isle Ornsay 150
L Hourn

Coastguard	MMSI	Met ev 3h
Stornoway	002320024	0110
Belfast	002320021	0110

Call on DSC, or VHF 16 and go to given working channel

Met After initial announcement on VHF 16 go to appropriate working channel

Barra

Mallaig* 150
L Nevis 150

Caledonian Canal

Castlebay*
164

Eigg 153

Arisaig 151

Corpach 154

Barra Head

Ardnamurchan Pt

L Na Droma Buidhe 153

L Linnhe

L Eatharna 160

Coll

Tobermory*
153

L Aline* 154

Lismore

Atlantic Ocean

Ulva
Staffa

Mull

Dunstaffnage 155

Oban* 156

SECTION B
p.153-160

L na Lathaich* 160

Iona

Puilladobhrain 157

Loch Melfort

Craobh Haven* 157
Ardfern* 158

Cuan Sound

Luing
Scarba

Stornoway CG
Belfast CG

Sound of Luing

Dorus Mor 156

Colonsay

Oronsay

Jura

Crinan 158
Ardrishaig 164

Kyles of Bute

West L Tarbert

Forth-Clyde Canal

Bowling* 165

Inverkip* 166

Craighouse 159

Tayvallich
158

East Loch Tarbert 164

Islay

Bute

Gigha*
159

Arran

Largs* 166

Ardrossan* 166

Port Ellen* 159

Troon* 167

Lamlash 167

Holy I

Mull of Kintyre

Campbeltown*
164

SECTION D
p.165-169

Rathlin Island

Sanda I

North Channel

Northern Ireland

Portpatrick* 168

Stranraer
168

Kirkcudbright 169

Note
Designated passage harbours are shown with *

Belfast

Mull of Galloway

Drummore
169

Isle of Whithorn 169

Burrow Head

8°
7°W
6°
5°
4°
3°

Page references are shown after locations, for example:
Oban 156. Bold type indicates that it is accompanied by a plan. *Italics* are used for rivers, lochs, bays, seas etc.

Scotland – West Coast

The West Coast of Scotland offers yachtsmen possibly the finest cruising area in Europe, with thousands of miles of highly scenic coastline, hundreds of secluded anchorages and extensive protected sailing waters. Some of the coast exposed to the W and N may suffer severe conditions with strong onshore winds and yachts sailing in these waters must be well found and crewed. However much of the more popular cruising is either protected by offshore islands or in sea lochs that extend many miles inland.

During the summer months the average wind strength is about the same as in the English Channel and there are marginally fewer gales. However the weather can change quickly and yachts must be prepared to clear out from some anchorages at short notice if the wind becomes on-shore. In the lee of high hills and mountains squally katabatic winds may be at least two forces greater than those prevailing in open waters. Fog is rare but misty conditions with visibility down to 1·0M is not uncommon. The best weather can usually be had from mid May to mid July. During this period there is the added bonus of few hours of darkness so that night sailing is seldom necessary.

The flood tide flows mainly N and W. The streams may be strong with associated overfalls off prominent headlands and in some of the sounds between the islands. Details are given in each section. Elsewhere the tidal streams are relatively weak. The tidal range varies from 0·3m at Islay to 4·9m at N Uist and is still more varied S of the Mull of Galloway.

Navigational aids are thinly spread and many harbours are unlit. GPS navigational system operates well in the area but with strong tides transits can be useful. Many large scale charts in this area are still on the old datum but give the correction to be applied to plot a satellite derived position (less than 0'·08).

The Navy notifies the sea areas in which submarines will be operating (*Subfacts*) by giving names which roughly correspond with a geographical name in the area. Details of *Subfacts/Gunfacts* are available twice daily at the end of the MSI (met) broadcast by Stornoway Coastguard at 0710 and 1910 LT and by Clyde Coastguard at 0810 and 2010 LT. Guard ships fly International Code flags NESS. Submarines monitor VHF 16 and may hear engines and depth sounders. Low-level lights are more easily seen by periscopes at night.

It would be impractical to give details in this almanac of all the numerous harbours and anchorages available. Some 34 harbours have been selected as Passage Harbours and are marked by *. These offer good access, secure anchorages, some facilities and are usually lit. Plans and pilotage information are provided for each. In addition a further 30 secondary harbours, suggested by members of the CA, are listed with pilotage information, 11 of which have plans. There are also plans of three passages with strong tides. As the West Coast of Scotland does not neatly fit into a coastline this information together with passage and tidal notes is given in the four separate sections listed below:

A. **Mainland coast from Cape Wrath to Ardnamurchan Point together with Skye, Canna and Rhum**

B. **Mainland coast from Ardnamurchan Point to Mull of Kintyre including Inner Hebrides S of Ardnamurchan**

C. **The Outer Hebrides**

D. **The Firth of Clyde and the S Galloway coast**

Any yacht cruising on the W coast of Scotland should carry the relevant volumes of the Clyde Cruising Club *Sailing Directions* (CCCSD) or Martin Lawrence's *The Yachtsman's Pilots to the*

A. Cape Wrath to Ardnamurchan Point

CAPE WRATH TO KYLE AKIN

Passage lights	BA No
Cape Wrath	3880
Fl(4)30s122m22M	
Stoer Head	3882
Fl.15s59m24M	
Ru Reidh (Re)	3900
Fl(4)15s37m24M AIS	
Rona (NE Point)	3904
Fl.12s69m19M AIS	

The coast from Cape Wrath to Ru Reidh (Re) is exposed to the W and in heavy weather big and dangerous seas build up particularly off the headlands of Stoerhead and Ru Re. There are many offshore rks and islets which make running for shelter hazardous. S of Ru Re some shelter is provided by Skye and the passage through the Inner Sound E of Rona and Raasay is free from hidden dangers. The passage down the E coast of Skye through the Sounds of Raasay, Scalpay and Pabay presents a number of hazards. Drying and submerged rocks extend nearly 1M N of Rona. The Sound of Raasay is clear as far as its S end where it narrows and the channel is marked by buoys. Caolas Scalpay is obstructed by narrows which are shoal and is not recommended without a large-scale chart.

Tidal streams.
All related to Dover
Cape Wrath
–0530 N –0045S
Stoerhead
+0015N HWD S (2½kn)
Ru Reidh
+0430NE –0115SW (3kn)
Raasay Narrows
–0500N +0200 S (2kn)
Kyle Akin
–0015W +0345E (sp 3kn)
+0145W –0415E (np 1½kn)

West coast of Scotland distances (miles)

	Bangor	Canna Harbour	Cape Wrath	Castle Bay	Corpach	Crinan	Croabh Haven	Kinlochbervie	Kyle of Lochalsh	Loch Boisdale	Lochinver	Loch Maddy	Mull of Kintyre	Oban	Plockton	Port Ellen	Portree	Stornoway	Tobermory	Ullapool
Bangor	0																			
Canna Harbour	153	0																		
Cape Wrath	266	119	0																	
Castle Bay	162	36	135	0																
Corpach	138	75	185	96	0															
Crinan	89	72	182	92	52	0														
Croabh Haven	95	66	175	89	46	9	0													
Kinlochbervie	257	111	15	124	177	174	167	0												
Kyle of Lochalsh	178	40	91	75	94	91	85	82	0											
Loch Boisdale	170	28	119	21	96	93	88	108	67	0										
Lochinver	238	94	37	107	158	154	148	29	64	90	0									
Loch Maddy	193	41	93	48	115	113	107	86	64	31	70	0								
Mull of Kintyre	39	113	228	122	98	50	56	220	137	140	201	160	0							
Oban	109	54	164	91	30	23	17	155	73	75	137	96	69	0						
Plockton	185	48	92	83	102	99	93	83	8	76	64	64	146	81	0					
Port Ellen	64	100	218	109	89	40	46	210	126	122	191	150	24	59	134	0				
Portree	195	59	84	94	114	111	104	75	20	87	56	50	157	93	22	147	0			
Stornoway	230	77	53	90	152	153	146	47	61	84	37	49	191	135	62	178	50	0		
Tobermory	128	32	142	52	45	42	35	133	51	53	114	73	88	24	59	81	70	109	0	
Ullapool	236	92	54	106	155	152	146	48	61	90	28	69	198	134	62	189	54	44	112	0

West Coast of Scotland (Imray). These with the appropriate medium-scale Admiralty charts will provide a basic minimum but large scale-charts where available are required in many areas, especially to gain access to the smaller anchorages. If space on the bookshelf allows, the *Admiralty Pilot* contains a wealth of information.

The spelling of Gaelic names varies widely and may cause confusion. The following abbreviations are used in this section of the Cruising Almanac.

Ru = Rubha or rudha	A headland
En = Eilean	An island
Bo = Bogha	A dangerous rock

Many villages have a PO/shop for provisions. Early closing days are often ignored in the summer months especially in places where there is a supermarket. Calor Gas is generally obtainable but not in all areas. It is prudent to carry a spare cylinder. Camping Gaz is not readily available. Diesel can be obtained at marinas and at most fishing harbours but not always by hose.

Many anchorages are remote with no facilities. Yachts contemplating crew changes may need to use public transport. Scotrail runs regularly to some ports e.g. Kyle of Lochalsh/Plockton; Mallaig; Oban and ports in the Firth of Clyde. There is a wide ranging bus network. The Scottish Tourist Board at Edinburgh, ☎ 0131 332 2433 is very helpful.

Yachts may be chartered from a number of centres.

Yacht marinas, though increasing in number, are still comparatively few except in the Clyde area. Apart from Dunstaffnage, there are none N of Oban. There are pontoons with some shoreside facilities at Loch Aline, Tobermory, Mallaig, Kyle Akin, Kyle of Lochalsh, Flowerdale, Stornoway, Kinlochbervie and Loch Inver. Repair facilities and chandlers are concentrated in these areas and at some fishing harbours. *Welcome Anchorages* published by a consortium including The Crown Estate lists visitors' moorings and berths, it is available from many marine outlets. A useful website is www.welcomeanchoragesscotland.com. Visitors' buoys are usually large, blue and labelled to give the safe gross weight or length.

Owing to the presence of heavy weed in some areas, anchoring with a CQR or a Danforth may present difficulties and yachts are recommended to carry a Fisherman, Bruce or modern high holding power anchor of sufficient weight. Shallow draught yachts, and especially those that can take the ground, can often find a clean sandy bottom (visible at 7m) as well as added protection, by going well up into an anchorage. An extra scope of chain may also be advisable for deep water anchoring.

Caution In recent years there has been a huge growth in marine farming. Many popular anchorages are now partially occupied by fish farms, these are moved regularly and debris may be left on the seabed. Not all are shown on either Admiralty charts or plans in this Almanac. Basically there are two types of marine farm:

1. Those for fin fish e.g. salmon, consisting of large floating cages.
2. Those for shellfish, consisting of a series of long cables suspended from buoys, sometimes in a radial manner to which the shellfish attach themselves.

Both types of farm are usually marked by special yellow can buoys, occasionally lit.

KINLOCHBERVIE*, Loch Inchard

Chart BA 2503; Imray C67
HW Ullapool +0020

MHWS	MHWN	MLWN	MLWS
4·9m	3·6m	1·9m	0·7m

A useful passage hbr for yachts rounding Cape Wrath.

Approach Entrance may be difficult to identify. Ru na Leacaig to N is bold and reddish with a W concrete Lt bn Fl(2)l0s30m8M. There is a group of rocky islets to SW of entrance to Loch Inchard.

Entrance Keep close to N shore to avoid Bo Ceann na Saile (3m). Kinlochbervie harbour is in a small inlet on N shore 1M E of Ru na Leacaig marked by DirWRG Lt. Narrow W sector 327° leads in. Dayglow Y framework tr and port and stb Lt bns, Fl.R.4s and Fl.G.4s, respectively. A back Lt at Creag Mhor DirIso.WRG.2s W sector 146·5°-147·5°.

Anchorages / Berthing
• Kinlochbervie. Berth on visitors' pontoon SE of ice factory.
• Rhiconich at head of loch. Shoals. Anchor according to depth. Fish farms may restrict anchoring.

Facilities Kinlochbervie: Diesel and water at pier. Chandlery. PO/shop, hotel. Rhiconich: PO, hotel. Bus to Lairg and rly to Inverness.

☎/VHF HM 01971 521235, *Mobile* 07901 514350; VHF 14.

LOCH LAXFORD

Chart BA 2503; Imray C67
HW Ullapool +0015.

MHWS	MHWN	MLWN	MLWS
4·9m	3·5m	1·9m	0·7m

A remote loch of easy access offering good shelter but no facilities.

Approach and Entrance Ru Ruadh the SW point of entrance is reddish. Keep N of islands off S shore of loch.

Anchorages
• Loch a Chadh-Fi. Beyond moorings of Adventure School. Pass W of En a Chadh-Fi.
• In bays behind islands off S shore. Beware fish farms.

Facilities None.

LOCH NEDD

Chart BA 2502; Imray C67
HW Ullapool HW

MHWS	MHWN	MLWN	MLWS
4·9m	3·7m	1·9m	0·7m

A very attractive safe anchorage in wooded surroundings.

Approach and Entrance From the S side of Eddrachillis Bay. Identify Ru na Maoile Point and approach down the coast on the E side of the entrance. Beware a reef which dries on the W half of the entrance. Keep closer to E shore.

Anchorage Anchor in mud, good holding in SW corner of loch in 3·7m. Trip line advisable owing to many empty moorings.

Facilities PO/shop, hotel at Drumbeg 1½M.

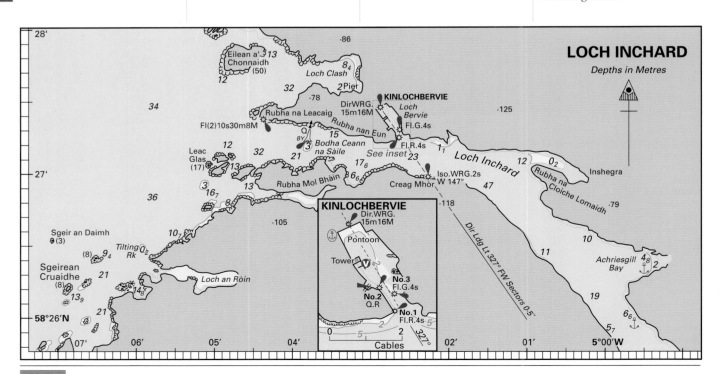

LOCH INCHARD
Depths in Metres

KINLOCHBERVIE
Dir.WRG.
15m16M
Pontoon
Tower
No.3 Fl.G.4s
No.2 Q.R
No.1 Fl.R.4s
Cables

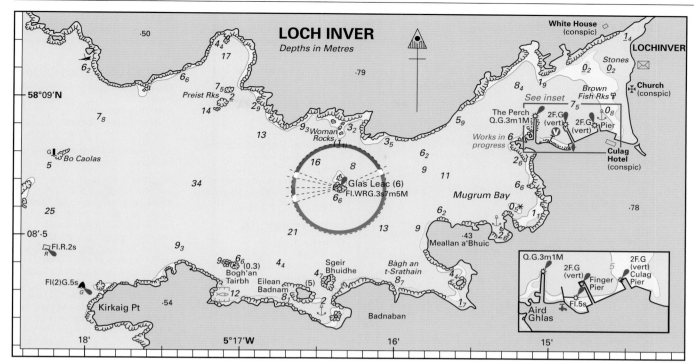

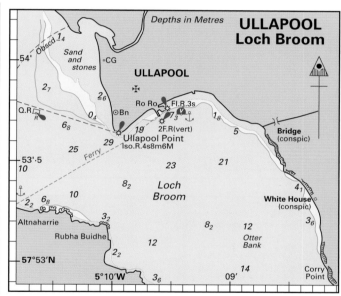

LOCH INVER*

Chart BA 2504;
Imray C67
HW Ullapool –0005

MHWS	MHWN	MLWN	MLWS
5·0m	3·9m	2·1m	0·8m

Approach In clear weather sugar loaf mountain, Suilven, 4M SE is a good landmark for entrance. From S give A'Chleit Is a wide berth to the W and pass close S of Soyea Is, Lt Fl(2)10s34m6M, and steer 075°.

Entrance Leave Glas Leac Lt Fl.WRG.3s to port. At night use W sector 243°–247° as a guide. Leave G bn Q.G to stb.

Berthing and Anchorages
• Visitors' pontoon between breakwater and main pier.
• Anchor off Culag Pier as directed by HM.

Facilities Water and diesel at pier. PO, bank, shops EC Tuesday, chandlery, showers in Harbour Office or at Leisure Centre. Bus to Ullapool and rly to Inverness at Lairg.

☏/VHF HM 01571 844247, *Mobile* 07787 151498; VHF 12.

SUMMER ISLES

Chart BA 2501;
Imray C67
HW Ullapool –0005

MHWS	MHWN	MLWN	MLWS
5·lm	4·0m	2·1m	0·8m

An attractive group of islands with several good anchorages. Large-scale chart desirable.

Approach From NW keep towards N of Dorney Sound to avoid drying rocks N of Tanera Beg but beware Iolla a Mealan (dr 0·8m) 2ca off mainland shore opposite N end of Tanera More. From S leave islands stretching 4½M SW of Tanera More to port.

Anchorages
• Tanera More. In bay to E either close to stone pier or possible mooring in 'Cabbage Garden' S of two islands and enter between them. Uncomfortable in swell from NNE.
• Tanera Beg. In bight to S of En Fada Mor or NE of Tanera Beg. If approaching from N keep close to En Fada Mor.
• Caolas En Ristol. To E of Is. Lt Fl.G.3s on mainland shore towards N end.

Facilities Tanera More: Water and diesel at new pier in SE corner of bay. Achiltibuie: Badentarbet Bay on mainland: PO/shop and Calor.

ULLAPOOL*, Loch Broom

Chart BA 2500;
Imray C67
HW Ullapool HW

MHWS	MHWN	MLWN	MLWS
5·2m	3·9m	2·1m	0·7m

A busy ferry and fishing port. Easy access. Good protection.

Approach and Entrance Straightforward. Ru Cadail (Fl.WRG.6s) marks the port hand entrance to Loch Broom 3·7M NW of Ullapool. Leave R can buoy Q.R and Ullapool Point Iso.R.4s8m6M to port.

Anchorages
• 16 visitors' buoys ENE of pier.
• Altnaharrie on SW shore of loch opposite Ullapool Point. Ferry to Ullapool.
• Loggie Bay on SW shore just beyond Narrows.

Facilities Water and diesel at fish pier. Showers at swimming pool. Chandlers, charts, some repairs, PO, shops, EC Tuesday, banks, hotel, laundry near supermarket. Ferry to Stornoway. Bus to rly at Inverness.

☏/VHF Harbour Office 01854 612091; VHF 16, 14.

LOCH EWE

Chart BA 3146;
Imray C66
HW Ullapool –0010

MHWS	MHWN	MLWN	MLWS
5·1m	3·8m	2·0m	0·7m

A large loch open to the N. The sound E of Is Ewe has a number of large unlit mooring buoys. There are some Naval establishments at Aultbea.

Approach and Entrance Straightforward.

Anchorages
• At head of loch off Poolewe, according to depth. Beware of Boor Rocks 2ca off W shore. If visiting gardens, anchor off small pier SW of Inverewe Ho, or in Loch Thuraig.
• Aultbea. To E of pier.

Facilities
Poolewe: water at pier SW of Inverewe Ho, PO, shops EC Thursday, garage, hotel.
Inverewe: Gardens are outstanding.

Aultbea: water at pier, PO, shops EC Wednesday, garage, hotel, Calor.

LOCH GAIRLOCH*

Chart BA 2528;
Imray C66
HW Ullapool –0020

MHWS	MHWN	MLWN	MLWS
5·2m	4·0m	1·8m	0·6m

Approach Pass S of Longa Is 3M NW of Glas En Fl.WRG.6s4M.

Anchorages
• Badachro SW of Horrisdale Is. A beautiful well-sheltered anchorage, crowded with many moorings. Keep to E side of channel. Anchor N or S of islets to SW. Note submerged wreck (dr 1·6m) ½ca E of rock (dr 3·7m) 1ca SE of islet. Visitors' mooring marked 'Inn'.
• SSE of Eilean Horrisdale
• Flowerdale Bay visitors' pontoon E of pier, or anchor SE of pier, subject to swell.

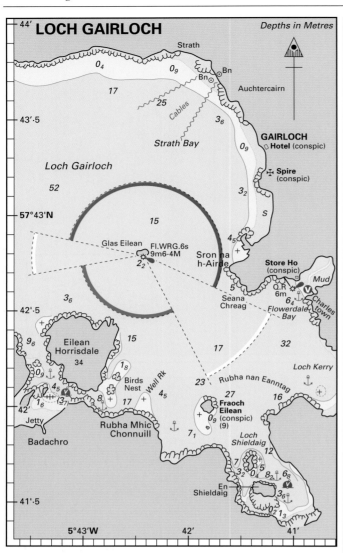

LOCH GAIRLOCH

Depths in Metres

• Loch Sheildaig E or W of En Shieldaig. Leave Fraoch En to stb and give middle island a wide berth.

Underwater rocks with less than 2m in the vicinity of En Horrisdale, SW of Fraoch En in Loch Shieldaig and off Rubha nan Eanntag.

Facilities
Badachro: Water, laundrette, Hotel with showers.
Flowerdale: Water and diesel, hotel/restaurant, showers at SC.
Strath: Bank, shops, laundrette.

☎ HM 01445 712140.

LOCH TORRIDON
Chart BA 2210;
Imray C66
HW Ullapool –0020

MHWS	MHWN	MLWS	MLWS
5·6	4·2	2·2	0·7

This loch comprises three lochs joined by narrows. Loch Torridon, Loch Shieldaig and Upper Loch Torridon.

Entrance 3M wide between Red Point and Ru na Fearn. Sgeir na Trian (2m) lies 1¼M SSE of Red Point. Entrance to L Shieldaig under ½M wide and narrows into Upper Loch Torridon only 2ca between N shore and En a Chaoil. Tide here runs at 2·3kn.

Anchorage
• In Loch a Chracaich off Kenmore in 5m clear of fish farm.
• In L Shieldaig two visitors' moorings E of Shieldaig Is or anchor clear of moorings or head of loch, poor holding.

• In Upper Loch Torridon there are many possible anchorages, the best being in the SE corner W of the jetty.

PLOCKTON*, Loch Carron
Chart BA 2528;
Imray C66
HW Ullapool –0015

MHWS	MHWN	MLWN	MLWS
5·7m	4·4m	2·6m	0·9m

An attractive hbr with many facilities.

Approach There are two approaches from SW.
• S of Sgeir a Chinn and Sgeir Bhuidhe (*not on plan*) then N of Golach and High Stone rocks giving them a clearance of 2ca and steering 065° on white bn (*see plan*). When Duncraig Castle conspic bears 164° alter course and steer towards castle to clear Hawk Rock (depth 0·1m) leaving Dubh Sgeir bn 2½ca to port.
• Mid-channel between the port bn marking High Stone rocks and the old LtHo on a heading to Bogha Dubh Sgeir bn.

Entrance Steer 164° towards castle conspic until hbr opens to SW. Beware Plockton Rks (dr 2·7m) extending 3ca NNW of Castle Point.

Anchorage In bay as marked on plan and clear of moorings. Large patches of kelp reported. Visitors' moorings with orange pick up buoys.

Facilities Short-stay pontoons for loading stores. PO, shop, EC Wednesday, water, diesel in cans,

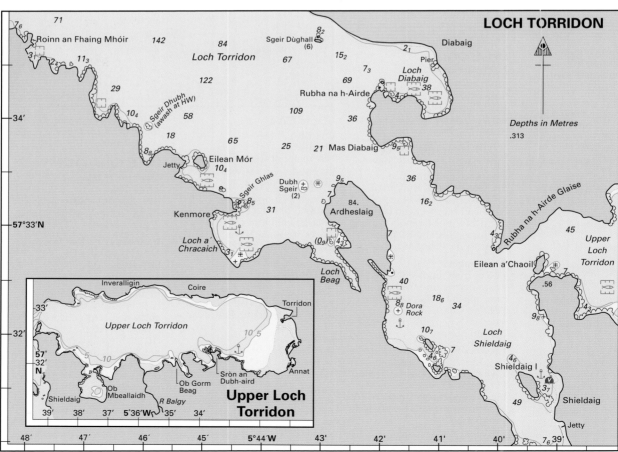

LOCH TORRIDON

Depths in Metres

Upper Loch Torridon

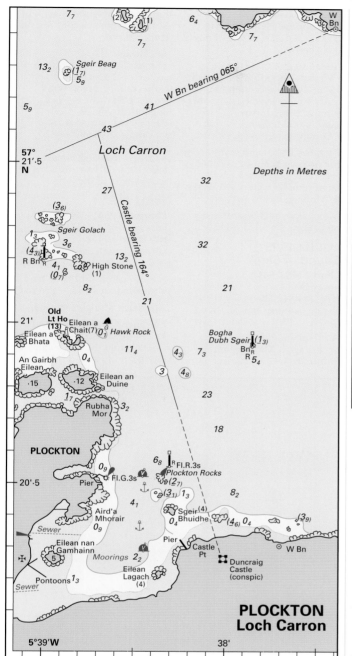

PLOCKTON
Loch Carron

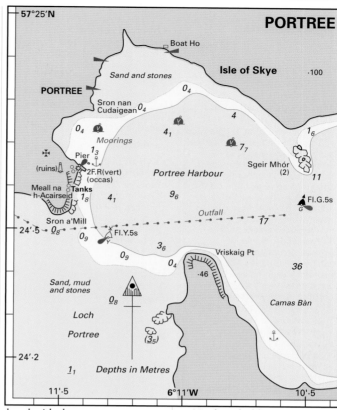

PORTREE

hotel with showers, restaurant, launderette. Rly to Inverness and to Kyle of Lochalsh.

PORTREE, SKYE*

Chart BA 2534;
Imray C66
HW Ullapool –0025

MHWS	MHWN	MLWN	MLWS
5·3m	3·7m	1·9m	0·7m

The principal town on Skye. Anchorage subject to squalls.

Approach and Entrance
Straightforward. 2F.R(vert) occas on pier.

Anchorages
• Visitors' moorings in N of bay, but subject to swell in S'lies.
• To NE of pier clear of moorings. Avoid mouth of burn to N where holding poor. Exposed to SW winds. Patches of kelp reported in anchorage.
• Camas Ban to SE. Protected from S.

Facilities Water and diesel at quay, engineer, Calor. Showers at swimming pool. PO, shops, launderette, EC Wednesday, hotels. Bus to Inverness. Rly to Inverness at Kyle of Lochalsh on mainland.

☎ HM 01478 612926.

KYLE AKIN

Charts BA 2540, 2498;
Imray C66
HW Ullapool –0030

MHWS	MHWN	MLWN	MLWS
5·3m	3·9m	2·1m	0·6m

KYLE AKIN

KYLE AKIN TO ARDNAMURCHAN

Passage lights	BA No
Isle Ornsay	3944
Oc·8s.18m15M	
Pt of Sleat	3952
Fl.3s20m9M	
Ardnamurchan Point	4082
Fl(2)20s55m24M	

The tides are strong in Kyle Akin and Kyle Rhea, but the channel is well marked and lit. It is essential to go with the tide in Kyle Rhea. Overfalls may be encountered at Glenelg on the ebb with a S'ly wind. From here the passage to Ardnamurchan is straightforward, though pass N of a dangerous rock, Bo Faskadale, 6M NE of Ardnamurchan, marked by a G con buoy Fl(3)G.18s AIS. At Ardnamurchan Point a big sea can build up with strong onshore winds and one is well advised to stand off at least 1M.

Tidal streams
All related to Dover

Kyle Akin
−0015W +0345E (sp 3kn)
+0145W −0415E (np 1½kn)
These can be significantly affected by climatic conditions

Kyle Rhea
+0145N −0415S (6–8kn)

Sound of Sleat
+0130NE −0430SW (1kn)

Ardnamurchan Point
+0130N −0430S (1½kn)

A temporary stopping place for stores and crew changing.

Approach There are numerous hazards in Kyle Akin (*see plan*), but these are well marked and lit. Tides run strongly. The channel under the br is 80m wide and has a clearance of 29m. *Bridge Control* VHF 12. There is a secondary passage (lit) to the N of the main channel with a clearance of 4·5m.

Berthing

• **Kyle of Lochalsh** Alongside pontoon, poor shelter in strong winds. Beware of dangerous rocky outcrop immediately W of pontoon.

• **Kyleakin** Alongside pontoon, can be crowded, good shelter. Three visitors' buoys on S shore between hbr and Skye br.

Facilities

• **Kyle of Lochalsh** Water on pontoon, diesel at pier. Showers at tourist office. Shops, bank, PO, chandler, calor. GRP repairs, engineer. Rly to Inverness.

• **Kyleakin** Small shop, hotel.

① Harbourmaster 01599 534167.

ISLE ORNSAY, Sound of Sleat, Skye

Chart BA 2208;
Imray C66
HW Oban +0017

MHWS	MHWN	MLWN	MLWS
5·0m	3·8m	2·0m	0·8m

Easy access. Convenient if awaiting a favourable tide to pass through Kyle Rhea going N.

Approach Enter to N of island.

Anchorages
• Towards head of bay according to depth and clear of moorings.
• Visitors' moorings off Duisdale Hotel (just N of plan).

Facilities PO, store 1M, hotel, showers (Duisdale).

ARMADALE

Chart BA 2208;
Imray C66
HW Oban +0017

MHWS	MHWN	MLWN	MLWS
5·0m	3·6m	2·1m	0·8m

On the W side of the Sound of Sleat a useful passage hbr open to NE.

Entrance Straightforward from the NE. From the S rocks off

Ru Phoil. Give a wide berth until hbr opens up. At night give Oc.R.6s Lt on end of pier a wide berth.

Anchorage
• Visitors' moorings subject to swell; distinguish from yacht charter moorings. Little room for anchoring further out in sand. Good holding.
• Alongside ferry pier.

Facilities Diesel and water from Isle of Skye Yachts workboat, general repairs. Showers, laundrette, PO/shop ¾M. Ferry to Mallaig; bus to Portree.

Isle of Skye Yachts administer moorings, ① 01471 844216.

LOCH NEVIS Sound of Sleat

Chart 2208, 2541;
Imray C66
HW Oban +0025

MHWS	MHWN	MLWN	MLWS
5·0m	3·8m	2·0m	0·7m

A useful and beautiful anchorage if Mallaig full. Subject to severe squalls.

Entrance Along the coast E of Mallaig keeping about 3ca out from S shore.

Anchorage
• En na Glasehoille in the NW corner of the loch gives protection from the W/SW.
• Inverie Bay 1M to the E, anchor off village. Restaurant/pub, visitors' moorings ① 01687 462267, VHF 12.
• Tarbert in the SE corner before the narrows into the second part of the loch.

MALLAIG*

Charts BA 2541, 2208;
Imray C66
HW Oban +0017

MHWS	MHWN	MLWN	MLWS
5·0m	3·6m	2·1m	0·8m

A busy fishing and ferry port with good facilities. Open to N.

Approach Straightforward.

Entrance Leave Sgeir Dhearg Fl(2)WG.8s to stb. At night in G sector and then W sector of pier head Lt Iso.WRG.4s and

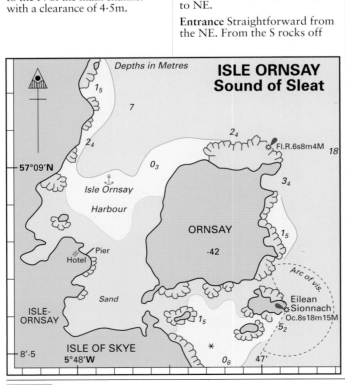

ISLE ORNSAY
Sound of Sleat

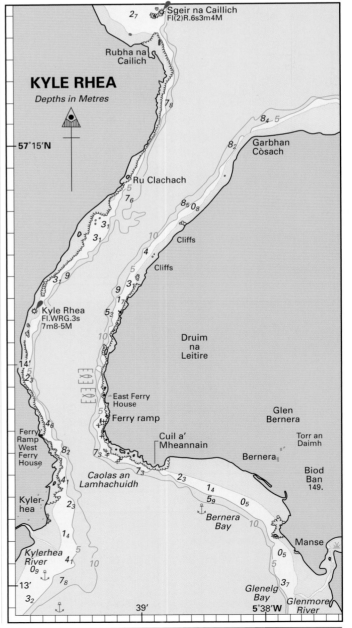

KYLE RHEA

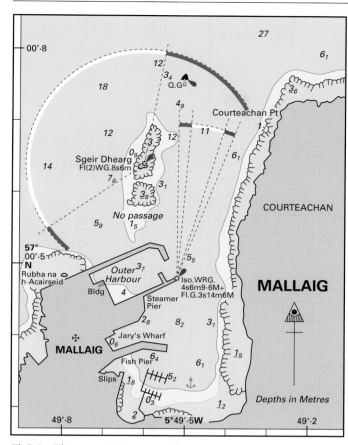

Fl.G.3s. Three vert R Lts mean a ferry is about to leave or enter, no other craft may leave or enter without HM permission.

Berthing

• On pontoons S of Fish Pier, as directed.

• Temporary berth alongside Fish Pier. Pier dues. HM will advise.

• There are 12 visitors' moorings in the inner harbour.

Facilities Water and electricity on pontoons. From 2012, showers, toilets and laundry in new reception building. Diesel at Fish Quay. Chandler, charts, slip, repairs. PO, shops EC Wednesday, hotels, launderette and showers (£3) at Seaman's Mission, banks. Ferry to islands. Rly to Glasgow. Minibus link to Oban. Bus to Fort William.

☎/VHF HM 01687 462154 (office hours); VHF 16, 09 call sign *Mallaig Harbour Radio*.

ARISAIG,
Loch Nan Ceall

Chart BA 2207;
Imray C65
HW Oban +0016

MHWS	MHWN	MLWN	MLWS
4·7m	2·8m	2·0m	0·9m

Approach this beautiful hbr with caution in clear weather as it is not easy to identify. The marked channel is winding with rocks (dr 0·2m) and has a fast tidal stream particularly towards LW. Enter HW±0400.

Approach Identify Rubh Arisaig, with W paint mark, S of channel, keeping ½M to W to avoid Meallan Odhar rocks, 1m high, *see plan*. Luinga Mor, 15m high, lies to the N of the channel with drying rocks extending ½M SE. A stone cottage known as the 'Waiting Room' lies 1M ENE of Ru Arisaig and to S of Torr Mor, 79m high, inside entrance.

Entrance Enter on a heading of 080°. Leave the first, second and third bns ½ca to port, avoiding Cave Rock to stb. Follow the curving channel leaving bns on appropriate side. Do not follow a straight course from one bn to the next. Then pass between R & G buoys and head ESE leaving the last R bn ½ca to N. Make E to village 1M away.

Anchorages
• Above Cave Rock 1M inside entrance.
• There are 50 visitors' moorings in various depths in Loch Nan Ceall.
• In bay SE of village at Camas an t-Salain, crowded with moorings.

Facilities Water at pontoon and diesel at pier. Showers, laundry, chandlery. Calor gas at shop, PO, hotels, restaurants. Repairs, 210-tonne crane. Rly to Glasgow. Bus to Fort William.

☎/VHF *Arisaig Marine* VHF 37, 01687 450224.

UIG BAY*,
Loch Snizort, Skye

Charts BA 1795, 2533;
Imray C66
HW Ullapool −0032

MHWS	MHWN	MLWN	MLWS
5·3m	3·5m	1·9m	0·7m

Bay on E side of Loch Snizort in the N of Skye. Easy access. Rather exposed to W.

Approach and Entrance Note spit extending 1ca S from Ru Idrigill (dr 2·6m).

Anchorage NNE of pier, Iso.WRG.4s, in 5m. Bottom reported foul, advisable to buoy anchor.

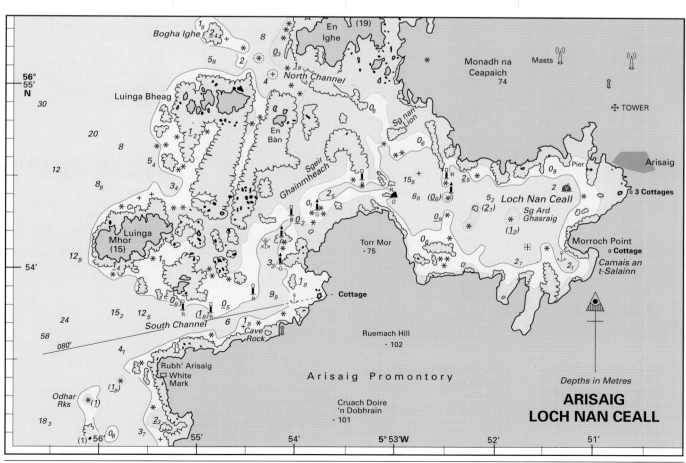

**ARISAIG
LOCH NAN CEALL**

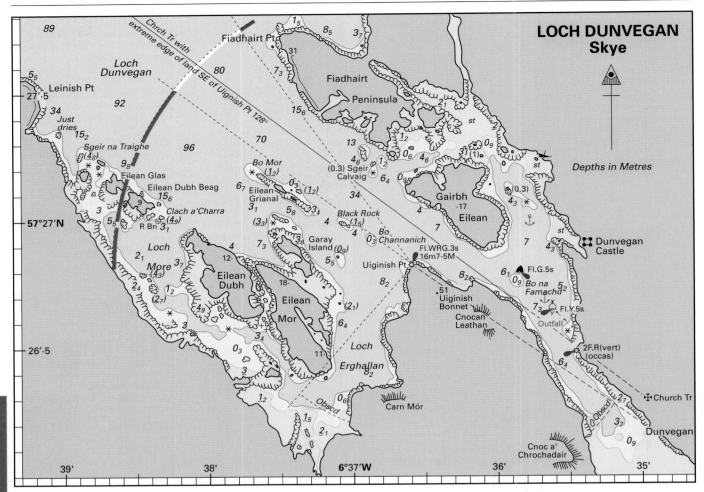

LOCH DUNVEGAN
Skye

Depths in Metres

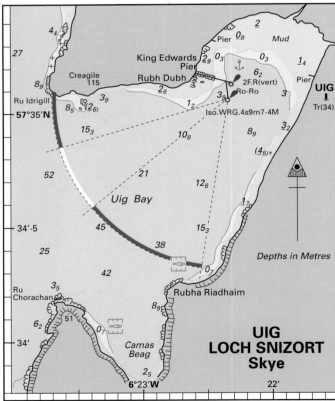

UIG
LOCH SNIZORT
Skye

Depths in Metres

Facilities Water and diesel at pier. PO, shops, hotels. Launderette at caravan park. Bus to Glasgow. Ferry to Harris.

☎ Harbourmaster 01470 542381.

LOCH DUNVEGAN*, Skye

Chart BA 2533;
Imray C66

HW Ullapool −0030sp −0105 np

MHWS	MHWN	MLWN	MLWS
5·2m	3·8m	2·1m	0·7m

Large loch in NW Skye. 2½ca between the Fiadairt peninsula to E and En Grianal to W. Note drying and submerged rocks extending 4ca SE of En to Bo Channanich (0·3m). *(See plan)*.

Entrance The shore SE of Uiginish Point in line with Dunvegan Church tr 128°, leads mid-channel. Leave Uiginish Point Lt (Fl.WRG.3s) and Bo na Famachd G con buoy to stb.

Anchorage
• Head of loch beyond pier. Leave Bo na Famachd buoy well to stb.
• E of Gairbh Eilean opposite the Castle. Note submerged and (dries 0·3) rocks to N. Poor shelter in strong SW'lies.
• L Erghallan, to S of En Mor obstructed by mussel beds.
• Loch More.

Facilities PO, shops, garage. Water and diesel at hotel jetty. Bus to Portree.

LOCH HARPORT, Skye

Chart BA 1795;
Imray C66

HW Ullapool −0055

MHWS	MHWN	MLWN	MLWS
5·1m	3·8m	2·1m	0·8m

Situated in the SE arm of Loch Bracadale in the S of Skye.

Approach and Entrance From NW note dangerous Dubh Sgeir (5m) 1½M S of Ru Ruadh. Enter between Oronsay and Ru nan Clach. Give the SW and E shore of Oronsay a berth of ¼M. Leave Ardtrech Point, Fl.6s18m9M, to stb.

Anchorages
• Portnalong. Space limited by fish farm. Useful if storm bound. Bottom reported foul.
• Carbost 1½M from head of loch. Good holding opposite Talisker Distillery, also distillery visitors' moorings. Sheltered except from the SE.

Facilities PO, shop EC Wednesday.

N AND W COASTS OF SKYE TO ARDNAMURCHAN

Passage lights	BA No
Neist Point	4064
Fl.5s43m16M AIS	
Oigh Sgeir, Hyskeir	4076
Fl(3)30s41m24M	

The N and W coasts of Skye present a series of prominent headlands with strong tides and overfalls, in the bays and lochs there may be back eddies. SW of Canna there are dangerous rks for over 7M and in bad weather the seas can be bad here. Around the Small Isles there are severe magnetic anomalies in places, particularly S of Muck.

Tidal streams
All related to Dover. Sp.Rates

Ru Hunish
+0415NE −0215SW   2½kn

Neist Poin
+0400N −0200S   1½kn

CANNA IS*

Chart BA 2208;
Imray C66
HW Ullapool −0037sp −0130np

MHWS	MHWN
4·8m	3·7m

A very beautiful hbr and useful passage port when bound for the Outer Hebrides. Easy access and sheltered except from E.

Approach from N and E is straightforward. Lt at E end of Sanday Is, Fl.10s32m9M. Steer to pass close S of Ru Carrinis. From S beware of drying reef to N of Sanday marked by R can buoy Fl.R.2s. Magnetic anomalies reported.

Entrance Beware of drying reef ¾ca SW of pier.

Anchorage Best in line between two churches. Much kelp, poor holding reported. Shoals. Hard sand suitable for bilge keelers.

Facilities PO opens as required. Tiny restaurant. Ferry to Mallaig.

LOCH SCRESORT
Isle of Rum

Chart BA 2208;
Imray C65
HW Oban +0015sp −0108np

MHWS	MHWN
4·8m	3·7m

Protection from all winds except the E and squalls from the W. Owned by Scottish Nature Conservancy.

Entrance Straightforward, keep to middle or N side. Reef on S side of entrance is marked by N Card buoy Q.

Anchorage Bay shallows towards the shore. Anchor according to depth. Moderate holding.

Facilities PO, Stores, water from pier. Hotel. Ferry to Mallaig. Showers in youth hostel.

EIGG

Chart BA 2207; Imray C65
HW Oban +0016

MHWS	MHWN	MLWN	MLWS
4·7m	2·8m	2·0m	0·9m

The Island of Eigg is a pleasant and convenient anchorage about half way between Mallaig and Ardnamurchan. Exposed to swell from N to E and S. Strong tides can be uncomfortable.

Approach Identify Sgurr(391m) conspic and En Chathastail Lt bn Fl.6s24m8M.

Entrance From NE identify two perches – circular topmark to N and triangular to S – and pass between them. Then head for stone pier. From S keep at least 1ca W of En Chathastail. Note rks extending 1½ca SW of En.

Anchorages
• To N of pier according to depth and clear of moorings. Sandy bottom shoals rapidly to W.
• S of Galmisdale Pt as close to shore as possible to avoid tide.

Facilities Water and café at pier, diesel, Calor. PO/store 2M. Hotel. Ferry to Arisaig and Mallaig.

B. Ardnamurchan to Mull of Kintyre and Inner Hebrides S of Ardnamurchan

ARDNAMURCHAN TO OBAN

Passage lights	BA No
Ardnamurchan Point	4082
Fl(2)20s55m24M AIS	
Ru nan Gall	4112
Fl.3s17m10M	
Lismore	4170
Fl.10s31m17M	

Entering the Sound of Mull from the N keep close to the Mull shore leaving the New Rocks G con buoy to port to avoid dangerous drying reefs towards entrance of Loch Sunart. All dangers in the Sound of Mull and the Firth of Lorne are well marked. Strong tides and overfalls may be encountered off Duart Point.

Tidal Streams.
All related to Dover. Sp rates

Ardnamurchan	
+0130N −0430S 1½kn	
Lismore Lt Ho	
+0115N −0500S 2kn	
Corran Narrows (L. Linnhe)	
+0600 NE −0530SW 5kn	
Firth of Lorne	
−0100NE +0500 SW 1½kn	

TOBERMORY*, Mull

Charts BA 2390, 2394, 2474; SC 5611;
Imray 2800, C65
HW Oban +0017

MHWS	MHWN	MLWN	MLWS
4·4m	3·3m	1·8m	0·7m

Sheltered, pretty town in the NE of Mull.

Approach From N keep close to Mull shore between Ru nan Gall LtHo Fl.3s17m9M, 1M to N and New Rocks G con buoy Fl.6s 1¼M N.

Entrance Main entrance N of Calve Is. No hazards.

The S entrance is a narrow drying channel with a sandy bottom passable at HW. Church spire on Aros Head 300°.

Anchorages/Berthing
• 20 pontoon berths near distillery. Free short stay for shopping by day.
• Off town as far S as furthest W mark on shore. Be prepared to anchor in up to 20m. Often crowded. Many visitors' moorings, marked THA.
• Aros Bay according to depth.
• Doirlinn Narrows (S entrance); fishing boats may use this at night.

Facilities Water and diesel at pontoons, showers and laundrette in Harbour Office building. Chandlery, charts,

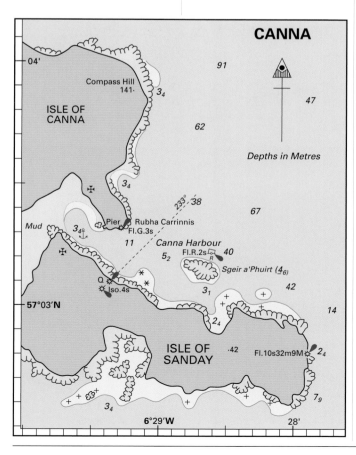

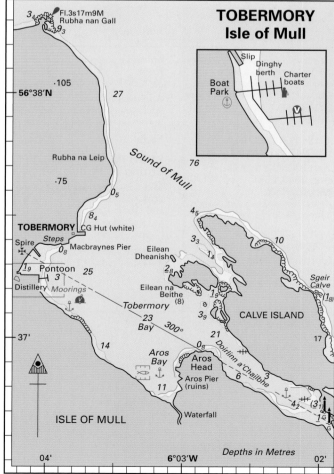

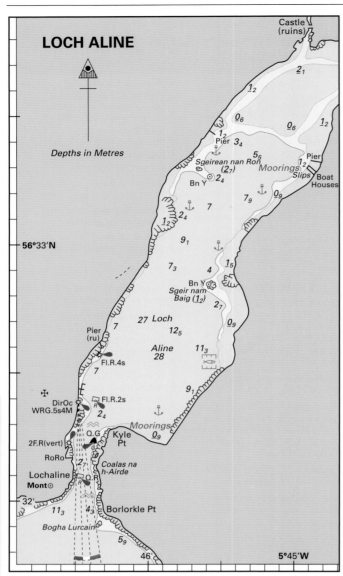

LOCH ALINE

Depths in Metres

Entrance Avoid reef off Bolorkle Point to E of entrance by keeping 2ca off-shore then keep in mid-channel. The channel is marked by two port and one stb Lt buoys. Ldg bns and Lts F 356°. The tide runs at 2½kn in the entrance. Keep a look out for the Loch Aline to Fishnish ferry.

Anchorages and Berthing
• 24 visitors' pontoon berths with min depth of 2·9m on the W side of the loch just N of the old jetty for the silica mine. Water and electricity, toilets and showers planned for 2013. Short walk to the village. VHF 80 call sign *Lochaline Harbour* ✆ 07583 800500.
• In SE corner of loch, partially obstructed by fish farm and moorings. Subject to squalls in SE winds.
• Head of loch: moorings or anchor according to depth.
• Moor to stone pier on W side of entrance. Short stay only.

Facilities PO/Store, water. Diesel, Petrol and Calor in village, laundrette, restaurant. Bus to Fort William.

CORPACH
Chart BA 2372, 2380; SC 5611; Imray C65
HW Oban +0010

MHWS	MHWN	MLWN	MLWS
4·0m	2·9m	1·6m	0·5m

Corpach is just beyond the SW entrance to the Caledonian canal. The approach through Loch Linnhe gives an impressive view of Ben Nevis.

Approach Through Loch Linnhe which is divided between the S and N parts of the loch by the Corran Narrows where the tide runs at up to 5kn at sp the in-going stream beginning at LW Oban and the outgoing stream at HW. After the Narrows leave the Corran shoal to port and continue up the loch which is buoyed towards Corpach. Leave En na Creiche to port and R can Lt buoy before turning W and coming round to canal entrance.

Anchorage If waiting to enter canal anchor W of entrance in 4·6m out of the way of canal traffic or at waiting pontoon. Or in Camus na Gall. One visitors' mooring off Lochaber Y.C., Fort William.

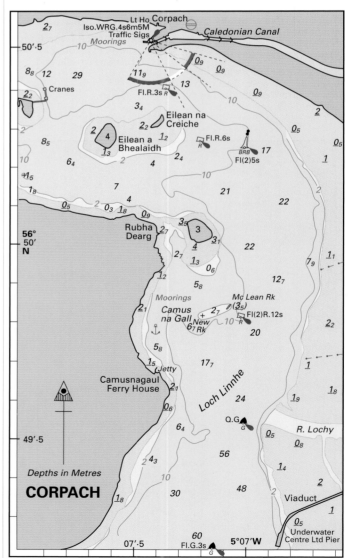

CORPACH

Depths in Metres

engineer, shops, free electricity and Wi-Fi, bank, hotels. Ferry to Kilchoan, Ardnamurchan; seaplane to Oban and Glasgow. ✆/VHF HM *Mobile* 07917 832497, VHF 12.

LOCH NA DROMA BUIDHE, SUNART
Chart BA 2394; SC 5611; Imray 2800, C64
HW Oban HW

MHWS	MHWN	MLWN	MLWS
4·4m	3·2m	1·8m	0·6m

Popular anchorage S of the Is of Oronsay sheltered in all winds.

Approach Beware of New and Red Rocks if coming from the W. From N beware rocks W of Oronsay.

Entrance Steep to, ½ca wide. Keep to N shore to avoid rock (0·3m) to S of E end of entrance.

Anchorages Suitable anchorages can be found in many parts of the loch.

Facilities None.

LOCH ALINE*, Sound of Mull
Chart BA 2390; SC 5611; Imray 2800, C65
HW Oban +0012

MHWS	MHWN
4·5m	3·2m

A useful and protected loch on mainland side of Sound of Mull. Frequent ferries use the channel.

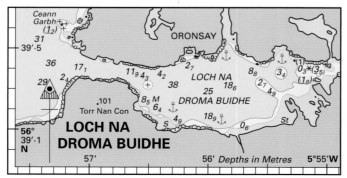

LOCH NA DROMA BUIDHE

Depths in Metres

CALEDONIAN CANAL

Charts BA 2380, 2372, 1791; Imray C23

The Caledonian Canal runs 60M NE from Corpach to Clachnaharry, near Inverness, via Lochs Lochy, Oich and Ness with 29 locks. Vessels up to 45m LOA, 10m beam and 4m draught can use the canal. The *Skipper's Guide* from www.scottishcanals.co.uk or Seaport Marina, Muirtown Wharf, Inverness IV3 5LS is invaluable.

Entrance Sea locks at Corpach at SW end and Clachnaharry at NW end normally operate HW±0400 within the operating hours 0800–1730 daily in summer, less at other periods. Waiting in the canal before transitting the canal is possible at Corpach or at Seaport Marina (NE end).

Transit All locks and bridges are manned with the same operating hours as above, but there may be a lunch break. Minimum passage time 2½days. Eight days transit time allowed. There are random spot checks, usually at sea lock, for boat safety, e.g. gas, electricity, fuel. There may be delays at Neptune's Staircase, a spectacular flight of seven locks at Banavie (near Corpach), and also at the Fort Augustus flight.

Facilities Shops at Corpach, Fort Augustus, and Muirtown. Diesel at Corpach and at Muirtown from Seaport or Caley Marinas. Showers, water, and pump out facilities.

☎ /**VHF** Sea locks, and most locks and bridges VHF 74; Corpach Sea Lock 01397 772249; Clachnaharry Sea Lock 01463 713896; Seaport Marina 01463 233140.

DUNSTAFFNAGE

Chart BA 2388, 2389; SC 5611; Imray C65

HW Oban +0002

MHWS	MHWN	MLWN	MLWS
4·1m	3·0m	1·9m	0·8m

A marina just N of Oban.

Entrance Channel between En Mor to stb and Rubha Garbh with castle ruins on headland.

To enter the marina follow the fairway (150°), after the 2nd G stb hand buoy turn on to 270° and the entrance should become apparent, but do not pass through moorings.

Berthing 200 berth marina with some moorings.

Facilities Full marina facilities, restaurant and accommodation. Shop (will deliver) and garage in Dunbeg ½M. Sailmaker 5M. Charter centre. Bus to Oban and Fort William.

☎ /**VHF** 01631 566555, VHF 37.

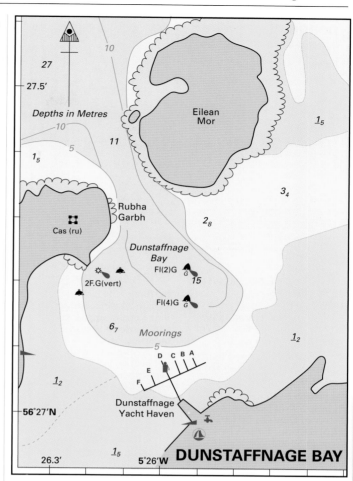

DUNSTAFFNAGE BAY

OBAN TO MULL OF KINTYRE

Passage lights	BA No
Fladda	4190
Fl(2)WRG.9s13m11-9M	
Skervuile	4230
Fl.15s22m9M	
McArthur's Head	4240
Fl(2)WR.10s39m13/10M	
Mull of Kintyre	4272
Fl(2)20s91m24M	

Strong tides will be experienced through the Fladda Narrows in Luing Sound, Cuan Sound and Dorus Mor, often with overfalls.

In the **Sound of Luing** pass midway between Fladda LtHo Fl(2)WRG.9s13m11-9M (sectors 169°-R-186°-W-337°-G-344°-W-356°-R-026°-obscd-169°) and Dubh Sgeir Fl.WRG.6s9m6-4M (sectors 000°-W-010°-R-025°-W-199°-G-000°) into the Sound of Luing.

Alternatively, **Cuan Sound** (*see plan on page 156*) provides a challenging passage, even at slack water, between the Firth of Lorne and Seil Sound and Loch Melfort. The tides run at 7kn springs, 5kn at neaps and there are numerous off-shore hazards. The NW entrance can be identified by overhead cables (clearance 35m) and their pylons. Overfalls may be experienced here in fresh W winds when coming through the Sound with the tide from the E. Coming from the W, beware Cullanach rks (dries 1·2m) (not on plan) SW of Cuan

Point entrance. Keep in mid-channel until An Cleiteadh (Cleit Rk) bn is identified and pass ¼ to ½ca N of bn. Note rock awash ¾ca from S point of Seil. Keep in mid-channel and pass either ¼ca or 3ca NE of Torsa. There are good anchorages clear of the tidal stream S of An Cleiteadh and at Ardinamar Bay. Leave G posts close to stb on entry.

In the Sound of Jura there are numerous islets and submerged rocks W and S of Craignish Peninsula terminating in Ruadh Sgeir Lt Fl.6s. If proceeding to Crinan or Ardfern pass S of Coiresa and Craignish Point through **Dorus Mor** (*see plan on page 156*). If keeping W on the flood beware of being swept into the very dangerous Gulf of Corryvreckan between Jura and Scarba.

Large-scale charts are advisable if approaching Gigha or the SE of Islay, owing to numerous off-lying rocks. Strong tides and heavy seas may be encountered between the Mull of Kintyre, Rathlin Is and the S coast of Islay.

Tidal Streams.
All related to Dover. Sp rates

Fladda Narrows
−0100N +0500S 7kn

Cuan Sound
−0100 NW +0530SE 7kn

Gulf of Corryvrechan
−0115W +0430E 8½kn

Dorus Mor
−0200NW +0445SE 8kn

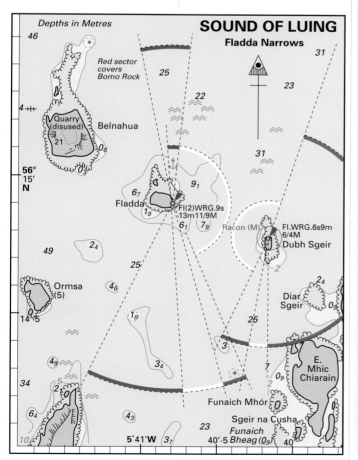

SOUND OF LUING
Fladda Narrows

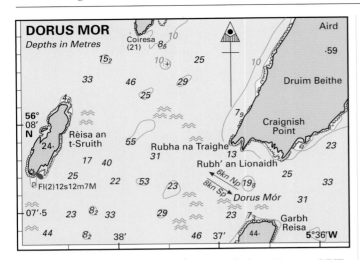

DORUS MOR

Depths in Metres

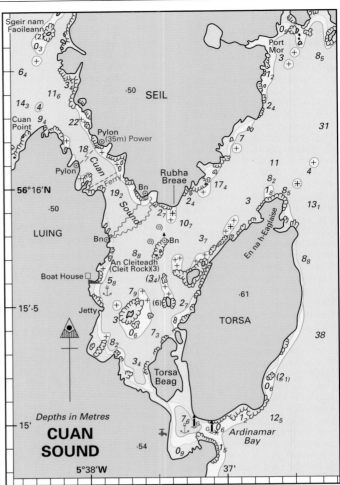

CUAN SOUND

Depths in Metres

OBAN*

Charts BA 1790, 2387; SC 5611; Imray 2800, C65

HW Oban HW

MHWS	MHWN	MLWN	MLWS
4·0m	2·9m	1·8m	0·7m

Large open bay. Rather exposed. Main hbr and tourist centre for the area. Busy ferry and fishing port.

Approach and Entrance From N keep SW of Maiden Is in W sector of Dunollie LtHo Fl(2)WRG.6s. From S by Kerrera Sound. Note Sgeir Rathaid marked by N and S card Lt buoys. A Voluntary Code of Practice is operated in the Oban Bay area. Vessels over 20m have right of way over smaller vessels when entering or leaving the bay. Listen on VHF 16/12 for vessel movements.

Berthing
• Oban Marina, Ardantrive Bay, Kerrera opposite Oban. 115 pontoon berths, 33 moorings capacity 20 tonnes, full facilities, boatyard, diesel, bar/grill open May to September. Free hourly ferry to Oban. VHF 80, ☎ 01631 565333.
• Visitors' buoys W of Port Beag, with short stay pontoon.
• Anchor N of N pier
• Temporarily at N pier or Fish Quay, by negotiation.

Facilities Busy town, chandlery, charts. Water at N pier, Fish quay. Rly and coaches to Glasgow. Ferries to Inner Hebrides, S Uist and Barra.

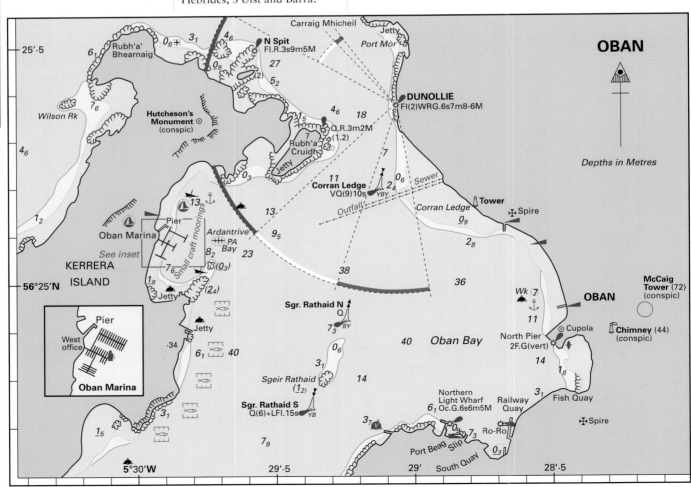

OBAN

Depths in Metres

Oban Bay

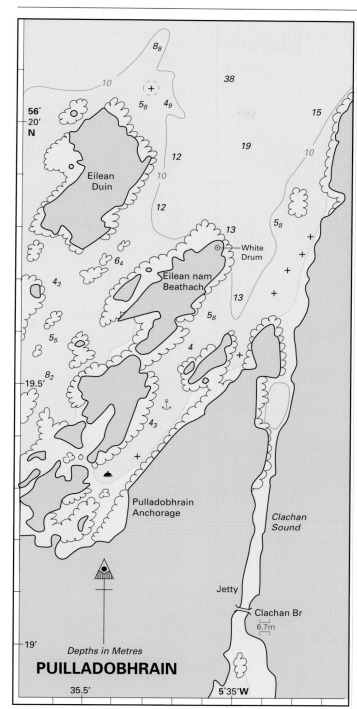

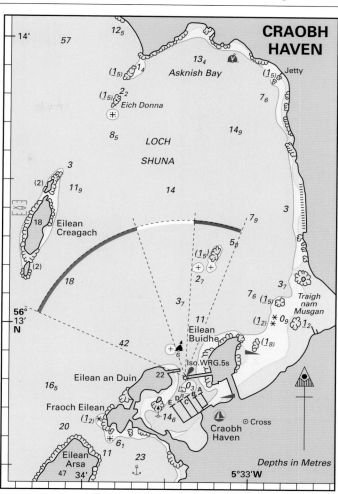

PUILLADOBHRAIN

56°19'·5N 5°35'·1W

Chart BA 2387; SC 5611; Imray 2800, C65
HW Oban –0015

MHWS	MHWN	MLWN	MLWS
4·0m	2·9m	1·8m	0·7m

Pronounced '*Pulldochran*', this anchorage provides excellent shelter from winds of all directions but in a severe W gale the low-lying rocks on its W side may be overwhelmed.

Approach and Entrance From the W and N avoid rocks awash N of En Duin. Entrance is close to En nam Beathach (W Drum on N end) avoiding rock which dries 2·7m off the mainland shore to the E. About 100m beyond the W Drum turn on to 215° down the anchorage.

Anchorage Anchor in 4m where room. A popular anchorage in summer. Holding has recently been reported as poor.

Facilities Inn at Clachan Br which is 18th century known as 'Bridge over the Atlantic'.

LOCH MELFORT

Chart BA 2326; SC 5611; Imray 2800, C65
HW Oban –0040

MHWS	MHWN	MLWN	MLWS
2·8m	2·1m	1·3m	0·6m

A very attractive and popular loch with many moorings and fish farms.

Entrance Note Campbell Rock 1·8m ¾M NE of Ru Chnaip. Also beware of covering rock marked by bn N of pontoon in L na Cille.

Anchorages
• Moorings in L na Cille at head of L Melfort. Apply Kilmelford Yacht Haven.
• Fearnach Bay. Moorings. Limited space for anchoring.

Facilities Kilmelford Yacht Haven ✆ 01852 200248. Full facilities. Shop/PO, hotel at Kilmelford 1½M. Bus to Oban. Fearnach Bay: Water, diesel and calor at pier.

CRAOBH HAVEN*, Loch Shuna

Chart BA 2326; SC 5611; Imray 2800, C65
HW Oban –0045.

MHWS	MHWN	MLWN	MLWS
5·1m	4·0m	1·3m	0·6m

Craobh Haven, pronounced 'Creuve', is a modern 250 berth marina 7M N of Crinan formed by the construction of breakwaters between off-shore islands and the mainland.

Approach Beware extensive reef (dries 1·5m) ¼M N of Eilean Buidhe.

Entrance From N leave G con buoy to stb. Inside to port R buoys mark a shoal patch between the entrance and the pontoons. On the W side of the Haven a perch marks a submerged spit, the rest of the Haven has sufficient depth.

Berthing Visitors' berths on pontoon C. Four visitors' moorings off Loch Melfort Hotel in Asknish Bay.

Facilities Full facilities. Shop, Chandlery, and Restaurant. Bus to Oban.

✆/VHF 01854 500222, VHF 80, 37.

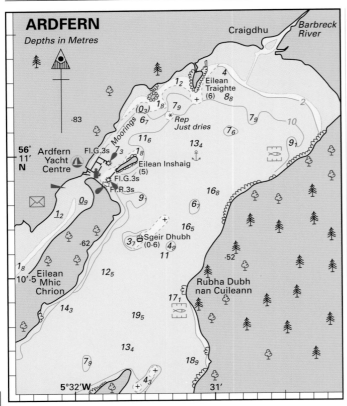

ARDFERN
Depths in Metres

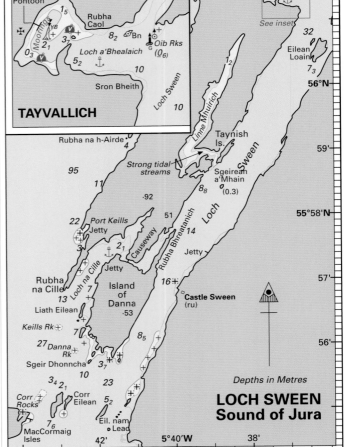

TAYVALLICH

LOCH SWEEN
Sound of Jura
Depths in Metres

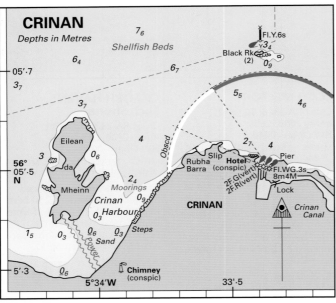

CRINAN
Depths in Metres

ARDFERN*,
Loch Craignish

Chart BA 2326; SC 5611;
Imray 2800, C65
HW Oban –0100

MHWS	MHWN	MLWN	MLWS
2·4m	1·7m	1·0m	0·3m

May be squally in strong N and
NE winds. Barometric pressure
and SW winds can alter tidal
height up to 1m.

Approach From N via Dorus
Mor S of Craignish Point. (Tide
8kn at springs). From S keep E
of Ruadh Sgeir Fl.6s then in
Loch Craignish give shore and
islands a berth of 1½ca. Note
Sgeir Dubh (0·6m) 2ca E of N
end of En Mhic Chrion.

Entrance to Ardfern is between
Ens Mhic Chrion and Inshaig
keeping well over to former.

There is a floating breakwater
extending SW from En Inshaig.

Facilities Ardfern Yacht Centre
with pontoon berths and
swinging moorings. Full
facilities and boatyard.
PO/shop and hotel. Bus to
Oban.

☎/VHF 01852 500247, VHF
80.

CRINAN*,

Charts BA 2326, 2476; SC 5611;
Imray 2800, C63
HW Oban –0100

MHWS	MHWN	MLWN	MLWS
2·4m	1·7m	1·1m	0·3m

Approach Straightforward. W
hotel conspic. LtHo Fl.WG.3s.

Entrance to canal E of hotel.
Note Black Rock 2ca N.

Anchorages
• Crinan Harbour: VHF 74. For
moorings Crinan Boats
☎ 01546 830232, VHF 12.
• Anchor off hotel in 4m.
Exposed to NW.
• Moor in canal basin.
• Alongside concrete pier to E
of Lt Ho.

Facilities
Crinan Harbour: Water, diesel,
café, hotel/restaurant with
showers.
Crinan Boats: Full facilities.
Bus to Lochgilphead,
connections to Oban and
Glasgow.

Crinan Canal runs across the
base of the Kintyre Peninsula to
Ardrishaig on Loch Fyne thus
saving a sometimes difficult
80M passage round the Mull to
the Clyde. Canal can be entered
at all states of tide from
0800–2100 daily in season,
unless there is a drought, when
entry confined to HW±0300.
The Canal is 9M long with 15
locks and seven swing bridges
and can take vessels up to
26·5m LOA, 6m beam and
2·9m draught. In summer,
June–August locks and bridges
open 0830–2000 daily, 2100
Friday, Saturday, Sunday. Other
periods shorter opening times.
Further information see
www.scottishcanals.co.uk.
Inland locks are operated by
boat's crew. Passage time at
least 6hrs. Yachts proceeding W

have right of way. Use horn
when approaching bridges.
Mooring pontoons established
at Bellanoch. Dues payable at
sea locks. Details from Crinan
Canal, Pier Square, Ardrishaig,
Argyll PA30 8DZ ☎ 01546
603210.

☎/VHF Sea Lock 01546
602458, VHF 74.

TAYVALLICH,
Loch Sween

Chart BA 2397; SC 5611;
Imray C64
HW Oban 1st –0330 / 2nd –0030

A popular and well protected
hbr at head of Loch Sween.
Many moorings.

Approach The tides run
strongly in this area. From N
care must be taken to avoid
Keills and Danna Rocks to port
and Corr Rocks to stb. The N
end of En Ghamhna on the Pt
of Knapp 155° leads clear but
landmarks may be difficult to
identify as Point is 2M away.
Avoid Sgeir Bun an Locha on
W side of entrance to L Sween.
In the loch, the shores are
mostly clean but avoid mid-
channel rock awash at HW
1½M N of Castle Sween, (see
plan). At head of loch keep
close to Sron Bheith.

Entrance Enter hbr through
narrow passage S of mid-
channel islet.

RUM TO ISLAY

Passage lights	BA No
Skerryvore	4096
Fl.10s46m23M	
Racon (M) (- -)	
Dubh Artach	4098
Fl(2)30s44m20M	
Orsay	
Fl.5s24M	

SW of both Tiree and Mull dangerous rks and an uneven bottom extend 10M causing a bad sea. Great care must be taken to avoid the Torran Rocks extending 5M SW of the Ross of Mull. The passage N of Colonsay to the Sound of Islay is clear.

Tidal Streams

All related to Dover. Sp rates.

Passage of Tiree	
+0100N −0515S	1½kn
Ross of Mull	
−0115N +0445S	1½kn
W of Islay	
−0030NE +0600SW	2kn
Sound of Islay	
−0100N +0515S	5kn
Race off Onsay, Sound of Islay	
HW NW −0615SE	8kn
Mull of Oa (S. Islay)	
HW NW −0615SE	5kn

Anchorages
- Anchor W of central reef between reef and moorings. Space limited.
- In Loch a' Bhealaich SE of entrance reef.
- Visitors' moorings may be found in the NE and S parts of the hbr.

Facilities Water on pontoon, short-stay only, shop, restaurant. Calor and showers in Caravan Park. Ferry to Craighouse, Jura. Bus to Lochgilphead.

CRAIGHOUSE, Loch Na Mile, Jura

Chart BA 2396; SC 5611; Imray C64
HW Oban −0240

MHWS	MHWN	MLWN	MLWS
1·0m	0·5m	0·5m	0·1m

A useful alternative to Gigha. Good shelter but subject to swell.

Approach and Entrance Na Cuilten Fl.10s9M lies 1½M SW of entrance. Enter between En nan Gabhar Lt bn Fl.5s to stb and perch to port.

Anchorages
- 16 visitors' moorings.
- Anchor clear of moorings off stone pier. Holding reported poor.
- In sandy cove at SW entrance of Lowlandmans Bay N of L na Mile.

Facilities PO/Shop, water, fuel, Calor, hotel.

GIGHA*

Chart BA 2475; SC 5611; Imray C64
HW Oban −0210 sp; −0450 np

MHWS	MHWN	MLWN	MLWS
1·5m	1·3m	0·8m	0·6m

A convenient and useful passage hbr for yachts proceeding to or from the Mull of Kintyre. Exposed from NE to SE.

Approach From S, keep about 2ca E of Gigalum, leave W card buoy Q(9)15s to stb. From N, keep 1M offshore to avoid Sgeir Nuadh (dr 1·3m), marked by R can buoy Fl.R.6s.

Entrance When jetty bears 270° head in, but beware of Kiln Rock (dr 1·5m) 1ca ENE of jetty.

Anchorage in Ardminish Bay, 11 visitors' moorings. Plenty of room to anchor, hard sand.

Facilities PO/shop, cycle hire, showers at hotel (½M), diesel at shop (300m), launderette and water at café. Ferry to Tayinloan connects with bus to Glasgow.

PORT ELLEN, Islay*

Chart BA 2474; SC 5611; Imray C64
HW Oban −0050 sp; −0530 np

MHWS	MHWN	MLWN	MLWS
0·9m	0·8m	0·5m	0·3m

A useful passage hbr on the S coast of Islay, if proceeding S to Mull of Kintyre or N Ireland. Exposed to swell from S. Note very small tidal range.

Approach From E keep 1½M off Islay shore and ¾M S of Texa to avoid offlying rks. From W beware of tide races and overfalls off the Oa. From S avoid breakers over Otter Rocks marked by S card buoy Q(6)+LFl.15s. Keep Carraig Fhada Lt Fl.WRG.3s in line with Ro masts 330° leaving G con buoy to stb.

Anchorages and Berthing
- Pontoons in hbr behind ferry terminal, uncomfortable in strong SW winds. Take care in final approach to pontoons, depth reduces rapidly outside channel buoys.
- 10 visitors' moorings established in two trots in NE of bay. Note three perches with topmarks over underwater rks.
- Kilnaughton Bay provides some shelter from the W, good holding.

Facilities PO, shops, hotels, water at pier head, diesel. Ferry with link to Glasgow.

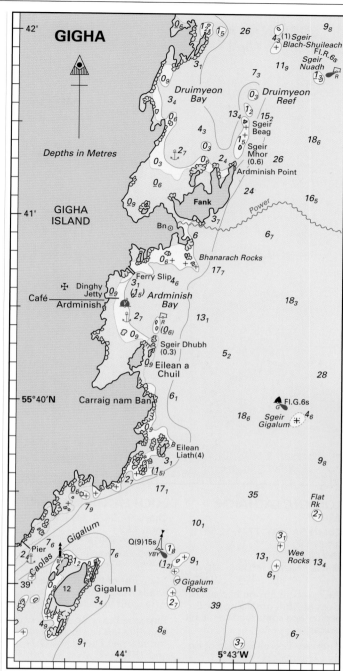

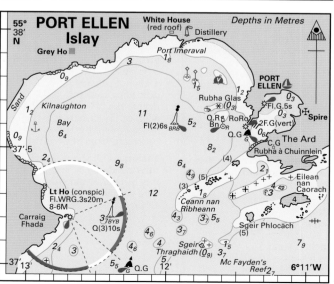

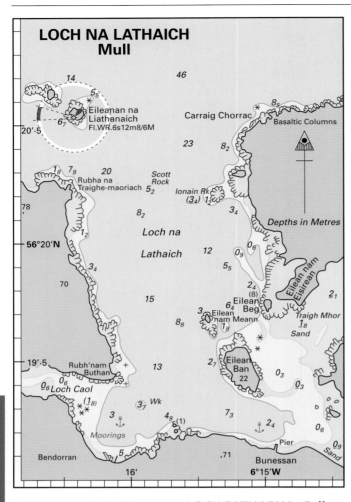

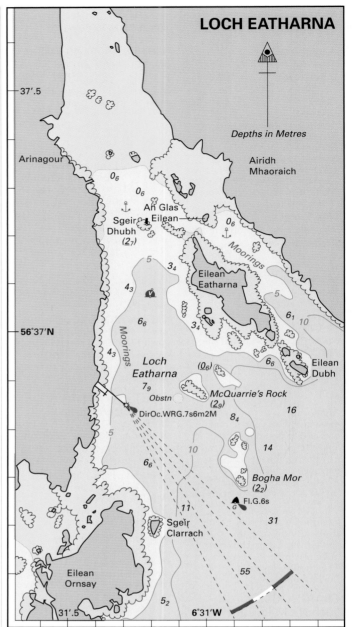

LOCH NA LATHAICH, Mull*

Charts BA 2617, 2771; SC 5611; Imray C65
HW Oban −0015

MHWS	MHWN	MLWN	MLWS
4·3m	3·0m	1·8m	0·6m

An excellent hbr on N coast of Ross of Mull providing good shelter and some facilities. Easy access.

Entrance Pass either side of En na Liathanaich, Fl.WR.6s12m8/6M. Give the En a berth of 2ca and keep to the W side of the loch.

Anchorages
• Entrance to L Caol to W.
• S of En Ban off pier.
• In bay off Bendorran, many moorings, trip line advised.
• Staffa (Fingals Cave) 5M N. Difficult anchorage off SE corner.

Facilities Bunessan: PO, shops, garage, hotel at 1½M. Bus to Craignure for ferry to Oban. Bus to Fionnphort for ferry to Iona.

LOCH EATHARNA, Coll

Charts BA 2474, 2171; SC 6511; Imray C65
HW Oban +0018

MHWS	MHWN
4·4m	3·2m

Main hbr of Coll. Exposed to winds from E to S. Village of Arinagour at head of loch.

Entrance Leave Bo Mor G con buoy Fl.G.6s to stb and make for new pier DirOc.WRG.7s and 2F.R(vert), then ½ca off W shore turn N towards old stone pier where loch shoals rapidly.

Anchorages
• Visitors' moorings to N of new pier. Untenable in winds greater than Force 4 from E to S because of swell.
• Anchor off stone pier according to depth. Note drying rks NW of En Eatharna.
• NE of En Eatharna. Swinging space limited but more protected from SE.

Facilities PO, shops, hotel offering showers, laundry and meals. Fuel, water from tap in field behind stone pier. Ferry to Oban.

C. The Outer Hebrides

Passage lights	BA No
Flannan Is	4028
Fl(2)30s101m20M AIS	
Butt of Lewis	3968
Fl.5s52m25M AIS	
Tiumpan Head	3972
Fl(2)15s55m25M	
En Glas E L Tarbert	3990
Fl(3)20s43m23M Racon	
Ushenish	4004
Fl.WR.20s 54m19/15M	
Barra Head	4020
Fl.15s208m18M	
Ru A'Mhail	4236
Fl(3)15s45m19M	

The navigation of the W side of the outer Hebrides should not be attempted without a crew capable of handling the yacht in severe conditions. Heavy seas are common along the whole 100M of the western seaboard and the coast should only be closed in settled weather with large-scale charts aboard. Shelter can be found by sailing either N or S of the chain into the lee of the islands. Off Harris, Benbecula and N and S Uist a vessel should stand off several miles. The land on the W is so low that an accurate visual fix may be difficult to obtain.

In order to make a passage to the W side of the Outer Hebrides the three possible passages are:

• Round the Butt of Lewis and passing down the W side between the coast and the Flannan Is.

• Through the Sound of Harris. This passage requires strict attention to the tides and the channel taken for which BA chart 2802 is absolutely essential. CCC Directions *Outer Hebrides*.

• From Castlebay at the S end through either the Sound of Barra or the Sound of Berneray for which BA charts 2770 or 2769 are required. Again CCC Directions are detailed.

The E coast of Lewis and Harris is clear from the Butt of Lewis to the Shiant Is. There are numerous dangerous rocks and islets with strong tides and overfalls extending from the Shiants to Ru Hunish (N Skye). Heavy seas may be experienced S of the Shiants. Between the Sound of Harris and the S end of N Uist the coast is clear beyond ½M off-shore but Benbecula and its islets should be given a berth of at least 1M. Dangerous rocks exist up to 2M S of Barra.

Tidal Streams

All related to Dover Sp rates

Ru Uisenish to Shiant Is
+0500NE −0100SW 3–4kn

En Glas (Harris) to Sgeir Inoc
+0500NE −0100SW 2½kn

Ru Hunish (Skye)
+0400NE −0200SW 2½kn

ST KILDA

Chart BA 2524;
Imray C66
HW Stornoway −0040

MHWS	MHWN	MLWN	MLWS
3·4m	2·5m	1·2m	0·4m

A small group of islands. The main island is owned by National Trust for Scotland and leased to the Scottish National Heritage and the Army. As a courtesy, visitors should report to the base, call sign *Kilda Radar* VHF 16, 08.

Approach Fine, settled weather is particularly desirable when undertaking the 35M+ journey to St Kilda. Rip tides form between the Islands of the group when wind and tide are opposed.

Anchorages
In Village Bay off concrete pier. Ldg Lts Oc.5s 270°. Subject to swell. Untenable in winds from ENE to SSW when Glen Bay to NW may be possible with line ashore, but subject to extreme squalls.

Facilities Water from well near landing. Seek assistance from Army.

WEST LOCH TARBERT, Harris

Chart BA 2841;
Imray C66
HW Stornoway −0015

MHWS	MHWN	MLWN	MLWS
3·7m	2·8m	1·5m	0·7m

One of the few harbours on the W coast of the outer Hebrides offering protection from all winds except those from the W.

Approach Either side of Taransay, the N being clearer. From S keep Toe Head and summit of Coppay Is in line. Once past Bo Ushig (dr 2m), ½M S of Taransay, keep to mid-channel to avoid sand spits on either side of the Sound.

Anchorages
• Head of loch at Tarbert.
• Taransay N of Corran Raah spit.
• Loch Leosavay: Beware drying rocks SW of jetty.
• Loch Bun Abhainn-eader: N of Ardhasaig. Anchor SW of chimney of old whaling station (swell) or off E bay. Telephone, store, garage (marine diesel) on main road. Land with permission, at fish farm in SE corner of bay.

Facilities Tarbert: Shops, PO, hotel. Ferry to Skye.

STORNOWAY, Lewis*

Chart BA 2529;
Imray C67
HW Stornoway HW

MHWS	MHWN	MLWN	MLWS
4·8m	3·7m	2·0m	0·7m

Busy ferry and fishing port.

Entrance Between Holm Point and Arnish Point. Beware of the Beasts of Holm, drying rocks marked by unlit G bn off Holm Point and Reef Rock off Arnish Point marked by port hand R can buoy Q.R. At night use the sectored lights shown on plan. Call *Stornoway Harbour* VHF 12 before entering.

Anchorages
• In bay NW of En na Gobhail. Shoals.
• 27 pontoon berths at inner harbour beyond lifeboat. Beware shallow water just outside the pontoons.
• Glumaig Harbour, 3M S of town. Advisable to buoy anchor.

Facilities PO, Launderette, shops closed all day Wednesday, charts, water, diesel, slip. Showers at Leisure Centre. Ferry to Ullapool.

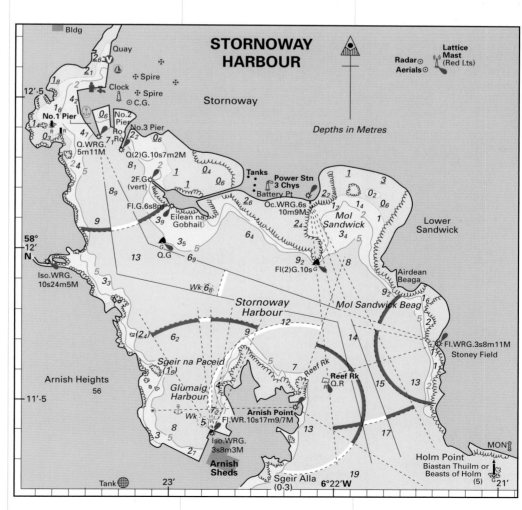

LOCH SHELL, Lewis

Chart BA 1794;
Imray C67
HW Stornoway −0006

MHWS	MHWN	MLWN	MLWS
4·8m	3·6m	1·9m	0·7m

Entrance Enter S of En Lubhard. Note drying rocks to NW of En.

Anchorages
• Head of loch. Shoals. Exposed to E. Fish farms developing.
• Tob Eisken.
• Tob Lemreway leaving En Lubbard to port.

Facilities None.

SCALPAY, East Loch Tarbert*

Charts BA 1794, 2905;
Imray C66
HW Stornoway −0015

MHWS	MHWN	MLWN	MLWS
5·0m	3·7m	2·1m	0·8m

Approach The Sound of Scalpay is clearer than the passage to the S of the island, the only danger being Elliot Rocks (2m) off the S shore. Pass under br (20m).

Entrance to Scalpay N hbr give Aird an Aiseg to NW a berth of ½ca. Ldg marks two W ▲s in line lead between G con buoy Fl.G.2s to stb and submerged rock 1·1m to port.

Anchorages
• N hbr off pier (2F.G(vert) Lts). Good shelter.
• S hbr, not easy to identify rocks off entrance.
• Tarbert 3M WNW of Scalpay. WSW of Ferry pier, not much room. Exposed to E.

Facilities Tarbert: PO, shops EC Thursday, hotel, diesel, water at pier. Ferry to Skye.

LOCH RODEL Poll an Tighmhail

Chart BA 2802;
Imray C66
HW Stornoway −0025

MHWS	MHWN	MLWN	MLWS
4·6m	3·5m	1·9m	0·6m

The unusual anchorage at Poll an Tighmhail offers complete protection but entrance only at HW±0100. Nearby, a fine example of a medieval church.

Entrance By way of Loch Rodel avoiding the Duncan rock 0·3m off the W shore. Although Tighmhail appears to have three entrances the only viable one is through Bay channel dries 1·9m, the most N'ly off Loch Rodel and to the N of Corr-eilean. Enter HW±0100 according to draught. Do not attempt to enter via the other two channels.

Anchorage Visitors' moorings are laid and anchoring is possible outside these although depth in parts deep, requiring kedge to avoid swinging. Use a trip line as bottom has fishing nets and gear.

Facilities None but hotel.

LOCHMADDY, North Uist*

Chart BA 2825;
Imray C66
HW Stornoway −0030

MHWS	MHWN	MLWN	MLWS
4·8m	3·6m	1·9m	0·7m

Approach From S pass either side of Madadh Mor (26m high). Note submerged rocks ½ca N of Leac nan Madah. From N pass between Weavers Point and Madadh Beag (6m). Thence by channel between Glas En Mor, Fl(2)G.4s and Ru Nam Pleac, Fl.R.4s and S of Ruig Liath Q.G to W sector of Lt Fl(3)WRG.8s. Follow Ldg Lts front 2F.G(vert), rear Oc.G.8s on 298° to pier.

Anchorages
• Visitors' moorings SW of pier in soft mud.
• SW corner of S Basin.
• Bagh Aird nan Madadh. (Heavy moorings for visitors).
• Loch Portain 2M NNE. Keep in mid-channel NE of Flodday and 1ca off Ru nam Gall. Good holding and protection.
• Tie up to pier if no ferry due but beware of surge.

Facilities PO, shop, water at pier, diesel, calor, showers at hotel. Ferry to Skye and Harris.

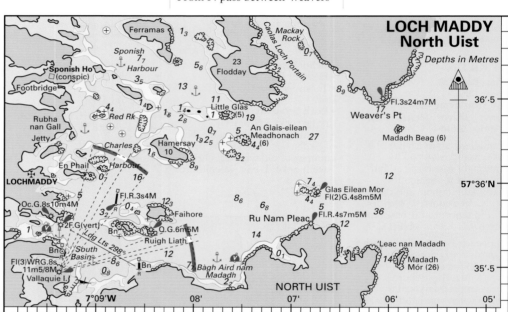

LOCH MADDY North Uist — Depths in Metres

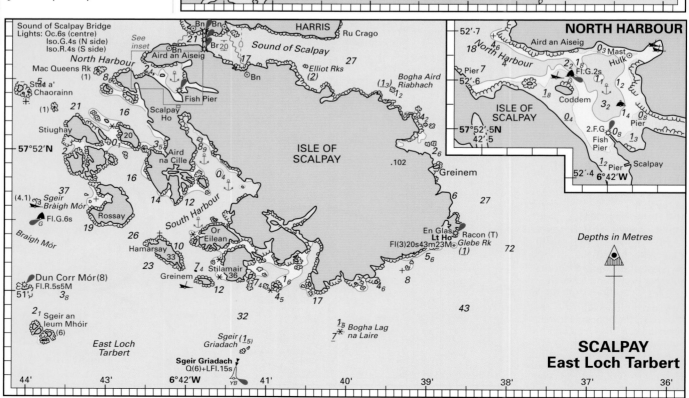

SCALPAY East Loch Tarbert

NORTH HARBOUR

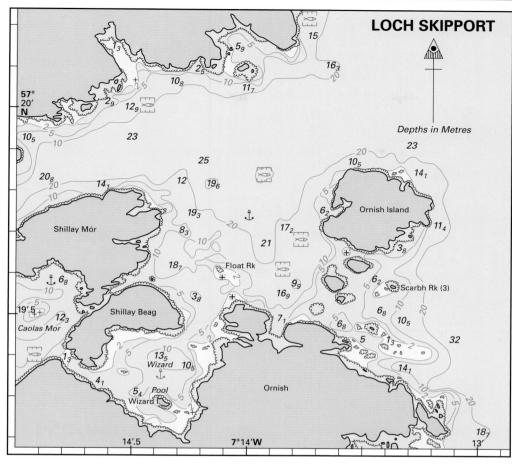

LOCH BOISDALE*

Chart BA 2770;
Imray C66
HW Stornoway –0042

MHWS	MHWN	MLWN	MLWS
4·1m	3·0m	1·7m	0·5m

Approach and Entrance Pass between Ru na Cruibe and Calvay Is Lt Fl(2)WRG.10s then N of Gasay Lt bn Fl.WR.5s at NE pt of island. Beware Gasay Rocks (dr 0·9m) and an obstruction extending 2½ca to E of end of Is. Follow marked channel to pier 2F.G.

Anchorages
• Six visitors' moorings NE of pier.
• SW of pier, clear of moorings and pier approach. Limited space and poor holding.
• S of loch NE of ruined pier. Note rocks 2ca NNW of pier and many marine farms in this area.

Facilities Tearoom with some supplies, hotel. Water at pier, fuel at garage. Shops at Daliburgh 3M. Ferry to mainland.

LOCH SKIPPORT, South Uist

Chart BA 2825;
Imray C66
HW Stornoway –0042

MHWS	MHWN	MLWN	MLWS
4·6m	3·3m	1·7m	0·5m

Easy access N of Ornish Is. Several remote anchorages.

Anchorages
• Wizard Pool: Keep well over towards the Shillays Mor and Beg to avoid Float Rock (dr 2·3m) thence mid-channel keeping Wizard Is just open of Skillay Beg. Note drying rock (0·3m) 1¼ca NW of Wizard Is.
• Bagh Charmaig: (NNW of Shillay Mor) Note reef ½ca off middle of W shore. Anchor at head of bay or just within E arm which shoals. Good holding.

Facilities None.

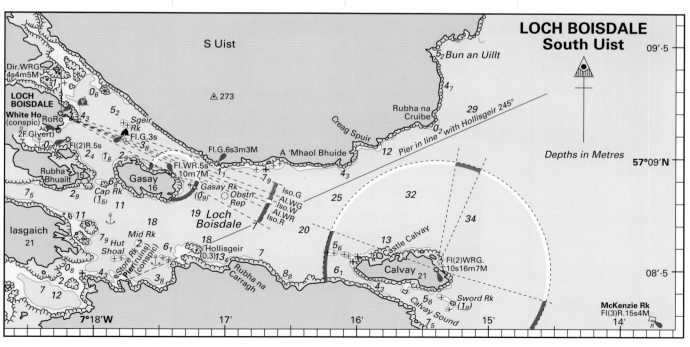

CASTLE BAY, BARRA*

Charts BA 1796, 2769;
Imray C65
HW Stornoway –0050

MHWS	MHWN	MLWN	MLWS
4·3m	3·1m	1·7m	0·6m

A valuable hbr at S end of
Outer Hebrides.

Approach and Entrance From
Bo Vich Chuan buoy,
Q(6)+LFl.15s, 2·2M E of Sgeir
a Scape, keep R can buoy,
Fl(2)R.8s, close to port and
head midway between Sgeir
Dubh Q(3)G.6s and Channel
Rock Fl.WR.6s. Pick up Ldg
line on Ru Glas 295°, Or and
W day marks, F.Bu Lts,
between these two bns by
steering 270° for not more than
½M from Sgeir a Scape. Leave
G con buoy, Fl.G.3s, to stb
until pier, 2F.G vert, opens W
of castle.

Anchorages
• 12 visitors' moorings.
• NW of castle in 6–10m.
• Vatersay Bay.

Facilities PO, shops, hotel.
Water at pier, diesel at garage,
Calor. Ferry to mainland.

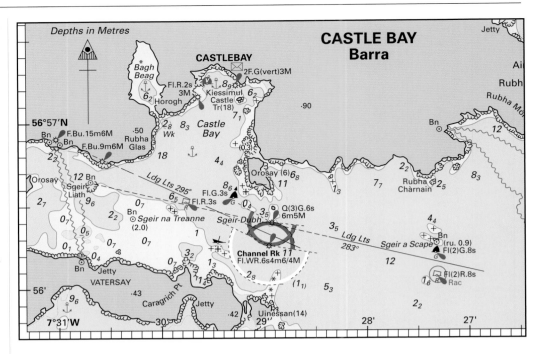

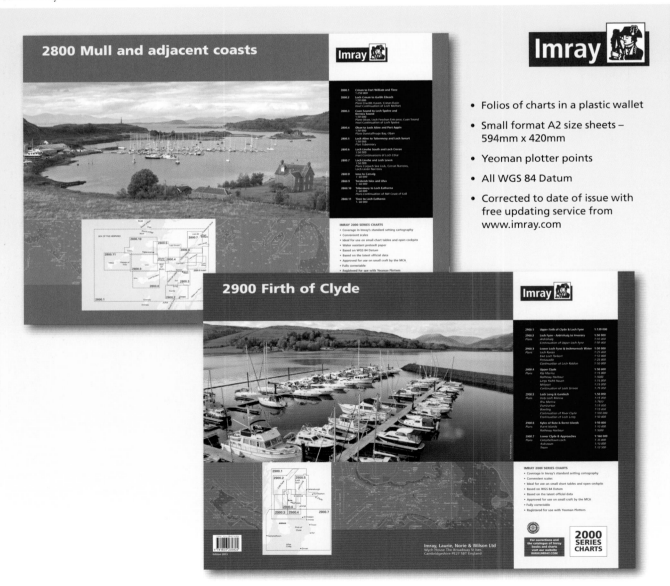

D. Firth of Clyde and S Coast of Galloway

CAMPBELTOWN TO PORT PATRICK

Passage lights	BA No
Mull of Kintyre Fl(2)20s91m24M	4272
Sanda Is Fl.10s50m15M	4274
Davaar Fl(2)10s37m23M	4276
Toward Point Fl.10s21m22M	4362
Little Cumbrae Fl.6s28m14M	4346
Holy Is, Pillar Rock Fl(2)20s38m25M	4330
Pladda Fl(3)30s40m17M	4326
Turnberry Point Fl.15s29m24M	4580
Ailsa Craig Fl.4s18m17M	4582
Corsewall Point Fl(5)30s34m22M	4604

The waters of the Clyde Estuary are very popular with many yachts and consequently there are more facilities for yachtsmen. The passages are protected and well marked. There are restrictions to the movement of vessels in Gareloch and Loch Long during submarine movements. The tidal streams are generally weak turning N'ly at HW Dover and S'ly at Dover +0600. There is a race with dangerous overfalls off the Mull of Kintyre and in Sanda Sound. Strong tides will also be encountered between Bennane Head (8M SSE of Ailsa Craig) and the Mull of Galloway. There is a dangerous race extending some 3M S of the Mull.

Tidal Streams
All related to Dover Sp rates
Sanda Sound
+0500E −0100W 5kn
Davaar Is
HWD N +0600S 4kn
Black Head
−0130N −0430S 5kn

CAMPBELTOWN*

Charts BA 1864, 2126; SC 5610; Imray C63
HW Greenock −0015

MHWS	MHWN	MLWN	MLWS
2·9m	2·5m	1·1m	0·5m

A well sheltered loch. Useful if waiting to round the Mull.

Approach and Entrance From N avoid Otterard Rock marked by E card Lt buoy, 1M N of entrance. From S pass to N of Davaar Is, Lt Fl(2)10s, then enter loch on 240° Ldg Lts F.Y. Thence to hbr entrance. Lts 2F.G(vert) and 2F.R(vert).

Anchorages
• Berth at pontoon just NW of N quay. Beware shallow water to NW of pontoon.

• Anchor S of hbr.

Facilities PO, shops EC Wednesday. Usual facilities at pontoon. Showers at Leisure Centre.

☏/VHF HM 01586 522522, VHF 16, 12, 13; Pontoon Berthing Master *Mobile* 07798 524821.

EAST LOCH TARBERT*, Loch Fyne

Chart BA 2381; SC 5610; Imray 2900, C63
HW Greenock −0005

MHWS	MHWN	MLWN	MLWS
3·6m	2·9m	1·0m	0·3m

An excellent, sheltered and popular hbr.

Entrance Pass N of bn, Fl.R.2·5s, and S of bn, Q.G, off En a Choic (ignoring buoys marking passage N of Choic). Leave stb bn VQ.G. S of Sgeir Bhuidhe to stb before turning NW towards visitors' pontoon and finger berths (row A).

Berths
• Pontoon and finger berths on NW side of hbr.
• Alongside fish quay, for taking on fuel only.
There is no anchoring space within hbr.

Facilities Shops EC Wednesday, PO, chandlers, charts. Slip, sailmaker, some marine and electronic repairs. Fuel, diesel on fish quay (weekdays only). Bus to Glasgow.

☏/VHF HM 01880 820344, VHF 14.

Inner Firth of Clyde distances (miles)

	Ardrishaig	Ardrossan	Bangor	Bowling	Campbeltown	Inverkip	Lamlash	Largs Marina	Mull of Kintyre	Portpatrick	Stranraer	Tarbert	Troon
Ardrishaig	0												
Ardrossan	33	0											
Bangor	84	66	0										
Bowling	54	37	97	0									
Campbeltown	40	35	49	65	0								
Inverkip	39	20	81	17	46	0							
Lamlash	33	12	57	41	25	25	0						
Largs Marina	33	11	72	25	41	9	18	0					
Mull of Kintyre	55	44	39	74	21	59	35	51	0				
Portpatrick	75	53	23	83	41	68	45	59	37	0			
Stranraer	71	46	39	78	39	62	40	54	38	22	0		
Tarbert	10	25	75	46	32	30	25	24	47	66	63	0	
Troon	39	8	64	43	34	26	15	18	44	49	43	31	0

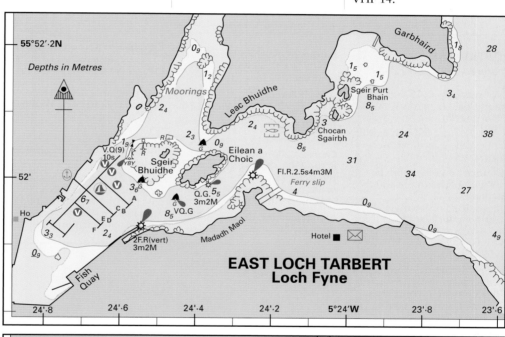

EAST LOCH TARBERT
Loch Fyne

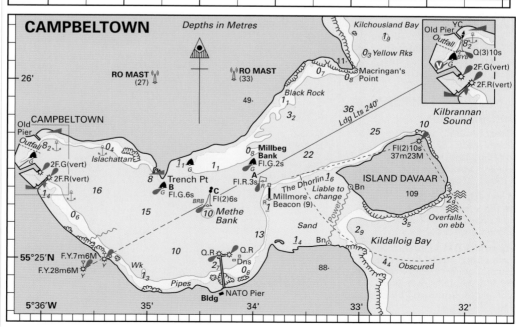

CAMPBELTOWN

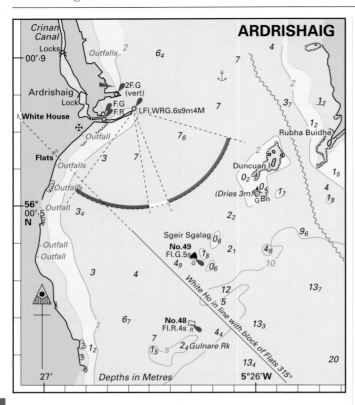

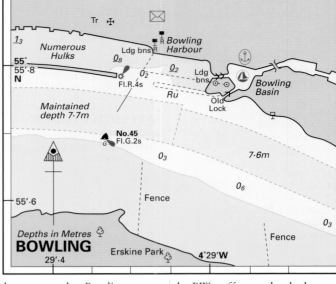

PORTAVADIE

Charts BA 2381; Imray 2900.3, C63

HW Greenock –0005

MHWS	MHWN	MLWN	MLWS
3·4m	2·9m	1·1m	0·3m

A fully serviced modern marina with excellent facilities. Access at all states of the tide.

Entrance From the south be aware of a fish farm just to the north of Rubah Stillaig, otherwise no problems identifying the entrance. Lit for easy access at night. Enter between breakwaters Fl.R.2s and Fl(2)G.8s.

Berths 230 fully serviced berths accommodating all sizes up to 70ft LOA with no restriction on draft. Diesel and petrol available from fuel berth.

Facilities Shop, selling basic provisions and gifts, Chandlery, Yard services, Bar/Restaurant, Range of self catering accommodation, Bike hire.
☎/VHF 01700 811075; VHF 80
www.portavadiemarina.com

ARDRISHAIG*

Chart BA 2381; SC 5610; Imray 2900, C63

HW Greenock +0005

MHWS	MHWN	MLWN	MLWS
3·4m	2·8m	1·1m	0·2m

This is the hbr at the entrance to the S end of the Crinan canal in Loch Gilp. *For Canal Directions see page 158.*

Approach 3M from the hbr pass either side of Big Rock 2·1m. Pass between Nos.48 and 49 R & G buoys, Ldg line conspic W house and block of flats, 315°.

Entrance Give the S breakwater a wide berth and wait on pontoon until lock gate opens.
☎/VHF Canal Office 01546 603210, VHF 74.

BOWLING*

Entrance to Forth-Clyde Canal

Chart BA 2007; SC 5610; Imray 2900, C63

HW Greenock +0015

MHWS	MHWN	MLWN	MLWS
4·0m	3·3m	1·3m	0·4m

In the canal the air draft is 3m; there are facilities for masts to be unstepped at Bowling. Locking HW±0200.

Approach From seaward contact estuary control tower VHF 12 or ☎ 01475 726221 prior to arrival at No.1 buoy off Greenock container terminal.

Entrance To port off the River Clyde opposite G con Lt buoy Fl.G.2s No.45 turn on to Ldg line 030° marked by R posts with topmarks. Once inside ruined breakwater marked by posts turn on to Ldg line 100° marked by R posts and topmarks. Follow lock keeper's instructions when entering lock mooring on port side.

Transit Allow three days. 39 locks including sea locks. To pass the Dumbarton road br a drop lock enables boats to pass under. Some locks are operated by BW staff, some by the boats crew with assistance and some entirely by the boats crew. Exit at Grangemouth into River Carron, step mast at Port Edgar. *See Scotland – E Coast section on page 122.* Bowling basin operates 0830–2100 June–August daily but shorter opening hours other periods. Transit time five days allowed. Further information www.scottishcanals.co.uk.

☎/VHF 01389 877969, VHF 74.

INVERKIP*

Chart BA 1907; SC 5610; Imray 2900, C63

HW Greenock –0015

MHWS	MHWN	MLWN	MLWS
3·3m	2·8m	1·0m	0·4m

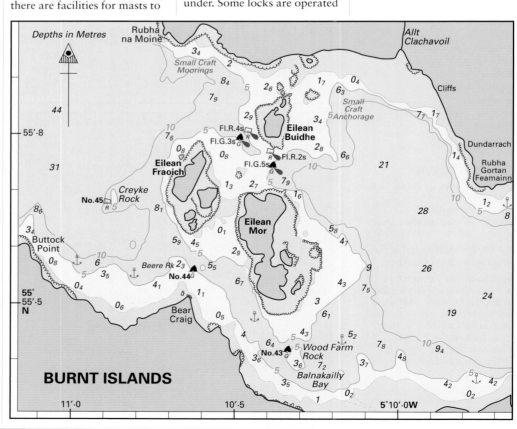

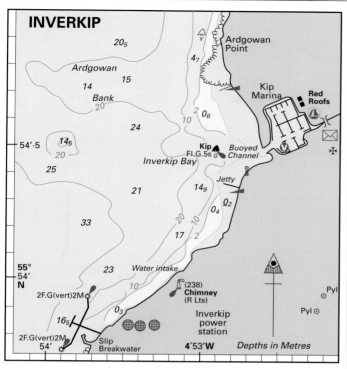

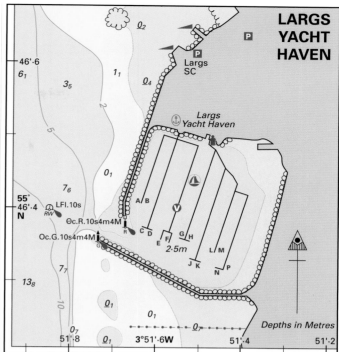

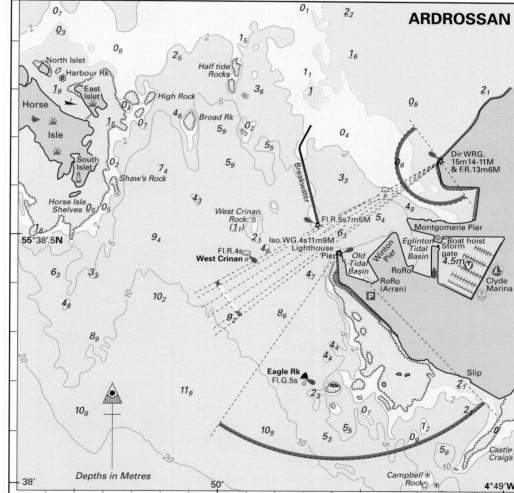

A large well-founded marina and convenient stopover before entering the Clyde.

Approach and Entrance ½M N of power station (conspic) head for G con buoy Fl.G.5s and follow buoyed channel into marina.

Berthing Kip marina with 600 berths and all facilities and chandlery.

Facilities Rly to Glasgow

☎/VHF 01475 521485, VHF 37, 80.

LARGS YACHT HAVEN*

Chart BA 1907; SC 5610; **Imray** 2900, C63

HW Greenock –0015

MHWS	MHWN	MLWN	MLWS
3·3m	2·8m	1·0m	0·4m

A convenient modern marina on the Firth of Clyde 1M S of Largs.

Approach Easy access. Pass close to RW sph buoy LFl.10s and enter between breakwaters (Oc.G.10s and Oc.R.10s) painted W.

Facilities Full marina facilities, PO, Shops EC Wednesday, hotels 1M, Rly to Glasgow.

☎/VHF Marina 01475 675333, VHF 37, 80.

ARDROSSAN*

Charts BA 2131,1866,SC5610; Imray C63

HW Greenock –0020

MHWS	MHWN	MLWN	MLWS
3·2m	2·6m	1·1m	0·4m

A well-protected deep water marina with 20 visitors' berths. Entrance closed by a storm gate in extreme weather. The outer harbour is the Cal Mac ferry port for Arran.

Approach From the W or NW keep clear of low-lying Horse Isle, conspic tr on S end, ringed by drying ledges. The passage between Horse Isle and the mainland should not be attempted. From S or SE make for 55°38'·0N 4°50'·2W. Head for entrance leaving G con buoy Eagle Rock Fl.G.5s to stb and R can buoy West Crinan Rock Fl.R.4s to port. Inside the hbr entrance, engines must be used, keep clear of commercial craft, monitor VHF 12/16.

Traffic Signals shown from control tr at entrance to marina.

• 3F.R.(vert) Hbr and Marina closed.

• 3F.G.(vert) Hbr closed, Marina open; pleasure craft may enter/leave marina.

• 2F.R. over 1F.G. Hbr open, Marina closed.

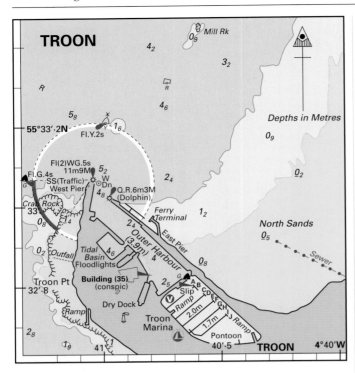

Entrance

DirWRG.15m14–11M, W sector, 055° leads to hbr entrance between the breakwaters.

Berthing As instructed by Clyde Marina or on the third pontoon from N.

Facilities as expected of a modern marina. Boatyard, chandlery, sail repairs. Large supermarket nearby. Wi-Fi. Rly to Glasgow.

☎/VHF 01294 607077, VHF 80, Call sign *Clyde Marina* (office hours seven days).

LAMLASH, Arran

Charts BA 1864, 2220; SC 5610; Imray 2900, C63
HW Greenock –0025

MHWS	MHWN
3·2m	2·6m

A large natural hbr on the E of Is of Arran opposite Holy Island.

Approach by either N or S passages lit by port and stb marks. The flood tide sets into the S and out of the N of the bay. In strong NW winds the S channel may be difficult. Pillar Rk Lt Fl(2)20s38m25M, is situated on SE of Holy Is.

Anchorages

• Off Lamlash. 25 Arran Y.C. visitors' buoys. Exposed to SE.
• W of Holy Island (Budhist sanctuary).
• In SW of hbr.

Facilities PO, shops EC Wednesday, hotels. Water near pier. Showers at Pier Head Café. Diesel in cans. Bus to Brodick for ferry to Ardrossan.

☎ Arran YC 01770 600705.

TROON*

Charts BA 1866, 2220; SC 5610; Imray C63
HW Greenock –0025

MHWS	MHWN	MLWN	MLWS
3·2m	2·6m	1·0m	0·3m

A useful hbr and marina at southern approach to Clyde. Easy access. Before arrival call marina on VHF 37/80.

Approach and Entrance Give shore an offing of 2ca. Leave G con buoy Fl.G.4s to stb and pass between pierheads. Lts Fl(2)WG.5s11m9M (shore-W-036°-G-090°-shore) on west and Q.R on E Port entry signals not applicable to yachts. Proceed through outer harbour to marina.

Facilities PO shops EC Wednesday. Full marina facilities. 50 visitors' berths. Rly to Glasgow. Prestwick Airport 4M.

☎/VHF HM 01292 313412, VHF 14; Marina 315553, VHF 37/M, 80.

LOCH RYAN*

Chart BA 1403; SC 5610; Imray C63
HW Greenock –0020

MHWS	MHWN	MLWN	MLWS
3·0m	2·4m	0·6m	0·1m

A busy ferry port, including HSS and superferries, operating from Old House Point or Cairnryan.

Approach and Entrance From S give N shore of Rhins of Galloway a good berth. The new ferry terminal, Loch Ryan Port, is in operation at Old House Point to the NW of Cairn Point. Pass the new ferry terminal and leave the S card buoy (VQ(6)+LFl.10s) to port, then head for the Spit buoy (Fl.G.6s). Keep a good lookout for ferries using both Loch

Ryan Port and Cairnryan Ferry Terminal. Listen on VHF 14 for all ferry movements.

Anchorages and Berthing
• Stranraer Marina. South of Spit buoy, three G Lt bns mark the W side of the channel leading into Stranraer Hbr and marina.
• Anchor 3ca NW of W pier. Holding good, Uncomfortable in strong northerlies.
• The Wig. Enter bay by passing midway between Spit G con buoy Fl.G.6s and No.1 bn Oc.G.6s. Holding poor.
• Lady Bay. W side of loch 1M S of entrance. Holding good.

Facilities Small marina, basic facilities. PO, shops EC Wednesday. Rly or coach to Glasgow and London.

☎/VHF HM *Mobile* 07734 073421, 07827 277247.

PORTPATRICK*

Chart BA 2198; Imray C63
HW Liverpool +0022

MHWS	MHWN	MLWN	MLWS
3·8m	3·0m	0·9m	0·3m

This small hbr 15M N of the Mull of Galloway provides good shelter. Strong tides across entrance. Do not approach in strong onshore winds. Busy at

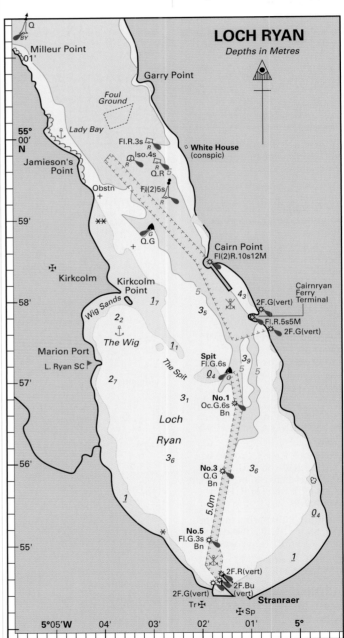

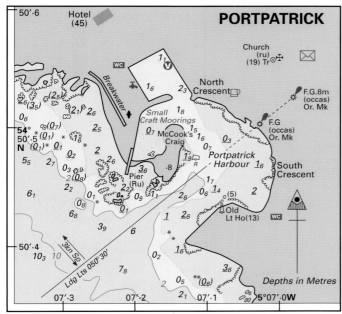

PORTPATRICK

Depths in Metres

PORTPATRICK TO KIRKCUDBRIGHT

Passage lights	BA No
Crammag Head Fl.10s35m18M	4608
Mull of Galloway Fl.20s99m28M	4610
Little Ross Fl.5s50m12M	4634
Hestan Is Fl(2)10s42m9M	4640

There are strong tides between Portpatrick and the Mull of Galloway off which there is a dangerous race extending some 3M S of the Mull. The Galloway coast is frequented by increasing commercial traffic. The few harbours are small and drying and there is limited refuge if caught out in a SW–SE blow. There are dangerous sand banks at the entrance to the Solway Firth. The tidal range is over 6m sp and there is a dangerous race in strong winds extending 3M S of the Mull. Note Scares Rocks 6M E of the Mull. Shelter for deep keeled yachts may best be found in Kirkcudbright.

Tidal Streams
All related to Dover sp rates

Black Head (Portpatrick)
–0110NNW +0500SSE 1·8kn

Mull of Galloway
+0040WSW –0535ESE 4·5kn

weekends in season with yachts from N Ireland 21M away.

Approach and Entrance TV mast behind hbr conspic. From N keep 1ca off. Narrow entrance opens suddenly. Ldg Lts 2Oc.G.5s, two orange lines by day bearing 050°, on wall and building behind, lead between ruined piers. Beware Half Tide Rock marked by a buoy, to port and enter inner hbr.

Berthing Alongside NE and NW walls of inner harbour. Fender plank desirable. HM will advise. Subject to swell from SW.

Facilities PO, shops EC Thursday, hotel/restaurants, water, fuel. Bus to Stranraer.

✆ HM 01776 810355.

DRUMMORE

Chart BA 2198;
Imray C62
HW Liverpool +0035

MHWS	MHWN	MLWN	MLWS
5·9	4·9	2·0	0·6

Small drying hbr 4M N of Mull of Galloway.

Approach and Entrance Enter after half tide, unmarked shingle bank extends W from pier head. The entrance can be very difficult to see through the mudbanks.

Berth Alongside pier. N end reserved for MoD range boat. Very limited space.

Facilities Water on pier. PO, shops, hotel.

ISLE OF WHITHORN

Chart BA 2094;
Imray C62
HW Liverpool +0022

MHWS	MHWN	MLWN	MLWS
6·9m	5·4m	2·1m	0·7m

A drying hbr with 2½m at half flood.

Entrance On the E side of the bay there is a conspic W low square tr. An isolated unmarked rock lies off shore. From the W side of the bay the Skerries reef extends E to R bn. The stream sets very strongly SW across entrance at all times when there is 2m or more in the hbr. Keep to the apparent middle third of the channel on entry. Conspic Ldg marks (Or diamonds) lie on a bearing 335° in the W of the hbr. At night these are replaced by Lts Oc.R.8s7M.

Anchorages
• Alongside quay in SE corner, HM will advise. Space limited.
• Anchor in entrance S of the slip on E side to lie well afloat. Subject to big swell in S'ly winds.

Facilities Water at pier. Showers, PO, shops, garage, hotel, chandlers.

✆ HM 01988 500468, *Mobile* 07734 073420.

Offshore Anchorage

Portyerrock Bay 1·5M north of Whithorn provides a safe anchorage in W and SW winds. Perhaps useful on passage to Whitehaven or Maryport while awaiting the tide.

KIRKCUDBRIGHT

Charts BA 1344, 1346, 2094;
Imray C62
HW Liverpool +0015

MHWS	MHWN	MLWN	MLWS
7·5	5·9	2·4	0·8

A 4M long narrow channel between sandbanks forming estuary of River Dee.

Approach and Entrance Beware of firing range at entrance, no restrictions on passage, safety boat always present when in use. Bar (0·5m) 5ca N of Torr Point. Ldg marks astern on Little Ross 201°. Channel (dries) is buoyed and lit.

Anchorages and **Berthing**
• At marina, alongside outside of floating pontoons.
• N end of Little Ross in position giving most shelter. Stream runs fast.
• Flint Bay. N of Torrs Point sheltered in E'lys.

Facilities PO, shops, EC Thursday. Diesel, chandlers.

✆/VHF HM 01557 331135, VHF 12. Range Safety Officer 0141 2248520, Range Safety Boat VHF 73.

KIRKCUDBRIGHT

Depths in Metres

Kirkcudbright
Buoyed Channel
Saint Mary's Isle
Inch
Manxman's Lake
River Dee
Milton Sands
Frenchman's Rock (2·6)
Fl.3s7m3M Lifeboat House (conspic)
Bar Pt
Ross Bay
Manor Pt
Torrs Pt
Howwell Bay
Gipsy Pt
Ross Roads
The Sound
Little Ross

SCOTLAND – WEST COAST

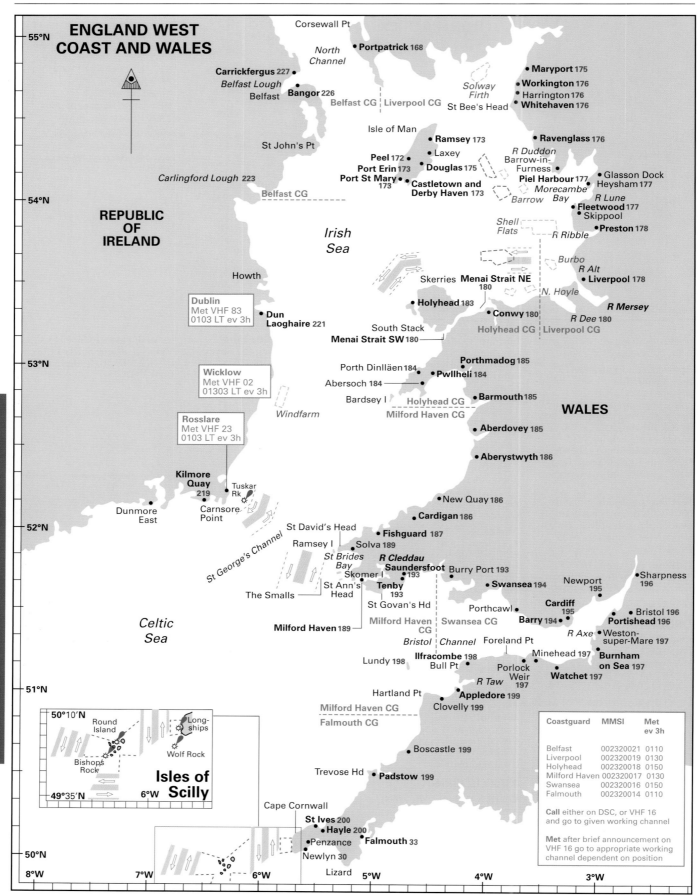

ENGLAND WEST COAST AND WALES

Corsewall Pt

55°N

North Channel

● **Portpatrick** 168

● **Maryport** 175

● **Carrickfergus** 227
Belfast Lough
Belfast ● **Bangor** 226

Solway Firth

● **Workington** 176
● Harrington 176
St Bee's Head ● **Whitehaven** 176

Belfast CG | Liverpool CG

St John's Pt

Isle of Man

● **Ramsey** 173
● Laxey

● **Ravenglass** 176

R Duddon
Barrow-in-
Furness

● **Peel** 172
Port Erin 173
Port St Mary 173
● Douglas 175
● **Castletown and
Derby Haven** 173

Piel Harbour 177
Barrow
Morecambe Bay

● Glasson Dock
Heysham 177

Carlingford Lough 223

54°N

**REPUBLIC
OF
IRELAND**

Belfast CG

R Lune
● **Fleetwood** 177
● Skippool

Shell Flats
R Ribble
● **Preston** 178

Irish Sea

Burbo
R Alt

Howth

Skerries
Menai Strait NE 180

● **Liverpool** 178

Dublin
Met VHF 83
0103 LT ev 3h

● **Dun Laoghaire** 221

N. Hoyle

● **Holyhead** 183

● **Conwy** 180

R Mersey

R Dee 180

South Stack
Menai Strait SW 180

Holyhead CG | Liverpool CG

53°N

Wicklow
Met VHF 02
01303 LT ev 3h

Porth Dinllaen 184

● **Porthmadog** 185

● **Pwllheli** 184

Abersoch 184

Rosslare
Met VHF 23
0103 LT ev 3h

Bardsey I

● **Barmouth** 185

Holyhead CG
Milford Haven CG

Windfarm

WALES

● **Aberdovey** 185

● **Aberystwyth** 186

**Kilmore
Quay**
219

Tuskar
Rk

● Dunmore
East

Carnsore
Point

52°N

St George's Channel

● New Quay 186

● **Cardigan** 186

St David's Head

Ramsey I

● **Fishguard** 187

*Celtic
Sea*

● Solva 189

St Brides Bay

R Cleddau
Saundersfoot
193

Burry Port 193

Sharpness
196

Skomer I

St Ann's
Head

● **Tenby**
193

● **Swansea** 194

Newport
195

The Smalls

St Govan's Hd

Porthcawl

Cardiff
195

● Bristol 196

Milford Haven 189

Milford Haven
CG

Swansea CG

Barry 194

Portishead 196

Bristol | *Channel*

R Axe

Weston-
super-Mare 197

Foreland Pt

Lundy 198

Ilfracombe 198
Bull Pt

Minehead 197

**Burnham
on Sea** 197

Porlock
Weir
197

Watchet 197

R Taw

51°N

Hartland Pt

● **Appledore** 199

Milford Haven CG
Falmouth CG

Clovelly 199

Coastguard	MMSI	Met ev 3h
Belfast	002320021	0110
Liverpool	002320019	0130
Holyhead	002320018	0150
Milford Haven	002320017	0130
Swansea	002320016	0150
Falmouth	002320014	0110

Call either on DSC, or VHF 16
and go to given working channel

Met after brief announcement on
VHF 16 go to appropriate working
channel dependent on position

Round Island

Long-
ships

50°10'N

Bishops
Rock

Wolf Rock

**Isles of
Scilly**

49°35'N   6°W

Boscastle 199

Trevose Hd ● **Padstow** 199

Cape Cornwall

St Ives 200
● **Hayle** 200
● Penzance
Newlyn 30

Falmouth 33

50°N

Lizard

8°W   7°W   6°W   5°W   4°W   3°W

Note The position of the Wind Farm Sites
is approximate

Round 1 Wind Farm Sites
Round 2 Wind Farm Sites

Page references are shown after locations, for example:
Padstow 199. Bold type indicates that it is accompanied by a plan. *Italics* are used for rivers, lochs, bays, seas etc.

England – West Coast and Wales

This coast, along with the Irish east coast, provides a beautiful collection of cruising areas as well as being the main through route to and from West Scotland. The most direct passage routes to/ from Scotland will normally be from Lands End via Milford Haven, Pwllheli, Holyhead, Peel (IOM), Portpatrick and on to the Clyde or round Kintyre, or along the East Irish Coast from Lands End via Kilmore Quay, Arklow, Dublin Bay, Ardglass, Belfast Lough, Glenarm and then to the Clyde or round Kintyre. If the outlook is for rough weather, vessels on passage to/from Scotland will find more refuge on the Irish East Coast (see page 219).

Tidal strategy plays a key role in these waters. Tides reach 3kn in St Georges Channel and 5kn in North Channel at springs. Tidal streams flood north to Liverpool/Dublin Bay, and flood south through the North Channel, with a slack area to the west of the Isle of Man, so it is possible to carry a fair tide for many miles and hours with judicious planning. Key tidal gates are the whole of the North Channel, Point of Ayre, Calf of Man, South Stack (Holyhead), Bardsey Island, Grassholm to Strumble Head, and Land's End.

Most harbours on the West Coast of England and Wales are tidal, with entrance bars or strong currents restricting access to a window either side of local high water, and with a prevailing onshore wind. On the entire coast from the Solway Firth to Lands End, only Holyhead, Fishguard and Milford Haven provide all tide, all weather access. Fishguard is only secure in winds from W through S to SE.

Douglas and Peel on the Isle of Man have marinas, accessible HW±2, which offer some shelter outside the marinas whilst waiting for tide – Douglas and Peel waiting areas are both exposed to NE. Although a major commercial port, Liverpool has strong currents and no sheltered waiting area. Pwllheli is secure in all winds but the entrance is dredged to 0·6m below datum.

The route down the English coast has a number of well-found marinas at Maryport, Whitehaven, Fleetwood and others in estuaries at Glasson Dock, Preston and Liverpool. The coast is a lee shore with extensive shoals, with wind farms, either completed or under construction. These should pose few problems except in poor visibility. There may be exclusion zones during construction. In North and West Wales there are marinas at Conwy, Holyhead, Port Dinorwic, Caernarfon, Pwllheli and Aberystwyth.

From Conwy there is a choice of going N of Anglesey, carrying the tide to Holyhead then taking the tide south past South Stack, or going through the Menai Strait, a beautiful route through The Swellies to Port Dinorwic, Caernarfon and out over Caernarfon Bar. Tides are critical to this passage.

Porth Dinllaen provides a sheltered anchorage in winds from S to W winds in settled weather, en route to Bardsey Sound and Cardigan Bay, where Abersoch and Pwllheli are major yachting centres.

Three well buoyed major shoals project west from the coast in Cardigan Bay – Sarn Padraig (St Patricks Causeway) running SW from Harlech, Sarn y Bwch running SW from S of Barmouth, and Cynfelyn Patches running SW from S of Aberdovey.

Porthmadog, Barmouth, Aberdovey, Aberystwyth and Fishguard are all good cruising destinations within day-sail of each other and Abersoch and Pwllheli.

From Fishguard south the next major harbour is Milford Haven, easily reached by taking the tide round Strumble Head then west of S Bishop light and via Skokholm/Skomer round St Annes Head.

Ramsey and Jack Sounds provide a slightly shorter route, albeit with challenging navigation in strong tidal streams.

In the Bristol Channel, Pembrokeshire, particularly the Gower peninsula, Devon and Cornwall have beautiful coastlines. However there are very few all-weather, all-tide harbours. The prevailing wind is from the SW or W, and strong winds invariably blow from the westerly sector. The area is exposed to frequent Atlantic swells and, being on the West side of the UK, receives its fair share of rain and poor visibility. There is relatively little commercial traffic and, perhaps because of limited berthing, there are few yachts on passage. Lundy (meaning 'Puffin' in Viking) is beautiful and an interesting place to explore. It is surrounded by the UK's first marine nature reserve. There are tidal races to the N and S of the Island, but the anchorage in the SE is useful in bad weather because it offers good protection from strong winds from S to W. Many hbrs in the Bristol Channel are small and dry, or have entrance bars that can be difficult or dangerous under the wrong conditions. Many popular tourist towns, like Ilfracombe, Clovelly, Boscastle, Newquay and St Ives have drying harbours that are vulnerable to a surge or run or 'scend' (a rise and fall combined with a sideways motion, repeated with say a 30-second period) in the hbr when there is a heavy ground swell running – usually off season. Clovelly is a unique and attractive village that clings to a steep cliff. The anchorage in its roads is sheltered from most strong winds.

Cardiff Bay has a barrage and offers good facilities. Milford Haven is very scenic and provides a large area for cruising, which is useful in bad weather.

There are lobster pot markers off the N Cornish coast well offshore and not always very visible. There are marinas at Milford Haven, Swansea, Cardiff, Bristol, Portishead, Watchet and Padstow. For crew changes, road and rail connections to Milford, Swansea, Cardiff and Bristol are good, but are poor along the N coast of Somerset, Devon and Cornwall.

Useful references for greater detail are *Irish Sea Pilot* by David Rainsbury, *Cruising Anglesey and Adjoining Waters* by Ralph Morris and *Bristol Channel and Severn Cruising Guide* by Peter Cumberlidge, all from Imray.

Irish Sea to St George's Channel distances (miles)

	Bangor (N.I.)	S. Rock	Whitehaven	Peel	Douglas	Carlingford	Liverpool Bar	Conwy Fairway	Holyhead Pier	Howth	Caernarfon Bar	Pwllheli	Aberystwyth	Fishguard	S Bishop 1M W	Arklow	Tuskar Rk 1M E
Bangor (N.I.)	0																
S. Rock	23	0															
Whitehaven	74	62	0														
Peel	47	26	46	0													
Douglas	69	47	39	27	0												
Carlingford	62	39	97	54	64	0											
Liverpool Bar	113	90	64	75	56	106	0										
Conwy Fairway	109	84	77	70	54	93	25	0									
Holyhead Pier	98	74	83	60	58	112	50	37	0								
Howth	88	66	112	100	74	42	99	80	53	0							
Caernarfon Bar	101	88	103	93	77	86	70	53	21	62	0						
Pwllheli	146	123	133	107	108	110	104	85	56	79	40	0					
Aberystwyth	181	137	148	122	106	126	119	99	70	93	55	33	0				
Fishguard	168	146	165	136	139	130	132	112	83	93	71	57	40	0			
S Bishop Lt Ho 1M W	175	153	160	146	143	137	136	124	95	96	86	73	60	23	0		
Arklow	124	102	142	99	102	81	114	93	64	40	66	72	80	64	62	0	
Tuskar Rk 1M E	159	137	171	135	133	115	139	126	90	74	86	80	79	47	36	36	0

North Channel to Milford Haven

Chart BA 1121; Imray C51, C52, C59, C60, C61, C62, C69, 2700	
Passage lights:	*BA No*
Mull of Galloway Fl.20s99m28M	4610
S Rock R pillar Fl(3)R.30s9M Racon (T) (–)	5966
South Stack Fl.10s60m24M Horn 30s	5204
Codling E card AIS Q(3)10s	5861
Bardsey Is Fl(5)15s39m26M Horn Mo(N) 45s (– ·)	5234
Wicklow Head Fl(3)15s37m23M	5850
Tuskar Rock Q(2)7·5s33m24M Racon (T) (–)	5838
Strumble Head Fl(4)15s45m26M	5274
S Bishop Fl.5s44m16M Horn(3)45s Racon (O) (– – –)	5276
The Smalls Fl(3)15s36m18M+ Iso.R.4s13M Horn(2)60s Racon (T) (–)	5278

There are two main routes from N Channel to Milford Haven and reverse. One can either take the English/Welsh side or the Irish side. If wishing to cut out night passages, the first route is possible going N, stopping at Fishguard, Holyhead, Isle of Man, Portpatrick, and Loch Ryan. Going N from the IoM it is not possible to get through the N Channel on one tide hence the stop at Port Patrick. Going S and leaving Corsewall Point (off Loch Ryan) at Dover +0600 one can get into the slack water off the W coast of the IoM for Peel or Port Erin on one tide. Then make for Holyhead, Fishguard and from there work the tides round Strumble Head, Ramsey and Jack Sounds to Milford Haven. This takes five days N and four days S. The other route is to leave Milford Haven to suit the tides through the Sounds (*see Passage Note Strumble Head to St Ann's Head*) and head straight for Belfast Lough (Bangor) which is 200M and can be accomplished with one night at sea. Leave Bangor at Dover +0500 on the last of the ebb for the S'ly passage. Ports of refuge on the Irish side are Ardglass, Howth or Dun Laoghaire and if needed Wicklow or Arklow.

Isle of Man

Chart BA 2094; SC 5613; Imray Y70, C62	
Passage lights	*BA No*
Point of Ayre Fl(4)20s32m19M Racon (M) (– –)	4720
Douglas Head Fl.10s32m24M	4770

Tidal Streams related to Dover (0015 before Liverpool)

Langness to Point of Ayre
–0330NE for 0900 +0530S for 0315

Point of Ayre
+0500S –0015W, race.

Contrary Head to Calf Sound
–0115N +0445S

S of Niarbyl Point stream nearly continuously N in an eddy close inshore.

Calf Sound
+0400S –0130N

Note the tidal races off Chicken Rock: Eddies and a race both E and W of Langness Lt Ho. Ayre Point has a race and a dangerous 2m shoal, the Whitestone Bank over which the sea breaks, 5ca E marked by a W card buoy. The inshore channel is ¾M wide. With SW winds and low barometer the rise of tide is increased by up to 1m. With high pressure and E and N winds the

tides are lowered to the same extent. None of the harbours where yachts can lie afloat is safe in all winds unless locked into a marina e.g. Douglas or Peel. Douglas is safe in all but NE gales. Douglas is a busy commercial and ferry port. If HMs are warned in advance of a yacht's probable time of arrival they take a lot of trouble to allot a suitable berth. Except at Douglas where a continuous service is maintained, it is the practice of HMs to be on duty 2hrs either side of HW and to meet incoming vessels and direct them to their berths. Harbour staff are extremely helpful. Hbr dues are moderate. In good weather vessels coming from the W can find shelter in Peel Hbr when there is sufficient rise. From the S make first for Port St Mary. From the N find a temporary anchorage at Ramsey at all states of the tide. These anchorages are all exposed to winds from certain directions. At the time of writing yachts may not be left unattended unless in the charge of an IOM resident. www.gov.im/transport/harbours gives much useful information on harbours and marinas.

PEEL

Chart BA 2696; SC 5613; Imray C62, Y70

HW Liverpool –0005

MHWS	MHWN	MLWN	MLWS
5·2m	4·3m	1·5m	0·4m

This is a picturesque hbr with a conspic castle on the W coast. It makes a pleasant port of call for supplies when on passage from one end of the Irish Sea to the other. The hbr has 3·3m at MHWN. It has a sill and a flapgate.

The new 120 berth marina also has 15 visitors' berths. A call on VHF 12 1h before entry smooths the approach.

Approach The breakwater should be given good clearance and vessels should not stand in too far towards the shore as a shoal lies between the breakwater and the shore and depths on it are variable. Strong NW'ly to NE'ly winds may cause heavy seas at the entrance.

Entrance There are Ldg marks. The training wall to the Fl.R Lt covers at half tide.

Entry to the Inner Hbr and Marina is through a flapgate, retaining a depth of 2·5m, and a swing foot br. Access HW±0200. Call *Peel Harbour* on VHF 12 upon approach to request an opening of the bridge. Outwith office hours (0800–1630), Douglas Harbour Control will answer and open the bridge for you. IPTS signals for entry and Fl amber Lts when gate or br are

Passage through **Calf Sound** should only be undertaken in quiet conditions as there are overfalls. There may be a distinct step in the water opposite Thousla Rock. Tide through the sound runs at about 3·5kn, the N going stream starts at Liverpool –0145 and the S-going stream at Liverpool +0345. The stream runs at 4kn sp (2kn np) and is maximal near HW and LW Liverpool. The main sound between Kitterland and Thousla rk with Lt bn Fl.R.3s is just over ½ca wide; beware the Clett rks extending 1ca from the Calf near S entrance. Little Sound should not be attempted except with local knowledge. BA chart 2696 essential.

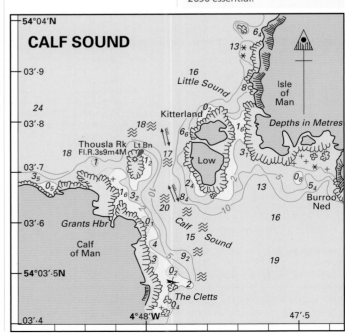

about to move. VHF 12 ☎ 01624 842338 or 495036 or Douglas Harbour Control.

There are three Or Vs buoys E of the Fl.R.5s Lt in 2m. All stores, fuel outside entrance to marina, card obtained from Manx Fishing Producers Organisation (MFPO) in marina. On the waterfront, the Peel Sailing and Cruising Club welcomes visitors, nearby there is a launderette. Buses to Ramsey and Douglas.

☎ HM 01624 842338.

PORT ERIN

Chart BA 2696; SC 5613; Imray C62, Y70

HW Liverpool +0010

MHWS	MHWN	MLWN	MLWS
5·2m	4·2m	1·6m	0·4m

This inlet affords secure anchorage in 4–9m and shelter in winds from N through E to SW. Raglan Pier (Oc.G.5s) on S side of bay forms a drying hbr with sandy bottom having 3·6m MHWN alongside.

Approach In the middle of the head of the bay are Ldg Lts F.R 099° W columns, R bands which lead into the middle of the bay.

Entrance A demolished breakwater, covered at HW, runs out N from the SW arm of the bay and is marked by an unlit G con buoy.

Berthing Anchor in 3–5m N off Raglan pier or use one of the two visitors' buoys W of this. A telegraph cable runs roughly E–W across S side of bay so care is necessary when anchoring. Good landing at jetty shown on plan. All stores. Buses to Castletown and Douglas.

☎ HM 01624 833206.

PORT ST MARY

Chart BA 2696, 2094; SC 5613; Imray Y70, C62

HW Liverpool +0010

MHWS	MHWN	MLWN	MLWS
5·9m	4·8m	1·6m	0·5m

The hbr dries to sand and mud. It has 3m at MHWN, 2m when the Carrick covers; good shelter off the entrance in 2–3·5m from NE through NW to SW winds. The bay should not be approached in strong S winds. Note that the Carrick should be given 1ca clearance from its bn in all directions but 2ca to the E.

Approach To clear The Carrick (Lt bn Q(2)5s) which dries 4·3m keep Langness Lt Ho well open of Scarlett Point Stack or at night when nearing the bay bring the Lts of the hbr in line 303°. Approaching from the E during the first of the ebb, from Stack of Scarlett to S of The Carrick, small craft should avoid standing inshore until The Carrick shows when the sea steadies. From SW give the shore a berth of 2ca and round in to N of the Alfred Pierhead (Lt Oc.R.10s).

Berthing Anchor 50–100m NW of Alfred Pier outside the line of the two Lts (one on Alfred Pier and the other on the inner pier). Take care to avoid reef NE of Alfred Pier marked by a G bn with con topmark. The outer part of Alfred Pier is often occupied by fishing vessels, but yachts may raft up afloat near its root. Inner harbour dries to channel, hard sand: centre is full of local moorings but yachts taking the ground can lie alongside. Four Y visitors' buoys off Chapel Bay in a line between ends of Alfred and Little Carrick which is the rock with the G bn near the small inner pier. There is a landing below the clubhouse of the IoM YC which has excellent facilities and is welcoming to visitors many of whom come over from Ireland for Saturday night.

Facilities All stores. Bus to Castletown and Douglas.

☎ /VHF HM 01624 833205, VHF 12 (if the Harbour Office is closed, HM Douglas will reply); YC 842088. IoM YC 932 088.

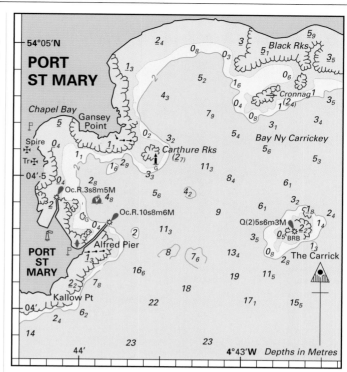

PORT ST MARY

54°05′N

PORT ST MARY

Chapel Bay
Gansey Point
Spire
Carthure Rks (2·7)
Oc.R.3s8m5M
Oc.R.10s8m6M
Alfred Pier
Kallow Pt
Black Rks
Cronnag
Bay Ny Carrickey
Q(2)5s6m3M
BRB
The Carrick
4°43′W *Depths in Metres*

CASTLETOWN

Chart BA 2696; SC 5613; Imray Y70, C62

HW Liverpool +0010

It is difficult to imagine a more romantic little hbr with its castle, quays and ancient buildings. Behind the sea-front is a busy modern town. The bay affords good shelter in NW through NE to E winds. The bottom is not good and the tidal streams are felt. The hbr dries.

Approach To avoid the race off Langness Pt give it a good berth in all winds. Approaching from E in heavy weather keep Clay Head well open of Douglas Head to clear rough ground 8ca SE of St Michael's Is where a race causes heavy overfalls.

Entrance Enter midway between Langness Point and the R can buoy Fl.R.3s which marks the Lheeah-Rio Rocks which should be left to port. From abreast the buoy steer 022° until the light house on the inner jetty comes open N of the pier head LtHo. Then steer 317° for the entrance to the hbr. At the end of the breakwater the ground consists of rocky ledges and large boulders. Beware of confusing the hbr bns with Ronaldsway airport landing Lts.

Berthing Anchor in 5·5m off the entrance to the hbr, King William College tr bearing 022°. One W can buoy 3ca SE of breakwater. The hbr has 2·7m MHWN; there is a basin between the outer swing and inner fixed bridges. Berth alongside the vertical NE face of the inner quay (Irish Quay). Bollards, ladders, water and electricity. Bottom is flat, hard sand.

Facilities All stores. Bus to Port Erin and Douglas. Steam train in the summer.

☎ /VHF HM 01624 823549, VHF 12 (usually answered from Douglas).

DERBY HAVEN

Chart BA 2696

HW Liverpool +0010

The bay affords shelter on a good bottom of sand and mud in 2–5m inside St Michaels Is and is available in N through W to S winds. Inside the breakwater the hbr which dries affords complete shelter in all winds. Bottom mud and sand, 2m MHWN. It is very close to Ronaldsway Airport which is busy and noisy.

Entrance With the S going stream which runs for 9hrs give N point of St Michael's Is a good berth as the stream sets hard across a shelving rock at the entrance point. For the hbr bring the Lt Iso.G.2s on SW end of breakwater to bear 262° and pass between it and the R perch marking a rk to S of it to enter the drying hbr.

Anchorage Two or 3ca from the S end of the breakwater. The bottom is foul 1ca out from it. Stores at Castletown 2M. No supplies at Derby Haven.

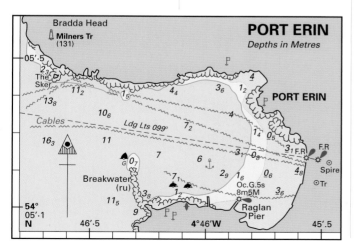

Bradda Head
Milners Tr (131)

PORT ERIN
Depths in Metres

05′·5

The Sker
Cables
Ldg Lts 099°
PORT ERIN
Breakwater (ru)
54° 05′·1 N
46′·5
Oc.G.5s 8m5M
Raglan Pier
Spire
Tr
F.R
4°46′W
45′·5

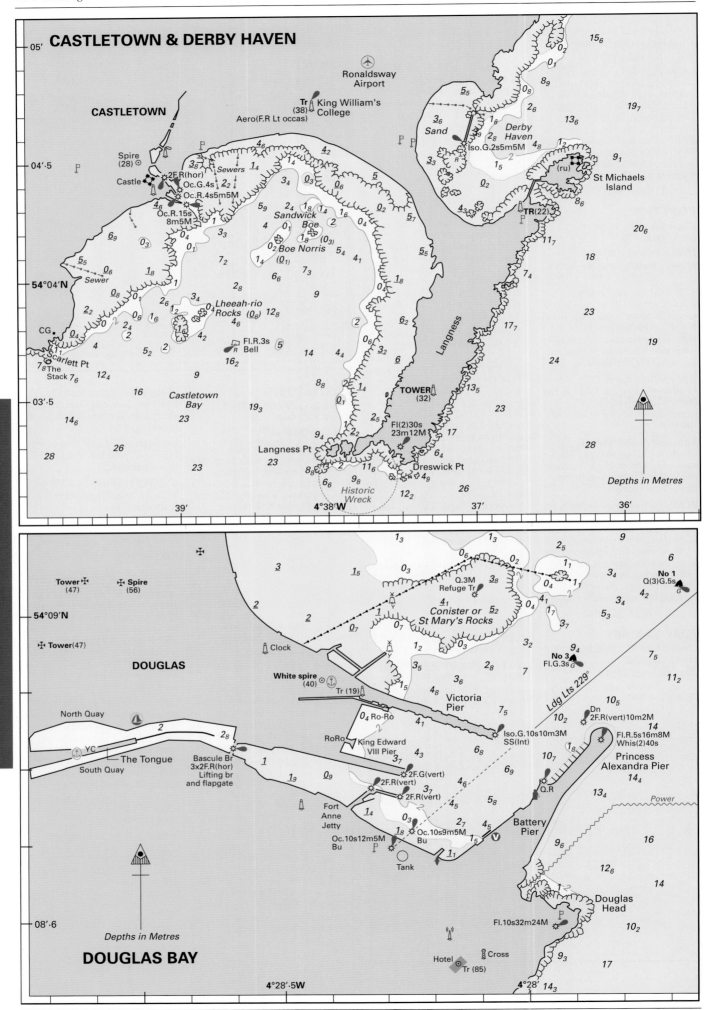

CASTLETOWN & DERBY HAVEN

ENGLAND – WEST COAST AND WALES

CASTLETOWN

Ronaldsway Airport

Tr (38) King William's College
Aero(F.R Lt occas)

Sand

Derby Haven
Iso.G.2s5m5M

St Michaels Island

Spire (28)
Castle
2F.R(hor)
Oc.G.4s
Oc.R.4s5m5M
Oc.R.15s 8m5M

TR(22)

Sandwick Boe
Boe Norris

Langness

Lheeah-rio Rocks

Fl.R.3s Bell

Castletown Bay

TOWER (32)
Fl(2)30s 23m12M

Langness Pt
Dreswick Pt

Historic Wreck

Scarlett Pt
The Stack
CG.
Sewer

54°04′N

Depths in Metres

4°38′W

DOUGLAS BAY

DOUGLAS

Tower (47) **Spire** (56)

Tower(47)

54°09′N

Clock

White spire (40)
Tr (19)

North Quay
YC
The Tongue
South Quay
Bascule Br 3x2F.R(hor) Lifting br and flapgate

Ro-Ro
RoRo
King Edward VIII Pier
2F.G(vert)
2F.R(vert)
2F.R(vert)

Fort Anne Jetty
Oc.10s12m5M Bu
Oc.10s9m5M Bu
Tank

Conister or St Mary's Rocks
Q.3M Refuge Tr

Victoria Pier

Iso.G.10s10m3M SS(Int)

No 1
Q(3)G.5s

No 3
Fl.G.3s

Ldg Lts 229°

Dn 2F.R(vert)10m2M
Fl.R.5s16m8M Whis(2)40s
Princess Alexandra Pier

Q.R

Battery Pier

Power

Douglas Head
Fl.10s32m24M

Hotel
Tr (85)
Cross

Depths in Metres

08′·6

4°28′·5W   4°28′

Depths in Metres

DOUGLAS

Chart BA 2696, 2094; SC 5613; Imray C62, Y70

HW Liverpool +0010

MHWS	MHWN	MLWN	MLWS
6·9m	5·4m	2·4m	0·8m

The outer harbour has 4–7m and a heavy sea runs in during NE gales.

Approach Request entry from Harbour Control. Come in on 229° along approach channel with Ldg marks front W ▲ and back W ▼ with both in R borders (Lts Oc.Bu.10s) past G con Lt buoys. Watch out for IPTS entry signals on Victoria Pier. Beware ferries and HSS and keep S of Ldg line. The only hazard is a dolphin 2F.R.

Berthing
• Inner harbour marina. Call *Douglas Inner Harbour* VHF 12 to book a bridge opening and request a berth. Access through flap-gate, which holds 2m water in the hbr, is approx HW±0200. If the gate is not open, berth temporarily alongside inner end of Battery Pier. Usual facilities. Shops nearby.
• Outer harbour. Alongside pontoon near steps at inner end of Battery Pier, subject to wash, or radially to a buoy close N of lifeboat.
• Anchor in bay, preferably N end, sheltered from N through W to S.

Facilities As expected, shops nearby. Fuel pump on Battery Pier, card from Manx YC.

☎/VHF Harbour Control 01624 686628 (24hrs), VHF 12, also broadcasts nav warnings every 4hrs from 0133; YC 673965.

LAXEY

Chart BA 2094; Imray Y70

Laxey Bay offers good anchorage in N to SW winds through W. The hbr dries and has about 2m MHWN. Care is needed in entering the hbr which is very crowded. There are seasonal visitors' buoys in Garwick Bay (1 mile S).

RAMSEY BAY

Chart BA 2696; SC 5613; Imray C62

HW Liverpool +0010

MHWS	MHWN	MLWN	MLWS
7·4m	5·9m	2·3m	0·9m

The bay affords secure anchorage and good holding ground, and is sheltered with winds from NW through W to S. The Queen's Pier extends 685m from the shore to the S of the hbr. Landing is prohibited on this pier which is partly derelict. Vessels waiting to enter should anchor between this pier and S pier clear of any moorings. There are two summer only waiting buoys. S and N piers are 90m inside LW mark. The hbr dries and has up to 5·5m at MHWS, 4m at MHWN. Vessels are advised not to attempt the entrance earlier than HW−0230 or later than HW+0200.

Approach From N rounding Point of Ayre (N point of Is) Fl(4)20s keep close inshore to avoid Whitestone Bank (7ca E of Ayre Point). The stream sets round the pt into Ramsey Bay at about LW Douglas, and runs for 3hrs. Watch for lobster pots.

Berthing Berth alongside quay as instructed by HM, usually in the channel between the piers. When entering, watch the stream which sets N across the entrance for 9hrs from half flood to LW approx. Most facilities. Buses to Peel and Douglas, tram to Douglas in summer.

☎/VHF HM VHF 12, 01624 812245 (24h).

MARYPORT

Chart BA 2013; SC 5613; Imray C62

HW Liverpool +0025

DS Dover −0430NE

MHWS	MHWN	MLWN	MLWS
8·6m	6·6m	2·5m	0·9m

The Senhouse Basin to seaward is a secure marina staffed 24hrs. Contact marina on VHF 12 before entry.

Solway Firth to Holyhead

This coast tends to be low but with high ground inland. The ports and harbours of N Lancashire are relics of the industrial revolution as many of the towns were connected with coal and iron. Their harbours have well constructed stone basins and quays. In some cases these have been converted to marinas. The strong tides carry much silt and the harbours mostly dry at low water. Further south are the shallow estuaries forming Morecambe Bay, the Ribble, the Mersey, the Dee and the N entrance to the Menai Strait. It is interesting for a boat which easily takes the ground as there is a lot of shallow water. It is a lee-shore for W and SW winds; rough seas and breakers easily occur.

SOLWAY FIRTH TO ST BEES HEAD

Charts BA 1346, 2013; Imray C62

Passage light	BA No
St Bees Head	4710

Fl(2)20s102m18M

The Solway Firth is difficult and dangerous without recent local knowledge as the streams run at 6kn between shifting sandbanks. In the upper estuary, the length of the flood stream shortens to about 2hrs and is associated with a bore wave at spring tides.

There are *Solway Sailing Directions* produced by the SW Scotland SC which may be obtained from Matheson Kidsdale, Whithorn, Newton Stewart DG8 8HZ. It is not possible to make the direct passage from Hestan Is to Maryport, nor should any attempt be made higher up the Firth where streams are strong, the shifting sands are hard and seas can be steep. When leaving Hestan Is for the English shore keep off Barnhourie Sand, Dumroof Bank and Robin Rigg by making 170° over the ground until S of the 'Two Feet Bank' W card buoy before turning E. Workington is the only port of refuge which can be entered at all states of the tide. Wind can raise a difficult sea over Workington Bank but the passage inside the Bank is safe. Going further S, the ebb will help to St Bees Head: aim to get there 1hr after LW and pick up the S-going flood from the head onwards. The streams run at 4kn round the point.

Ranges Firing of various weapons takes place at Eskmeals and Ravenglass about 10M S usually on weekdays with variable danger areas off St Bees Head. You are advised to call *Eskmeals Gun Range* on VHF 13 or ☎ 01229 712246.

Bar It dries for some distance W of S pier and is liable to change. There was a channel dredged to 1m and 25m wide from the end of the S pier. However as the hbr has no commercial traffic this has not been maintained. Beware the tidal set 2kn sp which starts at Dover −0400 and runs N for 5hrs.

Approach Keep at least 1M off coast until in the offing because the shelving bottom is clay, foul with large rocks. Open work pier is conspicuous.

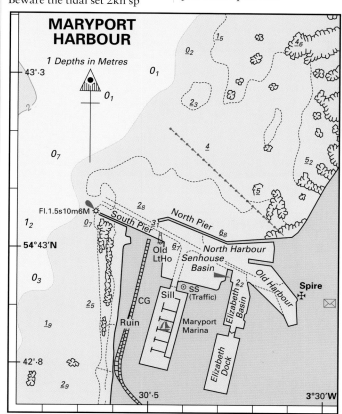

MARYPORT HARBOUR
1 Depths in Metres

RAMSEY
Depths in Metres

Entrance Lt Fl.1·5s10m, W tr on S pier head. Keep closer to S pier head on entry. Leading line is old LtHo in transit with the third window of the house close S of church spire. When square on to lock gate turn to stb. There are extensive quays outside the docks. These all dry and have a bank of silt. Entry to the marina is through a flap-gate which folds down into the lock and forms a sill at 0·5m above CD. Access is 2hrs either side of HW and the water level is maintained at 1·5m above the sill.

Facilities 25 tonne boat lift. MP Marine have extensive workshops and use of slipway with 100-tonne cradle and up to 8m beam.

☎/**VHF** Marina 01900 814431, VHF 12; MP Marine 01900 810299.

WORKINGTON

Chart BA 2013; SC 5613; Imray C62

HW Liverpool +0020

DS Dover –0430ENE

MHWS	MHWN	MLWN	MLWS
8·1m	6·3m	2·6m	0·9m

This is a commercial hbr for coasters at the mouth of the River Derwent. It is easily identified by the large wind farm 1M NE. There is a considerable current after heavy rain as well as a 2kn tidal set across the entrance. The only attraction to the yachtsman is that this is a safe hbr deep enough to enter at any state of the tide.

Bar Extends for 3ca N of R brick disused CG Lt Fl.5s near end of S pier. Localised steep seas occasionally.

Approach Clear when S pier head bears between 010° and 180°. From the S and W pick out Q.G Lt on end of S pier and head N until the Ldg Lts F.R on W pyramids are in line 132° clearly framed between two pairs of F.Bu Lts which mark the edge of the channel to the Turning Basin, dredged to 1·2m.

Entrance Marked by Q.R Lt on 'Bush' perch N of dredged channel. When 2F.R(vert) on end of N jetty abeam round up to port N into turning basin.

Berthing

• In offshore winds anchor 2ca NE or SE of CG.

• In Turning Basin sheltered from all winds but must not be left unattended as large ships pass through. Good shelter.

• Vanguard SC may have a half tide mooring free in the tidal dock S of Riverside Wharf. Trawlers, Pilot and Fishery Protection vessels take up all this dock's quay berths but try to negotiate a berth alongside.

• With short or lowering masts, drying moorings may be found on berths in tidal hbr inside rly br which no longer opens. Air draught 1·8m.

☎/**VHF** HM 01900 602301, VHF 16, 11, 14 *Workington Harbour Radio.*

HARRINGTON

Chart BA 2013; SC 5613; Imray C62

HW Liverpool +0025

A small drying hbr used by local boats.

☎ Contact Fishing and SC 01946 830600.

WHITEHAVEN

Chart BA 2013; SC 5613; Imray C62

HW Liverpool +0010

MHWS	MHWN	MLWN	MLWS
8·0m	6·3m	2·4m	1·0m

Bar 1ca N of W pier head.

Approach Easily identified from N by tall chimney and tall monuments on cliffs just S of hbr. No obstructions.

Entrance The outer harbour dries but there is a buoyed channel, dredged to 1m above CD, to the lock gates. Call *Whitehaven Harbour* VHF 12 for permission to enter. It may be possible to pass the lock at HW±0400 (IPTS shown). Hold towards the N pier head, Fl.R.5s, until lined up with the lock, do not pass too close to the W pier head, Fl.G.5s, since a bar is building up there. Beware being set to port by an anticlockwise rotation in the hbr. In rough westerly weather wait for more water and keep close to the W pier head. Near HW there may be a period of free flow, but in exceptional tidal surges the lock may

remain closed at HW to prevent flooding.

Berthing as instructed on entry. Max length of 13m on finger pontoons.

Facilities as expected of a modern marina. 45-tonne boat lift. Boatyard. Wi-Fi. Town nearby.

☎ /**VHF** HM and Marina 01946 692435 (24hrs); HM and Sealock VHF 12.

RAVENGLASS

Chart BA 1346; SC 5613; Imray C62

HW Liverpool +0005

This estuary is very shallow and requires local knowledge but provides shelter for vessels able to dry out. When approaching from the south contact Eskmeals Gun Range.

☎/**VHF** 01229 712246, VHF 13.

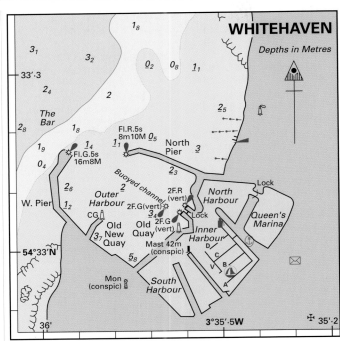

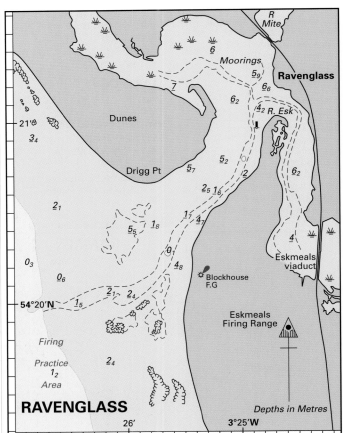

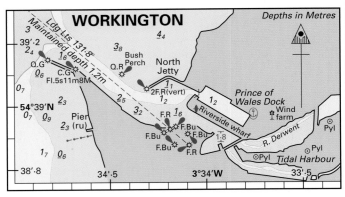

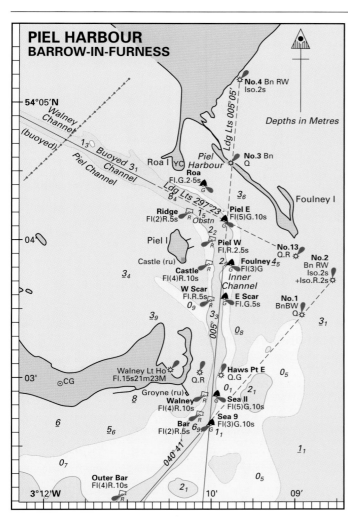

PIEL HARBOUR
BARROW-IN-FURNESS

Depths in Metres

54°05'N

No.4 Bn RW Iso.2s

Walney Channel
(buoyed)
Ldg Lts 005 05'

Buoyed
Channel

Piel Channel

Roa YC
Piel Harbour
Roa
Fl.G.2.5s

No.3 Bn Q

Foulney I

Ldg Lts 297 23'

Ridge
Fl(2)R.5s

Piel E
Fl(5)G.10s

Obstn

Piel I

Piel W
Fl.R.2.5s

No.13
Q.R

Castle (ru)

Castle
Fl(4)R.10s

Foulney
Fl(3)G

Inner Channel

No.2
Bn RW
Iso.2s
+Iso.R.2s

W Scar
Fl.R.5s

E Scar
Fl.G.5s

No.1
BnBW
Q

04'

03'

CG

Walney Lt Ho
Fl.15s21m23M

Haws Pt E
Q.G

Q.R

Groyne (ru)

Walney
Fl(4)R.10s

Sea II
Fl(5)G.10s

Sea 9
Fl(3)G.10s

Bar
Fl(2)R.5s

040 41'

Outer Bar
Fl(4)R.10s

3°12'W

10'

09'

PIEL HARBOUR AND BARROW-IN-FURNESS

Chart BA 3164; SC 5613; Imray C62

HW Liverpool +0015

MHWS	MHWN	MLWN	MLWS
9·3m	7·1m	3·0m	1·1m

Approach Strangers should take the entrance at half flood which runs from NW. The ebb runs from S. There are extensive shoals 5M offshore. Pick up Lightning Knoll RWVS Sph bell buoy LFl.10s and leaving it close to stb steer 041° on first Ldg Lts (No.1 Q, No.2 Iso.2s). Keep on this line for just over 3M leaving Halfway R can bn Q.R and Outer Bar R can buoy Fl(4)R.10s to port until Bar R can buoy Fl(2)R.5s

MORECAMBE BAY

Passage lights	*BA No*
Lune Deep	4870
S card Q(6)+LFl.15s5M	
Fleetwood Fairway	
No.1 N card Q Bell	
River Lune	
W card Q(9)15s	
Heysham Breakwater	4860
2F.G(vert)9m5M Siren 30s	

(Streams run hard, 5kn max, and raise a short steep sea on the ebb with W winds).

N Hoyle wind farm marked by four turbines 61m F.R and Fl.Y.2·5s11m5M Horn Mo(U) centred at 53°25'·0N 3°25'·5W.

is reached. Then bring Nos.3 & 4 Ldg Lts 005° (No.3 Q, No.4 Iso.2s) in transit and follow line for 1M till abreast of Piel Island.

Berthing Anchor clear of fairway. Channel to Barrow 3M is well marked with lateral buoyage and further sets of Ldg Lts. Some moorings off town. Landing at Piel Is and Roa Is.

Facilities All at Barrow. Water from HM.

RIVER LUNE AND GLASSON DOCK

Chart BA 1552; Imray C62

HW Liverpool −0003

Glasson Dock

MHWS	MHWN
6·6m	4·4m

Approach As for Fleetwood then continue to River Lune W card Lt buoy.

Entrance Much of the river dries so plan to arrive at River Lune No.1 W card Lt buoy 0115 before HW and proceed up channel at 4kn to be at Glasson Dock 45 minutes before HW Liverpool when gates open until HW. Channel marked by lateral buoys, course 084° but channel varies until Plover Scar W bn which has tide gauge for sill at Glasson. It turns N past Chapel Hill; then follow river round with training wall to port until

No.18 R can Q.R buoy whence make for lock with short length of training wall to stb.

Berthing Glasson Dock has good laying up berths and a boatyard with all facilities including electricity on quays, showers, boat storage under cover and chandlery. Glasson Basin Yacht Harbour lies E of swing br and has pontoons (British Waterways). Lancaster lies 5M above Glasson can be reached by small craft near HW. The channel is narrow and local knowledge advisable. The river has 1·5m at the town at HW.

☎/VHF HM 01524 751724, VHF 69; Marina 751491.

HEYSHAM

Chart BA 1552; Imray C62

HW Liverpool +0005

MHWS	MHWN	MLWN	MLWS
9·4m	7·4m	2·9m	1·1m

Although the hbr affords good shelter it is unavailable to yachts except in emergency.

Approach As for Fleetwood until past the Fairway buoy which is left to stb. Make No.1 Heysham buoy and then make good 045° to No.5 G con buoy Q.G and thence to hbr entrance. Beware ferries and HSS.

Entrance Or Ldg marks on S quay (not jetty) on a line 102° show the entry in middle of dredged channel. Front Lt F.Bu.11m, rear F.Bu.14m.

Berthing Berth as directed.

FLEETWOOD AND SKIPPOOL

Chart BA 2010, 1552; SC 5613; Imray C62

HW Liverpool −0008

MHWS	MHWN	MLWN	MLWS
9·2m	7·3m	3·0m	1·2m

Bar 2·7m to 3·7m in main channel to Isle of Man quay.

Approach and Entrance Arrival at N card Fairway buoy, Q. Bell, at HW−0100 is ideal for a stranger bound for the marina. Steer SE for G con buoy No.3, VQ.G, then follow the well buoyed channel. Beware of the flood tide which sets E across the channel. If bound for the marina call *Fleetwood Dock Radio* VHF 12 before passing Perch No.11, Q.G.4M Horn 15s. After passing R can No.18 follow the Fleetwood shore. Beware of ferries manoeuvring near Nos20 and 22 buoys. A revolving Y light is displayed 18m above quay level near the Ro-Ro berth when a large vessel is arriving or departing.

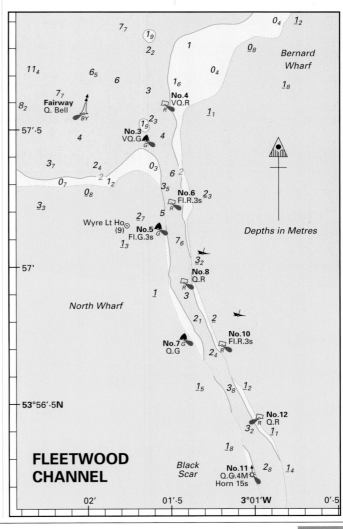

7.7

1.9
2.2

1

0.4
1.2

Bernard Wharf

11.4

6.5

6

1.6

0.4

1.8

8.2

Fairway
Q. Bell
BY

7.7

3

No.4
VQ.R

4

57'·5

No.3
VQ.G

4

1.9
2.3

1.1

3.7

2.4

0.3

0.7

0.8

2
1.2

0.5

6
3.5

1

No.6
Fl.R.3s

2.3

3.3

Wyre Lt Ho
(9)

No.5
Fl.G.3s

2.7

5

1.3

7.6

57'

No.8
Q.R

North Wharf

1

2.1
2

No.7
Q.G

No.10
Fl.R.3s

2.4

1.5

3.8
1.2

53°56'·5N

No.12

3.2
1.1

1.8

FLEETWOOD CHANNEL

Black Scar

No.11
Q.G.4M
Horn 15s

2.8
1.4

02'

01'·5

3°01'W

0'·5

Depths in Metres

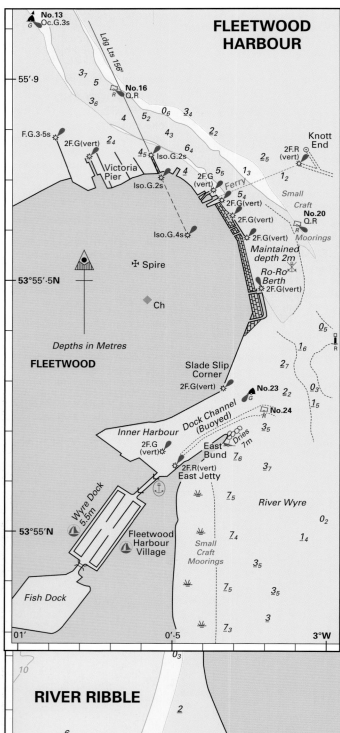

FLEETWOOD HARBOUR

FLEETWOOD

Berthing

• Fleetwood Haven Marina in Wyre Dock. Max length 17m. Dredged to 5m. Gates operate HW±0130. Usual marina facilities including diesel, calor gas and laundry. Tram and bus to Blackpool.

• Anchor out of channel at Knott End or at jetty (53°55'·70N 2°59'·73W) or at landing stage used by local yachts ½M S of Knott End. Land ferry slip, also on beach opposite No.2 IoM berth.

☎/VHF HM and Marina 01253 872323 *Fleetwood Dock Radio* VHF 12 (both Harbour Control and Marina).

Skippool is 5M above Fleetwood. Channel is not well marked and requires local knowledge.

☎ YC 01253 884205.

PRESTON/RIVER RIBBLE

Chart BA 1981; SC 5613; Imray 62

Approach and Entrance should not be attempted in strong W winds or heavy swell. Aim to arrive at fairway RW buoy, Gut, LFl.10s at HW Liverpool −0200. With boat speed of 5kn one should be at Preston within ½hr of HW. Make good 090° to 53°41'·7N 3°03'·4W, i.e. until due S of the outer perch, Fl.R.5s, on the N side of marked channel. Then, making due allowance for the tidal stream, make good 026° towards a waypoint 53°43'·3N 3°02'·1W in the marked channel. Follow the perches up to Preston (14M).

Berthing It may be possible to pick up a mooring at Lytham between LB and W windmill. Preston Marina lock gates open HW−0300 to HW+0200. There is a deep water waiting pontoon outside the gates.

☎/VHF Marina 01772 733595; Preston Lock *Riversway* VHF 14.

LIVERPOOL/RIVER MERSEY

Charts BA 1978, 1951, 3490; SC 5613; Imray C52, C62

HW Liverpool HW

MHWS	MHWN	MLWN	MLWS
9·3m	7·4m	2·9m	0·9m

Liverpool is a busy commercial port and was City of Culture 2008. It has much to offer visitors.

Approach The Anglican Cathedral is a land mark visible from 40 miles. The Bar light float (Fl.5s11m12M) marks the entry to the 10 mile long, well buoyed Queens/Crosby Channel. Be aware of tidal streams up to 5kn; training walls either side of channel; HS ferries; ships limited by draught; Rock Channel not recommended for use by visitors.

Berthing Liverpool Marina, at Coburg Dock is accessible HW±0200, call on VHF 37/M or ☎ 0151 707 6777. NB for arrival between 2200 and 0600 necessary to arrange in advance. 450 berths with full club facilities and limited on site chandlery, rigger, mechanical repairs, straddle carrier.
www.liverpoolmarina.com.

RIVER RIBBLE

RIBBLE LINK

PRESTON

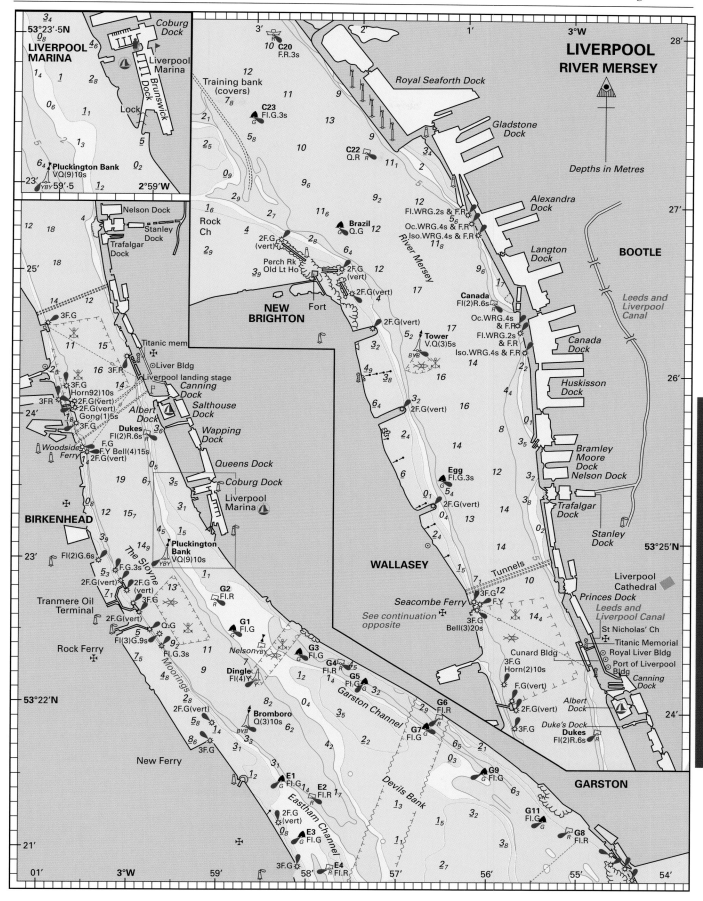

LIVERPOOL MARINA

53°23'·5N

Coburg Dock

Liverpool Marina

Brunswick Dock

Lock

Pluckington Bank
VQ(9)10s

23' 59'·5 2°59'W

LIVERPOOL
RIVER MERSEY

3°W 28'

Training bank (covers)

C20
F.R.3s

C23
Fl.G.3s

C22
Q.R

Royal Seaforth Dock

Gladstone Dock

Depths in Metres

Brazil
Q.G

Alexandra Dock 27'

Fl.WRG.2s & F.R
Oc.WRG.4s & F.R
Iso.WRG.4s & F.R

Langton Dock

BOOTLE

Rock Ch

Perch Rk Old Lt Ho

2F.G (vert)

2F.G (vert)

2F.G(vert)

NEW BRIGHTON

Fort

River Mersey

Canada
Fl(2)R.6s
Oc.WRG.4s & F.R
Fl.WRG.2s & F.R
Iso.WRG.4s & F.R

Canada Dock

Leeds and Liverpool Canal

2F.G(vert)

Tower
V.Q(3)5s

Huskisson Dock 26'

Nelson Dock
Stanley Dock
Trafalgar Dock

3F.G

Titanic mem

Liver Bldg

Liverpool landing stage

3F.G
Horn92)10s
3FR 2F.G(vert)
2F.G(vert)
Gong(1)5s
3F.G

Canning Dock
Salthouse Dock
Albert Dock

Dukes
Fl(2)R.6s
F.G
F.Y Bell(4)15s
2F.G(vert)

Woodside Ferry

Wapping Dock

Queens Dock

Coburg Dock

Liverpool Marina

WALLASEY

Egg
Fl.G.3s

2F.G(vert)

Bramley Moore Dock
Nelson Dock

Trafalgar Dock

Stanley Dock 53°25'N

Tunnels

Liverpool Cathedral

Princes Dock

Leeds and Liverpool Canal

St Nicholas' Ch
Titanic Memorial
Royal Liver Bldg
Port of Liverpool Bldg

Canning Dock

BIRKENHEAD

Fl(2)G.6s 23'

The Sloyne

F.G.3s
2F.G(vert)

Tranmere Oil Terminal

2F.G(vert)
2F.G(vert)
3F.G
2F.G(vert)

Q.G
Fl(3)G.9s
Fl.G.3s

Rock Ferry

Moorings

G2
Fl.R

G1
Fl.G

Nelson

Dingle
Fl(4)Y

G3
Fl.G

G4
Fl.R

G5
Fl.G

Garston Channel

Seacombe Ferry
See continuation opposite

Bell(3)20s

3F.G
F.Y
3F.G

Cunard Bldg
3F.G
Horn(2)10s

F.G(vert)

G6
Fl.R

2F.G(vert)

Albert Dock

3F.G

Duke's Dock 24'

Dukes
Fl(2)R.6s

53°22'N

2F.G(vert)

Bromboro
Q(3)10s

G7
Fl.G

New Ferry

E1
Fl.G

E2
Fl.R

Eastham Channel

2F.G(vert)

E3
Fl.G

Devils Bank

G9
Fl.G

GARSTON

G11
Fl.G

G8
Fl.R

3F.G

E4
Fl.R

01' 3°W 59' 58' 57' 56' 55' 54' 21'

LIVERPOOL TO CONWY

Charts BA 1978, 1977; Imray C52

Passage lights	BA No
RW Pillar Buoy	4942
Bar Fl.5s12M	

Tidal Streams between Great Orme Head and Formby Point run Dover +0100 to +0500W, –0500 to –0100E.

Do not attempt short cuts as the seaward edges of some sandbanks are not buoyed. Do not cut across the sands between Great Orme Head and Conwy without local knowledge.

Pass the N Hoyle buoy 1M off. The wind farm extends 20M W to NE, N of this line. The turbines have Lts F.R and Fl.Y.2·5s11m5M Horn Mo(U)30s.

Albert Dock is accessible HW –0200 to HW by prior arrangement but very expensive. ☏ 0151 709 6558. Langton Dock and Birkenhead Docks are commercial, access only with permission of Port Operations, VHF 12 ☏ 0151 949 6136. Similarly, Landing Stages are for commercial vessels only. Temporary mooring possible opposite Canada Dock at New Brighton but, more usefully, 1M SSW of Liverpool Marina, between Rock Ferry and New Ferry.

ESTUARY OF RIVER DEE

Charts BA 1953

HW Liverpool –0015

MHWS	MHWN	MLWN	MLWS
8·5m	6·7m	no data	no data

Broad and shallow with moving/drying sandbanks and ever growing spartina grass marsh as a consequence of canalisation on the Welsh side. The Dee may be of interest to nature lovers with Hilbre Island and its bird and seal life. Yachts usually pass by unless able to take the ground.

Approach From W and E by buoyed channels. Contact HM Dee Conservancy ☏ 01516 323355 or their website, or HM Mostyn Dock ☏ 01745 560335 for latest situation.

Berthing and Anchorages Yachts are not welcome at Mostyn Dock. There are no mooring buoys. Depending on wind, anchorage possible
• In Welsh Channel,
• SSE of Mostyn Dock if wind W to N,
• SW Hilbre Island if wind N to NE.

Access to Chester only possible with max air draught at MHWS of 3·8m due to four bridges at Connah's Quay. Access to Shropshire Union Canal, Chester, impossible at present due to seized lock gate.

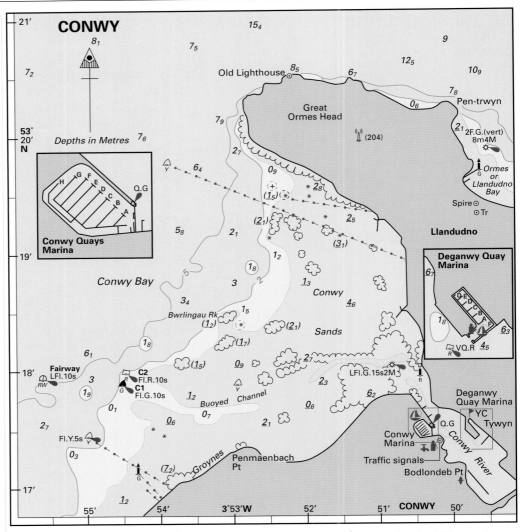

CONWY

Chart BA 1978; Imray C52, 2700

HW Holyhead +0030

MHWS	MHWN	MLWN	MLWS
7·9m	6·2m	2·6m	1·1m

An historic town in an area of outstanding natural beauty. 13th-century castle. Two modern marinas. Access HW–0300 to HW+0200.

Bar About 0·6m at MLWS. Flood runs for 5hrs, ebb 7hrs. Vessels drawing 1·8m enter at HW–0230. The channel shifts.

Entrance Make the Fairway RWVS sph buoy and turn on to 094° for 9ca to pass between C2 R can buoy Fl.R.10s and C1 G con buoy Fl.G.10s. Follow lit buoyed channel. Pass the buoys within 10 to 20m. It is very shallow to seaward of No.6 buoy less than 1m LWS. After passing B metal bn LFl.G.15s carry on for about 45m before turning on to 139° which will bring you into the Conwy River.

Berthing
• Conwy Marina, access HW±0330, opens when tide height >3·5m. Waiting pontoon, request berth before entering, RG traffic lights.
• Deganwy Quay Marina, access HW±0315 opens when

tide height >4·0m, request berth before entering.
• SE of Bodlondeb Pt there is a long pontoon. No shore access. Obtain permission from HM.
• Pick up vacant mooring and inform HM.
• Floating pontoon at town quay, only accessible HW±0200. Nearby shops.

Facilities As expected in the marinas. N Wales Cruising Club in Lower High Street.

☏/VHF Conwy Marina 01492 593000 (24hr), Deganwy Marina 576888, HM 596253, N Wales Cruising Club 593481. Both marinas www.quaymarinas.com VHF 80, HM VHF 14, NW Cruising Club and Water Taxi VHF 37/M. www.conwy.gov.uk/harbouran dseaboard contains very useful information.

MENAI STRAIT

Chart BA 1464; SC 5609; Imray C52, 2700

The Menai Strait between Anglesey and the mainland offers good shelter, except in strong NE or SW winds, excellent facilities and fine scenery. It runs NE/SW and can be entered at either end. There are two bridges, the Menai

Suspension Br (NE) and the Britannia rly br (SW) and an overhead cable, min vertical clearance 22m at HAT. Between the two bridges lie the rocks known as the Swellies where the tides run at speeds up to 8kn. The direction of buoyage changes at the S Card buoy called 'Change' off Caernarfon.

The NE part of the Strait leads in from Conwy Bay, leaving Puffin Island (landing prohibited) with the R bn on Perch Rock to port and Trwyn Du LtHo Fl.5s to stb. The stream starts to flow in here at Holyhead HW +0530 and out at HW –0145. To the S lie Dutchman's Bank and Lavan Sands which cover at half tide. The Anglesey shore should be cleared by at least 3ca. No.2. Float Fl(2)R.5s lies 1½M SW of the entrance. The channel has Lt buoys. Beaumaris pier has a Lt F.WG.5m6M

Beaumaris castle is conspicuous. Most of the moorings are private but there are 2Y visitors' buoys. It is possible to lie alongside the SW side of the pier to take on provisions. The Royal Anglesey YC is near the pier and the NW Venturers YC are at Gallows Point which dries 3ca offshore. There is a boat yard and chandlery at Gallows Point.

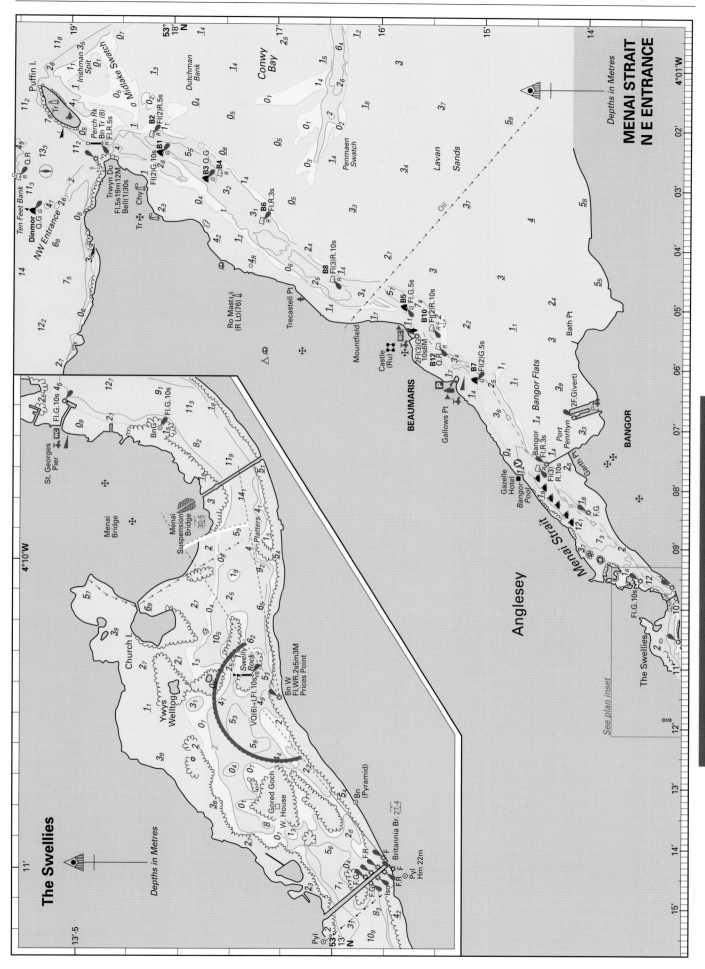

MENAI STRAIT
N E ENTRANCE

Depths in Metres

The Swellies

Depths in Metres

ENGLAND – WEST COAST AND WALES

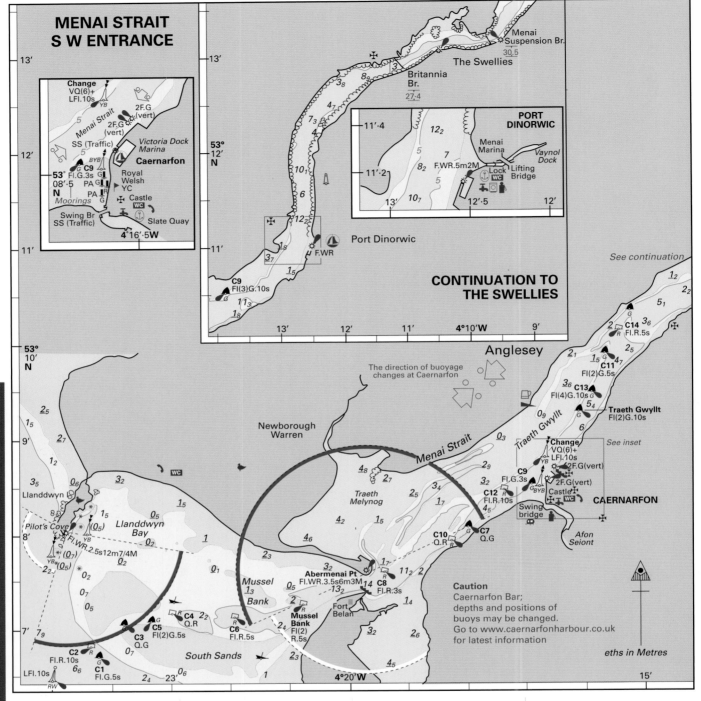

Anchorage SE of B10 buoy or outside moorings.

Bangor has a long pier with a bn Fl.R.3s. There are two drying docks at Port Penrhyn, for allocation of a berth/drying mooring contact Dickies boatyard ☎ 01248 363400 www.dickies.co.uk/office-info/bangor.

Facilities Toilets, showers, boatyard, chandlery, no diesel or gas. Opposite on the Anglesey shore, there is the Gazelle Hotel. There are two Y visitors' moorings here.

Menai Bridge Temporary swinging moorings, 2Y visitors' buoys or berth alongside St George's Pier which is the mooring of Bangor University's research ship. Only water and a public toilet.

The Swellies The tides run round Anglesey and into both entrances creating an area of slack water at the Swellies at Liverpool HW –0200 and LW –0200 lasting between 10–20 minutes. The tide is an hour later at the NE entrance of the Straits and the tide can be 1·8m higher. Timing is crucial to a safe passage and if the tide sets against your craft it is safer to abort the passage than to fight it as there is a risk of being set sideways onto the rocks. There is plenty of water between the rocks as coasters drawing 4·6m use it but the channel past the Swelly Rock is only 30m wide at LW and without local knowledge the HW passage is recommended. Advice from Menai Bridge piermaster ☎ 01248 712312 (Menai Pier),

THE SWELLIES

Passage from NE

Pass St Georges pier Fl.G.10s and the G bn on the rock to stb and move into midstream.

Pass under centre of Suspension Bridge.

Keep Swelly Rock S card Lt bn open on port bow to clear the Platters until Price's Point is on with the centre of Britannia Bridge. Steer on Price's Pt until Swelly Rock bn is abeam to stb.

Pass midway between Price's Pt and Swelly Rock bn with bow on Gored Goch Island which has a White house on it. When Price's Point is past, steer on lts at port end of Britannia Bridge until W pyramid is abeam to port.

Pass under centre span of Britannia Bridge and favour the N shore to Port Dinorwic.

Passage from SW

Pass under the middle of the S span of Britannia Bridge and steer on W pyramid on stb shore until F.G lts at base of S tower of bridge are in transit. Keep Swelly Rock Lt bn fine on stb bow until Price's Point bn is close abeam to stb. Pass midway between Price's Point bn and Swelly Rock bn until Price's Point shuts out centre tower of Britannia Bridge.

Steer on NW tower of Suspension Bridge until on a line between Swelly Rock and the middle of the Suspension Bridge to clear the Platters.

Finally turn to pass under the centre of the Suspension Bridge.

VHF 16, 69 or Victoria Dock ☎ 01286 672346, VHF 80.

HW Menai Br is Holyhead +0030 at sps and HW +0010 at nps.

HW Caernarfon is Holyhead HW –0030 at sps and HW –0030 at nps.

Times to leave Beaumaris
Dover HW –0240
Liverpool HW –0230
Holyhead HW –0140

Times to leave Caernarfon
Dover HW –0215
Liverpool –0235
Holyhead HW –0145

The slack at the Swellies is at Liverpool HW –0200, Holyhead HW –0115. These times allow for boats to carry the flood tide from the NE. If you are late you will be swept through very fast. If you are early you may find the end of the contrary tide. It would be prudent not to attempt the Caernarfon Bar on a falling tide so plan to stop at Port Dinorwic, Caernarfon or anchor.

From the SW the times are deliberately early because it helps to carry the flood through the Swellies and then the ebb past Bangor. Do not be late if travelling NE as the tide will set strongly against you before you pass the Swellies.

SW winds make the times of HW earlier and NE winds make it later.

On the N bank 2ca beyond the Britannia Br you will see Nelson's statue and a little further on you will catch glimpses of Plas Newydd, the home of the Marquis of Anglesey now in the care of the National Trust.

Port Dinorwic This old dock which was used to export slate is now a marina. 2m available through the lock HW±0230. Lock operates all tides, berthing alongside in freshwater. All facilities. The tidal basin outside dries HW±0300 at springs but has pontoons. Moorings available outside, free first 24h. Boatyard, engineer, rigger. Contact on VHF 80 before arrival. ☎ 01248 671500.

Leaving to the SW, remember to leave C9 and C7 G buoys to port. C10 and C8 R can buoys keep boats off shoals to starboard. Pass midway between Abermenai Point and Fort Belan. The R Mussel Bank buoy Fl(2)R.5s lies 5ca ahead on 260°. On the same bearing the first of the bar buoys should be 1M ahead. This is between the R and W sectors of the Abermenai Lt.

Caernarfon This spectacular town is dominated by its castle. The old hbr in the River Seiont dries and is crowded with moorings under the swing br

(opening signal is three short blasts. The br is left open between 2300 and 0700). Lie against wall or raft up and contact hbr office, ☎ 01286 672118. The Victoria Dock marina 2m entered through a flap gate which opens at half tide (October–March during daylight hours only). Port entry signals. There are two waiting buoys SW of C9 G con buoy. At half-tide there is a strong set across the Victoria Dock entrance. Chandlery but no diesel. VHF 80 (0700–2300 summer), ☎ 01286 672346. www.caernarfonharbour.co.uk.

Caernarfon Bar This is an area extending 3M out to sea where the charted depths are mostly less than 1m. The Fairway buoy, RWVS LFl.10s, lies 0·5M to SW of the outer bar buoys. There is a shifting buoyed channel winding across it. The Lt buoys are numbered C1 to C6. It is unsafe to cross the bar except in the top half of the tide, depending on sea state. Follow the buoys in sequence and do not pay much attention to chart. www.caernarfonharbour.co.uk gives latest positions of buoys. It is dangerous in SW winds more than Force 4 or in poor visibility. Advice about Caernarfon Bar at Harbour Office ☎ 01286 672118 or VHF 14, 16. As the channel narrows at Abermenai Pt the stream gets stronger, 3–4 knots, it starts to run NE at Holyhead HW +0430 and SW –0130.

Anchorages around Anglesey (see chart *1971*)
• SW Menai Straits; **Llanddwyn Island** at 53°08'·0N 4°24'·6W. Shelter from W to NE wind, Uncomfortable in SW. Fair to good holding. Approach with care from small S Card buoy 600m S of Llanddwyn Lt, anchor E of Lt in 2m or more. Beware sub rocks 150m NE and 400m E of Lt (latter marked by small S Card).
• **Abermenai Point** at 53°07'·6N 4°19'·6W in 2m or more 250m NE of Point Lt. Shelter from W.
Fort Belan This lies on the S side and close E of the fort. Sound in carefully as the water shoals rapidly in this bay.
• NE Menai Straits; **Puffin Island** at 53°18'·9N 4°01'·60W. Shelter from N wind, impossible in E. Good holding. Approach with care from N of B2 600m S of Perch Rock entrance bn, arcing right to left towards tr on Island. Anchor 200m off in 1·5–4m when CG Station and Perch Rock bn in line.
• E Coast; **Moelfre** at 53°21'·0N 4°13'·5W. Shelter from all but NE–SE wind. Good holding. Approach easy, anchor 200m off in 3m SE of RNLI slipway.
• N Coast; **Porth Eilian** at 53°24'·9N 4°17'·6W. Shelter from E–SW wind. Strong tidal stream off Point Lynas. Easy

approach. Anchor in 2–5m, ½ cable off, SSW of Lynas LtHo, holding fair to good.
Amlwch Dock at 53°25'·0N 4°19'·9W. Shelter from all winds but swell if from N. Small confined, rough/tall dock sides with ladders, plank/fenders in outer dock in 2m. Approach with care (possible overfalls and strong current) from NNE, entrance unclear until near to end of RH mole marked 2FRvert. No facilities.
Cemaes Bay at 53°25'·2N 4°27'·6W. Shelter from all wind depending on anchorage. Large swell possible in strong N wind. Good holding. Approach from Middle Mouse buoy only when fully open. Shoals 500m off E entrance. Rocks 200m off W entrance. No marks or buoys in bay.
Cemlyn at 53°25'·0N 4°30'·0W. Shelter from E through S to W, N winds deny access. Swell possible, holding varies in 2m. Approach on 180° from 250m E of Harry Furlong buoy.

HOLYHEAD

Chart BA 2011; SC 5609; Imray C52, 2700

HW Holyhead HW

MHWS	MHWN	MLWN	MLWS
5·6m	4·4m	2·0m	0·7m

The hbr of Holyhead lies between Holyhead Mountain a conspic landmark 213m and Carmel Head. It can be entered in all conditions. The large commercial harbour of Holyhead is used by High Speed (40kn) and large traditional ferries, cruise ships and other large commercial vessels. The focus of these vessels is the Old Harbour (south of Salt Island) and Jetties on and north of Salt Island. Yachts should keep clear of commercial traffic and monitor VHF 14 *Holyhead Port Radio*. The depth inside the new hbr is generally 5–15m, shoaling to 2m or under near the shore, and to just under 1m over the Platters on the E side of the hbr.

Approach From N give the Skerries a berth of at least 1M and keep S Stack well open of N Stack till breakwater LtHo bears SSE to avoid race over Langdon Ridge. Thence steer for breakwater. From SW give the Stacks a berth of at least 1M. Conspic chimney (the former Anglesey Aluminium Smelter) is a good mark. Holyhead race extending 1½M offshore is worst N of the Stacks in NW winds. At the breakwater the W going stream runs for 9hrs from half flood to LW by the shore.

Entrance Between the breakwater and Clipera Rocks R can bell buoy Fl(4)R.15s. The breakwater and the Aluminium jetty mark the entrance to New

SKERRIES/CARMEL HEAD AND STACKS PASSAGE

Passage lights:	BA No
Skerries	5168
Fl(2)15s36m20M & Iso.R.26m10M Horn(2)60s	
S Stack	5204
Fl.10s60m24M Horn 30s	

DS between Skerries and Carmel Head

Dover +0005NE –0100SW 5·6kn

DS N and S Stacks

Dover +0530NNE –0030SSW 5kn

Race up to 1½M NW of S Stack and ½M W of N Stack on NNE stream.

Race up to 5ca W of S Stack with SSW stream.

Harbour. Give breakwater ½ca clearance as there is foul ground close in.

Berthing In New Harbour only where a NE wind can make it very uncomfortable.

The conspic new apartment buildings at the W end of the Harbour are adjacent to the Marina and the Sailing Club.

• Holyhead Sailing Club has visitors' moorings – contact HSC on VHF 37 or HSC Bosun *Mobile* 07864 830004 for allocation of an available swinging mooring. Launch usually operates from 0900–2100 (later at weekends) summer only.

• Holyhead Marina. In the west end of the harbour, the 320 berth marina has full facilities and min. depth of 2m throughout. Contact Holyhead Marina on VHF 37 for allocation of berth. Visitors normally berth on outside of the north/south pontoon E, this can be very uncomfortable in NE winds – inside berths should be available on request.

Facilities Holyhead Sailing Club is very welcoming to visiting yachts. Good value catering is available: Monday, Wednesday–Saturday lunch and evening, and Sunday (lunch order in advance) ☎ 01407 769359, *Mobile* 07826 252133 to check availability/book. Launch service.

Holyhead Marina provides usual full facilities, with boatyard, chandlery, Wi-Fi at reception, mechanical/electrical/rigging services, Langdon restaurant, small shop/café, and health and beauty salon on site.

Holyhead Marine at Mackenzie Pier 500m E of HSC (where RNLI craft are serviced) with 30-tonne crane and boatyard facilities.

Shops in town 700m good ferry/train connections.

☎ /VHF Holyhead Sailing Club VHF 37, 01407 762526, HSC Bosun *Mobile* 07982 466913,

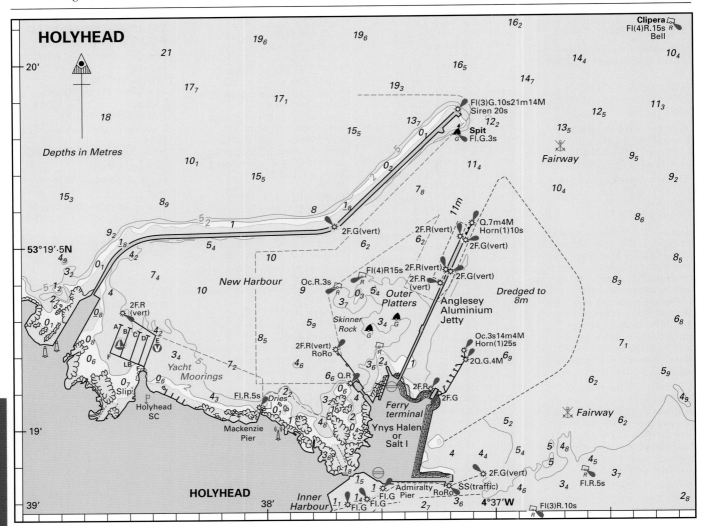

HOLYHEAD

HSC Catering 01407 769241
www.holyheadsc.org

Marina VHF 37, ☏ 01407
764242; out of hours *Mobile*
07714292 990
www.holyheadmarina.co.uk.

Port Control VHF 14, 01407
606700.

PORTH DINLLÄEN

Chart BA 1512; SC 5609;
Imray C52, 2700

This fine bay on the N side of
the Lleyn peninsula 15M SW of
Caernarvon affords the only
safe anchorage between there
and Pwllheli in S to W winds
and settled weather. With
strong NW winds some shelter
may be found by shallow
draught boats close to the point
but strong winds from NNW to
NNE send in a heavy sea.

Approach From W keep Yr Eifl
(twin conspic peaks 561m)
open of Porth Dinlläen Point to
clear Careg-y-Chad dries 2m
¾M W of Point. Give the rocks
off the point a fair berth.
Chwislen Rock, BRB bn,
extends ½ca to W. From
seaward steer for Boduan a
rounded wooded mountain
275m high 1M S of Nevin.

Anchorage About 1ca S of
lifeboat station in 1·5 to 3m.

Better holding further out in the
bay but less shelter. Groceries at
Morfa Nevin, Ty Coch pub on
beach. For petrol and general
stores Nevin 2M or in Nevin
Bay 1M to E. Anchorage in
Nevin Bay not recommended.

ABERSOCH AND
ST TUDWAL'S ROAD

Chart BA 1512; SC 5609;
Imray C52, 2700

HW Milford Haven +0150sp
+0250np

MHWS	MHWN	MLWN	MLWS
4·8m	3·3m	1·8m	0·5m

This sandy bay with fine
beaches is a very popular
summer yachting centre with
many moorings in St Tudwal's
Road. The village has a vibrant
beach/café culture with many
trendy shops and is well worth
a visit.

The anchorage offshore in St
Tudwal's Road offers
protection from S through W to
NE. Better shelter from the
South can be obtained at
Chapel Bay on the north side of
St Tudwal's Island East.

A heavy sea comes in with
strong winds from the E or SE

South Caernarfon YC on
Penbennar has three visitors'
moorings and a launch service
during the summer months.

BARDSEY SOUND

Tidal streams in the vicinity of
Bardsey Island are strong and
run at up to 7kn in the Sound.
Slack water occurs, turning NW
at HWD +0500 and SE at
HWD −0100 approx. The sound
can be extremely dangerous in
strong wind over tide situations
with severe overfalls. There are
two shallow ridges SE of
Bardsey, Bastram Shoal and the
Devil's Tail, where severe
overfalls may also be
encountered in adverse
conditions. There are also
overfalls to the N of Braich-Y-
Pwll at the north end of Bardsey
Sound. Aberdaron offers a
temporary anchorage to await
slack water for passage North
through Bardsey, shelter from
W through N to NE.

Without local knowledge
Bardsey Sound should only be
taken at slack water and in
winds Force 4 or less.

Contact SCYC on VHF 37.
www.scyc.co.uk. SCYC offers
catering facilities; contact club
for details.

Landing slip, water, small
boatyard and chandlery. All
stores and many restaurants in
Abersoch.

PWLLHELI

Chart BA 1512; SC 5609;
Imray C52, 2700

HW Milford Haven +0200sp
+0305np

MHWS	MHWN	MLWN	MLWS
5·0m	3·4m	1·9m	0·5m

The only 'all-weather' harbour
on the Welsh coast between
Holyhead and Milford Haven,
Pwllheli, in Tremadoc Bay is
home to the Welsh National
Sailing Academy and events
centre and welcomes visitors to
its safe and secure 420 berth
marina.

A popular yachting and holiday
centre with safe sandy beaches.
Pwllheli hosts many major
Dinghy Sailing Championships.

Bar The entrance channel has
been dredged to 0·6m below
CD. If awaiting the tide, shelter
from NE through N to W is
available off Abererch, to the E
of the harbour entrance, from
W through SW at Abersoch,
from S off St Tudwal's Islands,
6M SW of Pwllheli.

Approach Gimlet Rock (30m,
quarried) lies E of conspic row
of white houses on the
promenade. From the Fairway
Buoy, RW Iso.2s, (52°53'·0N
4°22'·9W) make good approx
294° towards the end of the
training arm, Q.G 3m3M.

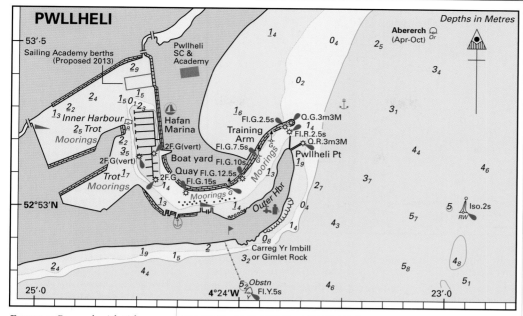

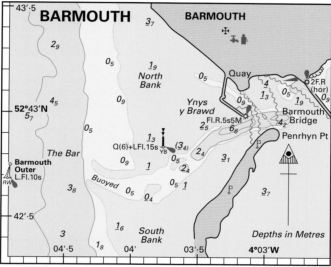

Cardigan Bay

Aberporth Range

An active firing area covering a large part of Cardigan Bay, with target floats, some unlit. The range is normally operational Monday–Friday 0900–1630, and occasionally at weekends. Contact *Aberporth Marine Control* on VHF Ch 13 or 16, or ☎ 01239 813760, or Aberporth Range Control on ☎ 01239 813480.

St Patricks Causeway Sarn Badrig

This rocky ridge extends 14M SW from just N of Barmouth. It includes many drying heights up to 1·5m above CD and is a major hazard for vessels sailing S from Pwllheli and St Tudwals. It is marked at its W end by a W card called Causeway. There is an unmarked twisting passage, East Passage, at the E end of St Patricks Causeway. This is used by local boats and local knowledge is required.

electricity. Anchoring in the hbr is NOT advised due to poor holding ground.

Facilities Water, electricity and diesel on quayside, Wi-Fi, bar and showers from Merioneth YC. Rly and all stores. Resident mechanic and launching/recovery for trailable boats.

☎ HM 01341 280671
Mobile 07795 012747
www.barmouthwebcam.co.uk includes weather site.

ABERDOVEY

Chart BA 1484; SC 5609; Imray C51, C61, 2700
HW Milford Haven +0207
DS HWDover S

MHWS	MHWN	MLWN	MLWS
5·0m	3·5m	2·0m	0·7m

This hbr is the first major inlet south of Cader Idris, it is a beautiful estuary with a lively town and well worth a visit.

Bar About 0·25m shifts continually. Entry ±0230. In stronger W winds a bad sea gets up on the ebb and advice should be sought from HM on VHF 12/16 prior to proposed entry. If entry is inadvisable, shelter can be found in St Tudwal's Roads or Pwllheli (over 30 miles to the NW).

Approach Identify the large spherical fairway buoy RWVS Iso.4s. At the fairway buoy turn due E and identify the G/R gate (Note Port Hand Mark is seasonal Apr–Sep) proceed through the gate and follow the buoyed channel (all stb marks) to the wooden jetty.

Berthing Advice on berthing/mooring should be sought prior to entry. Berths available on jetty 1·5m LW and three visitors' moorings in >3m, other free moorings may be made available. Advice should

---

Entrance Buoyed with tide gauge on N of entrance channel controlled by training wall on N side which covers around half-tide. Follow the channel marked by buoys and bns to the marina.

Berthing In Hafan Pwllheli Marina. Pile and drying moorings may be available, contact the marina who control all berthing in Pwllheli hbr.

Facilities Fuel, gas, boatyards, 50-tonne hoist, chandlers, sailmaker, sailing club (bar food may be available).
All stores and restaurants in Pwllheli town. Rly.

☎ /VHF Hafan Pwllheli (24 hrs) 01758 701219, VHF 80; Pwllheli Sailing Club 01758 614 442.
www.hafanpwllheli.co.uk;
www.pwllhelisailingclub.co.uk

PORTHMADOG

Chart BA 1512; SC 5609; Imray C52, 2700
HW Milford Haven +0225

MHWS	MHWN
5·1m	3·4m

A beautiful walled hbr in the middle of a bustling holiday town. Suitable for vessels up to 50ft, maximum draught 2m. Good shelter in inner hbr, outer exposed to S and SE'lies.

Bar with least depth about 0·5m lies across the entrance. Caution: seas break on the bar when winds from S to SW exceed Force 4. Access should only be attempted HW ±0200. Entry is not hazardous in up to Force 5–6 from E (Seek advice from HM before entry).

Approach Fairway Buoy RWVS LFl.10s, at 52°53′·01N 4°11′·10W

Entrance Follow the buoyed channel from Fairway buoy. The channel is well marked by small lit buoys, which may be moved without prior notice throughout the year to meet

---

frequent changes in the channel.

A sketch of the channel is available from the HM, by email if possible. If in doubt contact HM before entry, direct or via the CG.

Berthing Visitors who can take the ground should go alongside the N wall of inner hbr or at Madoc YC on Outer Drying Pontoon. Contact MYC for berth. At night, or boats which cannot take the ground, pick up a vacant mooring in main stream and await instructions. HM Office on N Wall of inner hbr (Oakley Wharf).

Facilities: Madoc Yacht Club – bar and food. Chandlery. Boatyard. Fuel (cans). All stores and restaurants in town. Rly.

Interest Narrow gauge Festiniog & Welsh Highland Railways. Closest hbr to Portmerion.

☎ /VHF HM 01766 512927, *Mobile* 07879 433147, *Email* daveoneill@gwynedd.gov.uk, VHF 12/16;
Madoc YC 01766 512976
www.madocyachtclub.co.uk

BARMOUTH

Chart BA 1484; SC 5609; Imray C52, C61
HW Milford Haven +0210

MHWS	MHWN	MLWN	MLWS
5·0m	2·5m	1·8m	0·7m

A very beautiful estuary and interesting town with cafés, pubs and restaurants overlooking the harbour.

Bar About 0·5m, 1M off the town, harbour is unapproachable in strong SW winds, advice should be sought from HM before entry in onshore winds over F4.

Approach Identify the large RW Barmouth Outer pillar buoy, LFl.10s, and leave the G Bar Buoy to stb then follow the buoyed lit channel into the hbr.

Berthing Good shelter is available in the hbr in winds between W and N. It is advisable to contact HM for berthing advice on VHF 12/16 before entry. Alongside drying berths and five deep water visitors' moorings available. A small pontoon (dries) max length 9m. Strict booking of berths in advance, no

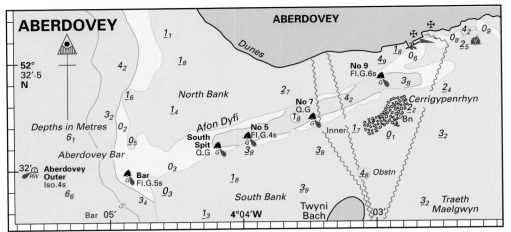

be sought from HM before anchoring.

Facilities Water, diesel and electric alongside wall at Harbour Office. All stores, pubs, restaurants, cafés, rly.

☎ HM 01654 767626, *Mobile* 07879 433148 www.aberdyfi.com.

ABERYSTWYTH

Chart BA 1484; SC 5620; Imray C51, C61, 2700

HW Milford Haven +0130sp +0145np

MHWS	MHWN	MLWN	MLWS
5·0m	3·5m	1·8m	0·7m

The hbr may be located by Pendinas, a conspic 120m hill with Wellington monument, S of entrance.

Bar 0·7m off the head of S pier. Can be dangerous in onshore winds access HW±0230. The hbr mostly dries but affords good shelter. Narrow entrance with right-angle turn inside the pier head.

Approach The approaches are dangerous in strong onshore winds. Beware of strong cross tides and boulders around the head of S pier and the Trap to the N of the N breakwater. The head of the N breakwater on Wellington's monument leads 140° and clears Castle Rocks which lie N of entrance which has 3m at half-tide.

Entrance By day make for a waypoint 52°24'·5N 4°06'·0W about 3ca W of the entrance. Identify the ldg ln, 100°, marked by a W card bn (front) seen between the piers near the far shore and a Y daymark (rear), the lower half of a lamp post. By night keep within the W sectors of both pierhead lights (R sector of Lt on N pier marking hazards to N and G sector on S pier marking hazard to S). When abeam of the N

pierhead turn 90° to port to head up river to the marina.

Berthing In marina as directed, usually Pontoons B or C. About 2m at LWS. Outside office hours, on hammerhead of Pontoon A/B which is the fuel berth. Marina office at NE end of marina. The long, most W'ly pontoon does not have visitors' berths.

Facilities as expected in marina. Small chandlery. Shops in town, EC. Wednesday. Launderette five minutes.

☎ /VHF Marina 01970 611422, VHF 80; HM VHF 14 www.abermarina.co.uk

Visit Talyllyn Railway and the Centre for Alternative Technology.

NEW QUAY CARDIGAN

Chart BA 1484; SC 5620; Imray C51, C61, 2700

HW Milford Haven +0132

Sheltered from winds W through S to NE; with N or NW wind a dangerous sea comes in. Hbr dries, bottom sand and clay. In fine weather vessels can lie head to anchor and stern to pier or outside the pier. The E side of bay off Ina Point is foul. Pier head has Fl.WG.3s Lt, 135°-W-252°-G-295°. An extension runs out 80m SSE from the end of the pier and is marked by a E card Lt bn Q(3)10s.

CARDIGAN

Chart BA 1484; SC 5620; Imray C51, C61, 2700

HW Milford Haven +0130

MHWS	MHWN	MLWN	MLWS
4·7m	3·4m	2·0m	0·7m

The hbr is at the mouth of the River Teifi. Entrance difficult, and dangerous in strong W to NW winds, but good shelter within. No special outlying dangers.

Bar Dries and shifts. There is over 2·5m at MHWS and about 1·5m a MHWN.

Approach Straightforward on a course approx SSE.

Entrance Prior inspection of the channel or local advice is desirable. Leave isolated danger Lt bn to stb, passing it about 6m off.

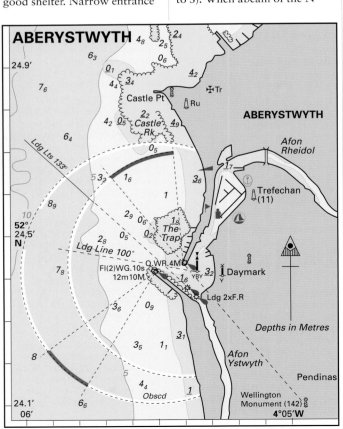

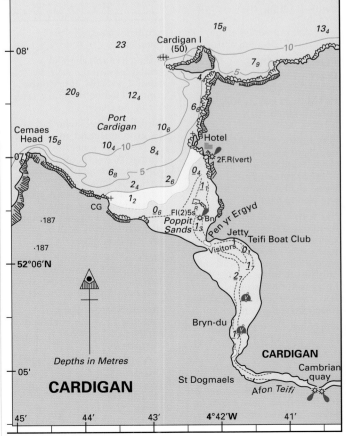

FISHGUARD TO ST ANN'S HEAD

Chart BA 1973, 1478; SC 5620; Imray C60

Strumble Head to St Ann's Head

Passage lights	BA No
Strumble Head Fl(4)15s45m26M	5274
South Bishop Fl.5s44m16M Horn(3)45s	5276
The Smalls Fl(3)15s36m18M+ Iso.R.4s33m13M Horn(2)60s	5278
Skokholm Is Fl.WR.10s54m19/8M	5282
St Ann's Head Fl.WR.5s48m18/14M, R(intens)17M Horn(3)60s	5284

This is an area of strong tides and turbulent seas. The streams run at 5kn near the Bishops, 4kn between Skomer and Grassholm and up to 6 or 7kn in the narrow parts of the inner sounds. 2–3M W of the Bishops and Smalls the streams are much weaker (2–3kn). Eddies and races form off the rks and islands, the Wild Goose Race W and SW of Skokholm being particularly dangerous.

Four routes are available:

• Outside the Smalls but staying between 1–2 M W of the Smalls LtHo to avoid the N going traffic separation lane and well S of Wild Goose Race. It clears all dangers and avoids the worst of the tidal stream. It is much the longest and is really more suitable for a passage from the middle of the Irish Sea.
• Outside the Bishops and between Skomer and Grassholm.
• Inside the Bishops along the W coast of Ramsay and between Skomer and Grassholm.
• Inshore through Ramsay and Jack Sounds.

For the second: pass N of N Bishop but do not turn S for S Bishop until at least 1¼M W of N Bishop to clear heavy overfalls. Then steer to pass midway between Skomer and Grassholm. One should take Broad Sound between Skomer and Skokholm to avoid the Wild Goose Race. Then steer to clear St Ann's Head.

The third route: From N pass between St David's Head and Carreg-trae (dries 4m) and steer to leave Gwahan to port. Pass down W coast of Ramsay Is leaving Lech Uchaf to stb and continue S across entrance to St Bride's Bay to pass W of Skomer Is. Continue as for the second. Do not attempt at night. Tides are weaker than in sounds.

The fourth route is a valuable short cut but should only be used by strangers in good visibility. Always go through at slack water or with a fair tide and avoid with wind over tide in Force 4 or over. Chart BA 1482 is absolutely essential. See separate entries for Ramsay Sound and Jack Sound on pages 188 and 189.

Bound S from Fishguard leave the harbour 1hr before local

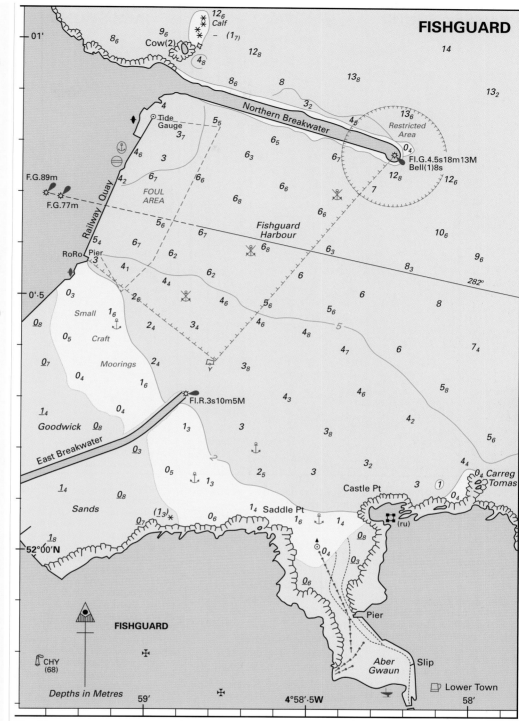

FISHGUARD

FOUL AREA

Fishguard Harbour

Railway Quay

RoRo Pier

Small Craft Moorings

Goodwick

East Breakwater

Fl.R.3s10m5M

Sands

FISHGUARD

CHY (68)

Depths in Metres

Castle Pt

Saddle Pt

Carreg Tomas

(ru)

Pier

Aber Gwaun

Slip

Lower Town

Fl.G.4.5s18m13M Bell(1)8s

Restricted Area

Northern Breakwater

Tide Gauge

F.G.89m

F.G.77m

282°

52°00'N

59'   4°58'·5W   58'

01'

0'·5

Berthing
• Good anchorage in soft mud with sufficient depth in several pools between St Dogmaels and Cardigan.
• Take ground on muddy sand alongside Spillers Quay on

HW. This will take you past the dangerous overfalls of Strumble Hd near slack water. Advantage can be taken of an inshore eddy by keeping fairly close to the land until Porthgain. Keep clear of rk awash off Penbwchdy Head. After Porthgain the coast must be left 7ca to clear outlying rocks. This helps to get through Ramsay Sound before the full strength of the tide develops and causes overfalls at the S end.

right bank, good shelter. Land on the beach below br.

Facilities Chandlery, provisions, hotels, PO and launderette in town, mainly on N side of river. EC Wednesday.

FISHGUARD

Chart BA 1484; SC 5620; Imray C60, 2700

HW Milford Haven +0107

MHWS	MHWN	MLWN	MLWS
4·8m	3·4m	2·0m	0·8m

Although this is the only harbour between Holyhead and Milford Haven that can be entered in any weather at any state of the tide, it is only secure in winds from W through S to SE. A considerable swell exists in winds above Force 5 in winds

from NNW through N to E. In E gales Pwll Gwaelod ¾M E inside Dinas Hd offers some shelter to small craft.

Approach Avoid the shoals off Strumble Head particularly in NW to NE winds. From NW after passing Pen Anglas on coast steer to leave the N breakwater Lt Fl.G.4·5s 200m to stb. This will clear the rocks, dry 1·7m, off Pen Cw near the root of the breakwater. Hold course until E breakwater Lt Fl.R.3s is well open then proceed to anchorage watching out for fishing nets.

Anchorage and Berthing
• **The Commercial Port and Goodwick** Access to the commercial port is controlled

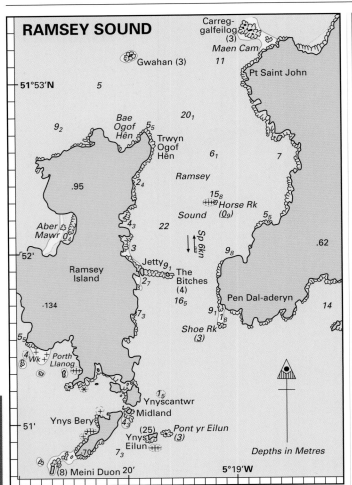

RAMSEY SOUND

Carreg-galfeilog (3)
Maen Cam
11
Pt Saint John
Gwahan (3)
51°53'N
5
20₁
9₂
Bae Ogof Hên
5₅
Trwyn Ogof Hên
6₁
7
Ramsey
2₄
15₈
Horse Rk (0₉)
Sound
5₅
Aber Mawr
4₃
22
3
9₈
.62
52'
Ramsey Island
Jetty 9₁
2₇
The Bitches (4)
Pen Dal-aderyn
.134
16₅
14
9₁ 1₈
Shoe Rk (3)
5₅
4 Wk + Porth Llanog
7₃
1₅
Ynyscantwr
51'
Ynys Bery
4₃
Midland
(25) Pont yr Eilun (3)
Ynys Eilun
7₃
(8) Meini Duon 20'
.95
.134
Depths in Metres
5°19'W

JACK SOUND

27
Tusker Rk (2)
11₆
7₃
15₅
44'·3 9
Woolltack Point
1₈
9₈
Sp 6 to 7kn
8₈
1₈
Midland Isle
9₁
Crabstones (3₇)
3₇
.45
+ 0₉ 1₈
The Cable (2₄)
7₃
3₁
Jack
Anvil Pt(34)
51°44'N
5₈
8₁
Sound
The Anvil
6₄
6₁
6₄
Limpet Rocks (3₇)
7₃
3₇
18₉
0₉+
11₉
Western Blackstone (2₁)
15₂
15₂
10₇
6₁
Blackstones (1·5)
15₂
The Bench
13₇
12₂
7₉
2₄
Depths in Metres
18₃
5°15'·5W
15'

by the Commercial Port HM. Entry to the quay for Fuel (own arrangements with tanker), water or shelter must be agreed with the HM. The quay has no facilities for yachts. Anchoring is prohibited N of the line from the RoRo pier to a large yellow buoy.

Anchorage is available to the S of the line from the RoRo Pier to a large yellow buoy, good holding, no stream. If draught permits anchorage is possible inside the E breakwater and between the breakwater and Saddle Pt. Any mooring buoys in this area cannot be trusted as no formal maintenance has been carried out.

•**Old Harbour** This sits between Saddle Pt and Castle Pt and is exposed to strong winds from the N and NE which cause dangerous seas. It has six visitors' buoys, without bridles, amongst the outer mooring buoys; they are free of charge and may also be used to await tide to enter the old harbour. These buoys are unsafe in N winds of Force 5 or over. The Old Harbour has six visitors' berths (drying, mud and clay) behind the main quay with water and free electricity. Charge £5 per night. For advice on entry and mooring/berthing enquiries contact Old Harbour HM.

Facilities Fishguard Bay Yacht Club has showers and toilets.

Shops, launderette, fuel and Rly in Fishguard town.

☎/**VHF** Commercial Port; HM 01348 404425 VHF 14: Old Harbour; HM 01348 873389, *Mobile* 07775 523846.

RAMSEY SOUND

Chart BA 1482; SC 5620; Imray C60, 2700

Tides

Milford Haven (Dover)

DS +0300   (−0200) S 6kn
   −0325   (+0400) N 6kn

Careful timing is essential. One should arrive at slack water. From N pass close to St David's Hd and steer to leave Carreg Gafeilog off the S end of Whitesand Bay 3ca to port. Leave Horse Rock (dr 1m) well to port. When Pen Dal-aderyn is abeam keep St David's Head in sight astern to avoid Shoe Rock (dr 2·7m).

From S leave Sylvia Rock to the W and when clear of it open St David's Head of Pen Dal-aderyn to clear Shoe Rock. Steer midway between E end of Bitches and the mainland and continue due N being careful to leave the Horse Rock 1ca to stb. Steer midway between Gwahan to port and Carreg Gafeilog to stb.

Ramsey Island Anchorage lies just N of the Bitches off a white farmhouse, close in to the steep

to cliffs. It is open to the N but sheltered from other directions. The tidal stream is weak (<1½kn at springs). The holding is good but an anchor buoy is essential due to the presence of old chains. This island is an RSPB Sanctuary. For permission to land call their Cardiff office ☎ 02920 353000 or the island warden, *Mobile* 07836 535733. To enter, if N bound stay in N going current until 3ca past the Bitches then turn to port into a S-going eddy that will carry you into the anchorage. If you turn too soon the eddy will carry you into the Bitches. If bound S sail over to the island shore and anchor off the farmhouse and its little hbr.

SOLVA

Chart BA 1478; SC 5620; Imray C60

HW Milford Haven +0012

MHWS	MHWN	MLWN	MLWS
5·5m	4·2m	2·3m	0·7m

A small creek on the N side of St Brides Bay, 4M inside entrance. Difficult to locate from seaward. Hbr dries to hard sand. 100m inside entrance rock. Complete shelter for craft that can take the ground, though swell in extreme weather. Hbr crowded.

Entrance 50m wide. Black Rock 4m showing at HW lies in centre; it is steep-to on its E side. Leave close to port and

proceed up the hbr keeping to outside of bend. Beware spit of stones just inside entrance on W side at Trwyn Caws.

Anchorage Temporary anchorage in calm weather may be found in 3m just behind Black Rock but there is little room. In N winds it is better to anchor outside or behind Dinas Fach 1M E. Small craft taking the ground can go further in and lie alongside the quay or pick up a visitors' mooring S of the old LB slip. Strong winds from the S render the entrance impassable. A charming village with some facilities, showers and stores.

ST BRIDE'S BAY

Chart BA 1478; SC 5620; Imray C60, 2700

HW Milford Haven +0100

MHWS	MHWN	MLWN	MLWS
5·9m	4·4m	2·3m	0·7m

It is possible to anchor in fine weather at various places in St Bride's Bay, especially in offshore winds. Avoid if any possibility of strong winds from the W, as although the tides in the bay are weak, to get out one has to go through the sounds or round Skomer Is or Ramsey Is, either way encountering strong tides.

Anchorages In N or E winds anchor between Solva and Dinas Fach.

Dinas Fach An inlet to the E of the second headland 1M E of Solva. Anchor in 3m on sand abeam of the middle of the headland.

Goultrop Roads 51°46'·20N 5°07'·50W, lies just E of Borough Head off Little Haven. It gives shelter from the E and S and, surprisingly, even from the W if one anchors close in. Unfortunately, the best places are taken up with small boat moorings. A tripping line is essential because of old mooring chains.

SKOMER ISLAND

Charts BA 1478, 1482; SC 5620; Imray 2600, C60

HW Milford Haven –0005

MHWS	MHWN	MLWN	MLWS
6·6m	5·1m	2·5m	0·7m

Skomer Is is a Marine Nature Reserve and the waters around it are protected. Care should be taken on the Is to respect wildlife particularly where nests are marked. No facilities.

North Haven is the only place where landing is permitted. There is a small charge. Beware of the reef on the E side on entry, keep well to the W of the bay. It is open to the N and NE. Visitors' mooring buoys are provided and you are expected to use them. Anchoring is not permitted shoreward of them because of a bed of rare seagrass. Land on the slip out of the way of the ferry. Close inshore beware of rock, the Loaf, 10m from the cliff, which shows at LW.

South Haven A small bay on the SE side of Skomer giving shelter in winds from W through N to E. This is a beautiful anchorage and although exposed to winds from the S it is normally an easy beat or fetch down to Milford Haven should winds come from this direction.

Entrance If coming from Milford Haven aim for the Mewstone a prominent rock 48m high off the S tip of Skomer. Beware of rocks extending SW from the Neck on the E side of entrance.

Anchorage Right up towards the head of the bay in about 6m, sand. Do not go further in at neaps as the ground becomes rocky. Landing is not permitted here.

JACK SOUND

Chart BA 1482 (essential); SC 5620; Imray C60, 2700

Tides

Milford Haven (Dover)

DS +0200 (–0300) S 7kn
    –0425 (+0300) N 7kn

It is a cable wide and at slack water, on a neap tide and in calm weather it presents no difficulty. It should be avoided in heavy weather, particularly with spring tides and especially if wind is against tide.

It is advisable to have to the engine running because even in fair weather, there are both wind eddies and strong tidal stream eddies. Timing is essential. Go through at slack water or with the stream very newly turned with you. You may await slack water in N or S Haven of Skomer Island, which lies immediately to W of Midland Isle.

From N identify Tuskar Rock (1·5m) ¾ca W of Wooltack Point and the Blackstones 2ca S of Middle Is before entering the sound. Pass W of Tuskar Rock and immediately bring the Blackstones on with the W end of Skokholm. Approach the Blackstones to pass 100m E of them. Rough water will be encountered on leaving the sound with a moderate S wind against tide. There are dangerous eddies around Tuskar Rock and S of Middle Is on the S going tide.

From S identify the Blackstones while still S of them and also Tuskar Rock. Leaving the Blackstones 100m to port steer for Tuskar Rock keeping the Blackstones on with the W end of Skokholm as a back bearing. When Garland Stone off the N point of Skomer opens N of Middle Is you are free of all dangers W of Tuskar Rock. Except, maybe, when bound N on a spring tide it is not possible to pass both Jack and Ramsay Sounds at slack water on the same tide.

Little Sound between Skomer and Middle Is is used by some locals but should not be attempted without BA *1482*.

MILFORD HAVEN

Charts BA 2878, 3274, 3275; SC 5620; Imray 2600, C60

HW Milford Haven HW

DS in offing:
Local HW –0130NW; +0450SE

MHWS	MHWN	MLWN	MLWS
7·0m	5·2m	2·5m	0·7m

Picturesque and one of the finest harbours in the British Isles. May be entered in any weather. From Dale to Lawrenny in the E is about 12M with width varying from 1½M to ½M. It is a major commercial, oil and LNG port with four terminals for very large tankers. In the entrance there are two deep-water channels and yachts must keep out of the way of deep-draught vessels, which are restricted to these channels and must maintain steerage-way. However, there is plenty of room to manoeuvre and tack inshore of these channels or between them.

Small craft, including sailing vessels, must keep out of the way of large vessels. No yachts may approach within 100m of any tanker or terminal. It is particularly important not to cross the channel ahead of a tanker under way.

It is highly recommended to maintain a listening watch on VHF 12, *Milford Haven Port Control*. Details of commercial vessel movements, a Leisure User Guide, Bylaws, Tide tables and lock times for the Milford Marina are available from www.mhpa.co.uk. The Authority's launches have green hulls and white upperworks. They are helpful, but their instructions must be obeyed.

Caution Tugs and pilot boats may travel at 10kn escorting vessels in the W Channel, producing a considerable wash in the bays between St Ann's Head and Dale Fort.

Approach The Turbot Bank 4M S of St Ann's Head, marked at its W end by a W card buoy, causes a heavy sea in bad weather. There is also a confused and sometimes dangerous sea close to St Ann's Head especially with a strong southwesterly against the ebb. Large yachts have capsized there. In these conditions quieter water and less traffic will be found in the E Channel near Sheep Is. At night the first Lt is as likely to be from the Valero oil refinery stack where gas is burned off. This can be seen from 30M, beyond the range of St Ann's LtHo.

Entrance The entrance offers no obstructions to yachts but Middle Channel Rocks 5m and Chapel Rocks 3m in the centre should be avoided in heavy weather.

Both E and W Channels are well buoyed and lit, W Channel being the deeper with three sets of leading lights before the channels combine. Yachts should not follow these but keep out of the channels. If the lights come on in the daytime it is warning that large vessels are moving. In poor visibility, at night, the Ldg Lts on W Blockhouse Point may be seen before St Ann's Head Lt.

The most noticeable mark in the entrance is the bn Fl(3)G.7s18m8M on Middle Channel Rocks.

Although there is never any necessity to go between Thorn Is and the shore the channel has 3m and an overhead cable clearance of 15m.

W of the line Dale Fort to Thorn Is the shores, on both sides are clean and steep to and can be safely approached within ½ca but note that Thorn Rock has only 2·6m at LAT.

For vessels going up to Neyland the channel is well buoyed. The water is very shallow off Chapel Bay, between Thorn Is and Angle Bay and it is obstructed by fishing buoys. Angle Bay is also shallow but it is possible to navigate outside the main channel as far as the gap between the Murco and Valero terminals. Thereafter one can skirt the Milford Shelf. Then it is wise to cross the channel and skirt Pwlcrochan Flats. These are very shallow and near LW one should not stray S of the N card LtF. Beware of Wear Spit (marked), Carr Rocks (marked), over which the tide sets strongly, and Neyland Spit (marked). When navigating the Haven it is best to keep out of the fairway or, failing that, keep to the side with an escape route should a large vessel appear.

If proceeding beyond the Cleddau Br (37m) pass under the arch marked by 2F.G and 2F.R Lts. The channel is remarkably deep but beware of unmarked spits on the inside of bends. Above Lawrenny do not approach Benton Castle closer than midstream to avoid rocks. The river shoals rapidly above Llangwm. The Cockle Ground extends almost to the rocky E shore. The river divides into the E and W Cleddau at Picton Point of which there is ample water on neap tides. This is a beautiful, peaceful river in complete contrast to the industry lower down. There is a firm landing slip near Landshipping just inside the entrance to the E Cleddau. Shallow draught vessels can sail up the E Cleddau to Slebech on the tide and dinghies back to Blackpool Mill. Shallow draught vessels with an air-draught of less than 6m can get to Haverfordwest on the tide. The br below the town is fixed. From Lawrenny Carew Mill and Creswell Quay can be reached by dinghy.

Berthing
• **Milford Marina** is approached from Milford Dock Lt buoy RGR Fl(2+1)R.6s along a channel in the mud dredged to 2·0m. The Ldg Lts are on 348° and the lock gates open approximately:

Entry HW–0400 Exit HW–0315

Entry and Exit free flow HW–0210 to HW–0010

Entry HW+0100 Exit HW+0130

Entry HW+0230 Exit HW+0320

www.milfordmarina.com gives more exact lock times.

Signal for gates open; 2Bu Lts vert by night displayed to E of entrance. Call *Pierhead* before entry. Waiting (only) pontoon 1·5m, E side of entrance, very exposed to S wind and wash of many passing vessels. Metal pontoon immediately to W is reserved for fishing vessels. Yachts should not be left

ENGLAND – WEST COAST AND WALES

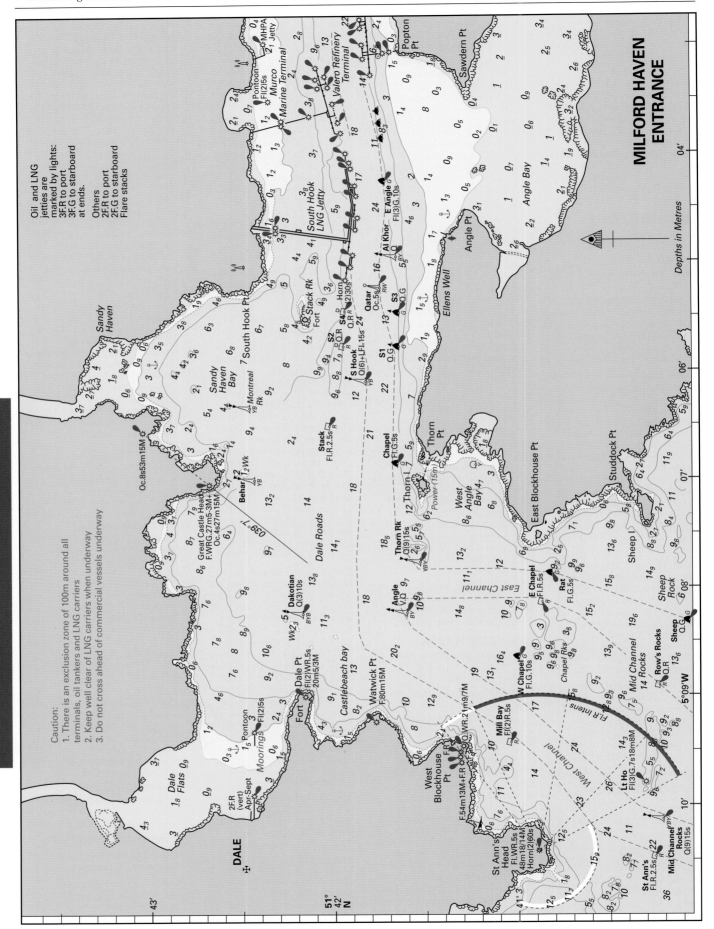

MILFORD HAVEN ENTRANCE

Depths in Metres

Caution:
1. There is an exclusion zone of 100m around all terminals, oil tankers and LNG carriers.
2. Keep well clear of LNG carriers when underway.
3. Do not cross ahead of commercial vessels underway

Oil and LNG jetties are marked by lights:
3F.R to port
3F.G to starboard at ends.
Others
2F.R to port
2F.G to starboard
Flare stacks

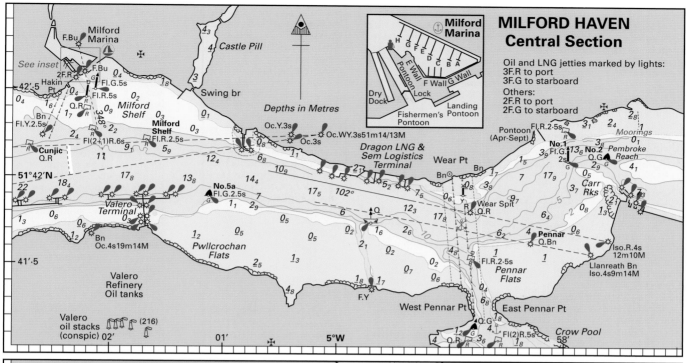

MILFORD HAVEN
Central Section

Oil and LNG jetties marked by lights:
3F.R to port
3F.G to starboard
Others:
2F.R to port
2F.G to starboard

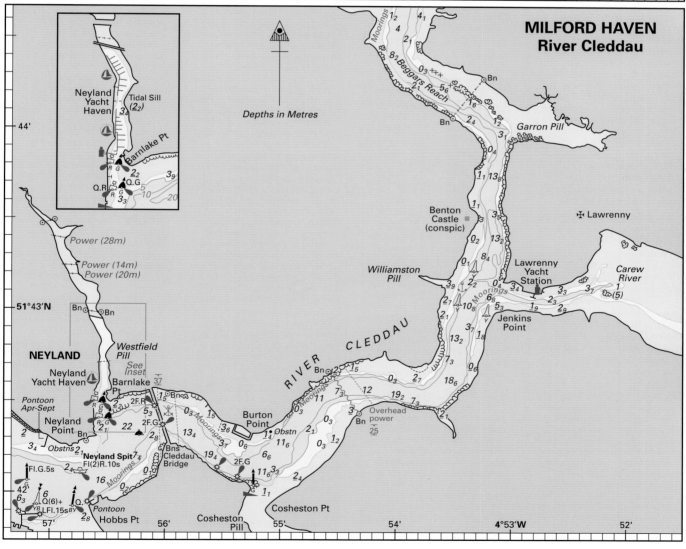

MILFORD HAVEN
River Cleddau

unattended. Fortunately the outer lock gates are often left open so wait at floating pontoon to stb in the lock. Call *Pierhead* 1h before departure. Remain on berth until directed.

Facilities Fuel, gas, chandlery, boat repairs, restaurants. Wi-Fi and internet available at HM and Martha's Vineyard. Supermarket with cashpoint. Rly five min walk.

☎ Milford Marina 696312, VHF 37; *Pierhead* VHF 14.

• **Neyland Yacht Haven** in Westfield Pill has 450 berths and normally room for visitors. It is dredged to 2m. Call on VHF 80, 37 when past Wear Point ☎ 01646 601601. There is Wi-Fi, café, restaurant and three chandlers. Dale Sailing Company ☎ 601636 can undertake all repairs including engine and have a fibreglass paint workshop. Stephen Ratsey Sailmakers ☎ 601561 have an extensive loft and can undertake repairs at short notice.

Anchorages from W to E
• **Dale** About 3ca NW of Dale Fort close to moorings. Comfortable in winds S to W. In strong N winds anchor off N shore or in Castlebeach Bay. In strong E winds very exposed and landing difficult. There is a detached pontoon (Apr–Sept) outside the moorings to which

one can moor. Damage may occur in strong winds or large wash; rigging of rafted boats could tangle. There is also a landing pontoon (Apr–Sept) dries 1m. Only very basic provisions in village. Showers at YC. Water on pontoon but no fuel, limited chandlery, PO has internet. Bus to Milford and Haverfordwest.
• **Sandy Haven** is sheltered from N and E but beware of Bull Rock.
• Off Ellen's Well and Angle Pt on S shore sheltered from S.
• With sufficient rise of tide Angle Bay may be entered. Useful for boats that can take the ground.
• At Milford off Hakin Point or off MHCB jetty W of town.

NAVIGATION IN THE BRISTOL CHANNEL EAST OF A LINE ST GOWAN'S HEAD – LUNDY – HARTLAND POINT

Chart BA 1179; SC 5608; Imray 2600, C58, C59, C60

Passage lights	BA No
Caldey Is	5328
Fl(3)WR.20s65m13/9M	
Mumbles Head	5358
Fl(4)20s35m15M Horn(3)60s	
Lundy N Point	5616
Fl.15s48m17M	
Lundy S Point	5618
Fl.5s53m15M	
Nash Point	5406
Fl(2)WR.15s56m21/16M	
Flatholm	5426
Fl(3)WR.10s50m15/12M	
Foreland Point	5590
Fl(4)15s67m18M	
Bull Point	5600
Fl(3)10s54m20M+F.R.48m12M	
Hartland Point	5621
Fl(6)15s30m8M	

The funnel shape of the Bristol Channel causes a larger range of tide, and thus stronger tidal streams as one goes further east. The change of tidal stream occurs within about 10 minutes of the time of local HW, except that in many bays the stream turns up to ½ hour earlier, especially on the new flood tide. If the tide turns against a strong wind, a short, steep sea soon builds up, which can be uncomfortable or even dangerous to small craft. With a strong wind against tide there will be overfalls off some headlands. Boats on passage will need to make full use of the tidal stream, particularly in the east of the Bristol Channel, where the tide may be carried for seven hours eastbound, but only five hours westbound, because of the difference in the time of local HW. Because of this and the prevailing winds, passage westbound is usually more difficult than passage eastbound.

• **Pennar Gut** on S side 1M W of Pembroke Dock, entrance marked by red can buoy. Sheltered anchorage in 4m, buoy anchor.
• **Pembroke Dock** above Hobb's Point close to moorings (tide runs strongly). Watch out for Irish ferry, which enters and leaves by channel E of Dockyard Bank. Kelpie Boat Services have an extensive chandlery and may be able to advise on moorings. Otherwise enquire at Pembroke Haven YC next door. Grid for drying inside slipway. Rly. Diesel from E. Llanion Marine (☎ 686021) HW±0130, telephone first.
• **Burton**, off and above Trinity House pier.
• **Williamston Pill** opposite Lawrenny.

Padstow to Clovellly (39M) **to Ilfracombe** (another 19M) Depart hbr before HW–0200 but could wait at The Pool for worst of ebb tide to ease. Beware overfalls off Hartland Pt and Lundy with wind against a strong stream. In offshore winds Hartland Pt has an inshore passage, almost clear of the race. Consider overnight at Lundy or Clovelly. If caught out in SW gales, Clovelly Roads offers an anchorage or possibly a mooring. Beware overfalls off Morte Pt and Bull Pt. The max stream is stronger further E; you must use it, not fight it.

Ilfracombe to Barry (34M) Depart hbr before half tide. Consider anchoring off Ilfracombe or Watermouth (¾M to E) and sail on last of ebb. The scenic route is to follow Devon-Somerset shoreline with Exmoor National Park and cross the channel at Foreland Pt avoiding overfalls. Ensure your ETA at Barry is before not much after HW because a strong stream will soon strengthen against you.

To sail from **Bristol to Sharpness**, leave Bristol at Bristol HW–0030 or as late as they will lock you out, and anchor in mud off Portishead, E of Marina ent, or SE of Firefly Rks, or on small neaps, anchor off Pill, a small drying creek in R. Avon and home of Portishead Cruising Club ☎ 01275 373988. Then leave Portishead at ½ flood to arrive Sharpness at HW–0030. BA chart *1166* essential. The channel is well marked and lit, but the stream is strong and there are numerous hazards, so do not navigate in poor visibility or at night on your first visit.

Outward bound **from Sharpness** lock out at HW–0030 and set off against the last of the flood, because the stream will already be ebbing in The Shoots, and more strongly by the time you reach there.

• **Lawrenny** moorings may be available off the jetty. Large yachts should select moorings with sufficient room to swing as space is tight. Secure temporarily to visitors' buoy at entrance to creek or to pontoon and go ashore to arrange a berth. Chandlery, restaurant and supplies available.
• Upper end of Beggars Reach (below moorings) very sheltered in W gales.

Yachts on passage requiring a night's shelter use Dale or Ellen's Well, otherwise any anchorage of choice, Pennar Gut and off Williamston Pill being the most peaceful. Neyland Marina is probably most convenient if fuel and water is required, unless Milford Marina is on free-flow.

To sail from **Barry to Ilfracombe**, leave Barry at HW–0100 and keep initially to the Welsh shore. To sail from **Barry to Bristol**, leave Barry at LW–0100. On neap tides you may only get enough tidal help to reach Portishead. Keep clear of commercial traffic (narrow channel). Tides inshore on the W side of Carmarthen Bay from Pendine to St Govan's Head are strong at 2–3kn especially in Caldey Sound; the SW going stream starts HW Milford Haven –0200. This means that a yacht on passage from **Milford to Tenby** has only 4h of fair tide. Fortunately there is a permanent E going eddy inside Turbot Bank and if the firing range allows one can compensate by making an early start.

There is a firing range at Castlemartin to the E of the entrance to Milford Haven. Firing extends up to 12M WNW from Linney Head in an arc to 12M S off St Govan's on most weekdays 0900–1700. Night firing is usually on Tuesdays and Thursdays. During these times it is necessary to proceed S of the Turbot Bank buoy before passage E. Often shorter-range weapons are used and it is necessary to keep as little as 3M off. ☎ 01646 662367 for recorded message about firing during next few days. Before approaching during times of firing call Castlemain Range Officer on this number or VHF 16.

There is a rocket range at Manorbier where it may be necessary to keep 12M off. Enquire on VHF Ch 16, 73 or ☎ 01834 871282 ext 209. You may be guided through close inshore.

Penally rifle range seldom causes a problem.

Pendine range sea danger area in Carmarthen Bay is normally N of 51°40'N and active Monday–Friday 0800–1800. Call CG prior to departure on day, or range safety vessel on VHF 16 before approach.

MILFORD HAVEN TO LAND'S END

Chart BA 1178; SC 5603, 5608; Imray 2600, C59, C58, C7

Passage lights	BA No
Skokholm Is	5282
Fl.WR.10s54m8M	
St Ann's Head	5284
Fl.WR.5s48m18/14M R(intens)17M Horn(2)60s	
Pendeen	5670
Fl(4)15s59m16M Horn 20s	
Seven Stones LtV	0020
Fl(3)30s15M Horn(3)60s Racon O (– – –)	
Longships	0028
Fl(2)WR.10s35m15/11M Horn 10s	

The tidal stream runs at right angles to the course to be made good although there is a slight advantage in leaving Milford Haven on the flood for the first 10M. As the coast of Cornwall is closed so the tide will be more in line with the course especially between Cape Cornwall and Land's End where the streams run up to 2kn. It is 110M from Milford Haven to Land's End and very little shelter offers. To the E of the direct track it can be found under the lee of Lundy in W or SW winds otherwise Padstow is the only harbour of refuge from the prevailing SW but entry over Doom Bar would be difficult at LW or at any time in strong W winds or big ground swell. St Ives Bay offers shelter in S and E winds only.

MILFORD HAVEN TO KILMORE QUAY

Distance 60M BA 1121; SC 5621

Best time to leave Milford Haven is at HW taking the ebb tide. Give St Ann's Head a wide berth as there is a dangerous sea near the head in strong SW'lies. Best course is to leave Skokholm to port avoiding the Wild Goose race on the SW side of the island. Then aim to leave Grassholm to port. Steer a course of 305° crossing just N of the shipping lanes to the W of the Smalls. From Grassholm to Carnsore Point is 43M. 13M from Carnsore Point you cross the shipping lanes off Tuskar Rock. At night you should be able to see the lights of the Smalls and S Bishop on the Welsh side and Tuskar Rock on the Irish side as the range of all three are 24M or over.

On the Irish side BA chart *2049*. From a position about 52°N 6°10'W alter course to 297° for St Patrick's Bridge. and pass between G con Lt buoy Fl.G.6s and R can Lt buoy Fl.R.6s. Carry on for a further 3ca before turning on to the ldg line 008°. Entrance is now 1M. Do not deviate from the ldg line as there is shallow water to starboard and just before the entrance rocks to port.

TENBY

Charts BA 1482; SC 5620; Imray 2600, C60

HW Milford Haven −0012

DS outside Caldey Is:

Dover −0500W +0100E

MHWS	MHWN	MLWN	MLWS
8·4m	6·3m	3·0m	0·9m

Delightful old tourist town. Hbr dries 1m at pier head to hard sand.

Approach

From the W by day through Caldey sound. Steer ENE for Giltar Pt giving St Margaret's Is a berth of at least 2ca. Pass between Giltar Spit R can and Eel Point G con buoys. Then make for N Highcliff N card Q buoy leaving it to stb. Steer due N until abreast of St Catherine's Is giving Sker Rock a berth of 1ca. The stream runs hard in Caldey Sound and power may be needed if it is foul. A weather going stream causes a tide rip at the W end of the sound. The Whitebank off S Beach extends seaward of the direct line Giltar Pt to Sker Rock. By night pass S of Caldey keeping ½M offshore.

From the S and E by day look out for the Woolhouse Rocks, marked by a S card buoy. St Mary's Church steeple on with the N side of St Catherine's Is, 275°, leads ½M N of them. DZ2 Y buoy is virtually on this transit. A vessel approaching from S at night should pass 2ca E of Caldey and then steer NE for DZ2 buoy, Fl.2·5s, keeping in the W sector of Caldey LtHo. From DZ2 steer 290° for Tenby Roads allowing for any SW going tide. Alternatively, having rounded Caldey Point a yacht can steer to pass close E of North Highcliff buoy, keeping well W of Woolhouse buoy. There is normally no need to pass E of E Spaniel E card Lt buoy.

Entering Tenby's North Bay keep outside moorings and beware of pick-up buoys on floating lines.

Berthing

• Anchor NNE of LB slip. You may have to go well towards First Point to avoid moorings. Beware of rk awash off First Pt. Good holding, sand over mud. Safe except in strong E winds.

• To enter hbr, accessible HW±0230, steer well towards iron post on shore S of Gosker Rock and when nearly on line joining rock and pier head round up and go alongside pier; apply to HM for berth. The hbr is crowded, busy and there are only two drying berths available alongside the pier. The wooden stairs at the pier head are in constant use by passenger launches. There are also stone steps and ladders. It is smooth except in strong E winds. Beware of being neaped.

• **Caldey** Small craft can anchor in Priory Bay outside moorings but as close inshore as draught permits to avoid the tide. Uncomfortable in any wind, it gives reasonable shelter from SE through S to WSW. In E winds shelter may be found in Sandtop Bay on the W side of the Is. Close in there is little swinging room between rocks but in moderate winds shelter extends offshore although there might be a swell.

Unusually, the Caldey foreshore belongs to the monks rather than the Crown. Landing is permitted only at Priory Bay and never on Sunday. A landing fee is payable at the post office.

Facilities at Tenby limited. Stores, water from tap below SC, diesel from garages in town, showers and bar in SC, rly. EC Wednesday. HM ☎ 01834 842717.

SAUNDERSFOOT

Chart BA 1482; SC 5620; Imray 2600, C60

HW Milford Haven −0012

DS Dover −0500W +0100E

MHWS	MHWN	MLWN	MLWS
8·4m	6·3m	3·0m	0·9m

A quiet hbr dries at 4hrs ebb but there is at least 3·5m at MHWS and 1·5m at MHWN. Yachts drawing 1m can enter at half tide. There is a good anchorage in 2·5m 5ca SE of hbr Lt, about 3ca offshore keeping the glasshouses on the W shore of the bay well open. Well sheltered from winds from NNE through W to SW good holding. Scend in W and SW gales.

Approach Keep about 100m NE of entrance until N pier head is abeam to stb. A variable sandbank (about 3m at MHWS) extends about 50m from S pier head. At night, once clear of Monkstone Pt (unlit) keep S pier head Lt Fl.R.5s due W then approach as above.

Berthing There may be room alongside against the NE pier, sharp to stb inside the entrance, or alongside the SE wall with ladders. A few moorings are available in the centre of the hbr. Enquire from HM whose office is next to SC at NW of hbr. Bottom level, sand and mud.

Yacht yard and laying up facilities, chandlery and provisions, water tap on SW wall. Concrete slip for vessels up to 15m, buses to Tenby and Haverfordwest, rly 1M, EC Wednesday.

☎/VHF HM 01834 812094, VHF 11.

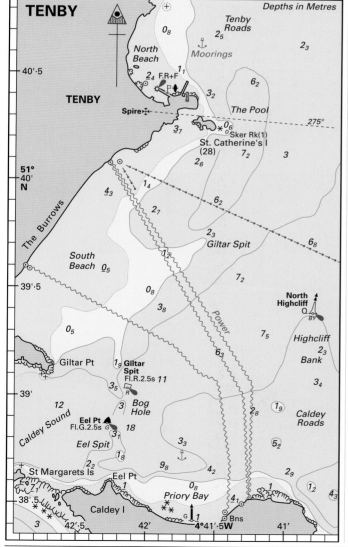

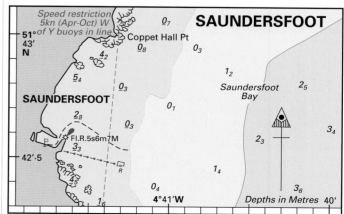

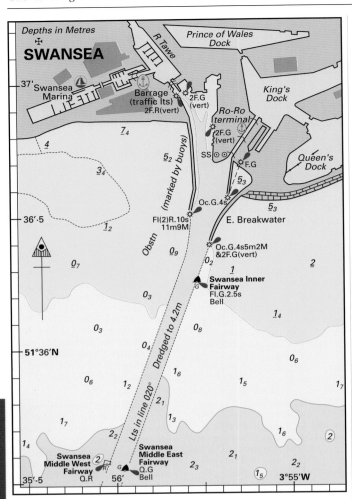

SWANSEA

Chart BA 1161; SC 5608; Imray 2600, C16, C59

HW Swansea HW

MHWS	MHWN	MLWN	MLWS
9·5m	7·2m	3·1m	1·0m

There is a barrage across the River Tawe and to reach the marina, which is in the city centre, one has to negotiate two locks.

Approach Make the SW Inner Green Grounds S card buoy and steer 020° keeping just to the W of buoyed channel, where practical. Give way to commercial vessels.

Vessels approaching the harbour will see nine signal lights displayed in three columns of three lights, just to the west of the dock entrance, marked SS on the plan. The centre light of the left hand column controls pleasure craft. When this light is R, craft must not enter the river and should hold SW of the western breakwater, G you may enter the river. Beware of bank extending from W pierhead. Once you have seen these lights call *Tawe Lock* on VHF 18.

In busy periods the lock operates a waiting list based on the time that a radio call was made on entering the river. Boats are to keep in the lower part of the river, or on a waiting buoy, until they are called

forward. Initial calls made from boats outside the river (covered by a camera) will be ignored.

Entrance The locks operate 0700–2200 (1900 weekdays in winter). Tawe Lock times: Entry on the half hour, exit on the hour. Last entry is half an hour before close of business. Beware of bank extending from W pier head. There are holding buoys outside the barrage lock but depths here are near chart datum. The barrage and marina locks employ identical signal Lts.

2R or no Lts – Lock not operating
1R – Wait
1G – Enter as directed
R and G – Free Flow in operation. During free flow vessels proceeding against the stream give way to those proceeding with it.

Call *Swansea Marina* VHF 80, on leaving Tawe Lock.

There is a large lagoon above the barrage. The pontoons here are owned by Swansea Yacht and Sub-Aqua Club and there are no visitors' berths. The entrance channel to the marina is to port, between quays, immediately before the first pontoon. Moor to chains hanging from walls to await lock entry. Yachts keep to port in lock.

Berthing As directed.

Facilities Include boatyard and chandlery. No Wi-Fi. No petrol but garage nearby. Rly and coach to London and Midlands

☎/**VHF** *Swansea marina* VHF 80, 01792 470310; SYSAC 469084; Wray Marine (engineering) 01903 963947.

OFFSHORE ANCHORAGES

Pwll Du and **Oxwich Bay** provide anchorages with good holding in sand to stay overnight or await the change of tide. Both are sheltered from SW to NE but unusable in S to E winds. The W side of Pwll Du has rocks that are not obvious at HW. At Oxwich avoid the moorings and a drying wreck, shown by BA and Imray, 200m off W shore and indicated by a white arrow painted on the rocks.

The Mumbles One can anchor N of the pier off the village. Sheltered from NW through W to S. A long row ashore against the tide that flows S except for 2hrs after LW.

RIVER NEATH

Chart BA 1161; SC 5608; Imray 2600, C59

Do not enter in gales from SE to SW even at HW. About 3M E of Swansea. Entry HW−0200 to HW between training walls marked by posts and buoys.

Monkstone Marina with an automatic gate lies to port just before motorway br (30m) Fl.R on W pier. Two waiting buoys in river upstream of entrance. If stream too strong to enter marina wait until near HW. YC ☎ 01792 812229 hbr.

PORTHCAWL

Charts BA 1169; SC 5608; Imray 2600, C59

HW Swansea +0007

MHWS	MHWN	MLWN	MLWS
9·9m	7·5m	3·3m	1·0m

A small hbr full of local boats on fore and aft moorings. Access HW±0200. Being developed into marina with gate. Limited visitors' berths.

Approach From W find Fairy W card buoy. From E Tuskar R can buoy Fl(2)R.5s and steer 315° to Fairy buoy making due allowance for the tide and avoiding Fairy Rocks. From Fairy buoy steer 010° to end of jetty (F.WRG). Tide runs at 6kn (springs) off end of breakwater.

Entrance Beware submerged old breakwater extending from E side of entrance marked by bn, also rocks off Lt on W entrance.

Berthing Hbr dries, soft mud. Anchorage possible in 7m 3ca SSE of LtHo but poor holding. ☎ HM 01656 782756.

BARRY

Chart BA 1182; SC 5608; Imray 2600, C59

HW Avonmouth −0022

DS in offing Dover −0500 W

MHWS	MHWN	MLWN	MLWS
11·4m	8·5m	4·0m	1·0m

The hbr is available at any state of the tide, but do not enter in SE gales. Yachts over 11m and multihulls not easily accommodated. Do not approach if ship approaching or departing. At LW craft may anchor in fairway but must move into the yacht area as soon as the tide serves. Keep clear of pilot launches, LB, and new pontoon N of the

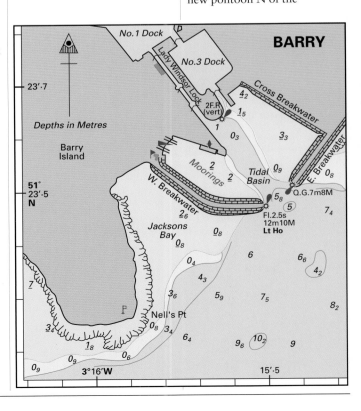

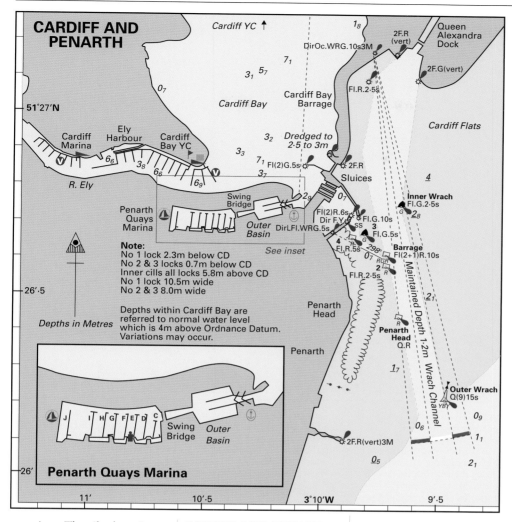

CARDIFF AND PENARTH

Cardiff YC ↑

DirOc.WRG.10s3M

2F.R (vert)

Queen Alexandra Dock

Cardiff Bay

Cardiff Bay Barrage

Cardiff Flats

Cardiff Marina

Ely Harbour

Cardiff Bay YC

51°27'N

R. Ely

Penarth Quays Marina

Swing Bridge

Outer Basin

See inset

Dredged to 2.5 to 3m

Fl(2)G.5s

Sluices

2F.R

Inner Wrach Fl.G.2·5s

Fl(2)R.6s
Dir F.Y
SS
Fl.G.10s
DirLFl.WRG.5s
Fl.G.5s
Fl.R.5s
Barrage
Fl(2+1)R.10s
RGR
Fl.R.5s
Fl.R.2·5s

Note:
No 1 lock 2.3m below CD
No 2 & 3 locks 0.7m below CD
Inner cills all locks 5.8m above CD
No 1 lock 10.5m wide
No 2 & 3 8.0m wide

Penarth Head

Penarth Head Q.R

Penarth

Depths within Cardiff Bay are referred to normal water level which is 4m above Ordnance Datum. Variations may occur.

Depths in Metres

26'·5

26'

Outer Wrach Q(9)15s YBY

2F.R(vert)3M

Swing Bridge

Outer Basin

Penarth Quays Marina

Maintained Depth 1·2m Wrach Channel

11'   10'·5   3°10'W   9'·5

---

moorings. The pilot boats' swinging mooring may be used with permission to await a rise of tide.

Approach Beware Bendrick rocks to E of ent, and overfalls on the ebb stream off Nell's Pt to W.

Entrance Beware cross-setting W-going stream off entrance at all times. Dredged channel initially has 3m but steep-sided.

Berthing Hbr is crowded but a berth can always be found. Tie up alongside moored boats in centre of hbr and enquire at YC for berth. Do not drop anchor W of pilot boats due to mooring chains and in any case a tripping line is advisable. Most moorings dry to soft mud below half tide. Some moorings suitable for fin keel vessels. Yachts must not be left unattended overnight. No charges. Diesel one mile. Wi-Fi, water and showers at YC. ☎ 01446 735511. www.barryyachtclub.co.uk. VHF. Shore access available at slip HW±0300. Town 1M but YC grounds locked. Drying out area. In emergency 12-tonne marine trolley and hoist. Technical and Marine Engineering *Mobile* 07811343466 have 40-tonne marine trolley.

CARDIFF AND PENARTH

Chart 1182; SC 5608; Imray 2600, C59

HW (Outside Barrage) Avonmouth –0015

MHWS	MHWN	MLWN	MLWS
12·2m	9·2m	3·9m	1·0m

See plan

Cardiff Bay Barrage has changed Cardiff Bay into a large, freshwater lagoon with a group of three entry locks, protected by an outer harbour, at the SW end of the barrage.

Approach From Cardiff and Penarth Roads locate Outer Wrach W card Lt buoy, 3ca ENE of Penarth pleasure pier head. Maintain a listening watch on VHF 69 for shipping movements, and steer 349° up the Wrach Channel keeping clear of commercial vessels, preferably on the Penarth side just clear of the dredged channel. At the Outer Wrach S Card buoy call *Cardiff Bay Barrage Control* on VHF 18 for permission to enter the outer harbour and one must not do so without it.

Entrance
• By night In Wrach Channel keep in W sector of Oc.RWG Lt situated on barrage just outside entrance to Queen Alexandra Dock. At buoy Fl.R.2·5s turn to port onto

298°, keeping in W sector of DirRWG Lt at root of S outer harbour breakwater. Immediately look out to stb for W chevron Ldg Lt which will guide you into the outer hbr.
• By day Turn to port between R can, No.2, and R can buoy with G stripe, Barrage.

Traffic signals are displayed on the N pier head:
3R(vert) Flashing – Emergency; Stop and contact *Barrage Control*.
3R(vert) – Do not proceed.
3G(vert) – Enter
GWG – Proceed on instruction from *Barrage Control*.

In outer harbour, which is dredged to 0·7m below chart datum, moor to a barge and listen on VHF 18 for permission to enter one of the three parallel locks. The locks operate throughout the 24hrs except at the highest spring tides. The outer sill of No.1 (E'most) lock is 2·3m below CD, the other two 0·7m above CD. Entry signals with same characteristics as that on pier head displayed on each lock. Lock-in times are 0015 and 0045, lock out 0000 and 0030. Enter lock dead slow, moor securely, in emergency inform *Barrage Control*.

Berthing
• **Penarth Quays Marina** immediately to port on leaving barrage lock. Marina lock normally open, inner gate closed to provide footpath. Call *Penarth Quays Marina* VHF 80. Entry signals from N pier:
Double R – Keep clear of lock. Danger
Single R – Lock in use
G – Proceed only on instructions from marina staff.
If swing br is closed call the marina. Berth as instructed. Usual marina facilities, pubs and restaurants nearby. Cycle hire.
• **Cardiff Marina** on N side of River, Ely, 50m beyond YC pontoons. Unless otherwise instructed, moor in a free berth and report to office at head of pontoons C and D. Usual facilities, diesel but no petrol.
• **Cardiff Bay YC** As you leave the barrage locks, the clubhouse is visible dead ahead, the visitors' pontoon is on the seaward side of Pontoon A, the first pontoon you encounter. Bar and meals.
• **Cardiff YC** near entrance to R. Taff.

Facilities Regular bus service to Cardiff. Rly. Airport 12M by road.

☎/VHF *Barrage Control* VHF 18, 02920 700234; *Penarth Quays Marina* VHF 80, 705021, Wi-Fi; Cardiff Marina 343459, Wi-Fi; CBYC VHF 37, 66627 (office); 226575 (club), Wi-Fi in bar; Cardiff YC 463697.

NEWPORT

Charts BA 1176; SC 5608; Imray 2600, C59

HW Avonmouth –0015

MHWS	MHWN	MLWN	MLWS
12·1m	8·8m	3·2m	0·3m

Bar There is a least depth of 0·2m on the bar between Newport Deep and No.1 buoys.

Approach Make for Newport Deep G con buoy Fl(3)G.10s and leave it about ½M to stb steering 021° to pass between No.1 Q.G and West Usk Q.R buoys at mouth of River Usk. Ldg Lts on E Usk Tr Fl(2)WRG+Oc.WRG.10s on same tr.

Entrance Possible within 1hr of LW but tide is strong 4–5kn. Follow buoyed channel (dredged 0·7m) to South Lock after which there is no buoyage but keep slightly to stb of centre of river.

Berthing Moorings on S side between jetty in front of power stn and SC which dry HW+0330. Anchoring possible in 1m outside line of moorings, essential to display anchor Lt.

SHARPNESS

Contact *Sharpness Radio* VHF 13 on passing Avonmouth and on approach. Beware of being swept above Sharpness by the strong flood tide without local knowledge. There is nowhere to anchor in the river. Enter Sharpness under engine and clear of commercial shipping by turning sharply to stb close to end of pier. The tidal stream is strong between the piers, which are not solid, and it sets the boat towards the northern pier. There is nowhere to anchor or tie up inside the piers before entering the lock. The canal leads to Gloucester Docks.

RIVER AVON AND BRISTOL

Charts BA 1859; SC 5608; Imray 2600, C59

HW Avonmouth HW

MHWS	MHWN	MLWN	MLWS
13·2m	9·8m	3·8m	1·0m

The booklet entitled *Bristol City Docks – Information for Owners of Pleasure Craft* obtainable from Bristol Harbour Office, Underfall Yard, Cumberland Road, Bristol BS1 6XG, ☎ 0117 9031484. Check with Dockmaster ☎ 9273633 to make sure there is a berth available.

Approach Find Cockburn can buoy and steer 098° for entry to River Avon at Swash Channel immediately S of south pier of Avonmouth Docks – just dries at MLWS. Tide across entrance may be 5kn.

Entrance Proceed up River Avon taking care to keep in channel. Chart *1859* or *SC 5608* is essential. The channel is marked by Ldg Lts at many points. Ashore there are G Lts to stb and R Lts to port. The characteristics of these G and R Lts vary. There are only two bridges, the M5 Br (30m) and Clifton Suspension Br (73m) until Plimsoll swing br at the Cumberland Basin at the entrance to the City Docks. From the Swash Channel to the Basin is 6·2M. Strict VTS, call *Avonmouth Radio* VHF 12 at English and Welsh Grounds RWVS safe water buoy and again at Welsh Hook S card buoy. Keep listening watch on VHF 12. After entering River Avon inform Avonmouth Signal Station that you are bound for the City Docks. Alternatively signal or flash R (▬·▬). When at Black Rock, 1M below lock, call Bristol City Docks on VHF 14. Signal Lts 1¼ca and 2½ca above Clifton Suspension Br, at Hotwells Pontoon on E bank before dock entrance indicate that the lock is open. If they are R you must tie up to the ladder on the tongue head just upstream of the entrance to the lock approach channel.

If too late to be locked in take the ground in soft mud opposite Survey Mark No.4 and certainly not any closer to the lock or against any other ladder as the bottom there will be foul as it is off Hotwells Pontoon. Locking in times are at HW−0235, −0125 and −0015, the lock gates remaining open for 30m after these times if other craft are expected. Plimsoll Br opens in conjunction with the inner lock gate but not 0800–0900 and 1700–1800. Once in the lock check your air draught for the swing bridges exiting the Cumberland Lock System. If the height of tide over the sill is over 9·4m you may be held in the Cumberland Basin until the river level has fallen.

Berthing At Bristol Marina ☎ 0117 921 3198 on the S side of Floating Harbour W of *SS Great Britain* or at E end of Floating Harbour. No Wi-Fi in Bristol City Docks.

PORTISHEAD

Charts BA 1859; SC 5608; Imray 2600, C59

HW Avonmouth −0001

MHWS	MHWN
13·1m	9·7m

The old dock is now a marina.

Approach Beware of high tidal range and heavy shipping. The same VTS rules apply as for Bristol. One must call *Avonmouth Radio* on VHF 12 at English and Welsh Grounds buoy and again at Welsh Hook buoy. Listen on VHF 12.

The stream turns W close inshore 2hrs before HW and runs fast outside Firefly buoy, which should be rounded close to. Beware Firefly Rock (0·3m). Head for pier (Lt at end Iso.G.2s5m3M and Y bns along it) which should be given a good berth. An eddy on the flood sweeps towards the pier end.

Entrance Call *Portishead Quays Marina* VHF 80 or ☎ 01275 841941 for permission to enter.

Access is possible for a vessel drawing 1·5m at MHWN±0430 and

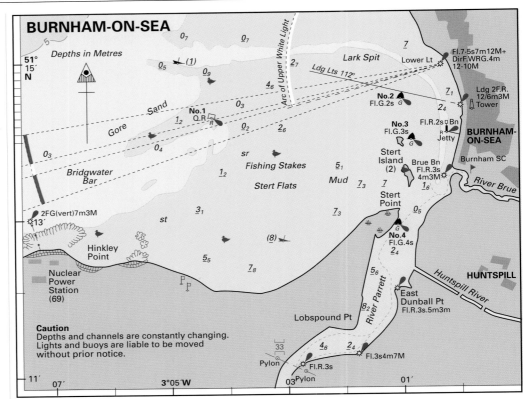

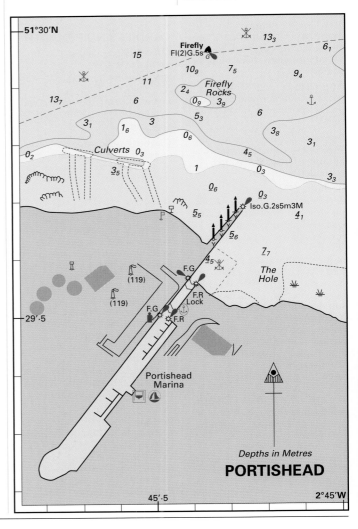

MHWS±0345. Yachts enter at 0015 and 0045 and exit at 0000 and 0030. Approach lock close to pier. Lock sides are marked by F.R and F.G Lts. Tidal gauges are provided at both ends of the lock showing depth over sill.

Entry signals are displayed on the port side of the entrance:

3R(vert) – Vessels shall not proceed and are requested to keep clear of lock gates.

GWG(vert) – Vessels may proceed on instruction from marina control.

Keep dead slow in lock and moor adequately.

During 'Free Flow' do not enter lock and do not manoeuvre within the marina without the advice of marina staff as the current can be violent.

Berthing as instructed by marina staff.

The usual marina facilities. Wi-Fi. Boat hoist, repairs. Pubs and restaurants in town.

WESTON-SUPER-MARE

Charts BA 1152; SC 5608; Imray 2600, C59

HW Avonmouth –0025

DS in offing Dover –0500W

MHWS	MHWN	MLWN	MLWS
12·0m	8·8m	3·0m	0·8m

Approach The causeway at the hbr entrance is marked by a bn and there are 2F.G(vert) Lts on the Grand Pier.

Berthing Anchorage is available from HW±0200 except at dead neaps but Knightstone harbour dries out and yachts normally use legs or make fast alongside two wooden dolphins. Shelter from all winds except S. Small yachts anchor S of old pier near the LB Ho in what is called the Cut or Sound; mainly dry at MLWS. Boatman will indicate the best berth. All stores, engine repairs, rly. EC Thursday.

RIVER AXE

Charts BA 1152; SC 5608; Imray 2600, C59

A half-tide hbr running into Weston Bay S of Weston. Fresh N'lies make the entrance difficult. To enter bring Black Rock into line with W mark on Uphill Hill. Approach the rk to within 1ca and leave it to port, then keep in mid channel. A Weston Bay YC buoy 'Juicy' indicates the bar 4ca from Brean Down about halfway along. There are withies along N side of channel. The river dries.

No room to anchor. Take vacant mooring or go alongside single pontoon and enquire ashore. Further up at the E end of Brean Down a bend in the channel is buoyed and thereafter bns mark the channel upstream. In moderate winds anchor in shallow bay under Brean Down. There is a boatyard at the top of Uphill

Pill; chandlery, fuel and repairs. Craft up to 14m and 15 tonnes can be handled.

BURNHAM-ON-SEA

Charts BA 1152; SC 5608; Imray 2600, C59

HW Avonmouth –0022

DS in offing: Dover –0500

MHWS	MHWN	MLWN
10·9m	7·9m	2·4m

Lies at the head of Bridgewater Bay. Shoals 5M out from the land which is flat and featureless except for Brent Knoll a conspic hill.

Bar Dries about 1·3m.

Approach and entrance Best approach is at HW–0200 when riverbanks are clearly distinguishable. After half flood vessels drawing 2m have enough water for Burnham in moderate weather. In strong winds and wind over tide the sea around Gore buoy suffers very broken water and there is often a pronounced sea breeze effect on summer evenings turning the bay into a lee shore. An approach in the morning with a midday tide is best for those visiting first time.

Make for 51°13'·5N 3°09'·8W, about 5ca S of Gore RWVS buoy, Iso.5s Bell. Proceed to No.1 R can buoy Q.R leaving it 2ca to N. Then steer 076° and keep in W sector of Burnham Lower Lt Fl.7·5s7m12M and DirF.WRG4m12–10M, a W structure on the beach with R vert stripe on piles (upper Lt disused), which indicates the channel. R sector indicates Gore sands, G the N edge of Stert Flats. Continue in W sector until 2 R Lts are in transit bearing 112° (back Lt on St Andrew's Church, front Lt in street). Daymarks are painted W rectangles with R vert stripe on sea wall and SW corner of St Andrew's Church. Continue on this transit until 4ca from sea wall, when No.2 buoy Fl.G.2s bears 265° and steer middle of River Parret. Entrance to River Brue is marked by Brue bn Fl.R.3s.

Berthing There are a few holes where yachts may lie afloat in the River Parret in quiet weather. Better to contact Burnham-on-Sea SC, ☎ 01278 781689, or occasional listening watch on VHF 80, for advice. The River Brue offers best shelter for yachts and and the SC have 20m of pontoons and occasional visitors' moorings all of which dry in soft mud. The yard upstream at Highbridge has repair facilities. All stores, fuel and facilities.

It is possible to go up River Parret to Combwich, a drying inlet accessible HW–0100, and to Dunball, although commercial shipping may be operating here particularly on spring tides.

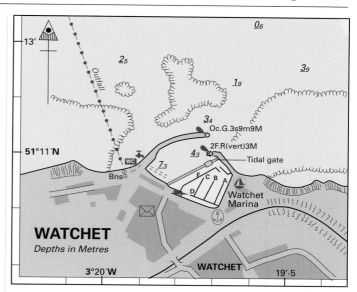

WATCHET
Depths in Metres

WATCHET

Chart BA 1160; SC 5608; Imray 2600, C59

HW Avonmouth –0042

DS in offing: Dover –0500

MHWS	MHWN	MLWN	MLWS
11·3m	8·3m	3·9m	1·1m

A delightful old village. The marina retains water using an automatic rising gate. It is subject to silting.

Approach Beware Culver Sand in mid channel NNE of hbr. Lilstock firing range extends in a semicircle offshore to Hinkley Point nuclear power station, 7·3M E. Hbr entrance lies 210° 3·2M from DZ No.2 buoy Fl.Y.10s. Two radio masts with R lights bear 208° 1·6M from hbr. The rocky shore dries ½M out.

There is an obstruction dries 2·8m on the foreshore NW of the pierhead and fishing stakes N of the hbr entrance.

Entrance Call *Watchet Harbour Marina* on VHF 80, ☎ 01984 631264. The outer harbour may be entered HW–0130. On entry leave R tr with G light on W pier to stb. Tidal gate with gauge showing depth over sill is sharp to port behind E pier head. The gate opens when there is 2½m in the entrance and up to 3m inside. Entry sigs:

3G(vert) – proceed
3R(vert) – stop.

Facilities Usual marina facilities. Wi-Fi. Small town. EC Wednesday.

MINEHEAD

Chart BA 1160; SC 5608; Imray 2600, C59

HW Avonmouth –0045

MHWS	MHWN	MLWN	MLWS
10·6m	7·9m	3·6m	1·0m

Hbr is formed by a single pier curving E to SE and dries. It should not be approached earlier than HW–0230 when there is 2·1m of water at the hbr steps alongside the quay. No bar.

Approach From seaward, if the tide too low to enter, approach the W mark on shore abreast the hilltop 5ca E of Greenaleigh Point and 5ca NW of the column on the foundations of the old pier and anchor abreast the mark 2ca offshore in about 3½m. The column shows 3m above HW. If approaching from E beware of Gables ridge extending 1M to NW of Warren Point.

Entrance From W round G stb hand bn with cone topmark Q.G and then round the pier head Fl(2)G.5s at least 10m off. Go slow as hbr is crowded.

Berthing As directed or as space allows, alongside pier or other vessels. The bottom is an easy slope upwards from the entrance. HM ☎ 01643 702566. All supplies. EC Wed.

PORLOCK WEIR

Chart BA 1160; SC 5608

HW Avonmouth -0050

MHWS	MHWN	MLWN	MLWS
10·2m	7·6m	3·7m	0·9m

A delightful privately-owned, small, crowded hbr in rural surroundings. Difficult and narrow entrance channel but safe once inside. Not lit. Hbr dries HW–0300 but moorings for small number of yachts in pool 1·5m. Beware terraced shorings round basin, only safe in middle. Exposed to N–NE winds near HW. Moorings in inner harbour by prior arrangement, contact HM first. No VHF. ☎ 01643 863187.

Entrance At the W end of Porlock Bay. The bar dries. The channel is about 10m wide and the entrance is marked by a pair of withies. Thereafter keep about 3m off the remaining two port-hand withies marking a timber-piled wall below water. There is a pebble bank to stb. Channel available HW–0130 to HW+0100 for 1·8m draught.

Berthing Anchor in Porlock Bay only in very settled

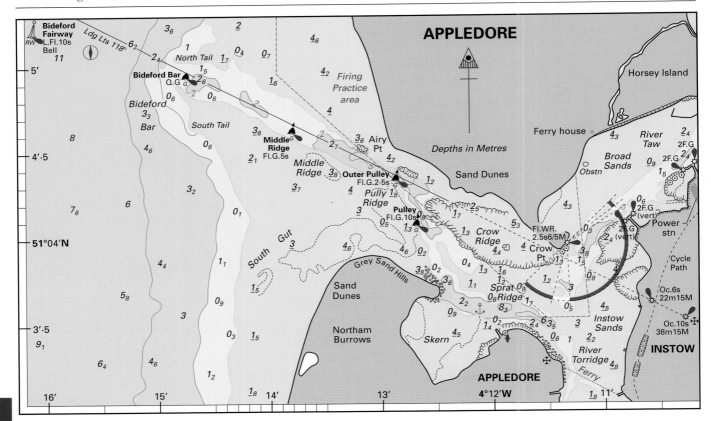

conditions; holding poor on pebbles except in patch of sand off thatched cottages to the W of entrance channel. Reverse stream on flood tide against W winds makes for uncomfortable anchorage.

Pub, hotel and small village store at hbr side, otherwise 1½M to village of Porlock where good shops, fuel and gas.

ILFRACOMBE

Charts BA 1160; SC 5608; Imray 2600, C58

HW Milford Haven –0016

DS in offing Dover –0520 W 3kn

MHWS	MHWN	MLWN	MLWS
9·3m	7·0m	3·1m	1·0m

A tourist town, crowded in summer, good shops, and a busy harbour.

Approach Beware of overfalls at Buggy Pit ¾M NE of entrance, where the stream turns 1h after local LW and HW. Ferry plies between hbr and Lundy Is and may return at HW day or night. Beware of fishing pot buoys to E of approach to ent. If arriving near LW springs in strong N or NE winds, there will be no sheltered anchorage to await rise of tide to enter hbr.

Berthing Inner hbr is full of fore and aft moorings which dry to flat sand after half tide. A mooring may be available but do not anchor here. N and S walls are mainly for visitors. Outer hbr dries to flat sand at LW springs and has one row of fore and aft moorings for visitors, or anchor in outer hbr but avoid commercial pier to N and fairway to inner hbr. Water on pier and S side of inner harbour. Chandlery, diesel,

marine engineer. Stores five minutes, petrol 20 minutes each way. ① 01271 862108, VHF 12. Wi-Fi.

LUNDY ISLAND

Charts BA 1164; SC 5608; Imray 2600, C58

HW Milford Haven –0025

MHWS	MHWN	MLWN	MLWS
8·0m	5·9m	2·7m	0·7m

DS in the vicinity, clear of the land: Dover +0030ENE –0500WSW.

Lundy is a marine nature reserve owned by the National Trust and administered by the Landmark Trust.

Approach Beware of tidal races. On E-going stream a heavy race extends 1M N from the N end of the Is and 1½M E of Rat Is in the S. The White Horses race over Stanley Bank NE of the Is is severe and should be avoided. Similar races form during the W-going stream extending 1M SW of Shutter Point but that over Stanley Bank is less violent.

Anchorage If caught out in gales from SSW to W, Lundy offers an anchorage of refuge with good holding and shelter. The anchorage is at the Landing Beach, just N of the SE point of Is, as far in as draft and tidal range permit. Keep clear of the commercial jetty (Fl.R.3s). Dinghy may land at slipway S of jetty, or at Landing Beach, but this latter is exposed to winds of any strength from NE to SE, which will make launching the dinghy difficult. In NW gales a swell enters the anchorage, which is also

completely exposed to any wind with E in it. If preferred, a privately-laid mooring might be available. Contact the *Lundy Warden* VHF 16, but do not leave your boat if mooring owner might return. Inn and shop (limited supplies) available at top of track from Landing Beach. In strong and persistent winds from E sector, shelter for a few boats in 10m at Jenny's

HARTLAND POINT TO LAND'S END

Charts BA 1178, 1168, 1149; SC 5608; Imray 2600, C7, C58

Passage lights	BA No
Hartland Point Bn Fl(6)15s30m8M	5622
Trevose Head Fl.7·5s62m21M	5638
Godrevy Fl.WR.10s8M	
Pendeen Fl(4)15s59m16M Horn 20s	5670
Longships Fl(2)WR.10s35m15/11M Horn 10s	0028

There is little shelter on the N Cornish coast if it blows up from any direction except from SE. In SW gales if Padstow cannot be reached then Milford Haven may be the best port of refuge. St Ives Bay is subject to swell but will afford some shelter from strong S winds. Clovelly Roads and Lundy's anchorage are sheltered in S and SW winds but beware of overfalls off Hartland Pt and off both ends of Lundy. Once round Land's End there is Newlyn and Penzance.

Beware of overfalls off Pendeen Pt.

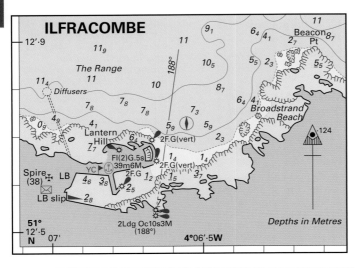

Cove on middle of W side of Is, provided no remaining swell from W. Dinghy access ashore is by landing on Pyramid Rock to N of anchorage, which is possible but not easy. In N winds try The Rattles anchorage off S of Is.

APPLEDORE

Charts BA 1160; SC 5608; Imray 2600, C58

HW Milford Haven –0022

MHWS	MHWN	MLWN	MLWS
7·5m	5·2m	1·6m	0·2m

Bar Bideford Bar has about 1m. Bar, sands and channel are continuously shifting. Buoys and Oc Ldg Lts are moved to suit the fairway. Entrance is dangerous if a heavy ground sea is running on the bar, especially against an ebb tide, in which case await a good rise of tide. The best time to enter (or depart) is usually on the last of the flood. Avoid entering (or leaving) on the ebb tide, especially if there is a strong W wind or a large ground swell against the ebb stream. Advice on the state of the bar can be obtained from Swansea CG. Under normal conditions expect breakers on the sands to port and stb just outside the channel. The tide may be awaited in Clovelly Bay, comfortably with winds S of W.

Approach After passing Outer Pulley buoy turn on to 160° to leave Pulley G con buoy Fl.G.10s to stb and continue to SE end of Grey Sand Hills. Then steer 102° through Appledore Pool towards lifeboat on a mooring buoy. After passing slip on stb watch out for three mooring buoys which may be partly submerged at HW.

Berthing Anchor close above or below lifeboat and other two buoys in fine weather, buoying anchor. The stream runs strongly in this pool and is uncomfortable in N winds during early ebb. In that event better to anchor in the River Taw to NE of Crow Point Lt Fl.WR.2·5s bearing 240° and Appledore church about 197° but holding is only moderate. Q.Y at Crow Point marks channel under br. Instow sands and R. Torridge offer many drying moorings.

BRAUNTON

Anchor close inshore abreast the Ferry House on Broad Sands; a boat of 1·8m draught can berth in very soft sand. The vessel will make its own berth but care should be taken not to be neaped. The position is excellent if a few days stay is desired but the berth should be located beforehand. Near midstream the sand is hard and anchor likely to drag.

BIDEFORD

The passage from Appledore to Bideford is easy for 1·8m draught at HW–0200. At Bideford anchor on sand in middle opposite the vertical section of the quay about ½ca downstream from the br; legs needed.

Alternatively, with permission, dry out alongside boat already alongside quay, but avoid quay near the bridge (too deep).

CLOVELLY

Extremely picturesque village with small drying hbr. Only two visitors' berths, each with ladder alongside hbr wall. Enter HW±0200.Stay only with no ground swell. Alternatively, anchor in Clovelly Roads with good protection from SW to E, and row ashore.
HM *Mobile* 07975501830.

BOSCASTLE

HW Milford Haven –0027

MHWS	MHWN	MLWN	MLWS
7·3m	5·6m	2·7m	0·9m

Picturesque; approach HW±0200 and stay only in fine settled weather. Difficult to locate from seaward. Beware lobster pot markers in approach. Unlit. Night entry dangerous. Essential to identify Meachard Rock before attempting to enter near HW. Narrow entrance with very sharp bend to stb. Berth against wall and dry out on hard sand over rock. Heavy bumping in any slight ground swell.

PADSTOW

Chart BA 1168; SC 5608; Imray C58

HW Milford Haven –0052

DS off Trevose Hd Dover HW NE, +0600 SW

MHWS	MHWN	MLWN	MLWS
7·3m	5·6m	2·6m	0·8m

An interesting tourist town, crowded in summer, with a secure floating harbour and all facilities.

Bar Under normal conditions the entrance is perfectly safe and is best approached about HW–0230 to HW+0200. Depth over bar likely to change. For latest survey, see www.padstow-harbour.co.uk. Do not attempt entry across the bar at any state of tide (even HW) when seas are breaking on the bar, e.g. near LW, in strong winds from W to N, or when there is a significant ground swell causing seas to break periodically especially below half tide. It will be difficult to tell from upwind if the waves are breaking. Be extra cautious at night. The breaking seas are usually worse on the ebb rather than the flood stream, and worse on spring rather than neap tides. To await the rise of tide: in good weather, anchor as

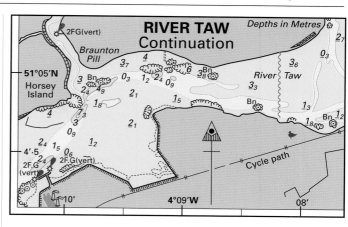

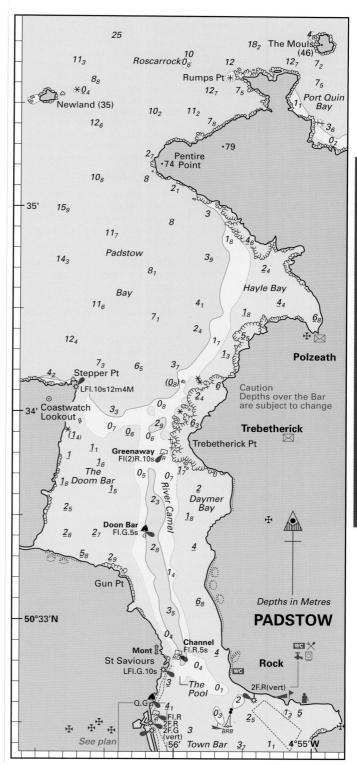

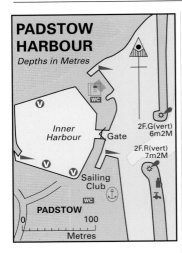

PADSTOW HARBOUR

Depths in Metres

2F.G(vert) 6m2M

2F.R(vert) 7m2M

Inner Harbour

Gate

Sailing Club

PADSTOW

0   100

Metres

close inshore as depth allows just inside Stepper Point, but beware of fishing gear. In strong winds from S to W, anchor in Polventon (or Mother Ivey's Bay) just SE of lifeboat slip in 3m on sand, or anchor in the W corner of Port Quin Bay, south of The Mouls (island), as close inshore as depth and tidal height allow to get clear of the tidal stream, but stay clear of rocks at LW. Here there is good holding and shelter.

Approach If approaching from the E or N beware of rocks close W and E of Newland Is and also Roscarrock 0·8m, which by day is cleared by keeping Stepper Pt, which has a daymark (just off plan) 12m high and 83m above sea level, well open of Pentire Pt. If approaching at night, you need to be N of W to see Stepper Pt light. Also, by night beware of Quies, Gull Rk, Gulland Is (off the plan to the W) and Newland Is, all unlit. Beware of lobster pots scattered in Padstow Bay on approach to hbr, dangerous at night.

Entrance The start of the entrance channel is about 2ca N of the first mark, a red can buoy, **Greenaway**, Fl(2)R.10s. The deepest water is on a track from Pentire Pt to **Greenaway**, so enter the channel with Pentire point bearing approx 000°T dead astern, and pass **Greenaway** close to port. Then pass very close to St Saviour's Pt, the extremity of which is marked by a stb bn. Here the deepest water is close inshore (20m off bn). If you stand too far off, a flood tide will set you S onto the town bar to port of the channel. When passing N pier and clear of vessels leaving hbr, turn sharply to stb and pass through dock ent between 2F.R(vert) and 2F.G(vert).

Berthing Dock gate is open HW±0200 approx, but if waiting to enter or to set sail outside gate opening times, pick up a mooring in The Pool (charged same rate as hbr).

Beware that The Pool shallows to the S and some moorings dry. The Pool and much of the river is subject to strong tidal streams and scouring. In narrow channels avoid obstructing vessels constrained by their draft. The Padstow-Rock ferry uses hbr near HW and St Saviour's Pt near LW. Shops, launderette, restaurants, Wi-Fi, webcam, and cycle hire, e.g. for Camel Trail. For diesel apply HM ☎ 01841 532239, VHF 12 (0900–1700 Monday–Friday and HW±2). Wi-Fi. EC Wed. See www.padstow-harbour.co.uk.

Wadebridge With careful sounding it is possible to take the tide up to this picturesque little market town. The R Camel is partially buoyed to Wadebridge, where a new long pontoon at Commissioners' Quay (to stb just before bridge) gives free shore access over HW to shops, etc, for occasional visitors with 1·2m draught at MHWN. The pontoon dries over LW. A fin keeler may dry out alongside wall with ladders between pontoon and bridge.

NEWQUAY

Small drying harbour next to surfing beach. Dry out against E quay. Avoid in winds W to NE above F3, and when there is any swell.

HAYLE

Chart BA 1168; SC 5608; Imray C7

HW Milford Haven –0100

MHWS	MHWN	MLWN	MLWS
6·6m	4·9m	2·4m	0·8m

The bar dries ½M offshore. The hbr dries and is only approachable HW±0100 with offshore winds in the absence of ground swell. There are plans to redevelop this historic port.

Entrance Identify N card buoy ½M N of entrance and leading marks, W boards with hor R bands F.17/23m4M, 180°, the church tr is also on this transit. Leave training wall marked by five Lt bns Oc.G.4s to stb. Off Chapel Anjou Point identify the shingle shore, marked by a bn Q at its N end, which is steep to separating River Hayle from the hbr channel to port. In this channel leave four perches marking the middle ground to port and when abeam the last perch alter hard to port and then stb to berth against quay.

Berthing Vessels dry at LW alongside quays. All stores. Rly. EC Thursday. ☎ 01736 754043 VHF 18, 14.

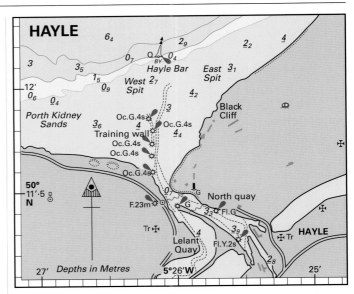

HAYLE

Hayle Bar

West Spit

East Spit

Porth Kidney Sands

Training wall

Oc.G.4s

Oc.G.4s

Oc.G.4s

Oc.G.4s

Oc.G.4s

50° 11'·5 N

F.23m

North quay

Fl.G

Lelant Quay

Fl.Y.2s

HAYLE

27'   *Depths in Metres*   5°26'W   25'

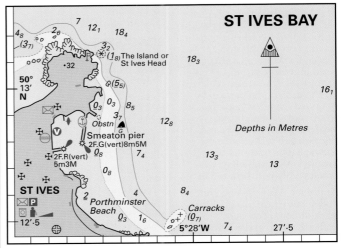

ST IVES BAY

The Island or St Ives Head

50° 13' N

Obstn

Smeaton pier 2F.G(vert)8m5M

2F.R(vert) 5m3M

ST IVES

Porthminster Beach

Carracks

12'·5   5°28'W   27'·5

Depths in Metres

ST IVES

Chart BA 1168; SC 5608; Imray C7

HW Milford Haven –0100

MHWS	MHWN	MLWN	MLWS
6·6m	4·9m	2·4m	0·8m

A pier hbr which dries 2m and is subject to heavy swell in onshore winds and when Atlantic lows are approaching or passing.

Approach and Entrance Hoe and Merran rks are cleared by keeping Knill's monument on with Tregenna Castle Hotel.

The ruins of the end of the outer breakwater are marked by a G con buoy. Round inner pier head close to and moor alongside. The hbr is crowded and it is difficult to find a place. At night the W pier shows 2F.R(vert) and the outer (Smeaton) pier 2F.G(vert). HM ☎ 01736 795018, VHF 14. Alternatively in offshore winds anchor in 3m between hbr and the Carracks or in Carbis Bay S of the Carracks. All stores. Rly. EC Thursday.

SW England and S Wales to Ireland distances (miles)

	Baltimore Ent	Old Hd Kinsale	Kilmore Quay	Arklow	Padstow Bar	Milford Haven ent.
Longships LtHo	163	143	131	166	47	100
Hugh Town	151	133	138	178	75	121
Padstow Bar	178	150	115	142	0	68
Swansea	210	175	113	129	74	51
Milford Haven ent.	159	126	62	79	68	0
S. Bishop Lt Ho	151	117	48	63	78	14

Ireland

This section of the almanac covers the whole of the coast of Ireland and gives directions for entering over 60 anchorages together with their facilities. The Irish Cruising Club *Sailing Directions* are published in two volumes, one for the South and West Coasts and one for the East and North. They are obtainable in Ireland from: Terry Johnson, ICC Publications, Frazerbank, Strathmore Road, Killiney, Co. Dublin. ☎ +353 (0) 1285 1439, *Email* johnson@gofree.indigo.com, or from Imray, www.imray.com who are agents for the UK and the rest of the world. They publish *Cruising Cork and Kerry* by Graham Swanson. These publications are recommended for those wishing to cover the area in greater detail and mention all anchorages known to yachtsmen, many of which are remote, secluded and sometimes difficult to find but very rewarding. BA Sailing Directions *Irish Coast Pilot* NP 40 is also useful.

Weather forecasts Forecasts for Irish coastal waters are broadcast four times daily by Radio Eireann (RTE1) on 567 and 729kHz at 0602, 1255, 1655 and 2355 hours BST, but times may be changed by as much as five minutes. Forecasts are for 24hrs with a 48hrs outlook and gale warnings. The forecasts go round the coast in a clockwise direction between various headlands. These are shown distinctively marked on the accompanying introductory plans of Ireland. Coast radio stations broadcast a weather forecast for shipping at 0103 and thence every three hours updated every sixth.

Ireland, Howth to Slyne Head north-about, distances (miles)

	Howth	Carlingford ent.	Strangford ent.	Bangor	Glenarm	Fairhead	Port Rush	Malin Head	Mullroy Bay ent.	Bloody Foreland	Aran More Island	Rathlin O'Birne	Sligo entrance	Broadhaven ent.	Erris Head	Blacksod Bay ent.	Achill Head	Westport ent.	Inishbofin Island Hbr	Slyne Head
Howth	0																			
Carlingford ent.	37	0																		
Strangford ent.	58	27	0																	
Bangor	87	57	26	0																
Glenarm	107	76	47	23	0															
Fairhead	124	93	64	46	23	0														
Port Rush	144	113	84	66	43	20	0													
Malin Head	189	138	109	91	68	45	29	0												
Mullroy Bay ent.	203	152	123	105	82	59	43	14	0											
Bloody Foreland	213	162	133	115	92	69	53	24	19	0										
Aran More Island	226	175	146	128	105	82	66	37	32	13	0									
Rathlin O'Birne	253	215	173	155	132	109	93	64	59	40	24	0								
Sligo entrance	279	241	199	186	158	135	119	90	85	66	50	26	0							
Broadhaven ent.	291	240	211	193	170	146	131	102	97	78	68	47	48	0						
Erris Head	294	243	214	196	173	150	134	103	100	81	71	49	50	6	0					
Blacksod Bay ent.	314	263	234	216	193	170	154	123	120	101	91	69	70	26	20	0				
Achill Head	318	287	238	220	197	174	158	127	124	105	95	73	74	30	24	12	0			
Westport ent.	342	312	262	244	221	198	182	151	148	129	119	97	98	54	48	36	24	0		
Inishbofin Island Harbour	342	312	262	244	221	198	182	151	148	129	119	97	98	54	48	36	24	25	0	
Slyne Head	355	325	275	257	234	211	195	164	161	142	132	111	112	67	61	49	37	38	13	0

Ireland, Howth to Slyne Head south-about, distances (miles)

	Howth	Dun Laoghaire	Wicklow Head	Arklow	Carnsore Point	Kilmore Quay ent.	Dunmore East ent.	Cork Harbour ent.	Old Head of Kinsale	Mizen Head	Lawrence Cove ent.	Dursey Head	Bray Head	Dingle ent.	Blasket Sound	Loop Head	Kilrush	Kilronan ent.	Roundstone	Slyne Head
Howth	0																			
Dun Laoghaire	8	0																		
Wicklow Head	28	22	0																	
Arklow	40	34	12	0																
Carnsore Point	77	71	49	39	0															
Kilmore Quay ent.	87	81	59	49	10	0														
Dunmore East ent.	102	96	74	64	25	16	0													
Cork Harbour ent.	152	146	124	114	75	68	54	0												
Old Head of Kinsale	166	160	138	128	89	81	66	15	0											
Mizen Head	217	211	189	179	140	132	117	66	51	0										
Lawrence Cove ent.	233	227	205	195	156	148	133	82	67	16	0									
Dursey Head	235	229	207	197	158	150	135	84	69	18	16	0								
Bray Head	255	249	227	217	178	170	155	104	89	38	36	20	0							
Dingle Ent.	271	265	243	233	194	186	171	120	105	54	52	36	16	0						
Blasket Sound	268	262	240	230	191	183	168	117	102	51	49	33	13	9	0					
Loop Head	302	296	264	254	225	217	202	151	136	85	83	67	47	43	34	0				
Kilrush	314	308	286	276	237	229	214	163	148	97	95	79	59	55	46	18	0			
Kilronan ent.	336	330	308	298	259	251	236	185	170	119	117	101	81	77	68	48	56	0		
Roundstone	348	342	320	310	271	263	248	197	182	131	129	113	93	89	80	36	67	22	0	
Slyne Head	346	340	318	308	269	261	246	195	180	129	127	111	91	87	78	42	69	27	13	0

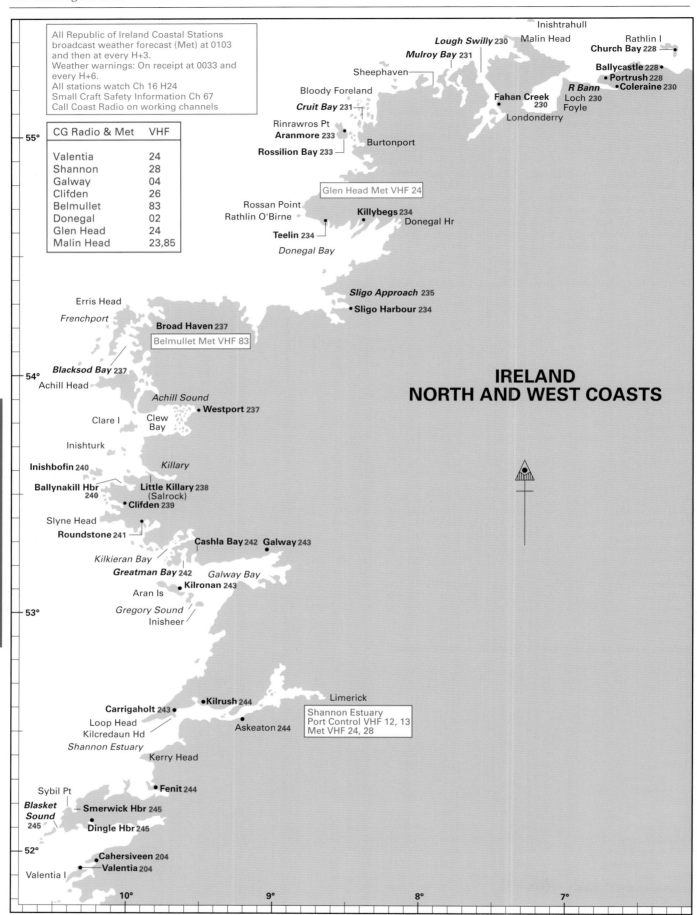

All Republic of Ireland Coastal Stations broadcast weather forecast (Met) at 0103 and then at every H+3.
Weather warnings: On receipt at 0033 and every H+6.
All stations watch Ch 16 H24
Small Craft Safety Information Ch 67
Call Coast Radio on working channels

CG Radio & Met	VHF
Valentia	24
Shannon	28
Galway	04
Clifden	26
Belmullet	83
Donegal	02
Glen Head	24
Malin Head	23,85

IRELAND
NORTH AND WEST COASTS

IRELAND

55°
54°
53°
52°

Inishtrahull
Lough Swilly 230   Malin Head   Rathlin I
Mulroy Bay 231   **Church Bay** 228
Sheephaven   **Ballycastle** 228
Bloody Foreland   **Fahan Creek**   **Portrush** 228
    230   • **Coleraine** 230
Cruit Bay 231   *R Bann*
Loch 230
Rinrawros Pt   Foyle
Aranmore 233   Burtonport   Londonderry
Rossilion Bay 233

Glen Head Met VHF 24

Rossan Point   **Killybegs** 234
Rathlin O'Birne   Donegal Hr
Teelin 234
Donegal Bay

Sligo Approach 235
• **Sligo Harbour** 234

Erris Head
Frenchport   **Broad Haven** 237
Belmullet Met VHF 83
Blacksod Bay 237
Achill Head
Achill Sound
Clare I   • **Westport** 237
    Clew Bay
Inishturk
Inishbofin 240   *Killary*
Ballynakill Hbr   **Little Killary** 238
    240   (Salrock)
    • **Clifden** 239
Slyne Head
Roundstone 241
    Cashla Bay 242   **Galway** 243
Kilkieran Bay
Greatman Bay 242   *Galway Bay*
Aran Is   **Kilronan** 243
Gregory Sound
Inisheer

Limerick
Carrigaholt 243 •   • **Kilrush** 244
Loop Head
Kilcredaun Hd   Askeaton 244
Shannon Estuary

Shannon Estuary
Port Control VHF 12, 13
Met VHF 24, 28

Kerry Head

Sybil Pt   • **Fenit** 244
Blasket   — **Smerwick Hbr** 245
Sound
245   • **Dingle Hbr** 245

• **Cahersiveen** 204
• **Valentia** 204
Valentia I

10°   9°   8°   7°

Page references are shown after locations, for example:
Valentia 204. Bold type indicates that it is accompanied by a plan. *Italics* are used for rivers, lochs, bays, seas etc

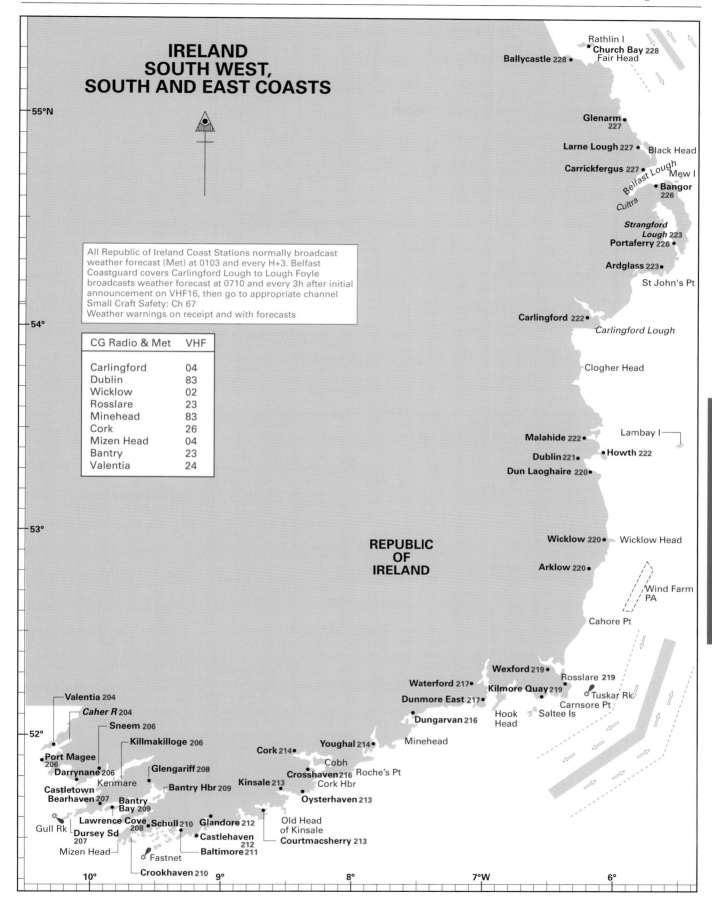

IRELAND
SOUTH WEST,
SOUTH AND EAST COASTS

All Republic of Ireland Coast Stations normally broadcast weather forecast (Met) at 0103 and every H+3. Belfast Coastguard covers Carlingford Lough to Lough Foyle broadcasts weather forecast at 0710 and every 3h after initial announcement on VHF16, then go to appropriate channel
Small Craft Safety: Ch 67
Weather warnings on receipt and with forecasts

CG Radio & Met	VHF
Carlingford	04
Dublin	83
Wicklow	02
Rosslare	23
Minehead	83
Cork	26
Mizen Head	04
Bantry	23
Valentia	24

55°N

54°

53°

REPUBLIC
OF
IRELAND

52°

Rathlin I
Church Bay 228
Fair Head
Ballycastle 228 •

Glenarm •
227

Larne Lough 227 •
Black Head

Carrickfergus 227 •
Belfast Lough
Mew I
Bangor
226

Cultra

Strangford Lough 223
Portaferry 226 •

Ardglass 223 •
St John's Pt

Carlingford 222 •
Carlingford Lough

Clogher Head

Malahide 222 •
Lambay I
Dublin 221 •
• **Howth 222**
Dun Laoghaire 220 •

Wicklow 220 •
Wicklow Head

Arklow 220 •

Wind Farm PA

Cahore Pt

Wexford 219 •
Rosslare **219**
Waterford 217 •
Kilmore Quay 219
Dunmore East 217 •
Tuskar Rk
Carnsore Pt
Hook
Head
Saltee Is
Dungarvan 216 •

Minehead

Youghal 214 •

Cobh
Roche's Pt

Cork 214 •

Crosshaven 216
Cork Hbr

Kinsale 213
Oysterhaven 213
Old Head
of Kinsale
Courtmacsherry 213

Valentia 204
Caher R 204
Sneem 206
Killmakilloge 206
Port Magee 206
Darrynane 206
Glengariff 208
Kenmare
Bantry Hbr 209
Castletown Bearhaven 207
Bantry Bay 209
Lawrence Cove
208
Schull 210
Glandore 212
Gull Rk
Dursey Sd 207
Mizen Head
Castlehaven 212
Baltimore 211
Fastnet
Crookhaven 210

10°   9°   8°   7°W   6°

Page references are shown after locations, for example:
Dublin 222. Bold type indicates that it is accompanied by a plan. *Italics* are used for rivers, lochs, bays, seas etc

IRELAND

VHF: Cork 26, Bantry 23, Valentia 24, Shannon 28, Clifden 26, Malin Head 23, Dublin 83, Wicklow Head 87, Rosslare 23, and Mine Head 83. The BBC shipping forecasts on 198kHz are easily picked up on the W coast and are essential for tracking incoming weather.

Warning – Nets Salmon drift net fishing is now illegal at sea, however it has been reported at night near headlands. It is permitted in some rivers and estuaries.

Lights Another reason for avoiding making smaller ports by night is that the lesser navigational lights, which are operated and maintained by the local authorities, have been reported as not showing from time to time. But this is becoming less frequent.

Gas Calor (Kosan) gas, though widely available, comes in yellow containers different from the usual 10lb containers supplied in the UK. Though still holding 10lb the container is about 5in taller when fitted with the supply tube, wider at the base and may not fit into existing gas lockers. It has a different connection which is provided for no extra charge if a British type container is exchanged for the Irish container. British Calor Gas containers can be refilled while you wait at the Whitegate Gas Depot on the SE side of Cork Harbour and filled or exchanged at Crosshaven. Standard Calor containers are available in Northern Ireland. Camping Gaz is widely available in the Republic. This is the same gas as Calor but one will need an adapter to connect to the Calor reducing valve. This will serve in many other European countries.

Customs The international boundary line between the Republic of Ireland (Eire) and Northern Ireland is at the inner end of Carlingford Lough and again at the inner end of Lough Foyle. It is marked on the charts. No action is required if arriving from an EU port unless you have anything to declare, such as firearms or non-EU nationals on board. If so or if arriving from a non-EU port fly Q flag. If no customs are immediately available, report by phone to the nearest police station – Garda in the Republic and the police service of Northern Ireland, in Northern Ireland. Courtesy ensigns are customary when in the Republic.

Naval patrol Off the coast of Northern Ireland there are a small number of Royal Naval patrol vessels, these are on anti-terrorist duties. If sighted you should listen out on VHF 16 and obey any instructions. Sometimes yachts are boarded but more frequently it is only an enquiry of your last and next ports of call.

Long term laying up Non-EU owners wishing to leave or lay up their vessels in the Republic need to obey the same rules as for other EU countries. They should contact the VAT authorities in Dublin Castle, Dublin 1 to obtain a copy of current regulations.

Hydrographic surveys Very little of the coast of the Republic of Ireland has been surveyed since 1914. In fact many of the surveys date back to the latter part of the 19th century. Yachtsmen are particularly warned about depths of water in river estuaries and of sandy bays where there may be considerably less water than shown on the charts, even if they are metric*. Tidal information on the West Coast is incomplete and in some places unreliable.

Fish farms These have been noted on plans where currently known but they are liable to movement without notice.

Imports To protect Irish agriculture; avoid importing any raw or cooked meats. Certainly never take any ashore. At prsent there is great anxiety about potato ring rot. Do not take potatoes ashore, not even the peelings.

Safety Following the loss of an angling fishing boat, regulations have been introduced to require that a lifejacket is carried for every person aboard. The regulation also requires that lifejackets will be worn outside the cockpit at all times. However, it is understood that a common-sense view will be taken of this in fair weather.

Vistors' Moorings can be found, especially in the S and W. They are usually large Y buoys, up to 15T. A charge of €5 may be made.

* But new surveys are being carried out and changes recorded in *Notices to Mariners*.

VALENTIA TO CROOKHAVEN

Charts BA 2423, 2424; SC 5623; Imray C56

Passage lights	BA No
Skelligs Rock Fl(3)15s53m12M AIS	6422
Bull Rock Fl.15s91m18M Racon (N) (–) AIS	6430
Sheep Head Fl(3)WR.15s83m18/15M AIS	6432
Mizen Head Iso.4s55m15M	6448

Direction of tidal streams (all related to Dover) between Skelligs and the shores

+0530S –0015N

between Bull Rock and Dursey Head

+0245S –0315N.

Dursey Sound is a useful channel between Dursey Is and the mainland, but be aware tides run up to 4kn.

DS Dover +0145S –0415N. *See later for plan and directions.*

In the Kenmare River above Sneem watch out for Maiden Rock in the middle, awash at LWS, marked by G con Lt buoy Fl.5s 3ca N of rock.

Between Three Castle Head and Mizen Head the streams run S and NW to N, becoming E and W between Mizen Head and Crookhaven Dover +0130S and E and –0430N and W. Off Mizen Head the spring rate is 4kn, and off Three Castle Head 3kn decreasing to 1·5kn when 4–5M offshore. The race off Mizen Head can be dangerous in windy weather and may extend to Three Castle Head. On S and E going stream it extends SE in a crescent. If caught in the race steer straight out to sea, then parallel to the edge of rough water.

VALENTIA

Chart BA 2125; SC 5623; Imray C56

HW Cobh –0118sp –0038np

MHWS	MHWN	MLWN	MLWS
3·5m	2·8m	1·2m	0·4m

The hbr affords shelter in all winds and may be entered from the NW at all states of the tide (exposed in NW gales), and, with sufficient rise, from SW through Portmagee channel. But obstructed by bridge with limited headroom and permanently closed opening span.

Bars By NW entrance: The Fort (Cromwell) Point entrance has 7m on the Ldg line.

By SW entrance: Until inside Reencaheragh Point there is 8m. Then there is down to 1·5m through the Portmagee Channel.

Approach NW entrance: make Doulus Head, avoiding the CG patch in severe conditions. Make toward Fort Point. Sectored Lt Fl.WR.2s16m17/15M 104°-W-304°-R-351°.

Entrance For Valentia Harbour, having located Fort Point, Fl.WR.2s keep in W sector (140°-142°) of Lt Dir.Oc.WRG.4s, leaving Harbour Rock bn Q(3)10s to stb, and thence to anchorage as convenient, avoiding the Caher bar 0·6m between E end of Beginish Is and Reenard Point near LW.

Berthing The floating pontoon/breakwater to a new marina is completed just south of the ferry ramp at approx 51°55'·2N 10°17'·1W. Mooring on the inside of the pontoon gives excellent shelter. Completion of marina fingers expected late summer 2013.

Anchorages In N winds, good anchorage off SE bight of Beginish Is, in 2–8m; or, according to wind, off Knight's Town to S of jetty, a marina is in the course of construction but is unlikely to be completed until 2012, or S of Reenard Point, or as convenient in Portmagee channel. There is a pier at Reenard Point with 3m on the SE side. 12 visitors' moorings off Knight's Town.

Caution Do not anchor S or W of the pecked lines S of Knight's Town owing to telegraph cables. Buoy anchor if near the lifeboat. Silting of the channel has been reported.

CAHER RIVER (VALENTIA RIVER)

If proceeding to Cahersiveen from Doulus Bay enter over Doulus bar, 3m, leaving Doulus Rocks (Or Black Rocks) to stb and Kay Rock to port, thence SSE passing a full ca from E end of Beginish Isl and ½ca E of Church Island. From Valentia harbour, cross Caher bar, 0·6 to 1m, then close the S shore of the river till Ballycarberry castle comes abeam N, then work towards N shore gradually until Cahersiveen barracks open and proceed in midstream to the marina on S shore or to the quay at Cahersiveen. There is a series of five Ldg lines up the Caher River, F.G Lts on rather inconspic telephone type poles One set gives a stern lead. It is very important to follow closely these Ldg marks as the channel is not wide, but the buoys are adequate. Streams run fast at springs. If anchoring off Cahersiveen it is not possible to lie clear of the current. Welcoming marina.

Supplies at Knight's Town, limited to bread, some general stores and fuel. Water on quay at Reenard Pt and an excellent fish restaurant. Beginish Is uninhabited. Cahersiveen, all requirements and a first class heritage museum.

☎/**VHF** Cahersiveen Marina 066 9472777, VHF M, 37.

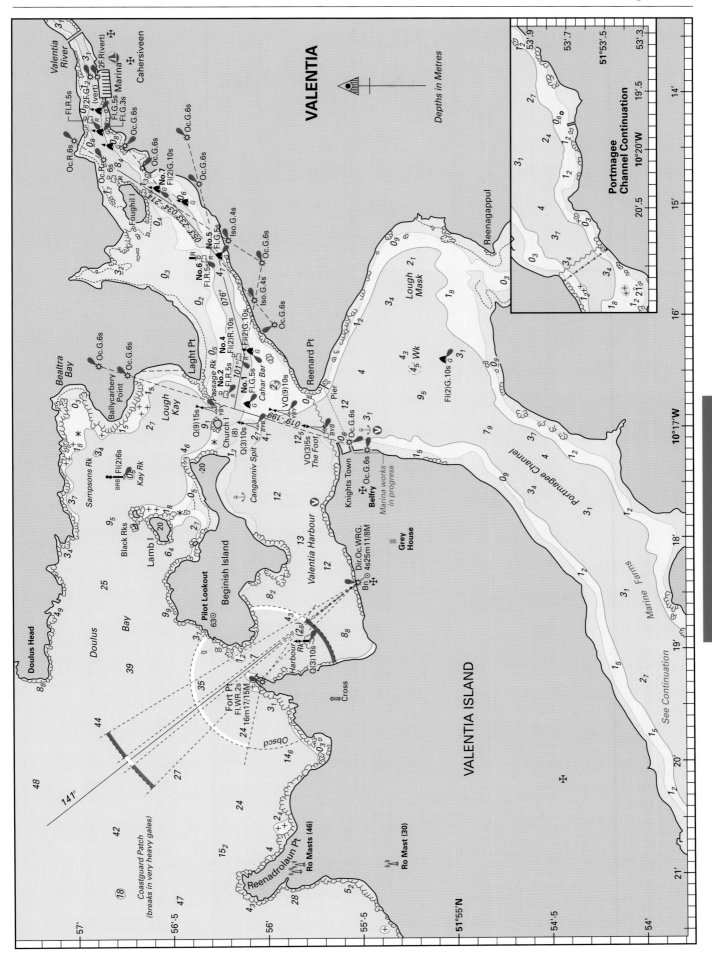

VALENTIA

Depths in Metres

Portmagee Channel Continuation

IRELAND

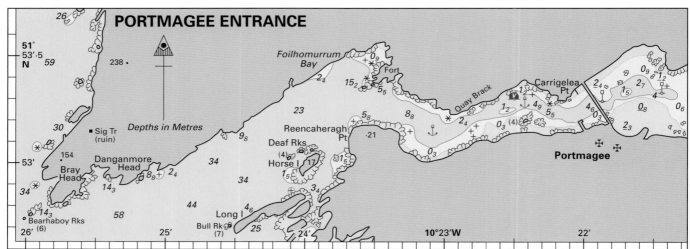

PORTMAGEE ENTRANCE

Depths in Metres

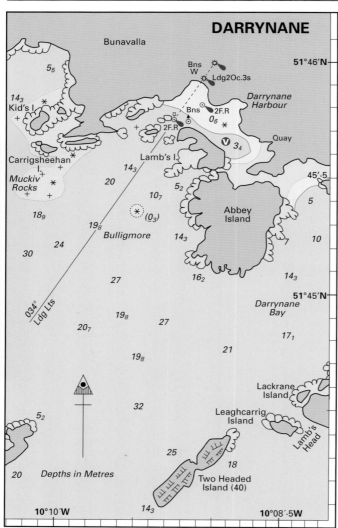

DARRYNANE

Depths in Metres

DARRYNANE

Chart BA 2495; SC 5623; Imray C56

HW Cobh −0119sp −0039np

MHWS	MHWN	MLWN	MLWS
3·6m	2·7m	1·2m	0·4m

A beautiful, natural hbr 1½M NW of Lamb's Head, Well sheltered in all weathers.

Avoid entering in heavy W'ly or SW'ly weather when the narrow entrance between rocks may be dangerous. Even impossible in bad weather.

Approach From S pass between Two Headed Is and Moylaun Is. Make north approx 1M and sight two conspicuous white Lt bns Oc.3s bearing 034°.

From SW pass between Moylaun Is and Deenish Is then steer ENE to sight the bns. From W or NW make to position 5ca N of Deenish Is then steer E to sight the bns. Steer carefully on the transit to avoid rocks close either side. When ½ca past Middle Rock (always shows) to stb alter course 030° to stb to pass between a lit R bn 2F.R. to port and a B topped bn to stb on Lamb's Rock to the N of Lamb's Is.

Entrance When past Lamb's Rock some ½ca, pass between it and Odd Rock bn 2F.R to the NE of it.

Anchorage Steer SE down into the hbr some 2ca to come to anchor clear of moorings in 3m. Three visitors' moorings.

Facilities Land at the quay in the SE corner or on the sandy beach. There are no shops nearby but, some 150m along the road from the quay, there is a friendly bar where they can direct you to shops some 2M distant and they offered to bring back some supplies when they were going themselves. There are fine sandy beaches in Darrynane bay to the SE of the hbr and Daniel O'Connell's House some 600m walk beyond the quay is well worth a visit.

SNEEM

Chart BA 2495; SC 5623; Imray C56

HW Cobh −0113sp −0033np

MHWS	MHWN	MLWN	MLWS
3·5m	2·7m	1·2m	0·4m

A small hbr on N side of the Kenmare River opposite Kilmakilloge; Affords sheltered anchorage for small craft in 3–6m and upwards in very beautiful surroundings.

Approach Close with the SE side of Sherky Is. To pass inside Sherky Is and avoid Cottoner Rock (dries 0·3m), keep nearer to Pigeon Is to port than to Sherky Is.

Entrance Thence steer 013° on the hotel. When well past the third Is, Inishkeragh, steer 318° on the NE extreme of Garinish Is, leaving it close to port.

Visitors' moorings Three Y visitors' moorings established 51°48'·7N 09°53'·6W.

Anchorage In 6m between Goat Is and the pier, or in 3m inside the bay at the NE end of Garinish known as 'The Bag'.

Facilities All necessities from Sneem, 1½M by water but only accessible by dinghy at half flood. Otherwise approximately 2M walk up the lane from the pier. Water at pier NW of anchorage symbol. Parknasilla Hotel, with restaurant, can be approached on foot from Goat Island.

KILMAKILLOGE

Chart BA 2495; SC 5623; Imray C56

HW Cobh −0113sp −0033np

MHWS	MHWN	MLWN	MLWS
3·5m	2·9m	1·2m	0·4m

Inside Kilmakilloge, there are three separate harbours: Kilmakilloge, Bunaw and Collorus.

Approach From E give Laughan Point a berth of over 2½ca give W side of entrance a berth of 1½ca.

Entrance Book Rocks, awash at LW, extends 3ca off E shore, R can Fl(2)R.10s, near a grassy

PORTMAGEE

Chart BA 2125; SC 5623; Imray C56

HW Cobh −0118sp −0038np

MHWS	MHWN	MLWN	MLWS
3·5m	2·8m	1·2m	0·3m

Approach Entrance inadvisable in heavy weather owing to violence of sea under Bray Head and baffling winds. No dangers in approach.

Entrance In strong SW winds the N entrance via Knightstown should be used. Approaching from SW for 1¼M inside

Reencaheragh Pt, navigation requires caution and the chart should be studied carefully.

Anchorage Below the br off the pier in 5m. There are visitors' moorings 3ca west of the fixed br. Alongside mooring may be possible on the pier for short periods and longer at pontoon on the N shore between Carrigalea Point and the br. Good restaurant and shop on S shore.

The br is now permanently closed.

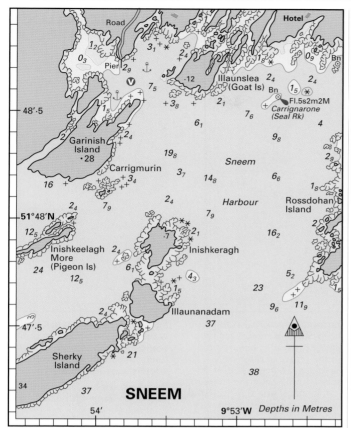

SNEEM 9°53'W *Depths in Metres*

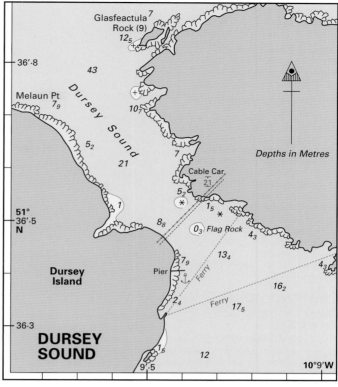

DURSEY SOUND 10°9'W *Depths in Metres*

precipice 53m high, off Collorus Point on W side dangers extend 1½ca. Enter on mid-channel course steering slightly W of Spanish Is. Thence according to anchorage.

Anchorages

• For Kilmakilloge harbour, once past Collorus Point alter course to 102° for the woods near Dereen Ho. Anchor in 4m SW of Yellow Rock, (Bn missing) awash at HW. Landing at Dereen, shop 1½M E at Lauragh. Good pub lunches.

• For Collorus harbour, round Collorus Point keeping a good ca off, and passing between the Pt and Spanish Is slightly nearer the former. Anchorage in middle of hbr in 5m, holding soft with kelp and unreliable. Look out for oyster fishing rafts. No shops, but some provisions might be obtained from farms.

• For Bunaw harbour, on NE side of entrance, is entered through channel 1ca wide between unmarked rocks, with pier-head bearing 041°. There are B & Y Ldg poles with Lts: Oc.R.3s9m (front) Iso.R.2s11m (back) on this bearing: front Lt on pier-head. Anchor near Ldg line in 4–6m. Limited stores and water available. There are numerous shrimp pots all over the hbr. Good pub.

CASTLETOWN BEARHAVEN

Charts BA 1840; SC 5623; Imray C56

HW Cobh –0048sp –0012np

MHWS	MHWN	MLWN	MLWS
3·2m	2·6m	1·2m	0·4m

A very busy fishing hbr.

Bar 3m W of Dinish Is.

Approach

From the W and S make for Ardnakinna Point Fl(2)WR.10s on the west end of Bear Is. In a position 2·5ca to W sight, on Dishnish Is, the light DirOc.WRG.5s15/12M which is above a W hut with vert R stripe. Now head in, between Naglas Pt to stb and Pipers Pt to port. The W sector of the light, centre 023·3°, is very narrow (0·5°); at night, it is safest to keep on the W/G boundary. This line takes you between Naglas Point to stb and Piper's Point to port, through Piper's Sound. When 4½ca short of Dinish Is sight Ldg bns Oc.Bu.6s 008° for entrance to Castletown.

From E leave Roancarrigmore Is Fl.WR.3s 3ca to stb. Steer 280° to leave Lonehort Point 3ca to port and enter Bearhaven Sound. Leave George Rock Lt buoy Fl(2)10s to stb. Continue down centre of sound leaving dangerous wreck (always showing), marked by N card Lt buoy to port. Leave Hornet Rock S card Lt buoy to stb and Walter Scott S card Lt buoy to stb. Proceed W until 3ca SSW of Dinish when sight hbr bns as above.

Entrance The entrance channel is less than 50m wide abreast Came Point. Perch Rock marked by a G con buoy Q.G to stb and Lt bn Q.R to port. Keep a little closer to this. Ldg bns R with W stripe Oc.Bu.6s in line 008° lead through the channel.

DURSEY SOUND

Chart BA 2495; SC 5623; Imray C56

Tidal Stream

Dover –0430 N-going, +0145 S-going. Spring rate 4kn with overfalls. It can be even swifter close to the shore on the spring stream. There are eddies on both sides of the S entrance during S-going stream. This is a narrow and useful channel between Dursey Island and the mainland. It is advisable to go through with a favourable tide or at least before it reaches its maximum rate. Entering the sound from the S a peculiarity about which strangers should be forewarned is that having rounded Crow Head the bay presents the appearance of a cul-de-sac as the similarity of colour of the island and the mainland shores prevents contrast where they overlap. There is a temporary anchorage off the pier on the E side of Dursey Is while waiting for the tide.

Having cleared the Bull's Forehead off Crow Head steer for Illanebeg on the island shore. Look out for lobster pots SW of the entrance. Keep very close to the island shore going through the narrows which are only 1ca wide. Flag Rock with only 0·3m over it at LW lies almost in mid-channel in the narrowest part of the sound, thus limiting the navigable part to 90m. The N-going tide sets directly on to the rock. There is deep water close to the shore of the island so a yacht should keep very close in. The E extremity of Scariff Is in line with the E shore of the island, 339°, leads W of the 0·3m rock. Note that Scariff Is, 252m, and Deenish Is, 141m, are the same shape viewed from the S. There is a cable car across the sound also a telephone wire; the least clearance at HWS is 21m under the car itself with 24m under the cables and 26m under the telephone wires. There is usually a disturbed sea at the N entrance which can become dangerous in strong to gale force N/NW winds. The sea rebounds from the cliffs of Glasfeactula Rock, 9m high, at the E side of the N entrance. Quite frequently a different wind is met on either side of the sound. Be prepared for sudden changes in wind direction going through the sound especially near the N entrance where heavy squalls from the high ground may be met. Salmon nets may be just N of the N entrance and it would be very dangerous to foul one here.

Berthing

• Anchor in area dredged to 2·4m centred 1·2ca W of quay (see RNLI mooring), or in a S blow closer to Dinish Is.

• A temporary berth may be available at W end of Quay or at NE end: avoid central part. Ask HM, VHF 16 and 14.

Facilities Water on quay. Petrol and diesel, good shops, hotels, banks, PO, gas and fuel. Limited chandlery. Engineer.

BEARHAVEN (SOUND)

Charts BA 1840; SC 5623; Imray C56

HW Cobh –0048sp –0012np

MHWS	MHWN	MLWN	MLWS
3·2m	2·6m	1·2m	0·4m

IRELAND

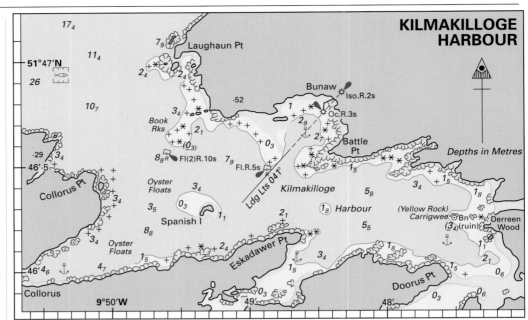

Stream in offing is negligible. In entrance at HWD tide floods, from +0615 ebbs, max rate 2kn.

Approach and Entrance
Bearhaven is on N shore of Bantry Bay. Approach from E or W *see Castletown, above.*

Anchorages As alternatives to Castletown.

• In Dunboy Bay on W side of Piper's Sound, S of rock drying. Two rocks now marked by 'occasional' buoy. Approach 58°38'·1N 9°55'·38W 1·5m; or go further up in E winds. Avoid Colt Rock R bn Fl(2)R.10s when entering. Beware of an oyster fishery using floating lines and nets.
• Visitors' moorings 1½ca NW of Minane Island
• See Lawrence Cove 7ca SSE of George Rock.

LAWRENCE COVE

Charts BA 1840; SC 5623; Imray C56

HW Cobh –0048sp –0012np

MHWS	MHWN	MLWN	MLWS
3·2m	2·6m	1·2m	0·4m

A secluded, picturesque haven in the north shore of Bear Island 8ca S by E of George Rock buoy offering good shelter in all weather except strong north winds. Further into the cove is a small, well run, marina that offers good shelter in all weathers.

Approach From E or W, in Bearhaven make for Ardnagh point (NNW of the Cove). From E keep 2½ca off shore to avoid Palmer Rock. From W keep 1ca off shore.

Entrance From Ardnagh point head SSE closing toward the next headland. There is a rock in the centre of the cove entrance. To keep clear of this stay within ½ca of the shore to stb. Come round this headland which forms the west side of the entrance keeping within 50m. There is a rocky island in the centre of the cove with a large cylindrical tank on it. The marina lies beyond this island some ½ca to SW. Seek instruction from the marina management where to berth.

Moorings and anchorage There are four visitors' buoys to the SSE of Ardnagh point.
• One may anchor near this point.
• Anchor within the entrance N or NE of the tank island in 5–6m but leave room for the small car ferry to enter to the N of you.

Facilities The marina has fuel, water and electricity. Travel-lift crane. Below waterline repairs undertaken and secure over-wintering, storage ashore.

Payphone (no mobile cover) and Craft-Shop with many boat needs.

Provision can be made for leaving the boat in care and the ferry can connect with buses to Cork enabling crew change. The nearby village shop PO has necessity provisions. There are two good restaurants and a pub. Large charge for rubbish disposal.

☎ Marina 027 750 444.

GLENGARRIFF

Chart BA 1838; SC 5623; Imray C56

HW Cobh –0045sp –0025np

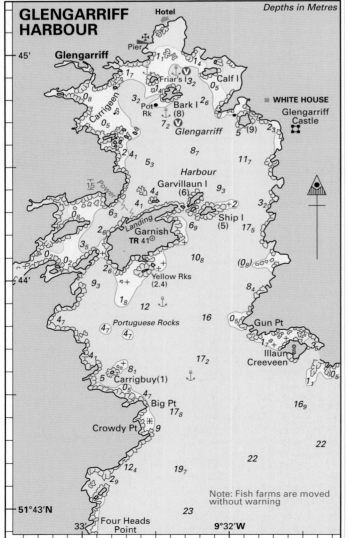

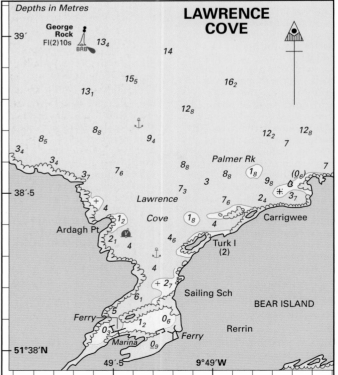

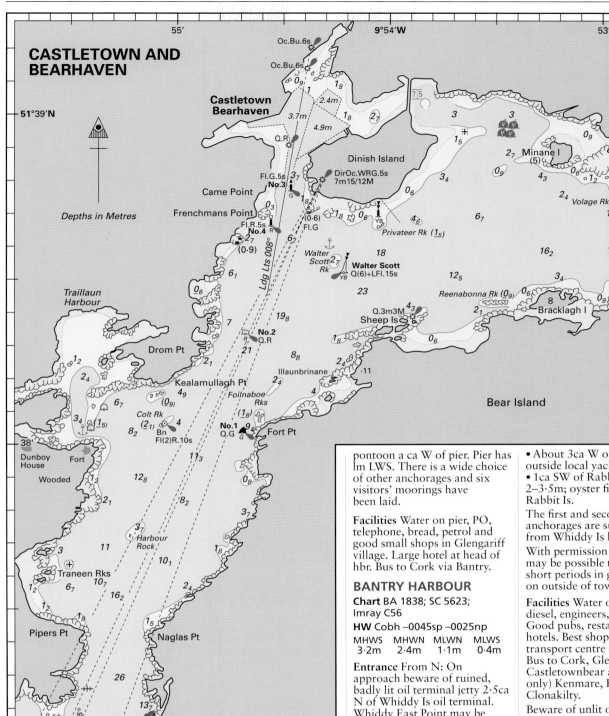

CASTLETOWN AND BEARHAVEN

Depths in Metres

Castletown Bearhaven

MHWS	MHWN	MLWN	MLWS
3·2m	2·4m	1·1m	0·4m

The hbr is situated at the E end of Bantry Bay and affords complete shelter in beautiful surroundings.

Approach Leave Corrid Point (Four Heads Point) about 3ca to W and steer 010°, leaving Gun Point 2ca to E.

Entrance From position off Gun Point head 015° toward a conspic house on shore NW of Glengariff castle. Beware of extensive mussel farms. Keep 1½ca E of Ship Is and ½ca clear

of the eastern shore. There is an uncharted patch of rock, having 3m at MLWS, 30m E of Ship Rocks. When 1ca or so to the N of Ship Is and Garvillaun Is the hbr is clear of submerged rocks.

Anchorages
• S of Bark Is This anchorage may have oyster rafts in it.
• NE or N of Bark Is in about 3m. The latter having easy access to a new concrete slip and steps available all tides, near symbol for church.
• For yachts of less than 1·8m draught, close to wooden pier N of Carrigeen Is or at floating

pontoon a ca W of pier. Pier has 1m LWS. There is a wide choice of other anchorages and six visitors' moorings have been laid.

Facilities Water on pier, PO, telephone, bread, petrol and good small shops in Glengariff village. Large hotel at head of hbr. Bus to Cork via Bantry.

BANTRY HARBOUR

Chart BA 1838; SC 5623; Imray C56

HW Cobh –0045sp –0025np

MHWS	MHWN	MLWN	MLWS
3·2m	2·4m	1·1m	0·4m

Entrance From N: On approach beware of ruined, badly lit oil terminal jetty 2·5ca N of Whiddy Is oil terminal. Whiddy East Point may be rounded close in, but islands in hbr are generally foul all round. Leave Horse Lt buoy Fl.G.6s to stb, Gurteenroe Lt buoy Fl.R.3s to port and Chapel Lt buoy Fl.G.3s to stb.

From W entrance: use only in good conditions. Bar has only 1·7m and sometimes breaks. Outside bar, Cracker Rock has only 1·7m. On an easterly course steer towards Relane Point, keeping approximately 150m off shore. Turn on to about 063° when the S side of Reenbeg Point is in line with the HW mark on South Beach, passing S of Cracker Rock.

Anchorages
• 1ca NW of town pier; keep over 1ca from pier on N side which is foul, but clear of fairway.

• About 3ca W of above, outside local yachts in 3·5m.
• 1ca SW of Rabbit Is in 2–3·5m; oyster fisheries inside Rabbit Is.

The first and second anchorages are subject to wash from Whiddy Is launches.

With permission from HM it may be possible to moor, for short periods in good weather, on outside of town pier.

Facilities Water on pier. Petrol, diesel, engineers, some repairs. Good pubs, restaurants and hotels. Best shopping and transport centre on this coast. Bus to Cork, Glengariff, Castletownbear and (summer only) Kenmare, Killarney, Clonakilty.

Beware of unlit oyster rafts in hbr and (September/October) shrimp pots. It is unsafe to pick up moorings without permission.

Mussel farming has started in the hbr. Rafts may be encountered in the area E of Whiddy Is, particularly outside the main buoyed channel, and sometimes quite close to it. They are low, unmarked and sometimes hard to see. Most are floating structures but some are lines of barrels. They can be moored in strings. Do not pass close as floating mooring lines may extend some distance.

CROOKHAVEN

Chart BA 2184; SC 5623; Imray C56

HW Cobh –0057sp, –0033np

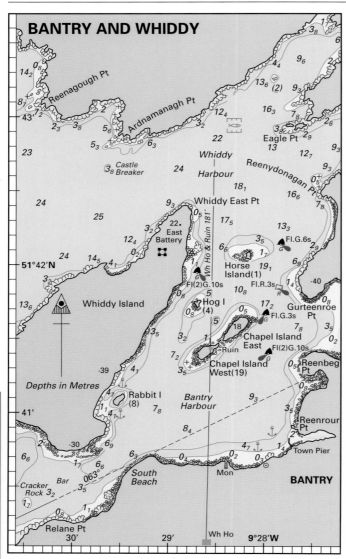

BANTRY AND WHIDDY

Depths in Metres

Reenagough Pt
Ardnamanagh Pt
Castle Breaker
Whiddy Harbour
Reenydonagan Pt
Eagle Pt
Whiddy East Pt
East Battery
Horse Island(1)
Fl.G.6s
Fl.R.3s
Fl(2)G.10s
Hog I
Gurteenroe Pt
Fl.G.3s
Chapel Island East
Fl(2)G.10s
Whiddy Island
Chapel Island West(19)
Reenbeg Pt
Rabbit I (8)
Bantry Harbour
Reenrour Pt
Town Pier
Cracker Rock
Bar
South Beach
Mon
Relane Pt
Wh Ho
BANTRY

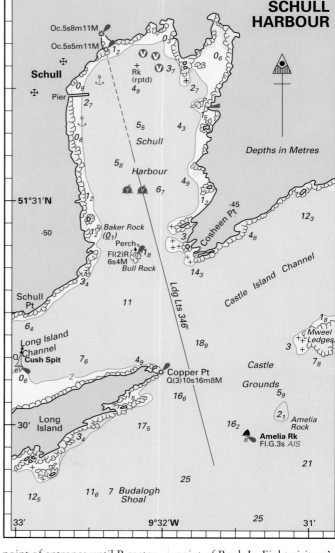

SCHULL HARBOUR

Oc.5s8m11M
Oc.5s5m11M
Schull
Pier
Rk (rptd)
Schull Harbour
Baker Rock (Q.1)
Perch
Fl(2)R 6s4M
Bull Rock
Schull Pt
Long Island Channel
Cush Spit
Long Island
Copper Pt Q(3)10s16m8M
Budalogh Shoal
Cosheen Pt
Depths in Metres
Castle Island Channel
Mweel Ledges
Castle Grounds
Amelia Rock
Amelia Rk Fl.G.3s *AIS*
Ldg Lts 346°

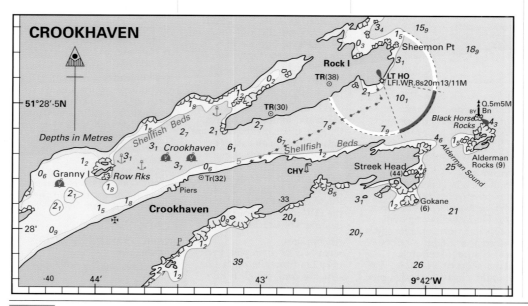

CROOKHAVEN

Depths in Metres
Rock I
TR(38)
TR(30)
LT HO
LFl.WR.8s20m13/11M
Shellfish Beds
Sheemon Pt
Crookhaven
Granny I
Row Rks
Piers
Tr(32)
Crookhaven
Shellfish Beds
CHY
Streek Head (44)
Gokane (6)
Q.5m5M Bn
Black Horse Rocks
Alderman Rocks (9)
Alderman Sound

MHWS	MHWN	MLWN	MLWS
3·3m	2·6m	0·9m	0·3m

An excellent hbr which may be entered at all states of the tide and in all weathers. 2M long, 2ca wide, 10m depth at entrance, 3m off Crookhaven village, shoaling thence gradually to its head.

Approach From the Fastnet Rock steer N to fetch the entrance. Beware salmon nets.

Give Alderman Rocks and Black Horse Rocks, which extend ½M to E of Streek Head (the latter marked by a N card QFl. bn), give both a good berth. Otherwise both shores are steep-to. Silting of the channel has been reported. Beware tidal set through Alderman Sound.

Entrance At night do not steer for the LtHo Fl.WR.8s at N point of entrance until R sector covering Alderman Rocks turns to W, then enter along N shore.

Anchorage Anchor abreast village in 3m. There is kelp in parts of this anchorage and holding only moderate. In a SW blow some shelter can be found behind Granny Is. In E blow shelter to be found N of W point of Rock Is. Eight visitors' moorings.

Facilities Water from taps on both piers, PO, some stores from village shops. Good pubs and restaurants.

SCHULL

Chart BA 2129, 2184; SC 5623; Imray C56

HW Cobh –0040sp, –0015np

MHWS	MHWN	MLWN	MLWS
3·2m	2·6m	1·1m	0·4m

The hbr is situated between Schull Pt and Cosheen Pt and is protected by Long Is and other islands from S. It affords good shelter and may be preferred to Crookhaven in W'ly or E'ly winds and at other times. However, it is untenable in a S gale and then shelter should be sought behind Long Is. Dig the anchor in well with engine to ensure that it is clear of kelp both in the hbr and Long Is Channel. Heavy fishing boat traffic.

Approach From S, when about 3ca S of Amelia Rock G Lt buoy Fl.G.3s marking the rocks W of Castle Is, steer 346° for entrance. From W, leave Cush Spit N card Lt buoy to stb, thence for entrance.

Entrance By day pass Bull Rock, dries at half-ebb, Lt bn Fl(2)R.6s. Pass on either side. W shore is then clear apart from Baker Rock 4·5ca N of Schull Point but E shore must be given a berth of at least 1ca. By night Ldg Lts Oc.5s lead 346° to E of Bull Rock. In season, beware salmon nets in approaches and fairway.

Anchorage To E and NE of pier but holding generally poor. Better clear of moorings to S of pier. But avoid track SSE of pier – fishing boat approach channel. Visitors' moorings NNE of pier and S of pier.

Facilities Good shops, hotels, pubs and restaurants. Water from tap on pier, Gas. For fuel see HM. Chandlery and sail repairs.

BALTIMORE

Chart BA 3725; SC 5623; Imray C56

HW Cobh −0025sp, −0005np

MHWS	MHWN	MLWN	MLWS
3.5m	2.9m	1.4m	0.6m

Approach The position of hbr may be recognised by a conspic W tr called Lot's Wife on E Point of entrance, Beacon Point, and by the W LtHo Fl(2)WR.6s on Barrack Point, the W pt of entrance. S of the LtHo, give the W shore a berth of fully ¾ca to clear Wilson Rock, awash at HW.

From N and W Baltimore harbour can be reached through channel S of Hare Is but careful pilotage between islands and rocks is required. The restricting electric cable over 'The Sound' has now been removed.

Entrance Steer in 340° between entrance points and give the inner E entrance point, Loo Point, a berth of ¾ca, leaving Lt buoy Fl.G.3s marking Loo Rock, 0·2m, to stb. Steer N, leaving Quarry Rock, 2·1m, to stb until the North Pier comes open N of Connor Pt, 060° Leave G. con buoy Q.G. to stb.

Anchorages
• N or W of North Pier.
• In Church Strand Bay beyond the RNLI slip, the safest place in gales – 'a hurricane hole'.
• Off Skerkin Is under Dunalong Castle ruins. Yachts can berth alongside pontoon S of this point for a fee at pub.
• Yachts can also berth alongside NW face of North Pier, 1·3m, for short periods in fine weather or at pontoon off S pier for a fee at pub.

Rocks Quarry Rock, 2·1m, lies 1¾ca 004° from Loo Point. Lousy Rocks, situated in the W centre of the hbr, dry, and are marked by a S card bn on the SE rock. Wallis Rock, 1·6m, in centre of the hbr, has a R can buoy SSE of the rock. Other rocks obstruct the NW corner of the hbr along the shore but not the passage to or from 'The Sound' which is an alternative route to Schull and Roaring waters bay.

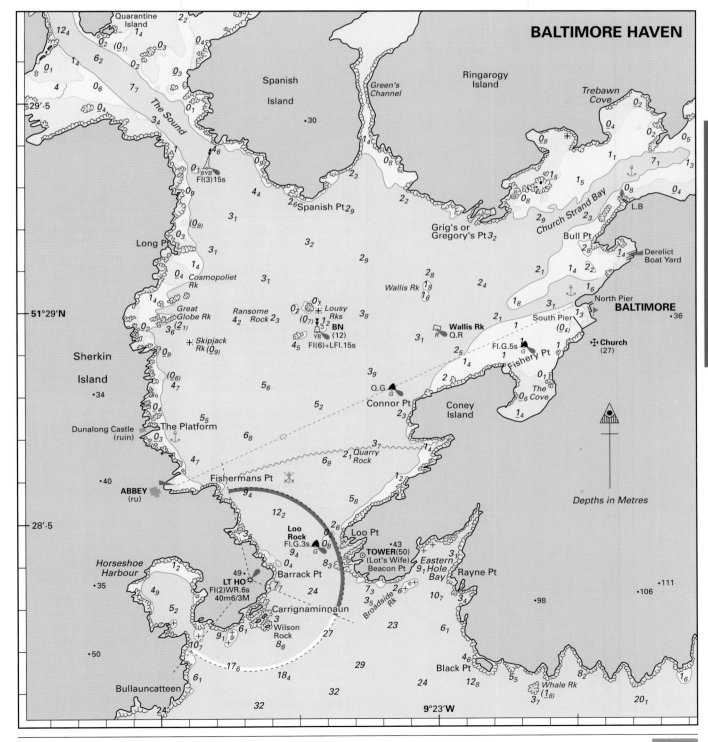

BALTIMORE HAVEN

Depths in Metres

Facilities Water on N Pier. Chandler and small yard, possible to leave boat here with Vincent O'Driscoll ☏ 028 20125. PO, hotels, showers at Baltimore YC, general store, fuel, bus to Skibbereen, 8M. Good pub restaurant on Sherkin Island.

CASTLEHAVEN

Chart BA 2092, 2129; SC 5623; Imray C56

HW Cobh −0020sp, −0030np
DS Dover +0200 E −0400W

MHWS	MHWN	MLWN	MLWS
3·7m	3·0m	1·4m	0·7m

Can be entered at all states of tide, and affords a protected and excellent anchorage in most weathers, with some swell in strong S or SW winds.

Approach Hbr lies 3M NE of Stag Rocks. Black Rock SE of

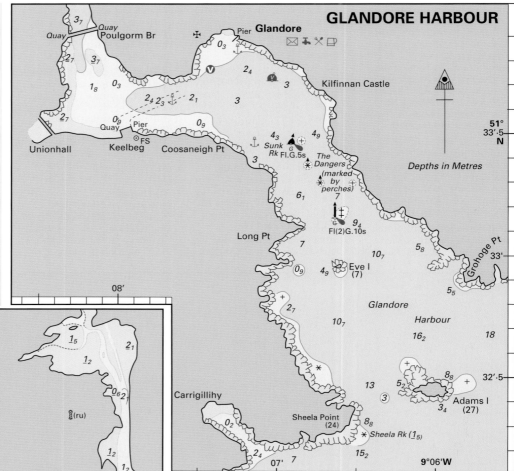

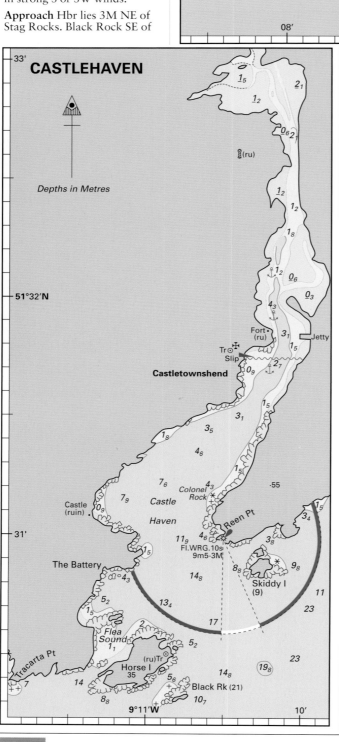

Horse Island is clean but sea can be turbulent in strong winds. Give a clearance of 1ca.

Entrance Steer in midway between Horse Is to port and Skiddy Is to stb. A Lt Fl.WRG.10s9m5–3M is shown from W tr on Reen Point, and at night the W sector leads in. Continue heading for NE shore until the Stags open through Flea Sound, to port, which line clears Colonel Rock, 1m, on SE shore. In hazy weather keep in mid-channel.

Anchorages Anchor abreast of Castletownshend in 3m or lower down clear of fishing boats, which enter at night along SE shore. In SW winds excellent shelter will be found upstream just above the Ruined Fort and Cat Is, where the fishermen go. Slip at Castletownsend renovated. Dinghy access at all tides. Jetty on opposite shore repaired and vessels may be able to berth alongside for FW hose.

Facilities A few adequate shops. Good pubs and one excellent pub/restaurant. Skibbereen, where all stores may be obtained, is 5M.

GLANDORE

Charts BA 2092; SC 5623; Imray C56

HW Cobh −0020sp, −0030np
DS Dover +0200E −0400W

MHWS	MHWN	MLWN	MLWS
3·7m	3·0m	1·4m	0·7m

A picturesque haven with an active yacht club. Well sheltered from all except winds from SE when shelter may be found at Unionhall.

Approach The entrance lies between Goats Head on E and Sheela Point on W and is divided into two channels by Adam Is. From SW give High Is a berth of 1ca. From E there are no dangers on the direct course from a position S of Doolic Rock off Galley Head.

Entrance Between Adam Is and Goats Head giving Adam Is a wide berth, or between Adam Is and Sheela Point; then steer to pass close to E of Eve Is. Turn to port a little to pass midway between W shore and the Dangers, three separate rocks in the middle of the channel. The Outer Danger is marked by a bn Fl(2)G on its W side, and a R port perch, can topmark, on its E side. The Middle Danger and the Inner Danger are each marked by one perch G, con topmark. Sunk Rock, about 1ca N of the Inner Danger, is marked by a lit G con buoy Fl.G.5s. Strangers should not attempt to sail between the Dangers and should particularly note that the perches on the Outer Danger mark the ends of what is in effect one rock.

CROOKHAVEN TO CORK

Charts BA 2424, 2184, 2129, 2092, 1765; SC 5623; Imray C56, C57

Passage lights	BA No
Fastnet	5702
Fl.5s.49m27M	
Racon (G) (——·) AIS	
Galley Head	5708
Fl(5)20s53m23M	
Old Hd Kinsale	5710
Fl(2)10s72m20M AIS	
Roche's Point	5718
Fl.WR.3s30m20/16M	

Tidal Streams All related to Dover. In general the streams up to 5M offshore change at nearly the same time from Crookhaven to Old Head of Kinsale: +0215 E-going stream –0400 W-going; spring rate 1 to 1·5kn, but 2–2·5kn off the Fastnet Rock and the main headlands. In Gascanane Sound: 0030SE; –0545NW. spring rate 3kn. Old Head of Kinsale to Cork Harbour: +0045E; –0500W.

The channel between Fastnet Rock and Cape Clear is free of dangers apart from a rock with 3m ¼M NE of Fastnet. Galley Head is fairly steep-to, but ½M WSW is Dhulic Rock, dries 3·4m, with Sunk Rock, less than 1·8m, 1·5ca to SSW of it. Tides set across Dhulic Rock and it must be given a wide berth.

With wind against tide there can be a bad sea close to Galley Head and to Seven Heads.

Off Old Head of Kinsale a potentially dangerous tide-race extends over 1M to SW on W-going stream, to SE on E-going stream. The race can be avoided by rounding the hd close up except in S winds or any strong winds; in these conditions give it a berth of over 2M.

Anchorages

• In SW through N to E winds off Glandore pier in 2·5m; or secure to a visitors' buoy.

• In S or SE winds off **Unionhall** in 2·5m; give Coosaneigh Point a good berth to avoid mudbank extending 1ca from it.

There is a new, large fishing boat pier at Keelbeg, Unionhall, with a dredged channel to it. Yachts may berth for short periods and use the water hose.

Facilities Water at both piers. Provisions, small supermarket, and some fuel at Unionhall, many pubs. Good pubs with food and excellent restaurant at The Old Rectory.

COURTMACSHERRY

Charts BA 2092; SC 5623; Imray C56

HW Cobh –0020

MHWS	MHWN	MLWN	MLWS
3·8m	3·0m	1·2m	0·4m

The entrance lies in the NW corner of the eponymous bay about 6M from Old Head of Kinsale. The Bar has only about 2m at LWS with constantly shifting sands. In strong to gale southerly to south-easterly winds seas break and the entrance should not be attempted. Otherwise, after half tide it is straightforward and, once inside, the hbr affords excellent shelter, has a picturesque charm and the unspoiled village is very welcoming.

Approach Hazards to avoid: Horse Rock, visible except HWS; Black Tom, marked by G con Lt buoy Fl(2)G.5s; Barrel Rock marked by unlit S card bn. Aim to leave Black Tom G con Lt buoy close to stb (*see appropriate chart*). At night enter on W sector of Wood Point Fl(2)WR.5s.

Entrance Make for close S of bar buoy, *Courtmacsherry*, Fl.G.3s, then steer approx due W for 5ca leaving the three lit G con buoys close to stb. Turn to port at the lit R can buoy, stay close to the line of moored boats on the village side of the channel toward the quay at the village. For advice phone the 'Sea Anglers' ☎ 023 46427.

Anchorage Either just north of the moored boats, leaving room for the lifeboat to pass, or 100m WNW of the pontoon at the quay. Caution: The tide runs hard here and there is a range of 3·4m at springs.

Moorings Secure to the pontoon just west of the pier. There is ample depth at the pontoon all tides. One may be charged a berthing fee. Try to leave the down-stream end of the pontoon free for angling boats.

Facilities Cosy bars at Inns and Hotel where there is excellent restaurant.

Fresh water tap and Diesel pump on the quay. Some stores. Other supplies from Timoleague 2M to the west.

KINSALE

Chart BA 1765, 2053; SC 5622; Imray C56

HW Cobh –0019sp, –0005np

MHWS	MHWN	MLWN	MLWS
3·9m	3·2m	1·4m	0·6m

Bar 3m, 2–3ca S of Charles Fort.

Approach From E keep outside the Bulman Rock S card Lt buoy off Preghane Point. The hbr will then open up to N and when Charles Fort is visible between Money Pt and Preghane Pt, steer for it. At night the W sector of Charles Fort Lt Fl.WRG.5s leads in.

Entrance Keep in mid-channel and cross the bar S of Charles Fort. At night enter on the White sector 358°–004° Lt Fl.WRG.5s. The W side of the channel from the bar round Blockhouse Point to the town is marked by three R can Lt buoys (Fl(2)R.6s, Q.R & Fl(3)R.10s) which must be left to port.

Berthing

• At Kinsale YC marina N of Town Quay; visitors' berths on outer pontoon, but a finger berth inside marina may be available. Berthing controlled by marina supervisor.

• Anchor on bank N of James Fort, 2–4m.

• Anchor in river between Town Quay and br outside prohibited area.

• At Castlepark Marina on opposite bank.

Facilities Chandlery and showers. Landing at Town Quay or on SE shore from Castlepark Marina. All stores, bus to Cork. EC Thursday. Cork airport 12M. Diesel available at Gibbons Quay and Castlepark marina, water at marina and pier head, electricity at marina. Showers, Wi-Fi in YC. Many good restaurants. 'The Gourmet Capital of Ireland'. Interesting maritime museum.

☎ /VHF HM 021 4772503, VHF 14. Kinsale YC Marina 4773433, VHF 37. Castle Park Marina 4774959, VHF 06.

OYSTER HAVEN

Chart BA 2053; SC 5622; Imray C56

HW Cobh –0019sp, –0005np

MHWS	MHWN	MLWN	MLWS
3·9m	3·2m	1·4m	0·6m

A picturesque, quiet, safe hbr 2M E of Kinsale, where shelter can be found from all weathers bar the strongest of south winds.

Entrance Approach either side of Big Sovereign. In quiet weather or above half tide there is safe passage between Little Sovereign and the shore. Make for centre of entrance. Give Ballymacus Point on W of entrance a berth of at least ¾ca. Inside the haven Harbour Rock, 0·9m, is 1·5ca E of Ferry Point and must be passed on its W side. To clear, keep 'Big Sovereign' open of Kinare Point.

Anchorages

• N of Ferry Point midway between N and S shore in 4–6m, soft mud and weed.

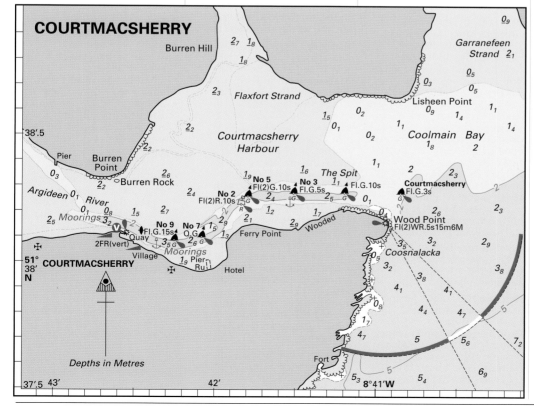

COURTMACSHERRY

Depths in Metres

IRELAND

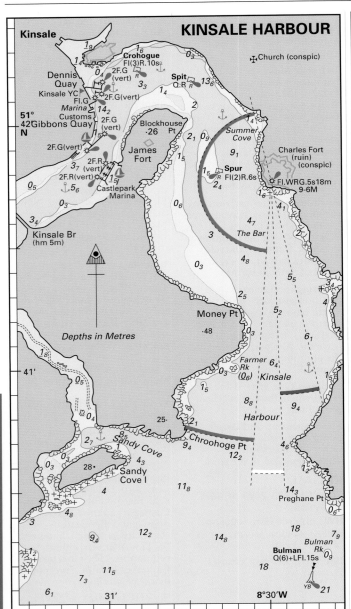

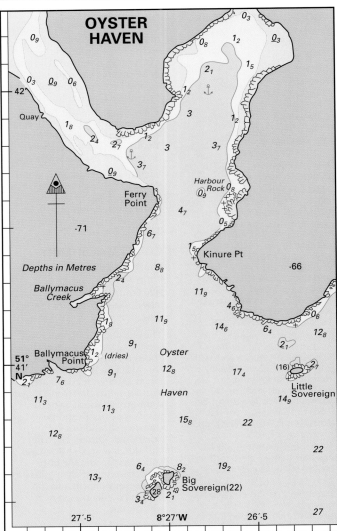

Keep Kinure Point on E side of entrance open of Ferry Point.

• In stronger southerly weather, clear of spring tides, better shelter can be found midstream in 2m 1½ca further up the W branch.

• In stronger SE'ly weather, in N branch of haven 5ca N by E of Kinure Point in 3m sand close to eastern shore. Scenery but no facilities.

CORK HARBOUR

Charts BA 1777, 1773; SC 5622; Imray C57

HW Cobh HW
DS Dover +0100E; –0430W

MHWS	MHWN	MLWN	MLWS
4·1m	3·2m	1·3m	0·4m
	Passage West		
4·4m	3·6m	1·5m	0·7m
	Cork		
4·4m	3·4m	1·3m	0·5m

Hbr is accessible at all times.

Approach From Old Head of Kinsale, Cork RWVS buoy, Fl.10s, off the entrance to the port of Cork bears 058°, 12½M. Thence Roche's Point, the E point of the entrance, 001°, 4¾M. The approach is clear of obstruction for small craft excepting Daunt Rock, 3·5m, marked by R buoy Fl(2)R.6s, 7ca 140° from Roberts Head: to leave this to W bring the high tr E of Roche's Point LtHo on with tree clump in rear, 018°. By day, having left Daunt Rock about 4ca to port, a course 009° made good will lead into the entrance between Weaver Point and the LtHo. By night, a R sector from Roche's Point LtHo Fl.WR.3s covers Daunt Rock, and this sector should be shut in after passing Daunt Rock R can Lt buoy before rounding up for Roche's Point LtHo 016°.

In offshore winds, awaiting tide, anchorage will be found outside the entrance in Ringabella Bay.

Entrance No dangers for small craft in entrance to Cork Harbour. To make for Crosshaven, the main yachting centre, round Rams Head at a distance of fully 2ca and steer for the G con Lt buoy Fl.G.10s C1 at entrance of Owenboy River. Leave R can Lt buoy Fl.R to port. Enter on 252° leaving G con Lt buoy Fl.G.5s C1A to stb and R can Lt buoy Fl.R.5s C2 to port then R can Lt buoy Fl.R.10s C4 to port. In the entrance the tidal streams follow the bends, the flood and ebb streams setting into White bay.

Berthing
Crosshaven
• At W end of RC & MYC Marina. (Interest: Royal Cork YC now amalgamated with Royal Munster RMYC is the oldest in the world). ② 021 483 1023.
• At Crosshaven Boat Yard marina, ② 0121 831161.
• At Salve marina at long pontoon E of RCYC. Visitors' berths marked on upstream portion. Diesel by hose.
• Anchor below Town Quay clear of telephone cables and out of busy fairway.
• Anchor beyond the bend ¾M up stream of the town in 3–5m. Good holding and peace, landing to road possible toward HW.
• Anchor a further ½M up stream in 2–4m in Drake's Pool.
• Ask Crosshaven Boat Yard for a mooring.

Facilities Good supplies, all facilities. Small supermarket and PO in village, sailmaker MacWilliam Sails ② 831505.

Bus to Cork Airport. Ferry Port Ringaskiddy.

Cobh
Follow main buoyed channel up the hbr.
• Anchor W of town clear of Fairway. Garage, shops, hotels, PO, bank. EC Wednesday.
Warning No yacht may approach within 50m of Whitegate oil jetty.
• In East Passage: **East Ferry Marina** S of Belgrove Quay.
• Anchor on W side to S or to E of Belgrove quay, 2–3m.
• On E side ½M further up East Passage 3–4m.

Cork
A berth may be obtained by permission of Port Operations Office, Cobh. Cork is the second city of the Republic of Ireland and has all facilities including rail to Dublin, airport to UK and ferry (from Ringaskiddy) to Swansea and France.

YOUGHAL

Chart BA 2071; SC 5622; Imray C57

HW Cobh +0000sp, +0010np
DS HWD W

MHWS	MHWN	MLWN	MLWS
3·9m	3·1m	1·2m	0·3m

The tidal stream sets into and out of hbr at 2·5 to 3kn springs.

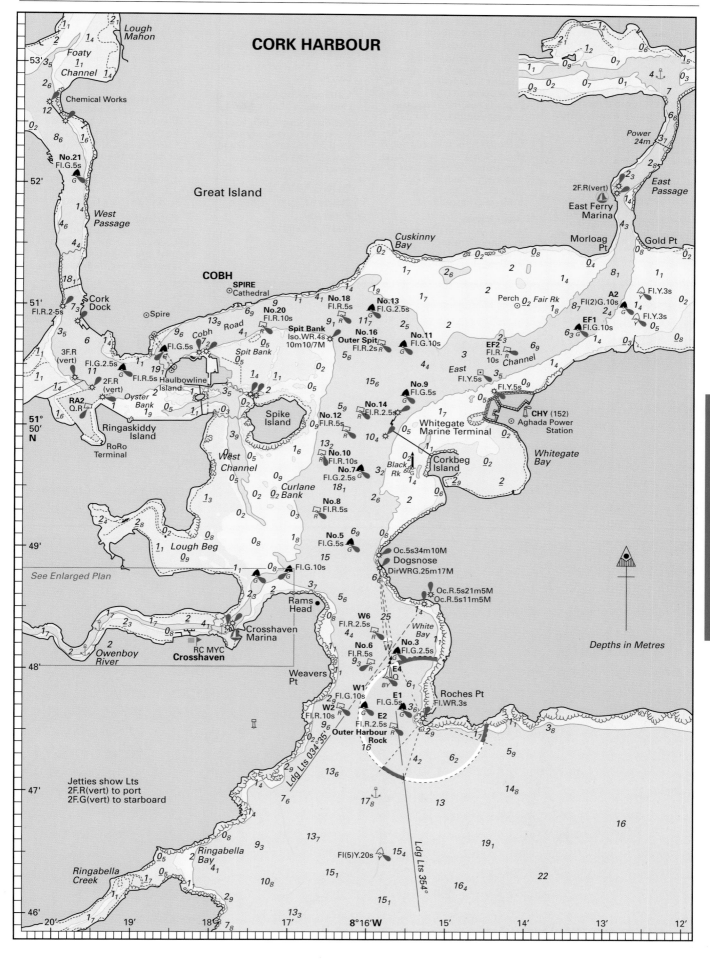

CORK HARBOUR

Lough Mahon

Foaty Channel

Chemical Works

No.21 Fl.G.5s

Great Island

West Passage

Cork Dock Fl.R.2·5s

COBH SPIRE Cathedral
Spire

No.20 Fl.R.10s
Cobh Road

Spit Bank Iso.WR.4s 10m10/7M

Spit Bank

Fl.G.5s

Fl.G.2·5s
2F.R (vert)
Fl.R.5s Haulbowline Island

RA2 Q.R

Oyster Bank

Ringaskiddy Island

RoRo Terminal

No.18 Fl.R.5s
No.13 Fl.G.2.5s

No.16 Outer Spit Fl.R.2s

Spike Island

No.12 Fl.R.5s

West Channel

No.10 Fl.R.10s

No.14 Fl.R.2.5s

No.9 Fl.G.5s

Whitegate Marine Terminal

Black Rk

Corkbeg Island

Curlane Bank

No.7 Fl.G.2.5s

No.8 Fl.R.5s

No.5 Fl.G.5s

Cuskinny Bay

Perch Fair Rk

A2 Fl.(2)G.10s

EF1 Fl.G.10s

Morloag Pt

East Ferry Marina
2F.R(vert)

East Passage

Gold Pt

EF2 Fl.R. 10s Channel

East Fl.Y.5s

Fl.Y.5s

CHY (152) Aghada Power Station

Whitegate Bay

Fl.Y.3s
Fl.Y.3s

Dogsnose Oc.5s34m10M
DirWRG.25m17M

Oc.R.5s21m5M
Oc.R.5s11m5M

Lough Beg

Fl.G.10s

See Enlarged Plan

Rams Head

W6 Fl.R.2.5s

White Bay

W2 Fl.R.10s
W1 Fl.G.10s

Crosshaven Marina
RC MYC
Crosshaven

Owenboy River

Weavers Pt

No.6 Fl.R.5s

No.3 Fl.G.2.5s

E4 Q
BY

E1 Fl.G.5s
E2 Fl.R.2.5s

Outer Harbour Rock

Roches Pt Fl.WR.3s

Jetties show Lts
2F.R(vert) to port
2F.G(vert) to starboard

Ringabella Bay

Ringabella Creek

Ldg Lts 034°35'

Ldg Lts 354°

Fl(5)Y.20s

Depths in Metres

IRELAND

Bar Should not be attempted in a big sea. The approach is divided by Bar Rocks, 0·6m and Blackball Ledge, 3·4m, into two channels, East Bar having least depth 2·8m, and West Bar, 1·8m. Over E Bar one may expect less sea and less stream. Strong E and S winds cause a heavy and dangerous sea in the bay. N winds reduce the tidal rise, and SW gales cause a swell inside; the ebb sets on to the W bar. Best approach is round Black Ball E card Lt buoy.

Approach From W, using the W bar channel, leave Bar Rocks S card Lt buoy marking Bar Rocks 0·6m about 2ca to stb, then steer direct for the entrance, about N.

Using E Bar channel, coming from S, leave Blackball Ledge E card Lt buoy to port.

From E, steer for LtHo Fl.WR.2·5s when it comes well open of Blackball Head and bears about 300°. Give East Point 1½ca offing before bearing round into the hbr.

Entrance Having passed the LtHo, keep in towards the W shore. The E side of entrance on a transit between East Point and Ferry Point is shoal. Streams run hard between LtHo and Ferry Point.

Anchorages
• On a 3m bank off the most N'ly warehouse.
• In 2–4m N of Ferry Point.
• Off market clock.

• ENE of clock, abeam of a building with conspic circular balconies, outside moorings in 2m LWS.
• N of LB slip off small landing beach.

Caution Depths continually changing in hbr.

Facilities Shops, PO, banks, pubs, hotels, restaurants. Boat yard for repairs to hull and machinery. Chandlery, electronics. Bus to Cork.

DUNGARVAN

Charts BA 2017; SC 5622; Imray C57

HW Cobh +0010

MHWS	MHWN	MLWN	MLWS
4·1m	3·2m	1·3m	0·4m

A large and attractive expanse of open water, much of it drying, sheltered from winds from N through W to S.

Approach between Helvick head to the S and Ballynacourty Point to the N. Between these lie three hazards: midway *Carrickpane*, always showing at least 2m, 5ca to its SSW, Helvick Rk guarded by *Helvick* E Card buoy Q(3)10s, and 2½ca W of the buoy a foul rocky area *The Gainers*.

Entrance
• Dungarvan Harbour. Give *Carrickpane* a good berth to port and make for a position 2½ca south of Ballynacourty

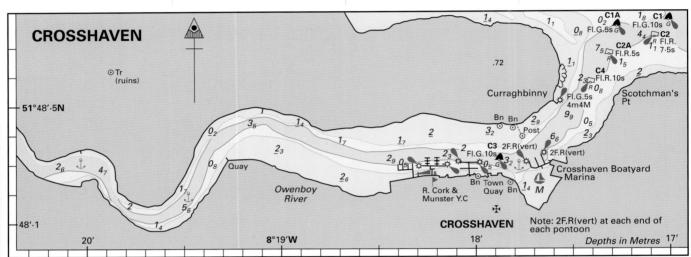

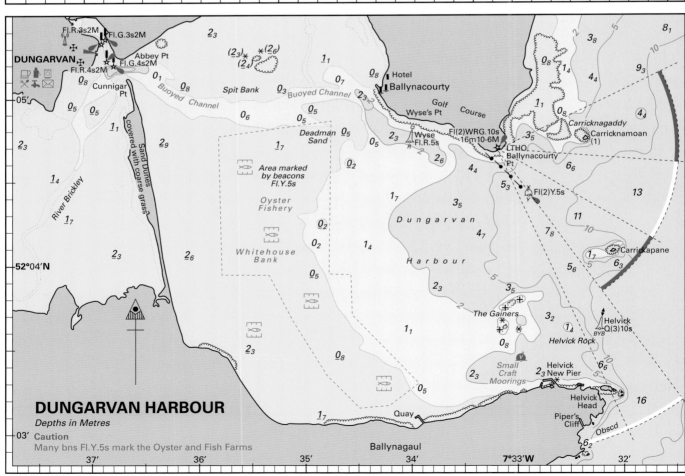

CORK TO TUSKAR ROCK

Charts BA 2049; SC 5622; Imray C57

Passage lights	*BA No.*

Mine Head
Fl(4)30s87m12M   5778

Ballycotton   5774
Fl.WR.10s59m21/17M AIS

Hook Head   5798
Fl.3s46m23M AIS
Racon(K) (–·–)

Coningbeg S card buoy 5832
Q(6)+LFl.15s9M
Racon(M) (––) AIS

Tuskar Rock   5838
Q(2)7·5s33m24M
Racon(T) (–) AIS

Tidal Streams All related to Dover. Cork to Waterford less than 0·5kn starting progressively later towards Waterford where they begin +0530ENE; –0100WSW. Between the Saltees and Carnsore Point +0515ENE, spring rate 2·4kn; –0045WSW, spring rate 2·6kn.

Off Hook Head there is a dangerous tidal race extending 1M S of the Head, especially in strong westerlies. To avoid this race keep outside the 20m line. The passage between the Tuskar Rock and Carnsore Point can become very rough in bad weather. Dangerously so in strong SW wind against tide and should be avoided.

E of Hook Head, Baginbun and Bannow Bays though exposed to SE give good shelter from W'lies. The recommended offshore anchorage is at the SW end of Bannow Bay just N of Ingard Point.

A yacht proceeding from Waterford to the E coast has the choice of the offshore or inshore passage. Using the offshore passage keep well clear of the dangerous rocks extending some 4M SW through S to E of Great Saltee, marked by the Conningbeg S card buoy (52°03'·12N 6°38'·57W) together with lit W and E card buoys. Thence go to a position S of South Rock Lt buoy, S card, and pass E of the Tuskar Rock giving it a good berth as the tide sets on to it, but avoiding the TSS.

For the inshore passage, pass between the Saltees or north of them through St Patrick's Bridge marked by G & R Lt buoys Fl.6s (April–September) There are two dangerous rocks and a wreck some 2M SW of Carnsore Point. In anything other than fair weather it would be wise to pass S of the buoys guarding them. Black Rock S card Lt and Barrels E card Lt. Then either S of South Rock, S card Lt and ½M E of Tuskar Rock Lt. Or in fair weather 1¼M W of Tuskar.

Warning The sea area off the SE corner of Ireland is to be avoided in bad weather especially wind against tide in the channel between the Tuskar Rock and Carnsore Point.

Light. At night enter in the W sector (274°–302°), but move to south when closing the light. Then steer 300° until identifying the buoyed channel which leads to Dungarvan town hbr. In the channel from Wyse's Point to Abbey Point at half tide there should be at least 1·8m between the buoys. Follow round Abbey point to stb to reach the town quay.
• Helvick Harbour. Go to Helvick Head then west along the coast for ½M.

Mooring and Anchorage

• Dungarvan town: Port side to, as the ebb runs strongly, alongside the club pontoon or alongside the quay but take soundings and be prepared to take the ground at LWS. Anchor in a deep hole NW of Cunnigar Point (at the N end of the long sand spit) but caution, sp tide runs at 2·5kn.

• Helvick: There are eight Y visitors' moorings NW of the hbr or inside the N pier if it is not occupied by fishing vessels. Anchor anywhere convenient N or NW of the hbr in more than 2m.

Facilities Dungarvan all supplies. Water on the pontoon. Fuel from garage. Good pubs, hotels and restaurants. Showers at the SC.

WATERFORD

Chart BA 2046; SC 5622; Imray C57

HW Cobh Dunmore +0005; Cheek Pt +0022; Waterford +0057

DS Dover –0200 to +0500W –0600 to –0300SSE

Waterford

MHWS	MHWN	MLWN	MLWS
4·5m	3·5m	1·2m	0·5m

Approach The summit of Slieve Coilte bears 000° from the entrance, which lies between Swines Head 60m and Hook Head, long and low lying, with conspic LtHo Fl.3s It bears 296° 11M from Coningbeg S Card Lanby. Coming from the W in hazy weather care must be taken to distinguish Tramore Bay, which has three W towers on the W point and two on the E. The approach is clear of obstructions except Falskirt Rock 2ca S of Swines Head, covers at ⅔ flood and Brecaun Reef, 2M NE of Hook Head,

3ca offshore 0·5m, to clear which keep Hook LtHo W of 233°. Tr Race extends 1M S of Hook Head, and should be given a wide berth. In strong W winds over tide conditions are severe.

Dunmore East This is a small artificial hbr on the W side of the entrance, which can afford a convenient port of call, but at times very busy with fishing vessels with no room for yachts.

LtHo on pier Fl.WR.8s. Lt on pier head Fl.R.2s & Lt on end of W pier Fl.G.2s. Moorings N of hbr are private, check with YC ☎ 051 83230 for vacant one. Berthing if free space along pontoons or fishing vessels on W quays. Water from YC. Diesel on E quay. Shops and PO above hbr. Showers at YC and heads next to LB office.

Anchor in bay opposite Strand Hotel, N of moorings at Dunmore East. Good holding but not sheltered in S–NE winds.

Bar 4M inside Hook Head, has 5·4m. The River Suir has 4m up to Waterford and the Barrow the same to New Ross. Below Duncannon the ebb follows E side and the flood the W side.

Waterford entrance Duncannon sectored Lt Oc.WRG.4s W 002° leads through Duncannon Bar. Keep in buoyed channel. Abreast Duncannon the channel lies on E side; avoid Drumroe Bank on W.

Waterford – River Suir Ldg Lts 255° over Cheek Point Bar. After Cheek Point take the bend wide passing close to Snowhill Point. New works W of Cheek Point for new port on N bank. Groynes cover at HW but marked by Y Lt buoys Nos1–4 Fl.6s, 4s, 2s, and 1s respectively. Then river has R can Lt buoys to port. Large wharfs on N bank near junction of King's and Queen's Channels. Then G con Lt buoys to stb and Ldg Lts at E end of Queen's Channel, bearing 098° astern, mark the fairway through the channel. Beware fish weir stumps extending over mud flats.

Two lifting bridges at Waterford, HM ☎ 051 74499. River Suir has 2·5m at Fiddown Is and dries 3M below Carrick.

Anchorages Just above Ballyhack Ferry ramp in 5m close in out of stream. Note: do not anchor at Cheek point due to silting between groynes, not shown on any chart. In W side of King's channel just N of the W bank ferry ramp. Approach only from N as there is no passage through the wires of the ferry.

Berthing
Marina: secure 370m pontoon in city 5ca below lifting br.

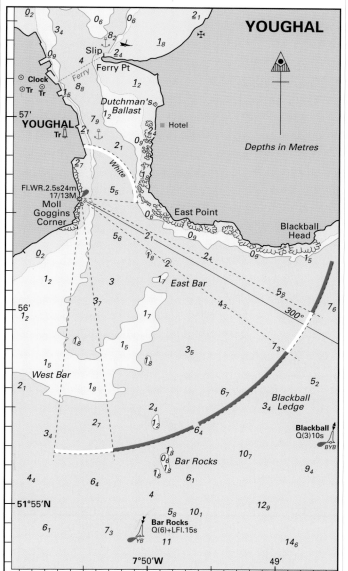

YOUGHAL

Depths in Metres

IRELAND

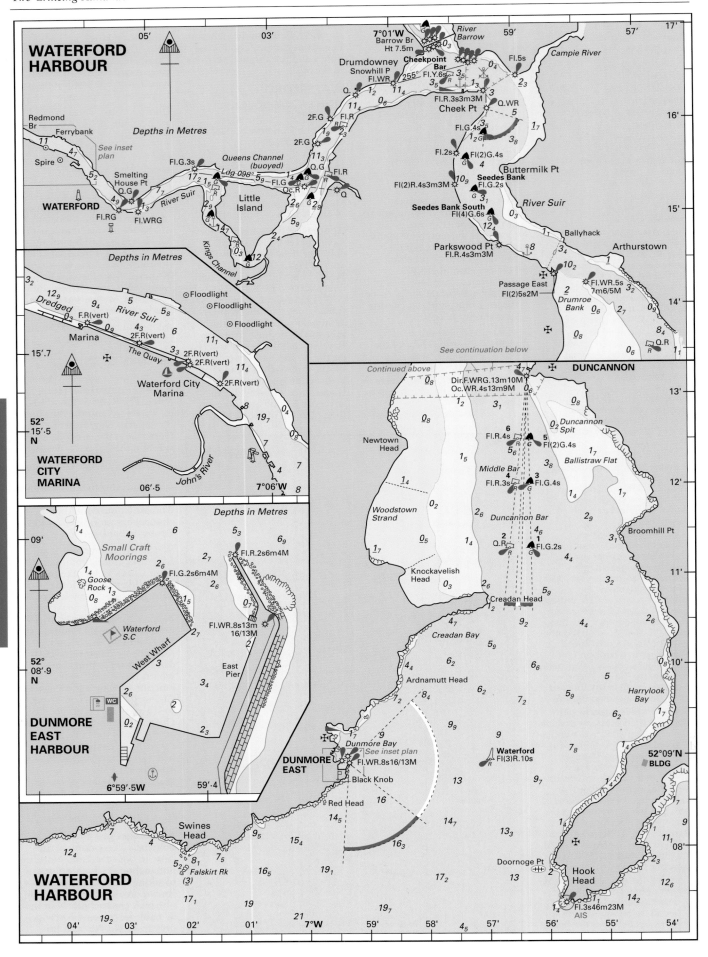

WATERFORD HARBOUR

Depths in Metres

WATERFORD

Redmond Br
Ferrybank
See inset plan
Spire
Smelting House Pt
Q.G
River Suir
Fl.RG
Fl.WRG

Queens Channel (buoyed)
Ldg 098°
Little Island
Fl.G.3s
Fl.G
Oc.R
2F.G
2F.G
Q.G
Fl.R

Kings Channel

7°01'W
Barrow Br
Ht 7.5m
Drumdowney
Snowhill P
Fl.WR
Cheekpoint Bar
River Barrow
Campie River
Fl.5s
255°
Fl.Y.6s
Cheek Pt
Fl.R.3s3m3M
Q.WR
Fl.G.4s
Fl.2s
Fl(2)G.4s
Buttermilk Pt
Fl(2)R.4s3m3M
Seedes Bank
Fl.G.2s
River Suir
Seedes Bank South
Fl(4)G.6s
Parkswood Pt
Fl.R.4s3m3M
Ballyhack
Arthurstown
Passage East
Fl(2)5s2M
Drumroe Bank
Fl.WR.5s 7m6/5M
Q.R

WATERFORD CITY MARINA

Depths in Metres

River Suir
Dredged
Marina
F.R(vert)
2F.R(vert)
The Quay
2F.R(vert)
2F.R(vert)
Waterford City Marina
2F.R(vert)
Floodlight
Floodlight
Floodlight

52°15'.7
52° 15'.5 N

06'.5
John's River
7°06'W

See continuation below

Continued above
DUNCANNON
Dir.F.WRG.13m10M
Oc.WR.4s13m9M
Newtown Head
Fl.R.4s 6
5
Fl(2)G.4s
Duncannon Spit
Middle Bar 4
Fl.R.3s 3 Fl.G.4s
Ballistraw Flat
Woodstown Strand
Duncannon Bar
2 4 6
Q.R Fl.G.2s
Knockavelish Head
1 Fl.G.2s
Creadan Head
Broomhill Pt
Creadan Bay
Ardnamutt Head
Harrylook Bay

DUNMORE EAST HARBOUR

Depths in Metres

Small Craft Moorings
Goose Rock
Fl.R.2s6m4M
Fl.G.2s6m4M
Fl.WR.8s13m 16/13M
Waterford S.C
West Wharf
East Pier
WC

52° 08'.9 N

6°59'.5W
59'.4

DUNMORE EAST
Fl.WR.8s16/13M
Black Knob
Red Head
Dunmore Bay
See inset plan
Waterford
Fl(3)R.10s
52°09'N
BLDG
Doornoge Pt

WATERFORD HARBOUR

Swines Head
Falskirt Rk (3)
Hook Head
Fl.3s46m23M
AIS

04' 03' 02' 01' **7°W** 59' 58' 57' 56' 55' 54'

Beware strong tide. Moor both sides. Minimum depth outside 2m. Access gate controlled by mobile phone, 051309900 0900–1700 Monday–Friday, otherwise ☎ 0872384944. Water and electricity. Showers 300m. All city facilities. Most repairs. No sailmaker.
☎ 051 309 900.

New Ross – River Barrow
Barrow swing br has 7m clearance, opens as required, three blasts or ☎ 051 88137. Enter E side, leave W side. Buoyed channel to New Ross, very narrow between Red Bank and the W side 6M upstream from Barrow br. Steer mid way between the W bank and the G con Lt buoys. 3½M below New Ross.

Mooring Berth alongside Harbour Office next to round tr in centre of town on E bank, or visitors' moorings at YC above fixed br, 7·7m clearance above CD.

Anchorage S of town on E side, or at Marsh pt 2M downstream.

Facilities City has all stores, no EC, late night Friday. Most repairs, no sailmaker.

KILMORE QUAY
Charts BA 2049, 2740; SC 5622; Imray C57

HW Cobh +0019sp, +0009np
DS Dover HW to +0500WSW
+0600 to –0100ENE

MHWS	MHWN	MLWN	MLWS
3·8m	2·8m	1·5m	0·6m

Visiting yachts are welcome, marina berths usually available. Kilmore quay is a pleasant village, the small fishing hbr providing excellent shelter to a 55 berth marina (20 visitors') in the north of the hbr. Dredged 3m. A good arrival port from Lands End, Scillies or S Wales.

Caution Hbr entrance exposed to SE and approach could be dangerous in strong SE'ly winds, particularly toward HW. Best time to approach HW–0200 when cross tide, wind against tide, element is taken out of the equation. If in doubt seek advice of HM VHF 9 and 16 or ☎ 053 9129955.

Approach Large-scale BA or Imray chart recommended. To avoid hazards lying off shore, approach is advised from position 52°09'·25N 06°35'·20W, 3ca west of St Patrick's Br, marked (April–September) by port and stb Lt buoys Fl.R & G.6s. Sight Ldg marks, white with red stripe, on foreshore (Oc.4s by night) bearing 007° for channel 1·9m CD. Reported to be silting. Shoaling steeply either side.

Entrance Approaching hbr entrance keep within 30m of western breakwater then turn to port to leave it and the south

quay to port. By night the breakwater light shows sectored Lt. Q 269°-R-354°-G-003°-R-077°. Approach on the lead lights.
Leave east quay to stb then bear round to stb to head N by W for the marina.

Berthing Finger pontoons with electricity and water.

Facilities Fuel, gas and chandlery available. Two mini-supermarkets. Good restaurants and pubs. Toilets and showers at Harbour Office. Showers and toilets at Stella Maris Centre.

Warning A sharp lookout should be kept for lobster pots.

(Kilmore Quay HM is also HM for Rosslare and Wexford.)

For passage notes Milford Haven to Kilmore Quay see page 193.

ROSSLARE
Not suitable for yachts and should only be used in emergency.

The only place to moor is at the quay furthest west from the ferry terminal. This is used by fishing boats and small commercial vessels so yachts should not be left un-attended. Uncomfortable in strong NE'lies.

☎ As Kilmore Quay, HM 053992995.

Ireland – East Coast

CARNSORE POINT TO DUBLIN BAY
Charts BA 1787, 1468; SC 5621; Imray C61, C62

Passage lights	*BA No*
Arklow S Superbuoy	5845
Q(6)+LFl.15s *AIS*	
Racon(O) (–––)	
Wicklow Head	5850
Fl(3)15s37m23M	
Kish Bank Lt Tower	5865
Fl(2)20s29m21M	
Racon(T) (–) AIS	
Dun Laoghaire	5872
Fl(2)R.8s16m17M	
(E breakwater)	

Tidal Streams DS (related to Dover) in middle of St George's Channel – +0600NE; HWD SW. Outside Tuskar Rock –0530 NE; HWD SW, 2·5kn; there is a strong set onto the rock. Streams change about 1½hrs earlier between the Irish banks and the shore. They set across these banks. From Land's End it can be dangerous to come in W of the Tuskar Rock, but coming from the W yachts need not leave this rock to port in settled weather.

WEXFORD HARBOUR
Chart BA 1772; SC 5621; Imray C61
HW Cobh +0126

MHWS	MHWN	MLWN	MLWS
1·7m	1·4m	0·5m	0·4m

Once entered, this hbr is completely safe, sheltered and charming but route in is

At night, the passage from Carnsore Point to Rosslare should only be attempted with care and competent navigation. Rosslare is not a comfortable harbour for yachts but, if need be, a berth may be found alongside a fishing boat at the quay west of the ferry terminals. From Tuskar to Dublin Bay the normal route is outside the Blackwater bank, inside the Arklow Superbuoy, thence past Wicklow Head and through Dalkey Sound, quite clean except close to island side, or through Muglins Sound, but this has rocks with under 2m on each side. By night go outside Muglins Lt Fl.5s14m11M.

Keep away from **Arklow Bank**, a dangerous shallow ridge with seven windfarm turbines Fl.Y.5s14m10M. Approaching Dublin Bay from E make Kish Bank Lt F, thence to S Burford S card Lt buoy, leaving N Kish N card Lt buoy to port. In Dublin Bay, yachts are required to yield clear channel to commercial shipping.

circuitous. The approach and entry channel are well marked, but subject to change: a 2m draught vessel should have no difficulty between HW–0300 and HW+0200.

Approach Dangerous in strong winds between S and E. Otherwise make for Wexford

IRELAND

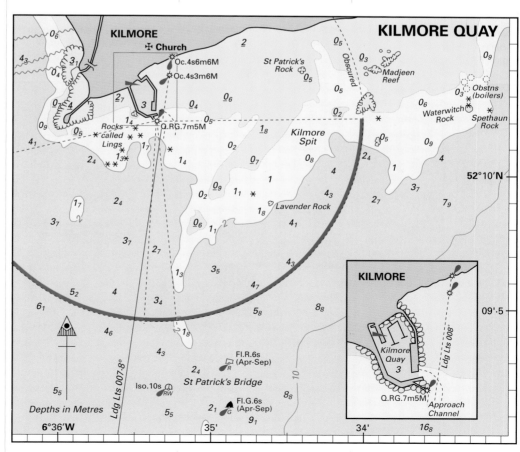

KILMORE

✝ Church
Oc.4s6m6M
Oc.4s3m6M

KILMORE QUAY

St Patrick's Rock

Obscured

Madjeen Reef

Obstns (boilers)

Waterwitch Rock

Spethaun Rock

Rocks called Lings

Q.RG.7m5M

Kilmore Spit

52°10'N

Lavender Rock

KILMORE

09'·5

Kilmore Quay

Ldg Lts 008°

Approach Channel

Q.RG.7m5M

Fl.R.6s (Apr–Sep)

St Patrick's Bridge

Iso.10s

Ldg Lts 007·8°

Fl.G.6s (Apr–Sep)

Depths in Metres

6°36'W   35'   34'   16

Bar, a RW safewater Lt buoy LFl.10s, approx position 52°19'.1N 6°19'.4W. From the N keep outside the 5m contour to avoid the Dogger Bank and the unmarked dangerous Slaney wreck which lies 8ca NW of Bar Buoy.

Entrance It is essential to find the bar buoy. The channel is marked with lateral lit buoys; head for No.4 (R can) about 8ca to the WSW, then follow the R and G buoys which may not agree with the plan, to 52°20'.13N 6°26'.8W to the S of the Black Man, a lit stb bn marking the end of the training wall which covers. Thereafter the water is deep to the quay. The banks in the entrance are variable in depth and the information in the plan must not be relied upon in detail. Strangers should contact, preferably in advance one of those listed below.

Berthing Four visitors' moorings marked 'Bank of Ireland' opposite Town Quay. Berthing against town quay not recommended; anchoring the other side of the channel is comfortable.

Facilities Good shops, restaurants, boatyard, YC, fuel and water along the quays.

Warning The banks in the entrance are variable in depth and position and the information on the plan must not be relied upon in detail. Strangers should telephone Wexford Boating Club who will give latest information and supply pilot if thought necessary.

☏/VHF HM (As Kilmore Quay) 053 992995 or VHF 16

(occas): Wexford Boating Club 053 9147504 (office hrs), 053 9122039 (evening or weekend) VHF 16, 69: John Sherwood, Rosslare 053 9122875 (shop hrs) or 9122713 (home).

ARKLOW

Chart BA 633; SC 5621; Imray C61

HW Dublin (North Wall) –0315sp –0200np
DS Dover –0100SSW

MHWS	MHWN	MLWN	MLWS
1·3m	1·2m	0·9m	0·6m

Bar and river to wharves dredged to not less than 3·5m. Dock dredged to 3·7m but there is a drying part on SW side between LB and ship hoist. Note very small tidal range.

Entrance Narrow and difficult under sail. Dangerous in gales from N through E to SE. S pierhead has 10m steel Tr, Fl.WR.6s11m13M. N pierhead Lt Fl.G.7s. The dock on S side with 10m wide entrance provides perfect shelter against SE quay. Lie alongside fishing boat, many are little used or layed-up. But keep clear of Pilot launch. There is approx 2m in centre of River to NW as far as ASC premises where there is a visitors' pontoon and a small slip has been built. Through a gap in the NE bank 1ca NW of the dock entrance there is access to a small marina with visitors' berths. Holding poor in river and liable to silting.

Facilities All facilities including boat yard, chandlers and engineers but no sailmaker. Showers by donation at RNLI shore building or at marina. EC Wednesday. Good pubs and restaurants.

☏ Marina 0402 39901

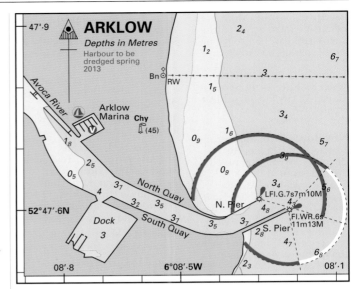

WICKLOW

Chart BA 633; SC 5621; Imray C61

HW Dublin (North Wall) –0019
DS HWD SW

MHWS	MHWN	MLWN	MLWS
2·7m	2·3m	1·1m	0·7m

The hbr faces N and is exposed in NE winds; inner part offers complete shelter.

Approach Pass between West pier head Iso.G.4s and East pier head Fl.WR.5s.

Entrance For inner harbour steer SSE between outer piers towards W boathouse; when face of ferry quay opens turn sharp to stb. Keep front of RNLI boathouse open to avoid shallows on SE side.

Berthing
• Anchorage in outer harbour midway between ends of W pier and quay in 2–3m outside YC moorings.

• In inner harbour the S side is being developed for use by fishing boats and yachts; if the quays there are not available a yacht may go alongside the steamer quay, beyond knuckle, with permission from HM – office in middle of pier.
• Moor against climbing frames on inside of East pier.

Facilities Fuel and water on S quay. All stores and facilities except sailmaker. EC Thursday.

DUN LAOGHAIRE

Chart BA 1447; SC 5621; Imray C61, C62

HW Dublin (North Wall) –0003
DS off entrance:
Dover –0130SE +0500NW

MHWS	MHWN	MLWN	MLWS
4·lm	3·4m	1·5m	0·8m

A large artificial hbr on S side of Dublin Bay, always available. Ferry port. Major

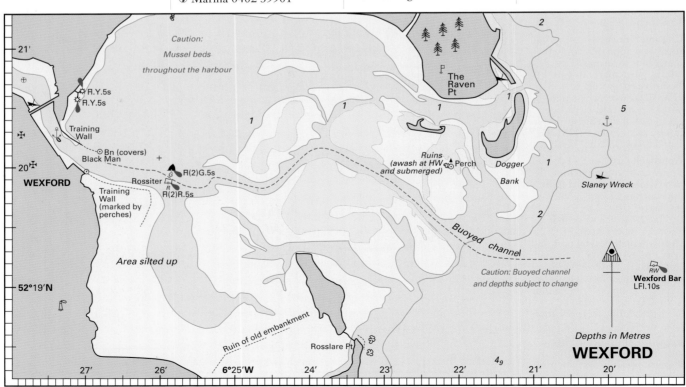

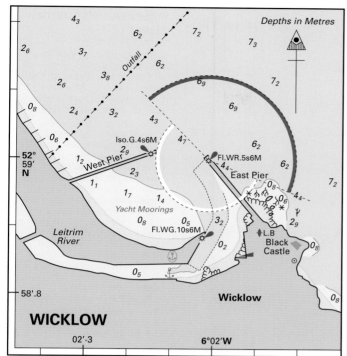

WICKLOW

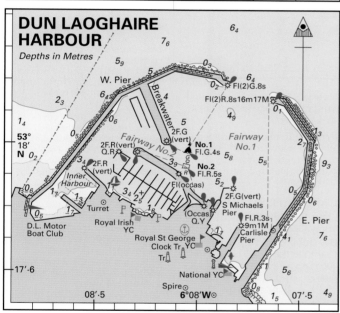

DUN LAOGHAIRE HARBOUR
Depths in Metres

DUBLIN

Charts BA 1415, 1447; SC 5621; Imray C61

HW Dublin (North Wall)

MHWS	MHWN	MLWN	MLWS
4·1m	3·4m	1·5m	0·7m

A major hbr in the River Liffey and its estuary. Deep water, all weather entrance with channel dredged to 7·8m through the bar. A capital city well worth a visit.

The former marina style pontoon, 'Dublin City Moorings' on the north bank of the Liffey a short distance below the O'Connell Street Bridge has been closed and at present there are no plans for re-opening. This reach of the river is still accessible to pleasure vessels through the lifting bridge 'East Link' and the elegant swing 'Samuel Beckett' bridge. But these are only opened at about 2000 and may be denied if heavy traffic is expected. 24hrs notice of a request to open is required, call *East Link* VHF 12 or, failing a response, *Dublin Port Control* VHF 12 (13). There are no facilities for yachts above the opening bridges.

Traffic control Dublin Bay is a large area of relatively shallow water and large commercial vessels comply with three TSS. These are:
1. The S Burford buoy to the Dublin Bay buoy Mo(A)10s.
2. The N Burford to the Dublin Bay buoy.
3. The Dublin Bay to Poolbeg LtHo Fl.R.4s10M (hbr entrance).

Small craft should keep to the stb side of the channel until just before the ferry terminals then,

crossing to the S side at the first terminal on the N bank. They are advised to avoid the triangle bounded by the Dublin Bay and the two Burford buoys. In these areas, and within the port, yachts should accord large vessels the freedom of manoeuvre required by Colregs Rule 9. Vessels should monitor Dublin VTS on VHF 12 (13) at all times.

✆ Dublin Port Office 003 53 1 887 6000.

Approach From north rounding Baily Head (Howth peninsula) endeavour to keep on or near a line to No.3 Bar buoy IQ.G. From south round Dalkey Island and south of the TSS to No.4 IQ.R. At No.4 cross directly to No.3.

Approaching from the east in heavy weather it is advisable to avoid the Burford and Kish banks over each of which seas can break heavily.

Entrance From No.3 Bar keep well to stb side of channel to avoid commercial and ferry traffic. Head 272° for No.5 Bar Fl.G.2s then leave North Bull Lt Fl.G.4s10M close to stb. Under power keep within the buoyed channel to enter the river. The main commercial docks indent the north shore of the river. Keep sharp lookout for ferries arriving and departing the RoRo docks; at No.14 buoy cross, at right angles, to the S quays and then stay to the port side.

Berthing Poolbeg Marina, ½ mile before the lifting bridge, on the S bank opposite the end of the docks offers a warm welcome to visitors. All marina facilities including Diesel.

yachting centre. Exposed to NE and E gales when the outer and eastern part of the hbr may become untenable to moored and anchored small craft.

Two new breakwaters have been built within the hbr, the ends of which are marked by 2F.G(vert) and 2F.R(vert) lights. These enclose a new marina in complete shelter.

Entrance Allow for tide across hbr mouth. Keep well clear of ferries, which have right of way. When through the main entrance make SSW to sight two fairway buoys, Dun Laoghaire No.1 G con Lt buoy Fl.G.4s and Dun Laoghaire No.2 R can Lt buoy Fl.R.5s. Pass between these and shape course to pass between the new breakwater heads to gain access to the marina.

Berthing Call marina control 80 and M for advice to visitors' berths.

Facilities All supplies. EC Wednesday. Chandlery and boatyard. Boat hoist. Hotels and restaurants. Frequent DART rly to Dublin. Maritime Museum within a few hundred yards.

✆ HM 280 1130; Marina 01 202 0040. Port VHF 14; Marina M, 37, 80.

DUBLIN BAY

This is only some 20-minute walk from the city centre: O'Connel Street, the heart of Dublin, shops, pubs, restaurants, theatres, museums and galleries.

☎/**VHF** 01 6889983, VHF 37/80.

Alternatively the marinas at both Dun Loaghaire and Howth offer a ready welcome, with quick and frequent access to Dublin City by the 'Dublin Light Railway' (The DART)

HOWTH

Chart BA 1415; SC 5621; Imray C61, C62

HW Dublin (North Wall) –0006

DS Dover –0600N HWD S

MHWS	MHWN	MLWN	MLWS
4·1m	3·3m	1·3m	0·5m

This hbr, fishing port to W, separate marina to E, affords excellent shelter and facilities.

Approach and Entrance From E leave to stb Rowan Rocks E card Lt buoy, Howth G con Lt buoy Fl.G.5s and South Rowan G con Lt buoy Q.G. Give E pier head Lt Fl(2)WR.7·5s a berth of at least 50m; do not turn into the hbr until it is well open; enter nearer W pier-head Lt Fl.G.3s. Keep watch for fishing boats leaving. Inside hbr is the Trawler Breakwater Head Q.R.

Berthing In marina operated by Howth YC. Yachts are recommended to call on VHF 37(M) or 80 (calling and working channel) before entering the hbr. Follow the port and stb-hand spar buoys marking the dredged channel toward the marina. A gabionade 30m long and 2m wide is positioned to shelter the marina. Leave this to port then follow berthing instructions received on VHF to take you to allocated mooring or secure at waiting berth, first pontoon.

Facilities Water, diesel, Wi-Fi, showers, clubhouse in hbr area. Grid and boat lift. Shops, hotels, restaurants and pubs within walking distance. Frequent 'DART' rly to Dublin.

☎ Marina 01 839 2777.

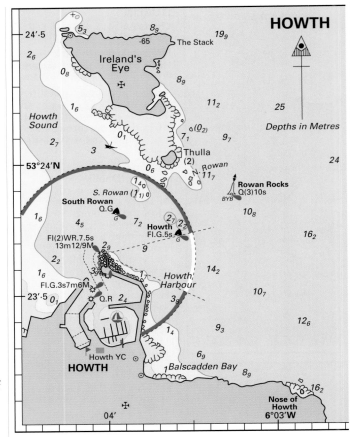

MALAHIDE

Chart BA 633; SC 5621; Imray C62

HW Dublin (North Wall) +0002

DS Dover –0600N HWD S

MHWS	MHWN	MLWN	MLWS
4·2m	3·2m	1·1m	0·5m

Approach Entry not advised in strong onshore winds and frequently shifting bar. Otherwise enter on adequate rise of tide. Make for small con RW safe water Lt buoy Fl.10s. Observe Malahide town chapel spire. Bearing 266° gives approximate dredged deepest water (min 0·3m) over bar but watch soundings.

Bar 0·3m. Less water reported 2008. Least water is approx 2m less than at fairway buoy.

Entrance Enter at HW±0300. Flood 3kn, ebb 3½kn. Outer channel is buoyed and dredged (1995). Follow transit of church spire and right hand edge of Grand Hotel and then between moorings. Bear round bend to stb. Marina will be seen to port.

Berthing In marina as directed VHF M. Showers and laundry facilities. Diesel at fuel pontoon. Depth 2·4m.
☎ 00 353(0) 184 54129.

CARLINGFORD LOUGH

Chart BA 2800; SC 5621; Imray C62

HW Dublin (North Wall)
Cranfield Point –0027sp, –0011np

MHWS	MHWN	MLWN	MLWS
4·8m	4·3m	1·8m	0·9m

Warrenpoint –0020sp, –0010np

MHWS	MHWN	MLWN	MLWS
5·1m	4·1m	1·7m	0·7m

HOLYHEAD TO DUBLIN

Charts BA 1411; Imray C61

A passage of some 55M. The tides ebb and flood on the Irish and Welsh coasts at much the same time. Thus, all other things being equal, the north and south sets will more or less balance.

However, leaving Holyhead, there is a westerly, helpful, component in the tide flow from about +0200 to +0500 HW Dover. Say +0300 to +0600 HW Holyhead. So there is a distance benefit in starting between these times. Additionally the tide will carry you away from the concentration of shipping at the southern end of the Holyhead traffic separation zone. But avoid allowing your vessel to be swept south of the North Stack as there are overfalls between that headland and the South Stack.

Once clear of the land set a tide corrected course to leave the Kish Bank Light tower to port. The waters to its south, over the Kish Bank, can be turbulent.

On reaching the Kish Tower one must decide whether one is to pass, dependent upon conditions, to the north or south of the Burford Bank. This is marked with the 'North' and with the 'South' Burford cardinal buoys.

Dublin Port Authority operates traffic separation schemes between these buoys and the Dublin Bay RW buoy. Yachts are strongly requested to keep well clear of the triangle formed by the three marks.

When a position is reached, either a mile to the north or to the south of the Dublin Bay buoy, head for the Poolbeg Light house. But keep outside the 'maintained channel' and enter Dublin port in accordance with the guidance to be found in the Dublin entry.

If ones arrival at the port is likely to be in darkness the recommendation is to divert either to Howth, to the north of, or to Dun Laoghaire, on the south side of, Dublin Bay then to enter Dublin Port in daylight.

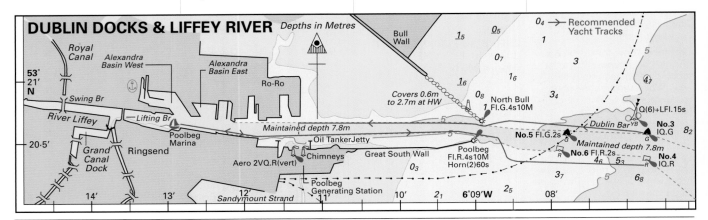

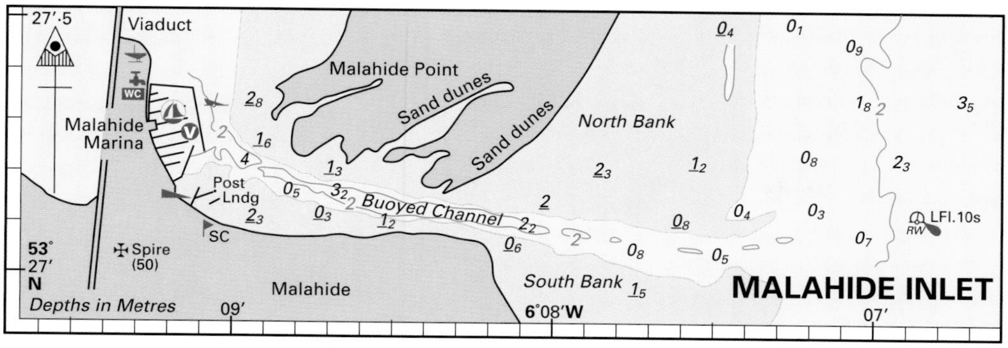
27'.5
Viaduct
Malahide Point
Sand dunes
Sand dunes
North Bank
Malahide Marina
Post Lndg
SC
Spire (50)
53° 27' N
Malahide
Depths in Metres
09'
Buoyed Channel
South Bank
6°08'W
LFl.10s
RW
07'
MALAHIDE INLET

Carlingford Lough lies 39M N of Dublin, 28M S of Strangford, and may be located by Carlingford Mt, 585m, some 5M NW of entrance and by the Mourne mountains to the N.

There are shoals E and W of the approach within 1M of the entrance points, Ballagan on W and Cranfield on E. The whole entrance is blocked inside at LW by the Limestone Rocks, except the Cut, a narrow channel 1M long on NE side.

Approach
Tidal streams Weak outside, 3·5kn in buoyed approach channel, 4·5kn just E of LtHo, 1·5kn between entrance and Greenore, 5kn off Greenore, 2·5kn between Stalka and Watson rks, 1·5kn off Carlingford, quiet above Killowen Point. Between LtHo and No.5 buoy the flood tends to N; there is a S-going eddy on flood along E side of Block House Is. Otherwise the streams follow channels. Small yachts cannot enter or leave against the tide and should have reliable power or leading wind even with fair tide. A heavy and disturbed sea occurs with a southerly wind against the ebb immediately outside the entrance. In onshore gales the entrance is impassable.

From NE or SE, leave to stb Hellyhunter S card Lt buoy, From S, keep a mile or more off Ballagan Point. Cranfield Point (not conspic) with houses bearing 016° or No.2 R can Lt buoy bearing N will lead to entrance.

Entrance Steer on Vidal Ldg Lts, Oc.3s on RW piles 1M inside the Point, 310°, along buoyed and lit channel, leaving Haulbowline LtHo ¼M to port, till Greenore lt, Fl.R7·5s, bears 287°, when steer for it. Proceed between further lighted lateral Lt buoys till abreast Killowen Pt, hence 355° to anchor off Wood House, or off Rostrevor quay, 1–4m. Alternatively turn to port at No.18 R can Lt buoy steer 185° to Carlingford marina or just beyond same to anchor off Carlingford village.

Anchorages
- ½M N of Carlingford Harbour in 3m, or berth alongside either pier in hbr, which dries.
- Between Killowen Point and Rostrevor.
- In SW wind, off Greer's quay.
- Carlingford Sailing Club have laid four complimentary visitors' moorings 4ca north of the hbr for deep draught vessels and four similar for shallow draught at about half the distance.

Berthing In Carlingford marina. Do not turn until No.18 port-hand buoy. Depth 3·5m, 30 visitors' berths.

Facilities at marina include launderette, restaurant and boat lift ✆ 042 9373073. Shopping in village 10 minutes' walk.

In S wind the lough is disturbed by squalls from the hills. Landing is impossible at Rostrevor pier at LW, but Carlingford Lough YC just N of Killowen Point has a slip where one can always land, though caution needed at LW. Water at Greenore and Warrenpoint; stores at Greenore and Carlingford, best at Warrenpoint, there are reasonable stores at Rostrevor.

Note The NE shore of the lough is Northern Ireland, the SW the Republic. EC: Carlingford Thursday, Warrenpoint Wednesday.

ARDGLASS

Chart BA 633; SC 5621; Imray C62

HW Belfast +0012

MHWS	MHWN	MLWN	MLWS
5·2m	4·2m	1·7m	0·7m

Pier Harbour 1M N of Ringfad Point, a conical hill with tr. Always available, has 2–3m. SE winds send in heavy swell. There is an inner basin with 3m at HW, bottom deep mud, affording perfect shelter at all times. A marina (20 visitors') has been dredged in the bay west of Churn Rock. Rocks extend from both sides of the shore outside the hbr entrance.

Approach Give shore on either side a fair berth. At night, approach in the W sector of WRG Lt Iso.4s on inner pier 311°.

Entrance Leave quay pier head Lt Fl.R.3s to port. For the fishing hbr turn to port leaving S card bn to stb. This bn marks rocks to the W of the pier head and W of fairway.

For the marina leave the S card well to port, R buoy to port, a W card buoy to stb, a R bn to port and turn to port at a R can Lt buoy Fl(2)R. Then buoyed and perched narrow channel to marina. Call VHF 80 or listen for verbal instructions, not 24hr.

Berthing In marina or, if no room, berth alongside and contact HM.

Anchorage In quiet weather, for overnight stop, space to anchor in 4m can be found 100m N of the pier head.

Facilities All supplies. Hotel, pubs, restaurant. Bus to Downpatrick.

✆/VHF Marina 028 44 842332, VHF 37, M, 80.

STRANGFORD LOUGH

Chart BA 2156, 2159 (Narrows); SC 5621;
Imray C62

HW Belfast

Killard Point +0011sp, +0021np

MHWS	MHWN	MLWN	MLWS
4·5m	3·8m	1·2m	0·5m

Strangford +0147sp, +0157np

MHWS	MHWN	MLWN	MLWS
3·6m	3·1m	0·9m	0·4m

Killyleagh +0200

MHWS	MHWN
3·8m	3·3m

Beyond Strangford Narrows lies Strangford Lough, a picturesque area of some 100km² of navigable water, magnificent for small craft.

Strangford Narrows

Approach In strong winds between SSW and E no yacht should approach or leave the entrance on the ebb, when the sea breaks heavily outside. In such conditions departure should be timed for the young flood. Otherwise enter with the flood and leave with the ebb. The stream runs true, out of the

DUBLIN BAY TO FAIR HEAD

Charts BA 44, 2093, 2198, 2199; SC 5621;
Imray C62, C64

Passage lights	*BA No.*
Ben of Howth–Baily Fl.15s41m18M	5898
Rockabill Fl.WR.12s45m17/13M AIS	5904
Carlingford-Haulbowline Fl(3)10s32m10M AIS	5928
St John's Point Q(2)7·5s37m25M Fl.WR.3s15/11M AIS	5958
South Rock R pillar buoy Fl(3)R.30s7m9M Racon(T) (–) *AIS*	5966
Mew Is Fl(4)30s37m24M Racon(O) (– – –) AIS	5976
Black Head Fl.3s45m27M AIS	6028
Maidens Fl(3)15s29m23M+Fl.R.5s8M Racon(M) (– –) AIS	6042

Tidal streams DS All related to Dover. Between Hill of Howth and St John's Point – +0600N; HWD S; strong S of Rockabill Point, weak further N and negligible S of St John's Point. Between St John's Point and Fair Head – HWD N and NW; +0600 S and SE; weak near St John's Point, strong N of Belfast Lough, reaching 4·5kn in entrance to North Channel. There is an inshore eddy on the SE stream between Torr Hd and Fair Hd, –0400NW for 10hrs.

TSS orientated NE to SW 1·3M SE of Bailey.

Ballyquintin Point, E of the entrance to Strangford Lough, should be given a berth of ½M.

There are extensive rocks off Kearney Point 3¼M NE of Ballyquintin Point. South Rock LtV is moored 2M E of South Rock, marked by a disused LtHo 18m high. North Rocks, 1½M E of Ringboy Point, must be passed at least 1½ca to E. Donaghadee Sound, *see plan*, inside Copeland Is is the normal passage for yachts sailing along the coast; S entrance marked by buoys.

SE of Muck Is there is a race which should be taken with the stream. The Maidens are two dangerous groups of rocks within 4M of Ballygalley Head separated by a channel 1M wide.

Rogerstown Inlet in the bay facing Lambay Is provides sheltered anchorage for up to 1·7m draught. Drogheda, on River Boyne, provides good shelter for a night but has no special berths for yachts. Portavogie, some 8M N of Strangford Lough, is at present so congested that yachts should use it only in emergency.

Carnlough Harbour, some 11M N of Larne, provides shelter for yachts drawing less than 1·5m, and for these is a useful port for a passage to or from the Scottish coast.

Similarly Red Bay, some 10 miles south of Fair Head can make a useful anchorage in its SW corner, S of Cushendall, when awaiting the tide on passage north or south. The tide swilling past outside the bay seems to shut out the swell. But it should not be used in strong onshore winds.

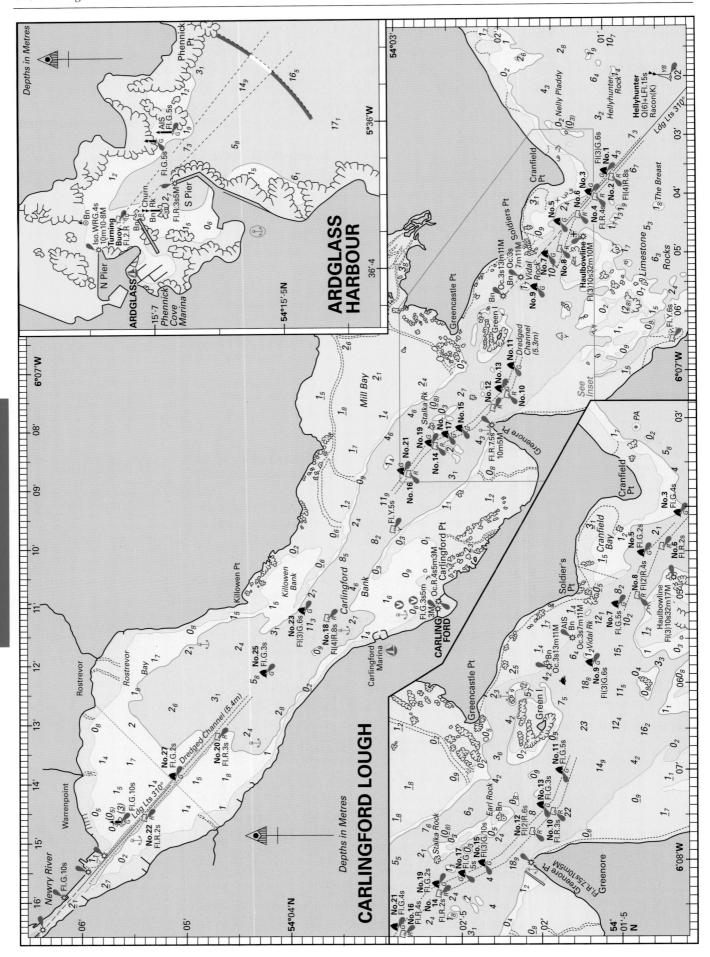

ARDGLASS HARBOUR

CARLINGFORD LOUGH

IRELAND

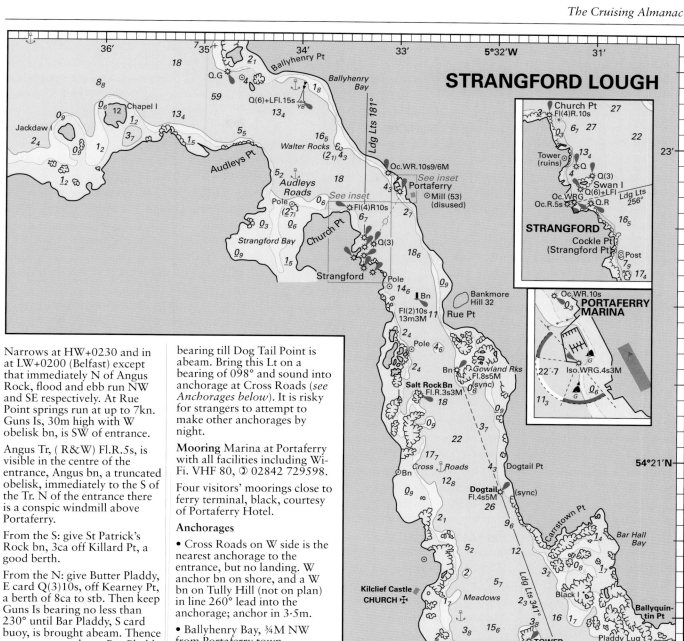

STRANGFORD LOUGH

STRANGFORD

PORTAFERRY MARINA

IRELAND

Narrows at HW+0230 and in at LW+0200 (Belfast) except that immediately N of Angus Rock, flood and ebb run NW and SE respectively. At Rue Point springs run at up to 7kn. Guns Is, 30m high with W obelisk bn, is SW of entrance.

Angus Tr, (R&W) Fl.R.5s, is visible in the centre of the entrance, Angus bn, a truncated obelisk, immediately to the S of the Tr. N of the entrance there is a conspic windmill above Portaferry.

From the S: give St Patrick's Rock bn, 3ca off Killard Pt, a good berth.

From the N: give Butter Pladdy, E card Q(3)10s, off Kearney Pt, a berth of 8ca to stb. Then keep Guns Is bearing no less than 230° until Bar Pladdy, S card buoy, is brought abeam. Thence turn to west to leave Bar Pladdy to stb. Stand on 2ca then turn to 324° to enter the Narrows.

From seaward: make for Strangford Fairway buoy RWVS, Fl.10s. Then steer to leave Bar Pladdy S card as above.

Entrance By E channel, when N end of Portaferry town comes open W of Bankmore Hill and Rue Point steer 341°, leaving Bar Pladdy buoy to stb and Pladdy Lug W pile bn at least 1ca to stb and Angus bn to port, into the Narrows until Kilclief castle bears 265°, then Meadows shoal has been left to port. Thence in mid-channel to pass between Gowland Rocks bn Fl.8s to stb, and poles and bns marking shoal water to port. NW of Gowland Rocks strong eddies in midstream. Then anchor as required.

By night keep Dog Tail Point Oc(4)G.10s in transit with Gowland Rocks LFl.8s 341° until Salt Rock bn Fl.R.3s bears 330°. Keep Salt Rock bn on this bearing till Dog Tail Point is abeam. Bring this Lt on a bearing of 098° and sound into anchorage at Cross Roads (*see Anchorages below*). It is risky for strangers to attempt to make other anchorages by night.

Mooring Marina at Portaferry with all facilities including Wi-Fi. VHF 80, ☏ 02842 729598.

Four visitors' moorings close to ferry terminal, black, courtesy of Portaferry Hotel.

Anchorages

• Cross Roads on W side is the nearest anchorage to the entrance, but no landing. W anchor bn on shore, and a W bn on Tully Hill (not on plan) in line 260° lead into the anchorage; anchor in 3·5m.

• Ballyhenry Bay, ¾M NW from Portaferry town

• In Audleys Roads between small stone pier and perch. S and W inside of this is all shoal.

Strangford Lough

Navigation in the Lough near LW is obstructed by numerous shoals, called Pladdies. It is highly advisable to use a large scale chart, such as BA2156. Many hazards are now marked by bns or buoys, a number of which are lit.

Leave the northern end of Strangford Narrows between Audley Pt to port and Ballyhenry Pt, marked with bn, Q.G, to stb; head 305° for some ½M, this brings you to the approach line 270° to Killyleagh Town Rock RW bn, Fl(2)WRG 5s.

• **Killyleagh** Leave the Town Rk bn to stb to take you to the town with pontoon, slip, YC and sail board centre. Anchor SSW of Town Rk bn in 2–4m, or secure to one on the Y visitors' buoys.

Facilities Water, fuel and gas at quay, available HW±0200. Stores, bus to Belfast. YC ☎ 028 9258 7200.

Alternatively, to proceed further north in the Lough, when ½M beyond Ballyhenry Pt turn to stb to 350° leaving Limestone Rk bn, Q.R., 2ca to port.

• **Ringhaddy** Cruising Club. After Limestone Rk turn to port and head for conspic White House keeping it on bearing 317°. Leave Prawle Island to stb then Warren Pt to port and Eagle Hill Pt (Islandmore) to stb. Follow Eagle Pt round at about ½ca distance into the enclosed, sheltered and attractive waters off Rinhaddy pontoon with Fl.R.5s end light. Deep water to anchor and the tide runs at 2kn. Secure temporarily to club pontoon and seek advice to secure to a vacant mooring. No facilities. ☎ 028 4483 0520 or 078 1285 6060.

• **Kircubbin** Sailing Club and Village. From about 2ca E of Limestone Rk head approx 005° to leave Long Sheelagh shoal, E card bn Q(3)10s to port. Then turn to 045° to leave Tip Reef S card Q(6) + LFl.15s to port. Follow the buoyed channel between Hoskyns Shoal and Sand Pladdy. Alter course to 005°, passing between Woman's Rk and Black Neb. Continue ¾M to anchor in 2–8m off the slip in Kircubbin Bay. This anchorage is completely exposed to the W.

Facilities Water at SC. Stores in village. Bus to Belfast with connections to both airports. SC ☎ 028 4277 1707.

• **Ballydorn** on the W side of the lough is the location of the Down Cruising Club. At Long Sheelagh bn turn to port and head 348° towards Mahee Pt on the extreme E tip of Mahee Is sectored lt. When some 6ca beyond Dead Man's Rk E card bn and some mile short of Mahee Pt turn W across Mahee Roads. (Caution: many racing buoys). Head for the channel between Rainey Is and Sketrick Is, only 1·5m at LW. Inside the sheltered and picturesque sound off the LtV clubhouse there is 3–4m. There are four visitors' moorings. Berth temporarily at the LtV for advice, water and fuel. ☎ 028 9754 1663.

These are but four places of interest. There are six other yacht clubs in the lough. The chart will reveal countless picturesque anchorages, islands and channels to be explored by both the long-distance cruiser and local potterer! Whatever the weather, a sheltered anchorage can always be found.

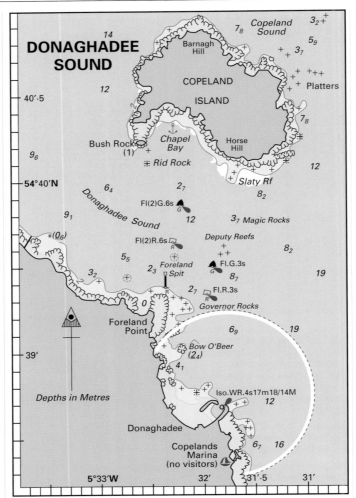

DONAGHADEE SOUND

Depths in Metres

BELFAST LOUGH

Chart BA 1753; SC 5621; Imray C64

HW Belfast.

MHWS	MHWN	MLWN	MLWS
3·5m	3·0m	1·1m	0·4m

Approach Tidal streams run strongly in the offing reaching 4·6kn at springs and may raise a big lop. The lough is 10M long, depths decreasing from 12–3m. From the south, when rounding Orlock Pt avoid Briggs Rocks ¾M offshore, R can buoy Fl(2)R.10s. Thence give the shores a reasonable offing. The navigable area is considerably reduced by shoal banks towards the head of the lough.

BELFAST HARBOUR

This is at the head of the Lough, with a marina 10 min walk from city centre.

Approach The RW Fairway buoy, Iso.4s6M AIS, in 54°42'·32N 5°42'·30W is at the entrance to the main channel, marked by two pairs of lateral buoys, followed by a narrow dredged channel marked by lit beacons. Before entering the beaconed channel call *Harbour Control* VHF 12 or ☎ 02890 553015 to state position and intention to berth in the marina. The channel can be entered between bns 11 and 12,

after which keep to the channel, the south side dries.

Entrance In the hbr take the centre of three channels. When approaching the first bridge the marina is to port in Abercorn Basin. It has finger berths and, alongside pontoons, berths for vessels up to 40m and 4m draft. Security gate access code will be given by mooring ticket machines on main pontoon at base of entry bridge. Payment by credit or debit card.

DONAGHADEE SOUND

Chart BA 1753; Imray C64

DS Dover HWD NW; +0600SE. The sp tide runs up to 4½kn

Whether making for Belfast Lough from South or coming from the lough bound south, passage through this sound can save nearly three miles in distance and, if favourable tides are taken, an hour or more on the voyage time.

From the SE identify R can Lt buoy Fl.R.3s and G con Lt buoy Fl.G.3s (Governor and Deputy respectively) passing obliquely midway between on a course of about 290°. When abreast the G buoy alter on to 340° to leave second R can Lt buoy Fl(2)R.6s Foreland Spit to port. When abreast of that alter to 310° which leads out of Sound.

From the NW enter Sound midway between Copeland Is and the coast and identify Foreland Spit R can Lt buoy which will be left to starboard. Pass within 1ca of it and when abreast alter course for the R can buoy Governor leaving the G con buoy Deputy to port. With a SE-going tide be careful not to let the Deputy and Governor buoys get in line as there is a reef close NNE of Deputy buoy.

Adjacent there is a plan showing route to city and facilities such as chandlery.

Facilities Electricity included. No fuel.

BANGOR MARINA

Marina with all facilities and services. Before approach call on VHF 80 for a berth, giving an ETA. You will be too busy later. Visitors' berths are normally on the south pointing fingers of pontoon E. On approach the entrance is obscured; from the north, leave the end of the North Breakwater, Iso.R.12s9M,

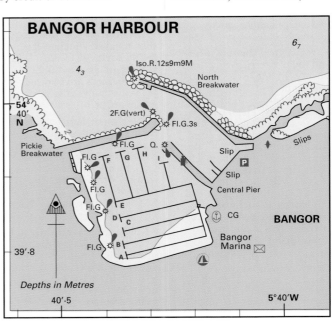

BANGOR HARBOUR

Depths in Metres

some 100m to port. At night, it is vital to identify this light amongst the many shore lights before making an approach. When to W of the pierhead turn to port to a position 75m S of it. The entrance will be visible; leave the dolphin 2F.G(vert) on the end of the Pickie Breakwater some 30m to stb, likewise the dolphin Fl.G.3s. There is then a very sharp turn to stb following round the S side of the breakwater to enter a well-lit marina. Leave the pontoons H, G, and F to port. Turn to port leaving all the Fl.G. marks to stb; the first opening to port is the access lane to pontoon E. Bangor is a prosperous town where all requirements can be obtained. Fuel on W side Central Pier. ☎ 02891 453297.

Anchorages

• Anchor in Ballyholme Bay in 3·5 to 5·5m exposed to winds from NW to NE.
• Cultra, 5M W of Bangor. Anchor in offshore winds in 3·5 to 4m outside yacht moorings. Water, diesel from RNIYC,

stores at Holywood 1M. Boatyard and slipping facilities. Contact Secretary on ☎ 01232 428041 for visitors' mooring and launch service.

CARRICKFERGUS

Carrickfergus Marina about 330m W of Carrickfergus harbour. Approach on 320° to marina retaining wall which has Ldg bns with top marks. Entrance is marked by Q.G and Q.R bns but the R is obscured by the breakwater from 205°-305°. Thus when using the Ldg

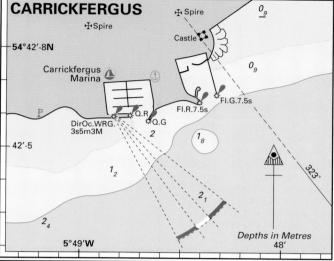

bns entrance will not open up until you are nearly opposite the stb mole. By night; the west wall has a sectored light Oc.WRG.3s near the pier head. Approach in W sector 320°. Turn sharply to stb to enter and, when in, to port.

Facilities as expected of a modern marina including chandlery and sailmaker. All stores in town.
☎ 028 9336 6666, VHF 37, 80.

Anchorage W of Carrickfergus Bank in 2m 2ca offshore at Greenisland.

LARNE LOUGH

Chart BA 1237; SC 5621; Imray C64

HW Belfast +0005 DS HWD N

MHWS	MHWN	MLWN	MLWS
2·8m	2·5m	0·8m	0·4m

Larne Lough affords the best anchorage shelter between Belfast Lough and Lough Foyle.

Approach The entrance lies 4M S of the Maidens. The approach is obstructed by Hunter Rock, 0·8m, marked by N and S card Lt buoys, situated 2½M 036° from Ferris Point, the E point of the entrance. On entering steer between quays to stb and two pile bns to port, Fl.R.3s and Fl(2)R.6s respectively. By night Ldg Lts, Oc.4s 184°, lead in through the entrance.

Anchorages

• In 5m ¾M S of Ferris Point, SW of the Yellow Stone (painted occasionally) 1ca E of the L-shaped wharf opposite No.7 buoy.
• Anchoring off Curran Pt is permitted NW of a line from the Pt to No.5 buoy and SW of a line from No.5 buoy to S end of ferry quays but local yachts leave no room for visitors; VHF 37 for berthing instructions.
• Outside a shallow bay 1M SE of first anchorage, ½ca offshore in 2–3m NW of moored boats. Beware wreck ¾ca off the shore of the bay and 1¼ca SE of its NW tip. Water at Wymers Pier, petrol and stores in town, diesel by arrangement with Harbour Office. Repairs. Ferry from Island Magee to Larne.

Moorings There are visitors' moorings in vicinity of the first anchorage above.

Caution This is a busy ferry port and it is advisable to call Larne Port Control VHF 14 before approaching.

Frequent ferry service up to 24 sailings per day to UK mainland at Cairnryan and Troon. Train to Belfast. International airport 20M.

GLENARM (MARINA)

Charts BA 2198, 2199; SC 5621; Imray C62, C64

HW Belfast –0010. DS HWD N

This small, well sheltered marina offers a convenient

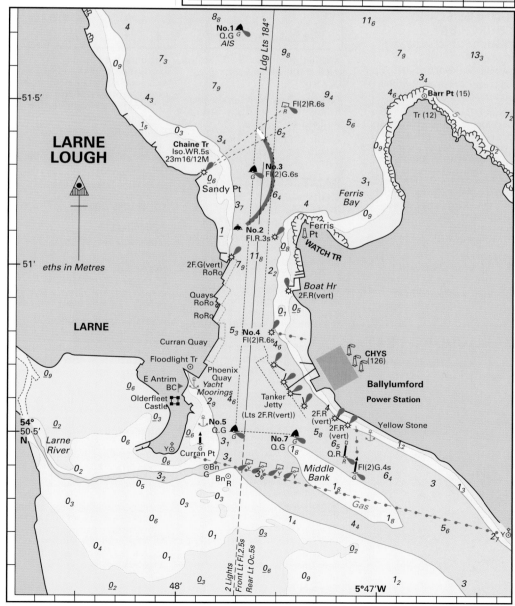

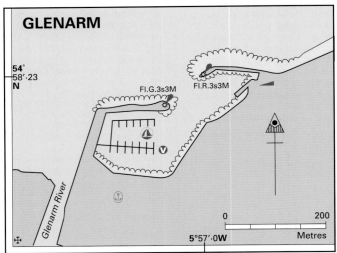

GLENARM

54° 58'·23 N

Fl.G.3s3M   Fl.R.3s3M

Glenarm River

0   200

5°57'·0W   Metres

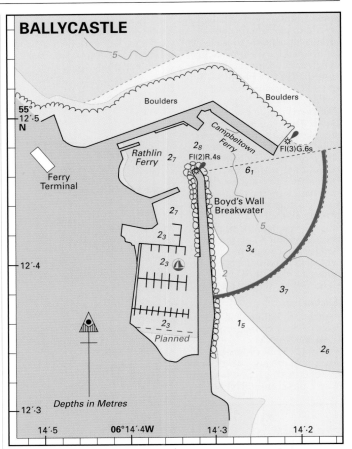

BALLYCASTLE

5

55° 12'·5 N

Boulders   Boulders

Campbeltown Ferry

Rathlin Ferry   2₈   Fl(2)R.4s   Fl(3)G.6s
              2₇
Ferry
Terminal   6₁

Boyd's Wall
2₇   Breakwater

12'·4   2₃   3₄

2₃

2   3₇

2₃   Planned   1₅

12'·3   *Depths in Metres*   2₆

14'·5   06°14'·4W   14'·3   14'·2

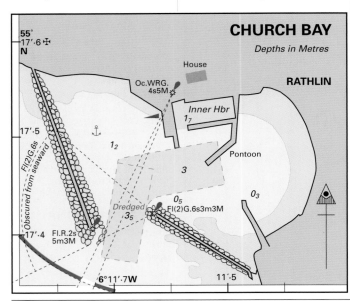

CHURCH BAY

55° 17'·6 N

Depths in Metres

House

RATHLIN

Oc.WRG. 4s5M

Inner Hbr
1₇

17'·5   Pontoon

1₂   3

Fl(2)G.6s (Obscured from seaward)

0₅   0₃
Dredged   Fl(2)G.6s3m3M
3₅

17'·4   Fl.R.2s 5m3M

6°11'·7W   11'·5

---

staging post and port of refuge for yachts traversing the North Channel.

Approach Entry is safe in all but severe NE gales. Tucked into the root of Glenarm Bay about 8ca W of Rath Head and 1M SE of Straidkilly Point, the hbr entrance is sheltered from all winds between ESE through S to NNW. It is out of the run of the strong North Channel tides and from N though to E approach is in deep water without natural hazard. The HM recommends entry from 54°58'·33N 05°57'·02W. This is exactly 1ca N of the entrance between the E and W hbr pier heads, marked with port and stb lights. In darkness, from 1M distant, approach on courses between 180° to 200° or 230° to 270° to avoid a marine farm that may be poorly marked.

Entry Between the pier heads which are constructed of random boulders so there is little reflected swell. There is a large, unobstructed area within the hbr to enable vessels to prepare in shelter for berthing. The well-lit marina is to the SW of the entrance.

Berthing Two hammer-head ended pontoons with well spaced finger pontoons for vessels up to 14m. 4m depth LW. 30 Visitors' berths.

Facilities Security coded gate access to pontoons. Water and electricity. (Fuel by can 3M). Shower at marina office. One mini-supermarket, several pubs. Bus to Coleraine, Larne, Belfast.
☎ 07703 606763.

RATHLIN ISLAND – CHURCH BAY

Charts BA 2798; SC 5621; Imray C64

HW Belfast –0450sp –0155np

DS Dover. Through Rathlin Sound –0500 E +0100 W

Church Bay Harbour has been developed, with two substantial breakwaters, as a sheltered ferry port for the island for ferries from Ballycastle. Yachts are welcomed and may anchor in the NW of the hbr, but beware there may be insufficient depth at LWS, or to lay alongside the pontoon or in the inner harbour for limited periods with the HM's approval.

Approach
By day from SW clear of dangers to the hbr entrance.
By night a sectored light Oc.WRG.4s is positioned within the village. The W sector leads to the hbr entrance 023°–026°.

Entrance Pass between the pier heads, West Lt Fl.R.2s, East Lt Fl(2)G.6s.

Facilities Limited, a small island, but a warm welcome. Ferry to Ballycastle.

BALLYCASTLE

Charts BA 2798; SC 5621; Imray C64

HW Belfast –0450sp –0155np

DS Dover. Along the near shore. –0300W +0200E

MHWS	MHWN	MLWN	MLWS
1·2M	0·9m	0·9m	0·3m

Ballycastle Harbour The hbr has been substantially improved to provide shelter for the Campbeltown and Rathlin Island ferry terminals. At the same time it encloses an area of complete shelter for a significant marina, ☎ 028 2076 8525. The North Quay, ferry berths, is protected by a large, random stone, breakwater against the strongest N'lies and carries a Lt Fl(3)G.6s. The S quay has a Lt Fl(2)R.4s at its head. Obscured north of bearing 261°.

Approach From E, Fair Head, along the coast keeping some 4ca offshore. Outside the 10m line it is clean. Keep south pier head open of north pier.

From N and W shape a course to leave the N quay a clearance of some ½ca. Turn to stb when the S quay is well open of the north. By night when it bears 275°.

Entrance Between the pier heads then bear round to port to leave the Old quay to stb and enter the marina. Berth as directed or in vacant berth to await instruction.

Facilities FW. Diesel. Gas. Supplies in the town EC Wednesday. Ferry to Church Bay, Rathlin.

☎ /VHF Marina 028 2076 8525, or *Mobile* 078 0350 5084; VHF 80.

PORTRUSH

Chart BA 2494; SC 5621; Imray C53

HW Belfast –0433

DS Dover +0600E HWD W

MHWS	MHWN	MLWN	MLWS
1·9m	1·4m	0·8m	0·4m

A small crowded hbr on W side of Ramore Head, good shelter. RNLI Station.

Approach From East there is ample water through Skerries Sound but beware small area of tidal disturbance. In poor weather approach from outside The Skerries. Swell can make entrance difficult in onshore winds over Force 4. Beware submerged breakwater (0·6m) projecting 20m SW from N pier Lt Fl.R.3s. S pier Lt Fl.G.3s.

Entrance Between pier heads hbr has 2m in entrance, 3–5m inside. By night (occas) Lead lights for hbr entrance sited in NE corner of hbr F.R. By day the ldg Lts have good red daymarks.

IRELAND

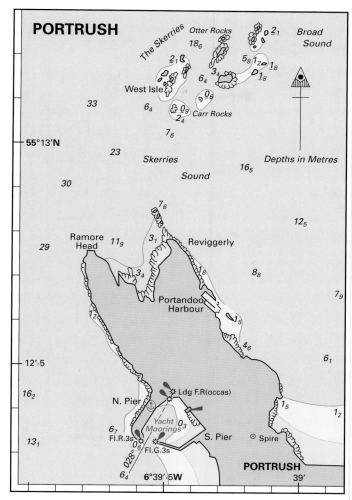

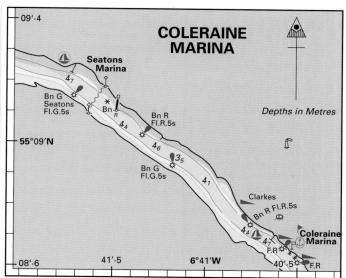

Berthing Berth alongside N quay and seek directions from Harbour Office, also temporary pontoon berthing in NW corner. Mooring may be available but congested.

Facilities FW and diesel on the quay. A busy and friendly little town. Rly to Belfast and Derry. All supplies including gas. EC Wednesday. Hotels, restaurants and pubs.

RIVER BANN

Chart BA 2494, 2798; SC 5621; Imray C53

HW Belfast −0440sp −0240np

MHWS	MHWN	MLWN	MLWS
2·2m	1·8m	0·9m	0·4m

Bar Maintained to 4m but subject to shoaling.

Approach River mouth is between stone training walls projecting 2ca N from beaches. It must not be attempted in strong onshore winds or if swell is breaking noticeably on ends of training walls. Pier heads have Lts, E Fl.R.5s, W Fl.G.5s. Ldg Lts 165° Oc.5s.6m & Oc.5s.14m.

FAIR HEAD TO BLOODY FORELAND

Chart BA 2723; SC 5621; Imray C53

Passage lights	BA No
Altacarry Head (Rathlin East)	6062
Fl(4)20s74m26M Racon(G) (−−·)	
Rathlin West	6064
Fl.R.5s62m22M AIS	
Inishtrahull	6164
Fl(3)15s59m19M Racon (T) (−) AIS	
Fanad Head	6168
Fl(5)WR.20s39m18/14M AIS	
Tory Island	6200
Fl(4)30s40m18M Racon(M) (−−) AIS	

Note A sharp lookout should be kept for salmon nets and lobster pots when navigating this coast.

Tidal steams DS (all related to Dover): Fair Head to Malin Head, +0100WNW, −0500ESE. Malin Hd to Bloody Foreland, inshore, −0230WSW, +0300ENE. Malin Hd to Horn Hd, offshore, −0530ENE, becoming E and SE; −0130SW, becoming W, slack −0230 and from +0300 to +0600. Streams are strong near Fair Hd but get progressively weaker to W; 6kn in Rathlin Sound, 4kn in Inishtrahull Sound, 2kn in Tory Sound. Rathlin Sound, 2–3M wide, is the normal approach to the N coast. A fair tide is essential; the NW-going tide commences HWD and the SE-going −0500. The overfalls SW of Rue Pt must be avoided from HW+0100 to +0300. Beware Carrickmannanon Rock 3ca NE of Kinbane Point, across which the tidal streams set. Skerries Sound is convenient in moderate conditions but keep outside in swell or strong offshore winds.

Inishtrahull Sound should not be attempted if there is a big sea running; in bad weather it is advisable to pass 3M N of Torr Rocks.

Entrance Keep towards E wall as W side is foul with boulders. Channel 45m wide, dredged to 3·4m, is marked with lights (which may be weak) and bns. Beware possible salmon nets

Between Lough Swilly and Mulroy Bay the coast should be given a wide berth using the clearing marks on chart BA 2699. An area of abnormal magnetic variation has been reported 1M 250° from Malin Head.

• Portstewart is a small harbour 2½M SW of Portrush which in quiet weather is convenient for a temporary visit. Advice may be obtained about entering the Bann and a berth arranged at Coleraine Marina.

• Culdaff Bay provides good anchorage in winds between SE and NNW, and is useful if awaiting favourable conditions for Inishtrahull Sound. Sheephaven anchorage offers a reasonable anchorage.

The N coast of Ireland is most beautiful, with many interesting geological formations, including the famous Giant's Causeway, and in ideal conditions it can be an idyllic cruising ground. However, it must never be forgotten that the whole length of the coast is completely exposed to the full weight of the Atlantic swell when the wind is from between W and N, and in established strong winds from this quarter, conditions can be such as to test even the most seaworthy and strongly crewed yacht. If conditions deteriorate suddenly, the most satisfactory refuge is Lough Swilly; it is easy to enter and there are a number of anchorages. Nevertheless, boats cruising the coast should be prepared to keep to sea for some time before shelter can be reached. Indeed, if a strong SW'ly wind begins to show any sign of veering, it is wise to consider putting in to shelter straightaway, to avoid the danger of being caught on a lee shore.

IRELAND

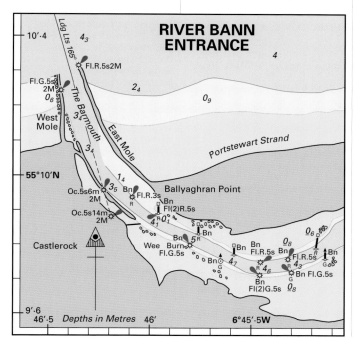

across full width of river. Ebb runs at 4kn.

Berthing
• In **Coleraine** marina on NE bank 4M from entrance. Water and fuel on pontoons, chandlery, 15-tonne travel-lift crane. ☎ 028 7034 4768.
• Anchor on NE side ½M upstream of old CG, clear of channel.

Facilities Shops ½M away in thriving town all supplies. EC Thursday. A possible place to leave a boat. Rly to Antrim for airport and Belfast.

LOUGH FOYLE AND LONDONDERRY

Chart BA2511;
Imray C64

HW Belfast –0330sp –0300np

MHWS	MHWN	MLWN	MLWS
2·7m	2·1m	1·2m	0·6m

Greencastle on the NW of the entrance is a large commercial hbr with no specific facilities for yachts. It is a port of refuge in foul weather when a mooring for visiting yachts may be found by rafting up alongside a resident. It is occasionally used by the RNLI. A small town, usual supplies, also a ferry across the lough to Magilligan which has busses to Colraine.

Lough Foyle Using appropriate coastal charts make your approach, taking care not to hamper large vessels, up the well buoyed channel to Londonderry which is a city of great historic and architectural interest. It is now largely free of sectarian conflict and visitors will feel perfectly safe: it was recently voted 'City of Culture'.

On entering the lough visitors should contact *Harbour Radio* VHF 14. You will be directed to Londonderry Port, Lisahally.

Berthing In the new Foyle Marina, in the centre of the city, 17M from the mouth of the lough. Vessels may berth either side of the Foyle Marina pontoon where there is a depth of 7m on the outside and 5m inside. Pay harbour dues, collect security access keys and tokens for electricity.

Anchorage Either side of the approach channel, well clear of

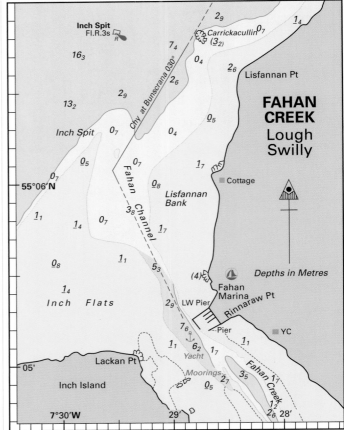

FAHAN CREEK
Lough Swilly

Depths in Metres

the approach channel, preferably on the more sheltered side near village of Carrowkeel. Seek advice from *Harbour Radio*.

Facilities Nearby chandlery. Launderette. City centre easy walking distance, shops, etc as expected of a large city.

☎/VHF +44(0)28 7186 0113, VHF 14 (24h), www.londonderryport.com/marina.htm

LOUGH SWILLY

Chart BA 2697; SC 5621; Imray C53

HW Galway Rathmullan +0125sp +0050np

MHWS	MHWN	MLWN	MLWS
4·3m	3·2m	1·9m	0·5m

The lough is entered between Fanad Head Lt Fl(5)WR.20s and the bold Head of Dunaff. It is 26M long, 3½M wide at entrance, and has 15 to 20m up to Fort Stewart; bottom sand and mud.

Approach From E care should be taken to carry tide through Inishtrahull Sound, NE of Malin Head, where the W-going stream runs 4hrs only. Dover +0100 to +0400.

From W give Fanad Head a berth of ½M and leave Swilly Rocks G con Lt buoy Fl.G.3s to stb. By night, keep out of the R sector of Fanad Lt.

Entrance Off Dunree Head up to Buncrana Bay, keep at least ½M clear to W, or keep Dunree Head Lt Fl(2)WR.5s and Fanad Lt in line.

Anchorages
• Pincher Bay, just south of Fanad Head. Exposed to E'lies.
• Ballymastocker Bay 4 ½M inside Fanad Head on W shore, anchor off the pier in 2–5m, small shop and pub. Exposed to E.
• Fahan Creek is the most sheltered anchorage although uncomfortable in NW winds. The bar is subject to silting and alteration; care should be taken on entry and exit which, except in very smooth conditions, should be between HW–0300 and HW+0200 when a least depth of 3m should be found. With a NW sea running extreme caution should be applied, particularly on the ebb. Anchor near moored yachts in 2–5·5m. Bus to Buncrana and Londonderry. Sometimes the entrance is buoyed by the local YC.
• W of Macamish Point sheltered from SW to N through W, 3–5m, sand.
• Rathmullan Road, N of pier off the town. The best place for visiting yachts; water at pier-head. Pontoon on south side of pier. Small grocery, petrol, good local hotels.
• This large lough offers many other anchorages and much exploration in beautiful scenery further inland.
Guest moorings at Portsalon. FW hose on pontoon at Rathmullan and Calor Gas at the pub.

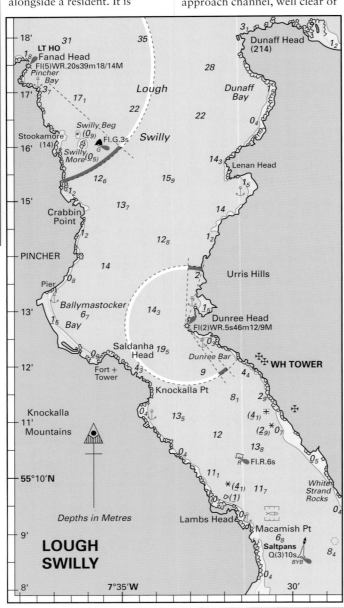

LOUGH SWILLY

Depths in Metres

Ireland – West Coast

This coast resembles the W coast of Scotland and the Scandinavian peninsula. In an uncharacteristically 'purple' passage: HJ Hanson, who compiled the early editions of *The Cruising Association Handbook* almost single-handed, wrote; 'The splendour of the mountains, their varying colours, whether in the rising or setting sunlight, by noonday or under the moon, the glory of the sea in fine weather at sundown, when it often resembles a lake of molten gold, the mighty cliffs, attaining in Donegal and Mayo to a height of nearly 2,000ft, and the secure hbrs scattered with few exceptions at easy intervals, will well repay the efforts required to reach these waters.' That is as true today as it was when it was written over eighty years ago.

The *ICC Sailing Directions* are essential for those exploring in detail the west coast and its many smaller anchorages.

Except when crossing the mouth of Donegal Bay and between Galway Bay and the Blaskets, there is usually an easily accessible harbour close by. In unsettled weather a yacht may be held up to leeward of one or other of the headlands, but on such occasions most hbrs afford facilities for dinghy sailing or excursions.

Although a careful and experienced skipper can in general navigate this coast with ease and confidence, it is fully exposed to the Atlantic swell. If overtaken by bad weather and poor visibility, unless a familiar anchorage is close at hand it may well be necessary to get clear of the land until the weather improves. This coast should therefore be cruised only by seaworthy yachts capable of making to windward and remaining at sea in any conditions.

Local opinion is that the sailing season starts well on in May and closes early in September, on account of the heavy swell which is usually running in the Atlantic at other times of the year. So long as there is swell in the offing, only a moderate onshore breeze is needed to bring it quickly into the coast, but from June the coast is usually subject only to such seas as may be caused by local breezes or a summer gale.

Many W coast anchorages have heavy growths of kelp on the bottom, and the CQR anchor (at least in weights below 30kg) tends to clog and drag, as does the Danforth. A large fisherman is the traditional solution: the Bruce is also well thought of in some quarters. Whatever is used, it is wise to ensure that the anchor is holding, particularly in calm conditions, by reversing the motor. Vessels are advised to moor on two anchors when left unattended on such ground.

Streams are not extensively charted, but are apt to be considerably stronger off headlands giving rise to confused and possibly breaking seas with any weight of wind. Headlands such as Bloody Foreland, Erris, Achill, Slyne and Loop Heads should be treated with the greatest respect and an offing of two to three miles lessens the chances of a shaking-up when rounding. Avoid, in all but calm periods, those areas in which the symbol for overfalls is indicated on the chart.

The ensuing pages of this almanac provide, in each of three sections of the coast between Bloody Foreland and Valentia, brief general notes followed by sailing directions on a selection of harbours. They indicate possible harbours of refuge although very bad weather may make it unsafe to approach any harbour.

The Rosses, extending 15M from the Bloody Foreland to Aranmore, afford a fascinating cruising area on the direct route for a yacht sailing round Ireland, sheltered by a string of islands and with several good anchorages. The Stag Rocks and more particularly the Bullogconnell shoals must be given a good berth.

The direct course between Rinrawros Pt on Aranmore and Rathlin O'Birne some 20M to S leads clear of dangers, but there is a strong set into Boylagh Bay.

Yachts proceeding S with insufficient time to explore Donegal Bay should make for Erris Head (47M from Rathlin O'Birne) with the option of putting into Broadhaven or carrying on.

Proceeding N on the direct passage, Rathlin O'Birne is the best landfall, with the options of making for Killybegs (or Teelin in favourable weather) or for Aranmore.

For those with more time Donegal Bay contains several interesting inlets between Sligo and Killybegs. Between Killala and Broadhaven there is a 24M stretch of inhospitable, but spectacularly scenic cliffs of the N Mayo coast but this should be given a wide berth if unsettled weather between WSW and N is forecast.

The best harbours of refuge are Killybegs, Aran Road in W winds and Rutland harbour inside Aranmore in S or E winds although passage into the latter is intricate.

BLOODY FORELAND TO ERRIS HEAD

Chart BA 2725;
Imray C53, C54

Passage lights	BA No.
Tory Island	6200
Fl(4)30s40m18M	
Racon(M) (– –)	
Bloody Foreland	6203
Fl.WG.7·5s14m6/4M	
Aranmore	
Rinrawros Point	6208
Fl(2)20s71m27M+Fl.R.3s13M	
Rathlin O'Birne Is	6216
Fl.WR.15s35m12/10M AIS	
Mullaghmore Head	6231
Fl.G.3s5m3M	
Eagle Is	6268
Fl(3)15s67m19M AIS	

MULROY BAY

Chart BA 2699;
Imray C53

HW Galway
Bar +0108sp, +0052np

MHWS	MHWN
3·9m	2·9m

Mulroy Bay affords 12M of navigable channel. A power cable across Moross channel, clearance 6m, bars North Water to most yachts. Some of the finest scenery in Ireland. Fanny's Bay, about 3½ miles from the entrance, is probably the best anchorage on the NW coast of Ireland.

Approach The coast both east and west of the entrance to the bay is foul and must be given an offing.

From West From a position some 4ca or more N of Frenchman's Rk (always visible) make for 55°16'·05N 7°47'·15W about ½M N of Melmore Hd, (to make sure that you are clearing the dangerous, submerged rocks keep Horn Hd will open to the N of Frenchman's Rk). Thence alter course to 150° to a position 55°15'·12N 7°46'·40W, 3ca E of the light on Ravedy Island, Fl.3s.

From East Keep the highest part of Dunaff Hd open of Fanad Hd, bearing 91°, steer 271° until the light on Ravedy Island bears 220° (55°17'·05N 7°45'·15W) then steer for it until some 4ca distant at which point alter course to 180° to the position 3ca to its east.

Entrance and Bar Least water is likely to be 2.8m at datum over the east bar, when seas break in onshore winds and/or there is a big swell running. Inspect before entry and watch your echo sounder. The Bar west of the 'Bar Rocks' has silted and the preferred entry is to the east of the rocks. The best time of entry is from ½ tide to HW–0100 when most of the rocks are well visible and the flood can be carried far inland. From the position 3ca E of the Ravendy Island Lt steer 165° to

a position 2ca E of High Bar Rk which only covers at HW springs and then the disturbance can usually be seen. This position is 2ca W of the Sessiagh Rks that very rarely covers. Be aware that the Low Bar Rk, which covers at about ¾ rise, is 1ca E of High Rk, so give it a berth. At this point turn to 210° toward the First Narrows. When 2ca off the Glinsk Pt shore gradually turn to stb and pass through the middle of the Narrows. Thereafter keep in mid channel until past the Dundooan rocks, Bn Q.G., then work toward the west shore.

Anchorages
• N of Dundooan Rocks in 3·5–5·5m, sand.
• Fanny's Bay on W side about 3M inside the bar in 2m affords complete shelter out of the stream at all times. PO and shop at Downings village, 1M across the peninsula dividing Sheep Haven from Mulroy. Excellent hotel at Rosapenna, ¾M. Bus to Londonderry.
• In Bullogfemule, a land-locked basin on E side just above the second narrows, where there is a road br vert clearance 19m. The third narrows or Hassans Pass has 8kn stream and should be taken at slack water. Flood begins at Galway –0230, ebb at +0325.

CRUIT BAY

(pronounced *Critch*)

Chart BA 1883; Imray C53

HW Galway +0042sp, +0055np

MHWS	MHWN	MLWN	MLWS
3·9m	2·9m	1·4m	0·5m

A good anchorage in all summer winds, and easy to enter, however, there is a swell particularly in N'ly winds. The ebb runs out strongly.

Approach from N. Leave Gola Island which has Knockaculleen 69m at the N end to port with a fair offing ½M and head due S to leave Inishfree also to port. This takes a yacht clear of all possible breakers. The transit for entering Cruit Bay is Gortnasate Point open E of Corillan Is 195°. The Is is well into the bay.

Entrance Keeping on the transit leave Nicholas Rock with bn to stb. This also clears the Yellow Rock. On closing Corillan turn to stb and round the islet close leaving it to port. Take care not to mistake the entrance with the bay to the W of Tordermot and Inishillintry which is very foul.

Anchorages
• Just S of Corillan in 2m sand.
• To W of the above and N of existing local boats, also in sand. Take care not to get N by W of Corillan as there is a bad rock just off an unmarked Is in this area.

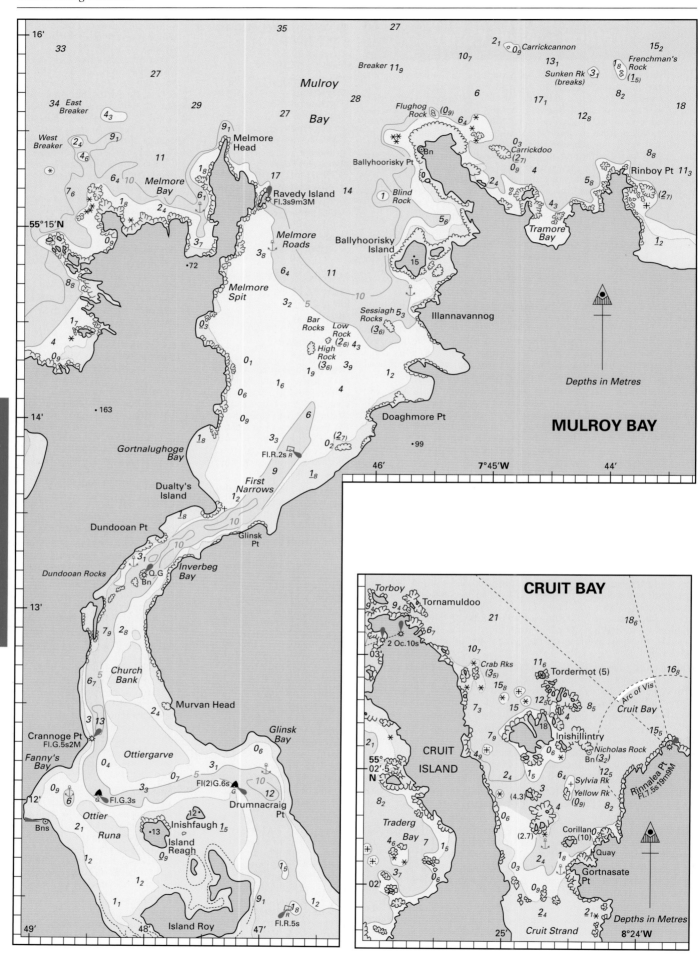

IRELAND

MULROY BAY

Depths in Metres

Mulroy Bay

East Breaker
West Breaker
Melmore Head
Melmore Bay
Melmore Spit
Melmore Roads
Ravedy Island Fl.3s9m3M
Bar Rocks
Low Rock
High Rock
Gortnalughoge Bay
First Narrows
Fl.R.2s
Dualty's Island
Dundooan Pt
Glinsk Pt
Inverbeg Bay
Dundooan Rocks
Q.G Bn
Church Bank
Murvan Head
Crannoge Pt Fl.G.5s2M
Fanny's Bay
Ottiergarve
Fl.G.3s
Ottier Runa
Bns
Inishfaugh
Island Reagh
Glinsk Bay
Fl(2)G.6s
Drumnacraig Pt
Island Roy
Fl.R.5s

Flughog Rock
Ballyhoorisky Pt
Bn
Blind Rock
Ballyhoorisky Island
Illannavannog
Sessiagh Rocks
Doaghmore Pt
Carrickcannon
Breaker
Sunken Rk (breaks)
Frenchman's Rock
Carrickdoo
Rinboy Pt
Tramore Bay

55°15'N

CRUIT BAY

Depths in Metres

Torboy
Tornamuldoo
2 Oc.10s
Crab Rks
Tordermot (5)
CRUIT ISLAND
Inishillintry
Nicholas Rock Bn
Sylvia Rk
Yellow Rk
Rinnalea Pt Fl.7.5s9m9M
Corillan
Quay
Gortnasate Pt
Traderg Bay
Cruit Strand
Arc of Vis Cruit Bay

55° 02'.5 N

25'

8°24'W

7°45'W

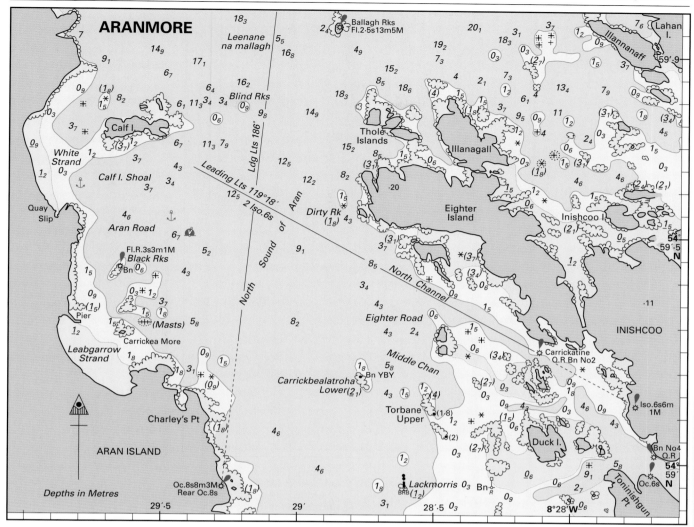

ARANMORE

Depths in Metres

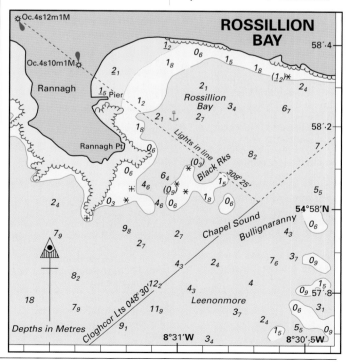

ROSSILLION BAY

Depths in Metres

• It is possible to go alongside Gortnasate Quay while getting stores.

• Town quay pontoon. HM ✆ 071 9111237 or 086 0890767 for gate code.

Facilities water at quay. PO and limited stores at Kincaslough ½M. Fuel 2M. Enquire from the locals who may be able to help with transport.

ARANMORE (ARAN ROADS) RUTLAND, BURTON AND ARAN ISLAND

Charts BA 1883, 2792; Imray C53

HW Galway +0042sp, +0055np

MHWS	MHWN	MLWN	MLWS
3·9m	2·9m	1·4m	0·5m

This is a very popular area of the W of Ireland having many good anchorages with good shelter. As there are many holiday homes in the area supplies and fuel are relatively easy. Most of the difficult parts of the roads are well marked by buoys, Ldg Lts and bns. Chart 1883 is essential and 2792 is essential for Burtonport and Rutland Harbour. The easiest passage in is through N Sound leaving Ballagh Rocks bn Fl.2·5s to port and Calf Is to stb. At, or before this point one can sight one of two Ldg lines:

The more W'ly 161° is the line of two bns. The front on Carrickbealatroha Rock and the rear on Lackmorris Rock. The E'ly lead line 186° on two lighted bns Oc.8s on the SE shore of Aran Island. Each line is safe water into North Sound of Aran. They cross just east of Calf Island. For the best anchorage off the E Aran shore turn to stb at this point to 241° on the transit of an obelisk on the shore with the summit of Moylecorragh 162m. When S or SW-by-S of Calf Is come to anchor in 3–4m some 2ca N of the Black Rock Fl.R.3s. Further S than this and you may hamper the Island ferry fairway which berths at a pier 2ca SSW of Black Rock. Good landing at the slip beside the obelisk.

Visitors' moorings may be found in this vicinity.

Facilities General store, Two small hotels, Well water.

To make for Rutland Harbour or Burtonport, both well sheltered. Continue on the N entry transit (161° or 186°) until two bns Iso.6s come in transit 119°. The channel is narrow with rks each side and busy with fishing vessels coming to and from Burtonport. Follow this lead until Carrickatine bn Q.R.

abeam to port, when turn gently to 137° on the transit of two bns Oc.6s on Rutland Island. Half way past Duck Is come to anchor in the wider part of the channel in 5–7m but avoid the centre line of the fairway for the ferry and fishing boats. Alternatively continue toward Inishcoo to come to

anchor in 4–5m some 75m WNW of the ruined quay, put a line ashore abreast the anchor to hold boat out of the fairway where the tide runs hard. Anchor lights essential here as fishing boats use the channel day and night. A further anchorage is Black Hole, just beyond the inner of Rutland Is

IRELAND

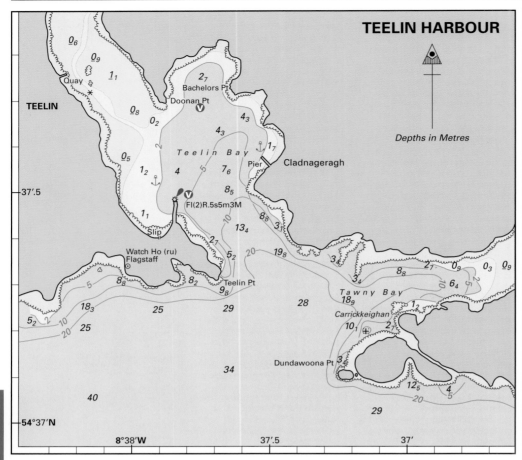

TEELIN HARBOUR

Depths in Metres

TEELIN

Quay

Bachelors Pt

Doonan Pt

Teelin Bay

Pier Cladnageragh

Fl(2)R.5s5m3M

Slip

Watch Ho (ru)
Flagstaff

Teelin Pt

Tawny Bay

Carrickkeighan

Dundawoona Pt

Ldg Lts. A little bay some 55m across and 35m deep with a depth of 4m one can anchor or secure with long lines fore and aft across the bay and breast ropes to hold in out of the tide or anchor. A secure and sheltered S to NW gale hole. For Burtonport continue up marked channel on sufficient rise (half tide) to reach the quay. It is possible to secure here alongside the pier or a fishing boat, with permission, in a least depth of 1·7m. Yachts now welcome. HM VHF 14, 16, ☎ 075 42046.

Facilities FW hose, diesel, petrol in cans. Shops, hotel and bar. Hull and engine repairs. Electronics. Bus to Donegal.

Approach from south Some 3ca S of Ranagh Pt, Aran Island, on transit 048° two Lt bns Iso.8s at head of Chapel Bay through Chapel Sound. Either turn to port on transit 308° of two bns Oc.4s but beware of Black Rocks, 0·3ca, to port of line. Come to anchor in 2m 1¼ca ESE of pier in Rossillion Bay, or continue toward the first bns, toward Chapel Bay, keeping clear of rocky foreshore to port to come to anchor in 4m 1ca SSW of the quay. Both these anchorage good in northerly breezes but may be troubled by westerly swell.

TEELIN

Charts BA 2702; Imray C53

HW Galway –0055

MHWS	MHWN	MLWN	MLWS
4·0m	2·9m	1·4m	0·7m

A naturally beautiful haven. Other than in strong S or SE winds, it offers a quiet anchorage or mooring.

Approach

From the W make for Carrigan Head, which has a conspicuous tr (101m) then easterly along the coast keeping 3ca offshore. After 2M the entrance will open up to port.

From SW or S approach the coast 1½M east of the conspicuous tr on Carrigan Hd.

From the E from Muckross Head shape a course for Dunawoona Point 1·3M. Close to this point Teelin will be seen ½M ahead to the NW.

Entrance is straightforward by day. There is no longer a light on Teelin Point. Pier head lit Fl(2)R.5s5m3M. Avoid making a first entry at night.

Anchorage Quiet anchorage can usually be found 100m NW of the pier. If a swell is chasing in, there may be quieter water on the eastern side of the bay close N of the old pier at Cladnageragh.

Moorings There are four yellow visitors' moorings between Teelin pier and Bachelors point, but these are exposed and not recommended.

Facilities The nearest shops are at Carrick, 3M, friendly pub ½M from Teelin pier. Water on the pier, but it can be busy with fishermen. Electricity on pier head, cards Paddy Byrne ☎ 0876284688, 0749739365. Taxi ☎ 0749739145.

KILLYBEGS

Charts BA 2702, 2792; Imray C53

HW Galway +0040sp, +0050np

MHWS	MHWN	MLWN	MLWS
4·1m	3·0m	1·5m	0·6m

A very busy fishing port, yachts should not be left unattended except for very short periods. However it does provide very good shelter and can be entered day or night. New quays recently built.

Approach

From the W Pass two miles S of Muckross Head and head E until the E side of Drumanoo Head bears NE, then turn in to pass SE of it, passing midway between Ellamore Shoal and the 14·3m shoal 1½M to the W. In heavy westerly weather it can break heavily on these shoals.

From the S Leave Inishmurray 2M to port and head for Bullockmore buoy which lies 3M W of St John's Point, then alter course for Drumanoo Head to leave Ellamore shoal to stb and follow the directions above.

Entrance Keep in the mid channel leaving Rotten Island

Fl.WR.4s to stb. Keeping mid-channel locate R Lt buoys Fl.R.3s and Fl.R.7s. Head for the S card Lt buoy on the Harbour Shoal and when ½ca S of this buoy turn in towards the quays. There is sectored Lt WRG.6s bearing 338° to lead to the quay.

Anchorages
• To the E of the town in 2·5–3·5m in mud, thus avoiding heavy fishing boat traffic. Sometimes poor in SW'ly weather.
• To the SW of W end of the town in 4–7m. Subject to fishing boat traffic.
• In Walkers Bay (SE of Rough Point) if the wind is S'ly. Off the slip to NW in 5–8m, avoiding local moorings.

Warning Do not anchor in Port Roshin, (½M NW of Rotten Is) holding poor and an uncharted rock. Beware of lost ground tackle in all anchorages.

Facilities All in town except sailmaker; buses to Donegal Town and Sligo. Call HM on VHF 16, 14 for a mooring. ☎ 073 31032.

SLIGO

Charts BA 2852; Imray C54

HW Galway +0043sp, +0055np

MHWS	MHWN	MLWN	MLWS
4·1m	3·0m	1·5m	0·5m

Sligo is a large estuary hbr the inner parts of which are well protected by sandy islands. The port itself is a long quay in the river just below the city. The city is a communication centre, which lends itself to crew change, and all supplies are readily obtainable. The Harbour Authority is eager to attract pleasure craft and have provided a pontoon with all facilities at the head of the quays just NW of the first city road bridge.

Approach Donegal Bay is relatively clear of hazards. Pass between Anghris Head to stb and Ballyconnel Point to port 5M apart. Make for Wheat Rock S card Lt buoy S of Raghly Pt. Beware The Ledge 2½M WSW of buoy and 1M off Anghris Point (Breaks in heavy weather). From 2½ca S of the card buoy sight 068° for Lower Rosses Lt bn Fl(2)WRG.10s.

Entrance Maintain this heading for 1·4M to N card buoy, Bungar Bank, then turn to stb on 125° transit Metal Man Rock bn Fl(3)6s (Metal Man actually is a metal statue of a sailor) and Oyster Is bn Fl(3)6s. Hold this course to Metal Man then leave the statue bn to stb and two perches to port. Turn to port round the south of Deadman's Point into the channel between Oyster Island and Deadman's Point keeping closer to the N shore.

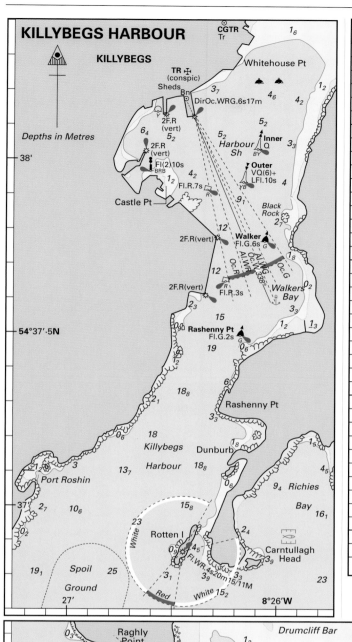

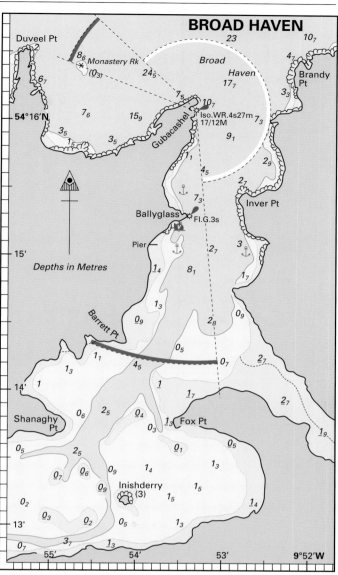

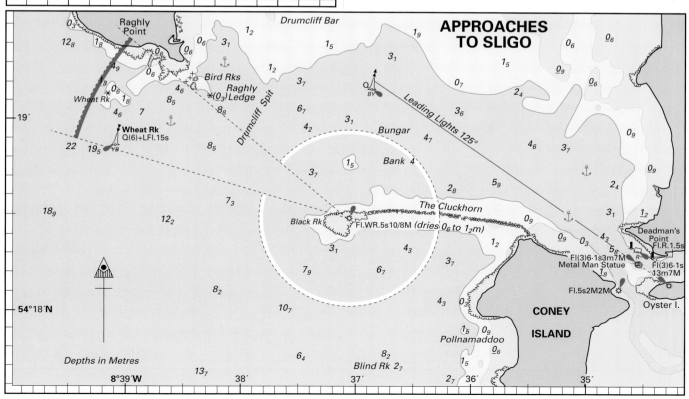

IRELAND

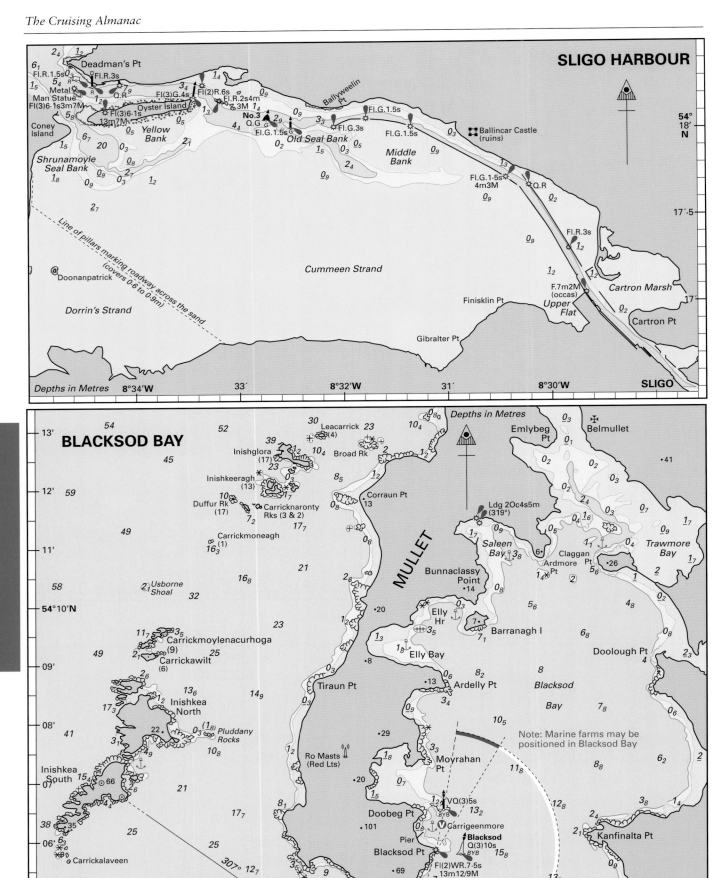

Anchorage One can anchor in this vicinity. Either 1ca to the SW of the pier in 2–3m but the holding is poor and the tide runs hard. Safer and more comfortable, in similar depth ¾ca WNW of the first port-hand Lt bn Fl.R.1·5s. These anchor points give access to the pier and to the yacht club. Showers and bar. Rosses village has some shops or take a bus to Sligo.

Continuing to Sligo The channel is marked with port and stb bns. After about 1M one reaches the bn marking the end of the training wall Fl.1·5s. Leave it to stb and continue keeping training wall 30m to stb until a port training wall appears when keep closer to it in 2m dredged channel. When first left to stb is seen some 2½ca ahead cross toward it and keep close to stb-hand bns. Beware: There is a mid-channel middle ground/rock marked by two stb bns. Do not pass between this and the SW quay. Beyond the second of these bns proceed up the channel parallel with the SW quays. The first city bridge will come into sight. At the head of the quays there is a 60m pontoon with depths; MHWS 4·0m MHWN 3·0m MLWN 2·0m MLWS 1·5m. Moor securely since the ebb can run quite quickly.

Facilities Water, fuel and electricity on the pontoon. Security by coded gate. All amenities of a modern conurbation. Rly to Dublin, long distance buses, and Knock Airport for international flights.

☎/**VHF** Hbr Office +353(0)719111237 VHF16/12 HW−0200 to HW+0100; HM *Mobile* +353(0)860890767.

BROADHAVEN

Chart BA 2703; Imray C54

HW Galway +0040sp, +0050np

MHWS	MHWN	MLWN	MLWS
3·7m	2·8m	1·6m	0·5m

A good safe hbr in all summer weather. It is 5M long and 1M wide in places. In bad NW and N gales the entrance breaks and should not be attempted.

Approach From N: Pass outside the Stags and give Kidd Island a 1M berth to avoid the race. Alter course for Gubacashel Lt Iso.WR.4s. This takes you clear of the rk off Doonanierin Point. From S: Leave Eagle Is light Fl(3)10s to stb and head for a point 1M N of Erris Head – again to avoid the race. Turn into Broad Haven Bay and head for Gubacasel Lt. Do not get inside a line between this point and Duvell Point as Monastery Rock is nasty.

Entrance The entrance is clear for 1M. After that there are shallow patches on each side.

Anchorages
• In bay N of Ballyglass in 3·5m. The line is Gubacashel Point in line with the W side of Kidd Is. Shelter from SW to NW.
• Off the pier in the next bay to stb in 3m with the outer end bearing 035°. The pier has 2m alongside and it is sometimes possible to lie alongside a trawler there. Bellmulet 6M. PO. Showers at LB station. Telephone. Friendly local transport.
• On port side ½M S of Inver Point in 3·5m off the hamlet. Best in E winds. Telephone 2M at Barnatra. The rest of the bay can be explored on a rising tide in a dinghy.

FRENCHPORT

A small inlet providing a port of call on the direct route for yachts sailing round Ireland. Not recommended if the W'ly swell is running high. No facilities, no water. Good pub and shops at Clough.

BLACKSOD BAY

Chart BA 2704; Imray C54

HW Galway +0025sp, +0035np

MHWS	MHWN	MLWN	MLWS
3·9m	2·9m	1·4m	0·4m

The tide runs strongly 2·5kn straight on to the two headlands Turduvillaun and Achill which guard the outer bay. In the bay itself the tide is weak.

This is a large open bay surrounded by low-lying land and sand hills. It is about 3M wide and 9M long. Off the main bay are many smaller bays, most of which are very shoal at their heads. It is always possible to select a bay for any wind so only the main places to anchor are mentioned below. The canal at Belmullet connecting through to Broadhaven is now closed.

Approach From N through Inishkea Sound, leading mark to avoid Pluddany Rocks to the E of Inishkea N is Turduvillaun in line with the Ears of Achill. It is possible in daylight to enter the bay through Duvillaun Sound. The Ldg bns are on Inishkea South. At night sail S until into the W sector of Black Rock Lt Fl.WR.12s then turn in to open up the W sector of Blacksod Lt Fl(2)7·5s. 3½ca abeam is an E card pillar Lt buoy Q(3)10s. Proceed due N until clear of the E Card bn VQ(3)5s with topmark on Carrigeenmore and anchor until daylight.

Anchorages
• On the bay NW of Blacksod Quay between it and Doobeg Point avoiding local boats, 3m sand. The quay itself dries and is foul, and the immediate area for 2ca around is shallow and poor holding. Visitors' moorings available.
• **Elly Bay** is one of the best anchorages. Give Ardelly Point a good berth. Anchor outside local boats.
• **Elly Harbour** just N of Elly Bay. Anchor in the middle in 3–4m. Subject to swell in southerlies. Visitors' moorings.
• **Saleen Bay** 1½M N of Elly Harbour. Tend towards the NE shore Ldg line 319° with Lts Oc.4s5M. There is 3m. Good landing. Subject to swell in S or SE'lies.
• **N of Claggan Point** If possible enter at LW in order to see the drying patches to N. Avoid the dangerous rock which lies 3ca S by E of Ardmore Point.

Facilities
• About 1½M inland, PO, petrol, diesel and limited groceries. Possible local friendly transport.
• At Belmullet 3M. Shops, PO, fuel, pub, RC Church. Possible friendly local transport or taxi.

WESTPORT

Chart BA 2057; Imray C54

HW Galway +0030

MHWS	MHWN	MLWN	MLWS
4·4m	3·4m	1·8m	0·8m

At half tide the following directions should find no less than 4m depth all the way to the final 'Entrance' to Westport Quay.

The approach channel has recently been buoyed but do not attempt without one of the charts above.

IRELAND

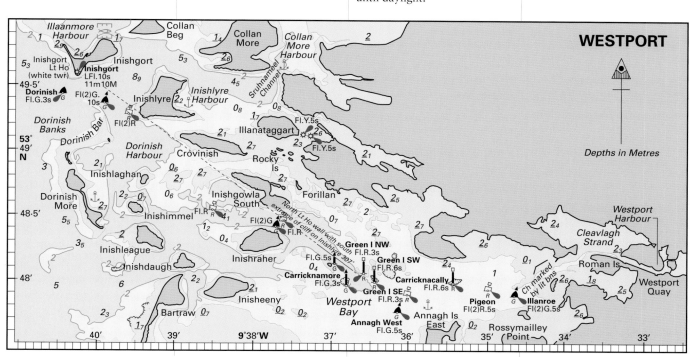

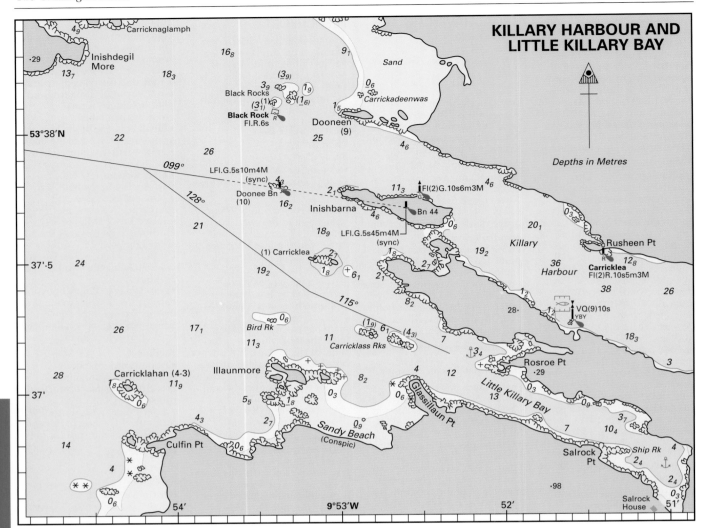

KILLARY HARBOUR AND LITTLE KILLARY BAY

Depths in Metres

IRELAND

Approach Pass between Inishgort LtHo Fl.10s and Dorinish buoy Fl.G. Steer ESE toward Inishlyre some 3ca and when the shore is about 2ca ahead a green buoy should be seen to stb marking the extent of the Dorinish Bar. Steer S toward two small islands; Inishlagen and Inishimmel. The channel between the two is buoyed. Then steer ESE toward Inishraher. There will be a port hand buoy then a stb to take you north of Inishraher on an E'ly course. As 'Inishgowla South' draws close on the port bow the south Cliff of Inishlyre will be seen to come in transit with the N end of the white wall at Inishgort LtHo bearing 307°, as shown on plan. Using this as an astern transit steer 127°, after some 6ca port and stb hand perches will be seen. Pass between these into Westport Bay. On reaching a position some 2ca south of Green Isle steer 080° to leave Carricknacally rock with R Lt bn to port and pick up the buoyed channel to Westport Quay.

Entrance Pass between Lt bn Fl.3s.G box on con stone bn and Monkellys Rocks into Westport Channel, marked by G perches to stb. Bear round Roman Island

to approach Westport Quay. Keep close to stb side. At HW –0200, mean tides, 2·2m can be found all the way to the quay with sandy bottom.

Berthing Against the quay near the 'Old Derrick Crane'. Prepare to dry out as tide falls. Soft mud on hard underlay.

Facilities At Westport Quay; pubs, restaurants, four-star hotel and medium-sized supermarket. Boatyard. Westport city; 1M with all facilities. Rly from Dublin.

Anchorages
• In the bay to the east of Dorinish More. Good holding
• In Inishlyre Harbour to the east of the island.
• In Collan More Harbour to the east of Collan More island.
• To the north of 'Annagh Island East' an all states of tide 'hole' can be found. Useful when awaiting tide to Westport Quay or departing same.

LITTLE KILLARY HARBOUR (SALROCK)

Chart BA 2706; Imray C54

HW Galway +0018

MHWS	MHWN	MLWN	MLWS
4·1m	3·1m	1·6m	0·5m

A very picturesque anchorage. Not easy in bad weather or low visibility as the various clearing lines marked on the chart are sometimes difficult to identify. There are quite a number of off-lying rocks and shoals. In that event adjacent Killary Harbour which itself is well worth a visit for its magnificent fjord-like scenery offers easier access. Although one has to travel 3M up the lough for shallow enough water to anchor at Derrynasliggan or a further mile to anchor on the N shore at Bundorraghan. Beware of large numbers of lobster pots and fish farms in this region.

Approach
From N the line astern is Mweelaun 19m high in line with the sloping top of Clare Island 341°. However it is necessary to come to the Eastward to avoid the patch to the E of Govern Island, likewise 1M later bear to the Westward to avoid the patch to W of

Inishdegil More, then turn in toward Little Killary Harbour.

From W give Inishbroon Island off Rinvyle Point a fair berth of approximately ½M to avoid Mweelaunatura. When Rinvyle Point shows N of Innishbroon alter course for Illaunananima (Live Island) until reaching the next transit of N side Freaghillaun with S islet of Shanvallybeg 089°. This clears the Puffin Rocks. The next transit is Cleggan Point over the E end of Inishbroon (051°) taking one clear of various dangers to stb. When the lit bns on Doonee and Inishbarna come in line alter course onto 099° and proceed until Doonee bn, the front mark is ½M distant. Then alter course to 128°, Carricklass rocks ahead. Hold course until Carricklea, always visible, is abeam 1ca to port. Alter course to 115° to leave Carricklass, always visible, 1ca to stb. The hbr entrance is then visible ahead of you fine on stb bow. Leave a fair berth to port off Rosroe Pt, submerged rock, and to stb off Ship Rk, a tapering reef.

Entrance All dangers are above water and should be given a fair berth.

ERRIS HEAD TO VALENTIA

Chart BA 2420; 2173, 2254
Imray C54

Passage lights	*BA No.*
Black Rk	6270
Fl.WR.12s86m19/14M AIS	
Achillbeg Is	6276
Fl.WR.5s56m18/15M AIS	
Slyne Head	6288
Fl(2)15s35m19M Racon (T) (–)	
Rock Island (Earagh)	6296
Fl.15s35m18M	
Innisheer	6334
Iso.WR.12s34m20/16M AIS	
Loop Head	6338
Fl(4)20s84m23M	
Inishtearaght	6408
Fl(2)20s84m19M	
Racon (O) (– – –) AIS	

The coast from Erris Head to Slyne Head is deeply indented, with long stretches fronted by islands affording some protection from the swell. It is a fine day-cruising area, although not well enough lit for sailing inshore at night. There are many sheltered bays, the pick of the anchorages being Blacksod Bay, Clew Bay, Killary and Little Killary, Ballynakill, Inishbofin and Clifden. Frenchport is handy if pressed for time.

It is theoretically possible for motor cruisers to pass through Achill Sound, some 15M E of Achill Head, given sufficient rise of tide and subject to mast height of less than 11m (check the clearance locally) but the channel is very intricate and local knowledge is needed.

Blacksod Bay is a good refuge in bad weather, with quite a number of anchorages. The South Connemara coast between Roundstone Bay, 15M E of Slyne Head, and Cashla, 32M from Slyne Head, affords a fascinating cruising ground with a wide choice of anchorages among several bays.

For 20M between Cashla and Galway the N shore of Galway Bay is exposed with no safe hbrs. The S side has a number of anchorages between Galway and Black Head. Thence the 45M of coast to Loop Head has no safe anchorage and should be given a good offing. Passages to or from the S can be shortened by spending a night at Kilronan, Aran Is, in most weather conditions.

If making a direct passage between the Aran Is and Blasket Sound, note that the course from the Gregory Sound to Sybil Pt passes 7M W of Loop Head. There is no light between Inisheer and Loop Head (33M SW of Inisheer) and at night it is important not to get to the E of the direct course. Nor is there any major light between Loop Hd and Inishtearaght (39M). In the prevailing swell there is a pronounced set to the E for which it is wise to allow 5°.

Yachts bound between the Mayo, Sligo or Donegal coasts and the S might consider a direct Inishbofin – Valentia passage, thus eliminating considerable deviation of course to hbrs on this coast. Direct course takes you within 1M of Slyne Head.

There are, however, possible anchorages between Loop Head and Sybil Point which, apart from Smerwick Harbour, involve varying deviations from the direct course.

If passing through or outside the Blaskets, it is especially important to note and respect those areas where overfalls are indicated on the large-scale chart. The magnetic anomaly to the N of the Blaskets is to be treated seriously: its influence is reported as very localised but extreme enough to spin the compass through 360°!

The best hbrs of refuge are, in the N of the area, Roundstone and Cashla Bays, and S of Loop Hd, Smerwick in S'ly gales and Dingle in N'lies. Yachts may also run for shelter in the River Shannon, notably to Carrigaholt or Kilrush.

Anchorages
• In 3–4m off Rosroe Point as shown on chart.
• Better still at the head beyond Ship Rock. Turn to stb to anchor as convenient in 2–3m (mud) ½ca SE of Ship rock or in the bay 1½ca NNE of Salrock House; a good berth in perfect shelter. A good anchor is required in strong blows. Water from well with permission of the owner of Salrock House. No other facilities.
• Killary eight visitors' moorings.

Killary Harbour
Alternatively, leave the bns and Inishbarna to stb to enter this dramatically picturesque 'fjord'. There are eight visitors' moorings near the top of the long hbr some seven miles beyond Inishbarna.

Caution Only attempt this area in good visibility during daylight. Chart 2706 essential.

CLIFDEN BAY

Chart BA 2708;
Imray C54

HW Galway +0005

MHWS	MHWN
4·4m	3·4m

This bay is well sheltered, but now has a number of fish farms with their attendant gear. The town of Clifden which can be approached by dinghy on a rising tide has all facilities and is one of the best places for victualling on this coast. EC Thursday.

Approach Pick up the conspic bn on Carrickrana Rock. Keep clear of the Corbet Shoal breakers. Approaching the Carrickrana rock alter course to stb to leave the Carrickrana bn at least 4ca to port, continue round the bn at this range until Clifden Castle (ruins) is just open of Fishery Point on a bearing of 080°. Steer this course, leaving the Doolick rocks and ledge well to stb, toward Fishery Point until it is 4ca distant, fine on the stb bow, then alter course to 045°.

Entrance Steer 045° until Fahy Point (to your NW) bears 289°. Turn to stb to 109° and maintain Fahy Point on the stern bearing 289°. This will take you over the Bar. 4m minimum at datum.

Caution Have your echo sounder on as silting is reported from the north.

Thence steer up the bay toward 'Double Rock' bn. There is a second bar, 'The Oyster Bank', (0·9m datum) a little S of the shallow creek that leads to Clifden town. From a position 50m west of Double Rock bn steer 160° for 2ca, then ease to port until the bn bears 340° over your stern. After a further 2ca you are into the deeper waters of Ardbear Bay. Continue up this bay but keep to stb to avoid the 'Yellow Slate Rock' (dr 1·2m) after which all hazards are visible.

Anchorages
• Off the bn which marks the entrance to Clifden Harbour, slightly to NW. Road to Clifden town approx 1½M. Mud.
• Off Drinagh Pt in 5m. Beware of ebb in overfall from Ardbear Bay. A good place to wait for the flood tide up to Clifden Harbour for shallow draught yachts.
• Any unoccupied place in Ardbear Bay (*see above for entrance transit*). Beware of Yellow Slate Rock which dries 1·2m about 5ca above Oyster Bank.
• The head of the bay has good shelter giving the shore a fair berth. No facilities.

Moorings There are moorings on the southshore of Ardbear Bay and eight visitors' moorings in Clifden Bay.

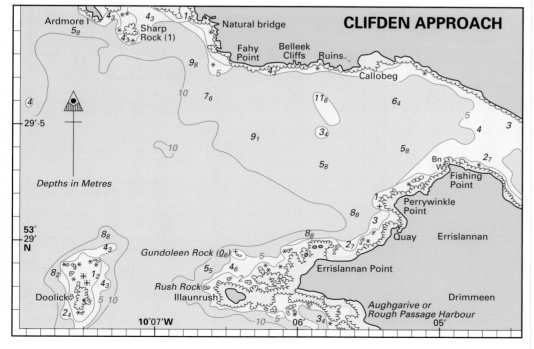

CLIFDEN APPROACH

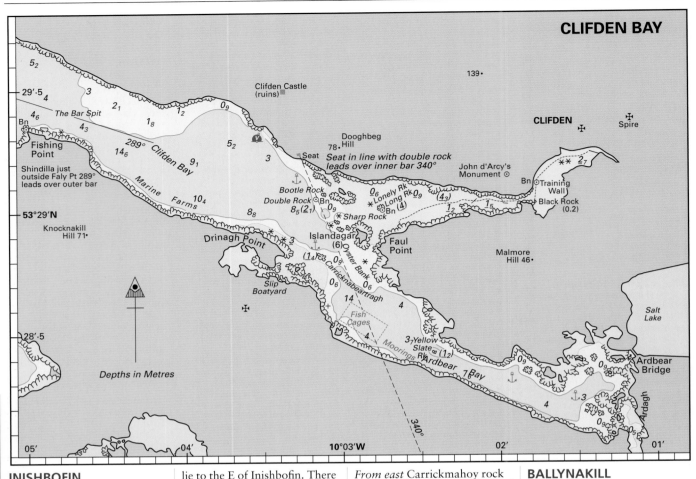

CLIFDEN BAY

CLIFDEN

Spire

139·

Clifden Castle
(ruins)

Dooghbeg
Hill

78·

Seat *Seat in line with double rock
leads over inner bar 340°*

John d'Arcy's
Monument ⊙

Bn ⊙ Training
Wall

Black Rock
(0.2)

29'·5

The Bar Spit

Bn

Fishing
Point

*Shindilla just
outside Faly Pt 289°
leads over outer bar*

289° Clifden Bay

Marine Farms

53°29'N

Knocknakill
Hill 71·

Drinagh Point

Bootle Rock
Double Rock

Lonely Rk

Long Rk

Bn
Bn (4)

*Sharp Rock

Islandagar

Oyster Bank

Carricknabeartragh

Faul
Point

Malmore
Hill 46·

Salt
Lake

Slip
Boatyard

Fish
Cages

Moorings

Yellow
Slate

Ardbear

Ardbear
Bay

Ardbear
Bridge

28'·5

Depths in Metres

340°

Ardagh

05'   04'   **10°03'W**   02'   01'

INISHBOFIN

Chart BA 2707;
Imray C54

HW Galway +0010

MHWS	MHWN	MLWN	MLWS
4·1m	3·1m	1·6m	0·5m

A favourite port of call for
yachts on passage N or S,
however the area is strewn with
rks so it must be approached
with caution. Whilst safe
inside, exit would be impossible
in S/SW gales.

Approach

From the N Leave Inishturk to
port – it is clear, and steer for
Davillaun Island. Pass between
it and the Black Rocks which
lie to the E of Inishbofin. There
is a dangerous rock to W of
Davillaun but it is close
inshore. Lyon Head is clean
with a sectored Lt Fl.WR.7·5s.
Keep close ½ca along the shore
steering to the W. When the hbr
opens up look for the new
sectored Lt DirOc.6s, about
130m to WSW of the nearest
conspic W tr. Once in the very
narrow W sector turn hard to
stb onto 021°. As you enter the
hbr this leads you very close to
a 1.2m patch. Do not enter the
R sector. Leave Gun Rk Fl(2)6s
close to stb. Should the sectored
Lt be extinguished enter on the
transit of the two W trs (032°)
but this leads you very close to
Gun Rk.

From east Carrickmahoy rock
lies 8ca due S of Lyon Head and
should be carefully avoided.
Then similar to above.

From south Good approach is
from between High Is and Friar
Is. Make 10° toward Gun Rock
to pick up transit as above.

At night Enter on 021° in the
narrow W sector of the
Dir.Oc.WRG.6s light.

Anchorage Having passed the
fort on Port Is turn to E and
anchor in the pool in 2–4m.
Leave fairway clear for access
of ferries to the new pier. Do
not go further E than abreast of
the building with three
chimneys, as the bay shelves
rapidly. Fishing boats moored
here have heavy ground tackle
running E–W. Holding good.
Can be gusty.

Facilities Dinghy landing at the
New quay, but keep clear of the
ferry berths, on the foreshore
or, above half tide, the old pier
at the E end of the hbr. Small
shop on hbr front. Two good
pubs, one with bar food, and a
good hotel. Water, with hose,
on the old stone quay. Work
has been completed to provide
2m LAT channel to the quay
and short-term mooring
alongside the quay. In addition
improved access to the dredged
inner hbr allows it to be used
for shelter in severe conditions.
Consult the HM or Day's Inn
for conditions. The islanders
are very friendly towards
visitors. Ferry to Cleggan.

BALLYNAKILL

Chart BA 2706;
Imray C54

HW Galway +0018

MHWS	MHWN	MLWN	MLWS
4·1m	3·1m	1·6m	0·5m

This bay is a good and
picturesque alternative to
Salrock (Little Killary). It is
easier to enter and if the
weather outside is bad affords a
number of sheltered bays to
explore. BA Chart 2706
desirable.

Approach Between Inishbroon
and Cleggan Point. Leave
Mullaghadrina rocks (covered
at HWS) to port and keep close
to Freaglillaun in order to avoid
the Ship Rock.

Entrance Leave Carrigeen
Rocks, always showing, and
Ardagh Rock, covers, marked
by small orange bn tr, to stb if
proceeding to Deryinver bay.
Otherwise to port. Fish farming
in the area.

Anchorages

• Fahy Bay in 2–3m. Good
holding. Eight visitors'
moorings. Enter over the bar
SSE of Ross point 2ca SSE of
the point 0·2m on sufficient rise
of tide using sounder.

• 1ca ENE of Ross Point 2–3m.
Tide rode, but good shelter
from W.

• Derryinver Bay about ½ca SSW
of pier in 2m (mud). Entry N of
Carrigeen and Ardagh Rocks.

• In the pool NW of
Doleengarve 3–4m. Accessible
at half tide.

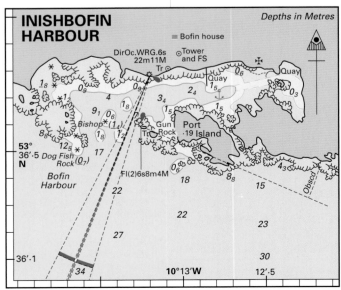

**INISHBOFIN
HARBOUR**

Depths in Metres

■ Bofin house

DirOc.WRG.6s
22m11M

⊙Tower
and FS
Tr

Quay

Quay

Bishop

Gun
Rock
Tr

Port
Island

**53°
36'·5
N**

Dog Fish
Rock

Fl(2)6s8m4M

Bofin
Harbour

Obscd

36'·1   **10°13'W**   **12'·5**

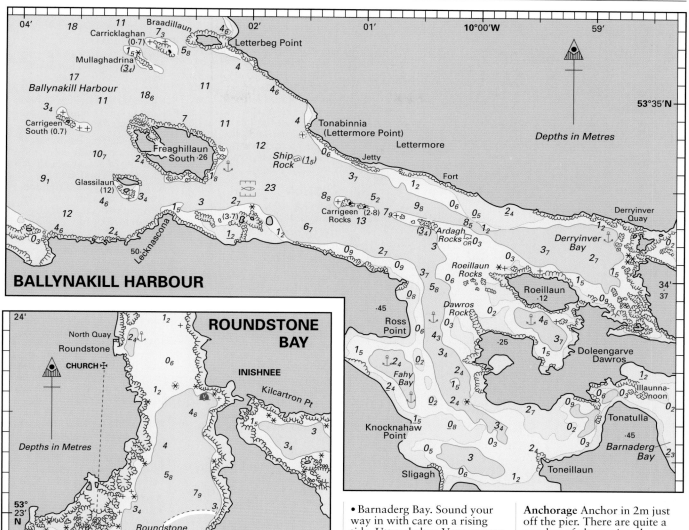

BALLYNAKILL HARBOUR

ROUNDSTONE BAY

Depths in Metres

- Barnaderg Bay. Sound your way in with care on a rising tide. Utter shelter. Very narrow entrance.

ROUNDSTONE

Chart BA 2709;
Imray C54

HW Galway +0003

MHWS	MHWN	MLWN	MLWS
4·4m	3·4m	1·7m	0·5m

A well-sheltered anchorage in shallow water exposed only to strong SSE winds when shelter could be found in Bertraghboy bay. A good base from which to explore the nearby bays: Bertraghboy and Cashel. The appropriate chart is recommended.

Approach From the W steer E to avoid Murvey and Caulty Rocks to be left to port. The Wild Billows Rock with Illunacroagh More and its outlying dangers to be left to stb.

When SE of Inishlackan alter course for Inishnee Pt sectored Lt Fl(2)WRG.10s, enter the bay giving a fair berth to both sides but tend towards the W side to avoid rock which lies 3½ca SE of pier.

Bar There is a bar with 0·9m some 1½ca SSE of the 2·4m pool outside Roundstone Harbour. Beware of salmon nets and fish farms.

Anchorage Anchor in 2m just off the pier. There are quite a number of alternative places to lie in the area which can best be ascertained from the chart.

Moorings Four visitors' moorings have been laid in the bay ½M SE of the hbr to avoid passage of the bar. Beware the Rock 1½ca NW. But these are in a more exposed location and leave a long dinghy ride to the village.

Facilities Water. A mini supermarket and other shops, good pubs with bar food, hotels, PO and bus to Galway. Diesel at local garage. Gaz in shops. Roundstone is fast becoming a dormitory for Clifden and a weekend residence for Galway but it retains much of its old charm. Zetland Hotel at the head of Cashel Bay is very well known.

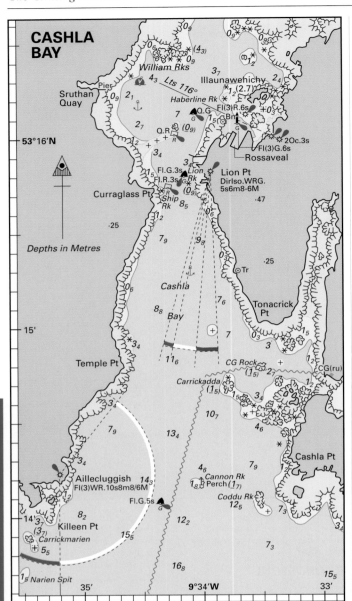

Facilities Supplies are limited, but there are groceries, telephone, church, bus to Galway and a pub about 1M where petrol can be obtained.

There is a further anchorage up the bay at Bealadangan which can be approached with great care on a rising tide. Again limited stores and pub. If time permits, the rest of this bay and the inlet to westward, Kilkieran, can be explored with care and a dinghy.

CASHLA

Chart BA 2096;
Imray C54

HW Galway –0008

MHWS	MHWN	MLWN	MLWS
4·7m	3·6m	1·8m	0·5m

One of the most sheltered anchorages on this part of the coast. It has the added advantage of being lit with two fixed lights and a number of lit and unlit buoys. Entry is possible in practically all weather. But it is the ferry port for the Aran Isles and with the growing tourist activity plus many fishing boats is becoming noisy and busy. If seclusion and scenery are sought Greatman's bay, though lacking facilities, may be preferred.

Approach
From W The North Sound, between Inishmore and Gorumna Is. 1M or more S of Golam tr steer 090°. Keep Golam tr open of Loughcarrick Is (S Point of Gorumna) 283° clears English Rock (dries 1m). When Greatman Bay (do not mistake this bay for Cashla) is clear open to N, alter to port toward Cashla keeping Killeen Point Fl(3)WR.10s on port bow and give the point at least 7ca offing. At night approach in the

W sector bearing <360°. Leave Cannon Rock G con Lt buoy Fl.G.5s to stb.

From S Killeany Bay, Gregory Sound, Foul Sound or South Sound. Head for Cashla Entrance keeping in W sector of Killeen Lt and leaving Cannon Rock G con Lt buoy Fl.G.5s close to starbord.

From E Galway Bay. Coast to stb (N) is generally clean. Give an offing of 5ca. When abreast Cloghmore Point steer for Killeen Point to find Cannon Rock G con Lt buoy. Beware off-lying rocks to W of Cloghmore Head.

Entrance Between Killeen Point with its outlying Narien Spit and Cannon Rock. Lion Point bn, DirIso.WRG.5s, by night in W sector, shows way in. Off Curraghglass Point is the dangerous Ship Rock to port R can Lt buoy Fl.R.3s and to stb Lion Rock G con Lt buoy Fl.G.3s off Lion Point. There is a drying patch 3ca due N of Lion Rock marked by a R can buoy Q.R and 1·5ca beyond it a G con Lt buoy Q.G. Give each a berth. 1ca beyond the G sight the Ldg Lts Oc.3s 116° to Rossaveal Harbour. Leave bn Fl(3)R.6s to port and G bn Fl(3)G.6s to stb. The transit takes care of the bn on the rock to W of the pier head and Haberline Rock 1ca due N of it.

Anchorages
• Rossaveal Harbour, which is a busy fishing port, clear of fishing boat fairways. (A marina is at project stage). It is possible to lie alongside a friendly boat.
• The alternative anchorage is off Struthan Quay to WNW of Rossaveal in 3m. Eight visitors' moorings.

GREATMAN BAY

Chart BA 2096;
Imray C54

HW Galway –0008

MHWS	MHWN	MLWN	MLWS
4·7m	3·6m	1·8m	0·5m

This bay lies between Gorumna Island and the mainland. It is immediately to the W of Cashla and can be confused with Cashla if care is not taken.

Entrance Its entrance, which has no lights, is relatively simple provided chart 2096 is on hand.

Anchorages There is an anchorage off the quay at Natawnay in approx 3m but it is a 2M walk to the village of Carrowe for the simplest of supplies. The best anchorage is off Maurmeen Quay approx 1½M further up the bay on the Gorumma side. It is guarded by a number of unmarked rocks. The best place to lay your anchor is 4ca NW of the quay in 3m.

Moorings Four visitors' moorings have been laid off Maurmeen.

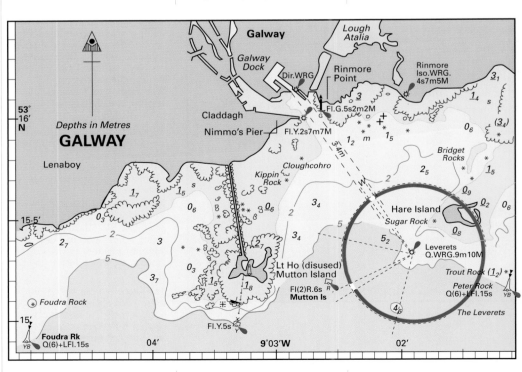

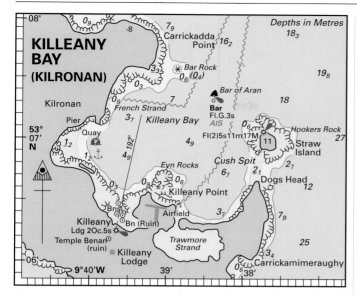

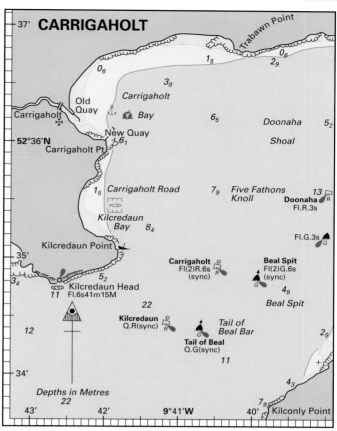

Facilities At Rossaveal: Small shop ½M, pub 1M, bus to Galway. Diesel and water available.

At Struthan: shops, hotel, church, telephone, and bus to Galway at Carraroe, 1M. Fuel 200yds. Water at quay.

GALWAY

Chart BA 1984;
Imray C55

HW Galway

MHWS	MHWN	MLWN	MLWS
5·1m	3·9m	2·0m	0·6m

The major city of western Ireland. It has an airport, excellent rail and road communications, and all the amenities one would expect, with a safe, sheltered entry in all but very strong S to SE winds.

Approaches From between the fairway buoys, Fl.R.3s and Fl.G.3s to the S of Black Rock. Head 054° for Hare Island or Levrets bn sectored light Q.WRG.9m10M. Stay within the W sector until within 2ca then head N until into the NW W sector of the same light. Turn to 325° toward the hbr entrance staying in the W sector. A conspicuous silo just inside the hbr is a useful guide.

Entrance Between Nimmo's Pier head Fl.Y.2s7m7M and Rinmore Point G bn Fl.G.5s, in the W sector of a fixed sectored light on the end of the dock pier. The narrow W sector has Alt.WG immediately to stb then F.G. To port there is Alt.WR immediately then F.R. The dock opens from HW–0200 to HW+0100. If waiting call HM VHF 16, 12 (but may only be available from HW–0200 to HW+0100) ① 353(0)91 562329 to lie alongside the SW side of the pier to the E of the lock or to the NE of this pier in the 'layby'. There is sufficient room to round up in the 'layby' and it is unsafe to use these points in strong S–SE winds. Yachts must not be left unattended as the

fishing fleet uses these berths and it becomes crowded. Enter through the lock to the Inner Dock then turn to port and moor in the SW basin, reserved for small craft, or to port against the SE wall for larger craft.

Facilities All facilities. Boat repairs but no slip. Some shops close all day Monday. The HM is welcoming but the hbr can be dirty. Diesel by can.

KILRONAN HARBOUR, KILLEANY BAY, ARAN IS

Chart BA 3339;
Imray C55

HW Galway –0008

MHWS	MHWN	MLWN	MLWS
4·7m	3·6m	1·8m	0·5m

Much the most sheltered anchorage in the Aran Islands. Major building works at Kilronan (2011).

Approach
From W through to N North Sd. Between Inishmore and Goruma Island. Keep at least 1M clear of the Inishmore shore line. A shoal extends N from Carrickadda Point over which swell may break. When Killeany Lodge opens clear of Carrickadda Point >192° shape course for Staw Is Lt Fl(2)5s leaving Killeany G con Lt buoy Fl.G.3s 1ca to stb.

From N through to ESE make for position 3ca N of Straw Is Lt then for G con buoy.

From S Gregory Sound. Keep 2ca clear of Inishmore shore and 3ca off Straw Is. Steer for G con buoy.

Entrance For best water 1ca E of Killeany G con buoy on transit of Temple Benan (ruin) in line with N edge of sand patch 226° on S shore of the bay. When 1ca S of the buoy turn to stb WSW for 1ca S of the pier.

Anchorage 1–2ca S of the pier in 3m. There are also several visitors' moorings. Well sheltered.

Facilities Diesel, water, groceries, pub, ferry and air service to Galway. There are excellent walks in the area. Bicycles and a sidecar can be hired to see the more remote parts of the island and particularly the outstanding 1000BC fort at Dunaengus.

CARRIGAHOLT

Chart BA 1547;
Imray C55

HW Galway –0015

MHWS	MHWN	MLWN	MLWS
4·9m	3·7m	1·9m	0·7m

This is a wide bay about 1½M N of Kilcredaun Point in the entrance to the River Shannon. Well sheltered from SSW through W to NNW. If going well into the bay to anchor off Old Quay, shallow draught only, take care regarding the soundings which date from 1842.

Approach The mouth of the Shannon is approx 11M wide lying between Loop Head and Kerry Head. It is well lit and all dangers are marked. In strong winds S through W to NW there are bad races during the ebb. Give both heads a good berth.

Entrance The inner entrance to the River is between Kilcredaun Head and Kilconly Point. Approx 1¾M wide. The main channel is marked by buoys. The coast to port is clear of dangers if given a cable offing to pass Ladder Rock under the light and the wreck which shows 1·2m at LW under the battery.

Anchorages
• E of the New Quay in 6m, sand. It is possible to lay alongside, but it is occupied by lobster boats most of the time.
• About 2ca SSW of above in 4m if the wind is NW.
• About 3ca E of the Old Quay in 2m, or use one of the visitors' buoys.

Berthing At the Old Quay for shallow draught boats. *See warning above.*

Facilities It's about 10 minutes' walk from the New Quay to the village of Carrigaholt. Groceries, fuel, meat, doctor, PO and telephone, restaurant in summer.

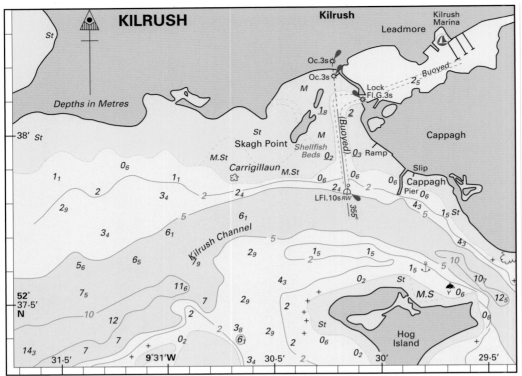

IRELAND

KILRUSH

Chart BA 1547;
Imray C55

HW Galway +0012sp, +0027np

MHWS	MHWN	MLWN	MLWS
5·0m	3·7m	1·7m	0·5m

The best place to leave a boat or for a crew change on the W coast. With an excellent marina accessible at all states.

Approach About 5M up the Shannon from Kilcreadaun Point on a course of 068° to Kilrush Channel. Leave Scattery Is and Hogg Is to stb. N of Hogg Is turn to port at a RW sph Lt buoy LFl.10s to enter the buoyed Kilrush marina channel.

Entrance Channel is dredged 1·5m and buoyed port and stb. Ldg Lts Oc.3s by night 355°. Then turn to stb to 070° in G sector of lock approach Lt Fl.G.3s to reach the lock. Lock available at all states of tide and free-flow if height sufficient. For lock opening and berthing instruction contact marina office VHF 80 (or ☎ 065 905 2072) or marina manager, Mr John Hehir, on *Mobile* 0862 313870 some 30 minutes before arrival. Through the night the lower gates of the lock will be left open so that arriving yachts can berth in the lock from midnight to 0900.

Berthing In well-found marina as directed.

Facilities Comprehensive marina with full services and laundry. The marina controls a fully operational boatyard with a full range of services provided by five nominated specialist contractors. A 45-tonne travel-lift crane with jib for mast lifting and stepping. Space for secure winter storage, open or covered, available. www.kilrushcreekmarina.ie

Flourishing town with pubs and restaurants. All supplies available in town 200m. Shannon International Airport 1hr, bus to Dublin (about 5hrs).

Anchorages
• Temporary or fair weather anchorage to the NE of Hogg Island. Tide runs hard.
• In the bays to the E and SE of Scattery Island. Check depths carefully on the shoaling shore.

ASKEATON

Chart BA 1549

Some 18 miles further up the well-marked Shannon, beyond Foynes Island on south shore is the River Deel tributary. RW pillar buoy at entrance to channel, marked by port hand perches, to pontoon berths with 1·7m LWS. But channel is only accessible HW –0100 through HW. Fully equipped boatyard, ☎ 061 392198, with specialist services, including GRP repairs and crane.

FENIT

Chart BA 2739;
Imray C55

HW Cobh –0057sp –0017np

MHWS	MHWN	MLWN	MLWS
4·6m	3·4m	1·6m	0·5m

The hbr is formed by a long breakwater connecting Great Samphire Island northward to the shore and a short breakwater projecting NE from the island for 1½ca. Within the enclosed angle an L-shaped breakwater with a short overlapping pier enclose a custom built marina.

Approach From seaward about midway between Mucklaghbeg and Mucklaghmore rocks. Keep in the W sector of a light on Little Samphire Island Fl.WRG.5s 17m16-13M. Head for the island 147° until within ½M then turn S to leave it comfortably to port. When Great Samphire Lt Q.R comes in sight turn to round it to port. Then along the NE aligned pier to round the pier head to a reciprocal course toward the marina. Watch depth carefully. Port Control VHF 16, 14.

Entrance Between the pier heads Iso.G.6s6m and Iso.R.6s6m. Berth as directed. VHF 80 or *Mobile* +353(0)97460516.

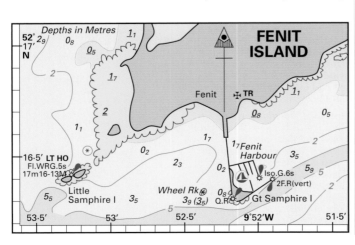

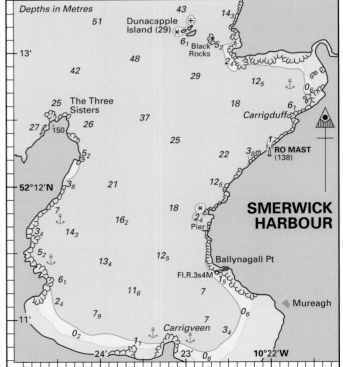

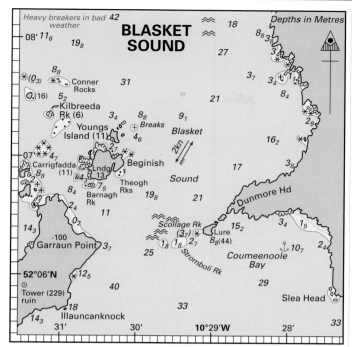

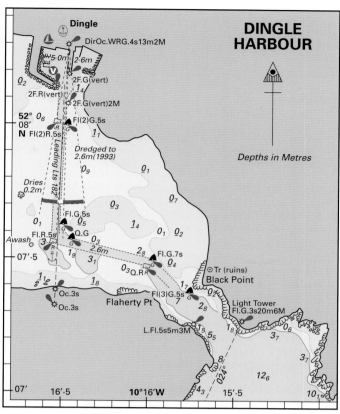

Anchorages Clear of the fairway to the marina or further east under the lee of the hbr. The bottom shoals rapidly northward.

Facilities Electricity and water on pontoons. Showers. Fuelling berth. Village: one general store/PO with limited supplies. Bar restaurant.

SMERWICK HARBOUR

Chart BA 2789;
Imray C55

HW Cobh –0107sp –0027np

MHWS	MHWN
3·8m	2·8m

Tide sets N across the entrance at Dover –0100 at 1kn. This wide bay is open to NW to NE and subject to swell in N winds, but some protection will be found close in on the W side in NW winds and tucked up in the NE corner in northeasterlies.

Approach The approach is clear from the N, but there are no lights in the area. From the S coming from Sybil Point a rk about 3ca due N of middle of the Three Sisters must be avoided. These cliffs are about 150m high.

Entrance Between Dunacapple Island and the northern most of the Three Sisters about 1M wide. Do not pass between Duncacapple Is and the mainland. There is a rock just to W of the island.

Anchorage
• In Smerwick Road just N of the Boat Harbour marked on the chart in good holding.
• In the bay to the NE corner of the hbr. Gives shelter in N winds. Do not go in beyond the 2m line as there are boulders. Beware of pots and nets. Pier on Ballynagall Point beware rocks at inshore end.

• In the bay just S of Ballynagall Point in order to get stores at Bulitsnitty. The bottom is rock just off the pier. Further to the SW in this bay is good holding in sand, in 2m just W of Carrigveen Point.

Facilities At Ballynagall (known locally as Ballydavid) there are limited shops, pub, and tel. At Carrigveen there is petrol beyond the sandhills.

BLASKET SOUND

Chart BA 2789;
Imray C55

DS Dover –0115 N +0445 S, 2–3kn

From the N steer 195° keeping the Tr on Sybil Head in line with Clogher Rock off Clogher Head making sure not to deviate to the W when passing the rocks off Youngs Is and Beginnish Is. South of Clogher Head and around Stromboli Rock off Dunmore Head there are overfalls which should be avoided.

DINGLE HARBOUR

Chart BA 2790;
Imray C55

HW Cobh –0111sp –0041np

MHWS	MHWN	MLWN	MLWS
4·0m	3·2m	1·0m	0·0m

Dingle is a large natural hbr with a fishing port on its N shore just to the W of which is a well sheltered marina with close access to the town.

Approach Identify Eask tr 195m conspic about 8ca W of entrance. Beware Crow Rock dries 3·7m 3ca off shore to W of entrance. A course of 024° with Lt tr Fl.G.3.s on NE side of entrance open of Reenbeg Point clears Crow Rock.

Entrance At the entrance you are likely to be met by the friendly local dolphin, Funji, that has brought tourist fame to Dingle. Keep slightly to port of centre of channel to avoid rocky foreshore of Black Point. Then follow a narrow buoyed channel round the S coast of hbr until Ldg Lts Oc.3s come abeam to port. Turn sharply to

stb to observe sectored light (Oc.WRG.4s bearing 002°) visible day and night. Keep in White sector N up a narrow, straight, dredged channel toward the pier head 2F.G(vert). When ½ca from the pier turn to port into the marina.

Anchorage There is safe anchorage to be found at 52°07'·50N 10°16'·55W just south of the red can buoy. But keep clear of pot markers.

Berthing VHF 80 is not watched continuously but the marina master keeps a sharp lookout at all likely times. Berth as he directs.

Facilities Dedicated marine sports building beside the marina with daytime restaurant/café, showers and laundry. Fuel. Marina master can supply diesel by can. Busy tourist-orientated town for all supplies. Hotels, good pubs and restaurants. Gas at Foxy John's Bar. Bus to trains at Trallee. Wi-Fi.

IRELAND

Belgium

Introduction

An excellent first call on the way to more distant places, but popular in its own right. Oostende has a spring maritime show, *Oostende vor Anchor*, and many period vessels accumulate there. Nieuwpoort presents a village atmosphere and copious berths. Zeebrugge offers good facilities, a serious fish market and numerous eating opportunities. Nearby is Blankenberg, a resort town with pleasant cafés, promenade and shopping facilities.

All are connected by the efficient tram service that spans the length of the coast, taking two hours in all, and making light of day tripping – just right for a rainy day!

Interior attractions within easy reach include Brugge and Ghent, even Brussels, by train or own vessel via the canals (see page 304).

Marine services are good throughout and berthing charges reasonable. Much has been made of the Belgian aversion to UK vessels running on red diesel, but the reality is that free passage is permitted, as elsewhere.

Passage along the coast between Oostende and Calais is somewhat constrained by sandbanks, but well marked channels make the whole coast passable in most conditions.

Entry requirements and regulations

Belgium is part of the Schengen system of countries having no internal borders, and vessels from the UK, which is not party to this scheme, must register their presence at the first port encountered. Schengen forms should be downloaded in advance free from the RYA site – they are rarely available from HMs abroad – and deposited in the marked boxes on first landing, retaining a copy on board. Compliance is mandatory, if rarely checked. All ports are recognised ports of entry. See www.rya.org.uk and also *page 16* for other necessary documents and fuel regulations.

Weather forecasts

Navtex is broadcast from Oostende on VHF M and T. Weather forecasts in English are broadcast on VHF 27 at 0720 LT and 0820 and 1720 UT. Gale warnings are issued on receipt and at H+55 on VHF 24.

Search and rescue

There is an MRCC based at Oostende VHF 16, for boats with DSC the MMSI No. is 002050480. ☎ 059 701100.

Language

Belgium is divided into two monolingual regions plus the capital, Brussels, which is bi-lingual. The northern Flemish speaking region includes the provences of West and Oost-Vlaanderen, Antwerpen, Vlaams-Brabant and Limburg; the southern Walloon district makes up most of the remainder. Although Flemish is officially the same as common Dutch, dialects account for a number of differences in spelling and pronunciation. In the Walloon region, French is easily understood. English is widely used by harbourmasters and lock operators on the coast and in large cities, but less so in the remoter areas.

Charts

BA and Imray charts provide coverage of the passages to Belgium and along the coast. If intending to continue to the Netherlands, the Dutch Hydrographic Folio *1801* also covers the Belgian coast from Nieuwpoort.

Other sources of information

The following guides may be found useful:

North Sea Passage Pilot by Brian Navin. (Imray).
Inland Waterways of Belgium Jacqueline Jones (Imray).
Cruising the Inland Waterways of France & Belgium by Roger Edgar & Iain Stitt (Cruising Association).

Smoothing the Way

Transport facilities in Belgium are very good. The coastal tramway connects all ports along the whole length of the Belgian coast and is valuable for the ferry ports (Oostende to Ramsgate, and Zeebrugge to Hull services) plus rail at Oostende (direct connection to Brussels) The motorway runs along the coast from Dunkerque to Oostende then inland to Brussels, Brugge and Gent. Except Blankenberge, all ports offer canal access to the interior.

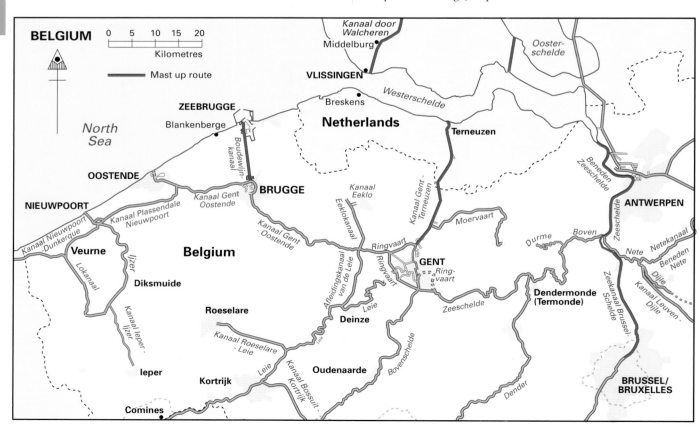

CROSSING THE SOUTHERN NORTH SEA TO BELGIUM

Charts BA 1872; F 6735; B 11; N 1801; Imray C30

The Belgian coast is mainly sand. The approach is strewn with shallows and banks, but buoyage and lights are excellent, so the approach from UK should be straightforward.

For further navigational guidance see Crossing the N Sea in the Netherlands section (page 251).

Nieuwpoort, Oostende, Zeebrugge and Blankenberge offer excellent shelter and facilities 24/7 but Blankenberge's entrance (*see page 246*) has depth restrictions. From the UK, Oostende and Zeebrugge/Blankenberge can be approached directly, the channels being well marked. But the approach to Nieuwpoort requires more careful navigation to avoid the off-lying banks.

From the Dover Strait the typical approach is via Dunkerque East, using the buoyed Chenal Intermediare. East of Dunkerque, divert through the Pass de la Zuydcoote (buoyed) into the Westdiep to avoid the Trapegeer sands. Thereafter the inshore channel to Oostende is buoyed. Further passage up the coast holds no major threats beyond navigating the huge moles at Zeebrugge at sufficient distance to avoid reflected waves in rough weather, and commercial traffic.

Shipping movements into Zeebrugge and along the coast to the Westerschelde River are heavy. East of Zeebrugge the Scheur/Wielingen deep water channel runs into the Westerschelde and small vessels should keep S of it as it closes the coast at Vlissingen. North of this waterway lies the Raan bank, to be avoided.

Approaches to Oostende and Zeebrugge are well marked, but at night the number of lit buoys in the area plus vessel movements can be distracting.

Many resorts along the coast present a similar appearance but Oostende can be distinguished by its very high Europa Centrum tower right next to the port entrance.

Tides run SW–NE along the coast, starting to the E at Dover –0015, and Dover +0445 to the W; the average rate is 2kn.

Note that E-going tides offer only 4hr 'lift' on this coast, W-going at least 7h; useful for the return trip to UK.

Southeast England to Northeast France, Belgium and Holland distances (miles)

	Dunkerque	Oostende	Breskens	Stellendam	IJmuiden	Den Helder	W Terschelling
Dover	40	63	80	149	151	175	203
Ramsgate	43	60	83	137	139	161	189
Sheerness	73	76	109	131	159	168	196
Burnham	90	93	107	125	148	163	191
Bradwell	89	94	105	121	143	164	192
Harwich	61	80	86	105	126	145	173
Lowestoft	101	87	95	97	104	118	146

NIEUWPOORT

Charts BA 1873; B 11; Imray C30, 2100

HW Vlissingen –0110sp –0050np

DS Dover –0130E +0545W.

MHWS	MHWN	MLWN	MLWS
5·3m	4·3m	1·2m	0·5m

A small historic port town, formerly a military base, now housing major marina facilities – arguably the premier small vessel facility in Belgium.

Approach and Entrance The Banc Smal and Nieuwpoort banks lie three miles off and should be skirted in rough conditions at LW when seas break over them. The approach from Dunkerque will be along the Chenal Intermediare, diverting through the Pass de la Zuydcoote (buoyed 3m min depth) into the Westdiep to avoid the Trapegeer sands. A firing range in Lombardsijde close E of the Entrance is in use from 15 September to 15 June. Firing is preceded by a W parachute flare. *Radio Lombardsijde* VHF 67. The harbour entrance between two lattice piers is dredged to more than 1·5m but is subject to silting particularly on the E side. The main LtHo Fl(2)R.14s26m16M is a R tower with W horizontal bands and is situated just E of the root of the E pier. Enter parallel to the piers between the two white entrance trs (F.R and F.G Lts). Beware cross-set off entrance. VHF 09.

Berthing The entrance channel divides after 1M. The Royal Nieuwpoort YC on the W branch has large premises with a good restaurant. Shops are more than 20 minutes walk away. Entering the narrow entrance close to stb wall, visitors should contact the HM on fuel pontoon to Pt just inside. HM ☎ 058 23 44 13. The second, much larger, yacht basin on the E branch (Novus Portus) houses the 2400-berth VVW Nieuwpoort marina. The town is reached by road and a bridge ½M away. However, bicycles are made available free of charge for shopping trips and can be hired for extended journeys. VHF 8. HM ☎ 058 23 52 32. In the NE corner of the basin, and directly ahead on entering, is the Royal Belgian Air Force YC which is a 10 minutes walk from shops in the village of Lombaerdsijde, VHF 23. HM ☎ 058 23 36 41. There are restaurants in both marinas. Fuel can be obtained from Royal Nieuwpoort YC and from a grey-painted barge belonging to VVW Nieuwpoort on the port side as you enter the fishing harbour which is 200m up-river from the yacht basin. Self service with credit card, but not all types accepted.

There is a frequent service to Oostende, Blankenberge and Zeebrugge on the coastal tramway which also gives access close to Oostende airport.

Inland connections There is access to the Kanaal Plassendale–Nieuwpoort and the Kanaal Nieuwpoort– Duinkerken via the locks and bridges of the Achterhaven that operate HW±0300 during the day. Onward passage on the River Yzer to the Kanaal Ieper–Yzer is via the Kanaal Plassendale– Nieuwpoort. All canals have fixed bridges restricting headroom (4m–5·5m).

OOSTENDE

Charts BA 1873, 1874; B 11; N 1801.2; Imray C30

HW Vlissingen –0055

DS Dover –0045E +0445W

MHWS	MHWN	MLWN	MLWS
5·1m	4·2m	1·2m	0·5m

A long established very busy fishing and ferry port, also a resort town with excellent beaches plus three marinas. A wide range of shops, restaurants, a casino, transport (including an airport) a good fish market and other tourist facilities justly support Oostende's claim to serious consideration by the cruising sailor.

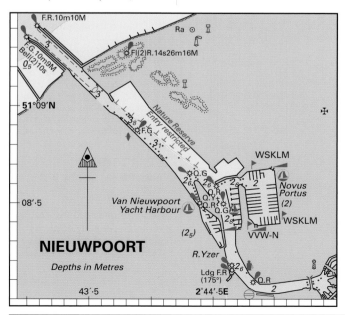

NIEUWPOORT
Depths in Metres

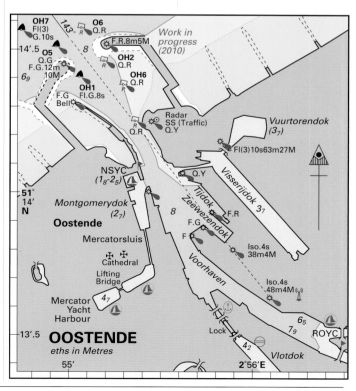

OOSTENDE
Depths in Metres

Approach and Entrance The approach to Oostende entrance is straightforward but the Stroombank 1M SW of the entrance is to be avoided in rough weather. Approaches from the W are inshore via the Kleine Rede, or further out using the Grote Rede. From the E the coastal passage is clear from Zeebrugge, whilst from the N the passage is buoyed through the banks until the N card Buitenstroombank and E card Binnenstroombank buoys are reached.

Two moles with an entrance 200m wide have been constructed, extending 4ca to seaward enclosing the old W pier and previous entrance. Oostende is a very busy commercial and ferry port: beware ship movements in the relatively confined waters of the harbour. Monitor port control VHF 09 and observe port entry lights.

Small vessel lights stand at the entrance to the Montgomery Dock and N Sea marina basin and prohibit exit when large vessels are moving in the main channel.

Berthing Three marinas offer convenient short and longer term mooring facilities. The Royal Yacht Club at the far end of the Voorhaven is quieter with pontoons, better security (gate with code lock) and a friendly clubhouse, but ship movements nearby can disturb sleep; shops close by, otherwise a 15 minute walk or a short tram ride back to town. The Mercator harbour (VHF 14 for berth reservation) in the centre of town is close to the action but access through the lock with its twin bridges is time consuming (daylight hours service): best for a longer stay. The Royal North Sea YC Harbour immediately to stb on entering is smaller; part alongside, and part bow to pontoon with an aft buoy; it is right alongside the pricier restaurants and suffers some disturbance from passing vessels.

Inland connections There is access to the Kanaal Gent–Oostende via the Demey lock, on the SW side of the Voorhaven. Operated at all times in conjunction with the brs either side. Canal has fixed bridges restricting headroom (7m).

BLANKENBERGE

Charts BA 1874; B 11; N 1801.2; Imray C30

HW Vlissingen –0040

DS HW Dover –0100E +0500W

MHWS	MHWN	MLWN	MLWS
4·9m	4·0m	1·0m	0·5m

An important yachting centre, with customs facilities available all year round.

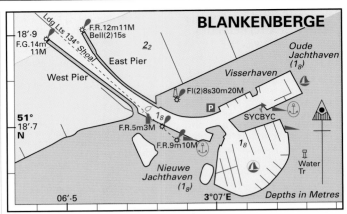

Approach and Entrance The approaches to this harbour are relatively shallow and uncomfortable, possibly even dangerous, in strong onshore winds. The entrance is narrow, between two piers (F.R and F.G), neither of which should be confused with the Casino pier at the E end of the town. The LtHo Fl(2)8s30m20M is near the root of the E pier. The channel is dredged to 1·5m in June each year but is subject to silting, especially after onshore gales. Ldg Lts (F.R) on 134° assist at night and are marked with red crosses for visibility during daylight. Actual minimum depth between the piers is shown in illuminated digits in decimetres from the end of the E pier, but is not visible to out-going vessels. If in doubt about conditions or depth, contact *Traffic Centre Zeebrugge* on VHF 69. All three yacht clubs listen on VHF 23 in season. VHF 8 is local rescue and emergency channel.

Berthing There is a marina in the old harbour which lies to port. A large marina is reached through a narrow passage to stb marked by dolphins, just after the main channel turns to port. Water, electricity and fuel available on pontoons. The three YCs which administer the marina all have good facilities in their own premises. Shops and restaurants are close at hand. Good bathing from the beaches. Fl.Bu Lt prohibits departure of craft of less than 6m LOA. HM ☽ VVW Blankenberge YC 050 41 75 36. Royal Scarphout YC 050 42 89 52, *Mobile* 0476 97 16 92. Free N Sea Sailers *Mobile* 0497 565565. Diesel and petrol available from stage in entrance channel.

ZEEBRUGGE

Charts BA 1872, 1874; B 11; N 1801.2; Imray C30

HW Vlissingen –0035sp –0015np

DS HW Dover E +0500W

MHWS	MHWN	MLWN	MLWS
4·8m	3·8m	1·1m	0·4m

A major facility with two massive moles built out into the N Sea and lit with high

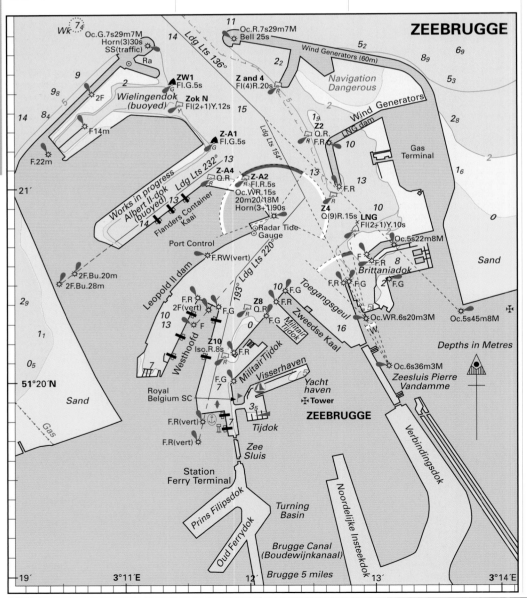

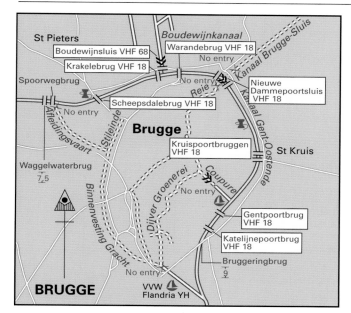

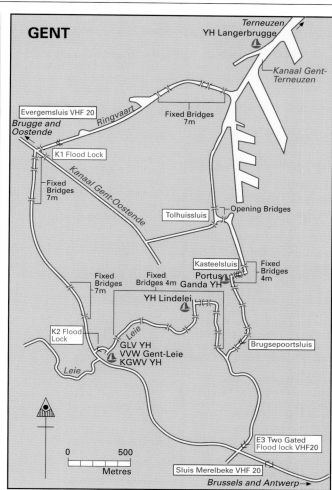

visibility arrays, plus port entry lights. The major fishing port of Belgium, and a fast growing centre for bulk and container traffic. Ferry to Hull. Excellent marina lying deep within the port.

Approach and Entrance If you have VHF radio it is mandatory to call *Zeebrugge Port Control* (VHF 71) before entering or leaving and to maintain a listening watch on that channel while inside the harbour. Because of reflected waves, confused seas may be encountered if approaching too close inshore from the W and to a lesser extent from the E. The entrance can be very rough in strong onshore winds. Tidal stream across the entrance up to 4kn. Occasionally the movement of all craft is prohibited for up to 45 minutes during the arrival/departure of bulk methane carriers.
Berthing A major installation, the marina is well over one mile away from the entrance in the old Visserhaven so not immediately obvious. On entering between the moles, maintain a distance from the outer wall and pass SSE leaving two major docks on stb. Approach old harbour wall (lit) dead slow in case of issuing traffic from beyond. With container quays to stb press on approx S towards lock gates. Note large circular waving base to port and shortly afterwards a narrow turning to port reveals the marina to stb. Reception pontoon and HM close by. Gated entry, code required for re-entry. Club house 400m left of gate: strongly recommended. Other cafés etc nearby.

Inland connections Entrance to the Boudewijn kanaal is usually through the very large Pierre Vandamme sea lock approached from the Toegangsgeul. The Zee Sluis is an alternative (to port after the marina). Check on VHF 68 for

information about operating times and charges. Boats with fixed masts can reach the centre of Brugge from Zeebrugge along this route through two lifting bridges which can be contacted on VHF 68. Speed limit on the Boudewijnkanaal is 7·2km/h (3·9kn). *See Inland Waterways section on page 304 for futher advice.*

BRUGGE
The Boudewijnkanaal joins the Kanaal Gent-Ostende (12km from Zeebrugge) at the Boudewijn lock which is operated Monday–Saturday 0800–1200 and 1300–1700. No service on Sunday and holidays. Bridges around the city are operated throughout the day subject to road traffic flow and normally in convoys starting at 1000 from Katelijnepoortbrug on the SE side, and 1430 from the Nieuwegebrug between Oostende and Brugge. Nieuwe Dammepoortsluis operates throughout the day but transit is normally in convoy or with a commercial vessel. Limited moorings without facilities available on the canal S of the Nieuwe Dammepoort lock (mast-up); in the Coupure (depth 1·5m) between Kruispoortbrug and Gentpoortbrug which have water and electricity and are convenient for the town centre, access restricted to 6m headroom; in Flandria YH (depth 1·6m) S of Brugge ringbrug, with all facilities and convenient for the rly station. HM ✆ 050 38 08 66. Water available at the Nieuwe Dammepoort lock.

GENT
Access from W is 40km along Kanaal Gent-Ostende with fixed bridges (7m). Speed limit 12km/hr (6·5kn). There are also two lifting bridges which do not operate 0750–0820, 1155–1225 and 1700–1730.

The Beernem flood lock normally stands open. Moorings half way at Beernem YC (maximum depth 2m) HM ✆ 0472 394593. Canal joins the Gent ringvaart west of the city (fixed bridges 7m). Turn N for the Kanaal Gent–Terneuzen and Westerschelde via Evergem lock (operates Monday–Saturday 0600–2200, Sunday and holidays 1000–1800) or S for city centre moorings, Brussels and Antwerp.

Access from the N is 32km along the Kanaal Gent-Terneuzen and all brs to the ringvaart, N of the city, are opening. Speed limit 16km/h (8·6kn). From E the ringvaart can be reached via the Schelde from Antwerp. Moorings with all facilities off the Kanaal Gent-Terneuzen at Royal Gent YC, Langerbrugge (mast-up) HM ✆ 09 253 7920; in the River Leie at YCs south of town (maximum depth 2·1m)

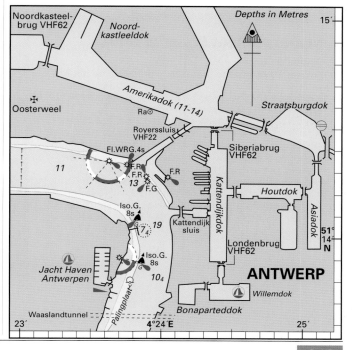

HM ② 09 220 4424 or in the centre at Lindelei (fixed bridges 4m, max depth 2·1m) HM ② 0479 246388 or Portus Ganda (fixed bridges 4m, max depth 2m) HM ② 0472 417843.

Yachting Merelbeke is convenient if entering or leaving the Zeeschelde via Sluis Merelbeke, but is a long way from the city centre.
② 09 245 16 57.

ANTWERP

Charts BA 128; N 1803
HW Vlissingen +0145

MHWS	MHWN	MLWN	MLWS
6·0m	4·9m	0·9m	0·3m

Approach via the Westerschelde some 45M from Vlissingen and 33M from Terneuzen. At the mouth of the Westerschelde spring tidal streams can exceed 4kn and rates are almost as high between sandbanks further into the estuary. Tidal timing is therefore critical and it may be desirable to break the passage at Terneuzen. At Nieuwe Sluis the in-going stream starts at HW Vlissingen −0500 and there is then 8hrs of favourable tide for the passage up river. There is between 4½ and 5hrs of favourable tide for the return passage. The river is well-buoyed and lit, but there is heavy commercial traffic, particularly between Terneuzen and Hansweert. Maintain listening watch on VTS radio channels shown on Dutch charts. Keep to starboard side of channel. Give way to commercial craft. Have engine ready for immediate use and hoist a cone if motor-sailing.

Antwerp Linkerover Yacht Harbour

Entrance Keep N of the Stroomleidam, the N end of which is marked by an 82m pylon, and follow the winding channel until a sharp bend to

starboard at the 107 G buoy (Iso.G.8s) brings the waterfront and churches of Antwerp into view. Keep the floating pontoon to starboard. The entrance to the Jachthaven Antwerpen is marked by a Y can buoy to starboard and a Y can buoy to port. The gate operates approx HW±0100 between 0800 and 2200 (April–October) as long as the level does not exceed 5·3m. Yachts may moor to the Y waiting buoy opposite the entrance, or moor at the floating pontoon about 1M downstream. All moored yachts must keep at least one crew member on board at all times. HM ② 03 219 08 95 There are 350 well-sheltered berths, 70 of which are reserved for visitors. On the return journey, yachts should leave the marina at the first opening of the hbr gate.

The marina offers good sheltered facilities and restaurants nearby. To reach Antwerp by foot, turn left out of the marina and proceed 800m to the Waaslandtunnel entrance building: the free lift descends to the 1km long foot tunnel under the Schelde. You emerge right in the centre of the ancient town. A large supermarket stands 400m opposite the west bank tunnel entrance.

Marina Willemdok

Entrance This harbour is closer to the centre of the city but more time-consuming to enter and leave. Every vessel entering the locks into the dock complex requires an FD number. This can be obtained in advance at www.jachthaven-antwerpen.be or at the time of arrival in the lock (which delays passage through the lock).
The Royersluis (VHF 22) leads to the Siberiabrug (VHF 62) which opens 24hrs except on working days between

0700–0815; 1315–1345 and between 1550–1715. The Londenbrug opens at 0630, 0830, 1000, 1130, 1415, 1530, 1715, 1845, 2015, 2145 and 2245. (VHF 62). The Willemdok is contacted on VHF 23. HM ② +0 3231 5066.

Entry to the docks can also be made through the Kruisschans lock further down river. This involves passage through an additional bridge, the Noordkasteelbrug, which opens 24hrs. VHF 62. Both locks open 24hrs a day. It is usually quicker to use the Kruisschans but both can be time-consuming.

Fuel is available in both harbours.

Inland connections Continuing up the Schelde river leads after 80km to Gent with fixed brs (minimum 5m at HW) beyond Rupelmonde. Speed limit upstream of Dendermonde, 12km/hr (6·5kn) for vessels of 1–2m draught. A strong tide of up to 4kn runs and it is wise to time your passage with the flood. The channel is partially buoyed as far as Temse br. S of Rupelmonde is the very large Wintham sealock up into the non-tidal Zeekanaal Brussel-Schelde. The lock operates 24hrs, though access may not be possible around LW, and leisure boats normally lock through with commercial vessels. It is also possible to lock up into the Zeekanaal from the River Rupel at Sluis Klein Willebroek, but only from HW±0300 during the day. SE of Gent the waterway joins the Gent ringvaart where the Merelbeke lock operates Monday–Saturday 0600–1930, Sunday and holidays 0600–1800.

BRUSSELS

The Zeekanaal Brussel–Schelde connects the Schelde river at Rupelmonde to Brussels (27km). Speed limit on the canal is 18km/hr (9·7kn) for vessels up to 1·5m draught. All bridges as far as the Brussels Royal YC N of the city are opening (maximum air draught when open of 32m) and operate Monday–Saturday 0600–2200. Duties are levied for passage on Sunday or holidays except in July and August 0800–1800. Leisure boats are normally bridged with commercial vessels or in convoys. All facilities including diesel and launderette available at BRYC HM ② 022 41 48 48. Nearby tram service to city centre attractions.

INLAND WATERWAYS OF BELGIUM

Jacqueline Jones

It is over 40 years since there was a guide to the navigable waterways of Belgium in the Imray's catalogue. *Inland Waterways of Belgium* by E E Benest was published at a time when the waterways were used mostly by commercial traffic but like everywhere else in Europe, waterways are no longer essential arteries for trade and are being used increasingly by pleasure craft.

Jacqueline Jones's new waterway-by-waterway guide provides all the essential information for navigation, as well as details about things to do and places to see in Belgium's historic cities. Fully illustrated with clear maps and the author's photography, this book is a must for anyone cruising Belgium or en route to the French or Dutch canals. It comes with a folded map of the Belgian Waterways system.

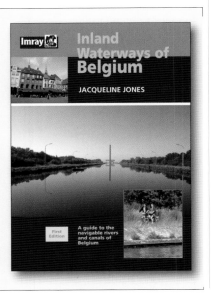

Netherlands

Outstanding cruising opportunities

Holland has a long and rich tradition of water transport, especially sail, and a great legacy of cruising facilities stretching from the major rivers of the south to the Frisian Islands of the north. Hundreds of miles of canals and waterways cross the country, with several hundred marinas, bustling in the summer months with Dutch families, so facilities are generally of a high order. Numerous small villages and old fishing ports provide a background of colour and entertainment that sustain all types of cruising.

Although only a few hours sail from Britain, the weather is noticeably more continental in type – warmer and drier in the summer than much of UK. Comfortable sailing is possible on more days on average, than on much of the UK coastline.

Dutch waters are manicured with buoyage and navigational landmarks, and the approach from the UK is straightforward. Off-lying sandbanks are well marked, and the tides running NE–SW along the coast can be used to good advantage. A large volume of heavy shipping passes along the coast and up the rivers: the Westerschelde and Maas are world class waterways and strict observance of procedures is absolutely essential.

The interior waterways are a unique system, intensively used for pleasure and commerce, much of it free for the visitor. The west of the country has a recognised system permitting boats with a draft of some 2m and an air draft of 18m to pass freely, called the Staande Mastroute. Bridges lift either on demand in quiet places, or to a controlled opening schedule. Passing though locks requires preparation with fenders and lines, but represents no challenge to the well tempered crew. In some towns, a small bridge fee is collected via a clog swung by the bridge master; watch for the signs. With a few words of Dutch, the visitor can take advantage of warning signs and advance service notices along the way, although almost all facilities respond in English.

See page 304 for further details of Inland Waterways.

Passanten (visitors) is the helpful sign denoting a facility open for passing cruisers. But *geen* in front of any word negatives what follows; *frei* means open; a berth so marked is open for use; one marked *bezet* is not. *Toegestaan* means permitted.

Hier melden (contact point) is often signposted on the outer pontoon of a marina – the required procedure to ensure the berth taken is indeed free for the night. Other marinas use green and red flags on each berth to signal free or occupied, and can usually be taken as a good guide to availability.

High season considerations

In the summer a huge range of old sailing barges (the brown armada) sets forth on the inland waterways, with parties of young people aboard. The boats make a fine picture and are very well sailed.

From mid July throughout August the Dutch set out in their boats with families and camp for days on end in certain attractive ports, the Frisian Isles being a prime example; entry to these marinas after midday is often impossible. Rafting in such hotspots and major attractions (Amsterdam etc) is to be expected; be prepared to shuffle the raft at about 0900 when departures normally begin. The Dutch are masters at this, and very helpful to strangers. Otherwise finding a berth is rarely impossible, given the huge number of boats and berths throughout Holland. A number of websites give up to date information on marina facilities eg: www.marina-guide.net

CROSSING THE NORTH SEA TO THE NETHERLANDS

Favourite destinations are: Breskens on the river Westerschelde; the Roompot & Stellendam which lock in to the Osterschelde and Haringvliet waterways; Scheveningen – the port for den Hague; Ijmuiden for the North Sea Canal to Amsterdam; Den Helder – gateway to the Wadden Zee and Ijsselmeer. All are 24/7 ports, well lit and buoyed, and navigable with confidence, with the usual caveat of extra care on approaching a lee shore.

Departure from the east coast of England requires planning to take into account the Thames banks, the tides, the gyratory system off Harwich and the North Sea TSS. From the Thames the optimum course is to head NE with the ebb tide, remaining west of the main North Sea TSS (see below) before striking east to the chosen destination.

From Essex and South Suffolk ports, the favoured course is, again employing the ebb tide, to clear the Long Sand Head and head E to clear the Galloper – taking care in crossing the Sunk Outer traffic system. But departing from mid Suffolk rivers, it is more usual to make for S Shipwash then navigate N or S of the Galloper depending on destination.

Many cruisers approach Holland via ports from the south. Departing Kent, Dunkerque East is the first port of call, using the buoyed Chenal Intermediare on the approach. Proceeding to Nieuwpoort in Belgium by the coast route requires a diversion via the Passe de Zuydcoote (buoyed) to avoid the Trapegeer sands. Thereafter the inshore channel to Oostende is buoyed, and passage onwards holds no major threats beyond passing the huge moles at Zeebrugge at sufficient distance to avoid reflected waves in rough weather, and commercial traffic. Note that east going tides offer only four hours 'lift' on this coast.

The Dutch coast is low sand dunes and shallow on the approach, throwing up short seas in breezy conditions, but approach channels are well marked. The Westerschelde estuary is not advisable in strong wind over tide conditions when a large sea builds, likewise the approach to Den Helder. A night approach to Dutch ports is helped by powerful lights, many visible over quite a distance to sea. Buoyage is exemplary. In any approach, vessels fitted with VHF are required to maintain a listening watch on Vessel Traffic System (VTS) channels. These channels are indicated on the Dutch 1800 series charts.

Wind farms are continuing to be established on several sites on both sides of the North Sea, some surprisingly far from shore. There are numerous gas well-heads off Ijmuiden and off Den Helder; all are clearly lit and charted.

The Harwich Gyratory – Sunk Outer

Lying some seven miles E of the old Sunk Inner Lightship, the Sunk Centre light is the focus of this gyratory system where very large vessels enter at the four points of the compass and circle anticlockwise en route to and from Felixstowe, Harwich and the River Orwell. TSS rules apply in part but minimal time should be spent in any part of the system.

The North Sea TSS

This is a major system for the many vessels passing through the North Sea and is subject to strict regulations. But it can be used to advantage by the cruising sailor. At North Hinder the system branches east to serve the heavy commercial traffic bound for the River Maas; vessels make major course changes here. The southern and northern edges of this junction are clearly marked and making passage to pass clear of it is very much to the navigator's advantage.

Significant changes to TSS took place on 01/08/2013. Carry up-to-date charts or consult www.rws.nl/newshippingroutes.

River Maas Approach

Likewise, approaching the river Maas from N or S is hazardous, as ships move in the approach channel at speed, often overtaking. For small vessels proceeding along the coast there is a recommended track to cross the Maas channel. Commercial vessels have priority so extra patience and care are required here; passage must be reported on VHF 03 to Maas Control.

Frisian Isles / TSS

From just SW of Den Helder stretching north and east, a complex of TSS zones runs along the Dutch coast into German waters, leading to the river Elbe. Considerable traffic can be expected in this area.

The W Friesland TSS and Texel TSS protect the well heads of the very large offshore Vlieland / Groningen gas fields. Approaching from the UK, a course may be shaped through the fields and across the TSS zones providing regulations are observed, and a 500m range is maintained from any well head.

Typically, a course for the Frisian Islands from Suffolk / Norfolk would head towards Den Helder keeping west of the offlying Noorderhaaks bank, to join the inshore traffic zone northwards. Allow for the shallows that reach out some way from SW of Terschelling and Ameland – all well buoyed and lit. Entrance to any of the gats between the islands requires special planning owing to tide and depth restrictions (see detail below). Passage in wind over tide conditions can be hazardous.

Southeast England to Northeast France, Belgium and Holland distances (miles)

	Dunkerque	Oostende	Breskens	Stellendam	Ijmuiden	Den Helder	W Terschelling
Dover	40	63	80	149	151	175	203
Ramsgate	43	60	83	137	139	161	189
Sheerness	73	76	109	131	159	168	196
Burnham	90	93	107	125	148	163	191
Bradwell	89	94	105	121	143	164	192
Harwich	61	80	86	105	126	145	173
Lowestoft	101	87	95	97	104	118	146

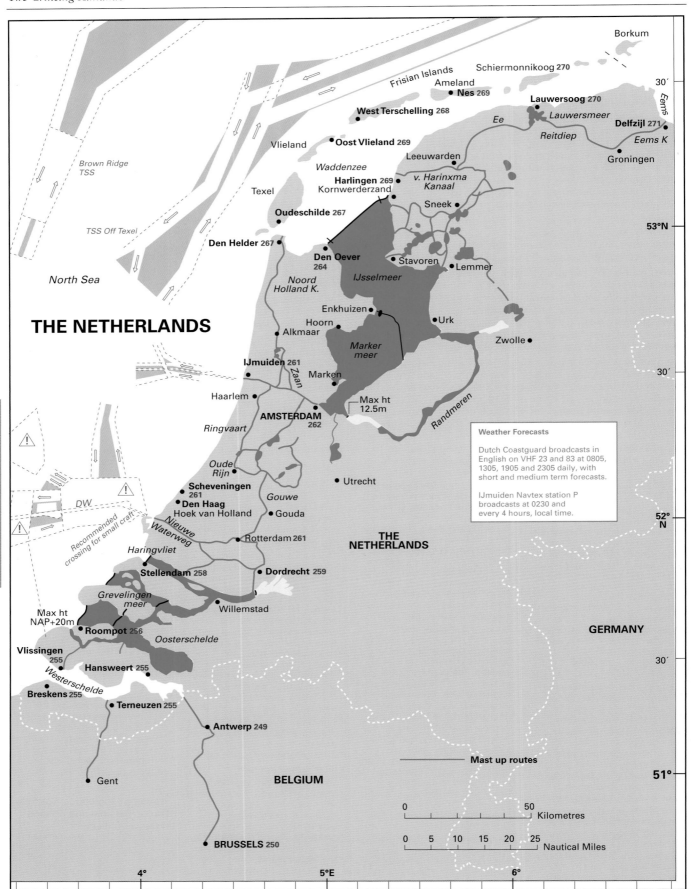

NETHERLANDS

Borkum

Frisian Islands

Schiermonnikoog 270

Ameland

Nes 269

West Terschelling 268

Lauwersoog 270

Lauwersmeer

Ee

Delfzijl 271

30′

Eems

Vlieland

Oost Vlieland 269

Leeuwarden

Reitdiep

Eems K

Waddenzee

Groningen

Harlingen 269

v. Harinxma

Texel

Kornwerderzand

Kanaal

Brown Ridge
TSS

Oudeschilde 267

Sneek

53°N

TSS Off Texel

Den Helder 267

Den Oever
264

Stavoren

IJsselmeer

Lemmer

North Sea

Noord
Holland K.

THE NETHERLANDS

Enkhuizen

Urk

Hoorn

Alkmaar

Marker
meer

Zwolle

30′

IJmuiden 261

Zaan

Marken

Haarlem

Max ht
12.5m

Randmeren

AMSTERDAM
262

Ringvaart

Oude
Rijn

Scheveningen
261

Gouwe

Utrecht

Den Haag
Hoek van Holland

Gouda

52°
N

Nieuwe
Waterweg

Rotterdam 261

THE
NETHERLANDS

DW

Haringvliet

Stellendam 258

Dordrecht 259

Recommended
crossing for small craft

Grevelingen
meer

Willemstad

Max ht
NAP+20m

GERMANY

Roompot 256

Oosterschelde

30′

Vlissingen
255

Hansweert 255

Westerschelde

Breskens 255

Terneuzen 255

Antwerp 249

———— **Mast up routes**

51°

Gent

BELGIUM

0   50
├──┼──┼──┼──┼──┤ Kilometres

BRUSSELS 250

0   5   10   15   20   25
├─┼─┼─┼─┼─┼─┤ Nautical Miles

4°   5°E   6°

Weather Forecasts

Dutch Coastguard broadcasts in
English on VHF 23 and 83 at 0805,
1305, 1905 and 2305 daily, with
short and medium term forecasts.

IJmuiden Navtex station P
broadcasts at 0230 and
every 4 hours, local time.

Page references are shown after locations, for example:
Antwerp 249. Bold type indicates that it is accompanied by a plan.
Italics are used for rivers, lochs, bays, seas etc.

Charts

The *1800 Series* of sheet charts published by the Dutch Hydrographic service in eight folios, covers in detail all main waterways in the west of Holland including the IJsselmeer. Folio 1801 is especially useful covering the coastal approaches to Belgium and mainland Holland. Available in the UK and everywhere in Holland. Strongly recommended, especially for travel north of Den Helder, and the Westerschelde.

Imray C30 fully covers the waters between Kent and S Suffolk to Holland as far N as the Maas, with useful port chartlets. C25 and C26 extend coverage N of the Maas.

BA charts cover the N Sea and Dutch coastal waters but lack port detail.

ANWB sector sheets (*Waterkaart*) are published for 14 areas in west Holland, giving buoyage, lights, depths, locks (Sluis) and movable bridge (Beweegbar Brug/BB) details. Available at chandlers and sports shops. Very desirable.

The *Wateratlas Staande Mastroute* published every spring gives details of the route passable for sailing boats from Willemstad in the mid-south all the way to Delfzijl on the northern coast. Detailed information on marinas en route, plus bridge and lock service times, makes this a valuable guide, and value for money. Stocked in chandlers.

Technically, all vessels are required to carry the *ANWB Wateralmanak* written totally in Dutch: *Volume 2* contains much useful data on waterway services to help smooth your passage, which can be understood by careful reading, but is in no way essential. The Wateratlas Staande Mastroute will suffice for many travellers in western Holland, except those going way off the beaten track in smaller vessels.

The combined tidal atlas and tide tables booklet published by the Dutch Hydrographic Office gives information on all tidal waters in and near Holland and is highly recommended. Look for *Waterstanden/Stromen HP33* in chandlers, guide notes in English.

Other sources of pilotage information:
North Sea Passage Pilot by Brian Navin (Imray)
Cruising Guide to the Netherlands – Brian Navin (Imray)
Inland waterways of the Netherlands Louise Busby & David Broad (Imray)

Official checks on crews, their boats and contents have increased in recent times and visiting vessels are strongly recommended to be prepared with documentation. See the Customs paragraph on *page 16*, note that vessels and crew from the UK, which is not party to the Schengen scheme, must register their presence at the first border port encountered. Schengen forms should be downloaded in advance free from the RYA site, www.rya.org.uk, and deposited in the marked boxes on first landing, retaining a copy on board. Compliance is mandatory.

If carrying duty-free goods, be prepared to demonstrate the on board stock does not exceed EU allowances. In the event of having a large quantity of dutiable goods on board, or crew without qualifying papers, it is a requirement to seek immigration on entry and gain clearance to the Schengen area before proceeding. Larger ports have Immigration/ Douane Offices: HMs are the best source of up to date info on office hours.

CEVNI – vessels under 15m and capable of not more than 10 knots are exempt from having a CEVNI qualified helmsman on board. However, many waterways employ CEVNI signage and familiarity with the meaning of the symbols is very much to the advantage of the navigator.

Radio communications

Dutch law does not stipulate that vessels must have VHF radio fitted but, where in use it is a requirement to listen in to the channel appropriate for every section of Dutch waterways as shown on navigation charts: this is especially important where commercial shipping is in motion.

VHF radios are required to be ATIS compliant, a facility that tags each broadcast with an individual identifying code based on the MMSI number. The ATIS code can be obtained free from the UK radio licensing authority. Many UK radios do not have ATIS capability, and ATIS is not actually legal in UK waters: if fitted it must be disabled before using the set on returning home. The Dutch authorities do not appear to be pursuing UK vessels that do not have ATIS compliant VHF radios, but this could change. In official communications expect to use your call sign rather than boat name.

VHF M or 37 must not be used in Dutch waters, as it is a commercial frequency. VHF 31 is sometimes specified but many UK radios do not offer this frequency. VHF 16 and high power are only used for emergencies and should be avoided.

Emergency services are obtainable on VHF 16. KNRM is the official lifeboat rescue service; other services responding to a call, including salvage services, will mostly make a charge for assistance.

Smoothing the way

Holding tanks are not yet mandatory for visiting vessels, but strict pollution controls are being introduced throughout Holland, and no sewage discharges in marinas or inland waters is the rule. More marinas now offer pay pump-out services, and all larger units can be expected to have one.

Holland's railway system is famously efficient, and is well connected with local bus services so putting most marinas in easy touch with airports and ferry terminals. Very fast inter-city rail service now available between Amsterdam / Rotterdam and Brussels, connecting with Eurostar to St Pancras (booking essential). Check out local routes and services in English via www.9292.nl or, for buses www.connexxion.nl or, Dutch railways www.ns.nl. Tickets available from machines at every station – there is a potential fine, 50% of the fare, for boarding a train without a valid ticket; inspectors are ubiquitous and speak excellent English.

Ferry services operate between Harwich and Hoek van Holland, Newcastle and Ijmuiden, Hull and Rotterdam.

Intercity buses ply between London and major Dutch and Belgian towns – competitive, and easier on the luggage allowance.

Telephone kiosks have been removed from many sites in Holland in response to the spread of mobile communications: be prepared. But more marinas now offer Wi-Fi connections.

VAT at 19% is applied to most transactions in Holland, and a tourist tax of up to €2.00 per head per night may be levied.

Most towns have a tourist bureau; look for the VVV sign in blue.

Weather forecasts

Dutch Coastguard broadcasts in English on Chs 23 or 83 at 0805, 1305, 1905 and 2305 daily, with short and medium term forecasts. Strongly recommended. Most marinas post a very useful synopsis.

Ijmuiden Navtex station P broadcasts at 0230 and every four hours, local time. Navtex station T operates from Oostende at 0310 and same intervals.

Gas supplies

Calor gas is not used on the Continent but Camping Gaz is widely available in hardware stores, supermarkets, and chandlers.

Language

Dutch people are generally very appreciative of foreign visitors attempts to speak their language and a little effort goes a long way towards making new friendships. It does not take long to discover that the town of Goes is pronounced 'hoose' or that IJmuiden is pronounced 'Ay-mowd-en'. The following translations may be found useful when trying to interpret notes in the almanacs or on Dutch charts:

aanlegplaatsen	= temporary berthing places	*brug*	= bridge
		douane	= customs
		gat	= channel
afval	= rubbish	*geen*	= no, none
ankerplaats	= anchorage	*gesloten*	= shut
bakboord	= port	*havengeld*	= harbour dues
bediening	= opening times of bridges and locks	*havenmeester*	= hbrmaster
		ligplaatsen	= overnight berths
ma. t/m zat	= Monday– Saturday	*oost (abbr. O)*	= east
		sluis	= lock
zo. en fd	= Sundays and public holidays	*spoorbrug*	= rly bridge
		vast	= fixed (bridge)
di, wo, do, vr	= Tues., Wed., Thurs., Fri.	*veer*	= ferry
		verboden	= forbidden
betonning	= buoyage	*wassalon*	= launderette
beweegbare	= opening (bridge)	*zuid (abbr. Z)*	= south

Zeeland

WESTERSCHELDE RIVER

A major river and waterway serving docks for 45M upstream to Antwerp. Its estuary has two large banks that are a hazard to navigation – the Raan on the seaward side, and the Hooge Platen upstream from Breskens – four navigable channels are buoyed to permit safe passage past them.

The NW approach channel (Oostgat) runs close along the Walcheren coast, the SW (Wielingen) along the Belgium coast. In the river, the Honte passes to the N side, and the lesser Waarwater Langs Hoofdplaat channel along the S of the river.

Approaching along the Belgian coast, stay S of the Wielingen channel until off Breskens. Coming in from the NW, stay close to the boundary of the narrow Oostgat or, take the less used Duerloo that runs in parallel until off Vlissingen where the two meet in a narrow chicane frequented by large vessels. Within the river, heavy traffic uses the Honte channel, but substantial barges can be

INLAND WATERWAYS OF THE NETHERLANDS

Louise Busby and
David Broad

This book is a user's guide to the whole network, covering all the mast-up routes and excluding only those waterways which offer less than 3·5m bridge height.

Navigational details are provided for each waterway; comprising dimensions and obstacles to be expected, including service arrangements for bridges and locks. This is followed by details of over 300 stopping places across all 12 provinces; some which are large or popular harbours, and others which are well off the beaten track. Comments on the significant features are expanded for nearly 100 'principal venues'.

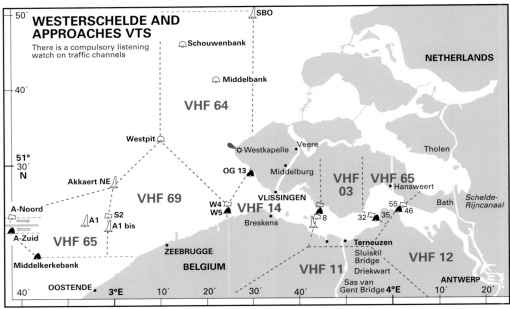

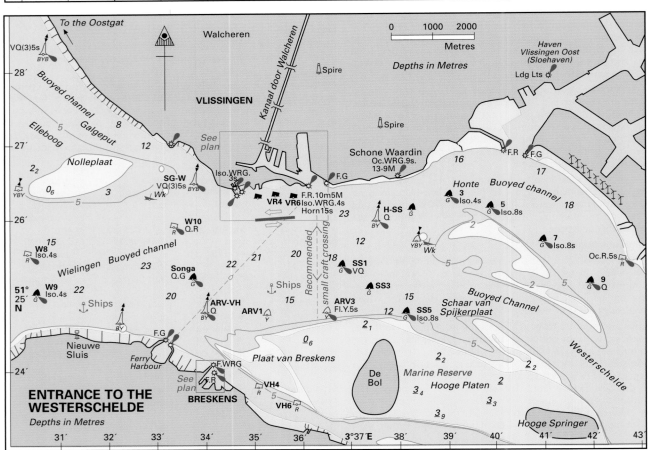

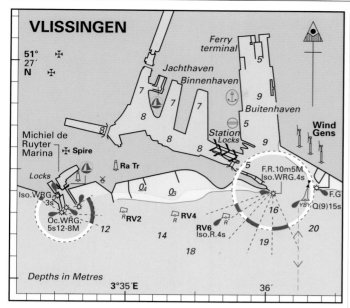

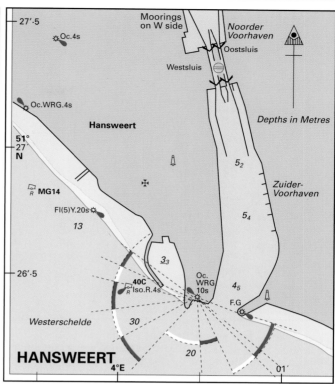

expected in the shallower Hoofdplat.

Heavy shipping converges in the estuary where pilots are taken on board, and ships can change direction and speed at any time. Tides flow up to 4kns, and strong wind over tide is something to behold.

Fast passenger ferries operate from a dock 500m W of Breskens to the locks entrance lying 1M E of Vlissingen.

The whole river is intensively buoyed to deal with the large areas of sandbanks. Chart number 1803 in the Dutch 1800 Hydrographic Series lays it out nicely.

BRESKENS

Charts BA 120, 1874: N 1803; Imray C30

HW Vlissingen HW

DS Dover −0315E +0300W, up to 4kn

MHWS	MHWN	MLWN	MLWS
4·8m	3·9m	0·9m	0·3m

A favoured port with a large marina accessible 24/7, with all facilities and pontoon berths capable of taking larger vessels, plus a well-known clubhouse and restaurant. More cafés and restaurants 300m away in town, a useful supermarket, and excellent seafood markets, a superior stopover to Vlissingen.

Expect strong streams right up to the entrance with shallows W of the mole. Inside, a barge to port acts as a wave break; turn to port round the barge and enter the reception pen where the HM can be contacted via phone on pontoon to allocate a berth. Clubhouse and facilities are on the other side of the marina. Note: seaport marinas in Holland are noticeably more expensive than inland facilities.

Passage upstream towards Antwerp is best made from Breskens using the S (Hoofdplaat) channel which joins the main river 5M upstream and is well marked. Departing just before LW and maintaining a steady speed it is possible to reach Antwerp on one tide. Terneuzen is otherwise a good stopping off port 12M up from Breskens.

Passage westwards from Breskens benefits from 7+ hours favourable tide so is a popular departure port for the UK.

VLISSINGEN

Charts BA 1872, 120; N 1801, 1803; Imray C30

Tidal data as for Breskens

Crossing the river between Breskens and Vlissingen, observe the traffic scheme, and be alert that the flood tide does not press you onto the banks upstream of Breskens. Beware heavy shipping and keep the required radio watch on VHF 14. Small vessels must maintain a minimum speed of 3·5kns, cross lanes at 90° and not obstruct shipping.

Entrance The Michiel de Ruyter Marina in the former Visserhaven shares an entrance with the pilot launch hbr, just W of the conspic public observation tr. The marina is tidal but there is normally a minimum depth of 1m over the sill at the entrance (0·7m at LAT). There is a footbridge over the entrance (min. air draught 6m when closed) which can be opened throughout the day by the HM, and stands open at night. There is no VHF but traffic lights indicate when the br will open. The flood lock may be closed between 1 November and 1 April and the marina is then not accessible.

Vlissingen Marina has over 100 berths and the HM allocates space on passing though the entrance. Showers and launderette but no fuel. Vlissingen town is close to hand with shops and restaurants.

HANSWEERT

Chart N 1803.3

HW Vlissingen +0056

20M upstream on the N bank of the river is the entrance to the S Beveland canal, giving easy access to the Oosterschelde via large locks. Lock control VHF 22 to ask for passage. Limited waiting pontoons at lifting bridges along the canal; mooring only possible at Wemeldinge. Expect heavy barge traffic.

No yacht facilities at Hansweert but customs post manned May–October.

Wemeldinge lies at the N end of the Beveland canal; good facilities in the marina and basic shops in a modern development.

TERNEUZEN

Charts BA 120; N 1803

HW Vlissingen +0020

DS Dover −0130ENE −0030W

MHWS	MHWN	MLWN	MLWS
5·1m	4·2m	0·9m	0·3m

An historic town 12M up river from Breskens on the Westerschelde; useful stopover facilities – a good range of shops and market. Also access to Gent, 18M distant, via locks and a canal; three lifting bridges make passage with mast up possible. (Detail Dutch Hydrographic chart 1803.)

On the approach, beware heavy traffic issuing from the W harbour (Westbuitenhaven). The E lock (Oostsluis accessed through the Oostebuitenhaven) is designated for yachts staying over or moving on to Gent. Contact locks on VHF 18,

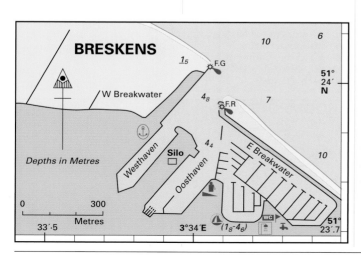

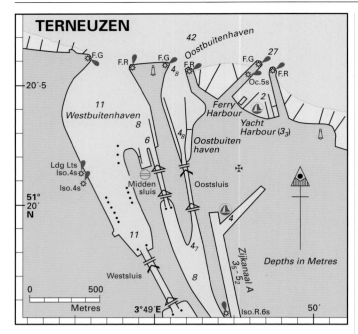

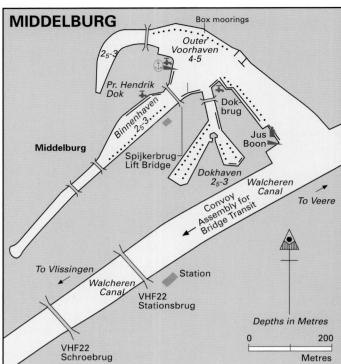

operates 24/7 at HW ±0100. Through the locks, make a 180° turn to port after 800m for moorings at the YC at the N end of the Zijkanaal A.

Alternatively, the Yacht Harbour, the most easterly facility, is for cruising vessels seeking ready access to town and river. Two marinas are sited in this basin, Yachthaven WV Neusen, and Jachthaven Terneuzen, with regular facilities, but some disturbance can be expected from tugs and ferries using the W side.

ANTWERP

See Belgium section on page 250.

WALCHEREN CANAL – VLISSINGEN TO VEERE

Travelling N via the Walcheren canal system (max depth 3·5m) make for the lock entrance 1M upstream from Vlissingen town, keeping watch for passenger ferries. Locks (VHF 18) operate 24/7. Proceed through the RH small vessel lock, setting fenders low for the timber baulks on either side. Then bear to stb towards the remote controlled bridge into the canal.

To stb, the **Schelde Yacht Club**: all facilities including diesel, and just 10 minutes' walk to Vlissingen town, and five minutes' walk to the rail terminal serving all Holland: trains every 30 minutes. A good refuge when arriving late.

MIDDELBURG

Three remote controlled bridges lie between Vlissingen and **Middelburg**, where two town bridges operate alternately in conjunction with the half hourly train service. Service hours 0900–2100 Sunday and holidays, otherwise 0600–2200.

The popular and capacious town marina lies to port 400m N of the swing bridge: register with the HM at reception pontoon, adjacent the bridge. Fuel and chandlery on barge to port at entry. Well known clubhouse and all facilities in historic town. With its handy (every 30 minutes) train connections, Middleburg is a natural for crew changes.

Free run N of Middelburg to locks (operating 0530–2300) gives entry to **Veerse Meer**, and **Veere** town, formerly open to the sea, with its small alongside berthing marina 90° to port on leaving locks: very limited services, but excellent clubhouse and picturesque setting.

VEERSE MEER

An extensive if somewhat shallow waterway formed by damming the sea entrance: numerous attractive (many free) mooring opportunities throughout, and two large marinas in the upper section with extensive facilities for the holiday trade. The Delta marina offers mechanical services and is handier for shops.

Reception pontoon to port when approaching, with HM cabin nearby.

A commercial waterway linking the Oosterschelde to the Westerschelde, the main channel is fully buoyed throughout; also note the small port and stb stick markers signifying the 2m contour. Nature reserves are marked and must be respected.

At the north end, a lock (Zandkreeksluis) issues into tidal Oosterschelde; many shellfish farms marked by withies, strictly to be avoided.

OOSTERSCHELDE

Charts N 1801, 1805

HW Vlissingen Roompot Buiten –0010

MHWS	MHWN	MLWN	MLWS
3·6m	2·9m	0·6m	0·3m

Roompotsluis approach With tidal streams running at up to 2½kn it is worth planning to arrive at the Middelbank buoy between HW Zierikzee +0300 and +0600 to carry the tidal stream towards the lock and into the Oosterschelde. Both the Roompot and Oude Roompot channels are well buoyed from over 6M to sea and mark the safe approaches from W and NW, skirting the Hompels banks. The no-go area in front of the barrage is well marked with yellow buoys and is kept to stb when making the final approach to the locking basin. Fishing vessels ply this route, so be prepared to share the lock (VHF 18).

The massive **Roompotsluis** barrage controls the tidal flow into the Oosterschelde but creates dangerous currents and shallows in the approaches. Hazards are clearly buoyed off on both sides of the barrage, and cruisers are strongly advised to stay within the marked, relatively shallow, approach channels.

One mile inside the locks to stb is a marina, otherwise the mooring options are at **Zierikzee** on the N bank or **Colijnsplaat marina**, just 6M distant on the S bank.

ZIERIKZEE

A famous old fishing town, now a centre of mussel culture, reached via a shallow canal (2·4m max depth) passing through old lock gates. Strong tides and very deep water at the seaward entrance. Very busy in season with very few box moorings available, visiting vessels are directed by the HM to turn and moor alongside, often in rafts. Power available.

Excellent eating and shopping opportunities amongst buildings of splendour and quality. Good chandlery on quay.

COLIJNSPLAAT

Subject to strong tides on the narrow approach, a large modern marina with a small characterful village nearby offering a range of eating possibilities. Good facilities.

ZEELANDBRUG

Beyond Zierikzee and Colijnsplaat this elegant bridge, some 2M long spans the Oosterschelde. The marked traffic spans offer air draughts

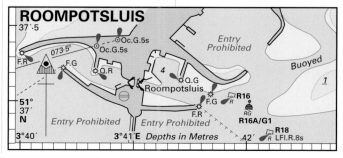

between 13 and 16m – actual clearance shown by gauge on the approach. Otherwise, at the N end of the bridge is an opening span (VHF 18) operating usually on the hour 0700–2130 (0900 start at weekends and holidays). Note the marked shallows in the vicinity of the bridge.

Beyond the bridge lies the main section of the Oosterschelde, a large waterway offering excellent sailing and busy with commercial vessels. An extensive area of shallows occupies the centre and is buoyed: mussel farming takes place on this bank and is forbidden territory.

The marked channels split north and south from the bridge:
To the north, locks to port at **Bruinisse** give entrance to the **Grevelingenmeer**, offering excellent cruising waters. At the far north end of the Oosterschelde the Krammer locks open onto the **Volkerak** waterway and central Holland.

Along the S shore of the Oosterschelde, the route passes the N entrance to the **Veerse Meer**, then the lock entrance leading to **Goes**; close by is **Wemeldinge** at the N end of the Beveland canal, finally reaching the small fishing town of **Yerseke**. Opposite lies the small village and port of **Tholen**, reached through the Bergsediepsluis lock (VHF 18) which also leads on to Bergen op Zoom.

GOES

A fine town with two marinas and facilities, good train connections, and markets on the square. Goes is reached via a locked shallow canal (2·4m max) running through picturesque countryside. Lock hours 0600–2100 summer months (VHF 18); small unattended marina inside lock is useful for a short break. Lifting bridge at Wilheminadorp operates on approach. At Goes, take right fork towards town; the HM operates the major road bridge (Ringbrug) at the edge of town

opening on the hour 0900–1100 and 1600–2000 in summer, with high season/weekend variations: quayside waiting moorings before bridge.

Inside the bridge to port, an unusual garden-style marina (WV de Werf) for 12m max vessels with less than 2.2m draught. Straight ahead and beyond a hand drawn footbridge lies the alongside berth and box marina, right in the centre of town. All facilities except fuel; useful DIY supermarket right next to Ringbrug.

WEMELDINGE

South side of Oosterschelde, at head of S Beveland canal (24/7) leading to Westerschelde.

Pleasant sheltered marina with some restaurants, and good supplies in town. Most facilities.

SOUTH BEVELAND CANAL

Very useful means of accessing the Westerschelde quickly from

the Oosterschelde. Heavy commercial use 24/7. Waiting pontoons at two bridges leading to locks at Hansweert; call control on VHF 22 for service. Departure from Hansweert at HW Vlissingen +0100 gives 5h run downriver; departure upriver at HW Vlissingen –0400 should put Antwerp within reach on one tide.

GREVELINGEN MEER

Accessed via lock operating daylight hours, at Bruinisse. This enclosed waterway is a delight for cruisers, lying away from the main commercial traffic. Navigable channels are well marked throughout, with extensive shallows against the N shore. Mooring is permitted in selected island sites, for which there may be a fee.

Bruinisse A resort town with modern developments and a large modern marina on the port bank just outside the lock basin, with facilities, chandlery and restaurants. Visitors pull in immediately to HM office on entering marina for berth allocation.

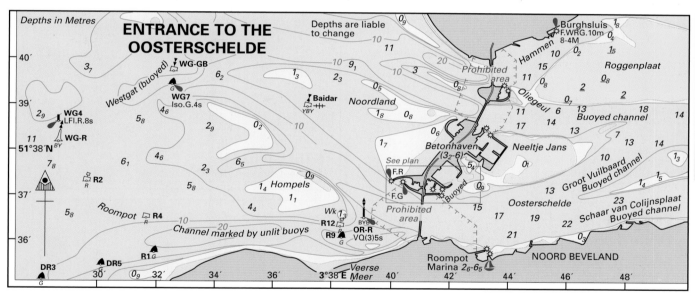

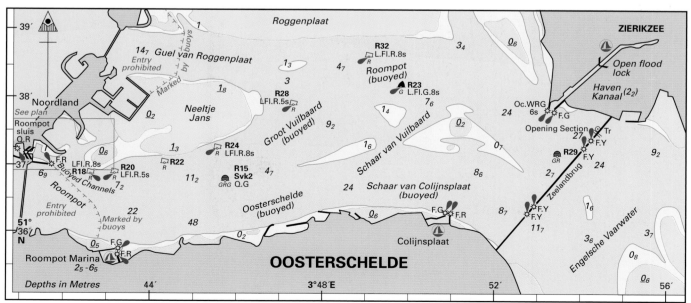

Also, in the lock basin a smaller marina lies to port.

Brouwershaven is at the W end of the waterway with its marina and alongside berths in quiet and historic settings. Approach the entrance with care; observe buoyage to avoid stranding, and HM signal controlling the narrow entrance. Go alongside pontoon before the old lock gate and report to HM for berthing. Chandlery, fuel and most facilities.

Herkingen on the N shore offers two marinas approached through a narrow shallow channel, with good facilities; a pretty, small town offering shopping and cafés.

On leaving the Grevelingen meer, the locks to the Volkerak lie to port past a large mussel farm. The 'Sport' sign directs to the smaller yacht lock on the left, north of the complex.

VOLKERAK

The Krammersluis locks (24/7) are often busy; an electric sign shows the max air draft (approx 18·4m) under the fixed bridge. The opening bridge in the commercial lock can be requested by vessels having greater air draft.

In the Volkerak, the channel forks past Noorderplaat island, the lesser north track is bounded on either side by 2m contour markers – most cruising vessels use this track. Otherwise to the south lies the main channel.

At the north end, the (Volkeraksluisen) locks, again with c.18·4m posted max air draft, give onto the Hollandsch

Diep, a major artery into East Holland. To port under the long Haringvliet bridge lies the Haringvliet, and to stb the delightful town of Willemstad.

HARINGVLIET

Another major controlled waterway, formed when the Stellendam barrage was erected in the '50s. The main sea approach is a by a long well marked channel, sometimes shallow, running W–E from SG Haven Buoy, ending in a sharp turn to port into outer harbour. Strong tidal flows through the barrage create turbulence – hazardous zones are well marked; staying in channel is strongly recommended. Waiting pontoon before the locks in the outer harbour (Buitenhaven) where fishing boats use the quays to the south.

The shallower approach route from the N (Rak van Scheelhoek) is hazardous owing to movements in the Hinderplaat sands.

Locks operate 24h weekdays April–November, but 0800–2000 at weekends (VHF 20). Twin opening road bridges straddle the locks but the seaward br offers just 14m clearance when closed, so yachts with higher masts must contact control for bridge service on entry. In high winds bridge movements may be suspended.

STELLENDAM

Chart N 1801

HW Vlissingen +0015

MHWS	MHWN	MLWN	MLWS
3·0m	2·3m	0·4m	0·3m

After the locks, a marina lies on the S bank with most facilities. Ahead lie some 15M of water with excellent cruising opportunities; numerous shallows all well marked, and two well-known former fishing ports – Hellevoetsluis and Middelharnis. The river Spui leads off N towards Dordrecht – a valuable but tidal route towards middle Holland.

HELLEVOETSLUIS

A major sailing centre, the small town offers three marinas – the large full facility marina is some 20 minutes' walk away west of the town, the Heliushaven.

Many visiting yachtsmen moor in the approach canal right in the centre of everything with basic alongside facilities, or pass through the swing bridge (daylight hourly service only, on the hour except 1200 and 1600) to quieter pontoon facilities in the Hellevoetsluis YC or Arie de Boom marinas beyond in the Groote Dok.

East of town lies the Voornekanaal, the entrance of which has mooring facilities in the outer Tramhaven, and beyond the lock alongside berths.

Small selection of restaurants and cafés, plus bus connections to Rotterdam – useful for crew changes.

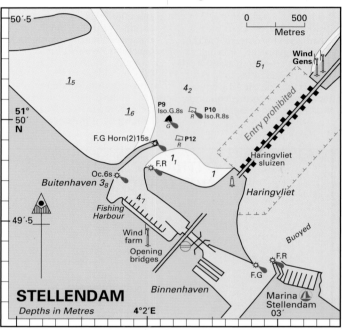

STELLENDAM
Depths in Metres

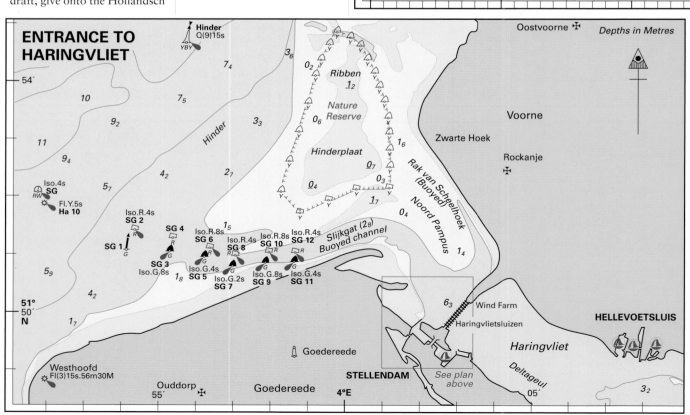

ENTRANCE TO HARINGVLIET

MIDDELHARNIS

Entry via a lock, open daylight hours (VHF 12) over which an extendable pedestrian walkway operates. Town is 1M distant along narrow canal lined with quays and moorings to the attractive village. All facilities, shops and a range of interesting restaurants.

Mooring in boxes on the east side and alongside on the west, just before the town proper.

RIVER SPUI

Tidal waterway departing N bank of Haringvliet to join Oude Maas beyond Beyerland (small town and marina with restricted (1·8m min) cill clearance, suitable for overnight and supplies) en route to Dordrecht. Pleasant country vista but caution required – heavy river traffic.

Note: E-going tide in Spui starts Hoek v Holland HW+0500, but E-going tide in Oude Maas begins HW Hoek v Holland.

HOLLANDSCH DIEP TO AMSTERDAM

Leaving the Volkeraksluis, the cruiser has two routes to Amsterdam, to port through the Haringvliet out to sea to Ijmuiden and along the N Sea Canal (2–3 days) or straight ahead through the canals via Dordrecht, Gouda, Haarlem / Aalsmeer to the N Sea Canal (4–5 days) The sea route entails two locks and one bridge, the inland route is slower because of the numerous bridges and locks, but has otherwise much of the essence of Holland to offer.

HOLLANDSCH DIEP AND DORDTSE KILL

Hollandsch Diep is tidal and carries heavy traffic from the interior; passable in its entire length only to yachts with up to 9m air draft, it opens up areas of special interest – the Biesbosch, leading to the R Maas, Venlo, Maastrict, and the canals of Belgium and France.

The Staande Maastroute going N takes in the first section of **Hollandsch Diep**, bearing N into the **Dordtse Kil**, where N flowing tides begin Hoek v Holland HW+0600.

WILLEMSTAD

To stb on entering Hollandsch Diep, a very attractive, formerly fortified, town with most facilities including diesel. HM in glasshouse to port on entering, allocates berths either alongside in town harbour ahead or in marina to port. Also, 400m W of narrow harbour entrance, another marina.

NEUMANSDORP

Small village opposite Willemstad with two marinas; quiet with shops and cafés. An alternative to Willemstad at height of the season. Bus service to Rotterdam and Dordrecht.

DORDRECHT

A major centre of commerce with a long history, standing at the confluence of three waterways, the old town is a delight of warehouses, shops and restaurants. Approached from the S via the impressive twin lifting road and rail bridges which operate to a fixed schedule, 0616 and every two hours from 0916, more often weekends and holidays (VHF 79). Waiting pontoon 800m S to stb in side water.

Several marinas in Dordrecht. One popular choice, the **Kon. Dordrechtsche R & Z.V**, lies 600m N of bridges on stb side, narrow entrance next to fire tug leads under lifting Engelenburgerbrug (summon via button on woodwork next bridge) into reception area, where HM allocates pontoon berths. All facilities. Chandlery on nearby quayside. Diesel from bunker boats on riverfront.

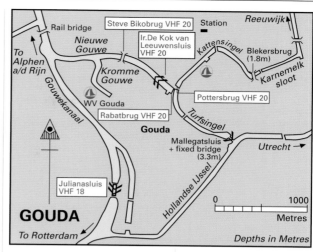

Moving N, take the Noord channel under the lifting **Alblasserdam bridge** (opens 08, 28, 48 minutes in each hour between 0700–1900) Small marina just beyond br to stb for o/night and provisions.

Heavy traffic in **Noord**; bear to port into **Nieuwe Maas** for 3M then take sharp turn to stb into **Hollandsche Ijssel**. Massive **Algera Flood barrier** passable for low air draft boats, otherwise wait on pontoon for bridge opening to port side (VHF 22)

Beyond the barrier, river runs through industrial hinterland of Rotterdam to **Julianasluis** 1M before Gouda. Operates daylight hours on demand.

GOUDA

1M after the lock, one of the difficult railway bridges, only opening briefly 0559, 1012, 1312, 1612, 2112. Waiting pontoon. For entry to outer Gouda moorings turn stb immediately before bridge into Nieuwe Gouwe through lock and opening bridges: opening daylight hours on demand. Few facilities.

Alternate YC marina found in Kromme Gouwe, a small cut to stb 300m before town lock, past industrial site. Alongside and box moorings: HM lives in facilities block close to entry. Short walk to town and historic sights, shops and restaurants.

Continuing N, a further five bridges open on demand, arriving in Alphen A/D Rijn. Passing the town bridges leads to the main junction heading either W along the Oude Rijn to Leiden or, N via Woubrugge and Brassemermeer (moorings, and marinas) to Oude Wetering. Here a T junction leads W to Kaag and the route to Haarlem, or N via the Westeinder Plas for the direct route (overnight passage only) to Amsterdam.

LEIDEN

The city, famous for historic buildings, and university life is accessible on foot from outer moorings. Can be approached via the Kager Plassen lake to the north or, the Oude Rijn from the SE. All bridges operate throughout the day, although some are closed briefly at the rush hour. From the Oude Rijn continue on under two bridges for central moorings offering facilities. Or turn N on the Zijl for a comfortable marina to the N of the city at YC Zijlzicht.

Lakes and waterways N of Leiden, the Kager Plassen, mostly passable with care, are home to much sailing activity in green surroundings.

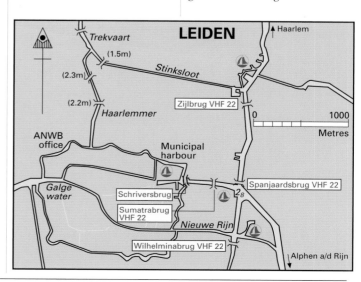

Heading onwards to Haarlem plan carefully to pass the Sassenheim rly and road bridges which present another pinch point, heavily congested at peak times. Opening briefly at 0558, 0628, 0658, 1228, 1258, 1328, 1828, 1858, 1928 weekdays, and fewer services at weekends April–November only. Good marina to port just before right turn to bridges. All facilities.

HAARLEM

The Spaarne through Haarlem turns N just E of the Cruquiusbrug and an interesting visit can be made to this steam pump museum. There are eight bridges through Haarlem which are worked by one or more mobile br operators in a convoy system, and a transit toll is collected at the furthest N town bridge. First convoy departs 0900 and on demand thereafter. No service 1600–1800 in rush hour. Rly bridge in N of city opens reluctantly.

Haarlem city a major centre of culture, restaurants and cafés: excellent atmosphere and famous cathedral dominating scene from all parts.

Moorings alongside all along through city; power and limited toilet / shower facilities.

As canal widens, some mooring possibilities to be found, also at Haarlemsche YC to port, before Spaarndam lock (daylight service, toll payable) all facilities.

1M beyond lock, another barrier to the cruiser – the remote controlled A9 motorway bridge which operates only between 0500–0600, 1200–1300, 1930–2030; air daft 6·9m closed. Limited waiting pontoon facilities.

Marina, WV Wymond, to port. Good facilities. Popular place to o/night before Amsterdam.

One lesser road bridge (Zijkanaal C), opening on demand (0500–2300) gives entry to the impressive N Sea Canal.

BRAASSEMERMEER TO AMSTERDAM

The route travels anti-clockwise on the Ringvaart van de Haarlemmermeerpolder across the Westeinderplassen to the Nieuwe Meer S of Amsterdam. Brs on this section operate throughout the day except the final br at Schiphol which opens early morning, lunchtime and evening. The harbours on the Nieuwe Meer are within a short bus ride of the city and make a convenient alternative for those intending to return S, avoiding the difficult route through 14 opening bridges, two of which are rly bridges which open only between 0100 and 0430.

Vessels over 5m air draught take this route in convoy during the night. It is an interesting experience, but keep a watch for plastic debris on the water to avoid propeller problems. Vessels travelling N towards

Amsterdam must gather at the Nieuwemeersluis at 2300. If you are travelling S from Amsterdam, go into the SE corner of the Oude Houthaven where there is a pontoon, pay dues at the br office and pass into the Westerkanaal to await the opening of the rly br. The Authorities prefer yachts to enter the Westerkanaal not later than approx 2200 so that they can determine the size of the convoy and make arrangements for all the bridges to be opened by the mobile team of br keepers. Contact the Nieuwemeersluis or Westerkeersluis on VHF 22 for instructions. Vessels must keep pace with the convoy but, after crossing the Nieuwe Meer at dawn and passing under the Schiphol motorway br at its early morning opening, you could anchor in the Westeinder plassen to recover.

Craft with less than 9m air-draught may use the Amsterdam-Rijn canal as an alternative route. Entrance is through a buoyed channel opening to the S from the IJ just W of the Oranjesluizen.

HOEK VAN HOLLAND AND NIEUWE WATERWEG

Charts BA 122, 132; N 1801, 1809.2;
Imray C30

HW Vlissingen +0040

MHWS	MHWN	MLWN	MLWS
1·9m	1·5m	0·2m	0·0m

Yachts crossing the approach are required to report to *sector Maasmond* on VHF 03 and to listen on that channel until clear of the Europoort approaches. A prohibited area marked by W card buoys has been established west of Maasvlakte extending approx 2M offshore. Weather information every hour on VHF 21. The Europoort is prohibited to pleasure craft and yachts are not welcome at the Berghaven.

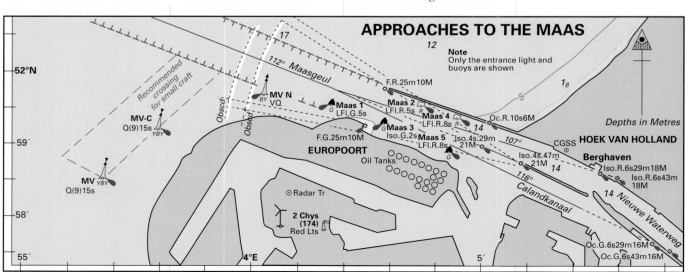

Inland connections The Nieuwe Waterweg, which becomes the Nieuwe Maas east of Vlaardingen, serves the harbours of Maasluis, Vlaardingen, Schiedam and Rotterdam. Vessels entering the Nieuwe Waterweg are required to maintain a listening watch on VHF 65 from km1030. Heading E, the following VHF channels must be monitored between the relevant km posts:

1028 and 1017 – VHF 80
1017 and 1011 – VHF 61
1011 and 1007 – VHF 63
1007 and 1003 – VHF 60
1003 and 993 – VHF 81

MAASSLUIS

Chart N 1809.2

Entrance on N bank just E of km post 1019. Enter Binnenhaven from Buitenhaven through a road br and rly br. Water and fuel are available. HM ☎ 0105 93 19 82.

VLAARDINGEN

Chart N 1809.4

Entrance on N bank just after km post 1011 – E of Delta Hotel. Buitenhaven is uncomfortable; continue through Keersluis, railway br and Prinses Julianabrug to Oude Haven. HM ☎ 0620 83 35 46.

SCHIEDAM

Chart N 1809.4

Entrance to Spuihaven at km post 1007 on N bank. Yacht Haven of WV Nieuwe Waterweg and Jachtclub Schiedam. Toilets and showers. Launderette at 750m. Close to shops, restaurants, rly station. 10 minutes by taxi to airport. HM ☎ 0104 26 39 05.

ROTTERDAM

Two bridges cross the Nieuwe Maas at Rotterdam, the Erasmus lifting br (air draught 12·5m when closed) which opens on the hour at 1000, 1100, 1400 and 1500 (VHF 20), and the fixed Nieuwe Willemsbrug which restricts headroom to 10·5m at HW. Moorings downstream of Erasmus br on the N bank at the Veerhaven HM ☎ 010 436 5446 or upstream at City Marina in Binnenhaven via lifting br which opens on request (VHF 20). All facilities. HM ☎ 010 485 40 96.

SCHEVENINGEN

Charts BA 122, 1631; N 1801.5; Imray C25

HW Vlissingen +0105

DS Dover −0500SW +0100NE

MHWS	MHWN	MLWN	MLWS
2·2m	1·8m	0·3m	0·2m

A busy fishing port. There is no access to the inland waterways but it is a lively seaside resort and convenient for visiting The Hague. Customs post. The outer harbour entrance faces NW, is uncomfortable in strong N to E winds and dangerous in NW winds of Force 6 or more when swell can run in through the entrance. Tidal streams, especially the N-going stream near the time of HW, run strongly across the entrance.

Approach Scheveningen LtHo Fl(2)10s48m29M lies ½M E of the entrance. The area between the N hbr wall and the pier shallows sharply so be sure to round the safe water buoy (Iso.4s2M) 2M NW of the hbr and then follow a course of 156° on Ldg Lts (Iso.4s) into the outer harbour.

Entrance Call *Scheveningen port* on VHF 21 to ensure clear passage. On entering the Voorhaven, Basin No.1 to NE is mostly for commercial vessels. Proceed hard stb through narrow cut to No.2 basin: marina HM and facilities to stb – visitors mainly alongside. Basin to NE available for mooring in busy periods.

Restaurants and all facilities close to hand. Fine beach, entertainment and shops a few minutes' walk N of marina. Supermarket and chandlery on E side of No.2 Basin where tram service runs direct to Den Hague with major rail connections, including Schiphol airport.

☎ HM 0703 52 00 17.

NORTH SEA CANAL

A major waterway, 15m deep and 15M long from massive locks at **Ijmuiden** to Amsterdam, with huge quays and alongside ship repair services en route. Major cargo and cruise shipping frequently seen. Several ferry services cross the canal, and high speed hydrofoils operate along its length. Sailing permitted but commercial shipping has priority.

IJMUIDEN

Charts BA 1631,124; N 1801 Imray C25

HW Vlissingen +0145

DS Dover −0400S +0200N, max 2kn

MHWS	MHWN	MLWN	MLWS
2·0m	1·7m	0·3m	0·2m

Useful entry port for Amsterdam along the Noordzee Kanaal, and then through to the Markermeer and IJsselmeer.

VTS Monitor VHF 61 from 5M off.

Approach There are steel works N of the town and the coloured smoke often provides the first positive identification by day. Keep a good look-out for fishing vessels entering and leaving. Vessels fitted with VHF should report to IJmuiden Traffic Control (VHF 61) on approach when 5M from the hbr. The S arm of the hbr extends 1M offshore. Strong tidal streams run across the entrance.

Entrance From the IJmuiden IJM racon buoy Morse(A)8s a course of 100·5° on the Ldg Lts for 5M leads through the outermost pierheads and the Buitenhaven towards the Zuider Buitenkanaal. IJmuiden Port Control should be contacted on VHF 61 when approaching from seaward. The approach and outer harbour and even the Buitenhaven can be rough in onshore winds. The Customs office ☎ 020 25 81 36 14 is

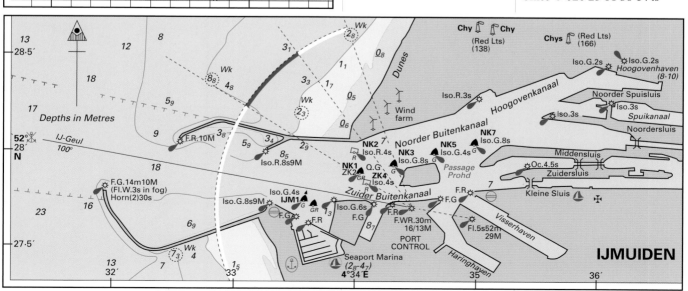

situated on the ground floor of a grey tr block between the Zuider Buiten Kanaal and the Visserhaven, W of the Kleine Sluis (☎ 0255 52 33 09). Take care before leaving that conditions are suitable outside.

Berthing The Seaport Marina IJmuiden is on the seaward side of the locks and has a capacity of 600 boats. Entrance is from the S side of the Buitenhaven between IJM3 (Iso.G.4s) and IJM5 R/G buoys and then along a buoyed but unlit channel, to the marina entrance which is marked by F.R and F.G lights. VHF 74. HM ☎ 0255 56 03 00. Diesel and petrol available.

Marina has restaurants and chandlery / services and good beach, but is 1M from Ijmuiden town and few shops. Berthing charges above average. Bus connection to Schiphol via Haarlem.

North Sea Canal From sea, enter by sports lock (Kleine Sluis) to S side (24/7). Vessels monitor VHF 22 in the locks and VHF 03 to 10km inland, then VHF 04 to Amsterdam.

After locks, limited waiting alongside on quay to stb.

5M from Ijmuiden, **Zijkanaal C** enters from S and route to Haarlem. Buitenrust road br opens on demand (0500–2300) giving access to marina, **WV Wymond**, to stb. Good facilities. Popular place to overnight before Amsterdam / N Sea voyage.

Further 10M to Amsterdam, passing major docks and port installations / traffic.

Hout harbour on S side close to town is gathering point for daily (not Sunday) night convoy S through Amsterdam canals and lifting bridges heading S via Gouda.

AMSTERDAM

Charts BA 124; ANWB G and I

This principal city of The Netherlands is a natural mecca for all visitors to Holland. Among many other attractions the Maritime Museum, the Rijksmuseum, the Vincent van Gogh Museum, the Rembrandthuis and Anne Frank House are worth a visit. The Noordzee Kanaal continues through the city as the R Het IJ.

Locks on N bank lead to **Noord-Hollands Kanaal** which runs to den Helder through historic landscapes and Alkmaar. An alternative connection to this canal for mast-up vessels starts at Km18, the Zijkanaal G routing through Zaandam, and connecting at the Alkmaarder Meer.

Approaching Amsterdam, the long low rounded roof to stb is the central rail station. Opposite, behind a wave barrier is entrance to **Sixhaven**, a small popular marina, good facilities, mainly alongside, rafting in high season, likely to be closed from early pm at busy times. Supermarket five minutes right out of gates. For Amsterdam town and onward transport, walk left, over N Holland canal lock gates and take (free) ferry to Centraal Station – excellent point for train service to Schiphol airport (20 minutes)

and pedestrian access to downtown Amsterdam.

Aeolus marina, 300m beyond Sixhaven, is alternative overnight alongside and pontoon berthing, good facilities, but small. Supermarket outside gates.

E of Amsterdam the waterway splits, bearing stb to the RijnKanaal, or straight ahead to the **Markermeer** via the **Oranjesluis** (VHF 18). For the lock, hold to port and enter 'sport' waiting area for the N lock. Beware: commercial traffic has priority. Often a busy lock, be prepared.

Beyond lock wait for road bridge (Schellingwouderbrug VHF 18) opening on demand, and stay in dredged channel.

The small hbr of Durgerdam is reached through a narrow buoyed channel to the N. HM ☎ 020 4904 717. It is only a short bus ride from the city centre. Anchoring is possible in the bay if the hbr is full.

MARKERMEER AND IJSSELMEER

Originally open to the sea, until the outer Afsluitdijk was built in 1932 forming an inland sea: 1975 this was cut in two by the Houtribdijk, linking Enkhuisen in the W with Lelystadt in the E. The inner Markermeer is semi-fresh, and the outer Ijsselmeer is partly open to the sea through small sluices. Previous sea-going ports all around are now protected from surges but keep their locks and infrastructure, offering charming settings and excellent mooring opportunities.

Commercial channels are maintained throughout the two waterways, and the remainder is freely passable to vessels drawing no more than 2·0m, and 2·5m with careful navigation. In winds over Force 5 the shallow conditions throw up a short sea that makes progress wet and slow, but a port is always near to hand. Polderisation, or land recovery, ceased some years ago, but straight sea walls indicate where land was recovered, especially (as in Flevoland) where it lies some metres below the level of the lake.

A circuit of the waterways has much to offer, but taking the quiet and peaceful route round Flevoland has limitations – the 12·7m max clearance under the fixed Hollandse Brug near Naarden, prevents a full circuit of the polder to larger vessels.

MARKEN

Between 1164 and 1957 Marken was an Is but is now joined to the mainland by a causeway. From the N end of the Is there is a wall stretching 1M NNW to the 2m contour, and on the E tip there is a prominent white LtHo. Enter the Gouwzee from N of Marken and follow the buoyed channel (2·2m) into any of the three hbrs, avoiding the busy ferry quay.
HM ☎ 0299 60 13 82.

MONNICKENDAM

A picturesque town with four marinas. However, the closest berths to the town are beyond the marinas in the Town Harbour which has toilets and

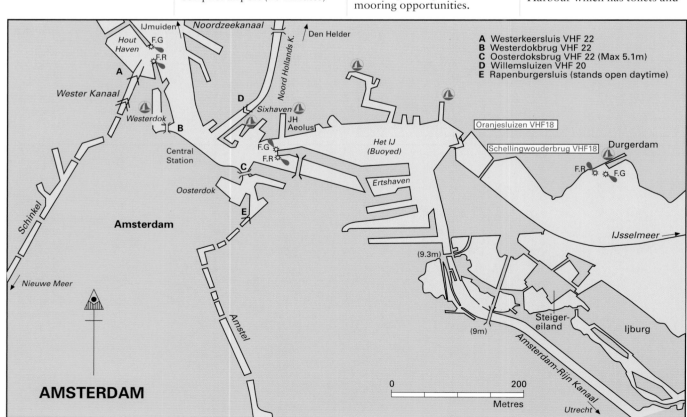

A Westerkeersluis VHF 22
B Westerdokbrug VHF 22
C Oosterdoksbrug VHF 22 (Max 5.1m)
D Willemsluizen VHF 20
E Rapenburgersluis (stands open daytime)

AMSTERDAM

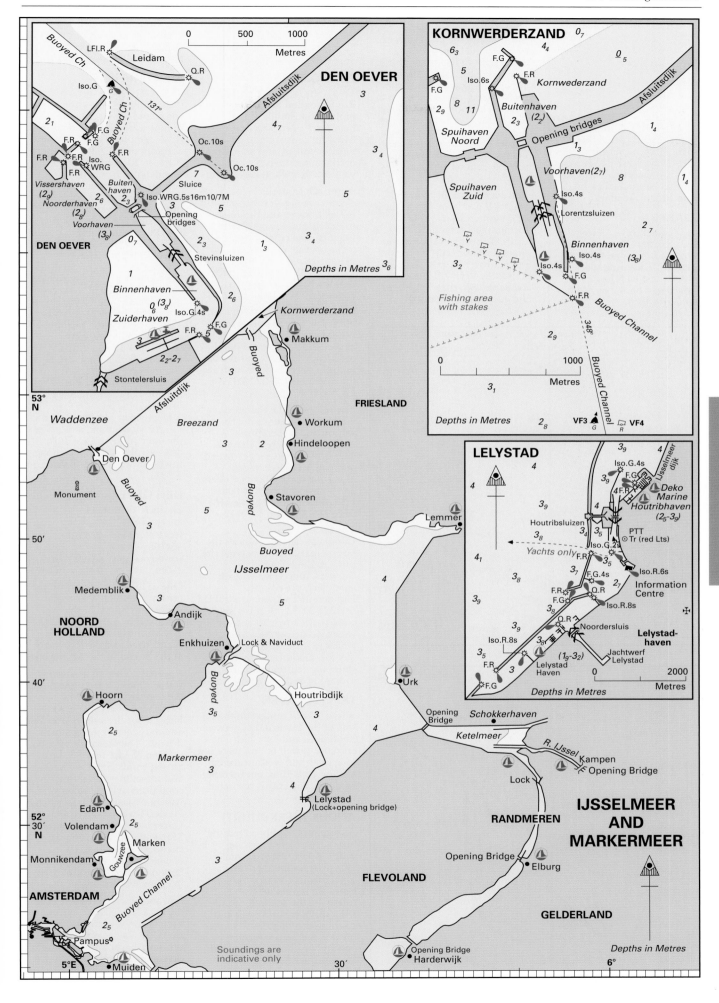

DEN OEVER

0 500 1000
Metres

Buoyed Ch
LFl.R
Leidam
Q.R
Iso.G
131°
Oc.10s
Oc.10s
Sluice
7
2₁
F.G
F.G
F.R
F.R
Iso.
F.R WRG
Buiten
haven 2₃ Iso.WRG.5s16m10/7M
Vissershaven
(2₉)
2₆
Noorderhaven
(2₈)
Voorhaven(3₈)
0₇
Opening
bridges
2₃
1₃
DEN OEVER
Stevinsluizen
1
Binnenhaven
0₆(3₈)
Iso.G.4s
Zuiderhaven
2₆
F.R F.G 5
3
2₂-2₇
Stontelersluis

3
4₇
3
3₄
5
3₄
Depths in Metres 3₆
2₃
1₃
3
3₄

KORNWERDERZAND
0₇
6₃
4₄
0₅
F.G
5
F.R Iso.6s
Kornwederzand
F.G
2₉ 8 11
2₃ *Buitenhaven*
(2₂)
Opening bridges
1₄
1₃
Spuihaven
Noord
Voorhaven(2₇)
8
1₄
Spuihaven
Zuid
Iso.4s
Lorentzsluizen
2₇
Binnenhaven
Y Y Iso.4s Iso.4s (3₈)
Y Y Iso.4s F.G
3₂
F.R
Fishing area
with stakes
2₉
348°
Buoyed Channel
0 1000
Metres
3₁
Depths in Metres 2₈ **VF3** **VF4**
G R

Afsluitdijk

Kornwerderzand
• Makkum
Buoyed

FRIESLAND

53°
N
Waddenzee
Breezand
• Workum
Den Oever
• Hindeloopen
Monument
Buoyed
• Stavoren
5
Buoyed
Lemmer
50'
Buoyed
IJsselmeer
4
Medemblik
3
5
NOORD
HOLLAND
• Andijk
Enkhuizen
Lock & Naviduct
4
40'
Hoorn
Buoyed
3₅
Houtribdijk
3
Urk

LELYSTAD
3₉
4
IJsselmeer dijk
Iso.G.4s
F.G
4
4 F.R
Deko
Marine
Houtribhaven
(2₅-3₉)
Houtribsluizen
3₄
3₅
PTT
Tr (red Lts)
4
3₈
Iso.G.2s
Yachts only
4₁
F.R
3₅
3₈
3₇ F.G.4s Iso.R.6s
F.R
F.G Q.R
2₇ *Information*
Centre
3₉
3₈
Iso.R.8s
3₉
Q.R
Iso.R.8s
3₈
Noordersluis
Lelystad-
haven
3₅
F.R
3
Jachtwerf
Lelystad
Lelystad
Haven
(1₉-3₂)
0 2000
F.G
Metres
Depths in Metres

Opening
Bridge
Schokkerhaven
Ketelmeer
4
R. IJssel Kampen
Lock Opening Bridge

Buoyed
3

4
Houtribdijk

Lelystad
(Lock+opening bridge)
4

RANDMEREN

Edam
2₅
52°
30'
N
Volendam
2₅
Marken
Monnikendam
3
Gouwzee
FLEVOLAND

Opening Bridge
• Elburg

IJSSELMEER
AND
MARKERMEER

AMSTERDAM
Buoyed Channel
2₅
GELDERLAND
Pampus
2₅
5°E
Muiden
Soundings are
indicative only
30'
Opening Bridge
Harderwijk
6°
Depths in Metres

Markermeer
3

NETHERLANDS

showers. Diesel is available in Marina Monnickendam. VHF 31. HM ② 0299 65 25 95.

VOLENDAM

Visitors' moorings on the quayside in the NE half of the hbr. HM ② 0299 36 96 20. A new marina to SW of the town has excellent facilities for visitors, or as a longer term berth. Harbourmaster ② 06 1276 2921, VHF 31. Town and eel market worth a visit and can also be reached by bike from Monnickendam.

EDAM

Small, quiet town. Narrow entrance, max depth 2m, through a lock and br to a canal with mooring space on both banks; Jachthaven Galgenveld on the port side before the lock.

HOORN

The home of the first European to sail round Cape Horn has many signs of its former glory as a Hanseatic town. The streets are brimming with history and the Westfries Museum is worth a visit. The former warehouses now serve as private dwellings or restaurants, and the bronze statues of the 'Boys from the Bontekoe' still look out for a suitable ship on which to stow away.

Entrance From the S on 352° from a R can buoy 1ca to the S of the rough stone walls forming the outer harbour walls. You may anchor in the outer harbour (2m) or raft out in the town hbr. HM ② 0229 21 40 12. VHF 74. Diesel available. Alternatively, there are quieter box moorings

available in the Grashaven on the port side (HM ② 0229 21 52 08) or to stb in the Hoorn YC (HM ② 0229 21 35 40).

ENKHUIZEN

This is the largest port of the Zuiderzee and lies at the N end of the Houtribdijk. It is also a busy ferry port. The Zuiderzee Museum consisting of an outdoor village and an indoor marine museum is superb and well worth a whole day's visit.

Approach from the S, the channel to the Krabbersgatsluis is well buoyed and the course to the entrance is marked by Ldg Lts. The two new yacht locks operate on VHF 22. The N approach is from the EZ1/KG2 (Iso.RGR.2s) buoy into the Krabbersgat on a course of 230° (Ldg Lts Iso.8s).

Entrance There are three yacht hbrs. The first to port is the Buyshaven which has a marina at the S side. There is a good toilet/shower block but the box moorings are the furthest from the town. HM ② 0228 31 56 60. VHF 31.

The second is the Buitenhaven which is adjacent to the rly station and is therefore convenient for crew changes. This hbr is often very crowded and you may have to raft alongside several boats. Toilets and showers are next to the HM office on the N side. HM ② 0228 31 24 44. VHF 12.

The third hbr, the Compagnieshaven, houses the largest marina. It is beyond the town to the NE and has showers, toilets, water, fuel, chandlery, provisions, launderette and restaurant. HM ② 0228 31 33 53. It is a short walk to the town and next door to the Zuiderzee Museum which is worth staying an extra day for. Enkhuizen has a good shopping centre, boatyards, sailmaker and engine repairs.

TRINTELHAVEN

A free 'hbr of refuge' on the N side of the Houtribdyk between Enkhuizen and Lelystad. The entrance is well lit and there is a long quay and well-protected anchorage within, but no other facilities, and stay is restricted to three days.

ANDIJK (KERKBUURT)

A large, well equipped marina but fairly isolated (visiting shop). Apart from the small village of Andijk there are no other attractions nearby. Entrance is obtained by following the sea wall round from the N tip at Andijk and continuing along the W of the breakwater before turning its S end and heading N through the hbr entrance between breakwaters. A sharp turn to stb brings one to the end of the first pontoon where a reporting

telephone is provided. Chandlery and restaurant. HM ② 0228 59 30 75. VHF 31. Diesel available.

MEDEMBLIK

3M to the NW is identified at a distance by its collection of spires and the large white pumping house building just to the N. Approach the narrow entrance on 232° (Oc.5s Lt between F.R and F.G on wooden piers). There are submerged rocks either side. The first turning to port, almost opposite the ferry berth, leads to the modern marina in the Pekelharinghaven HM ② 0227 54 21 75; VHF 31. Diesel and petrol available. The Middenhaven has no facilities but yachts can lie alongside on either side of the hbr. Access to the marina in the Westerhaven is through an opening road br. The HM office and facilities are all in one building. HM ② 0227 54 18 61. VHF 09. The Noordhollands canal can be entered here via the Westerhavensluis at the SW of the hbr, but there are fixed bridges.

A large yacht hbr, the Regatta Centre Medemblik, is 2ca S of the main hbr entrance. It is, however, the furthest from the town. VHF 31. HM ② 0227 54 77 81.

DEN OEVER

Charts N 1810, 1811; Imray C26

HW Helgoland –0245sp –0410np

MHWS	MHWN	MLWN	MLWS
1·9m	1·7m	0·4m	0·2m

One of four old villages on the former island of Wieringen which was joined to the mainland by a dyke in 1924. The Stevinsluis links the Waddenzee and the IJsselmeer at the W end of the Afsluitdijk.

Approach There is no deep water approach from the E on the seaward side of the Afsluitdijk. This area is well-buoyed but the streams run fast and the edges of the channels dry out. The mean spring rates off Den Helder reach 3½kn. Strong winds create difficult and sometimes dangerous conditions in these shallow waters. Passage from Den Helder/Texelstroom to Den Oever locks is by buoyed Malzwin and Visjagergatje channels, departing HW Helder –0400. Visibility here is famously variable and staying in channel is essential.

Entrance Turn to stb just before the O12 buoy (Iso.R.4s) and keep in the W sector of the Iso.GWR.2s Lt on the end of the inner harbour wall, entering the outer harbour between F.R and F.G Lts. The outer harbour is well sheltered by moles on each side. Turn to port, keeping

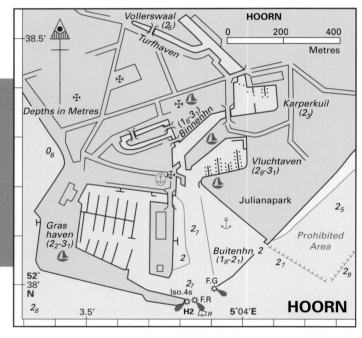

between the port and stb buoys, towards the Afsluitdijk where it may be necessary to tie up to the piles while waiting for the two bridges to open. Enter the Voorhaven and the lock (VHF 20). The channels are lit, but a first-time passage at night is inadvisable. The fishing hbr N of the locks has limited facilities for yachts. After passing through the locks a temporary berth may be found on the W side of Binnenhaven. For overnight stays the Jachthaven Den Oever, with all facilities, is at the S end of the Zuiderhaven. HM ☎ 0227 51 17 89. Diesel available.

KORNWERDERZAND

Charts N 1810.6, 1811

HW Helgoland –0210sp –0315np DS –0545SW +0200NE

MHWS	MHWN	MLWN	MLWS
2·2m	1·4m	0·3m	0·2m

The NE entry point for the IJsselmeer.

Approach From the E by the Boontjes channel from Harlingen with a minimum depth of 1·8m at LW. The channel is well marked at regular intervals, but very narrow. From the N by the Inschot and Zuidoostrak with a turn to the E at the KWZ W card buoy, 12ca W of the entrance. The sea-dyke is featureless with the occasional ch spire showing above.
Entrance There are two apparent entrances but only the smaller one to the E leads to the locks. The W or Spuihaven is not used for navigation. The Buitenhaven piers have F.R and F.G Lts. Enter on a course of 225° taking care to avoid the shoal to port. Before the swing bridges there are waiting pontoons to stb if it is necessary to wait for a lock opening. The Lorentzsluizen operate 24hrs VHF 18. On the S side are mooring posts with good shelter which may be used for a few hours or overnight. No facilities. HM ☎ 0517 57 81 70. Customs ☎ 0582 94 94 44.

MAKKUM

Chart N 1810.6

Only 2M SE from Kornwerderzand locks.

Entrance From the Kornwerderzand lock there is a buoyed channel leading between shoals to the start of the entrance channel proper which has Ldg Lts on 090·5°. Several marinas to stb, first YC Makkum, HM ☎ 0515 23 14 08. Small marina, but supermarket, chandler, sailmaker and beach nearby. Then marina Makkum, ½M along the entrance channel to stb, has 500 residents berths plus 100 for visitors. HM ☎ 0515 23 23 55. There are also marina berths at the Prins YC HM ☎ 0515 23 29 30.

Vessels may continue to the end of the entrance canal where there are box moorings in the town hbr (closest to town). For craft drawing less than 1·5m it is possible to enter the Friesland canal system here and join the fixed mast route to Leeuwarden and beyond. There is a chandler, a supermarket and fried fish take-away in the town. Diesel available from several outlets.

WORKUM

5M further S is entered from the Workum-Hindeloopen middle-ground buoy H2/W1 Iso.RGR.2s through a narrow buoyed channel and 1M long entrance canal with Ldg Lts on 081·5° Oc.6s. The steam rising from the tall chimney of a crop-drying plant often makes a good landmark. This is another entrance to the Frisian canals and lakes. A large marina on the N bank (It Soal) has all facilities. HM ☎ 0515 54 29 37. Between It Soal and the lock are a number of additional moorings. The entrance canal, Het Zool, has a min depth of 1·7m and ends in a quaint circular basin before the lock where it is possible to moor overnight. The basin has a toilet block and it is just a short walk into the town. It is hardly worth entering the lock unless proceeding to the lakes.

HINDELOOPEN

This beautiful town is famous for its enamelled woodware. No access to the inland waterways, but the small canals and tiny bridges are very attractive.

Entrance Enter from the H2/W1 buoy (Iso.RGR.2s) on a general SE course, keeping to the buoyed but unlit channel. Enter between high wooden piers and turn to port immediately for the large Jachthaven Hindeloopen, which has all facilities including fuel, launderette, 20-tonne travel-lift, swimming pool and engineers. HM ☎ 0514 52 45 54. Moorings can also be found in the old hbr to the S of the entrance. VHF 10. HM ☎ 0514 52 20 09. Stores from the town close by. The Church with its leaning tr and graves of servicemen from both sides from the 1939–45 war should not be missed. Although there is full shelter from the seas in the marina, strong winds from the N blow right across.

STAVOREN

4M S of Hindeloopen offers access to the Friesland canals for craft not over 2m draught. There are several harbours, two of which do not involve passing through the locks into the canal system. The one to the N is the Oude haven where a small ferry to Enkhuizen operates every

two hours. The S side of the Oude haven is suitable for yachts; it is close to town and the rly station but can be very crowded. HM ☎ 0514 68 12 16 VHF 74. The S hbr is the 500-berth Marina Stavoren Buitenhaven which has its entrance just S of the E end of the entrance to the Nieuwe Voorhaven. HM ☎ 0514 68 46 74. VHF 74. Diesel available. Access to the canal system is via the Johan Frisosluis at the NE end of the Nieuwe Voorhaven. From off-shore, the distinctive concave roof of the pumping station provides a useful steering mark. Inside the lock, a turning almost immediately to port leads to the Jachthaven Stavoren, while the entrance to the 425-berth Marina Stavoren is on the stb side of the canal (HM ☎ 0514 68 46 86) and the 170-berth Jachthaven de Roggebroek about 150m further up on the port side. HM ☎ 0514 68 14 69. Stores from shops in the town. Fuel alongside.

LEMMER

The Prinses Margriet canal, 1M W of the town harbours, provides access to the Friesland canals for craft not exceeding 3m draught via the Prinses Margrietsluis (VHF 20 no fee, open all days). However, there is also a route via the town which is well worth visiting.

Approach is E between Friesland and the Nordoost Polder with a buoyed channel close to the S shore. The small Friese Hoek LtHo on the NW corner of the Noordoost polder provides a steering mark until the channel buoys, less than 2ca from the steep-to shore, can be identified. Lemmer is a large yachting centre and there are ten yacht harbours, plus mooring places both outside and inside the locks through the town. Full facilities. Fuel is

available at the Marine Center in the Industrie haven on the N shore outside the locks and at the marinas on either side of the canal after the Zijlroedebrug. Opening times for the locks are: Monday–Friday 0700–2100, Saturday 0700–2000, Sunday, holidays 0830–1200, 1400–1730, 1800–2000. VHF 11. All the town brs open on approach. A fee for the lock and town bridges is collected by the HM in the lock.

Lemmer leads inland to the many delights of Friesland and Groningen via the canal system. Sneek, Leeuwarden, Dokkum and Lauwersoog, Groningen are rewarding destinations; bridges opening along the way (small bridge tolls in Leeuwarden and Dokkum and Burdaard) during daylight hours, often closed for an hour midday and evening rush hour – so timing is important, especially in busy Leeuwarden with its railway bridge on the S approach.

URK

A former island, now linked by dykes to the polders, Urk retains its individuality – which includes steep streets! A large fishing fleet operates mainly from coastal ports, but some boats still work from here. The entrance, which is only possible from the S, requires care. There are more mooring places than the single marina symbol on the chart indicates. Visiting yachts can moor on the N, S and W sides of the Nieuwe Haven, all three walls of the Westhaven and the S wall of the Oosthaven. VHF 12. HM ☎ 0527 68 99 70. Fuel is available in the Westhaven. Small shopping centre and an interesting memorial to fishermen lost at sea.

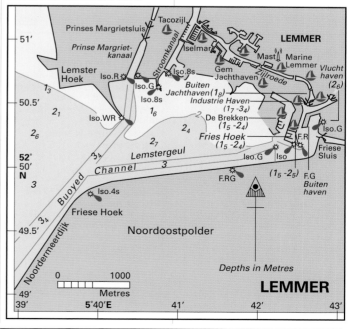

Depths in Metres

LEMMER

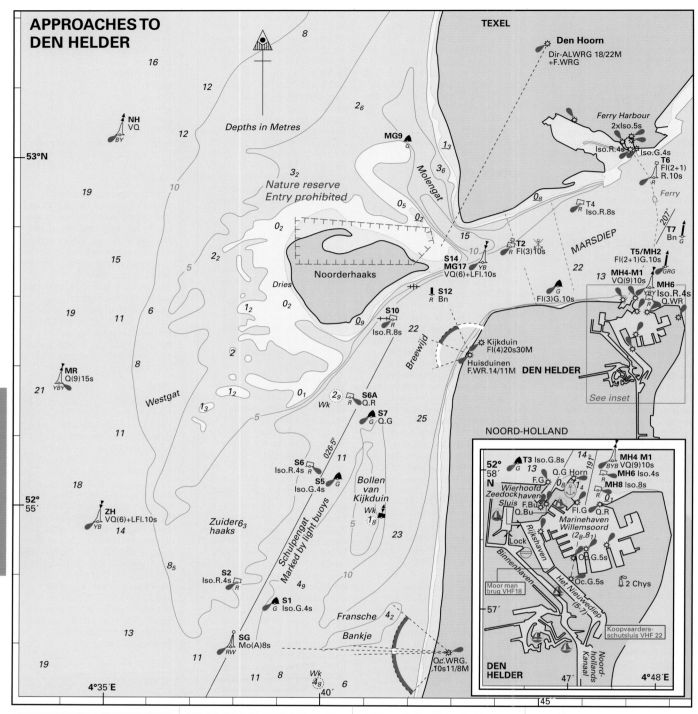

UK TO N HOLLAND & R ELBE

Passage to the River Elbe, gateway to the Baltic, can take only a few days from E England via the Frisian Islands. A satisfying journey offering a variety of colourful stopping points, and not taxing in reasonable conditions; part of the passage can be taken via the Dutch canal system or less exposed Waddenzee.

UK to N Holland

Lowestoft offers the shortest passage 104M to **Den Helder / Oudeschildt** (Texel) popular first ports for N Holland. Using at least two full NE going tides will speed the journey. Approach the lit Schulpengat on the ingoing tide.

Alternatively, make first landfall 40M further south at **IJmuiden** where access to the inland waterways is also possible.

Harwich is another good point of departure, 125M to **IJmuiden** and 140M to **Den Helder**. Depart Harwich HW-0100 to optimise tidal lift.

Coastal Route N from Den Helder

Den Helder to the Elbe / Cuxhaven can be made comfortably in five stages calling at Oost Vlieland / West Terschelling, Lauwersoog, Borkum, Norderney, Cuxhaven, each port offering scenic or practical advantages and lit for 24h access.

Den Helder to Borkum, (93M) the westernmost German island, is also feasible direct; the islands en route are well lit, with only light traffic in the inshore traffic zone. Depart NE from Den Helder at Hoek van Holland HW+0055 and return SW from Borkum at Hoek van Holland HW-0400. Spring rate up to 1·5kn.

Alternative Sheltered Routes:

Waddenzee route: Den Helder to Oost Vlieland is accessible by careful use of the Scheurrak channel (max 2m draft at HW) to the Inschot; otherwise route via Harlingen and the Blauwe Slenk channel – a longer but less restrictive passage.

Canal Route: the Friesland canal system connects Harlingen to Lauwersoog, or further N still via Groningen to Delfzijl, exiting on the R Eems to Borkum. All passable for mast up vessels drawing no more than 2m. See page 270.

LELYSTAD

This port has a lock, the Houtribsluis (VHF 20), through the dyke separating the IJsselmeer from the Markermeer. There are large marinas both N and S of the lock. Jachthaven Lelystad HM ☎ 0320 26 03 26, WV Lelystad HM ☎ 0320 26 01 98. VHF 31. Deko Marine HM ☎ 0320 26 02 48. VHF 31. IJsselmeer museum close by.

Approach This is clearly defined by the dyke and the seawall whilst the two very conspic chimneys of the electricity generating station are passed close to port. These chimneys provide an excellent navigating mark for the whole of the S part of the IJsselmeer. The S exit from the locks is between the sea-wall and offshore training dykes. There is a yacht hbr 1½M further S by the Noordersluis.

MUIDEN

At the S end of the IJsselmeer, Muiden is approached from the main shipping channel leading to Amsterdam by leaving the channel at the P8/IJM27 RG buoy, 11ca N of the old fort of Pampus Is. The narrow buoyed channel is then followed on 142° until the Pampus is abeam to stb. A course of 202° for a further 12ca leads to the spar buoys marking the channel into Muiden. The E mole (port hand on entry) is submerged for the first 2ca and considerable caution should be exercised in keeping on 181° in the entrance and close to the W training wall. Even greater care is needed on leaving if other vessels are entering. There are several yacht hbrs including the Royal Netherlands Sailing and Rowing Club. HM ☏ 0294 26 14 50. Fuel available in the hbr. N of the Pampus the buoyed channel leads SW to the Buiten IJ. Through the Muiden lock (small fee payable) a motorway bridge (limited openings) and railway bridge, the Vecht provides a short route to the very pretty town of Weesp. Marina and services.

THE RANDMEREN

3M SE from Urk, the Ketelbrug – clearance 12·9m, but with a lifting span – separates the IJsselmeer from the Ketelmeer and Randmeren.

VHF 18. The Randmeren is all that is left of the SE part of the Zuiderzee after reclamation of the Noordoost and Flevoland polders. It provides a continuous navigable waterway, with a buoyed channel 3m deep, between the Flevoland polder and the original Zuiderzee coast. However, yachts with more than 12·5m air-draught will not be able to pass under the fixed Hollandse br at Muiderberg and so would have to retrace their track to the Ketelmeer.

KAMPEN

This interesting medieval town, about 6M up the R IJssel from the Ketelmeer, has four yacht marinas and a good shopping centre. The channel has a minimum depth of 3·2m and is well marked. The Eilandbrug, completed in 2003, has a clearance of 15·8m, and an opening span.

ELBURG, HARDERWIJK, SPAKENBURG AND HUIZEN

Elburg is a 13th-century town with impressive ramparts and a moat. Moorings alongside the S bank of the canal and in the town hbr. Harderwijk is an old Zuiderzee trading port with several 13th and 14th-century buildings and a choice of three hbrs. Spakenburg has a very picturesque old hbr with many traditional Dutch sailing barges. The townsfolk are noted for their wearing of traditional dress. Huizen has two buoyed entrance channels, the W one leading to three marinas while

the E leads through an opening br to the old fishing hbr. The town has suffered considerable development.

FRISIAN ISLANDS AND THE WADDENZEE

The Waddenzee, an area of sandbanks and shallow channels, is the tidal remnant of the former Zuider Zee. The non-tidal S section became the IJsselmeer with the completion of the Afsluitdijk in 1932. It is an inhospitable expanse of wild seascape and frequently-changing channels which, although buoyed, can be difficult to follow. It requires particularly careful concentration in the reduced visibility to which this area is liable during the summer. For yachts with fixed keels, the only

Return Passage from R Elbe

Departing Cuxhaven at Helgoland HW+0220 taking maximum advantage of the tide, turn SW at the Elbe No.1 buoy from which in favourable conditions Norderney (50M) can be made direct. A passage break can also be taken at Spiekeroog Island. Alternatively, make for Helgoland and head S from there on following tide. Great care has to be exercised in German waters to stay well clear of shipping lanes (at least one mile) whenever possible, making meticulous log entries to present a convincing defence should a German coastguard cutter challenge your navigation.

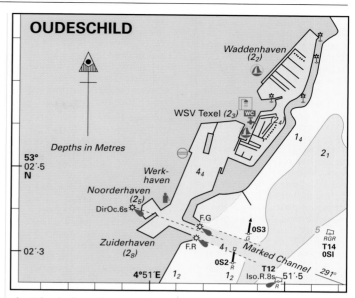

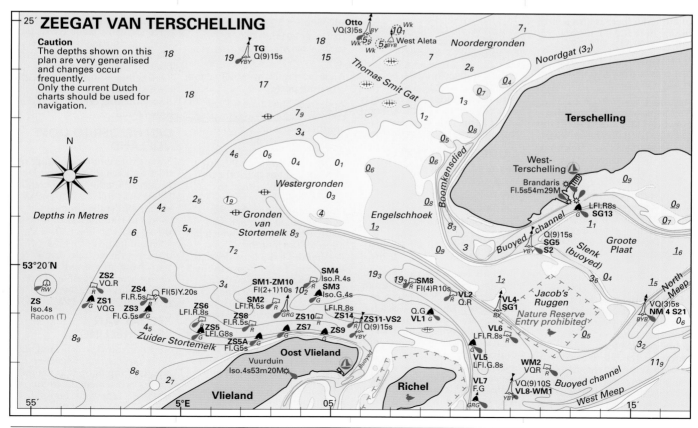

NETHERLANDS

area for reasonable sailing until one has acquired some local knowledge, is the area between Terschelling, Texel (pronounced '*Tessel*') and the mainland from Harlingen to Den Helder. From Terschelling or Vlieland the Vliestroom leads S and after 4M divides into the Blauwe Slenk, leading to Harlingen, and the Inschot which leads via the Verversaat to Kornwerderzand and the locks into the IJsselmeer. On the flood tide either route may be taken, but in the reverse direction proceeding N from Kornwerderzand, departure must either be made 1–2 hours before HW, or a diversion taken through the Boontjes close to the dykes to join the channel from Harlingen. This avoids the Zuidoostrak which at one point dries at LW.

It is slow but interesting to pass close inside the Frisian Islands. Every island has a drying height where the HW depth is about 2m at neaps extending for a mile or more and marked by withies. There are buoyed channels into the small drying hbrs and the islands have beautiful sands. You must not stray outside the marked channels because if you ground, you may be fined, as the Waddenzee is a conservation area.

DEN HELDER

Charts BA 1546; N 1811; Imray C26

HW Helgoland –0410sp –0520np

DS Dover +0315E –0300W

MHWS	MHWN	MLWN	MLWS
1·7m	1·5m	0·4m	0·2m

This is the principal naval hbr of Holland: there is also a large fishing fleet and a Customs office (☎ 0223 65 75 15).

VTS Monitor VHF 62 from 5M seawards to M13 buoy about 2M E.

Approach From the N the Molengat buoyed channel lies between 1M and ½M W off the coast of Texel and has at least 6m. From the S the Schulpengat buoyage commences at the SG buoy situated 3M W of the Grote Kaap Oc.RWG.10s LtHo and is within the narrow W sector. There is a Dir.WRG. Lt on Texel (026·5°). The channel runs NE through the Breewijd for 7M to join the Marsdiep between Texel and the mainland. The Noorderhaaks is an uninhabited area of sand with off-lying banks to the W of Marsdiep and presents a major hazard in the approach. There is a S card Lt buoy off the E end of Noorderhaaks from which an E course for 2M leads to the entrance. The North Sea coasts of both Texel and the mainland are low-lying and fringed by dunes with few landmarks. This area is now covered by a Vessel Traffic System (VTS) and all

vessels in the Schulpengat, Molengat and Marsdiep are required to monitor VHF 62. This rule also applies when leaving hbr. Keep a look-out for busy ferry traffic as you cross between the ferry harbours of Den Helder and Texel.

Entrance There are two sets of Ldg Lts, one on 207° (Iso.2s) for the ferry hbr to the W of the main hbr and the other on 191° (Oc.G.5s) for the Marinehaven. Signals apply to all vessels and permission to enter should be requested on VHF 62, call sign *Den Helder Traffic Centre*. Tidal streams run fast across the Marinehaven entrance and reference to Dutch *Waterstanden/Stromen HP33* is recommended. There are two successive sets of port and stb Lts marking the hbr entrance.

Berthing The KMJC yacht hbr is to stb after entering the main hbr piers and has water and electricity to the pontoons. Diesel available. The Koninklijke Marine Jachtclub is part of the Dutch Navy and toilets and showers are in the Officers' Mess. HM ☎ 0223 65 26 45. VHF 31. Customs office in the YH. ☎ 0205 81 36 14. Bicycles available for hire from the HM. At the north end of the Rijkshaven, the Zeedock Sluis gives access to the Passantenhaven Willemsoord. All facilities including diesel. HM ☎ 06 51181879. Alternatively pass through the Vice-Admiral H.V. Moorman Bridge (VHF 18) into the Nieuwe Diep and lock through the Koopvaardersschutsluis (VHF 22) into the Noord-Hollands canal. There are three YCs to the N in the Binnenhaven. Going N they are: WSOV Breewijd (☎ 0223 61 55 00); WV Marine (☎ 0223 65 21 73 and WV Helder-Willemsoord-N (☎ 0223 62 44 22). The Noord-Hollands canal connects with Alkmaar and Amsterdam to the S (opening bridges throughout).

OUDESCHILD (TEXEL)

Charts BA 1546; N 1811; Imray C26

HW Helgoland –0310sp –0420np

DS Dover +0400NE –0145SW up to 3kn

MHWS	MHWN	MLWN	MLWS
1·7m	1·5m	0·4m	0·2m

The only harbour available to cruisers – the car ferry harbour with service to Den Helder, to the SW, is prohibited. Good bus services and bikes for hire. Den Bourg is the pretty capital of the island, busy in summer with tourist trade, but never overwhelmed. N side beaches are magnificent sand, and much of the island is farmed / nature reserve behind massive dikes.

Approach

Flood tide begins Den Helder LW +0200

From seaward through the Molengat or the Schulpengat leading to the wide and deep Marsdiep. From SE and the Den Oever locks at the NW corner of the IJsselmeer. From the E from Kornwerderzand or from the ENE via an intricate channel from Terschelling. All routes lead into the Texelstroom. This is a naval exercise area and submarines may be encountered on the surface.

Entrance is from between a R Lt buoy (T12) and a RGR buoy (T14/OS1) followed by R and G spar buoys on the NW side of the Texelstroom. Keep the Oc.6s Lt between the 2F.R and 2F.G pier head Lts for approach of 291° through the moles. Strong currents across the entrance. On entering harbour, area to port is for ferries and 'brown armada'. To stb is pool for fishing vessels with large chandlery. 100m to stb is entry to small channel leading through sharp 90° turn N to large visitors' pontoon marina with all facilities; locals moor in first section. Buy electronic key at HM to access facilities. Bike hire and small shops to hand. Several rather good restaurants around small village.

Note: Mid July– end August is very busy in the visitors' moorings, leaving newcomers to raft against fishing boats in main pool.

HARLINGEN

Charts BA 1633, 112; N 1811; Imray C26

HW Helgoland –0155sp –0245np

DS Dover –0115S –0600N

MHWS	MHWN	MLWN	MLWS
2·3m	2·0m	0·3m	0·2m

An important ship-building and repairing port.

Approach The Blauwe Slenk continues into the main approach channel which runs along the S side of the Pollendam. This training wall is awash at half-tide and the row of R topped bns mark the top of the wall. It is critical to approach the S side of the Pollendam from within the buoyed and lit channel. The centre of the channel, which lies approx 50m S of the Pollendam, has a least depth of 6m. Small Y spar buoys to the S of the main channel mark a two-way channel for small craft with at least 1·8m. When the tide covers the wall, the stream sets strongly across it. The final approach is marked by Ldg Lts (Iso.6s) on 112°. Port VHF 11. HM ☎ 0517 41 25 12. Customs ☎ 058 29 49 49 44. Channel from S (Boontjes) is narrow and shallow (3m).

Entrance Through mole heads, watching for ferries and fishing vessels. Short term alongside moorings to stb in exposed outer harbour.

N Harbour reached through lock gates (Keersluis) and split swing bridge (service on demand, but closed at HW springs for one hour) Note moorings to port for 'brown armada'. Under lifting bridge to N harbour, some pontoons, mostly alongside; normal facilities. Otherwise, S Harbour reached under stb lifting bridge, AB and small quiet marina. Electricity and water only. Supermarket on RH side of S Harbour.

From outer harbour, waterway to port leads to large commercial facility. Hold to stb in Oude Buitenhaven past ferry loading positions towards lock for van Harinxma canal (daylight hours) and route to Leeuwarden. Just beyond lock, hard stb for small quiet marina (Harlingen Yachthaven) 4m max beam and 1·9m draft max.

COASTAL PASSAGE NORTH

From Den Helder the route NE is not demanding in fair weather. The coast is sandy and low, the shallows aplenty but good water is found just a little way offshore, and islands are clearly lit. Zeegats between the islands are fast running waterways leading to havens of varying value to the cruiser; approaches where feasible are well marked.

In the Waddenzee when sands are uncovered, streams tend to flow in the direction of the channels, but when covered the direction can change across the sands. Anchoring behind the islands is possible but shelter is limited. Texel, Vlieland, and Terschelling islands have good marinas and offer much to the discriminating cruiser should time permit.

DEN HELDER TO OOST VLIELAND

Taking maximum advantage of tides for each stage, depart Den Helder or Oudeschild (Texel) at Hoek van Holland HW+0055 via the Molengat channel (buoyed) running close along the W coast of Texel. Oost Vlieland (page 269) 35M distant is the next accessible port, lying off the well marked Zeegat van Terschelling. Enter with the flood tide (begins HW Hoek van Holland HW +0055)

ZEEGAT VAN TERSCHELLING

Approach to Oost Vlieland and West Terschelling, whether coming from N or W is via the Zuider Stortemelk; from the Iso.4s ZS safe water buoy (53°19'·75N 4°55'·80E) a

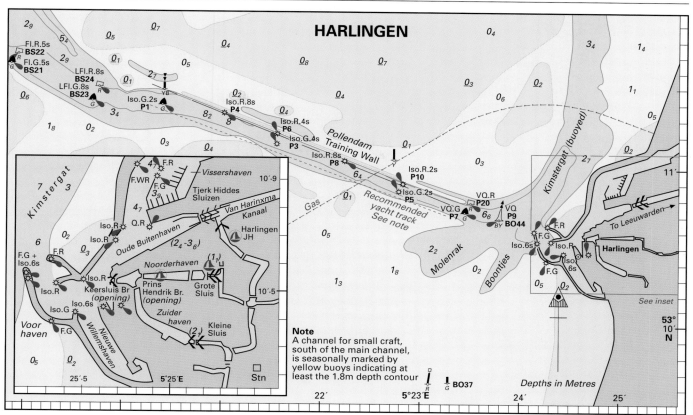

HARLINGEN

Note
A channel for small craft, south of the main channel, is seasonally marked by yellow buoys indicating at least the 1.8m depth contour

Depths in Metres

See inset

Stn

53°
10′
N

course of 110° leads into the buoyed channel, uncomfortable in strong winds from W to NW. Channels are constantly shifting and buoyage changes are made frequently and should be followed.

Call VHF 02 for the latest navigational information. Call sign *Verkeerscentrale Brandaris*. VHF 04 for the Dutch Waddenzee.

The Eierlandsche Gat between Vlieland and Texel is sparsely marked and should not be attempted without local knowledge. No facilities.

OOST VLIELAND

Charts BA 112;
N 1811;
Imray C26

HW Helgoland −0250sp −0320np

Approach From the Zuider Stortemelk, the ZS11–VS2 N card Lt marks the entrance to the Vliesloot buoyed and partly lit channel. Keep to the middle of the channel until approaching VS14 R buoy Iso.R.4s before making for the hbr entrance avoiding shallows E of the E mole. HM ☎ 0562 45 1729; VHF 12.

Entrance is lit. HM office only opens for short periods morning and evening. Very busy late July and all of August. Anchoring off is feasible W of harbour entrance. Beware not to leave the vessel unattended until satisfied it will remain afloat at LW! The sand is hard.

Facilities. Superb beaches, excellent walks, wonderful views from LtHo, and the scent of the pines on a summer evening make this the pearl of

the Frisian Islands. Small shops and restaurants in the town, 15 minutes' walk away. Bicycles and trailers may be hired from HM. Fuel may be ordered from the HM for delivery by tanker. Visitors' cars prohibited. Ferries ply to Harlingen. Customs office (1 May–1 November) is at the NW end of the yacht hbr ☎ 058 294 94 44.

WEST TERSCHELLING

Charts BA 112;
N 1811;
Imray C26

HW Helgoland −0230
DS Dover −0100E +0500W

MHWS	MHWN	MLWN	MLWS
2·3m	2·1m	0·5m	0·2m

VTS VHF 02 for 20M out to sea and 10M in the Waddenzee.

Approach from the S (Vliestroom), turn E into the W Meep and make for narrow buoyed and lit Slenk channel. Beware ferries. No safe route across the sands from the SW into the Schuitengat. The Boomkensdiep channel leading round the SW end of Terschelling is unreliable: take local advice.

Entrance between lit piers. E mole covers at HW. Yacht hbr with pontoons for visitors at N end of hbr. Good facilities, including launderette. Diesel available. Stagings near entrance are for ferries and large commercial sailing vessels. Berth alongside by arrangement. HM ☎ 0562 44 33 37. VHF 31. HM is also authorised Customs Officer. Good selection of shops and restaurants in the town. Very picturesque landscape and

magnificent beaches. Bicycles are available for hire from HM.

OOST VLIELAND TO LAUWERSOOG

From Oost Vlieland, back track along the Stortemelk for four miles to avoid the Westergronden shallows; departing Helgoland HW +0320, the turn of the tide will then carry NE past Terschelling and Ameland for 40M before turning S into the Westgat for Lauwersoog harbour and marina; note the yellow small craft channel markers giving passage S of the Plaatgat shallows into the Westgat entrance.

AMELAND (NES)

Charts N 1811;
Imray C26

HW Helgoland −0119sp −0209np

Approach a stopover in Nes is possible on the flood tide, but access is not straightforward, and facilities are limited. The marked approach into the Zeegat van Ameland leads in a loop to the Borndiep channel, with two routes (Dantziggat and Molengat) leading off NE to Nes hbr entrance in the mid-S of the Is. Yachts settle on the firm bottom against the N end of E hbr wall with permission of HM. Shelter except in strong S winds. HM ☎ 0519 54 21 59. Diesel and petrol available from nearby garage.

LAUWERSOOG

Charts BA 1631, 1633;
N 1812;
Imray C26

HW Helgoland −0140

MHWS	MHWN	MLWN	MLWS
2·9m	2·6m	0·7m	0·3m

Approach from the W for small craft is possible via the yellow cans marking a channel ESE past the Plaatgat to the Westgat. Otherwise enter via the Westgat heading SE into the Zoutkamperlaag for 7m, turning stbd at the R Z18 buoy through the lit piers to the large commercial harbour. Ahead lies a small marina close to the Robbengatsluis lock (VHF 84). Through the lock (open Monday–Saturday 0700–1900, and Sunday 0900–2000, April–October) to the pastoral delights of the Lauwersmeer for berths and good facilities at the Noordergat YH (HM ☎ 0519 349040) and YH Het Booze Wijf (HM ☎ 0519349133). Diesel available at YH Noordergat.

Immediately to the W of the lock is a Customs office (☎ 0598 69 6560). On the N side of the sea wall, E of the lock, are a restaurant, fish cafés, chandlers and a small supermarket. Bus connections to Groningen.

Onward cruising routes to the interior – Groningen via Zoutkamp, or Leeuwarden and Harlingen via the Dokkumer ei.

SCHIERMONNIKOOG ISLAND

Charts BA 1633, 1635;
N 1812;
Imray C26

HW Helgoland −0103sp −0153np

Hbr lies in the SW of the island at the end of the causeway across the sands. From the Zoutkamperlaag follow the

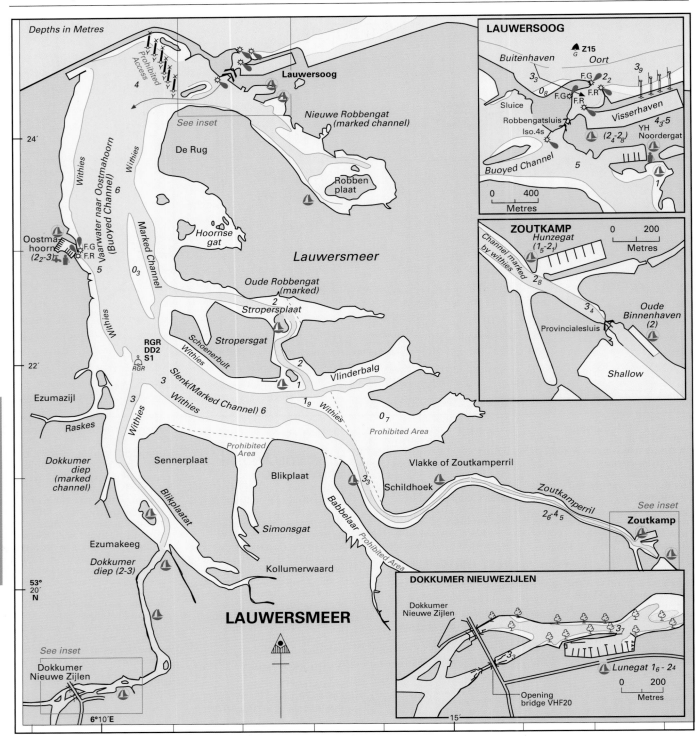

Depths in Metres

LAUWERSOOG

Prohibited Access

Lauwersoog

Nieuwe Robbengat (marked channel)

See inset

24′

De Rug

Withies

Withies

6

Robben plaat

Hoornse gat

Lauwersmeer

Oostma hoorn (2₂-3) F.G F.R

Vaarwater naar Oostmahoorn (Buoyed Channel)

5

Marked Channel 0₃

Withies

Oude Robbengat (marked)

2

Stropersplaat

22′

RGR DD2 S1 RGR

Stropersgat

Schoenerbult

Withies

Slenk (Marked Channel) 6

Withies

2

Vlinderbalg

2

1

1₉ *Withies*

0₇

Prohibited Area

Ezumazijl

3

3

Withies

Withies

Raskes

Prohibited Area

Sennerplaat

Dokkumer diep (marked channel)

Blikplaat

Vlakke of Zoutkamperril

3₃

Schildhoek

Zoutkamperril

2₆-4₅

See inset

Zoutkamp

53° 20′ N

Blikplaatat

Simonsgat

Babbelaar *Prohibited Area*

Ezumakeeg

Dokkumer diep (2-3)

Kollumerwaard

LAUWERSMEER

See inset

Dokkumer Nieuwe Zijlen

6°10′E

15′

LAUWERSOOG (inset)

Buitenhaven Z15 *Oort*

3₉

3₃ F.G 2₂

0₈ F.G F.R

Sluice

Robbengatsluis Iso.4s

Visserhaven 4₃-5

YH Noordergat (2₄-2₈)

Buoyed Channel 5

YH 1

0 400 Metres

ZOUTKAMP (inset)

Hunzegat (1₅-2₁) 0 200 Metres

Channel marked by withies

2₈

3₄

Oude Binnenhaven (2)

Provincialesluis

Shallow

DOKKUMER NIEUWEZIJLEN (inset)

Dokkumer Nieuwe Zijlen

3₇

3₃

Lunegat 1₆ - 2₄

Opening bridge VHF20

0 200 Metres

---

buoyed Gat van Schiermonnikoog to the RGR GVS/R1 buoy. Head N to leave R3 G buoy to stb and follow withies across the 'Siege wal' drying area. It is advisable to approach and leave on a rising tide within 2hrs of HW. No entrance Lts. The hbr has min depth of 1·3m and max 1·5m. Necessary to reserve a berth in busy summer months. HM ☎ 0519 53 15 44 or VHF 31 from 3hr before to 2hr after HW.

LAUWERSOOG TO BORKUM (G)

From Lauwersoog return N via the Westgat, departing near the tail end of the ebb, about Helgoland +0300, then head NE to clear Rottumerplaat

island (no landing permitted). Join the marked Huibertgat E–W channel for 7m before turning into the R Eems.

Cross the R Eems for the harbour on **Borkum** (Germany, see page 278) or carry on SE for 13M to **Delfzijl** via the well marked Doekegat channel: stay close to the marks to avoid the Randzelgat shallows and other banks.

ONWARD PASSAGE TO R ELBE (G)

Departing Borkum on passage E, stay with the Riffgat channel markings for at least 5m before rounding the Borkum Riff shallows. **Norderney** is an easy one tide ride past Juist island.

From Norderney the **R Elbe** entrance, or a detour to **Helgoland**, are one long tidal ride away. The flood tide will make light of the trip up the Elbe to Cuxhaven, taking precautions against the wash of large ships passing at full speed. Great care should be exercised when navigating close to or crossing shipping lanes: keep a detailed log. German patrol cutters are known to levy large fines for perceived deviations from regulations. For more detail see the next section 'Approaches to the Baltic'.

Mast-up route

HARLINGEN TO DELFZIJL
Charts ANWB A, B

From **Harlingen** (*see page 269*) to **Lauwersoog** takes two days via the canal systems of Friesland and Groningen – a unique panorama of town and country life in N Holland, and a delightful contrast to the modernity and industry of SW Holland.

Take the van Harinxma canal, maintained to 3·8m depth to busy Leeuwarden, pass through town and exit on shallower (2·2m) Dokkumer Ei to rustic Dokkum. Onwards via the Dokkumer Grutdjip; wander through the fields to the open waters, reed beds and country peace of Lauwersmeer. All bridges en route open on demand, daylight hours, some closed for lunch break. Diesel at several points along canal. Whole route passable for 2m draught, but some moorings may offer less. Note: canal gates at Harlingen operate free flow at LW to purge canal – care required on entering.

Franeker Small club marina to port 1M before town centre. Shops and banks 15 minutes' walk in pleasant setting. Alongside mooring in town centre.

Leeuwarden The van Harinxma canal swings S on approach to town, leading to Sneek and Lemmer, well signed. Ahead into Leeuwarden, marvel at ingenuity of first lifting bridge, and pass six more conventional bridges; toll collected at 5th bridge by swinging clog. Bridge service on demand 0900–1600 and 1800–2000 on summer weekdays but closed 1200–1300 at weekends.

Alongside mooring through picturesque town centre, but variable depth under trees; some facilities.

Van Harinxma route to Sneek and Lemmer – note restricted service at Leeuwarden railway bridges S of town – 0500–0700, 0900–1600, 1800–2100. YC (Leeuwarden yachthaven) to port after railway bridges, via remote-controlled swing bridge. Quiet, but 20 minutes' walk to town: basic facilities.

Leeuwarden to Lauwersmeer via Dokkum is a canalized river, passable for 2m draft with care; many side waters and moorings no more than 1·5m. Toll at

pretty village of Burdaard, collected by clog at 2nd bridge.

Dokkum A very pretty town. mooring along canal bank, with most facilities. 2m draft moorings best found on staging beyond 3rd bridge. Bridge toll collected at 2nd bridge. Service hours as for Leeuwarden.

Further box marina beyond 3rd bridge to port. Supermarket and bus services to Groningen / train connection.

Entry to Lauwersmeer is via lock at Dokkumer Nieuwe Zijlen. Large marina to stb on exit, all facilities.

Lauwersmeer formed when dam constructed – now a large shallow nature reserve with much on-water activity. Part of standing mast route to Groningen.

Channel wanders N through reed beds, marked by withies. Several nature reserves – off limits to boats. Buoyage requires close observation to avoid stranding.

Good facilities at Jachthaven Oostmahorn, at NW side of Lauwersmeer, and Yachthaven Noordergat close to the lock. Diesel. Restaurants nearby. Short walk to dam, sea views and village.

Lauwersoog A small fishing village on dike with ferries to Schiermonnikoog island. Exit to Wadden Zee via Robbengatsluis lock (daylight hours VHF 84). Marina on sea side of dam, but rather exposed boxes. Large fishing fleet in industrial harbour. Good facilities. Bus service to Groningen.

Access canal route to Groningen via narrow waterway (Slenk) at S end of

Lauwersmeer. Locks at Zoutkamp. Large friendly marina (Yachthaven Hunzegat) before lock to port – suitable for longer term mooring.

Zoutkamp Small marina and restaurants / shops. Onwards via canalized Reitdiep (2·4m max depth) crossing van Staarkenborgh canal, into approaches to Groningen.

Groningen Major regional centre, university town with long history and museums, shops and restaurants. Good onward train connections.

Multiple bridges to navigate round S side of town centre for mast up vessels; bridges work in sequence – service hours 0900–1200, 1300–1600, 1730–1900. Jachthaven Oosterhaven lies E of ring, close to railway station, all facilities and very close to shops / cafés.

Eemskanaal From Groningen to Delfzijl the Eemskanaal (5·4m draft) runs straight, forking at Delfzijl. Town and small marina to port. Bypass S to locks (VHF 26) for R Eems. Immediately past lock to port lies ZV Neptunus marina, chandlery and shops, cafés.

DELFZIJL

Charts BA 3632; N 1812; Imray C26

HW Helgoland +0020sp –0005np

MHWS	MHWN	MLWN	MLWS
3·6m	3·2m	0·7m	0·3m

This is the most important commercial and fishing port in the N of Holland. Customs post. Eems Kanaal leads via Groningen along a fixed mast route to the IJsselmeer. A resort town with a small selection of shops plus rail service via Groningen to S.

Marina boxes and most facilities in the Abel Tasman marina, close to town.

VTS Monitor VHF 20.
Going N change to VHF 18 at buoy 35.

Approach The outer part of the Eems estuary is divided by the island of Borkum and large drying areas in the Westereems and Oostereems. From the Oostereems buoy there is a difficult passage across the shoals S of Memmert to join the Westereems 7M N of Delfzijl. A safer approach from the E is to continue to the Riffgat or Westereems, both of which are marked at their seaward ends by safe-water buoys bearing the names of their respective channels. (The Huibertgat channel is now marked by a series of unlit safe water buoys and the fixed W sector Lt which used to guide vessels along this channel has been extinguished). From the W the main approach channel is the Westereems which is well buoyed. After the Noll pillar buoy (Q.G), follow the Ranselgat buoyed channel SE guided by the leading sector Lt of Campen LtHo, keeping just outside the shipping channel. Change course slightly to stb after the No.27 G pillar buoy (Fl.G.4s) to follow the buoyed and lit Doekegat channel into the Oostfriesche Gaatje. After the second R sector of the multi-sector Knock LtHo, the W sector guides you towards the Ldg Lts on a heading of 203°. In any event, keep N of the PS3/BW26 GRG buoy Fl.G(2+1)12s on approach.

Entrance is between F.R and F.G pier head Lts followed by a turn to stb between bns exhibiting G Lts to stb and R to port for 3M. The pontoons of the yacht hbr lie against the W wall of the Handelshaven. The HM office is halfway along the W wall ☎ 0596 61 50 04. Diesel available at the marina.

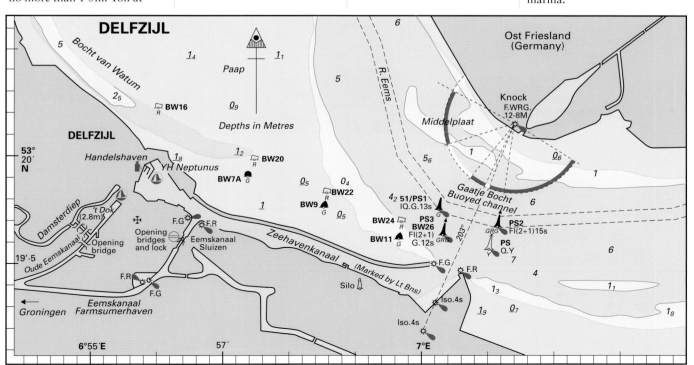

ROUTES AND PORTS

APPROACHES TO THE BALTIC

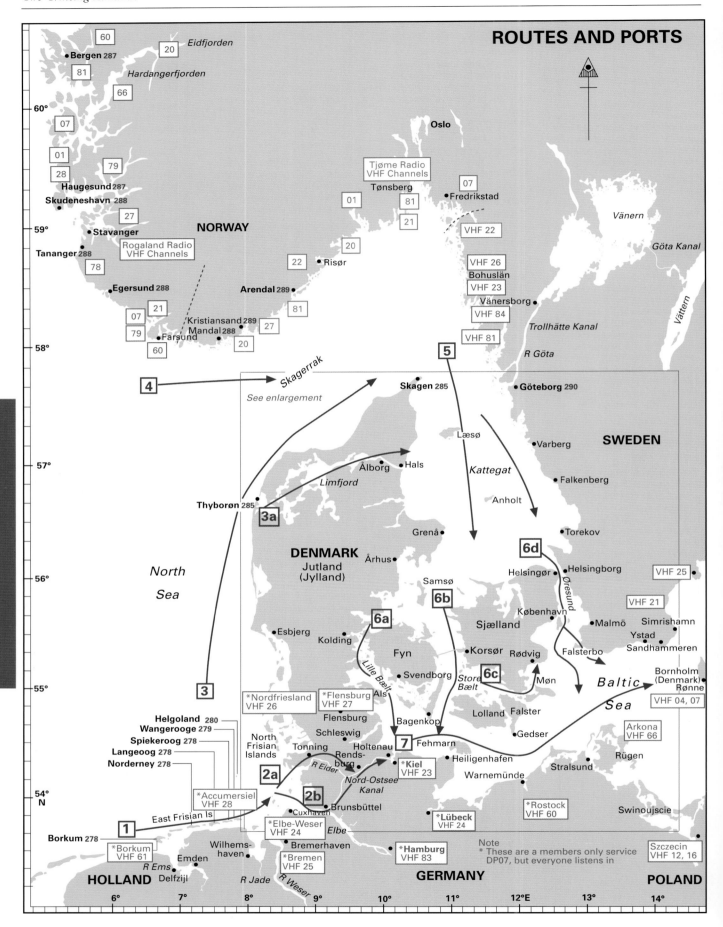

60

20 *Eidfjorden*

Bergen 287

81

Hardangerfjorden

66

60°

07

01

28

79

Haugesund 287

Skudeneshavn 288

27

59°

Stavanger

NORWAY

Rogaland Radio VHF Channels

Tananger 288

78

Egersund 288

21

07

79

60

Farsund

Kristiansand 289

Mandal 288

27

20

58°

22 Risør

Arendal 289

81

Oslo

Tjøme Radio VHF Channels

Tønsberg

01

81

21

07

• Fredrikstad

VHF 22

VHF 26

Bohuslän

VHF 23

Vänersborg

VHF 84

VHF 81

20

Vänern

Göta Kanal

Trollhätte Kanal

R Göta

Vättern

4 → *Skagerrak*

See enlargement

5

Skagen 285

Göteborg 290

SWEDEN

Læsø

Varberg

Kattegat

Falkenberg

57°

Ålborg • Hals

Limfjord

Thyborøn 285

3a

Anholt

Torekov

Grenå •

Helsingør • Helsingborg

VHF 25

6d

Øresund

DENMARK
Jutland (Jylland)

Århus •

56°

Samsø

VHF 21

6b

København •

Malmö • Simrishamn

Sjælland

Ystad

North

Sea

6a

Esbjerg •

Kolding

Fyn

Svendborg

Korsør • Rødvig

Store Bælt

6c

Falsterbo

Sandhammeren

Bornholm (Denmark)

Rønne

3

55°

Lille Bælt

Als

Møn

Baltic

VHF 04, 07

*Nordfriesland VHF 26

*Flensburg VHF 27

Helgoland 280

Wangerooge 279

Spiekeroog 278

Langeoog 278

Norderney 278

Flensburg

Schleswig

North Frisian Islands

Tonning

R Eider

Rends-burg

Holtenau

Nord-Ostsee Kanal

2a

2b

Bagenkop

7

Fehmarn

Lolland Falster

Gedser

Sea

Arkona VHF 66

Rügen

Kiel VHF 23

Heiligenhafen

Warnemünde

Stralsund

Lübeck VHF 24

*Rostock VHF 60

Swinoujscie

54°
N

Cuxhaven •

Brunsbüttel

*Elbe-Weser VHF 24

Elbe

East Frisian Is

1 →

Borkum 278

*Borkum VHF 61

Wilhems-haven •

*Bremen VHF 25

Bremerhaven •

*Hamburg VHF 83

Note
* These are a members only service
DP07, but everyone listens in

Szczecin VHF 12, 16

Emden

R Ems

R Jade

R Weser

HOLLAND

Delfzijl

GERMANY

POLAND

6° 7° 8° 9° 10° 11° 12°E 13° 14°

Page references are shown after some locations, for example:
Ålborg 285. Bold type indicates that it is accompanied by a plan.
Italics are used for rivers, lochs, bays, seas etc.

Approaches to the Baltic

Introduction

The sea area known in English as the Baltic comprises the Skagerrak, the Kattegat, the Sound, the Belts, the Baltic proper (the East Sea in the languages of the littoral states), the Gulf of Bothnia, the Gulf of Finland and the waters of the Baltic States. This is a popular cruising ground with negligible tides and usually warmer summers than in the North Sea. Facilities are good but harbours tend to be crowded in July and August. This section provides suggestions for routes to the Baltic. It does not pretend to be comprehensive – some of the routes described are cruising grounds in their own right. Crews wishing to explore further will want more detailed literature. There is a wide selection of boatyards in the Baltic, and many British boats winter here. The Cruising Association has a very active Baltic Section, and members will find much useful and updated information in the Baltic section pages at www.cruising.org.uk.

Approaching the Baltic from the N Sea there are two main routes: through the German Bight and the Nord-Ostsee Kanal or through the Skagerrak passing to the N of Jylland (Jutland). There is a variation of the Nord-Ostsee-Kanal route which uses the river Eider for part of the passage or one may pass through the scenic Limfjord in N Jylland. For a crossing of S part of the N Sea and the mast-up inland route through the Dutch canals see previous section.

1. S approach: through the German Bight

a) Along the E Frisian Islands

The Nord-Ostsee-Kanal route will be the route usually preferred by yachtsmen from the UK S and E coast. Following this route it is feasible to reach the Baltic by day sailing from the English Channel. The Dutch, German and Danish coasts of the N Sea however have few hbrs of refuge and there are extensive offlying shoals and a formidable lee shore to be avoided in strong winds from the W through to the N. The rivers Ems, Jade, Weser and particularly the Elbe have strong tidal streams and detailed passage planning is necessary. The waters are busy with large ships and are closely monitored by authorities. Shallow draft vessels may do part of the passage inshore, passing S of the East Frisian Islands between rivers Ems and Jade. It is worth noting during planning that the prevailing winds being from the W, the return journey may be longer and wetter than the outward trip. Nowhere is this more true than in the Elbe, which becomes so rough in fresh W winds that passage to seaward is not possible.

b) Direct crossing

Yachts from UK E coast may consider a direct passage to Elbe approaches, passing N of the German Bight Western Approach TSS. Crossing the TSS should only be considered after consultation with German Bight VTS (VHF 79/80). Helgoland is an all-weather all-tide hbr and ideally located for final approach up the Elbe. From Grimsby to Helgoland is 285M, from Whitby 300M. Updated charts should be consulted for position of oilrigs and wind farms under construction. Oil rigs enforce a 500m safety zone. Listen VHF 16 for information from guard vessels. A point-down cone must be shown when motor-sailing in German waters.

2. N approach: through the Skagerrak

This approach avoids the TSS and large tides of the German Bight, but you will need to spend at least one night at sea. The passage from Peterhead to Egersund is 255M, to Mandal 310M. From Lerwick to Tananger is 220M, from Lerwick to Marstein LtHo in the approaches to Bergen 185M. On the crossing a keen lookout is required for fishing boats, whose often changing courses may be confusing especially in the dark. Not all have AIS transmitters. Updated charts should be consulted for position of oil rigs. With the exception of Danish W coast there are small tides. The Norwegian coast with its many offlying islands has many harbours that can be approached in all weathers. Where the Skagerrak enters the Kattegat lies Skagen hbr which can be entered in all weather conditions. When planning a passage across the North Sea note that web sites such as www.yr.no provide detailed 48hr forecasts for many of the oil installations.

Tides

Tides in the approaches to the Baltic vary from more than 3m in the German Bight to less than 1m in the Skagerrak. Surges caused by persistent strong winds and changes in barometric pressure lead to marked changes in tidal heights. In the German Bight E'ly winds will generally give less water than indicated in tide tables. See Route 1 for sources of detailed tidal predictions. The Baltic Sea is almost landlocked. Its salinity is variable but is about half that of the ocean. Because it is fed by many rivers there is a tendency for a N-flowing current between the Danish islands and this is accentuated by a tendency for the warmer, lighter Baltic water to run N and for deeper, colder and denser water to run back into the Baltic. There are few true tides in the Baltic but like in the North Sea massive movements of water may take place as the result of changes in barometric pressure and wind. In the W Baltic strong W'lies will cause lower water levels than indicated in tide tables. Danish Met Office web site www.dmi.dk has a useful graphic display of predicted currents next 48hrs: [sitemap] [farvandsutsikter] choose area then [strøm].

Immigration

For list of documents that should be carried aboard see Chapter 1 (General Information). All countries in this section are members of the Schengen scheme. Holders of non-EU/EEA passports should establish beforehand whether there are any visa requirements. UK is not a signatory to the Schengen agreement, hence a yacht on passage from the UK directly to a country in this section will be crossing a Schengen outer border. Formalities vary between countries. In *Germany* Hamburg Bundespolizei will advise on ☎ (+49) 4066995050. In *Denmark* notify the HM upon arrival. Formally a crew list should be supplied. Landfall in Norway after a North Sea crossing from UK should be made at an authorized Port of Entry. Apart from Skudeneshavn all Norwegian hbrs described in the *Almanac* are authorised Ports of Entry. Enquire with local police on arrival ☎ (+47 02800). Formal legislation suggests Norwegian authorities be notified 24hrs before landfall, this appears largely ignored. If you plan to spend more than 90 days in any of the countries covered enquire about application/registration formalities. For entry procedures on return passage to the UK, see Chapter 1 General Information.

APPROACHES TO THE BALTIC

North Sea, southeast part distances (miles)

	Borkum	Norderney	Helgoland	Cuxhaven	Brunsbüttel	Esbjerg	Thyborøn
Borkum	0						
Norderney	34	0					
Helgoland	75	45	0				
Cuxhaven	94	64	35	0			
Brunsbüttel	109	79	52	17	0		
Esbjerg	137	121	85	109	124	0	
Thyborøn	204	188	162	182	203	96	0

(Distance Borkum to Helgoland passing W of the Riffgat RW buoy.
Distances from Borkum and Norderney to Helgoland are measured passing E of buoy TG19.)

North Sea, north and Skagerrak distances (miles)

	Bergen	Tananger	Egersund	Mandal	Arendal	Thyborøn	Skagen
Bergen	0						
Tananger	101	0					
Egersund	136	40	0				
Mandal	175	96	60	0			
Arendal	231	151	119	58	0		
Thyborøn	262	166	128	85	109	0	
Skagen	303	206	170	118	80	122	0

Skagerrak, Kattegat distances (miles)

	Skagen	Göteborg	Hals	Grenå	Helsingør	Korsør	Kolding
Skagen	0						
Göteborg	44	0					
Hals	51	72	0				
Grenå	88	87	43	0			
Helsingør	124	107	97	62	0		
Korsør	158	158	112	70	101	0	
Kolding	169	172	126	91	116	66	0

(Distance Göteborg measured to/from Långedrag)

DENMARK AND SWEDEN

TSS
Traffic Separation Scheme
DWR
Deep Water Route
[ ] Offshore Wind Farm
Denmark
All call sign *Lyngby Radio*
Sweden
All call sign *Stockholm Radio*

Customs

Germany, Denmark and Sweden are members of the EU. Norway is not a member of the EU but is in the EEA. Helgoland is duty free but in the EU. The import of alcohol and tobacco into the EU countries in this section is restricted to reasonable quantities for personal consumption. The amount of alcohol allowed into Norway is limited to one litre of strong liquor or three litres of wine per crew member. Leaving a boat behind in Norway for more than six weeks should only be done after arrangement with Customs about VAT exemption; application form can be downloaded from www.toll.no [skjema] [RD 0027].

Health

For First Aid see General Information. Ticks carrying borrelia (Lyme disease) may be found throughout the Baltic and approaches. Tick born encephalitis (TBE) has been reported in all countries in this region but is uncommon. Vaccination against TBE is available. General advice is to wear long sleeved shirts and long trousers tucked into socks when walking in infested areas. Ticks should be removed intact; special tweezers are available from local pharmacies. Should a red ring develop around a tick bite or any other unexplainable symptom appear, seek medical attention. The common adder (Vipera Berus) is found in the Baltic as far north as the Arctic Circle. If bitten keep afflicted body part at rest and seek medical advice. ☎ 112 for emergency services in all countries

COAST RADIO STATIONS

Working channels supplied in plan are to relay stations, from where calls are passed on to a central unit.

Denmark: Call sign for all working channels *Lyngby Radio* (MMSI 002191000)

Germany: Search and Rescue VHF16 and 70 (DSC) call sign *Bremen Rescue* (MMSI 002111240). Working channels supplied in plan serviced by DP07 Seefunk, a 'members only' service funded by membership fees (www.dp07.com)

SW Norway: Call sign all working channels *Rogaland Radio* (MMSI 002570300)

SE Norway: Call sign all working channels *Tjøme Radio* (MMSI 002570100)

Sweden: Call sign all working channels *Stockholm Radio* (MMSI 002652000).

For latest information on VHF working channels see www.stockholmradio.se [För abonnenter][Kartor och kanalplan - VHF] then choose relevant region. For contact information Rescue Coordination Centers see Chapter 1 General Information.

WEATHER FORECASTS

1. **VHF** (working channels) DP07 Seefunk weather forecast in German at 0745, 0945, 1245, 1645 and 1945 (LT).

Stockholm Radio inshore weather forecast in Swedish: S coast 0915, 1715 and 2215. W coast 15 minutes later (May–October, local time)

Stockhom radio shipping forecast in English 0600 and 1800 (UTC).

Rogaland and Tjøme radio weather forecast in Norwegian at 0900, 1200, 1500, 1800 and 2100 (local time).

2. **Public radio** (local language, local time)

Denmark: Danmarks radio (P4, Kalundborg) 243 kHz 0545, 0845, 1145, 1745, 2245

Germany: Deutschlandfunk FM, 1269 and 6190 kHz: 0105, 0640, 1105, (2105 summer only) Deutschlandradio kultur FM, 177 kHz Same times as for Deutschlandfunk

Norddeutscher Rundfunk FM, 702 and 972 kHz 0005, 0830, 2205

Norway: Norsk Rikskringkasting (P1) FM 0545, 1330 (1726 Sunday), 2030

Sweden: Sveriges radio (P1) FM 0555, 0755, 1250, 1555, 2150

3. **HF radio**
Deutsche Wetter Dienst (DWD) publish 1-, 3- and 5-day forecasts for those with dedicated receiver or SSB and computer.

4. **Navtex**
Pinneberg (S), Rogaland (L), Jeløy (M), Stockholm (Grimeton, I) and Stockholm (Gislövshammer, J) transmit in English on 518kHz. Pinneberg (L) transmit in German on 490kHz.

5. **Internet**
Although many of the national weather websites do some information in English, the local language links will be more comprehensive.

Denmark: www.dmi.dk. Follow link to Sitemap – Farvandsutsikter then choose from menu and chart

Germany: www.dwd.de. Follow links in German: Wetter + Warnungen; Seewetter; seewetter aktuell; then choose from options list.

Norway: www.yr.no. Follow links Sea and Coast then choose relevant area.

Sweden: www.smhi.se follow link to översikt Sverige then kustväder. The Swedish publication *Väderkortet* is a useful resource for weather forecasts in the Nordic countries. Available from marinas and chandlers, less reliably at www.transportstyrelsen.se (*vaderkortet* in search box).

Mobile devices: Apps are available for Scandinavian met offices indicated above, but accessing the full site will always give more information. Among popular weather-apps are weatherpro, windguru, windfinder, klart.se and kustväder.

For further information on acquiring weather forecasts in the Baltic see Brian Gay's summary of English language forecasts on www.cruising.org.uk (Baltic section, members only), Frank Singleton's website at www.weather.mailasail.com/Franks-Weather

covered, in Norway ☎ 113 for emergency medical services. All crew should carry a valid European Health Insurance Card (www.ehic.org.uk).

Rescue services

In Denmark rescue services are offered by Søværnets Operative Kommando (a public service) and the voluntary Dansk Søredningsselskab (www.dsrs.net). Sea rescue operations in Germany are offered by Deutsche Gesellschaft zur Rettung Schiffbrüchiger (DGzRS). This is a voluntary organization, dependent on memberships and private contributions. Further information at www.dgzrs.de. In Norway Redningsselskapet (www.redningsselskapet.no) is run on similar lines, in Sweden the service is supplied by Sjöräddningsselskapet (www.ssrs.se). These latter two offer a membership service, giving a member in one organisation equal benefits in the sister organisation.

Authorities monitor VHF 16 and 70 (DSC), see Chapter 1 (General Information). ☎ 112 is the emergency tel no in the countries covered.

Offshore wind farms

Offshore wind farms are operating, being constructed or projected throughout all the waters of the approaches to the Baltic. For example, such farms exist (or are planned) for the Dogger Bank, the German North Sea coast, west of Jutland, The Sound, east of Fehmarn, the Mecklenburger Bucht, north and east of Rügen and southwest of Gedser. They represent a significant hazard to navigation and mariners should proceed with caution using fully corrected charts.

Charts

Chart information throughout this chapter refers to the officially approved printed charts from the Danish (Dk), German (G), Norwegian (N) and Swedish (S) Hydrographic offices. British Admiralty (BA) or Imray charts are referred to where relevant. For much of the area covered there are cost-efficient small craft portfolios available which will be preferred by most yachtsmen. There is also a wide coverage of electronic charts for navigators with suitable plotters or portable device. Charts for much of the area can – with patience – be viewed online at www.nv-pedia.de, http://kartor.eniro.se and www.statkart.no [Norgeskart] [Sjøkart] [Hovedkartserien].

It is usually not possible to obtain foreign charts ex-stock from chart agents in Britain. Requirements should be discussed with Imray, Kelvin Hughes or other suppliers well in advance of departure. The small craft portfolios are widely available at dealers throughout the region.

For index of officially approved printed charts see website of national Hydrograph offices:

Denmark: www.gst.dk [søkart og navigation] [papirsøkort] [indeks over Danske søkort]
Germany: www.bsh.de [produkte] [karten] [seekarten] then select region
Norway: www.sjokart.no [sjøkart på papir] [produkt katalog]
Sweden: www.sjofartsverket.se [maritime sector] [recreational boating] [charts & nautical publications]

Pilots and Harbour Guides in English

The British Admiralty publishes pilots, sailing directions, list of radio signals and maritime communications relevant for the region, for details see www.ukho.gov.uk. Other useful literature published in English:

Cruising Guide to Germany and Denmark Brian Navin (Imray)
The Baltic Sea RCC Pilotage Foundation (Imray)
Norway RCC Pilotage Foundation/Judy Lomax (Imray)
The Norwegian Cruising Guide Phyllis Nickel and John Harries (also available as e-book from www.norwegiancruisingguide.com)
Havneguiden vol 10 Scandinavia Hanne and Jørn Engvik
Cruising Guide Booklets from the Cruising Association include publications covering all countries in this section. Some are for sale to non-members from CA house, all are available for members as free downloads from www.cruising.org.uk, together with a number of other useful documents such as *Leaving Your Home*, *Routes to the Baltic*, *Formalities* and *Baltic Lay-up Directory*. Much of this can also be accessed from your portable device using the Captain's Mate app from the CA.

Pilots and Harbour Guides in local languages

National Hydrographic offices publish pilots mostly targeting commercial shipping. Some yachtsmen find these useful, for titles see websites given for charts. There is a wide range of harbour guides published locally. Many of these are richly illustrated and may be useful even with no knowledge of German or a Scandinavian language. These will be available at local dealers or from websites such as www.weilbach.dk, www.naudi.de, www.nautiskfritid.no and www.nautiska.se. These will also supply the full range of national charts. Harbours in the Havneguiden series can be downloaded as single harbours, saving you buying a whole book (www.havneguiden.no, app available). Free printed harbour guides such as *Sejlerens* (www.sejlerens.no), *Gästhamnsguiden* (www.gasthamnsguiden.se) and *Baltic Sailing* (www.balticsailing.com) are distributed through marinas as well as being available online. Baltic sailing also has text in English.

APPROACHES TO THE BALTIC

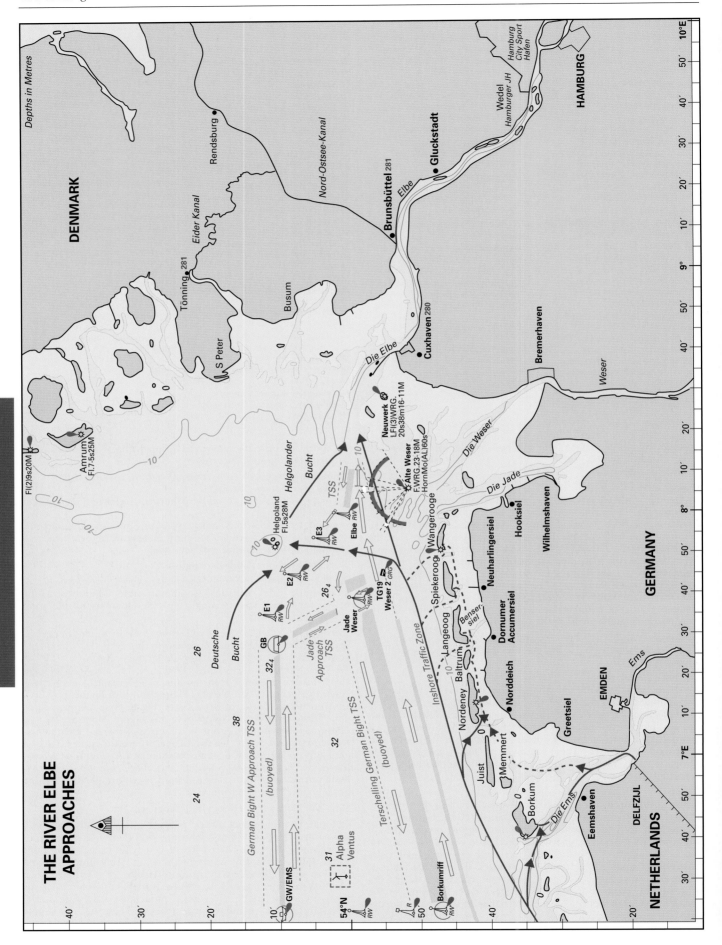

THE RIVER ELBE
APPROACHES

Depths in Metres

DENMARK

GERMANY

NETHERLANDS

HAMBURG

Hamburg
City Sport
Hafen

Hamburger JH

Wedel

Gluckstadt

Brunsbüttel 281

Elbe

Nord-Ostsee-Kanal

Eider Kanal

Rendsburg

Tönning 281

S Peter

Busum

Die Elbe

Cuxhaven 280

Bremerhaven

Weser

Die Weser

Die Jade

Neuwerk
LFl(3)WRG.
20s38m16-11M

Alte Weser
F.WRG.23-18M
HornMo(AL)60s

Wangerooge

Spiekeroog

Wilhelmshaven

Hooksiel

Neuharlingersiel

Dornumer
Accumersiel

Benser-
siel

Langeoog

Baltrum

Nordeney

Norddeich

Greetsiel

EMDEN

Ems

Juist

Memmert

Borkum

Die Ems

Eemshaven

DELFZIJL

Amrum
Fl.7.5s25M

Fl(2)9s20M

Helgolander
Bucht

Helgoland
Fl.5s28M

TSS

E3
RW

Elbe RW

E2
RW

E1
RW

GB

32₄

GW/EMS

German Bight W Approach TSS
(buoyed)

Jade
Approach
TSS

TG19
Weser 2 GRG
RW

Jade
Weser

Inshore Traffic Zone

Terschelling German Bight TSS
(buoyed)

Borkumriff
RW

R

54°N
RW

Alpha
Ventus

26₄

Deutsche
Bucht

24

26

38

26

32

31

10

10

10

10

10

Other useful online resources, local language:
www.wattsegler.de
www.wattenschipper.de
www.dendanskehavnelods.dk
www.portpilot.de
www.yourportpilot.com
www.velihavn.no
www.gjestehavner.no
www.havna.com

Accessing internet
Wi-Fi will be found in many marinas, cafés, public libraries and tourist information facilities. GSM and 3G services are widely available in the region, increasingly also 4G. In Scandinavia data traffic is also available through the NSM 450 system (www.ice.no). To minimise charges ensure your subscription is appropriate for the planned cruise, and enable 'data roaming' on your device only when needed. If spending a long time in an area enquire about local sim card/pre-paid dongle. Many network providers only offer their services to residents with national ID number. Bring your passport to supplier and make certain your device is up and running before leaving shop.

Spelling
There are minor (occasionally major) differences in the spelling of geographical names in the different languages. For example, The Sound is Øresund in Danish and Öresund in Swedish (sometimes Sundet in both languages) and the capital of Denmark could be called København, Köpenhamn, Kopenhagen or Copenhagen. As far as possible the spelling in the local language has been used throughout the text with the English equivalent occasionally given.

Note that there are three additional letters in the Scandinavian languages (Norwegian and Danish: æ, ø, å; Swedish: å, ä, ö). In telephone directories, gazetteers etc these letters appear alphabetically after z. In Danish the letter å is often written aa.

Marina telephone numbers and VHF channels
Information in text is liable to change. Marinas are usually staffed once or twice daily for a few hours. Few marinas in this area listen to VHF and most do not accept berth reservations by telephone. For information about hbrs offering pre-booking of berths and booking online see www.dockspot.com.

Fuel
Diesel is widely available throughout this region. Not road-taxed (dyed) diesel is not available to yachts in mainland EU. Yachts entering Germany with tanks containing dyed fuel should retain receipts. Diesel sold from marinas in the EU will contain biodiesel (FAME). Boat owners should consider using appropriate additive, especially if planning winter lay up in the Baltic. Non road-taxed diesel dyed green is, at time of writing, available to yachts in Norway. This is reportedly free of biodiesel.

Gas
All the Baltic countries use propane gas routinely but some butane (Camping Gaz) is found in Germany, Denmark and S Sweden. Calor butane and propane gas are not available and spare bottles should be taken. It may be possible to have propane cylinders refilled at outlets of LPG Norge and Primagaz Sverige, see www.lpgnorge.no and www.primagaz.se for retailers. An adaptor fitting your cylinder should be carried. Calor discourages refilling of their cylinders outside of the UK. For a longer stay in the Baltic a change to local cylinder may be necessary. For 5kg composite propane cylinders there is an exchange agreement between AGA and Kosan dealers in the Nordic countries, adaptor required. For further information see Baltic General Cruising Information on Cruising Association web page (www.cruising.org.uk, members only).

Holding tanks
Many countries in the Baltic have restrictions on discharging black water directly overboard. In Germany, Denmark and Sweden discharging black water to sea may only be done when more than 12M from shore. There are exemptions for older yachts and foreign flagged yachts, but at time of writing regulations are not clear. In Norway holding tanks may be emptied 300m from shore in non-congested waters. Crews should use shore-based toilet facilities when available. Popular anchorages in Norway and Sweden often have basic (composting) toilets ashore.

Berthing
In German and Danish hbrs in the Baltic a 'box' mooring is common, bows to pontoon or quay with long warps to piles from the stern. Boats with wide beam may have difficulty fitting between piles, fenders best removed. It is worth preparing two long lines

with large bowlines before entering hbr. Locals often cross stern lines to minimise sideways movement: line from stb cleat to port pile. In other areas pontoons with outriggers are the norm. Some hbrs supply lazy lines or mooring buoys for stern lines, few hbrs now require use of stern anchor. Vacant berths are usually indicated by green tag. Some marinas charge more for collecting mooring fees at the boat, so it is worth while visiting the HM or pay at the ticket machine where available. A sticker is sometimes given as receipt to be displayed on the pulpit. Some hbrs have berths that can be pre-booked (www.dockspot.com).

Anchorages, moorings
Mooring buoys outside settlements are available in the Scandinavian countries courtesy of local clubs, notably Svenska Kryssarklubben (SXK – Sweden), Kongelig Norsk Båtforbund and Oslo Friluftsråd (Norway) and Dansk Sejlunion (Denmark). This is generally a service to members only. The Cruising Association is affiliated with SXK and members can apply for one of the seasonal stickers. There are many anchorages along Norwegian and Swedish coasts of Skagerrak and Kattegat. These get crowded in season and yachts usually anchor from stern and take lines ashore from bow.

ROUTES

ROUTE 1 GERMAN FRISIAN ISLANDS – RIVER ELBE
Charts BA 1633, 1635, 1423, 2182A;
Imray C70, C26

Offshore
Borkum can be reached through the Westerems at all states of the tide, but in strong onshore winds approach should be made on the flood. Norderney can most seasons be reached at all states of the tide, but the two approach channels are shallow, they frequently change course and entry is not advisable in onshore winds above Force 4. Helgoland can be entered in all weather conditions. The *Seegats* to Langeoog, Spiekeroog and Wangerooge have shallow bars and should only be attempted in calm weather on last 2hrs of rising tide. The Elbe, with its strong tidal streams, is usually approached from Norderney or Helgoland. Yachts should keep well clear of TSSs in the German Bight. The waters are closely monitored by authorities and on-the-spot fines are issued for infringement of regulations. On passage N of the Frisian Islands yachts should stay in the Inshore Traffic Zone and keep at least 1M S of the TSS. Contact German Bight Traffic VHF 79 (W) or 80 (E) if you need to pass closer than this or want to cross the TSS. On passage from E Frisian Islands to Helgoland passing E of buoy TG 19 will keep you clear of TSS. When motor-sailing point-down cone must be shown.

Inshore
The Wattensee S of the E Frisian Islands is well known to yachtsmen as the scene of Erskine Childers' *Riddle of the Sands* and Sam Llewellyn's follow-up *The Shadow in the Sands*. The channels behind the islands offer an interesting passage for yachts with limited draft. Much of the Wattensee is a Nature Reserve. Passage is generally allowed HW ±3hrs (Zone 1), but there are conservation areas for birds and seals where entry is not permitted in summer months. There is a distinct pattern to the channels, with a watershed towards the E end of each island with a drying height of approx 1m. The channels are marked by buoys except for drying areas which are marked by withies. Boats with draft 1·5m can usually pass S of the islands Langeoog, Spiekeroog and Wangerooge at *mittleren Tide- Hochwasser* (MHW), while even deeper draft boats pass S of the islands between river Ems and Norderney. The passage S of Baltrum, between Norderney and Langeooge, has less water and boats with draft >1.3m will struggle. It is usually not possible to pass more than one watershed on each tide. The channels are constantly changing and charts may be unreliable. Local information should be sought before attempting these passages. There is a canal system connecting the rivers Weser and Elbe but with limited depths and height restriction of approx 2·7m.

River Elbe
The Elbe is bounded by shoals and sandbanks that run far out to sea. Very severe seas occur in wind over tide conditions and with W or NW winds the river should not be entered until the flood has begun. Until then keep W of the Elbe RW Lt buoy. A vessel passing the Elbe RW buoy at Helgoland HW -0500 will normally carry the flood up the 25M to Cuxhaven for 7hrs or the 40M to Brunsbüttel for 8hrs. Stay well clear of the Elbe Approach TSS. The channel E of the TSS is well buoyed but traffic is heavy. Keep right over to stb side of channel outside but close to the buoys and if necessary

cross the shipping lanes at right angles. Monitor VHF 80 (German Bight Traffic) in approaches, as you pass up the river VHF 71 (Cuxhaven Elbe Traffic) then VHF 68 (Brunsbüttel Elbe Traffic).

Current water depths and tidal predictions

Depths at Seegats at MLW and the watersheds in the Watts at MHW are regularly monitored by surveying vessel *Lütjeoog*. The information is posted at hbr offices in the islands and usually published on local websites such as www.wattsegler.de and www.wattenschipper.de. Information may also be had from HM at Norderney. For a passage S of the islands information of current tidal heights and 24h predictions essential and usually posted at hbr offices. Also available from www.bsh.de [Meeresdaten] [Vorhersagen] [Wasserstand], or as link from local websites. Tidal information weather transmitted in German on VHF from DP07 Seefunk after weather forecast on working channels as listed in plan, from Jade Traffic VHF 20 (H+10) and EMS Traffic VHF 18/20 (H+50) (limited range). Generally expect less water in winds from E, more in winds from W/NW.

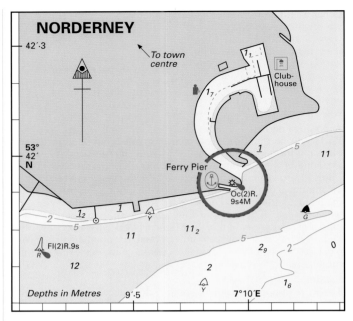

NORDERNEY

Depths in Metres

BORKUM

Charts BA 3631; G 90; G 3015 (portfolio)

HW Helgoland -0050

MHWS	MHWN	MLWN	MLWS
2·7m	2·4m	0·4m	0·0m

DS (offshore) Helgoland +0000ENE +0600ESE

Borkum Island has two areas of high dunes and the W end of the island is distinguished by the Großer Borkum Lt Ho 63m, located in Borkum town.

Approach This hbr can be approached from the W by the buoyed Westerems fairway in onshore gales. Wind over tide conditions should be avoided if possible. From the Fischerbalje Bn Oc(2)16s, a narrow buoyed channel leads along S side of training wall, covered at HW.

Berthing There are two hbrs with three berthing options:

• Sporthafen Bahlman 'Port Henry' first hbr to port. Yachts with draft <1·4m can usually enter at all states of tide, but may have to wait inside moles before able to come alongside pontoon. Deeper draft yachts should enter and leave at HW ±0200. Many berths dry to soft mud: yachts sink in and stay upright. Scenic surroundings, some noise from windmills.

• Burkana Hafen second hbr to port. Old navy hbr with large pontoons N in hbr. Deep with room for large yachts. Uncomfortable in S'lies. Industrial surroundings. Smaller boats will be more comfortable at club pontoons W in hbr, report to Burkana Hafen Café.

Passage lights	BA No
Borkum (Grosser Lt)	0970
Fl(2)12s63m24M+F.WRG	
Norderney	1054
Fl(3)12s59m23M	
Wangerooge	1112
Fl.R.5s60m23M+F.WR+ Dir.WRG	
GB (German Bight) LtF	1052
Iso.8s12m17M	
Horn 30s (R) (·‒·)	
Helgoland	1312
Fl.5s82m28M	
Elbe RW Lt buoy	
Iso.10s Racon (T) (‒)	

Facilities Diesel in Burkana Hafen by can. Restaurants and bars. Bicycle rental. Resort town 7km with shops and restaurants, buses from hbr and train from ferry terminal.

☏ YC +49 (0) 15154274088 www.borkum-hafen.de

NORDERNEY

Charts G 89; G 3015 (portfolio) Imray C26

HW Helgoland –0026

MHWS	MHWN	MLWN	MLWS
2·8m	2·4m	0·4m	0·0m

DS (offshore) Helgoland –0400E +0200W

Town at W end of island has conspic skyline. The Lt Ho is a R octagonal tr 59m middle of island.

Approach From the N through the buoyed Schluchter and Dovetief channels. Depths vary and can be <2m. In 2013 least depths at *Mittleres Niedrigwasser* (MLW) in

Schluchter 2·60m between buoys S4 and D5/S8 when keeping near R buoys, Dovetief 3·10m between buoys D2 and D10 when keeping near red buoys. Neither approach should be attempted in onshore winds >Force 4. On passage from Delfzijl yachts with limited draft may consider the inshore passage through the Dukegat/Osterems and Memmeret Wattfahrwasser. Local advice should be sought for this passage. For information on current tidal predictions see Route 1 above.

Berthing Hbr is on SW corner of island, a 90° turn to port after ferry terminal. Hbr is secure. Moor at vacant finger berth (green tag) or along quay as available. Like in the other E Frisian islands a tourist tax (kur taxe) is charged per crew member, in addition to the regular hbr fee.

Facilities Wi-Fi. Restaurant in YC building. Diesel on N quay. Supermarket by ferry terminal. Bicycle rental. Town 1M worth visiting as imperial spa. Many shops, mostly clothing and accessories.

☏ HM +49 (0) 493 28 35 45 www.norderney-hafen.de

LANGEOOG

Charts G 89; G 3015 (portfolio)

HW Helgoland +0001

MHWS	MHWN	MLWN	MLWS
3·1m	2·6m	0·4m	0·0m

DS (offshore) Helgoland –0400E +0100W

From offshore Langeoog water tower is conspicuous.

Approach From the Accumer Ee RW Iso.8s Lt buoy enter the buoyed channel with depths less than 2m. Enter on last two hours of the flood. Entry not advised in strong onshore winds. On the last half of the

ebb there are breakers over the bar even in settled weather. Position of buoys changes regularly. Once over the bar enter the deep channel passing around SW end of island.

Berthing A well sheltered hbr at the SW corner of the island has a small marina. Enter between pierheads, final part of approach marked with withies (twigs fanning downwards = stb/green, fanning upwards = port/red). Fairway to marina dredged to 1·5m, but many berths dry to soft mud at LW – yachts sink in and stay upright. Visitors' berths at E fingerberth pontoons or enquire about vacant berths elsewhere.

Facilities Two restaurants in hbr. Wi-Fi. Shops and restaurants in town 2kms from hbr, train, horse carriage, bicycle rental or ½hr walk. Langeooge has no cars, hence no fuel available. Peaceful resort island with lovely beaches.

☏ HM +49 (0) 173 8832 567 www.sv-langeoog.de

SPIEKEROOG

Charts G 89; G 3015 (portfolio); Imray C26

HW Helgoland +0002

Arguably said to be the most beautiful of the E Frisian islands. The town is small and located near the hbr, without the large tourist developments seen on many of the other islands.

Approach Apart from a windmill on E end, the low island is featureless from offshore. From the Ozumer Balje safewater mark Iso.4s follow the marked channel. The channel changes frequently and even the most recent charts may not be correct. There is a bar and the approach should only be made on last half of the

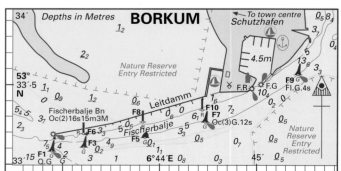

BORKUM

Depths in Metres

To town centre Schutzhafen

Nature Reserve Entry Restricted

Leitdamm

Fischerbalje

Fischerbalje Bn Oc(2)16s15m3M

Nature Reserve Entry Restricted

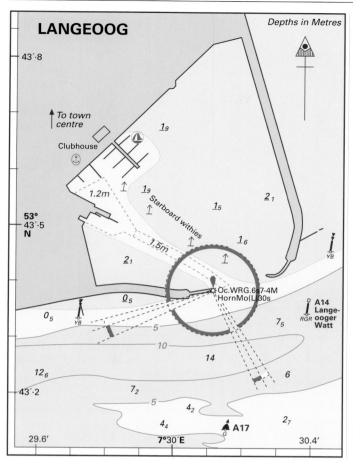

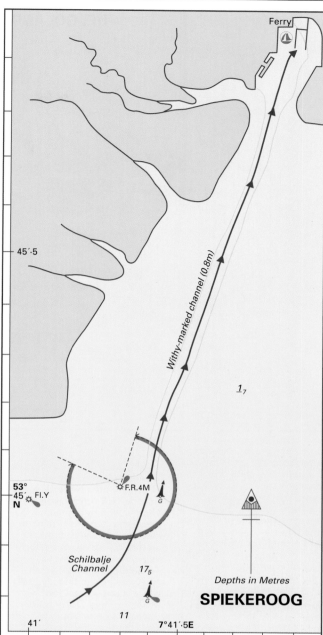

APPROACHES TO THE BALTIC

flood. Approach should not be attempted in strong onshore winds or in poor visibility. From SW end of island there is a long narrow approach channel to the hbr. Beginning of channel marked with G and R buoys, remainder with withies. Be aware ferry traffic.

Berthing At fingerberths without red tag, or alongside S side of N pontoon. Most berths dry to soft mud – yachts sink in but stay upright. Yachts >12m enquire about mooring at docks W of pontoon SW in hbr. Hbr uncomfortable at HW in strong winds from S.

Facilities Usual marina facilities. Short walk to pretty town with 17th-century church, many restaurants. Swimming pool. Limited supplies, provisioning best done elsewhere. No cars on island, hence no fuel available.

✆ HM +49 (0) 1788 7977 41
www.spiekerooger-segelclub.de

WANGEROOGE

Charts BA 1635, 1875, 3617; Imray C26; G 2; G 3015 (portfolio)

HW Wilhelmshaven –0100

MHWS	MHWN	MLWN	MLWS
3·3	2·8m	0·4m	0·0m

DS (5M N) Helgoland –0500ENE +0100WNW

Approach The tall Wangerooge LtHo and old tr (Westturm) are on W end of the island. From the offshore Harle Lt buoy enter buoyed Harle channel.

Position of buoys changes regularly. Enter on last two hours of the flood. Entry not advised in strong onshore winds. Mole ends marked with red and green bns, W 'mole' mostly rocks on a sandy spit. Moles cover at HW , only bns visible. Keep W in final part of approach, near the W2 red buoy and W mole. Final approach marked with port-hand withies.

Berthing Marina E of ferry terminal. Moor at vacant fingerberth (G tag) or alongside guest pontoon E in hbr. Large yachts moor alongside piles N in hbr or in main hbr N of ferries. Despite regular dredging depths at guest pontoon at times 1m and yachts touch bottom at LW. Hbr uncomfortable at HW in strong winds from SE through SW.

Facilities Bar at Wangerooge Yacht Club. Pleasant resort town at centre of island 5km from hbr. Infrequent trains corresponding with ferry arrival/departure at HW±0200. Bicycles for rent at Westturm Youth Hostel 1km from hbr. No cars on island. Basic shopping in village, several restaurants, no fuel.

✆ +49 (0) 4469 240,
+49 (0) 172 2622 705
www.wyc-wangerooge.de

HELGOLAND

Charts BA 1875; G88; G 3014, G 3015 (portfolio); Imray C26

HW Helgoland HW

MHWS	MHWN	MLWN	MLWS
2·7m	2·4m	0·4m	0·0m

DS (5M SE) Helgoland –0400ENE +0200W

A conspic red rock with a conspic tall radio mast. Although described as an all-weather hbr, there is an uncomfortable swell in E gales.

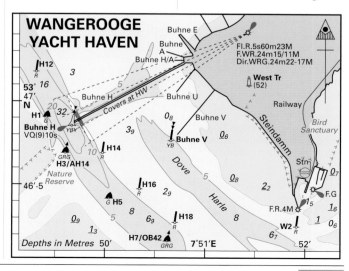

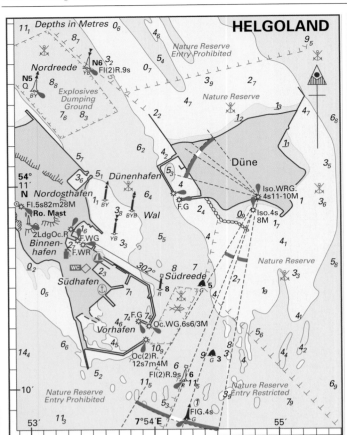

HELGOLAND

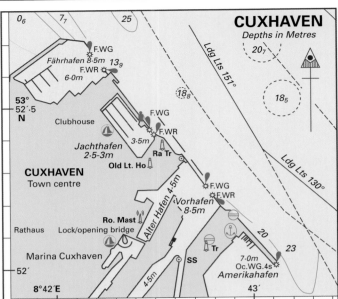

CUXHAVEN
Depths in Metres

Strong winds from S also makes hbr uncomfortable, especially during large raft-ups. One or other approach should be sufficiently sheltered and hence a useful port of refuge. Good place from where to begin passage up the Elbe or Eider or to the E Frisian islands. The island is duty free and popular with day trippers. Worthwhile walk on the cliffs giving close-up views of the bird colonies. No bicycles allowed.

Approach On passage from E Frisian islands passing E of buoy TG19 will keep you clear of TSS (but not of traffic!). Channels from NW and S are well buoyed. It is important to stay in the channels which are narrow, to avoid offlying hazards and the Nature Reserves. Enter Vorhafen between mole heads then turn stb for Südhafen. Be aware high speed vessel, mooring inside W mole in Südhafen.

Berthing Alongside pontoons in Südhafen. Buoys are to take pressure off during large raft-ups. Yachts <10m may find vacant berth in private YC to NE of projecting pier in Südhafen or enquire about vacant berth in Nordosthafen (Wassersportclub Helgoland). Binnenhafen usually for fuelling only. Hbr very crowded at weekends. Nordseewoche regatta takes place on Pentecostal weekend when hbr best avoided. If hbr full enquire with HM about anchoring in Vorhafen. Yachts are not allowed into the hbr at Düne

(shuttle boat to Düne for beaches and seal colony).

Facilities Service building with laundry. Coin-operated electricity outlets. Fresh water outside HM office, against charge. Fuel in Binnenhafen, deepest water along quay on S side – enquire with bunker station before moving your vessel from Südhafen to Binnenhafen. DWD weather forecasts posted outside HM office. Longer term forecast available from DWD office above HM office but against a fee. Charts and some chandlery at Jörn Rickmers in Hafenstrasse 1105. Goods available duty free, however basic supplies other than alcohol not cheap.

☎/VHF HM +49 (0) 815 93 583 Wassersportclub Helgoland +49 (0) 1604 2094 82, *Helgoland Port* VHF 67. www.wsc-helgoland.de

CUXHAVEN

Charts BA 3619; G 44; G 3014 (portfolio) Imray C26

HW Cuxhaven HW

MHWS	MHWN	MLWN	MLWS
3·3m	2·9m	0·4m	0·0m

DS Cuxhaven –0410 upstream +0130 downstream

This hbr has one of the largest of all the German N Sea yacht fleets.

Approach The channel is well buoyed from both directions, and the yacht hbr entrances lie close to the conspic radar tr in front of the 23m former LtHo. At night the conspic Ro-Ro

terminal is easier to see than the radar tr. Upriver traffic should have no problem, but travelling down from Brunsbüttel with the ebb, considerable anticipation and reliable engine power is needed to cut across the busy traffic lane.

Entrance Beware of the strong stream across the entrances which can reach 5kn. There is room inside to round up and lower sails.

Berthing Pontoon berths in the YC marina NW of the radar tr. For longer stay consider City

Marina Cuxhaven which is accessed through the Vorhafen and the Alter Hafen. There is a lock and opening br before the City Marina Cuxhaven.

Facilities All facilities of a major town including chandlery. Wi-Fi in YC. Diesel.

☎/VHF Cuxhaven YC HM +49 (0) 4721 34111; City Marina HM +49 (0) 175 902 0015; Bridge +49 (0)4721 500 120, VHF 69. www.svc-cux.de, www.marina-cux.de

ROUTE 2A RIVER EIDER – NORD-OSTSEE-KANAL

Charts BA 1423; G 104; Imray C26

The Eider connects with the Nord-Ostsee-Kanal through a number of locks. This is slower, longer and more picturesque than using the Nord-Ostsee-Kanal for the entire passage. It adds 30M to the distance. Above the Eidersperrwerk dam the locks and bridges are operated only for limited hours on Sundays and public holidays. For details enquire from HM Tönning or visit www.wsa-toenning.wsv.de (links to Schiffart – Schleusen – Eider). From Nordfeld lock to the Gieslau lock on the Nord-Ostsee-Kanal, the canalized river is peaceful with numerous mooring opportunities.

TÖNNING

Chart G104; G 3014 (portfolio)

HW Helgoland +0243

MHWS	MHWN	MLWN	MLWS
3·5m	3·0m	0·4m	0·0m

DS (R Eider approach) Helgoland –0430 S to E (Flood) +0125 NE to W (Ebb)

Approach This should only be attempted on a rising tide in calm weather. A course of 078° from Helgoland 23M brings a boat to Eider RW Iso.4s Lt buoy. The winding channel is then clearly buoyed and should be carefully followed. Buoys are moved regularly. Bend in channel N of Linnenplatte may have <1m at LW. The Eidersperrwerk Dam must be passed by a lock on the N side. The dam is for flood relief and is usually open. The river continues to be tidal for a

further 16M to the Nordfeld lock (beyond Tönning).

Entrance The Eidersperrwerk lock (VHF 14 or ☎ +49 (0) 4833 4535 – 0) operates 24 hrs. Tönning 5M above the lock has a depth of 3m at MHW. Silting takes place in approaches, usually from W mole so keep well to stb.

For a passage from Tönning to North Sea local advice is to depart Tönning HW–0100. This will leave you fighting the flood initially, but gives sufficient water in approaches to the lock, at the Linnenplatte and over the bar.

Berthing Visitor's berth to port as you enter the hbr, in front of the old storage house. Moor alongside. Hbr dries to soft mud – yachts sink in and stay upright. Smaller vessels may look for vacant outrigger berth

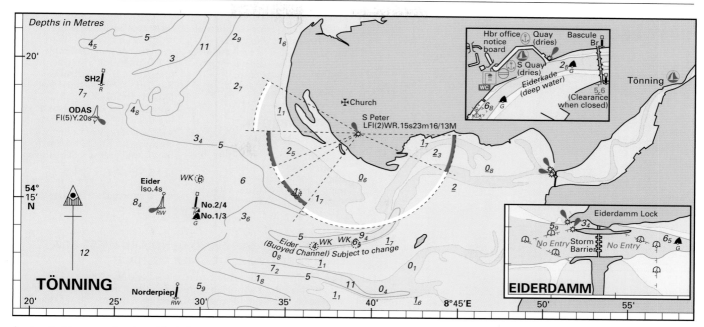

further in hbr, some berths with 1·5m at LW.

Facilities Several cafés, restaurants. Coin-operated internet stations at local game shop. Wattenmeer National Park visitors' centre (Multimar Wattforum).

ROUTE 2B RIVER ELBE – NORD-OSTSEE-KANAL

Charts BA 3625, 2469;
Imray C26; G 42

The river is under continuous radar surveillance and police launches enforce strict obedience to the regulations. *German Bight Traffic* transmits information on weather and ship movements on VHF 79 (W) and 80 (E) H+00, *Cuxhaven Elbe Traffic* on VHF 71 H+35 and *Brunsbüttel Elbe Traffic* on VHF 68 H+05. *Kiel kanal II* VHF 02 transmits information on ship movements H+15, H+45, *Kiel kanal III* VHF 03 H+20, H+50. The Nord-Ostsee- Kanal (Kiel Canal) extends for 54M to Kiel-Holtenau. The only locks are at Brunsbüttel and Holtenau. The canal is a busy commercial waterway. Yachts must have their engines running but may motor sail if the wind is free. A black cone, point down, must be displayed when motor sailing. Yachts may not navigate at night or in limited visibility, except when heading for the hbrs at Brunsbüttel and Holtenau or locking out into the Elbe or Kieler Förde (by arrangement with the lockmaster).

Berthing in the canal

Overnight mooring is permitted only at Brunsbüttel (inside the locks), Brunsbüttel inner hbr 2·7km, Dükerswish 20·5km, Gieslau lock entrance 40·5km, Rendsburg (Obereidersee) 66km, Borgstedter Enge 70km, Flemhudersee 85·5km, and Holtenau 99km. When visibility is unexpectedly reduced, yachts may moor behind the dolphins at the 'sidings' (passing places).

Lt signals at sidings

Q.R entrance prohibited, 3Oc.R(vert) exit prohibited, 2Iso(vert) exit prohibited for small vessels. A graphic display of this and other useful information from www.kiel-canal.org [pleasure craft].

VHF channels on the canal

Brunsbüttel locks	VHF 13 (call *Kiel canal I*)
Brunsbüttel-Breiholz	VHF 02 (call *Kiel canal II*)
Breiholz-Holtenau	VHF 03 (call *Kiel canal III*)
Holtenau locks	VHF 12 (call *Kiel canal IV*)

BRUNSBÜTTEL

Chart BA 2469 (plan);
Imray C26; G 42
HW Cuxhaven +0100

MHWS	MHWN	MLWN	MLWS
3·1m	2·7m	0·2m	0·0m

HM +49 (0) 4861 749, +49(0)16098476999
www.toenninger-yacht-club.de

Passage light	BA No
Tönning (St Peter)	1624
LFl(2)WR.15s23m15/12M	

commercial shipping. There is a waiting area in the Elbe E of the locks but it is unsheltered and the stream runs strongly. Bottom is reported to be foul. Yachts may enter the lock approaches when an Oc.W Lt is shown from mast on lock island, and enter the lock when Oc.W Lt is shown from mast on lock. The locks have narrow floating pontoons.

Berthing Just inside the locks to port is the small Binnenhafen with pontoons. Some noise from big ships passing through locks 24hrs. Mooring also possible N bank ½ M further E. Brunsbüttel Alter Hafen is approached from the Elbe W of the locks. Approach last half of flood. Guest pontoons N end of hbr, dries. Scenic and peaceful.

Facilities Supermarket 100m from Kanal Yachthafen. Diesel N of Kanal Yachthafen on W bank.

www.nok-wsa.de (general information).

RENDSBURG

Chart BA 2469 (plan);
G 42

This town is N of the canal at km66.

Approach The yacht hbr is in the dammed section of the Upper

Eider River and is approached by a buoyed channel from the canal at the E end of the town, passing shipyards.

Berthing The yacht hbr lies to port, 1½M along this channel and has bows-to moorings with piles. Some alongside berths for larger yachts, signposted.

Facilities Diesel fuel supply in marina. Diesel may also be obtained by pump from the commercial wharf on the main canal.

Beware a transporter br near this town, the main structure has a clearance of 40m but the conveyer itself passes only about 2m above water when lowered.

At km85·4 beyond some dolphins on the S side is the beautiful Flemhudersee where it is possible to anchor in 2–3m (5m at the N end) overnight.

HM +49 (0) 433 123 961
www.rvr1888.de

HOLTENAU

Charts BA 2469 (plan), 2113, 2341; G 30

This is the town at the junction of the canal and the Kieler Förde. Yachts usually pass through into the Baltic at one of the older pair of locks on the N side of the canal on an Oc.W

Approach From the Elbe yachts usually pass through the E locks (Alte Schleusen). Lock keeper monitors VHF 13, call sign *Kiel kanal I*. The lock approach is reserved for

DS Cuxhaven –0300 upstream +0220 downstream

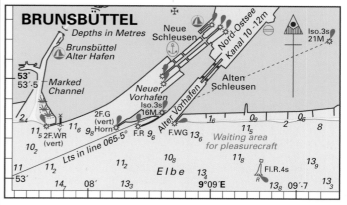

APPROACHES TO THE BALTIC

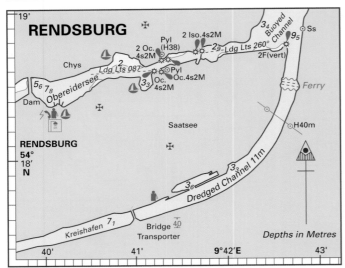

RENDSBURG

Depths in Metres

Lt being shown. Payment of canal dues for both E and W passage is made directly to the lockmaster at the old locks or at the kiosk on the new locks. The entrance to the canal from the sea is often crowded and it is wise to clear the area as soon as practical. Beware large ships manoeuvering.

Berthing There are some yacht pontoons at the N bank in Kieler Förde after the lock.

Facilities Supermarket. Charts may be obtained from Nautische Dienst (Kapitän Stegman) at Mäklerstrasse 8 (www.naudi.de). Shop is inside Holtenau lock security zone and passport needed. www.kiel-kanal.org (general information).

STICKENHÖRN

Charts BA 2113; G 34

The British Kiel Yacht Club is a military establishment to provide adventurous training for British Forces. Civilians are made very welcome. Charges are reasonable and security is excellent. It is situated at the

head of a deep bay just over 1M N of Holtenau. It is 4ca NW of the E card Stickenhörn buoy, passing W of the breakwater. Boats are moored to a T-shaped pontoon bow or stern to piles. The shore-end of the main pontoon is very shallow and some berths are reserved for club boats. Report to the duty watch. Laying up and other yard facilities may be available by negotiation but there is no diesel. (Floating fuel pump north of Schilksee at Strande, cash only). A regular bus runs into Kiel. Local shops and restaurants are half a mile away. A large German marina is on the E side of the breakwater.

☎ /VHF +49 (0) 431 398 833, *Sailtrain* VHF 06 www.bkyc.de

MÖLTENORT

Charts BA 2113; G 34

Möltenort is a fishing port and yacht hbr on the E coast of Kieler Forde opposite Stickenhörn. Yachts normally moor bow or stern-to piles in the S basin (least depth 2·8m) but larger vessels can moor on the

inner side of the mole of the N basin. Good facilities at hbr and in town centre (500m). Ferry service to Kiel. The Heikendorfer YC welcomes visitors at their club ship in the N basin.

☎ HM +49 (0) 431 243 560, www.hyc86.de

DÜSTERNBROOK

Chart BA 2344; G 34

Located near Kiel city centre, this is the former Olympic Marina from 1936. Largest marina in inner part of Kiel fjord. Home of Kieler YC. Vacant berths marked

with green tags. Northern basin for yachts >13m. Additional moorings for vessels up to 25m available at northern mole. HM at Düstenbrook also operates marinas at Blücherbrüke, Reventlou and Seeburg S of Düsternbrook. Kieler YC organise Kiel Woche usually the last full week of June. During this week hundreds of racing yachts converge on Kiel Fjord and room for visiting yachts will be limited.

☎ +49 (0) 431 2604 8426
Mobile +49 (0) 172 802 4354
www.sporthafen-kiel.de

ROUTE 3 GERMANY AND DENMARK WEST COAST

Charts BA 3767, 2182B, 1402, 1422, 1423, Dk 93

This route avoids the often crowded W Baltic. Hbrs are commercial and facilities for cruising sailors are limited. In strong W'lies this coast is a formidable lee shore. The only all-weather hbr is Esbjerg, and even this can be dangerous on the ebb in strong onshore winds. Cruisers considering this route should have time to wait for appropriate weather. The coast is tidal. Current gets weaker as you go north, and is greatly affected by wind, 48hr predictions at www.dmi.dk (sitemap – farvandsutsikter – choose area then choose graphic display for 'strøm'). *Blåvandshuk* shooting range N of Esbjerg extends 4·3M offshore, on occasion more. Passage though *Slugen and Nordmands Dyb* will normally keep you outside the 4·3M limit. For firing times and range enquire Lyngby radio VHF 23 or call *Oksbøl* camp at ☎ +45 7654 1213. Firing times and required security distance posted (in English) at http://forsvaret.dk/OKSBL [skydninger].

Passage lights	BA No
Blåvandshuk (Esbjerg) Fl(3)20s55m22M	1848
Thyborøn Fl(3)10s24m12M	1890
Hantsholm Fl(3)20s65m24M	2084
Hirtshals FFl.30s57m18/25M	2106
Skagen W Fl(3)WR.10s31m14/11M	0001
Skagen Fl.4s44m20M	0002

HÖRNUM

Charts G107; G 3013 (portfolio)
HW Helgoland +0220

MHWS	MHWN	MLWN	MLWS
0.5m	0.3m	0.2m	0.0m

Ferry hbr with friendly YC. All weather protection but there is a bar to cross. The long approach makes it a rather substantial detour on passage to or from the Danish hbrs.

Approach From S through the Vortrapptief seegat. From Vortrapptief deep water buoy find well marked passage across bar with approx 4m, less in

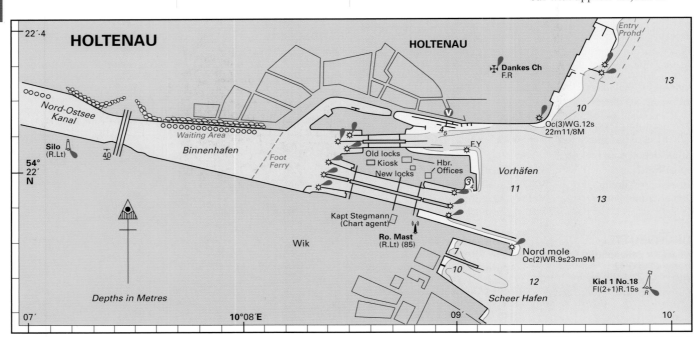

HOLTENAU

Depths in Metres

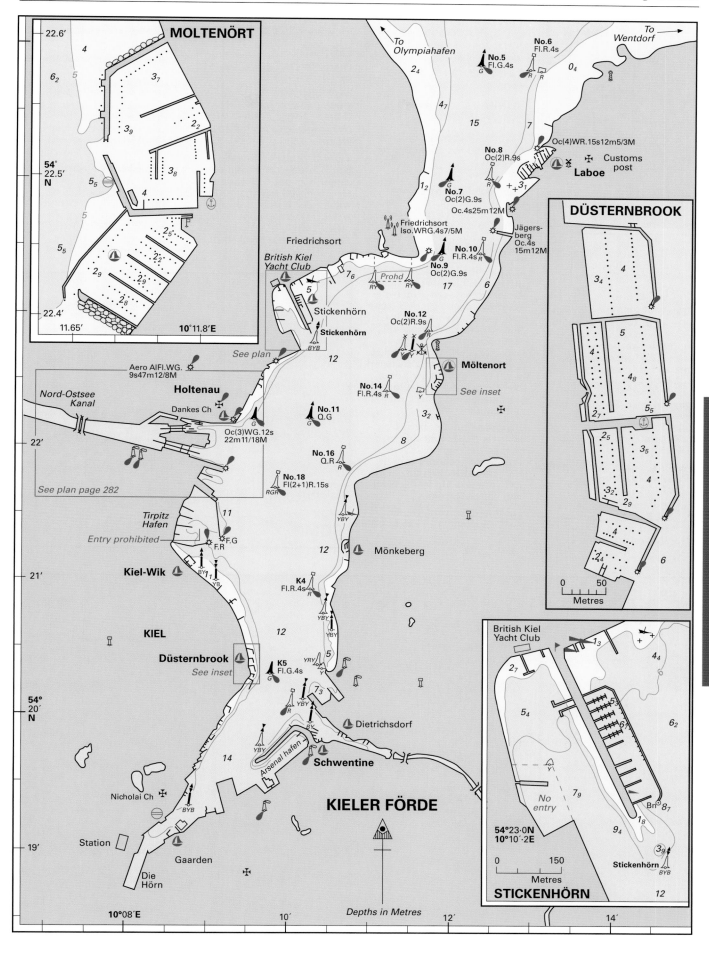

MOLTENÖRT

22.6′

4

6₂ 5

3₇

3₉ 2₂

54°
22.5′
N

5₅

4

5

5₅ 2₅
2₂
2₉
2₉
2₈

22.4′

11.65′ 10°11.8′E

To Olympiahafen

To Wentdorf

No.5 Fl.G.4s G
No.6 Fl.R.4s R R

2₄

4₇

15

0₄

7

Oc(4)WR.15s12m5/3M

No.8 Oc(2)R.9s

1₂ G
No.7 Oc(2)G.9s
Oc.4s25m12M

3₁

Customs post

Laboe

Friedrichsort Iso.WRG.4s7/5M

Jägersberg Oc.4s 15m12M

Friedrichsort

British Kiel Yacht Club

No.10 Fl.R.4s R

No.9 Oc(2)G.9s

17 6

7₆ Prohd

5

Stickenhörn

Stickenhörn BYB

No.12 Oc(2)R.9s R

12

Möltenort
See inset

No.14 Fl.R.4s R

Y

3₂

No.11 Q.G G

8

No.16 Q.R R

No.18 Fl(2+1)R.15s RGR

YBY

Aero AlFl.WG. 9s47m12/8M

Holtenau

Dankes Ch

Oc(3)WG.12s 22m11/18M

Nord-Ostsee Kanal

22′

See plan page 282

Tirpitz Hafen
Entry prohibited

11

F.G
F.R

Kiel-Wik

BY YB

21′

KIEL

Düsternbrook
See inset

12

K4 Fl.R.4s R

YBY

K5 Fl.G.4s G

YRY

5

Mönkeberg

12

7₃

YBY

Dietrichsdorf

BY

54°
20′
N

14

YBY

Arsenal hafen

Schwentine

Nicholai Ch

BYB

Station

Die Hörn

Gaarden

19′

KIELER FÖRDE

Depths in Metres

10°08′E 10′ 12′ 14′

DÜSTERNBROOK

3₄ 4

5

4 4₈

2₇ 5₅

2₅ 3₅

4

3₂ 4

2₉

4

2₄ 6

0 50
Metres

STICKENHÖRN

British Kiel Yacht Club

1₃ 4₄

2₇

5₄ 6₁ 6₂

Y

7₉

No entry

Bn 8₇

9₄ 1₈

54°23·0N
10°10′·2E

0 150
Metres

3₉ BYB

Stickenhörn

12

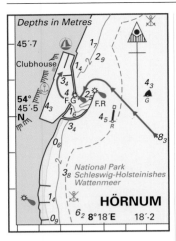

HÖRNUM

E'lies. Flood at bar begins HW Helgoland -0330, current initially setting E across the approach route. You may wish to wait until HW Helgoland −0100, which leaves three hours for passage to hbr before ebb begins. Final approach S-shape around low outer breakwater. From W approach through the Holtknobsloch seegat, marked with R buoys placed at quite some distance. Approach passes near shallows with breakers, suitable fair weather only. Flood Holtknobsloch begins HW Helgoland -0350.

Berthing At pontoons N in hbr. HM will usually assist on arrival.

Facilities Service building at YC. No fuel. Basic shopping and several restaurants in pleasant village. Bicycle rental.

Buses to Westerland which has all the attractions and distractions of a major tourist resort.

☎ HM +49 (0) 171 3300327
www.sylter-yachtclub.de

RØMØ

Charts D 60
HW Esbjerg +0035

Fishing and ferry hbr offering all-weather protection. Town tourist resort.

Approach Lister Tief is considered among the safest seegats in the North Frisian islands as it is quite wide and deep. Currents in excess of 3kn, approach should be made on the flood which begins HW Helgoland +0300 (barely ½h after LW Esbjerg). From the Lister Tief safe water buoy the waterway does a gentle S-curve and is marked with mostly Gn buoys, some lit. Alternative approach from S through buoyed Lister Landtief, settled weather only. Once in sheltered water N of Sylt follow Romø Dyb (buoys and lit bns) to mole opening. Strong cross current in hbr mouth.

Berthing Pontoons berths courtesy local yacht club to port as you enter inner hbr. Possible to anchor N of mole hbr (alternative berthing at List on Sylt where hbr is small and with limited facilities).

Facilities Boat yard. Diesel. Basic shopping. Ferry to List on Sylt.

☎ HM +45 40783354
www.portromo.dk

ESBJERG

Charts BA 3766, 420; Dk 60, 61, 94, 95
HW Esbjerg HW

MHWS	MHWN	MLWN	MLWS
1·8m	1·4m	0·4m	0·0m

DS Helgoland −0305 ESE +0315 WSW

This is Denmark's largest North Sea port and a busy commercial hbr with ships serving the oil rigs and offshore windfarms. It is the only all weather port and hbr of refuge on the Danish N Sea coast and even this hbr has breakers in the channel in a W Force 8 and entry may be dangerous.

Approach The Grådyb approach channel is 200m wide and dredged to 9·5m. It is well marked for approach day and night. In strong onshore winds enter on the flood. Large vessels with limited margins for maneuvering use this channel. Monitor VHF 12 for information on ship movements.

Berthing Pontoon berths at Esbjerg Søsport by the veteran Horns Rev Lt Vessel, N of Trafikhavnen. Enter between mole heads with consp R and G bns, turning sharply to port once inside mole opening. Be

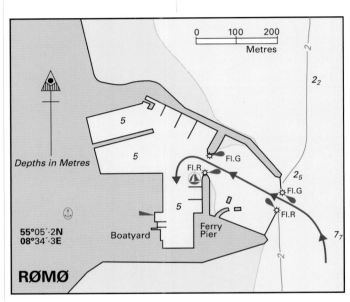

RØMØ

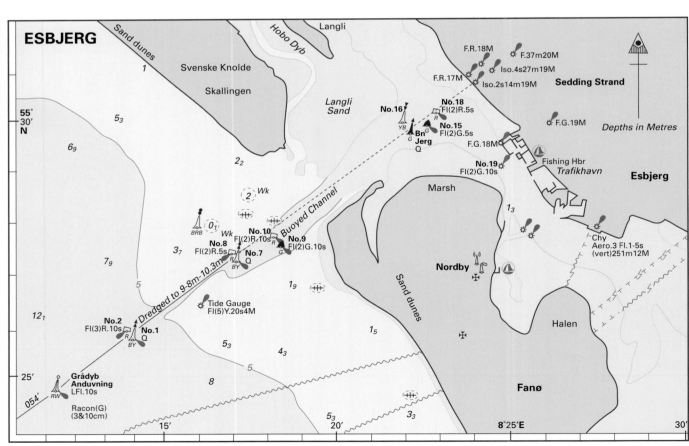

ESBJERG

aware unlit wavebreaker N of pontoons. Green tag indicates vacant berth. Hbr in industrial surroundings, 1·5km from city centre. Alternative berthing at pretty Nordby on Fanø island: large vessels alongside rough docks in village, smaller boats at boat club pontoons approached through dredged channel (1·8m, prone to silting). Beware frequent ferries.

Facilities Wide range of repair facilities. Diesel by cans from road pump approx 500m from hbr, trollies provided. For large quantities enquire about fuel from barge. Rly, ferry to Harwich.

☎ /VHF YC +45 7513 8486; *Esbjerg Port* VHF 12
www.essoesport.dk
www.portesbjerg.dk
www.fanoesejlklub.fnshare.com

HVIDE SANDE

Charts Dk 99

HW Esbjerg +0005

MHWS	MHWN	MLWN	MLWS
1·8m	0·7m	0·2m	0·0m

DS (9M offshore) Dover –0500W –0400SE +0100NE +0200NW

Busy fishing and industrial hbr. Town tourist resort popular with surfers and anglers.

Approach On passage from S note current regularly >2kn in the Slugen channel inside Horns Rev, generally flowing NW from HW Esbjerg +0315. Three conspic wind turbines on shore N of hbr. Approach channel dredged to 4·5m, but may be less after NW gales. Regular dredging carried out throughout the year. Approach dangerous in strong onshore winds – enquire HM about conditions. Signal mast N side of drainage lock indicating current (triangle point down = strong current inflowing, point up = strong current outflowing). HM will advise.

Berthing Visitors' berths at pontoons in S basin. For longer stay enquire about locking into Ringkøbing Fjord and berthing at boat club.

Facilities Service building incl laundry facilities as provided for fishing fleet. Diesel from truck, will also supply small quantities, contact HM. Ship yards, wide range of repair facilities. Chandlery with diesel engineer by small marina on Ringköbing fjord 15 mins' walk from hbr. Restaurants and shops catering for the many tourists.

☎ /VHF HM/lock keeper +45 9731 1633 (24hrs); VHF 12, 16. www.hvidesandehavn.dk

THYBORØN

Chart BA 426, DK 108

HW Esbjerg +0120sp +0230np

MHWS	MHWN	MLWN	MLWS
0·4m	0·3m	0·1m	0·0m

DS Helgoland –0400N +0100S

There is a 2kn tidal stream which can be increased to 6kn by strong winds.

Approach From W find the Lt buoy LFl.10s. There is a church N of entrance and conspic industrial complex and windmills S of entrance. Ldg bns with triangulated top markers, lower bn is the sector lt – red structure with peaked top. Ldg lts Oc.WRG.4s & Iso.4s, 082°.

Final part of approach into Søndre Dyb well buoyed with Ldg bns and Lts Iso.2s 120°. Channel tends to vary according to dredging. Seas break in onshore strong winds especially on the ebb when entry is dangerous.

Berthing Enter hbr by lit entrance, turn to stb and go to northernmost basin. Pile moorings or moor alongside. The hbr is commercial – for longer stay consider Lemvig 10 miles S. (Lystbådehavnen/Thyborøn YC S of commercial hbr with shallow approach and not advisable for first time visitors).

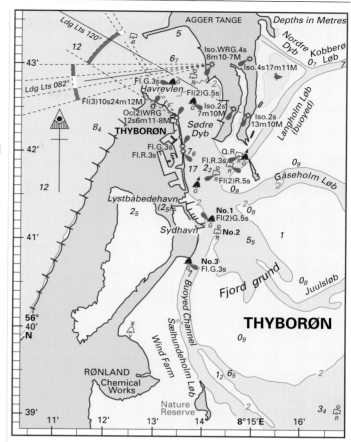

Facilities Service building. Wi-Fi locked to Danish Met Office web forecast for Fisher. Some chandlery, sailmaker.

☎ Marina +45 9783 1288; Harbour office +45 9783 1188 www.thyboronport.dk

SKAGEN

Charts BA 2107; DK 101

This is a large fishing and commercial hbr just E of the Skagen peninsula (The Skaw). Like rest of Danish E coast, tides are negligible, but strong E winds can reduce water levels by nearly 1 m. Hbr is popular with Swedish and Norwegian sailors and crowded in season. The town is a busy tourist resort.

Approach From SE, avoiding fish stakes which may extend 3M from shore. In daylight,

conspic Lt Houses on mole ends, Ldg Lts Iso.R.4s.

Berthing Visitors' berths in basins W of the old pier (gamle pier). Moor alongside docks or bows to pontoons with anchor from stern. Many of the visitors' berths are overlooked by restaurants. For more peaceful berthing look for vacant berth (green tag) at Skagen Sejlclub to port after 2nd mole.

Facilities Diesel, some chandlery, wide range of mechanical repairs available. Wi-Fi. Rly to Fredrikshavn.

☎ /VHF +45 98443341; VHF 12 Skagen port (commercial hbr) www.skagen-havn.dk www.skagen-tourist.dk [search 'lystbaadehavn'] www.skagensejlklub.dk

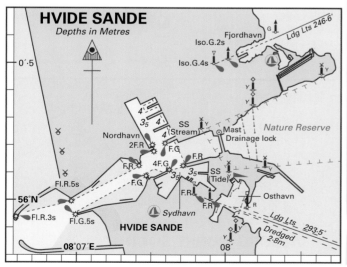

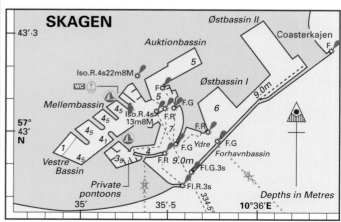

ROUTE 3A LIMFJORD

Charts BA 426, 427, 428, 429

The Limfjord from Thyborøn to Hals passes through several wide expanses of water (Bredning) and the pleasant city of Ålborg. It is a cruising ground in its own right and a pleasant alternative to passing N round Skagen. Main passageway dredged to 4m, but many harbours have <2m, less water in W'lies. There is one fixed bridge with a clearance of 26m (can be avoided by choosing the longer passage N of Mors). For opening bridges Lt signals are: 1F.R. Lt bridge closed, 2F.R. Lts bridge open for vessels from N or E, 3F.R. Lts bridge open for vessel from S or W and 5F.R. Lts bridge open to pleasure craft both directions. For more detailed pilotage see Navin.

THYBORØN

See Route 3

LEMVIG

Chart BA 426 (plan); DK 108

This is an interesting and picturesque town with a large marina lying 10 miles S across the bredning (broad) from Thyborøn. There is a clear water mark at the start of a 4m dredged channel and R triangular ldg marks (F.R Lts at night); the channel turns to port. Lemvig marina has a lit entrance. Room for visiting yachts N in the marina, by the clubhouse. The marina is on the W side of the bay, the town, shops, fuel are on the S. It may be possible to moor on the N or W quays of the W fishing hbr or in the E Gammelhavn.

☎ /VHF HM Marina +45 9782 0106 (2–3pm), *Lemvig Port* VHF 12, 13; www.visitlemvig.dk (from sitemap, choose harbours).

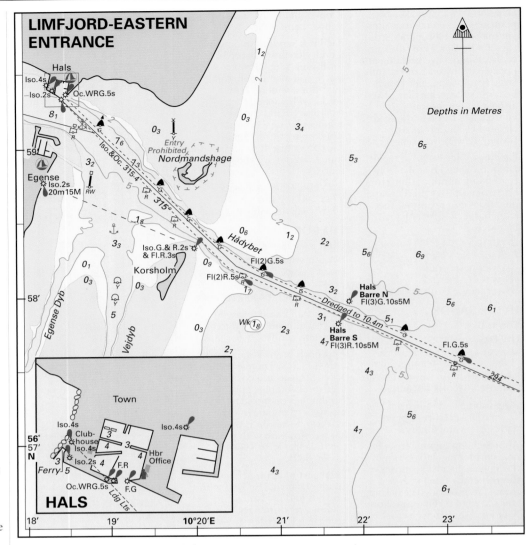

LIMFJORD-EASTERN ENTRANCE

Depths in Metres

HALS

ÅLBORG

Chart BA 430; DK 107/105

Ålborg is a picturesque and interesting place with all the facilities of a substantial town. It has good rail connections to other parts of Denmark and to Germany. Passage through Ålborg may be slow due to the two opening bridges (one road and one rail).

Berthing There are three marinas on the S side, all with visitors' berths. Vestre Baadehavn in pleasant surroundings with good restaurant and short walk to town but limited space, especially for larger boats. Marina Fjordparken, home of Aalborg YC, long-term berthing for visitors available at favourable price (see webpage in English).

Facilities Diesel E and W-most marina, chandlery in Vestre Baadehavn.

☎ HM Marina Fjordparken (YC) +45 9810 2575; Skudehavn and Vestre Bådehavn +45 9813 7034; Ålborg port +45 9930 1500, VHF 16.
www.sejlklubbenlimfjorden.dk
www.vestrebaadelaug.dk
www.anf-adm.dk
www.aalborg-sejlklub.dk

HALS

Charts BA 429, 2107; DK 106, 122

Old fishing port, now a pilot station and yacht hbr, located at E end of Limfjorden.

LEMVIG MARINA

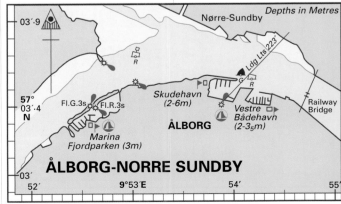

ÅLBORG-NORRE SUNDBY

Approach From E there is a deep water ch marked by buoys and an offshore Lt Ho (Hals Barre Fl.10s and Iso.WRG.2s). In settled weather, yachts avoid the deep water ch heading straight for R and G Lts at Hals Barre N Fl(3)R10s/Fl(3)G10s. The Lts look like cranes from a distance. From here buoyed ch, ldg Lts Iso.W.2s kept between Iso.R.2s and Iso.G.2s. Ldg Lts also for final approach to mole opening, see plan.

Berthing At vacant berths W in hbr or as indicated by HM. Alternative berthing at Egense across the fjord or anchor at Vejdyb 2M SSE.

Facilities Diesel available but very limited opening hrs. Limited shopping. Shuttle ferry to Egense.

☎ Hals +45 9825 9370; Egense +45 9831 0057
www.halsbaadelaug.dk
www.egense-sejlklub.dk

ROUTE 4 NORTH SEA – SKAGERRAK
Chart BA 1402, 2182B, 2182C, 2107 and others

This relatively tideless route to the Baltic takes you from the N Sea into the Skagerrak. The Norwegian SW coast between Egersund and Tananger is exposed, with Sirevåg being the only port of refuge. Between Egersund and Mandal the hbrs at Rekefjord, Flekkefjord and Farsund can be entered in most weather conditions although Rekefjord should be avoided in SW gales. On the Danish coast Thyborøn should not be approached in strong onshore winds. Between Thyborøn and Skagen the commercial hbrs of Hantsholm and Hirtshals are useful ports of refuge. Skagen can be entered in all weather conditions. On a direct crossing of the N Sea note that web sites such as www.yr.no give detailed 48h forecasts for the oil installations.

Passage lights	BA No
Denmark	
Thyborøn	1890
Fl(3)10s24m12M	
Hantsholm	2084
Fl(3)20s65m24M	
Hirtshals	2106
FFl.30s57m18/25M	
Skagen W	0001
Fl(3)WR.10s31m14/11M	
Skagen	0002
Fl.4s44m20M Racon (G)	
Norway	
Marstein	3780
Iso.WR.4s37m11M	
Racon (M)	
Slåtterøy	3752
Fl(2)30s18M Racon(T)	
Utsira	3540
FFl(3)30s10M Racon (O)	
Kvitsøy	3246
Fl(4)40s18M	
Feistein	3228
FFl(2)20s37m11M	
(Feistein, same structure)	
Iso.RG.6s21m11M	
Racon(T) (–)	
Jærens Rev Lt buoy	N/A
Q(9)15s7M	
Obrestad	3220·1
FFl.30s38m18MRacon(O) (– – –)	
Kvassheim	3217
Oc(2)WRG.8s11m10–7M	
Eigerøy	3184
Fl(3)30s45m19M	
Lista	3112
Fl.4s38m17MRacon(G) (– – ·)	
Lindesnes	3058·1
FFl.20s49m18M	
Ryvingen (Mandal)	3014
Fl(4)40s51m19M	
Racon(M) (– –)	
Oksøy (Kristiansand)	2926
Fl(2)45s46m19M	
Racon(O) (– – –)	
Store (ytre)	2798
Torungen	
Fl.20s42m18M Racon(T) (–)	

BERGEN
Chart N 21, 23; BA 3553, 3555

Bergen is Norway's second biggest city and the west coast capital. Scenic hbr front dating back to the Hansa league.

Approach From offshore enter Korsfjorden passing N of Marstein LtHo (Iso.4s), then N through the well marked fjords W or E of Tyssøyna/Bjorøyna. Current in narrows N-going on rising tide, S on falling tide. Pass under bridges to Sotra (49m) and to Askøy (63m). Enter Vågen between G buoy and molehead with sector Lt.

Berthing Yachts moor alongside SE in Vågen, large raft ups common. Wash from express boat traffic, noise as expected with inner city location. More peaceful alternatives are Strusshamn 3·5M W, Kvitturspollen (Bergen YC) (60°15'·7N 05°15'·0E) or Lysevågen (60°12'·9N 05°21'·5E).

Facilities Water, diesel, some electricity outlets, service building. Chandlery, sailmaker, fish market.

☎ HM +47 5556 8980, +47 95 98 99 80;
www.bergenhavn.no
YC +47 5552 7270;
www.bergens-seilforening.no

HAUGESUND
Chart BA 3539 N 17

Town with many facilities supporting fisheries and offshore oil industry. Hbr offers all weather protection. Good place to wait for suitable conditions for passage N across the exposed sea area Sletta.

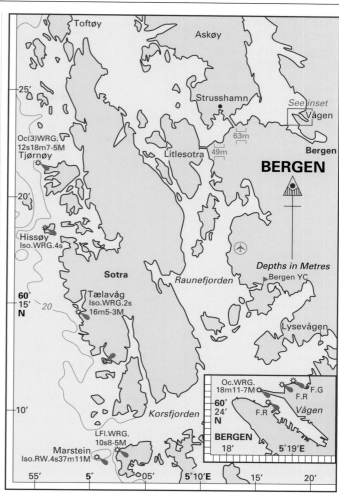

Approach From N using the main shipping channel passing between NE Karmøy and Vibrandøya or the small craft approach passing E of Sørhaugøy and Gardsøy. From S up Karmsundet under 45m bridge in Salhusstraumen. Current greatly influenced by wind but generally S going current from 3hrs before HW, N going from 3hrs after HW. Final approach from W between Hasseløya and Risøya or from S between Østre Storesundflu and mainland.

Berthing Berth alongside on E side of Smedasundet, the sound between Risøya and mainland. There is berthing N and S of 22m bridge. Busy with large raft-ups in July and during film-festival mid/late August. Some visitors' berths at private marina N of 13m bridge. Boats with mast approach from W where no bridge.

Facilities Water and electricity at some berths. Service rooms by Rica Maritim Hotel. Diesel S on Hasseløy. Some chandlery in town. Most repairs can be carried out in the region but few mechanical shops in town.

☎ HM +47 5270 3750
www.karmsund-havn.no

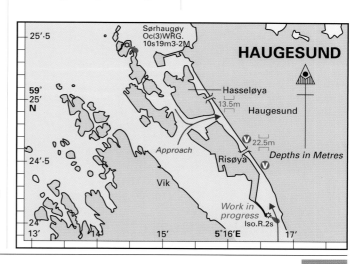

SKUDENESHAVN
Chart BA 3539, N 16

Old fishing harbour S on Karmøy. Well preserved town centre dating from rich herring fisheries. All weather protection but approach difficult in strong winds from S. Nearest official Port of Entry is Kopervik (E Karmøy).

Approach From offshore pass S of Geitungen Lt. Depending on weather conditions pass N of Treboen rock or S of Austboen rock, both marked by perches. For first time visit final approach best made from SE following well marked ferry lead, passing N of Vikeholmane.

Berthing Visitors' berths in inner hbr basin, opening up to stb N in hbr. First weekend in July local boating festival and hbr very crowded.

Facilities Water and electricity in inner hbr, diesel pump in approaches. Several shops and restaurants.

www.visitskudeneshavn.no

TANANGER
Chart BA 3538; N 14, 16

Tananger old hbr WNW of the new large oil hbr has retained much of its charm. Mole connecting Melingsholmen to mainland provides all weather protection.

Approach From Jærens Rev Lt buoy lay a course W of Feistein Lt Ho and into W sector at Kolneshl Lt Ho and sheltered water. Remaining approach taking you S and E of Melingsholmen keeping Melingshl Lt and perch to port.

Berthing Alongside mole S of pilot boat and lifeboat. Alongside wood dock and pontoon by service building NW in hbr. At vacant pontoon berths at local boat club N in

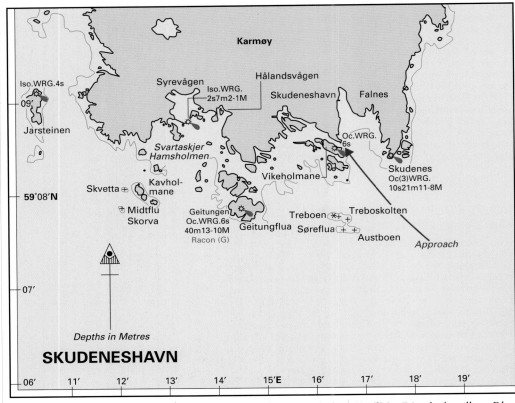

hbr. Outside Hummeren Hotel NE in hbr.

Facilities Diesel – key for pump at Hummeren hotel. Wi-Fi in hotel lobby. Shops, restaurant, bus to Sola Airport and Stavanger.

EGERSUND
Chart BA 2987; N 13

Useful hbr offering all weather protection on an otherwise exposed coast. Ship building and repair facilities serving fishing fleet.

Approaches From W and N through Nordregabet, passing S of cairn on Guleholmen and N of perch on Tryet, in W sector of Ruskodden Lt. Yachts with air draught >22m use S

approach due to br. S approach through Søragabet, keeping clear of Stabbsædet and shallows E of this before passing between Skarvøy Lt and mainland. S approach preferable in strong westerlies.

Berthing Pontoons NE in hbr past church, marked 'Gjestebrygge'. Larger yachts moor alongside docks NE of lifeboat and pilot vessel. Anchorage in public recreation area at Gyrahamn in Nordregabet, position 58°28'·0N 05°51'·1E

Facilities Diesel, chandlery, Rly. Customs.

☎ HM +47 4815 2573
www.egersund.gjestehavn.com

MANDAL
Chart BA 2982; N 10

No significant tidal rise or tidal stream although wind generated currents may occur. It is a landlocked river hbr, totally protected and available in all weathers.

Approach From the seaward, identify Ryvingen LtHo conspic

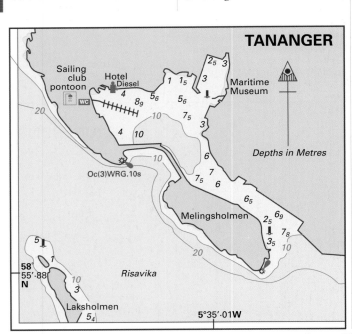

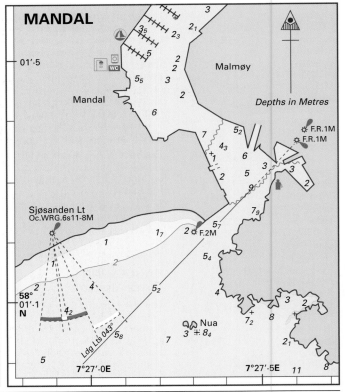

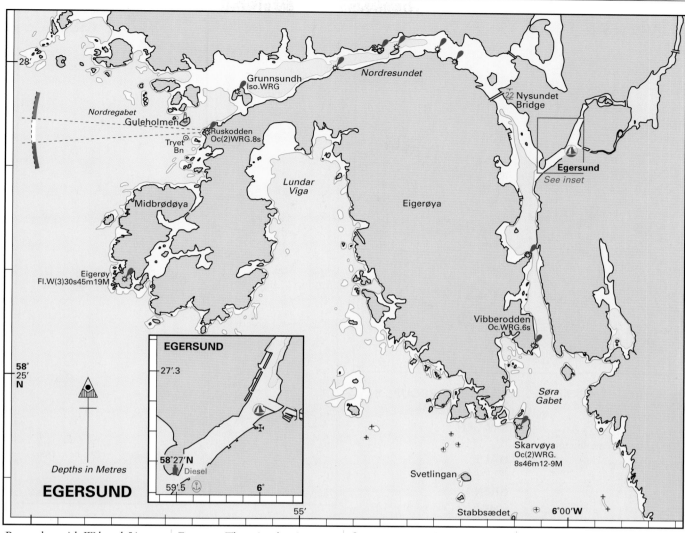

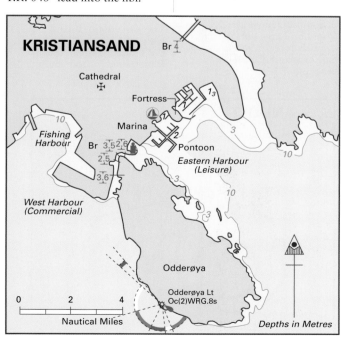

R metal tr with W band 51m. Steer 350° with major islands to stb and rocks and skerries to port, altering slightly as necessary. This will lead in safely, as all relevant hazards show above water. The Hattholmen LtHo Fl(2)WRG.10s and Sjøsanden Lt Oc.WRG.6s and the Ldg Lts F.R. 043° lead into the hbr.

Entrance There is a bar in sheltered water with 3m. In the channel keep to stb until channel turns NW, then keep to port side as stb side shoals.

Berthing Room for visiting yachts in N of hbr. Mooring at five floating stages with finger pontoons. Larger yachts may moor alongside docks NE of floating stages. A planned pedestrian bridge to Malmøy may limit access.

Facilities Wi-Fi. Ship and yacht repair facilities. Diesel SE in hbr by Nautic Marine.

⏱ HM +47 4000 5152
www.mandal.kommune.no/mandalhavn

KRISTIANSAND

Chart BA 2987; N 9

A double hbr set in a deep bay and available in all weathers.

Approach From offshore through Østergapet leaving Oksøy Lt (W metal tr with R bands Fl(2)45s) to port and Grønningen Lt (Fl(2)WRG.10s) to stb. From SW through the narrow Vestergabet between Flekkerøy and mainland.

Berthing Facilities for visiting yachts located near city centre E of Odderøya. SW of old fort (Christiansholm). Fort floodlit at night. Lt (F.R) end of mole. Inside mole two pontoons and pile moorings 2m most places, less alongside mole. Pontoons outside mole untenable in strong S'lies.

Facilities Wi-Fi. Diesel W of marina. Chandlery. Wide range of shopping. Rly, airport, ferries to Denmark.

⏱ HM +47 3802 0715,
www.kristiansandgjestehavn.no

A lovely cruising area lies E of Kristiansand towards Lillesand called the Blindleia. It lies among and behind offshore islands.

ARENDAL

Chart BA 3515; N 7, 8

Approaches LHos on Store (ytre) Torungen and Lille (indre) Torungen both conspic. Pass E of Store Torungen. Lille Torungen sector light can be passed either side but note shallows S of Mærdø if passing E of lighthouse. All hazards in further approach well marked. Accessible in all weather conditions.

Berthing Best all weather protection in city centre hbr (Pollen), but notorious for noise in summer season. Main visitors' pontoons SW on Tyholmen, further development planned for 2014.

Facilities Wi-Fi, diesel on mainland E of city. Arendal is a commercial centre with several boat builders and ship building industry. Hbr busy in July. YC has facilities at Bratholmen S of Rægevig in approaches to Arendal with room for visiting yachts. In settled conditions consider anchorage outside

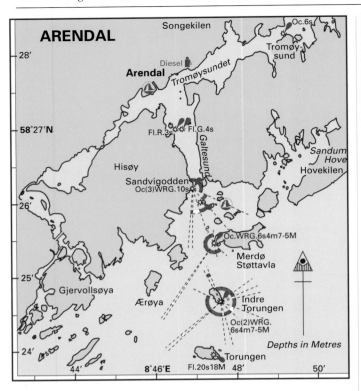

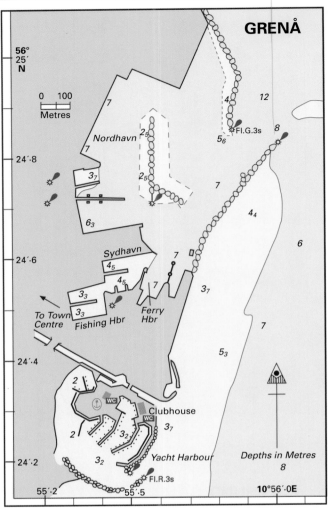

APPROACHES TO THE BALTIC

small settlement on N shore of Mærdø. Museum and small café.

☎ Arendal HM +47 9752 7000, www.arendalhavn.no

THYBORØN

see Route 3

ROUTE 5 KATTEGAT

Charts BA 2107, 2108; D101, 102; DK100

Kattegat lies E of Jylland and W of the W coast of Sweden. It is continuous with the Skagerrak N of Skagen. The Danish coast tends to be shallow and sandy while the Swedish coast tends to be rocky with islands and skerries particularly N of Göteborg. Selected hbrs only are mentioned as ports of passage or refuge.

Passage lights	BA No
Hirsholm Fl(3)30s30m22M+F.WR	0020
Syrodde Fl.WR.3s12m8/5M	0057
Hals Barre Fl.10s18m18M+ Iso.WRG.2s10-5M	0066
Sjællands Rev N Iso.WRG.2s25m16-13M	1478
Trubaduren LFl(3)WRG.30s24m20-17M+ F.R	0569
Fladen LFl.8s24m9M+Fl.Y.3s	0671
Kullen Västra Oc(3)WG.20s12m14/10M	2262
Anholt Harbour Iso.WRG.4s8m14-10M	0166
Anholt (East) Fl.15s.40m14M	0164

DANISH HARBOURS IN THE KATTEGAT

SKAGEN
see Route 3

HALS
see Route 3a

GRENÅ

Chart BA 2108 (plans); D124

The busy fishing and ferry port lies 2M S of the conspic round tr of Fornæs LtHo Fl.20s32m23M but this is exclusively commercial. The yacht hbr with visitors' berths lies 1M S.

From the RW buoy Iso.8s steer S to leave the Kalkgrund N card buoy and S card Lt buoy to stb. Then steer towards the yacht hbr which is entered between W pyramids with R and G tops Fl.R&G.3s. From the S leave Y con buoy E of Naveren shallows to port.

Berthing Yachts >13m moor inside N mole, otherwise as indicated by HM.

Facilities Shops, chandlery, sailmaker in commercial hbr. Kategatcenteret aquarium near marina worth seeing. Old village 2kms.

☎ HM +45 8632 7255 www.grenaamarina.dk

ANHOLT

Charts BA 2108, DK 124

Popular resort island with well protected mole hbr on W shore. Conspic radar tr above hbr and LtHo on N mole.

Approach From N identify W card buoy marking NW end of Nordvestrevet. Possible approach in good weather through Nordvestrevet at Slussen, unmarked. From S

keep clear extensive shallows along SE shore. Sector lt on N mole. Breaking seas in approaches in strong W'lies.

Berthing To stb after second mole, room for up to 250 yachts moored fore-aft. 3·5m shallowing to 1·5m towards mole. Anchor in outer harbour only after agreement with HM. In calm weather yachts anchor off beach S of hbr.

Facilities Wi-Fi. Diesel. Shops, café and PO in village 2·5km from hbr. Large part of island is a nature reserve. Seal colony E part of island. Extensive beaches.

☎ +45 86 31 90 08 www.anholt.dk (links to transport – Anholt Havn).

SWEDISH HARBOURS IN THE KATTEGAT

GÖTEBORG

Chart BA 857, 858, 2107; S 931, 9312, 9313

This is the second largest city in Sweden situated on the R Göta. There are numerous marinas but not all welcome visitors. There is a major inland waterway via the Göta river, the Trollhättekanal, the lakes Vänern and Vättern and the

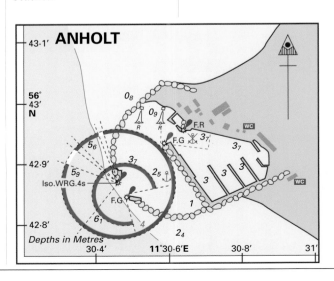

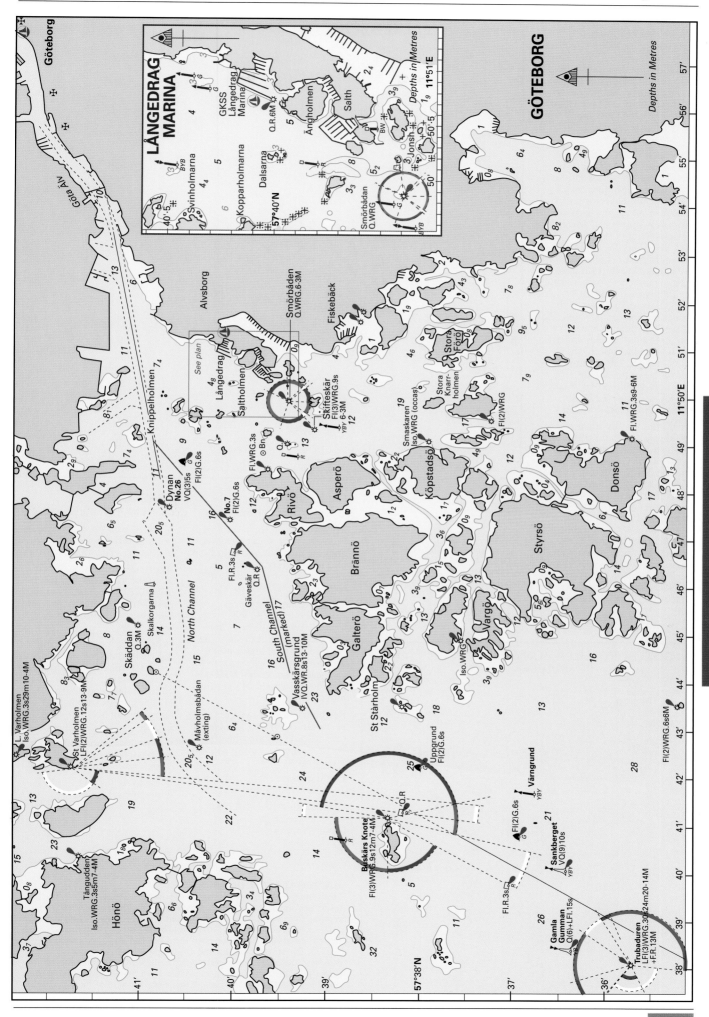

Götakanal to Mem near Stockholm. For further information on Göta kanal see www.gotakanal.se. Bohuslän is a challenging archipelago with many small fishing harbours and delightful anchorages lying N of Göteborg. Detailed charts are essential to taste the flavour of Swedish skärgård (archipelago) sailing.

Approach From offshore the Trubaduren LtHo (24m) is conspic by day as it stands in clear water. At night it has a wide SW White sector and a narrower NE White sector. From here steer 030° towards Buskärs Knöte LtHo Fl(3)WRG.9s12m 3½M away. Leave this to port. From NE of Buskärs Knöte the two deep water channels (North and South channel) are clearly marked. Both are busy with commercial shipping. Note that some of the lateral markers resemble small cranes and are flood lit in addition to the R and G Lts. To Långedrag marina an approach in darkness should be made from the SW using sector Lts on Skifteskär and Smörbåden.

Berthing Lilla Bommen (Lisebergs Gästhamn) is located on the S bank in city centre, between the Göteborg opera and the barque 'Viking'. Some wash from ferries and express boats that dock nearby. No anchoring, use provided lazy lines. Just a footbridge away from a large shopping centre. Excellent if preparing for a passage up the Trollhätte and Göta canals. Open year-round. Berths can be pre-booked at www.dockspot.com. More peace and quiet will be found at

Långedrag, an artificial hbr 5M WSW of the city and HQ of Royal Göteborg YC. Green tag indicates vacant berth.

☎ Långedrag +46 (0) 3129 1145, +46 (0) 70339 9398; VHF 68. www.gkss.se (links Hamn/Flottilj – Gästhamn).

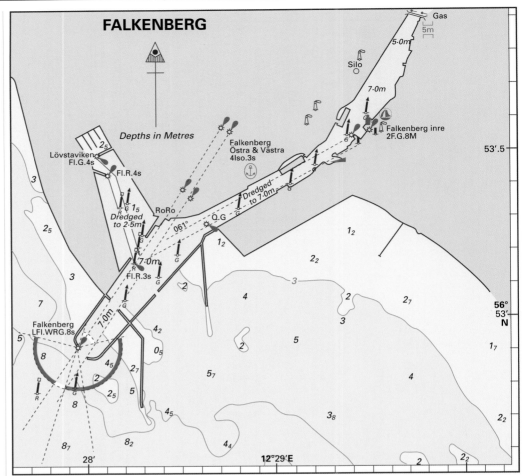

FALKENBERG

Charts BA 874 (& plan); S 924

Major town on the river Ätran. Industrial hbr with extensive docking facilities and ship yard. Old town pretty, nice walks along river above bridge and a large beach 500 m S of YC.

Approach and Entrance Approach from the SW. Conspic windmills N of hbr entrance. Sector lt on W mole. Buoyed channel inside mole. The current in the hbr narrows can reach 4kn. Listen VHF 16 for announcement of big ship movements.

Berthing There are visitors' berths at YC on SE side. Green tag indicates vacant finger/pile berth, or moor alongside wood dock upriver of YC.

Facilities Diesel at YC. Shopping and many restaurants in town.

☎ HM +46 (0) 3468 4124 www.falkenbergs-batsallskap.nu

TOREKOV

Charts BA 875 (and plan); S 923

A pretty, well protected hbr in popular resort town. Crowded in season.

Approach From N or S in W sector of Vingaskär LtHo (Fl(3)WRG9s). Ldg Lts until past W mole then stb between G/R buoys and mole ends.

Berthing Alongside in inner hbr, expect to raft up. Inside outer mole with piles for stern lines. In settled weather moor alongside wavebreaker in E of hbr. Yachts >12m should enquire to the HM about vacancy before approaching hbr.

Facilities Diesel. Several restaurants, grocery store. There is a passenger ferry to Hallands Väderö, a nature reserve.

☎ HM +46 (0) 4313 63534 www.tbss.se

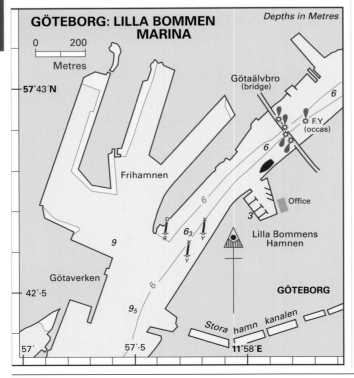

KATTEGAT SOUTHWARDS

From the S end of the Kattegat there are three channels into the Baltic proper, in the Lillebælt to the W lies Kolding which has a pleasant fjord and is a major town with good communications to Esbjerg for crew changes. Further S are Sønderborg and the German hbr of Maasholm. The Storebælt between Fyn and Sjælland leads past Korsør and Bagenkop. The Øresund to the E is the busy channel between Denmark and Sweden with Helsingør, København and Rødvig on the Danish side and Limhamn on the Swedish side. In the middle of the Sund is the delightful Swedish island of Ven.

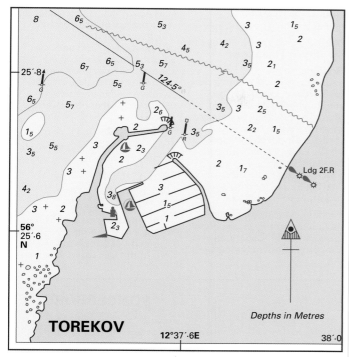

TOREKOV

12°37'·6E   38'·0

ROUTE 6A LILLEBÆLT

Charts BA 2106, 2592, 2532;
Dk 151, 152

KOLDING

Chart BA 900 (and plan);
DK 158, 151

A major town located 5M up a pleasant fjord from the N end of Lillebælt. Many sites of historic and cultural interest.

Passage lights	BA No
Trelde Næs	0894
Iso.WRG.2s26m8-6M	
Æbelø	0893·5
Fl.15s20m14M	
Strib	0922
Oc.WRG.5s21m13-10M	
Bågø	0972
Oc(2)WRG.6s12m12-9M	
Assens	0977
Oc.WRG.10s5m14-11M	
Helnæs Lindehoved	0988
Fl.WRG.5s30m13-10M	
Nordborg	1030
Oc.WRG.5s27m12-9M	
Taksensand	1034
Oc(2)WRG.12s15m15-12M	
Skjoldnæs	1070
Fl.30s32m22M	
Gammel-Pøl	1100
Oc(3)WRG.15s20m11-8M	
Vejsnæs Nakke	1082
Fl.5s23m12M	
Schleimünde	1186
LFl(3)WR.20s14m14/6M	
Horn Mo(SN)30s (···/−·)	

The current can run strongly through Lillebælt, especially so in the N end (Snævringen) where it can reach 4 knots. Flow is largely dictated by wind: S flow in winds from N and W, N flowing in winds from E and S. In spring, flow generally N wards out of the Baltic. Detailed graphic predictions found at www.dmi.dk (Sitemap – Farvandsvarsler – Bælthavet og Sundet – Strøm).

Approach A buoyed channel leads up Kolding Fjord. The main hbr has 2F.R. Lts 267°. Buoyed channel to Sørhavnen leads off SW from main channel ½M before mole.

Berthing There are two marinas, Nordhavnen and Sydhavnen, both nearly 500 berths. Nordhavnen approached from commercial hbr hence deep water in approach and ample room for manœuvering. Sørhavnen approached through channel dredged to 2·5m, but less depth in strong winds from N and W. Sørhavnen located in green surroundings and less noise from road and railway. Both hbrs 1,500m to town centre, from Sørhavnen reasonably pleasant walk along river.

Facilities Diesel in Sørhavnen. Chandleries. Wide range of shopping in town. Railway station with trains to Esbjerg useful for crew change, buses to Billund airport.

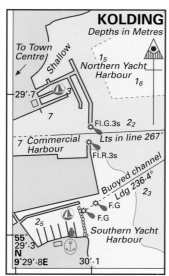

KOLDING
Depths in Metres

To Town Centre
Shallow
Northern Yacht Harbour
29'·7
Commercial Harbour
Fl.G.3s
Lts in line 267°
Fl.R.3s
Buoyed channel
Ldg 236·4°
F.G
F.G
Southern Yacht Harbour
55° 29'·3N
9°29'·8E   30'·1

☾ Marina +45 7553 2722
www.koldinglystbaadehavn.dk

ASSENS

Chart BA 2592 (plan); DK 151

Assens is SW on island of Fyn, in S end of Lillebælt. Large well protected marina in harbour shared with a shipyard. 10 minutes' walk to picturesque town centre.

Approach From NNW, identify the N card mark at N end of Asnæs Rev. Sectored Lt and ldg Lts for approach at night.

Berthing Pile berthing, green tag indicating vacant berth.

Facilities Diesel, chandlery, small restaurant and pub in marina. Usual range of shopping in town.

☾ HM +45 6471 3580,
+45 2169 1567
www.assens-marina.dk

FÅBORG

Chart BA 2532 (plan); DK 152

Fåborg lies some miles E of the main Lillebælt route on the island of Fyn. It is at the entrance to route 6C but it is still a useful port if bound N or S.

Approach From the Lillebælt Fåborg may be approached either N or S of the island of

Lyø. From the SW approach in the W sector of Bjørnø LtHo IsoWRG.4s and then steer NW on Sisserodde LtHo DirIso.WRG.2s before turning to 047° on the F.G Ldg Lts and finally to 336·5° on F.R Ldg Lts.

Facilities It is an attractive town and a busy commercial and ferry port with connections to the local islands. There is a yacht hbr to the NW of the commercial hbr but yachts can also lie alongside in the commercial port.

☾ HM +45 7253 0260
www.faaborghavn.dk

SØNDERBORG

Charts DK 155, 152

Picturesque hbr on SE shore of Als Sund.

Approach From the N leave the Alsfjord into the clearly buoyed Als Sund. Before the town the sound is crossed by the opening King Christian X's Br. From the S leave the Østerhage W card Lt buoy to stb and Vesterhage R can to port.

Signals for bridge 1F.R. no passage. 2F.R. Lts pass N to S. 3F.R.Lts pass S to N. 2+3F.R. Lts: pass both directions. Long sound from horn indicates stay

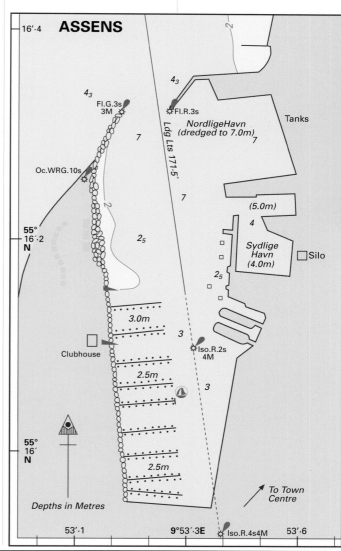

ASSENS

16'·4

Fl.G.3s 3M
Fl.R.3s
NordligeHavn (dredged to 7.0m)
Tanks
Oc.WRG.10s
Ldg Lts 171·5
(5.0m)
Sydlige Havn (4.0m)
Silo
3.0m
Clubhouse
Iso.R.2s 4M
2.5m
2.5m
To Town Centre
Depths in Metres
53'·1   9°53'·3E   53'·6
Iso.R.4s4M

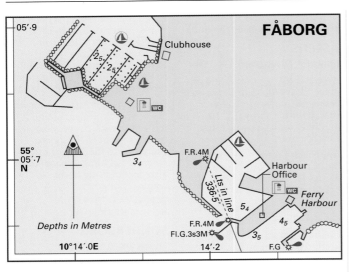

FÅBORG

Depths in Metres

clear of br. Time of next opening shown on light board.

NB The br marks the change in the direction of buoyage.

Berthing
• Along city docks S of opening br, E side of sound. Rather rough wooden docks, good fendering essential. Some wash in strong winds from SW through SE. Electricity and water. Large yachts will prefer these docks.
• Sønderborg Lystbådehavn. Marina SE of city with pile moorings for stern lines.

Facilities Marina all facilities including 5-tonne crane, diesel, laundry, Wi-Fi. Usual range of shopping in town. Sønderborg

has many historic sites relating to centuries of strife between the two neighbouring nations Denmark and Germany. Nearby Augustenborg in bottom of Augestenborgfjord two fully serviced boatyards, winter storage under cover (www.augustenborg-yachthavn. dk, www.mj-vaerft.dk).

☎ Marina +45 7442 9392; Port +45 7442 2765, VHF 16, 12.

BAGENKOP

Charts BA 2597, 2113; Dk 142, 195

This small marina and fishing hbr is situated on the W side of the S end of Langeland, 30M NE of the Kiel LtHo. It is also

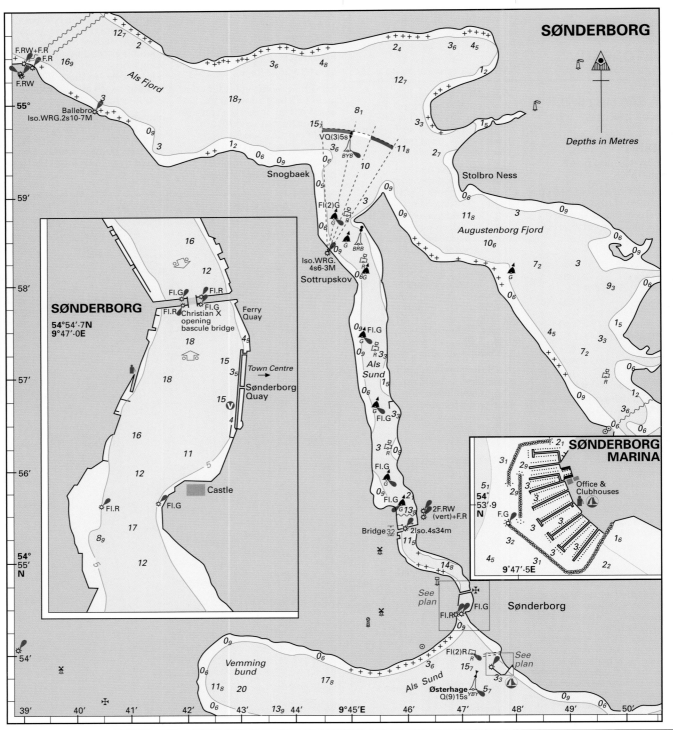

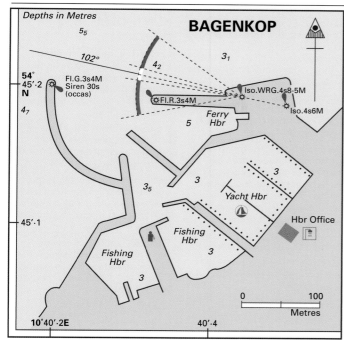

Depths in Metres

BAGENKOP

convenient for vessels on passage through the Storebælt.

Approach Shoals may make the approach rough in W winds but there are no hazards and it is safe to follow the 10m contour N to the Fl(2)R offing buoy. Steer 102° on the Ldg Lts on the N mole (W sector of Iso.WRG.4s & Iso.4s) to clear the W mole head.

Entrance The hbr faces N. Just inside the N breakwater lies the disued ferry hbr. The yacht hbr is in the NE basin of the inner harbour. Additional moorings in the S basin.

Facilities Customs, water, diesel and shops.

✆ HM +45 6256 1861 (0800–1000).

MAASHOLM

Charts BA 2113; G41
The river Schlei is a cruising ground in its own right. Maasholm is a small fishing village and tourist resort, 1½M inside the Schleimünde. It is the largest marina on the river.

Approach Schleimünde Seegat is a buoyed channel dredged to 5m. From the safe water buoy follow buoyed channel to the entrance between two moles. N mole has conspic W tower with black band. Approach dangerous in strong E'lies. Pass Schleimünde with small hbr to stb then follow buoyed channel. Hbr subject to considerable tidal surges depending on wind directions, less water in strong W'lies.

Berthing Vacant pile berths indicated by green tag. Alternative berthing in old hbr NW of village or anchor NW of this or S of passageway in Olpenitzer Noor.

Facilities Diesel in the fishing hbr, several restaurants. The town Kappeln 3M up-river has a wide range of services available to yachts, and several berthing options down-river of the opening bridge.

✆ HM +49 (0) 4642 6571
www.maasholm.de

ROUTE 6B STOREBÆLT

Charts BA 938, 2106, 2596, 2597; Dk 141, 142

This is a major shipping channel between the Kattegat and Kieler Bucht crossed by the Great Belt br. Direction of buoyage is to the S. When passing the br yachts should if possible use the Vesterrenden channel between Nyborg and Sprogø (clearance 18m). In the Østerrenden vessels of less than 20m in length and sailing vessels are recommended to avoid using the TSS traffic lanes and instead use the other br spans. Vertical clearances in the eastern spans towards Sjælland range from 53m to 8m and in the western spans towards Sprogø vary from 52m to 20m. If in doubt contact VTS *Great Belt Traffic* on VHF 16 and 11 or ✆ +45 45 5837 6868. Reporting is compulsory for vessels of 50 GRT and over and for vessels with a masthead clearance of 15m and over. This formal requirement seems lightly enforced and largely ignored by yachts cruising the area in good visibility.

KORSØR

An old ferry and naval port with interesting streets.

Approach From the Badstue Rev W card buoy steer NE leaving two G con buoys to stb. The Badstue reef 200m S of the hbr entrance has less than 0·2m depth over stones. S of the reef there are stones between the 2m and 4m contours. The yacht hbr entrance is lit (Iso.WRG.4s to port, Fl.G.3s to stb).

Berthing In the yacht hbr (S of the naval hbr) with perfect shelter. Berthing by HM whose office is at the base of the S wall.

Supplies Water, fuel, showers, chandler, restaurant and shops.

✆ +45 5837 5930
www.korsoerlystbaadehavn.com

BAGENKOP

see Route 6a on page 294.

Passage lights	BA No
Romsø Tue	1526
Fl.WRG.3s10m11-8M	
Østerrenden East Bridge Centre	
N side	1532.6
Fl.R.3s71m7M	
Østerrenden S	1534
Fl(3)R.10s10m8M	
Knudshoved	1556
Oc.WRG.10s16m12-10M	
Langelandsøre (Omø)	1640
Oc(2)WRG.12s21m17-14M	
Spodsbjerg SE	1673
Fl.WRG.3s10m11-7M	
Højbjerg E	1673.2
Fl.RG.5s10m8M	
Keldsnor	1706
Fl(2)15s39m17M	
Oc.WRG.5s22m12-9M	

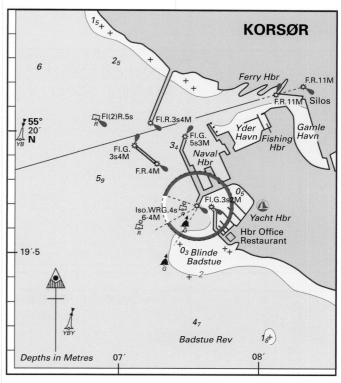

KORSØR

MAASHOLM   Depths in Metres

ROUTE 6C SOUTH OF FYN AND SJÆLLAND

Charts BA 2532, 2597, 2583, 940, 2115; Dk 103, Dk 104

This inshore route from Fåborg, through the islands S of Fyn and Sjælland passing N of Langeland to Vordingborg and Rødvig, is a pleasant sheltered alternative to continuing S on the Lille Bælt. Crossing the Storebælt the route leads directly to København. It may also be joined from Route 7 by sailing E of Langeland.

Passage lights	BA No
Helnæs Lindehoved Fl.WRG.5s30m13-10M	0988
Skjoldnæs LFl.30s32m22M	1070
Frankeklint (Langeland) Oc.RG.5s16m8M	1656
Langelandsøre (Omø) Oc(2)WRG.12s21m17-14M	1640

FÅBORG
see Route 6a

SVENDBORG

Charts DK 171

Svendborg Sund is an attractive sheltered waterway winding between Fyn and the offshore islands. It is often called the 'Danish Riviera'. There are a number of yacht harbours on the N and S banks. They are often crowded and it is usually better to proceed to the main commercial hbr at Svendborg where moorings are available in the inner harbour (Nordre Havn) and at various jetties around the port. Svendborg is a large town with a distinguished maritime history and the usual facilities.

℡ +45 6223 3080
www.svendborg-havn.dk

VORDINGBORG

Charts BA 2365; Dk161

After passing N of Langeland and crossing the Storebælt the wide inlet of Smålandsfarvandet leads S of Sjælland to the narrows at Vordingborg. The town is on the N bank and can be reached either through the Masnedsund opening br (road and rail) or by passing under the Storstrøm Br (clearance 26m) and crossing the Middelgrund (least depth 2·5m). There are two small marinas immediately E of the opening br but yachts usually proceed to the Nordhavn which is convenient for the town.

Facilities Wi-Fi. Chandlery and diesel at Masnedø Marinecenter SE of lifting br.

℡ +45 2218 1549
www.sejlklubben-snekken.dk

RØDVIG

Charts Dk 190

The route continues N of the island of Møn under two fixed bridges (20 and 26m clearance). The Bøgestrøm channel then leads out to the deeper waters of Fakse Bugt. Navigation of the Bøgestrøm should only be attempted in daylight. Least depth is around 2m. Rødvig lies across the Fakse Bugt on the S side of Sjælland. It is a charming old fishing village and a convenient passage port.

Approach From SW through mole opening with R and G Lts. There are fishing stakes E of approach.

Berthing Yacht hbr to stb on approach, limited room for manœuvering once inside. Piles for stern lines, some alongside berths. When crowded, yachts use the fishing hbr to port. Large yachts will prefer the fishing hbr.

Regular trains to Copenhagen.

Facilities There is a boatyard and a couple of shops, several restaurants.

℡ +45 5650 6007.

KLINTHOLM

Charts D 198

Located SE on the island of Møn, this is a popular landfall or point of departure for German Baltic hbrs. E side of Møn with conspic white chalk cliffs Møns Klint.

Approach From SW avoiding fish stakes both sides of hbr approach. Approach hazardous in strong winds from SW.

Berthing Large marina to port upon entry. Piles for stern lines. Large vessels moor alongside in fishing (east) hbr, or as directed by HM.

Facilities There is a general food store and a fish shop, bicycle rental useful if wishing to visit the geological centre at Møns Klint.

℡ HM +45 55819044.

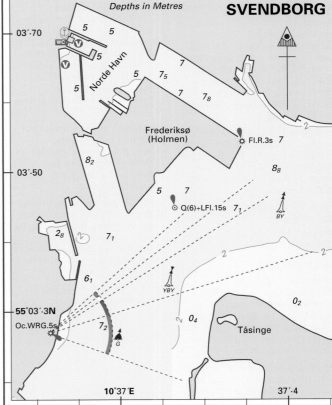

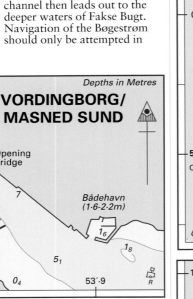

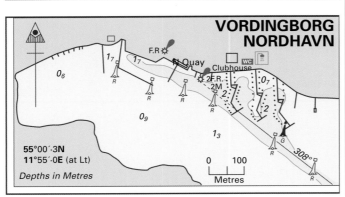

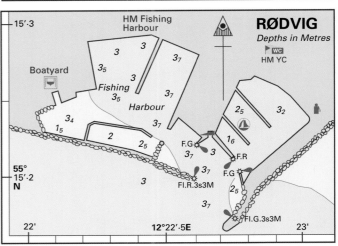

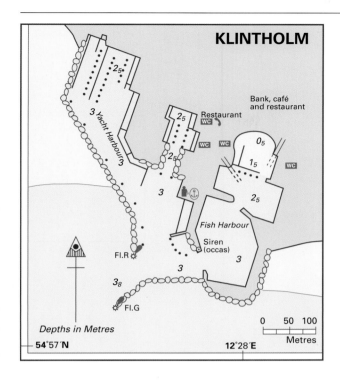

KLINTHOLM

Bank, café and restaurant
Restaurant
Yacht Harbour
Fish Harbour
Siren (occas)
Fl.R
Fl.G
Depths in Metres
54°57′N
12°28′E
0 50 100
Metres

ROUTE 6D ØRESUND (THE SOUND)
Charts BA 2115, 2594, 2595, 903; Dk 133, 131, S921, 922

This important deep waterway between Denmark and Sweden has very heavy commercial traffic and ferry-links. The road/railway link between Denmark and Sweden is in way of a tunnel on the Danish side, so there is no headroom restriction in the Øresund. There are many hbrs and marinas on both shores but they tend to be busy in season.

Passage lights	BA No
Kronborg (Helsingør) Oc(2)WRG.6s34m15-12M	1908
Helsingborg Oc.WRG.15s17m18-13M	2288
Ven LFl.WRG.10s24m16-12M	1928
Middelgrunds Fort E Oc(2)WRG.12s11m12-10M	1965
Middelgrunds Fort W Oc.WRG.5s11m12-10M	1964
Trekroner Iso.WRG.2s20m17-13M	1978
Nordre Røse Oc(2)WRG.6s14m17-13M	2042
Drogden Oc(3)WRG.15s18m18-13M Horn Mo(U)30s (··−)	2060
Falsterborev Fl(4)WR.12s29m14−12M	2417

DANISH PORTS IN THE ØRESUND

HELSINGØR
Chart BA 2594 (plan); Dk 131

Yachts <15m are not allowed in the commercial and ferry S hbr.

Approach N hbr, near spectacular Kronborg castle, has no hazards and has deep water to the entrance, but is crowded despite 1000 berths and it may be difficult to find a vacant mooring. There are plans for an expansion of the hbr to the NW. Beware of the heavy ferry traffic between Helsingør and Helsingborg. Note that the Kronborg Lt is on the NE tr of the castle.

Facilities All marina facilities. Interesting town with good shops. Maritime museum. Castle on the supposed site of Shakespeare's Elsinore has not been a Royal residence for 200 years. Trains to København.

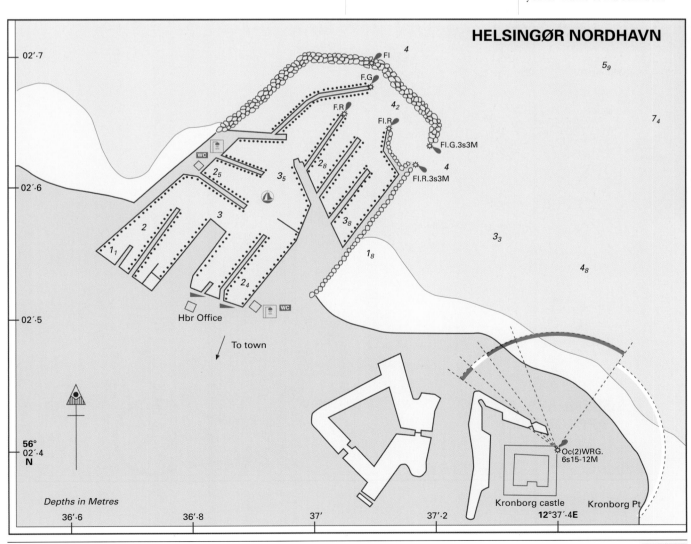

HELSINGØR NORDHAVN

Hbr Office
To town
Kronborg castle
Kronborg Pt
Oc(2)WRG. 6s15-12M
Depths in Metres
56° 02′.4 N
12°37′.4E

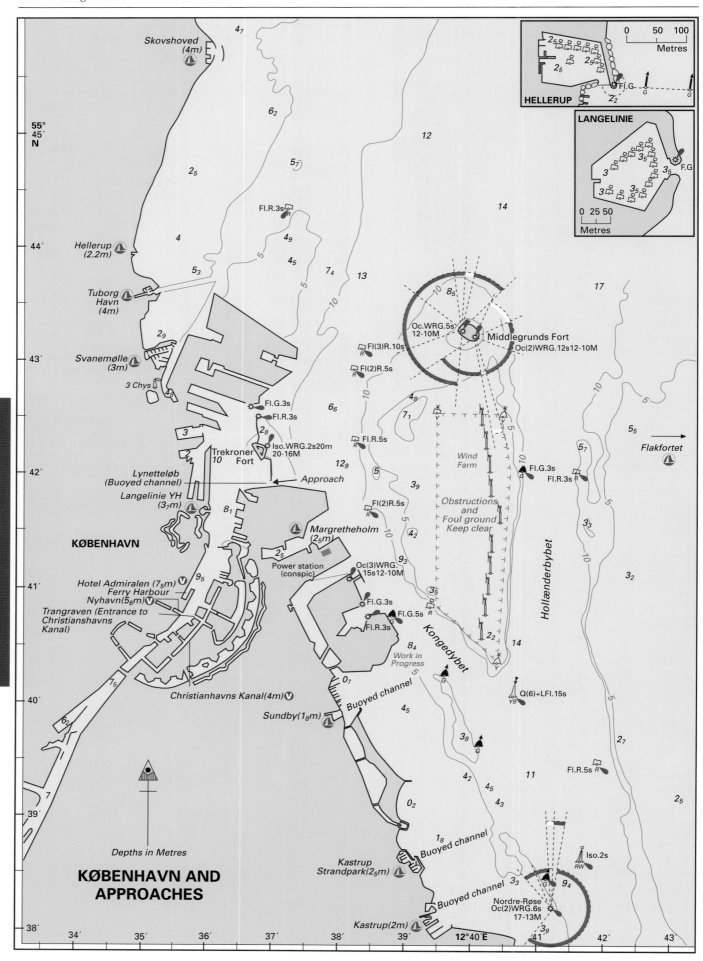

APPROACHES TO THE BALTIC

HELLERUP

0 50 100
Metres

Fl.G.
G   G

LANGELINIE

0 25 50
Metres

F.G

Skovshoved
(4m)

55°
45′
N

12

14

17

Hellerup
(2.2m)

Fl.R.3s
R

Tuborg
Havn
(4m)

Svanemølle
(3m)

3 Chys

Fl.G.3s

Fl.R.3s

Iso.WRG.2s20m
20-16M

Trekroner
Fort

Lynetteløb
(Buoyed channel)

Langelinie YH
(3₇m)

KØBENHAVN

Approach

Margretheholm
(2₅m)

Power station
(conspic)

Hotel Admiralen (7₅m) Ⓥ
Ferry Harbour
Nyhavn(5₆m) Ⓥ
Trangraven (Entrance to
Christianshavns
Kanal)

Christianhavns Kanal(4m) Ⓥ

Sundby(1₈m)

Oc.WRG.5s
12-10M

Middlegrunds Fort
Oc(2)WRG.12s12-10M

Fl(3)R.10s
R

Fl(2)R.5s
R

Fl.R.5s
R

Wind
Farm

Obstructions
and
Foul ground
Keep clear

Fl(2)R.5s
R

Oc(3)WRG.
15s12-10M

Fl.G.3s

Fl.G.5s
R
Fl.R.3s

Work in
Progress

Kongedybet

Fl.G.3s
G
Fl.R.3s
R

Flakfortet

Hollænderbybet

Q(6)+LFl.15s
YB

Buoyed channel

Depths in Metres

**KØBENHAVN AND
APPROACHES**

Kastrup
Strandpark(2₅m)

Buoyed channel

Kastrup(2m)

12°40′E

Buoyed channel

Iso.2s
RW

Nordre-Røse
Oc(2)WRG.6s
17-13M

34′   35′   36′   37′   38′   39′   41   42′   43′

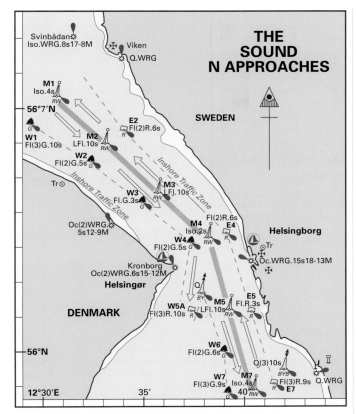

On the Swedish side of the Sound at Helsingborg opposite Helsingør there is a marina ½M N of main hbr. 240 berths and usual facilities.

☏ Marina +45 2531 1080
www.helsingor-havne.
helsingor.dk

KØBENHAVN

Charts BA 902;
Dk 131, 132, 133, 134

Approach København is on Kongedybet, the W branch of the Øresund S of the Middelgrund island. All marinas are approached from this fairway. Traffic passing N or S uses Hollænderdybet, the E fairway.

Berthing There are numerous marinas in the København area. Those nearest the centre are the most expensive and most crowded. There is an excellent public transport system and peripheral marinas may be more peaceful.

To the N lie four marinas: Skovshoved, Tuborg, Hellerup and Svanemølle. In strong N winds it is prudent to avoid the shoal patch N of the hbr complex.

Skovshoved is an artificial basin 3M N of Tuborg. Entrance between F.G and F.R Lts. There is a detached breakwater sheltering the entrance with a Fl.R Lt at the N end and a Fl.G Lt at the S end. All facilities incl fuel. Bus to København. An expansion of the hbr is planned for 2014.

Hellerup is a small marina, ½M N of Tuborg. It is approached from the E along a short channel with unlit buoys. Fl.G.3s Lt on mole. The marina has a depth of 2·2m.

Tuborg Havn Home of Royal Danish Yacht Club (KDY). Approach from SE passing first between off-lying breakwaters with R/G Lts then passing WSW between mole heads. Visitors' berth to port in outer basin.

Svanemølle ½M S of Tuborg is approached on Iso.R.2s & 4s Ldg Lts 208° along a buoyed channel starting at the E card buoy 5ca E of Tuborg. It is the home port of three sailing clubs and has about 1100 berths, bow to pontoon, long stern ropes to piles, the best facilities can found on the pontoons to stb. Vacant spaces are marked with a green ticket usually stating when the owner will be back. Diesel, Shops, launderette, banks and the metro station approximately 1km. About 4km to the city centre.

Four berthing possibilities are situated in the inner harbour, S and W of the Trekroner fort. Yachts must use the S entrance called Lynetteløbet which is buoyed and has a sectored light on the S end of the breakwater. (The N entrance is reserved for commercial shipping.

Langelinie Marina is set in parks and gardens near the Little Mermaid Statue (Den lille Havfrue). It is small; berth with bows to pontoon, stern to buoy. In high season arrival by noon is advised to have a chance of a place. 1km to city centre. The chart agent Iver Weilbach & co is near here at Toldbodgate 35.

Hotel Admiralen is for large yachts. It is exposed to wash from shipping.

Nyhavn is a canal in city centre, surrounded by restaurants and buzzing with life day and night. Visiting yachts berth outside lifting bridge. Exposed to wash from shipping hence smaller vessels tend to moor elsewhere. Expect the usual noise that goes with an inner city berth.

Christianshavns Kanal Entrance lies opposite Nyhavn. It is picturesque but crowded and with limited facilities. Three pedestrian bridges, all opening, were under construction in 2013.

Several marinas lie to the S and E of the city:

Margreteholm is situated on the N point of the island of Amager and is approached from the main shipping channel near the conspic power station. This large quiet marina is the home port of Lynetten sailing club and lies 3M from the city centre on a bus route. Access to city centre also with shuttle boat 10 minutes' walk from marina (shuttle boat in operation until bridge completed). All facilities and large chandlery.

Flakfortet is an artificial island fort 4M E of the hbr entrance. It has an encircling breakwater and a restaurant. Quiet, good shelter and usually plenty of room.

Dragør located SE on the island of Amager, this is a charming town with frequent buses to Copenhagen. Moor in old fishing hbr (north) or new marina (south). The old ferry hbr between these is not open for yachts.

☏ HM Skovshoved +45 3964 1388 (1100–1200)
Hellerup tel as for Skovshoved
Tuborg +45 2013 3787
Svanemøllen +45 3920 2221
Langelinie +45 3526 2338
Margreteholm +45 3257 5778
Flakfortet +45 3296 0800
Dragør +45 32891570

www.skovshovedhavn.dk
www.helleruphavn.dk
www.kdy.dk
www.langeliniehavn.dk
www.smhavn.dk
www.lynetten.dk
www.flakfortet.dk
www.dragoerhavn.dk

RØDVIG

see Route 6c

SWEDISH PORTS IN THE ØRESUND

VEN

Charts S 922

This small island 20M N of København is Swedish and the former home of the astronomer Tyco Brahe (d.1597). Pretty island with three hbrs:

Kyrkbacken on W side of island is principal yacht hbr. Good protection but reports of only 2m in approaches, 2·5m in hbr. Pile mooring or stern anchor, if mooring alongside expect large raft-ups.

Bäckviken on E shore is ferry hbr and exposed to wash from commercial shipping passing close to hbr. Pile moorings.

Norreborg on N shore small hbr with limited room to maneuver inside mole, smaller boats may find vacant berth. Pile or alongside berthing.

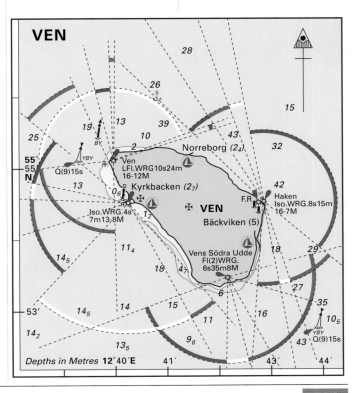

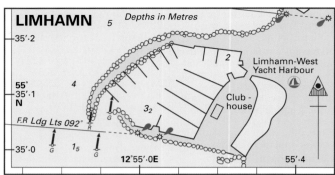

LIMHAMN

Depths in Metres

LAGUNEN YACHT HARBOUR

Depths in Metres

Facilities Diesel in Kyrkbacken, restaurants at Kyrkbackan and Bäckviken. Shops and Tyco Brahe museum in village on middle of island.

☎ HM Bäckviken +46 (0) 418 721 12; Kyrkbacken +46 (0) 418 72400; www.kyrkbacken.se

LIMHAMN
Charts S921, 8141

A large yacht hbr 3M SW of Malmö harbour and just S of the main Limhamn harbour. Another marina, Lagunen, to the N (*see plan*).

Approach From NW to avoid shoal S of hbr entrance which is marked by two G buoys. The entrance faces S. Visitors' berth on pontoon F. Vacant berths are also indicated by G card.

Facilities Fuel both hbrs, pump-out station and chandlery in S hbr (Limhamn). 3km to Malmö city centre with all facilities of a big city.

☎ HM +46 (0) 4015 2024
www.smabatshamnen.nu
www.lagunen.nu

FALSTERBOKANALEN
Charts S921

On passage from Øresund to the Baltic proper this route avoids the Falsterborev TSS

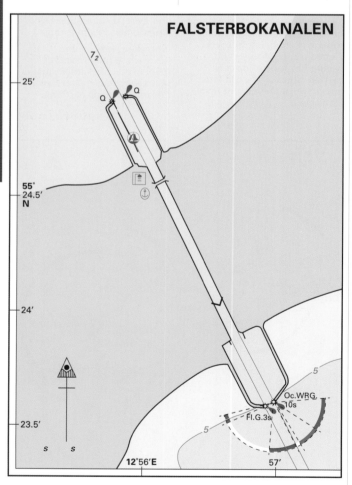

FALSTERBOKANALEN

roundabout. The canal sees little commercial traffic. Min depth 4m. Bridge opens every hour on the hour 0600–2200 during summer, except 0800 and 1700. Lock usually open.

Approach From N or S along buoyed and lit channel.

Berthing At berths with green tags at boatclub N of bridge.

Facilities Diesel, holding tank pump-out. Bicycles available.

☎ /**VHF** (bridge) +46 (0) 104785660; VHF 11 (call *Falsterbokanalen*) www.falsterbokanalen.se

ROUTE 7 WEST BALTIC
Charts BA 2106, 2113, 2117, 2365, 2360; G30, 35

This route leads from the E end of the Nord-Ostsee-Kanal S of the Danish islands and between Germany and Sweden to the southern parts of the Baltic Sea. The routes through the Lillebælt, Storebælt and Øresund join the northern side of the route.

Construction of a tunnel between Lolland in Denmark and Fehmarn in Germany is expected to begin in 2015, the Fehmarn Belt Fixed Link.

Passage lights	BA No
Kiel	1215
Iso.WRG.6s29m17-13M	
Horn Mo(KI)30s (−·−/··)	
Bülk	1216
Fl.WRG.3s29m14-10M	
Friedrichsort	1230
Iso.WRG.4s32m7–5M+aux Lts	
Flügge (Fehmarn)	1288.1
F.37m25M+Oc(4)20s38m17M	
Westermarkelsdorf	1280
LFl.WR.10s16m18/14M	
Marienleuchte	1284
Fl(4)WR.15s40m22/18M	
Staberhuk	1286
Oc(2)WG.16s25m18/14M	
Buk	1400
LFl(4)WR.45s95m24/20M	
Warnemünde	1404
Fl(3+1)24s34m20M	
Darsser Ort	1440
Fl(2+4)22s33m23M	

GERMAN PORTS IN THE W BALTIC

STICKENHÖRN
see Route 2b

SCHILKSEE – OLYMPIAHAFEN
Charts G 33

This large marina lies 4M N of Holtenau on the W side of the Kieler Förde. The Kieler Woche regatta takes place usually last full week of June, during which participating yachts have priority to berths.

Approach The approach is marked by the N card buoy Grasberg and the S card buoy Kleverberg–S. From between these buoys steer E towards marina. Lt on NE corner of the breakwater Oc.WRG.6s8–5M. All facilities. There is also a small marina close N of Schilksee at Strande.

☎ +49 (0) 431 26048421/22
Mobile +49 (0) 172 802 43 52
www.sporthafen-kiel.de

HEILIGENHAFEN
Charts G43

Lies 30M E of Kiel on the mainland opposite Fehmarn. W of Heiligenhafen there are firing ranges extending up to 7M offshore. Firing announced VHF 16/11. Usually no activity during main holiday season June 20–August 20, details available from local HMs.

Approach The area has extensive shoals. The Heiligenhafen-O E card Lt buoy marks the NE extremity of these. From this buoy steer towards the Heiligenhafen LtHo before entering buoyed channel with two sets of Ldg Lts.

Berthing Heiligenhafen marina is one of the largest in W Baltic with nearly 1,000 spaces. Many charter companies are based here. YC SE of fishing hbr offers a more intimate atmosphere when berths available.

Facilities Diesel in marina (no loose cans allowed due to Nature Reserve restrictions). Chandlery, sailmaker,

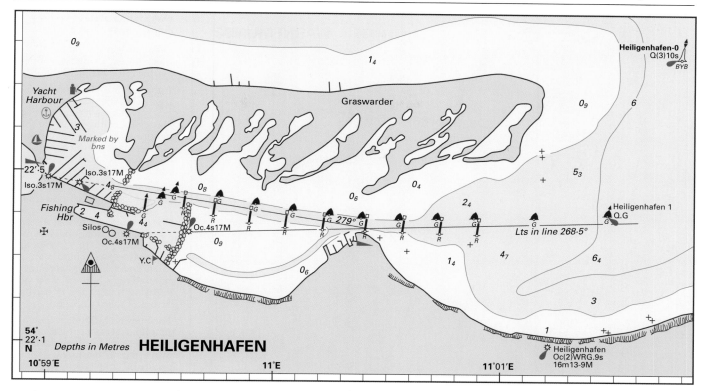

HEILIGENHAFEN

mechanical repairs. Usual range of shopping.

☎ HM +49 (0) 43 6250 3424
www.marina-heiligenhafen.de
www.svh-ssch.de

BURGTIEFE
Charts G 31

Located S on Fehmarn, 3M E of the 22m bridge. Fehmarn is a popular holiday resort and there are several smaller marinas. Burgtiefe is a large well protected marina that will usually have vacant berths even during high season. Neighbour to a major tourist resort, but 2km to Burg which is an interesting town with buildings dating back to 13th century.

Approach Approach from SE, three conspic large hotel buildings on Fehmarn E of buoyed channel. Sectored Lt E mole, Burgstaaken Oc(3)WR.12s, and W of Burgtiefe peninsula, Burger See Iso.WRG.4s. Buoyed channel divides at Burgtiefe buoys 1(G) and 2(GRG), turn 90° stb between these for Burgtiefe marina.

Berthing Green tag indicates vacant berth, pile moorings. Large yachts moor alongside concrete wave breakers to E.

Facilities Fuel, chandlery, 20-ton boat lift. Several restaurants and bars. Bicycles for hire. Indoor water sports centre. Beach (access small fee). Basic groceries, buses to Burg with wide range of shopping. Railway station in Burg. Burgstaake hbr ½M NW has boatyard with repair facilities and winter storage.

☎ HM +49 (0) 4371 5063 60.

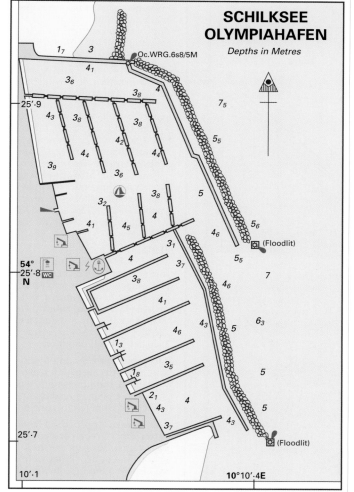

SCHILKSEE OLYMPIAHAFEN

Depths in Metres

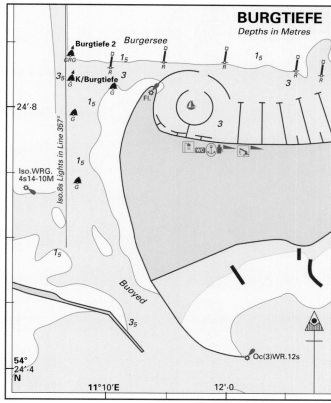

BURGTIEFE

Depths in Metres

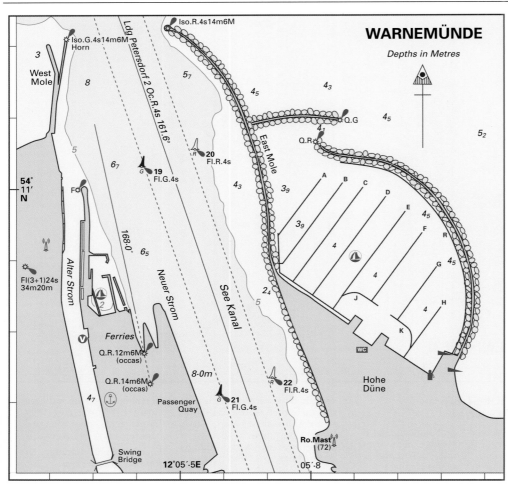

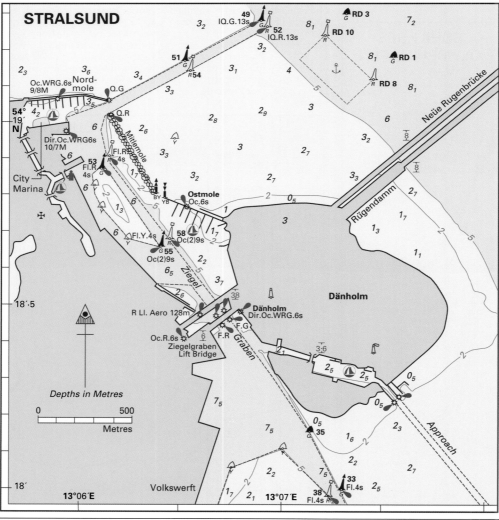

WARNEMÜNDE
Charts G1671, 1672 (plan)

Old seaside resort on the Mecklingburger Bucht, with new la marina (Hohe Düne) E of old port.

Approach For Hohe Düne approac from NE. Note that on approach fr N the W mole overlaps E mole, wh may cause confusion in darkness w lights appear wrong way around. F Warnemünde between mole heads a charted, keeping clear of commercia traffic to Rostock.

Berthing Hohe Düne usually has ma places for visitors, also in season. Fo or shuttle boat to Warnemünde. In Warnemünde some visitors' berths Alter Strom (alongside, pile moorin SE in canal) and in YC, E of inner mole. Alter Strom busy with tourist boats and fishing vessels but you ar moored right in front of the old captains' houses. Outer berths in A Strom exposed to N'lies.

Facilities Höhe Düne is a high qual marina development with modern facilities, in Alte Strum facilities at Warnemünde has many restaurants and bars, large beach. Ferries to Gedser and Trelleborg, Rly to Rost

☎ Marina Hohe Düne +49 (0) 381 5040 8000
www.yachthafen-hohe-duene.de
www.wscev.de

STRALSUND
Charts G 1621, 1622

On passage from Warnemünde the of Darsser Ort hbr may be used in emergencies. A rescue vessel is stationed here. While attempts are made to maintain depths to 1·8m th approach to Darsser Ort is suscepti to silting and the hbr is at times clo (hbr closed 2012 and 2013.)

Approach From W and N from Gel safe water buoy, following buoyed channel W of Hiddensee. In settled weather part of the channel can be b passed by following white sector of Gellen LtHo, depth 3m. Boats on passage from N or E often use the buoyed channel E of Hiddensee, wh Vitte is a useful hbr before further passage up the Strelasund. Approac from S passing under opening bridg Ziegelgraben brücke (opening times yachts: 0520; 0820; 1220; 1720 and 2130 changes posted at YC website (see below).

Berthing
NordMole (Citymarina) fingerberth and some alongside berths, visitors E most pontoons as sign posted. Ne city centre hence popular and often crowded. Docks by tallship *Gorch Foch* may be used after agreement v HM. A few berths also inside lifting bridge by diesel pump.

Ost mole Large marina that often h vacant berths even high season. Rat austere surroundings but friendly cl atmosphere. Small restaurant, sailmaker. 3km to city centre.

Dänholmen Approached from SE (after Ziegelgraben bridge on passa eastwards). Visitors' berths at sailin school and at YC. Peaceful hbr in scenic surroundings. Pub in YC. 3k to city centre.

Facilities Wide range of companies offering services to yachts including several small chandleries and a couple of sailmakers. Many sites of historic interest. The Altstadt (old town) is a UNESCO World Heritage Site.

☎ Citymarina
+49 (0) 3831 444 978
YC +49 (0) 3831 297 300
www.ycstr.de

DANISH AND SWEDISH PORTS IN THE W BALTIC

Passage lights	BA No
Keldsnor	1706
Fl(2)15s39m17M+Oc.WRG.5s	
Møn	2142
Fl(4)30s25m21M	
Falsterborev	2417
Fl(4)WR.12s29m14/12M	
Kullagrund	2445
Iso.WRG.4s18m16-12M	

BAGENKOP

see Route 6a

GEDSER

Charts D 197

This is a useful passage hbr. It is situated on the S tip of the Danish island of Falster and has a tall LtHo 26m.

Approach The main hbr is for the ferry to Rostock/Warnemünde in

Germany and yachts are not welcome there. The marina lies 1M NW along a narrow buoyed channel skirting the coast which starts near the entrance to the main hbr. Depth 2·5–3m. It is sheltered from the E but is rather exposed from the W being protected only by reefs and a hbr wall. Usual marina facilities including fuel but somewhat remote.

☎ HM +45 5417 9245.

YSTAD

Charts BA 2360 (plan); S 839

Hbr on the S Swedish coast in the NW corner of the outer harbour. The ferry port to Bornholm and Poland and a commercial hbr are nearby. There are some old houses and a 13th-century monastery.

Approach From the offshore R Lt buoy Fl(2)R.6s the Ldg Lts F.R 019° lead to the yacht hbr.

Berthing Visitors moor at most W'ly pontoon or at vacant berth as indicated by HM. Depth 2–4m. Visitors' pontoon can be uncomfortable in strong S winds, but protection has improved with recent extension of mole. Shops and chandlery near hbr. Wi-Fi.

☎ HM +46 (0) 702 55 29 32
www.ystad.se (links Fritid – Småbåtshamnar – Ystads marina).

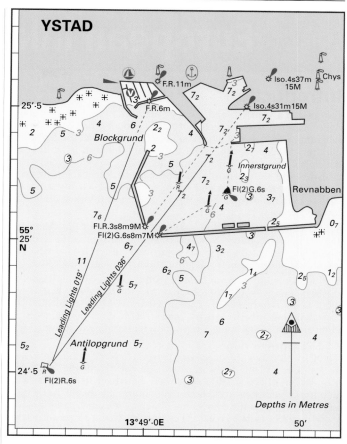

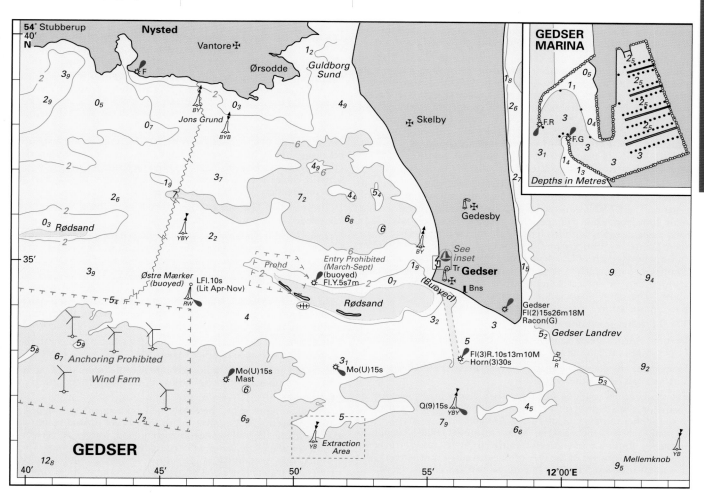

European Inland Waterways

Introduction

Europe has a vigorous and growing network of inland waterways, which can easily be entered through Germany, the Netherlands, Belgium or France and which connects to the Baltic, the Black Sea and the Mediterranean. Whilst it was built and is still being developed primarily for commercial traffic, it offers interesting cruising into northern, middle and eastern Europe for pleasure craft. The scale of locks and other works is sufficiently generous for use by a majority of both motor cruisers and sailing craft with lowered masts.

Whilst detailed information is beyond the scope of this Almanac, the following country by country notes introduce the cruising potential, ports of entry, licensing and other formalities and sources of information for the four countries mentioned above.

For other countries, from Ireland to the west, as far as Russia to the east, a useful source of information is the *European Waterways Map and Directory* by David Edwards-May, published by Euromapping (distributed by Imray). This contains data on 30 countries, including some information on standing mast routes.

CEVNI and other rules

The CEVNI (*Code Européen des Voies de la Navigation Intérieure*) Rules are an inland waterway equivalent of the Collision Regulations (IRPCS).They are closely based on IRPCS, but with important additions to reflect that almost all inland navigation takes place within the constraints of narrow channels, and involves close quarters manoeuvring. They also provide a range of marks, signs and signals intended to be understood internationally.

In most of Europe, it is a requirement that UK helmsmen navigating inland waterways should hold an International Certificate of Competence (ICC) with a CEVNI rules endorsement. In the UK, tests on the CEVNI rules are administered by the RYA, and may be taken as written tests at many RYA approved sailing schools, with a number now offering an option to take the test online. The ICC so issued states that it is in accordance with the relevant (United Nations) resolution on Inland Water Transport.

A copy of the CEVNI Rules should be carried on board. The full rules as published by the UN run to over 190 pages, and can be purchased via the Stationery Office or downloaded from the UN publications website. They contain much material that is irrelevant to pleasure craft, but there are several competent summaries of that which is relevant, published as *The RYA Book of European Waterways Regulations (the CEVNI Rules explained)* by Tam Murrell, 2004, *Euroregs for Inland Waterways* by Marion Martin, 3rd edition 2008 from Adlard Coles Nautical, and *RYA CEVNI Handbook* by Roy Gibson, 2011.

Slowly European countries are modifying their rules and signs to comply with CEVNI, although some regional variations still remain. The CEVNI equivalent of Rule 9, requiring craft of less than 20m length not to impede the passage of vessels which can only navigate safely within a narrow channel is one instance where there are local variations, and in some countries the corresponding rule applies to craft of less than 15m. On some waterways in some countries, particularly Germany, larger craft used for pleasure cruising may be subject to more stringent control than indicated above. The Barge Association – formerly the (UK based) Dutch Barge Association – is aware of the latest position.

The following are important aspects of CEVNI.

Do not obstruct the passage of commercial vessels, whether freight or passenger-carrying at any time.

Keep to the stb side of the channel unless directed by signs or other ship's signals to do otherwise.

Especially on rivers, look out for vessels displaying a blue flag or board on the stb side of the wheelhouse. This indicates that the vessel wishes to pass you stb to stb. At night or in poor visibility a flashing white light has the same meaning. Blue flagging is normally (but not exclusively) initiated by a vessel travelling upstream, to stay out of the way of one travelling downstream, but it may also be used to stay out of, or to take advantage of, the current, or to provide a better alignment on the approach to a quay, a bend, or a bridge or similar obstruction of the channel.

The navigable span of a fixed bridge is normally indicated by a yellow diamond (and a fixed yellow light at night). A single diamond/light indicates that the passage in both directions through the arch is permitted: if there are two diamonds/lights, then traffic in the opposite direction through the arch is not permitted.

Two red and white diamond shapes on a bridge span indicate an obligation to pass between them (possibly to avoid underwater obstructions) and two green and white diamond shapes indicate a recommendation to pass between them.

Light signals at locks and moveable bridges are increasingly standardised. A single R Lt means wait, a R Lt above a G Lt means prepare to proceed, and a single or double G means proceed. Two R Lts means no passage possible. (On smaller waterways, all lights may well be extinguished outside the scheduled operating hours of the lock or bridge.)

Vessels designed to transport dangerous cargoes display blue downward pointing cones (fixed blue lights at night). In France, some vessels still display an earlier alternative of red lights and cones, although most now comply with the blue of CEVNI. There may be one, two or three depending on the degree of hazard. Keep well clear and note that you may not be permitted to share locks with such vessels, especially when they are laden.

Whilst sound signals are not greatly used in inland navigation, when they are, a quick understanding is essential. CEVNI sound signals are generally the same as those of IRPCS, but there are additional signals for use when approaching junctions, and the CEVNI signals for acknowledging intention to overtake differ from those of IRPCS.

Code flag A, 'I have a diver down' is quite commonly used on inland waterways: stay well clear and proceed dead slow.

Hints and Tips for Inland Cruising

Especially on the larger waterways, and the great rivers (Rhine, Schelde, Rhône, Seine etc) keep a good all-round lookout; powerful 'pusher' tugs, propelling four or more barges each of up to 4,000 tonnes are the equivalent of a ship of up to 18,000 tonnes and need to be treated with extreme caution. Always keep well clear and never attempt to race them to a lock or through a bridge.

Following larger vessels is a good idea as you may well be able to use lock operations and bridge openings that are timed for their benefit, but note that they will create less wash than a smaller boat for the same speed, so you may not be able to keep up without creating excessive wash.

On arrival at a lock check astern befor entering. Unless instructed otherwise by the lock-keeper, always enter after larger commercial craft. It may not be possible to decide which side to moor until you actually enter the lock, so make sure that you have adequate length lines and fenders for both sides of your boat.

Do not make fast to another vessel in a lock without the knowledge and approval of its skipper.

Occasionally (and contrary to regulations) barges hold their position in locks by motoring against a single spring, in which case stay as far astern of them as you can to minimise the effect of their wash.

In locks secure lines as soon as possible and keep them secure until after the turbulence caused by departing ships has subsided. If you are secure enough to switch your engine off in a lock, do so – it is quieter, cleaner and cheaper, and especially in regions where there may be numbers of smaller craft sharing the lock, it may well be obligatory.

Towed dinghies in a lock can be a source of embarrassment to their owner and a nuisance to other vessels.

On inland waterways radio communications should be at low power, and unless otherwise indicated, intership communications use Channel 10.

In 2000, an agreement (the RAINWAT agreement) was signed in Basel, whereby 16 countries with significant inland waterway traffic agreed that all vessels in their inland waterway networks would communicate using ATIS equipped radio telephones. These automatically send out a unique vessel identifying number as part of every transmission. This improves communications on waterways such as the Rhine and Danube, which are used by vessels of many different countries, since shore based ATIS

Inland Waterways of Germany

— Large scale waterway(class IV or larger)
— Waterway for 300t barges(class I or II)
— Waterway for small barges(class 0) or Light Craft

receivers can automatically recognise the identity and nationality of the transmitting vessel.

The time scale for implementation of this was left in the hands of the national navigation authorities, and most of them had made it compulsory by January 2013.

In April 2012, an updated RAINWAT agreement was signed and anyone using ATIS capable equipment should now carry a copy of this agreement on board.

It may be downloaded, in Dutch, English, French or German from the website of the BIPT, a Belgian based organisation that administers the system, and which maintains the international data base of vessels. A comprehensive explanation of ATIS, RAINWAT and the UK licensing procedures that allow UK vessels to comply is available on the Ofcom website.

DSC activated radios must not be used on European Inland Waterways, and ATIS must not be used within 14 miles of the coastline of the UK, the Isle of Man and the Channel Islands.

Clearly anyone planning to replace or supplement their VHF radiotelephone would be prudent to make sure that their new equipment is ATIS capable, and ideally, switchable between DSC and ATIS modes.

When navigating in longer tidal estuaries, such as the Scheldte in Belgium, note that the tidal predictions from an almanac, which are necessarily based on average river flow figures, become increasingly unreliable as one moves further upstream. Strong river flows increase the duration of the ebb and delay the time of LW, and thereby reduce the duration of the flood.

GERMANY

Cruising potential As well as being accessible from the North Sea and the Baltic, German Inland Waterways interconnect to those of Poland, the Czech Republic, Austria, Switzerland, France and the Netherlands.

From the North Sea, the major routes for inland entry are via the Ems, Weser and Elbe estuaries. Shallower draught craft can also cruise several smaller northern canals with entry via Emden or Wilhelmshaven.

From the Baltic, as well as the Nordostsee Kanal (Kiel Canal) and the smaller linked Eider and Gieselaukanal to Tönning, there is a possibility of entry from the sea to the Elbe-Lübeck Kanal at Travemünde, which takes one south to the Elbe.

The mast-up entry to Emden by way of the Friesland Canal is noted in the 'Approaches to the Baltic' section. There are two further connections from the Netherlands to Germany, the minor Haren-Rütenbrock Kanal in the north with a limited depth of 1·5m, and the lower Rhine south east of Arnhem.

The Moselle and its tributary, the Saar, link the French canals to German routes at Schengen and Saarguemines. For about 38km the Moselle is bounded by Luxembourg to the northwest, and Germany to the southeast.

The Rhine forms the boundary between France and Germany for about 184km of its navigable length and between Switzerland and Germany for a further 20km.

Northeastern links are provided by the Elbe which flows down through Prague in the Czech Republic (albeit with variable and limited depth) and the Oder-Spree Canal which runs east from Berlin to join the R Oder in western Poland which then flows north to enter the Baltic at Szczecin (Stettin). Southeast, the Main-Donau Canal links the Rhine to the Danube, and provides a route into Austria, Hungary and eventually to the Black Sea between Romania and Bulgaria.

The key north–south route is of course the Rhine, which in spite of carrying more freight than any road or railway in Europe, offers spectacular scenery and fascinating cruising. Since most of it is free flowing river, downstream cruising is much easier than upstream, and a useful strategy is to travel southeast through the French canals, and enter the Rhine at Strasbourg, upstream of its most dramatic stretch.

Berlin and its surroundings are a diverse and fascinating cruising ground, with the River Spree running right through the historic city centre past the Reichstag and close to the Brandenburg Gate. The former East Germany maintained and extended its canal network, and the Mecklenburg area northeast of Berlin with several hundred km of navigable waterways (which also links to the Elbe upstream of Hamburg) is one of several areas where facilities for cruising are steadily being improved.

Formalities Save for a number of smaller waterways, the German system is administered by regional water and shipping authorities and no licence or other fees are levied on visiting foreign craft. No charges are made when locks are shared with commercial craft, but pleasure craft (universally referred to as 'sportboats' in Germany) may be required to pay for the exclusive use of large locks, such as those on the Moselle. Unlike the Netherlands, most yacht harbours are either privately owned or run by boat clubs. These are normally very welcoming, but since they are required to contribute to the costs of maintaining navigation, they will charge (usually modestly) for moorings.

Particularly on the busier rivers and canals, expect checks by Water Police, which may include ship's and crew's papers, VHF licence. Sobriety of helmsman and active crew is also taken seriously. The permissible blood alcohol level for Rhine navigation is lower than the permissible level for car drivers. Checks may also be made on the usual safety related equipment, lifejackets, lifebuoys, fire extinguishers, anchor and first aid kit.

See the previous note towards the end of *Hints and Tips for Inland Cruising* about the requirement for VHF radiotelephone equipment to be ATIS capable as from January 2013.

Sources of information In English, a good general account of the whole network is given by Barry Sheffield in *Inland Waterways of Germany* published by Imray. *Through the German Waterways* by Philip Bristow, published by Adlard Coles Nautical provides less comprehensive coverage.

Two German Publishers, DSV-Verlag and Edition Maritim, both of Hamburg, publish chart-guides in book form, suitable for navigation. The DSV-Verlag publications (of which 20 cover the whole country) are the more detailed, and generally show all buoyage, as well as training walls and similar hazards. Edition Maritim provide less map detail but do show the points at which large craft may cross to the left side of the channel, to stay out of the current, or to take advantage of it, or to provide a better line of approach to a bridge, a bend or other hazard.

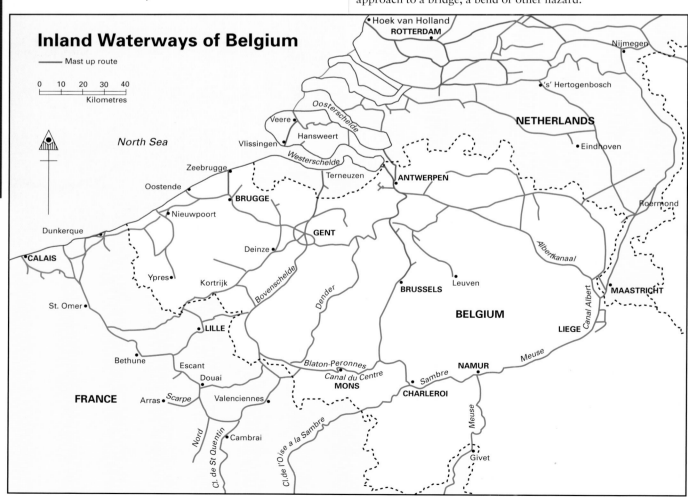

A third publisher, Nautische Veröffentlichung of Arnis, publishes inland cruising guides which cover almost all the area east of Hamburg and north from Berlin, as well as guides to Poland.

A fourth, Verlag Rheinschiffahrt, of Bad Soden also produces guides, primarily to the Rhein and its tributaries.

THE NETHERLANDS

Cruising potential The fixed mast routes are described in the Netherlands section, but there is also a vast network of navigable waterways ranging from major rivers capable of accommodating 2,000-tonne barges, right down to navigable drainage channels barely wide enough to row a dinghy.

In some parts of the country, older mobile bridges on small waterways have been replaced by fixed bridges with headroom of 2·5m, so craft with low air draught have a greater choice of route.

Of the major seaports of the Netherlands, only Scheveningen does not connect into the inland waterway system.

There are three links between the Dutch and German canal systems, and several others to Belgium, from which the French canals and eventually the Mediterranean can be reached.

Formalities Most of the network is open to navigation without licences or formality.

Especially on the busier routes which carry large commercial vessels, police checks may be carried out, as described above for Germany.

In some rural areas, small waterways, and areas of water opening off rivers may be designated as nature reserves from which powered craft are excluded. These restrictions are usually well signed, and shown on the *Waterkaarten* and should of course be respected.

Smoothing the way – the Dutch canal system All opening bridges and locks display red and green lights. Double red means the service is closed, either for lunch or the night, or during the rush hour. Single red means the service is ready: combined with a green indicates it will operate imminently and you should be prepared to move through smartly. Green is the go. If a bridge or lock opens and no green is seen, hold back – a commercial vessel may be given priority by radio. Public address loudspeaker announcements will be more valuable to you if you show clearly your national ensign on approaching.

All bridge and lock facilities have a VHF channel: calling the name of the lock or bridge and asking for the next opening will usually provide the guidance you seek. Using the Dutch for 'please' encourages even better responses – phonetically *Als tu blieft* often shortened to AUB on signs. Thank you – *Dank U Vell* – rounds off communications with a nice touch! Most facilities will respond in English.

Many bridges these days are remotely operated: positioning your craft within easy view of the surveillance cameras will produce a faster response when facing a red. Alert the controller to your presence by calling on the posted VHF channel the name of the bridge and AUB eg. "Ruck Brug, Ruck Brug, Als tu Blieft." Within a few minutes the red over green lights will appear and you can line up for clearance. In rural areas a call button is sometimes mounted on a post near the bridge and must be used to initiate the service.

Railway bridges (Spoorbrug) are subject to strict schedules, and may open only three to four times a day, and briefly at that. Close attention to opening times can save hours of waiting. Traffic congregates at these critical openings, so be prepared and move through swiftly or risk the bridge closing in your face.

Waiting before locks and bridges is often encountered at the height of the season. Be prepared with copious fenders on both sides and raft as directed, moving ahead slowly into the lock. Getting one aft or centre mooring line ashore quickly, then fine tuning your position, makes for a more orderly landing.

Major facilities operate 24/7 during the summer months, many others between 0800–2000. In winter much of the non-commercial waterway network closes to pleasure craft or has heavily restricted hours of service – see notices on each facility for up to date details.

Many Dutch marinas moor bow-to in 'boxes', employing poles to secure the aft cleats. Often these poles are set for 3·5m beam, or even less. So, on allocation of a berth, it pays to make your beam known to avoid an untenable berth. And on berthing, have an aft mooring line ready to drop over the upwind pole on entry.

Sources of information A majority of the system is covered by a series of *Waterkaarten* maps published by the ANWB and usually revised every two years. These show all major navigation features, and also useful detail relating to the surrounding landscape. Most importantly, they show water depths and heights of fixed bridges. Whilst they are in Dutch, with no multilingual glossary, the style and quality of the graphics used makes them easy to understand.

Unfortunately, the *Waterkaarten* series does not cover much of the south and east of the country. In some such areas local maps may be available from the tourist offices.

The most comprehensive information available is contained in of the *ANWB Wateralmanak 2* which gives water depths, bridge heights, moveable bridge and lock operating times, hbr facilities and much more. It is worth noting that although the *Wateralmanak* gives depths and heights in metres, the *Waterkaarten* maps use decimetres (dm).

Inland Waterways of the Netherlands by Louise Busby and David Broad, Imrays 2007, is a valuable guide to routes with 3·5m air draught.

BELGIUM

Cruising potential From seaward, the Belgian waterway network can be entered at Nieuwpoort, Zeebrugge, and Oostende. The Scheldte estuary permits access at Terneuzen and Antwerp, and upstream of Antwerp the Scheldte remains tidal as far as Gent. Brugge is accessible from Zeebrugge with a fixed mast and similarly Brussels can be reached by way of the Brussels Maritime Canal which leaves the Scheldte near Rupelmonde and has lifting bridges providing 30m headroom.

With few exceptions, the network is heavily used by commercial craft, and so water depth is rarely an issue. The Albert Canal, running east from Antwerp across the Dutch border to join the Maas near Maastricht is probably the busiest, with lock chambers tripled to handle the volume of 2,000-tonne barges. However, there are quieter and more pleasant alternative routes.

In the south, five Belgian canals link into the French system. Whilst these are on a smaller scale (300-tonne), several of them still handle significant freight, including large tonnages of French grain shipped to the Belgian breweries in summer and autumn. The most westerly link connects to Dunkerque, the most easterly to the Meuse.

Formalities Boats navigating the Belgian waterways must be licensed. Unfortunately, the Flemish and Walloon regions of the country have different requirements. Roughly speaking, Flanders is the part of the country north of about 50°45′N, (which is just south of Brussels conurbation,) and Wallonia is the remainder.

In Flanders, a licence disc is purchased which must be displayed on the boat. The charge, usually payable at the first lock or lifting bridge, depends on the duration of the licence, boat size and its maximum speed. Fortunately, even for a large boat, a 12 month licence is unlikely to cost more than about €130.

In Wallonia, there is no longer any charge for the use of the system, but it is still necessary to declare the route that you plan to take and be issued with a permit. It is possible to reduce the frequency with which you will need to present this permit, by obtaining a MET Number from one of the lock offices that is described as a *Bureau de Perception*, which are usually at the beginning or end of a waterway, or at a junction. You can quote this number to the lock by VHF, avoiding the need to physically present the permit.

The requirement for vessels underway to fly a red flag with a white rectangle to indicate intention to pass through locks was abolished in 2007, although many local vessels still fly such a flag.

There are normally no customs checks when crossing between Belgium and its neighbours, except in the Schelde Estuary, where you might have arrived from seaward rather than another Schengen country.

Since 2005 it has been illegal for yachts to use untaxed (red) diesel in Belgium. Since 2008 the UK has permitted yachts to refuel with red diesel in UK harbours and marinas on condition that they paid duty on it, or at least that fraction of the diesel that was used for propulsion.

The Belgian authorities contend that even if duty is paid in this way, the use of red diesel remains illegal in Belgium, and there have been instances of checks on UK craft by the Belgian authorities, resulting in financial penalties being imposed of their

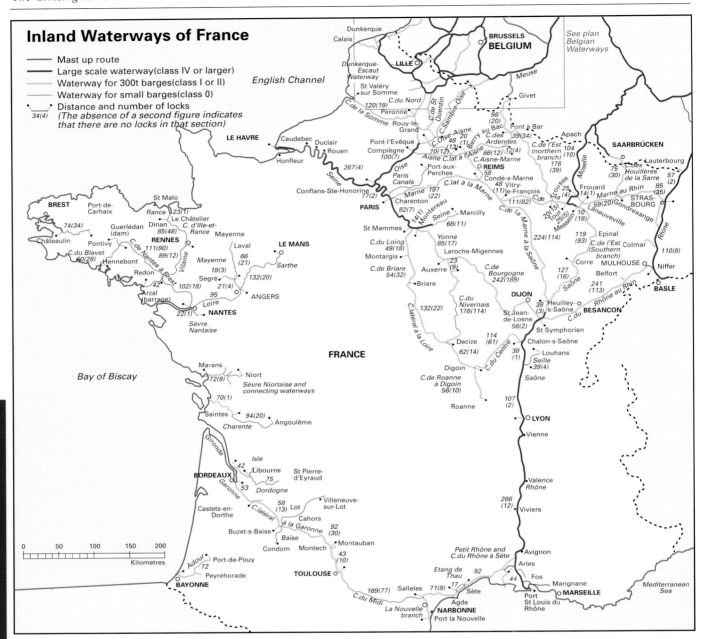

owners. Both Belgium and the UK have complained about each other's interpretation of the European law. Until such time as this dispute is resolved, you are advised not to cruise in Belgium with any significant level of red diesel in your tanks.

Also note that in Belgium there are only a limited number of waterside refuelling points that offer white duty paid diesel. (These include Antwerp, Antoing, Bocholt, Brussels, Comines, Dijksmuide, Givet, Liège, Namur and Nieuwpoort.)

Sources of information

Inland Waterways of Belgium by Jacqueline Jones, published by Imray in 2006 is an excellent and very comprehensive guide to the Belgian network.

Cruising the Inland Waterways of France and Belgium published by the Cruising Association (CA) in 2013, contains a wealth of information not published elsewhere on boatyards, moorings and other facilities.

The Dutch *ANWB Wateralmanak* contains a chapter with information about the Belgian waterways, in the same format as the Dutch data noted above.

Fluviacarte No. 23, Belgium, useful map published by Editions Fluviale, but out of print at December 2012.

FRANCE

Cruising potential For more detailed information than this brief summary, see the CA publication *Cruising the Inland Waterways of France and Belgium* and the other sources of information given below.

From a yachtsman's point of view, France has a twofold attraction, offering routes between sea cruising areas, and as an interesting cruising area in its own right.

From seawards, the northern and central parts of the network can be entered from Dunkerque, Gravelines, Calais, the Somme estuary or by way of the Seine estuary.

All inland routes south converge on the Saône, and in turn the Rhône, which enters the Mediterranean at Port St Louis, some 40km west of Marseille.

The waterways of Brittany, which do not connect to the main routes, offer interesting cruising for smaller craft, however restricted headroom (2·5m) and water depth (between 1·2m and 1·0m or less at times of drought) prevent most seagoing craft from using them.

In the southwest, the Midi route provides a link from Atlantic to Mediterranean, albeit with limited depth.

The canal links between France and Belgium to the north, and Germany to the east have already been noted; crossing these borders involves no more formality than a change of courtesy ensign.

Formalities The main navigable waterways in France are under the management of Voies Navigables de France, (VNF), who issue licenses and a *vignette*, that must be displayed on the boat. From January 2013 charges are based on the length of the boat (and no longer take into account its beam) and licences are available for the full year, for the four months from June to September, for 30 consecutive days, and for one or three specified days, all at reasonable cost. They are sold at VNF offices including the main ports of entry from sea or by canal, but many only open for limited hours. Thus it may be easier to apply well in advance by post. Internet payment is now possible, via the VNF website www.vnf.fr.

Licences are not needed for the Brittany waterways and the navigable part of the R Somme, both of which are under local control.

When planning to use an inland route through France, note that stretches of canal or locks are sometimes closed for maintenance or repair. A list of the scheduled stoppages or *chomages* is available from the offices that issue licences. It is available on the VNF website, and in principle from the French Government Tourist Office, Lincoln House, High Holborn, London WC1V 7JH. The VNF website also list the prices of the various *vignette* options, the addresses of the VNF offices and other information about navigation conditions, moorings etc. The list is normally published in March for the following 12 months, and is usually fairly reliable. Nonetheless unscheduled stoppages can occur, and it is a good idea to check when passing any VNF office.

Dimensions The maximum dimensions for a yacht going from the UK to the Mediterranean via the main canals are: length 38·5m, beam 5·00m, draught 1·80m and air draught 3·50m. On the Burgundy route the maximum depth is only 1·40m, beam 4·50 and air draught 3·10m. The alternative Canal du Nivernais only offers 1·20m depth and 2·70m air draught.

For the Canal du Midi between Atlantic and Mediterranean maximum dimensions are: length 30m, beam 5·45m, water draught 1·40m and height 3·10m at the centre of bridge arches, reducing to 2·10m over 5·0m of beam.

Do not place too much reliance on published depths. On many canals dredging has not kept pace with silting up. Thus the nominal depth may only be available in the centre of the cut, and there are few mooring places with full depth alongside.

Through routes (see map)
The popular routes southwards through France pass through Paris, either entering the canal system at Dunkerque, Calais or via the Somme and selecting one of several possible routes; joining the Oise at Compiègne, and then south to Paris, or alternatively travelling up the tidal Seine from Le Havre or Honfleur to Rouen and then to Paris.

Navigation of the Seine is described in outline in Imrays *Map of the Inland Waterways of France* or CA *Cruising the Inland Waterways of France and Belgium* and also in Fluviacarte No.1 *La Seine Aval du Havre à Paris. Paris by Boat* by David Jefferson (Adlard Coles Nautical) provides very full information including tidal curves and a discussion of passage planning for both upstream and downstream voyages. This is important because yachts are prohibited from navigating the tidal Seine upstream of buoys 27 and 28 (about 6km upstream of Honfleur) during the hours of darkness, and there are very few satisfactory moorings or anchorages. (Caudebec-en-Caux has pontoons which may be used if they are not required by passenger craft. The town tourist office will advise.)

Yachts travelling between Honfleur and Rouen must log in and out to the Port de Rouen at Honfleur, and Port Fluvial de Rouen, both on VHF 73, giving estimated time of arrival and confirming arrival.

Between Le Havre and Rouen, three spectacular bridges provide headroom of over 50m, so the route is navigable with masts stepped as far as Bassin St Gervais, where a new marina was opened in 2012 with all facilities including haul-out, repairs and lowering and storage of masts available. Alternatively masts may be unstepped and stored at the yacht hbr at Le Havre. Several French transport companies offer a service that transports masts between the Channel or Seine ports, and those of the French Mediterranean. This can be a useful alternative to transporting a mast on deck, which can be a stressful experience in locks, especially if there is considerable overhang.

After Rouen, the Seine offers good depth and 6m of headroom all the way to Paris. Once through Paris there is a choice of three main routes to the Saône.

The Bourbonnais (western) route Paris to Lyon via Canal de Briare, 643km and 158 locks, with moderate commercial and pleasure traffic. This is the easiest and quickest route, but check before starting, since in several recent years, problems with water supply to the southern end restricted passage to shallow draught boats, especially in late summer.

The Burgundy route Paris to Lyon via Dijon, 629km and 219 locks. Beautiful but slow, with little commercial traffic but many hire boats in summer season.

The Marne (eastern) route Paris to Lyon via Vitry-le-François, 713km and 155 locks. This carries a fair amount of commercial traffic, especially between Paris and Vitry, and is probably the best route if draught is close to the limit.

All three routes converge by Chalon-sur-Saône, and join the Rhône at Lyon. From Lyon, south to the Mediterranean is 310km with 13 locks. Whilst the Rhône is canalised, there is still a considerable current in some stretches, up to 3kns in normal times, but exceeding 6kns at times of flood. Coupled with strong winds that funnel along the river valley, dangerous conditions can be created, so unlike most inland cruising, it is important to heed weather forecasts. Do not try to enter the Mediterranean by way of the Rhône delta, which is shallow and also has restricted headroom. Either lock out at Port St Louis, or if west bound take the Petit Rhône and then enter the Canal du Rhône à Sète, from which there are several ways to the sea, including a recently opened cut at Frontignan.

The Midi route from the Gironde estuary through Bordeaux and Toulouse to Port la Nouvelle, Agde or Sète, is about 480km long with about 135 locks. This direct route from the Atlantic to Mediterranean offers some magnificent scenery and fascinating industrial and other architecture. The disadvantages are that parts of it are shallow and have limited headroom, and that especially in the months of July and August the Canal du Midi is overcrowded with hire boats.

Sources of information
Fluviacarte Carte-Guides More than 20 published, with English, French & German text and clear maps. *No.1* essential for the tidal Seine, *No.16* essential for the Rhône. *No.21* is a good route planning chart.
Carte-Guides Chagnon not such a comprehensive range as Fluviacarte, although fairly similar.
Editions du Breil – Waterway Guides A series of 19 guides, tri-lingual, which now covers the whole of the French network save the lower Seine and the north (Pas de Calais). Excellent maps and generally up to date.
Cruising the Inland Waterways of France and Belgium published by the CA, 16th edition, 2013.
Inland Waterways of France, 8th edition David Edwards-May. Imray, 2010.
Cruising French Waterways by Hugh McKnight (Adlard Coles Nautical).
Waterway Routes through France. Map by Jane Cumberlidge (Imray).

The VNF website www.vnf.fr is sometimes useful, but suffers from infrequent revision and maintenance, so check the date of any information derived from it.

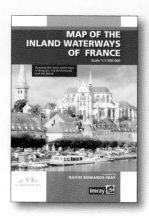
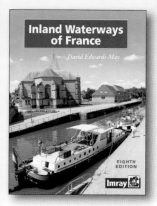

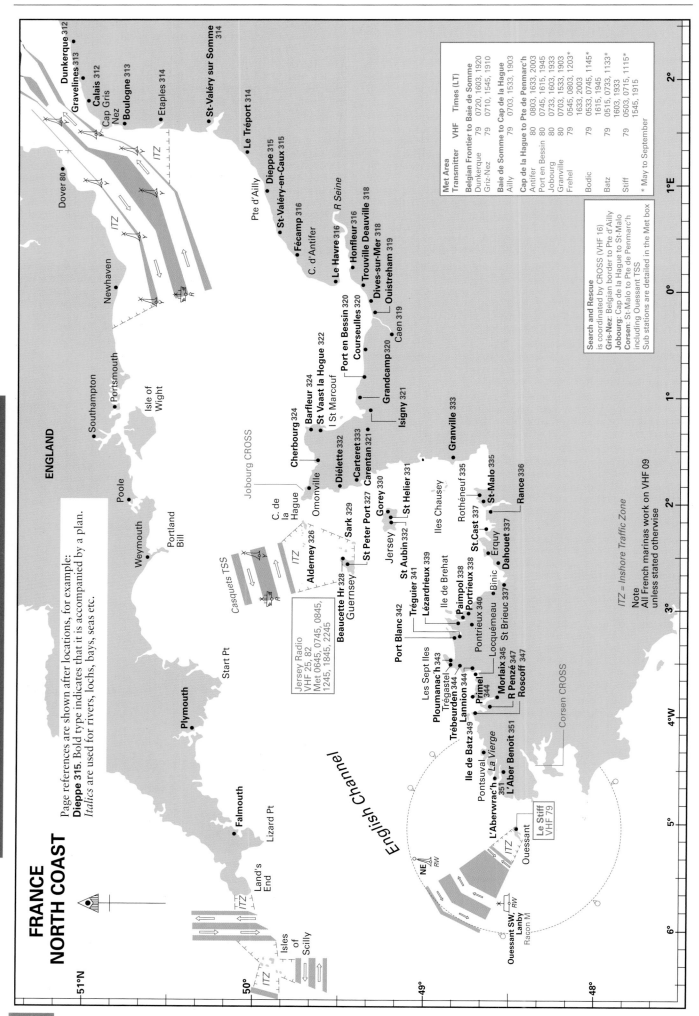

FRANCE – NORTH COAST AND CHANNEL ISLANDS

FRANCE NORTH COAST

Page references are shown after locations, for example: **Dieppe 315**. Bold type indicates that it is accompanied by a plan. *Italics* are used for rivers, lochs, bays, seas etc.

ENGLAND

51°N

Dover 80

Newhaven

Southampton

Portsmouth

Isle of Wight

Poole

Weymouth

Portland Bill

Start Pt

Plymouth

Falmouth

Lizard Pt

Land's End

Isles of Scilly

50°

ITZ

English Channel

Dunkerque 312
Gravelines 313
Calais 312
Cap Gris Nez
Boulogne 313
Etaples 314
St-Valéry sur Somme 314

Le Tréport 314

Dieppe 315
St-Valéry-en-Caux 315
Fécamp 316
C. d'Antifer
Pte d'Ailly

Le Havre 316
Honfleur 316
Trouville Deauville 318
Dives-sur-Mer 318
Ouistreham 319
Caen 319

R Seine

Port en Bessin 320
Courseulles 320
Grandcamp 320
Isigny 321

Barfleur 324
St Vaast la Hogue 322
I St Marcouf

Cherbourg 324

Diélette 332
Carteret 333
Carentan 321

Jobourg CROSS

C. de la Hague
Omonville

Alderney 326
ITZ

Beaucette Hr 328
Guernsey

Sark 329

St Peter Port 327
Gorey 330
Jersey
St Helier 331
St Aubin 332

Granville 333

Rothéneuf 335
St-Malo 335
St Cast 337
Erquy
Dahouet 337
Rance 336

Iles Chausey

Port Blanc 342
Tréguier 341
Lézardrieux 339
Ile de Brehat
Paimpol 338
Portrieux 338
Pontrieux 340
Locquémeau
Binic
St Brieuc 337

Les Sept Iles
Ploumanac'h 343
Trégastel
Trébeurden 344
Lannion 344
Primel 344
Morlaix 345
R Penzé 347
Roscoff 347

Ile de Batz 349
Pontusval
La Vierge 351
L'Aber Benoît 351
L'Aberwrac'h 350

Ouessant SW Lanby
Racon M

NE
RW

Le Stiff VHF 79

Ouessant

Ouessant SW
Lanby
RW

ITZ

Corsen CROSS

48°

49°

ITZ = Inshore Traffic Zone

Note
All French marinas work on VHF 09 unless stated otherwise

Jersey Radio
VHF 25, 82
Met 0645, 0745, 0845,
1245, 1845, 2245

Casquets TSS

Met Area

Transmitter	VHF	Times (LT)
Belgian Frontier to Baie de Somme		
Dunkerque	79	0720, 1603, 1920
Griz-Nez	79	0710, 1545, 1910
Baie de Somme to Cap de la Hague		
Ailly	79	0703, 1533, 1903
Cap de la Hague to Pte de Penmarc'h		
Antifer	80	0803, 1633, 2003
Port en Bessin	80	0745, 1615, 1945
Jobourg	80	0733, 1603, 1933
Granville	80	0703, 1533, 1903
Frehel	79	0545, 0803, 1203*
		1633, 2003
Bodic	79	0533, 0745, 1145*
		1615, 1945
Batz	79	0515, 0733, 1133*
		1603, 1933
Stiff	79	0503, 0715, 1115*
		1545, 1915

* May to September

Search and Rescue

is coordinated by CROSS (VHF 16)
Gris-Nez: Belgian border to Pte d'Ailly
Jobourg: Cap de la Hague to St-Malo
Corsen: St-Malo to Pte de Penmarc'h including Ouessant TSS
Sub stations are detailed in the Met box

France – North Coast and Channel Islands

This cruising ground covers the French coast from Dunkerque in the NE to Brest in the west and includes the Channel Islands. The varied landscape and culture are a delight. The cliffs from Calais to Boulogne give way to low land across the Bay of the Somme. Once past Boulogne there is much less cross-channel traffic and also the tides are less strong. From Le Tréport to Le Havre, high land with harbours such as Dieppe, St-Valery-en-Caux, and Fécamp nestling in gaps in the chalk cliffs give way to low cliffs and sandy beaches south of the Seine estuary starting in Honfleur through to Barfleur. The fascinating and thought-provoking history of the D-Day landings makes this particular part of Normandy memorable.

For many people, Cherbourg, with a harbour accessible in virtually all weathers, is the first port of call having crossed the Channel. It is a convenient place to start cruising the coast to the east or to the west towards the Channel Islands. The Channel Islands and adjacent coast of France combine superb sailing with excellent opportunities to use the tides to advantage and to hone your pilotage skills.

The rocky coastline of North Brittany is stunning with plenty of options: rocks and islands extend well offshore; there are many attractive harbours, secluded anchorages, and rivers. Tides are strong and the further west you go, the Atlantic swell becomes more noticeable.

Formalities For craft registered in EU countries and whose last port of call was in an EU country there is no requirement to clear in. France does not operate Schengen declarations. However, boats may be subject to random inspection by French Customs at any time both at sea and in hbr. NB The Channel Islands are not part of the EU. For documents to be carried, see *Customs* on page 16.

Crossing to France E of the Greenwich meridian the Dover Strait Traffic Separation lanes must be crossed and the rules observed.

Similarly there is the Casquets TSS to the E of the Channel LtV. Lanes must be crossed at right angles as defined by the course to steer, not the course made good. In the Dover Strait listen on VHF 16 or 11 for broadcasts from the Channel Information service. Avoid the voluntary separation scheme used by cross-channel ferries. High speed ferries demand extra vigilance especially when approaching from astern. Where International Port Signals are in use it is vital to obey them even though some fishing vessels or local craft may be ignoring them. A listening watch on VHF is advised at all commercial ports.

Boats may be scrubbed only in approved areas with the proper facilities for collecting the residue. It is an offence to have out of date flares on board.

Marinas and Pilotage

French marinas use VHF 09 unless stated otherwise, many do not provide hoses from taps on pontoons. Diesel (*gazole*) is widely available, in some ports by self-service only, requiring a credit or debit card. Marinas do not normally pre-allocate berths. Enquire at the *capitainerie* on arrival. Pump-out facilities are being installed in many marinas.

The following pilots may be of value supplementing the information in this *Almanac*.
The Shell Channel Pilot Tom Cunliffe (Imray)
North Brittany RCC Pilotage Foundation (Imray)
The Channel Islands RCC Pilotage Foundation (Imray)
Bloc – Mer du Nord – Manche Atlantique published annually (contains English translation).

The datum on some old charts may still be ED 50. Position derived from a GPS must be adjusted otherwise it may be up to 100m out.

France, Dunkerque to Cherbourg and cross Channel to England distances (miles)

	Dunkerque	Calais	Boulogne	Dieppe	Fécamp	Le Havre	Ouistreham	St Vaast	Cherbourg	Dover	Sovereign Hbr	Brighton	Nab Tr
Dunkerque	0												
Calais	28	0											
Boulogne	43	21	0										
Dieppe	95	74	53	0									
Fécamp	117	97	77	33	0								
Le Havre	142	124	101	57	26	0							
Ouistreham	156	134	114	71	40	21	0						
St Vaast	174	154	133	94	66	54	47	0					
Cherbourg	184	161	142	107	79	70	65	29	0				
Dover	42	22	27	89	98	125	140	139	143	0			
Sovereign Hbr	85	65	48	59	63	83	93	125	101	44	0		
Brighton	109	90	73	74	71	83	92	86	87	68	25	0	
Nab Tr	135	115	113	65	74	83	75	72	65	95	52	29	0

BELGIUM TO CALAIS

Charts BA 323, 2449 SC5605.1;
F 6651;
Imray C30, C31

Passage lights	BA No
W Hinder LtV	0145
Fl(4)30s21m12M	
Horn Mo(U)30s (··—)	
Dunkerque	1114
Fl(2)10s 59m26M	
Calais Main	1144
Fl(4)15s59m22M	
Calais Approche Lt buoy	1162
VQ(9)10s8m6M	

STREAMS RELATED TO DOVER

Mainly parallel to banks; generally 1½–2kn.
HW Dover –0100 E to NE. HW +0500 W-going.

A series of sandbanks running roughly SW to NE, on which the sea breaks heavily with wind against tide, lies off this section of the coast. The banks shelve gently on the seaward side but are steep-to on the land side. Cross in the gaps between the banks rather than crossing the banks themselves, except possibly at HW in light winds. The coast is low-lying with few readily identifiable features. On the approach, course should be set for buoys marking the banks rather than attempting to pick up a shore landmark.

The inshore approach from Belgium is via Passe de Zuydcoote (2°30'E), entering between E12 S card buoy and E11 buoy, Fl.G.4s, to port then steering SW, leaving E10, 8 and 6 Lt buoys to N and E9 to S, to the inshore buoyed channel to Dunkerque.

From the N take the Banc de Flandre route (9m). Cross the West Hinder traffic lanes to enter it W of Oost Dyck N Card Lt buoy at N end of Oost Dyck bank. Some six miles SW steer W between Bergues-S S card and Ruytingen-E N card buoy. Thence SW to leave Ruytingen-SE E card buoy and Dyck-E E card buoy to stb and the W card buoy off Haut-Fond de Gravelines to port to enter the buoyed and lighted Calais-Dunkerque channel.

Alternatively the Banc de Flandre route can be approached further W and entered between Ruytingen-N and Ruytingen-E N card buoys.

The inshore channel W from Dunkerque is clearly marked and lit.

France – Channel Ports

DUNKERQUE

Charts BA 1350, 323; SC5605;
F 6651, 7057;
Imray 2100, C30

HW Dunkerque HW

DS Dover −0200E;+0400W

MHWS	MHWN	MLWN	MLWS
6·0m	5·0m	1·5m	0·6m

A commercial hbr, good shelter for yachts and good facilities at two tidal marinas. Two locked marinas for large vessels rather than short-term visiting yachts. A possible entry to the canal system.

Approach from E or W along one of the inshore buoyed channels. The offshore banks dry in places at LAT and should only be crossed having verified water depth available, and in light winds.

Signals Three pairs of Lts are shown in Avant Port, the top pair for the large W lock, the middle for the S (Wattier) lock, and the bottom for Trystram. A listening watch on VHF 73 is advised.

Entrance Straightforward except for strong cross-set across entrance. At night enter between two ldg lines 179° and 185° (both F.Vi.4M) and then keep along E breakwater on Ldg Lts both Q, 137°, through Avant Port and continue to tidal marinas.

Locks The W lock out of Avant Port leads into W hbr – yachts not allowed. Trystram lock, just past LtHo on stb, leads into inner basins, canal system and non-tidal marinas. For times call *Dunkerque VTS* VHF 73.

Berthing Tidal
• **Port du Grand Large** tidal marina to port. Pontoons will take large and multi-hull yachts, 3m draught, 25 visitors'. Moor anywhere on visitors' pontoon.
• **Yacht Club de la Mer du Nord** tidal marina. About 70 visitors' berths. 3·85m. HM monitors VHF 09 when on duty. Moor at visitors' pontoon initially and enquire at *capitainerie*. Engineers, chandlers and sailmakers.

Non-tidal

Enter via Trystram lock, then make for the lifting br (opening co-ordinated with locking). About 1½ cables before the far lock turn to port under a second lifting br (opens a few minutes after the first). Now turn to stb for Bassin de la Marine, or to port under a third br into Bassin du Commerce. Moor at first pontoon. Advisable to book in first week in June when racers congregate. Office opens only 1700–1900 Monday–Friday and 1000–1700 Saturday–Sunday.

Facilities Fuel at YCMN on inner end of visitors' pontoon and Port du Grand Large. Long walk to shops from Port du Grand Large.

☎/VHF Port Control 03 28 29 70 70. VHF 73, Port du Grand Large 03 28 63 23 00, both non-tidal marinas 03 28 24 58 80. YCMN 03 28 66 79 90.

Items of interest *Duchesse Anne* square-rigger, maritime museum, lighthouse, St Eloi church, town hall, numerous war memorials.

DUNKERQUE OUEST

7M W of Dunkerque is a tanker and ferry terminal; yachts are forbidden to enter except in an emergency.

GRAVELINES

Chart BA 1350, 323, SC5605;
F 6651, 7057;
Imray C30

HW Dunkerque −0010

DS Dover +0600W; −0100E

MHWS	MHWN	MLWN	MLWS
5·7m	4·9m	1·4m	0·5m

A small fishing port on the mouth of River Aa with long drying entrance, a non-tidal small marina and access to canal system.

Approach Six conspicuous 60m buildings 1·5M to the east and the spire of Petit-Fort-Phillippe identify the entrance.

Entrance Dries with variable sandbanks. On no account attempt to pass between the N card bn and E pierhead due to a submerged training wall. On entry, for the first 100m keep nearer to the E pier. Without local knowledge access is only possible from HW−0200 to HW, is difficult in fresh onshore winds and should not be attempted in such winds over Force 5. Entrance to marina in Bassin Vauban has single pair of lock gates which open approx HW±0300, when the depth,over the lock sill is about 2·0m. Possible to lock into canal system at far end of the basin but requires 48h notice and only if free flow is possible; ☎ 03 59 73 42 42.

Berthing Visitors' berths are on the first pontoon to stb; most dry to very soft mud. Single keel boats remain upright. HM may direct you to a berth.

Facilities. Fuel from garage. Large supermarket 1km, small supermarket on site. Good restaurants in town.

☎ *Capitainerie* 03 2865 4524; Lock 03 2823 1945.

Items of interest Vauban fortifications, arsenal museum.

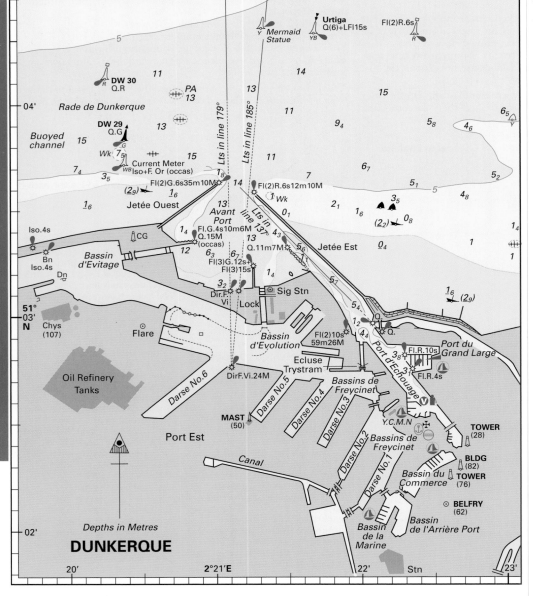

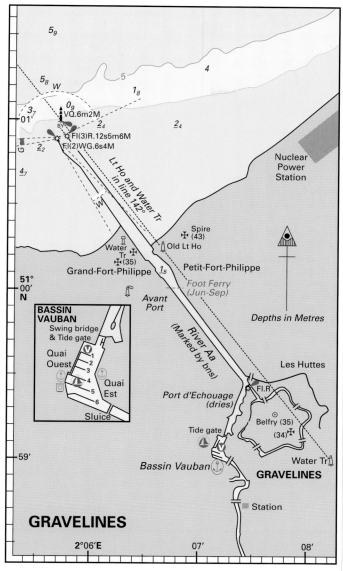

GRAVELINES

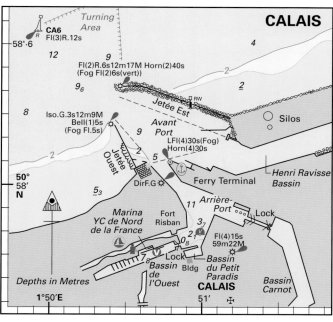

CALAIS

CALAIS

Charts BA 1351, SC5605;
F 6651, 7258;
Imray 2100, C8
HW Calais HW
DS Dover −0200E +0330W

MHWS	MHWN	MLWN	MLWS
7·2m	5·9m	2·1m	0·9m

A very busy ferry port geared to British visitors, with a non-tidal basin for yachts and access to the canal system.

Approach To the N of the entrance is the bank Ridens de la Rade which at MLWS has only ½m in places. In winds of Force 6 or more from NW to NE it is wiser to make for Boulogne; otherwise the bank may be crossed safely at HW±0300. With less water keep S of the R buoys S of the shoal when coming from W; from E keep at least 2M offshore and do not make for the entrance until the W jetty head bears about 100° – in bad weather keep on round SW end of the bank. The banks 1M to the NE of the outer end of the Jetée Est continue to move.

Signals IPTS shown to seaward from E jetty for entry to Avant Port, and at foot of W jetty for entry to Arrière Port. Signals are also shown for exit to stb on leaving Bassin de l'Ouest as well as foregoing. These signals must be obeyed, with no exemptions for small craft. Attempts to transgress receive loudspeaker-amplified rebukes. Call *Calaisport* on VHF 17 to request permission and monitor. Enter at best speed with engine assistance.

Entrance If asked by Port Control to wait outside, avoid the fairway. Some protection on the ebb may be found behind tip of W jetty. Beware strong current past E jetty; on entry, keep W jetty close to stb and bear to stb round Fort Risban (beware shallows) for entrance to yacht basin. For the canals lock into Bassin Carnot, then through a second lock into Bassin de la Batellerie and thence under br to port.

Berthing Waiting buoys in Arrière Port. Concrete blocks reported at foot of wall opposite Fort Risban, dangerous at less than half tide. Berth in Marina YC de Nord de la France, max draught permitted is 3m. Illuminated signs on each side of the bridge show when there is 2m of water over the sill, which dries 2·0m. Red and orange lights are shown 15 mins before br opening which is HW −0200, −0100, HW, HW+0100, HW+0200, HW+0300. Ship's Papers and Insurance may be required.

Facilities Diesel. Crane for demasting at YC. Wide range of bars and restaurants. Rly to Paris. Wi-Fi.

DOVER TO CALAIS

See page 81.

CALAIS TO LE HAVRE

Passage lights	BA No
Cap Gris Nez Fl.5s72m29M Racon RG	1166
Cap d'Alprech Fl(3)15s62m23M	1190
Pointe d'Ailly Fl(3)20s95m31M	1234
Cap d'Antifer Fl20s128m29M	1250
Cap de la Hève Fl.5s123m24M	1256

The approach to Boulogne is impeded to the NW by the Bassure de Bas, marked by N and S cardinals over which steep seas develop in wind.

The features of concern outside the 10m contour after Boulogne are the Vergoyer, Bassure de Baas and Ridens de Dieppe banks which throw up breaking big seas with wind. The latter two are not buoyed. Inshore, drying banks are found until Ault after which the coast is more steep-to until Le Havre.

The approach channel to Cap d'Antifer must be crossed at right angles and not inshore of buoys A21 and A22. The approach channels to Le Havre and the Seine should be crossed with care.

☎/**VHF** *Calaisport* VHF 17; Port de Plaisance 03 2134 5523; Yacht Club de Calais 03 21 97 02 34.

Items of interest Town hall, lighthouse, belfry.

BOULOGNE

Charts BA 438, 1892;
F 7247, 7416;
Imray C8
HW Calais −0025
DS Dover +0330S −0200N

MHWS	MHWN	MLWN	MLWS
8·8m	7·2m	2·6m	1·1m

A high speed ferry, fishing and commercial port with tidal marina. Accessible at all times except in very strong W–NW winds.

Approach The sea breaks heavily on the Bassure de Baas shoals, N and S of the entrance in gales from SW to NW, when it is best to keep 3M offshore until entrance bears E; otherwise from S keep about 1½M offshore inside the shoal. From W make for ZC1 Y buoy, Fl(4)Y.15s, and head E. The church tr is prominent behind the town as is the tall Colonne de la Grande Armeé (145m).

Signals Yachts must obey the IPTS shown from SW pierhead of inner harbour for entry to the latter and from signal mast at Darse Sarraz Bournet for exit to outer harbour. Call *Boulogne Port* on VHF 12.

Entrance The N breakwater is submerged for its outer ½M

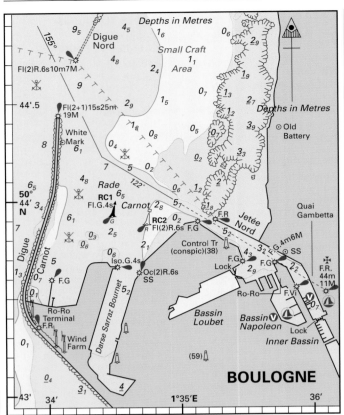

BOULOGNE

with the outer end marked by a tr, Fl(2)R.6s (Ldg Lts F.G and F.R, 197°, lead to Ro Ro berth). 1ca inside S pier steer S until inner piers open (Ldg Lts front F.G with neon ▲, rear DirF.R, 123°), then steer for inner

harbour. Follow round the N side for the marina.

Berthing The all-tide visitors' marina is on the south bank just before the lock to the Inner Bassin. Some fingers have been removed; beware of metal projections from the main

pontoon. Don't go beyond last pontoon. The locked Bassin Napoleon, access ±0300HW, is used for long stay visitors.

Facilities Fish market; scrubbing grid. Free Wi-Fi.

☏/VHF Port control VHF 12; Marina 03 21 99 66 50.

Items of interest Interesting old town, church, Nausicaa Aquarium.

ÉTAPLES

Charts BA 2451; F 7416; Imray C31

HW Dieppe +0010

DS Dover −0245N +0315 S

MHWS	MHWN	MLWN	MLWS
9·5m	7·7m	2·9m	1·2m

The drying estuary of the River Canche. Le Touquet is a popular holiday resort: beware sailboards, dinghies and swimmers.

Approach The approach is impracticable with strong winds from SW through W to NE because of breakers. It should be attempted only in daylight, in settled weather between HW±0200 according to tide and preferably before springs to avoid the risk of being neaped. (There is 3m at springs but only 1m at neaps.) Identify La Canche Lt tr (Or oct with brown band) at Le Touquet, S of entrance, and the heights of Terres de Tourmont, 175m, to N.

Entrance Channel is marked by buoys and bns, altered to meet changes. The first pair is usually about ½M W of Pte de Lornel, whence the course is on the N side of the estuary. After the buoys, currently seven pairs, the channel to Étaples is marked by port bns.

Berthing Small drying basin at Le Touquet is no longer used. At Étaples, there is a marina for yachts up to 13m but only 1.3m draught; some moorings for visitors. Current makes mooring difficult except at slack HW. Accessible HW±0200, open to NW.

Facilities Pump-out. Fuel from garages. Good shops at Le Touquet. Shipyard.

☏/VHF *Capitainerie* 03 21 84 54 33. VHF 09 (HW±0200).

Items of interest Le Touquet-Paris-Plage has much human interest during high season.

SOMME ESTUARY

Charts BA 2451; F 7416; Imray C31

HW Le Hourdel, Dieppe +0020; St Valéry +0035

DS Dover −0215NNE +0315SW

MHWS (St Valéry)	MHWN
10·2m	8·1m

The approaches and the estuary to St-Valéry dry; Le Crotoy is a small fishing village. St-Valéry is somewhat larger with a marina and a lock giving access via the Canal Maritime

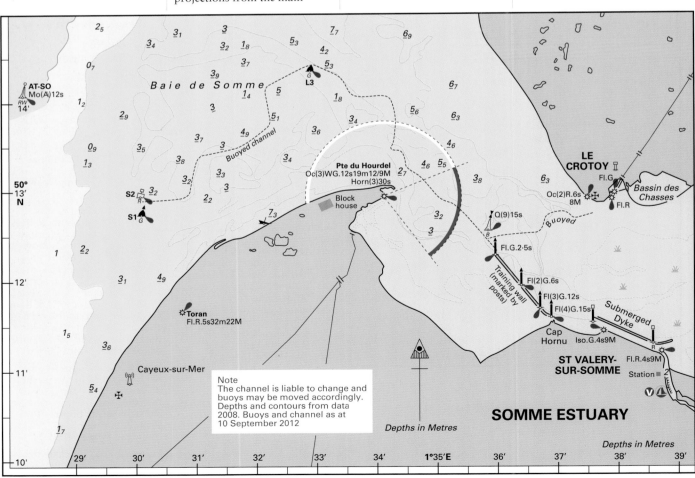

SOMME ESTUARY

Note
The channel is liable to change and buoys may be moved accordingly. Depths and contours from data 2008. Buoys and channel as at 10 September 2012

Depths in Metres

Depths in Metres

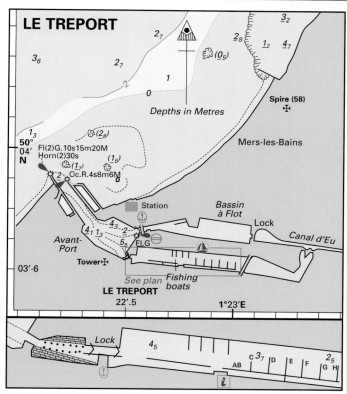

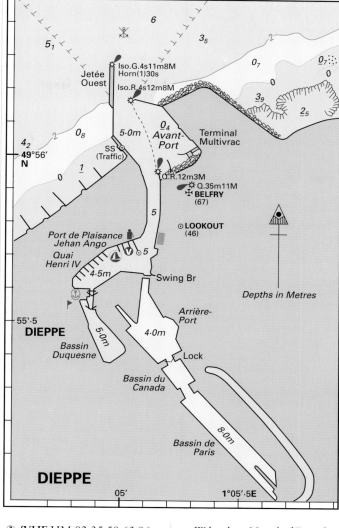

d'Abbeville to the main canal system.

Approach should not be attempted in onshore winds, at night or in poor visibility. Coast is low-lying, prominent features being the LtHo of Ault (W tr, R top, 95m) 8M S of entrance and Toran (W tr, R top, 32m) about 3M SE of landfall buoy. Accurate navigation and timing are essential, to allow 2hrs (at 4kn) to reach St Valéry from the entrance. Approach S1 at HW−0100 suggested.

Entrance Make for the Baie de Somme RW buoy AT-SO, Mo(A)12s, about 3M 325° from Toran LtHo. The positions of the channel buoys vary from year to year. The first pair (S1 and S2) at time of publication are SE of the card buoy. The channel winds – it is easy to mistake which pair to make for. It approaches the blockhouse on Pte du Hourdel, after which the Crotoy channel (1m MHWS), with buoys marked C, runs NE. The major channel runs SE towards the training wall, St Valery marina, and canal lock. Go to www.portsaintvalery.fr for latest information.

Berthing Anchor at Le Hourdel (dries, sand) or Le Crotoy pontoons (shallow draught boats only). St-Valéry marina is after the quay. Visitors' moorings (maximum 12m) on hammerhead of each pontoon, 2·1m, accessible HW±0100; mooring difficult when stream running. If waiting for lock it is sometimes possible to tie alongside a work boat opposite the marina. Enquire at the *bureau du port* because the canal is frequently closed due to lack of water.

Facilities Water and petrol at marina. Diesel at garage. Shops at St-Valéry and Crotoy; nothing at Le Hourdel.

☎ St-Valéry-sur-Somme Marina 03 22 60 24 80.

LE TRÉPORT
Charts BA 1354, 2147; F 7207; Imray C31

HW Dieppe +0002

DS Dover +0200 SW −0430NE

MHWS	MHWN	MLWN	MLWS
9·4mm	7·5m	2·5m	0·9m

A small drying commercial port and holiday resort with wet basins and yacht berths.

Approach Difficult to identify by day. Distinguishable from adjacent towns by two clock towers or at night by west jetty Lt Fl(2)G.10s15m20M Horn(2)30s. Difficult in strong onshore winds; severe scend in outer harbour in such conditions.

Entrance dries 2m, Avant Port dries 4·3m in centre, 2m in lock approaches. From W keep E pierhead, Lt Oc.R.4s, open of W pierhead, Fl(2)G, to clear off-lying rocks. Allow for NE set, and squalls in entrance. Call on VHF 12 before entry.

Berthing Enquire at *capitainerie*. Yacht berths at far end of S basin (Port de Pêche), 2·2m. Crowded and difficult for more than 12m. Strong current at times through the pontoons. Gates open approx HW±0400, entry lights. If full may have to use Bassin du Commerce, N basin.

Facilities Water on pontoons and on quay; stores; fuel from garage.

☎/VHF HM 02 35 50 63 06, VHF 12.

DIEPPE
Charts BA 1355; F 7317, 7417; Imray C31

HW Dieppe HW

DS Dover −0515ENE +0015WSW

MHWS	MHWN	MLWN	MLWS
9·3m	7·4m	2·5m	0·8m

A commercial, fishing, and ferry hbr with a large tidal marina which welcomes visitors. Accessible at all states of the tide though there can be a large swell in the entrance with strong N'ly winds.

Approach is straightforward, but the entrance is exposed to winds from NW to NE, causing a heavy scend. Entrance channel and Avant Port are dredged to 5m. Beware strong tidal stream across entrance. The east jetty has a W tr with R top, Iso.R.4s12m8M while the west has W tr with G top Iso.G.4s11m8M, Horn30s.

Signals IPTS signals control entry/exit during ferry movements. Yachts are required to request entry before entering hbr on VHF 12 and to request permission to exit before leaving marina. Signals displayed on W jetty ½ca from seaward; for leaving, display is on W bank at N end of Port de Plaisance, opposite signal mast; additional Lts may be shown above normal signals; R or G for ferry entering or leaving, W for dock gates open, 2R dredger in channel. Simplified code at entry to inner basins. In fog there is a blast on fog signal on Jetée Ouest every 30s when a ferry is expected.

Entrance Listen on VHF 12; do not attempt when a ferry is entering or leaving. On the flood make for the up-tide jetty at entrance, passing the ferry terminal at the E side of port entrance, and then follow W wall around fixed wavebreak close W of entrance to Arrière Port (prohibited to yachts) into marina Jehan Ango at Quai Henri IV.

Berthing Port de Plaisance (marina Jehan Ango) at the Quai Henri IV (50 berths for visitors). Call on VHF 09 because pontoons are access controlled from shore. In high season there are pontoons alongside entrance to Ango lock; some scend in winds NW to NE.

Facilities Fuel, shops, good restaurants. Saturday market. Rly to Paris. Wi-Fi.

☎/VHF Port de Commerce
02 35 84 10 55; Harbour
Control (*Dieppe Port*) VHF 12.
Marina Jehan Ango 02 35 40
19 79, VHF 09.

Items of interest Maritime
museum, museum in castle.

ST-VALÉRY-EN-CAUX

Charts BA 2148; F 7417;
Imray C31

HW Dieppe -0005

DS Dover –0500ENE +0030WSW

MHWS	MHWN	MLWN	MLWS
8·8m	7·0m	2·4m	0·7m

A holiday resort with locked
marina.

Approach Dangerous in strong
winds from NW to NE. From
NE keep 1½M off to avoid
shoals (0·6m) ENE of entrance
which can be identified by the
four dome-roofed buildings of
Paluel nuclear power station
3M to the W and six conspic
wind turbines immediately to
the E. The west jetty has G tr
and the E a W mast.

Entrance dries 2·5m. Leave R
posts marking wave-break
ramp close to port to avoid
shingle bank off W pier, then
keep to mid-channel. On the
flood there is an eddy across the
entrance from E to W until
HW+0030.

Berthing Avant Port accessible
HW±0300, moor on buoys to
wait for gates to inner harbour
to open. Gate operates

HW±0215 (day), ±0030 (night,
April–October only). Inside tie
to pontoon on stb and report to
hbr office. 40 visitors' berths.

Facilities Fuel from service
station, shops, especially fish.
Choice of restaurants.

☎ Marina 02 35 97 01 30.

Items of interest Henry IV
house, cliffs.

FÉCAMP

Charts BA 1354; F 7207;
Imray C31

HW Dieppe –0012;

DS Dover +0015SW –0500NE

MHWS	MHWN	MLWN	MLWS
8·3m	6·8m	2·8m	1·2m

A fishing port with good tidal
yacht marina and locked basin.

Approach Dangerous in strong
onshore winds. SW of hbr are
two square church towers (one
with sloping top) and a water tr
(conspic). Give wide berth to
rocks N of entrance: Pte Fagnet
semaphore in view guarantees
3·7m. Jetty marked by Grey tr
with R top Fl(2)10s15m16M
Horn(2)30s.

Signals IPTS on tr by Avant-
Port show when Bassin Bérigny
is open.

Entrance is dredged 1·5m, but
is subject to shoaling. Heavy
swell frequent: in strong
onshore winds attempt only
from HW–0200 to +0100. Best
approach on ldg ln 082°,

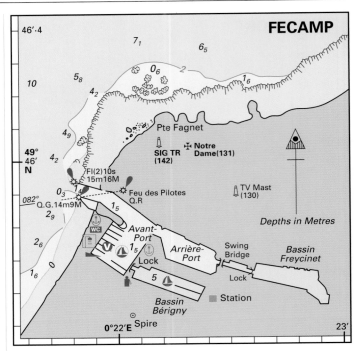

Q.R.10m4M (rear) and Q.G.
14m9M on SW jetty head;
beware spit running W from
latter and cross-set onto rocks
during flood which flows
strongly (ebb is weak). At end
of entrance channel turn to stb
for yacht berths.

Berthing 75 visitors' berths at
pontoons in Avant Port
(Pontoon C, 1·2m, severe scend
at times) or in Bassin Bérigny
(gates open HW–0200 to
HW+0045). If Avant Port berths
full report to *capitainerie*.

Facilities Fuel with card,
chandlery, supermarkets,
restaurants.

☎ Marina 02 3528 1358;
Bérigny lock 02 3528 2376.

Items of interest Bénédictine
distillery.

LE HAVRE

Charts BA 2990, 2146;
F 6683, 7418;
Imray C31

HW Le Havre HW

MHWS	MHWN	MLWN	MLWS
7·9m	6·6m	2·8m	1·2m

DS off Le Havre is complicated
by the flow from the Seine and
an eddy close N of the entrance.

DS 3M W of Cap de la Hève:
Dover –0415NE +0045SE;
+0245SW –0515SE

Close inshore of Cap de la Hève:
Dover –0315NE +0045NW
+0345S

2M S of entrance:
Dover –0615S –0415E –0215NE
–0015 slack +0045W

A busy commercial and ferry
port and a major yachting
centre, well sheltered tidal
marina.

Approach The main hazards
are the Banc de l'Éclat, 1m,
which lies approx 2M WNW of
the entrance, and the shallows
at the mouth of the Seine.

From the NE aim to pass 1½M
off Cap de la Hève and enter
the main channel W of LH12.

From the S or the Seine pass to
the W of Duncan L. Clinch W
card buoy and proceed with
caution to the main channel.

From the W make for LHA
safewater mark Mo(A)12s AIS

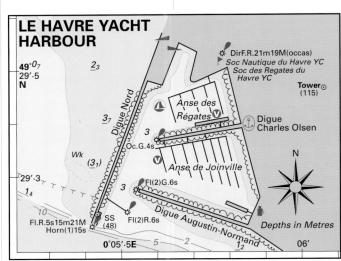

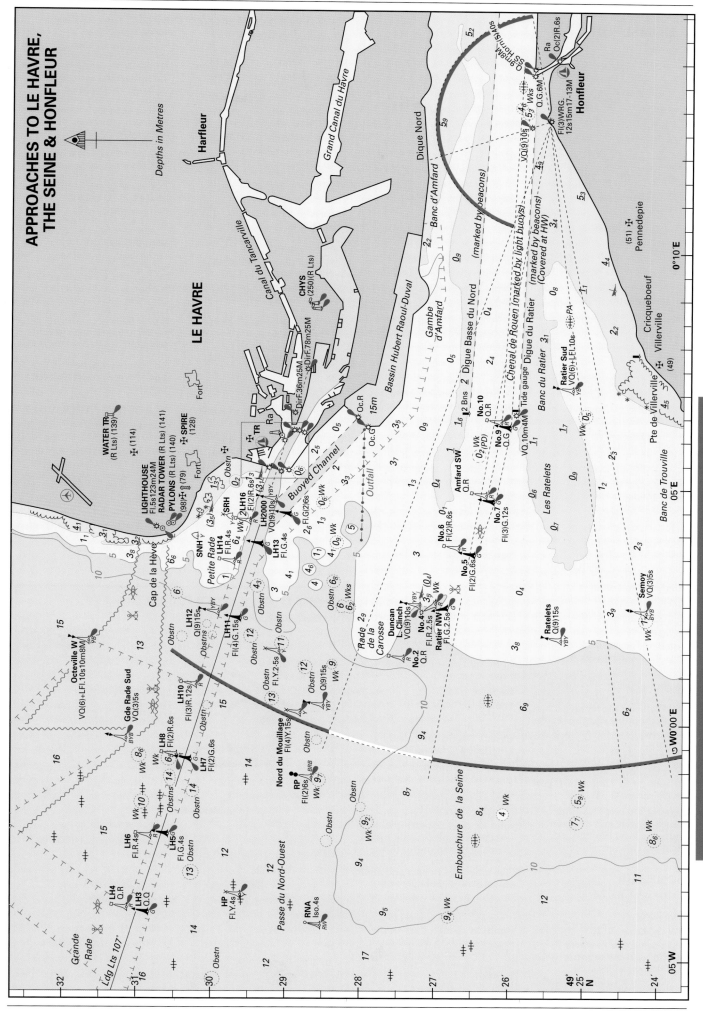

APPROACHES TO LE HAVRE, THE SEINE & HONFLEUR

Depths in Metres

Harfleur

Grand Canal du Hâvre

Canal du Tancarville

LE HAVRE

CHYS DirF.78m25M (250)(R Lts)

DirF.36m25M

WATER TR (R Lts) (139)
‡ (114)

LIGHTHOUSE Fl.5s123m24M
RADAR TOWER (R Lts) (141)
PYLONS (R Lts) (140)
‡ **SPIRE** (128)
(98)‡ ₪ (79)

Fort

Cap de la Hève

Octeville W VQ(6)+LFl.10s10m8M

Gde Rade Sud VQ(3)5s

LH12 Q(9)15s

LH11 Fl(4)G.15s

LH10 Fl(3)R.12s

LH8 Fl(2)R.6s

LH7 Fl(2)G.6s

LH6 Fl.R.4s

LH5 Fl.G.4s

LH4 Q.R

LH3 Q.Q

HP Fl.Y.4s

RNA Iso.4s

HP Fl.Y.4s

Grande Rade

Ldg Lts 107°

Passe du Nord-Ouest

Nord du Mouillage Fl(4)Y.15s

RP Fl(2)6s

No.2 Q.R

Duncan L.Clinch VQ(9)10s

No.4 Fl.R.2.5s

Ratier NW Fl.G.2.5s

No.5 Fl(2)G.6s

Ratelets Q(9)15s

Semoy VQ(3)5s

Rade de la Carosse

Petite Rade

SNH Fl.R.4s

SRH

LH14 Fl.R.4s

2LH16 Fl(2)R.6s

LH13 Fl.G.4s

LH2000 VQ(9)10s

Buoyed Channel

Oc.R 15m

Oc.G

Outfall

Bassin Hubert Raoul-Duval

Gambe d'Amfard

Banc d'Amfard

Amfard SW Q.R

No.6 Fl(2)R.6s

No.5 Fl(2)G.6s

No.7 Fl(3)G.12s

Les Ratelets

Digue Basse du Nord 2 Bns

No.10 Q.R

No.9 Q.G

VQ.10m4M Tide gauge

Ratier Sud VQ(6)+LFl.10s

Banc du Ratier

Chenal de Rouen (marked by light buoys)

(marked by beacons)

(marked by beacons)
(Covered at HW)

Digue du Ratier

Dique Nord

SS Horn(15s)

VQ(9)10s

Ra Oc(2)R.6s

Honfleur Fl(3)WRG.12s15m17-13M Q.G.6M

Wks

Pennedepie (51)

Cricqueboeuf (49)

Villerville

Pte de Villerville

Banc de Trouville

Embouchure de la Seine

Wk

0°00'E / W

0°10'E

05'E

0°05'W

49°25'N

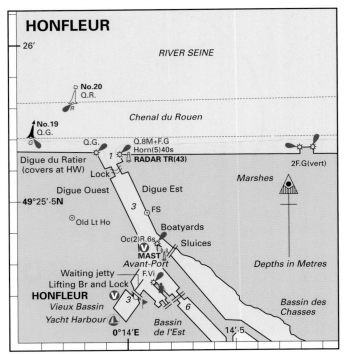

HONFLEUR

RIVER SEINE

No.20
Q.R.

Chenal du Rouen

No.19
Q.G.

Digue du Ratier
(covers at HW)

Lock

Digue Ouest   Digue Est

49°25'·5N

Old Lt Ho

Boatyards

Oc(2)R.6s

MAST

Waiting jetty

Lifting Br and Lock

HONFLEUR

Vieux Bassin

Yacht Harbour

Q.8M+F.G
Horn(5)40s
RADAR TR(43)

2F.G(vert)

Marshes

FS

Sluices

Avant-Port

F.Vi

Bassin des
Chasses

Bassin
de l'Est

0°14'E   14'·5

Depths in Metres

---

at 49°31'·4N 0°09'·8W and follow the main channel.

In all cases leave LH 2000 W card buoy to stb; give way to commercial traffic by keeping just outside the main channel, crossing it if necessary at right angles, and monitoring VHF 12.

Entrance and Berthing For the marina, pass the end of Digue Nord and leave the short spur breakwater Fl(2)R.6s to port, but do not leave the main channel until W end of Digue Augustin-Normand becomes visible. Unless directed otherwise find a berth (often rafting) on the marked visitors' pontoons and report to the *capitainerie*. If making for Le Havre from the Seine when conditions in the outer estuary are bad, it is better to enter the Canal at Tancarville: locks open HW (Le Havre) –0400 to +0315.

Facilities Fuel at SE corner of outer basin of yacht hbr; grid, and crane for unstepping masts. Good shopping near Les Halles Centrales to E of marina. Rly and bus connections, ferry to UK and Ireland.

☎/VHF Port control VHF 12, 20 callsign *Le Havre Port*; Port de Plaisance 02 35 21 23 95.

Items of interest Maritime museums, fine arts museum (includes local boy Monet), amazing concrete church by Auguste Perret.

HONFLEUR

Charts BA 1349, 2879;
F 6683, 7420;
Imray C32

HW Le Havre –0135

DS in Seine: LW Le Havre +0130E +0700W (approx HWD –0500 at sps +0530nps)

MHWS	MHWN	MLWN	MLWS
8·0m	6·7m	2·9m	1·5m

A locked fishing port with several non-tidal basins, one for yachts. A picturesque town and popular tourist attraction. Very busy in high season.

Approach Via Chenal de Rouen, buoyed and lit with submerged training banks either side marked by bns. Yachts are required to keep outside the buoyed channel, close N of R buoys (2m). Coming from W, round Ratier NW G buoy, Fl.G.2·5s to clear Banc du Ratier.

Signals IPTS code shown to E of entrance. Locks 2R(vert) or 2G(vert).

Entrance Conspic Radar Tr on E side. Pass E of buoys 19 and 20. Wait in Chenal de Rouen until entry permitted. No waiting facilities outside. Lock opens on the hour for ingoing traffic and on the half hour for exit.

Berthing
• **Avant Port** raft up to pontoons on west side, best for large yachts
• **Vieux Bassin** controlled by Honfleur YC (max. 20m)

There is a lifting br across the entrance which opens in season at 0830, 0930, 1030, 1130, 1630, 1730, 1830, 1930. Be ready to enter or leave on time – it does not wait for ditherers. While waiting for the br, make fast to one of three metal ladders on the W side. The moorings to port and at far end are for local boats only; immediately to stb is an area reserved for fishing boats. Visitors raft up alongside pontoon about a third of the way down the SW (stb) quay. Wait afloat in outer harbour; beware rush of boats leaving as br opens.

LE HAVRE TO CHERBOURG

Charts BA 2613 F 6857; Imray C32

Passage lights	*BA No*
Pointe de Ver	1396
Fl(3)15s42m26M (obscured when bearing >275°)	
Iles St Marcouf	1424
VQ(3)5s18m8M	
Pointe de Saire	1442
Oc(2+1)10s11m10M	
Cap Barfleur	1454
Fl(2)10s72m24M	
Cap Lévi	1462
Fl.R.5s36m22M	

STREAMS RELATED TO HW DOVER

9M WSW of Cap de la Hève –0515E +0045W, 1½kn

9M NE of Grandcamp –0515SE; +0045NW; 2kn

Inshore W of Iles St Marcouf: –0515 S-going to SE –0015 NE-going to NW, 1kn

Between Pte de Saire and Pte de Barfleur +0415SSE –0315 NNW, 2¾kn

3M N of Pte de Barfleur –0515SE +0045 WNW, 5¼kn

Larger boats may lie in Bassin de l'Est – consult HM.

Facilities Water on pontoons; fuel only at garages. Good shops; boatyard.

☎/VHF *Capitainerie* 02 3114 6109; Honfleur Sea Lock 02 3198 7282, VHF 17. See www.cnh-honfleur.net for details.

Pte de Barfleur: slack water. +0430 and –0200.

In strong onshore winds there is no easily accessible port of refuge between the Seine and St Vaast. Tidal streams can run at up to 4kns in the Seine approaches. With onshore winds against ebb seas are steep and break. The streams in Baie de la Seine are weak until rounding Pte de Barfleur. Approaching Iles St Marcouf keep clear of Banc du Cardonnet, extending 6M to SE, marked by E card buoy, VQ(3)5s at SE end, with another E card (wreck) buoy Q(3)10s halfway along N edge; and of Banc de St Marcouf extending 2½M NW, marked at NW end by W card buoy VQ(9)10s.

In the Barfleur race the sea breaks heavily, especially at Springs with wind against tide. It extends 3–4M E and NE from the point and should be given a wide berth. From Basse de Rénier buoy to Cherbourg, keep well N of Pierre Noire W card buoy, Q(9)15s to clear the shoals off Cap Lévi. (Leaving Cherbourg with the E-going tide, the stream sets hard onto the shoals).

DEAUVILLE / TROUVILLE

Charts BA 1349, 2146; F 7420; Imray C32

HW Le Havre 0100sp –0010np.
DS Dover +0530NE –0215SW

MHWS	MHWN	MLWN	MLWS
8·3m	6·9m	3·1m	1·3m

Deauville is a sophisticated and expensive holiday resort with a private marina. Trouville offers a municipal hbr with basic facilities, but a practical town.

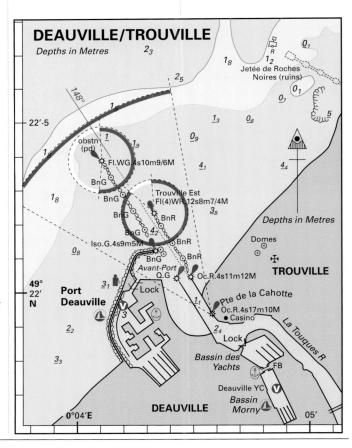

DEAUVILLE/TROUVILLE

Depths in Metres

148°

22'·5

obstn
(pd)

Fl.WG.4s10m9/6M

BnG

BnG

BnG

BnG

Iso.G.4s9m5M

BnG

49°
22'
N

**Port
Deauville**

Lock

DEAUVILLE

0°04'E

Jetée de Roches
Noires (ruins)

Trouville Est
Fl(4)WR.12s8m7/4M

BnR

BnR

BnR

Q.G

Domes

TROUVILLE

Depths in Metres

Pte de la Cahotte
Oc.R.4s11m12M

Oc.R.4s17m10M

Casino

Lock

*Bassin des
Yachts*

FB

Deauville YC

*Bassin
Morny*

La Touques R.

05'

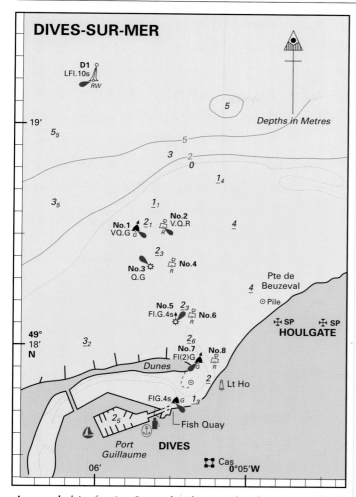

DIVES-SUR-MER

Approach dries for 6ca. In good weather, approach can be made after half-tide; in strong onshore winds, from HW−0200 to HW or avoid altogether. From N keep W of the town to avoid Banc du Ratier (S side of Seine estuary) and inshore shoals. From W keep 1½M offing to Trouville SW buoy, W card VQ(9)10s 49°22'·6N 0°2'·6E, then steer about 100° for the entrance. At night keep in W sectors of two outer Lts until on ldg line 148° Oc.R.4s. The front Ldg Lt is obscured NE of the line of the E outer breakwater; coming from N it will not be seen until close in.

Entrance At night keep on the ldg line, 148°; by day clear the posts on E and W training walls, and obstruction ½ ca NW of W training wall. Turn to stb round end of Digue du Large, Iso.G, use buoyed channel for lock to Port-Deauville, or straight on for gate to Trouville basin, avoiding shoals at the sides. (Do not continue up-river past the Trouville entrance).

Signals at municipal hbr: 3F.R(vert) closed; 2G/1W two-way traffic; 3G(vert) proceed, one-way traffic.

Berthing
• **Port-Deauville** lies to stb on entry, seaward of a modern housing development. There is accommodation for 100 visitors at pontoons alongside the outer breakwater. 3m depth in basin. Approach through Avant Port (dries) where there are two waiting buoys for the lock which functions when there is 3·50m depth, approx HW±0400. Free flow when water 7m.
• **Port de Deauville** is the municipal hbr which has two basins: Bassin des Yachts for residents and Bassin Morny where visitors raft on the E side. Gate opens and closes when depth is 5·50m, approx HW±0230.

Facilities Fuel, water at both harbours (Bassin Morny fuel point closes Tuesdays). Deauville is Paris-on-Sea in season, market. High quality bars and restaurants. Trouville has supermarkets and more practical items. Airport 7km.

☎ Port-Deauville 02 3198 3001. Deauville Port (municipal hbr) 02 3198 5040, Lock 02 3188 9566.

Items of interest Casino, boardwalk, horse racing, bars, Deauville market.

DIVES SUR MER

Charts BA 1349, 2146; F 7420; Imray C32

HW Le Havre −0100sp, −0010np

MHWS	MHWN	MLWN	MLWS
8·2m	6·8m	3·0m	1·3m

Port Guillaume is a large recently built marina, surrounded by holiday homes.

The estuary of River Dives dries 3m but is accessible to small craft HW±0230. Should not be approached in strong onshore winds. Make for RW con safewater Lt buoy, LFl.10s, DI then steer 166° for entrance marked by four pairs of buoys and dir Lt Oc(2+1)WRG.12s, 157-W-162°. The estuary quays are occupied by fishing boats; the drying area is almost fully taken up by moorings. Up-river at Cabourg it is possible to anchor in soft mud but landing is impossible below half-tide.

Port Guillaume Marina lies to port after entering estuary.

Entrance Lock opening according to tidal range, roughly HW±0300, but for 2m+ enter HW±0230.

Berthing on pontoons for 25 visitors, 17m x 2m draught max in locked basin.

Facilities Fuel, water, electricity. Shops Dives 1M.

☎ Marina 02 3124 4800.

Items of interest Grand Hotel in Cabourg (Proust's Balbec).

OUISTREHAM AND CAEN

Charts BA 1349, 2136; F 7420, 7421;
Imray C32

HW Le Havre −0025

DS Dover −0600ESE; HWD WNW

MHWS	MHWN	MLWN	MLWS
7·6mm	6·3m	2·6m	0·9m

A ferry hbr accessible all states of the tide with access to rural marina after locks. Canal to Caen marina. The only hbr

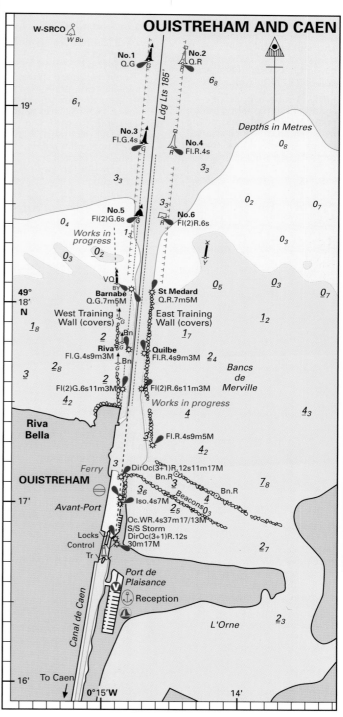

between Le Havre and Cherbourg with deep water access at all times. Useful for crew changes. Estuary of River Orne non-navigable.

Approach Prominent LtHo: W tr, R top, Oc.WR.4s37m17/13M (115°-R-151°, W elsewhere). Sands dry for 2M but approach channel is dredged 3m; make for E card pillar buoy Ouistreham, VQ(3)5s 49°20'·4N 0°14'·7W, and steer 175° for entrance, 2½M.

Signals IPTS code for locks; small craft enter when 3F.G(vert) displayed with W alongside. (W left or right of G indicates which lock to use). W alone means lock will open 1hr before usual time.

Entrance Channel buoyed, Ldg Lts DirOc(3+1)R.12s, 185°. E training wall covers, with Lt Q.R at head on pylon, nearly 1M N of head of main jetty. W training wall also covers and has Lt Q.G offset to E at head and Fl(2)G.6s at root.

Locks A waiting pontoon connected to the shore, lies to port, beyond and opposite the ferry terminal. Notice ashore indicates planned lock opening times. Upstream lock opens HW−0200; last downstream exit HW+0215; small craft generally use smaller E lock, entrance dredged to CD. From 15 June to 15 September, and at weekends in April to October incl, lock opens upstream at HW−0215, −0115, +0030 +0215, and +0315; and downstream at HW −0245 −0145, HW, +0145 and +0245. Congested on summer Sunday evenings. Lock openings may vary according to tidal conditions. Lock turbulent near low water. Vertical cables along the sides.

Canal de Caen is 7½M long, dredged to 7·8m and has three moveable bridges and a viaduct with over 22m clearance. Yachts go free in convoy at 5kn. Usual departure times are to Caen 1010, 1330 and 1630 at Pegasus Br (4·5km from Ouistreham), and from Caen 0845, 1200 and 1500 at first br. Enquire at Ouistreham marina for variations and extra convoys.

Berthing
• Marina to E of canal just to port after the locks: 16 visitors' berths on pontoon D.
• Caen: in Bassin St Pierre (dredged to 3·8m). 20 visitors' berths on 2nd pontoon to stb.

Facilities Limited shops in Ouistreham across canal: fuel N of marina entrance. Caen: wide range of shops and restaurants.

✆ /VHF Port HM 02 31 36 22 00, Locks VHF 68. Ouistreham Marina 02 31 96 91 37, VHF

09 (or VHF 74 after hours). Canal VHF 68. Caen port HM 02 31 95 24 47, VHF 68, 12.

Items of interest Museums of landings and Grand Bunker in Ouistreham; Caen has a castle built by William the Conqueror, many interesting churches, museums and a Sunday morning market around marina basin. Train to Bayeux for tapestry.

COURSEULLES

Charts BA 1349, 2136; F 7420; Imray C32

HW Le Havre −0030

DS Dover +0530E −0115W

MHWS	MHWN	MLWN	MLWS
7·4m	6·1m	2·7m	1·1m

A drying approach with congested locked yacht basin surrounded by modern holiday flats; entrance dangerous in strong onshore winds.

Approach Courseulles lies 2½M E of Pte de Ver LtHo, W square tr, Fl(3)15s42m26M, and 1½M W of Bernières church spire. Calvados Plateau shoals extend 2M off shore and dry to ½M off pier-heads. From W steer with Bernières spire on with twin towers of Délivrandes, 134° to Fosse de Courseulles pillar buoy, Iso.4s. If necessary anchor there (6m) to await rise in tide for entry.

Entrance Dries 3·5m. Enter between HW−0200 and +0100. There are training walls either side of entrance marked by bns, leading to a jetty on E and a spur on W. W side has a wooden tr, brown with G top, Iso.WG.4s (135°-W-235°) on dolphin at head of W training wall; E side has brown pylon, R top, Oc(2)R.6s at head of E jetty. Keep to E side until the end of the wooden part of the E pier, then continue in mid channel.

Berthing
• Yacht basin in River La Seulles for shallow draught local boats only.
• In Bassin Joinville marina at end of Avant Port, 2m. Gates open HW±0200. 20 visitors' berths, but full in season.

Facilities Fuel Rue Foch (800m), varied shops, restaurants. Boat yard.

✆ Port Control 02 3137 4603, *Capitainerie* 02 31 37 51 69.

ARROMANCHES

Charts BA 2136, 2613; F 7420; Imray C32

HW Le Havre −0040

MHWS	MHWN	MLWN	MLWS
7·3m	6·0m	2·6m	1·0m

Remains of wartime Mulberry harbour provide an interesting daytime anchorage, uncomfortable in strong onshore winds, particularly when the caissons cover. Approach from E has Roche du

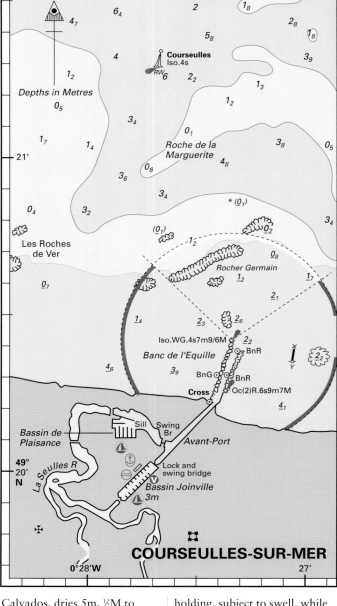

Calvados, dries 5m, ½M to NNE. Keep 2M offshore until near approach because of fishing pot chains. Make for E card BY wreck buoy Harpagas then steer 160° for entrance marked by port and stb buoys near W end of N side of hbr. Avoid wrecks on E side and anchor near the W end, sand, gradually shoaling, clear of obstruction marked by W buoys. Foul patches, buoy anchor. E part is foul with wrecks.

PORT-EN-BESSIN

Charts BA 1349, 2136; F 7420; Imray C32

HW Le Havre −0040

DS Dover +0200W −0400E

MHWS	MHWN	MLWN	MLWS
7·2m	5·9m	2·6m	1·1m

A drying fishing port with very limited accommodation for visiting yachts in wet basin.

Approach should not be attempted in winds from NW to NE over Force 5; otherwise approach at over half-tide. Anchor off in 3m, good

holding, subject to swell, while waiting.

Entrance Pier heads are painted white, visible a long way off. Ldg Lts Oc(3)12s 204°. Channel through Avant Port dries 2m; at end is a long passage, 10m wide, leading through a lock into wet basins. Beware the rock breakwater (covers) to port between entrance and lock.

Signals R over G lock gates closed. Signal station ½M W of entrance shows traffic signals on simplified code.

Berthing There are buoys in the outer harbour (dries). Wet basin is crowded with fishing boats but in principle there are berths for six visitors in the NW corner of the first basin. May have to raft up to fishing vessel in practice. Locks open HW±0200 but swing br only opens on demand. Call on VHF 18. After gates close, level may fall by 1m if sluices are opened to scour outer harbour (24hrs warning is given by blue flag at

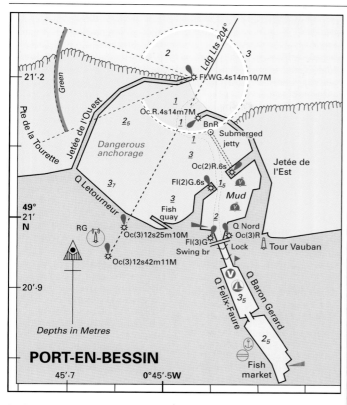

PORT-EN-BESSIN

GRANDCAMP-MAISY

Charts BA 1349, 2135;
F 7420, 7422;
Imray C32

HW Rade de la Capelle
Cherbourg +0100

DS Dover +0200NW; −0500SE

MHWS	MHWN
7·2m	5·9m

A fishing port with a wet basin, which welcomes yachts.

Approach Roches de Grandcamp dry 1·6m for 1M. N limit marked by three BY N card unlighted buoys marked Nos.1, 3, 5 from E to W. Approach from any of these at HW±0200.

Signals IPTS shown from control tr on E side of lock. These apply to entrance to hbr as well as inner basin.

Entrance is exposed to winds from NW to NE, has Lts Fl.G.4s6M and Oc(2)R.6s9M on towers 50m beyond the jetty heads with obstruction between. Two sets of Ldg Lts DirQ.15M 146°. Much Japanese seaweed reported.

Berthing Do not wait in front of the gates: considerable surge. Berths for 12 visitors at pontoon C in wet basin. Gates open HW±0230. If coeff <40

gates may close HW+0130 or earlier. Sill dries 2m; basin has 2m. Mass exodus when gates open, so hang back.

Facilities Fuel at garage, shops, restaurants. Bus to Bayeux.

☎ Port de Plaisance 02 3122 6316. Lock 02 3122 1917.

ISIGNY

Charts BA 2135, 2613; F 6857, 7422;
Imray C32

HW Rade de la Capelle. Cherbourg +0100 (sp; maybe later at np)

DS in Rade de la Capelle, off the entrance: Dover +0500SSW −0130NNE

In Chenal d'Isigny: Dover +0500S −0130NNE

E-going stream begins S and quickly changes to E; W-going stream begins SW and quickly changes to W.

MHWS	MHWN
7·3m	6·0m

LW is at HW−0245: tide comes in with a rush.

Small town famous for cream and cheese, with drying quays on River Aure.

Approach should not be attempted in winds of Force 5 or more; otherwise approach

lock gates). Yachts may be limited to 48hrs stay.

Facilities Water on quay; fuel at garage. Shops, fish, scallops.

☎ /VHF Lock 02 3121 7177, VHF 18.

Items of interest Fish market.

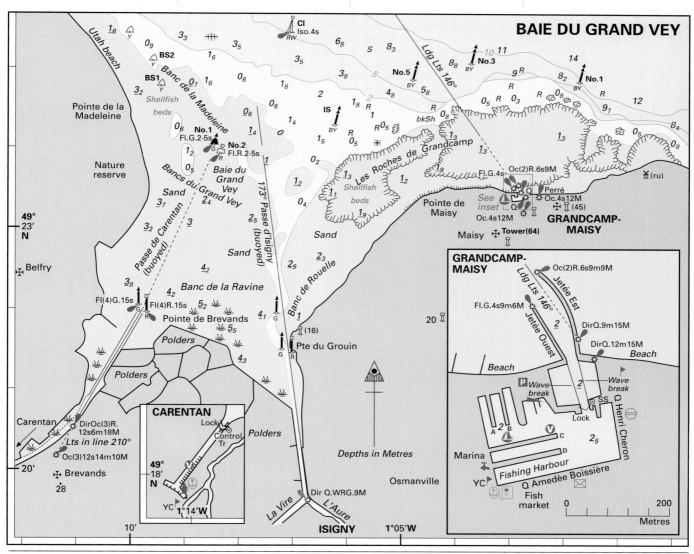

BAIE DU GRAND VEY

CARENTAN

GRANDCAMP-MAISY

ISIGNY

HW±0300. From E make for the three BY N card buoys N of Grandcamp (marked 1, 3, 5); from No.5 (W-most) bear SW for N card buoy IS 1M N of W end of Roches de Grandcamp. From NW make for CI RW pillar buoy, Iso.4s and then steer SE for the IS buoy.

Entrance dries in parts, but more water than Carentan approach; passable for 2·7m at half-tide. From IS buoy the channel is marked by buoys and bns. At G tripod, channel follows S shape and then enters canal. At junction with River Vire turn to port for Isigny but beware mud bank off left bank just short of the division.

Berthing Five visitors' berths (soft mud; dries 4m) at pontoon on W bank. Quai Neuf, near Spar warehouse. E bank quay slopes, hard bottom, and spaces mostly taken by work boats.

Facilities Water and fuel on quay. Shops, restaurants.

☎ Mairie 02 3151 2401.

CARENTAN

Charts BA 2135, 2613; Imray C32

HW Rade de la Capelle Cherbourg +0100

DS in Rade de la Capelle: Dover +0500SSW –0130NNE

MHWS	MHWN
7·2m	5·9m

Flood lasts for 2hrs sp, 3hrs np.

A small town with pleasant marina of rural aspect at end of long canal with good rail connections.

Approach Aim to be at the C1 RW safewater buoy Iso.4s at 49°25'·5N 1°07'·1W by HW–0200, then make good approx 200° toward the Passe de Carentan, marked at its seaward end by G and R buoys, No.1 and No.2, Fl.G.2·5s and Fl.R.2·5s. The channel is marked by at least a further two pairs of lit buoys. There is about 1·2m at half tide. All these buoys may be moved should the sands shift. NB The Ldg Lts for the canalised section are not appropriate for the approach channel.

Entrance The canal section is marked by bns or perches with its entrance bns Fl(4)G.15s and Fl(4)R.15s. The canal is dredged to 3·2m, at night follow the ldg Lts Dir.Oc(3)R.12s and Oc(3)12s on 210°.

Immediately in front of the lock gates (8M from the safewater buoy) River Douve enters from stb and River Taute from port: there can be a strong cross current. A waiting pontoon for small boats only.

Gates open HW–0200 to +0300; sill 1·8m above CD. Staffed 1 June to 31 August. At other times use telephone to contact lock-keeper. On

departure aim to lock out at HW–0200.

Berthing At pontoon K in ¾M long locked section of canal; 50 visitors' berths, maximum 37m.

Facilities Water on pontoons; fuel (0900–1000 weekdays); shops.

☎ Marina 02 3342 2444; Lock 02 3371 1085.

Items of interest Boat trips through marshes. Cheese.

ILES SAINT-MARCOUF

Charts BA 2135, 2613; Imray C32

HW Cherbourg +0100

MHWS	MHWN	MLWN	MLWS
7·0m	5·7m	2·6m	1·2m

Two uninhabited fortified islands, which sea birds dominate. Avoid in bad weather, especially from SW.

Approach Keep clear of Banc de Saint-Marcouf, extending 2½M to NW, on which there are breakers with fresh winds from N to NE; and of Banc du Cardonnet running 6M SE.

Anchorage 3–4m, to SE of S card bn, on rocks 1ca WSW of larger Is, Ile du Large, and SW of Lt Ho. Buoy anchor, stream strong. Land between

HW±0200 at boat hbr on W side of Is; when rocks to bn are awash there is 1·3m in entrance. Expect gull attacks. Ile de Terre, smaller Is, is a bird sanctuary; landing forbidden without permission.

Facilities None.

Items of interest Birds.

SAINT-VAAST

Charts BA 2135; F 7090; Imray C32

HW Cherbourg +0105

DS in Grande Rade: Dover +0530SW –0200NE, 1kn

An eddy runs N during the English Channel E-going stream.

MHWS	MHWN	MLWN	MLWS
6·7m	5·5m	2·5m	1·0m

A delightful fishing port with marina in wet basin; wide range of restaurants, bars and shops.

Approach From N leave Pte de Saire 1M to stb and continue for 1¾M W of S past Ile Tatihou (broad tr on S end with low detached fort to S); steer W round one lit and one unlit S card pillar buoys, then bear NW for end of jetty. From S go between Iles St-Marcouf and mainland to leave to port two E

card buoys, E of Fort de la Hougue. The approach, Le Run, used by local boats to N of Tatiou is not recommended since it crosses oyster beds.

By night From N keep Barfleur-Gatteville Lt, Fl(2)10s, open until on the line La Hougue Lt Oc.4s with Morsalines Oc(4)WRG.12s, 267°. Keep on the latter until in W sector of St Vaast Lt Oc(2)WRG.6s10–7M bearing NW. From S leave Quinéville W card Lt buoy, well to stb; do not cross La Houge-Morsalines line until in W sector of St Vaast Lt. Leave this Lt to port and enter between Oc(4)R.12s and Iso.G.4s lts to lock.

Entrance Port side of approach to the jetty head from S is marked by buoys and bns; exposed to strong winds from NE and SE. Dries 1½m but sandbank outside the gates covers at half flood – draught over 1·6m will touch; stay within 15m of wall until just past first (stone) bollard. Lock opens from HW–0215 to HW+0300, but may be extended during depressions or decreased if coeff <50.

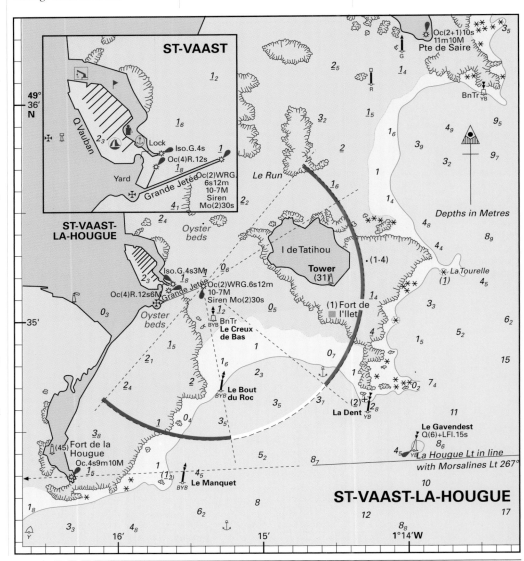

FRANCE – NORTH COAST AND CHANNEL ISLANDS

Berthing
• To await lock opening, anchor SSW of Ile Tatihou clear of the E half of W sector of Oc.WRG Lt, but open from S to SE.
• Waiting on N side of jetty inadvisable as this is used by fishing boats to unload.
• Marina. 100 visitors' on pontoon B >14m, C 12–14m, E <12m or as directed.

Facilities Good shops. Restaurants at all price levels, shellfish a speciality.

☎ *Capitainerie* 02 3323 6100.

Items of interest Île de Tatiou maritime museum, Gosselin shop, coastal walks.

BARFLEUR

Charts BA 2135; F 6857, 7090; Imray C32

HW Cherbourg +0105

DS Dover −0445N +0430S

MHWS	MHWN	MLWN	MLWS
6·5m	5·3m	2·5m	1·1m

A small picturesque drying hbr. Access HW±0200.

Approach *See Passage Notes re Barfleur Race.* From a position about 1¼M ESE of Pte de Barfleur, steer 219° on the 7m W square Lt tr (Ldg Lts Oc(3)12s). Do not confuse this tr with the squat W tr at end of S breakwater: ldg line passes about 50m S of the latter.

Entrance Ldg line is 219°, front W square tr Oc(3)12s7m; rear Grey and W square tr, G top, Oc(3)12s13m, synchronised. Channel is marked by buoys

and bns and has a strong cross-current. Near HW adjacent rocks are awash and it is most important to keep on the ldg line and not steer direct for the entrance. When two or 3ca off the entrance the Ldg Lts will be hidden by the hbr wall; at this point, about abreast of the last port bn, head for the entrance. There is a tide gauge on concrete base close SW of lifeboat slip: when the base is covered there is 1·6m along the quay.

When leaving at night have compass course prepared as Ldg Lts are not visible for first 250m.

Anchoring Waiting to enter, near the ldg line, 5–6m, sand and mud, poor holding. Also in bay N of town, except with winds E to NE. Approach 256° from La Roche à l'Anglais G con buoy.

Berthing along SW part of NW quay, dries 2–3m, level mud, sand and gravel. Room for 10 visitors, in principle but may have to moor alongside fishing boats which use space allocated for yachts. E side is rocky. There is a strong surge with fresh winds E to NE.

Facilities Water on quay; fuel delivered; shops. Hôtel Moderne has restaurant.

☎ *Capitainerie* 02 3354 0829. No VHF.

Items of interest Charming village, church, Gatteville 1hr, coastal walks.

CHERBOURG

See plan on next page

Charts BA1114, 1112; F 7086, 7092; Imray C32

HW Cherbourg HW

DS Dover +0600E −0100W

Tidal streams change 2–3hrs later in mid-channel than along the shore.

MHWS	MHWN	MLWN	MLWS
6·4m	5·0m	2·5m	1·1m

An enormous commercial, ferry, naval and yachting hbr, which is a true port of refuge and can be entered at all times. Tides outside the hbr are very strong and so they are in the Grande Rade.

Approach To E and W keep at least 2½M off the land; and keep well clear of Raz de Lévi in E, end of which is marked by W card YBY Lt buoy. Cherbourg can be located by atomic power station on high ground to W, a cliff behind the town, a long low breakwater with prominent circular forts, and Cap Lévi LtHo (36m) to the E. Note that the entrances are 3M apart and large vessels tend to prefer the W.

West Entrance Follow leading lts Dir.2Q through the entrance which is marked on its E side by Fort de l'Ouest Fl(3)WR.15s, and on the W side by Querqueville Lt Fl(2)G.6s. There is a R port buoy Fl.R.4s close inside the entrance. Keep well to stb on entry to avoid emerging craft. From here the Ldg line for Petite Rade is 124°, front F.G, rear Iso.G.4s leaving front Lt on Digue du Homet to stb.

East Entrance Ldg line, twin spires of Notre Dame and small tr of Ste Trinité, 212°, clear the shoals near Ile Pelée. At night Fort des Flamandes Dir.Q and Jetée des Flamands Q.,189°, serves the same purpose. The shoals are marked by two R buoys Fl.R.2.5s and Fl(4)R.15s. Enter between these buoys and Fort de l'Est Iso.G.4s. Steer 220° for the Petite Rade.

Passe Cabart-Danneville at E end of Grande Rade is narrow with strong streams; not recommended.

Petite Rade The NE breakwater, Jetée des Flamands, covers. Its W end is marked by R pillar buoy, VQ.R. Once clear of breakwater, steer 196° for marina and entrance to inner harbour (at night marked by Fl(3)G.12s and Fl(3)R.12s).

Departing If heading for Passe de l'Est it is imperative to leave to stb the R pillar buoy VQ.R in the entrance to clear Jetée des Flamands.

Berthing At Port Chantereyne marina, tidal, 250 visitors' berths: take any space available

according to length, pontoons N, P and Q are marked with length, east side of H and J max 25m, K <9m. If arriving at night and outer berths are full, raft up on waiting pontoon (30 spaces). In high season, a waterborne HM will direct boats. Anchoring is possible in Petite Rade close N of marina breakwater (wash and uncomfortable in N winds) or at W end of Grande Rade (isolated and considerable swell).

Facilities Hypermarket within walking distance. Market Tuesday, Thursday, Saturday. Restaurants. Ferry. Wi-Fi.

☎ /**VHF** Port Chantereyne 02 3387 6570; Port control VHF 12.

Items of interest Fort, maritime museum, Park Liais.

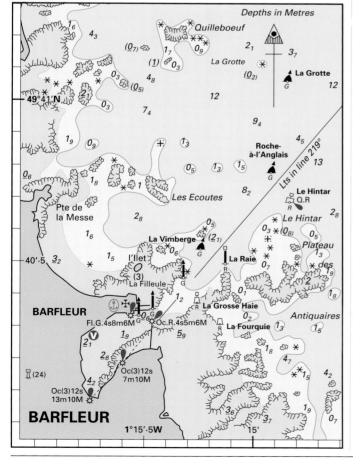

BARFLEUR

FRANCE – NORTH COAST AND CHANNEL ISLANDS

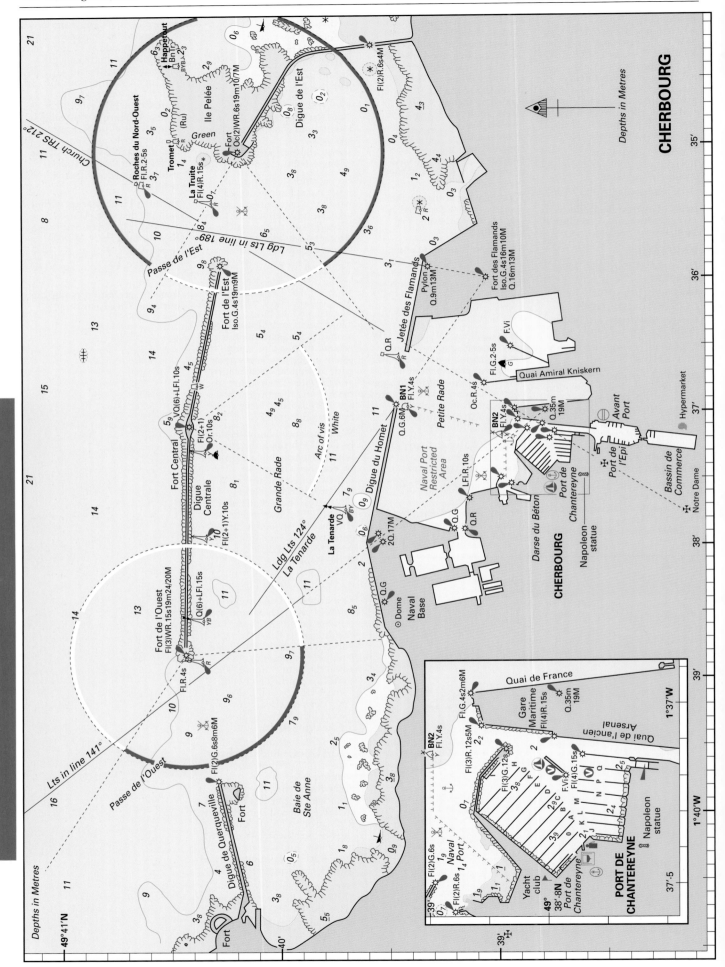

CHERBOURG

Depths in Metres

Church TRS 212°

Roches du Nord-Ouest
FI.R.2.5s

Happecurt
BnTr
BYB

Ile Pelée

Tromet
(Ru)

La Truite
FI(4)R.15s

Fort
Oc(2)WR.6s19m10/7M

Digue de l'Est

Passe de l'Est

Ldg Lts in line 189°

Fort de l'Est
Iso.G.4s19m9M

Jetée des Flamands

Pylon
Q.9m13M

Fort des Flamands
Iso.G.4s16m10M
Q.16m13M

Quai Amiral Kniskern

FI.G.2.5s

F.Vi

Fort Central

VQ(6)+LFI.10s

FI(2+1)
Oc.10s

Arc of vis
White

Digue Centrale
FI(2+1)Y.10s

Grande Rade

BN1
Q.G.6M
FI.Y.4s

Digue du Homet

Petite Rade

Oc.R.4s

Q.R

BN2
FI.Y.4s

Q.35m
19M

Naval Port
Restricted
Area

LFI.R.10s

Port de
Chantereyne

Avant
Port

Hypermarket

La Tenarde
VQ

Ldg Lts 124°
La Tenarde

2Q.17M

Q.G

Q.R

Port de
l'Epi

Bassin de
Commerce

Notre Dame

CHERBOURG

Darse du Béton

Napoleon
statue

Fort de l'Ouest
FI(3)WR.15s19m24/20M

Q(6)+LFI.15s

FI.R.4s

Dome

Naval Base

Q.G

Lts in line 141°

Passe de l'Ouest

FI(2)G.6s8m6M

Digue de Querqueville
Fort

Baie de
Ste Anne

Fort

Depths in Metres

49°41'N

PORT DE
CHANTEREYNE

Quai de France

FI.G.4s2m6M

Gare
Maritime

FI(4)R.15s

Q.35m
19M

BN2
FI.Y.4s

FI(3)R.12s5M

Quai de l'ancien
Arsenal

FI(3)G.12s

F.Vi

FI(4)G.15s

Yacht
club

Napoleon
statue

FI(2)G.6s

Naval
Port

FI(2)R.6s

Port de
Chantereyne

49°
38'.8N

1°40'W   1°37'W

Channel Islands

Chart BA 2669, SC 5604;
Imray 2500, C33A, C33B

These islands afford fascinating sailing for the well-equipped yacht with an experienced navigator. The hazards are concealed rocks, strong tidal streams and poor visibility. Good up-to-date charts are essential. BA 2669 gives the outlines of the Channel Islands and is adequate if passing round them; but for inter-island navigation larger scales are needed, as shown at the head of each island entry. The Small Craft Folio *SC 5604* has 10 charts of a convenient size. A good pilot guide is also highly desirable because of the importance of transit lines when navigating in these waters; in some places the difference between a course steered and the course made good can be as much as 60°. *The Admiralty Channel Pilot* is a mine of detailed information. For those wishing to make the most of inshore routes and anchorages the RCC Pilotage Foundation's *The Channel Islands* (Imray) is exceptionally well provided with sketches of transit lines and marks.

The *Admiralty Tidal Atlas for Channel Islands and Adjacent Coasts of France* (NP 264) or a good equivalent is also essential. The range of mean spring tides shows a remarkable variation from 5·5m to 11·5m within the area of the Islands and the adjacent French coast; within the islands the range varies from 9·8m at springs to only 2·1m at neaps. Tides make and take off rapidly; streams run rapidly even at neaps; and there may be considerable variation from predictions due to weather. There may also be many local variations in streams, particularly eddies, not shown on the tidal atlas. Of the 25 harbours with quays for berthing alongside, only five do not dry.

The Admiralty Pilot shows an incidence of fog on only two days a month in the summer: this is deceptive because there are also many days of morning mist when poor visibility makes it impossible to pick up some leading marks. Radar and a GPS are most helpful if caught by mist or fog when at sea; but neither is sufficiently reliable to keep on transit lines and their possession does not justify leaving hbr in poor visibility.

There is complete shelter at all times at St Peter Port or Beaucette in Guernsey and at St Helier in Jersey. Elsewhere there are very many anchorages which provide shelter in settled weather or offshore winds, but all are subject to swell.

Search and Rescue
VHF 16 or DSC will connect to Jersey Coastguard (MMSI 002320060), St Peter Port Radio (MMSI 002320064) or Joburg CROSS (MMSI 002275200). Lifeboats operate from Braye, St Peter Port and St Helier.

Weather
Jersey Radio VHF 25, 82 at 0645, 0745, 0845LT, and 1245, 1845 and 2245UTC.
BBC Radio Guernsey 1116kHz, 93·2mHz at 0807, 1235, 1710LT weekdays and 0810LT weekends.
BBC Radio Jersey FM 88.8mHz, MW 1116kHz at 0725, 0825, 1725 weekdays, 0825 Saturday/Sunday, all LT.
Island FM 93·7mHz (Alderney) on the half hour.
St Helier Pierheads gives current conditions on VHF 18 every two minutes.

Navtex
This area is covered from Niton Areas S and K also by Corsen Area A. It is probably sufficient to use Area K alone. This will give two forecasts at 0840 and 2040 UTC. Gale and Navigational warnings are updated every 4hrs.

Link calls
These can only be made through St Peter Port on working channel VHF 62, payment being made through the vessel's accounting authority.

Customs
The Channel Islands are Crown Dependencies but they are not part of UK nor of EU. Customs requirements for yachts are more rigorous than in France: Q flags must be flown and it is necessary to report to customs (usually by depositing a form) not only when arriving from France but also from UK and when moving from one Island administration to another (e.g. from Guernsey to Jersey). Clearance can be given at Braye in Alderney; St Peter Port, St Sampson or Beaucette marina in Guernsey; and St Helier or Gorey in Jersey. Normal EU duty-free limits apply.

In practice the French customs are not very interested in the arrival and departure of yachts provided that the yacht has evidence of having paid VAT in the EU and is not carrying non-European nationals, animals, drugs, firearms or duty-free stores. Duty-free includes alcohol and tobacco purchased in the Channel Islands in excess of personal allowances. It is really only in these circumstances that it is necessary to fly a yellow flag and report. Evidence is the VAT receipt, not a photocopy.

On return to UK from the CI it is necessary to fly the yellow flag from the 12M limit. You must then attempt to contact a customs officer by telephone and follow any instructions on the pre-recorded message. Use the National Yachtline ✆ 0845 723 1110 (24hr). Customs notice No.8 gives full details and this may be found in all hbrs and marinas together with Form C1331 which should be completed and posted in the special customs boxes. The customs are usually very helpful provided you comply with the regulations and do not attempt to smuggle drugs, animals, firearms or foreign nationals into the country. It is helpful to have receipts for dutiable goods, fuel and an original VAT certificate for the boat. Island airports shut in fog which makes crew changes unreliable.

Health Insurance
Since the United Kingdom NHS no longer has a reciprocal agreement with the Channel Islands, do not expect free health care even if carrying an EHIC. Medical Insurance is strongly recommended. The same applies to CI residents visiting the UK.

Diesel
Diesel fuel is available at a low rate of duty. Keep receipts and do not carry duty-free fuel in loose containers.

CHERBOURG AND THE CHANNEL ISLANDS

Charts BA2669, SC5604; Imray 2500, C33A

Passage lights	BA No
Cap de la Hague Fl.5s48m23M Horn30s	1512
ALDERNEY	
Quénard Point Fl(4)15s37m12M	1536
Casquets Fl(5)30s37m18M	1532
C.de Carteret Fl(2+1)15s81m26M	1638
SARK	
Pt Robert Fl.15s65m20M Horn(2)30s	1544
GUERNSEY	
Platte Fougère Fl.WR.10s15m16M Horn 45s Racon(P)(·——·) R sector over rks to NW	1548
Les Hanois Fl(2)13s33m20M Horn(2)60s	1580
St Martin's Point Fl(3)WR.10s15m14M Horn(3)30s R sector over rks to SW	1574
JERSEY	
Grosnez Point Fl(2)WR.15s50m19/17M R sector over rks to NE.	1622
Corbière Iso.WR.10s36m18/16M Horn Mo(C)60s (—·—·) R sectors over rks to N and SE	1620
Roches Douvres Fl.5s60m24M Siren 60s	1734

STREAMS RELATED TO DOVER
Alderney Race HWD –0020 SW; +0540 NE.

Between Guernsey and Jersey the stream is rotatory anti-clockwise, HWD W; +0300 S; +0600 E; –0300 N.

The Alderney Race is 7M wide and presents no difficulty in reasonable weather although there are overfalls, marked on the chart, which should be avoided, especially with wind against tide. Tidal streams can reach 10kn and it is essential to time a passage carefully taking advantage where necessary of the inshore eddies round Alderney.

From Cherbourg to Channel Islands, leave Cherbourg at about HWD –0300 to catch the start of the inshore W-bound eddy. Between Cherbourg and CI, Omonville is a convenient passage port: the eddy running W inshore from there begins at HWD –0500. If bound for Alderney or the Casquets, a generous allowance must be made for tidal set. If bound through the Race for Jersey or Guernsey, the most comfortable passage will be made at HWD before the overfalls have built up.

Southbound from Alderney, the shortest route to Guernsey is through the Swinge. Depart Braye Hbr at local HW+0200 to 0230 (Dover –0200 to –0130) to avoid the overfalls S of Burhou. Leave Corbet Rk about 100m to port and then change course to keep Great Nannel just open E of Burhou, 003°, until Les Etacs are on the port beam.

Northbound from St Peter Port Leave as soon as the stream in the Little Russel turns N at about HWD+0430. This should give a favourable tide through the Swinge or the Alderney Race. If bound for Alderney note that the tide runs NE in the Race longer than in the Swinge and change course if you run out of tide before entering the Swinge. Approaching the Swinge keep Great Nannel just open E of Burhou, 003°, to clear Pierre au Vraic (dries 1·2m) and to clear Les Etacs at SW end of Alderney. Keep to E side of Swinge to avoid the overfalls, about 100m W of Corbet Rock.

To Cherbourg from Alderney leave at about HWD+0500 to catch the start of the NE-going stream. If coming from Guernsey note that the early W-going stream along N coast of Cherbourg Peninsula is stronger than suggested in *Tidal Atlas*. Avoid it by keeping well offshore.

Alderney

BRAYE

Charts BA 2845, 60, SC 5604;
Imray 2500, C33A

HW St Helier+0045

DS (Race):HWD SW+0600NE

MHWS	MHWN	MLWN	MLWS
6·3m	4·7m	2·6m	0·8m

Alderney is an unspoilt island with reasonable facilities. The artificial hbr is exposed to NE. No animals may be landed. Air connections to UK, Cherbourg and other islands.

Approach is best from NE at HWD+0500 when the stream off the entrance is least. From NW either pass N of the Casquets and Burhou Is or, if the SW stream is running, leave them to N, pass S of Alderney and go NE through the Race with flood tide.

From S see Passage Notes; but at night it is prudent to use the Race approach rather than the Swinge because in the latter it is difficult to establish the clearance off rocks to the side.

Entrance Beware sunken continuation of the breakwater running NE for 3ca. The W-going stream sets strongly onto it for 0930hrs. When rounding it, if coming from SW, keep E of Ldg line of two bns: front W with W globe on islet on W side of Saye Bay, rear BW ▲, 142°; then bring W cone near head of Old Harbour pier on with St Anne's spire, 210° (this transit leads 1ca E of the submerged breakwater).

At night to clear the breakwater extension keep in W sector of Château à L'Etoc Lt Iso.WR (071°-R-111°-W-151°) the R sector covers the shoals W of Saye Bay. Then sight the Ldg Lts into the hbr (215°) which are both Q., visible 210° to 220°. The port radar can assist vessels in poor visibility.

Berthing There are about 80 Y visitors' buoys max LOA 15m or anchor clear of moorings with a riding Lt, 8m. There are some patches of rock and weed with poor holding. The rings on the buoys are rough and with a little swell will easily chafe through a warp. Little Crabby Harbour is used for local boats except for visitors when re-fuelling, HW±0200. Land at pontoon below HM office (keep it clear), not on the slip.

Facilities Fuel, water, gas, chandler. Restaurants, small supermarket at hbr, otherwise 1M up the hill at St Anne.

☎/**VHF** HM 01481 822620. VHF 16, 74, call sign *Alderney Radio* (0800–2000 June–September). Call *St Peter Port* when closed. Water taxi *Mainbrayce* VHF 37, 80 and *Mobile* 07781 415420 or 01481 822772. Runs 0800–2359.

N.B **Burhou** Landing prohibited 15 March–27 July.

In distress call VHF 16, 74 for Radio Direction Finding Service and radar VTS.

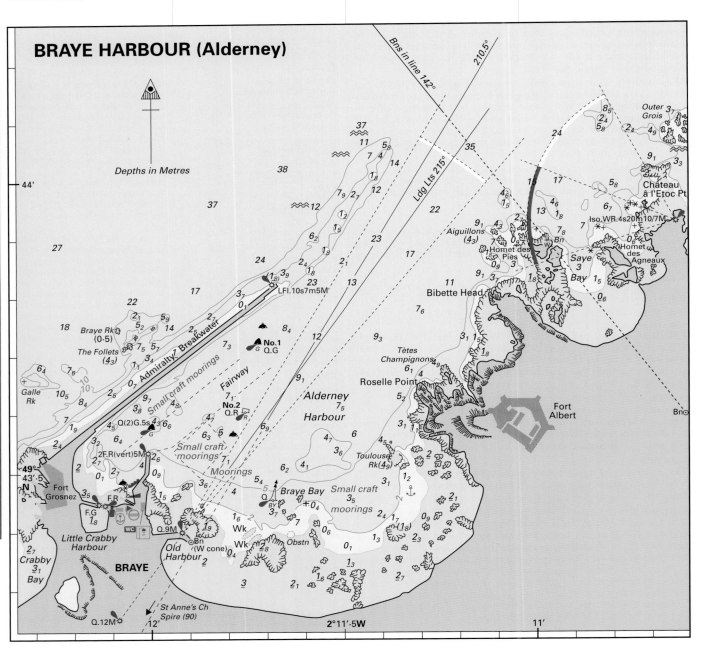

FRANCE – NORTH COAST AND CHANNEL ISLANDS

Guernsey

Chart BA 3654, SC 5604;
Imray 2500, C33A

HW St Peter Port HW

DS off E side:
Dover −0100SW +0500NE

off W side: HWD SW;+0600NE

The W coast is rocky and inhospitable; the E coast offers better shelter and facilities.

Approach There are three main lines of approach to the E coast and St Peter Port:
• by Little Russel channel;
• by Great Russel channel;
• from W and S.

Approaching from N, as from the Solent, the traditional pilotage is to make for the Casquets, then make good 224° down W coast to Les Hanois LtHo and follow S coast 1M off to pick up approach from W and S. In bad visibility this route is strongly to be preferred. Warning: with the SW-going tide there is a considerable inset SE across the N end of Guernsey.
• Little Russel Channel entrance is marked on W by Platte Fougère octagonal tr with B hor band, Fl.WR.10s (085°-R-

155°) and on E by Tautenay Lt tr, BW vert stripes Q(3)WR.6s (R over area to E, 215° to 050°). It provides the most direct route from N, and can be used at LW with good visibility, but the streams run at up to 6kn and it can be very rough, with overfalls, with wind against tide. At NE end of channel, between the Braye Rocks and Amfroque, the stream sets directly towards the N end of Herm from Dover +0100 to +0345. Do not approach Platte Fougère octagonal tr with B and W hor bands, from W on a bearing less than 165° or from E on a bearing greater than 255°. Make for a position about 2M NE of Platte Fougère and then bring Brehon tr (low, squat) just to the E of St Martin's Point, 208°. Keep on this line until Roustel tr, BW, is 1¼ca to stb, then get on transit of Belvedere House, W, on with Castle Breakwater Lt tr, white on NE side, 220°. If these latter marks are difficult to pick out against the sun or in poor visibility, steer 220° from Tautenay, adjusting as necessary to clear Roustel tr, BW chequered stone, to port;

Platte tr, G con stone, to stb; and Brehon tr, squat circular fort, ½M to port.
At night from a position NE of Platte Fougère Fl.WR.10s, pick up Ldg Lts front Castle Breakwater Al.WR.10s16M, rear Belvedere Ho Oc.10s14M, 220°. When St Sampson front Ldg Lt F.R is obscured, bear to E of line to open Castle Breakwater and Belvedere Lts by about 2° to clear Agenor shoal, 1·8m.
• Great Russel Channel is 2M wide, easy of access, and has weaker streams than Little Russel. In rough weather or poor visibility it is safer. Enter it with W edge of Little Sark open E of the E side of Brecqhou. When St Martin's Point comes well open S of Goubinière Rock (½M SE of Jethou) 243°, make good 230°, allowing for tide, round Lower Heads S card buoy to make for St Peter Port. At night keep in the W sector of Noire Pute lt, Fl(2)WR.15s (W 220°–040°) as far as Lower Heads S card buoy. Leave this close to stb and make directly for the Castle Breakwater Lt, Al.WR.10s16M.
• From W and S give the NW shore of Guernsey a berth of

3½M, Les Hanois Lt 1½M and the S shore about 1M. At night do not let Les Hanois Lt bear more than 164° until Casquet Lt bears 051°. Round St Martin's Point about a mile off and bring E side of Castle Cornet in line with White Rock LtHo (round, 11m) 350° and make good this line to clear the drying rocks to port. If beating, keep Brehon tr E of N to avoid being set E into the Great Russell. Remember that the E-going tide does not set N round St Martin's Point till about Dover +0300.

At night, from a position off St Martin's Lt, Fl(3)WR.10s, keep the Victoria Marina Lt Oc.R.5s, just open of Terres Point, 342°. When St Martin's Lt bears 215°, steer 015° until White Rock Pier Lt, Oc.G.5s,

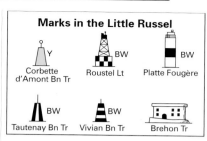

Marks in the Little Russel

| Corbette d'Amont Bn Tr (Y) | Roustel Lt (BW) | Platte Fougère (BW) |
| Tautenay Bn Tr (BW) | Vivian Bn Tr (BW) | Brehon Tr |

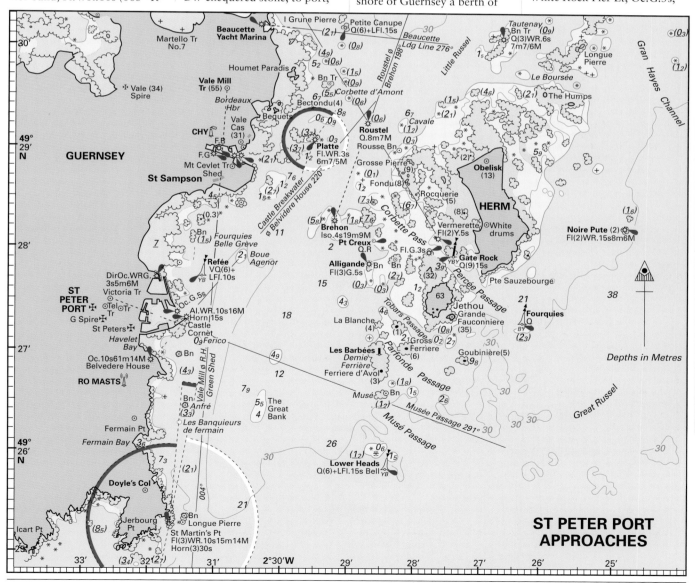

ST PETER PORT APPROACHES

Depths in Metres

comes on with Castle Breakwater Lt, Al.WR.10s, 308°, when steer 330° until the Victoria Marina Lt bears 265°, thence enter.

Anchorages There are several anchorages suitable for use in offshore winds:
• **Icart Bay and Petit Port** on SE (each has drying rocks and is subject to swell);
• **Havelet Bay** adjacent and S of St Peter Port is useful when the latter is crowded, but swell can be a problem;
• **Grande Havre and L'Ancress Bay** on N side, the latter being more protected from SW winds. Clearance at St Peter Port or Beaucette is required before anchoring in any of these places.

ST PETER PORT

Chart BA 3140; SC 5604; Imray 2500, C33A
HW St Peter Port HW
DS Dover −0200S +0400N

MHWS	MHWN	MLWN	MLWS
9·3m	7·0m	3·6m	1·5m

A good centre with all facilities.

Signals
R Lt from White Rock Pierhead and New Jetty, entry and exit from main hbr prohibited except for craft less than 15m under power in the small craft fairway.

Small craft should enter by the buoyed small craft fairway 100m S of the Ldg line.

R Lt from S pier of Victoria Marina: entry/exit from marina prohibited.

Entrance Monitor Port Control on VHF 12. Yachts are generally met by Harbour Patrol on or soon after entering. If waiting for marina opening, go straight ahead to holding pontoon at entrance.

Berthing Victoria Marina in old hbr is for visitors (max 12·8m, 1·8m draught); it has a sill, drying 4·2m. Open HW−0230 to +0200. Albert Marina immediately to the S of it and Queen Elizabeth Marina immediately N of main hbr are for local craft only.

Larger craft and those wishing to depart before half tide may

ask to be allocated a buoy or pontoon NE of the marina entrance.

Regulations Do not use marine toilets in marina, hbr or Havelet Bay; nor use outboards on tenders. Fly a Q flag on approach unless coming from Alderney.

Facilities Fuel point on S side of hbr, dries 2·5m; water in marina, at fuel pt and at root of Victoria Pier. All supplies and services. Wi-Fi at Ship & Crown and Visitor Information Centre.

☎ /VHF Harbour office 01481 720229; Marina 725987. Port control VHF 12; Customs 726911. Link calls VHF 62. CG (St Peter Port Radio) call direct on VHF 20.

ST SAMPSON

Entrance dries 3·6m. Marina behind gate (1·8m depth). For local boats, visitors may only enter by prior arrangement for commercial services.

BEAUCETTE MARINA

Charts BA 807, 808; Imray 2500, C33A

Approach from the NW in daylight by the Doyle Passage from 1M W of Platte Fougère tr get Corbette Amont Y con bn midway between Herm and Jethou 146° depth 15m.

From the Little Russel leaving Tautenay astern, on 276° pass S of Petite Canupe S card lit bn to find R and W approach buoy LFl.10s, 1ca SE of Grune Pierre. There are two lit porthand buoys and one lit stb buoy. Ldg Lts are both F.R. on W column with R arrow and R column with W arrow rear near windsock. Call *Beaucette Marina* before entry.

Entrance This is narrow and the rocks are painted white. Boats leaving have right of way. The sill dries 2·4m and has about 2·7m at half tide. Y waiting buoys N of entrance. Inside, turn to port.

Note this entrance is dangerous in NE or E winds.

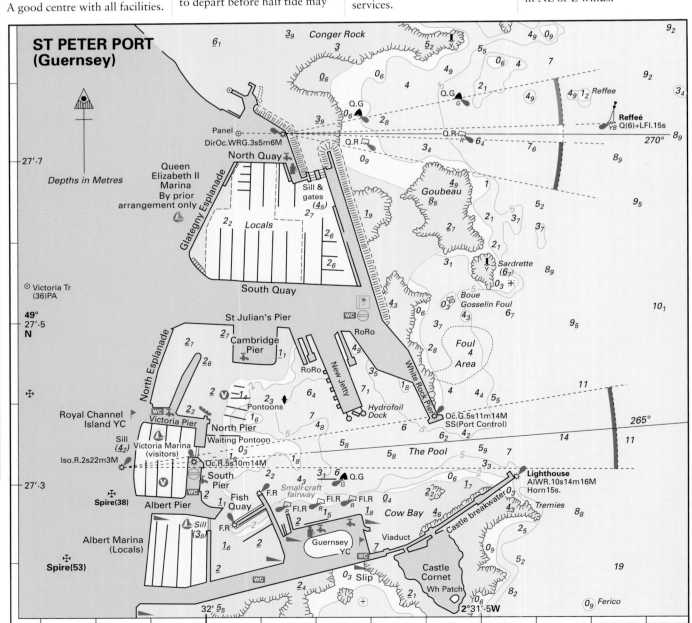

ST PETER PORT (Guernsey)

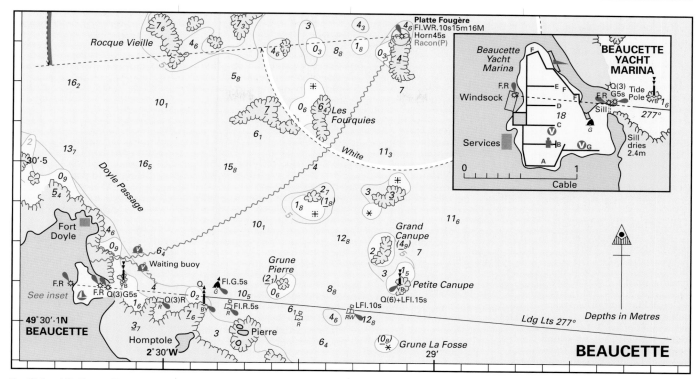

Facilities All. Shops ½M. Free Wi-Fi.

☎/VHF Marina 01481 245000, VHF 80
www.beaucettemarina.com.

Sark

Chart BA 808, SC 5604; Imray 2500, C33A

HW St Helier+ 0010

DS NE coast is slack at half-tide and HW; SW coast is slack at half-tide and LW

Off W coast:
Dover +0500NE –0100SW

Off E coast:
+0600NE; –0100SW

At Maseline Pier:

MHWS	MHWN	MLWN	MLWS
9·0m	6·8m	3·5m	1·0m

An island with basic facilities and good anchorages, sometimes subject to swell.

Approach Should not be attempted by night. The safest, but longest route from St Peter Port is to go S, round Lower Heads S card buoy. Bound for La Grande Grève, Musé Passage (29m), Victoria Tr in line with N face of Castle Cornet 291°, is more direct; but if going N of Sark, use the mailboat route, Tobars passage. The transits are:
• **Grande Fauconnière** bn (or, better, Bec du Nez of Sark) seen just over the S slope of Jethou, 090° (or 093°).
• 2ca short of Jethou, get Vale Mill in line with W edge of Brehon tr, 321°; hold this course for 2ca.
• **Noire Pute** just SE of Grande Fauconnière, 061°, leaving Quarter rocks of Jethou ½ca to port, and bearing off to leave

Grande Fauconnière (steep-to) also ½ca to port. Beware cross tides; these shorter routes are best taken near slack water.

Anchorages All may be subject to swell. None should be considered in onshore winds except the lightest. Most have laid moorings, many of which are private. Expect to pay for a visitors' buoy which have been laid in Havre Gosselin and La Gréve de la Ville.
• **La Grande Grève** on W coast has good sandy bottom but

with a rock drying 0·3m in the middle and a group of drying rocks in the S. Approaching from W keep S end of La Coupée on with N end of Point Le Jeu, 090°. From the S, first round Les Hautes Boues by keeping W end of Givaude

bearing at least 355° or, if visible, on with middle of Grande Amfroque, 355°. Anchor 1ca NE of Point Le Jeu. Long steep flights of steps to the top. 12 visitors' moorings.

• **Havre Gosselin** Approach from N with W'ly rock of Little Sark seen through Gouliot Passage 188° (half-tide is slack). Through Gouliot, head E leaving Moie de Gouliot (50m) ½ca to port. Hbr is clear of dangers, no stream. Anchor in 5m, shingle and sand, as near to landing (300 steps) as convenient. Y visitors' buoys, pay.

• **Dixcart and Derrible Bays** From SE with Sark Mill (no vanes) open W of Point Chateau in Dixcart Bay 337°. Both are clear of danger in middle, sand 3–5m. Path at Dixcart to hotels and village.

• **Creux Harbour** dries and is full of local boats. It is sometimes possible for yachts to lie, with HM's permission, against one of the walls. Anchoring outside is difficult, owing to local moorings and

the need to leave a passage for launches from Guernsey.

• **Maseline Harbour** is the main arrival place for supply ships and tourist boats. There is no room for yachts at the quay but it is possible to anchor in the bay, 10m. Approach from NE with E side of L'Etac de Sark in line with W side of Les Burons, 211°. When Point Robert LtHo opens to S of Grande Moie, alter course to leave Grande Moie 1ca maximum to N.

• **Grève de la Ville** is a good anchorage with cliff path to village. Approach from N with Noire Pierre (3·7m) midway between Grande Moie (30m) and NE face of Les Burons (22m) 153°. Noire Pierre is clean all round beyond 10m so pass either side and anchor in the bay, 11m sand. There are 12 visitors' buoys.

Supplies Diesel is available in cans from the electricity company above Creux; water is difficult – there is a pipe in Creux. General stores, butcher, bank, pub and hotels.

Jersey

Chart BA 3655, SC 5604; Imray 2500, C33A, C33B

A very popular holiday island, Jersey has a large marina, a number of drying harbours and several good anchorages for offshore winds.

The SE corner has reefs extending for over 3M but the Is may be readily approached from SW to NW, and from N between the Paternosters and Dirouilles groups.

At N and S of Jersey it is slack water at local HW and HW+0500 by the shore. At E and W ends of the Is, it is slack water at about half-tide by the shore.

Yachts arriving from outside the Bailiwick, unless from the Minquiers or Ecrehous, must fly a Q flag and clear at either St Helier or Gorey.

Coastguard: for routine traffic, passage reports etc, call direct on VHF 82.

GOREY

Charts BA 1138, 3655, SC 5604; Imray 2500, C33A, C33B

An attractive drying (3–5m) hbr but generally very crowded.

Approach From NE, the Ldg line is Grouville white mill (rear) over SE slope of Mont Orgeuil Castle (front), 230°. At night use the Ldg Lts (see Entrance). From SE, at a position 1M E of Grande Anquette Refuge BW bn, steer on line pierhead with Gorey ch spire, 305°. When abeam of Le Giffard R can buoy, alter course to N for leading line.

Entrance Ldg line 298°, front W frame tr Oc.RG.5s8m, rear WOr patch on stone wall of house. When leaving, if bound N go at half flood with N-going inshore eddy.

Anchorage There are some drying visitors' moorings. Otherwise anchor E of pier, stream runs fast; or take the ground inside, hard sand, mooring bow and stern; or lie

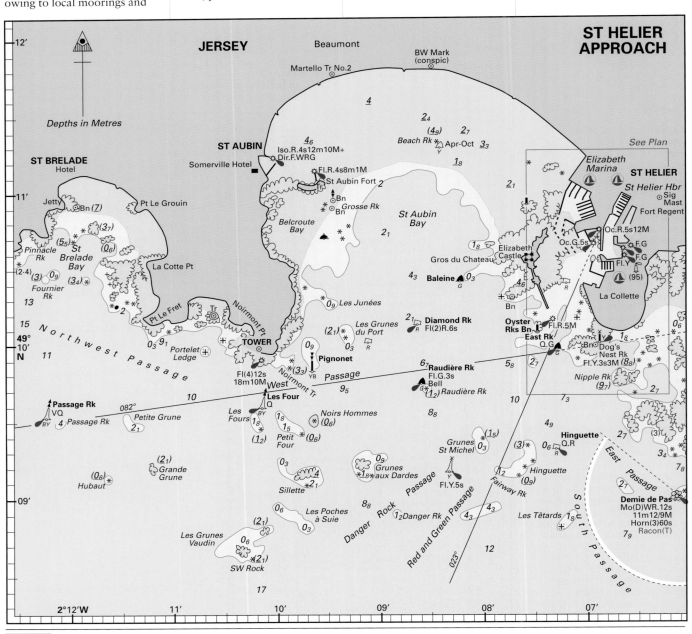

alongside pier inside staging at pierhead. Also at St Catherine's Bay inside breakwater off Verclut Point, sand and weed, 3–9m, moderate holding.

Supplies Fuel and Water at end of pier. Shops.

☎/VHF 01534 853616, VHF 74.

ST HELIER

Chart BA 1137, 3278, SC 5604; Imray 2500, C33A, C33B

HW St Helier HW

DS (2M S):

Dover –0400W+0200E

MHWS	MHWN	MLWN	MLWS
11·1m	8·1m	4·1m	1·3m

Approach from NW, rounding La Corbière, keep the summit of Jersey high land in line with or above the lantern of the LtHo, but in bad NW weather keep 1½M off; at night keep the F.R Lt to the NE at the level of Corbière lantern. Once round keep ½M off S coast until just E of Noirmont Point it is possible to get on the Western Passage Ldg line, front Dog's Nest W bn, globe top; rear Grève d'Azette RW Lt tr, 082°.

At night
• Keep Noirmont Point LtHo bearing 095° until La Corbière LtHo is touching La Moye Point, 290°.
• Then steer 110° on that back bearing to pass about 2ca S of Noirmont Point.
• When Noirmont Point is abeam, steer 082° on Western Passage Ldg Lts: front La Grève d'Azette LtHo, Oc.5s; rear Mont Ubé Lt tr Oc.R.5s. This

passage passes N of Les Fours N card buoy; N of Ruaudière G bell buoy, Fl.G.3s; and S of RW Oyster Rock bn.
• Soon after passing Oyster Rock bn, and before reaching East Rock G con buoy Q.G, alter course to port round Platte bn, Fl.R.1·5s to bring Ldg Lts in transit: front Oc.G.5s, rear Oc.R.5s synchronised (R daymarks), 023°. Port side of entrance is well marked by BW diagonal bands visible by day before Ldg marks in haze.

From Gorey come down E coast on line La Coupé Turret open E of Verclut Pt 332° until about ½M N of Violet pillar buoy, RWVS Fl.10s. Steer about 240° to leave this buoy close to port and continue to pick up the line Icho BW tr, 14m, open S of Conchière bn, 2m, disc top. After about ½M on this line steer W to pass midway between Conchière bn and Canger W card Lt buoy, and continue so as to pick up line Noirmont LtHo B tr W band, Fl(4)12s open S of Demie de Pas YB tr 11m Mo(D) (–··) WR.12s, (R 130° to 303°), Racon, 290°. Follow this line until ½M from Demie de Pas, then pass 2ca to the S to get St Aubin Fort bearing 314°. Keep on this bearing, leaving Hinguette R can buoy, Q.R. to port and East Rock G con buoy, Q.G, to stb until on hbr Ldg line, 023°.

IPTS at Victoria Pier Head: Q amber in addition: power craft under 25m may proceed

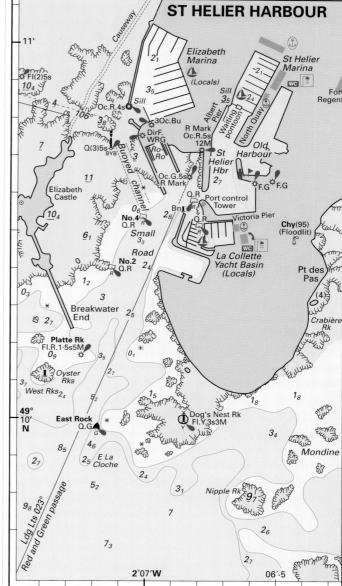

contrary to signals, keeping to stb.

Entrance Yachts exceeding 14m LOA or 1·8m draught should call St Helier VTS on VHF 14 to confirm there is berthing space. All should watch on this channel. Keep on Ldg marks until entrance opens: two G Lts in line 078°. Beware strong cross-set. Speed 5kn.

Berthing Visitors are directed by port control to marina in N part of hbr. There is a fixed sill 3·6m above CD; on this a hinged gate rises 1·4m to maintain a depth of 2·5m inside. The flap is lowered/raised when there is 2·2m of water. IPTS on E side of entrance. Depth gauges and an electric indicator board show when entry and exit are possible, approx HW±0300. Visitors normally berth at piers E, F or G at N end. Marina sometimes full in August. Two weeks maximum stay.

When marina is closed yachts should go to the waiting

pontoon alongside the Albert pier outside the marina with rafting.

Anchoring outside in Small Roads is not recommended owing to shipping movements and fish storage boxes. Elizabeth Marina is not available to short stay visitors.

Supplies Fuel at E side of main hbr, opposite entrance. No pontoon, note drying height at base of quay. All facilities.

☎/VHF Marina office 01534 885588. St Helier VTS VHF 14. Customs 73561. Weather VHF 25. MMSI 02329960. Jersey Coastguard VHF 82. NB: VHF 37/M is not used in Jersey.

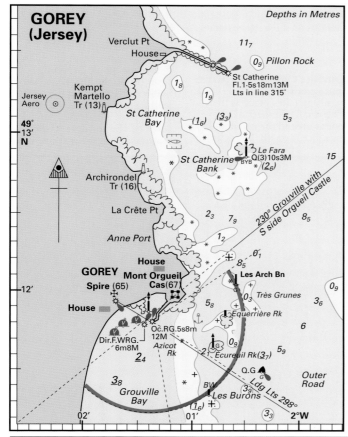

ST AUBIN

Chart BA 1137;
Imray 2500, C33A, C33B

A pleasant but drying hbr, much quieter than St Helier.

Approach as for St Helier but from Ruaudière G con buoy, Fl.G.3s, turn N to leave Diamond R can buoy, Fl(2)R.6s, close to port and steer 332° for 1·3M leaving two bns SSE of fort well to port.

Entrance A causeway between the fort and the shore dries 5·1m. The channel, leaving fort to port, has small port and stb buoys. At night round the fort pierhead, Fl.R.4s, and steer 254° in W sector of Lt DirF.WRG on N pier head (with Lt Iso.R.4s on same structure). Tide gauge on N pierhead; enter HW±0130.

Berthing There are berths for about 10 visiting yachts alongside N quay: dry, mud.

Anchorage E of Platte Rock bn SE of fort, 2m. RCIYC has three moorings for visitors in Belcroute Bay, 3½ca S of fort, 0·9m.

Supplies Water on quay; fuel; shops; boatyard.

☎ RCIYC 01534 41023.

France – Northwest Coast

W COAST OF THE CHERBOURG PENINSULA

Charts BA 2669; F 6966;
Imray C33A, C33B

Passage lights	BA No
Cap de la Hague	1512
Fl.5s48m23M Horn 30s	
Alderney	1536
Fl(4)15s37m12M	
Cap de Carteret	1638
Fl(2+1)15s81m26M	
Le Sénéquet	1648
Fl(3)WR.12s18m11/8M	
Iles Chaussey	1654
Fl.5s39m23M	
Horn 30s	
Pte du Roc	1660
Fl(4)15s49m23M	
La Pierre de Herpin	1670
Iso.4s20m13M	
Siren Mo(N)60s (–·)	

STREAMS RELATED TO DOVER

Alderney Race HWD SW; +0600NE

5M NW of Cap de Carteret: Rotary anti-clockwise, +0530N –0100S, each 3¾kn.

Between Les Écrehou and Chaussée des Boeufs: rotary anti-clockwise –0445N 1·2kn, +0145S 0·5kn.

Entré de la Déroute –0500NE, 1·2kn; –0300NW, 2·1kn; –0100W 0·5kn; +0200S 1·0kn.

The W side of the Cherbourg Peninsula is an inhospitable and rocky coast, with shoals and mussel and oyster parks extending far offshore, exposed to winds with any W in them. There are now three marinas but these can be approached only after half tide in reasonable weather. Fog may occur at any season. Tides run strongly and the W'ly swell breaks heavily on the shoals.

DIÉLETTE

Charts BA 3653; F 7133;
Imray C33A

HW St-Malo +0040

MHWS	MHWN	MLWN	MLWS
9·7m	7·4m	3·5m	1·2m

Diélette is a hbr about 11M S of Cap de la Hague, sheltered between ENE and S. Entrance dredged to –0·5m. It has a marina (2·5m) with a flap gate sill at +3·5m and 70 berths for visitors. Gate opens when there is 1·5m over the sill. There is a waiting pontoon, a tide gauge showing height over sill and IPTS entrance Lts for the marina. Dangerous to approach and uncomfortable in strong W or SW winds.

Approach The approach is without hazard but keep outside the W card lying 1½M WSW which marks the prohibited zone off the conspic nuclear power station. W card buoy unlit close W of Rocher Piernier.

There is an area of abnormal magnetic variation around Cap Flamanville.

Nevertheless, although it is simpler to go W of Jersey and Les Minquiers, this inshore passage provides the most direct route between Cherbourg, Granville and St-Malo, for which there are two channels: Passage de la Déroute and Déroute de Terre. Only the latter is possible by night.

Passage de la Déroute leads from Cap de la Hague between Les Écrehou and Basses de Taillepied; between Basse Occidentale des Boeufs and S Anquette (beware dangerous wreck position (doubtful) 49°05'·00N, 1°50'·00W); W of Basse Le Marié; E of Les Ardentes; over Banc de la Corbière and through Entrée de la Déroute between Les Minquiers and Iles Chausey. In the narrows the flood runs at 4–5kn, the ebb at 3½–4kn. Fishing buoys are common on this passage and some of these are linked by stout rope lying just beneath the surface.

Déroute de Terre should be attempted only near HW there being only 0·9m at the S end. It passes inshore between Trois Grunes and Cap Carteret; between Bancs Félés and Basses de Portbail; between Basse Jourdan Lt buoy and the W card buoy NW of Le Sénéquet; close E of special buoy, Internationale F, marking outer edge of oyster beds, 4M SW of Sénéquet Lt; E of La Catheue buoy; E of a wreck buoy to 1M W of Pte du Roc at Granville.

The night passage involves eight transits on shore lights: details in *Admiralty Pilot*.

Entrance On entering give the inner pier to port a wide berth as silting takes place at the end. The small commercial hbr opens up and the marina entrance is to stb. Dredging in

progress. –2m in Bassin de Commerce. –1·5m in approach channel. 70 visitors' berths. Extra moorings on waiting pontoons. May ground.

Facilities Chandler, sailmaker, laundry, pump out. Small shop behind café. Restaurants. Cycle Hire. Free shuttle bus to Flamanville (6km) and Le Pieux for supermarkets, etc. weekdays July/August.

☎ HM 02 33 53 68 78.
Taxi 02 33 52 53 53.

CARTERET

Charts BA 3655; F 7157, 7133;
Imray C33A

HW St-Malo +0025

MHWS	MHWN	MLWN	MLWS
10·6m	8·1m	3·7m	1·3m

Carteret, 10M S of Cap de Flamanville, is a small fishing port used also by vedettes to Jersey. The hbr dries apart from a marina with 60 visitors' berths.

HW St-Malo tide runs when access possible, near local HW NW across the entrance, 4kn.

Approach Do not approach from N as there are rks 1M offshore. From W dries 5ca off-shore. Steer for a W building with R roof on the shore at Barneville, 1½M E of Cap Carteret LtHo until it is possible to see inside the estuary, with the white head of W breakwater to port. Steer N for the entrance.

Entrance Dries. Dangerous in S to W winds. It is best to enter HW–0100. Port breakwater has Lt bn Oc.R.4s at head. Keep 50m off. To stb is a training wall, Fl.G.2·5s. This and a parallel training wall inside it both cover. The entrance channel dries 4m. Move to centre of channel just before the bn on E training wall. Inside the hbr the deeper water is to port, near the quays leading to basin. There are R and G piles where the channel turns E. The entrance to the marina is dangerous at opening

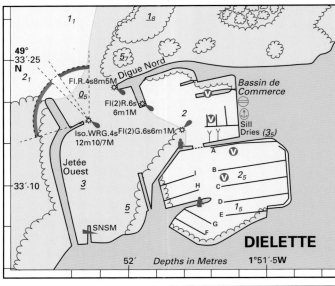

DIELETTE

49° 33'·25 N

2₁

0₅

Fl.R.4s8m5M

Fl(2)R.6s 6m1M

Iso.WRG.4s 12m10/7M   Fl(2)G.6s6m1M

Digue Nord

Bassin de Commerce

Sill Dries (3₅)

33'·10

Jetée Ouest 3

33'·10

SNSM

52'   Depths in Metres   1°51'·5W

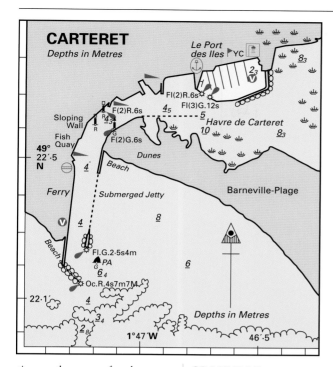

time as there are often boats waiting and a very fast current runs out.

Berthing Marina (2·3m) is on port side beyond town. Sill +5m between R & G Lt bns. The gate opens when there is +1·3m over it. Fl.R or G Lts indicate whether the gate is up or down. Depth inside from 2·3 to 8m according to tide. Visitors at far end on pontoon 'F' often with rafting.

Facilities All. Small town.

☎ Port de Plaisance 02 33 04 70 84.

GRANVILLE

Charts BA 3672; F 7156; Imray C33B

HW St-Malo +0005

DS (1½M offshore): Dover −0500NE HWD SW

MHWS	MHWN	MLWN	MLWS
12·9m	9·8m	4·5m	1·6m

A commercial and fishing port; also a popular holiday resort and yachting centre. Accessible only after half-flood. Note the huge range of tide.

Approach is rough in strong winds between W and NW. Pte du Roc has a steep cliff under grey, circular Lt tr with R top, Fl(4)15s. 3½M to W is a W card Lt buoy marking Videcoq Rk (dries 1m).

Entrance Best to arrive at HW−0130. From Videcoq buoy steer 090° to leave Le Loup BR Lt tr, Fl(2)6s to stb and W jetty head, Fl.R.2·5s, to port. Continue easterly past Avant Port and double back round the southern breakwater, Fl(2)R.6s, leading to the Port de Hérel marina basin. Keep clear of line of R posts, Fl.Bu.4s, marking the submersible breakwater of the dinghy basin.

Berthing Access to the Hérel marina is over a hinged gate, 16m wide, sill dries 4·5m, between R and G bns, Oc(2)R or Oc(2)G.6s. The gate opens and closes at HW±0300 to ±0330 when there is 1·4m on the sill. An illuminated panel on the breakwater shows the depth of water on the sill. If the panel shows 'O', entry is forbidden as the gate is closed. Moor to ends of first two pontoons, in front of office, 2·5m (but only 1·3m in N end of basin). Maximum 15m by 1¾m draught. 150 visitors.

Supplies Fuel on quay; water on pontoons. All facilities. Railway.

☎ Marina 02 33 50 20 06.

ÎLES CHAUSEY

Charts BA 3656; F 7156

HW St-Malo +0005

DS 1M N and S:

Dover +0130E −0500W

1M E and W:

Dover +0415N −0230S

Up to 3·7kn

MHWS	MHWN	MLWN	MLWS
11·2m	9·3m	4·2m	1·5m

A beautiful archipelago of islets and rocks. Grande Ile, the largest island, with anchorage and moorings in the Sound on its NE side. Much frequented in summer.

Note If coming from the Channel Islands, customs must be cleared at Granville or St-Malo.

Approach is straightforward from the S. The N is more difficult: marks are harder to distinguish and the approach dries.

Entrance from a position SE of the grey square LtHo, Fl.5s39m Horn 30s, on SE tip of Grande Ile, steer 332° with La Crabière Est bn, Dir.Oc(3)RWG.12s (329°-W-335°) in line with L'Enseigne W tr, to leave Epiettes G con bell buoy, Fl.G.2s, to stb. Keep La Crabière close to stb, and bear 030° to port to leave next RW bn to stb.

Berthing Moorings are normally available in the Sound, sheltered at LW, apart from swell from SE winds; but exposed at HW and uncomfortable with wind against tide. Anchorage is restricted by moorings but craft that dry out can find large stretches of flat sand, but beware rocky outcrops and poor holding with strong streams. The N part dries at springs but there is 2m in S. Anchorage is also possible in the bay to the W of the LtHo, sheltered from NW to E.

ST-MALO TO LES HÉAUX DE BRÉHAT

Passage lights	BA No
Cap Fréhel Fl(2)10s85m29M	1698
Le Grand Léjon Fl(5)WR.20s17m18/14M	1716
Barnouic VQ(3)5s15m7M	1730
Roches Douvres Fl.5s60m24M	1734
Les Héaux Fl(4)WRG.15s48m15-11M	1738

STREAMS RELATED TO DOVER

1½M N of Cap Fréhel HW Dover +0200ESE −0530WNW, both 3¾kn

Near La Horaine +0130 ESE 4kn −0445WNW 3¾kn

Near Les Héaux +0115E −0500W both 3¾kn

Keeping well offshore this passage presents no particular difficulties, apart from the strength of streams. Further inshore Cap Fréhel can be uncomfortable with wind against tide, which approaches 4kn at springs.

An area of magnetic anomaly is reported SE of Grand Léjon.

Going to Trieux river or further W, keep N of Grand Léjon.

Anchorages in offshore winds can be found in several places, including Erquy, Rade de Portrieux and W of Le Taureau bn tower (2°55'W).

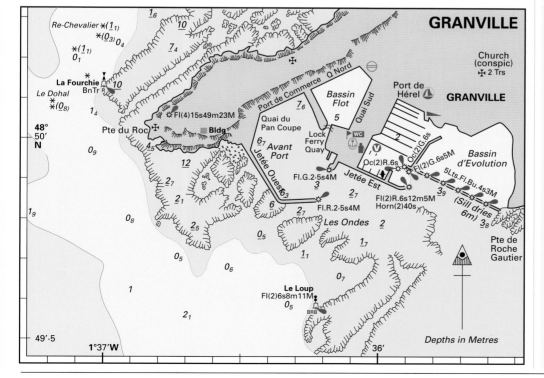

FRANCE – NORTH COAST AND CHANNEL ISLANDS

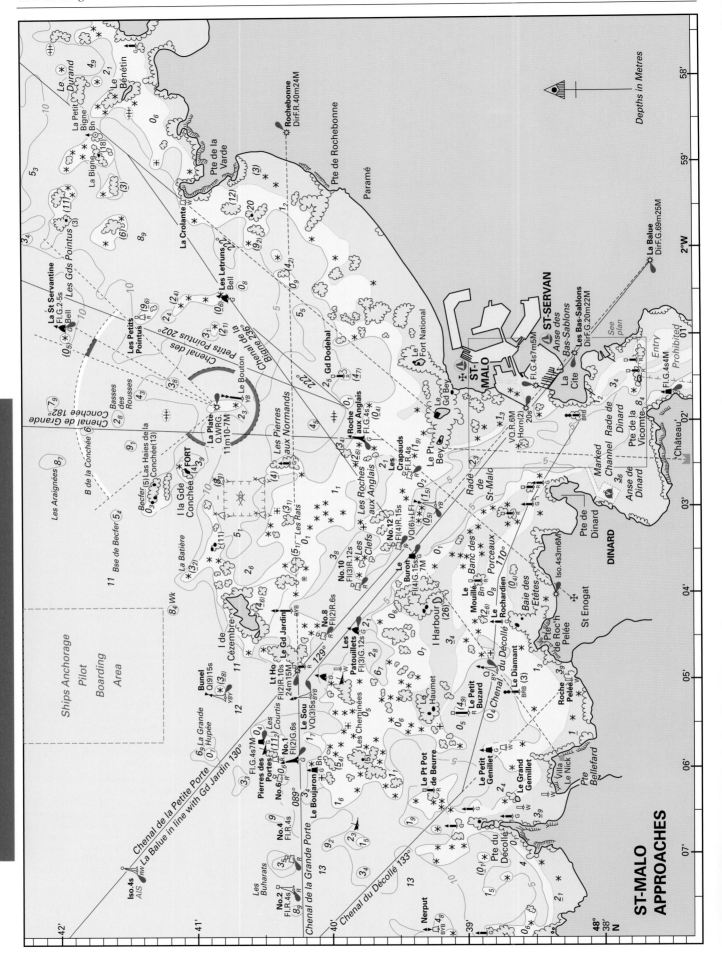

Depths in Metres

ST-MALO APPROACHES

ROTHÉNEUF

Chart BA 2700

HW St-Malo HW

DS (Chenal de la Bigne):
Dover +0145NE −0500SW

MHWS	MHWN	MLWN	MLWS
12·2m	9·3m	4·2m	1·5m

A drying hbr about 3M E of St-Malo, offering good shelter.

Approach and Entrance The approach is dangerous near HW when the rks are covered; and the flood, crossing the approach, is at its strongest just after half-tide. It is best to approach before then and if necessary anchor outside to await more water.

Leave St-Malo by Chenal de la Bigne; after passing La Petite Bigne G bn 50m to port, continue on that line (042°) to leave Le Durand (dr 10m) and le Roger (dr 4·7m) to stb, until the entrance bn, G cone up, is about 7ca off bearing 162°. Steer on that course to leave the bn close to stb. If too early to enter, anchor to await the tide about 50m N of this bn, 3–4m.

Anchorage The whole hbr dries about 8m, good flat sand. Supplies, shops in village.

ST-MALO

Charts BA 2700, 3659;
F 7130, 7155;
Imray C33B

HW St-Malo HW

For DS see various approach channels.

MHWS	MHWN	MLWN	MLWS
12·2m	9·3m	4·2m	1·5

St-Malo is an attractive old town with good shops and yacht moorings in the locked docks and a tidal marina.

Approach There are six approach channels, of which only the second and third are lighted. Beware strong cross-streams. From E to W they are as follows:

Chenal de la Bigne

(0·5m. DS Dover +0200ENE −0500SW)

A useful short cut bound for Granville or Cancale. Start about ¾M E of Rochefort bn tr and steer 222° with La Crolante W bn tr in line with N edge of Grand Bey. Be careful to be on this line when passing the narrow gap E of La Bigne stb bn. ¼M after La Bigne bn, steer 236° with Le Buron G Lt tr in line with W stripe under a villa on Pte Bellefard (if the latter not visible, keep Buron just left of Ile Harbour fort behind Buron). In rounding La Crolante keep at least 200m to NW to clear unmarked drying rock (3·2m) to SW of it. When La Plate tr comes on with Conchée fort, bear to port, 222°, to S of Roche aux Anglais buoy to join Chenal des Petits Pointus.

Chenal des Petits Pointus

DS Dover +0145E −0500WSW
This is another day channel for good visibility, with 0·3m but is the most direct from Iles Chausey. From a position 1¼M W of Rochefort bn tr steer 202° on line of W edge of small fort on Petit Bey with either high W house with four chimneys or with bell tr of Dinard ch to join Chenal de la Bigne E of Roche aux Anglais.

Chenal de la Grande Conchée

DS as for Chenal des Petits Pointus

Can be taken by day at all times save LWS; least depth 0·5m. Identify La Grande Conchée, a rock with round ruined fort on top, 5m, 1M E of Ile Cézembre.

From a position 3ca E, steer 182° to leave La Plate N card Lt tr, Y with B top, Q.WRG, to port. At night keep in W sector; R sector covers La Servantine Rock. Beware strong cross-stream and alter course if necessary to leave Roche aux Anglais G con, Fl.G.4s, clear to stb and bear SW to leave Les Crapauds R can buoy to port to join Chenal de la Petite Porte. Shallows are E and SE of Roche aux Anglais and W of Les Crapauds – about 0·5m, but easily passable after half-tide.

Chenal de la Petite Porte

7·2m. DS Dover: +0215E −0430W
Is the approach from NW. From the RW safewater buoy, Iso.4s, get Le Jardin Lt tr in line with La Balue grey square Lt tr (on high ground behind town), DirF.G, 129°. Beware strong cross-streams. When about 4ca off Le Jardin, bear S to get Bas-Sablons W square Lt tr, B top, DirF.G (intense 127°–130°) 20m, in line with La Balue, 129°. Beware ferries.

Chenal de la Grande Porte

7·2m. DS Dover: +0215E −0430W
Is the main approach from W. Le Grand Jardin grey tr, R top, Fl(2)R.10s24m, in line with Rochebonne W square tr, R top, DirF.R.40m 088°-intens-090°, 089°. The latter is difficult to distinguish by day: the buoyed channel can be followed. Finally No.3 Le Sou E card buoy VQ(3)5s marks the turn into Chenal de la Petite Porte.

Chenal du Décollé (regard as drying 1·2m) is the shortest approach from the W but is unlit. Tidal streams as in Chenal de la Grande Porte. Starting about 3½ca SW of No.2 R buoy, get W pyramid on Roche Pelée in line with W bn tr Grand Genillet, 134°. From this line steer with Pte de Dinard bn on with Rochardien bn 105°, altering course to N to round the latter to get on line of Ste-Croix ch round belfry with Pourceaux bn, 110° to round

Pte de Dinard, marked by two stb bns.

Entrance In the main channel get Ldg Lts, front Bas-Sablons W square tr, B top; rear La Balue grey square tr, both DirF.G, in line 129°; channel is well marked. This leads N of N card Rance Lt buoy, to head of Môle des Noirs, VQ.R. Port des Bas-Sablons (St Servan marina) is to stb of approach to the locks (dredged 2m).

Berthing
• **Port des Bas-Sablons** Pontoon berths max 12m. Entrance via narrow channel S of ferry catwalk. A sill, drying 2m, runs SW–NE across entrance to marina. Entry is possible at LW+0100 to −0130 with tidal coefficient over 70. Passage is possible at all times at neaps (coefficient 40). There are two 'Sablons' waiting buoys, 2m depth, at S edge of dredged channel. All other outside anchoring or mooring is forbidden or reserved. A tide gauge at the head of the ferry pier, with large illuminated repeater on W breakwater, shows depth on the sill, which is unmarked when covered. The head of the breakwater is lit, Fl.G.4s, but there is no corresponding R Lt at the far end

of the sill. Visitors moor to pontoon A in season, pontoon B out of it. Sheltered at LW but surge when sill is covered, especially with strong NW winds. Note that fuel can only be bought with card with chip, no cash, no Visa.
• **Bassin Vauban** in the docks, reached via L'écluse du Naye, Ldg line 070°, Lts F.R. Gates work between HW±0230, varied according to tide. Simplified code of signals. Possible to wait for opening in Port des Bas-Sablons. Yachts enter after ships and fishing boats; high lock sides require keepers' help with mooring lines. Yachts are moored to quay and pontoons at N end of Bassin Vauban; when full it is necessary to pass the lifting br into bassin Duguay-Trouin and moor to quay immediately to left after the br. Well protected and near old town.

Supplies Fuel from garages. (Fuel at Bas-Sablons marina with French credit cards only). Water on pontoons at both marinas. Visit Old City (Intra Muros).

☎ /VHF HM 02 99 20 25 01 VHF 12. Les Bas-Sablons 02 99 81 71 34. Basin Vauban 02 99 56 51 91.

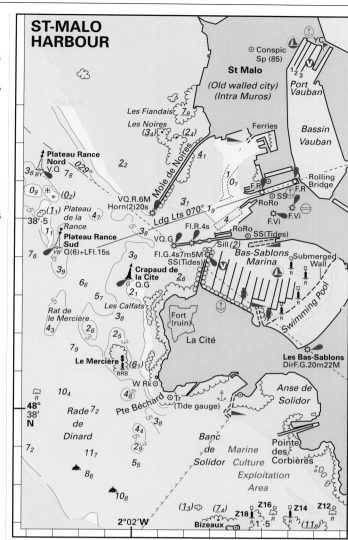

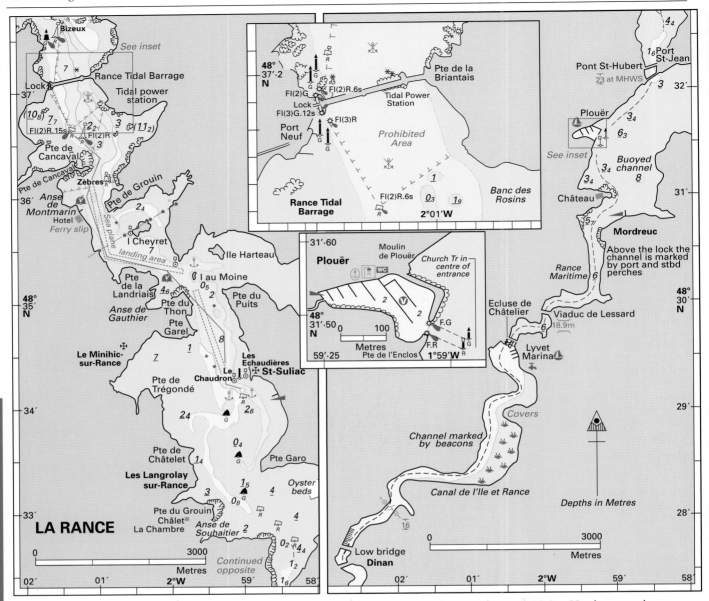

DINARD

Charts BA 2669, 2700; F 7130, 4233; Imray C33B

Berthing sometimes available in basin S of Pte de Dinard, dredged 1–2m with approach channel (1m) from Rade de Dinard. 150 berths, buoys sometimes available in bay (NR5 & 7).

Supplies water and fuel on quay.

☎ HM 02 99 46 65 55.

RIVER RANCE

Chart F 4233

The Rance is dammed by a hydro-electric barrage 1M above St Servan. A lock at the W end gives access to the river which with a reasonable engine and less than 1·6m draught and 16m head height is navigable to Dinan, above Le Châtelier lock, and thence to Brittany canal system. Above Dinan the canal has max 1·2m draught and 2·5m headroom. Do not go above Plouër (½M S of Pont St Hubert) when sea HW less than 9m. Remember that you need an ICC endorsed for Inland Waterways and a CEVNI rule book.

Approach, dredged 2m, is along W shore by La Jument G Lt tr, Fl(5)G.20s, leaving to port an exclusion safety zone below the barrage, marked by R conical buoys, cylinder topmarks, lettered ZI with a number. ZI12 is lit, Fl.R.4s.

Signals at the lock
3R Lts: No entry. 3G Lts vessels may pass. 2G 1 W act as instructed.

Signals near the centre of the barrage
W cone over B cone, pts up or G over W Lts:
Flood stream through sluices.
B cone over W cone, points down ebb stream through sluices.

Entrance The lock is 65m by 13m with 2m depth on the sill. It works from 0430–2030 and opens on the hour when height of tide on each side of it exceeds 4m. Yachts should arrive 20 minutes before opening (30 minutes if leaving). Locks open on the hour from seaward and on the half hour from the river. There are three mooring buoys to port in the approach from seaward. Boats with no masts enter last (first when descending) as they may otherwise be berthed under the lowered br. Enter as soon as there is room or gates may close. Ropes in lock.

Water levels do not follow the tide times. They are given 48hrs in advance at St-Malo office and at the locks at the barrage and at Châtelier. The channel dries at LW between St Suliac and Le Châtelier. Do not go above Plouër (½M S of Pont St Hubert) when sea HW is less than 9m. Le Châtelier lock, 3M below Dinan, opens when the river depth exceeds 8·5m, giving about 5hrs working per tide. When the lock is working there is 2m in the approach. Boats with 1·8m draught can lock through and berth to stb, but cannot get to Dinan. To Châtelier from seaward, leave HW–0300 to have the best conditions above Mordreuc. From Châtelier to the sea, leave at HW.

Headroom: Pont St Hubert 23m; De Lessard viaduct 18·9m. Headroom under power cable above Châtelier lock reported as 15m.

Anchorage anywhere up to St Suliac clear of main channel; holding variable.

Moorings
• Off St Suliac (1·5m).
• Small marina at Plouër on W bank just above Pont St Hubert. Enter between R and G Lts (lit when entry possible) on 284° with church midway between Lts. Sill gives 2m depth. 10 visitors' berths max 13m; two outside waiting buoys and visitors' buoys in approach.
• Boats with 1·4m draught may proceed to Dinan where visitors' berths are available in small marina on stb side. Local shops. HM and showers in half-timbered building.

☎/VHF Lock La Pointe de la Brebis 02 99 46 21 87. VHF 13; Plouër Port de Plaisance 02 96 86 83 15. VHF 09; Chatelier lock 02 96 39 55 66.

ST-CAST (LE GUILDO)

Charts BA 3659; F 7129; Imray C33B

HW St-Malo –0002

MHWS	MHWN	MLWN	MLWS
12·2m	9·3m	4·2m	1·5m

A 780 berth marina has been built by extending the east mole in a WSW direction for approximately 350m, the end of which, is marked by a light Fl.G. It has been dredged to 2m. 24h access. There is a substantial tidal range similar to St Malo. The main shops are in the town, pleasant walk 1M. Extensive sandy beach.

Approach By day, either side of Les Bourdinots, drying rocks 1M E of Pointe de St-Cast, marked by E cardinal buoy. At night, approach in either W sector of the hbr light Iso.WG.4s.

Entrance Follow round to the south of the new mole. The access channel is marked by small lit R and G buoys.

Berthing 40 visitors' berths. As directed. Alternatively 10 visitors' swinging moorings.

Facilities As expected of a modern marina. Capitainerie, showers etc near visitors' berths. Slip, boat hoist, pump out, chandler. Small shops nearby, 10 mins' walk to town. High speed ferry to St Malo.

◑ Marina Office 02 9681 0443; HM *Mobile* 06 0763 1092.

BAIE DE SAINT BRIEUC

Charts BA 2029; F 7154; Imray C34

The hbrs dry except Dahouet, Le Légué and Binic which have wet basins. The best anchorage in westerly winds is in the Anse de Bréhec, 48°43′N, 2°56′W.

ERQUY

Charts BA 3672; F 7310, 7154; Imray C34

HW St-Malo –0007. DS (Chenal d'Erquy):
Dover +0145ENE 3kn
–0500WSW 2½kn

MHWS	MHWN	MLWN	MLWS
11·2m	8·6m	4·0m	1·4m

A drying hbr whose roadstead provides a useful passage anchorage open SW.

Approach From E, steer 229° through Chenal d'Erquy (dangerous with strong wind against tide) with Cap d'Erquy in line with Le Verdelet Rock, leaving two S card Lt buoys to stb, La Justière 15s and Basse de Courant 10s. When Rohein YBY W card Lt tr is behind La Basse de Courant S card buoy, bear to stb to round the headland about 2ca off. From W, from 1ca S of Rohein Lt tr make good 100° until the jetty W Lt tr, R top, Fl(2)WRG.6s, bears 090°. Enter in W sector (081°-094°); beware lobster pots in R sector.

Anchorage Good holding ½M W of jetty. Not recommended with W or SW winds. Berths at or in lee of jetty are taken by fishing boats. Drying anchorage for visitors to E of the two moles. Anchoring in the W sector of the jetty Lt is forbidden.

Supplies Fuel.

◑ /VHF HM 02 96 72 19 32.

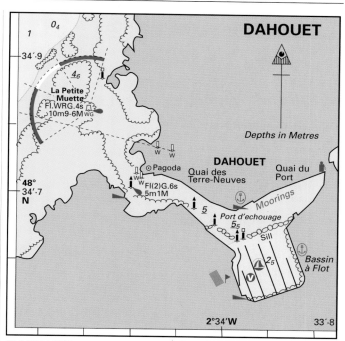

DAHOUET

Depths in Metres

DAHOUET

Charts BA 2029; F 7310, 7154; Imray C34

HW St-Malo –0002

DS Plateau des Jaunes: Dover +0130ESE 3kn, –0500W 2½kn

MHWS	MHWN	MLWN	MLWS
11·3 m	8·6m	4·0m	1·4m

A small fishing port with drying anchorage and wet basin open to the NW.

Approach from NW leaving Rohein W card bn tr, VQ(9)WRG.10s8M, and Plateau des Jaunes W card bn tr both to port and Dahouet N card buoy to stb. At night keep in W sector, 114°–146°, of Petite Muette Lt Fl.WRG.4s9–6M.

Entrance lies in a gap in the cliffs 1M SW of Pte Pléneuf. Bar is dangerous with strong NW winds and on the ebb with any sea. Await HW for entry, otherwise accessible at half-tide with 1m draught. La Petite Muette Lt tr may be passed on either side but locals use Ldg line 133°, pagoda just open N of tr, leaving it to stb, then steering S between tr and port bn at edge of shore, then to SE as entrance opens. The S approach with tr to port is on line of two Ldg bns, 100°. La Muette tr stands on a rocky platform and should be given 100m clearance.

Berthing Avant Port reserved for fishing boats. NE branch of inner harbour has 180 drying moorings on buoys. On the S side the wet basin has pontoons with 20 visitors' berths up to 12m o.a. and 2·4m draught at neaps. Sill passable HW±0200, dries 5·5m. Fair weather anchorage W of Petite Muette 2m.

Supplies Water, fuel (only at HW), gas. provisions.

◑ /VHF HM 02 96 72 82 85, VHF 16.

ST BRIEUC (LE LÉGUÉ)

Charts BA 2029; F 7154; Imray C34

HW St-Malo –0005

MHWS	MHWN	MLWN	MLWS
11·4m	8·7m	4·1m	1·4m

Approach W of Grand Léjon RW Lt tr, Fl(5)RW.20s17m, and 1½M W of Le Rohein YB W card Lt tr. At night keep in W sector of Grand Léjon (350°-015°) leading between Roches de St Quay and Le Rohein, to the landfall RW buoy, Mo(A)10s (·−); thence make good 210° for the entrance channel.

Entrance Channel which has some bends, dries about 5m, buoyed and lit. Entrance lock opening times between HW–0200 and +0130 according to tide. Blue flag from lock indicates sluicing of channel.

Berthing at end of W basin (turning br) beyond the swinging bay. Maximum 15m.

Supplies Fuel, water on quay; shops.

◑/VHF HM 02 96 33 35 41, VHF 16, 12 (during locking times).

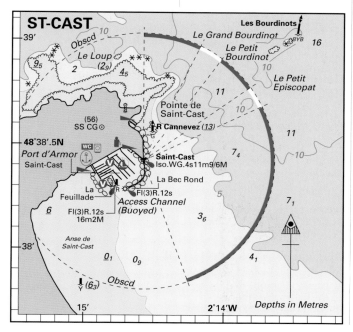

ST-CAST

Depths in Metres

BINIC

Charts BA 2029; F 7128, 7154; Imray C34

HW St-Malo –0008

MHWS	MHWN	MLWN	MLWS
11·6m	9·6m	4·0m	1·3m

A small port with drying avant port and wet basin.

Approach from the NW is easier offshore of St Quay Portrieux rocky plateau rather than by the inshore passage.

Entrance to Avant Port dries 5m; W tr, Oc(3)12s on N mole. Wet basin has a single pair of gates; gates open HW–0215 to HW+0015 sp less at nps. Gates stay shut if coefficient is 40 or less.

Berthing In wet basin alongside long pontoon on N side of hbr, rafting as necessary or as directed at lock gate. Maximum 16m LOA. Space for 50 visitors dependent on length. Outer harbour, hard flat sand, space limited. S jetty has rocky base.

Supplies Fuel in town, water, shops.

☎ *Capitainerie* 02 96 73 61 86.

ST-QUAY-PORTRIEUX

Charts BA 3672; F7154, 7128; Imray C34

HW St-Malo –0007

DS W of Roches St Quay: Dover +0100SSE; –0515NNW, 2kn.

MHWS	MHWN	MLWN	MLWS
11·2m	8·6m	4·0m	1·4m

The 1,000 berth marina is sheltered, lit and available at all states of the tide. The entrance faces SE.

Approach Drying rocks lie 6ca off-shore and the channel inside these can be approached from N or SE.

From the N, 5ca W of Madeaux W card tr in the W sector of the DirIso Lt on the elbow of the hbr wall steer 153° towards Les Noires W card buoy. When La Moulière tr is abeam, (at night alter course on entering the G sector of the Herflux Lt) steer 185° for the entrance Fl(3)G.12s giving the hbr wall 1ca clearance.

The SE approach is from 3ca SE of La Roselière W card Lt buoy. A course of 317° leads to the entrance Fl(3)G.12s in the W sector of the DirIso.WRG. Lt.

This approach is narrow and is bounded by shoals and oyster beds. It needs good visibility.

Entrance to the marina accessible at all states of the tide; entrance lts are Fl(3)G and Fl(3)R.12s. Entrance to the old hbr dries 3m. Berthing to pontoons max 18m LOA. Reception pontoon No.7. In season, a dory directs.

Anchorage possible in the Rade

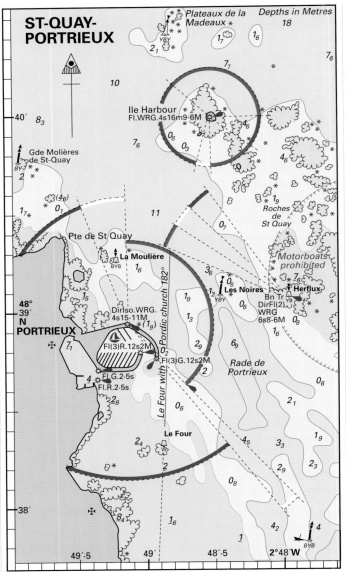

ST-QUAY-PORTRIEUX

Plateaux de la Madeaux

Depths in Metres

SE side of marina. Good holding but exposed at HW to N through E to S. Avoid oyster beds.

☎ Marina 02 96 70 81 30.
Old Harbour 02 96 70 95 31.

PAIMPOL

Charts BA 3673; F 7127; Imray C34

HW St-Malo –0007

DS La Jument channel: Dover +0100SSE 2¾kn, –0530NNW 2½kn

In Chenal du Denou Dover +0045SE –0545NW both 2¾kn

MHWS	MHWN	MLWN	MLWS
10·8m	8·4m	3·8m	1·4m

A pleasant small town with marina in wet basins.

Approach From the E by Chenal de la Jument. At 1¾M NE of L'Ost Pic Lt, 2 W towers R tops, Fl(4)WR.15s (105°-W-116°-R-221°-W-253-R-291°-W-329°), follow line of Paimpol spire over wooded Pte de Brividic, 260°, but N of La Jument R tr steer 262° on Ldg line, front W hut R top, Q.R.5m7M; rear W pylon R

top, Q.R12m14M (260°-264°). By night keep in W sector of Porz Don, Oc(2)WR.6s, past R sector of Lost Pic until the latter changes to W when the Ldg Lts can be followed. From N by Chenal du Denou (2·8m). At ¾M E of Men-Gam BYB E card tr, make good 193°, allowing for cross-set, with W Denou tr in line with Plouézec church spire. ¾M N of Denou tr it is essential near LW to keep on this line which passes E of Garap stb bn and only 50m E of a rock drying 1m close E of Garap, and W of Rohan-Hier port bn. Pass about ½ca W of Denou bn.

Alternatively, Chenal de La Trinité is well marked by bns but start from position at least 1ca E of Les Piliers BY bn (*see plan*) to avoid drying rks E of bn.

Anchor to await at least half tide 1ca SW of La Jument.

Entrance Continue on Ldg line to the buoys marking last 800m. Front Ldg mark is small Lt bn W with R top. Channel very narrow between buoys. Banks dry 6m. Lock gates open between HW±0230 (less at

neaps) with sometimes free flow around HW, with a current up to 2kn. Channel dries 6m in places and should not be attempted before half tide.

Berthing Boats under 10m moor in NW No.2 basin, immediately after the lock; larger ones (max 20m) go through the narrow passage to port into SE No.1 basin and moor at pontoons at the far end. If in doubt enquire at office on central mole between the two basins.

Supplies Water at entrance jetty and in No.2 basin; fuel. Good shops.

☎ /VHF Port office 02 96 20 80 77/2; Lock 02 96 20 90 02, VHF 09.

ILE DE BRÉHAT

Charts BA 3673; F 7127; Imray C34

Coming inshore from E take the Ferlas Channel

DS Dover +0100E –0545W, both 3¾kn

Transit lines are Bréhat chapel to the left of Quistillic W pyramid 296°; La Croix LtHo (two trs joined) in line with S side of Raguenez-Bras (small islet off SW tip of Bréhat) 277° and into well-marked Ferlas channel. At night, steer for Paon Lt, Oc.WRG (307°-W-316°) in its W sector until in W sector of Men-Joliguet Lt, Fl(2)WRG.6s (279°-W-283°). Steer in this sector past unlit Piliers tr and pick up the narrow W sector of Quinonec Lt, DirQ.WRG, (257°-W-257·7°). Near Rompa tr pick up the W sector of a third dir Lt on W bank of Trieux River – Kermouster DirFl.WRG.2s (270°-W-272°) which comes onto Coatmer Ldg line.

Ile de Bréhat has three main anchorages.
• **La Chambre,** off Ferlas channel, E of Men Joliguet tr. Very popular but uncomfortable at HW with a strong N wind. Anchor as far in as tide height allows.
• **La Corderie,** off the N end of the Kerpont channel which dries 1·5m and leads off Ferlas channel past SW tip of the island; it is passable only after 2hrs of flood. The tide runs at up to 5kn. Enter leaving Pierres Noires bn to port. (Note: There is no passage between Pierres Noires bn and Pierre Jaune bn to SW). Steer 352° for 2ca and then slightly W of N between visible rocks and bns (leave cones to W, cans to E). La Corderie is well marked with bns. At springs it is impossible to stay afloat out of the strong tide in the Kerpont, but at neaps a quiet berth can be found. Yachts can take the ground on hard flat sand. Four W visitors' buoys,

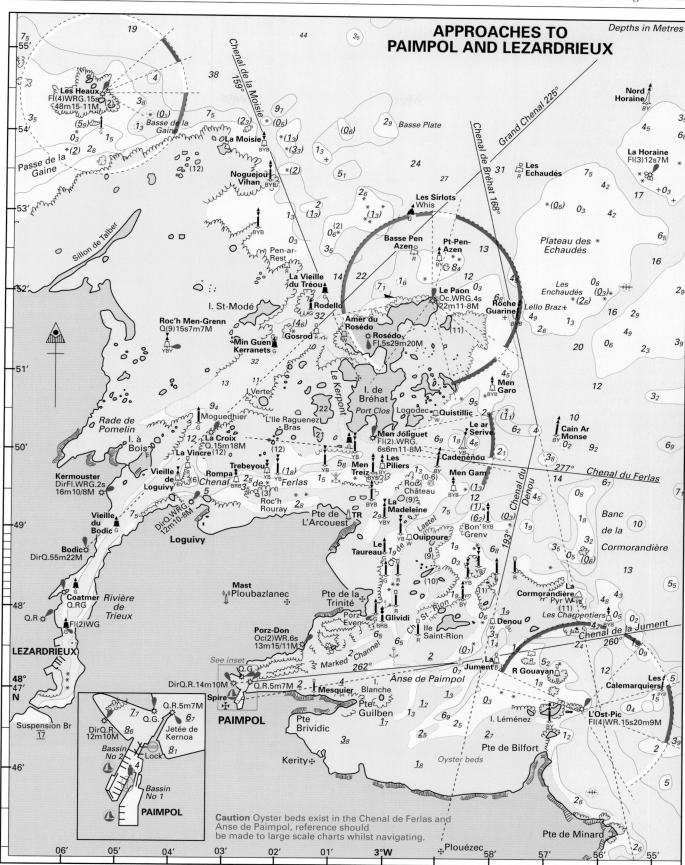

APPROACHES TO PAIMPOL AND LEZARDRIEUX

Depths in Metres

FRANCE – NORTH COAST AND CHANNEL ISLANDS

the inner two nearly dry at springs.
• **Port Clos** at the SW tip of Bréhat is the main landing place for tripper launches and room to anchor is limited. Not recommended.

TRIEUX RIVER, LÉZARDRIEUX

Charts BA 2027, 3673; F 7127; Imray C34

HW Les Héaux St-Malo –0010

DS (near La Horaine):
Dover +0130ESE, 4kn
–0345WNW, 3¾kn

MHWS	MHWN	MLWN	MLS
10·5m	8·0m	8·7m	1·3m

A beautiful river with many anchorages and good shelter.

Approaches The coastline is low-lying and the marks are not easily distinguished against the sun or in a haze.

The main approach channels are the Grand Chenal (6m)

from NE; the Chenal du Ferlas (2·4m) from the E and Chenal de la Moisie (less than 2m), unlit, from NW.

From the N, if W of Roches Douvres, get in the W sector of Le Paon square Lt tr, Oc.WRG.4s22m11-8M (181°- W-196°) and head S until on Ldg Lts of Grand Chenal, 225°.

Coming from N, E of Roches Douvres, or coming offshore from E, get in W sector of Les Héaux grey Lt tr, Fl(4)WRG.15s48m15-11M (247°-W-270°) until on Grand Chenal Ldg line. Both of these approaches leave to port La Horaine grey octagonal Lt tr, B diagonal stripes, Fl(3)12s.

By day make for a position 9ca NW of Nord Horaine N card buoy, 1M N of La Horaine, thence make good SW to Grand Chenal.

From NW, there is a more direct daytime approach via the Moisie Passage, dangerous in strong onshore winds.

DS Dover +0015S –0600N both 3¾kn.

At 1¾M E of Les Héaux Lt tr, steer 159° with Rosédo W pyramid in line with the chapel, both on Ile de Bréhat. Keep exactly on this line when passing close NE of La Moisie bn tr and Noguejou bn, both E card, to clear drying rocks to port, until in the Grand Chenal.

Le Grand Chenal

DS Dover +0100 inward; –0515 outward, both 3¾kn.

From Les Sirlots G con whistle buoy the Channel is clearly marked by day. At night the Ldg Lts are front La Croix (two towers joined) Q15m18M (215°-intens-235°); rear Bodic W ho with gable, DirQ.55m22M (221°-intens-229°). When Bodic dips behind La Croix, bear slightly W to keep it at the W edge of the tr. When Men-Grenn Lt Q(9)15s is abeam to stb, steer 235° until on Coatmer Ldg line, front Q.RG (220°-R-250° to seaward; 250°-G-053° up-river); rear Q.R.7M (219°). When Olenoyère unlit R tr is abeam to port head for W sector of Perdrix Lt Fl(2)WG.6s, (197°-W-203°). Leave Perdrix about 60m to stb; F Bu Lts ahead mark marina pontoons.

Berthing pontoons at Lézardrieux marinas maximum 15m. S marina has drying entrance. There are W visitors' buoys on west edge of channel N of Perdrix and fore and aft buoys off Lézardrieux marina. With care it is possible to anchor in the estuary between Ferlas channel and Perdrix (although the best places are taken by buoys); above the suspension br (17·7m above MHWS, 28m above CD) at Lézardrieux; and in the Ferlas Channel off Loguivy.

Rivière de Pontrieux is navigable at HW to Pontrieux lock and quays above it. The channel is straightforward (keep to outside of bends) and is navigable, except at LWS, to Roche Jagu chateau, visitors' buoys, 4M above Lézardrieux. Above that, passage best

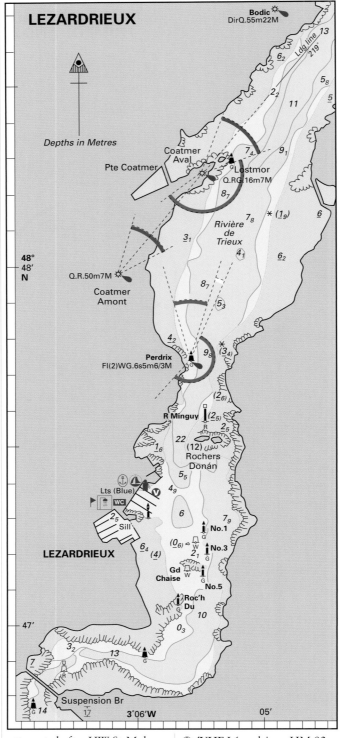

LEZARDRIEUX

Depths in Metres

48° 48' N

Q.R.50m7M ☼
Coatmer Amont

Pte Coatmer

Coatmer Aval

Lostmor
Q.RG.16m7M

Rivière de Trieux

Bodic ☼
DirQ.55m22M

Ldg line 13

219°

Perdrix
Fl(2)WG.6s5m6/3M

R Minguy

Rochers
Donán

Lts (Blue)
WC

Sill

LEZARDRIEUX

Gd
Chaise

No.1

No.3

No.5

Roc'h
Du

Suspension Br

47'

3°06'W   05'

attempted after HW St-Malo –0230. Keep to stb at the next two branches to Pontrieux lock (sill 3·5m above CD): gates open by day nominally HW±0215. Waiting buoy. Lock is open by day and night with a free flow when tide exceeds 8·8m. Moor to town quay (100 boats, rafting), port side ¾M above the lock, as directed by HM. Clearance under cable at Pontrieux lock reported as 25m.

Supplies Fuel and water at N marina. Water and fuel at Pontrieux. Shops at Lézardrieux, Pontrieux and Loguivy and some small ones on Ile Bréhat.

☎/VHF Lézardrieux HM 02 96 20 14 22, VHF 09; Lock Ecluse de Pontrieux 02 96 95 60 70, VHF 12.

LES HEAUX TO ILE DE BATZ

Passage lights	BA No.
Les Heaux	1738
Fl(4)WRG.15s48m15–11M	
Perros Guirec	
Kerjean	1770
DirOc(2+1)WRG.78m15–12M	
Les Sept-Iles	1786
Fl(3)20s59m24M	
Mean Ruz	1784
Oc.WR.4s26m12/9M	
Les Triagoz	1790
Fl(2)WR.6s31m14–11M	
Le Lande	1800
Fl.5s85m23M	
Ile Louet	1800.1
Oc(3)WG.12s17m15/10M	
Ile de Batz	1816
Fl(4)25s69m23M+F.R	

STREAMS RELATED TO DOVER

Plateau de Triagoz and Canal des Sept-Iles Dover+0145 ENE, –0430 WSW, both 3¾kn.

Baie de Lannion (centre) Dover +0130S-E-S 1kn, –0530 S-W-S 1½kn

Plateau des Duons (to E of Roscoff) Dover+0600 SSE, –0530 NNW, both 2¾kn

This is the most difficult section of the N Brittany coast, especially at night or in poor visibility. Inshore the coast has off-lying rocks which although buoyed are often not lit. Offshore are three main hazards: Les Sept-Iles, LtHo but off-lying rocks for 3M to NE; Plateau des Triagoz, LtHo but rocks and shoals to W; Plateau de la Méloine, rocks and shoals extending for 5M, unlit and only a W card buoy at one end. Between these the streams run strongly.

Bound for Chenal du Four it may be wiser, apart from settled weather and good visibility, to go N of these hazards. For Chenal de Batz go N or S of Les Sept-Iles, S of Triagoz, continuing W to pick up the main approach for Batz. For Baie de Lannion it is possible to go inshore by the Canal des Sept-Iles, in which there are 'high seas with wind against tide' (*Channel Pilot*).

At night approach from E in W sector of Méan Ruz Lt; when in the W sector of Kerjean Dir Lt (near Perros Guirec) steer 270°, leading S of Triagoz.

Anchorages are to be found with suitable winds E of Ile Tomé; Trégastel; off the slipway E of Sept-Iles LtHo; N of Ile Milliau; between Pte de Bihit and Rivière de Lannion.

Search and rescue From Les Heaux westwards the CROSS is based at Corsen. In distress call VHF 16 or DSC (MMSI No 002275300). There are six repeater substations.

Weather Navtex Area A is also based here.

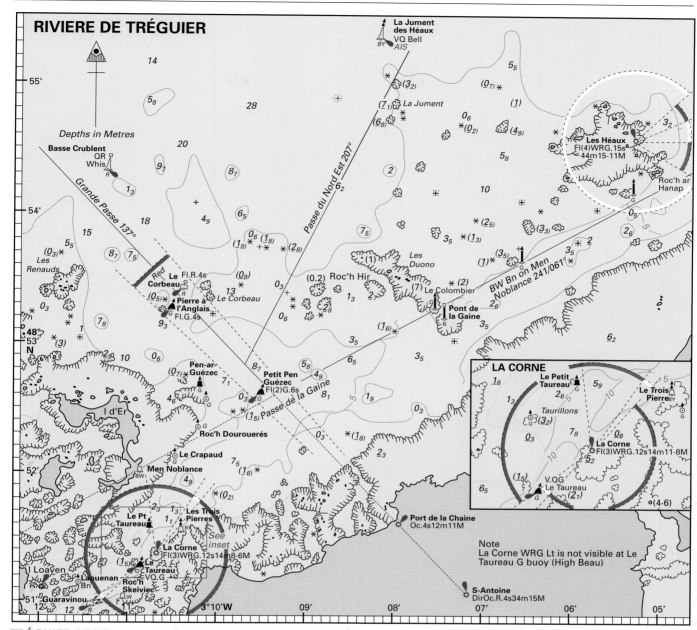

The Cruising Almanac

RIVIERE DE TRÉGUIER

TRÉGUIER RIVER

Charts BA 3672; F 7126; Imray C34

HW (Tréguier) St-Malo −0007

MHWS	MHWN	MLWN	MLWS
9·9m	7·7m	3·6m	1·3m

TIDAL STREAMS

5M N of Les Héaux:
Dover +0145 E −0430 W, 4kn

La Jument buoy:
Dover +0115 E −0500 W, 4kn

A pleasant sheltered river leading to the old cathedral town of Tréguier and marina.

Approach From the N and E the dominant feature is Les Héaux grey LtHo, Fl(4)WRG.15s44m15-11M. From W get 7M WNW and enter by Grande Passe. From E, either pass N of the LtHo and La Jument des Héaux N card bell buoy VQ to enter by Grande Passe or by day and in good visibility, get 2M ENE of Les Héaux and enter by Passe de la Gaine. The latter is shorter and may seem more attractive if conditions round

Les Héaux are uncomfortable, but the marks are difficult to see and the line must be strictly followed. From Trieux River, in good weather leave by the Moisie Passage (*details under Trieux*) for Passe de la Gaine.

Entrance There are two main entrances, only one lit, and a third more difficult.

La Grande Passe (4·4m)

DS N of Les Renauds:
Dover +0030 E, −0545 W, 4kn.
It can be taken at any time with reasonable visibility. From Basse Crublent R buoy, Q.R Whis, the Ldg line is 137°: front, Port de la Chaine W ho Oc.4s12m, and rear, Ste Antoine W ho, R roof, DirOc.R.4s34m. It can be hard to identify by day, in which case pick up the entrance buoys (Pierre à l'Anglais G con and Corbeau R can) and steer 137°, to Petit Pen ar Guezec G con buoy and alter course to stb when La Corne bears 217°. There is a strong cross-set from Crublent buoy to well past

Corbeau, dangerous at springs, 3¾kn, Dover +0030E, −0545W.

Passe de la Gaine (0·3m)

DS Dover +0015 ENE; +0445 WSW, 3kn

It is not easy and is unlit; the Ldg marks require 8M good visibility, but if there is enough, about 1M, to see the first bn before starting the passage, after half flood there are few difficulties. At 1¾ca S of Roche ar Hanap (7m), which is 3ca SE of the LtHo, get Men Noblance BW pyramid in line with Plougrescant mark (W wall with B vert band, 1¾M behind it), 242°. Pass two stb bns into the Duono narrows between port and stb bns to Petit Pen ar Guezec G con buoy.

Chenal du Nord-Est (0·8m) is to the E of Corbeau rocks. W and NW seas break across it; the Ldg marks are often not visible and with a strong cross-tide this entrance can be dangerous. At a position SW of La Jument N card Lt buoy, Ldg line is Roc'h Skeiviec W tr in line with Tréguier cathedral

spire, 207°. When the latter disappears, follow buoys and bns. Not recommended.

River

DS N of La Corne Lt tower: Dover +0030 SW, −0545 NE, 3kn.
From La Corne the channel is clearly buoyed. At night on the Grande Passe line, when G sector of La Corne light, Fl(3)WRG.12s, changes to W, steer in that sector 217°. The W sector Lt is focussed high, so not seen near Le Taureau buoy. Leave La Corne on junction of RW sectors 239° leaving VQ.G con buoy Le Taureau 40m to stb. Proceed to Guarivinou Lt buoy, Fl.R.4s (each of these two buoys is near E edge of the white sector of Corne Lt), whence come S into the lit channel. Approaching the marina, the channel follows the E bank on outside of the bend: do not aim straight for the marina Lts. The br has 3m headroom at HW, when river is navigable for 3M above it.

On leaving remember that from S La Corne has R sectors on either side of W sector.

Berthing There is a marina at Tréguier (maximum 12m) on stb side before the br over the main channel. The stream is strong around half-tide: it is essential not to attempt to enter between the lines of pontoons across the stream. If the stream is too strong go alongside the waiting pontoon in mid-channel to the North of the Marina. It is equally important not to leave other than at slack water. At LWS there may only be 1·5m between the waiting pontoon and the marina. Shallow berths near bank. Temporary anchoring only is permitted in sight of the town but is otherwise possible in the river, out of the fairway, especially off Roche Jaune village (off small shingle beach 1½ca S of ramp); at Pen Paluc on W bank 1½M to the N; or anchor close inshore under the château 1ca to seaward of No.10 buoy, 5m (crowded in season; charge). Strong stream, dig in anchor.

Supplies Water at marina and Roche Jaune; diesel at marina. Shops at Tréguier and Roche Jaune. Well-stocked chandlery over the br. Wednesday market. Launderette.

☏ HM 02 96 92 42 37.

PORT BLANC

Charts BA 3672; F 7125; Imray C34

HW St-Malo –0035

DS Dover +0015E –0600W, 2½kn

MHWS	MHWN	MLWN	MLWS
9·3m	7·4m	3·4m	1·3m

Beautiful and unspoilt small village, open NW to NE.

Approach To the E are rks extending 1½M offshore as far as Pte du Château, and Ile Ziliec with a large house. To NW the Plateau du Four has a R can whistle buoy on its NW side.

Entrance (7m) lies between Ile du Château Neuf to W and Ile St Gildas to E, both with conspic W pyramids. Enter with Le Voleur W tr DirFl.WRG.4s14–11M, 150°. Marks in gap in trees are difficult to see until on the line. Best line is with Ile St Gildas twice as far to port as Ile du Château Neuf is to stb.

Berthing Available space is being taken up by buoys; subject to this anchor SW of Ldg line, SW of Roc'h Ruz R

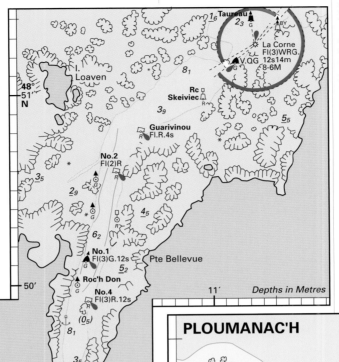

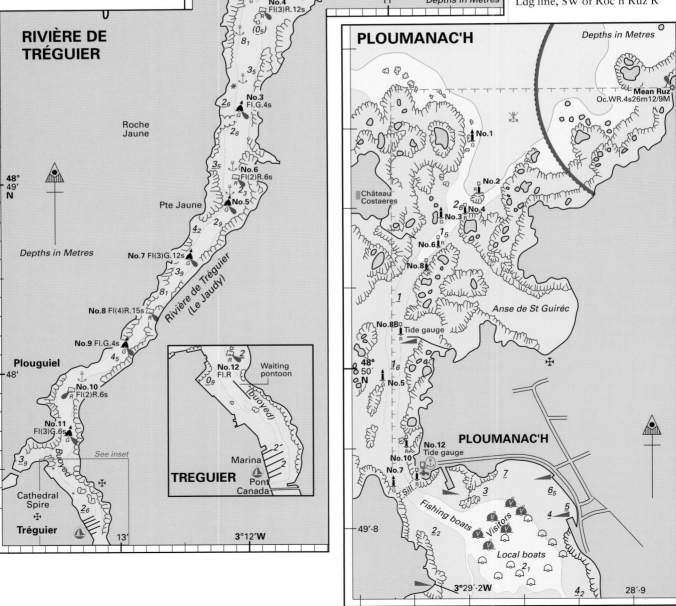

RIVIÈRE DE TRÉGUIER

TRÉGUIER

PLOUMANAC'H

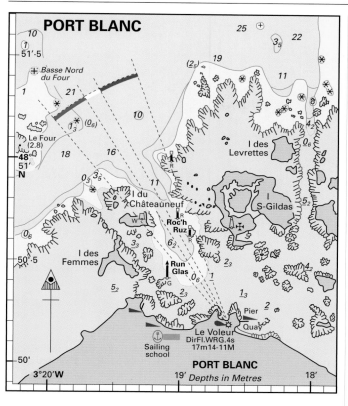

bn, 7m, or closer in, sand and shell. There are W visitors' buoys in the W part of the hbr, offshore of small craft moorings, and also in the E, drying, part of the hbr with room to anchor clear of them. Very uncomfortable at HW with a W or NW sea. If taking the ground in shallower area, beware of some deep holes.

Supplies Water from tap on drying ramp E of the Lt tr. Small shop in village.

☎ *Capitainerie* (Sailing School) 02 96 92 64 96.

PLOUMANAC'H

Charts BA 2027; F 7125; Imray C34

HW St-Malo –0035

DS Dover +0030E 0615W 2¾kn

MHWS	MHWN	MLWN	MLWS
9·3m	7·4m	3·6m	1·4m

A village with wet inner harbour with sill and drying outer harbour. There are fantastic shapes in the wind eroded rose pink granite in the entrance.

Approach By day make for W side of peninsula on which is Ploumanac'h Mean Ruz pink square Lt tr, not conspic, Oc.WR.4s26m12/9M.

Entrance between the LtHo and Ile Costaeres (towered château, conspic) is well marked by bns. S end dries 1·6m. At LW keep No.2 and No.4 in transit to avoid rocks near No.1.

Berthing Anchoring in outer harbour is not permitted. Two W waiting buoys. Inner harbour has sill drying 2·5m. There are two lines of moorings for visitors, 1·3 to 2·2m. Shore access at slipway save at LWS. Tide gauge on port bn by sill; when base is covered there is 2·5m on sill.

There is a large digital gauge showing clearance over the sill on the ferry wall to the north, in line with pontoon E, but visible from most berths.

PERROS-GUIREC

Charts BA 2027; F 7125; Imray C34

HW St-Malo –0035

DS NW of Ile Tomé:

Dover +0100E –0430W, both 3¼kn

MHWS	MHWN	MLWN	MLWS
9·3m	7·4m	3·4m	1·3m

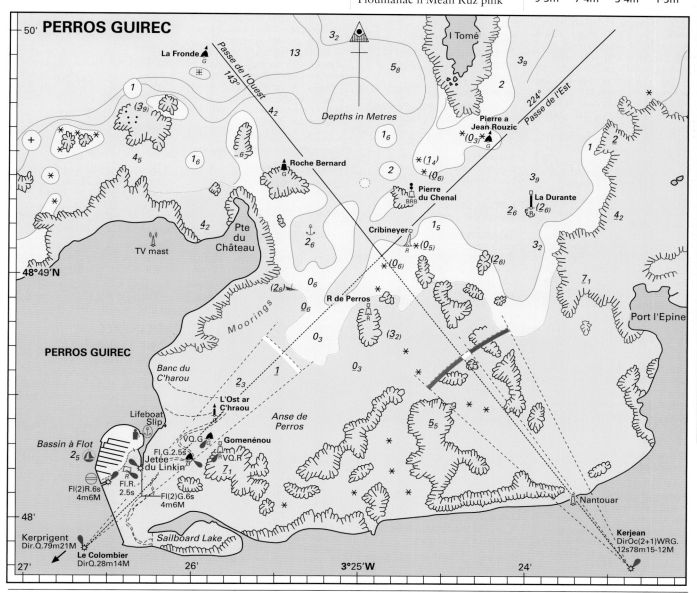

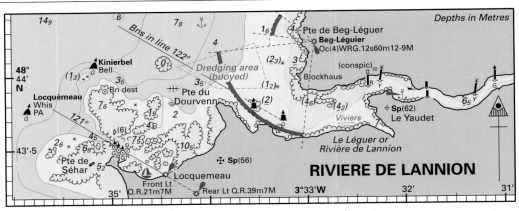

A popular holiday resort with a marina and drying approach.

Approach Ile Tomé with its surrounding plateau separate the E and W channels.

Passe de l'Est

DS Dover +0030ENE −0430WSW, both 3kn

From Guazer R whistle buoy, 2½M NE of Ile Tomé, pick up Ldg line 224°: front Le Colombier W ho DirQ.28m14M (217°-intens-233°); rear Kerprigent W tr, DirQ.79m21M (221°-228°).

Passe de l'Ouest

(0·9m) DS Dover +0030SE, −0430NW, both 2¾kn
Enter between Bilzic R tr and La Fronde G con buoy with Kerjean W tr, B top, DirOc(2+1)WRG.12s78m15-13M (143°-W-144°), bearing 144°. By day have it in line with Nantouar W disused LtHo on the shore, 143°. When ¼M SW of Pierre du Chenal BR bn tr, turn SW into Passe de l'Est. Moorings cross Ldg line, lights may be lost once past R. de Perros.

Entrance The Passe de l'Est leads to the hbr to stb. Entry is possible after half-flood with 1·5m draught. There are some waiting buoys. The basin has a sill on the SE side, drying 7m, marked by R and G perches and a gate 6m usable width, at E end. The gate is open by day at springs between HW−0200 and +0130; at neaps between HW−0030 and HW. At night it is open only at HW. At low neaps, coefficient less than 40, it may not open at all. Sometimes shorter opening at weekends. Beware of strong current as the gate opens.

Berthing On entry turn to port for pontoons. Depth 2·4m decreasing to NW and towards the shore. Or anchor to NE of port according to height of tide; on E side of peninsula, S of Roche Bernard (swell with NE winds); or on E side of Ile Tomé (beware Platier du Tomé, 0·6m, 1ca off middle of Is). Trots of W buoys have been laid N of the marina many of these dry at spring tides.

Facilities Water on pontoons. Fuel station at E end of basin serves when gate is open. Shops on quay and up hill to town where there is a fine church.

☎ Marina 02 96 23 37 82.

LES SEPT ILES

Charts BA 2027; F 7125; Imray C34

A fair weather open anchorage. Approach on 285° towards the E end of Ile aux Moines from Les Dervinis S card buoy, avoiding isolated rocks. When Ile de Bono bears 345° steer on this bearing into anchorage Anchor E of LtHo on Is. Landing on steps at end of slip; this is the only landing place allowed. Path to LtHo and old fort at W end of Is. Bird sanctuary.

TRÉGASTEL

Charts BA 2026, F7125; Imray C34

About a mile W of Ploumanac'h, this hbr provides moorings afloat. Rock La Pierre Pendue conspic E of entrance which is marked by bns. Inner buoys dry but outer ones have 2m; 10 are for visitors. Uncomfortable in winds between W and N, especially near HW when outer rocks cover. Some shops.

LANNION RIVER

Charts BA 2026; F 7151, 7124; Imray C34

HW Brest +0102

DS at Le Crapeau:

Dover +0100ESE +0500WSW,

MHWS	MHWN	MLWN	MLWS
9·0m	7·1m	3·4m	1·3m

A mainly drying river in a wooded valley leading to Lannion about 4½M from the entrance.
Le Taureau rock, 2m, 2M offshore is a good guide.

Approach should not be attempted with winds from WNW to NW, when shelter can be sought under Pte de Locquirec, 3M to SW. From W keep Ben Leguer W LtHo, R top, Oc(4)WRG.12s60m12–9M, bearing 090° (at night keep in the W sector, 084°-098°), leaving Kinierbel G bell buoy to stb. From NW the two G towers in the entrance in line, 123°, lead N of Le Taureau rocks (11m), but the line leaves close to stb the Ar Boulier rock, 4·9m, 4ca N of Le Taureau. When Ben Léguier LtHo bears 095° make for it and follow instructions for entrance.
By night keep W of R sector (339°-010°) of Triagoz Lt, Fl(2)WR.6s, leaving Le Crapaud W card Lt buoy, Q(9)15s, to port, to pick up Locquémeau Ldg Lts 121°, Q.R.7M, and then follow W sector of Ben Leguer.

Entrance dries 0·4m and the sea bed may be marked by dredgers digging gravel. Do not come S of Ben Leguer, or into its G sector, until Locquémeau Q.R Lt is just W of S to miss rk drying 0·1m ¾M to its N; then bear SE to leave two G towers close to stb. If waiting for the tide to rise, anchor in the bay N of Locquémeau front Lt, keeping E of N of it. River is clearly marked to Lannion but is unlit. There is a br at Lannion, headroom 2·5m. If going above the br by dinghy, beware large masonry blocks in the channel which are used as a canoe slalom.

Berthing There is room for two boats to anchor in a pool not used by local boats which has 2m. The pools just upstream of it, 1–3m, have many moorings leaving little swinging room, two anchors necessary. At Lannion moor to short quay on S bank by the first houses, dries 5m. There is a wrecked fishing boat at the W end.

Supplies Water on quay, fuel from garage, shops at Lannion.

TRÉBEURDEN

Charts BA 2026; F 7151, 7125; Imray C34

HW Brest +0105

DS at Basse Blanche buoy:
Dover +0100 SE–E +0500 SW–W, both 2kn

MHWS	MHWN	MLWN	MLWS
9·2m	7·3m	3·5m	1·4m

A popular holiday resort with marina, and good anchorages except in W and NW winds.

Approach on the W side of Le Crapaud shoal. The marks for the passage to the E are difficult to identify and it cannot be recommended. By night keep W of R sector of Triagoz Lt Fl(2)WR.6s and steer 064° on junction of W and G sectors of Lan Kerellec Lt Iso.WRG.4s8-5M (48°46·8N 3°35·0W). Warning: the flood sets strongly from S onto the rocks near Ar Gouredec buoy.

Entrance Steer 064°on Lan Kerellec Lt (grey tr) to pick up buoyed and lit channel to entrance on N side of marina. Enter over sill between G and R lit bns with signal Lts: GGW Lts vert: entry permitted; 3R(vert): entry prohibited.

Berthing at pontoons in marina (maximum 16m, 1·5 to 3·4m depth) or to W visitors' buoys outside, uncomfortable around HW with W swell. There are anchorages
• N of Ile de Milliau, W of a line joining the Is slipway to the white high-rise apartment block at Trébeurden, 2m.
• NW of that, as close in as tide allows to the edge of the beach SE of Ile Molène. Exposed at HW.
• 1½M N of the marina is a neap tide anchorage for deep draught boats or for bilge keelers. Large-scale charts SHOM 7124, 7125 are needed for the interesting approach to this anchorage which is free of swell.

Facilities All. Shops. Wi-Fi.

☎ HM 02 96 23 64 00.

LOCQUÉMEAU

Charts BA 2026; F 7151; Imray C34

A drying hbr with anchorage open to winds W to NW.

Approach At ¾M S of Le Crapaud W card buoy, steer 121° on Ldg line: W frame, R top, Q.R (068°-228°) 21m front; W gabled ho Q.R.39m7M (016°–232°).

Entrance Leave Locquémeau G con whistle buoy close to stb and enter N of G Séhar bn.

Berthing Anchor E of bn off end of slipway, 1·5m; or dry further in E of second, short, slipway.

LOCQUIREC

Charts BA 2026; F 7125

Drying hbr at head of bay (3°38'·5W) with deep water moorings, including visitors. Report to Mairie. Considerable surf in onshore winds.

Supplies Water on quay. Shops.

☎ HM 02 96 91 44 31.

PRIMEL

Charts BA 2745; F 7124, 7151; Imray C34

HW Brest +0107

DS see Morlaix

MHWS	MHWN	MLWN	MLWS
9·0m	7·1m	3·4m	1·3m

A small fishing village in a rocky bay exposed to NW.

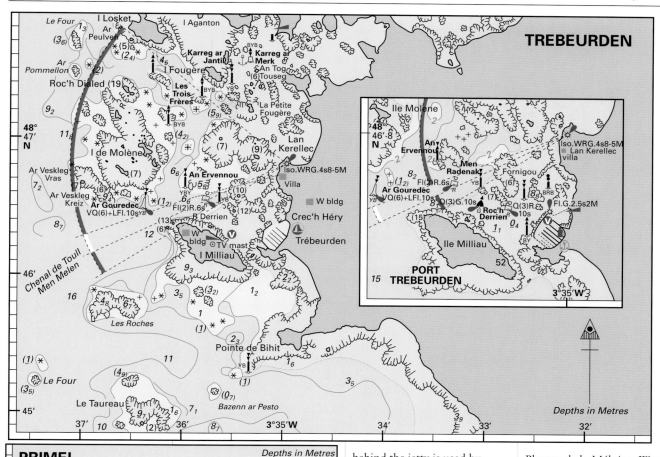

TREBEURDEN

PORT TREBEURDEN

Depths in Metres

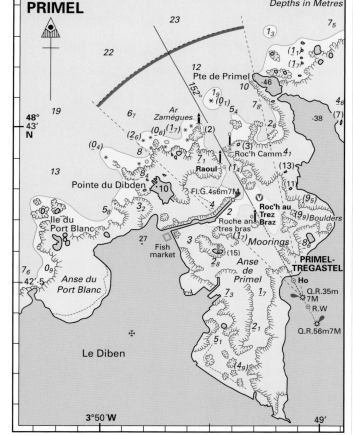

PRIMEL

Depths in Metres

Approach At ½M NW of Pte de Primel pick up Ldg marks, three W rectangles with vert R stripes, two lit Q.R, 35 and 56m, (134°-vis-168°), 152°.

Entrance Leave Zamégue rk (painted bright GW on seaward side with con top mark) to stb and enter between two conspic

rocks marked by bns. Gap is 27m wide, 7m depth.

Berthing Some visitors' buoys, 10 in deep water. Reported rolling in SW Force 4/5+. Anchor in channel, 2–9m, but not more than 2ca inside the entrance, or dry out clear of the outcrops. The dredged area

behind the jetty is used by fishing boats; the rest of the jetty is rocky.

Supplies Water on quay. No shops at Primel.

☎ HM 02 98 62 28 40.

MORLAIX ROADSTEAD AND RIVER

Charts BA 2745; F 7095, 7151; Imray C35

HW Brest +0100

DS Plat. des Duons:

Dover +0600W; +0100E both 2¾kn

MHWS	MHWN	MLWN	MLWS
8·9m	7·1m	3·4m	1·3m

A wide estuary, available at all times except by night in strong onshore winds, leading by a drying channel to Morlaix, where there is a wet basin with marina.

Approach Prominent marks are: Ile de Callot with chapel, 18m, and small W tr off Carantec peninsula; Château de Taureau, a large square fort; Ile Noire W Lt tr, R top, Oc(2)WRG.6s15m11–8M, 4ca ESE of Le Taureau; and Ile Louet W Lt tr, Oc(3)WG.12s17m15/10M.

From Roscoff keep Piguet W bn tr in line with steeple of Notre Dâme among trees on Ile de Batz 293° (at night in W sector of Charden Lt Q(6)+LFl.WR.15s (289°-W-294°) until on Ldg line of Grand Chenal, just W of Stolvezen R buoy. From the N pass between Plateau des Duons, grey bn tr 10m, and

Plateau de la Méloine, W card whistle buoy, for any of the three entrance channels.

From NE pass between La Méloine and Pte de Primel. At night from the E keep in W sector of Triagoz Lt Fl(2)WR.6s, bearing at least 063° astern to pass N of Méloine bank.

Entrance There are three main entrance channels, of which only the first is available at all times, and even that is difficult at night, especially with strong onshore winds.

• **Grand Chenal** E of Ile Ricard 2m

DS: Dover +0015 in-going; –0615 out-going, 2½kn

Get Ile Louet Lt tr in line with La Lande rear W Lt tr, B top, Fl.5s85m23M, behind it, 176°. On this line, abreast Calhic G bn tr, steer 160°, leaving Corbeau G tr to stb and pass between Château de Taureau and Ile Louet. Hence keep edge of the Château on with W edge of Ile Ricard astern steering 153° past La Barre de Flot stb buoy into the estuary. At night get the two Ldg Lts, front Ile Louet Oc(3)WG.12s15M, rear La Lande Fl.5s23M, in line 176°, leaving Ile Ricard G tr close to stb. When Ile Noire Lt, Oc(2)WRG.6s, changes from R to G, steer 160°, leaving Taureau fort and bn to port and entering G sector of Louet. It is then prudent to round the Lt at just over 1ca off, leaving unlit Barre de Flot buoy well clear to port and anchor or pick up W

FRANCE – NORTH COAST AND CHANNEL ISLANDS

345

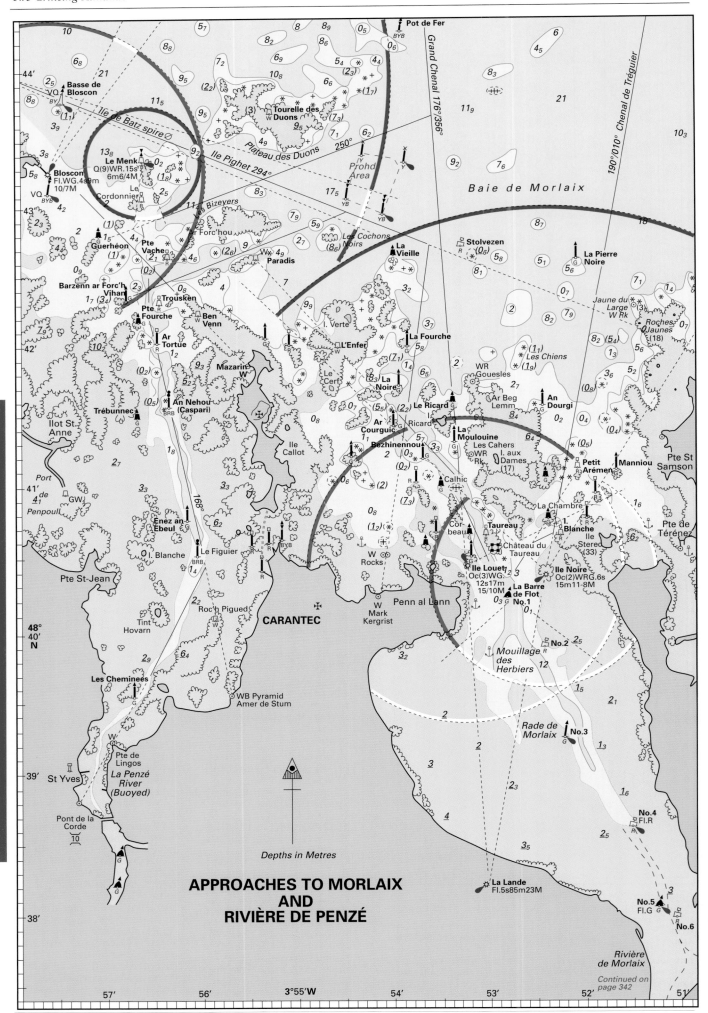

APPROACHES TO MORLAIX
AND
RIVIÈRE DE PENZÉ

Depths in Metres

Continued on page 342

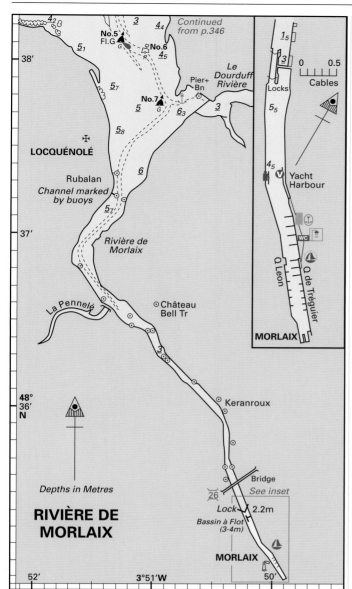

RIVIÈRE DE MORLAIX

Depths in Metres

---

buoy off Pen Lann until daylight.

• **Chenal de Ricard**, 5·8m, is a wider variant of Grand Chenal going W of Ile Ricard. It is a safer choice when an onshore swell is breaking on the rks bordering Grand Chenal but it is unlit. From a position on the Grand Chenal Ldg line, N of Stolvezen R buoy, bring La Pierre de Carantec, an isolated double rk, in line with a W mark, Kergrist, 4ca E of Carantec church tr, 188°. The channel is well marked by G stb bns. After La Noire stb bn bear round to SSE with a back bearing of L'Enfer W bn tr in line with Paradis W bn tr, 319° to join Grand Chenal NE of Calhic bn.

• **Chenal de Tréguier** dries 0·8m and should not be attempted before half-tide. DS as for Grand Chenal. Steer with Ile Noire W Lt tr, R top, in line with La Lande W Lt tr, B top, 190°. Having passed between La Chambre G tr and Ile Blanche R tr, steer SW until E edge of Château de Taureau comes on with W edge of Ile

Ricard and with this line astern continue past Barre de Flot buoy into the estuary. By night keep Ile Noire Lt Oc(2)WRG and La Lande Lt Fl.5s in line 190° until Ile Louet Lt Oc(3)WG changes from W to G, 244°, then steer for it until Ile Noire lt, Oc(2)WRG.6s, turns from R to G, 135°, then round to 180°. Leaving Barre de Flot to stb, Ile Noire will change from G to W. 051°; continue for 1ca. The channel continues 153°: find a berth as convenient either side.

Morlaix River From Barre de Flot the river is marked by buoys and stakes, including two G and two R Lt buoys, Fl(2)G.2s/Fl(2)R.2s. The channel dries about 1M NNW of Dourduff. It is 5½M from Pen Lann anchorage to Morlaix lock. Leaving at half-tide or HW–0200 will give sufficient time. The narrow part is entered at Dourduff and is clearly buoyed; unlit but many of the buoys have reflectors. As the river narrows there are Ldg marks, with St Andrew crosses, showing the deeper water.

Below Morlaix are an overhead cable (32m) and a viaduct (30m).

Anchorages
• Between **Barre de Flot** and **Pen Lann**. Land near NE corner or at fish quay on S side of Pen Lann. Do not pick up buoys marking oyster beds.
• **Mouillage des Herbiers**, a creek between mud banks, ½M S of Barre de Flot, on W side of channel, 4m.
• Between **Barre de Flot** and **Dourduff**, just outside the channel clear of oyster beds; exposed to NW.
• At neaps, in the entrance to **Dourduff** river; br has 3m headroom.
• Off **Locquénolé**, on W side, if space allows among the moorings. Sand barges pass close and good anchor Lt is essential. Anchoring is forbidden above this point.
• **Morlaix** The wet basin, 2·50m, is formed by a weir with lock at W side; the inner sill is 3·1m above CD, the lock 63m by 16m. The gates operate only by day at HW–0130, HW and HW+0100. Moor to quay on E side (dries 3m) while waiting. N part of the basin is for commercial use; yachts moor to pontoons in S part, max 12m, run by Morlaix YC; larger craft moor on W quay. If leaving after HW, clear the river before ebb sets hard.

Facilities Fuel from HM. Large town. Rly to Paris.

☎/VHF Locks 02 98 88 15 10; Marina 02 98 62 13 14, VHF 9, 16 (HW±0200); YC 02 98 88 38 00.

PENZÉ RIVER

Charts BA 2745; F 7095, 7151
HW Brest +0100
DS Dover –0015 ingoing; +0515 outgoing, 1kn

MHWS	MHWN	MLWN	MLWS
8·9m	7·1m	3·4m	1·3m

A wide estuary, approached through a maze of rocks. The narrow channel has good depths but is open to N and the banks dry. Small drying hbr of Penpoul is convenient for St Pol-de-Léon.

Approach With the aid of a large-scale chart various lines of approach can be followed.

Entrance From Bloscon N card Lt buoy, the transits are Guerheon G tr with Trébunnec G tr, 169°; Benven W tr with Mazarine W tr, 137°; La Tortue R tr perch with Caspari isolated danger bn 171°, to pass midway between Trousken R tr and La Petite Fourche G tr. Leave Trébunnec tr 2ca to stb and when about 3ca S of it with enough water make for the trumpet-shaped bn off the end of the breakwater at Penpoul.

The river dries below La Corde br (10m) with 1m at the first of the St Yves slipways. At HW it is navigable above the br as far as Penzé; small quay dries 5m.

Berthing Swell in winds N-NE. Anchor:
• In channel, 11m, poor holding. Off Penpoul; drying hbr is full of moorings.
• Mouillage de Carantec, S of Figuier isolated danger bn, 4m sand; difficult to land at low water.
• Off St Yves, 1–2m. Crowded, but room to anchor ¼M below slip.

Supplies Fuel from garage at Carantec. Shops at St Pol-de-Léon, 2M.

ROSCOFF MARINA (PORT DE BLOSCON)

Charts and tidal data as on page 349.

A hbr on the NE side of the Roscoff peninsula built primarily for car ferries and commercial shipping but with a new 625 berth marina, with 50 visitors' berths, approx 2ca S of the ferry terminal. Anchoring is now prohibited in the vicinity of the commercial port and marina. Infrastructure will not be complete until spring 2013. For latest information go to www.morlaix.cci.fr.

Approach Like most of this coast there are many drying rocky areas, however in good visibility, using suitable charts, it should present no problems except in strong onshore weather. From seaward, the grey 69m LtHo at the W end of the Ile de Batz is a prominent landmark. From the N make for 48°44′N 3°57′W, leaving Astan N card buoy well clear to stb. Monitor VHF 12 for ferry movements.

Entrance From N leave Basse de Bloscon N card Lt buoy to stb. The ferry port entrance, ½M south of it has a pier with a light Fl.GW.4s on a W column with G top at its east end. The ferry terminal is on the S side of this pier. At night enter in the W sector, 200–210°. The marina entrance is between the fishing port pierhead, Fl(2)G.6s, and the northern end of the marina outer breakwater, Fl(2)R.6s. Call marina on VHF 9 before entry/exit, controlled by IPTS lights.

Berthing In the marina, as directed.

☎/VHF Port HM 02 98 61 27 86, VHF 12, 16.

FRANCE – NORTH COAST AND CHANNEL ISLANDS

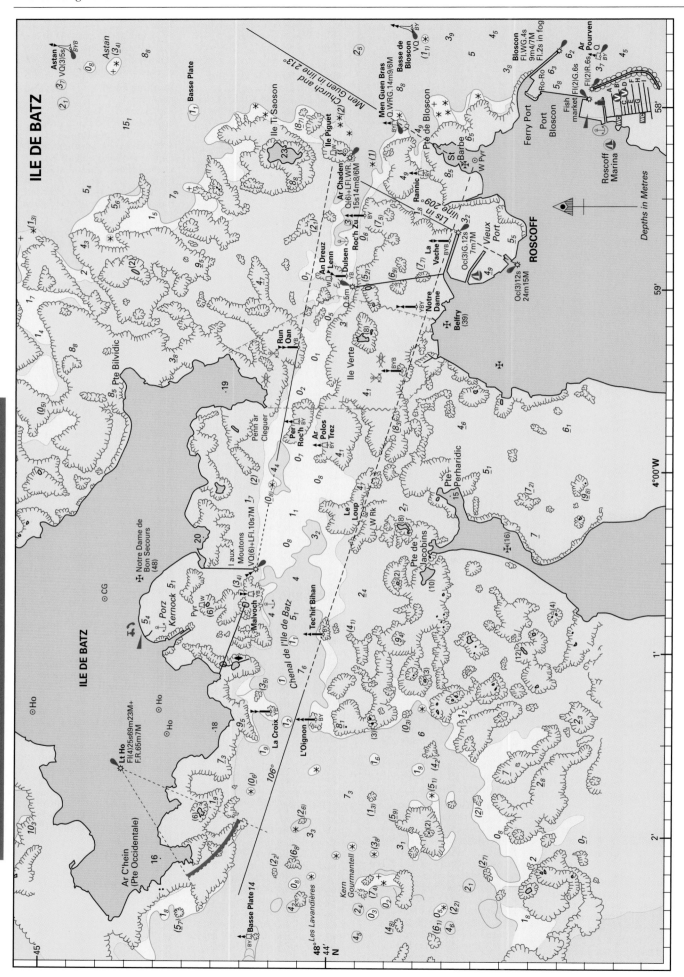

ILE DE BATZ

ROSCOFF

ROSCOFF (OLD PORT)

Charts BA 2745, 2026;
F 7095, 7151;
Imray C35

HW Brest +0100

DS in Chenal de Batz: Dover
+0030E; −0600W, 3¾kn

MHWS	MHWN	MLWN	MLWS
8·8m	7·0m	3·4m	1·3m

An interesting old town and
popular holiday resort, with
drying hbr.

Approach From W by Chenal
de Batz. From N leave Astan E
card buoy, VQ(3)5s8M, clear
to stb and then approach in W
sector (197°–257°) of Men-
Guen Bras BY N card Lt tr,
Q.WRG. Align it with Roscoff
rear Ldg Lt Oc(3)12s (grey tr,
W on NE side) and when Ar
Chaden R Lt appears,
Q(6)+LFl.WR.15s, steer to
leave that close to stb. Continue
for a short distance to W for
the Ldg Lts 209°. From Baie de
Morlaix follow above
directions for Chenal de l'Ile de
Batz; by night approach in W
sector of Ar Chaden
Q(6)+LFl.WR, 291°.

Entrance dries 3·2m and should
not be attempted until after
half-tide. Six W waiting buoys
available west of Ar Chaden bn
NE of entrance. Steer on the
Ldg Lts 209°, front W rectangle
with B stripe on W column
with G top at head of NW
mole, Oc(3)G.12s7m; rear grey
tr, W on NE side, Oc(3)12s
(synchronised with front), 2ca
to SW. This line leaves rks
drying 7m close to port.
Nearing the front Lt, bear away
to leave it to stb and round
second pierhead to Vieux Port.

Berthing in outer harbour (Port
Neuf) is discouraged as quays
are for fishing vessels. Inner
harbour, drying 3–5m, is
available for yachts. Moor
alongside rough jetty or anchor
in centre. Jetty to E has rocks at
base. Surge in strong NE winds.

Anchoring outside possible
while awaiting tide on line
between Roch Zhu N perch
and Ar Chaden Lt tr, 2–3m, but
uncomfortable with weather-
going tide. Buoys sometimes
available.

Supplies Water on quay. Fuel
from tanker. Shops.

☎ /VHF Old Port (Port de
Plaisance) 02 98 69 76 37,
VHF 09.

CHENAL DE L'ILE DE BATZ

Charts BA 2745, 2026;
F 7095, 7151;
Imray C35

HW Brest +0050

DS W entrance, Basse Platte:
Dover −0415SSW; +0015NE,
1–2½kn, reaching 3kn on ebb

MHWS	MHWN	MLWN	MLWS
8·9m	7·0m	3·5m	1·4m

The channel is unlit W of
Roscoff. The transits pass close
to shoals and one almost dries
in the area of Per Roc'h, ½M
NW of Roscoff landing stage.
It should not be attempted 2hrs
either side of LWS. Only E
entrance is practicable at night.

Directions From E to W the
transits are as follows, with E-
most mark of each pair quoted
first:
• Duslen W tr with Malvoc'h S
card tr 282°. Passes close S of
Ar Chaden S card YB Lt tr,
Q(6)+LFl.WR.15s, and N of
Men Guen Bras N card BY Lt
tr, Q.WRG. Before coming
abreast of Roc'h Zu N card bn
steer 270° to clear rocks from
Duslen W tr to mid-stream N
of long Roscoff landing stage,
conspic. Keep close to the
former to:
• W pyramid in Kernoc'h
harbour in line with E-most of
the two mills (named Moulin
de l'Ouest) SE of Batz LtHo,
291°. This leaves Per Roc'h N
card BW bn to port.
• About 1ca past Per Roc'h,
steer on rear bearing 078° with
Pte Pen Ar Cléguer in line with
Horville rock (dr 15m) to just
N of Tehi Bihan N card bn.
• At Tehi Bihan bn steer W to
get on rear bearing 106° with
Le Loup W rock in line with W
pyramid at Ste Barbe to clear
the entrance.

From W to E the transits are
reversed.

Anchorages
• While awaiting the tide to
enter at the W end, off Ar Skeul
W card YBY bn tr SW of Ile de
Siec; beware drying rock to its
SW.
• Porz Kernoch on Ile de Batz.
Level ground N and NW of W
Kernoch pyramid, dries 5m.
Area S of pyramid has rocks.
Slipway to E used by passenger
boats.
• W of Roscoff entrance on line
joining Roc'h Zu bn and Ar-
Chaden tr.

Supplies Small shops in
Kernoch village on Ile de Batz.

PONTUSVAL (BRIGNOGAN)

HW Brest+0100

MHWS	MHWN
8·8m	7·0

Useful day hbr

Dries 2–5m

Open to N and accessible only
by day after half-tide. Lies 1M
to E of Pontusval Lt tr with
conspic W lookout tr to W of
entrance. From a position
48°41'·43N 4°19'·20W, about
1ca E of Port de Pontusval E
card buoy, approach on 178°
with Coat Tanguy W tr in line
with Plounéour-Trez spire
passing G con buoy and R An
Neudden tr. Anchor SW of the
latter, 4m, or dry further in. Six
W visitors' buoys, some in deep
water. Stores at Brignogan.

Books from

SECRET ANCHORAGES OF BRITTANY

Peter Cumberlidge

Secret Anchorages is not just a
pilot but also a cruising
companion in the true sense
which conveys the essence of
Brittany to the cruising
yachtsman. It is a wonderful
reference, not just in the
cockpit but for anyone
contemplating a Brittany
cruise. It is in full colour and is
lavishly illustrated with sea
level and aerial photographs.

246 x 189mm. 288pp. Soft
cover. Full colour
978 085288 757 8 2nd ed. 2005

RCC PILOTAGE FOUNDATION

NORTH BRITTANY

Cherbourg to Ouessant and
the Channel Islands

John Lawson

This pilot covers the west side
of the Cotentin peninsula from
Cherbourg, the Channel
Islands, and the previously
covered coast from St-Malo to
Ouessant. The pilot is
published in full colour with
superbly detailed charts and
nearly 200 photographs from
both the air and sea level.

This is the essential cruising
companion for yachts
exploring the drying harbours
and ports little more than a
day or two's sailing from the
south coast of England.

A4. 200 pp. Hard cover. Full colour.
978 184623 069 1 2nd ed. 2008

RCC PILOTAGE FOUNDATION

ATLANTIC FRANCE

North Biscay to the Spanish border

Jeremy Parkinson

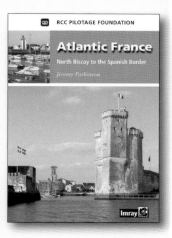

North Biscay has been
renamed *Atlantic France* to
reflect the extended coverage
to the Spanish border. The
Brittany harbour of
L'Aberwrac'h, the key to
entering the Chenal du Four, is
now included. At the south
end the guide now covers
Arcachon, Cap Breton,
Bayonne, St Jean de Luz and
the Rada de Higuer up to the
Spanish border.

Atlantic France is the
authoritative cruising guide for
this long and varied coastline,
and its revision will be
welcomed by both first time
visitors and old west coast of
France hands.

A4. 330 pp. Hard cover. Full colour.
978 184623 280 0 1st ed. 2010

FRANCE – NORTH COAST AND CHANNEL ISLANDS

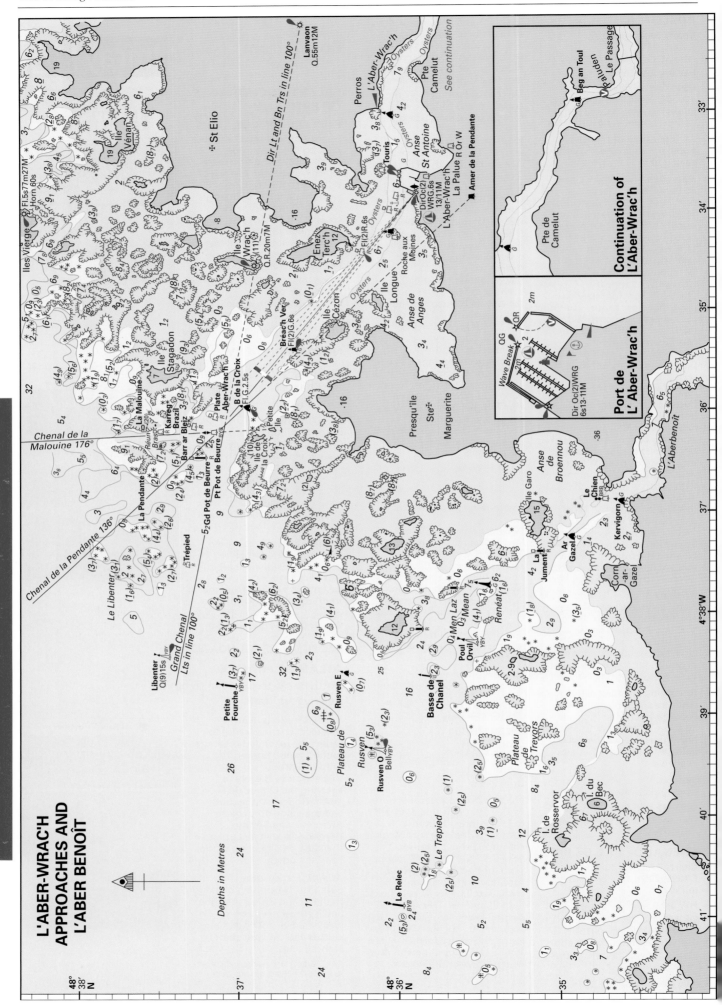

L'ABER-WRAC'H
APPROACHES AND
L'ABER BENOÎT

Continuation of
L'Aber-Wrac'h

Port de
L'Aber-Wrac'h

L'ABER-WRAC'H

Charts BA 1432; F 7150, 7094; Imray C35

HW Brest +0030

DS at entrance to Grand Chenal: Dover HW SE; +0600NW, 1½kn

MHWS	MHWN	MLWN	MLWS
7·7m	6·1m	2·8m	1·0m

An estuary accessible at all times, open to NW but with shelter in the upper reaches.

Approach From W or N make for a position ½M W of Libenter W card Lt buoy, whistle, 3M WSW of Ile Vierge lt. From NE, with good visibility and reasonable sea, make a position 1½M W of the light for the Malouine channel.

Entrance There are three entrance channels of which only the first is usable at all times.

• **Grand Chenal** (3m) From 1ca SW of Libenter buoy pick up the Ldg line, 100°, of front, Ile Vrac W LtHo, R top, Q.R.20m7M; rear Lanvaon W Lt tr with Or ▲, Q.55m 12M (090°-110°); and also on this line, Plouguerneau belfry. Beware of cross tide in entrance. The flood sets hard on Libenter. After Petit Pot de Beurre E card bn tr, steer 128° following the line of buoys and towers; at night change course from 100° at La Croix Lt buoy, Fl.G.2·5s, and follow W sector of La Palue molehead lt, DirOc(2)WRG.6s (127°-W-129°). This leads past Breac'h Ver G stb tr, Fl(2)G.6s, Fort Cézon and Roche aux Moines G tr (ignore the W tr to SW of it) all to stb; and then bear E for marina and moorings.

• **Chenal de la Malouine** (3m, ½ca wide at entrance). Coming from E this saves the distance round Libenter. 4M visibility is needed. It passes between La Pendante rock (6m) to W and La Malouine (17m) to the E. At 1½M W of Ile Vierge Lt pick up the Ldg marks 176°: front BY E card tr, 5m, and rear Petite Ile de la Croix W tr, 6m and 4ca to its S. Beware strong cross tide, up to 3kn, in entrance and pass ¼ca W of Karreg Brazil R tr. At Bar-ar-Bleiz R buoy bear SSE between Plate Aber-Wrac'h and Petit Pot de Beurre, at which steer 128° as in Grand Chenal.

• **Chenal de la Pendante** (0·3m) can be used only by day with good visibility. At 2½M W of Ile Vierge, leave La Pendante 1½ca to port, making good 136° (cross-set 2½kn) on line of front W mark on Fort Cézon, rear Amer de la Pendante B tr 1¼M SE. When 1½ca off Grand Pot de Beurre R bn, 2m, come to port and make for Bar-ar-Bleiz R buoy; when close, steer SSE past Plate Aber-Wrac'h R buoy into the main channel.

The river is navigable (2·7m) to Paluden which is more sheltered with winds from W to NW. When past Touris R tr, steer for the quay upriver on N shore. Nearing it turn to stb up centre of river, with stakes on the edges. Give Beg-an-Toul a wide berth and keep to W side of channel until near the quays.

Berthing In the marina for boats under 12m at La Palue; otherwise there are 30 visitors' buoys on which rafting is permitted. Anchoring is allowed only to W of life-boat slip (not in NE winds); otherwise it is prohibited within hbr limits, including Beg an Toul. In bad weather, especially from W to N, it is more comfortable to moor up the river at Paluden where there are dumbbell moorings for visitors, good shelter.

Facilities Fuel (ask HM). Water at the quay and pontoons. Small shop in the village; more at Landéda, 1M. Restaurant at Paluden.

① /VHF *capitainerie* 02 98 04 91 62, VHF 16, 09. Customs 02 98 85 07 40; Harbour launch VHF 09. Paluden 02980 46312. Bus to Brest.

L'ABER BENOIT

Charts BA 1432; F 7150, 7094; Imray C35

HW Brest +0024

DS Dover +0030 in-going; +0615 out-going, 3kn

MHWS	MHWN	MLWN	MLWS
7·8m	6·1m	2·9	1·1m

A wide estuary, less developed than L'Abervrac'h. Unlit but providing good shelter.

Approach by the W of Le Libenter W card Lt bn, whistle, which is 3M WSW of Ile Vierge Lt.

Entrance should not be attempted in strong NW winds. From close W of Petite Fourche W card buoy, ½M SSW of Libenter buoy, make good 170°. From about 2ca S of Rusven Est G con buoy, at Basse du Chenal G con buoy (Rusven Sud on some charts), steer 141° on line of Le Chien BRB bn tr just open to right of white topped La Jument rock west of Ile Garo (4m). Bear to port to clear stb buoy marking Mean Renéat rocks, then steer for Le Chien, leaving La Jument to port.

Alternatively from Rusven Est G buoy steer 190° on line of front Ven Bihan rock (19m) in line with Lampaul-Ploudalmezeau spire (W-most of two). When Orvil W card buoy is in line with Jument de Garo alter course to leave the buoy close to port, 130°. Bear to port to clear Ar Gazel G buoy SE of La Jument de Garo and leave Le Chien BR isolated danger tr to port. Thereafter follow the channel.

Berthing Anchor clear of moorings by Le Passage (old ferry site) about 6ca past Le Chien, or round the bend to S. Depths greater than shown due to sand dredging. The inter-tidal zone has extensive oyster beds. It may be best to pick up a buoy.

CHENAL DE BATZ TO L'ABER-WRAC'H

Charts BA 2647 or 2025 and 2026; Imray C35

Passage lights	*BA No*
Ile de Batz	1816
Fl(4)25s69m23M+ F.R.65m7M (024°-059°)	
Pontusval	1820
Oc(3)WR.12s16m10/7M (R over rks to SW)	
Amann Ar Rouz N card Lt buoy Q.7M Whis	
Lizen van Ouest	1821·3
W card Lt buoy VQ(9)10s5M	
Ile Vierge	1822
Fl.5s77m27M Horn 60s	
Libenter buoy W card Lt buoy Q(9)15s8m6M	
Le Four	1854
Fl(5)15s28m22M	

STREAMS RELATED TO HW DOVER

2M N of Ile de Batz +0115E –0515W, 3¾kn. Off Le Libenter +0015E; –0600 W, 2½kn

On arriving from or leaving to UK allowance must be made for the tidal streams which are stronger nearer the coast. There are no sheltered harbours or anchorages in this 26M stretch; such harbours as there are, dry, the best being:

Mogueriec SW of Ile de Siec. Rocks to NE are in Ile de Batz R sector. Ldg Lts 162° front W tower G top Iso.WG.4s9m11/6M, rear W column G top F.G.22m7M. Shelter by quay taken by fishing boats. Entrance impossible LW±0200 or with fresh N winds. There is a shoal in the middle of the harbour.

Supplies Small shops up the hill on S side of the ferry. Water on S quay. Large oyster centre on S side.

THE WEST COUNTRY TO L'ABER-WRAC'H

From Plymouth the overall distance is 107M, bearing 189°.

The streams run strongly on the headlands outside the Eddystone and the Lizard. Streams run W from HW Dover –2 and E from HW Dover +4. Max stream 2kn sp and 1kn np and run E/W.

Tidal streams increase near the French coast to 2·5kn sp and 1·2kn np and run SW from HW Dover –4 and NE from HW Dover +2.

Shipping will be encountered throughout the passage. Naval vessels exercise off Plymouth and coastal shipping heading for Lands End TSS will be encountered S of Eddystone. The recommended traffic route between Casquets TSS and Ouessant TSS lies 50M out, with the W going ships in the N lane. Fishing boats are found near the Brittany coast.

Do not close the French coast in poor visibility as rocky shoals extend 3M out.

The Ile Vierge Lt Ho is one of the tallest in the world and lies 3M NNE of the Libenter W card Lt buoy. Libenter Shoal lies NE of the buoy, approach from N.

In good weather La Malouine is an easy passage. At night or in poor visibility use the Grand Chenal starting 2ca S of the Libenter buoy. L'Aber-wrac'h is available in any weather at any state of the tide.

NW France, Channel Islands and cross Channel to England

	Cherbourg	Alderney	St Peter Port	St Helier	St Malo	Lezardrieux	Roscoff	L'Aberwrac'h	Longships 1M W	Falmouth	Plymouth BW	Dartmouth	Portland Bill 2M S
Cherbourg	0												
Alderney	23	0											
St Peter Port	42	22	0										
St Helier	60	37	32	0									
St Malo	89	68	54	39	0								
Lezardrieux	88	75	47	46	48	0							
Roscoff	119	84	73	79	83	51	0						
L'Aberwrac'h	149	124	103	109	114	83	36	0					
Longships 1M W	164	145	139	154	212	139	108	101	0				
Falmouth	141	133	112	129	150	119	93	97	41	0			
Plymouth BW	111	88	87	107	139	106	98	108	72	38	0		
Dartmouth	85	70	64	94	131	98	99	117	96	63	35	0	
Portland Bill 2M S	58	47	63	88	132	112	122	146	135	102	72	44	0

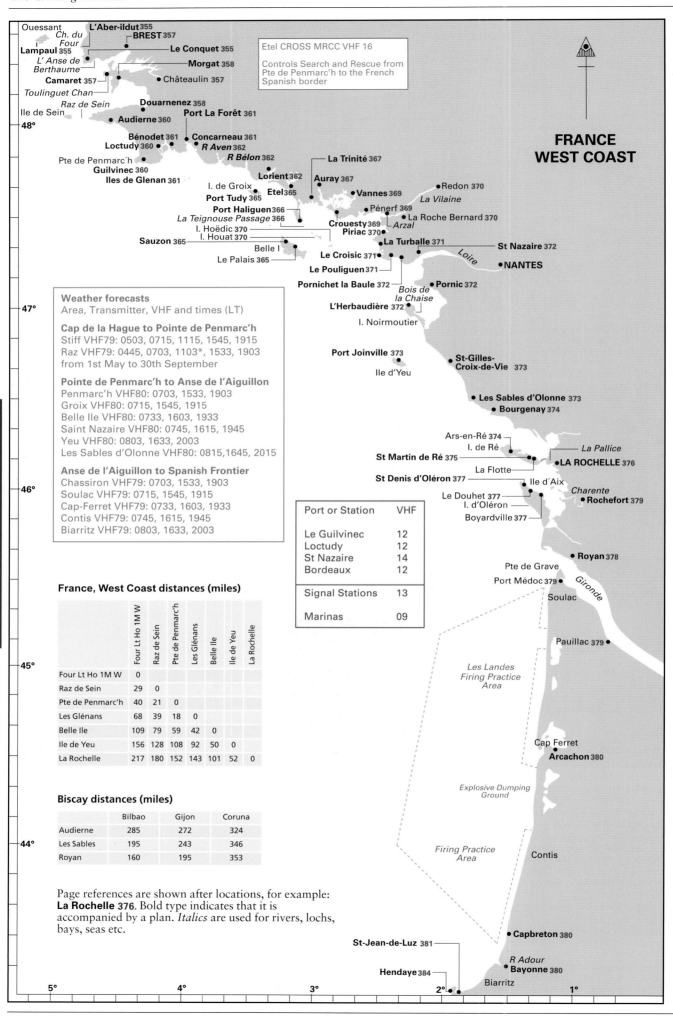

FRANCE – WEST COAST

FRANCE
WEST COAST

Ouessant
Ch. du Four
L'Aber-ildut 355
BREST 357
Lampaul 355
Le Conquet 355
L' Anse de Berthaume
Morgat 358
Camaret 357
Châteaulin 357
Toulinguet Chan
Raz de Sein
Ile de Sein
Douarnenez 358
Port La Forêt 361
Audierne 360
Bénodet 361
Concarneau 361
Loctudy 360
R Aven 362
Pte de Penmarc'h
R Bélon 362
La Trinité 367
Guilvinec 360
Lorient 362
Auray 367
Iles de Glenan 361
I. de Groix
Etel 365
Vannes 369
Redon 370
Port Tudy 365
La Vilaine
Port Haliguen 366
Pénerf 369
La Teignouse Passage 366
Crouesty 369
La Roche Bernard 370
I. Hoëdic 370
Piriac 370
Arzal
I. Houat 370
La Turballe 371
St Nazaire 372
Sauzon 365
Belle I
Le Croisic 371
Loire
Le Palais 365
Le Pouliguen 371
•NANTES
Pornichet la Baule 372
Pornic 372
Bois de la Chaise
L'Herbaudière 372
I. Noirmoutier

Etel CROSS MRCC VHF 16
Controls Search and Rescue from Pte de Penmarc'h to the French Spanish border

Port Joinville 373
St-Gilles-Croix-de-Vie 373
Ile d'Yeu
Les Sables d'Olonne 373
Bourgenay 374
Ars-en-Ré 374
I. de Ré
La Pallice
St Martin de Ré 375
LA ROCHELLE 376
La Flotte
St Denis d'Oléron 377
Ile d'Aix
Charente
Le Douhet 377
Rochefort 379
I. d'Oléron
Boyardville 377
Royan 378
Pte de Grave
Port Médoc 379
Gironde
Soulac
Pauillac 379
Cap Ferret
Arcachon 380
Capbreton 380
St-Jean-de-Luz 381
R Adour
Bayonne 380
Hendaye 384
Biarritz

Les Landes Firing Practice Area

Explosive Dumping Ground

Firing Practice Area

Contis

Weather forecasts
Area, Transmitter, VHF and times (LT)

Cap de la Hague to Pointe de Penmarc'h
Stiff VHF79: 0503, 0715, 1115, 1545, 1915
Raz VHF79: 0445, 0703, 1103*, 1533, 1903
from 1st May to 30th September

Pointe de Penmarc'h to Anse de l'Aiguillon
Penmarc'h VHF80: 0703, 1533, 1903
Groix VHF80: 0715, 1545, 1915
Belle Ile VHF80: 0733, 1603, 1933
Saint Nazaire VHF80: 0745, 1615, 1945
Yeu VHF80: 0803, 1633, 2003
Les Sables d'Olonne VHF80: 0815,1645, 2015

Anse de l'Aiguillon to Spanish Frontier
Chassiron VHF79: 0703, 1533, 1903
Soulac VHF79: 0715, 1545, 1915
Cap-Ferret VHF79: 0733, 1603, 1933
Contis VHF79: 0745, 1615, 1945
Biarritz VHF79: 0803, 1633, 2003

Port or Station	VHF
Le Guilvinec	12
Loctudy	12
St Nazaire	14
Bordeaux	12
Signal Stations	13
Marinas	09

France, West Coast distances (miles)

	Four Lt Ho 1M W	Raz de Sein	Pte de Penmarc'h	Les Glénans	Belle Ile	Ile de Yeu	La Rochelle
Four Lt Ho 1M W	0						
Raz de Sein	29	0					
Pte de Penmarc'h	40	21	0				
Les Glénans	68	39	18	0			
Belle Ile	109	79	59	42	0		
Ile de Yeu	156	128	108	92	50	0	
La Rochelle	217	180	152	143	101	52	0

Biscay distances (miles)

	Bilbao	Gijon	Coruna
Audierne	285	272	324
Les Sables	195	243	346
Royan	160	195	353

Page references are shown after locations, for example:
La Rochelle 376. Bold type indicates that it is accompanied by a plan. *Italics* are used for rivers, lochs, bays, seas etc.

France – West Coast

Given a three week cruising period, the harbours of Southern Brittany are within reach of the South and West Coasts of England and Wales. The Rade de Brest together with the Bays of Camaret and Douarnenez and off-shore islands of Ushant, Molène and Sein provide an excellent introduction to the attractions of South Brittany.

South of the Pointe de Penmarc'h, the weather is warmer and sunnier. The jewel of the Breton cruising grounds lies within the shelter of the Quiberon Peninsula. Together with Belle Île, three weeks could easily be spent exploring the islands in the bay, the Morbihan and the ports on the mainland. The marina at Vannes is close to its mediaeval centre and across the bay from the entrance to the Morbihan lies the pretty town of Piriac.

For those able to make a longer cruise, or who decide to sails further south, the Vendée ports can be reached within four day sail from L'Aber-Wrac'h. The Ile d'Yeu is sufficiently far off shore to have retained its identity and the bicycle is king. Further south lie the delightful islands of Ré, Oléron and Aix, La Rochelle and the Charente. This cruising ground has the advantage of excellent connections to the UK from the airport at La Rochelle.

The alternative to crossing Biscay is to follow the coast south from the Gironde and conditions may permit entry into Arcachon Bay. Although a shallow draught boat will allow an exploration into the smaller ports and harbours around the Bay, there are also deeper water anchorages.

With rare exceptions, it is very easy to access supplies from all harbours and anchorages; even on small islands like Houat and Hoëdic. The traditional markets continue and sometimes fish can be bought directly from the boats. Wi-Fi and laundry facilities are widely available. French traffic laws and cycle tracks make cycling a pleasure. Marina charges, although they have risen are usually more modest than those on the South coast of the UK. In May and June, charges are lower than high season; anchorages are less crowded, except at weekends on the islands.

Currents and Tidal Streams

South of the Raz de Sein, apart from few exceptions, tidal streams are relatively weak. South of the Gironde, there is a north-going current 0·5–1kn extending up to five or six miles offshore; prolonged W'ly gales often increase its rate. Inshore of this, a south-going current may be found.

Weather and Swell

Most forecasts give information on swell (*houle*) indicating height in metres and frequency in seconds as well as the effect of wind on sea (*vent du mer*).

In spring and summer prevailing winds between Ouessant and the Gironde are from between W and NE through N, but in the neighbourhood of Brest SW winds are often experienced. Gales are not frequent during June through August, but at no time can freedom from W gales be relied on, and in unsettled weather small craft are well advised not to stray too far from shelter. In the autumn, E winds are slightly more frequent. Fog rarely lasts long on most of this coast but is quite frequent around Ouessant at all times.

Le Vent Solaire

Warm, sunny weather often produces this cycle of sea breezes. Beginning in the early afternoon, the wind goes into the northwest, strengthening to Force 4; after which it veers to the north, dying away towards dusk, to be replaced by a fresh NE wind. The latter may blow with enough force to make anchorages uncomfortable. By morning, this wind dies completely. This phenomenon is particularly noticeable S of Penmarc'h.

Pilots and Charts

Votre Livre de Bord; *Atlantique Manche – Mer du Nord* published annually by Bloc Marine, *Almanach du Marin Breton*.
Atlantic France: North Biscay to the Spanish Border RCC Pilotage Foundation (Imray).
SHOM *tidal atlases 558, 559, 560*.

CHANNELS BETWEEN OUESSANT AND THE MAINLAND

Charts BA 3345, 2356; F 7149; Imray C36

There are three channels between the Is and the mainland; the Fromveur, where the streams run at 9kn at springs, the Helle, the channel of approach from NW and Land's End, and the Chenal du Four from the English Channel. The last two are well buoyed. At the N end of the Chenal du Four, the stream runs at 3·5kn at springs. Where the channels unite near the Grand Vinotière the tidal stream reaches 6–7kn at springs. By using either the Helle or Four, boats may avoid the traffic separation zone to the NW of Ouessant, as well as the heavy swell often found there. Use VHF Ch 13 to report position if crossing the Ouessant TSS. Avoid taking these passages in poor visibility, strong winds, high swell or wind against tide.

CHENAL DU FOUR (FOUR CHANNEL)

Charts BA 2356, 3345; F 7122; Imray C36

HW (Ouessant) Brest +0005

MHWS	MHWN	MLWN	MLWS
6·9m	5·3m	2·5m	1·0m

Approach

From the North At the North end of the Channel, slack water is at HW Brest; the south-going stream running from Brest HW+0100 to Brest HW+0500. Arrival time at Le Four depends on passage plans. If making a passage from L'Aberwrac'h to Camaret or Brest, leave no later than Brest HW+0215 to arrive off Le Four at Brest HW+0445. From L'Aberwrac'h to beyond the Raz de Sein, leave Brest HW–0300 in order to be off Le Four at slack water (HW Brest), thus making the passage through the Raz at slack water.

Coming directly from the UK, it may be difficult to time the arrival at the Chenal du Four to coincide with the tide. As the streams are weaker in the Northern end of the channel in calm conditions, a boat could reach either the Anse de Porsmoguer or Anse des Blancs Sablons and wait for the tide. It may even be possible, in quiet weather and good visibility, to skirt inside the Grande Vinotière.

By night Remain in the white sector of Kermorvan, until in the white sector of Pte de Corsen. Change course to remain in this sector until R pillar buoy, Tournant et Lochrist, has been passed. Then steer a course that will lead between G con buoy, La Fourmi, and R bn tr, Les Vieux Moines.

From the South

If making for L'Aberwrac'h from Brest, be off Les Vieux Moines at Brest HW–0500. A boat bound northwards from south of the Raz, entering the Raz at Brest HW+0530 and with the help of the north-going stream, should be entering the Chenal du Four Brest HW–0400; thus having a fair tide from the N end of the Chenal to L'Aberwrac'h.

The channel is well buoyed and, in good conditions, the marks are easy to follow. It is easier to check progress noting the buoys as they are passed, rather than trying to align lights and marks.

Anchorages

• Anse de Porsmoguer
• Anse des Blancs Sablons

Useful anchorages when on passage through the Chenal du Four. The holding in both is sand. The latter is appropriate in fine weather as it is exposed to the W and N, and has an eddy stream in the S of the bay.

Passage lights	BA No
La Vierge Fl.5s77m27M Horn 60s	1822
Le Stiff Fl(2)R.20s85m24M	1842
Créac'h Fl(2)10s70m32M Horn(2)120s	1844
La Jument Fl(3)R.15s36m22M Horn(3)60s	1848
Le Four Fl(5)15s28m22M	1854
L'Aber-Ildut DirOc(2)WR.6s12m25/20M	1856
Trézien DirOc(2)6s84m20M	1873·9
Kermorvan Fl.5s20m22M	1874
St Mathieu Fl.15s56m29M (Rear) DirF	1874·1
La Grande Vinotière LFl.R.10s12m5M	1872

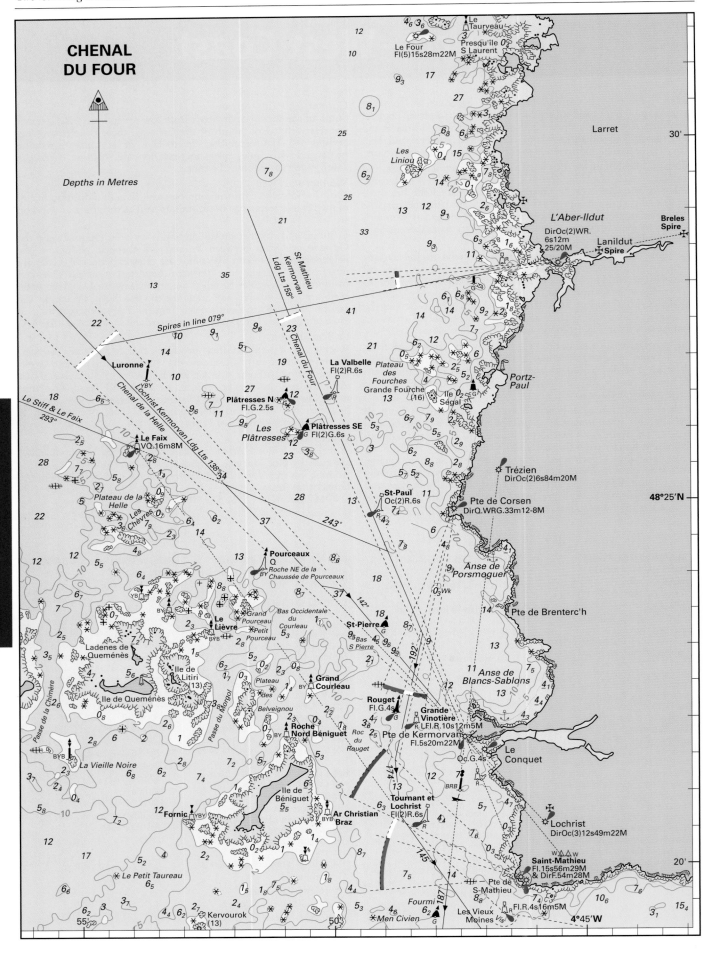

CHENAL DU FOUR

Depths in Metres

FRANCE – WEST COAST

Larret

Le Taurveau

Le Four
Fl(5)15s28m22M

Presqu'ile
S Laurent

Les Liniou

L'Aber-Ildut
DirOc(2)WR.
6s12m
25/20M

Lanildut
Spire

Breles
Spire

Portz-Paul

St Mathieu
Kermorvan
Ldg Lts 158°

Spires in line 079°

Chenal du Four

Luronne
Lochrist Kermorvan Ldg Lts 138°

La Valbelle
Fl(2)R.6s

Plateau
des
Fourches
Grande Fourche
(16)

Ile de
Ségal

Chenal de la Helle

Plâtresses N
Fl.G.2.5s

Plâtresses SE
Fl(2)G.6s

Les
Plâtresses

Le Stiff & Le Faix
293°

Le Faix
VQ.16m8M

Trézien
DirOc(2)6s84m20M

Pte de Corsen
DirQ.WRG.33m12-8M

48°25'N

St-Paul
Oc(2)R.6s

Plateau de la
Helle

Les
Chèvres

Pourceaux
Q
Roche NE de la
Chaussée de Pourceaux

Anse de
Porsmoguer

Pte de Brenterc'h

Grand
Pourceau
Petit
Pourceau

Bas Occidental
du
Courleau

St-Pierre

Bas
S Pierre

142°

192°

Le Lièvre

Ladenes de
Quéménès

Anse de
Blancs-Sablons

Ile de
Litiri
(13)

Plateau
des
Belveignou

Grand
Courleau

Passe du Margol

Ile de Quéménès

Passe de la Chimère

Rouget
Fl.G.4s

Grande
Vinotière
LFl.R.10s12m5M

Roche
Nord Béniguet

Roc
du
Rouget

Pte de Kermorvan
Fl.5s20m22M

Le Conquet

Oc.G.4s

La Vieille Noire

BRB

Ile de
Béniguet

Fornic

Ar Christian
Braz

Tournant et
Lochrist
Fl(2)R.6s

Lochrist
DirOc(3)12s49m22M

Saint-Mathieu
Fl.15s56m29M
& DirF.54m28M

Le Petit Taureau

Pte de
S-Mathieu

Fl.R.4s16m5M

55'

Kervourok
(13)

Fourmi

Men Civien

Les Vieux
Moines

Vis

4°45'W

30'

20'

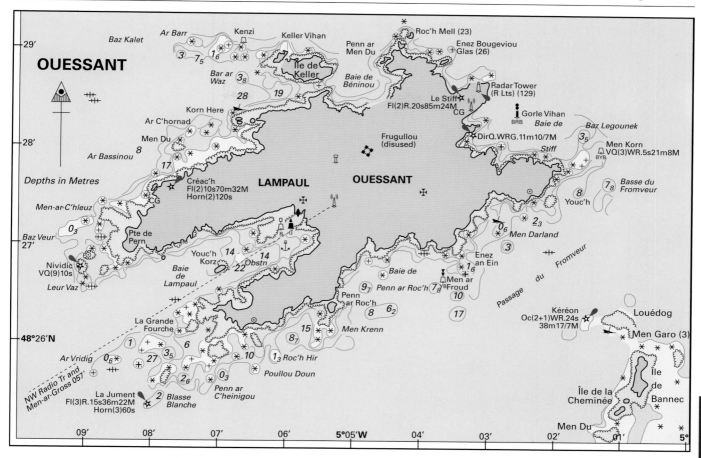

OUESSANT (USHANT)

Charts BA 2356; F 7123, 7149; Imray C36

HW Brest +0005

MHWS	MHWN	MLWN	MLWS
6·9m	5·3m	2·5m	1·0m

A fascinating place to visit in settled weather, with a picturesque anchorage at Lampaul.

Approach The tidal stream runs very strongly in the Passage du Fromveur; it is best taken at slack water, Brest +0030 or Brest −0530. On rounding La Jument, take care to allow for a southwesterly current.

Entrance Leading line, NW radio tr and Men-ar-Gross G bn tr 057°.

Anchorage Lampaul Bay provides more shelter than might be imagined; there is no current at the head of the bay where there are 24 white, visitors' mooring buoys. When the inner harbour Pors-Pol dries, go alongside either the lifeboat slipway or the end of the wharf to its west.

Facilities Water, fuel in small quantities from garage, PO, hotels, restaurants, shops, supermarkets with ATMs. Cycle hire.

ÎLE DE MOLÈNE

An attractive island whose anchorage is sheltered in winds from E through S to WSW. Due to strong currents and numerous rocks, best approached from the N. Leading marks, Bn on S hbr mole Dir.Fl(3)WRG12s in line with Mill on the South of island, 190°.

L'ABER-ILDUT

Charts BA 3345; F 7122; Imray C36

HW Brest +0010

MHWS	MHWN
7·6m	6·0m

DS as Chenal du Four

Bar 2m approx at LW.

Approach Transit of 078·5°on the spires of Lanildut and Brélès churches, taking care to avoid the shoals of 1·8m and 2·3m, by leaving Le Lieu R. bn tr 100m to port. Then steer for the small lighthouse on the N side of the L'Aber-ildut shore. Steer to leave Le Lieu R close to port, then follow the buoyed channel.

Anchorage 20 visitors' moorings (<12m) on lines V and G. Contact Harbour Office ☾ 02 98 04 36 40 prior to arrival. 15 June–15 September: 0800–1145, 1400–1900.

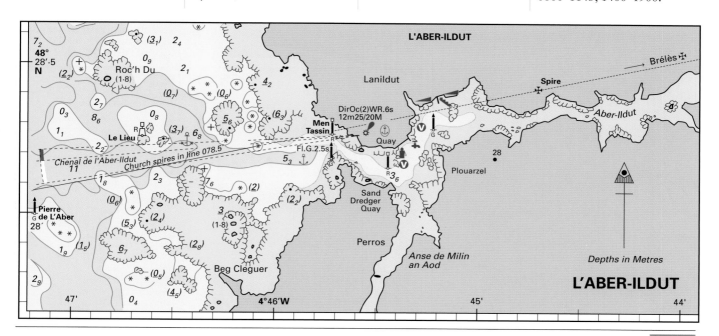

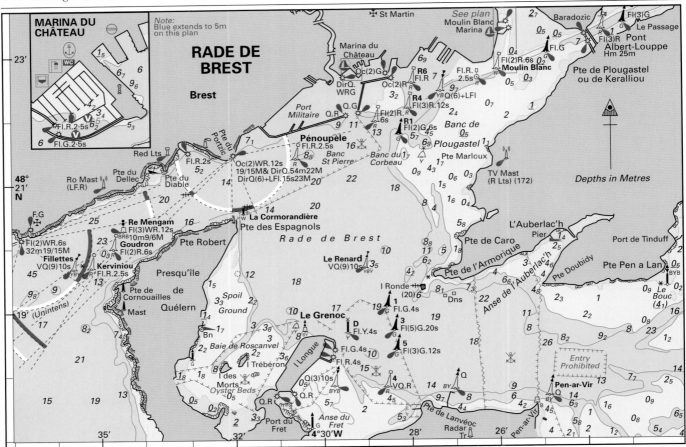

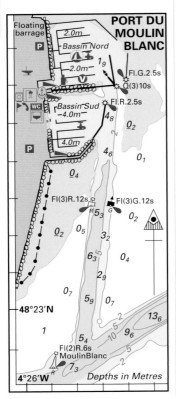

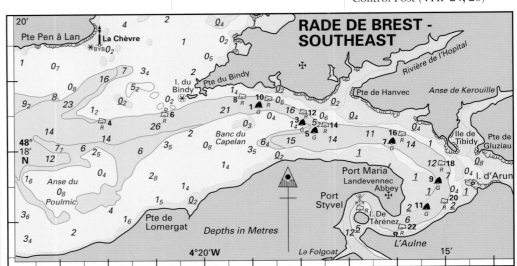

Low season: 0800–1200 except Sunday and Monday. Use of pontoon limited to two hours.

Facilities Water and electricity on pontoon at Combarelle quay. WC, showers, fuel, boatyard, chandlery, supermarket, restaurant.

LE CONQUET

Charts BA 3345;
F 7122, 7148, 7149;
Imray C36

HW Brest –0002

MHWS	MHWN	MLWN	MLWS
6·8m	5·3m	2·5m	1·0m

A picturesque hbr between Kermorvan and Point St Barbe for visiting in settled conditions.

Entrance There are strong cross tides in entrance. Hbr dredged to 2m.

Anchorage Yachts may not anchor in the outer harbour. Vessels that can take the ground may anchor in the inner, drying hbr. Beware of strong streams across the entrance at springs.

Facilities All stores and restaurants.

L'ANSE DE BERTHEAUME

Charts BA 3427; F 7148, 7149;
Imray C36

Anse d'Bertheaume anchorage. Useful stopover to await favourable streams through Goulet de Brest or Le Four channel. Exposed to S and E, give a wide berth to the SW corner to avoid Le Chat rock close to the fort. Many small craft moorings off Plougonvelin with some visitors' buoys, anchor in one of the two bays N of le Chat in 2–3m on sand. Avoid NE part of Anse, foul ground and rocks.

BREST AND THE RADE DE BREST

Charts BA 3427, 3428;
F 7400, 7401;
Imray C36

HW Brest

MHWS	MHWN	MLWN	MLWS
7·4m	5·8m	3·0m	1·3m

The Rade de Brest offers an excellent cruising ground with the rivers Élorn and Aulne to explore and many anchorages. Yachts are unwelcome in the Naval and commercial ports.

Approach

This is straightforward and well buoyed.

In the Goulet de Brest naval ships and other large vessels have priority. Vessels over 25m need permission from the Control Post (VHF 24, 28)

TIDAL STREAMS IN THE GOULET DE BREST

In Passe Sud the flood stream begins ½hr after local LW and flows E; the ebb soon after HW, to W. The ebb sets obliquely between Point des Espagnols and Pt de Dellec. During the ebb an E-running eddy flows inshore along the S side of the Goulet, attaining its greatest strength during the latter half. In the Passe Nord the streams begin about ½hr later. Contrary wind and tide produce a steep sea.

THE TOULINGUET CHANNEL

Chart BA 3427; F 7401; Imray C36

At Brest +0015 the stream sets S, and at –0550 N. The passage is 3ca wide, but may be made with care by day or night with a fair tide, in clear weather, as the tide sets straight through the fairway at 2–3kn. From N, pass midway between La Louve rock tower and Pohen rock on a course of 156°. Channel has 4·5m.

From the S make W of Les Tas de Pois allowing for the inset into Douarnenez Bay. Hence steer for Toulinguet Lt Oc(3)WR.12s with the Petit Minou LtHo Fl(2)WR.6s a little open to W of Toulinguet Point, 011°. Abreast of Toulinguet rocks at night when St Mathieu Lt is hidden behind them, steer about 335° to pass between Pohen and La Louve tower. When clear to the N of them, round up to E as soon as Portzic LtHo Oc(2)WR.12s comes open from the S side of the Goulet, but if bound for the N channel (Goulet de Brest) hold on for the Minou Lt till well clear to N of the Fillettes, onto which the flood tide sets. There are fair weather anchorages in the Anse de Penhir and Anse de Dinan sheltered NW to E through N after rounding Les Tas de Pois heading S.

before passing through. Smaller vessels should monitor VHF 24 and obey instructions from patrol boats. Passage through the Goulet may be restricted by military operations.

BREST

• Marina du Château

Approach and entrance At night remain in the white sector of Dir.VQ.WRG.24m10–5M on shore, by day 344°. Take care to respect the limits of the Military Port to port. Head for conspic G pile at entrance beneath naval signal station on château.

Berthing On pontoon near the outer wall or the most easterly pontoon.

Facilities Fuel, launching and lifting. Some repairs. Wi-Fi. Restaurants, stores and in town centre. Chandleries at Moulin Blanc. Rail and Air connections. ☎ HM 02 98 00 96 00.

• Le Moulin Blanc Marina

Approach Turn to port after Moulin Blanc R can Fl(3)R12s and follow buoyed channel.

Berthing On the wave baffle or visitors' pontoon.

Interest Océanopolis-Acquarium close to Moulin Blanc Marina. Ferries to Ouessant and Île Molène.

Facilities All marina and boatyard facilities. Restaurants. Small supermarket. Bus service into Brest. TGV and air connections. HM ☎ 02 98 01 20 20.

Anchorages There are many delightful anchorages in the Rade de Brest, in some of which there are also moorings.

• Élorn River With suitable charts and rise of tide this river

may be explored, but only boats that can take the ground will be able to stay at Landerneau 12M. 24m clearance under the br; use the N arch. It is advisable to leave early on the ebb or before HW. There is much mud exposed at LW and a permanent barrier which covers at half tide between the sand quays and the main town quay.

Anchorages
Sheltered anchorages at Le Passage and St Jean. Lie alongside the quay at Landerneau.

• Anse de L'Auberlac'h
Excellent anchorage at the end of the bay in 3–5m, equidistant from the shores. Jetty on W bank, dries 1·3m at end of jetty and 2·7m at end of slip. No supplies in village, only a bar.

• Daoulas River Vessels of 2·7m draught can reach Daoulas at HWS.

• Anse de Poulimic Good holding to the E of the Pen-ar-Vir Point, marked by N Card bn of the same name. Avoid oyster beds.

• Baie de Roscanvel On W side about half way down prominent headland in 2m (mud) exposed from N through E. Southeast area of bay prohibited anchorage due to French naval activity.

• River Aulne Probably the prettiest river running into the Rade with abundant wildlife. The lower reaches of the river are buoyed and there is a good depth of water at all states of the tide to just above the br at Terenez. Above the lock at Guily-Glaz, there is 3m of water to Port Launay, and rather less to Châteaulin. Best

water above the lock nearer to port bank. About 1km above Port Launay, unlit stb hand bn, marking underwater mid-channel obstruction, reported as unreliable.

Anchorages Port Styval and on S bank near the creek to Le Folgoat.

Lock Opens local HW–0200 to HW+0130, (HW Brest –0130 to +0200).

Facilities Restaurants at lock, Port Launay, and Châteaulin. Water and bread at Port Launay. Water, electricity and all shops including large supermarket near to pontoon on stb bank as you approach at Châteaulin.

CAMARET-SUR-MER

Charts BA 3427; F 7401; Imray C36

HW Brest –0010

MHWS	MHWN	MLWN	MLWS
6·6m	5·1m	2·5m	1·0m

Exceedingly popular with British yachts because of its convenient position. Weak tidal streams within the bay, good beaches. Megaliths.

Approach and Entrance Easy by day; at night remain in white sector of Lt Iso.WG.4s, on N Mole. Avoid fish farm.

Marina Visitors' berths in Port Vauban, the outer marina. Exposed to E winds. Large vessels berth on the wave baffle. By arrangement, visitors may berth on the outer pontoons in Port de Notic.

Anchoring No anchoring in either the hbr or channels. Visitors' buoys to SE of Port Vauban.

Facilities Fuel, Wi-Fi, shops and restaurants in town. Good beaches. HM Port Vauban ☎ 02 98 27 95 99.

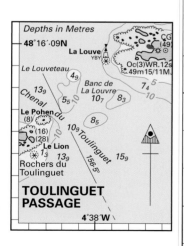

TOULINGUET PASSAGE

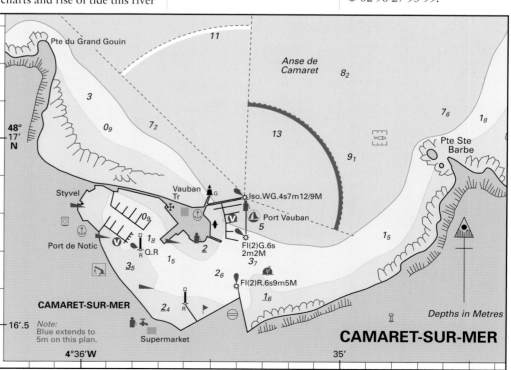

CAMARET-SUR-MER

CAP DE LA CHÈVRE
Rounding Cap de la Chèvre beware of uneven bottom as far as Basse Vieille BRB Lt buoy Fl(2)6s.

MORGAT
Charts BA 2349; F 7121; Imray C36

HW Brest –0008

MHWS	MHWN	MLWN	MLWS
6·5m	5·0m	2·4m	1·0m

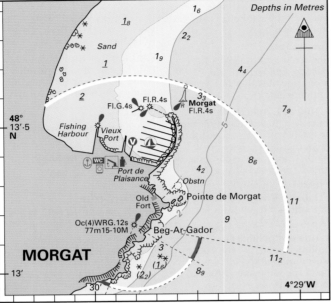

Typical French seaside town set in a wide, sandy bay.

Entrance After passing Pte de Morgat make for the Morgat R can Lt buoy.

Anchorage To the N of the Morgat buoy in 2m sheltered except from S and E.

Berthing Leave Morgat buoy to port and enter marina dredged to 2m. Visitors use pontoon extending from a point adjacent to crane and fuel berth at right angles to other pontoons. Marina is small and often full.

Facilities All supplies in town.

☏ HM 02 98 27 10 28.

DOUARNENEZ – TRÉBOUL
Charts BA 2349; F 7121; Imray C36

HW Brest –0012

MHWS	MHWN	MLWN	MLWS
6·4m	4·9m	2·3m	0·9m

A fascinating spot, 17M E of Pte du Raz. Marina at Tréboul. An excellent maritime museum ashore and afloat at Port Rhu. Megaliths. Beaches.

Approach At night, avoid the two shallow patches Basses Neuve and Basse Veur which are in the red sector of the Tristan Lt Oc(3)WR.12s.

Entrance At all states of the tide.

Berthing Visitors' pontoon to stb before entrance to marina at Tréboul, may be affected by swell.

Facilities 15-tonne travel lift, chandleries, shops, daily market.

☏ HM 02 98 74 02 56.

• **Port Rhu**

30 visitors' berths at Port Rhu. Sill 1·1m above CD. 16·5m headroom at coeff 80. HM ☏ 02 98 92 00 67 for lock times.

Anchorage Yachts are not allowed in fishing hbr. Rade de Guet anchorage is not recommended in north and easterly winds. Anchoring in Port de Rosmeur may be possible by arrangement with HM ☏ 02 98 92 14 85, VHF 12.

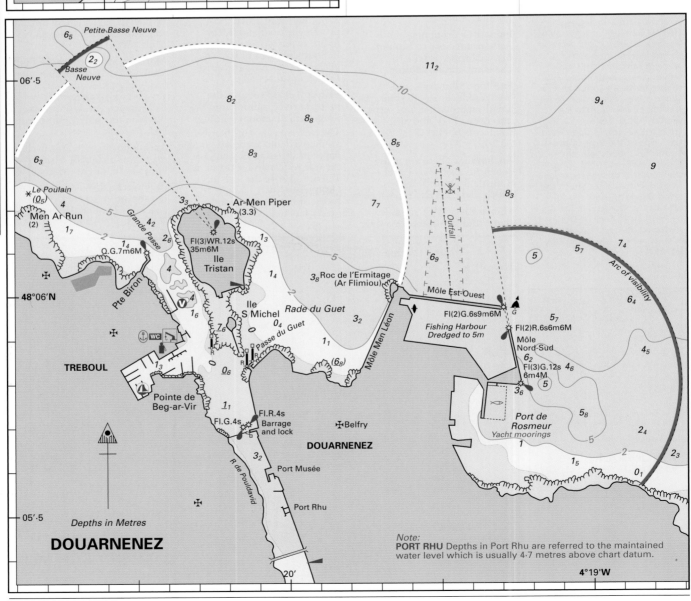

Note:
PORT RHU Depths in Port Rhu are referred to the maintained water level which is usually 4·7 metres above chart datum.

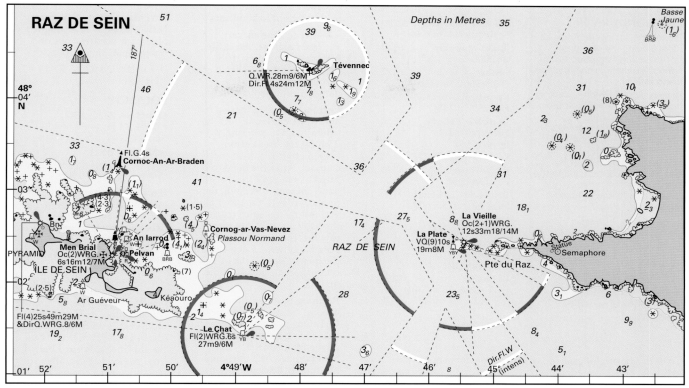

RAZ DE SEIN

Charts BA 2348; F 7148, 7423; Imray C37

Slack water, which lasts for about 30 minutes, is Brest −0100 and Brest +0530. The Raz presents few problems if it is taken at these times and when conditions are calm and visibility is good. Quite moderate winds can produce rough conditions, as can wind against tide or swell. Even when conditions are calm and windless, fighting the tide is time consuming because of the strength of the streams. Keep at least 6ca off Tévennec and a respectable distance off La Platte W Card bn tower.

If coming from the North, a yacht may wait for slack water in the Baie des Trépassés: from the South, use Ste-Evette.

Passage lights	BA No
Île de Sein Main Lt	0856
Fl(4)25s29M and DirQ.WRG	
Tévennec	0866
Q.WR.28m9/6M+	
DirFl.4s24m12M	
La Vieille	0870
Oc(2+1)WRG.12s33m18-14M	
La Plate	0872
VQ(9)10s19m8M	
Le Chat	0862
Fl(2)WRG.6s27m9-6M	

ÎLE DE SEIN

Charts BA 2348; F 7423; Imray C37

An interesting port of call if the weather is settled but chart BA *2351* or *F 5252* essential. Approach is best made by the N channel guarded by a whistle buoy, Fl.G.4s. Anchor in 4–6m, sand and rock, 3ca N of Men Brial Lt Ho, or take the ground

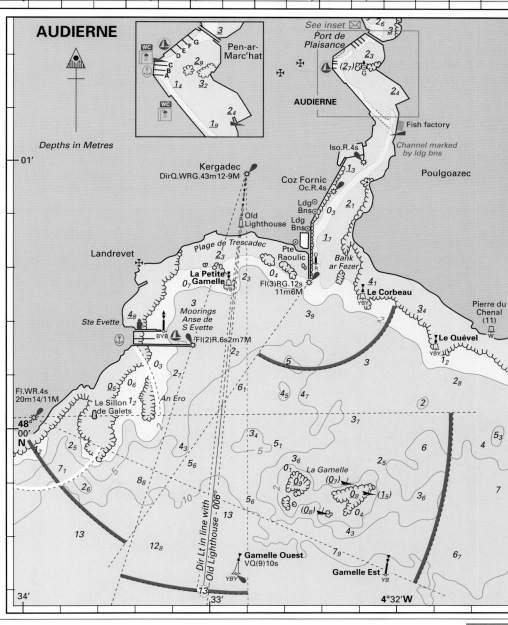

FRANCE – WEST COAST

PENMARC'H POINT TO LA GIRONDE RIVER

Penmarc'h lies low and may be identified by the octagonal LtHo 60m high standing 120m from the old tr, which is shorter and smaller.

Between Pte de Penmarc'h and Îles de Glénan the tidal streams are rotary clockwise. SW of Penmarc'h Pte the flood sets N changing to NE and the ebb SE changing to SW Max 1½–2kn.

The general direction of the tidal streams offshore along the coast between Penmarc'h and the R Gironde is as follows:

Time and direction

Brest	Brest
HW Slack/S	–0600NW
+0100SW/SE	–0500NE/NW
+0200SW	–0400NNE
+0300SW by W	–0300NE/E
+0400SW by W	–0200E
+0500NW by W	–0100ESE
+0600NW	

Passage lights	BA No
Pointe de Penmarc'h	0890
Fl.5s60m23M Horn 60s	
Ils aux Moutons	0918
Iso.WRG.2s15–11M	
Penfret	0922
Fl.R.5s36m21M+Q.11M	
Ile de Groix, Pen Men	0962
Fl(4)25s60m29M	
Goulphar, Belle Ile	1032
Fl(2)10s87m27M	
Ile du Pillier	1152
Fl(3)20s33m29M+Q.R	
Petite Foule, Ile D'Yeu	1176
Fl.5s56m24M	
Pointe des Corbeaux	1186
Fl(2+1)R.15s25m20M	
Les Baleines	1218
Fl(4)15s53m27M	
Chassiron, Ile d'Oléron	1270
Fl.10s50m28M	
La Coubre	1290
Fl(2)10s64m28M+F.RG	

in SW of hbr or alongside quay on S side. Better visited at neaps and with winds other than from the N. Entrance channel may be buoyed in season.

AUDIERNE AND STE–EVETTE ANCHORAGE

Charts BA 3640, 2819; F 7067, 7147
HW Brest –0033

MHWS	MHWN	MLWN	MLWS
5·2m	4·1m	2·0m	0·8m

A charming, friendly town with a small marina. Also moorings at Ste-Evette. A useful place to wait for a fair tide through the Raz.

Approach From N, leave Plateau de Gamelle, marked by two Cardinal buoys, W and S to stb, keeping a safe distance off Le Sillon de Galets. Keep at least ½ca from the mole of Ste-Evette.

Anchorage
• **Ste-Evette** White visitors' buoys, sheltered by the Mole. Those closer to the LB slip are less exposed to the swell. Vedettes use the landing slips. Anchor E of the buoys. Safe, except in strong SE winds.

☎ HM 02 98 70 00 28

Facilities Fuel, water from tap ashore. Shops, restaurants
• **Audierne Marina** Very sheltered marina. Accessible HW–0300 to HW+0100, depending on draught, in good conditions. The bar is dangerous in strong winds.

Entrance Leading marks, red and white chevrons, indicate safe water. On entering, keep 25m off the breakwater, keeping to this side of the channel. After the bend in the breakwater, steer for the stb hand chevrons. Keeping these in line, cross to the other bank and follow this until reaching the fish factory. Now steer towards the slipway on the port-hand bank. Keep close to the boats (3m) on the quay and on the hammerheads of the marina.

Berthing Berth as directed. May need to raft on hammerheads of G+F. On spring tides, there may be a strong current just downstream of the hammerhead of F. Although the hbr mostly dries, the pontoons remain afloat.

Facilities Fuel (at Audierne from garage). Shops and restaurants.

☎ HM 02 98 75 04 93.

LE GUILVINEC

Charts BA 2820, 3640; F 7146, 7147; Imray C47
HW Brest –0020

MHWS	MHWN	MLWN	MLWS
5·1m	4·0m	2·0m	0·8m

A crowded fishing hbr and interesting town. Entrance not

difficult with large scale chart. No entry or exit for yachts between 1600–1830. Eight places for visitors, four on buoys, four on pontoon.

☎/**VHF** HM 02 98 58 14 47, VHF 12.

LOCTUDY

Charts BA 2820, 3641; F 6649, 7146; Imray C37
HW Brest –0023

MHWS	MHWN	MLWN	MLWS
5·0m	3·9m	1·9m	0·8m

Bar Outside the entrance the S part of the bar has about 1½m; the N part almost dries. Moorings in 3·5m inside; a charming spot.

Approach Strong swell from the W can result in breaking seas between the Îles Aux Moutons and the Lesconil headland. From the W, use the transit Pointe de Combrit Oc(3+1)12s with La Pyramide Oc(2+1)12s (Benodet), until Bse du Chenal E Card buoy has been passed to port. Steer to pass mid-way between Karek-Saoz bn tr Fl.R.2·5s3m1M and Ru unlit G bn tr, to avoid rocks close to these two marks. The port is easily identified by the black and white chequered Le Perdrix Tr.

Entrance Leave No.2 R can buoy Fl(2)R.6s that marks the entrance to Loctudy close to port. At No.3 G con buoy, Fl(3)G.12s, steer towards the fish quay to port, then alter course to NW for the marina. When the fishing fleet returns, between 1630 and 1830, engines must be used in the channel and the hbr.

Berthing Ebb runs at 3kn. Visitors' berths on A pontoon and inside the wave-baffle. Hbr dory usually allocates a berth. Visitors' buoys N of the marina. If berthing further into marina keep close to hammerheads.

Facilities Good marina. Wi-Fi. Boatyard. Shops and restaurants. Important port for langoustines. Rail and bus connections for Pont L'Abbé.

☎ HM 02 98 87 51 36.

BÉNODET AND ODET RIVER

Charts BA 2820, 3641; F 6649, 6679, 7146; Imray C37
HW Brest –0010

MHWS	MHWN	MLWN	MLWS
5·2m	4·1m	2·1m	0·9m

An attractive river with marinas on both banks near the entrance. The river upstream of Bénodet deserves exploration. At Pte de Kersabiec the current can run at 4–6kn. Sound signals are required from boats at these bends in the river. Buoyage extends to Quimper, with a minimum depth in the channel

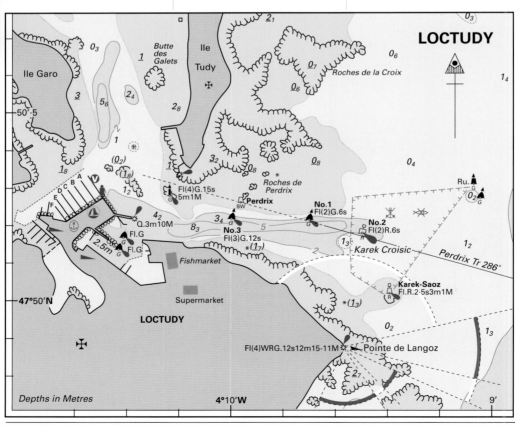

LOCTUDY

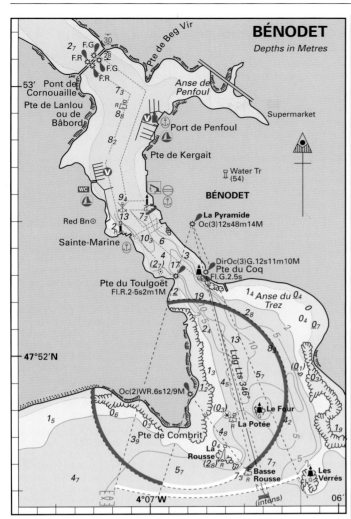

BÉNODET
Depths in Metres

of 2m up to Lanroz, above which it is too shallow for most yachts. Low br just downstream of Quimper.

Approach and Entrance The transit 346° on the Pte du Coq DirOc(3)G.12s11m10M and La Pyramide Oc(3)12s48m14M leads clear of all dangers. Beware, sea can break off the Pointe de Mousterin in SW winds.

Anchorage Outside the channel in Anse de Trez. Anchoring forbidden in the fairway between Pte de Coq and Anse de Penfoul. Private moorings downstream of both marinas and above the br (clearance 30m). Anchorages upstream of the br: Anse de Kérandraon (stb), Anses de Combrit and Kérautren (port). Narrow inlet to stb, just downstream of Lanroz. There are a few moorings on W bank by Lanroz.

Berthing Tidal flows can be very strong through both marinas. If necessary, wait on a mooring for slack water. Ste-Marine, visitors on pontoon A and the hammerheads of other pontoons. Penfoul, visitors on the wave baffle.

Interest Quimper upstream. Moorings downstream of Baie de Kerogan, continue by dinghy.

Facilities All facilities expected of a modern marina. Shops and restaurants. Fuel at Penfoul.

☎ HM Ste Marine 02 98 56 38 72; Penfoul 02 98 57 05 78.

PORT LA FORÊT

Charts BA 2820, 3641;
F 6650, 7146;
Imray C38

HW Brest −0020

MHWS	MHWN	MLWN	MLWS
5·0m	3·9m	1·9m	0·8m

A picturesque village with a large marina.

Approach Beware many rocks off Beg Meil on W point of La Fôret Bay. Keep to W of centre line of bay leaving (difficult to identify) Le Score stb bn to stb. Identify Cap Coz. There are four conspic W waiting buoys S of it.

Note shoal patch 0·9m between waiting buoys and Cap. No entry at LWS.

Entrance Round Cap Coz following the channel, dredged 1·2m, marked by R and B buoys or bns.

Leave long pontoon to port and near inner end turn to stb to enter marina. Visitors' pontoon facing.

Facilities Excellent. Fuel, boatyard, sailmaker, mechanical and electrical

repairs, Wi-Fi and chandlery. Shops, restaurants, bar and small grocers. Bus services to Quimper and Concarneau.

☎ HM 02 98 56 98 45.

CONCARNEAU

Charts BA 2820, 3641;
F 6650, 7146;
Imray C38

HW Brest −0020

MHWS	MHWN	MLWN	MLWS
5·0m	3·9m	1·9	0·8m

A splendid walled town built by Vauban enclosing the fishing hbr and yacht marina.

Approach From S, to clear the Corven de Trévignon and Soldats do not let Point de la Jumet W pyramid bear less than 005°; at night keep in the intensified sector of the Ldg Lts. When Point de la Jumet is abeam bring the Ldg Lts (front Q.14m13M, rear Q) in line, 029°. By day the front Ldg mark is a W tr on the quay outside a small chapel with a dark roof. The rear mark will be seen over the top of a large block of flats. This leads between Basse du Chenal bn to port and Le Cochon tr, Fl(3)WRG.12s, to stb. Continue until past Men Fall buoy, Fl(2)G.6s until Maison Feu de Lanriec Lt Q.G becomes visible.

Entrance Steer towards Maison Feu de Lanriec Lt Q.G. until channel to the marina, marked by Le Médée Fl(3)R.12s opens to port.

Berthing Visitors on D pontoon or inside the wave break. Berths nearer the hammerhead exposed to wash from fishing vessels. Many berths occupied by boats of Glénans sailing school. Avoid marina during strong onshore winds.

Anchorage Anse de Kersos if space is available, or outside, off La Croix mole in 5·5m. Ebb runs hard, but good holding in mud. In inner harbour on N side of La Ville Close double-ended mooring buoys, 2·4m; quays reserved for fishing and commercial vessels.

Facilities Fuel, shops, restaurants. Rail and bus connections. Mkt daily (am), outdoors Monday and Friday.

☎ HM 02 98 97 57 96.

ÎLES DE GLÉNAN

Charts BA 3640; F 6648;
Imray C38

HW Brest −0018

MHWS	MHWN	MLWN	MLWS
5·0m	3·9m	1·9m	0·8m

A picturesque archipelago, well sheltered in summer, that has the only coral beach in Europe. It is the home of the famous

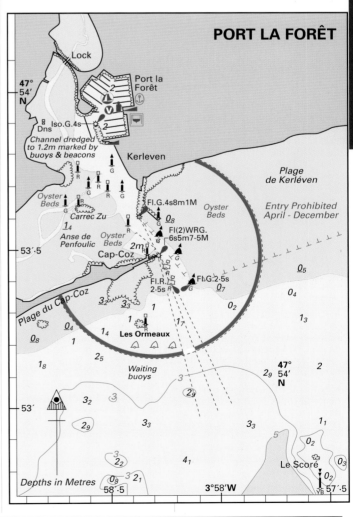

PORT LA FORÊT

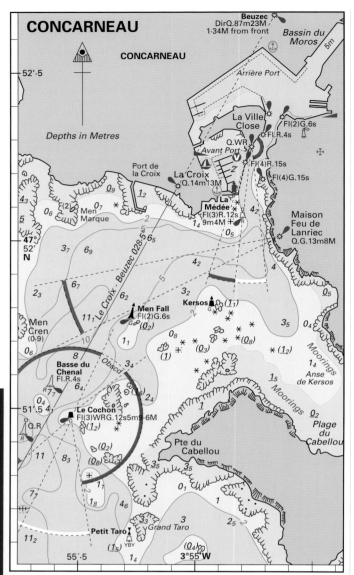

CONCARNEAU

RIVERS BETWEEN CONCARNEAU AND LORIENT

Cruising eastwards from Concarneau there are six small hbrs which may be visited in settled weather. They are all protected by bars which vary in position and should only be entered with the help of the RCC Pilotage Foundation's *Atlantic France* or *Pilote Cotier 5A* by Alain Rondeau. The best known of these harbours to cruising yachtsmen are the Aven and Bélon rivers, details of which are given below.

The other four harbours are:
• **Brigneau** a half tide port for 5/6 visitors, entry on 329°–339°. Not in strong W and SW winds.
• **Merrien** very pretty. Outer pool on six buoys (<9m) but limited shelter.
• **Doëlan** In outer harbour, eight fore and aft moorings, marked P1–4 <12m. Allocated by HM in season, 1630–2100. Inner harbour dries. Access dangerous in strong SW winds.
• **Le Pouldu** bar shifts and strong streams. Small marina on E bank.

RIVER AVEN

Charts BA 2821; F 7138; Imray C38

HW Brest –0020

MHWS	MHWN	MLWN	MLWS
5·0m	3·9m	1·9m	0·8m

The River is very beautiful and in calm conditions offers shelter at Port Manec'h. Access is dangerous in SE winds. The 3½M channel to Pont Aven is marked with unlit buoys. All quays on the river dry at LW.

Approach The bay into which the Rivers Aven and Bélon flow is marked to p by Port Manec'h Lt Ho Oc(4)WRG.12s and to stb G unlit buoy on E shore. At night remain in W sector to clear lying dangers to SE.

Anchorages
• **Port Manec'h** Five visitors' moorings at Port Manac'h 1ca off breakwater or anchor to E of moorings in greater depths. ☏ 02 98 06 81 23.
• **Kerdruc** Further fore and aft moorings (rafting) in varying depths may be available upstream of the bar ☏ 06 32 21 68 01
• **Rosbras en Riec sur Bélon** Fore and aft moorings. No official visitors' moorings, rafting alongside for one night may be possible. Flood 2kn, ebb 3kn ☏ 02 98 06 91 04.
• **Pont Aven** Drying berths on quays; best is on last straight below footbridge.

Interest Pont Aven where Gaugin painted.

Facilities Small shop up hill.

RIVER BÉLON

Charts BA 2821; F 7138; Imray C38

HW Brest –0020

MHWS	MHWN	MLWN	MLWS
5·0m	3·9m	1·9m	0·8m

The entrance is open to SW, and the bar which dries 1·5m is much more exposed than that of the River Aven and impassable in bad weather. There is an inner bar, same depth, abreast the first bend in the river, ½M inside the entrance. Beautiful scenery and Bélon oysters.

Approach Leave the bn on Bec-Lerzou rock off Point Kerhermen to stb, and steer to pass ½ca off the next point, Point Kerfany, on the stb side (caution off-lying rocks).

Entrance The channel then crosses to the N shore, whence bring Port Manec'h Lt to bear 240° astern until abreast next point to stb, where the channel turns somewhat S of E and then 030°; when the next bend comes open to stb, round the point, keeping close to moorings and proceed thereafter in mid-stream.

Anchorage Moor fore and aft to either dumb-buoys to port on entry downstream of Bélon, or to smaller fore and aft buoys at Bélon Lanriot in 2–3·5m rafting if necessary. No marked fairway through anchorage at Lanriot. Some room to anchor at neaps below moorings. Quay dries 1·7m. Oyster beds above Bélon. Stream runs 2kn on the flood and 3kn on the ebb. Restaurant at Lanriot. Bélon oysters.

LORIENT

Charts BA 304, 2821; F 7032, 7140; Imray C38

HW Brest –0010

MHWS	MHWN	MLWN	MLWS
5·1m	4·0m	2·0m	0·8m

See plan on page 364

A major commercial and fishing hbr and an outstanding sailing centre. Previously a major naval base, now with laid-up warships. The approach is sheltered from Atlantic swell by the Ile de Groix. Ferry link between all marinas and Lorient.

Approach Both the Passe de l'Ouest and the Passe Sud are well marked.

Berthing There are four marinas in the hbr with facilities for visitors.

• **To stb on entry:**
• **Port Louis** In Anse de Driasker 0·4M to stb after Citadel. Leave three G con buoys to stb. Visitors and reception on pontoon to stb after fishing boat pontoons.

Facilities Shops and restaurants in Port Louis. Supermarket between Port Louis and Locmiquélic. Bicycles available

---

Centre Nautique de Glénans Sailing School, whose boats are in evidence everywhere among the Is. To explore the interior of the archipelago, a large-scale chart is essential. Between the islands there are rocks and drying patches. With care, and suitable conditions of weather and tide, an exploration can be very rewarding.

Approach A safe approach can be made from the N to Île de Penfret, the eastern Is, recognised by the LtHo Fl.R.5s, which has no dangers until within ½ mile.

Anchorages Anchoring is permitted off all the islands. Often crowded, especially at weekends. Fenced nature area on St-Nicolas to protect rare narcissus.

• **St-Nicolas** The easiest, but exposed to the N, is N of the bay formed by St Nicolas and Ile de Bananec. La Pie, isolated danger bn Fl(2)6s3M, marks a drying rock to the W side of the entrance to the bay. W visitors' mooring buoys.

• **La Chambre (South of St-Nicolas)** The most sheltered of

all anchorages, but exposed to swell in southerlies.

From the E, follow the W coast of Île de Penfret until off the coral beach about halfway down the W shore. From here, above half tide, steer for houses on Île St-Nicolas, about 260°.

From the N, leaving Le Pie isolated danger bn Fl(2)6s3M, follow a course of 135° until abeam of the E card bn on the SE corner of Île de Bananec.

From the SE, the leading line 311°, gable end of large Ho on Île St-Nicolas with the NE edge of fort on Île Cigogne.

From the W, after half flood, as part of the channel dries, the Chenal des Bluiniers, Penfret LtHo in line with le Broc'h N Card bn tr 088°. With a sufficient rise of tide, this transit may be followed into the W end of the anchorage, depending on draught.

W visitors' buoys closer to the Is. Anchoring permitted outside fairway.

Facilities In season, two restaurants on St Nicolas, reservations advised. Weather forecast. No water or supplies.

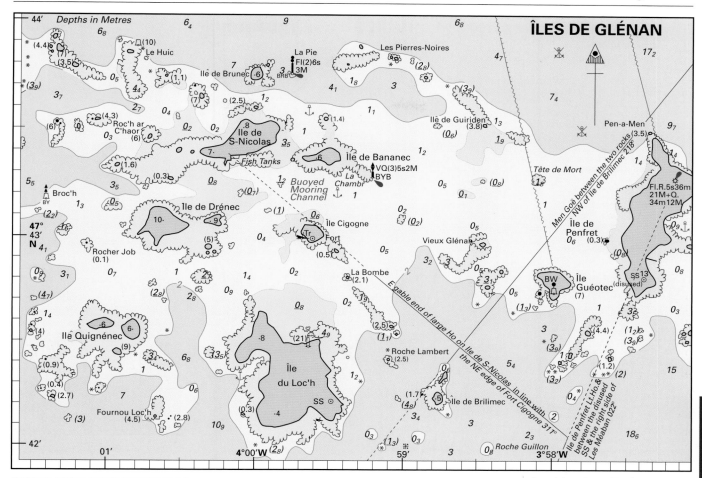

ÎLES DE GLÉNAN

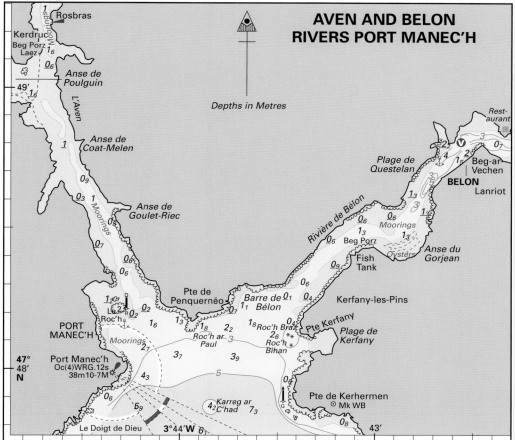

AVEN AND BELON RIVERS PORT MANEC'H

Depths in Metres

for visitors' use. Fuel at Kernével. Wi-Fi. Mkt Sat.

Interest Port Louis Citadel and its Museums.

☏ HM 02 97 82 59 55.

• **Locmiquélic Ste-Catherine** Channel to stb of Île St-Michel. Entrance NE of M5 G con buoy. Visitors on pontoon A.

Facilities Fuel, Wi-Fi, shops, supermarket towards Port Louis. Mkt Fri. Some bars and restaurants near marina.

☏ HM 02 97 33 59 51.

• **To port on entry:**
• **Kernével** The largest marina in the river, 0·7M to port beyond the Citadel. The entrance is at the N end of the marina. Visitors' berth in the northern section of the marina. On entry, the first section of the inside of the wave baffle is reserved for catamarans, visiting yachts may also berth beyond this and on the pontoon to stb.

Facilities Fuel. 45-tonne lift. Restaurant. Some shops at Larmor-Plage. Bus service to Larmor Plage. Chandlery. Wi-Fi.

☏ HM 02 97 65 48 25.

• **Lorient** After passing Kernével Marina leave Île St-Michel to stb. The entrance to Lorient is to port after Pen Mané marina to stb. Beware of ferries. Max speed in outer harbour 3kn. Contact capitainerie on arrival. Visitors' pontoon at head of the inlet, to port below the br.

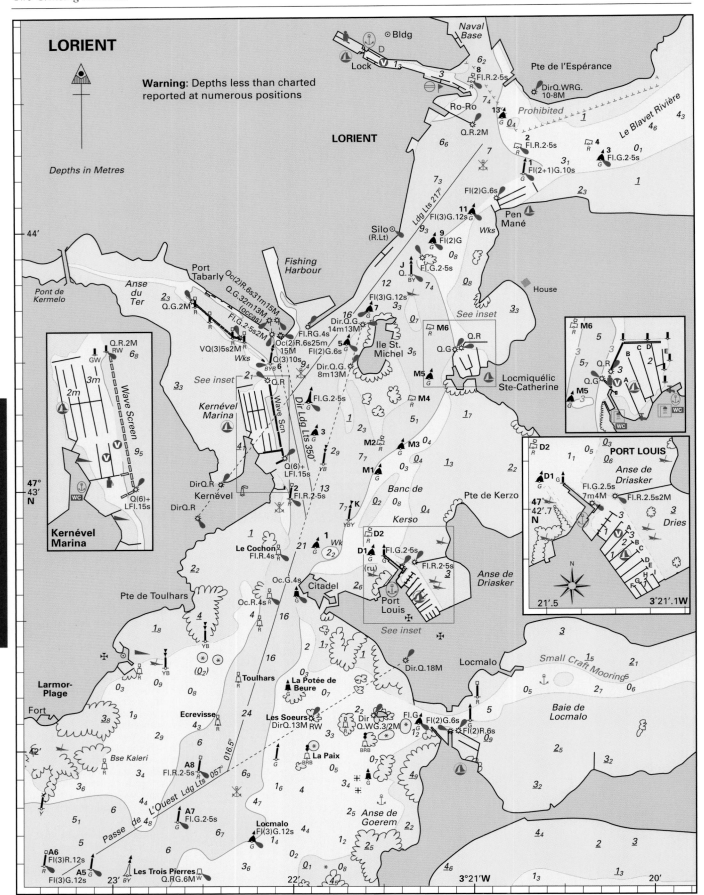

LORIENT

Warning: Depths less than charted reported at numerous positions

Depths in Metres

Kernével Marina

PORT LOUIS

Anse de Driasker

Dries

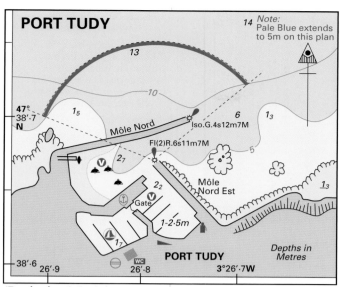

PORT TUDY

14 Note: Pale Blue extends to 5m on this plan

13

10

47° 38'·7 N

1₅

Môle Nord

Iso.G.4s12m7M

6

1₃

Fl(2)R.6s11m7M

5

2₇

Môle Nord Est

Gate

1·2·5m

1₃

1₇

38'·6 26'·9

wc

PORT TUDY

Depths in Metres

26'·8

3°26'·7W

(Dredged to 2·5m.) Access to inner basin; HW±0030, depending on coefficient, only during the day. Depth in basin, 2·5m. Sill dries 1m. Contact capitainerie on arrival.

Facilities Mobile crane. Chandleries, boatyards. Shops and restaurants. Rly. HM and lock ☎ 02 97 21 10 14.

Interest Cité de Voile Eric Tabarly, Musée Sous Marin and Sous Marin Flore. Ferries to Groix.

PORT TUDY ÎLE DE GROIX

Charts BA 2821, 2822; F 7139; Imray C38

HW Brest −0012

MHWS	MHWN	MLWN	MLWS
5·1m	4·0m	2·0m	0·8m

A small hbr affording shelter in 3m, but some swell in NE winds in avant port

Entrance Available in all weathers; use the transit of the LtHo on the N and E jetties of the hbr. Rocky promontories to the E of the entrance marked by N and E Card buoys. Mooring buoy reserved for the French Navy in the N of the hbr. Ferries have priority.

Berthing Lie to buoys in outer harbour, on fingers on the first two pontoons in the inner harbour, or raft on hammerheads. Charges from midday. Locked inner basin, HW±0200 unless coefficient very low.

Facilities Showers at limited times only. Restaurants near hbr, shops up the hill in town.

☎ HM 02 97 86 54 62.

ÉTEL RIVER

Charts BA 2822; F 7032, 7138; Imray C38

HW Brest +0005

MHWS	MHWN	MLWN	MLWS
4·9m	4·1m	2·2m	0·5m

The entrance is a few miles SE of Lorient, with moving sandbanks and drying bar which varies in depth and position. Entrance is forbidden at night and inadvisable on the ebb.

Approach Not before Brest HW−0300; from a position to the south of the entrance call *Étel Signal Station* VHF 13 or ☎ 02 97 55 35 59 for entry instructions. Entrance not advised in strong on-shore winds or swell. Semaphore signals; Cross-bar. No vessels may enter or leave. Black Ball: Vessels <8m may not enter or leave. Red flag: No entry or exit due to lack of water. Do not use leading marks until over the bar.

Entrance After crossing the bar, follow the buoyed channel until upstream of R can buoy Fl(2)R.6s. Then keep to middle or river. Marina to stb.

Berthing Yachts usually met by dory and directed to berth. Tidal flows weaker in marina.

Anchorage Above marina or off Magouer, not recommended because of strong tidal streams, 4–5kn. Anchoring prohibited offshore within ½M centred on LtHo near SS, Oc(2)WRG.6s.

Facilities Shops and restaurants. Chandleries. Fuel.

☎ /VHF HM 02 97 55 46 62, *Mobile* 06 83 99 92 39, VHF 13 – according to tide. Out of season Tuesday–Friday and Saturday mornings.

PORT MARIA

Charts BA 2357, 2822; F 7141; Imray C38

HW Brest −0005

MHWS	MHWN	MLWN	MLWS
5·3m	4·1m	2·1m	0·9m

Drying hbr. Except in an emergency, forbidden to yachts. Entrance dangerous in high swell from SW to SE.

SAUZON, BELLE ÎLE

Charts BA 2822; F 7142; Imray C39

HW Brest −0010

MHWS	MHWN	MLWN	MLWS
5·1m	4·0m	1·9m	0·7m

A delightful place with good restaurants. Open to the N/NE.

Anchorage 22 white visitors' moorings in W side of bay, Port Bellec, outside the hbr. Two ropes to buoy. Anchoring forbidden here. 40 berths for monohulls <12m and draught <2m, rafting on fore and aft buoys in outer harbour.

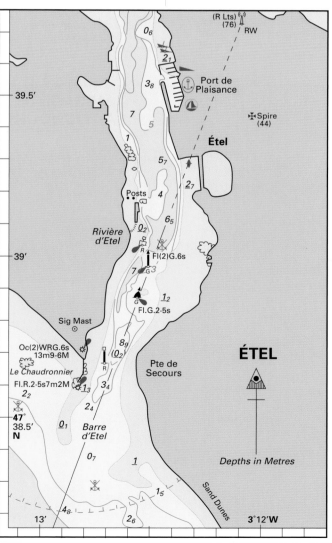

(R Lts) (76) RW

0₆

2₁

3₈

Port de Plaisance

7

5

Étel

5₇

☩ Spire (44)

2₇

Posts

4

6₅

Rivière d'Etel

0₂

Fl(2)G.6s

7 G 3

1₂

G

Fl.G.2·5s

Sig Mast

8₉

0₂

Oc(2)WRG.6s 13m9–6M

R

Le Chaudronnier

Fl.R.2·5s7m2M

1₃

3₄

Pte de Secours

ÉTEL

Depths in Metres

2₂

47° 38.5' N

0₁

Barre d'Etel

2₄

0₇

1

13'

4₈

2₆

Sand Dunes

3°12'W

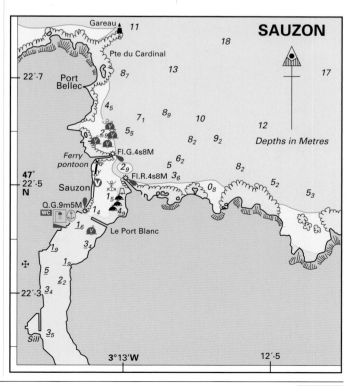

Gareau 11

18

Pte du Cardinal

22'·7

Port Bellec

8₇

13

SAUZON

17

4₅

7₁

5₅

8₉

10

12

Depths in Metres

8₂

9₂

Fl.G.4s8M

6₂

8₂

Ferry pontoon

2₉

47° 22'·5 N

Fl.R.4s8M

3₆

0₈

5₂

5₃

Sauzon

Q.G.9m5M

wc

1₅

1₄

4₉

Le Port Blanc

1₆

1₉

3₄

22'·3

3₄

5

1₉

5

2₂

3₅

Sill

3°13'W

12'·5

ARCHIPELAGO SE OF QUIBERON PENINSULA

Charts BA 2357; F 7141; Imray C39

There are four passages through the many islands and rocks which string out for 15M SE from the Quiberon peninsula:

- La Teignouse passage
- Passage du Béniguet
- Passage de L'Île aux Chevaux
- Passage des Sœurs

Of these the La Teignouse is the most N'ly, lit and probably the easiest; the Béniguet is the shortest, narrow and all right in good visibilty in daylight; the Chevaux is the longest but a useful passage in fine weather from Belle Isle to Hoëdic; the Sœur is perhaps the most difficult. Directions below are given only for the Teignouse passage.

From the SW identify the Guoé Vaz Sud S card Lt buoy and the Básse du Milieu G pillar Lt buoy Fl(2)G.6s and pass between on a course of 036° until past the Goué Vas Est pillar buoy Fl(3)R.12s. Alter course to 068° to pass in 1½M between the Basse Nouvelle R pillar buoy Fl.R.2·5s and the NE Teignouse G pillar buoy Fl(3)G.12s. NE stream commences HW Brest –0600 1·7kn max and SW stream at HW Brest +0100. 2kn maximum.

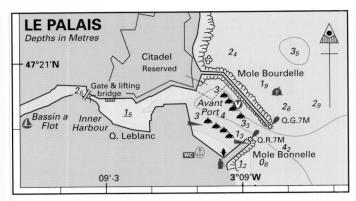

LE PALAIS
Depths in Metres

47°21'N

Citadel Reserved

Gate & lifting bridge

Bassin a Flot

Inner Harbour

Q. Leblanc

Avant Port

Mole Bourdelle

Mole Bonnelle

Q.G.7M

Q.R.7M

wc

09'·3

3°09'W

Visitors' buoys to port in drying, inner harbour. Moor fore and aft. Anchoring possible clear of these buoys, ground hard mud.

Facilities Some shops and a good range of restaurants. Showers and WCs near HM Office ☎ 02 97 31 63 40.

LE PALAIS, BELLE ÎLE

Charts BA 2822, 2823; F 7142; Imray C39

HW Brest –0010

MHWS	MHWN	MLWN	MLWS
5·2m	4·0m	1·9m	0·7m

A popular town, often crowded as it is a convenient port when passage-making and an excellent base from which to explore the island. Citadel dominates the entrance to the hbr.

Entrance Five unlit buoys to NE of Mole Bourdelle. Beware of the frequent ferries entering and leaving the hbr from 0600 to 2200.

Anchorage The anchorage to the E of Mole Bourdelle restricted by large buoys laid for commercial craft. Anchoring not advised in winds from SE/E/NE. These conditions produce swell in the outer harbour. On entry to outer harbour, boats are directed to fore and aft buoys, where rafting is the norm. Boats lie either between two buoys or between buoy and chains down hbr wall. In season, hbr staff assist with mooring.

Berthing Lock to the inner harbour opens HW–0130 to +0100 between 0600 and 2200. Berth, or more normally, raft, as directed alongside quays in Bassin à Flot. If requested, a berth may be available in the marina, Bassin de la Saline. The br between the two basins opens at the same time as that over the lock. White stripes

indicate that a berth is reserved for commercial boats only.

Facilities Water from Môle Bonnelle in outer harbour. Shops, chandleries and restaurants. Daily morning market. Ferries to mainland. Cycle and car hire. Wi-Fi.

Interest Citadel.

☎ HM 02 97 31 42 90.

PORT HALIGUEN

Charts BA 2357, 2822, 2823; F 7141; Imray C39

HW Brest –0005

MHWS	MHWN	MLWN	MLWS
5·2m	4·1m	2·0m	0·7m

Pleasant yacht hbr with moorings and marina, 3·5m in entrance, to E of old drying hbr and village on E side of Quiberon peninsula. Complete shelter. Adjacent beach. Ferries to Belle Île.

Approach Hazards: unlit buoys, E of entrance S Card buoy *Port-Haliguen*, N of entrance S Card buoy *SE Olibarte*. At night keep in W sectors of LtHo on outer mole Oc(2)WR.6s.

Entrance Accessible in all weathers and all states of the tide. No anchoring within the hbr.

Berthing Visitors' pontoon inside harbour wall in West Basin. Either report to office or the hbr dory if it is on duty.

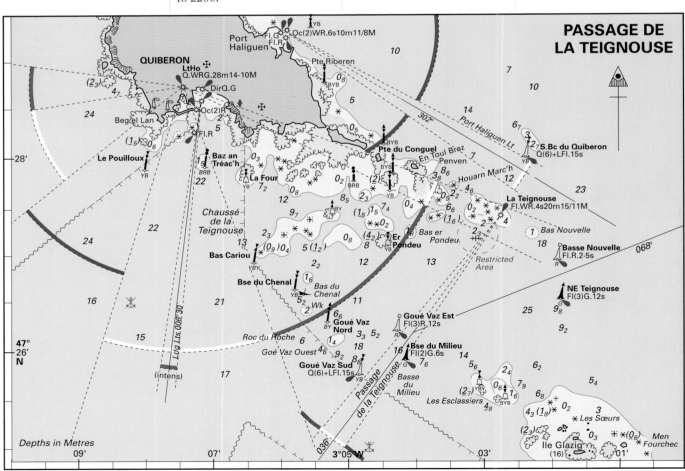

PASSAGE DE LA TEIGNOUSE

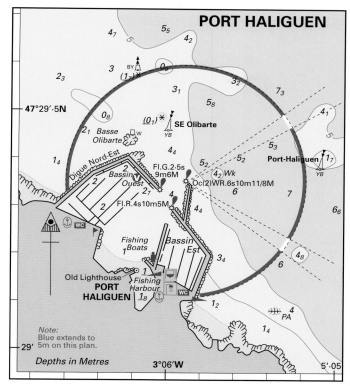

PORT HALIGUEN

Depths in Metres

Note: Blue extends to 5m on this plan.

47°29'·5N

3°06'W   5'·05

29'

RIVER AURAY WESTERN ARM

HW (Auray)

Brest HW sp +0005 np +0015

MHWS	MHWN	MLWN	MLWS
4·9m	4·0m	1·8m	0·8m

See plan on page 369.

The river is buoyed to Auray, which may be reached on the flood if draught and air-draught permit, the br below St Goustan has a clearance of 14m. Pass E of the island, Le Grand Huernic, and its two R can buoys; here in the narrows tidal streams can reach 4kn. Much of the river further upstream is lined with moorings. In the reach below Baie de Kerdréan, deeper water is to be found towards the W bank. At Auray at HW, there is a stand, after which the ebb runs quickly. It is advisable not to wait for the ebb when leaving Auray.

• **Le Rocher** Shallow draught boats may be able to anchor above moorings.

Facilities Restaurants and a few shops at Bono.

• **Auray – St-Goustan** Only 1·5m CD between Le Rocher and Auray. Good shelter at St-Goustan/Auray, on fore and aft buoys in 3·6m <12m, 200m upstream of br, clearances LW 16·5m HW 14m. Height indicated on scale to stb before br.

Crowded in season. Alongside quay at St-Goustan, dries.

☎ HM 02 97 56 29 08.

Facilities Restaurants, shops. Market in Auray, open mornings only. Rly TGV.

Facilities Shops in Quiberon and small épicerie near marina in season. Restaurants and bars nr marina and in town. Wi-Fi. Chandleries. Rly connection from Quiberon to Auray.

☎ HM 02 97 50 20 56.

LA TRINITÉ SUR MER CRAC'H RIVER

Charts BA 2357, 2358; F 7141; Imray C39

HW Brest –0005

MHWS	MHWN	MLWN	MLWS
5·4m	4·3m	2·1m	0·8m

Large marina, an ocean racing centre with good support facilities. Marina sheltered in all conditions except when certain high tides produce a large swell. Very busy in season. Megaliths at Carnac.

Entrance In all weathers and states of tide. Beware of oyster beds. Even at high tide, remain within the buoyed channel.

Berthing Visitors' pontoon next to S mole.

Facilities Chandleries, Wi-Fi, boatyards, shops and restaurants. Rly connection to Auray.

GOLFE DU MORBIHAN (THE MORBIHAN)

Charts BA 2371; F 7137, 6992; Imray C39

HW (Pt Navalo) Brest –0005sp; +0030np

MHWS	MHWN	MLWN	MLWS
4·9m	3·9m	1·8m	0·7m

The Morbihan is a large inland sea with two main rivers, the Auray and the Vannes, together with many islands, some inhabited, and numerous anchorages. A large scale chart is essential.

Tides These are very strong, particularly near and just inside the entrance, where the stream off N end of Grand Mouton reaches 8kn at sp on the ebb and 6kn on the flood. Off Point de Navalo, the ingoing stream begins at Brest –0445 4½kn on E side and 3½kn on W side and the outgoing stream at HW+0115. 5¾kn sp on E side and 4¼kn on W side. In Auray R, the flood stream begins at Brest –0455, the ebb at +0020; both attain about 3kn at springs.

Approach Identified by the two hillocks on Île Méaban to port and, if it is visible through the trees, the white Port Navalo lighthouse.

Entrance Inadvisable on the ebb. The official leading line of the white pyramid, Petit Vezid, with the Church spire of Baden is not easy to see as the spire is 5M inland. The port hand side of the entrance channel is marked by three large towers, the E Card Bagen Hir, the R Kerpenhir tr and R Goémorent tr. Keeping to mid-channel as they are passed, the stb Grand Mouton buoy, QG and the S Card Grégan will come into view. The flood sets strongly onto the latter. If entering the Morbihan, pass between these. The S Card buoys marking the shallows to the W of the Île Aux Moines are small. If going to Auray, leave Grégan and the pyramid to stb.

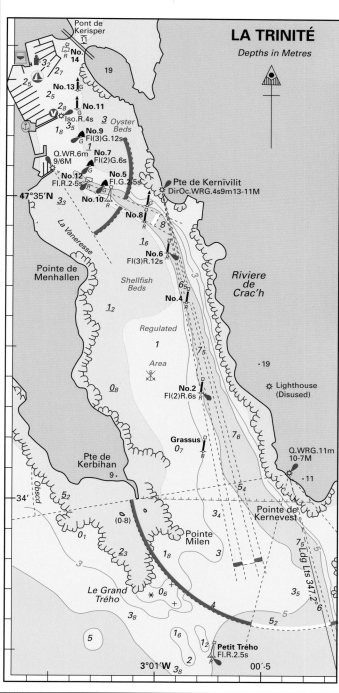

LA TRINITÉ

Depths in Metres

47°35'N

34'

3°01'W   00'·5

FRANCE – WEST COAST

GOLFE DU MORBIHAN

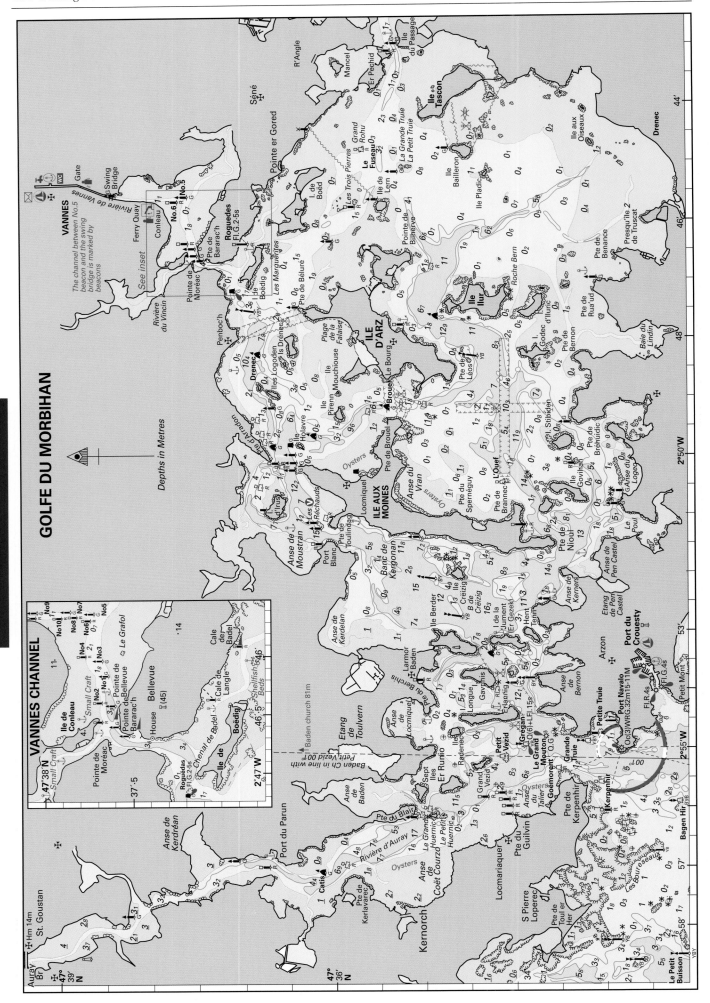

Depths in Metres

VANNES CHANNEL

The channel between No.5 beacon and the swing bridge is marked by beacons

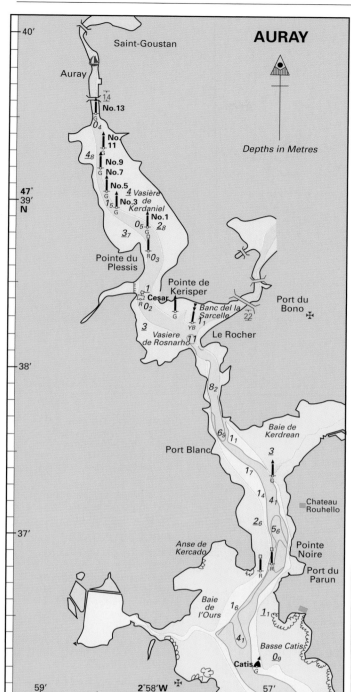

AURAY

Depths in Metres

Saint-Goustan

Auray

No.13

No. 11

No.9

No.7

No.5

Vasière de Kerdaniel

No.3

No.1

Pointe du Plessis

Cesar

Pointe de Kerisper

Banc del la Sarcelle

Vasiere de Rosnarho

Pointe du Bono

Le Rocher

Baie de Kerdrean

Port Blanc

Chateau Rouhello

Anse de Kercado

Pointe Noire

Port du Parun

Baie de l'Ours

Basse Catis

Catis

Morbihan. It is available at Le Crouesty, where there is also a large supermarket. Free short stays are permitted here for shopping.

VANNES

HW Brest + 0210

MHWS	MHWN	MLWN	MLWS
3·3m	2·7m	1·0m	0·5m

A delightful, historic town, worth a visit of several days. For most boats, the channel up to Vannes may be taken only on the flood. HW at Vannes is approx. 2hrs after that at Port Navalo. The area around the marina has been redeveloped. Capitainerie to stb on entry.

Approach Usually enough water at HW−0300 in channel beyond Conleau. At the sharp port turn (by the pink cottage) better water is towards the stb bank.

Entrance Waiting pontoons upstream and downstream of the lock. Lock and br open June–September HW −0230 to HW+0200 from 0800 to 2200 with a tidal height of 2m. Boats leaving the marina have priority.

Berthing Berth as directed. Visitors may have to raft unless they have pre-booked a berth.

Facilities Indoor market daily each morning. Market days Wednesday and Saturday. Good shore facilities, chandlery at ZA St Léonard N. Shops, restaurants, museums. Rly, TGV. ☎ 02 97 54 16 08 (not Sundays).

Port Navalo Hbr exposed to W and NW. Five visitors' moorings for boats <10m. ☎ 02 97 53 82 12.

PORT DU CROUESTY

Chart BA 2371; F7034, 6992; Imray C39

HW Brest +0020

MHWS	MHWN	MLWN	MLWS
4·9m	3·9m	1·8m	0·7m

A large marina to the E of the entrance to the Morbihan. Useful if waiting for flood to set into the Morbihan.

Approach. *See entrance to Golfe du Morbihan page 367.*

Entrance Buoyed channel into the hbr 1·8m. Pass between the breakwaters and watch for G and R bns marking ends of obstacles.

Berthing Visitors' berths in third bay to stb.

Facilities Excellent marina facilities, sailmaker and all repairs. Fuel, chandleries, supermarket, restaurants. Wi-Fi. ☎ HM 02 97 53 73 33.

PÉNERF

Charts BA 2823
Imray C39

HW Brest −0005

MHWS	MHWN	MLWN	MLWS
5·4m	4·3m	2·0m	0·7m

The river enters Quiberon Bay 3M W of Vilaine River.

Approach The mouth of the river is marked by Le Penvin R can and Borénis G con buoys.

Entrance The buoyage of the E entrance has been improved. R and G bns precede Pignon R tr. Do not pass too close to the first stb bn. After the last pair of bns has been passed, the channel widens.

Anchorage May find a space outside the moorings but avoid the oyster beds on either shore.

Facilities Minimal. Hotel.

LA VILAINE

Charts BA 2823; F 7144; Imray C39

HW Brest −0020 sp +0035 np

MHWS	MHWN	MLWN	MLWS
5·5m	4·4m	2·1m	0·7m

The river is 135M long, and is dammed at Arzal where one can lock into a non-tidal river as far as Redon. Entry to the

ANCHORAGES WITHIN THE GOLFE DU MORBIHAN

Fewer anchorages are now available to visiting yachts, and many that are marked on the chart will be full of moorings; especially those close to the mainland. Take care to avoid bathing areas which are marked by yellow buoys.

• **Île Longue** E of island in 2–5m. Sheltered from the west.

• **Île de la Jument** East of the island in 2–3m.

• **Île aux Moines** SE of the island between Pointe du Nioul and Pointe de Brannec, in 2–5m.

• **Île Pirenn** In 3–5m, mud, 0·2M S of the island. Slip accessible from half tide on

the E point of Île aux Moines; and another which also dries on W side of Île d'Arz.

• **Île d'Arz** S of the island but N of the G con buoy and R can buoy Bilhervé in 2–5m of water. Moorings closer in.

Moorings

• **Île aux Moines** A few visitors' moorings and two visitors' pontoons which are not connected to the shore, (expensive). ☎ 02 97 26 30 57.

• **Arradon** 10 visitors' buoys for craft <18m and some berths on a pontoon for shallow-drafted craft. ☎ 02 97 44 01 23.

Facilities Small supermarkets, restaurants and créperies on Île Aux Moines and Île d'Arz. Fuel is not available at any marina or hbr within the Golfe du

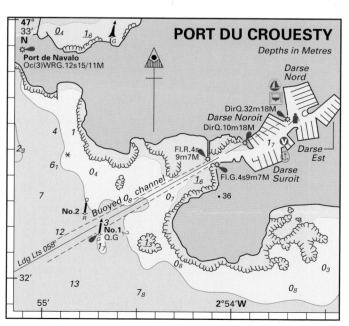

PORT DU CROUESTY

Depths in Metres

Port de Navalo
Oc(3)WRG.12s15/11M

Darse Nord

DirQ.32m18M

Darse Noroit

DirQ.10m18M

Darse Est

Fl.R.4s 9m7M

Darse Suroit

Fl.G.4s9m7M

Buoyed channel

No.2

No.1
Q.G

Ldg Lts 058°

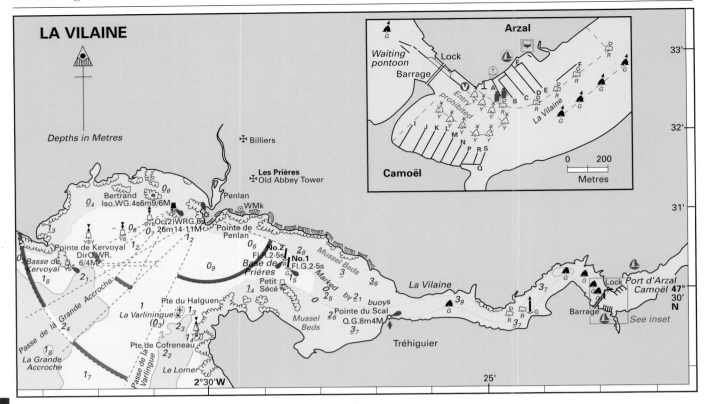

LA VILAINE

Brittany canal system can be made at Bellions Lock, a little below Redon.

Entrance Seas can break on the bar, which has 1m, in W'ly winds. Usually sufficient water at half flood. By day there are two entrance passages:

• **La Grande Accroche** The Tr of Les Prières with the Penlan LtHo 052°. Maintain this bearing until abeam of Bse Kervoyal S Card tr, then turn steer 090° to reach the buoyed channel.

• **Passe de la Varlingue** W of the Varlingue rock, Ldg ln 025° Billiers Church Spire with Penlan Lt Ho. E of the Varlingue, Ldg ln Tr of Les Prières with WMk (a white painted rock).

At night keep in the white sector of the Penlan LtHo, until in the white sector of Bse Kervoyal S Card tr. Keep the latter astern until the buoyed channel has been reached.

Anchorage At Tréhiguier, beyond the moorings, visitors' buoys to stb, or in greater shelter just below the lock, outside the moorings where there is a waiting pontoon.

Arzal Lock Hourly opening times from 0700–2200 (July/August). 0800–2000 the rest of the year, times not always adhered to. Waiting pontoons downstream of lock. Recorded message ✆ 02 97 45 01 15 (24hrs).

Berthing

• **Arzal** Report to HM office for a berth.

Facilities Wi-Fi. Best range of boatyard and chandleries on the River. Fuel. Restaurant and bars near marina, limited shops in village. HM ✆ 02 97 45 02 97.

• **La Roche Bernard** Visitors' berth on downstream side of first pontoon.

Facilities Chandlery. Wi-Fi. Good range of shops and restaurants. HM ✆ 02 99 90 62 17.

• **Foleux** Visitors' berth/raft on N bank.

Facilities Créperie. No shops ✆ 02 99 91 80 87.

• **Béganne** Single pontoon without power or water. Stay limited to 24hrs. Shops, bar and restaurant in village. Above Pont de Cran Br, which lifts at 0900, 1100, 1430, 1630, 1830, two waiting buoys downstream or moor alongside quay. Restaurant. Waiting pontoon upstream with no access ashore.

• **Rieux** Two pontoons, water and power available. Contact the campsite or Mairie to organise the latter. Modest charges. Restaurant, (reservations required for dinner) boulangerie, bars in village and restaurant near pontoons.

• **Redon** Take the port fork of the river. Visitors' berths immediately to port on entry.

Facilities Limited chandlery, all shops and restaurants of a town. Rly TGV. HM ✆ 02 99 71 35 28.

ÎLE DE HOËDIC

Charts BA 2823, 2835; F 7143; Imray C39

HW Brest –0010

MHWS	MHWN	MLWN	MLWS
5·1m	4·0m	1·9m	0·7m

Anchorage

• On the N coast, Port Angol, often crowded, moor to communal buoys if no room on pontoon. Not in N'ly winds.

• Off the Plage du Canot, to W of the port avoiding underwater cables. Exposed to N.

Facilities Shop, restaurants, ferry to mainland.

ÎLE DE HOUAT

Charts BA 2823, 2835; F 7143; Imray C39

HW Brest –0005.

MHWS	MHWN	MLWN	MLWS
5·2m	4·1m	2·0m	0·8m

Anchorages

• **St-Gildas** If approaching from the N, avoid the mussel park to the N of La Vieille and the zone of aquaculture to the S. Do not get too close to the breakwater when rounding it to enter the hbr. Raft to fore and aft buoys. S end of hbr dries. Few places for visitors. Alternatively, anchor or take a buoy outside the hbr. Mairie ✆ 02 97 30 68 04.

• **Treac'h er Béniguet** Very uncomfortable in W winds but sheltered from E. Leave le Roulou S Card tr to stb. Anchor in 3–4m sand.

• **Treac'h an Gouret** Popular anchorage in fine, settled weather; the NE part of this bay is a bird reserve and anchoring here is forbidden. Exposed to E. Bathing area marked by yellow buoys in season.

Facilities Hotels, restaurants and shops in the small town. Ferry to mainland.

PIRIAC-SUR-MER

Charts BA 2823; F 7033; Imray C39

HW Brest –0030sp +0015np

MHWS	MHWN	MLWN	MLWS
5·4m	4·3m	2·0m	0·7m

About 6M S of the Vilaine River; a fishing hbr with a marina built on to the east with lifting sill. 2·4m inside sill. Very attractive town.

Approach only after half tide. From the west there are many rocks, Grand Norven rock marked by N card bn dries 1·8m.

Entrance From a position 3·5ca E of Grand Norven turn on to 197°, at night W sector 194°–210°. Enter between R and G bns. Turn sharply to port after E–W mole and enter over sill. R flashing lights indicate sill is closed. Usually met by harbour dory. Visitors normally berth at northern ends of D and E, or raft on C.

Facilities Chandleries, shops, Wi-Fi, restaurants. Market Saturday or Tuesday. Beaches.

✆ HM 02 40 23 52 32.

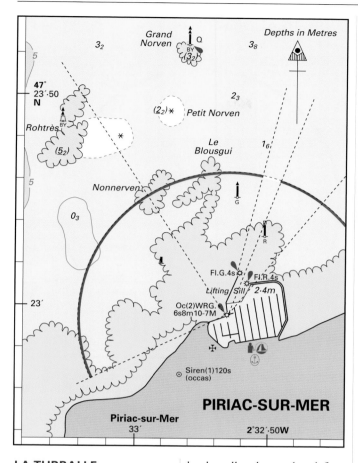

PIRIAC-SUR-MER

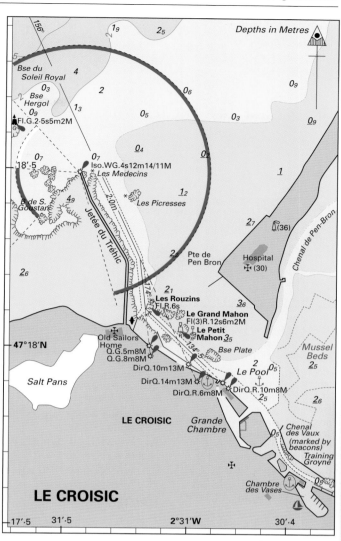

LE CROISIC

LA TURBALLE

Charts BA 2823; F 7033; Imray C39

HW Brest −0040sp +0015np

MHWS	MHWN	MLWN	MLWS
5·4m	4·3m	2·0m	0·7m

Two miles N of Le Croisic, a fishing hbr with a pleasant town worth a visit. Strong swell in S/SW winds.

Approach Easily identified by Trescalan large water tr. Rocky shoals to N. Ldg marks, Pierhead Lts 060°. In season, the approach channel is marked by the yellow buoys that define the bathing area.

Entrance 006° R bn Iso.R.4s11m3M to W of fish market, with the lt behind it, Iso.R.4s19m3M. This will lead clear of the rocks to stb.

Berthing In season, usually met by harbour dory. Visitors' berth in box S off B.

Facilities Fuel, chandlery, shops, restaurants, daily indoor market, main market day Saturday.

☏ HM 02 40 23 41 65.

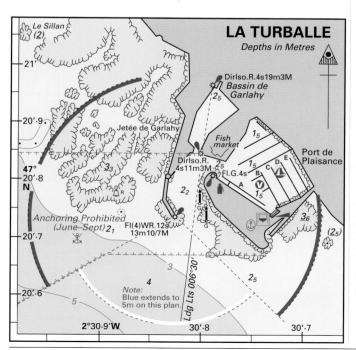

LA TURBALLE

LE CROISIC

Charts BA 2823; F7145; Imray C39

HW Brest−0040sp +0015np

MHWS	MHWN	MLWN	MLWS
5·4m	4·3m	2·0m	0·7m

A popular holiday resort and fishing hbr which dries. Limited provision for yachts that can take the ground. Anchoring in the pool only permitted with prior agreement from HM. The entrance channel is dredged to 1·2m but the tides are strong, exceeding 4kn at springs, when entry should be made 1hr before HW. At neaps, entry possible at any time. There is a gauge (difficult to read) at the head of the Tréhic jetty indicating depth of water at quayside.

Approach and Entrance Keep on the bearing 156°, until it is possible to identify the ldg Lts DirQ.13M on the W bank marked with orange dayglo chevrons. At the bend on the Jettée du Tréhic, bear 174°, ldg marks, two DirQ.G.8M on shore. Abeam Les Rouzins R can buoy, bear 135°, leading line on the two Lts. DirQ.R. until reaching the pool.

Mooring In the hbr, on pontoons with legs, or anchor as previously agreed with HM.

Facilities Fuel in town. Chandleries.

☏ HM 02 40 23 10 95.

LA BAULE – LE POULIGUEN

Charts BA 2986; F7145; Imray C39

HW Brest −0045sp +0020np

MHWS	MHWN	MLWN	MLWS
5·4m	4·3m	2·0m	0·7m

Hbr sheltered from all winds except SE, access after half-tide. Depth 1·2m at LW±0230. Possibility of grounding with a swell.

Approach Marked by Penchâteau Fl.R.2.5s and Martineau R can buoys.

Entrance The entrance to the channel is marked by R bn and la Vieille G bn. The position of the channel changes. Marked by bns.

Berthing Contact HM on arrival. VHF 09, ☏ 02 40 11 97 97.

Facilities Fuel. Shops and restaurants. Daily market in season. Rly.

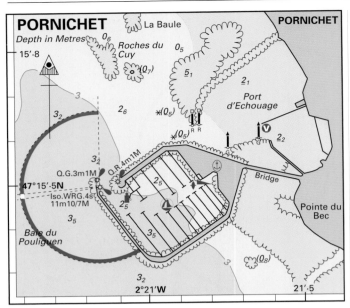

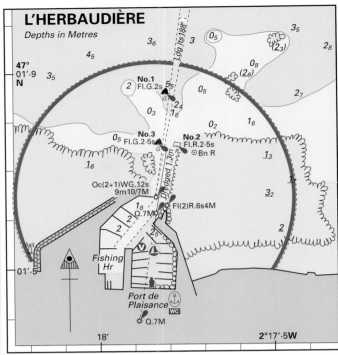

PORNICHET – LA BAULE

Charts BA 2986; F7145; Imray C40

HW Brest −0045sp + 0020np

MHWS	MHWN	MLWN	MLWS
5·5m	4·4m	2·1m	0·8m

Deepwater, large yacht hbr, protected from all winds and accessible at all states of the tide except at LW Springs. Crowded in season.

Entrance Easy by day, but hbr lights difficult to distinguish against shore lights.

Berthing Visitors' berths on hammerheads except H, J and K.

Facilities Fuel and all marina facilities. Market days Wednesday and Saturday. Shops, restaurants. Good beaches. Rly.

☎ HM 02 40 61 03 20.

ENTRANCE TO RIVER LOIRE, ST NAZAIRE

Charts BA 2986, 2989, 2985; F 6797, 7396; Imray C40

HW Brest −0040sp + 0020np

MHWS	MHWN	MLWN	MLWS
5·8m	4·6m	2·2m	0·8m

There are two approach channels, one to the N, the other to the S. In strong winds, especially westerly, seas can break in the relatively shallow entrance to the river. In these conditions, wait until half flood before entering. Some of the marks difficult to distinguish in poor visibility. There are some facilities for yachts. Yachts may make a brief stay in the St Nazaire Lock Basin, but salvage insurance is required. Unless in emergency, there are no facilities for visiting yachts at Trentemoult. The entrance to the Inland Waterway System at Nantes can be reached within the flood.

Approach and Entrance Off-lying dangers, rocks and shallows off the coast between Pornic and the Pte du Chémoulin, marked by cardinal buoys, the Plateau de la Lambarde to the SW, and a shallow bank SW of Pte de St-Gildas. Channel buoyed.

Anchorages Bonne Anse in 3m 2M S of St-Nazaire.

Facilities Minimal yachting facilities.

☎ HM St Nazaire 02 40 00 45 89.

NANTES

Pontoon Anne de Bretagne.

On N bank upstream of Anne de Bretagne br, stays of <72h.

☎ 02 40 37 04 62 for entry system. Water and electricity on request.

PORNIC

Charts BA 2981; F 7394; Imray C40

HW Brest −0050sp +0030np

MHWS	MHWN	MLWN	MLWS
5·8m	4·6m	2·2m	0·8m

The marina is a short walk from the cobbled streets of the town centre. The old port dries 1·8m, sand and mud. The N side is rocky and there is a breakwater off Gourmalon Point which covers at HW. The end is marked by a bn. The extended breakwater off Noëvéillard encloses a large marina.

Entrance Access possible at most states of the tide, except ±0200 MLWS.

Berthing Visitors' pontoons P1, P2, P3 to stb on entry and PA at W end of marina. Berth allocated at Reception.

Facilities Chandleries, Wi-Fi, restaurants, shops in town. Beaches nearby.

☎ HM 02 40 82 05 40.

ÎLE DE NOIRMOUTIER

Charts BA 2981; F 7394; Imray C40

HW Brest −0047sp +0023np

MHWS	MHWN	MLWN	MLWS
5·5m	4·4m	2·1m	0·8m

BOIS DE LA CHAISE

Anchor outside local moorings as close as possible. Uncomfortable in easterlies.

L'HERBAUDIÈRE

An excellent passage hbr modern marina, depth 2–3m. Berths close to entrance exposed to swell and N'ly winds.

Approach and Entrance Least depth 1·3m marked by R and G buoys and bns. Ldg Lts 188°. Idenify Basse du Martroger N card Lt bn tr and come in from about 4ca W of this tr. Keep close to stb-hand buoys with E end of breakwater in line with L'Herbaudière church clock tr (if not obscured by trees).

Berthing On visitors' pontoon, ahead on entry and adjacent to the fairway or, with permission, on hammerheads.

Facilities Wi-Fi, chandlery, caretaking. Shops, PO and restaurants. Mkt Monday in season.

☎ HM 02 51 39 05 05.

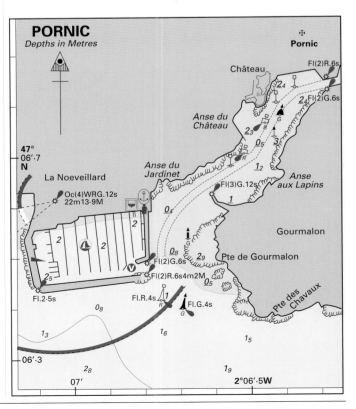

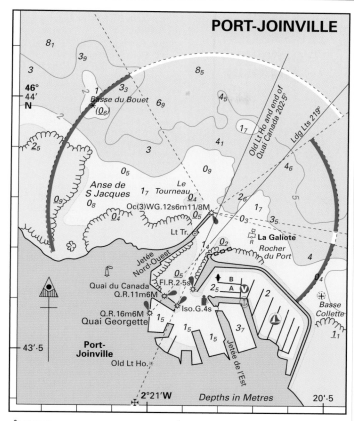

PORT-JOINVILLE

ÎLE D'YEU, JOINVILLE

Charts BA 2997, 2663, 3640; F 7410; Imray C40

HW Brest −0025sp +0010np

MHWS	MHWN	MLWN	MLWS
5·2m	4·1m	2·0m	0·8m

An attractive island, very busy in high season. Joinville is the only town of any significance on the island. There are some excellent beaches, especially on the S coast. The high water tr just W of the town is more conspic than the LtHo. The marina has 2·5m.

Approach Leading line 202·5° of Ch, former Lt Ho and end of Quai du Canada. At night, Ldg Lts Q.R 219°.

Entrance Marina entrance immediately to port at end of mole. Beware of ferries and vessels leaving marina.

Berthing Anchoring forbidden in outer harbour which is exposed to wind and swell from NW to NE, except to wait for tide. Visitors berth on the A, B and Accueil pontoons; in season often met by hbr dory. May need to raft. In exceptional circumstances, yachts may be directed into inner basin, usually reserved for fishing vessels. Lock opens HW±0200.

Facilities Fuel, chandleries, Wi-Fi, shop, restaurants, market daily. Ferry and helicopter connections to mainland. No hospital.

☎ HM 02 51 58 38 11.

Anchorages Anse de Ker Chalon in 3·5m, 6 ca SE of entrance to Port Joinville. To the S of the island, La Vieille and La Meule. The latter is a drying hbr but there are a few visitors' buoys outside.

ST-GILLES-CROIX-DE-VIE

Charts BA 2663, 2997, 3640; F 7402; Imray C40

HW Brest −0032sp +0013np

MHWS	MHWN	MLWN	MLWS
5·1m	4·1m	2·0m	0·7m

A sheltered marina accessible at most states of the tide and in most conditions. Swell breaks in S/SW winds Force 7, when great care is needed. Boats drawing more than 1·5m should not attempt to enter ±0200 LWS when the coefficient is high. Current in the channel runs hard, 4–6kn reported. Care need when berthing mid-tide. There have been reports of silting in the entrance channel. Identified by the Pointe de Grosse Terre LtHo, and white water tr.

Approach From the W, leave Pilours S card to port. Leading marks on shore, two white towers with red topmarks, 43·5°. (Not easily distinguished). By night, DirQ.7m15M with DirQ.28m12M.

Entrance Keep mid-channel to avoid rocks and shallows on the edge of the marked channel.

Berthing Visitors' pontoon, (rafting in season) to port on entrance past pontoon 6. Extra berths in season.

Anchoring Only possible offshore in fine weather, not in strong S/SW winds.

Facilities Chandleries, shops, Wi-Fi and restaurants in town. Rly.

☎ HM 02 51 55 30 83.

LES SABLES D'OLONNE

Charts BA 3638; F 7411, 7403; Imray C40

HW Brest −0030sp +0015np

MHWS	MHWN	MLWN	MLWS
5·2m	4·1m	2·0m	0·7m

An important fishing port; major yacht hbr and popular holiday resort. The hbr has 1·5m throughout.

Approach From the N and W, leave the Nouch Sud S card buoy and Nouch Nord, N card buoy to port. In strong onshore winds, follow the ldg ln 032·5°, La Potence Iso.4s33m16M and Iso.4s12m16M, and then follow the E approach. From the E and S, follow ldg ln 320°, the head of the Jetée des Sables, Q.G., with the Tour Arundel, Q., large tr with castellated top.

Entrance When Jean Marthe, BRB buoy is abeam, bear a little to port, and follow leading line of 328°. Day marks, two white towers with red topmarks, difficult to distinguish. Do not get too close to either jetty. Beware of foot ferries running between banks.

Berthing

• **Quai Garnier** First basin to stb on the approach. Marina on the S bank, convenient for Les Sables. Visitors' pontoon by Capitainerie.

☎ HM 02 51 45 32 71.

• **Port Olona** Continue past the two basins to stb, reception pontoon, to port. Berth here, and report to HM office, where a finger berth will probably be allocated.

☎ HM 02 51 32 51 16.

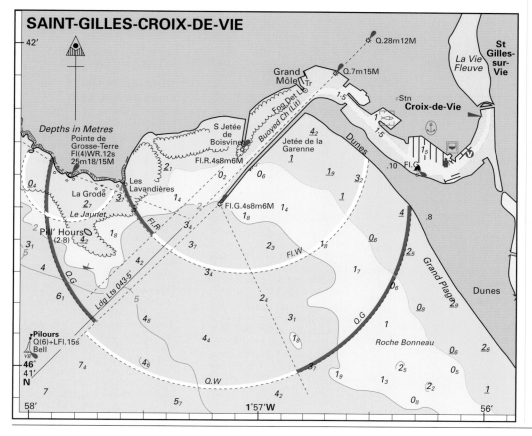

SAINT-GILLES-CROIX-DE-VIE

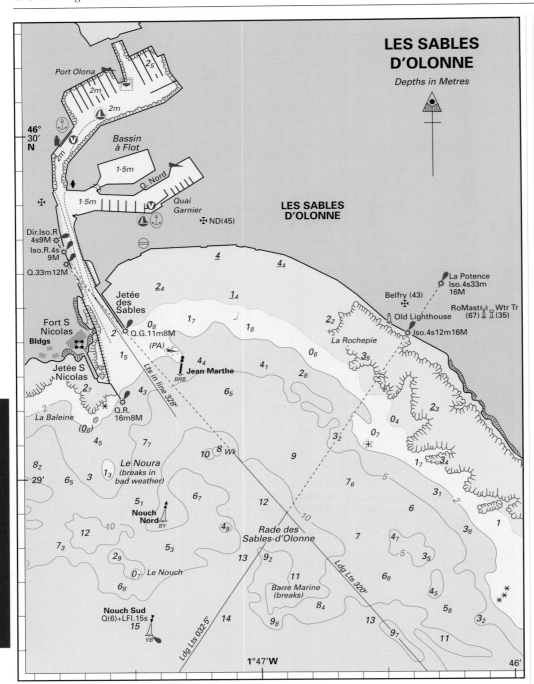

LES SABLES D'OLONNE

Depths in Metres

Port Olona
Bassin à Flot
Q. Nord
Quai Garnier
ND(45)
LES SABLES D'OLONNE
Dir.Iso.R 4s9M
Iso.R.4s 9M
Q.33m12M
Jetée des Sables
Fort S Nicolas
Bldgs
Jetée S Nicolas
La Baleine
Q.G.11m8M (PA)
Jean Marthe BRB
Q.R. 16m8M
Le Noura (breaks in bad weather)
Lts in line 328°
Le Nouch
Nouch Nord BY
Rade des Sables-d'Olonne
Barre Marine (breaks)
Nouch Sud Q(6)+LFl.15s 15 YB
Ldg Lts 032·5°
Ldg Lts 320°
La Potence Iso.4s33m 16M
Belfry (43)
Old Lighthouse
RoMast (67) Wtr Tr (35)
Iso.4s12m16M
La Rochepie

46°30'N
29'
46'
1°47'W

FRANCE – WEST COAST

Facilities A major yachting centre with a good range of chandleries and repair facilities. Fuel at Port Olona. If on pontoons A–G, Port Olona, bread available from newsagent and épicerie on shopping parade. Restaurants and bars near to marinas. Shops and markets in La Chaume, Tuesday, Thursday and Sunday, and Les Sables d'Olonne daily except Monday. Rly. Wi-Fi.

PORT DE BOURGENAY

Charts BA 2663, 2998; F 7403; Imray C41

HWBrest –0030sp +0015np

MHWS	MHWN	MLWN	MLWS
5·2m	4·1m	2·0m	0·7m

Purpose built marina and holiday resort 6m SE of Les Sables d'Olonne.

Approach Safe water buoy 46°25'·33N 1°41'·83W

immediately SW of marina entrance. Ldg Lts Q.G.7M, 040°, not easy to see. Left-hand corner of conspic large W building to E of marina, easier to see and 040° on this approximates to ldg bearing.

Entrance Stb edge of channel marked by G can and G bn. Entry channel dredged to 1m below CD. Entry not recommended in swell or in on-shore winds. Keep to mid-channel to avoid rocks near hbr moles.

Berthing Reception pontoon to stb on entry inside Jetée Est.

Facilities Fuel, chandlery, Wi-Fi. In Season, shops nearby and in holiday village. Swimming pool in holiday village. Bars and restaurants. Supermarket at Talmont St-Hilaire.

☎ HM 02 51 22 20 36.

ARS-EN-RÉ

Charts BA 2998, 2999; F 7404, 7412; Imray C41

HW Pointe de Grave –0032sp +0007np

MHWS	MHWN	MLWN	MLWS
5·9m	4·7m	2·3m	0·9m

An attractive small town which has become very fashionable. Makes a good base from which to explore the N of the island, especially the nature reserve. Some very good beaches within cycling distance.

Approach and Entrance Best on a rising tide, from HW–0230, according to draft and tidal coefficient. Good visibility recommended and a night entry to be avoided. From a position to the N of Les Islette N Card tr, make good a course to pass S of

PERTUIS BRETON TO LA PALLICE
DS in Pertuis Breton: the flood or ESE stream begins HW–0600 Pte de Grave; the ebb stream begins at or shortly after HW. A marine farm, length 2½M in NW/SE direction has been established approx 4M N of Ile de Ré, marked by four card buoys. There is restricted passage between La Pallice and Ile de Ré due to road bridge (30m clearance). Controlled passage, S bound between piers Nos.10 and 11, and N-bound between piers Nos.13 and 14, buoyed channels each marked by port and starboard pillar buoys with topmarks.

the Bûcheron buoys. Continue on this course past the stb bn for ½M until the buoyed channel can be seen to port. The black and white spire of the church is a useful landmark at this point. The leading marks, red trellis in front of a rectangle 232°, difficult to see. Channel well buoyed and reputed to be dredged. Check with HM. Tidal streams can reach over 4kn near Bûcheron buoys and at the entrance to the Fiers D'Ars.

Berthing In both basins as directed by HMs.

Basin de la Criée to stb. Visitors' pontoons to port immediately after crossing sill.

Basin de la Prée, at the head of the entrance channel. Visitors berth on D.

Anchoring Some moorings, outside marina, shallow draught vessels may find a space to anchor.

Facilities Small chandlery. Shops, restaurants and excellent daily morning market. Cycle hire, beaches.

☎ HM (Criée) 05 46 29 25 10; HM (Prée) 05 46 29 08 52.

ST-MARTIN-DE-RÉ

Charts BA 2998, 2999; F 7412, 7412; Imray C41

HW Pointe de Grave –0032sp +0007np

MHWS	MHWN	MLWN	MLWS
5·9m	4·7m	2·3m	0·9m

One of the most picturesque harbours in W France. Very sheltered in inner harbour. Space is at a premium, but HM accommodates a large number of vessels in the small space available. Multihulls not allowed in marina.

Approach Four W buoys for waiting vessels. Lock opens HW–0300 to HW+0230: July/August within 0500–2300; May, June and September 0630–2200; March/October 0800–1900 (2000 at weekend). Entry difficult in strong NW winds, which produce swell in outer harbour. Leading marks, Fl.G.2·5s on Grande Môle with

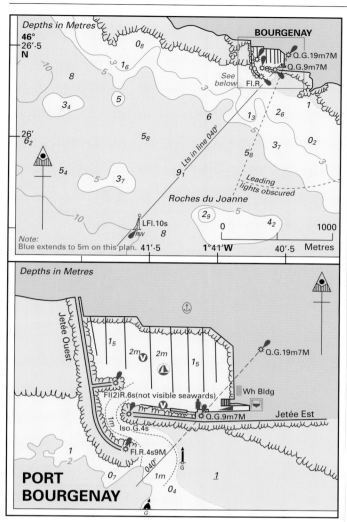

PORT BOURGENAY

(Plan - BOURGENAY)

Depths in Metres

46° 26'·5 N

Lts in line 040°

See below Fl.R.

Q.G.19m7M
Q.G.9m7M

26' 6·2

Roches du Joanne

Leading lights obscured

LFl.10s RW

Note:
Blue extends to 5m on this plan.

41'·5   1°41'W   40'·5

0   1000
Metres

(Plan - PORT BOURGENAY)

Depths in Metres

Jetée Ouest

Q.G.19m7M

Fl(2)R.6s(not visible seawards)

Iso.G.4s

Wh Bldg

Jetée Est

Q.G.9m7M

Fl.R.4s9M

040°

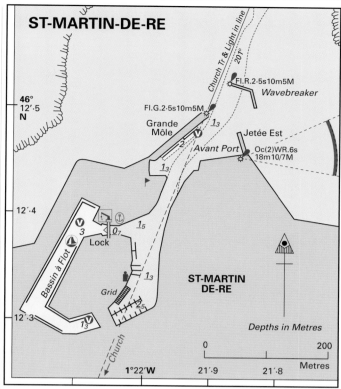

ST-MARTIN-DE-RE

Church Tr & Light in line 201°

Fl.R.2·5s10m5M
Wavebreaker

46° 12'·5 N

Fl.G.2·5s10m5M

Grande Môle

Jetée Est

Avant Port

Oc(2)WR.6s 18m10/7M

12'·4

Lock

ST-MARTIN DE-RE

Bassin à Flot

Grid

12'·3

Depths in Metres

1°22'W   21'·9   21'·8

0   200
Metres

the square church tr 201·5° to N end of the outer breakwater.

Entrance Turn into outer harbour, and pass between the Grande Môle and Jetée Est. Follow the line of the Grande Môle, to the entrance to inner harbour. Steer to stb on entering inner harbour to pass into inner basin. Entry Lts.

Berthing On Grande Môle in outer harbour (exposed to swell) or in locked marina. Follow directions of HM. Visitors' pontoon, boats >10m immediately ahead of entrance, expect to raft. Further berths at head of basin.

Facilities Restaurants, Wi-Fi, daily morning market.

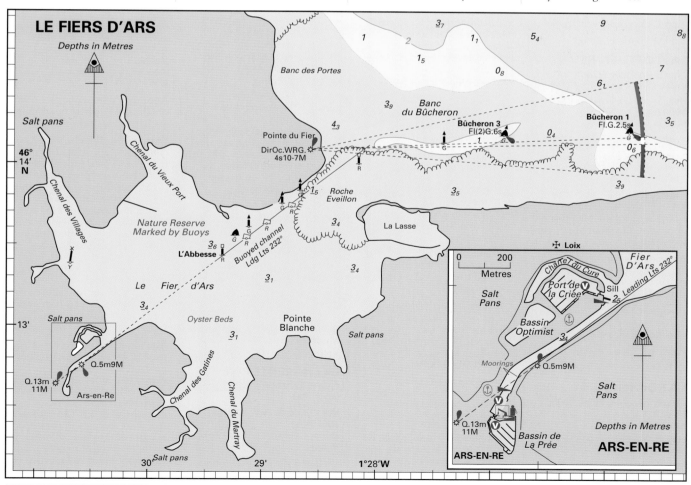

LE FIERS D'ARS

Depths in Metres

Salt pans

46° 14' N

Chenal du Vieux Port

Chenal des Villages

Banc des Portes

Banc du Bûcheron

Pointe du Fier

DirOc.WRG. 4s10-7M

Bûcheron 3 Fl(2)G.6s

Bûcheron 1 Fl.G.2.5s

Roche Eveillon

L'Abbesse

Buoyed channel Ldg Lts 232°

Nature Reserve Marked by Buoys

La Lasse

Le   Fier   d'Ars

13'

Salt pans

Oyster Beds

Pointe Blanche

Salt pans

Q.5m9M

Q.13m 11M

Ars-en-Re

Chenal des Gatines

Chenal du Martray

30'   29'   1°28'W

ARS-EN-RE

0   200
Metres

Loix

Chenal du Cure

Port de la Criée

Sill

Fier D'Ars

Salt Pans

Bassin Optimist

Leading Lts 232°

Moorings

Q.5m9M

Q.13m 11M

ARS-EN-RE

Bassin de La Prée

Salt Pans

Depths in Metres

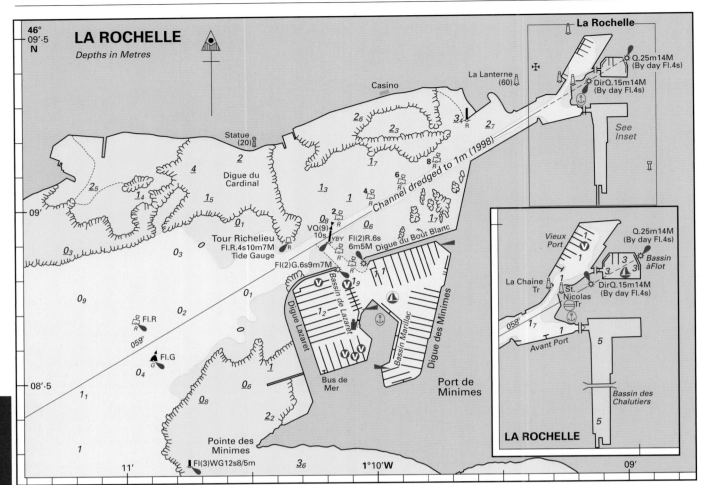

Supermarkets towards La Flotte. Beaches (nearest beyond the prison), museum, cycle hire. Buses to mainland and around island. Excellent cycle tracks.

☏ HM 05 46 09 26 69.

LA FLOTTE-EN-RÉ

Charts BA 2998; F 7404, 7412; Imray C41

HW Pointe de Grave –0032sp +0007np

MHWS	MHWN	MLWN	MLWS
5·9m	4·7m	2·3m	0·9m

Small drying hbr. Delightful town but smaller than St Martin.

Entrance 212° on La Flotte LtHo FlWG.4s10m12/9M. Chevrons indicate final line of approach. Limits of oyster park indicated by bns.

Berthing Visitors berth on the hammerheads immediately to stb on entry on either side of the Jetée Nord.

Anchorage Five W visitors' buoys in good depth of water outside hbr. Exposed to N.

Facilities Shops, restaurants.

☏ HM 05 46 09 67 66.

LA ROCHELLE

Charts BA 2743, 2999, 3000; F 7413; Imray C41

HW Pte de Grave –0030sp +0015np

MHWS	MHWN	MLWN	MLWS
6·0m	4·9m	2·4m	0·9m

An important historic town renowned for its architecture and arcades. Yachts may berth in either Minimes, the large marina that may be entered in most states of the tide, or in the Vieux Port. The marinas provide excellent shelter. However, during the grand Pavois, usually in September, and the weeks before and after it, visiting yachts are not permitted in the Vieux Port and may find it difficult to find a berth in Minimes.

Approach Tour Richelieu (R tr), is easy to identify; the W bn Fl(3)WG.12s8M, near S edge of plan, looks like a Chinese bandstand. Ldg Lts, 059°, by day two white towers, (not easy to distinguish) Fl.4s; by night DirQ. and Q.

Entrance At LWS there may be insufficient depth of water to proceed to either Minimes or the Vieux Port.

• **Minimes** Shortly after passing the Richelieu, R tr, the buoys marking the entrance to Minimes, W Card Buoy, and two R can buoys, will be seen. Leave these to port.

• **Vieux Port** The channel from Minimes to Vieux Port is clearly buoyed. Beware of ferries.

Berthing

• **Minimes** In season; check in at the hammerhead to stb on entry, where an office is manned. A berth will be

allocated. Otherwise go to visitors' pontoons 13, 14, 15, the pontoon inside the NW hbr mole, or the W side of the welcome pontoon. Unless planning an extended stay, visitors are expected to find a space for themselves on the visitors' pontoons and to report to HM office.

• **Vieux Port** After passing between the towers, find a berth on the N side of the first pontoon, or either side of the second pontoon. For a longer stay, it may be possible to berth by arrangement in either the Bassin à Flot or the Ancien Basin des Chalutiers.

Facilities Bus and ferry service between Minimes and Vieux Port. Daily morning indoor mkt in La Rochelle. Excellent yachting support services. Good rail and air connections. Network of cycle tracks. Beaches close to both marinas. Ferries to offshore islands. Cycle hire. Wi-Fi.

☏ HMs:
Minimes 05 46 44 41 20.
Vieux Port 05 46 41 32 05.

LA CHARENTE RIVER

Charts BA 2747; F 7415; Imray C41

HW Pte de Grave –0020sp +0020np

MHWS	MHWN	MLWN	MLWS
6·4m	5·1m	2·2m	1·4m

Sheltered river in which the streams can be strong,

especially on a spring ebb. Navigation in the river is forbidden at night when the banks cannot be seen.

Bar The bar can be crossed at HW–0300, which will allow sufficient time to arrive at Rochefort to lock into the marina at approximately HW–0030.

Approach From either E or W of L'Île d'Aix where boats may anchor to await the tide.

Entrance Marked by three G con buoys. The white leading towers, with red tops, on the north bank are easily identified, (115°) but the next pair on the southern shore are more difficult. A course of 135° from the second stb buoy will bring the deep-water channel marked by the moorings at Port des Barques to port. Beyond here, the channel is indicated by pairs of lettered bns on shore. Downstream of Rochefort there is the Transponder which now takes only tourists across the river.

Anchorages Mooring areas are marked by yellow buoys. Boats may anchor outside the designated mooring areas but the river is used by commercial craft which have priority, monitor VHF 12. The stream runs very strongly in the upper reaches of the river (4kn) and it might be prudent to take a vacant mooring. White visitors' buoy above the landing

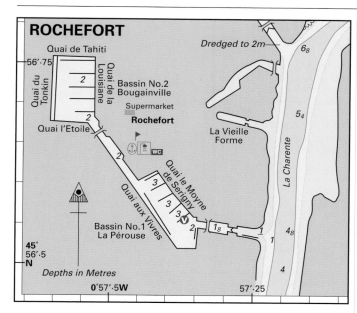

ROCHEFORT

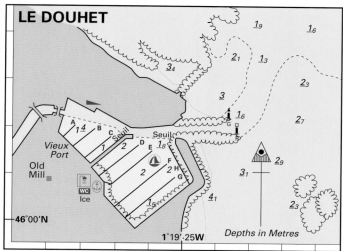

LE DOUHET

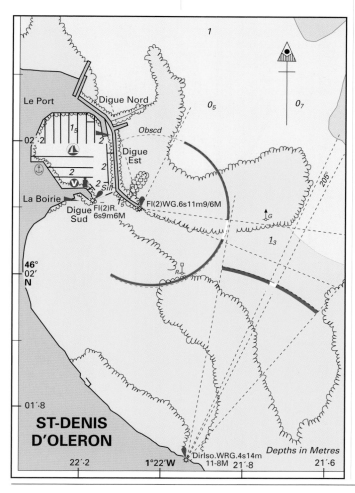

ST-DENIS D'OLERON

pontoon at Port des Barques, and pontoons at Soubise, where boats may ground at LWS.

ROCHEFORT

Charts BA 2747; F 7415, 7070; Imray C41

HW Pointe de Grave –0010sp +0035 np LW +0125np +0030sp

MHWS	MHWN	MLWN	MLWS
6·5m	5·3m	2·2m	0·8m

This historic town, well worth visiting, was where France built her navy. Europe's longest building, La Corderie, is now home to a museum, library and other organisations. Interesting

architecture and range of museums. Protected marina with very helpful staff.

Entrance To port just beyond the pontoon of La Corderie Hotel is the entrance to the marina. Waiting pontoon to port. Take care to keep close to the port side as metal poles protrude to stb. Boats may also wait on the Corderie Royale pontoon; avoid berth reserved for the Vedette.

Berthing Lock opens May to August 0500 to 2300, April and September 0630–2100, October to March by prior

arrangement 24 hrs in advance, at approximately local HW –0030 to HW, unless the coefficient is exceptionally low. Berths allocated prior to entering marina.

Facilities Most marina facilities, 16-ton crane, Wi-Fi, chandleries, but no fuel or garage within a sensible distance. Market days, Tuesday, Thursday and Saturday. Rly. Airport at La Rochelle.

✆ HM 05 46 83 99 96 open high season 0800–1200, 1400–1900; low season 0900–1200, 1400–1700.

ST-DENIS D'OLERON

Charts BA 3000, 2663; F 7405, 7414; Imray C41

HW Pte de Grave –0040sp +0015np

MHWS	MHWN	MLWN	MLWS
6·1m	4·9m	2·4m	0·9m

Sheltered marina behind a sill, 1·5m CD. At half-tide 1·9m on sill. White waiting buoys outside the hbr. At springs may be necessary to anchor further out.

Approach and Entrance Entrance dries and the approach is over shallows. Keep to mid-channel. Tide gauge by fuel pontoon.

Berthing Visitors' pontoon to port on entry, <11m on fingers, >11m, alongside or on hammerhead. Usually a reception dory on duty.

Facilities Fuel (cards), Wi-Fi, cycle hire, beaches, bars and restaurants near marina, shops and daily morning market in town. Buses. Ferry service to mainland in season.

✆ HM 05 46 47 97 97.

LE DOUHET

Charts BA 3000, 2663; F 7405, 7414; Imray C41

HW Pte de Grave –0040sp +0015np

MHWS	MHWN	MLWN	MLWS
6·1m	4·9m	2·4m	0·9m

Marina behind a sill, (1·8m in S basin, 2·9m in N basin). Sheltered from W winds. Entry difficult in NE winds, channel subject to silting in winter. Night entry not advised. Waiting buoys outside.

Approach The 300m entrance channel is marked by R and G buoys with reflective bands. Water level gauge to port before sill to S basin.

Access Tidal coefficient 80:

Draught 1·0m HW–0345 to HW+0330

Draught 1·50m HW–0315 to HW+0300

Draught 2·0m m HW–0240 to HW+0200

Berthing On visitors' pontoon and report to Capitainerie.

Facilities No fuel. Chandlery. Bakery and cycle hire. Shops at St-Georges-d'Oléron, and Le Brée les Bains. Market days Le Brée Wednesday, Friday and Sunday out of season. In season every morning. Pleasant cycle rides. Restaurant near marina. Beaches.

✆ HM 05 46 76 71 13.

BOYARDVILLE

Charts BA 3000, 2663; F 7405, 7414; Imray C41

HW Pte de Grave –0040sp +0015np

MHWS	MHWN	MLWN	MLWS
6·1m	4·9m	2·4m	0·9m

Sheltered marina behind an automatic gate whose approach is across drying sandbanks. Gate to marina opens at HW±0300 with a coefficient of 100 and from HW–0230 to HW +0130 with a coefficient of 35. Waiting pontoon to stb above the lock.

Approach With a sufficient rise of water, track from La Perrotine G con buoy 0·4M ENE of La Perrotine Jetty to LtHo on La Perrotine Jetty, Fl(2)R.6s8m5M, to avoid the drying banks.

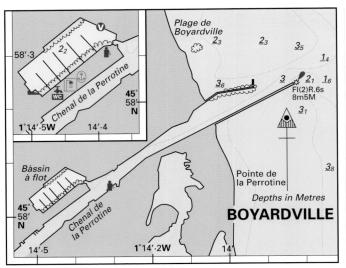

BOYARDVILLE

Depths in Metres

Entrance Keep 10m from the Perrotine Jetty. When the first slip to stb is abeam, move to mid-channel. Marina to stb.

Berthing Visitors' pontoon to stb on entrance.

Facilities Some shops and small morning market in season. Restaurants nr marina. Cycle hire, beaches. Buses and ferries to mainland in season.

☎ HM 05 46 47 23 71.

ÎLE D'OLÉRON TO GIRONDE RIVER

Charts BA 3000, 3057 F 7070; Imray C41

The passage through the Pertuis de Maumusson is not recommended. Complete details are given in the *Bay of Biscay Pilot NP22*. Without local knowledge it is preferable to make the open sea passage rounding the north end of the Île de Oléron at a suitable distance from the N card bn tower *Antioche* Q.20m11M.

GIRONDE RIVER

Charts BA 3068, 3069; F 7426, 7427; Imray C42

HW entrance Pte de Grave HW At **No.9** N card buoy in Passe de L'Ouest HW –0300 SE 2·5kn HW +0400 NW 4kn

Flood 2·5kn, ebb 4kn

MHWS	MHWN	MLWN	MLWS
5·1m	4·2m	2·1m	1·0m

Approach and Entrance Steep seas occur from swell, strong currents (3–5kn at springs) winds from NW to SW over Force 5 and conditions producing contrary directions of wind, current and or swell. Dangerous seas break on the sandbanks which shift. Current charts essential and the buoyage should be respected. No attempt should be made to enter on the ebb. Height of tide given at five minute intervals from gauges within the river (VHF 16 for broadcast frequency). Two entrance channels, Passe de l'Ouest and Passe Sud. The latter should only be used if coming from the S, and preferably not for the first entry.

• **Passe de l'Ouest** Used by commercial and fishing vessels. The flood may be delayed, entry after LW +0100 or later advised. From the N, leave No.2a Fl.R.2·5s to port, avoiding Banc de la Mauvaise, and follow the stb edge of the channel until after No.11 Iso.G.4s, when yachts may safely navigate between the channel and the N bank of the river.

• **Passe du Sud** Enter only if there is no swell and not before HW Pte de Grave –0430. To avoid all dangers make for Graves RW safewater buoy and follow the buoyed channel. The change of course prior to G3 must be made promptly, or a yacht may be set on the shallows to S of the channel. Leading marks difficult to see unless visibility is good. If proceeding to Royan, keep upstream after passing No.12 Fl(3)R.12s, to avoid being set on Banc de St Georges.

Anchorages

• N shore, in Bonne Anse. Sand, mud, drying area, anchor according to draught. Rade de Royan, only if weather good and no swell, SE of hbr entrance.

• S shore, Verdon-sur-mer, N of Pointe de la Chambrette.

Upstream of Royan, other anchorages may be found in soft mud and strong currents.

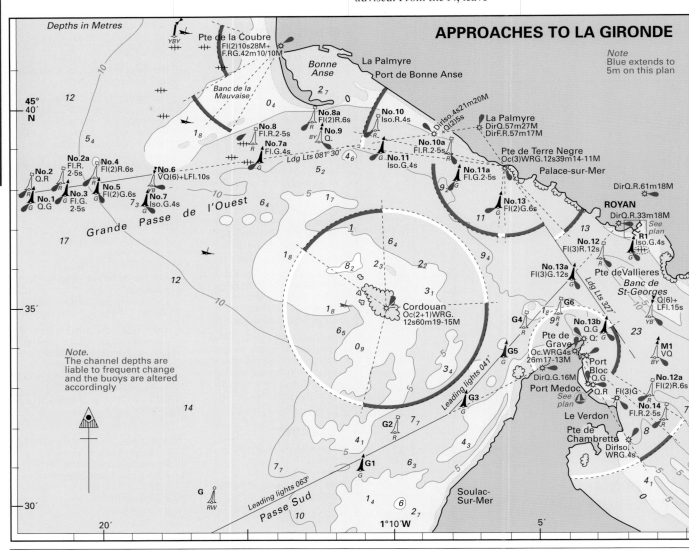

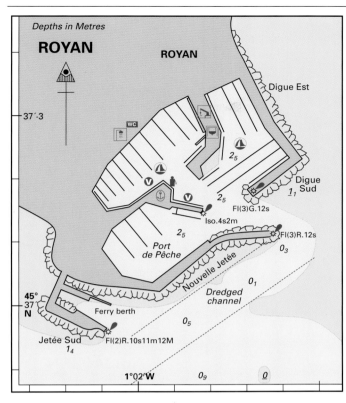

ROYAN

Depths in Metres

37´·3

45°
37
N

Port
de Pêche

WC

Nouvelle Jetée

Dredged
channel

Ferry berth

Jetée Sud
1₄

Fl(2)R.10s11m12M

1°02′W

ROYAN

Digue Est

Digue
Sud
1₁

Fl(3)G.12s

Iso.4s2m

Fl(3)R.12s

0₃

0₁

0₅

0₉

0

ROYAN

Charts BA 3057, 3068, 3069;
F 7425;
Imray C42

HW Pte de Grave HW

MHWS	MHWN	MLWN	MLWS
5·1m	4·2m	2·1m	1·0m

Marina sheltered from all winds.

Entrance Access possible in all conditions and states of the tide, draught permitting. Leave R1 Iso.G.4s to stb. Marina entrance on port side of dredged channel marked by Lts on Jetée Sud Fl(2)R.10s11m12M and Nouvelle Jetée Fl(3)R.12s.

Berthing In season, visiting vessels given berthing instructions from hbr dory. Otherwise, reception pontoon, marked V, is to port on entry.

Facilities Chandleries, boatyard and a good range of support services. Excellent daily indoor mkt. Shops and services of a seaside town.

☎ HM 05 46 38 72 22.

PORT MÉDOC

Ponton Cantier
Naval

45°
33′·5
N

Ponton
d'Accueil
E A
F B
G C
H D
I
J D
K
L
M
N

Quai Ouest

Channel dredged
to 3m

Pontoon
Catamarans
2

Digue Sud

Plage de la
Chambrette

1₅

Estuaire
de la
Gironde

Fl.G

Fl.R

Digue de la
Chambrette

1₅

1°03′·5W

Depths in Metres

MORTAGNE-SUR-GIRONDE

Charts BA 3057, 3068

Small yacht hbr, in attractive town. Lock to inner basin opens from 1 May–31 September HW±0100. Telephone in advance to verify times and to give 48hrs notice for weekends in low season, when the lock may not open after HW.

Entrance R can Mortagne buoy, close to E Card buoy, narrow channel marked by bns.

Berthing Boats that may take the ground, may berth on the visitors' and reception pontoon on the N bank. If proceeding to inner basin, berth as directed.

Facilities No fuel, restaurants. Stores. HM ☎ 05 46 90 63 15. HW±0100.

BLAYE

Charts BA 3068

In season 80m pontoon in up to 3m. 24hr stay permitted. Double springs required, moor head to wind. Citadel and resources of a town.

PORT MÉDOC

Charts BA 3057, 3068;
F 7425 7426;
Imray C42

HW Pte de Grave HW

MHWS	MHWN	MLWN	MLWS
5·1m	4·2m	2·1m	1·0m

Large, well-sheltered marina accessible in all weathers and states of the tide, 2–3m depth, situated on S bank of River Gironde, S of Pte de Grave.

Entrance By a dredged channel, jetty heads painted white, Q.G. and Q.R. Turn to stb after passing the fuel pontoon.

Berthing Reception pontoon for monohulls at far N end of marina. Pontoon for multihulls extends from S side of marina.

Facilities Chandleries, boatyard and restaurants. No supplies. Ferries to Royan from Port Bloc.

☎ HM 05 56 09 69 75.

PAUILLAC

Charts BA 3068; F 7427;
Imray C42

HW Pointe de Grave +0100

MHWS	MHWN	MLWN	MLWS
5·55m	4·40m	1·05m	0·55m

Town renowned for its wine rather than yachting facilities. Marina staff very helpful. Eddies and a strong current run through the marina.

Approach and Entrance Port jetty marked by a large wine bottle with red top. W buoys upstream of entrance for vessels waiting for slack water.

Berthing The two upstream pontoons reserved for visitors. Care is needed when berthing.

BORDEAUX TO CASTETS

At Castets is the first lock into the Canal Latéral à la Garonne which joins the Canal du Midi at Toulouse.

The R Garonne to Castets, 35M, is unbuoyed with extensive mudbanks, and rocky ledges. Garonne pilots do not operate above Bordeaux. Without a detailed chart or a pilot, a barge should be followed; barges moor just above the Bordeaux bridge. Castets can generally be reached on one tide. The flood comes up at over 5kn, the water suddenly rising 0·3m with a 1·5m wave; the last of the ebb goes down at 2kn.

The lock at Castets is to starboard. With the Garonne in spate and the upstream current therefore weakened, it could prove impossible to make Castets on one tide. Ask permission to tie to a barge (they do not move overnight) or to moor alongside the pontoon at Cadillac.

GIRONDE TO CAPBRETON WARNING

The firing range (CELM) with limits of:
45°28′N 1°14′W,
45°11′N 2°04′W,
43°56′N 2°17′W and
43°41′N 1°31′W
operates from Monday to Friday from 0800. Within this area, there is a forbidden zone:
44°23′·57N 1°26′·22W,
44°23′·57N 1°24′·72W,
44°21′·97N 1°24′·72W and
44°21′·97N 1°26′·22W.

Navigation is forbidden in or near any sector where firing is taking place. Information on firing activity is broadcast on VHF Ch 06 and VHF Ch 10 at 0703, 0715, 0733, 0745, 0803, 0815 and 1615. (This last being for the following day). Information on firing times and GPS positions of the extent of the areas to be used may also be obtained from the Semaphore stations, Chassiron, Pointe de Grave, Cap Ferret, Messanges, Socoa or Cross Etel or ☎ 02 97 55 35 35. Firing may occur anywhere within the zone and yachtsmen transiting the firing range should ignore any previous information regarding safety channels.

Passage lights	BA No
Cap Ferret	1378
Fl.R.5s53m22M+Oc(3)12s	
Contis	1382
Fl(4)25s50m23M	
Pointe Saint-Martin	1410
Fl(2)10s73m27M	

Facilities No fuel (2011). No chandleries but vineyards, restaurants and supplies, Rly. Mast lifting for boats heading for Canal du Midi.

☎ HM 05 56 59 12 16.

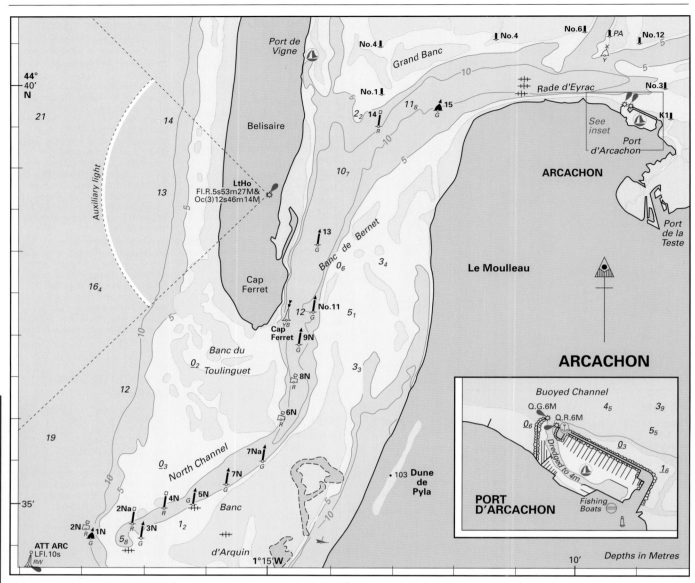

BORDEAUX

Charts BA 3068, 3069;
F 7030, 7427;
Imray C42
HW Pte de Grave +0212

MHWS	MHWN	MLWN	MLWS
5·3m	4·2m	0·6m	0·0m

•Marina, Pont du Jour
(suspension br) 4M outside city
on W bank opposite Lormont.
Contact HM when br comes
into view. Berth on outer
pontoon preferably inside to
avoid strong current, quite
secure and landing easy; Rly
(10 minutes). Shower, toilets
and restaurant in YC. Water by
hose. Crane on jetty head
operated very efficiently by HM
for masts. To organise access
call HM at least 24hrs or
preferably 2–3 days in advance.
Lock opens, Tues, Thurs, Sat
and Sun, once per day. The new
bridge, just upstream of the
basins has the same air draught
as the Pont de Pierre.

✆ / VHF HM 05 56 90 59 34,
05 56 91 58 64,
VHF 12.

• Dock basin, No.2 at
Bordeaux is dirty and charges
are high. Lock opens

HW−0200 to +0030. Canal
pilot book available from
HM office.

BASSIN D'ARCACHON

Charts F 7428, 7076;
Imray C42
HW Pte de Grave +0015

MHWS	MHWN	MLWN	MLWS
4·3m	3·4m	1·3m	0·4m

Approach and Entrance
Fairway entrance is about 2½M
S of Cap Ferret at the ATT
ARC pillar buoy LFl.10s. The
position of the channel
frequently changes and the
buoyage must be observed.
Enter in calm conditions, as
swell and onshore winds
produce breaking seas on the
banks, during daylight as the
buoys are not lit.

Enter at Pte de Grave
HW−0245 to HW. Currents in
the Bassin d'Arcachon are
strong, 3·5kn on a spring ebb.
The effect of the flood may be
delayed by an hour. Channel
dredged to 4m. Information on
sea state Cap Ferrat Semaphore
VHF 16: buoyage, depths and
positions of sand banks, Le
Service Maritime.

✆ 05 56 83 32 97.

Anchorages N of Port de Vigne.
There are a number of small
ports and other anchorages
which may be accessible to
vessels, depending on draught.
Large scale charts essential.
Channels marked by numbered
and lettered bns.

Berthing
Port d'Arcachon for vessels
<20m. Possibility of grounding.
A modern marina in a very
smart seaside town. Can be
entered at all hours and state of
the tide. Telephone to reserve
berth. Do not take a mooring
close to marina entrance.

Facilities All marine support
facilities and those of a town.
Rly.

✆ HM 08 90 71 17 33.

CAPBRETON

Charts BA 1292; F 7440
HW Pointe de Grave −0035

MHWS	MHWN	MLWN	MLWS
4·2m	3·3m	1·7m	0·7m

Large marina, divided into
three basins. Entrance after
half-flood, but not in strong onshore winds or swell. From
June to September, a foot ferry
may operate between the
basins.

Entrance The very narrow
entrance lies between a stone
jetty to the N and a wooden
jetty to the S. The latter has a
30m extension which is
underwater after half-tide.
Beware of strong currents and
surf. Keep closer to N
breakwater until level with the
statue. Then cross to just S of
mid-stream. When entering
marina, beware of cross current
from Canal d'Hossegor; this is
more noticeable on the ebb.

Berthing Reception on first
pontoon to stb on entry, and
report to Capitainerie. May
ground at LWS on visitors'
berth.

Facilities Chandleries, Wi-Fi.
No fuel Wednesday in low
season. A seaside town,
beaches. Rly Bayone 10M,
Airport Biarritz 16M. Ferry
across marina in season.

✆ HM 05 58 72 21 23.

ANGLET, BAYONNE AND
RIVER ADOUR

Charts BA 1170, 1175;
F 7430, 7440;
HW (Boucau)
Pte de Grave −0032.

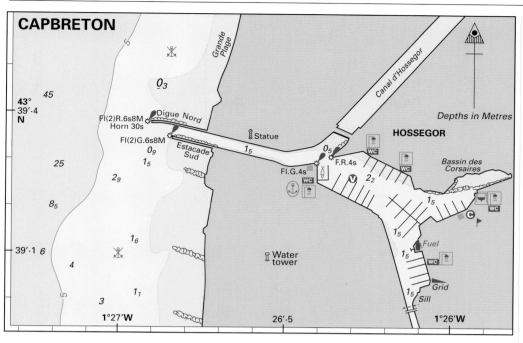

CAPBRETON

Grande Plage

Canal d'Hossegor

Depths in Metres

HOSSEGOR

43° 39'·4 N

Fl(2)R.6s8M
Horn 30s

Digue Nord

Fl(2)G.6s8M

Estacade Sud

Statue

Fl.G.4s

F.R.4s

Bassin des Corsaires

25

8·5

1·6

39'·1 6

4

3

1·1

Water tower

Fuel

Grid

Sill

1°27'W

26'·5

1°26'W

A delightful historic town in a sheltered bay. Superb beaches and scenery.

Approach and Entrance Enter the bay between the Digue des Criques and Digue D'Artha. The entrance to Larraldenia Marina at Ciboure is buoyed.

Berthing Marina directly ahead after passing into the inner harbour at Ciboure. Do not enter fishing port to port. Marina is small, crowded but friendly. Use anchorage at Socoa if no berths are available.

Facilities Rail connections, all facilities of a town. Chandlery. Airport at Biarritz

① HM 05 59 47 26 81 (not lunchtime).

See N coast of Spain section, page 384, for Hendaye.

MHWS	MHWN	MLWN	MLWS
4·2m	3·3m	1·7m	0·7m

Approach RW safewater buoy Fl.10s approx. 1M NNW of entrance.

Entrance Digue Jean Lesbordes extends to N of entrance channel. River entrance marked by N and S jetties; the S jetty marked by a W square tr with a G top and ADOUR S in black. Beware of fishing boats that extend their nets across the entrance channel. If proceeding upriver to Bayonne, above Port d'Anglet, best water to stb. Commercial vessels have priority.

Berthing
• **Port d'Anglet** on S bank. Port de Plaisance Brise-Lames. Opposite an industrial area but cleaner than might be expected. Reception on pontoon E.

Facilities Chandleries, travel-lift. Shops and Rly at Bayonne. Buses to Bayonne and Biarritz (airport). HM ① 05 59 63 05 45.

• **Bayonne** Historic town within easy cycling distance of Port Anglet. Good art gallery at Musée Bonnat.

Facilities Good rail and bus connections. Airport at Biarritz.

Anchorage Upstream of Port d'Anglet off N bank opposite G con Iso.4s. Out of the channel at Bouclou. Holding good but may be noisy. A mooring may be available, consult Capitainerie or Yacht Club.

ST-JEAN-DE-LUZ
Charts BA 1170, 1175; F 7431;
HW Pte de Grave –0042

MHWS	MHWN	MLWN	MLWS
4·3m	3·3m	1·7m	0·6m

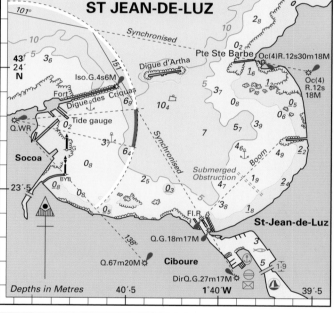

ST JEAN-DE-LUZ

Synchronised

Pte Ste Barbe

Oc(4)R.12s30m18M

Oc(4) R.12s 18M

43° 24' N

Digue d'Artha

Iso.G.4s6M

Fort

Digue des Criques

Q.WR

Socoa

Tide gauge

Synchronised

Boom

Submerged Obstruction

BYB

23'·5

Fl.R

St-Jean-de-Luz

Q.G.18m17M

Ciboure

Q.67m20M

DirQ.G.27m17M

Depths in Metres

40'·5

1°40'W

39'·5

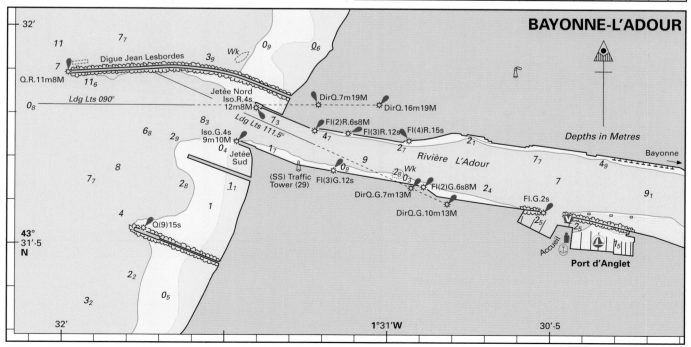

BAYONNE-L'ADOUR

32'

11

Wk

Digue Jean Lesbordes

Q.R.11m8M

Ldg Lts 090°

Jetée Nord
Iso.R.4s
12m8M

DirQ.7m19M

DirQ.16m19M

Ldg Lts 111·5°

Iso.G.4s
9m10M

Jetée Sud

Fl(2)R.6s8M

Fl(3)R.12s

Fl(4)R.15s

Depths in Metres

Bayonne

Rivière L'Adour

(SS) Traffic Tower (29)

Fl(3)G.12s

Wk

DirQ.G.7m13M

Fl(2)G.6s8M

DirQ.G.10m13M

Fl.G.2s

43° 31'·5 N

Q(9)15s

Accueil

Port d'Anglet

1°31'W

30'·5

SPAIN AND PORTUGAL

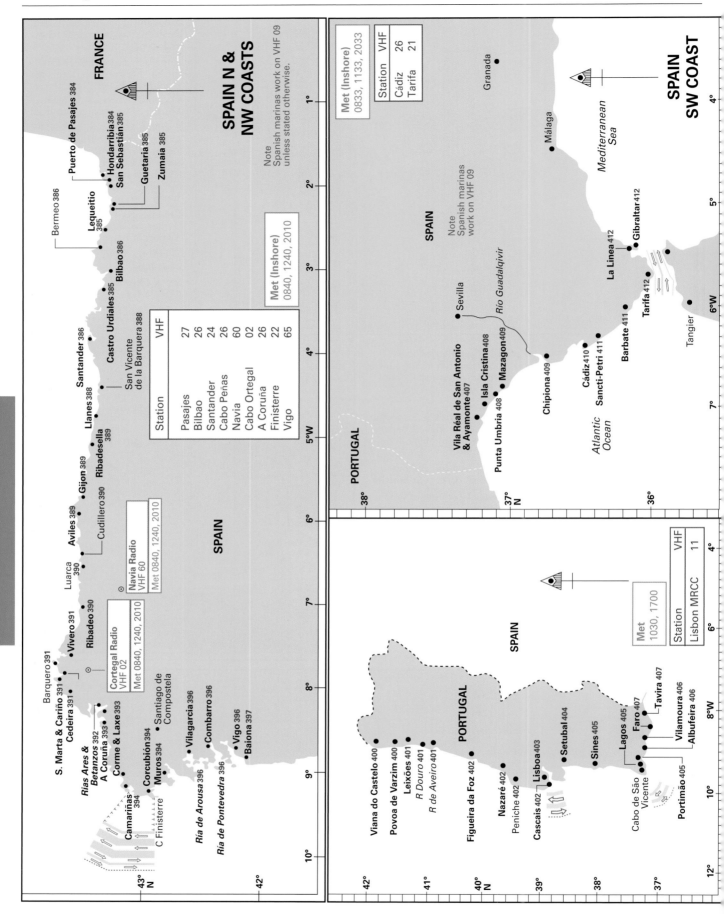

SPAIN N & NW COASTS

Note
Spanish marinas work on VHF 09 unless stated otherwise.

FRANCE

SPAIN

Puerto de Pasajes 384
Hondarribia 384
San Sebastián 385
Guetaria 385
Zumaia 385
Bermeo 386
Lequeitio 385
Bilbao 386
Castro Urdiales 385
Santander 386
San Vicente de la Barquera 388
Llanes 388
Ribadesella 389
Gijon 389
Aviles 389
Cudillero 390
Luarca 390
Ribadeo 390
Vivero 391
Barquero 391
S. Marta & Cariño 391
Cedeira 391
Rias Ares & Betanzos 392
A Coruña 393
Corme & Laxe 393
Corcubión 394
Camariñas 394
Muros 394
C Finisterre
Santiago de Compostela
Vilagarcia 396
Combarro 396
Ria de Arousa 396
Ria de Pontevedra 396
Vigo 396
Baiona 397

Met (Inshore)
0840, 1240, 2010

Station	VHF
Pasajes	27
Bilbao	26
Santander	24
Cabo Peñas	26
Navia	60
Cabo Ortegal	02
A Coruña	26
Finisterre	22
Vigo	65

Navia Radio
VHF 60
Met 0840, 1240, 2010

Cortegal Radio
VHF 02
Met 0840, 1240, 2010

SPAIN SW COAST

Met (Inshore)
0833, 1133, 2033

Station	VHF
Cádiz	26
Tarifa	21

SPAIN

Granada
Málaga
Mediterranean Sea
Gibraltar 412
La Linea 412
Tarifa 412
Barbate 411
Sancti-Petri 411
Cádiz 410
Chipiona 409
Mazagon 409
Punta Umbria 408
Isla Cristina 408
Vila Réal de San Antonio & Ayamonte 407
Sevilla
Río Guadalquivir
Atlantic Ocean
Tangier

Note
Spanish marinas work on VHF 09

PORTUGAL

PORTUGAL

Met
1030, 1700

Station	VHF
Lisbon MRCC	11

SPAIN

Viana do Castelo 400
Povoa de Varzim 400
Leixões 401
R Douro 401
R de Aveiro 401
Figueira da Foz 402
Nazaré 402
Peniche 402
Cascais 402
Lisboa 403
Setubal 404
Sines 405
Cabo de São Vicente
Lagos 405
Portimão 405
Albufeira 406
Vilamoura 406
Faro 407
Tavira 407

Page references are shown after locations, for example:
Vigo **394**. Bold type indicates that it is accompanied by a plan.
Italics are used for rivers, lochs, bays, seas etc.

Spain and Portugal

Routes from the UK to Spain and Portugal

• Outside the shipping lanes, directly from Cornwall to the Ría de Vigo or further south; this may be the fastest route, but is an ocean voyage, taking too long for forecasts to be dependable, and requires a yacht to be equipped and crewed for both storms and calms; the distance from the Lizard to Cabo Finisterre is about 450 miles

• To a point around the Rade de Brest, then to NW Spain, maybe Cedeira or A Coruña; this voyage is shorter, and can be made in two or three days, within the scope of reliable forecasts; if the winds are contrary, the yacht can cruise down the French coast until they become favourable; Pointe du Raz to Cabo Ortegal is about 290 miles, and La Rochelle to Santander 190 miles

• Coast hopping all the way, with only the passage between the Gironde and Capbreton providing a challenge with no safe harbours and the Landes firing range; this route is delightful, but takes a long time, especially as one is tempted to linger along the way; from the mouth of the Gironde to Capbreton is about 120 miles.

The destinations The coast of Atlantic Spain and Portugal can conveniently be divided into six stretches, each with its own characteristics:

• The north coast, from Hondarribia, on the Spanish/French border to Vivero, the most easterly ría alta. This has glorious mountain scenery, especially at the eastern end, numerous small ports where you moor alongside or anchor at no charge, and very little provision for visiting yachts (significant marinas only at Hondarribia, Santander and Gijon). In summer, winds are mainly limited to gentle sea breezes, air temperatures are higher than the UK, but you do get some rain and fog. Highlights are the bay of San Sebastián and the snow covered Picos de Europea between Santander and Ribadesella

• The Rías Altas and Costa da Morte, from Vivero to Fisterra, with more stunning scenery, though not mountainous, ample free anchorages and plenty of good marinas. The summer weather is similar to the north coast, except that, in July and August, the north easterly sea breezes in the afternoons are incessant and often strong, making passages up the coast a challenge. The sea water is freezing, even at the height of summer! The Costa da Morte is dangerous in winter – hence its name

• The Rías Baixas, from Muros to Baiona. This is one of the great cruising areas, offering as much as, say, Devon and Cornwall, or the south coast of Brittany. All the rías have numerous anchorages, all have useful marinas. The scenery is gentler than further north, but still beautiful. The afternoon sea breezes are a bit gentler as well, and the lie of the coast gives shelter and means that the seas are comparatively flat. Many cruisers heading for the Mediterranean linger here for a season or two, and some go no further. Winter cruising here is a possibility, as there is plenty of sailing to be had in sheltered waters. Highlights are the Atlantic islands of Cies and Ons

• The Portuguese west coast, which, frankly, is not an area to linger in. Many of the port towns, if not the ports themselves are attractive, but there are few places to anchor, and the incessant north wind from June to September makes a voyage north a bit of a trial. From October to April, there are fairly frequent fierce south-westerly gales

• The Algarve, from Cabo São Vicente to, say, Sancti Petri, just south of Cadiz in Andalucía. As you round Cabo São Vicente from the north, both the air and sea temperatures jump 5°, the fog lifts, the wind moderates, and suddenly you have a foretaste of Mediterranean weather. Much of this stretch of coast is attractive, with deeply indented cliffs hiding tiny beaches, but much is also despoiled by high-rise holiday apartments and hotels. There are sufficient anchorages to avoid marinas altogether, which is fortunate, because the marinas are very pricey in high season. Most days in summer, the sea breeze starts late morning from the north east, and veers steadily, reaching Force 4 or so, until it dies away in the evening as a northwesterly. From time to time an easterly Levanter sets in, giving fairly strong east winds in the morning and calms in the afternoon, when the sea breeze opposes it. From November to the end of April there are usually several gales – westerly, southerly and easterly. Highlights are the Río

Formosa, a 30-mile long lagoon behind sand dunes running east from Faro, and the Río Guadiana, between Portugal and Spain

• From Sancti Petri to Gibraltar. The scenery becomes more dramatic until you reach the stunning straights of Gibraltar. But the cruising is also more challenging, with nowhere sheltered to anchor, stronger winds, and only Barbate as a port of refuge. A strong headwind here brings a contrary current and fierce seas, and makes progress difficult for a small cruiser.

In general, there are fewer tourists and lower prices further north. In the Algarve and Andalucia anyone who works with tourists speaks some English, whereas in smaller places in northern Spain it certainly helps to have some Spanish. The best regional dishes are to be found further north, as are the best wines. Some people argue that the friendliest reception is also to be found further north, but the writer has found the people of both Spain and Portugal to be welcoming and totally honest throughout. For some reason, notwithstanding the EU, big chandlery items such as inflatables are stupidly expensive, and it usually pays to ship from the UK.

Formalities in Spain Yachts should be prepared to provide the normal ship's papers, insurance certificates (with a Spanish translation), passports for skipper and crew, and RYA certificate of competence for the skipper. The Spanish courtesy flag should be flown but in the area E of Bilbao to the French border a Basque courtesy flag is appreciated. If long-term cruising, be aware that the Spanish authorities deem anyone (not any boat) spending more than six months cumulatively in a calendar year in Spain as a resident, with expensive consequences.

Supplies Only diesel *Gasoleo A,* which is taxed, is available for yachts. This can generally be found in marinas or hbrs with yacht facilities. Water is plentiful, piped to most jetties and is safe. A charge is seldom made.

Calor gas is not available but cylinders can be refilled with butane. The Spanish alternative and Camping Gaz are universally available and cheap.

Repairs can be undertaken in most hbrs as can diesel engines. The price of spares is often less than in the UK.

Books If you wish to visit smaller ports, volumes to have on board are:

South Biscay: A Gironde to La Coruña RCC Pilotage Foundation (Imray)

Atlantic Spain and Portugal: El Ferrol to Gibraltar RCC Pilotage Foundation (Imray)

Spain N & NW distances (miles)

	Hondarribia	Bilbao	Gijon	Cabo Prior	A Coruña	C Vilano	C. Finisterre
Hondarribia	0						
Bilbao	60	0					
Gijon	157	115	0				
Cabo Prior	291	282	124	0			
A Coruña	305	295	138	14	0		
C Vilano	353	344	187	62	45	0	
C. Finisterre	371	362	204	80	63	17	0

W and S Spain & Portugal distances (miles)

	C. Finisterre	Baiona	Viana Castelo	C. Roca	C. Vicente	Cádiz	Gibraltar
C. Finisterre	0						
Baiona	53	0					
Viana Castelo	76	33	0				
C. Roca	210	208	176	0			
C. Vicente	320	318	286	110	0		
Cádiz	453	450	419	242	132	0	
Gibraltar	515	512	481	305	194	71	0

Cruising Galicia Carlos Rojas & Robert Bailey (Imray).

Good helpful brochures are available for every region from:
Spanish National Tourist Office, 23 Manchester Square, London W1A 6NB ℡ 020 7486 8077 *Fax* 020 7486 8034
The Portuguese National Tourist Office, 22 Sackville St, London W1X 2LY ℡ 020 7494 1441, Fax 020 7494 1868.

Plans Deep water is coloured blue. In some parts of this coast it is not possible to include a 2m contour line. Where this is so, the light blue will extend to the 5m line.

Order Text and plans on this coast are sometimes out of the natural sequence E to W in order to achieve maximum correlation between text and plans.

Passage charts	
Charts BA 89, 1104, 1292, 1291, 1290, 1111, 3633;	
S 40 to 49 inclusive, 59;	
Imray C18, C19, C42, C43, C48, C49, C50	

Principal lights	BA No
Igueldo San Sebastián Fl(2+1)15s132m26M	1483
Cabo Machichaco Fl.7s120m24M Siren Mo(M)60s (– –)	1520
Pta Estaca de Bares Fl(2)7.5s99m25M	1686

	BA No
Cabo Prior Fl(1+2)15s105m22M	1692
Torre de Hércules, Fl(4)20s104m23M AIS	1704
Cabo Villano Fl(2)15s103m28M AIS Racon M (– –)	1736
Cabo Toriñana Fl(2+1)15s63m24M	1740
Cabo Finisterre Fl.5s142m23M Siren(2)60s	1742
Cabo Silleiro Fl(2+1)15s83m24M	1916

HONDARRIBIA – HENDAYE

Charts BA 1171; S 3910

HW Pte de Grave –0042

MHWS	MHWN	MLWN	MLWS
4·4m	3·2m	1·5m	0·6m

An old fortified Spanish town on E side of Rio de Bidasoa opposite the sophisticated resort of Hendaye on the French side. Customs officials may be very active. Strong ebb tide at springs at mouth of Rio de Bidasoa.

Approach Conspic LtHo Fl(2)10s on Cabo Higuer at W end of bay. Give wide berth to Les Briquets in E of bay.

Entrance Enter river on top half of tide, no difficulties except in heavy swell from N, sp ebb is very strong. Enter between breakwater heads Fl(3)G and LFl.R.10s. Keep close to stb training wall until its root at Roca Punta where turn to port and follow dredged channel 3m with mooring buoys.

Anchorage
• 1ca SW of landing place at Hendaye Plage near YC in 3·5m clear of buoys.
• In the river N or S of Roca Punta in 3m.
• 1–2ca S of Puerto Gurutzeaundi (½M S of Cabo Higuer) W of extended breakwater Fl.G.3s in 2·5m clear of buoys (or inside hbr if room, F.G & F.R at entrance).
• In the river 2ca S of entrance to Hendaye Marina (most sheltered).

A first time night entry to the Rio de Bidasoa is not recommended. Use last anchorage given.

Berthing There are two marinas – the E side French the W side Spanish, visitors welcome.

℡/VHF Hendaye 05 5948 0600; Hondarribia 943 641 711; both VHF 09.

PUERTO DE PASAJES

Charts BA 1171; S 3911

HW Pte de Grave –0040

MHWS	MHWN	MLWN	MLWS
4·2m	3·1m	1·6m	0·5m

A busy commercial hbr which can be entered in all conditions. In heavy swell enter in the last quarter of flood. Well-sheltered but subject to wash from large vessels.

Approach There is a LtHo (conspic from E) on Cabo La Plata Oc.4s above Pta de Arando Chico, and on opposite E headland a conspic rock El Fraile. IPTS.

Entrance is straightforward once identified, however it is narrow. It is marked, just off shore by two towers, Fl.R.5s and Fl.G.5s. Enter on 155° on transit of Dir Lt Oc(2)WRG.12s. After entry the channel is well marked.

Anchorages
• Off village of Pasajes the San Juan, on both sides of the river, outside moorings in 4m mud. Very crowded.
• In cove opposite Pta de las Cruces (Ensenada de Cala Bursa) in quiet weather only.
• On W side of dunes off Pta del Puntal del Pasajes, moorings.

Berthing It may be possible to go alongside a fishing vessel at the Muelle de Pesquero.

VHF VHF 06.

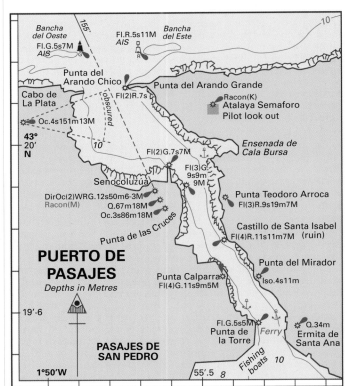

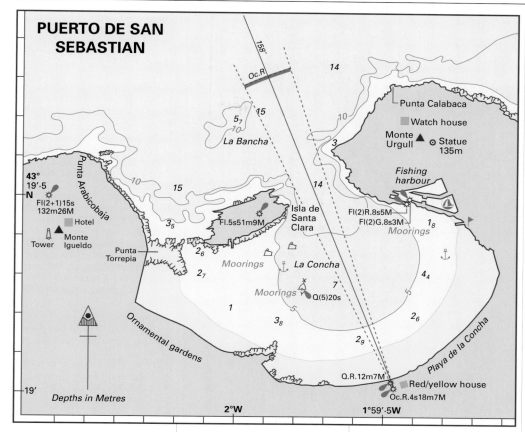

PUERTO DE SAN SEBASTIAN

Depths in Metres

43° 19'·5 N
Fl(2+1)15s
132m26M
Hotel
Tower ▲ Monte Igueldo
Punta Arabicobaja
Punta Torrepia
Ornamental gardens
La Bancha
5₇ 15
10 15 3₅
2₆
2₇
Moorings
158°
Oc.R
14
5₇
Fl.5s51m9M
Isla de Santa Clara
Moorings
La Concha
Moorings
1
3₈
2₉
Q(5)20s
7
4₄
2₆
Punta Calabaca
Watch house
Monte Urgull ▲ ● Statue 135m
Fishing harbour
Fl(2)R.8s5M
Fl(2)G.8s3M
Moorings
1₈
Playa de la Concha
Q.R.12m7M
Red/yellow house
Oc.R.4s18m7M
19'
2°W
1°59'·5W

SAN SEBASTIÁN

Charts BA 1171; S 3910

HW Pte de Grave –0030sp –0110np

MHWS	MHWN	MLWN	MLWS
4·2m	3·2m	1·6m	0·6m

An elegant city around a beautiful bay. Crowded in summer.

Approach Identify Mte Urgull with large statue, Mte Igueldo Fl(2+1)15s and Isla de Santa Clara Fl.5s. In poor visibility take care not to confuse Mte Urgull and Is de Santa Clara. Avoid La Bancha shoal in heavy swell.

Entrance From a position ½M off, follow centre of passage between Mte Urgull and Is de Santa Clara on 158°. By night, intensified ldg Lts Oc.R.4s and front Q.R on 158°.

Anchorage S of Is de Santa Clara on sand 4m, clear of local moorings, close in to avoid swell. Buoy anchor. YC provides visitors' moorings in summer and water taxi.

Berthing Very restricted space in yacht hbr Darsena de la Concha, E mole F.G, W mole F.R. TC pontoon in hbr available for visitors.

☎ 992 141 769.

PUERTO DE CASTRO URDIALES

Charts BA 1171; S 394A

HW Pte de Grave –0120sp –0040np

MHWS	MHWN	MLWN	MLWS
4·0m	2·9m	1·5m	0·4m

A picturesque and interesting old town.

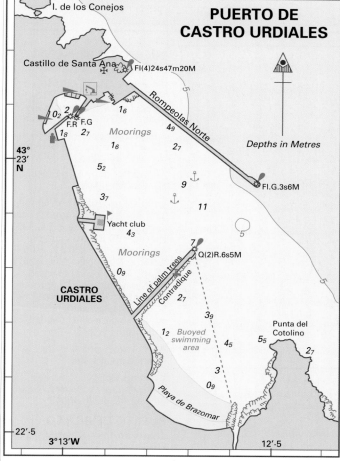

PUERTO DE CASTRO URDIALES

I. de los Conejos
Castillo de Santa Ana ✠ Fl(4)24s47m20M
Rompeolas Norte
Depths in Metres
1₀ 0₂ 2 F.R F.G
1₆
Moorings
4₉
2₇
Fl.G.3s6M
43° 23' N
1₈
2₇
1₆
5₂
9
11
3₇
Yacht club
4₃
Moorings
CASTRO URDIALES
0₉
7
Q(2)R.6s5M
Line of palm trees
Contradique
2₇
3₉
1₂ Buoyed swimming area
4₅
5₅
Punta del Cotolino
2₇
3
0₉
Playa de Brazomar
22'·5
3°13'W
12'·5

Approach From W Castro Urdiales is not seen until Pta del Rabanal is rounded. From E the buildings, castle and church are conspic. By night use the LtHo of Castillo de Santa Ana Fl(4)24s. Entrance From a position where

LtHo on Castillo de Santa Ana bears W ½M steer 230° and pass between mole heads Fl.G.3s to stb and Q(2)R.6s to port. Give a clearance of 25m.

Anchorage In entrance of outer harbour E of moorings in 11m.

Buoy anchor. YC water taxi VHF 09 (summer 0800–2100). Not recommended in strong easterlies. NW swell refracts in.

Berthing
• Alongside moles of inner harbour much of which dries.
• Inside N breakwater Rompeolas Norte of outer harbour in very calm weather.

PUERTO DE GUETARIA

Charts BA 1171; S 3921; Imray C42

HW Pte de Grave –0030sp –0110np

MHWS	MHWN	MLWN	MLWS
4·4m	3·4m	1·6m	0·6m

A small fishing port with easy entrance.

Approach Mte Igueldo Fl(2+1)15s is 9M to E. Conspic LtHo Zumaya Oc(1+3)12s is 2¼M to W.

Entrance Identify conspic Is de San Anton, Fl(4)15s and leave to stb.

Anchorage Behind Dique Exterior F.G in up to 8m. Affected by strong gusts from NW over Is de San Anton.

Berthing The marina sometimes has space on pontoon G, or it may be possible to get permission to moor between buoys in NE basin of harbour.

Facilities YC.
☎ 943 896 129.

PUERTO DE ZUMAIA

Charts BA 1171; S 3921; Imray C42

HW Pte de Grave –0035sp –0115np

See plan on page 386.

A small coast resort town with good yacht facilities inc repairs and laundry.

Approach The grey octagonal LtHo Oc(1+3)12s on its island is conspic. The breakwater head is to the E and below it. Do not approach too far E towards the cliffs as the sea breaks for a considerable distance out. Best entrance HW±0300, depends on swell.

Entrance Round the breakwater head Fl(2)G.7s keeping more to stb as there is shallow water towards the E training wall head Fl(2)R.7s. After entry keep to mid river. Least depth 2·5m.

Berthing In marina, reception by fuel berth. All usual facilities, including laundry.
☎ 943 860938.

PUERTO DE LEQUEITIO

Charts BA 1171; S 393

HW Pte de Grave –0035sp –0115np

MHWS	MHWN	MLWN	MLWS
4·2m	3·2m	1·6m	0·6m

A small picturesque fishing port and holiday resort.

Approach From W, identify Pta de Santa Catalina Fl(1+3)20s.

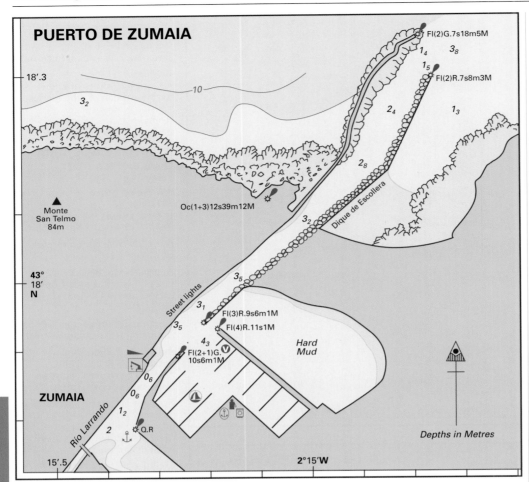

PUERTO DE ZUMAIA

Fl(2)G.7s18m5M

1₄ 3₈

18'.3 1₅

Fl(2)R.7s8m3M

3₂ 2₄ 1₃

Monte
San Telmo
84m

Oc(1+3)12s39m12M

2₈

3₂

Dique de Escollera

43°
18'
N

3₅

Street lights 3₁

3₅ Fl(3)R.9s6m1M

Fl(4)R.11s1M

4₃ Hard
Mud

Fl(2+1)G.
10s6m1M

0₆

ZUMAIA

Río Larrando 0₆

1₂

Q.R 2

15'.5 2°15'W

Depths in Metres

PUERTO DE LEQUEITIO

43°
22'
N

7₇

.47

8₅

Pta Amandarri 7

Isla de
San Nicolas

Fl.G.4s
8m5M

Yacht Club Bajo de la
Barra

2₈ 4m 3₈

Dredged
4.0m 4

Muelle de Tinglado

Aislado
Rock
Fl(2)R.8s

0₈ 3₅

F.R

6 1₈

Moorings F.G

1₂

Muelle Sur 0₆

Covers at HW

Playa del Carraspio

21'·7

Line of trees on quay

Pta
Currucho

LEQUEITIO

Río Lequeitio

Monte Calvario
117m Yard

Yard

Depths in Metres 2°30'W 29'·7

Entrance From a position 2ca N of Is de San Nicolas steer 212° on end of breakwater Rompeolas de Amandarri Fl.G.4s. Beware shoal patch Bajo de la Barra to port. Entrance channel dredged to 4m. Follow the breakwater leaving it 30m to stb and bn tr Dirque Aislado Fl(2)R.8s to port. Round the head of N mole of hbr F.G at a distance of 3m, leaving head of S mole F.R to port.

Anchorage
Outer harbour clear of entrance to inner harbour. Open to swell from N.

Berthing Inside Muelle de Tinglado as directed, normally turn to std on entry. Crowded in season.

☎ 946 840 500.

PUERTO DE BERMEO

Charts BA 1171; S 3931

HW Pte de Grave –0015Sp –0055np

MHWS	MHWN	MLWN	MLWS
4·6m	3·7m	1·6m	0·6m

A busy fishing port with a well-protected hbr and easy entrance but swell in E'lies.

Approach Cabo Machichaco Fl.7s is 2M to NW.

Entrance Approach hbr between 150° and 270° and round the end of the new breakwater Fl.G.4·5s, leaving it 50m to stb, into the Antepuerto. By night use white sector of Rosape Pta Lamiaren Fl(2)WR.10s for approach to breakwater Lt. Enter Puerto Mayor between moleheads F.G & F.R. The Puerto Menor is to stb but shallow and crowded with fishing boats.

Anchorage N or S side of Antepuerto in 4–6m.

Berthing Alongside wall just inside entrance to inner basin to port or stb, depth 3m.

PUERTO DE BILBAO

Charts BA 1173; S 3941; Imray C42

HW Pte de Grave –0045sp –0125np

MHWS	MHWN	MLWN	MLWS
4·2m	3·2m	1·6m	0·6m

A large commercial port which can be entered in most conditions for shelter.

Approach Cabo Machichaco Fl.7s is 15M to E. From W identify Pta Lucero and outer breakwater head Fl.G.5s. From E identify Pta Galea with light-coloured cliffs and LtHo Fl(3)8s, and outer breakwater head Fl.R.5s. Dique de Punta Galea is mainly submerged; do not cross.

Entrance Between breakwater heads and steer SE down middle of outer harbour. Give inner breakwater heads clearance of 25m leaving Dique de Santurce to stb Fl(3)G.10s and Contramuelle de Algorta to port Fl.R.5s. By night follow the white sector 119° to 135° in middle of E breakwater Oc.WR.4s and pass near R buoy Fl(4)R.12s before entering between inner breakwaters. Do not enter the River Nervion without contacting port control on VHF 06, 12 or 16.

Anchorages
• 100m N or NW of Las Arenas landing pier clear of moorings in 4m near YCs.
• 200m W of boat hbr at root of Contramuelle de Algorta.
• Club Maritimo del Abra stern buoy and line to pontoon.

Berthing
• In Getxo Marina at Algorta, S of E breakwater. All facilities.
• Marina at Real Club Maritimo at Las Arenas.

☎ /VHF Getxo 944 912 2367, Las Arenas 944 637 600; Marinas VHF 09, Port VHF 12.

Note See page 385 for Castro Urdiales and Lequeitio.

SANTANDER

Charts BA 1145; S 4011; Imray C43

HW Pte de Grave –0100sp –0020np

MHWS	MHWN	MLWN	MLWS
4·1m	3·0m	1·5m	0·4m

A pleasant city and large port on an estuary which can be entered by day or night under all conditions. Ebb stream can reach 3kn at Springs. New marina developments on S of river.

Approach Cabo Mayor conspic LtHo W round stone tr Fl(2)10s89m21M is 2M NW of entrance to Santander. Cabo Ajo Oc(3)16s is 7M NE.

Entrance Identify Is de Mouro Fl(3)16s.
• From W pass between Is de Mouro and Peninsula de la Magdalena with conspic Palace (now a University).
• From E pass ¼M E of Is de Mouro.

From both entrances pass 1–2ca S of La Cerda LtHo on Pta del Puerto Fl(1+4)20s, then S of Is Horadada Fl(2)7s into lighted buoyed channel. By night enter S of Isla de Mouro on ldg lts 236° front Q, rear Iso.R.4s and when S of Isla Horadada turn on to Lts 260°. Dir WRG.

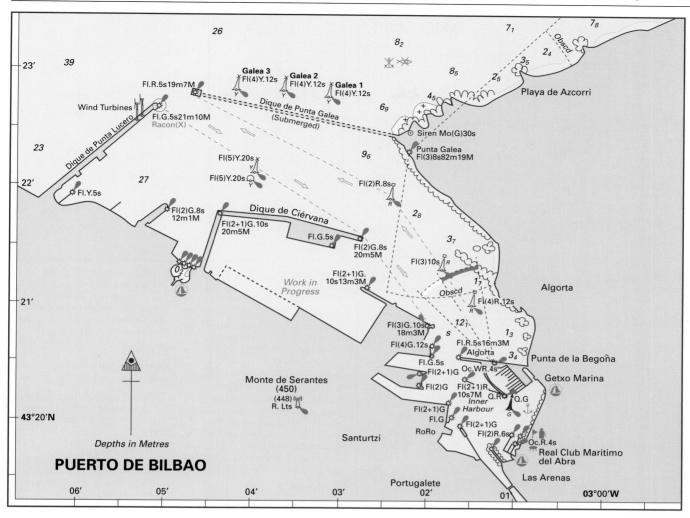

PUERTO DE BILBAO

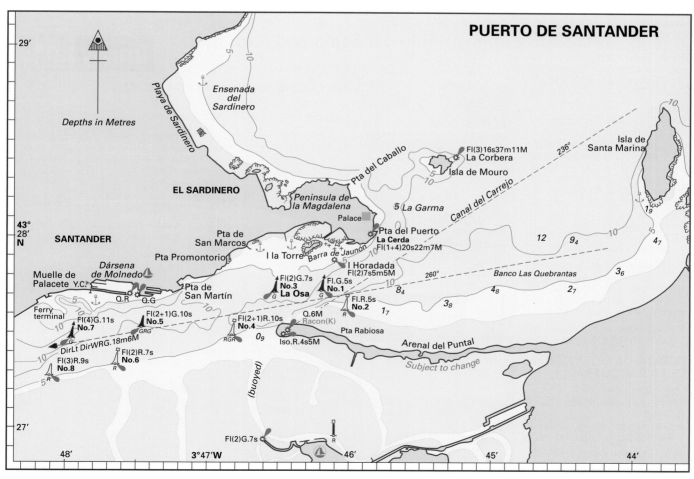

PUERTO DE SANTANDER

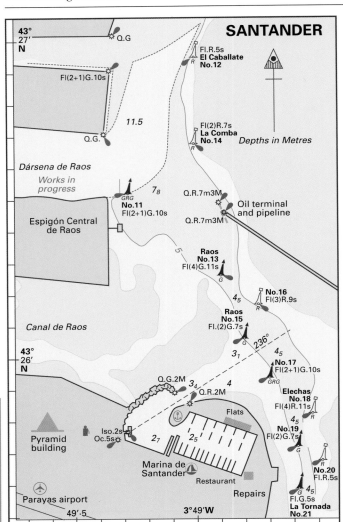

SANTANDER

43°27'N

Q.G

Fl.R.5s
El Caballate
No.12

Fl(2+1)G.10s

Q.G.

11.5

Fl(2)R.7s
La Comba
No.14

Depths in Metres

Dársena de Raos
Works in progress

7₈

GRG
No.11
Fl(2+1)G.10s

Q.R.7m3M

Oil terminal and pipeline

Q.R.7m3M

Espigón Central de Raos

Raos
No.13
Fl(4)G.11s

No.16
Fl(3)R.9s

Raos
No.15
Fl.(2)G.7s

Canal de Raos

43°26'N

236°

3₁

4₅

No.17
Fl(2+1)G.10s

GRG

Q.G.2M

3₄

Q.R.2M

4

Elechas
No.18
Fl(4)R.11s

Flats

Iso.2s
Oc.5s

2₇

2₅

4₅

No.19
Fl(2)G.7s

Pyramid building

Marina de Santander

Restaurant

Repairs

No.20
Fl.R.5s

Parayas airport

49'.5

3°49'W

Fl.G.5s
La Tornada
No.21

4₅

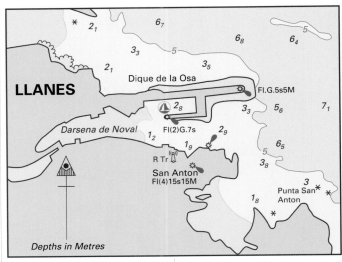

LLANES

2₁   6₇

3₃   5   6₈   6₄

2₁   3₅   5

Dique de la Osa

Fl.G.5s5M

2₈   3₃   5₆   7₁

Darsena de Noval

1₂   Fl(2)G.7s   2₉

1₉   6₅

R Tr   3₈

San Anton
Fl(4)15s15M   3

1₈   Punta San Anton

Depths in Metres

Enter at or near HW by day in the absence of swell. Few inner lights for night entry the first time.

Approach Pta Silla Oc.3·5s is ½M to W and Pta San Emeterio Fl.5s is 6M to W. Both are conspic. Steer to a position where hbr entrance bears SW ½M.

Entrance Enter on 225° halfway between breakwater head Fl.WG.2s to stb and training wall (can be submerged at HW) end Fl(2)R.8s to port. Follow round the small cliffs of Pta de la Espina F.G to stb at a distance of 25m and then steer for fish quay on 237° which is well lit.

Berthing
• Alongside fish quay if room. HM will allocate berth if asked.

• It may be possible to moor alongside a fishing boat on a buoy below the br. It is not recommended to anchor and take bow warps to the br piers. Strong current on spring ebb.

LLANES
Charts BA 1105; Imray C18
HW As Ribadesella

Tiny, but safe harbour, suitable for deep-draft yachts, providing a useful stopover. Attractive town.

Approach Identify the lighthouse and breakwater, surrounded by gayly coloured contrete blocks. Start approach from a point 1ca SE of breakwater, to clear rocks and breakers to E and N.

Anchorage Off Pta de San Marcos. 50–100m to SW or SE of YC near Darsena de Molnedo in 3m clear of moorings and race start line. Convenient to town but subject to wash from ferries. Land at YC.

Berthing
• At Marina Puerto Deportivo 2M upriver. Follow buoyed channel as far as conspic head of oil terminal to port then turn SSW, pass between the G and R buoys to avoid sand bank, to marina entrance leaving two G buoys Fl(2)7s to stb. Sheltered. Take taxi, bus to town 2M. Marina has all facilities.
• Dársena de Molnedo occasionally has space.

Facilities Good English-speaking chandler, 'Yates & Cosas' near E end of Dársena de Molnedo. Brittany Ferries two to three times a week to Plymouth.

☎ /**VHF** Marina Deportivo 679 715 479, VHF 09. Port VHF 12.

PUERTO DE SAN VICENTE DE LA BARQUERA
Charts BA 1150; S 4021
HW Pte de Grave –0100sp –0020np

MHWS	MHWN	MLWN	MLWS
3·9m	2·9m	1·5m	0·4m

A pleasant town with a Gaudi building at Comillas about 4M and ría in beautiful surroundings.

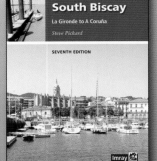
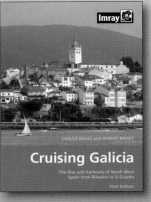

Entrance Head W into bay leaving breakwater to stb, until harbour entrance opens to stb.

Berthing Secure to N or E wall, wherever there is space. It may be necessary to raft up.

PUERTO DE RIBADESELLA

Charts BA 1150; S 4031; Imray C43

HW Pte de Grave –0008

MHWS	MHWN	MLWN	MLWS
4·0m	3·1m	1·5m	0·6m

Small fishing port with a bar 1·7m but good shelter inside. Enter HW–0200 to HW. A beautiful mountainous setting.

Approach Conspic LtHo Pta de Somos Fl(2+1)12s is ¾M to W. Conspic flat sloping cliffs off Pta del Caballo with white hermitage on top immediately to E of entrance. Steer to a position where Pta de Somos LtHo is due W and the concrete LtHo Fl(4)R.6s on the breakwater head at Pta del Caballo bears 140° ½M off.

Entrance Approach the breakwater head on 140°, leave it 25m to port and follow the quay round at a distance of 20m for 4ca into the hbr. Do not attempt in a heavy swell.

Berthing Visitors raft up on harbour wall on E side just before the section with pilings. May be possible to negotiate space in marina on W side.

PUERTO DE GIJÓN

Charts BA 1154; S 4042; Imray C43

HW Pte de Grave –0018

MHWS	MHWN	MLWN	MLWS
4·0m	3·1m	1·5m	0·6m

There is a choice of marinas: the original Puerto Deportivo near the Old Town, or the new Marina Yates, situated to the south of the commercial Puerto del Musel, on the Muelle de la Osa. The latter is a bike ride from town (free bike hire available 2011), but is highly praised and reported to be much cheaper. It is also probably easier to enter in adverse conditions.

Approach Cabo Peñas Fl(3)15s115m35M is 9M to NW. Cabo de Torres Fl(2)10s80m18M and the high exterior breakwater Digue Principe de Asturias of Puerto de Musel Fl.G.4s are conspic.

Marina Yates
Entrance From a position near the end of Dique Principe, sail south for a mile for the east corner of Dique de la Osa (Q(3)10s), then follow the wall SW for 0·6M to the end (Fl(4)G.20s). The marina is to stb.

Berthing The waiting pontoon is G, furthest W next to the dique, or on the ends of B, C or D. Usual facilities, inc diesel, but no yard. Cycle hire, 15 mins to town.

Puerto Deportivo
Entrance From a position near end of Digue Principe sail S for 1¼M and then leave Sacramento a G Lt bn Fl(2)G.6s to stb. Enter hbr between Digue de Liquerica Fl(2)R.6s to port and Malecon de Fomento Fl(3)G.10s to stb.

Berthing Marina pontoon berths inside Dique de Liquerica

dredged to 3m down to 1·3m. Water, electricity, showers, YC, diesel from near *capitanía*.

☎/VHF Marina Yates ☎ 985 30 97 48. Puerto Deportivo ☎ 985 34 45 43 Marinas VHF 09, Port VHF 14.

RÍA DE AVILÉS

Charts BA 1133; S 4052

HW Pte de Grave –0050.

MHWS	MHWN	MLWN	MLWS
3·9m	3·0m	1·4m	0·5m

A commercial hbr surrounded by heavy industry but with an easy approach and entrance, and a useful marina.

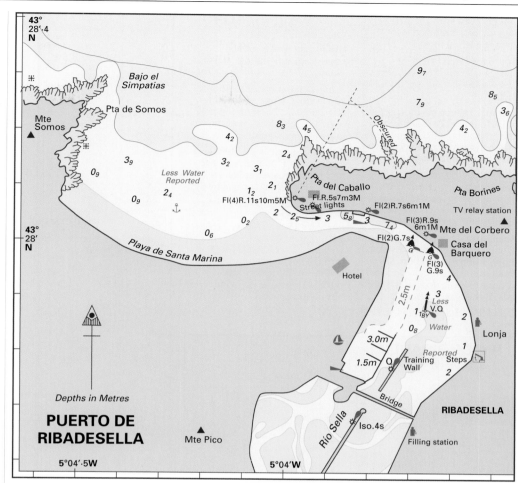

PUERTO DE RIBADESELLA

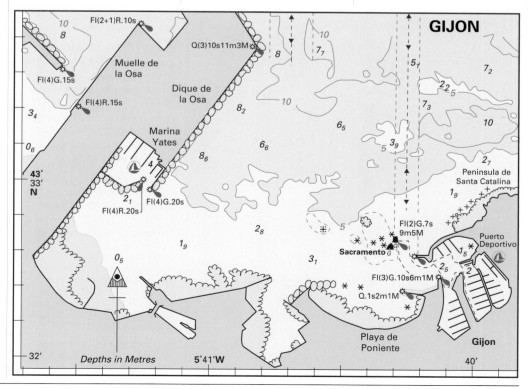

GIJON

On this coast with a strong N'ly a good port of refuge. Picturesque old town.

Approach Cabo Peñas Fl(3)15s115m35M to NE. Pta de Castillo Oc.WR.5s at entrance to Aviles.

Entrance From a position 2ca W of LtHo on Pta de Castillo enter lighted channel on 095°, in white sector, midway between cliffs to port and training wall and breakwater to stb.

Berthing New marina on W bank at end of channel had space in 2011 and welcomed visitors; telephone to get key.

Anchorage At Fondeadero del Monumento 1½M from entrance on port side in 4m, 100m SW of small café. Take dinghy to S end of quay (Muelle de Raices) on stb side of channel. Buses to Avilés.

☎/VHF 985 565 479, Port VHF 06.

PUERTO DE CUDILLERO

Chart BA 1290; S 405A
HW Pte de Grave –0035

MHWS	MHWN	MLWN	MLWS
4·0m	3·1m	1·5m	0·4m

A tiny picturesque old hbr in a gap in cliffs. Huge new fishing hbr 2ca to W. Enter on top half of tide. Swell breaks in entrance in strong NE winds.

Approach Identify Pta Rebollera Oc(4)16s at E of entrance. The new high breakwater Nuevo Dique del Oeste is conspic by day.

Entrance From a position where Pta Rebollera LtHo bears 200° at ½M steer 200° and leave LtHo to port, E breakwater F.G to stb. For new hbr turn hard to stb through narrow entrance behind Is Osa, swell breaks in the entrance in strong NE wind. Old hbr no longer used.

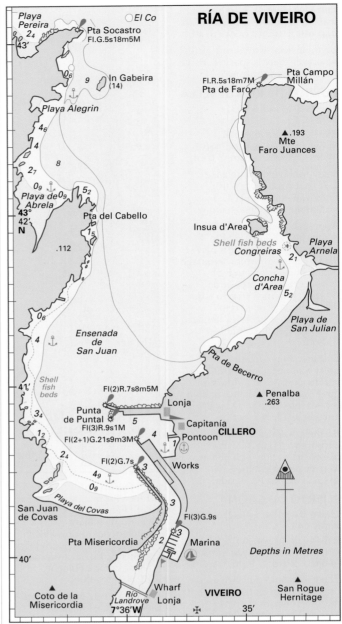

RÍA DE VIVEIRO

Berthing Fore and aft visitors' moorings in centre of harbour.

PUERTO DE LUARCA

Charts BA 1133; S 4061
HW Pte de Grave –0002

MHWS	MHWN	MLWN	MLWS
4·2m	3·3m	1·6m	0·7m

A fishing port and attractive town in a steep-sided valley.

Approach Identify low LtHo Oc(3)15s and conspic tall church tr on Pta Blanca 2ca E of hbr entrance, and Pta Mujeres 4ca NNW of hbr. By night car headlights around LtHo may confuse.

Entrance From a position 3ca N of Pta Mujeres steer on end of port-hand breakwater 170°. By night ldg Lts front Fl.5s rear Oc.4s, 170°. Enter between breakwaters Fl(3)R.9s to port, Fl(3)G.9s to stb. Turn to port and follow breakwater and port-hand quay 25m off.

Berthing Visitors' moorings inside Dique de Canouco; take bow line to quay.

RÍA DE RIBADEO

Charts BA 1096; S 4071
HW Pte de Grave –0002

MHWS	MHWN	MLWN	MLWS
4·0m	3·1m	1·5m	0·6m

The first of the Rias of Galicia, in a lovely setting.

Approach Is Pancha LtHo Fl(3+1)20s is conspic on W side of entrance to ría. Pta de la Cruz Fl(4)R.11s is on E side. Beware fish havens 2·5m high in approaches. Ebb tide can reach 3kn.

Entrance From a position ½M N of LtHo on Is Pancha follow first set of ldg marks on 140°, R diamond on W towers. By night, Front Iso.R, Rear Oc.R.4s. After 1M, turn on to second set of ldg marks 205°, R diamond on W structures. By night, front VQ.R, rear Oc.R.2s. These lead through the W span of the high-level road br (30m). Leave the quay close to stb and steer for the quay of Muelle de Mirasol Fl(2)R.7s.

Berthing The marina in Dársena de Porcillan has been expanded

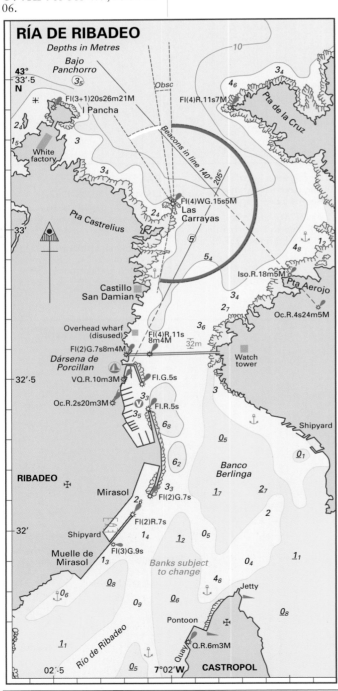

RÍA DE RIBADEO

and refurbished and welcomes visitors.

Anchorage Beware of marine farms which may be unmarked or unlit.
• Figueras in 4m, 250m W of shipyard.
• 100m W of Castropol, area becoming shallow. Castropol has a pontoon 1·4m for landing.

☎ 982 12 04 28.

RÍA DE VIVEIRO
Charts BA 1122; S 4082
HW Pte de Grave –0002

MHWS	MHWN	MLWN	MLWS
4·0m	3·1m	1·5m	0·6m

A beautiful ría with an easy entrance.

Approach Pta de la Estaca de Bares Fl(2)7·5s is 6M to NW. Is Coelleira Fl(4)24s is 3M to NW. Conspic high headland Mte Faro Juances on E side of ría.

Entrance Leave Pta de Faro Fl.R.5s to port, Pta Socastro Fl.G.5s to stb and steer towards Celeiro breakwater head Fl(2)R.7s5M to S.

Anchorages All rather exposed, open to N and swell.
• Off Playa del Covas in 5m. Convenient dinghy slip just upstream of marina.
• In Concha d'Area S of the rock Congreiras in up to 6m.
• Off Playa de Abrela in up to 10m. Open to NE.
• Ensenada de San Juan in up to 8m. Beware of shellfish beds.

Berthing
• The river is dredged to 3m to the marina which is nearly in the centre of town. Few marine facilities. Fuel. Visitors welcome.

☎ /VHF 982 57 06 10, VHF 09.

RÍA DEL BARQUERO
Charts BA 1122; S 4082
HW Pte de Grave –0002

MHWS	MHWN	MLWN	MLWS
4·1m	3·1m	1·5m	0·6m

A beautiful ría with easy entrance and steep-to sides.

Approach Pta de la Estaca de Bares Fl(2)7·5s is 2M to NW. Is Coelleira Fl(4)16s is ½M to E.

Entrance By night identify position of Pta del Castro Q(2)R.6s on port hand and Pta de la Barra Fl.WRG.3s on stb.

Anchorages
• Puerto de Bares in 6m. Open to NE.
• Is Vilela in 5m. Open to NE.
• Playa Campelo in 6m. Open to NE.
• Pta del Castro in 5m NNE of LtHo. Open to W and NW.
• Playa Arenal de Valle in 5m. Open to W–NW–N.
• Río Sor in 3m. Enter río near HW from Pta de Barra and follow stb bank to small cove beyond Puerto de El Barquero. Limited swinging room.
• Dry out alongside quay at Puerto de El Barquero.

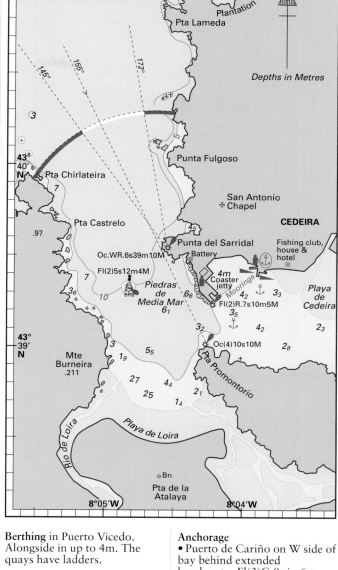

Berthing in Puerto Vicedo. Alongside in up to 4m. The quays have ladders.

ENSENADA DE SANTA MARTA AND PUERTO DE CARIÑO
Charts BA 1122
HW Pte de Grave –0005

MHWS	MHWN	MLWN	MLWS
4·1m	3·1m	1·5m	0·6m

A large bay and ría with wide entrance, and a beautiful Río to Santa Marta.

Approach Pta de la Estaca de Bares Fl(2)7·5s on E side, beware of shallows and rocks off Pta Banjeda, Cabo Ortegal Oc.8s on W side. Conspic line of sharp-pointed rocks Los Aguillones off Cabo Ortegal.

Entrance to Río de Mera has a bar and is not buoyed, so only possible for visitors HW–0200 to HW. Leave Isla de San Vicente close to port, then follow channel to stb behind the line of breakers, along line of yellow buoys. The river is buoyed further up.

Berthing Alongside pontoon in Cariño or on inside of mole.
• In marina in Santa Marta.

☎ 630 183 901.

Anchorage
• Puerto de Cariño on W side of bay behind extended breakwater Fl(3)G.9s in 6m.
• Ensenada de Espasante in 6m in SE of bay. Open to W or in hbr in N of bay.
• In Ría de Santa Marta at Santa Marta de Ortiguera.

RÍA DE CEDEIRA
Charts BA 1122; S 930
HW Pte de Grave –0030

MHWS	MHWN	MLWN	MLWS
4·4m	3·0m	1·6m	0·3m

Attractive ría with easy access and a small fishing port. Superb secure anchorage makes this a good arrival/departure point for Biscay.

Approach From N leave Pta Candelaria, conspic LtHo Fl(3+1)24s, to port. For 3M keep ¼M offshore until ría opens up. From SW steer 055° towards Pta Candelaria and when 2M from this headland identify to stb Pta Chirlateira and its off-lying rocky shoals. Steer towards Pta Lameda on 070° until the Lt on Pta Promontoiro Oc(4)10s is just clear of Pta del Sarridal Oc.WR.6s, on 160°.

Entrance Pass close to Pta del Sarridal to avoid the rocky shoal Piedras de Media Mar, isolated

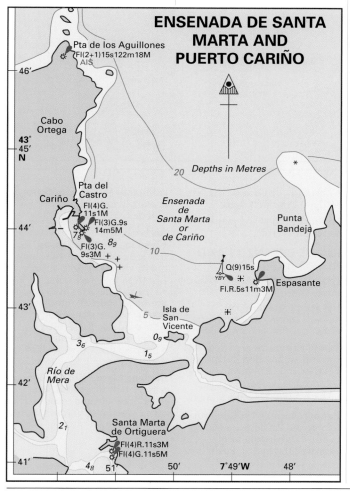

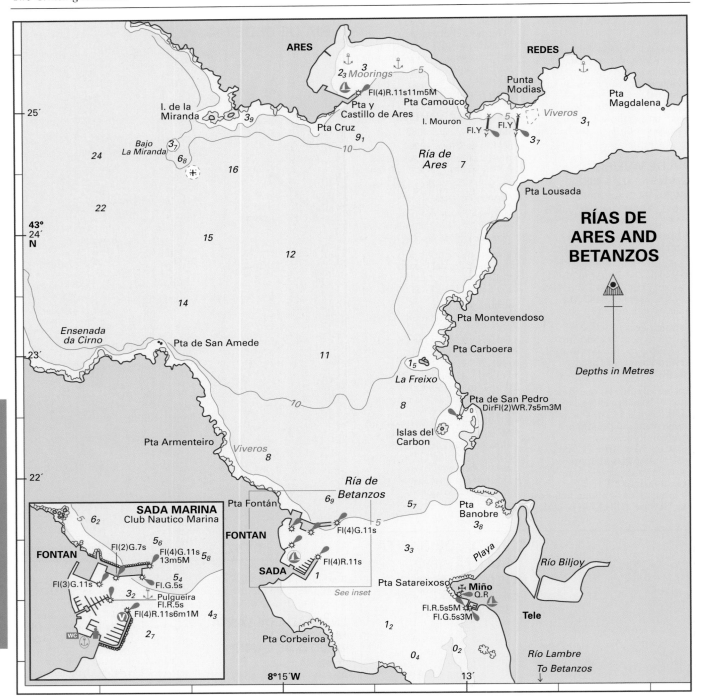

danger bn Fl(2)5s, to stb in centre of ría, and round the breakwater Fl(2)R.7s to port.

Anchorage E of jetty in 4m, clear of fishing boats. Supplies at Cedeira ½M.

Berthing E side of W jetty. Also at end of the old jetty by the *capitanía* ✆ 981 480 389.

RÍA DE EL FERROL
Charts BA 1118; S 412A

HW Pte de Grave −0045

MHWS	MHWN	MLWN	MLWS
3·8m	3·0m	1·5m	0·6m

An attractive steep-sided ría with a large port and naval base.

Approach Cabo Prior Fl(1+2)15s is 6M to NNE. Torre de Hercules Fl(4)20s is 5M to SW. From N in rough weather the sea breaks on banks S of Cabo Prior up to 4M off.

Entrance Identify Cabo Prioriño Grande and, ½M to S, LtHo on Cabo Prioriño Chico Fl.5s and leave 2ca to port. The entrance to the ría bears E, with Pta de Segaño to stb. A mole extends 0·5M SE of Cabo Prior with Lt Fl.R.5s at seaward end. By night use W sector of Bateria de San Cristobal Oc(2)WR.10s until ldg Lts on Pta de San Martin, Front Fl.1·5s Rear Oc.4s lead into ría and lighted buoyed channel.

Berthing in marina at La Graña – limited facilities.

Anchorages Subject to naval toleration.
• Ensenada de Baño, E of Pta Redonda.
• E of Castillo de San Felipe inside R can buoy No.4 clear of moorings.

• Ensenada de Cariño, 1M NE of Cabo Prioriño Chico.

Facilities Repairs and piped diesel at El Ferrol.

RÍA DE BETANZOS AND RÍA DE ARES
Charts BA 1094, S 412A; Imray C43

HW Pte de Grave −0050

MHWS	MHWN	MLWN	MLWS
3·8m	2·8m	1·5m	0·5m

Two quiet attractive rías with easy entrance within short distance of El Ferrol and La Coruña.

Approach Cabo Prioriño Chico Fl.5s. Torre de Hercules Fl(4)20s.

Entrance Identify Pta Coitelada to port and Pta del Seijo Blanco to stb. Pass between them, clearing coast by 2ca. Leave Is de

la Miranda well to port. Beware, unmarked isolated rock 5ca SW of Is de la Miranda.

Anchorages
• Fontán, Ría de Betanzos. Inside new hbr, clear of fishing boats. Holiday resort of Sada ¾M to S.
• Ensenada de Ares in 2–3m off hbr on W shore. Pontoon berths may be available.
• Ensenada de Redes, 4ca E of village off beach, sheltered NE.
• Ensenada de Cirno, inshore of mussel rafts.

Berthing Marina Sada, a modern marina with all facilities. Berth on outer pontoons and report to office. Good transport to Coruña.

✆ 981 619 015.

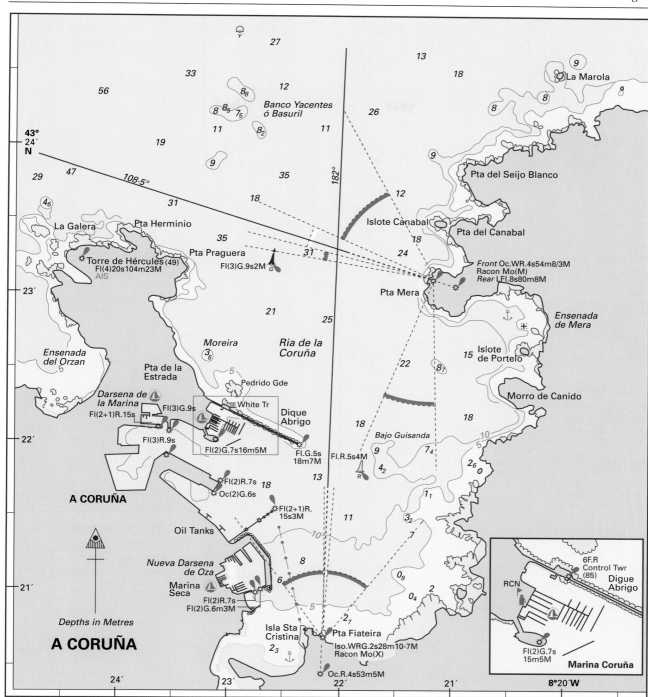

A CORUÑA

Charts BA 1094; S 412A, 4126; Imray C18, C48

HW Pte de Grave –0100

MHWS	MHWN	MLWN	MLWS
4·2m	2·8m	1·6m	0·3m

The major port on the NW coast of Spain with an easy entrance by day or night. Subject to swell in strong winds from N and NW. Picturesque old city.

Approach From N leave Cabo Prior Fl(1+2)15s and Cabo Prioriño Chico Fl.5s to port 1M off. Enter in mid-ría on S leaving Pta del Seijo Blanco to port and the conspic Torre de Hercules Fl(4)20s to stb. Steer 182°on Ldg marks (W sector) on Pta Fiaiteira front Iso.WRG.2s, rear Oc.R.4s. In heavy weather when the sea breaks across this channel use W approach. From W steer 108° on

Pta Mera Ldg marks front Oc.WR.4s rear Fl.4s leaving Pta Herminio with Torre de Hercules 2ca to stb. Turn on to Ldg marks on Pta Fiaiteira 182°.

Entrance Round end of breakwater Dique de Abrigo Fl.G.3s to stb and follow SW side of mole towards new marina 1ca N of Castillo de San Anton Fl(2)G.7s.

Anchorage
• SW of Is de Santa Cristina clear of slip and rocks.
• Ensenada de Mera, clear of rock off head of jetty. Sheltered N through E to SE.

Berthing
• Marina Coruña. A modern fully serviced marina at the root of Digue de Abrigo. All repairs. ☎ 981 920 482.

• Real Club Nautico de la Coruña Marina in Darsena Deportiva. In the heart of the city. Reception pontoon 10, near entrance. ☎ 981 914 142.
• Marina Seca in Dársena de Oza. Full facilities. Boatyard. ☎ 981 913651.

Facilities of a city, market. International airport at Santiago de Compostela, 1hr by bus.

VHF Port VHF 12; Marinas VHF 09.

RÍA DE CORME AND LAXE

Charts BA 1113; S 927

HW Pte de Grave HW –0015

MHWS	MHWN	MLWN	MLWS
3·7m	2·8m	1·5m	0·5m

Two small fishing villages. Choose anchorage according to wind.

Approach From N identify Pta del Roncudo Fl.6s and pass 1M offshore before turning S to Pta de Laxe Fl(5)20s. From SW keep 1M off coast NE of Cabo Villano Fl(2)15s Racon M (– –), and round Pta Lae between ½M and 1M off.

Entrance Avoid Bajo de la Averia shoal in heavy weather. From a position 1M N of Pta de Laxe steer E until Corme mole Fl(2)R.5s bears less than 045°.

Anchorages
• Corme 100–200m NE–E–SE of molehead 12 to 14m sand clear of moorings and reefs inshore marked by bn. Beware of fish farm. Exposed SW–W and to NW swell.
• Laxe SE end of mole Fl.G.3s clear of hbr entrance in 6–8m sand.

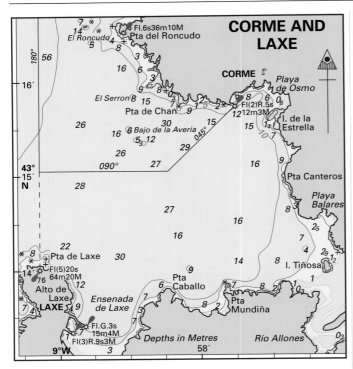

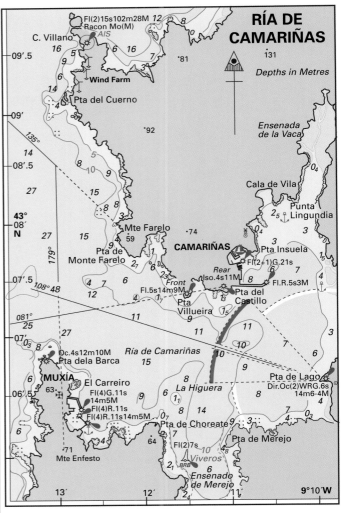

RÍA DE CAMARIÑAS

Charts BA 1113

HW Pte de Grave −0100

MHWS	MHWN	MLWN	MLWS
3·8m	2·8m	1·5m	0·5m

An attractive ría with two villages. Entry by day or night in reasonable visibility. Note Traffic Separation Scheme Cabo Villano to Cabo Finisterre.

Approach Cabo Villano conspic LtHo Fl(2)15s is 2M N of ría. Pass outside or inside El Bufardo, rock awash 3ca off Cabo Villano.

Entrance by day
• From NE round Cabo Villano and steer SW to avoid Las Quebrantas shoal until white hermitage on Mte Farelo bears E and the middle of the ría entrance is open on 108°, the line of Pta de Lago Ldg marks, two concrete towers in line but difficult to see. By night, steer for W sector of Pta de Lago Lt Oc(2)WRG.6s 107°-109°.
• From NE pass inshore of Las Quebrantas by heading 135° towards hermitage on Mte Farelo until ¾M from shore. Then steer for Pta de la Barca until Pta de Lago Ldg marks come in line on 108°.
• From SW pass ½M NW of Pta de la Barca to join Pta de Lago Ldg line.

By night
• From NE pass 1½M NW of Cabo Villano to clear isolated rock El Bufardo, then steer not less than 200° until the W sector of Pta de Lago Lt is visible on 108°. If Pta de Lago cannot be seen continue on 200° until the more powerful Ldg Lts of Pta Villueira Fl.5s and Pta del Castillo Iso.4s come into line on 080°. Follow this line until Pta de Lago Ldg Lts are seen.
• From SW steer to pass ½M NW of Pta de la Barca Oc.4s. Follow

Ldg Lts on Pta Villueira and Pta Castillo, and Pta de Lago.

Anchorage
• Camariñas (Heavy weed reported 2011) From Pta de Lago Ldg line steer for Camariñas molehead Fl.R.5s when it bears 340°. Mole gives good shelter.
• S of Cala de Vila, sheltered N.
• Ensenada de Merejo. Exposed to N and NW.
• Muxía From Pta de Lago Ldg line steer for Muxía molehead Fl(4)G.11s when it bears 220°. Anchor in 3–4m S of end of new breakwater. Beware two rocks off beach to S.

Berthing
• In the marina in Caramiñas ☎ 981 737 130.
• In the new marina in Muxía, located in the SE corner of the harbour under the lee of the new breakwater. Reported complete but apparently abandoned 2011 ☎ 981 742 030.

FINISTERRE AND RÍA DE CORCUBIÓN

Charts BA 3764; S 414

HW Lisboa +0100

MHWS	MHWN	MLWN	MLWS
3·3m	2·6m	1·2m	0·5m

A large bay, with the rather industrial Ría de Corcubión in the NE corner. All exposed to S, but offering shelter from the predominant summer NE'lies. The walk to the lighthouse of Finisterre is exhilerating.

Approach From the N, pass outside Centola de Finisterra and leave Cabo Finisterre at least ½M to port. There are often sudden squalls off Finisterre. From the S, there are numerous shoals and rocks. With a suitable chart and settled weather, a yacht can thread its way along the shore. Otherwise, approach Cabo Finisterre from a point 8M due S.

Anchorages
• Off Puerto de Finisterre, outside moorings, with some shelter from the mole
• Off the N end of the beach of Ensenada de Llagosteira
• In the NW or NE corners of Ensenada de Sardineiro, clear of mussel raft in NE corner
• Head of Ría de Corcubión, clear of mussel raft on W shore near head of ría.

RÍA DE MUROS

Charts BA 1756; S 415

HW Lisboa +0100

MHWS	MHWN	MLWN	MLWS
3·5m	2·6m	1·3m	0·5m

A delightful ría, with two marinas and several sheltered anchorages.

Approach From Cabo Finisterre in the N, with a large-scale chart, take a course of 140° leading to the Canal de los Meixidos, between the Piedras las Minarzos

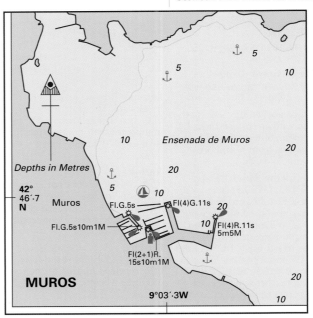

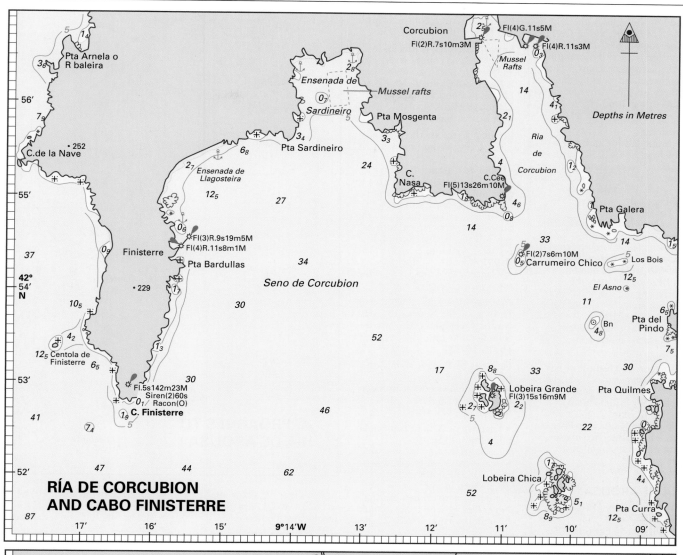

RÍA DE CORCUBION
AND CABO FINISTERRE

SPAIN AND PORTUGAL

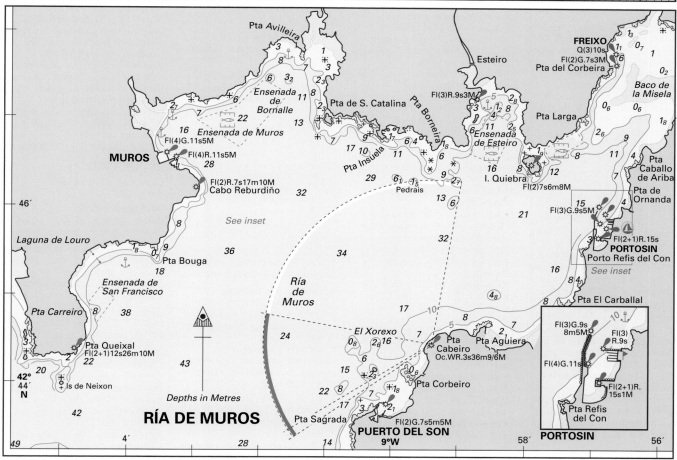

RÍA DE MUROS

Depths in Metres

PORTOSIN

and Los Meixidos. Otherwise pass S of Los Meixidos. Give the Islotes de Neixon ¼M offing – there are outliers. From the S, with a large-scale chart, a yacht can thread the rocks up the coast. Otherwise, give Cabo Corrubedo a 2M offing, head N for 6M, then head into the ría on 045°.

Anchorage
• Muros, outside harbour, NW of molehead Fl(4)G.11s. Pontoon for small boats outside N mole. Exposed to NE. Water, diesel on quayside, key holders near fishing shed
• N of Portosin hbr
• 5ca N of Muros hbr, close to shore, sheltered N
• Ensenada de Bornalle, clear of rocks. Sheltered from NE
• Freixo, 100m N of mole Fl(2)R.5s. From here the interesting old town of Noya 2½M to E can be reached by dinghy HW±0100
• Ensenada de San Francisco
• Ensenada de Esteiro.

Berthing
• The port of Muros now has a full-service marina. Yachts berth in the E half of the port. Facilities include Wi-Fi and laundry.
☎ 981 82 76 60
• The Club Nautico de Portosin also has a full-service marina, with fuel and a launderette, and a 32t travel-lift
☎ 981 766 598

RÍA DE AROUSA

Charts BA 1734, 1755, 1764; S 415, 4152

HW Vilagarcia Lisboa +0050

MHWS	MHWN	MLWN	MLWS
3·5m	2·8m	1·3m	0·5m

A large ría with buoyed channels, sheltered waters for sailing, and a variety of attractive anchorages. Night entry possibly into Vilagarcía and Pobra de Caramiñal. If you want to explore off the main channels, you will need a large-scale chart (Spanish *415*, *BA 1764* or, recommended, *Mapes de Navigacío CPP-28*, available locally), as there are numerous isolated rocks.

Approach The Canal Principal between Is Salvora and Pomberiño is the easiest and safest approach.

From N pass 5M offshore from Cabo Corrubedo Fl(2+3)WR.20s Racon K (−·−) to clear rocky shoal patch Bajos de Corrubedo situated within red sector 347°-040°. Leave Is Salvora LtHo Fl(3+1)20s+Fl(3)20s (sectored) to N at a distance of 1M.

Coming from S steer to a position mid-way between Is Salvora and Pombeiriño bn tr Fl(2)G.12s. Two alternatives, Canal de Sagres and Canal del Norte to the NW of Is Salvora and Is Vionta are best explored on leaving the ría and require a large-scale chart, passing N of

Piedras del Sargo conspic white con bn tr with G band Q.G.

Entrance Steer for Is Rua LtHo Fl(2)WR.7s on conspic rocky islet and leave to port, passing between Is Rua and Bajo Piedra Seca W tr Fl(3)G.9s. Continue on 030° for 2M to clear bank Sinal del Maño with R pillar buoy Fl(2)R.7s.

Berthing There are three main, easily accessible marinas with all facilities:
• **Pobra do Caramiñal** Leave bn tr Sinal de Ostreira Fl.R.5s 1ca to port and head for the outer mole Fl(3)G.9s. Leave R can buoy Fl(3)R.9s, marking the end of the mussel bed, to port, and turn in towards the marina. Reception on outer pontoon.
☎ 981 832 504. No fuel.
• **Vilagarcía de Arousa** is an active town with a sheltered marina.

Approach Use Pta Caballo LtHo Fl(4)11s on the N shore of I. de Arousa, steer about 055° past El Seijo G pillar buoy Fl(3)G.10s5M.

Facilities Berthing is mainly on fingers. Good shopping. International airport at Santiago de Compostela. Buses, trains. No fuel. ☎ 986 501 340.

• **Vilanova de Arousa** Leaving G pillar buoy, El Seijo Fl(3)G.10s5M to port, steer due S to avoid the fish farms. When the commercial hbr entrance is abeam turn in towards this well sheltered relatively new marina. Note: Bajo el Seijo rocks marked by unlit bn. Fuel. ☎ 670 623 084.

Anchorages
• **Sta Uxia de Ribiera** A busy fishing port with a small YC marina to the N of the hbr. Anchor outside harbour mole Fl(2)R.7s. Beware Bajo Camouco marked by Bn Q.G.
• **Pobra do Caramiñal** S or SE of marina. Sheltered S to W.
• **Cabo Cruz** To E of rocky peninsula in centre of bay, or N of new hbr on W side of peninsula, exposed to N.
• **Rianxo** A shallow hbr, pontoons for small yachts or anchor about 5ca E off Playa de Quenxo, sheltered N.
• **San Xulian** On I. de Arosa, in bay N of village.
• I. de Arousa, SW of Pta Caballo Fl(4)11s inshore of mussel rafts and inside Pta Barbafeita. Exposed to W. Reported that yellow buoys now take most of the space.
• **Cambados** With deep keel, N hbr only. With shallow draft, there is room to anchor S of pontoons in S hbr.
• **I. Toja Grande** On E side, in 4–6m. Attractive but requires BA 1768 and careful pilotage on top half of tide.
• **San Martin del Grove** Approach as above. Anchor S of end of breakwater in fair weather.
• **Puerto Pedro Negras** On S side of Peninsular del Grove.

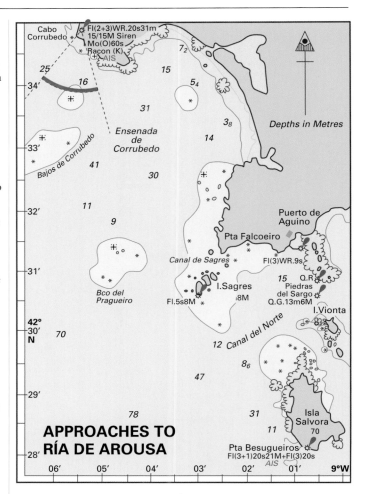
APPROACHES TO RÍA DE AROUSA

Approach on W sector 305°-315° to Lt Fl(4)WR.11s at root of breakwater. Pontoons.

RÍA DE PONTEVEDRA

Charts BA 1732; S 416A
Imray C48

HW Marin Lisboa +0100

MHWS	MHWN	MLWN	MLWS
3·3m	2·6m	1·2m	0·5m

A ría with several anchorages, and a naval college at Marin. No landing on Is Tambo (military zone).

Approach Identify Is Ons Fl(4)24s.
• N of Is Ons through Paso de la Fagilda, leaving R Lt buoy Q.R to port and Picamillo bn tr Fl.G.5s to stb. Leave Los Camoucos rocky shoal Fl(3)R.18s to stb.
• S of I. Ons. Steer 040° halfway between I. Ons and Pta Couso Fl(3)WG.10·5s.

Entrance Between Pta Cabicastro on N side and Cabo de Udra on S.

Anchorage and Berthing
• **Porto Novo** Moorings may be available see club or anchor E of small bay, clear of fishing boats.
☎ 986 723 266.
• **Sanxenxo** A large well-equipped marina with room for visitors. All facilities. Possible to overwinter here.
VHF 09 ☎ 986 720517.
• **Combarro** A delightful if touristy fishing village. Convenient for visiting Pontevedra. Berth in new marina,

or anchor E of harbour.
☎ 986 778 415.
• **Aguete** Small marina, exposed to the N. ☎ 986 702 373
• **Bueu** Small pleasant fishing port. E of E jetty Fl(2)R.6s, and N jetty Fl.G.3s clear of fishing boats on buoys, close to beach in 3–4m. Not much room in hbr. Good shelter from SW–W.
• **I. Ons** Pleasant day anchorages on E side. This is now a National Park, permission to anchor can be obtained directly from http://reddeparquesnacionales.mma.es/en/parques/cies/guia_auto.htm.
• **Ría de Aldan** Bays on S side.

RÍA DE VIGO

Charts BA 1730 S 416B
Imray C48

HW Lisboa +0050

MHWS	MHWN	MLWN	MLWS
3·4m	2·7m	1·3m	0·5m

The ría is dominated by the large commercial port of Vigo but has attractive anchorages. Baiona is delightful. It is also convenient, with easy access by day or night.

Approach Use Cabo del Horne Fl(2)WR.7·5s on N, Mte Faro Fl(2)8s on conspic Is Cies and Cabo Silleiro Fl(2+1)15s from S.

Entrance Note the TSS in both entrance channels and also the Precautionary Area N or Toralla.
• From the S use the wide deep water entrance, Canal del Sur. Round Cabo Silleiro ¾M off, leave Las Serreillas W card buoy Q(9)15s to stb and make for the

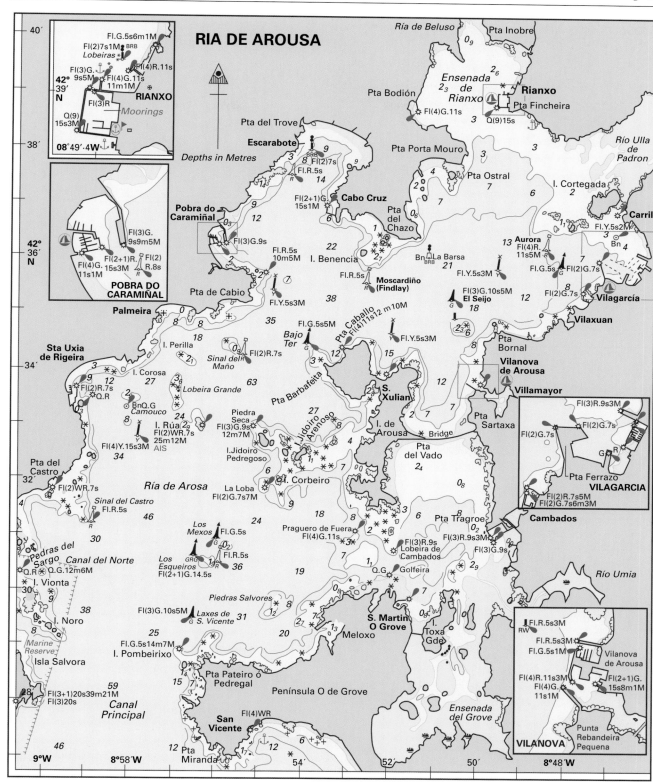

RIA DE AROUSA

G stb hand buoy Fl(3)G.9s off I. de Toralla.

• From the N use the Canal de Norte, avoiding the TSS, giving a good offing to the next four headlands clearly marked by port hand buoys or bns.

Anchorages

• E of Is Cies, N or S of Pta Muxiero or NE of Is de San Martin, off beach. Delightful. Part of the National Park, see web address under Pontevedra, above.

• Ensenada de Barra, sheltered NE.

• Cangas, outer harbour, little room. Pleasant town.

• Ensenada de Cangas, off beach.

• Ensenada de San Simón, beyond the suspension br; beware shellfish beds. Well sheltered.

• Baiona, S of Puerto Deportivo.

Berthing

• **Cangas** A small marina, some room for visitors. Ferry to Vigo. Laundry, Chandlery. ☎ 986 30 42 46, VHF 06.

• **Moaña** Relatively new marina ☎ 986 311 140.

• **Ensenada de San Simón** New marina 1ca N of Pta S Adrián welcomes visitors ☎ 986 874 007.

• **Punta Lagoa** Crowded in season. All facilities. ☎ 986 374 305.

• **Vigo** RCNV in basin immediately beyond conspic former transatlantic terminal buildings. Laundry. Marina expansion should be complete 2012. ☎ 986 449 694.

• **Bouzas** Marina Davila Sport is well equipped with good repair facilities. Chandlery. Beware frequent ferries to

Cangas from adjacent basin. ☎ 986 244 612. Major repairs at Astilleros Lago Carsi.

• **Baiona** Enter between Cabo Silleiro and Las Serralleiras on 084°. Sectored lt Oc.WRG.4s leads in. Steer for molehead Q.G. on not less than 160°. Either berth at YC (Monte Real Club de Yates) at NW side of hbr, crowded. Good YC. ☎ 986 385 000 VHF 71 or at the larger, modern Puerto Deportivo de Baiona. ☎ 986 385 107.

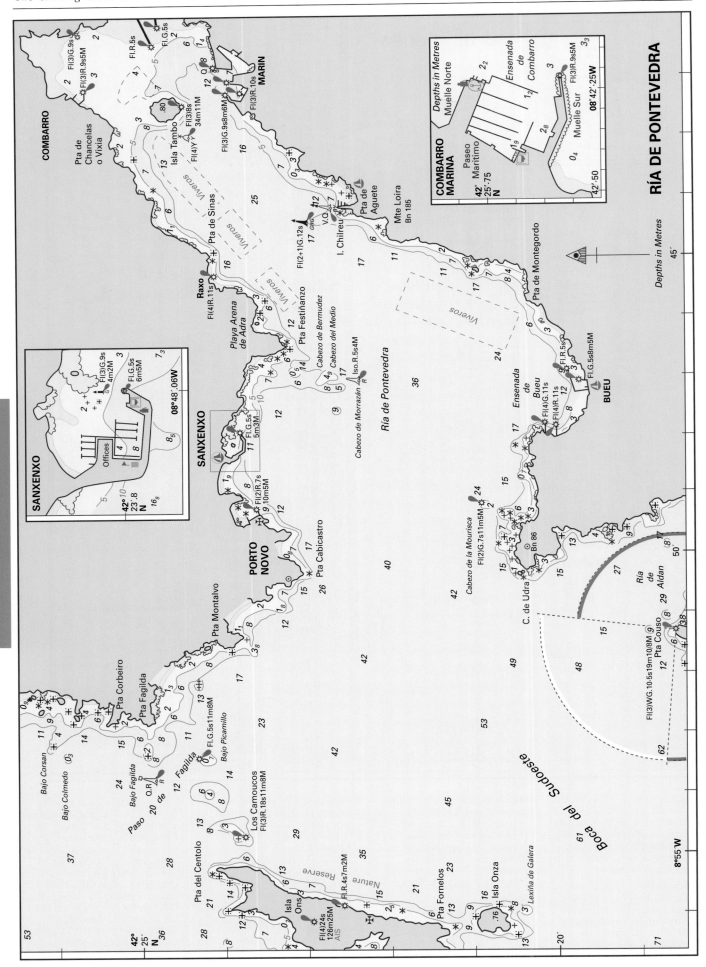

COMBARRO

Pta de Chancelas o Vixía

Fl(3)G.9s

Fl(3)R.9s5M

Fl.R.5s

Fl.G.5s

MARIN

Fl(3)R.10s

Fl(3)G.9s8m6M

Isla Tambo
Fl(3)8s
34m11M
Fl(4)Y

Viveros

Pta de Sinas

Raxo

Fl(4)R.11s

Viveros

Pta Festiñanzo

Playa Arena de Adra

Cabezo de Bermudez

Cabezo del Medio

Iso.R.5s4M

Cabezo de Morrazán

Ría de Pontevedra

SANXENXO

Fl.G.5s 5m3M

Fl(2)R.7s 9.10m5M

PORTO NOVO

Pta Cabicastro

Pta Montalvo

Pta Corbeiro

Pta Fagilda

Fl.G.5s11m8M

Fagilda

Bajo Picamillo

Bajo Fagilda
Q.R.

Paso

Bajo Corsan

Bajo Colmedo

20 de

Los Camoucos
Fl(3)R.18s11m8M

Pta del Centolo

Isla Ons

Fl(4)24s
126m25M
AIS

Fl.R.4s7m2M

Nature Reserve

Pta Fornelos

Isla Onza

Lexiña de Galera

Boca del Sudoeste

SANXENXO

Fl(3)G.9s 4m2M
Fl.G.5s 6m5M

Offices

08°48'.06W

42°
23.8
N

I. Chilreu
V.Q.
GRG
Fl(2+1)G.12s

Pta de Aguete

Mte Loira
Bn 185

Pta de Montegordo

Viveros

Fl.R.5s

Fl.G.5s8m5M

BUEU

Ensenada de Bueu

Fl(4)G.11s

Fl(4)R.11s

Cabezo de la Mourisca
Fl(2)G.7s11m5M

Bn 86

C. de Udra

Ría de Aldan

Pta Couso

Fl(3)WG.10.5s19m10/8M

COMBARRO MARINA

Depths in Metres

Muelle Norte

Ensenada de Combarro

Fl(3)R.9s5M

Muelle Sur

Paseo Marítimo

42° 25.75 N

08° 42'.25W

RÍA DE PONTEVEDRA

Depths in Metres

45'

8°55'W

42°
25'
N

50'

20'

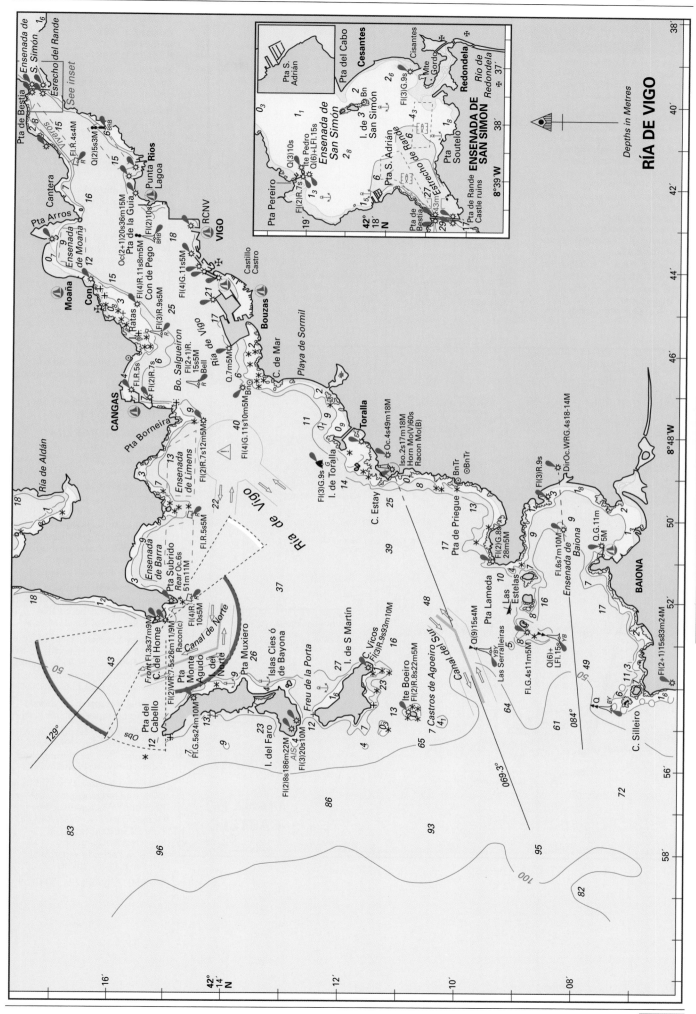

SPAIN AND PORTUGAL

RÍA DE VIGO

Depths in Metres

ENSENADA DE SAN SIMÓN

Portugal

From the Rio Miñho southwards to São Vicente the coast flattens progressively and becomes one of sand beaches backed by dunes or low cliffs. The rivers have sand bars and in any swell should only be entered with great care. Some of the fishing harbours have been improved and extended; ports free of a bar include Leixões, Sines, Nazaré and Peniche.

When conditions are not safe for any port, the authorities close the entrance. www.marinha.pt/PT/extra/Pages/EstadodasBarras.aspx gives up-to-date details.

There are TSS off Cabo da Roca and Cabo de São Vicente.

With the exception of Nazaré, where a separate police office needs to be visited, it now appears sufficient to fill out the usual forms in marinas, and not to bother the authorities if anchored. However, there are numerous reports that the authorities, especially around Faro, are visiting yachts and demanding that they be equipped to Portuguese ocean-going standards, pay light dues (a trivial sum), and have proof that all equipment, including fire extinguishers, is in-date. To avoid fines or threats of fines, anchor balls and lights should be used and the boat's name and port of registry (invent one for SSR) must be displayed.

Diesel is available at most ports. Calor Gas not readily obtainable but Camping Gaz is widely available. There may be a charge for water.

Note: Portuguese time is one hour behind Spanish time, i.e. same as UK.

Passage charts

The Portuguese *Instito Hidrografico* now offer a range of economical 1:150,000 coastal charts, from 25R01 to 25R12, as well as the conventional shipping charts.
BA 3634, 3635, 3636, 89
Imray C19, C48, C49, C50

Principal lights	BA No
Leça	2032
Fl(3)14s56m28M	
I Berlenga	2086
Fl.10s120m16M	
Horn 28s	
C da Roca	2108
Fl(4)17s164m26M	
C Espichel	2139
Fl.4s167m26M Horn 31s	
C de Sines	2160
Fl(2)15s55m26M	
C de São Vicente	2168
Fl.5s85m32M Horn Mo(I)30s (··)	

VIANA DO CASTELO

Charts BA 3257;
Imray C48
P 26401, P 25R01

HW Lisboa –0010

MHWS	MHWN	MLWN	MLWS
3·5m	2·7m	1·4m	0·5m

A fishing port and marina with good shelter. Entrance dredged but in heavy swell the sea may break on bar.

Approach Montedor Fl(2)9·5s Horn Mo(S)25s (···) is 5M to N.

Entrance Enter on the stb side of the channel, keep well clear of the W mole. Once abeam of the E mole follow the buoyed channel to Viana Marina before low level br. There is a footbridge across the entrance, call on VHF 12, waiting pontoon in river. Beware cross tide at the entrance.

Berthing Visitors use first pontoon to stb, bow on and pick up stern buoy. Reception pontoon opposite entrance.

Facilities Picturesque old town. Laundry. Rly. Porto International Airport, 30M.

☎/VHF Marina 258 359 546, VHF 12; Port VHF 11.

PÓVOA DE VARZIM

Charts BA 3634;
Imray C48
P 25R01

HW Lisboa –0010

MHWS	MHWN	MLWN	MLWS
3·5m	2·7m	1·4m	0·5m

A reasonably well-sheltered marina, reserving 40 berths for visitors. With heavy onshore swell the entrance can be dangerous and may be closed.

Approach Remain outside 20m contour. Distinctive white tr block stands N of hbr. Leca LtHo Fl(3)14s56m28M is 21M to S.

Entrance Keep well clear of broken water and hazards up to 40m off W mole Fl.R.3s; heading 023°. Turn stb into marina on clearing E mole, LFl.G.6s.

Berthing Reception on short hammerhead pontoon on N side.

Anchorage May be possible in NE corner of hbr, clear of all moorings. Beware of unmarked and possibly rocky shallows.

Facilities Laundry. First Aid Post in marina bldg, hospital in town. Boat hoist. Visitors welcomed by Clube Naval Póvoense, Rua da Ponte 2 (restaurant). Supermarket 2km. Buses and trains to Porto. International airport at Porto 20km.

☎/VHF 252 688 121, VHF 09.

VIANA DO CASTELO

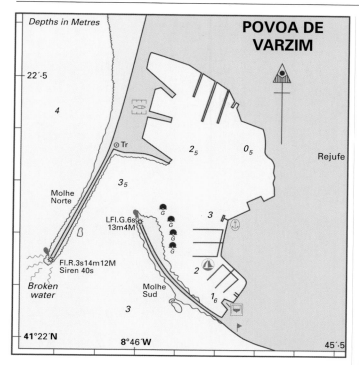

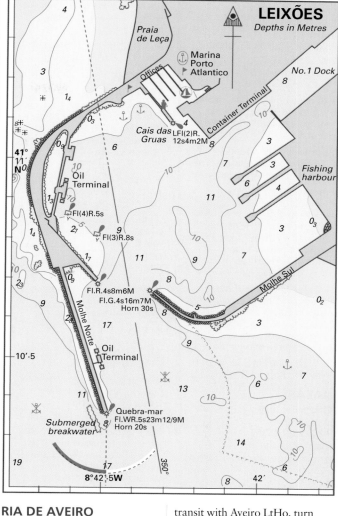

LEIXÕES

Charts BA 3258;
P 26402, P 25R02

HW Lisboa –0015

MHWS	MHWN	MLWN	MLWS
3·5m	2·7m	1·3m	0·5m

As a refuge, better than Póvoa de Varzim, but even Leixões closes in severe storms.

Approach Oil refinery 2M to N conspic by day and night. Leça LtHo Fl(3)14s is 1½M to N. From N round end of extended breakwater Fl.WR.5s (001°-R-180°-W-001°) Horn 20s, at distance of 200m.

Entrance Steer 350° between inner moleheads, Fl.G.4s and Fl.R.4s.

Berthing At marina in N corner of hbr (old fishing hbr); crowded. Berthing is bows on and stern buoy. Water and electricity at berths. YC and showers ashore.

Anchorage W of marina. No landing on Cais das Gruas – use the marina.

Facilities Launderette, free Wi-Fi. Bus to Porto from behind YC. Facilities for repairs nearby. Shops and market in Matosinhos.

☎ /VHF Marina 22 996 4895, VHF 09; Port 995 3000, VHF 12.

RIO DOURO

Charts BA 3258 (shows new mole);
P 26402, N25R02;
Imray C48

HW Lisboa +0015

MHWS	MHWN	MLWN	MLWSS
-0·6m	-0·4m	-0·1m	0·1m

The new Douro Marina offers a more convenient port for exploring Porto than Leixões or Póvoa de Varzim. There is a new mole across the entrance, to give enhanced shelter inside. In heavy weather Leixõs is a safer destination.

Approach The bar has at least 4m. However, caution is needed on the ebb and/or with significant swell and/or with a strong onshore wind. The (new) leading marks/Lts (Oc.Y.5s) are aligned on a course of 059° through the entrance. Thereafter, there is a dredged and buoyed channel to beyond the marina. At low water, there is a shallow spit between the channel and the marina with its E extremity marked by the G No.5 buoy.

Entrance Leave the mole to stb. The fuel berth, with access to reception, is straight ahead.

Berthing as directed. A dory will escort if you call ahead. Marineros are on-call from 0800 to 2030 in summer.

Facilities include fuel, Wi-Fi, laundry, water taxi to town, bike hire. 10% discount CA members.

RIA DE AVEIRO

Charts BA 3227;
P 24201, P 25R02, P 25R03

HW Lisboa +0007

MHWS	MHWN	MLWN	MLWS
3·2m	2·6m	1·4m	0·6m

Enter only in daylight in good weather just before HW. Strong tidal streams. Strong winds SW–NW produce a dangerous sea.

Approach There are few marks along the low sandy coast. Identify Aveiro LtHo Fl(4)13s, R tr, W bands. Keep at least 1M off shore. With S pierhead (W column G bands Fl.G.3s) in transit with Aveiro LtHo, turn onto 086° until inside N pierhead.

Entrance Between extended N mole Fl.R.3s and S mole Fl.G.3s; follow channel for 1½M to Baia de San Jacinto to port.

Anchorage Entry difficult into Baia de San Jacinto, cross currents. Enter between training walls and sph buoys to anchorage in N end of Baia.

Berthing It is possible to go up the Canal Principal de Navegação to Aveiro where the yacht club welcomes visitors to its pontoon if there is space.

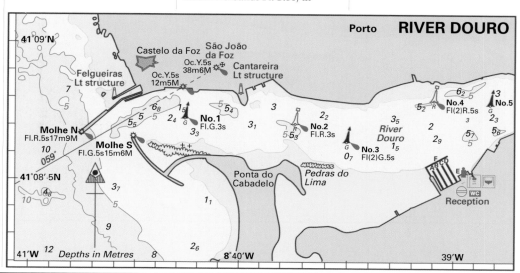

FIGUEIRA DA FOZ

Charts BA 3228;
Imray C49
P 26404, P 25R03, P 25R04
HW Lisboa –0007

MHWS	MHWN	MLWN	MLWS
3·5m	2·7m	1·3m	0·5m

Extended breakwaters and recent dredging of bar to 5m have improved the entrance. Strong ebb at Sp.

Approach Cabo Mondego Fl.5s is 2½M to N. Conspic suspension br 1½M upriver from entrance.

Entrance Between N mole Fl.R.6s Horn 35s and S mole Fl.G.6s on Ldg Lts front, Iso.R.5s, rear, Oc.R.6s, 082°. Ldg marks difficult to see by day. Keep to N shore. When ¾M inside moleheads turn to port into Marina da Figueira.

Berthing In W end of Marina da Figueira da Foz. Electricity and water at berths and showers ashore. Good security. Diesel from fish hbr to stb on entry. Good covered market alongside.

☎ /VHF Marina 233 402 901, VHF 08; Port VHF 11.

NAZARÉ

Charts BA 3635;
Imray C49
P 26302, P 25R05
HW Lisboa –0022

MHWS	MHWN	MLWN	MLWS
3·3m	2·6m	1·4m	0·6m

A new, well-sheltered major fishing port 1M to S of old town and beach. Useful as a port of refuge.

Approach Pontal da Nazaré Oc.3s is 1M to N.

Entrance Straightforward between N mole LFl.R.5s and S mole LFl.G.5s.

Berthing In one of two small marinas. In NE of inner harbour run by YC or in SW corner for visitors. Diesel and usual facilities.

☎/VHF Marina 262 561 401, VHF 09; Port VHF 11.

PENICHE

Charts BA 3635;
Imray C49
P 24202, P 25R05, P 25R06
HW Lisboa –0025

MHWS	MHWN	MLWN	MLWS
3·5m	2·6m	1·3m	0·5m

A large, well-sheltered fishing port with easy entrance on S side of peninsula of Peniche.

Approach From N identify two islands, Os Farilhão Fl(2)5s and Ilha Berlenga Fl.10s, 8/5M respectively NW of Peniche and Cabo Carvoeiro Fl(3)R.15s. By day, the peninsula of Peniche can be mistaken for an island. TSS to W of islands.

Entrance The W mole Fl.R.3s extends 1ca S of E mole Fl.G.3s. Narrow entrance 100m, approach on 345°.

Berthing Finger pontoons near YC fuel and showers (Not available in 2010).

Anchorage
• Inside harbour, in bay N of E mole, or alongside new jetty on E side of bay. Water and diesel at N end of W mole. Little room, buoy anchor.
• On N side of peninsula in 3–5m at Peniche de Cima. Open to N, and to swell from NW.
• SE of Ilha Berlenga near LtHo Fl(3)20s in 15m.

☎/VHF 262 781 153, VHF 62.

CASCAIS

Charts BA 3220
P 25R07, P 27504
Imray C49
HW Lisboa –0030

MHWS	MHWN	MLWN	MLWS
3·5m,	2·7m	1·4m	0·7m

Port of refuge. Cheap and frequent trains to Lisbon.

Approach As for Lisboa and Rio Tejo.

Entrance Three S card Lt buoys MC1, 2, and 3 guard the mole enclosing marina. Clear R can buoy Fl.R.4s before entering marina.

Berthing In marina. Reception to stb on entry below marina office.

Anchorage N of marina entrance on 5m contour outside moorings, open to SE.

☎/VHF 214 824 857, VHF 09.

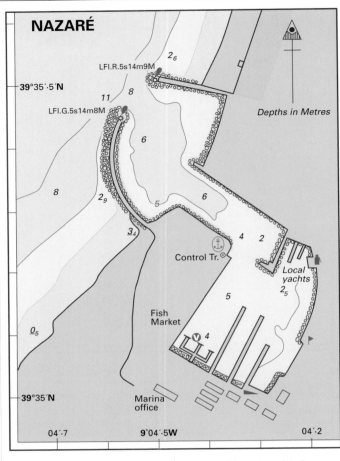

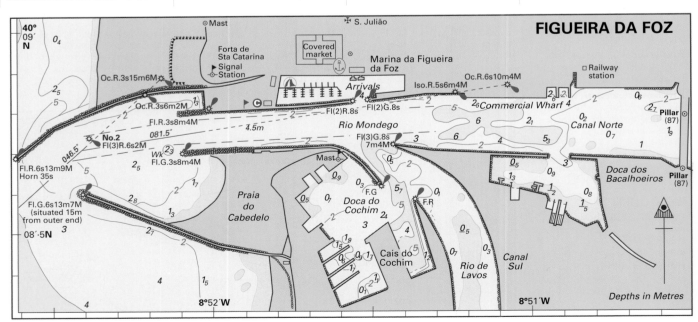

SPAIN AND PORTUGAL

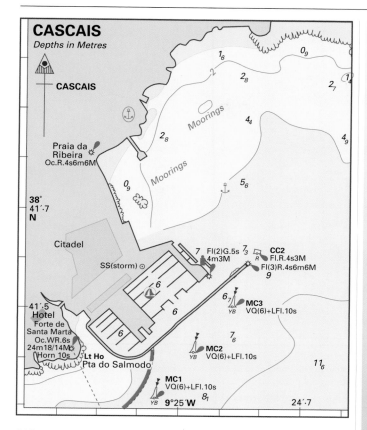

CASCAIS
Depths in Metres

CASCAIS

Moorings

Moorings

Praia da Ribeira
Oc.R.4s6m6M

38°
41′.7
N

Citadel

SS(storm)

7 Fl(2)G.5s
4m3M
CC2
Fl.R.4s3M
Fl(3)R.4s6m6M
9

MC3
VQ(6)+LFl.10s
YB

41′.5
Hotel
Forte de
Santa Marta
Oc.WR.6s
24m18/14M
Horn 10s
Lt Ho
Pta do Salmodo

MC2
VQ(6)+LFl.10s
YB

11₆

MC1
VQ(6)+LFl.10s
YB
8₁
9°25′W
24′.7

Charts for
Spain and Portugal

www.imray.com

SPAIN AND PORTUGAL

LISBOA AND RIO TEJO

Charts BA 3221, 3222, 3220;
Imray C49;
P 26305, 26306, 26307, 25R07

HW Lisboa HW

MHWS	MHWN	MLWN	MLWS
3·8m	3·0m	1·5m	0·5m

A great historically interesting maritime and capital city, with international and national air, rail and bus connections. Tidal streams in river 2–3kn at springs, more after heavy rain. In strong SW winds, enter only on flood.

Approach From N identify Cabo da Roca conspic LtHo Fl(4)18s, 26M NW of Lisbon, Cabo Raso Fl(3)9s and Guia Iso.WR.2s. From S, Cabo Espichel Fl.4s, 26M from Lisboa, TSS 9M to W of Cabo da Roca.

Entrance Steer between conspic Fort Bugio Fl.G.5s on a sandbank to stb and Fort São Julião Oc.R.5s to port. By night Gibalta Oc.R.3s and Esteiro Oc.R.6s give Ldg Lts 047° between Bugio and São Julião. Keep well on to Gibalta before turning upriver.

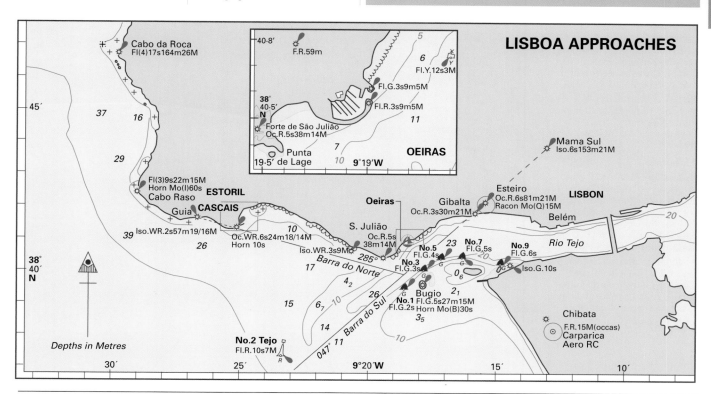

LISBOA APPROACHES

Cabo da Roca
Fl(4)17s164m26M

40·8′
F.R.59m

6
Fl.Y.12s3M

38°
40·5′
N

Fl.G.3s9m5M

Fl.R.3s9m5M

11

Mama Sul
Iso.6s153m21M

Forte de São Julião
Oc.R.5s38m14M

OEIRAS

7

10
Punta
19·5′ de Lage
9°19′W

45′

37

16

Fl(3)9s22m15M
Horn Mo(I)60s
Cabo Raso
ESTORIL

29

Guia
Iso.WR.2s57m19/16M

39

Oc.WR.6s24m18/14M
Horn 10s
CASCAIS

Iso.WR.3s9M

26

10

Esteiro
Oc.R.6s81m21M
Racon Mo(Q)15M

LISBON

Gibalta
Oc.R.3s30m21M

Belém

Oeiras

S. Julião
Oc.R.5s
38m14M

285°

23

No.5
Fl.G.4s
G

No.7
Fl.G.5s

No.9
Fl.G.6s

Iso.G.10s

Rio Tejo

20

Barra do Norte

17

No.3
Fl.G.3s

0·6

4₂

Bugio

2₁

Chibata
F.R.15M(occas)
Carparica
Aero RC

15

6₇

26

10

No.1
Fl.G.5s27m15M
Fl.G.2s Horn Mo(B)30s

3₅

14

Barra do Sul

047° 11

No.2 Tejo
Fl.R.10s7M

Depths in Metres

38°
40′
N

10

30′

25′

9°20′W

15′

10′

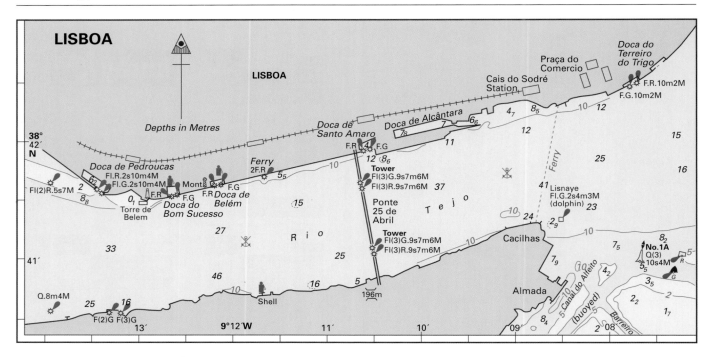

Berthing There are four harbours on N bank of river of interest to visiting yachts. All have cross currents at entrance.

• Oerias Marina with good facilities. Fuel. Rly to Lisbon (12km). ☎ 214 401 510, VHF 09.

• Doca de Belém, in 3m, 4ca E of Bom Sucesso, just past conspic floodlit Monument to the Discoverers. Reserved for local yachts but some spaces for visitors.

Water and diesel on fuelling pontoon. YC, showers, telephone. Travel-lift. Scrubbing grid. ☎ 213 922 203, VHF 12.

• Doca de Alcântara. Lifting br at entrance, currently fixed open for yachts, but if not call VHF 12 for opening times. Water and electricity on pontoons but no fuel (*See Doca de Belém earlier*). Excellent security but high deposit for magnetic card for entry and exit system ☎ 213 922 048.

• Marina Parque das Naçoes on W bank 1·5M downstream of Ponte Vasco de Gama. All facilities ☎ 218 949 066, VHF 09.

Anchorage

• Canal do Montijo. Round Ponta de Cacilhas 1½M E of suspension br and steer 108° for buoyed Canal da Cuf. After 1M the buoyed Canal do Montijo leads off at 073°. No landing at military airfield.

• Seixal. As above but turn S into Canal do Alfeite, and Canal do Barreiro and Canal do Seixal. Anchor clear of channel. Ferry and bus to Lisboa.

VHF Port VHF 64.

SETÚBAL

Charts BA 3635, 3636, 3259, 3260;
Imray C49;
P 25R08, 24204
HW Lisboa −0015

MHWS	MHWN	MLWN	MLWS
3·5m	2·7m	1·3m	0·5m

New marina within busy industrial port.

Approach Attempt entry only on flood in fine weather. Identify No.2 R Lt bn Fl(2)R.10s, Racon at SW entrance to buoyed channel. Keep at least 5ca clear of shore.

Entrance Between R Lt bn No.2 Fl(2)R.10s Racon B (−···) and Lt buoy No.1 Fl.G.3s. Ldg Lts on 040°, front Iso.Y.6s on entrance to fish hbr, rear Iso.Y.6s. Keep to N side of channel off Forte de Ontao. Beware car ferries leaving berth facing marina entrance.

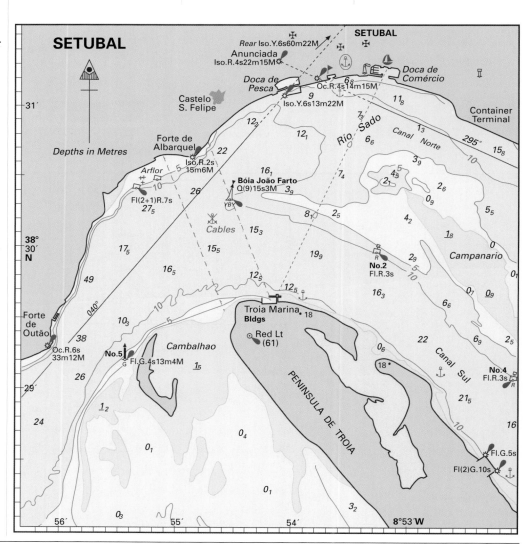

Anchorages

• SE of Castelo de S Filipe (conspic), in 10–12m.

• Off YC basin (*see Facilities, below*).

• In S winds, shift to E side of ferry berth at Punta do Adoxe on Peninsula de Troia.

Berthing

• **Setubal** in Doca de Comércio. Reception on central hammerhead, report to office near security gate. Visitors' berths scarce. Clube Nautico de Setúbal overlooks small basin to W of marina. Supermarket, fish and produce markets nearby. Buses and trains to Lisboa. International airport 35km.

• **Troia** marina on S side of river. Reception to stb on entry.

①/VHF 265 499 333, VHF 09.

SINES

Charts BA 3224
Imray C50
P 24204, 26408, 25R09, 24205

HW Lisboa –0040

MHWS	MHWN	MLWN	MLWS
3·4m	2·6m	1·4m	0·6m

A new port and oil terminal, well protected except from SW, surrounds the old fishing hbr. Interesting old town, birthplace of Vasco da Gama.

Approach 1½M to N is Cabo de Sines Fl(2)15s.

Entrance From N keep 1M offshore and leave to port R pillar buoy Fl.R.3s off unlit end of submerged breakwater. From S the entrance is wide. At night a variety of sectored lights lead into hbr and may confuse. Ldg

Lts front Iso.R.6s rear Oc.R.5·6s bearing 358° on inner pier.

Anchorage

• Off Praia Vasco da Gama, leaving channels to Porto de Pesca and marina free.

Berthing Marina on E side of hbr. Berth at hammerhead of fuel pontoon and report to the office.

Facilities Chandlery and repairs in fish dock. Camping Gaz in town. Groceries some 2km walk from marina, closer by dinghy (land on beach).

①/VHF Marina 269 860 612, VHF 09; Port VHF 11, 13.

LAGOS

Charts BA 89, 91;
P 24206, 25R11
Imray C50

HW Lisboa –0050

MHWS	MHWN	MLWN	MLWS
3·4m	2·6m	1·4m	0·6m

Situated 25M E of C St Vincent, a popular and well-furnished marina, with convenient rail connection to Faro airport.

Approach Find Pta da Piedade which features a Y LtHo tr (Fl.7s) with conspic palm trees either side. Hbr entrance is marked by two moles Fl.R.6s & Fl(2)G.6s.

Entrance Straightforward up 3m dredged channel, past fishing hbr, moor to reception pontoon to stb just before lifting br. Little turning room, beware onshore wind with ebb tide. Call VHF 09 to open br.

Berthing Report to reception. Finger pontoons. Good facilities. Fuel by reception. Washing machines. Provisioning close.

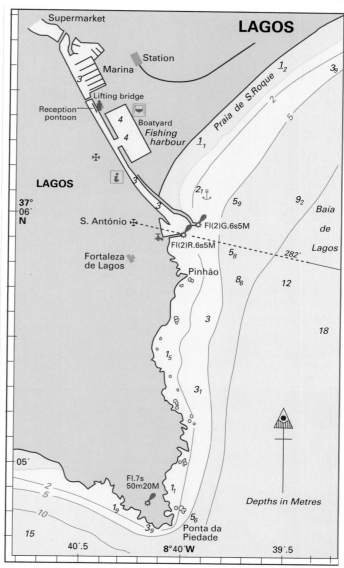

Good yard for storage and all repairs. Free Wi-Fi. Good security. English widely spoken. Weather forecast on notice board, also broadcast on VHF 12, in Portuguese and English, 1000 and 1600 during high season.

①/VHF Marina 282 770 210, VHF 09; Port VHF 11.

PORTIMÃO

Charts BA 83;
P 25R11, 24206
Imray C50

HW Lisboa –0050

MHWS	MHWN	MLWN	MLWS
3·3m	2·6m	1·4m	0·7m

A busy fishing port and resort town on the Algarve coast.

Approach Ponta da Piedade LtHo Fl.7s is 7½M to W. Alfanzina LtHo Fl(2)15s is 4½M to E.

Entrance Ponta do Altar LtHo LFl.5s is ½M to E of hbr entrance. Conspic communications tr just E of entrance. Pass between W mole Fl.R.5s and E mole Fl.G.5s on Ldg Lts 021°, front Iso.R.6s rear Iso.R.6s Ldg to port-hand buoy Fl.R.4s and buoyed channel. If

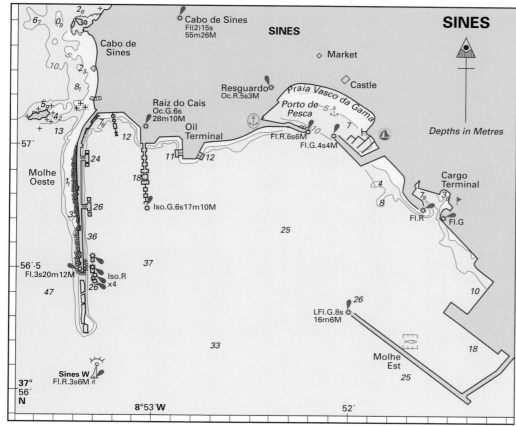

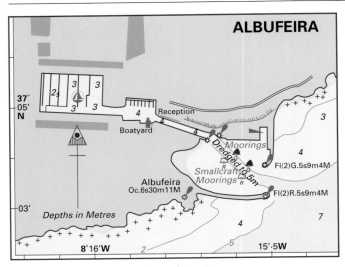

ALBUFEIRA

Charts BA 89; P 24206, 25R11
Imray C50

HW Lisboa –0050

MHWS	MHWN	MLWN	MLWS
3·5m	2·7m	1·5m	0·7m

A marina within a purpose built resort. Good shelter and facilities.

Approach Approximately 315° to enter between the sea walls of the hbr.

Entrance E mole with tr (hor G and W stripes, Fl(2)G). W mole with tr (hor R and W, Fl(2)R).

After passing through the sea walls, proceed along the navigational channel until the entrance to the marina channel (indicated by two cylindrical tr bns with wide G and W stripes to stb, R and W stripes to port). The channel is dredged to 4m.

Berthing The reception quay is situated at the end of the channel on the stb side. There are 475 berths for vessels up to 26m.

Facilities Water, power, fuel, ice, travel-lift, boatyard, pump out.

☎/VHF 289 514 282, Call *Marina de Albufeira* on VHF 09.

VILAMOURA

Charts BA 89;
Imray C50;
P 25R11, 24206, 25R12

HW Lisboa –0050

MHWS	MHWN	MLWN	MLWS
3·6m	2·8m	1·5m	0·7m

A well-developed marina with good facilities, including laying-up. English spoken. Formalities will be observed strictly. Exit at night not possible.

Approach Vilamoura Lt Fl.5s17m19M on control tr of marina.

Entrance Between W molehead Fl.R.4s and E molehead Fl.G.4s. In strong winds and swell seas may break at LW near W molehead. Width between moles 100m. Steer for entrance to inner basin 60m wide and moor to first pontoon to port alongside control tr to obtain clearance.

Facilities Diesel, repairs, chandler, scrubbing grid, hoist,

entering at night anchor at the first anchorage given below until daylight. Strong tidal streams but room to manœuvre in marina.

Berthing Reception at N end of marina. Finger pontoons, well sheltered. Good facilities. Wi-Fi (charged), free Ethernet connection. Limited provisioning at marina.

Anchorage
• Inside the E mole, clear of rocks along mole.
• Off Ferragudo on E shore in 3m mud. Supplies at Ferragudo. 1M from town quay for landing at Portimão.

☎/VHF Marina 282 400 680, VHF 09.

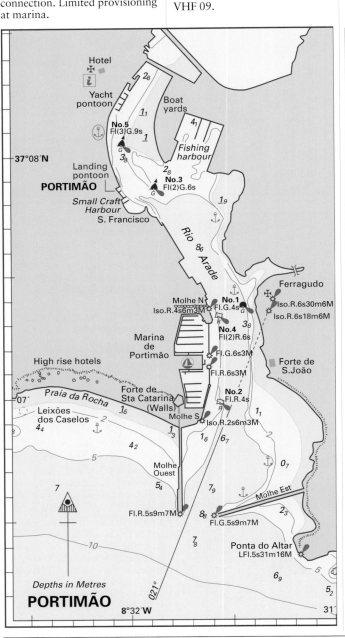

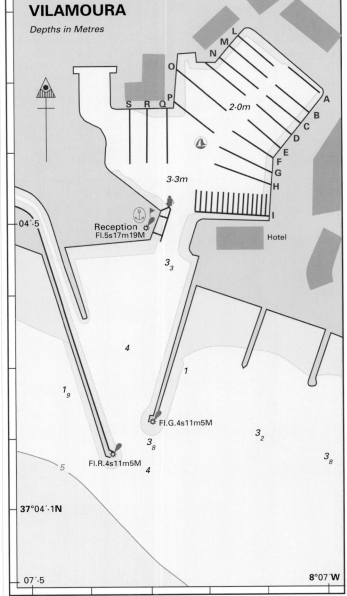

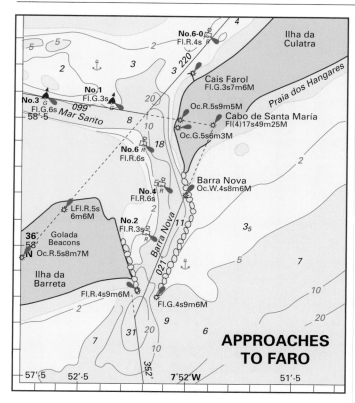

APPROACHES
TO FARO

crane, Camping Gaz and butane refills. YC next to marina office. International airport at Faro, ½ to 1hr by taxi/bus.

☎/VHF 289 310 560, VHF 09.

FARO AND OLHÂO

Charts BA 89; Imray C19, C50
P 25R12, 26311

HW Lisboa −0040

MHWS	MHWN	MLWN	MLWS
−0·4m	−0·4m	−0·1m	0·0m

The Faro lagoon has extensive and attractive anchorages, access to the regional capital, Faro, and charming Olhâo, yards in Faro and Olhâo, and two marinas in Olhâo.

Approach Identify Cabo de Santa Maria lighthouse Fl(4)17s. Approach from the SE quadrant to avoid the shoals W of entrance, extending nearly 1M offshore.

Entrance Breakwater ends are lit. Access at all states of the tide, although the ebb runs strongly and can be dangerous with onshore wind or swell. Once inside the breakwaters, the channel is buoyed. From No.6 either:

• Anchor about 2ca N of No.1 in the Canal De Faro to await favourable tide or daylight
• Follow the buoyed Canal De Faro W, then NW

• Follow the buoyed Canal De Olhâo NE.

Anchorages Numerous, including:

• 2ca N of buoy No.1, as noted above.
• Canal De Faro between buoys No.19 and No.22, for access to Faro.
• N of Culatra, anywhere in the channel N and E of the fishing harbour at Arraiaís.
• Olhâo between the two marinas in front of the market, room for four or five yachts.
• Olhâo, E of fishing harbour, clear of channel on N side.

Berthing Nothing in Faro. The E marina in Olhâo sometimes has space for short visits.

TAVIRA

Charts BA 89; Imray C19, C50
P 25R12, 24206

HW Lisboa −0035

MHWS	MHWN	MLWN	MLWS
3·1m	2·4m	1·4m	0·4m

Despite development around it, the centre of Tavira and the countryside around are as attractive as any in the Algarve.

Approach and Entrance Identify W breakwater Fl(1)R.2·5s. Enter between breakwaters on 325°, avoiding the shoal E.

Anchorages

• About 4ca into the river, where the main channel turns W. Tide runs hard, and there is much traffic.
• Follow the channel W, past the shallow channel leading N to Tavira itself, to anchor W of moorings. Land and find water at YC.
• Continue about 1·4M beyond YC along the beaconed channel SW then W, to anchor just below Santa Luzia.

The coast between the Río Guadalquivir and Tarifa is still comparatively undeveloped. Tunny nets are sometimes laid, from May to September, stretching 6–7M out to sea at right angles to the coast. Towards the Strait of Gibraltar the winds tend to be either easterly (more common in summer) or westerly. There may be an E-going current at the Strait of 2–3kn. Tidal streams can also run up to 3kn at springs. TSS in the Strait: the S limit of the inshore passage is only 1½M off Tarifa Lt. The range of tides at Cádiz is approximately 2·9m at springs and 1·3m at neaps.

Passage charts

Charts BA 89, 93, 142; S 44B, 44C, 4453A, 443B	
Principal lights	*BA No*
Vila Real Fl.6·5s51m26M	2246
El Rompido Fl(2)10s42m24M	2312
Picacho Fl(2+4)30s50m25M	2320
Chipiona (Pta del Perro) Fl.10s67m25M	2351
Castillo de San Sebastián Fl(2)10s37m25M Horn Mo(N)20s (− ·)	2362
Cabo Trafalgar Fl(2+1)15s49m22M	2406
Tarifa Fl(3)WR.10s41m26/18M Mo(O)60s (− − −)	2414
Europa Point, Gibraltar Iso.10s49m19M+Oc.R.10s49m 19M+F.R.44m15M Horn 20s	2438

VILA REAL DE SANTO ANTONIO AND AYAMONTE

Chart BA 89; S441A; Imray C50; P 25R12, 24206

HW Lisboa +0010

MHWS	MHMN	MLWN	MLWS
3·1m	2·4m	1·4m	0·4m

Vila Real (Portugal) and Ayamonte overlook each other across the River Guadiana.

Approach From the W Vila Real can be identified by the lt ho in the town (Fl.6.5s) and by the conspic buildings at Monte Gordo about 2M to the W. From the E the resort at Ilha de Canela can be identified about 2M E of the entrance. Avoid shoals to E of River Guardiana entrance, which extend over 1M from shore.

Entrance The entrance has approx. 2m at LW and can be dangerous when strong onshore winds are against an ebb tide. The outer entrance of the channel is marked by two buoys Fl.R.4s and

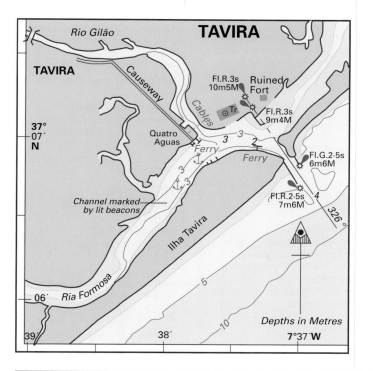

TAVIRA

SPAIN AND PORTUGAL

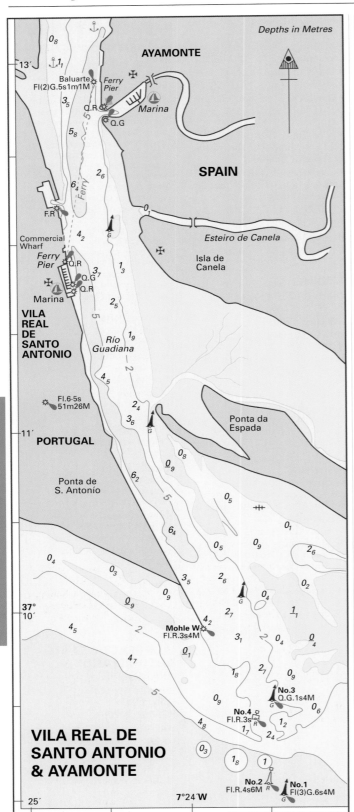

VILA REAL DE SANTO ANTONIO & AYAMONTE

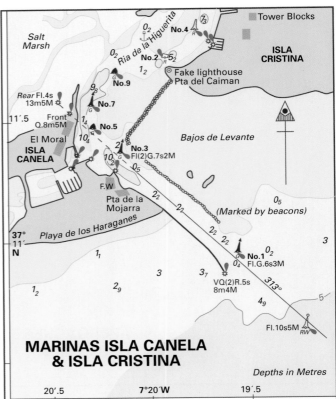

MARINAS ISLA CANELA & ISLA CRISTINA

Depths in Metres

ISLA CRISTINA

Chart BA 89; Imray C50

HW Lisboa HW

MHWS	MHWN	HLWN	MLWS
3·1m	2·4m	1·4m	0·4m

Pleasant town and small, well protected marina with the usual facilities (including haul out and repairs). Shops, bars and restaurants in the town.

Approach From the W avoid shoals between River Guadiana and River Carreras that extend over 1M from the shore. Ría de la Higuerita can be identified by the new resort on Isla Canela.

Entrance The entrance is marked by Lt buoys VQ(2)R.5s and Fl.G.2s. Avoid shallows either side. The W side of the channel has a sea wall and the E, a training wall. Ldg lts 313°. The channel in the ria is buoyed.

Berthing The marina has pontoon berths (max LOA 15m). The max. depth in the marina is quoted as 2m. Some swell from fishing vessels. No fuel.

☎ 959 34 35 01.

There is a marina at the resort on Isla de Canela. Fuel.

☎ 959 47 90 00.

Anchorage

• With shallow draft, most comfortable and convenient is 2ca NW of entrance to Isla Cristina marina.

• 5ca N of marina in entrance to Cano Canela.

PUNTA UMBRIA

Charts BA 90; Imray C19, C50

HW Lisboa +0010

MHWS	MHWN	MLWN	MLWS
3·7m	2·4m	1·4m	0·2m

A pleasant town, with three marinas and ample space for anchorage. Good general chandlers.

Approach Identify the fairway buoy, whose position varies from time to time, but lies in about 5m. It can be approached safely along the coast from either direction.

Entrance Possible HW ±0300 in good conditions. Follow the buoyed channel.

Anchorage Upstream of the third marina, and the town, on W side, in depth to suit yacht. Convenient landing.

Berthing There are three marinas:

• Real Club Marítimo.

• Puerto Deportivo de Punta Umbría – This EPPA marina has been extended.

• Club Deportivo Náutico Punta Umbria.

MAZAGON

Chart BA 73; Imray C50

HW Lisboa +0007

MHWS	MHWN	MLWN	MLWS
3·7m	2·4m	1·4m	0·2m

Large, well protected marina with usual facilities (including haul out and repairs) and nearby good beaches. Short walk to shops in the town.

Approach The Ria de Huelva can be identified by the Picacho LtHo Fl(2+4)30s.

Fl(3)G.6s either side of which are shoals. The inner entrance is marked by Fl.R.5s at the outer end of the sea wall. There are shoals on the E side.

Berthing and Anchorage Finger pontoons at both marinas. Strong tidal stream through outer Vila Real berths, little turning room inside. Good facilities and provisioning at both. Free Wi-Fi at Vila Real. Good anchoring off both, show anchor light and ball.

Facilities At Vila Real, modern boatyard. No fuel in Ayamonte. www.marinaguadiana.com
☎ /VHF 281 542 069
Ayamonte 959 32 16 94, VHF 09 (both).

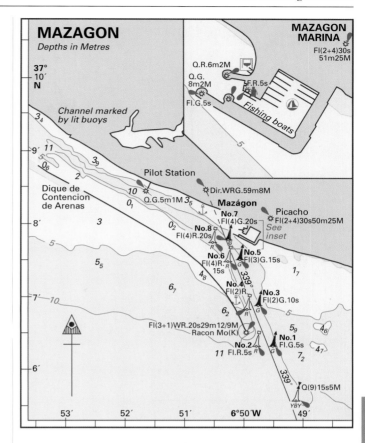

MAZAGON
Depths in Metres

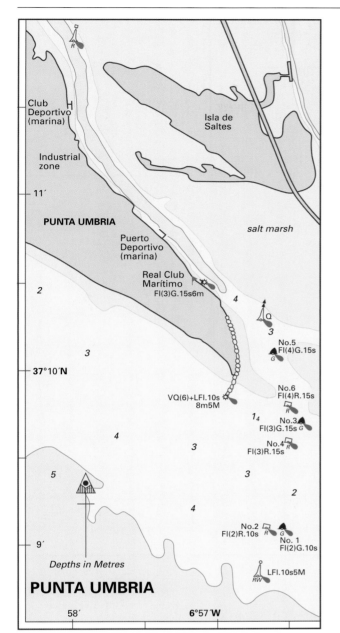

PUNTA UMBRIA

Entrance The entrance to the ria is well buoyed and protected from the E by a large breakwater. Entry should be possible in nearly all conditions. The marina is on the E side of the ria with its entrance facing NW (marked by Q.R. and Q.G.).

Berthing and Anchorage
Reception pontoon below marina office to port, shortly after marina entrance.

☎ 959 52 44 90.

It is possible to anchor just NW of the marina entrance clear of local moorings. Exposed to the NW.

CHIPIONA
Chart BA 93; S442, 443; Imray C50

HW Lisboa HW

MHWS	MHWN	MLWN	MLWS
3·2m	2·5m	1·3m	0·4m

Pleasant town with good beaches and marina. All facilities, including haul out, laundry and repairs. Good base to depart for Sevilla (approximately 50M up the River Guadalquivir).

Approach Chipiona is identifiable from the large lighthouse (Fl.10s) in the town. From N keep well clear of shoals N of the entrance to the Guadalquivir river that are marked by W card Lt buoy Q(9)10s and conspic wreck to E. From S keep W of card marker Q(9)15s marking Salmedina drying patch.

Entrance Leave No.2 Fl(2)R.7s and No.4 Fl(3)R.11s buoys to port and then turn 090° to stb into the marina entrance Fl(4)R.11s & Fl(2)G.10s.

Berthing and Anchorage
Reception pontoon below marina office to port, shortly after marina entrance. Fuel at reception. Good facilities.

☎ 956 37 38 44.

It is possible to anchor in the River Guadalquivir W of Bonanza out of main channel and on the west side. The tidal stream can run strongly but the holding is good.

☎ 956 373 844.

CÁDIZ AND CÁDIZ BAY
Charts BA 86; S 443A, 443B, 4430; Imray C50

HW Lisboa −0100

MHWS	MHWN	MLWN	MLWS
3·3m	2·5m	1·2m	0·5m

Approach From N pass 2M off Pta del Chipiona Fl.10s. A buoy Fl(2)R.9s marks Bajo El Quemado at 36°36′N 6°24′W. From S keep more than ¾M off conspic Castillo de San Sebastián Fl(2)10s.

Entrance The main lighted channel into Cádiz lies close N of bn tr Las Puercas (unlit). Make for RW fairway buoy L.Fl.10s at 36°34′N 6°20′W and follow buoyed channel. From S make well up to No.1 buoy Fl.G.3s before turning into channel, dredged 13m.

Berthing Cádiz Mole heads to main hbr Fl.G.3s and Fl.R.2s. Enter on W side and turn to stb into marina Puerto America

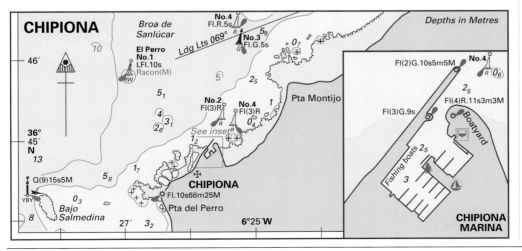

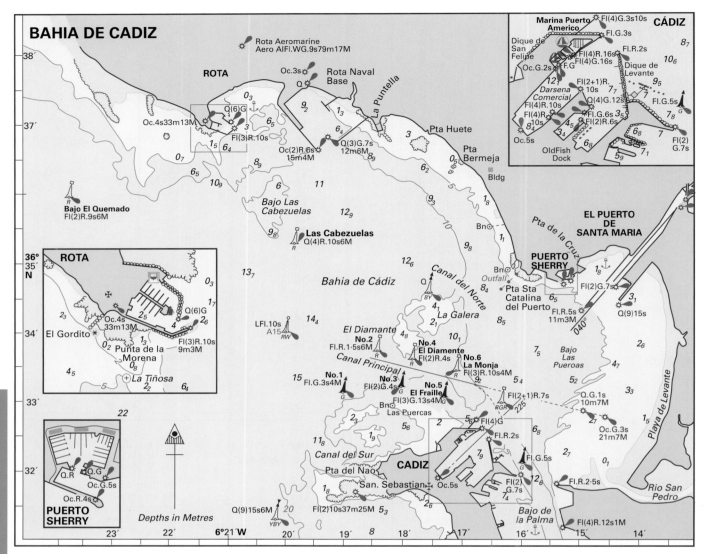

between heads Fl(4)RG.16s. Five pontoons with finger pontoons for each berth. Good facilities. Fuel available by appointment at YC; good restaurant there. Spanish charts available from Instituto Hidrografico, Tolosa Latour 1, Cadiz. Take passport for entry.

☎/VHF Marina 956 223 666, VHF 09; Port VHF 14, 11, 12.
Rota Marina 1M W of Naval Base. Entrance faces NE and shoals under 2m up to 5ca off. Enter between moles F.G and Fl(3)R.10s. Reception on fuel pontoon by entrance. Fuel,

boatyard, travel hoist and laundry. Bus to airport.
☎ 956 84 00 69.

Puerto Sherry A large well-founded marina to NW of training walls of Puerto Santa Maria. Conspic W tr at end of S mole Oc.R.4s. Inner lights on N

mole reported to be difficult to see. All facilities in marina including petrol and diesel, 50-tonne travel-lift and major repair facilities.

☎ 956 870 103.
Puerto Santa Maria At night Ldg Lts Iso.G.4s back, Q.G

Digital Charts

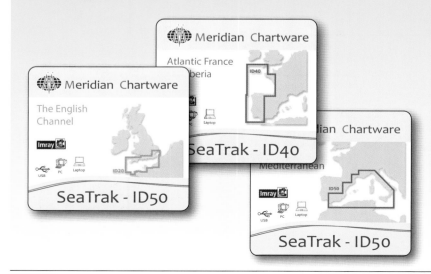

Imray Digital Charts are electronic editions of standard Imray charts published on USB sticks in PC format with integrated GPS plotter software.

The plotter enables high-resolution raster images of Imray charts to be used for simple navigation. The clear interface provides an ideal starting point for electronic navigation and provides the navigator with all the essential tools for using Imray charts on a PC.

Each Chart Pack comes with on line corrections and upgrades for a year.

Imray Digital Charts are published by Meridian Chartware as Meridian Digital Charts who will provide full support to users at www.meridian-chartware.co.uk.

Orders can be supplied direct from:

www.imray.com

or Meridian Chartware:
www.meridian-chartware.co.uk
50 Unthank Road, Norwich, Norfolk, NR2 2RF, UK
☎ +44 (0) 1603 216104
Fax +44 (0) 1603 765253
Email enquiries@meridian-chartware.co.uk

SPAIN AND PORTUGAL

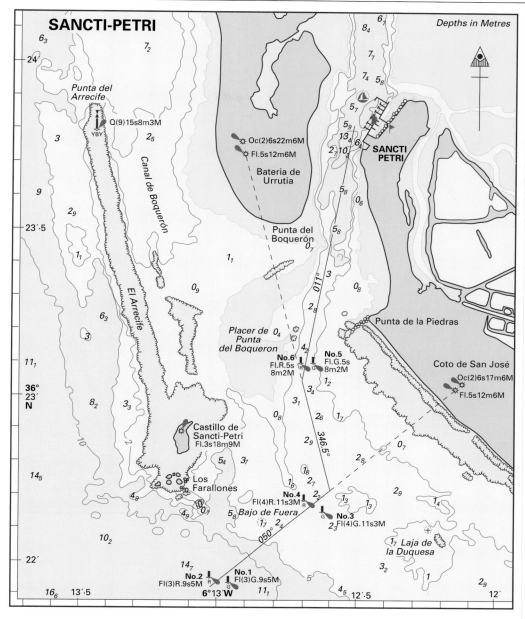

SANCTI-PETRI

Depths in Metres

Punta del Arrecife
Q(9)15s8m3M
YBY

Canal de Boquerón

El Arrecife

Oc(2)6s22m6M
Fl.5s12m6M

Bateria de Urrutia

SANCTI PETRI

Punta del Boquerón

011°

Placer de Punta del Boqueron

3

No.6
Fl.R.5s
8m2M
R

No.5
Fl.G.5s
8m2M
G

Punta de la Piedras

Coto de San José

Oc(2)6s17m6M
Fl.5s12m6M

346.5°

Castillo de Sancti-Petri
Fl.3s18m9M

Los Farallones

No.4
Fl(4)R.11s3M
R

No.3
Fl(4)G.11s3M
G

Bajo de Fuera

050°

Laja de la Duquesa

No.2
Fl(3)R.9s5M
R

No.1
Fl(3)G.9s5M
G

6°13'W

12'.5

12'

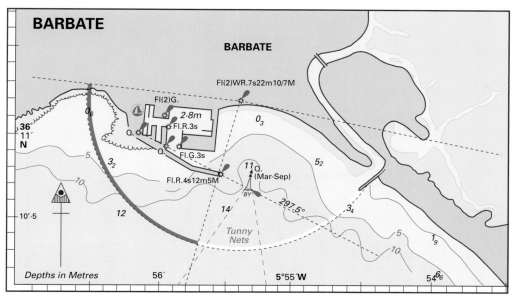

BARBATE

BARBATE

Fl(2)WR.7s22m10/7M

Fl(2)G.
2·8m
Fl.R.3s
Q.
Fl.G.3s
Fl.R.4s12m5M

Q.
(Mar-Sep)
BY

297.5°

Tunny Nets

Depths in Metres
56'
5°55'W
54'

---

front on 040°. Call YC on VHF 09 on approach for possible berth at pontoons on W side about 1M up. Possible anchorage 7ca beyond YC, just below bridge, in 3m.

Exceptional shell fish restaurant in town, passenger ferry to Cádiz.

Anchorages The following have been reported as good anchorages in suitable weather:

• Bay NE of Rota Marina.

• Bay E of Puerto Sherry.

• Bajo de la Palma, S of Cadiz hbr.

• up the Rio san Pedro, drying entrance, excellent shelter inside.

☎ 956 852 527.

SANCTI-PETRI

Chart BA 93; S 443B

HW Lisboa –0100

MHWS	MHWN	HLWN	MLWS
2·8m	2·1m	1·0m	0·4m

Delightful lagoon with good beaches, anchorage and small marina (no haul out but some mechanical repairs). Two or three restaurants. Interesting deserted fishing village. No other facilities. Bus to shops.

Approach Beware onshore swell. Choose settled weather and rising tide to avoid difficulties at the bar in the entrance.

From N pass well clear of reef extending from Punta del Arrecife Q(9)15s to Sancti Petri Castle Fl.3s. Stay at least ½M S of the castle to avoid Los Farallones rocks.

Entrance The buoys have been replaced by beacons. Pick up outer pair, and follow the channel.

Berthing and Anchorage Two small marinas, both crowded. Second marina, belonging to YC has swinging moorings which may be available to visitors.

Anchor about 5ca N of marinas in main chanel or channel branching E, to get clear of moorings.

☎ Club Nautico 956 496 169.

BARBATE

Chart BA 142; S 4441

HW Lisboa –0050

MHWS	MHWN	MLWN	MLWS
2·6m	1·7m	0·9m	0·2m

A new fishing hbr with well protected yacht marina 1M W of shallow Rio de Barbate.

Approach From W keep 3M off Cabo Trafalgar Fl(2+1)15s. From E clear the shoal Los Cabezos with conspic wreck 3M to S of Pta Paloma Oc.WR.5s. Unlit tunny nets May to September.

Entrance Steer on Ldg Lts 298°, both Q on white posts, and enter between W molehead Fl.R.4s and E molehead Fl(2)G.7s. Turn to stb round E molehead into hbr.

SPAIN AND PORTUGAL

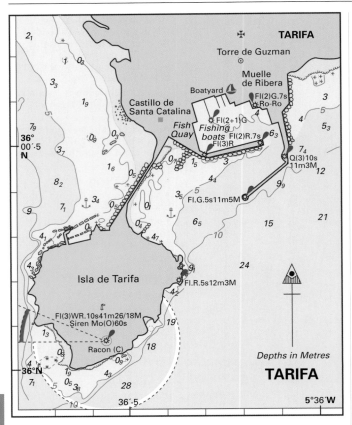

TARIFA

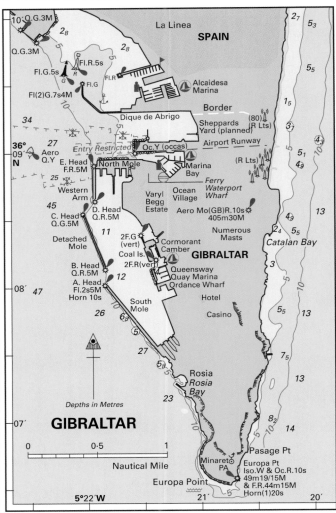

GIBRALTAR

Berthing Reception pontoon for marina on E side of hbr. Pontoon berths in two bays further W. Diesel. 30 minutes' walk to town.

☎ 956 431 907.

TARIFA

Charts BA 142; S 4450, 445B

HW Gibraltar –0038

MHWS	MHWN	MLWN	MLWS
1·4m	1·0m	0·6m	0·3m

A large fishing port 16M from Gibraltar.

Approach From W beware the shoal Los Cabezos with conspic wreck 5M to W of Tarifa, covered by R sector of conspic LtHo on Is de Tarifa Fl(3)WR.10s. From E clear Pta Carnero Fl(4)WR.20s by 1M. The S limit of the inshore passage of the TSS in the Strait of Gibraltar is 1½M to S of Tarifa LtHo. Unlit tunny nets May to September.

Entrance Steer for head of outer (E) mole Fl.G.5s of hbr on NE side of Is de Tarifa.

Anchorage Anchor E or W of causeway according to wind.

LA LINEA

Charts BA 45, 144, 1448; S 445

HW Gibraltar HW

MHWS	MHWN	MLWN	MLWS
1·0m	0·7m	0·3m	0·1m

A modern marina, now a viable alternative to Gibraltar for mooring, laying up and yard services. Nearby supermarket.

Approach As for Gibraltar.

Entrance Round the outer breakwater, Fl(2)G.7s, then inner mole with control tower.

Berthing No waiting pontoon (2011). Lie alongside mole by fuel point to visit control tower.

Anchorage Is possible inside outer breakwater, but the police sometimes tell yachts to move. Recommended to pay fee for leaving dinghy in marina.

☎ 956 02 16 60.

GIBRALTAR

Charts BA 45, 144, 1448; S 445

HW Gibraltar HW

MHWS	MHWN	MLWN	MLWS
1·0m	0·7m	0·3m	0·1m

A convenient port of call on passage to and from the Mediterranean, and a good place to fit out, repair and to lay up ashore unattended.

Approach Gibraltar Europa Point LtHo main Lt Iso.10s. Conspic buildings on reclaimed land on approach.

From April to August whales may be encountered in the Strait of Gibraltar.

Entrance Fly Q flag and report to Customs at N end of the Rock, just to the S of airfield runway. Pass round the N end of the N mole or so-called 'E' Head. Customs station flies 'Q' flag. Alternatively, go direct to Queensway Quay where you can clear customs in and out.

Berthing Marina Bay is in the N end of the hbr just S of the airport runway. It has comprehensive boat repair facilities and is close to shops and restaurants. Queensway Quay marina is in the centre of the main hbr N of Gunwharf (former RN base). It is quieter but some swell when big ships move. Queensway Quay is closed with a boom between 2100 and 0800. Probably best to anchor off La Linea if arriving between those times. Usual facilities. Diesel available.

Sheppard's Marina is closed, but chandlery in Ocean Village is still open; lifting out can be arranged. Both Queensway and Marina Bay are very full. It is possible to anchor at La Linea Bay but security is very bad, or possibly to berth against the old Customs berth. Contact by telephone or VHF before arrival.

Anchorage Immediately N of runway is not always permitted. In any case yachts must clear Customs in one of the marinas.

Facilities BA chart agent. Air services to UK.

☎/VHF Queensway Quay +350 2004 47000, Marina Bay/Ocean Village +350 2007 33000. All marinas VHF 71; Port +350 2007 7254, VHF 06, 12 .

Tides and tidal streams

Tides and Tidal Streams

Definitions

Chart Datum (CD) is the level from which the depth of water or drying height is measured and is approximately the same as Lowest Astronomical Tide (LAT). BA charts and this almanac use this datum.

Mean High Water Springs (MHWS) is the average height of Spring Tides throughout the year. Spring Tides occur about 36 hours after Full and New Moons. These are higher at the Spring and Autumn Equinoxes and lower in midsummer and winter.

Highest Astronomical Tide (HAT) is the highest level that can be expected to occur under average meteorological conditions and under any combination of astronomical conditions. In practice this is slightly higher than MHWS.

Mean High Water Neaps (MHWN), *Mean Low Water Neaps* (MLWS) and *Mean Low Water Springs* are similar averages.

Variation from the predicted height of tides

Barometric Pressure A rise of 34hPA (millibars) from the average (1013) lowers the predicted height of the tide by 0·3m, a fall in pressure will cause a similar higher tide.

Wind A strong wind blowing on to a coast will cause a higher tide and an offshore wind will cause a lower one. This is very noticeable in the Baltic where tides are minimal.

Seiches The passage of an intense local depression or a line squall may set up a wave having a period from a few minutes to an hour. Some harbours are more prone to this, Fishguard and Wick are examples.

Storm surges occur in the North Sea where a constant Northerly gale causes a surge up to 2·5m. Less marked negative surges may also occur. It is prudent, not only to consider the weather, but also to allow a safe margin when anchoring or making a passage in shallow water.

High Water The time of high and low water at Standard ports may be found in the Tide Tables. It should be noted that most of these are given in Universal Time and will need correction for local time. Most European countries use European Standard Time which is UT+1 in the winter and daylight saving time which is UT+2 from the last Sunday in March to the last Sunday October. Exceptions to this are UK, Ireland and Portugal who use UT in the winter and UT+1 in the summer. It must be noted that the corrections for secondary ports are based on UT.

Direction of Stream (DS) On entering or leaving some harbours a vessel may encounter a strong tidal set in what has traditionally been called 'the Offing'. When this is significant it is noted under the title of the harbour as DS with the direction of stream usually referred to HW Dover.

Tidal range The mean spring range at Dover is 6.0m and the neap range is 3·2m. MHWS springs will take place anywhere in Europe when the Dover range is 6·0m. Larger ranges occur at the Equinoxes.

The French base their tidal calculations on the range at Brest which is converted to tidal coefficients in which the Mean Spring Range at Brest is taken as 100 (*vive eau*) and the Mean Neap Range is 45 (*morte eau*). Be careful not confuse this with HW (*pleine mer*) and LW (*basse mer*). In some French harbours the lock gates do not function when the range is very small.

Depths refer to the depth at chart datum and the height of the tide should be added to this.

Bridges, Cables and Vertical Clearances

In the UK all vertical clearances are measured above HAT. In Europe the measurement is from Mean Tidal Level which is about half way between HW and LW.

Anchoring It is customary to use about 5x the depth of chain at HW. More will needed for warp, in swell, high winds, strong tidal streams, depending on the nature of the bottom. The catenary of the anchor chain reduces snatching

Corrections to Tidal Height according to Barometric Pressure

Millibars	Correction	Millibars	Correction
963	+0·50m	1003	+0·10m
968	+0·45m	1008	+0·05m
973	+0·40m	1013	+0·00m
978	+0·35m	1018	−0·05m
983	+0·30m	1023	−0·10m
988	+0·25m	1028	−0·15m
993	+0·20m	1033	−0·20m
998	+0·15m	1038	−0·25m

Tidal heights can in theory be precisely calculated using the tidal curves for the standard ports (*see Index on page 449*) corrected when necessary by the secondary port information. Such accuracy is only occasionally required and is only valid at mean atmospheric pressure, little wind and absence of swell. The Rule of 12ths is usually sufficiently accurate for practical purposes. This says that the tide rises or falls by one-twelfth during the first and last hour of the tide, by two-twelfths during the second and fifth hours and by three-twelfths during each of the third and fourth hours. This is very accurate in ports where the curve is near normal but is unsatisfactory when it is not. Le Havre, Poole and the Solent all have a 'stand' at HW or sometimes a double HW.

Tidal Curves

From the tidal curves and the tide tables it is possible to calculate the depth of water at any time in any charted position near any standard port and with the use of secondary port corrections the same can be found. (*See following page for an example*).

Tidal Stream Charts These are copied from BA *Tidal Atlases* most of which are based on Dover and are in the following pages. The speeds are for Spring and Neap tides separated by a comma and give the speed in tenths of a knot. Thus 11, 19 is 1·1 knots at neaps and 1·9 knots at springs. It should be noted that at the equinoxes the tidal streams run faster than the spring rate in proportion to the range of tide. In some places the tides build up to a maximum and then fall off to slack water. In other places flood and ebb alternate reaching their maximum rapidly, this is most likely to take place when a tidal lagoon fills and empties through a narrow entrance.

TIDAL STREAMS AND CURVES

A craft drawing 2m anchors in Dale Bay in Milford Haven at HW in a depth of 6·4m on 9th March 2008. The charted depth shows a drying height of 1m. To calculate the times of grounding and refloating.

HW	0714	7.4m	Range of tide	7·1m
LW	1334	0.3m	Draught of vessel	2m
HW	1932	7.2m		

Drying Height at LAT from the chart is 1m but LW is 0·3 above this so the actual drying height is 0·7m.

The boat will ground when the tide has fallen 4·4m to 3·0m (draught of vessel plus drying height). To find the time when this occurs mark the points HW 7·4m and LW0·3m on the horizontal scales. Draw a line between these points. From the point at which this line intersects the vertical line representing the grounding height (3·0m) of the tide, draw a horizontal line across to the ebbing (right) side of the curve. Drop a vertical line from this point and read off the time of grounding. It helps if the times of HW, HW +1hr etc have already been written down as shown.

To find the time of refloating the oblique line must be adjusted to the next HW which is 7·2m and the horizontal line drawn to the rising (left hand) part of the curve.

If the boat moves to Solva, the times will be later and the tidal heights less. The details can be found in the Secondary ports list beneath the tidal curve for Milford Haven but need to be extrapolated for the point in the tidal cycle.

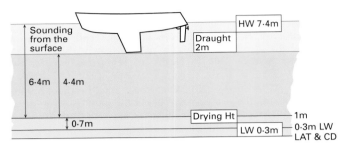

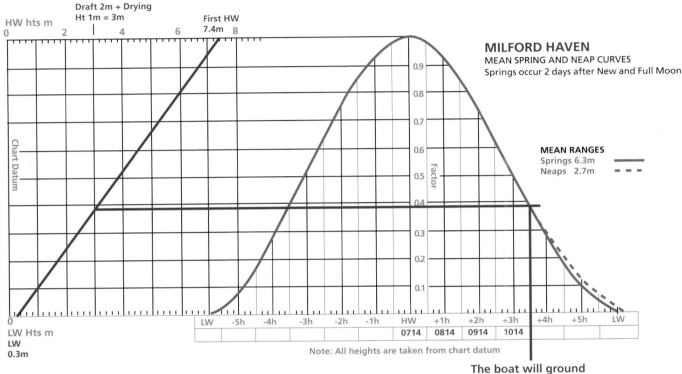

MILFORD HAVEN
MEAN SPRING AND NEAP CURVES
Springs occur 2 days after New and Full Moon

MEAN RANGES
Springs 6.3m
Neaps 2.7m

Note: All heights are taken from chart datum

The boat will ground at 1044 UT

5 HRS BEFORE HW DOVER

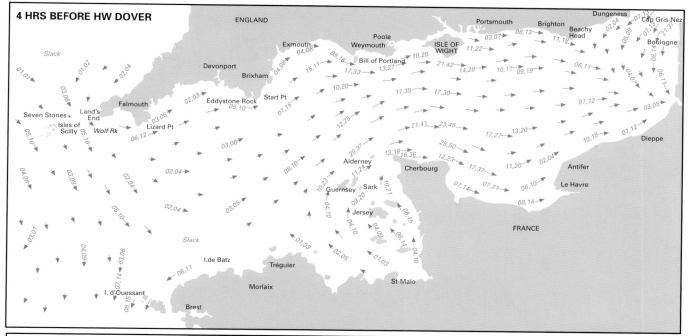

4 HRS BEFORE HW DOVER

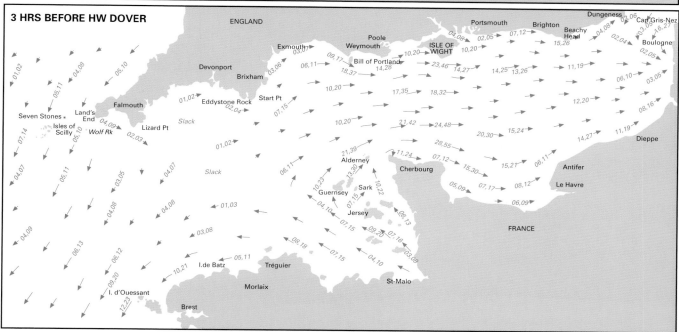

3 HRS BEFORE HW DOVER

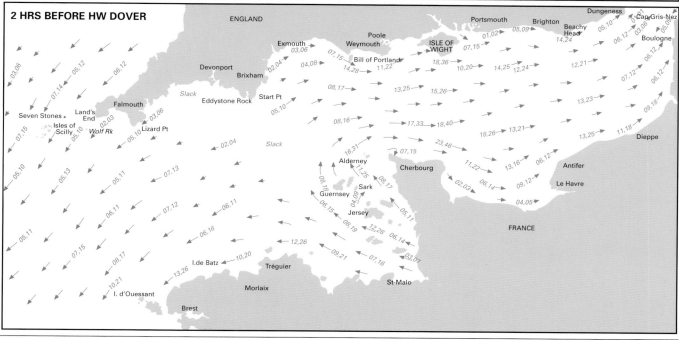

2 HRS BEFORE HW DOVER

TIDAL STREAMS AND CURVES

TIDAL STREAMS AND CURVES

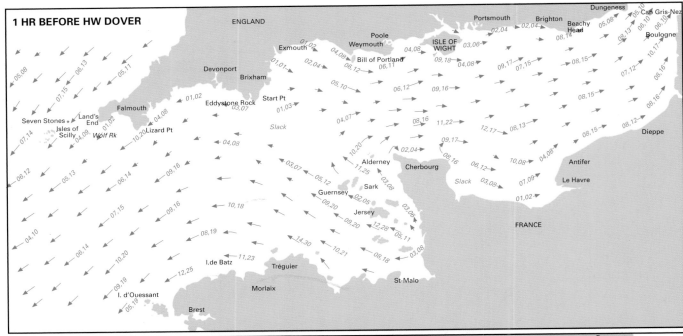

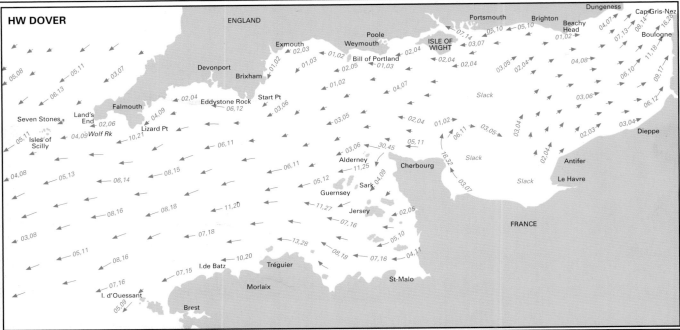

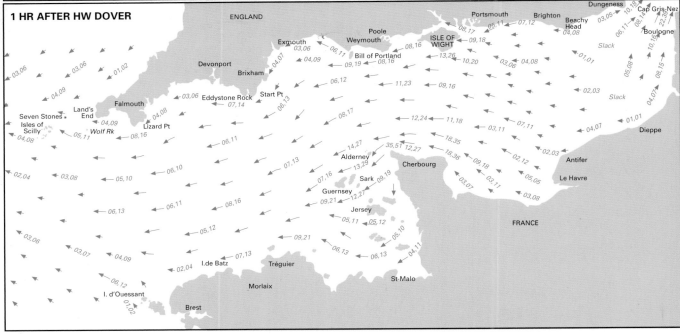

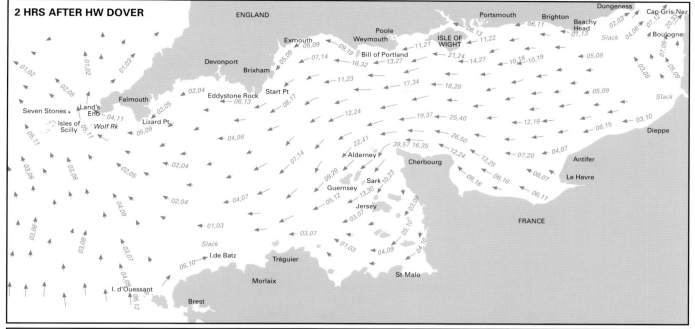

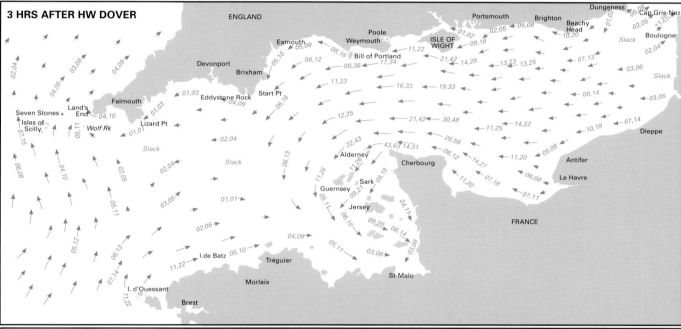

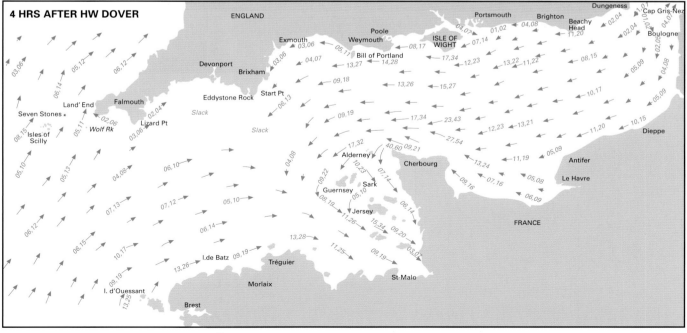

TIDAL STREAMS AND CURVES

TIDAL STREAMS AND CURVES

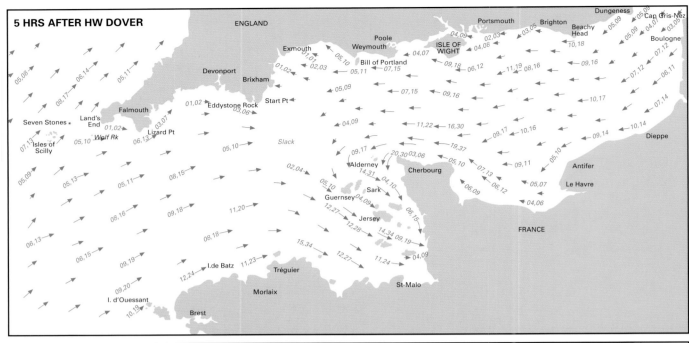

5 HRS AFTER HW DOVER

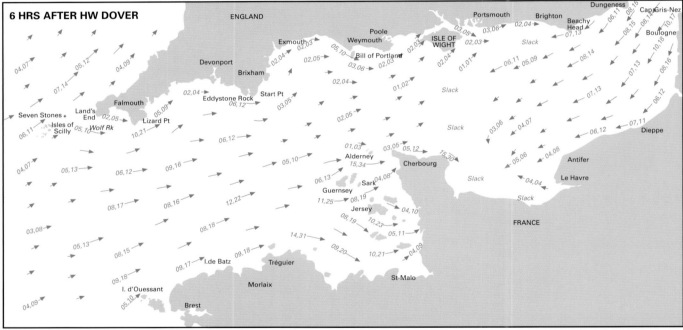

6 HRS AFTER HW DOVER

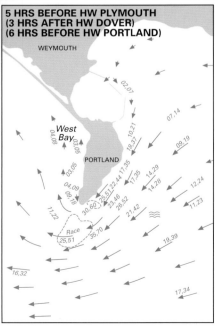

5 HRS BEFORE HW PLYMOUTH
(3 HRS AFTER HW DOVER)
(6 HRS BEFORE HW PORTLAND)

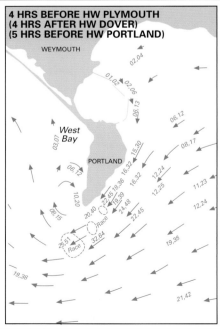

4 HRS BEFORE HW PLYMOUTH
(4 HRS AFTER HW DOVER)
(5 HRS BEFORE HW PORTLAND)

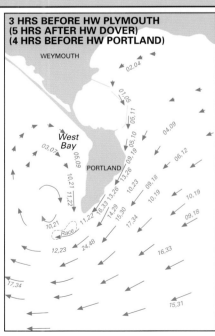

3 HRS BEFORE HW PLYMOUTH
(5 HRS AFTER HW DOVER)
(4 HRS BEFORE HW PORTLAND)

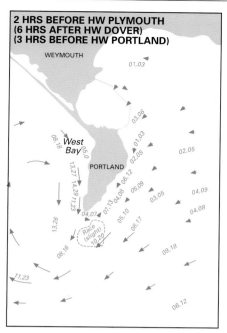

**2 HRS BEFORE HW PLYMOUTH
(6 HRS AFTER HW DOVER)
(3 HRS BEFORE HW PORTLAND)**

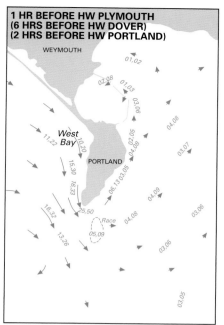

**1 HR BEFORE HW PLYMOUTH
(6 HRS BEFORE HW DOVER)
(2 HRS BEFORE HW PORTLAND)**

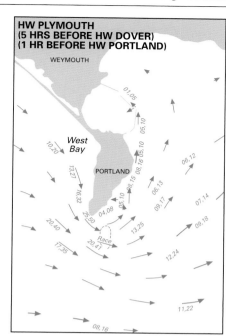

**HW PLYMOUTH
(5 HRS BEFORE HW DOVER)
(1 HR BEFORE HW PORTLAND)**

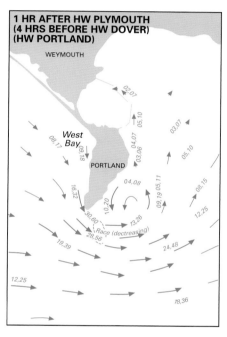

**1 HR AFTER HW PLYMOUTH
(4 HRS BEFORE HW DOVER)
(HW PORTLAND)**

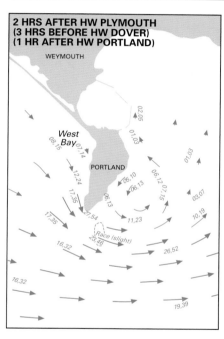

**2 HRS AFTER HW PLYMOUTH
(3 HRS BEFORE HW DOVER)
(1 HR AFTER HW PORTLAND)**

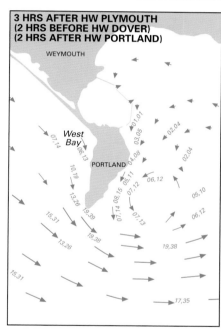

**3 HRS AFTER HW PLYMOUTH
(2 HRS BEFORE HW DOVER)
(2 HRS AFTER HW PORTLAND)**

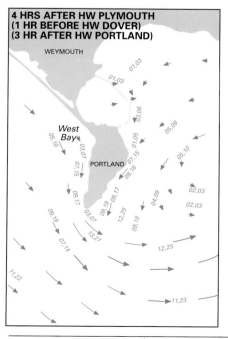

**4 HRS AFTER HW PLYMOUTH
(1 HR BEFORE HW DOVER)
(3 HR AFTER HW PORTLAND)**

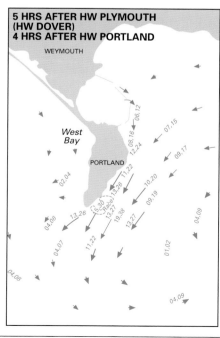

**5 HRS AFTER HW PLYMOUTH
(HW DOVER)
4 HRS AFTER HW PORTLAND**

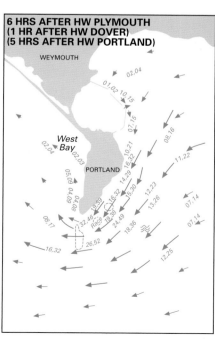

**6 HRS AFTER HW PLYMOUTH
(1 HR AFTER HW DOVER)
(5 HRS AFTER HW PORTLAND)**

TIDAL STREAMS AND CURVES

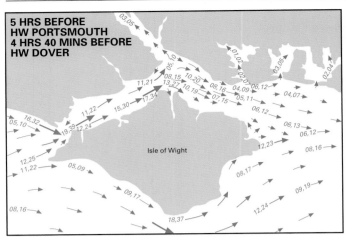

5 HRS BEFORE HW PORTSMOUTH 4 HRS 40 MINS BEFORE HW DOVER

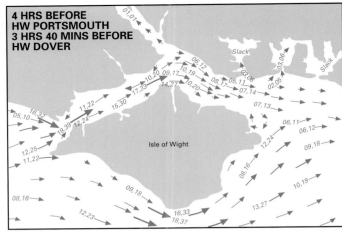

4 HRS BEFORE HW PORTSMOUTH 3 HRS 40 MINS BEFORE HW DOVER

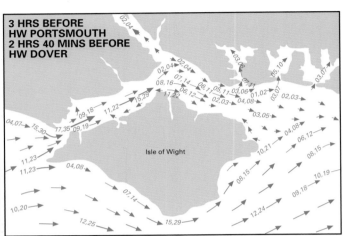

3 HRS BEFORE HW PORTSMOUTH 2 HRS 40 MINS BEFORE HW DOVER

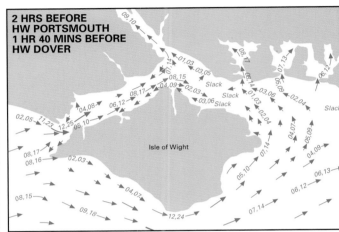

2 HRS BEFORE HW PORTSMOUTH 1 HR 40 MINS BEFORE HW DOVER

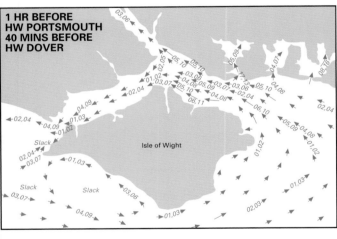

1 HR BEFORE HW PORTSMOUTH 40 MINS BEFORE HW DOVER

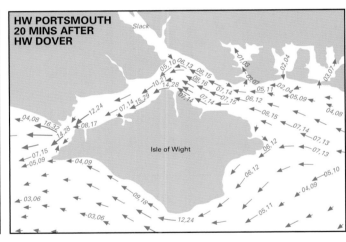

HW PORTSMOUTH 20 MINS AFTER HW DOVER

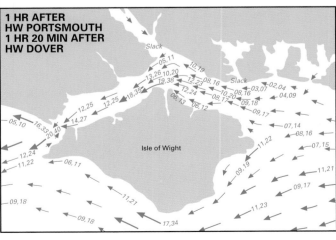

1 HR AFTER HW PORTSMOUTH 1 HR 20 MIN AFTER HW DOVER

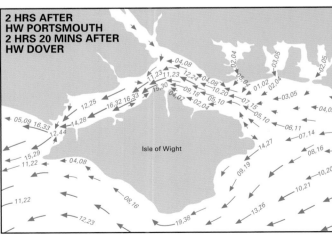

2 HRS AFTER HW PORTSMOUTH 2 HRS 20 MINS AFTER HW DOVER

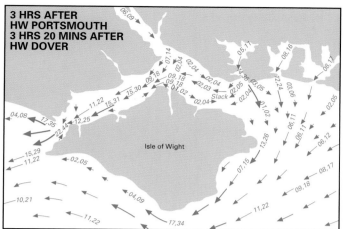

3 HRS AFTER HW PORTSMOUTH
3 HRS 20 MINS AFTER HW DOVER

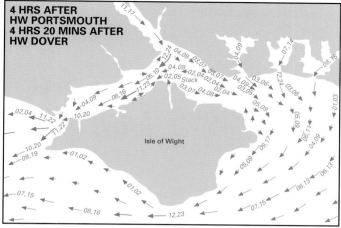

4 HRS AFTER HW PORTSMOUTH
4 HRS 20 MINS AFTER HW DOVER

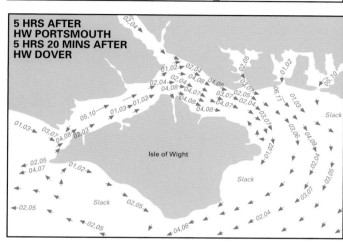

5 HRS AFTER HW PORTSMOUTH
5 HRS 20 MINS AFTER HW DOVER

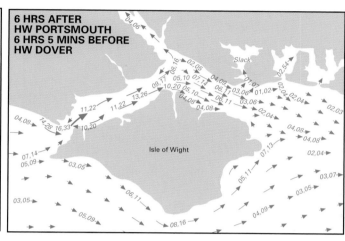

6 HRS AFTER HW PORTSMOUTH
6 HRS 5 MINS BEFORE HW DOVER

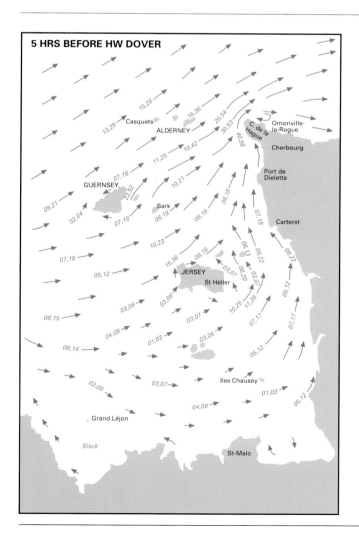

5 HRS BEFORE HW DOVER

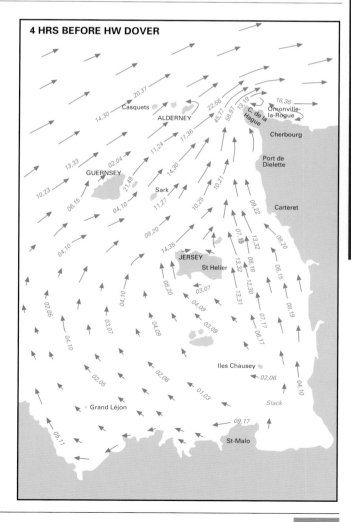

4 HRS BEFORE HW DOVER

TIDAL STREAMS AND CURVES

421

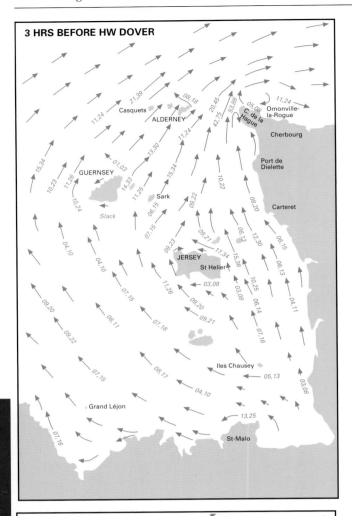

3 HRS BEFORE HW DOVER

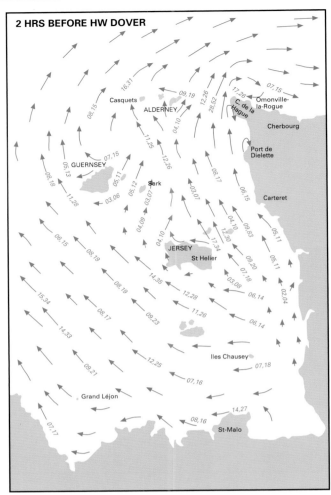

2 HRS BEFORE HW DOVER

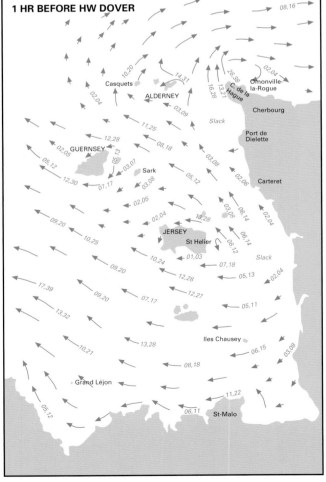

1 HR BEFORE HW DOVER

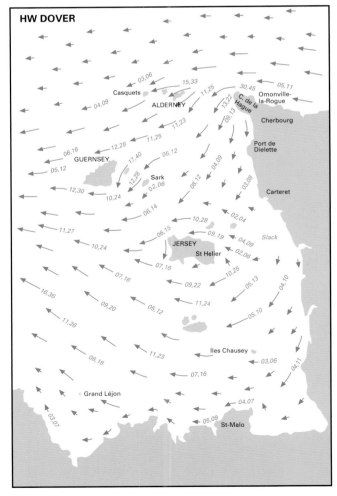

HW DOVER

TIDAL STREAMS AND CURVES

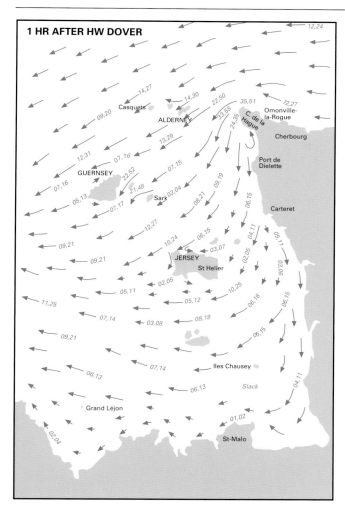

1 HR AFTER HW DOVER

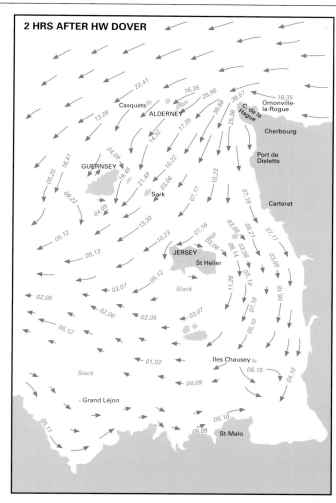

2 HRS AFTER HW DOVER

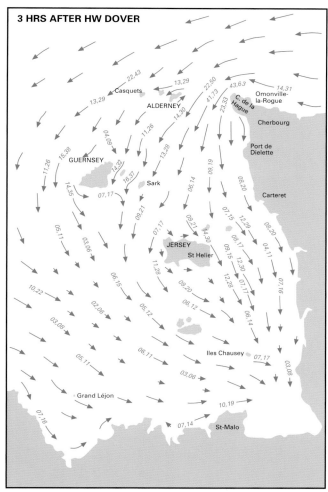

3 HRS AFTER HW DOVER

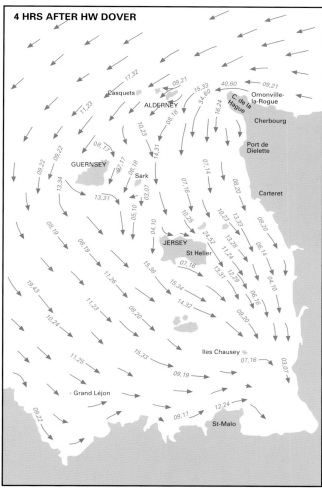

4 HRS AFTER HW DOVER

TIDAL STREAMS AND CURVES

TIDAL STREAMS AND CURVES

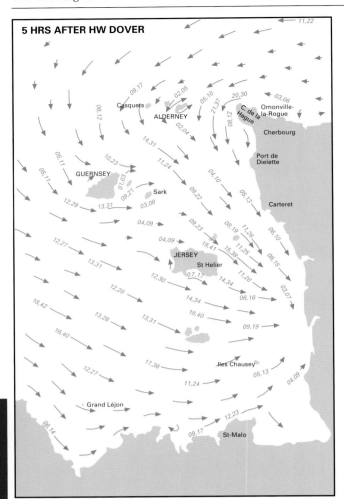

5 HRS AFTER HW DOVER

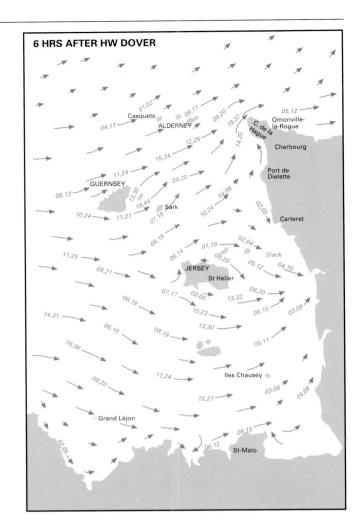

6 HRS AFTER HW DOVER

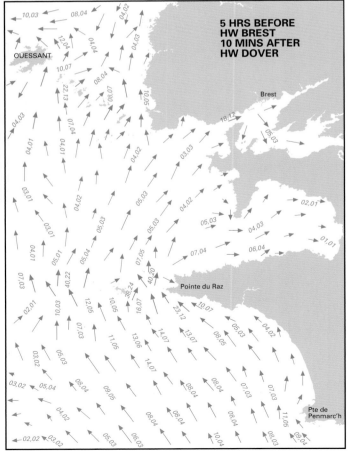

**5 HRS BEFORE
HW BREST
10 MINS AFTER
HW DOVER**

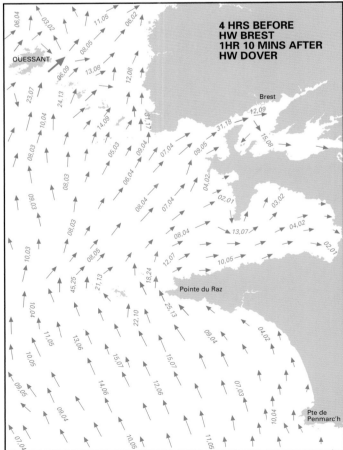

**4 HRS BEFORE
HW BREST
1HR 10 MINS AFTER
HW DOVER**

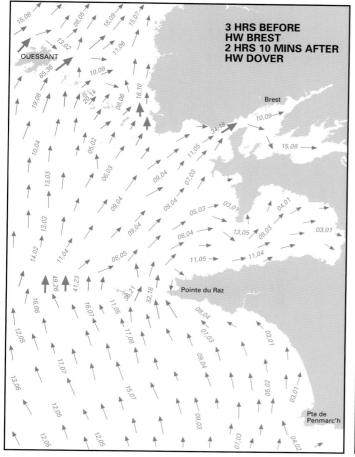

**3 HRS BEFORE
HW BREST
2 HRS 10 MINS AFTER
HW DOVER**

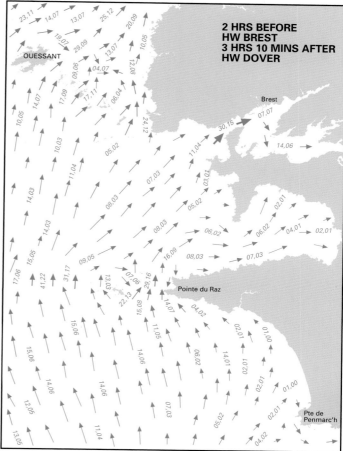

**2 HRS BEFORE
HW BREST
3 HRS 10 MINS AFTER
HW DOVER**

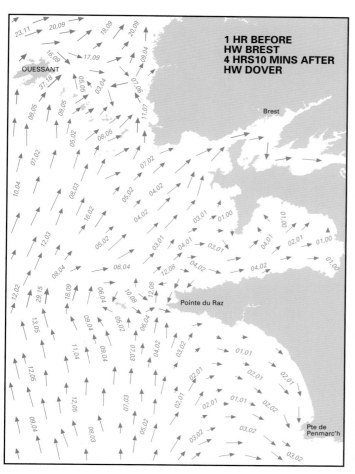

**1 HR BEFORE
HW BREST
4 HRS10 MINS AFTER
HW DOVER**

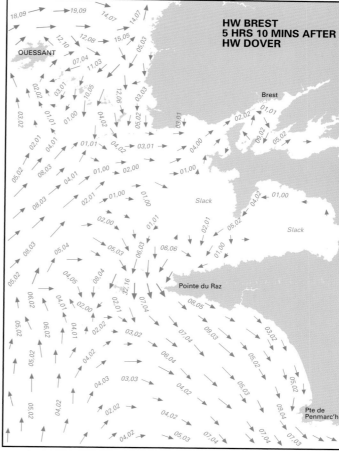

**HW BREST
5 HRS 10 MINS AFTER
HW DOVER**

TIDAL STREAMS AND CURVES

TIDAL STREAMS AND CURVES

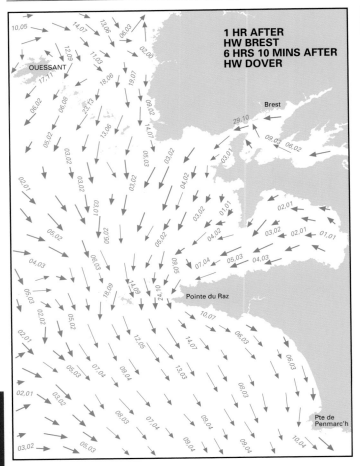

1 HR AFTER
HW BREST
6 HRS 10 MINS AFTER
HW DOVER

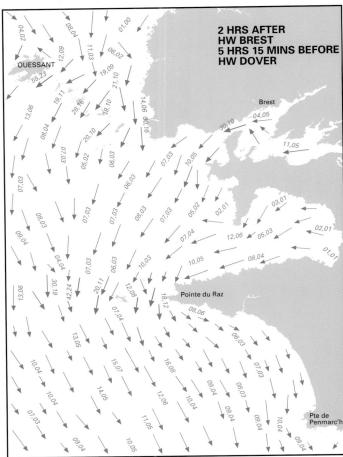

2 HRS AFTER
HW BREST
5 HRS 15 MINS BEFORE
HW DOVER

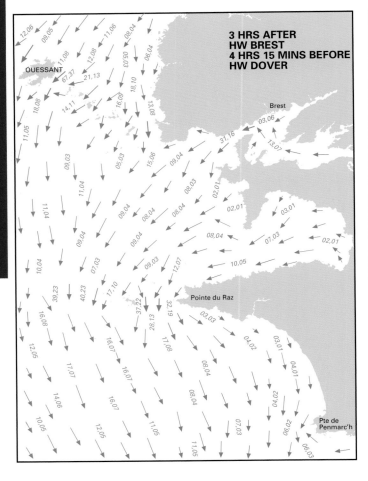

3 HRS AFTER
HW BREST
4 HRS 15 MINS BEFORE
HW DOVER

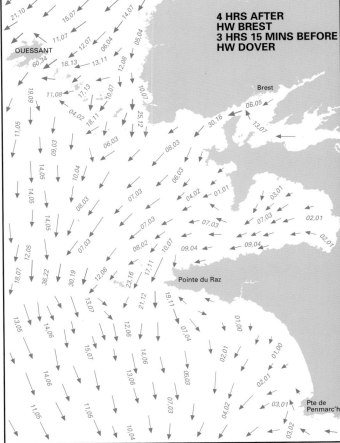

4 HRS AFTER
HW BREST
3 HRS 15 MINS BEFORE
HW DOVER

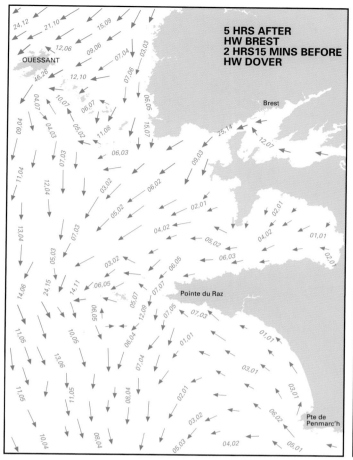

**5 HRS AFTER
HW BREST
2 HRS 15 MINS BEFORE
HW DOVER**

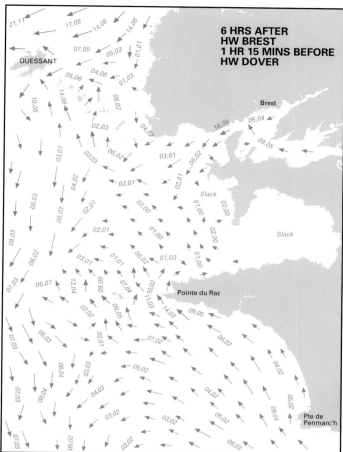

**6 HRS AFTER
HW BREST
1 HR 15 MINS BEFORE
HW DOVER**

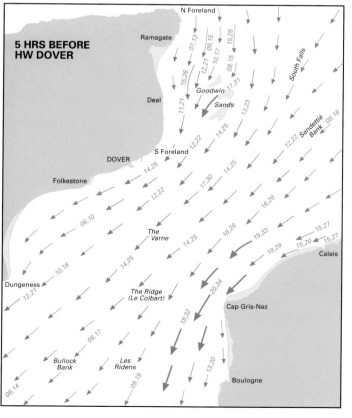

**5 HRS BEFORE
HW DOVER**

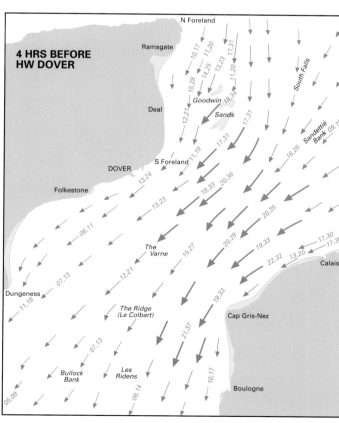

**4 HRS BEFORE
HW DOVER**

TIDAL STREAMS AND CURVES

427

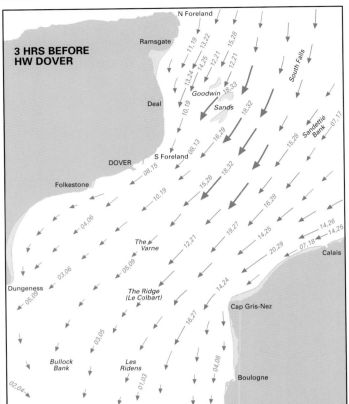

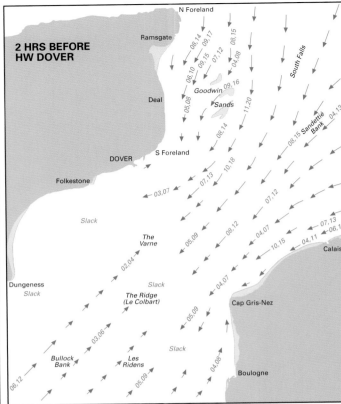

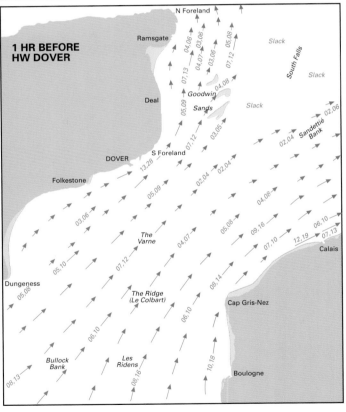

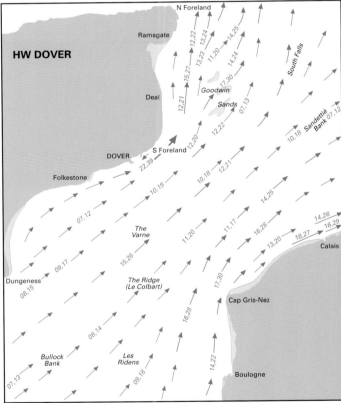

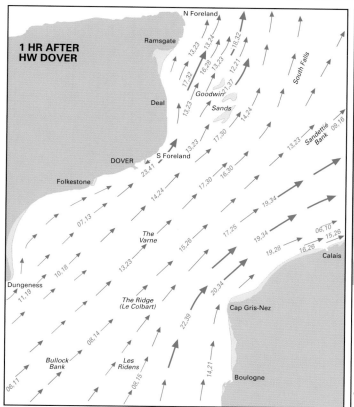

1 HR AFTER HW DOVER

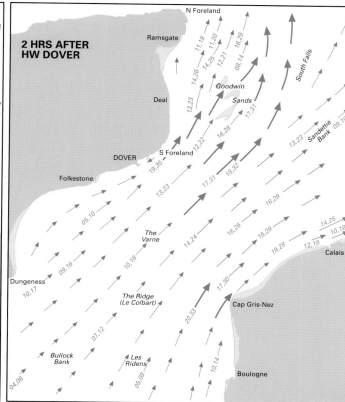

2 HRS AFTER HW DOVER

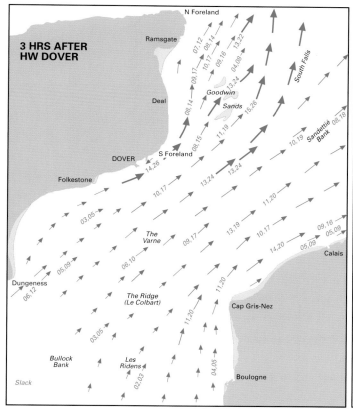

3 HRS AFTER HW DOVER

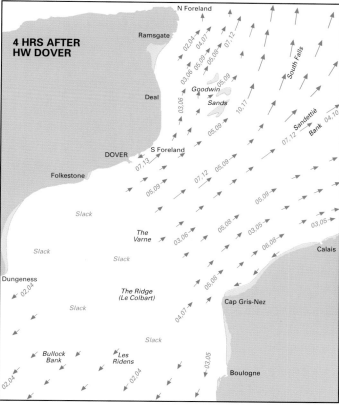

4 HRS AFTER HW DOVER

TIDAL STREAMS AND CURVES

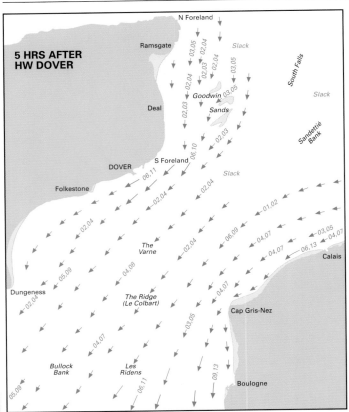

5 HRS AFTER HW DOVER

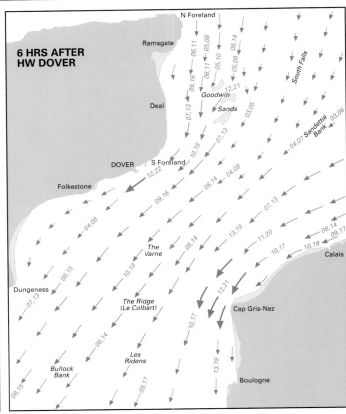

6 HRS AFTER HW DOVER

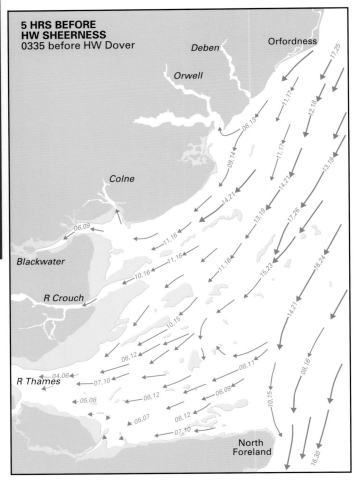

5 HRS BEFORE HW SHEERNESS
0335 before HW Dover

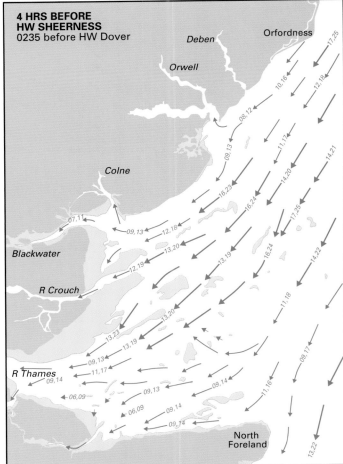

4 HRS BEFORE HW SHEERNESS
0235 before HW Dover

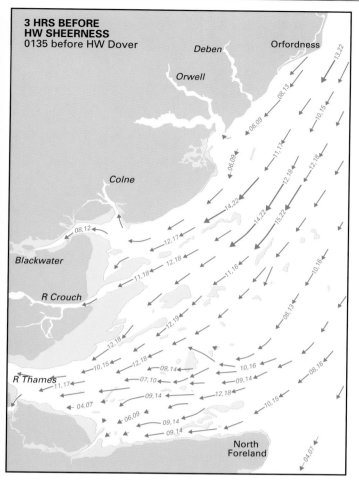

**3 HRS BEFORE
HW SHEERNESS**
0135 before HW Dover

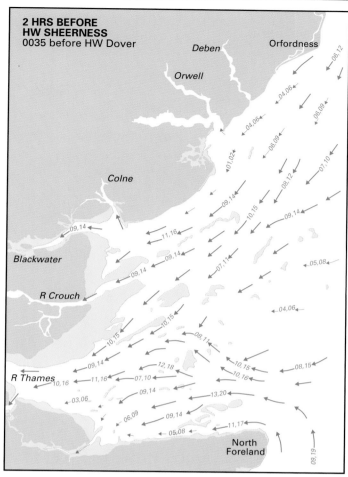

**2 HRS BEFORE
HW SHEERNESS**
0035 before HW Dover

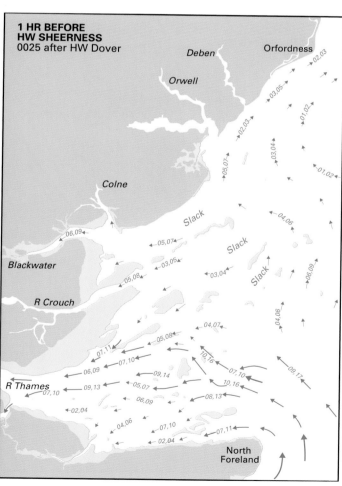

**1 HR BEFORE
HW SHEERNESS**
0025 after HW Dover

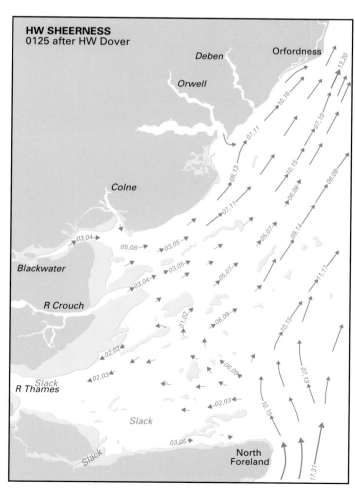

HW SHEERNESS
0125 after HW Dover

TIDAL STREAMS AND CURVES

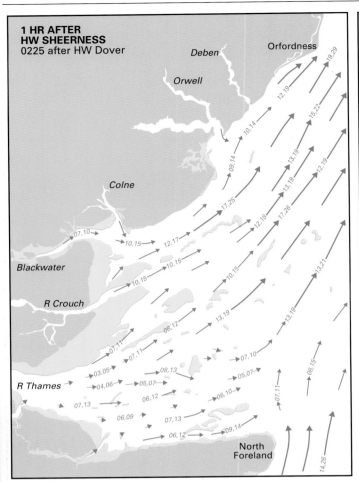

1 HR AFTER HW SHEERNESS
0225 after HW Dover

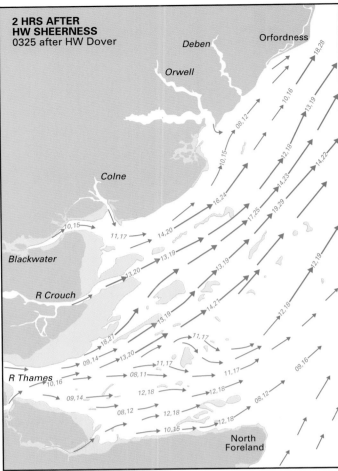

2 HRS AFTER HW SHEERNESS
0325 after HW Dover

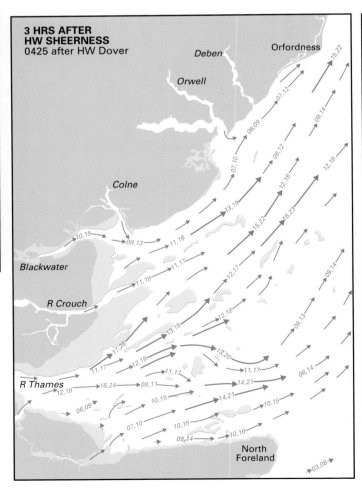

3 HRS AFTER HW SHEERNESS
0425 after HW Dover

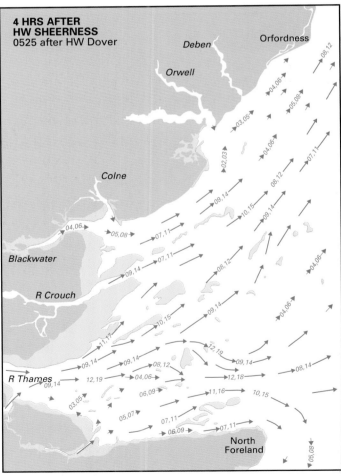

4 HRS AFTER HW SHEERNESS
0525 after HW Dover

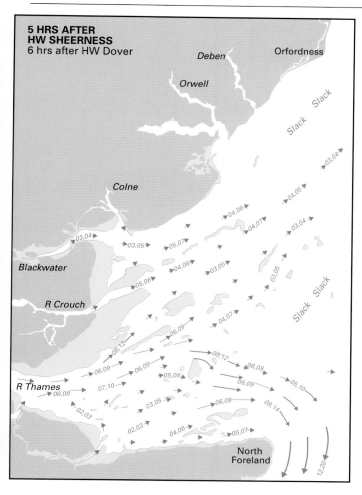

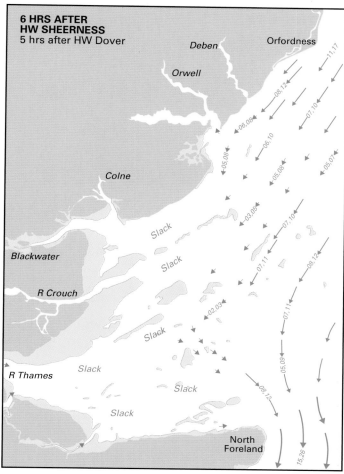

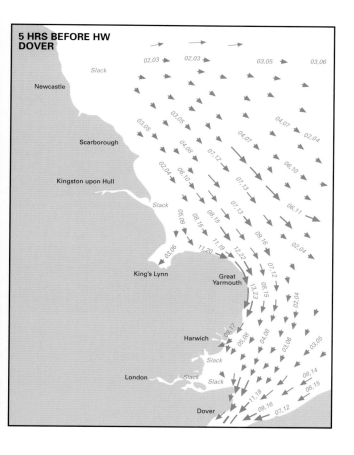

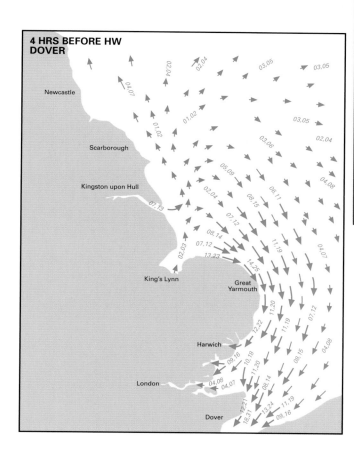

TIDAL STREAMS AND CURVES

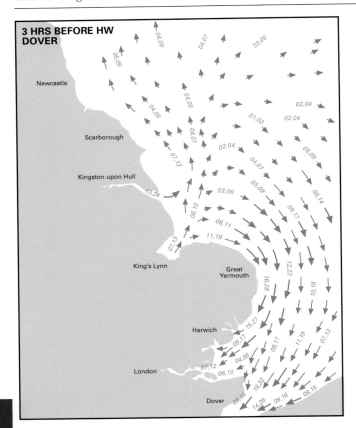

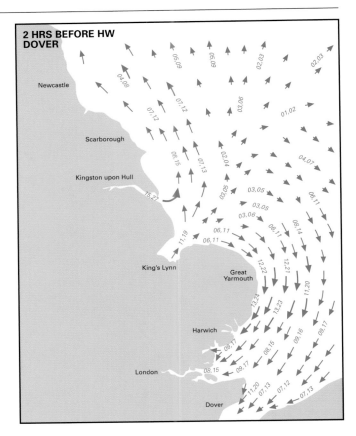

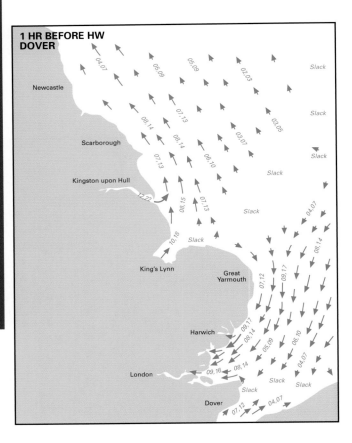

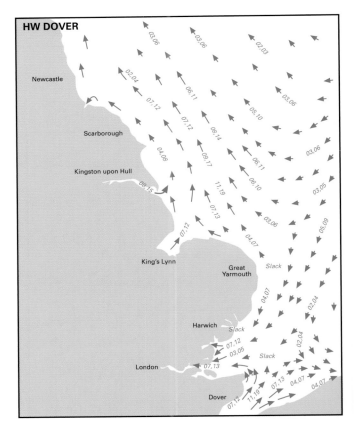

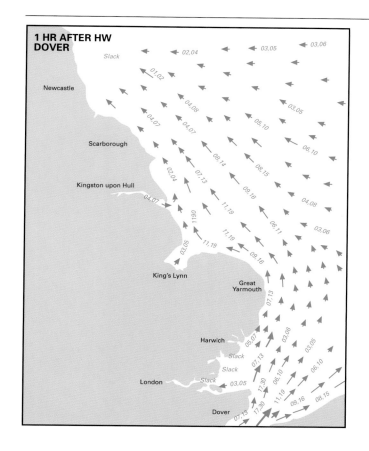

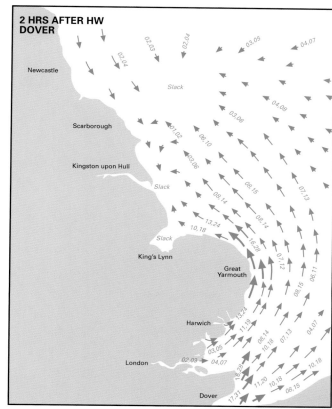

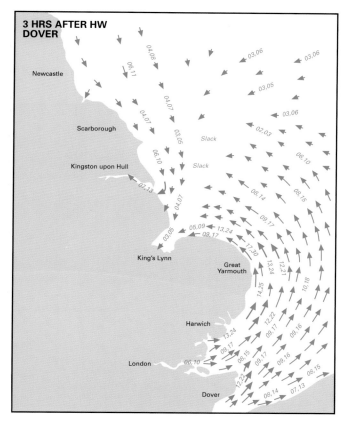

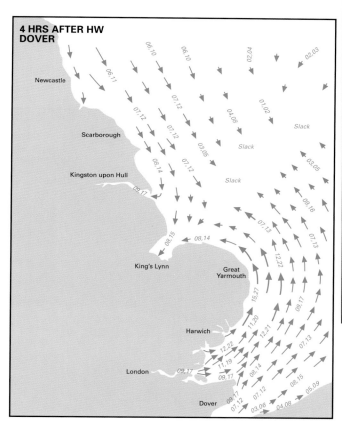

TIDAL STREAMS AND CURVES

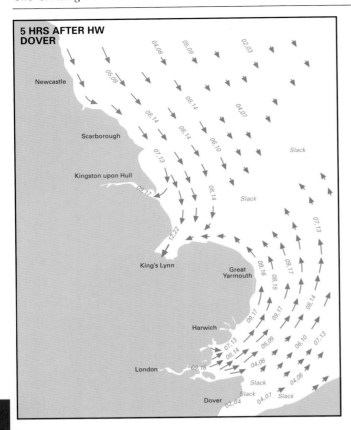

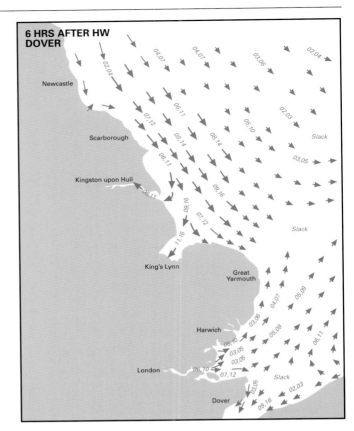

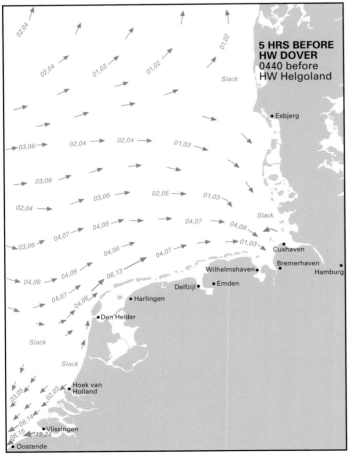

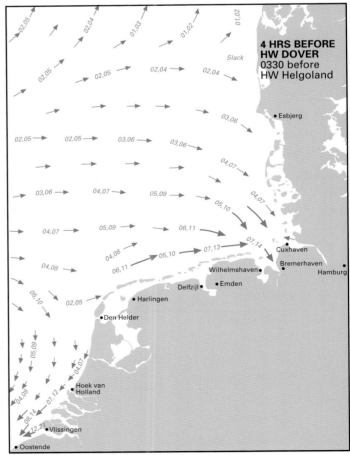

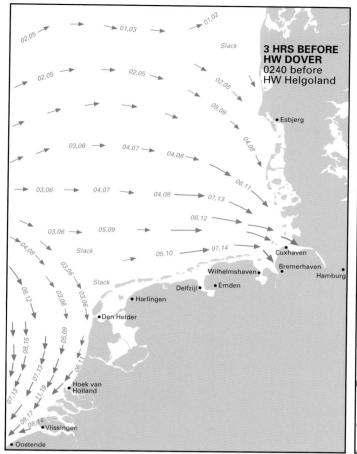

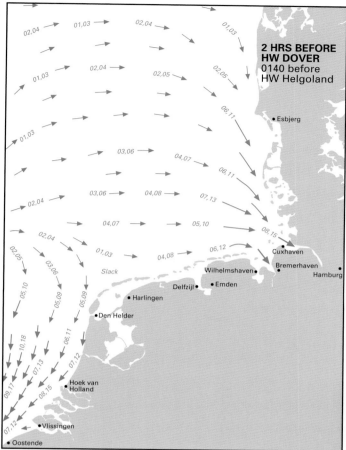

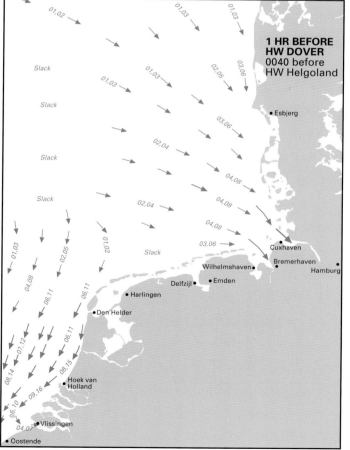

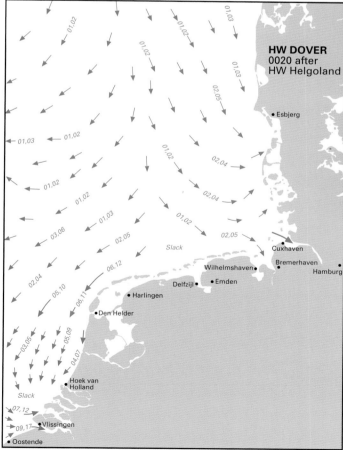

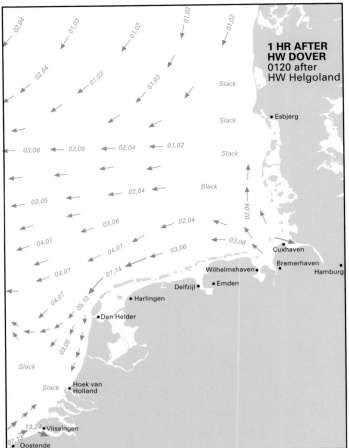

**1 HR AFTER
HW DOVER**
0120 after
HW Helgoland

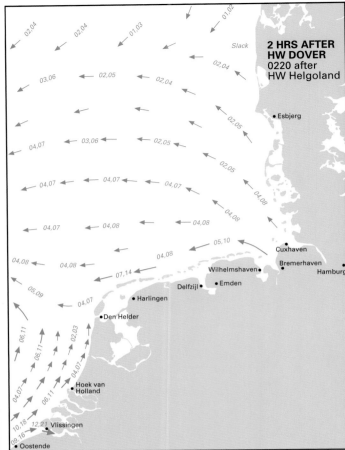

**2 HRS AFTER
HW DOVER**
0220 after
HW Helgoland

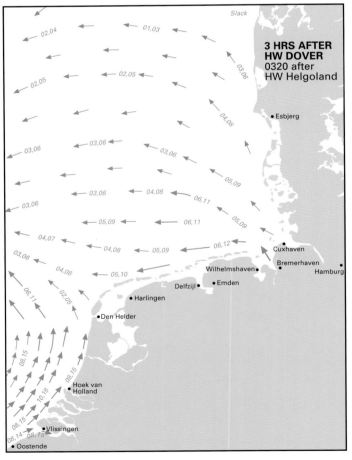

**3 HRS AFTER
HW DOVER**
0320 after
HW Helgoland

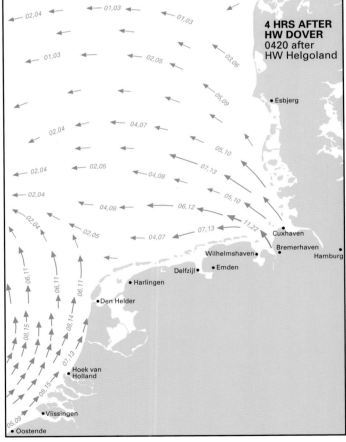

**4 HRS AFTER
HW DOVER**
0420 after
HW Helgoland

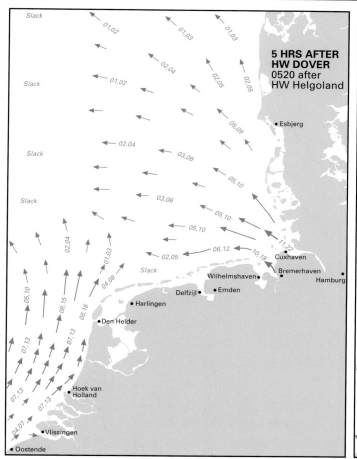

5 HRS AFTER HW DOVER
0520 after HW Helgoland

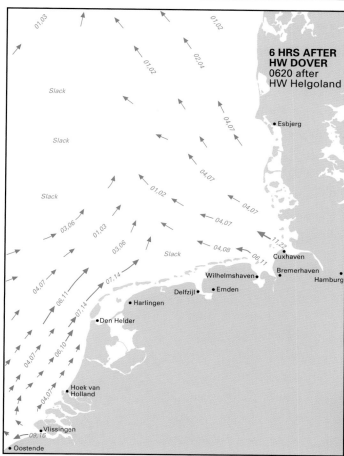

6 HRS AFTER HW DOVER
0620 after HW Helgoland

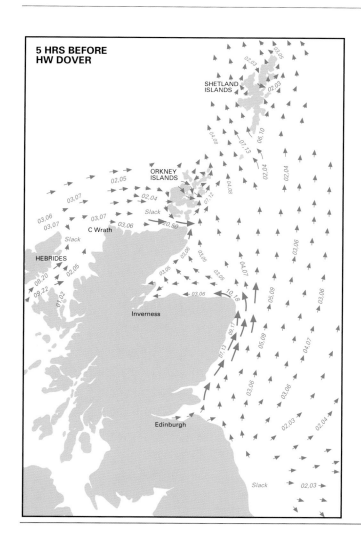

5 HRS BEFORE HW DOVER

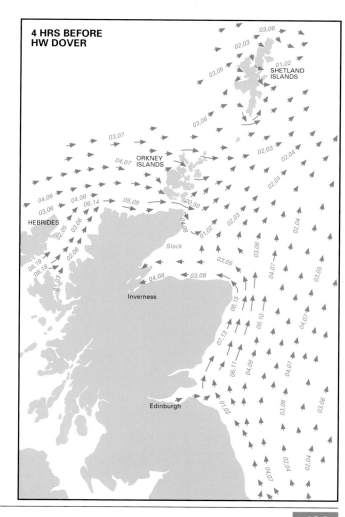

4 HRS BEFORE HW DOVER

TIDAL STREAMS AND CURVES

TIDAL STREAMS AND CURVES

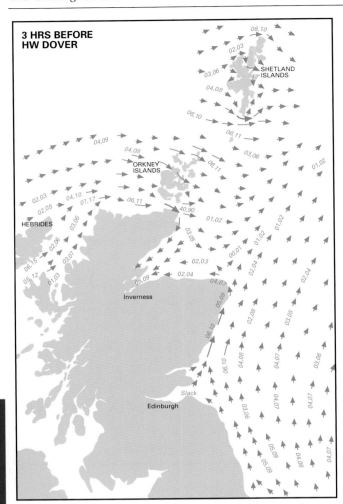

3 HRS BEFORE HW DOVER

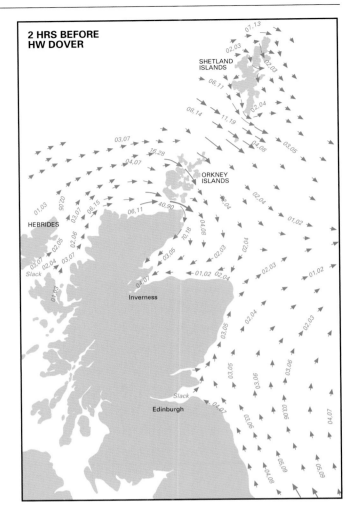

2 HRS BEFORE HW DOVER

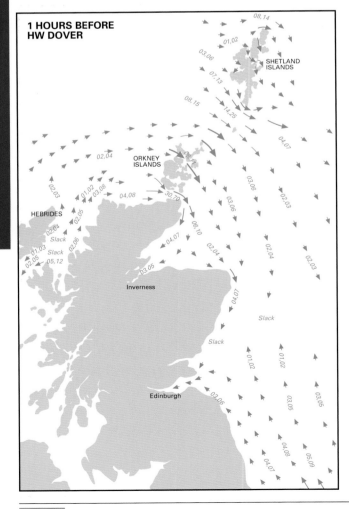

1 HOURS BEFORE HW DOVER

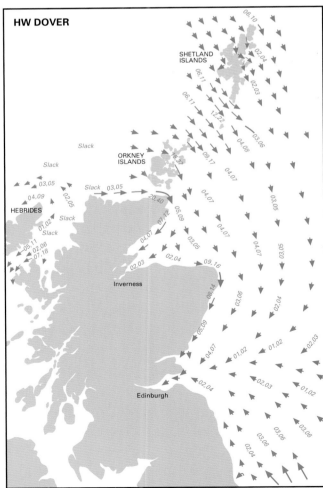

HW DOVER

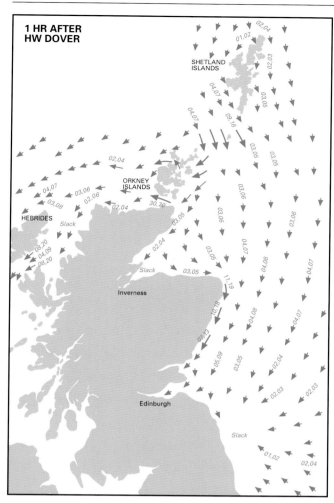

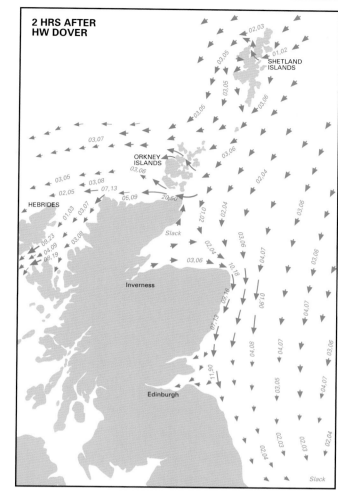

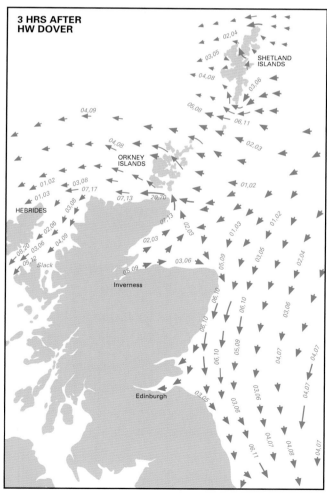

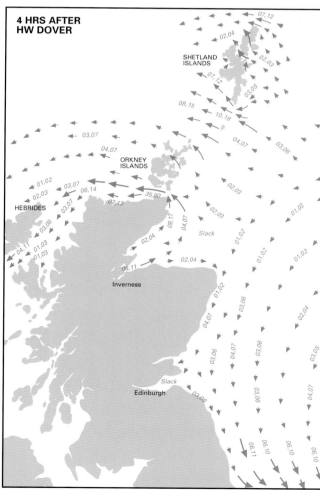

TIDAL STREAMS AND CURVES

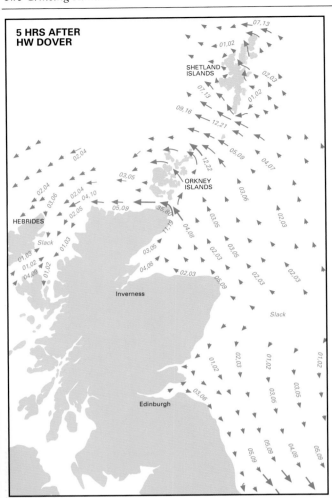

5 HRS AFTER HW DOVER

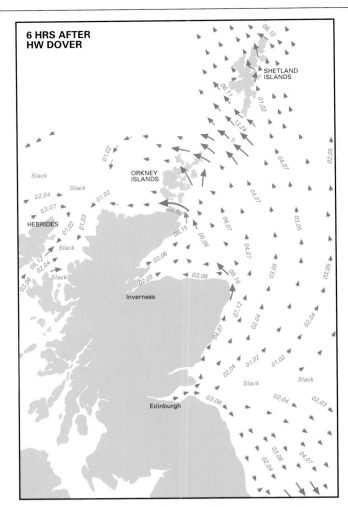

6 HRS AFTER HW DOVER

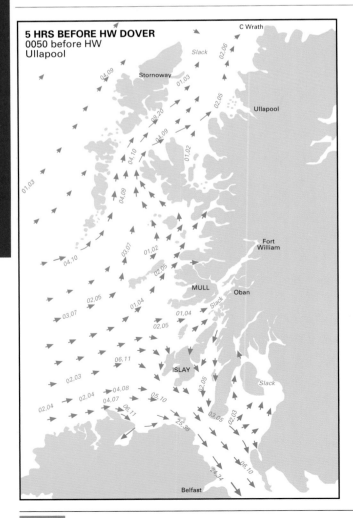

5 HRS BEFORE HW DOVER
0050 before HW
Ullapool

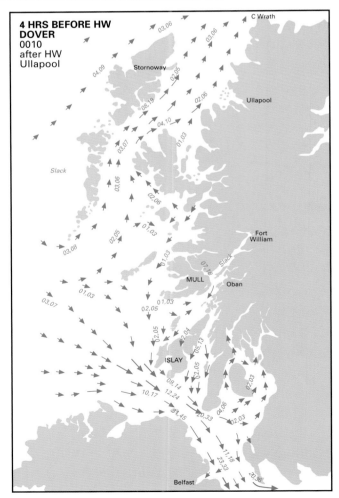

4 HRS BEFORE HW DOVER
0010 after HW
Ullapool

TIDAL STREAMS AND CURVES

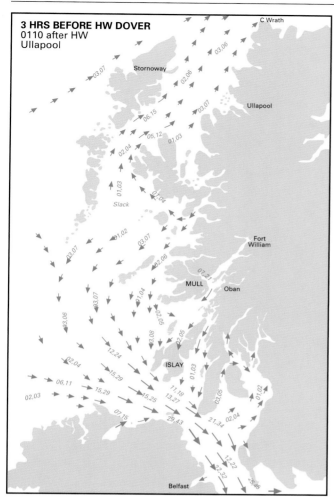

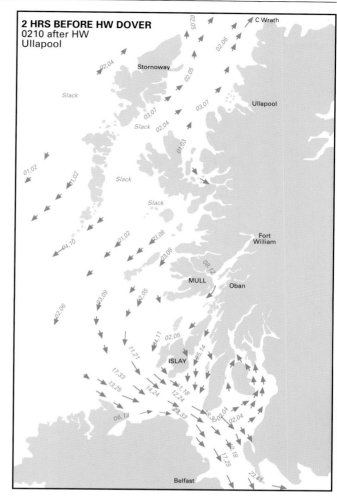

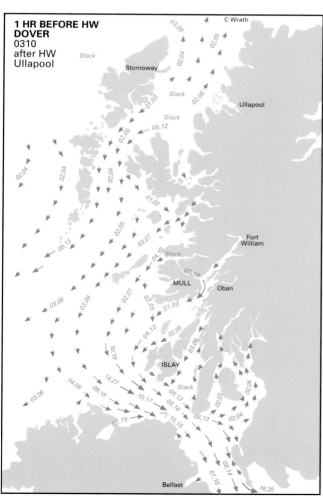

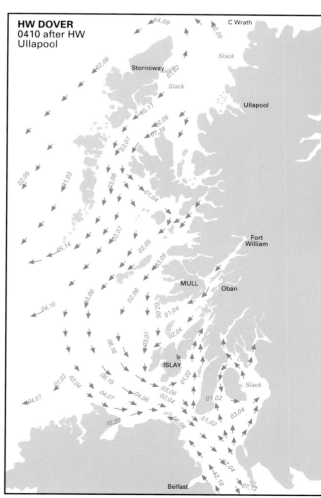

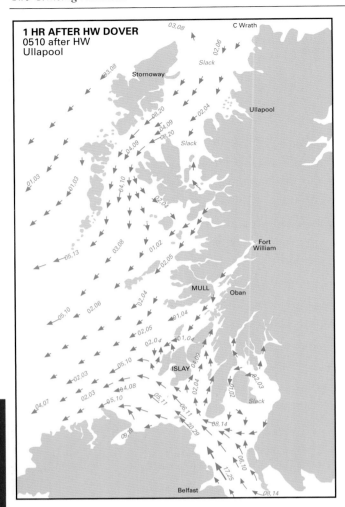

1 HR AFTER HW DOVER
0510 after HW
Ullapool

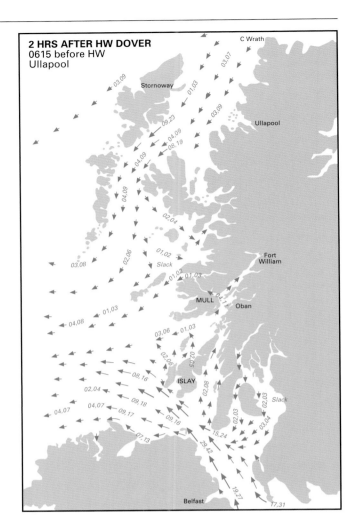

2 HRS AFTER HW DOVER
0615 before HW
Ullapool

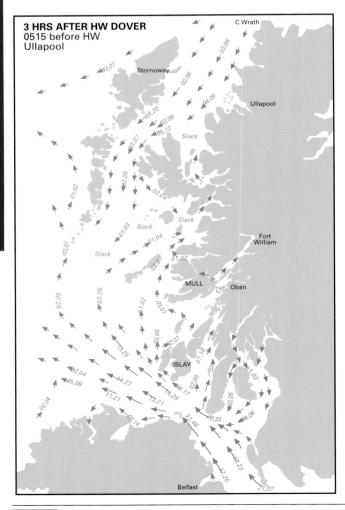

3 HRS AFTER HW DOVER
0515 before HW
Ullapool

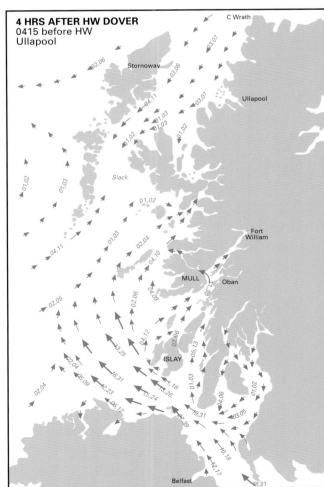

4 HRS AFTER HW DOVER
0415 before HW
Ullapool

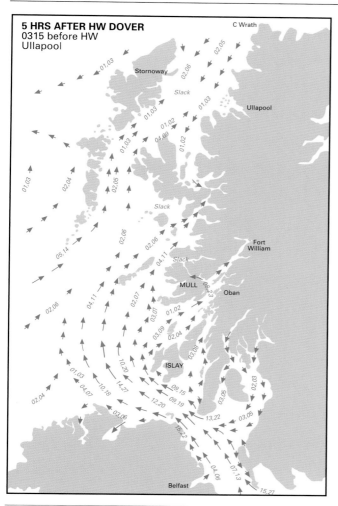

5 HRS AFTER HW DOVER
0315 before HW
Ullapool

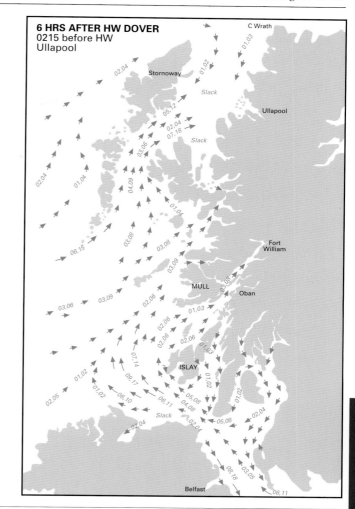

6 HRS AFTER HW DOVER
0215 before HW
Ullapool

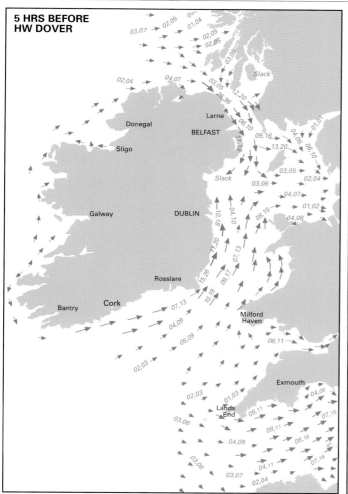

**5 HRS BEFORE
HW DOVER**

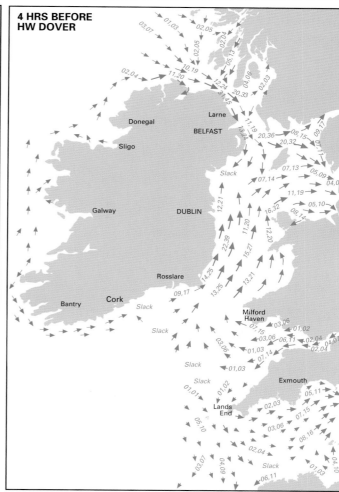

**4 HRS BEFORE
HW DOVER**

TIDAL STREAMS AND CURVES

TIDAL STREAMS AND CURVES

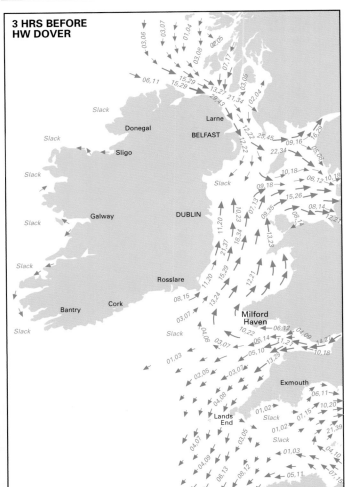

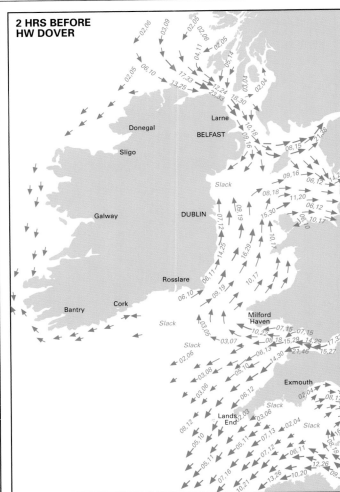

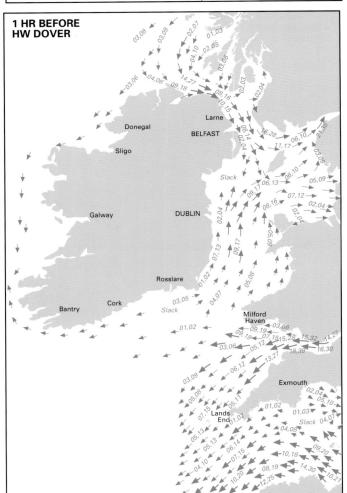

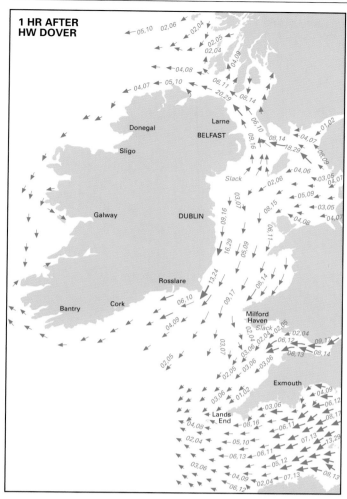

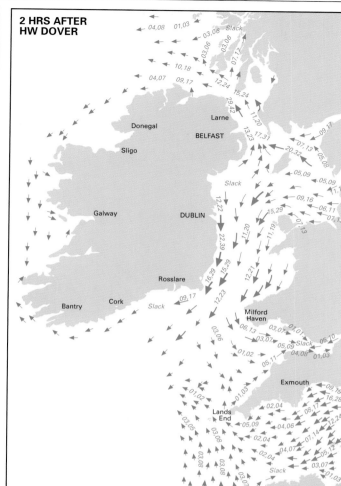

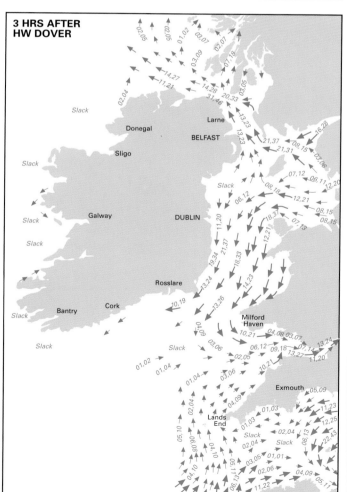

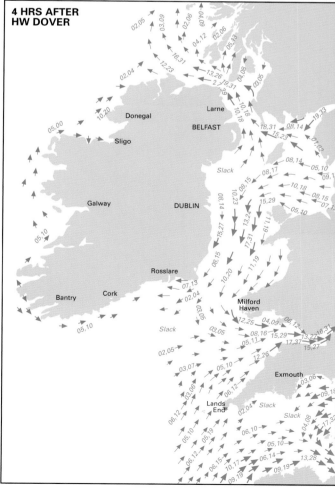

TIDAL STREAMS AND CURVES

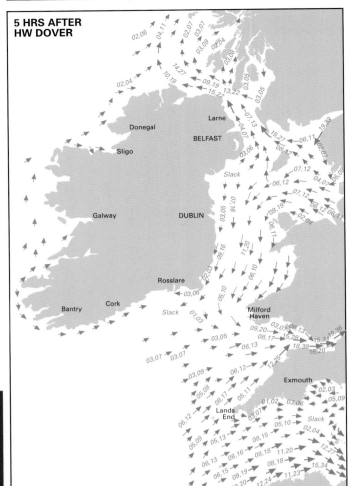

5 HRS AFTER HW DOVER

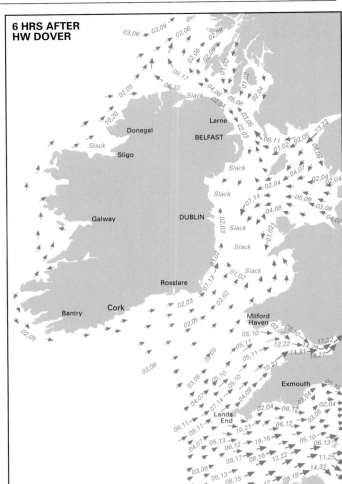

6 HRS AFTER HW DOVER

Index of Tidal Curves

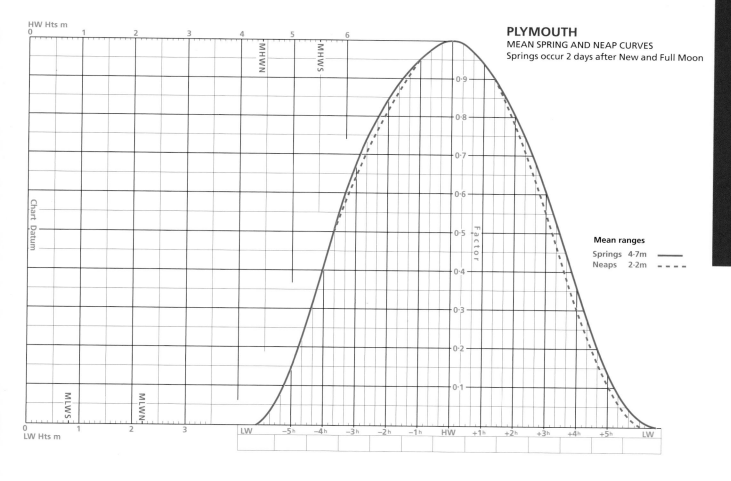

PLYMOUTH MEAN SPRING AND NEAP CURVES. Springs occur 2 days after New and Full Moon

TIDAL STREAMS AND CURVES

Left table

	Time differences HW		LW		Height differences in metres MHWS	MHWN	MLWN	MLWS
PLYMOUTH	0000 and 1200	0600 and 1800	0000 and 1200	0600 and 1800	5·5	4·4	2·2	0·8
Isles of Scilly								
St Mary's	−0035	−0100	−0040	−0025	+0·2	−0·1	−0·2	−0·1
Penzance (Newlyn)	−0040	−0110	−0035	−0025	+0·1	0·0	−0·2	0·0
Helford R (Entrance)	−0030	−0035	−0015	−0010	−0·2	−0·2	−0·3	−0·2
River Fal								
Falmouth	−0025	−0045	−0010	−0010	−0·2	−0·2	−0·3	−0·2
Truro	−0020	−0025	–	–	−2·0	−2·0	dries	dries
Mevagissey	−0015	−0020	−0010	−0005	−0·1	−0·1	−0·2	−0·1
River Fowey								
Fowey	−0010	−0015	−0010	−0005	−0·1	−0·1	−0·2	−0·2
Looe	−0010	−0010	−0005	−0005	−0·1	−0·2	−0·2	−0·2
River Yealm								
Entrance	+0006	+0006	+0002	+0002	−0·1	−0·1	−0·1	−0·1
PLYMOUTH	0100 and 1300	0600 and 1800	0100 and 1300	0600 and 1800	5·5	4·4	2·2	0·8
Salcombe River								
Salcombe	0000	+0010	+0005	−0005	−0·2	−0·3	−0·1	−0·1
River Dart								
Dartmouth	+0015	+0025	0000	−0005	−0·6	−0·6	−0·2	−0·2
Totnes	+0030	+0040	+0115	+0030	−2·1	−2·1	dries	dries
Torquay	+0025	+0045	+0010	0000	−0·6	−0·7	−0·2	−0·1
Teignmouth (Apps)	+0020	+0050	+0025	0000	−0·9	−0·8	−0·2	−0·1
Teignmouth (New Quay)	+0025	+0055	+0040	+0005	−0·8	−0·8	−0·2	+0·1

Right table

	Time differences HW		LW		Height differences in metres MHWS	MHWN	MLWN	MLWS
PLYMOUTH	0100 and 1300	0600 and 1800	0100 and 1300	0600 and 1800	5·5	4·4	2·2	0·8
Exmouth (Apps)	+0030	+0050	+0015	+0005	−0·9	−1·0	−0·5	−0·3
Lyme Regis	+0040	+0100	+0005	−0005	−1·2	−1·3	−0·5	−0·2
Bridport (West Bay)	+0025	+0040	0000	0000	−1·4	−1·4	−0·6	−0·2
River Exe								
Exmouth Dock	+0035	+0055	+0050	+0020	−1·5	−1·6	−0·9	−0·6
Topsham	+0045	+0105	–	–	−1·5	−1·6	–	–
PORTLAND	0100 and 1300	0700 and 1900	0100 and 1300	0700 and 1900	2·1	1·4	0·8	0·1
Lulworth Cove	+0005	+0015	−0005	0000	+0·1	+0·1	+0·2	+0·1
POOLE HARBOUR (RoRo Terminal)	–	–	0500 and 1700	1100 and 2300	2·2	1·7	1·2	0·6
Swanage	–	–	−0045	−0055	−0·2	−0·1	0·0	−0·1
Poole Harbour								
Entrance	–	–	−0025	−0010	0·0	0·0	0·0	0·0
Pottery Pier	–	–	+0010	+0010	−0·2	0·0	+0·1	+0·2
Wareham	–	–	+0130	+0045	0·0	0·0	0·0	+0·3
SOUTHAMPTON	0400 and 1600	1100 and 2300	0000 and 1200	0600 and 1800	4·5	3·7	1·8	0·5
River Hamble								
Warsash	+0020	+0010	+0010	0000	0·0	+0·1	+0·1	+0·3

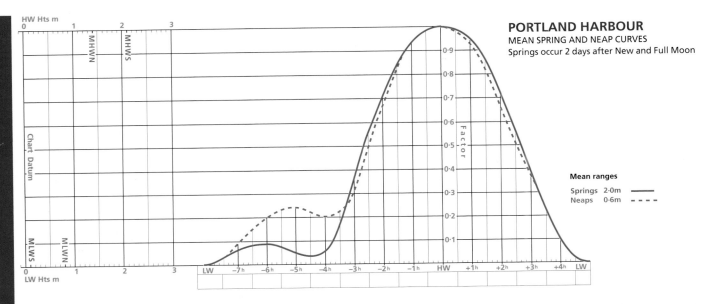

PORTLAND HARBOUR
MEAN SPRING AND NEAP CURVES
Springs occur 2 days after New and Full Moon

Mean ranges
Springs 2·0m ——
Neaps 0·6m ----

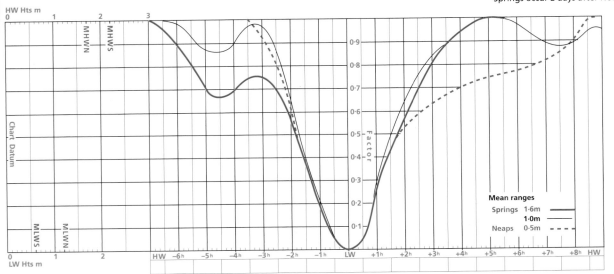

POOLE HARBOUR
MEAN SPRING AND NEAP CURVES
Springs occur 2 days after New and Full Moon

Mean ranges
Springs 1·6m ——
1·0m
Neaps 0·5m ----

TIDAL STREAMS AND CURVES

BOURNEMOUTH TO CHRISTCHURCH

Tides from Poole Harbour to Selsey Bill are based on LW except those related to Portsmouth which uses HW. Ports based on Portsmouth include Christchurch, Lymington, Beaulieu, Cowes, Bembridge and Chichester although some can also be related to the LW curve at Poole.

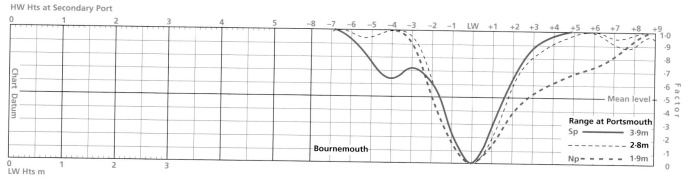

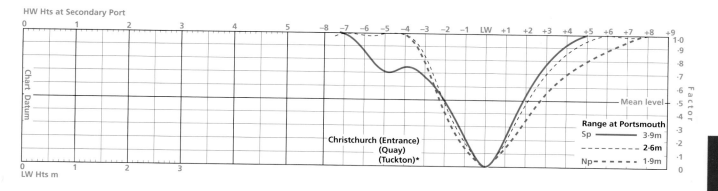

LYMINGTON TO COWES

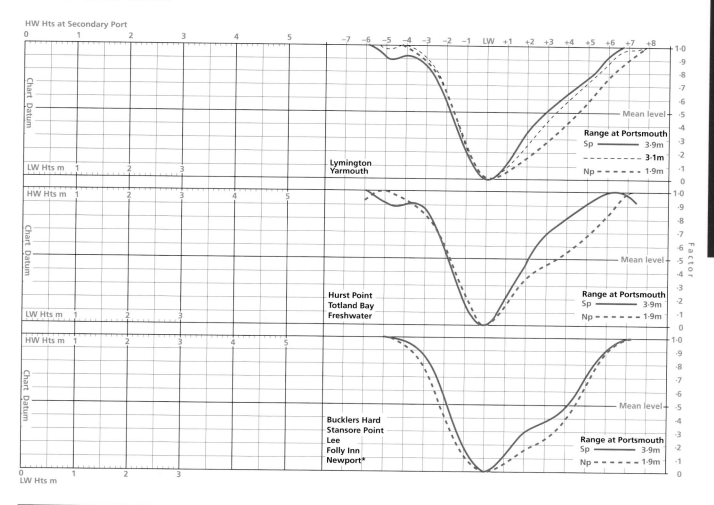

RYDE TO SELSEY

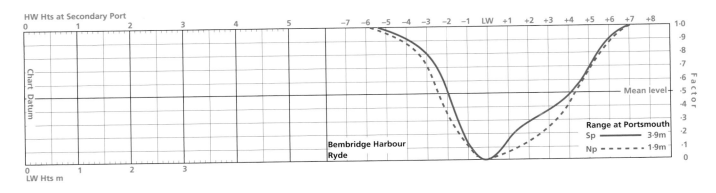

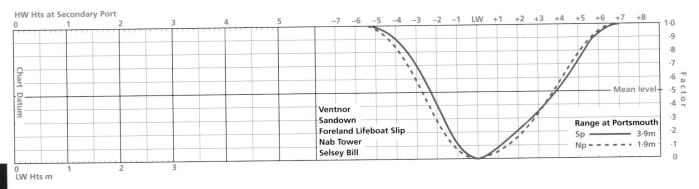

SOUTHAMPTON
MEAN SPRING AND NEAP CURVES
Springs occur 2 days after New and Full Moon

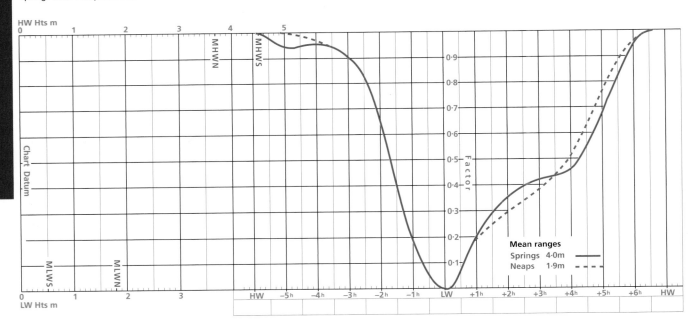

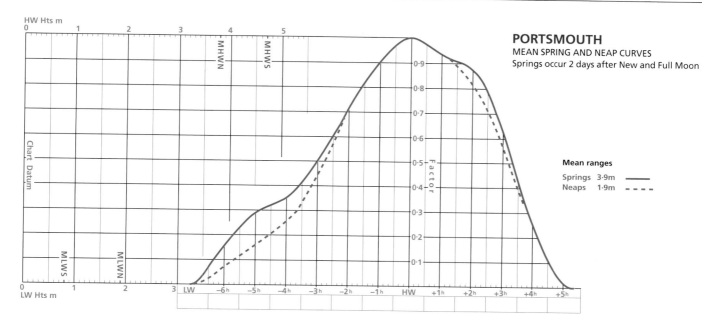

PORTSMOUTH
MEAN SPRING AND NEAP CURVES
Springs occur 2 days after New and Full Moon

Mean ranges
Springs 3·9m ———
Neaps 1·9m - - - -

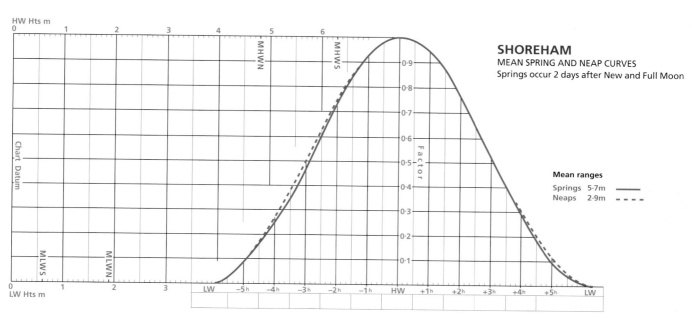

SHOREHAM
MEAN SPRING AND NEAP CURVES
Springs occur 2 days after New and Full Moon

Mean ranges
Springs 5·7m ———
Neaps 2·9m - - - -

TIDAL STREAMS AND CURVES

	Time differences				Height differences in metres			
	HW		LW		MHWS	MHWN	MLWN	MLWS
	0000	0600	0500	1100				
PORTSMOUTH	and	and	and	and	4·7	3·8	1·9	0·8
	1200	1800	1700	2300				
Christchurch (Ent)	−0230	+0030	−0035	−0035	−2·9	−2·4	−1·2	−0·2
Lymington	−0110	+0005	−0020	−0020	−1·7	−1·2	−0·5	−0·1
Bucklers Hard	−0040	−0010	+0010	−0010	−1·0	−0·8	−0·2	−0·3
Stansore Point	−0050	−0010	−0005	−0010	−0·8	−0·5	−0·3	−0·1
Isle of Wight								
Yarmouth	−0105	+0005	−0025	−0030	−1·7	−1·2	−0·3	0·0
Bembridge Hbr	+0020	0000	+0100	+0020	−1·5	−1·4	−1·3	−1·0
Cowes	−0015	+0015	0000	−0020	−0·5	−0·3	−0·1	0·0

	Time differences				Height differences in metres			
	HW		LW		MHWS	MHWN	MLWN	MLWS
	0500	1000	0000	0600				
PORTSMOUTH	and	and	and	and	4·7	3·8	1·9	0·8
	1700	2200	1200	1800				
Chichester Harbour								
Entrance	−0010	+0005	+0015	+0020	+0·2	+0·2	0·0	+0·1
Northney	+0010	+0015	+0015	+0025	+0·2	0·0	−0·2	−0·3
Bosham	0000	+0010	−	−	+0·2	+0·1	−	−
Itchenor	−0005	+0005	+0005	+0025	+0·1	0·0	−0·2	−0·2
Dell Quay	+0005	+0015	−	−	+0·2	+0·1	−	−
Selsey Bill	−0005	−0005	+0035	+0035	+0·6	+0·6	0·0	0·0

	Time differences				Height differences in metres			
	HW		LW		MHWS	MHWN	MLWN	MLWS
	0500	1000	0000	0600				
SHOREHAM	and	and	and	and	6·3	4·8	1·9	0·6
	1700	2200	1200	1800				
River Arun								
Littlehampton (Ent)	+0010	0000	−0005	−0010	−0·4	−0·4	−0·2	−0·2
Brighton	0000	−0005	0000	0000	+0·3	+0·2	+0·1	0·0
Newhaven	−0015	−0010	0000	0000	+0·2	+0·1	−0·1	−0·2
Eastbourne	−0010	−0005	+0015	+0020	+1·1	+0·6	+0·2	+0·1

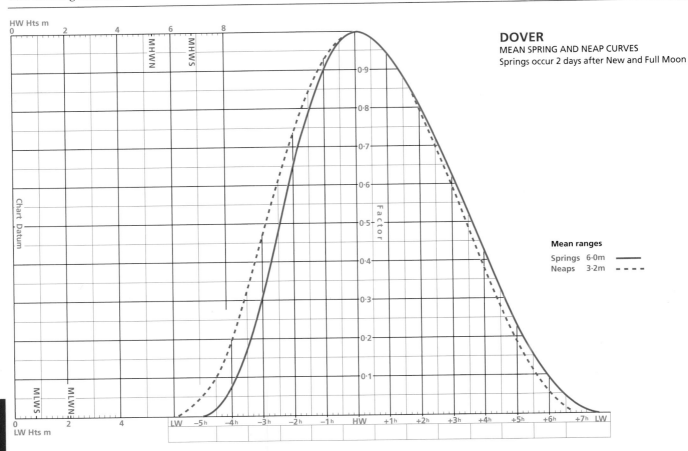

DOVER
MEAN SPRING AND NEAP CURVES
Springs occur 2 days after New and Full Moon

Mean ranges
Springs 6·0m
Neaps 3·2m

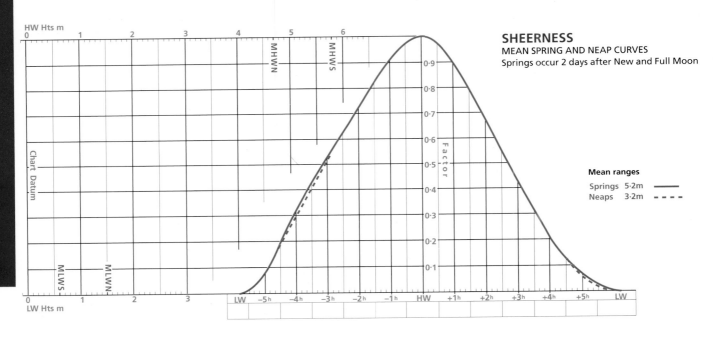

SHEERNESS
MEAN SPRING AND NEAP CURVES
Springs occur 2 days after New and Full Moon

Mean ranges
Springs 5·2m
Neaps 3·2m

	Time differences HW		LW		Height differences in metres MHWS MHWN MLWN MLWS			
DOVER	0000 and 1200	0600 and 1800	0100 and 1700	0700 and 1900	6·8	5·3	2·1	0·8
Rye (Approaches)	+0005	−0010	–	–	+1·0	+0·7	–	–
Rye (Harbour)	+0005	−0010	–	–	−1·4	−1·7	dries	dries
Folkestone	−0020	−0005	−0010	−0010	+0·4	+0·4	0·0	−0·1
Ramsgate	+0030	+0030	+0017	+0007	−1·6	−1·3	−0·7	−0·2

	Time differences HW		LW		Height differences in metres MHWS MHWN MLWN MLWS			
SHEERNESS	0200 and 1400	0800 and 2000	0200 and 1400	0700 and 1900	5·8	4·7	1·5	0·6
Margate	−0045	−0040	−0025	−0040	−1·0	−0·8	−0·1	−0·1
Whitstable (Apps)	+0017	+0004	−0005	−0020	−0·4	−0·2	0·0	−0·1
Faversham	–	–	–	–	−0·2	−0·2	–	–
Chatham (Lock Apps)	+0010	+0012	+0012	+0018	+0·3	+0·1	−0·1	−0·2
Upnor	+0015	+0015	+0015	+0025	+0·2	+0·2	−0·1	−0·1
Southend-on-Sea	−0005	0000	0000	+0005	0·0	0·0	−0·1	−0·1

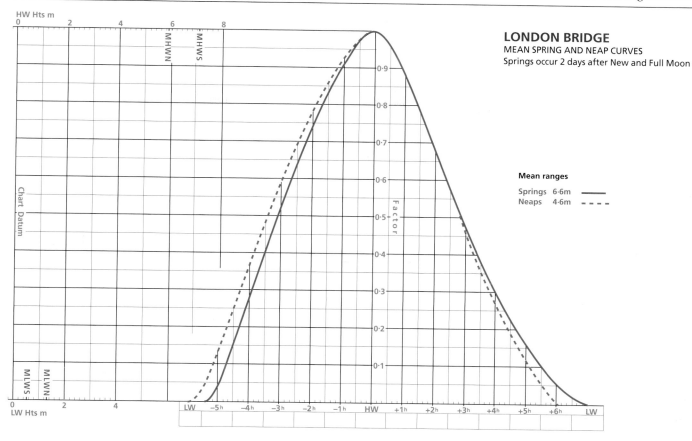

LONDON BRIDGE
MEAN SPRING AND NEAP CURVES
Springs occur 2 days after New and Full Moon

Mean ranges

Springs 6·6m ———
Neaps 4·6m – – –

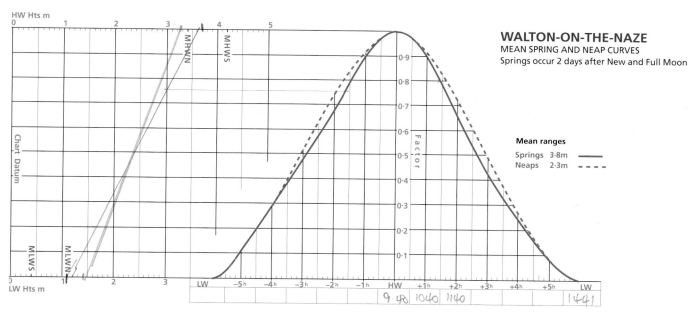

WALTON-ON-THE-NAZE
MEAN SPRING AND NEAP CURVES
Springs occur 2 days after New and Full Moon

Mean ranges

Springs 3·8m ———
Neaps 2·3m – – –

TIDAL STREAMS AND CURVES

	Time differences HW		LW		Height differences in metres MHWS	MHWN	MLWN	MLWS
LONDON BRIDGE	0300 and 1500	0900 and 2100	0400 and 1600	1100 and 2300	7·1	5·9	1·3	0·5
Albert Bridge	+0025	+0020	+0105	+0110	−0·9	−0·8	−0·7	−0·5
Hammersmith Bridge	+0040	+0035	+0205	+0155	−1·4	−1·3	−1·0	−0·5
Kew Bridge	+0055	+0050	+0255	+0235	−1·8	−1·8	−1·2	−0·5
Richmond Lock	+0105	+0055	+0325	+0305	−2·2	−2·2	−1·3	−0·5
WALTON-ON-THE-NAZE	0000 and 1200	0600 and 1800	0500 and 1700	1100 and 2300	4·2	3·4	1·1	0·4
River Crouch								
Burnham-on-Crouch	+0050	+0035	+0115	+0050	+1·0	+0·8	−0·1	−0·2
North Fambridge	+0115	+0050	+0130	+0100	+1·1	+0·8	0·0	−0·1
River Blackwater								
Osea Island	+0057	+0045	+0050	+0007	+1·1	+0·9	+0·1	0·0
Maldon	+0107	+0055	–	–	−1·3	−1·1	–	–
West Mersea	+0035	+0015	+0055	+0010	+0·96	+0·4	+0·1	+0·1
River Colne								
Brightlingsea	+0025	+0021	+0046	+0004	+0·8	+0·4	+0·1	0·0
Colchester	+0035	+0025	–	–	0·0	−0·3	dries	dries

	Time differences HW		LW		Height differences in metres MHWS	MHWN	MLWN	MLWS
WALTON-ON-THE-NAZE	0000 and 1200	0600 and 1800	0500 and 1700	1100 and 2300	4·2	3·4	1·1	0·4
River Stour								
Mistley	+0025	+0025	0000	+0020	0·0	0·0	−0·1	−0·1
River Orwell								
Ipswich	+0015	+0025	0000	+0010	0·0	0·0	−0·1	−0·1
WALTON-ON-THE-NAZE	0100 and 1300	0700 and 1900	0100 and 1300	0700 and 1900	4·2	3·4	1·1	0·4
River Deben								
Woodbridge Haven	0000	−0005	−0020	−0025	−0·5	−0·5	−0·1	+0·1
Woodbridge	+0045	+0025	+0025	−0020	−0·2	−0·3	−0·2	0·0
Rivers Ore & Alde								
Orford Haven Bar	−0026	−0030	−0036	−0038	−1·0	−0·8	−0·1	0·0
Orford Quay	+0040	+0040	+0055	+0055	−1·4	−1·1	0·0	+0·2
Slaughden Quay	+0105	+0105	+0125	+0125	−1·3	−0·8	−0·1	+0·2
Iken Cliffs	+0130	+0130	+0155	+0155	−1·3	−1·0	0·0	+0·2

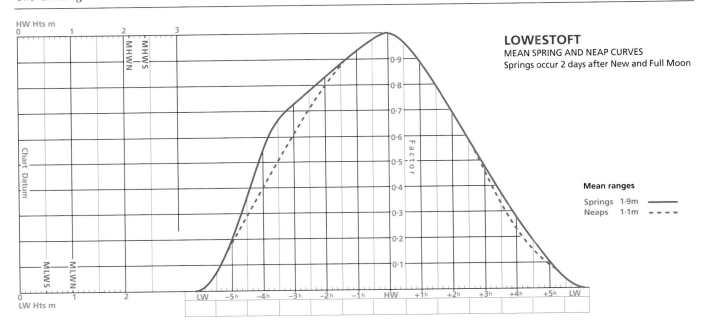

LOWESTOFT
MEAN SPRING AND NEAP CURVES
Springs occur 2 days after New and Full Moon

Mean ranges

Springs	1·9m	——
Neaps	1·1m	- - - -

TIDAL STREAMS AND CURVES

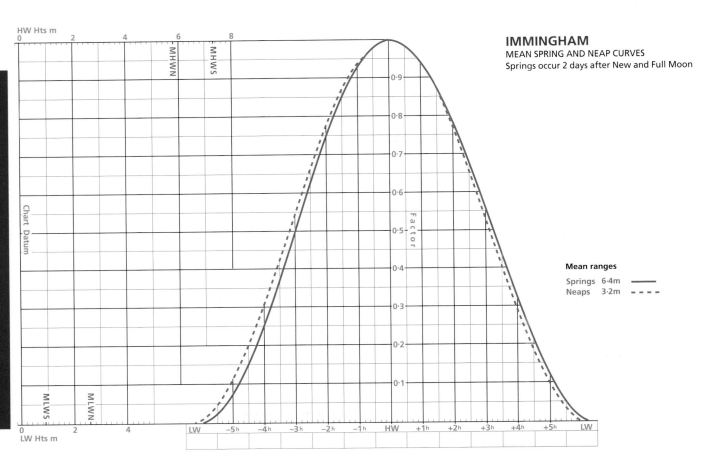

IMMINGHAM
MEAN SPRING AND NEAP CURVES
Springs occur 2 days after New and Full Moon

Mean ranges

Springs	6·4m	——
Neaps	3·2m	- - - -

LOWESTOFT	Time differences HW		LW		Height differences in metres MHWS	MHWN	MLWN	MLWS
	0300 and 1500	0900 and 2100	0200 and 1400	0800 and 2000	2·4	2·1	1·0	0·5
Aldeburgh (coast)	+0130	+0130	+0115	+0120	+0·3	+0·2	−0·1	−0·2
Southwold	+0105	+0105	+0055	+0055	0·0	0·0	−0·1	0·0
Great Yarmouth Gorleston–on–Sea	−0035	−0035	−0030	−0030	0·0	0·0	0·0	0·0

IMMINGHAM	Time differences HW		LW		Height differences in metres MHWS	MHWN	MLWN	MLWS
	0100 and 1300	0700 and 1900	0100 and 1300	0700 and 1900	7·3	5·8	2·6	0·9
Blakeney Bar	+0035	+0025	+0030	+0040	−1·6	−1·3	–	–
Wells Bar	+0020	+0020	+0020	+0020	−1·3	−1·0	–	–
King's Lynn	+0030	+0030	+0305	+0140	−0·5	−0·8	−0·8	+0·1
Wisbech Cut	+0020	+0025	+0200	+0030	−0·3	−0·7	−0·4	–
Boston	0000	+0010	+0140	+0050	−0·5	−1·0	−0·9	−0·5
Grimsby	−0012	−0012	−0015	−0015	−0·2	−0·1	0·0	+0·2
Hull	+0019	+0019	+0033	+0027	+0·3	+0·1	−0·1	−0·2

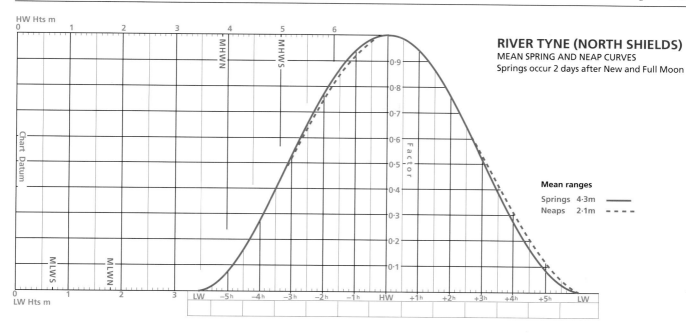

RIVER TYNE (NORTH SHIELDS)
MEAN SPRING AND NEAP CURVES
Springs occur 2 days after New and Full Moon

Mean ranges

Springs 4·3m ——
Neaps 2·1m - - - -

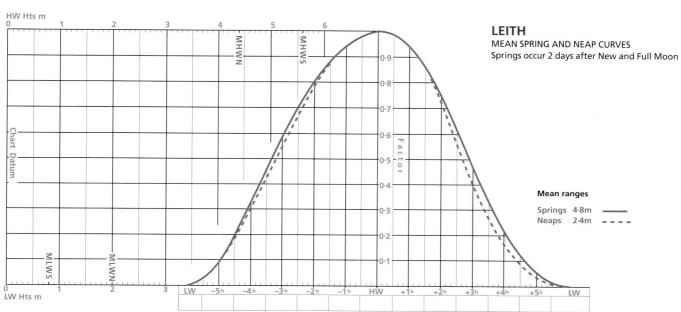

LEITH
MEAN SPRING AND NEAP CURVES
Springs occur 2 days after New and Full Moon

Mean ranges

Springs 4·8m ——
Neaps 2·4m - - - -

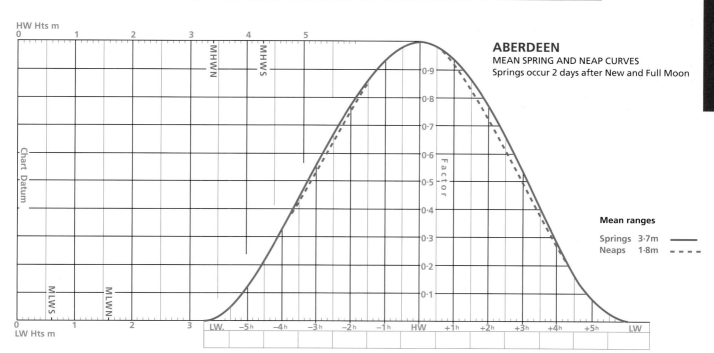

ABERDEEN
MEAN SPRING AND NEAP CURVES
Springs occur 2 days after New and Full Moon

Mean ranges

Springs 3·7m ——
Neaps 1·8m - - - -

TIDAL STREAMS AND CURVES

R. TYNE (N SHIELDS)	Time differences				Height differences in metres			
	HW		LW		MHWS	MHWN	MLWN	MLWS
	0200 and 1400	0800 and 2000	0100 and 1300	0800 and 2000	5.0	3.9	1.8	0.7
Bridlington	+0110	+0107	+0109	+0104	+1.1	+0.8	+0.5	+0.4
Scarborough	+0053	+0053	+0045	+0050	+0.7	+0.7	+0.5	+0.2
Whitby	+0033	+0054	+0033	+0020	+0.6	+0.4	+0.1	+0.1
R· Tees Entrance	+0014	+0016	+0013	+0010	+0.5	+0.6	+0.3	+0.1
Hartlepool	+0009	+0010	+0009	+0006	+0.4	+0.3	0.0	+0.1
Seaham	−0002	−0001	0000	−0003	+0.2	+0.2	+0.2	0.0
Sunderland	+0004	−0003	−0001	−0004	+0.2	+0.3	+0.2	+0.1
Newcastle-upon-Tyne	+0003	+0003	+0008	+0008	+0.3	+0.2	+0.1	+0.1
Blyth	+0005	−0007	−0001	+0009	0.0	0.0	−0.1	+0.1
Amble	−0013	−0013	−0016	−0020	0.0	0.0	+0.1	+0.1
Holy Island	−0043	−0039	−0105	−0110	−0.2	−0.2	−0.3	−0.1
Berwick	−0053	−0053	−0109	−0109	−0.3	−0.1	−0.5	−0.1

LEITH	HW		LW		MHWS	MHWN	MLWN	MLWS
	0300 and 1500	0900 and 2100	0300 and 1500	0900 and 2100	5.6	4.4	2.0	0.8
Eyemouth	−0003	+0008	+0011	+0005	−0.5	−0.4	−0.1	0.0
Dunbar	−0003	+0003	+0003	−0003	−0.3	−0.3	0.0	+0.1
Granton	0000	0000	0000	0000	0.0	0.0	0.0	0.0
Grangemouth	+0025	+0010	−0052	−0015	−0.1	−0.2	−0.3	−0.3
Burntisland	+0013	+0004	−0002	+0007	+0.1	0.0	+0.1	+0.2
Methill	−0005	−0001	−0001	−0001	−0.1	−0.1	−0.1	−0.1
Anstruther Easter	−0018	−0012	−0006	−0008	−0.3	−0.2	0.0	0.0

ABERDEEN	Time differences				Height differences in metres			
	HW		LW		MHWS	MHWN	MLWN	MLWS
	0000 and 1200	0600 and 1800	0100 and 1300	0700 and 1900	4.3	3.4	1.6	0.6
River Tay								
Bar	+0100	+0100	+0050	+0110	+0.9	+0.8	+0.3	+0.1
Dundee	+0140	+0120	+0055	+0145	+1.1	+0.9	+0.3	+0.1
Arbroath	+0056	+0037	+0034	+0055	+0.7	+0.7	+0.2	+0.1
Montrose	+0055	+0055	+0030	+0040	+0.5	+0.4	+0.2	0.0
Stonehaven	+0013	+0008	+0013	+0009	+0.2	+0.2	+0.1	0.0
Peterhead	−0035	−0045	−0035	−0040	−0.5	−0.3	−0.1	−0.1
Fraserburgh	−0105	−0115	−0120	−0110	−0.6	−0.5	−0.2	0.0

ABERDEEN	Time differences				Height differences in metres			
	HW		LW		MHWS	MHWN	MLWN	MLWS
	0200 and 1400	0900 and 2100	0400 and 1600	0900 and 2100	4.3	3.4	1.6	0.6
Banff	−0100	−0150	−0150	−0050	−0.4	−0.2	−0.1	+0.2
Whitehills	−0122	−0137	−0117	−0127	−0.4	−0.3	+0.1	+0.1
Buckie	−0130	−0145	−0125	−0140	−0.2	−0.2	0.0	+0.1
Lossiemouth	−0125	−0200	−0130	−0130	−0.2	−0.2	0.0	0.0
Burghead	−0120	−0150	−0135	−0120	−0.2	−0.2	0.0	0.0

ABERDEEN	HW		LW		MHWS	MHWN	MLWN	MLWS
	0300 and 1500	1000 and 2200	0000 and 1200	0700 and 1900	4.3	3.4	1.6	0.6
Inverness	−0050	−0150	−0200	−0105	+0.5	+0.3	+0.2	+0.1

WICK	HW		LW		MHWS	MHWN	MLWN	MLWS
	0000 and 1200	0700 and 1900	0200 and 1400	0700 and 1900	3.5	2.8	1.4	0.7
Helmsdale	+0025	+0015	+0035	+0030	+0.4	+0.3	+0.1	0.0
Kirkwall	−0042	−0041	−0041	−0041	−0.5	−0.4	−0.1	−0.1
Pierowall	−0150	−0150	−0145	−0145	+0.2	0.0	0.0	−0.1
Stromness	−0225	−0135	−0205	−0205	+0.1	−0.1	0.0	0.0

WICK	HW		LW		MHWS	MHWN	MLWN	MLWS
	0200 and 1400	0700 and 1900	0100 and 1300	0700 and 1900	3.5	2.8	1.4	0.7
Scrabster	−0255	−0225	−0240	−0230	+1.5	+1.2	+0.8	+0.3
Loch Eriboll Portnancon	−0340	−0255	−0315	−0255	+1.6	+1.3	+0.8	+0.4

WICK

MEAN SPRING AND NEAP CURVES

Springs occur 2 days after New and Full Moon

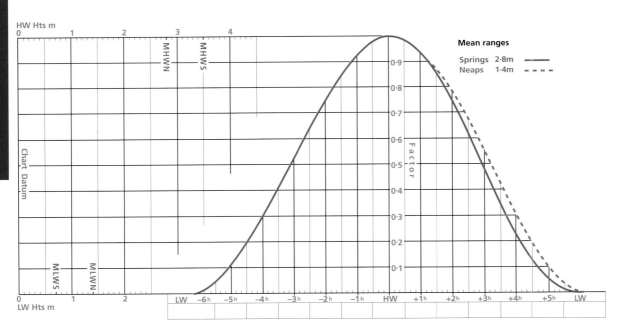

Mean ranges

Springs 2·8m
Neaps 1·4m

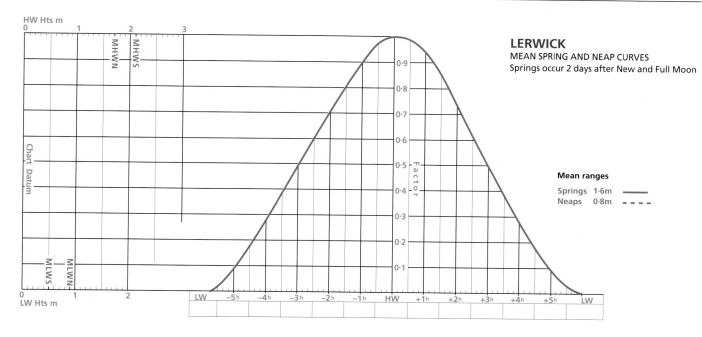

LERWICK
MEAN SPRING AND NEAP CURVES
Springs occur 2 days after New and Full Moon

Mean ranges

Springs 1·6m
Neaps 0·8m

	Time differences				Height differences in metres			
	HW		LW		MHWS	MHWN	MLWN	MLWS
LERWICK	0000 and 1200	0600 and 1800	0100 and 1300	0800 and 2000	2·1	1·7	0·9	0·5
Fair Isle	−0006	−0015	−0031	−0037	+0.1	0.0	+0.1	+0.1
Sumburgh (Grutness Voe)	+0006	+0008	+0004	−0002	−0.3	−0.3	−0.2	−0.1
Balta Sound	−0055	−0055	−0045	−0045	+0.2	+0.1	0.0	−0.1
Hillswick	−0220	−0220	−0200	−0200	−0.1	−0.1	−0.1	−0.1
Scalloway	−0150	−0150	−0150	−0150	−0.5	−0.4	−0.3	0.0
ULLAPOOL	0000 and 1200	0600 and 1800	0300 and 1500	0900 and 2100	5·2	3·9	2·1	0·7
Loch Bervie	+0030	+0010	+0010	+0020	−0.3	−0.3	−0.2	0.0
Loch Laxford	+0015	+0015	+0005	+0005	−0.3	−0.4	−0.2	0.0
Loch Nedd	0000	0000	0000	0000	−0.3	−0.2	−0.2	0.0
Loch Inver	−0005	−0005	−0005	−0005	−0.2	0.0	0.0	+0.1
Summer Isles								
Tanera Mor	−0005	−0005	−0010	−0010	−0.1	+0.1	0.0	+0.1
Loch Ewe								
Mellon Charles	−0010	−0010	−0010	−0010	−0.1	−0.1	−0.1	0.0
Loch Gairloch								
Gairloch	−0020	−0020	−0010	−0010	0.0	+0.1	−0.3	−0.1

	Time differences				Height differences in metres			
	HW		LW		MHWS	MHWN	MLWN	MLWS
ULLAPOOL	0000 and 1200	0600 and 1800	0300 and 1500	0900 and 2100	5·2	3·9	2·1	0·7
Loch Torridon								
Shieldaig	−0020	−0020	−0015	−0015	+0.4	+0.3	+0.1	0.0
Loch Carron								
Plockton	+0005	−0025	−0005	−0010	+0.5	+0.5	+0.5	+0.2
Portree	−0025	−0025	−0025	−0025	+0.1	−0.2	−0.2	0.0
Loch Snizort								
Uig Bay	−0045	−0020	−0005	−0025	+0.1	−0.4	−0.2	0.0
Loch Dunvegan	−0105	−0030	−0020	−0040	0.0	−0.1	0.0	0.0
Loch Harport	−0115	−0035	−0020	−0100	−0.1	−0.1	0.0	+0.1
Kyle of Lochalsh	−0040	−0020	−0005	−0025	+0.1	0.0	0.0	−0.1

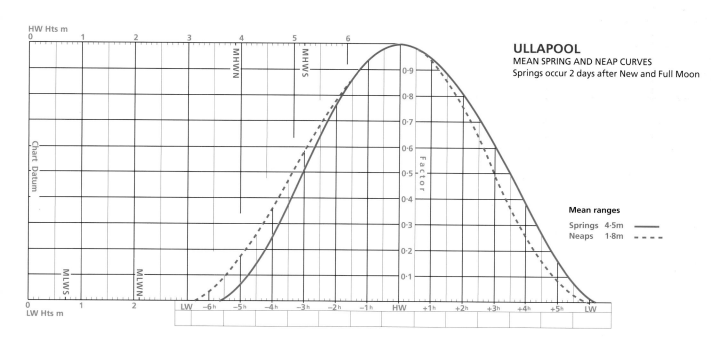

ULLAPOOL
MEAN SPRING AND NEAP CURVES
Springs occur 2 days after New and Full Moon

Mean ranges

Springs 4·5m
Neaps 1·8m

TIDAL STREAMS AND CURVES

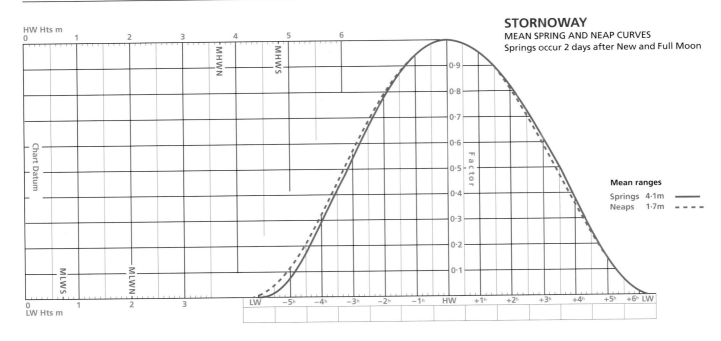

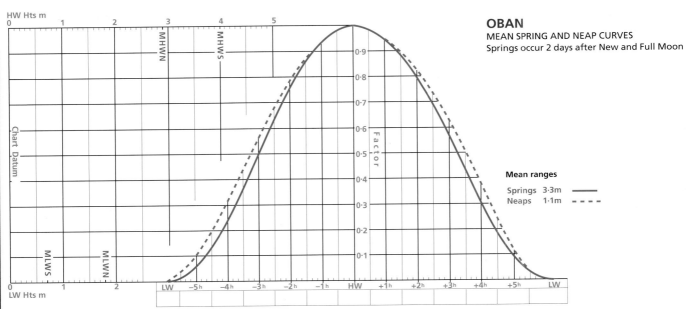

TIDAL STREAMS AND CURVES

	Time differences				Height differences in metres			
	HW		LW		MHWS	MHWN	MLWN	MLWS
STORNOWAY	0100 and 1300	0700 and 1900	0300 and 1500	0900 and 2100	4·8	3·7	2·0	0·7
Loch Shell	−0013	0000	0000	−0017	0·0	−0·1	−0·1	0·0
East Loch Tarbert	−0025	−0010	−0010	−0020	+0·2	0·0	+0·1	+0·1
Loch Maddy	−0044	−0014	−0016	−0030	0·0	−0·1	−0·1	0·0
Loch Skiport	−0100	−0025	−0024	−0024	−0·2	−0·4	−0·3	−0·2
Loch Boisdale	−0055	−0030	−0020	−0040	−0·7	−0·7	−0·3	−0·2
Castle Bay	−0115	−0040	−0045	−0100	−0·5	−0·6	−0·3	−0·1
St Kilda								
Village Bay	−0040	−0040	−0045	−0045	−1·4	−1·2	−0·8	−0·3

	Time differences				Height differences in metres			
	HW		LW		MHWS	MHWN	MLWN	MLWS
OBAN	0000 and 1200	0600 and 1800	0100 and 1300	0700 and 1900	4·0	2·0	1·8	0·7
Loch Nevis								
Mallaig	+0017	+0017	+0017	+0017	+1·0	+0·7	+0·3	+0·1
Eigg								
Bay of Laig	+0015	+0030	+0040	+0005	+0·7	+0·6	−0·2	−0·2
Glamisdale Pier	+0016	+0016	+0026	+0022	+0·7	+0·6	+0·2	+0·2
Coll								
Loch Eatharna	+0025	+0010	+0015	+0025	+0·4	+0·3	–	–
	0100 and 1300	0700 and 1900	0100 and 1300	0700 and 1900	4·0	2·0	1·8	0·7
Tobermory	+0025	+0010	+0015	+0025	+0·4	+0·4	0·0	0·0
Loch Aline	+0012	+0012	–	–	+0·5	+0·3	–	–
Corpach	0000	+0020	+0040	0000	0·0	0·0	−0·2	−0·2
Dunstaffnage Bay	+0005	0000	0000	+0005	−0·1	+0·1	+0·1	+0·1
Port Ellen	−0530	−0050	−0045	−0530	−3·1	−2·1	−1·3	−0·4
Loch Melfort	−0055	−0025	−0040	−0035	−1·2	−0·8	−0·5	−0·1
Loch Beag	−0110	−0045	−0035	−0045	−1·6	−1·2	−0·8	−0·4
Sound of Gigha	−0450	−0210	−0130	−0410	−2·5	−1·6	−1·0	−0·1

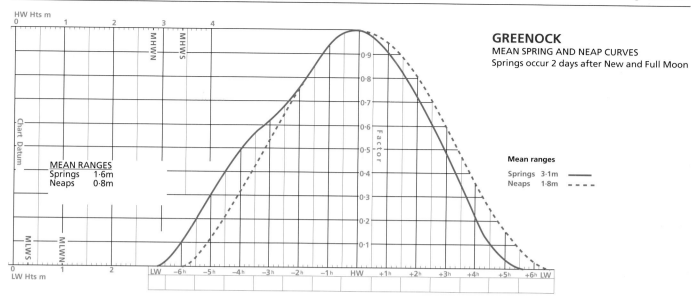

GREENOCK
MEAN SPRING AND NEAP CURVES
Springs occur 2 days after New and Full Moon

MEAN RANGES
Springs 1·6m
Neaps 0·8m

Mean ranges
Springs 3·1m ————
Neaps 1·8m - - - -

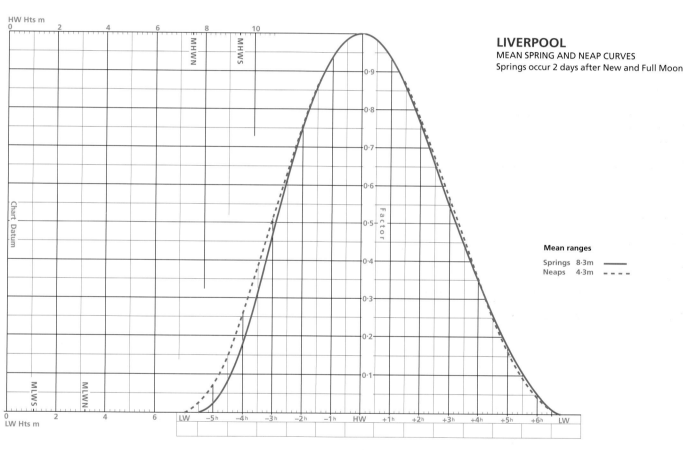

LIVERPOOL
MEAN SPRING AND NEAP CURVES
Springs occur 2 days after New and Full Moon

Mean ranges
Springs 8·3m ————
Neaps 4·3m - - - -

	Time differences HW		LW		Height differences in metres MHWS	MHWN	MLWN	MLWS
GREENOCK	0000 and 1200	0600 and 1800	0000 and 1200	0600 and 1800	3·4	2·8	1·0	0·3
Campbeltown	−0025	−0005	−0015	+0005	−0·5	−0·3	+0·1	+0·2
East Loch Tarbert	−0005	−0005	0000	−0005	+0·2	+0·1	0·0	0·0
Bowling	+0020	+0010	+0030	+0055	+0·6	+0·5	+0·3	+0·1
Lamlash	−0016	−0036	−0024	−0004	−0·2	−0·2	−	−
Troon	−0025	−0025	−0020	−0020	−0·2	−0·2	0·0	0·0
Loch Ryan								
Stranraer	−0030	−0025	−0010	−0010	−0·2	−0·1	0·0	+0·1
LIVERPOOL	0000 and 1200	0600 and 1800	0200 and 1400	0800 and 2000	9·3	7·4	2·9	0·9
Portpatrick	+0018	+0026	0000	−0035	−5·5	−4·4	−2·0	−0·6
Drummore	+0030	+0040	+0015	+0020	−3·4	−2·5	−0·9	−0·3
Kirkudbright Bay	+0015	+0015	+0010	0000	−1·8	−1·5	−0·5	−0·1
Maryport	+0017	+0032	+0020	+0005	−0·7	−0·8	−0·4	0·0
Workington	+0020	+0020	+0020	+0010	−1·2	−1·1	−0·3	0·0
Whitehaven	+0005	+0015	+0010	+0005	−1·3	−1·1	−0·5	+0·1

	Time differences HW		LW		Height differences in metres MHWS	MHWN	MLWN	MLWS
LIVERPOOL	0000 and 1200	0600 and 1800	0200 and 1400	0700 and 1900	9·3	7·4	2·9	0·9
Piel Harbour Barrow	+0015	+0015	+0020	+0020	−0·2	−0·3	−0·1	+0·1
Heysham	+0005	+0005	+0015	0000	+0·1	0·0	0·0	+0·2
River Lune								
Glasson Dock	+0020	+0030	+0220	+0240	−2·7	−3·0	−	−
Fleetwood	−0008	−0008	−0003	−0003	−0·1	−0·1	+0·1	+0·3
River Ribble								
Preston	+0010	+0010	+0335	+0310	−4·0	−4·1	−2·8	−0·8
Isle of Man								
Peel	+0005	+0005	−0015	−0025	−4·1	−3·1	−1·4	−0·5
Ramsey	+0005	+0015	−0005	−0015	−1·9	−1·5	−0·6	0·0
Douglas	+0005	+0015	−0015	−0025	−2·4	−2·0	−0·5	−0·1
Port St Mary	+0005	+0015	−0010	−0030	−3·4	−2·6	−1·3	−0·4
Calf Sound	+0005	+0005	−0015	−0025	−3·2	−2·6	−0·9	−0·3
Port Erin	−0005	+0015	−0010	−0050	−4·1	−3·2	−1·3	−0·5

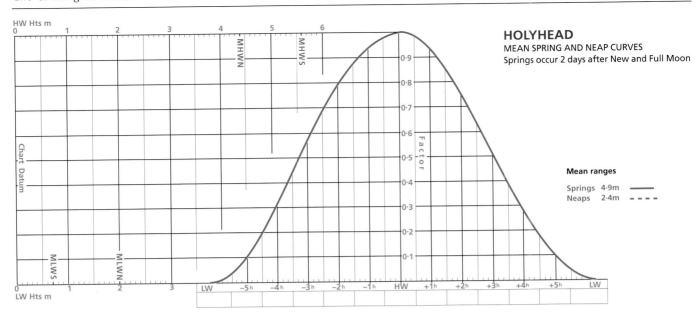

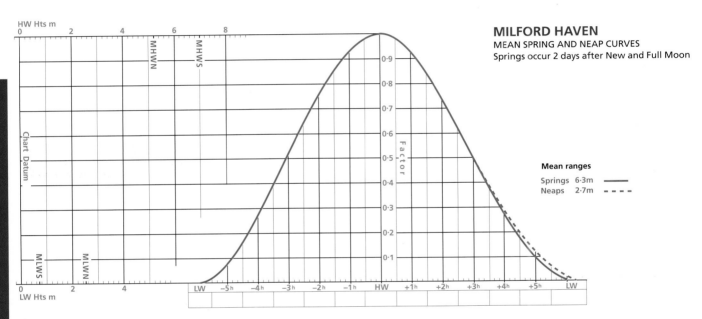

TIDAL STREAMS AND CURVES

	Time differences				Height differences in metres			
	HW		LW		MHWS	MHWN	MLWN	MLWS
HOLYHEAD	0000	0600	0500	1100	5·6	4·4	2·0	0·7
	and	and	and	and				
	1200	1800	1700	2300				
Conwy	+0025	+0035	+0120	+0105	+2·3	+1·8	+0·6	+0·4
Beaumaris	+0025	+0010	+0055	+0035	+2·0	+1·6	+0·5	+0·1
Menai Bridge	+0030	+0010	+0100	+0035	+1·7	+1·4	+0·3	0·0
Port Dinorwic	−0015	−0025	+0030	0000	0·0	0·0	0·0	+0·1
Caernarfon	−0030	−0030	+0015	−0005	−0·4	−0·4	−0·1	−0·1
Fort Belan	−0040	−0015	−0025	−0005	−1·0	−0·9	−0·2	−0·1
Cemaes Bay	+0020	+0025	+0040	+0035	+1·0	+0·7	+0·3	+0·1
Llanddwyn Island	−0115	−0055	−0030	−0020	−0·7	−0·5	−0·1	0·0
Porth Dinllaen	−0120	−0105	−0035	−0025	−1·0	−1·0	−0·2	−0·2
	0100	0800	0100	0700				
MILFORD HAVEN	and	and	and	and	7·0	5·2	2·5	0·7
	1300	2000	1300	1900				
St Tudwal's Roads	+0155	+0145	+0240	+0310	−2·2	−1·9	−0·7	−0·2
Pwllheli	+0210	+0150	+0245	+0320	−2·0	−1·8	−0·6	−0·2
Porthmadog	+0235	+0210	–	–	−1·9	−1·8	–	–
Barmouth	+0215	+0205	+0310	+0320	−2·0	−1·7	−0·7	0·0
Aberdovey	+0215	+0200	+0230	+0305	−2·0	−1·7	−0·5	0·0
Aberystwyth	+0145	+0130	+0210	+0245	−2·0	−1·7	−0·7	0·0
New Quay	+0150	+0125	+0155	+0230	−2·1	−1·8	−0·6	−0·1
Port Cardigan	+0140	+0120	+0220	+0130	−2·3	−1·8	−0·5	0·0
Fishguard	+0115	+0100	+0110	+0135	−2·2	−1·8	−0·5	+0·1
Ramsey Sound	+0030	+0030	+0030	+0030	−1·9	−1·3	−0·3	0·0
Solva	+0015	+0010	+0035	+0015	−1·5	−1·0	−0·2	0·0
Skomer Island	−0005	−0005	+0005	+0005	−0·4	−0·1	0·0	0·0
Tenby	−0015	−0010	−0015	−0020	+1·4	+1·1	+0·5	+0·2
Burry Port	+0003	+0003	+0007	+0007	+1·6	+1·4	+0·5	+0·4
Porthcawl	+0005	+0010	−0010	−0005	+2·9	+2·3	+0·8	+0·3

	Time differences				Height differences in metres			
	HW		LW		MHWS	MHWN	MLWN	MLWS
MILFORD HAVEN	0100	0700	0100	0700	7·0	5·2	2·5	0·7
	and	and	and	and				
	1300	1900	1300	1900				
Ilfracombe	−0016	−0016	−0041	−0031	+2·3	+1·8	+0·6	+0·3
Appledore	−0020	−0025	+0015	−0045	+0·5	0·0	−0·9	−0·5
Lundy	−0025	−0025	−0020	−0035	+1·0	+0·7	+0·2	0·0
Boscastle	−0045	−0010	−0110	−0100	+0·3	+0·4	+0·2	+0·2
Padstow	−0055	−0050	−0040	−0050	+0·3	+0·4	+0·1	+0·1
St Ives	−0050	−0115	−0105	−0040	−0·4	−0·3	−0·1	+0·1

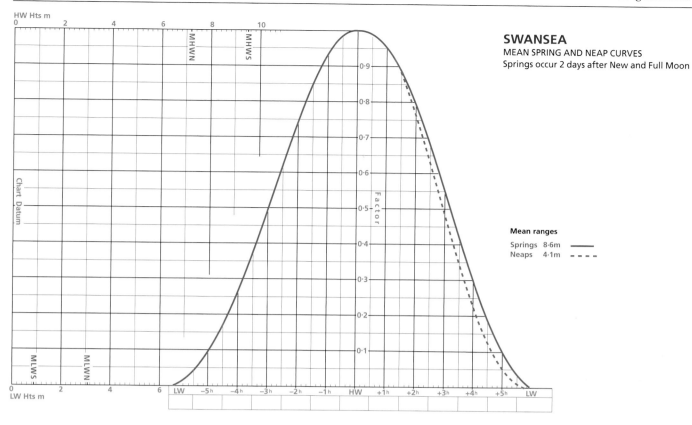

SWANSEA

MEAN SPRING AND NEAP CURVES
Springs occur 2 days after New and Full Moon

Mean ranges

| Springs | 8·6m | ——— |
| Neaps | 4·1m | - - - - |

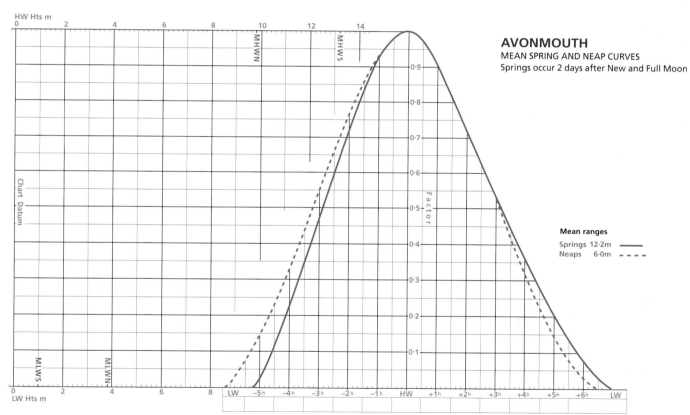

AVONMOUTH

MEAN SPRING AND NEAP CURVES
Springs occur 2 days after New and Full Moon

Mean ranges

| Springs | 12·2m | ——— |
| Neaps | 6·0m | - - - - |

TIDAL STREAMS AND CURVES

	Time differences				Height differences in metres			
	HW		LW		MHWS	MHWN	MLWN	MLWS
SWANSEA					9·5	7·2	3·1	1·0
No secondary ports related to Swansea								
BRISTOL	0600	1100	0300	0800	13·2	9·8	3·6	1·0
(AVONMOUTH)	and	and	and	and				
	1800	2300	1500	2000				
Barry	−0030	−0015	−0125	−0030	−1·8	−1·3	+0·2	0·0
Newport	−0020	−0010	0000	−0020	−1·1	−1·0	−0·6	−0·7

	Time differences				Height differences in metres			
	HW		LW		MHWS	MHWN	MLWN	MLWS
BRISTOL	0200	0800	0300	0800	13·2	9·8	3·8	1·0
(AVONMOUTH)	and	and	and	and				
	1400	2000	1500	2000				
Portishead	−0002	0000	–	–	−0·1	−0·1	–	–
River Parett								
Burnham–on–Sea	−0020	−0025	−0030	0000	−2·3	−1·9	−1·4	−1·1
Watchet	−0035	−0050	−0145	−0040	−1·9	−1·5	+0·1	+0·1
Minehead	−0037	−0052	−0155	−0045	−2·6	−1·9	−0·2	0·0
Porlock Bay	−0045	−0055	−0205	−0050	−3·0	−2·2	−0·1	−0·1

TIDAL STREAMS AND CURVES

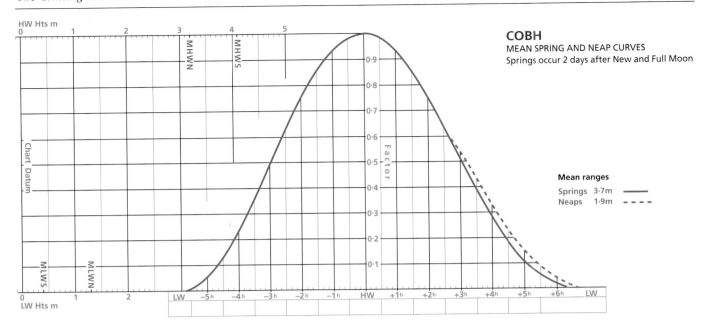

COBH
MEAN SPRING AND NEAP CURVES
Springs occur 2 days after New and Full Moon

Mean ranges
Springs 3·7m
Neaps 1·9m

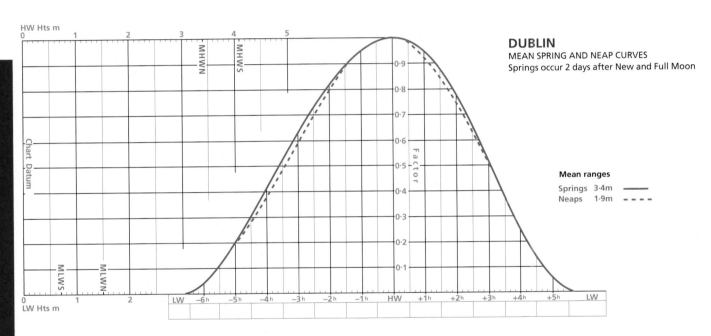

DUBLIN
MEAN SPRING AND NEAP CURVES
Springs occur 2 days after New and Full Moon

Mean ranges
Springs 3·4m
Neaps 1·9m

COBH	HW		LW		MHWS	MHWN	MLWN	MLWS
	0500	1100	0500	1100	4·1	3·2	1·3	0·4
	and	and	and	and				
	1700	2300	1700	2300				
Tralee Bay								
Fenit Pier	–0057	–0017	–0029	–0109	+0·5	+0·2	+0·3	+0·1
Smerwick Harbour	–0107	–0027	–0041	–0121	–0·3	–0·4	–	–
Dingle Harbour	–0111	–0041	–0049	–0119	–0·1	0·0	+0·3	+0·4
Valentia Harbour								
Knights Town	–0118	–0038	–0056	–0136	–0·6	–0·4	–0·1	0·0
Bantry Bay								
Castletown								
Bearhaven	–0048	–0012	–0025	–0101	–0·9	–0·6	–0·1	0·0
Bantry	–0045	–0025	–0040	–0105	–0·9	–0·8	–0·2	0·0
Crookhaven	–0057	–0033	–0048	–0112	–0·8	–0·6	–0·4	–0·1
Skull	–0040	–0015	–0015	–0110	–0·9	–0·6	–0·2	0·0
Baltimore	–0025	–0005	–0010	–0050	–0·6	–0·3	+0·1	+0·2
Castletownshend	–0020	–0030	–0020	–0050	–0·4	–0·2	+0·1	+0·3
Kinsale	–0019	–0005	–0009	–0023	–0·2	0·0	+0·1	+0·2
Youghal	0000	+0010	+0010	0000	–0·2	–0·1	–0·1	–0·1
Waterford Harbour								
Dunmore East	+0008	+0003	0000	0000	+0·1	0·0	+0·1	+0·2
Waterford	+0057	+0057	+0046	+0046	+0·4	+0·3	–0·1	+0·1
Great Saltee	+0019	+0009	–0004	+0006	–0·3	–0·4	–	–
Wexford Harbour	+0126	+0126	+0118	+0108	–2·1	–1·7	–0·3	+0·1

DUBLIN	HW		LW		MHWS	MHWN	MLWN	MLWS
	0000	0700	0000	0500	4·1	3·4	1·5	0·7
	and	and	and	and				
	1200	1900	1200	1700				
Arklow	–0315	–0201	–0140	–0134	–2·7	–2·2	–0·6	–0·1
Wicklow	–0019	–0019	–0024	–0026	–1·4	–1·1	–0·4	0·0
Dun Laoghaire	–0006	–0001	–0002	–0003	0·0	0·0	0·0	+0·1
Howth	–0007	–0005	+0001	+0005	0·0	–0·1	–0·2	–0·2
Malahide	+0002	+0003	+0009	+0009	+0·1	–0·2	–0·4	–0·2
Carlingford Lough								
Cranfield Point	–0027	–0011	+0005	–0010	+0·7	+0·9	+0·3	+0·2
Warrenpoint	–0020	–0010	+0025	+0035	+1·0	+0·7	+0·2	0·0
Newry								
(Victoria Lock)	+0005	+0015	+0045	–	+1·2	+0·9	+0·1	dries

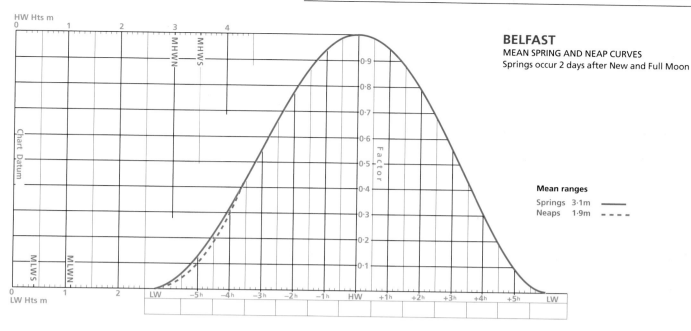

BELFAST
MEAN SPRING AND NEAP CURVES
Springs occur 2 days after New and Full Moon

Mean ranges
Springs 3·1m ————
Neaps   1·9m - - - -

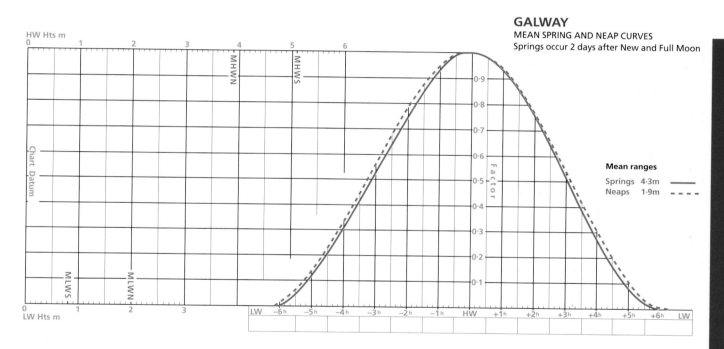

GALWAY
MEAN SPRING AND NEAP CURVES
Springs occur 2 days after New and Full Moon

Mean ranges
Springs 4·3m ————
Neaps   1·9m - - - -

TIDAL STREAMS AND CURVES

	Time differences HW		Time differences LW		Height differences in metres MHWS	MHWN	MLWN	MLWS
BELFAST	0100 and 1300	0700 and 1900	0000 and 1200	0600 and 1800	3·5	3·0	1·1	0·4
Ardglass	+0010	+0015	+0005	+0010	+1·7	+1·2	0·6	+0·3
Strangford Lough								
Killard Point	+0011	+0021	+0005	+0025	+1·0	+0·8	+0·1	+0·1
Strangford	+0147	+0157	+0148	+0208	+0·1	+0·1	−0·2	0·0
Killyleagh	+0157	+0207	+0211	+0230	+0·3	+0·3	–	–
Donaghadee	+0020	+0020	+0023	+0023	+0·5	+0·4	0·0	+0·1
Carrickfergus	+0005	+0005	+0005	+0005	−0·3	−0·3	−0·2	−0·1
Larne	+0005	0000	+0010	−0005	−0·7	−0·5	−0·3	0·0
GALWAY	0200 and 1400	0900 and 2100	0200 and 1400	0800 and 2000	5·1	3·9	2·0	0·6
Lough Swilly								
Fanad Head	+0115	+0040	+0125	+0120	−1·1	−0·9	−0·5	−0·1
Mulroy Bay								
Bar	+0108	+0052	+0102	+0118	−1·2	−1·0	–	–
Fanny's Bay	+0145	+0129	+0151	+0207	−2·2	−1·7	–	–

	Time differences HW		Time differences LW		Height differences in metres MHWS	MHWN	MLWN	MLWS
GALWAY	0600 and 1800	1100 and 2300	0000 and 1200	0700 and 1900	5·1	3·9	2·0	0·6
Burtonport	+0042	+0055	+0115	+0055	−1·2	−1·0	−0·6	−0·1
Killybegs	+0040	+0050	+0055	+0035	−1·0	−0·9	−0·5	0·0
Sligo Harbour								
(Oyster Island)	+0043	+0055	+0042	+0054	−1·0	−0·9	−0·5	−0·1
Broadhaven	+0040	+0050	+0040	+0050	−1·4	−1·1	−0·4	−0·1
Blacksod Bay								
Blacksod Quay	+0025	+0035	+0040	+0040	−1·2	−1·0	−0·6	−0·2
Westport (Inishgort)	+0035	+0045	+0115	+0100	−0·7	−0·5	−0·2	+0·2
Killary Harbour	+0021	+0015	+0035	+0029	−1·0	−0·8	−0·4	−0·1
Inishbofin								
Bofin Harbour	+0013	+0009	+0021	+0017	−1·0	−0·8	−0·4	−0·1
Roundstone Bay	+0003	+0003	+0008	+0008	−0·7	−0·5	−0·3	−0·1
Aran Island								
Killeany Bay	−0008	−0008	+0003	+0003	−0·4	−0·3	−0·2	−0·1
Kilrush	−0005	+0025	+0100	−0015	−0·1	−0·2	−0·3	−0·1

TIDAL STREAMS AND CURVES

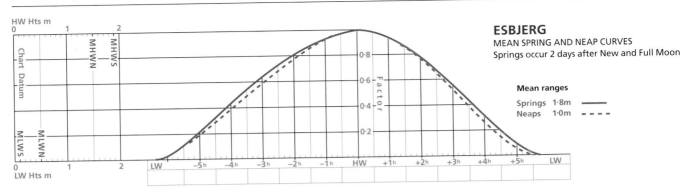

ESBJERG
MEAN SPRING AND NEAP CURVES
Springs occur 2 days after New and Full Moon

Mean ranges
Springs 1·8m ——————
Neaps 1·0m - - - - -

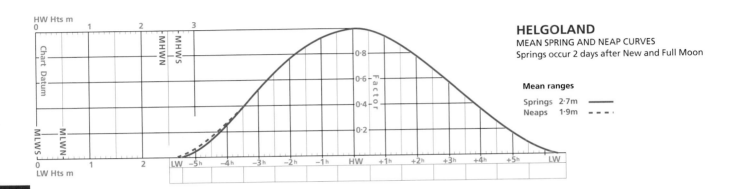

HELGOLAND
MEAN SPRING AND NEAP CURVES
Springs occur 2 days after New and Full Moon

Mean ranges
Springs 2·7m ——————
Neaps 1·9m - - - - -

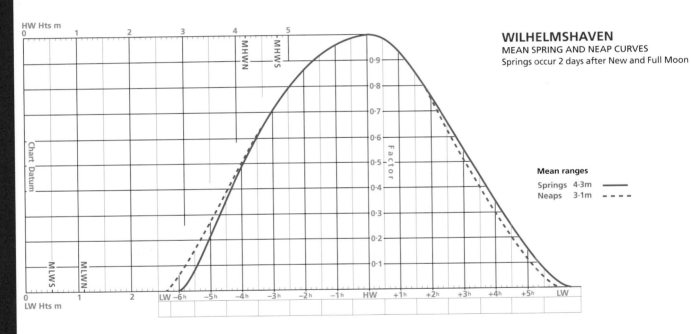

WILHELMSHAVEN
MEAN SPRING AND NEAP CURVES
Springs occur 2 days after New and Full Moon

Mean ranges
Springs 4·3m ——————
Neaps 3·1m - - - - -

	Time differences		Height differences in metres			
	HW	LW	MHWS	MHWN	MLWN	MLWS
HÔRNUM	+0223 +0218	+0131 +0137	−0.5	−0.3	−0.2	0.0
ESBJERG	0300 0700 and and 1500 1900	0100 0800 and and 1300 2000	1.9	1.5	0.5	0.1
Thyboron	+0120 +0230	+0410 +0210	−1.5	−1.2	−0.4	−0.1
Hvide Sands	0000 +0010	−0015 −0025	−1.1	−0.8	−0.3	−0.1
HELGOLAND	0100 0600 and and 1300 1800	0100 0800 and and 1300 2000	3.2	2.8	0.9	0.5

	Time differences		Height differences in metres			
	HW	LW	MHWS	MHWN	MLWN	MLWS
Langeoog	+0003 −0001	−0034 −0018	+0.4	+0.2	0.0	0.0
Norderney (Riffgat)	−0024 −0030	−0056 −0045	+0.1	0.0	0.0	0.0
Borkum (Fischerbalje)	−0048 −0052	−0124 −0105	0.0	0.0	0.0	0.0
Delfzijl	+0020 −0005	−0040 0000	+0.8	+0.8	+0.2	+0.2
Lauwersoog	−0130 −0145	−0235 −0220	+0.1	+0.1	+0.2	+0.2
West Terschelling	−0220 −0250	−0335 −0310	−0.4	−0.4	+0.1	+0.2
Harlingen	−0155 −0245	−0210 −0130	−0.5	−0.5	−0.1	+0.2
Kornwerderzand	−0210 −0315	−0300 −0215	−0.5	−0.5	−0.1	+0.2
Den Oever	−0245 −0410	−0400 −0305	−0.8	−0.7	0.0	+0.2
Oude Schild	−0310 −0420	−0445 −0400	−1.0	−0.8	0.0	+0.2
Den Helder	−0410 −0520	−0520 −0430	−1.0	−0.8	0.0	+0.2

	Time differences		Height differences in metres			
	HW	LW	MHWS	MHWN	MLWN	MLWS
WILHELMSHAVEN	0200 0800 and and 1400 2000	0200 0900 and and 1400 2100	4.3	3.8	0.6	0.0
Wangerooge West	−0101 −0058	−0035 −0045	−1.0	−1.0	−0.2	0.0

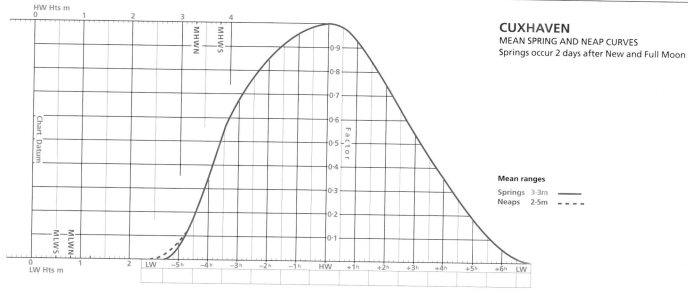

CUXHAVEN
MEAN SPRING AND NEAP CURVES
Springs occur 2 days after New and Full Moon

Mean ranges

Springs 3·3m ———
Neaps 2·5m - - - -

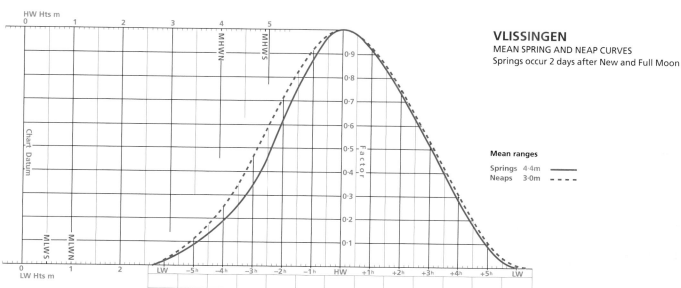

VLISSINGEN
MEAN SPRING AND NEAP CURVES
Springs occur 2 days after New and Full Moon

Mean ranges

Springs 4·4m ———
Neaps 3·0m - - - -

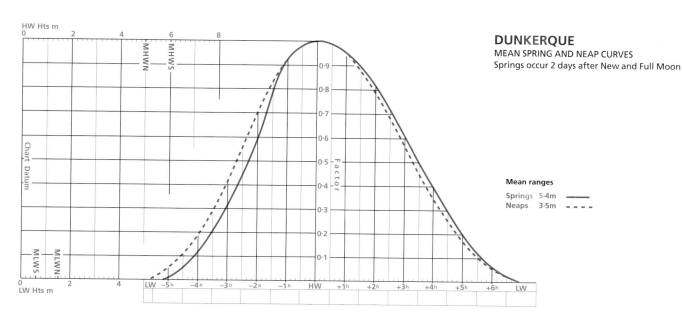

DUNKERQUE
MEAN SPRING AND NEAP CURVES
Springs occur 2 days after New and Full Moon

Mean ranges

Springs 5·4m ———
Neaps 3·5m - - - -

TIDAL STREAMS AND CURVES

	Time differences				Height differences in metres			
	HW		LW		MHWS	MHWN	MLWN	MLWS
CUXHAVEN	0200	0800	0200	0900				
	and	and	and	and	3·3	2·9	0·4	0·0
	1400	2000	1400	2100				
Brunsbuttel	+0057	+0105	+0121	+0112	−0.2	−0.2	−0.1	0.0

	Time differences				Height differences in metres			
	HW		LW		MHWS	MHWN	MLWN	MLWS
	0200	0800	0200	0900				
	1400	2000	1400	2100				
Gluckstadt	+0205	+0214	+0220	+0213	−0.3	−0.2	−0.2	0.0
Hamburg	+0338	+0346	+0422	+0406	+0.3	+0.4	−0.4	−0.3

	Time differences				Height differences in metres			
	HW		LW		MHWS	MHWN	MLWN	MLWS
	0300	0900	0400	1000	4·7	3·8	0·8	0·2
	and	and	and	and				
VLISSINGEN	1500	2100	1600	2200				
(FLUSHING)								
IJmuiden	+0145	+0140	+0305	+0325	−2·6	−2·1	−0·5	0·0
Scheveningen	+0105	+0100	+0220	+0245	−2·6	−2·1	−0·6	0·0
Hoek van H	+0043	+0046	+0039	+0046	+1·9	+1·5	+0·2	0·0
Oosterschelde								
Roompot Buiten	−0015	+0005	+0005	−0020	−1·1	−0·9	−0·2	+0·1
Terneuzen	+0020	+0020	+0020	+0030	+0·4	+0·4	0·0	+0·1
Hansweert	+0100	+0050	+0040	+0100	+0·6	+0·7	0·0	+0·1
Antwerp (Royersluis)	+0148	+0140	+0208	+0226	+1·3	+1·1	+0·1	0·0
Rupelmonde	+0235	+0225	+0215	+0225	n/a	n/a	n/a	n/a
Dendermonde	+0350	+0340	+0405	+0415	n/a	n/a	n/a	n/a
Gent (Merelbeke)	+0600	+0545	+0810	+0800	n/a	n/a	n/a	n/a
Lier	+0345	+0330	+0505	+0555	n/a	n/a	n/a	n/a

	Time differences		Height differences in metres					
	HW		LW		MHWS	MHWN	MLWN	MLWS
0200	0800	0200	0900		6·0	5·0	1·5	0·6
DUNKERQUE	and	and	and	and				
	1400	2000	1400	2100				
Gravelines	−0005	−0015	−0005	+0005	+0·3	+0·1	−0·1	−0·1
CALAIS					7·3	6·0	2·1	0·8
No secondary ports related to Calais								
	0100	0600	0100	0700				
DIEPPE	and	and	and	and	9·3	7·4	2·5	0·8
	1300	1800	1300	1900				
Le Touquet, Etaples	+0007	+0017	+0032	+0032	+0·2	+0·3	+0·4	+0·4
La Somme								
Le Hourdel	+0020	+0020	–	–	+0·8	+0·6	–	–
St Valery	+0035	+0035	–	–	+0·9	+0·7	–	–
Le Treport	+0005	0000	+0007	+0007	+0·1	+0·1	0·0	+0·1
St Valéry–en–Caux	−0005	−0005	−0015	−0020	−0·5	−0·4	−0·1	−0·1
Fecamp	−0015	−0010	−0030	−0040	−1·0	−0·6	+0·3	+0·4

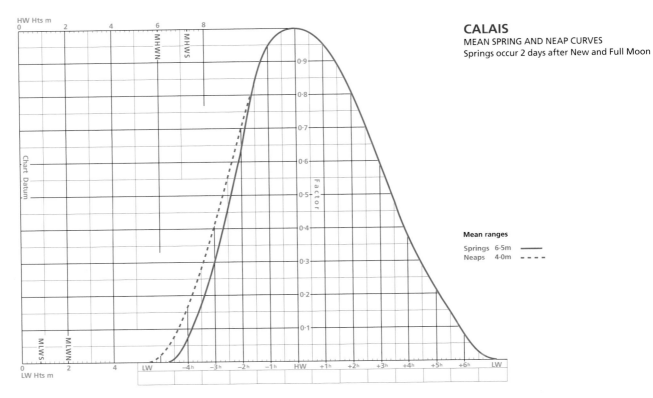

CALAIS
MEAN SPRING AND NEAP CURVES
Springs occur 2 days after New and Full Moon

Mean ranges
Springs 6·5m
Neaps 4·0m

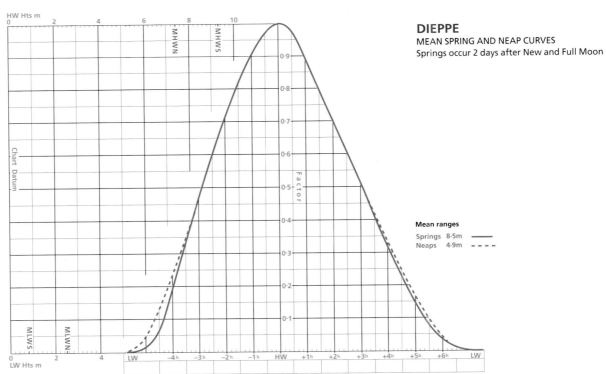

DIEPPE
MEAN SPRING AND NEAP CURVES
Springs occur 2 days after New and Full Moon

Mean ranges
Springs 8·5m
Neaps 4·9m

TIDAL STREAMS AND CURVES

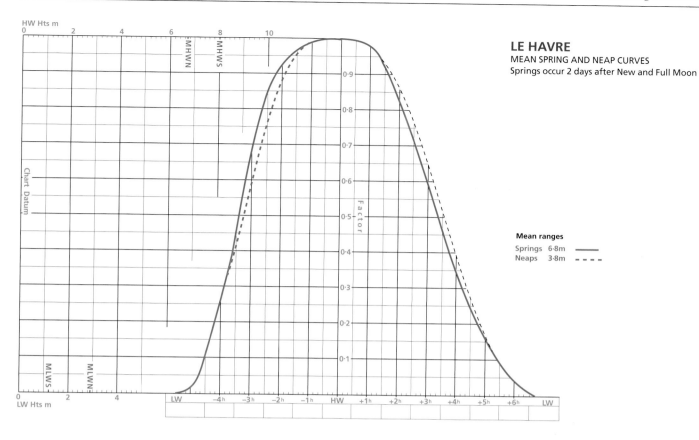

LE HAVRE
MEAN SPRING AND NEAP CURVES
Springs occur 2 days after New and Full Moon

Mean ranges
Springs 6·8m ——
Neaps 3·8m - - - -

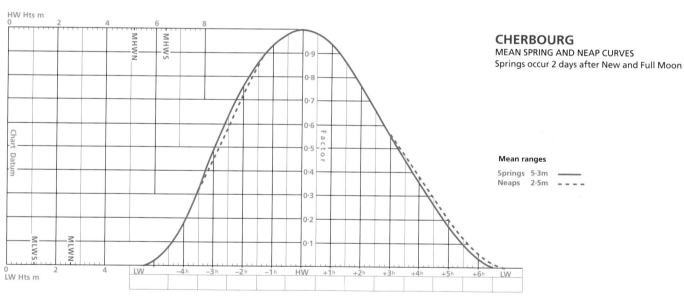

CHERBOURG
MEAN SPRING AND NEAP CURVES
Springs occur 2 days after New and Full Moon

Mean ranges
Springs 5·3m ——
Neaps 2·5m - - - -

	Time differences				Height differences in metres			
	HW		LW		MHWS	MHWN	MLWN	MLWS
LE HAVRE	0000 and 1200	0500 and 1700	0000 and 1200	0700 and 1900	7·9	6·6	2·8	1·2
Honfleur	−0135	−0135	+0015	+0040	+0·1	+0·1	+0·1	+0·3
Trouville	−0100	−0010	0000	+0005	+0·4	+0·3	+0·3	+0·1
Dives	−0100	−0010	0000	0000	+0·3	+0·2	+0·2	+0·1
Ouistreham	−0045	−0010	−0005	0000	−0·3	−0·3	−0·2	−0·3
Courseulles–sur–Mer	−0045	−0015	−0020	−0025	−0·5	−0·5	−0·1	−0·1
Arromanches	−0055	−0025	−0027	−0035	−0·6	−0·6	−0·2	−0·2
Port–en–Bessin	−0055	−0030	−0030	−0035	−0·7	−0·7	−0·2	−0·1
CHERBOURG	0300 and 1500	1000 and 2200	0400 and 1600	1000 and 2200	6·4	5·0	2·5	1·1
Iles Saint Marcouf	+1118	+0052	+0125	+0110	+0·6	+0·7	+0·1	+0·1
St Vaast–la Hougue	+0120	+0050	+0120	+0115	+0·3	+0·5	0·0	−0·1
Barfleur	+0110	+0055	+0052	+0115	+0·1	+0·3	0·0	0·0

	Time differences				Height differences in metres			
	HW		LW		MHWS	MHWN	MLWN	MLWS
LE HAVRE	0000 and 1200	0500 and 1700	0000 and 1200	0700 and 1900	7·9	6·6	2·8	1·2
Tancarville	+0105	−0100	+0105	+0140	−0·1	−0·1	0·0	+1·0
Caudebec	+0200	−0015	+0230	+0300	−0·3	−0·2	+0·9	+2·4
Duclair	+0225	+0150	+0355	+0410	−0·4	−0·3	+1·4	+3·3
Rouen	+0440	+0415	+0525	+0525	−0·2	−0·1	+1·6	+3·6

TIDAL STREAMS AND CURVES

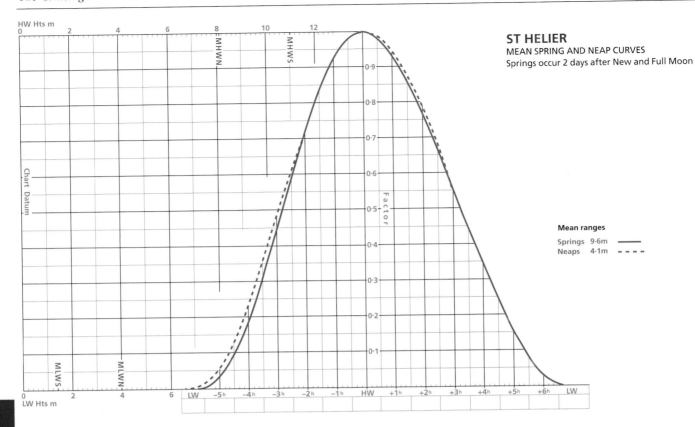

ST HELIER
MEAN SPRING AND NEAP CURVES
Springs occur 2 days after New and Full Moon

Mean ranges

Springs 9·6m ———
Neaps 4·1m - - - -

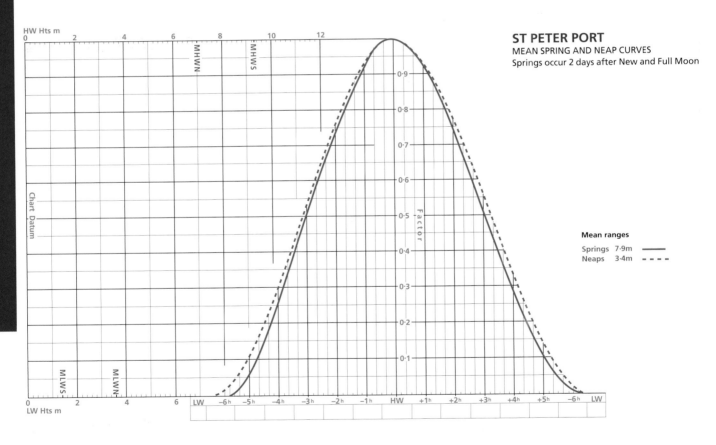

ST PETER PORT
MEAN SPRING AND NEAP CURVES
Springs occur 2 days after New and Full Moon

Mean ranges

Springs 7·9m ———
Neaps 3·4m - - - -

	Time differences				Height differences in metres			
	HW		LW		MHWS	MHWN	MLWN	MLWS
ST PETER PORT					9·3	7·0	3·6	1·4
No secondary ports related to St Peter Port								
ST HELIER	0300 and 1500	0900 and 2100	0200 and 1400	0900 and 2100	11·0	8·1	4·0	1·4
Alderney								
Braye	+0050	+0040	+0025	+0105	–4·8	–3·4	–1·5	–0·5
Sark								
Maseline Pier	+0005	+0015	+0005	+0010	–2·1	–1·5	–0·6	–0·3

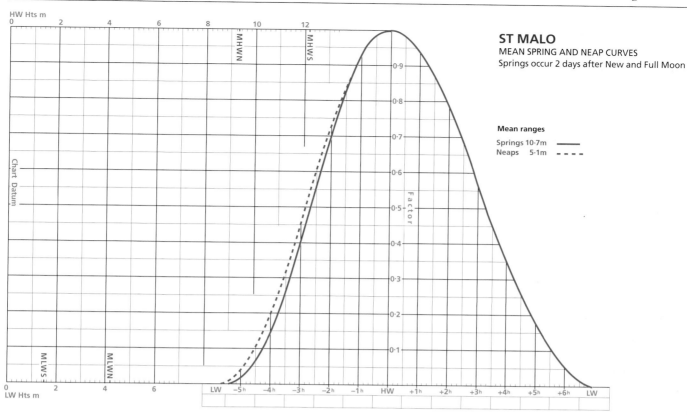

ST MALO
MEAN SPRING AND NEAP CURVES
Springs occur 2 days after New and Full Moon

Mean ranges

Springs 10·7m ⎯⎯⎯
Neaps   5·1m - - - -

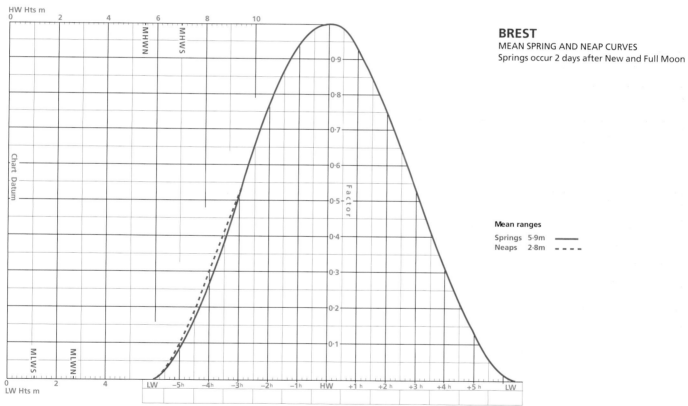

BREST
MEAN SPRING AND NEAP CURVES
Springs occur 2 days after New and Full Moon

Mean ranges

Springs 5·9m ⎯⎯⎯
Neaps   2·8m - - - -

TIDAL STREAMS AND CURVES

ST MALO	Time differences HW 0100 and 1300	0800 and 2000	LW 0300 and 1500	0800 and 2000	Height differences in metres MHWS 12·2	MHWN 9·3	MLWN 4·2	MLWS 1·5
Iles Chausey	+0005	+0005	+0015	+0015	+0·8	+0·7	+0·6	+0·4
Dielette	+0045	+0035	+0020	+0035	−2·5	−1·9	−0·7	−0·3
Carteret	+0030	+0020	+0015	+0030	−1·6	−1·2	−0·5	−0·2
Granville	+0005	+0005	+0020	+0010	+0·7	+0·5	+0·3	+0·1
St Cast	−0002	−0002	−0005	−0005	−0·2	−0·2	−0·1	−0·1
Dahouet	−0010	−0010	−0025	−0020	−0·9	−0·7	−0·2	−0·2
St Brieuc Le Legue	−0010	−0005	−0020	−0015	−0·8	−0·5	−0·2	−0·1
Binic	−0008	−0008	−0030	−0015	−0·8	−0·7	−0·2	−0·2

ST MALO	Time differences HW 0100 and 1300	0800 and 2000	LW 0300 and 1500	0800 and 2000	Height differences in metres MHWS 12·2	MHWN 9·3	MLWN 4·2	MLWS 1·5
Portrieux	−0010	−0005	−0025	−0020	−0·9	−0·7	−0·2	−0·1
Paimpol	−0010	−0005	−0035	−0025	−1·4	−1·0	−0·4	−0·2
Ile de Brehat	−0015	−0010	−0045	−0035	−1·9	−1·4	−0·6	−0·3
Lezardrieux	−0020	−0015	−0055	−0045	−1·7	−1·3	−0·5	−0·2
Treguier	−0020	−0020	−0100	−0045	−2·3	−1·6	−0·6	−0·2
Perros-Guirec	−0040	−0045	−0120	−0105	−2·9	−2·0	−0·8	−0·3
Ploumanac'h	−0035	−0040	−0120	−0100	−2·9	−2·0	−0·7	−0·2

BREST	Time differences HW		LW		Height differences in metres MHWS	MHWN	MLWN	MLWS
	0000 and 1200	0600 and 1800	0000 and 1200	0600 and 1800	6·9	5·4	2·6	1·0
Trebeurden	+0100	+0110	+0120	+0100	+2·3	+1·9	+0·9	+0·4
Anse de Primel	+0100	+0110	+0120	+0100	+2·1	+1·7	+0·8	+0·3
Bade de Morlaix								
Morlaix (Chateau du Taureau)	+0055	+0105	+0115	+0055	+2·0	+1·7	+0·8	+0·3
Roscoff	+0055	+0105	+0115	+0055	+1·9	+1·6	+0·8	+0·3
Ile de Batz	+0045	+0100	+0105	+0055	+2·0	+1·6	+0·9	+0·4
L'Aber Vrac'h								
Ile Cezon	+0030	+0030	+0040	+0035	+0·8	+0·7	+0·2	0·0
L'Aber Benoit	+0022	+0025	+0035	+0020	+0·9	+0·7	+0·3	+0·1
Portsall	+0015	+0020	+0025	+0015	+0·6	+0·5	+0·1	0·0
L'Aber–Ildut	+0010	+0010	+0023	+0010	+0·4	+0·3	0·0	–0·1
Ushant (Ouessant)								
Baie de Lampaul	+0005	+0005	–0005	+0003	0·0	–0·1	–0·1	0·0
Le Conquet	–0005	0000	+0007	+0007	–0·1	–0·1	–0·1	0·0
Cameret	–0010	–0010	–0013	–0013	–0·3	–0·3	–0·1	0·0
Morgat	–0008	–0008	–0020	–0010	–0·4	–0·4	–0·2	0·0
Douarnenez	–0010	–0015	–0018	–0008	–0·5	–0·5	–0·3	–0·1
Ile de Sein	–0005	–0005	–0010	–0005	–0·7	–0·6	–0·2	–0·1
Audierne	–0035	–0030	–0035	–0030	–1·7	–1·3	–0·6	–0·2
Le Guilvinec	–0010	–0025	–0025	–0015	–1·8	–1·4	–0·6	–0·1
Lesconil	–0008	–0028	–0028	–0018	–1·9	–1·4	–0·6	–0·1
Loctudy	–0010	–0030	–0030	–0020	–2·0	–1·6	–0·7	–0·3
Benodet	0000	–0020	–0023	–0013	–1·8	–1·4	–0·6	–0·2
Concarneau	–0010	–0030	–0030	–0020	–1·9	–1·5	–0·7	–0·2
Iles de Glenan								
Ile de Penfret	–0005	–0030	–0028	–0018	–1·9	–1·5	–0·7	–0·2
Lorient	+0003	–0022	–0020	–0010	–1·8	–1·4	–0·6	–0·2
Ile de Groix								
Port Tudy	0000	–0025	–0025	–0015	–1·8	–1·4	–0·6	–0·1

BREST	Time differences HW		LW		Height differences in metres MHWS	MHWN	MLWN	MLWS
	0000 and 1200	0600 and 1800	0000 and 1200	0600 and 1800	6·9	5·4	2·6	1·0
Port d'etel	+0020	–0010	+0030	+0010	–2·0	–1·3	–0·4	+0·5
Port Haliguen	+0015	–0020	–0015	–0010	–1·7	–1·3	–0·6	–0·3
Port Maria	+0010	–0025	–0025	–0015	–1·6	–1·3	–0·6	–0·1
Belle Ile								
Le Palais	+0007	–0028	–0025	–0020	–1·8	–1·4	–0·7	–0·3
Crac'h River								
La Trinité	+0020	–0020	–0015	–0005	–1·5	–1·1	–0·5	–0·2
Port Navalo	+0030	–0005	–0010	–0005	–2·0	–1·5	–0·8	–0·3
Auray	+0055	0000	+0020	+0005	–2·0	–1·4	–0·8	–0·2
Vannes	+0220	+0200	+0200	+0125	–3·6	–2·7	–1·6	–0·5
Port du Crouesty	+0013	–0022	–0017	–0012	–1·6	–1·2	–0·6	–0·2
Ile de Houat	+0010	–0025	–0020	–0015	–1·7	–1·3	–0·6	–0·2
Ile de Hoedic	+0010	–0035	–0027	–0022	–1·8	–1·4	–0·7	–0·3
Penerf	+0020	–0025	–0015	–0015	–1·5	–1·1	–0·6	–0·3
Le Croisic	+0015	–0040	–0020	–0015	–1·5	–1·1	–0·6	–0·3
Le Pouliguen	+0020	–0025	–0020	–0025	–1·5	–1·1	–0·6	–0·3
Pornichet	+0020	–0045	–0022	–0022	–1·4	–1·0	–0·5	–0·2
St Nazaire	+0030	–0040	–0010	–0010	–1·1	–0·8	–0·4	–0·2

BREST	0500 and 1700	1100 and 2300	0500 and 1700	1100 and 2300	6·9	5·4	2·6	1·0
Pornic	–0050	+0030	–0010	–0010	–1·1	–0·8	–0·4	–0·2
Ile de Noirmoutier								
L'Herbaudiere	–0047	+0023	–0020	–0020	–1·4	–1·0	–0·5	–0·2
Ile d'Yeu								
Port Joinville	–0040	+0015	–0030	–0035	–1·9	–1·4	–0·7	–0·3
St Giles Croix–de–Vie	–0030	+0015	–0032	–0032	–1·8	–1·3	–0·6	–0·3
Les Sables d'Olonne	–0030	+0015	–0035	–0035	–1·7	–1·3	–0·6	–0·3

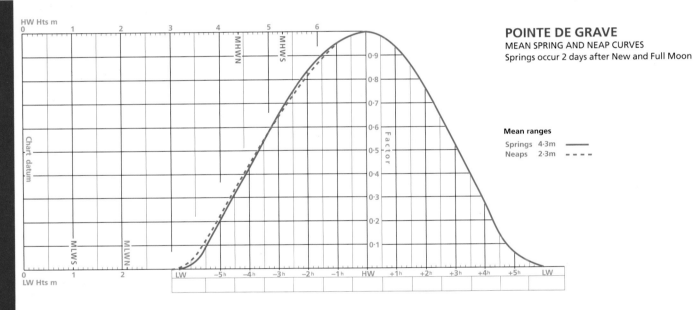

POINTE DE GRAVE
MEAN SPRING AND NEAP CURVES
Springs occur 2 days after New and Full Moon

Mean ranges
Springs 4·3m
Neaps 2·3m

POINTE DE GRAVE	Time differences HW		LW		Height differences in metres MHWS	MHWN	MLWN	MLWS
	0000 and 1200	0600 and 1800	0500 and 1700	1200 and 2400	5·4	4·4	2·1	1·0
Ile de Ré								
St Martin	+0015	–0030	–0025	–0020	+0·6	+0·5	+0·3	–0·1
La Pallice	+0015	–0030	–0025	–0020	+0·6	+0·5	+0·3	–0·1
La Rochelle	+0015	–0030	–0025	–0020	+0·6	+0·5	+0·3	–0·1
La Charente								
Rochefort	+0035	–0010	+0030	+0125	+1·1	+0·9	+0·1	–0·2
La Gironde								
Royan	0000	–0005	–0005	–0005	–0·3	–0·2	0·0	0·0
Pauillac	+0100	+0010	+0205	+0135	+0·1	0·0	–1·0	–0·5
Bordeaux	+0200	+0225	+0405	+0330	–0·1	–0·2	–1·7	–1·0
Portets	+0230	+0315	+0525	+0505	–0·3	–0·3	–1·9	–1·0
Cadillac	+0250	+0345	+0645	+0600	–1·3	–1·0	–2·0	–1·3
Langon	+0310	+0415	+0745	+0710	–3·0	–2·9	–1·8	–1·0
Castets en Dorthe	n/a	+0435	n/a	+0840	–4·0	n/a	n/a	–1·0
Arcachon	+0010	+0025	0000	+0020	–1·1	–1·0	–0·8	–0·6
L'Adour								
Bayonne	–0030	–0035	–0025	–0040	–1·2	–1·1	–0·4	–0·3
St Jean de Luz								
Socoa	–0040	–0045	–0030	–0045	–1·1	–1·1	–0·6	–0·4
Pasajes	–0050	–0030	–0015	–0045	–1·2	–1·3	–0·5	–0·5
San Sebastian	–0110	–0030	–0020	–0040	–1·2	–1·2	–0·5	–0·4
Guetaria	–0110	–0030	–0020	–0040	–1·0	–1·0	–0·5	–0·4

POINTE DE GRAVE	Time differences HW		LW		Height differences in metres MHWS	MHWN	MLWN	MLWS
	0000 and 1200	0600 and 1800	0500 and 1700	1200 and 2400	5·4	4·4	2·1	1·0
Lequeitio	–0115	–0035	–0025	–0045	–1·2	–1·2	–0·5	–0·4
Bermeo	–0055	–0015	–0005	–0025	–0·8	–0·7	–0·5	–0·4
Abra de Bilbao	–0125	–0045	–0035	–0055	–1·2	–1·2	–0·5	–0·4
Castro Urdiales	–0040	–0120	–0020	–0110	–1·4	–1·5	–0·6	–0·6
Santander	–0020	–0100	0000	–0050	–0·7	–1·2	–0·3	–0·7
San Vicente de la Barquera	–0020	–0100	0000	–0050	–1·5	–1·5	–0·6	–0·6
Ribadesella	+0005	–0020	+0020	–0020	–1·4	–1·3	–0·6	–0·6
Gijon	–0005	–0030	+0010	–0030	–1·0	–1·4	–0·4	–0·7
Aviles	–0100	–0040	–0015	–0050	–1·2	–1·6	–0·5	–0·7
Luarca	+0010	–0015	+0025	–0015	–1·2	–1·1	–0·5	–0·3
Ribadeo	+0010	–0015	+0025	–0015	–1·3	–1·5	–0·7	–0·8
Ria de Vivero	+0010	–0015	+0025	–0015	–1·4	–1·3	–0·6	–0·4
A Coruña	–0110	–0050	–0030	–0110	–1·6	–1·6	–0·6	–0·5
Ria de Corme	–0025	–0005	+0015	–0015	–1·7	–1·6	–0·6	–0·5
Ria de Camarinas	–0120	–0055	–0030	–0100	–1·6	–1·6	–0·6	–0·5

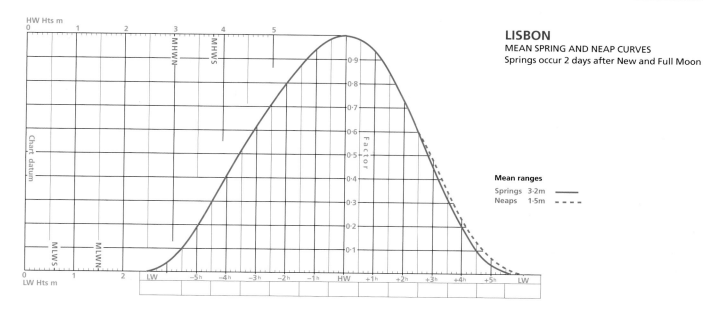

LISBON
MEAN SPRING AND NEAP CURVES
Springs occur 2 days after New and Full Moon

Mean ranges
Springs 3·2m
Neaps 1·5m

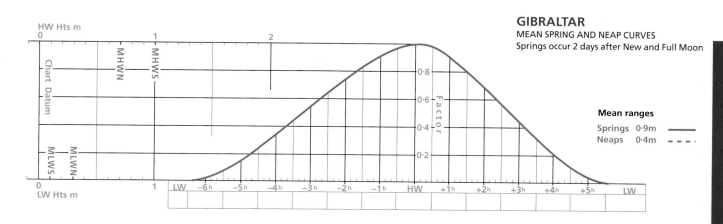

GIBRALTAR
MEAN SPRING AND NEAP CURVES
Springs occur 2 days after New and Full Moon

Mean ranges
Springs 0·9m
Neaps 0·4m

	Time differences HW		Time differences LW		Height differences in metres MHWS	MHWN	MLWN	MLWS
LISBON	0500 and 1600	1000 and 2100	0300 and 1600	0800 and 2000	3·8	3·0	1·5	0·6
Corcubion	+0055	+0110	+0120	+0135	−0·5	−0·4	−0·3	−0·1
Muros	+0050	+0105	+0115	+0130	−0·3	−0·3	−0·2	−0·1
Ria de Arosa								
Vilagarcia	+0040	+0100	+0110	+0120	−0·3	−0·2	−0·2	−0·1
Ria de Pontevedra								
Marin	+0050	+0110	+0120	+0130	−0·5	−0·4	−0·3	−0·1
Vigo	+0040	+0100	+0105	+0125	−0·4	−0·3	−0·2	−0·1
Baiona	+0035	+0050	+0100	+0115	−0·3	−0·3	−0·2	−0·1
LISBON	0400 and 1600	0900 and 2100	0400 and 1600	0900 and 2100	3·8	3·0	1·5	0·6
Viana do Castelo	−0020	0000	+0010	+0015	−0·3	−0·4	−0·1	−0·1
Povoa de Varzim	−0020	0000	+0010	+0015	−0·3	−0·3	−0·1	−0·1
Porto de Leixoes	−0025	−0010	0000	+0010	−0·3	−0·4	−0·1	−0·1
River Douro	−0010	+0005	+0015	+0025	−0·6	−0·4	−0·1	+0·1
Figueira da Foz	−0015	0000	+0010	+0020	−0·4	−0·4	−0·1	−0·1
Nazare (Pederneira)	−0030	−0015	−0005	+0005	−0·5	−0·4	−0·1	0·0
Peniche	−0035	−0015	−0005	0000	−0·3	−0·4	−0·1	0·0
Cascais	−0040	−0025	−0015	−0010	−0·3	−0·3	0·0	+0·1
Setubal	+0020	−0015	−0005	+0005	−0·4	−0·4	−0·1	−0·1
Lagos	−0100	−0040	−0030	−0025	−0·4	−0·4	−0·1	0·0
Portimao	−0100	−0040	−0030	−0025	−0·5	−0·4	−0·1	+0·1
Río Guadiana								
Vila Real de Santo Antonio	−0050	−0015	−0010	0000	−0·4	−0·4	−0·1	+0·1

	Time differences HW		Time differences LW		Height differences in metres MHWS	MHWN	MLWN	MLWS
LISBON	0500 and 1700	1000 and 2200	0500 and 1700	1100 and 2300	3·8	3·0	1·5	0·6
Faro	−0050	−0030	−0015	+0005	−0·4	−0·4	−0·1	0·0
Ayamonte	+0005	+0015	+0025	+0045	−0·7	−0·6	−0·1	−0·2
Ria de Huelva								
Bar	0000	+0015	+0035	+0030	−0·1	−0·6	−0·1	−0·4
Cadiz	−0100	−0040	−0020	−0035	−0·5	−0·5	−0·2	0·0
Barbate	−0044	−0044	−0015	−0015	−1·9	−1·5	0·4	+0·1
GIBRALTAR	0000 and 1200	0700 and 1900	0100 and 1300	0600 and 1800	1·0	0·7	0·3	0·1
Tarifa	−0038	−0038	−0042	−0042	+0·3	+0·3	+0·2	+0·1

Index

INDEX

INDEX

INDEX